D0508436

BISON
BOOKS

THE Midsu

mmer CLASSIC

THE COMPLETE HISTORY OF BASEBALL'S ALL-STAR GAME

David Vincent, Lyle Spatz, and David W. Smith

★ ★ ★ ★ ★ ★ ★ ★ ★ ★ ★

FOREWORD BY LEONARD KOPPETT

UNIVERSITY OF NEBRASKA PRESS LINCOLN & LONDON

© 2001 by the University of Nebraska Press
All rights reserved
Manufactured in the United States of America
♾
Library of Congress Cataloging-in-Publication Data
Vincent, David, 1949 July 26–
The midsummer classic : the complete history of
baseball's All-Star Game / David Vincent, Lyle Spatz,
and David W. Smith.
    p.   cm.
Includes bibliographical references and index.
ISBN 0-8032-9273-2 (pbk. : alk. paper)
1. All-Star Baseball Game — History.   2. Baseball — United
States — History.   3. Baseball — Records — United
States.   I. Spatz, Lyle, 1937–   II. Smith, David W., 1948–
III. Title.
GV878.V56 2001
796.357′648′09 — dc21   00-059964

𝒩

For

Shelley Vincent,

Marilyn Spatz,

and

Amy Tetlow Smith

CONTENTS

ILLUSTRATIONS

FOREWORD

Baseball's All-Star Game was conceived (as "How It All Started" describes) as a one-shot special event in conjunction with the Chicago's World's Fair of 1933. Significantly, no one connected with baseball thought it up—a newspaper editor did. The baseball people, to their credit, found it an attractive idea but never thought it would be repeated. One of those who voiced an objection (Sam Breadon of St. Louis) put his finger on what others also thought but didn't say: such an event, with money earmarked for charity, "might set a precedent."

Of course, it did—and most of the time, most baseball people have hated it ever since. Players appreciate the honor, but the risk of injury "in a game that doesn't count" is real, and they miss the midseason three-day vacation, welcomed (and often needed) by all the players not chosen. Club owners hate it even worse, because an injury will damage one of their best and highest paid players. It's no fun for the administrators of the commissioner's office or the individual clubs, who have to do all the logistic work. Managers get no special pleasure out of having their season-long procedures and rhythms interrupted.

Nobody likes it but the fans.

And they *love* it. They love it so much that various desires to get rid of it—always expressed privately—have never had a chance.

As time went on, however, all concerned recognized its assets, reluctantly or not. Players have come to appreciate not only the honor but the distinction of gathering with other stars in a festive atmosphere. When television came in and considered it a prime attraction, increasing the value of the national package, the club owners overcame their inherent resistance to support a game that brought them no income and some risk. And when the player contracts and marketing fallout began translating the All-Star identity into dollars, no one was left to object.

But the fans, as they usually do, got it right from the very beginning. Imagine: the best players, gathered together on one field, to display their special talents against one another. The phrase "dream team" was not in use yet, but the idea was unmistakable.

And baseball, by its nature, was the ideal game for such a display. Each star does his own thing one at a time, in full view. Unlike in other games, the batter, the pitcher, and the fielder can't be helped by a teammate who can block for him or pass the ball. Babe Ruth batting against Carl Hubbell is an ultimate confrontation, just like Mark McGwire facing Pedro Martinez two-thirds of a century later.

Other sports didn't miss the lesson. In 1934 the National Football League (NFL) produced a preseason game between college All-Stars (more respected then than their pro counterparts) and the previous year's NFL champion, the Chicago Bears. (They played a scoreless tie.) From 1938 through 1942 a game between the NFL champions and pro All-Stars was tried, but it wasn't until 1951 that the present Pro Bowl pattern along Conference lines came into being.

The National Basketball Association played its first All-Star Game in 1951, its fifth season. The National Hockey League started its in 1947, when it was thirty years old.

None of those all-star games, however, has the panache and record of baseball's. The *Retrosheet* people, with their purest of the pure devotion to detailed baseball research that money can't buy, have produced the data for the most complete compendium of everything one could imagine about the All-Star Series—not just every statistic but every single play, batter by batter. In addition the authors have provided compilations of all sorts of categories, from replacement players to families to presidential appearances—and, notably, injuries.

Anyone interested in baseball—for purposes of research, nostalgia, enlightenment, or trivia—can wallow in the material this book contains. For someone like me, who can use it as a working reference as well as for pleasure, it's out-and-out awesome, something that I not only never expected to see but never even dared imagine.

Use it in good health.

Leonard Koppett

The All-Star Game, that glorious midsummer contest between the American and National Leagues, is now an accepted part of each baseball season's calendar. The fans love it, and for the vast majority of them, a season without an All-Star Game is beyond the reach of memory. Since the first game in 1933, we've had one (two in some years) in every season except the war year of 1945. Yet it's worth noting that the first game almost didn't happen, and when it did it was viewed by many as a one-time phenomenon.

The 1933 game at Chicago's Comiskey Park was primarily the result of the efforts of Arch Ward, a *Chicago Tribune* sports editor. Chicago was hosting a World's Fair called the Century of Progress Exposition in 1933, and fair officials had asked the local sports editors to think of an athletic event that would bring sports fans to Chicago.

Ward thought a game matching the best players in the American League against the best players in the National League, a battle he called "the game of the century," would be a certain success. His idea was to have the fans select the players, and to do that he suggested enlisting fifty-five sportswriters in cities around the country to help with the voting. Editors at the *Tribune* thought it unlikely that other newspapers would do anything to help publicize another newspaper, but they changed their minds when all fifty-five accepted.

Yet before any voting could begin, or even any announcement of such a game could be made, Ward had to determine whether his dream was even feasible. On April 20, 1933, he broached the idea to American League president Will Harridge using these five arguments: (1) It was an opportunity to show that baseball was not, as some had suggested, in a state of decadence; (2) the Century of Progress Exposition was an ideal setting for baseball to show itself off; (3) all profits from the game would be donated to a charity — the Association of Professional Baseball Players of America; (4) the nation's fans would pick the teams; and (5) the *Chicago Tribune* guaranteed all expenses in case the game was rained out.

No one else had been consulted, and if Harridge were to say that a midseason game between the stars of the two leagues was impractical and out of the question, Ward and his colleagues were prepared to drop the whole scheme. But Harridge said no such thing; instead, he said, "I am all for it. While there has never been anything like it, I know no reason why it is impossible." Harridge promised to talk to the American League club owners to get their opinions.

Heartened by Harridge's response, the next day Ward's group explained their plan to William E. Veeck, president of the Chicago Cubs. When Veeck heard that the starting lineups would be selected by the fans, he was ecstatic. "That's the greatest idea that has come into baseball in my time," he said, while also promising to lobby for the game with the other National League owners. A call by Ward to NL president John Heydler elicited a promise to discuss the proposed game with the National League owners.

On May 9, the American League owners enthusiastically approved of the game at a special meeting in Cleveland. They chose July 6 as the date and instructed Harridge to adjust the AL schedule accordingly. However, a few days later, Ward received a telegram from Heydler informing him that three NL owners had turned down the idea. The three were Charles Stoneham of the New York Giants, Charles Adams of the Boston Braves, and Sam Breadon of the St. Louis Cardinals. Breadon based his opposition on the fear that the game would set a precedent, and also that any future games would be forced, like this one, to donate the proceeds to charity. Stoneham and Adams opposed the idea because their teams were scheduled to play doubleheaders in Boston on both July 4 and July 5. They pointed out that it would be impossible for Braves and Giants players to participate in a doubleheader on July 5 and be in Comiskey Park, Chicago, in time to play on July 6.

It wasn't until Ward convinced Breadon that other cities, including St. Louis, could benefit by hosting a future All-Star Game that Breadon dropped his opposition. The only obstacle remaining was the July 5 Giants-Braves doubleheader in Boston. Heydler was presented with a telegram from all eight National League owners supporting the game if he would postpone that doubleheader. He agreed, and within hours a contract was signed by Ward, representing the *Tribune*, Heydler, and Harridge.

All-Star Results

Date	Location		Winner
1933 (7-6)	Comiskey Park, Chicago	AL	4–2
1934 (7-10)	Polo Grounds, New York	AL	9–7
1935 (7-8)	Municipal Stadium, Cleveland	AL	4–1
1936 (7-7)	National League Park, Boston	NL	4–3
1937 (7-7)	Griffith Stadium, Washington	AL	8–3
1938 (7-6)	Crosley Field, Cincinnati	NL	4–1
1939 (7-11)	Yankee Stadium, New York	AL	3–1
1940 (7-9)	Sportsman's Park, St. Louis	NL	4–0
1941 (7-8)	Brigg's Stadium, Detroit	AL	7–5
1942 (7-6)	Polo Grounds, New York	AL	3–1
1943 (7-13)	Shibe Park, Philadelphia	AL	5–3
1944 (7-11)	Forbes Field, Pittsburgh	NL	7–1
1945	No game		
1946 (7-9)	Fenway Park, Boston	AL	12–0
1947 (7-8)	Wrigley Field, Chicago	AL	2–1
1948 (7-13)	Sportsman's Park, St. Louis	AL	5–2
1949 (7-12)	Ebbets Field, Brooklyn	AL	11–7
1950 (7-11)	Comiskey Park, Chicago	NL	4–3 (14 inn)
1951 (7-10)	Briggs Stadium, Detroit	NL	8–3
1952 (7-8)	Shibe Park, Philadelphia	NL	3–2 (5 inn)
1953 (7-14)	Crosley Field, Cincinnati	NL	5–1
1954 (7-13)	Municipal Stadium, Cleveland	AL	11–9
1955 (7-12)	County Stadium, Milwaukee	NL	6–5 (12 inn)
1956 (7-10)	Griffith Stadium, Washington	NL	7–3
1957 (7-9)	Busch Stadium, St. Louis	AL	6–5
1958 (7-8)	Memorial Stadium, Baltimore	AL	4–3
1959 (7-7)	Forbes Field, Pittsburgh	NL	5–4
1959 (8-3)	Memorial Coliseum, Los Angeles	AL	5–3
1960 (7-11)	Municipal Stadium, Kansas City	NL	5–3
1960 (7-13)	Yankee Stadium, New York	NL	6–0
1961 (7-11)	Candlestick Park, San Francisco	NL	5–4 (10 inn)
1961 (7-31)	Fenway Park, Boston	Tie	1–1
1962 (7-10)	D.C. Stadium, Washington	NL	3–1
1962 (7-30)	Wrigley Field, Chicago	AL	9–4
1963 (7-9)	Municipal Stadium, Cleveland	NL	5–3
1964 (7-7)	Shea Stadium, New York	NL	7–4
1965 (7-13)	Metropolitan Stadium, Minnesota	NL	6–5
1966 (7-12)	Busch Stadium, St. Louis	NL	2–1 (10 inn)
1967 (7-11)	Anaheim Stadium, Anaheim	NL	2–1 (15 inn)
1968 (7-9)	Astrodome, Houston	NL	1–0
1969 (7-23)	RFK Stadium, Washington	NL	9–3
1970 (7-14)	Riverfront Stadium, Cincinnati	NL	5–4 (12 inn)
1971 (7-13)	Tiger Stadium, Detroit	AL	6–4
1972 (7-25)	Atlanta Stadium, Atlanta	NL	4–3 (10 inn)
1973 (7-24)	Royals Stadium, Kansas City	NL	7–1
1974 (7-23)	Three Rivers Stadium, Pittsburgh	NL	7–2
1975 (7-15)	County Stadium, Milwaukee	NL	6–3
1976 (7-13)	Veterans' Stadium, Philadelphia	NL	7–1
1977 (7-19)	Yankee Stadium, New York	NL	7–5
1978 (7-11)	San Diego Stadium, San Diego	NL	7–3
1979 (7-17)	Kingdome. Seattle	NL	7–6

1980 (7-8)	Dodger Stadium, Los Angeles	NL	4–2
1981 (8-9)	Municipal Stadium, Cleveland	NL	5–4
1982 (7-13)	Olympic Stadium, Montreal	NL	4–1
1983 (7-6)	Comiskey Park, Chicago	AL	13–3
1984 (7-10)	Candlestick Park, San Francisco	NL	3–1
1985 (7-16)	Metrodome, Minnesota	NL	6–1
1986 (7-15)	Astrodome, Houston	AL	3–2
1987 (7-14)	Oakland Coliseum, Oakland	NL	2–0 (13 inn)
1988 (7-12)	Riverfront Stadium, Cincinnati	AL	2–1
1989 (7-11)	Anaheim Stadium, Anaheim	AL	5–3
1990 (7-10)	Wrigley Field, Chicago	AL	2–0
1991 (7-9)	SkyDome, Toronto	AL	4–2
1992 (7-14)	Jack Murphy Stadium, San Diego	AL	13–6
1993 (7-13)	Oriole Park at Camden Yards, Baltimore	AL	9–3
1994 (7-12)	Three Rivers Stadium, Pittsburgh	NL	8–7 (10 inn)
1995 (7-11)	The Ballpark in Arlington, Texas	NL	3–2
1996 (7-9)	Veterans' Stadium, Philadelphia	NL	6–0
1997 (7-8)	Jacobs Field, Cleveland	AL	3–1
1998 (7-7)	Coors Field, Denver	AL	13–8
1999 (7-13)	Fenway Park, Boston	AL	4–1
2000 (7-11)	Turner Field, Atlanta	AL	6–3

THE GAMES

Thursday, July 6, 1933

Comiskey Park, Chicago

American League 4, National League 2

SERIES RESULTS: AL 1, NL 0

A Dream Realized

The more than 49,000 fans who watched this battle between the greatest stars of the American and National Leagues went home satisfied that they indeed had witnessed "the baseball game of the century." The Americans won it, 4–2, but both sides thrilled Comiskey Park's capacity crowd with strong pitching, solid hitting, and nearly flawless defense. Yankees first baseman Lou Gehrig's drop of Phillies shortstop Dick Bartell's foul pop in the fifth inning was the game's only error; however, it didn't affect the scoring because Bartell then popped another one in the same area, which Gehrig grabbed for the third out of the inning.

Babe Ruth, thirty-eight years old and nearing the end of his career, provided the AL's margin of victory with a third-inning, two-run homer off National League starter Bill Hallahan of St. Louis. Ruth's blast, which increased the American League's lead to 3–0, was the first home run in All-Star competition and was for many in the crowd the event they most wanted to see.

Chicago Tribune sports editor Arch Ward had conceived this "game of the century" to coincide with the city's Century of Progress Exposition. The idea captured the imaginations of fans everywhere, who then took the opportunity to vote for the players they most wanted to see. In a gesture of cooperation unusual in the highly competitive newspaper business, fifty-five sportswriters from cities around the country volunteered to help in the polling. Outfielder Al Simmons got the most votes, 346,291. Simmons, then with the Chicago White Sox after nine spectacular seasons with the Philadelphia Athletics, was tied with Washington manager Joe Cronin for the league lead in batting, at .368. Philadelphia Phillies outfielder Chuck Klein, the National League's leading hitter, was also its leading vote getter, with 342,283. The final teams, eighteen players per league, were formed by a combination of the fans' votes and the selections of the respective managers. And while the players wouldn't be paid for participating, they did feel their pride was at stake — particularly the National Leaguers, whose Chicago Cubs had been swept in four games by the New York Yankees in the 1932 World Series. They would also benefit indirectly by the net receipts of $46,506 the game raised for the Association of Professional Baseball Players of America.

John McGraw had stepped down in June 1932 after thirty years at the helm of the New York Giants, but the National League called him out of retirement to manage this one game. The Americans gave the managerial honors to Connie Mack, who had led the Athletics since the league's birth. Beginning in 1934, the managers of the previous year's pennant winners would have the privilege of managing their league's All-Star team, but for this first game, each team was being led by its league's patriarch.

The players came to Chicago following their regularly scheduled games of the day before. The season was set to resume the following day, although the owners had agreed that if the All-Star Game was rained out, they would cancel the next day's schedule and play it then. That precaution proved to be unnecessary; the weather was perfect and every seat was filled, including 2,250 bleacher seats that had gone on sale only two days earlier. The country was struggling through the worst economic crisis in its history, but those bleacher seats were gone in forty-five minutes. For all sections of the park, patrons had been allowed to buy only four tickets, and there was no standing room. All seats were priced the same as for regular season games at Comiskey Park, and because the game was played under "World Series rules," no spectators would be allowed on the field. The crowd conducted itself in an exemplary manner, as if the fans knew they were witnessing something special. In the opinion of veteran Chicago baseball watchers, it was as well-behaved a gathering as any they could remember.

Five days before the game, McGraw and Mack

had announced that the starting pitchers would be baseball's two best left-handers: Carl Hubbell of the Giants and Lefty Grove of the A's. But both managers changed their minds on game day, although both stayed with left-handers: McGraw went with Hallahan (10-4), while Mack chose the Yankees' Lefty Gomez (9-6). McGraw said he planned for Hallahan, Hubbell, and the Cubs' Lon Warneke to each pitch three innings; however, he didn't say in what order he would use them nor would he reveal his starting lineup. "Wait until I see the other lineup," he said. Neither the crowd nor those in the press box would know the National League's batting order until all the players had batted. Current Giants manager Bill Terry captained the National Leaguers, who had the words "NATIONAL LEAGUE" on the fronts of their gray road uniforms and an "NL" emblazoned on their caps. Tigers second baseman Charlie Gehringer captained the Americans, who wore the regular home uniforms of their respective teams.

The managers of the defending league champions in 1933 were Charlie Grimm of the Cubs and Joe McCarthy of the Yankees, who had also managed the Cubs from 1926 through 1930. McCarthy sat in at a pregame meeting of Mack and his players at Chicago's Del Prado Hotel to give them tips about the National League players they would be facing. To further become accustomed to the other league, both teams used the other's ball during batting practice to familiarize themselves with the different construction. An American League ball, reputed to be more lively, would be used for the first four and a half innings, before switching to the thicker-covered National League ball.

At 1:15 P.M., home plate umpire Bill Dinneen of the American League called "Play ball," and Cardinals third baseman Pepper Martin stepped in as the first All-Star batter. Gomez got him on a ground ball to shortstop Cronin, and the "dream game" had become reality. In the second inning, the American Leaguers scored the first All-Star run, helped along by the wildness of Hallahan — who for good reason was known as "Wild Bill." Hallahan walked five in his two innings plus, to this day the most walks given up by a pitcher in one All-Star Game. After getting Simmons on a fly to left fielder Chick Hafey to open the second, Hallahan walked White Sox third baseman Jimmy Dykes and Cronin. Catcher Rick Ferrell of the Red Sox flied out to right fielder Klein for the second out, but then Gomez lined a single to center, scoring Dykes. Gomez, an historically weak batter, had just an .093 average this season.

Ruth's two-run homer in the third, a low liner into the right-field seats, followed a lead-off walk to Gehringer and preceded another walk to Gehrig. The Yankee Iron Man was playing, despite some early fears by the club that he might not have time to get back to New York for the following afternoon's game with Detroit. If that were to happen, Gehrig's opportunity to break Everett Scott's consecutive-games-played streak, which stood at 1,307, would be over. A month earlier, when reporters first raised the question, Gehrig had stated that if he were selected for the All-Star Game, he would play.

"Certainly!" Gehrig insisted. "If Colonel (Jacob) Ruppert and Joe McCarthy want me to play in the Century of Progress game I will go gladly and give up my chance at Scott's mark. It is not at all certain that the fans will pick me. They may like some other first baseman better. But if I am nominated I will prize the honor highly, and if the Colonel and Joe say 'Go' you will find me on that train for Chicago. Don't misunderstand my attitude toward that consecutive game record. I want to make it." (Gehrig got back to New York to play the following day against the Tigers, and he broke Scott's record on August 17.)

Gomez held the National Leaguers scoreless in his three innings, as did Washington's Alvin Crowder in the fourth and fifth. The Nationals finally broke through in the sixth. Warneke, who had replaced Hallahan after the walk to Gehrig, hit a one-out triple. The ball, a long fly down the right-field line, landed safely, then was poorly handled by Ruth, who with more agility might have held it to a single. Warneke scored the NL's first-ever run as Martin was grounding out to Dykes. Frankie Frisch, second baseman and manager of the Cardinals, then cut the AL's lead to 3–2 by driving a Crowder pitch into the right-field seats.

Despite having pitched three full innings and having raced around the bases in the top of the sixth, Warneke was sent out by McGraw to pitch the home half. The American Leaguers quickly got a run back on a single by Cronin, a sacrifice by Ferrell, and a single by Cleveland's Earl Averill, batting for Crowder. Ferrell, who had begun the season with St. Louis, had been traded to Boston on May 9 and was the Red Sox's representative in the game. He would catch the entire nine innings, despite having finished third in the voting behind the Yanks' Bill Dickey and Philadelphia's Mickey Cochrane, neither of whom was available that day. Cochrane had broken two ribs in a game against Cleveland ten days earlier, and Dickey had injured his thumb during pregame batting practice.

Hubbell and Grove, both of whom would lead their league in wins this season, came on in the seventh. Hubbell, who had shut out St. Louis, 1–0,

Ruth scoring on his home run, 1933
Babe Ruth crosses the plate after his third-inning home run off Bill Hallahan, the first home run in All-Star history.
National Baseball Hall of Fame Library and Archive, Cooperstown, New York.

in eighteen innings four days earlier, pitched the seventh and eighth, blanking the American Leaguers on one hit. Meanwhile, Grove pitched the final three innings also without allowing any runs, although the National Leaguers threatened to score against him in both the seventh and the eighth.

The National League had runners on second and third in the seventh, with just one out and Chicago's North Side fans screaming, as two Cubs waited to bat. But Grove struck out Gabby Hartnett and got Woody English, batting for Warneke, on a fly ball. Then, in the eighth, with two out and Frisch (who had singled) on first, Hafey hit what appeared to be a game-tying home run. It likely would have been a home run in most other big league parks but not in spacious Comiskey. Ruth

ran it down and caught it with his back pressed to the right-field wall. Grove retired the National Leaguers one-two-three in the ninth, and the "game of the century" was over.

McGraw went to the winners' locker room to congratulate Mack, his longtime rival. In the past, he had often denigrated Ruth but not today. "He was marvelous. That old boy certainly came through when they needed him," the sixty-year-old McGraw said of the thirty-eight-year-old Ruth.

McGraw used seventeen of his players, all but Giants pitcher Hal Schumacher. Mack used only thirteen, making just one nonpitching change; the Browns' Sam West replaced Ruth in the ninth inning.

Both managers said they hoped the game would be repeated annually.

	AL		NL	
P	Lefty Gomez	NYA	Bill Hallahan	SLN
C	Rick Ferrell	BOS	Jimmy Wilson	SLN
1B	Lou Gehrig	NYA	Bill Terry	NY
2B	Charlie Gehringer	DET	Frankie Frisch	SLN
3B	Jimmy Dykes	CHA	Pepper Martin	SLN
SS	Joe Cronin	WAS	Dick Bartell	PHI
OF	Ben Chapman	NYA	Wally Berger	BSN
OF	Babe Ruth	NYA	Chick Hafey	CIN
OF	Al Simmons	CHA	Chuck Klein	PHI
	Earl Averill	CLE	Tony Cuccinello	BRO
	General Crowder	WAS	Woody English	CHN
	Bill Dickey	NYA	Gabby Hartnett	CHN
	Wes Ferrell	CLE	Carl Hubbell	NY
	Jimmie Foxx	PHA	Lefty O'Doul	NY
	Lefty Grove	PHA	Hal Schumacher	NY
	Oral Hildebrand	CLE	Pie Traynor	PIT
	Tony Lazzeri	NYA	Paul Waner	PIT
	Sam West	SLA	Lon Warneke	CHN

```
National League     000  002  000- 2
American League     012  001  00x- 4
```

NATIONAL LEAGUE

	ab	r	h	bi	bb	so	po	a
P.Martin, 3b	4	0	0	1	0	1	0	3
F.Frisch, 2b	4	1	2	1	0	0	5	3
C.Klein, rf	4	0	1	0	0	0	3	0
P.Waner, rf	0	0	0	0	0	0	0	0
C.Hafey, lf	4	0	1	0	0	0	1	0
B.Terry, 1b	4	0	2	0	0	0	7	2
W.Berger, cf	4	0	0	0	0	0	3	0
D.Bartell, ss	2	0	0	0	0	1	0	3
P.Traynor, ph	1	0	1	0	0	0	0	0
C.Hubbell, p	0	0	0	0	0	0	0	0
T.Cuccinello, ph	1	0	0	0	0	1	0	0
J.Wilson, c	1	0	0	0	0	0	2	0
L.O'Doul, ph	1	0	0	0	0	0	0	0
G.Hartnett, c	1	0	0	0	0	1	2	0
B.Hallahan, p	1	0	0	0	0	0	1	0
L.Warneke, p	1	1	1	0	0	0	0	0
W.English, ph-ss	1	0	0	0	0	0	0	0
Totals	34	2	8	2	0	4	24	11

BATTING
2B: P.Traynor (off L.Grove).
3B: L.Warneke (off A.Crowder).
HR: F.Frisch (6th inning off A.Crowder, 0 on, 2 out).
2-out RBI: F.Frisch.
RBI, scoring position, less than 2 outs: P.Martin 1–1;
    W.Berger 0–1; G.Hartnett 0–2.
GDP: W.Berger.

BASERUNNING
Team LOB: 5

FIELDING
DP: (1). D.Bartell-F.Frisch-B.Terry.

AMERICAN LEAGUE

	ab	r	h	bi	bb	so	po	a
B.Chapman, lf-rf	5	0	1	0	0	1	1	0
C.Gehringer, 2b	3	1	0	0	2	0	1	4
B.Ruth, rf	4	1	2	2	0	2	1	0
S.West, cf	0	0	0	0	0	0	0	0
L.Gehrig, 1b	2	0	0	0	2	1	12	0
A.Simmons, cf-lf	4	0	1	0	0	0	4	0
J.Dykes, 3b	3	1	2	0	1	0	2	4
J.Cronin, ss	3	1	1	0	1	0	2	3
R.Ferrell, c	3	0	0	0	0	0	4	0
L.Gomez, p	1	0	1	1	0	0	0	0
A.Crowder, p	1	0	0	0	0	0	0	0
E.Averill, ph	1	0	1	1	0	0	0	0
L.Grove, p	1	0	0	0	0	0	0	0
Totals	31	4	9	4	6	4	27	11

BATTING
HR: B.Ruth (3rd inning off B.Hallahan, 1 on, 0 out).
2-out RBI: L.Gomez.
RBI, scoring position, less than 2 outs: C.Gehringer
    0–1; J.Cronin 0–1; R.Ferrell 0–1; E.Averill 1–1.
S: R.Ferrell.
GDP: A.Simmons.

BASERUNNING
SB: C.Gehringer (2nd base off B.Hallahan/J.Wilson).
Team LOB: 10

FIELDING
E: L.Gehrig (dropped foul ball).
DP: (1). J.Dykes-L.Gehrig.

PITCHING	ip	h	r	er	bb	so
National League						
B.Hallahan (L)	* 2.0	2	3	3	5	1
L.Warneke	4.0	6	1	1	0	2
C.Hubbell	2.0	1	0	0	1	1
American League						
L.Gomez (W)	3.0	2	0	0	0	1
A.Crowder	3.0	3	2	2	0	0
L.Grove (S)	3.0	3	0	0	0	3

*Pitched to 3 batters in 3rd

Inherited Runners—Scored:
    L.Warneke 1–0; C.Hubbell 0–0;
    A.Crowder 0–0; L.Grove 0–0.

GAME DATA—T: 2:05; A: 47595; Temp: Unknown;
Wind: Unknown direction, Speed: Unknown

UMPIRES—HP: Bill Dinneen (AL), 1B: Bill Klem (NL),
2B: Bill McGowan (AL), 3B: Cy Rigler (NL)

STARTING LINEUPS

	National League	*American League*
1.	P.Martin, 3b	B.Chapman, lf
2.	F.Frisch, 2b	C.Gehringer, 2b
3.	C.Klein, rf	B.Ruth, rf
4.	C.Hafey, lf	L.Gehrig, 1b
5.	B.Terry, 1b	A.Simmons, cf
6.	W.Berger, cf	J.Dykes, 3b
7.	D.Bartell, ss	J.Cronin, ss
8.	J.Wilson, c	R.Ferrell, c
9.	B.Hallahan, p	L.Gomez, p

NL 1ST: P.Martin grounded out (J.Cronin-ss to L.Gehrig-1b); F.Frisch grounded out (C.Gehringer-2b to L.Gehrig-1b); C.Klein lined to J.Cronin-ss; 0 R, 0 H, 0 E, 0 LOB. NL 0, AL 0.

AL 1ST: B.Chapman grounded out (P.Martin-3b to B.Terry-1b); C.Gehringer walked; B.Ruth was called out on strikes while C.Gehringer stole second; L.Gehrig grounded out (B.Terry-1b to B.Hallahan-p); 0 R, 0 H, 0 E, 1 LOB. NL 0, AL 0.

NL 2ND: C.Hafey singled to second base; B.Terry singled to left field [C.Hafey to second]; W.Berger grounded into a double play (J.Dykes-3b to L.Gehrig-1b) [C.Hafey out at third, B.Terry to second]; D.Bartell struck out; 0 R, 2 H, 0 E, 1 LOB. NL 0, AL 0.

AL 2ND: A.Simmons flied to C.Hafey-lf; J.Dykes walked; J.Cronin walked [J.Dykes to second]; R.Ferrell flied to C.Klein-rf; L.Gomez singled to center field [J.Dykes scored, J.Cronin to second]; B.Chapman forced L.Gomez (D.Bartell-ss to F.Frisch-2b) [B.Chapman to first]; 1 R, 1 H, 0 E, 2 LOB. NL 0, AL 1.

NL 3RD: J.Wilson grounded out (J.Dykes-3b to L.Gehrig-1b); B.Hallahan flied to A.Simmons-cf; P.Martin popped to J.Cronin-ss; 0 R, 0 H, 0 E, 0 LOB. NL 0, AL 1.

AL 3RD: C.Gehringer walked; B.Ruth homered to deep rightfield [C.Gehringer scored]; L.Gehrig walked; **L.Warneke replaced B.Hallahan (pitching);** A.Simmons grounded into a double play (D.Bartell-ss to F.Frisch-2b to B.Terry-1b) [L.Gehrig out at second]; J.Dykes singled to left field; J.Cronin flied to W.Berger-cf; 2 R, 2 H, 0 E, 1 LOB. NL 0, AL 3.

NL 4TH: **A.Crowder replaced L.Gomez (pitching);** F.Frisch lined to A.Simmons-cf; C.Klein grounded out (L.Gehrig-1b unassisted); C.Hafey popped to J.Dykes-3b in foul territory; 0 R, 0 H, 0 E, 0 LOB. NL 0, AL 3.

AL 4TH: R.Ferrell flied to C.Klein-rf; A.Crowder grounded out (F.Frisch-2b to B.Terry-1b); B.Chapman grounded out (P.Martin-3b to B.Terry-1b); 0 R, 0 H, 0 E, 0 LOB. NL 0, AL 3.

NL 5TH: B.Terry grounded out (C.Gehringer-2b to L.Gehrig-1b); W.Berger grounded out (J.Cronin-ss to L.Gehrig-1b); L.Gehrig-1b dropped a foul fly hit by D.Bartell; D.Bartell popped to L.Gehrig-1b in foul territory; 0 R, 0 H, 1 E, 0 LOB. NL 0, AL 3.

AL 5TH: Umpires move: Klem (hp), McGowan (1b), Rigler (2b), Dinneen (3b); the AL ball was replaced by an NL ball; C.Gehringer flied to W.Berger-cf; B.Ruth singled to center field; L.Gehrig struck out; A.Simmons singled to left field (it was the 0–2 pitch) [B.Ruth to second]; J.Dykes forced A.Simmons (D.Bartell-ss to F.Frisch-2b) [J.Dykes to first]; 0 R, 2 H, 0 E, 2 LOB. NL 0, AL 3.

NL 6TH: **L.O'Doul batted for J.Wilson;** L.O'Doul grounded out (C.Gehringer-2b to L.Gehrig-1b); L.Warneke tripled to right field; P.Martin grounded out (J.Dykes-3b to L.Gehrig-1b) [L.Warneke scored]; F.Frisch homered to deep rightfield; C.Klein singled to left-center; C.Hafey grounded out (J.Dykes-3b to L.Gehrig-1b); 2 R, 3 H, 0 E, 1 LOB. NL 2, AL 3.

AL 6TH: **G.Hartnett replaced L.O'Doul (playing c);** J.Cronin singled to center field; R.Ferrell out on a sacrifice bunt (B.Terry-1b to F.Frisch-2b) [J.Cronin to second]; **E.Averill batted for A.Crowder;** E.Averill singled to center field [J.Cronin scored]; On a bunt B.Chapman singled to third base [E.Averill to second]; C.Gehringer flied to C.Klein-rf in foul territory [E.Averill to third]; B.Ruth struck out; 1 R, 3 H, 0 E, 2 LOB. NL 2, AL 4.

NL 7TH: **L.Grove replaced E.Averill (pitching);** B.Terry singled to left field; W.Berger forced B.Terry (J.Cronin-ss to C.Gehringer-2b) [W.Berger to first]; **P.Traynor batted for D.Bartell;** P.Traynor doubled to center field [W.Berger to third]; G.Hartnett struck out; **W.English batted for L.Warneke;** W.English flied to A.Simmons-cf; 0 R, 2 H, 0 E, 2 LOB. NL 2, AL 4.

AL 7TH: **W.English stayed in game (playing ss); C.Hubbell replaced P.Traynor (pitching);** L.Gehrig walked; A.Simmons forced L.Gehrig (P.Martin-3b to F.Frisch-2b) [A.Simmons to first]; J.Dykes singled to left field [A.Simmons to second]; J.Cronin popped to B.Terry-1b in foul territory; R.Ferrell grounded out (F.Frisch-2b to B.Terry-1b); 0 R, 1 H, 0 E, 2 LOB. NL 2, AL 4.

NL 8TH: P.Martin was called out on strikes; F.Frisch singled to first base; C.Klein flied to A.Simmons-cf; C.Hafey lined to B.Ruth-rf; 0 R, 1 H, 0 E, 1 LOB. NL 2, AL 4.

AL 8TH: Ruth caught this with his hand over the wall; **P.Waner replaced C.Klein (playing rf);** L.Grove grounded out (B.Terry-1b unassisted); B.Chapman struck out; C.Gehringer lined to W.Berger-cf; 0 R, 0 H, 0 E, 0 LOB. NL 2, AL 4.

NL 9TH: **B.Chapman changed positions (playing rf); A.Simmons changed positions (playing lf); S.West replaced B.Ruth (playing cf);** B.Terry grounded out (C.Gehringer-2b to L.Gehrig-1b); W.Berger lined to B.Chapman-rf; **T.Cuccinello batted for C.Hubbell;** T.Cuccinello struck out; 0 R, 0 H, 0 E, 0 LOB. NL 2, AL 4.

Final Totals	R	H	E	LOB
National League	2	8	0	5
American League	4	9	1	10

* Thanks to Tim Cashion, who entered the majority of the play-by-play accounts into the computer, using data files obtained from Retrosheet (www.retrosheet.org).

GAME **2**

Tuesday, July 10, 1934

The Polo Grounds, New York City

American League 9, National League 7

SERIES RESULTS: AL 2, NL 0

Hubbell Makes History

Baseball fans had so enjoyed everything about the 1933 All-Star Game that the owners chose to do it again in 1934. The consensus among the executives in both leagues was that if the second game proved as popular as the first, they would make the contest an annual affair. Still, it was May before the leagues, at Commissioner Kenesaw Mountain Landis's insistence, agreed to hold the game at a National League park. American League president Will Harridge argued that a coin toss should decide the site, but Landis prevailed. The commissioner believed that playing the game in a National League park would set a precedent of rotating leagues for possible future games. The Polo Grounds, home of the New York Giants and the park with the largest seating capacity in the National League, was eventually chosen.

Both leagues would also set another precedent in 1934. Expected to choose Connie Mack and Bill McKechnie, the senior managers of the American and National Leagues respectively, Harridge and NL president John Heydler instead selected Joe Cronin and Bill Terry to manage for this game. Cronin, of the Washington Senators, and Terry, of the Giants, were the managers of the 1933 pennant winners.

The 1934 All-Star Game was an offense lover's delight in which the best hitters from the American and National Leagues combined for twenty-two hits and eighteen runs, scoring six runs in one inning and three runs in two others. Yet, despite all the hits and runs, the game would be forever remembered for the spectacular performances turned in by a pair of pitchers: the Giants' Carl Hubbell and Cleveland's Mel Harder. Hubbell successively fanned five of the most feared hitters in the game, while Harder pitched five scoreless innings to preserve the AL's 9–7 victory.

Like the first game at Comiskey Park in 1933, this second interleague clash was a sellout. In fact, when the gates were locked fifteen minutes before

game time, a crowd of more than fifteen thousand was still clamoring to get in. Receipts from the 48,363 fans that did attend resulted in a net contribution close to $52,982 for the game's chief beneficiary, the Association of Professional Baseball Players of America.

The first All-Star Game had been played as part of Chicago's Century of Progress Exposition, and this game too had a local tie-in. It was being played in commemoration of three hundred years of organized sport in New York City, which began in 1634 with the leasing of an area for bowling at the Battery, on the southern tip of Manhattan Island. John McGraw, the longtime Giants manager and the National League manager in the first All-Star Game, had died that winter. The pregame ceremonies included the unveiling of a memorial to McGraw, as Mrs. Blanche McGraw and Christy Mathewson Jr., the son of McGraw's greatest pitcher, looked on. Also in attendance were New York mayor Fiorello La Guardia, Landis, Heydler, and Harridge.

Hubbell took the mound shortly after receiving a plaque honoring his selection as the National League's Most Valuable Player in 1933. Facing an American League starting lineup that featured nine future Hall of Famers, Hubbell quickly found himself in trouble. Detroit's Charlie Gehringer, the American League's top vote getter, led off with a single and took second when center fielder Wally Berger (the only National League starter not destined for Cooperstown) failed to come up with the ball cleanly. (Gehringer, with two singles and three walks, would reach base five times in this game.)

Batting second was Washington's Heinie Manush, the Major Leagues' leading hitter at .403. Manush walked, putting runners at first and second, which led to a conference on the mound among Hubbell, his catcher Gabby Hartnett, and all four of his infielders. Three of the men in the huddle were managers: first baseman Terry, who was both Hubbell's and the National League's manager, third baseman Pie Traynor, of the Pirates, and second baseman Frankie Frisch, of the Cardinals.

As Babe Ruth stepped in to bat, the New York crowd roared in anticipation of the confrontation between these two local icons. Ruth was nearing the end of his career yet was still an extremely dangerous hitter. Two days earlier, he had slugged his 13th home run of the season and the 699th of his glorious career. Facing Hubbell for the first time ever, the Babe had a count of one ball and two strikes when he took a screwball that caught the outside corner for strike three.

Next up was Lou Gehrig, now even more dangerous than his teammate Ruth; however, after working the count full, Gehrig went down swinging. As he did, Gehringer and Manush executed a double steal. Runners were now at second and third with Philadelphia's Jimmie Foxx, the AL home run leader with twenty-six, due up. Foxx had finished a distant second to Gehrig in the voting for first baseman and in third place behind Chicago's Jimmy Dykes and Foxx's teammate Pinky Higgins at third base. Nevertheless, Cronin had chosen to start Foxx at third, and as Foxx approached the plate Terry again convened a conference at the mound. The NL had to decide whether to pitch to Foxx or to walk him to load the bases and take their chances against Chicago's Al Simmons. They chose to pitch to Foxx, who — like Gehrig — went down swinging.

The fans set partisanship aside as all present gave Hubbell a tremendous ovation in recognition of his having fanned consecutively three of the greatest sluggers in the game. Those rooting for the National League were soon up and cheering again when Frisch led off the home first by driving Lefty Gomez's second pitch into the right-field upper deck. The switch-hitting Frisch, who had homered left-handed against Alvin Crowder in the first All-Star Game, hit this one batting from the right side. Gomez, with three scoreless innings as the starter in that first game, then got the next three batters. But as Hubbell went out for the second inning, he now had a 1–0 lead to protect. He did so by again striking out the side, getting Simmons and Cronin on four pitches each to give him five strikeouts in a row. Hubbell also had a count of 1-2 on the next batter, Bill Dickey, but Dickey ended the run of consecutive strikeouts at five by singling. Hubbell then ended the inning by fanning Gomez.

In the third, Hubbell didn't strike out anyone, but he easily disposed of Gehringer and Manush and, after walking Ruth, got Gehrig on a fly ball. (It would be a long day for Gehrig, who would go hitless in four at bats, strike out three times, and for the second consecutive year make the AL's only

error.) Again the fans rose to cheer the great Giants left-hander as he headed for the center-field clubhouse. The Cubs' Billy Herman batted for Hubbell in the home third, and after he made the second out it appeared that Gomez would leave trailing by just one run. But after complaining to plate umpire Cy Pfirman on a pitch that he thought was strike three, Gomez walked Frisch. Traynor followed with a single up the middle, and he and Frisch both rode home on Cardinals slugger Joe Medwick's three-run blast into the left-field upper deck.

With the NL now leading, 4–0, Terry brought Lon Warneke in to pitch, and the Cubs right-hander promptly surrendered half that lead. A double by Simmons and a single by Cronin scored one run, and a two-out triple by Cleveland's Earl Averill, batting for Gomez, scored the other. Averill's drive went 460 feet to the bullpen, which was on the playing field in right-center. Old-timers judged it to be among the longest balls ever hit at the Polo Grounds.

Red Ruffing replaced his Yankee teammate Gomez in the home fourth and set the National Leaguers down, keeping the score at 4–2. Then came the fifth, which would be the All-Star Game's most productive inning ever. A record-setting nineteen batters would come to the plate, and a record-setting nine runs would score, six by the Americans and three by the Nationals. By the time the fifth inning ended, any thoughts that this game would be remembered solely for great pitching had vanished.

Ruth started the American League half quietly enough by drawing a walk. Actually, the start wasn't that quiet, as both Ruth and Hartnett, Warneke's regular season Cubs battery mate, took turns complaining about Pfirman's ball and strike calls. The complaints by the Nationals continued after Warneke walked Gehrig. After yet another meeting on the mound, Terry replaced Warneke with Van Mungo. Foxx greeted the Brooklyn right-hander by hitting his first pitch into center field for a run-scoring single. Gehrig went to third and then scored the tying run on an infield hit by Simmons.

One out later, Mungo walked Dickey to load the bases. Averill followed with another clutch hit, a double to left, scoring Foxx and Simmons and putting the American League ahead, 6–4. With Averill at second and Dickey at third, Terry had Mungo intentionally walk Gehringer to pitch to Ruffing, who was now batting in the number two position. The count went full before Ruffing, one of the game's best-hitting pitchers, smacked a two-run single to left, making the score 8–4.

The pitchers switched to the American League

ball in the home fifth, but it didn't matter because this was the first season in which both leagues were allegedly using the same ball. Using the ball with the American League label, the Nationals drove out Ruffing before he could retire a batter. Following a lead-off walk to Pepper Martin, Frisch, Traynor, and Chuck Klein singled in succession. Two runs were in and two men were on with nobody out and Mel Ott at the plate. Cronin replaced Ruffing with Harder, who got Ott to line to the Yankees' Ben Chapman in left. Chapman dropped the ball but recovered in time to force Klein at second, while Traynor took third. With Paul Waner, batting for Berger, at the plate, Ott broke for second. Dickey's throw failed to get him; meanwhile, Traynor scored standing up, accomplishing the only steal of home in All-Star history.

Their lead cut to a single run, the Americans added another run against Dizzy Dean in the sixth on doubles by Simmons and Cronin. It was Simmons's third hit of the day and his second double; he remains the only American Leaguer to have two doubles in one game. The run made it a 9–7 game, and although three innings remained, that would be the final score. Dean and Boston's Fred Frankhouse held the Americans, while Harder limited the Nationals to just one hit in his five-inning stint—Herman's two-out double in the ninth.

Herman, of course, had already been in the game, serving as a pinch hitter for Hubbell back in the third inning. He then sat around until the seventh, when he went in to play second base in place of Frisch, who had suffered a small sprain to his right foot while scoring a run in the fifth inning. The Nationals had used all their players except Frankhouse by the seventh, and the Americans graciously allowed Herman to replace the thirty-five-year-old Frisch. Frankhouse later came in to pitch, which meant that Terry got his entire roster of twenty players into the game. By contrast, Cronin, who had said he planned to use everyone, kept pitchers Tommy Bridges of Detroit and Jack Russell of Washington, catcher Rick Ferrell of Boston, and Higgins on the bench.

While happy at what he interpreted as his league's superiority, Cronin still had high praise for Hubbell after the game. "Hubbell is unquestionably the greatest pitcher I have ever seen," he said. "He showed himself out there today. He has something no other pitcher has—a screwball with which you just can't do a thing."

Meanwhile, American League coach Walter Johnson, the former great Washington pitcher and now the manager of the Cleveland Indians, paid tribute to his pitcher Harder. "I purposely gave Harder a five-day rest period for this game, and I had my reward this afternoon," Johnson said.

For the National Leaguers, their only consolation was harking back to the victory by Terry's Giants over Cronin's Senators in the 1933 World Series. "We'll get 'em in the fall, the way we did last year," Terry predicted. He would prove himself correct when the NL repeated as Series winners in 1934. However, a rash preseason statement by Terry disparaging Brooklyn's pennant chances would return to haunt him. In a season-ending series, the Dodgers would knock the Giants out of the race, and it would be Frisch's Cardinals, rather than Terry's Giants, who would win the National League pennant and go on to be the world champions.

	AL		NL		
P	Lefty Gomez	NYA	Carl Hubbell		NY
C	Bill Dickey	NYA	Gabby Hartnett		CHN
1B	Lou Gehrig	NYA	Bill Terry		NY
2B	Charlie Gehringer	DET	Frankie Frisch		SLN
3B	Jimmie Foxx	PHA	Pie Traynor		PIT
SS	Joe Cronin	WAS	Travis Jackson		NY
OF	Heinie Manush	WAS	Wally Berger		BSN
OF	Babe Ruth	NYA	Joe Medwick		SLN
OF	Al Simmons	CHA	Jo-Jo Moore	+	NY
	Earl Averill	CLE	Kiki Cuyler		CHN
	Tommy Bridges	DET	Dizzy Dean		SLN
	Ben Chapman	NYA	Fred Frankhouse		BSN
	Mickey Cochrane	DET	Billy Herman		CHN
	Jimmy Dykes	CHA	Chuck Klein		CHN
	Rick Ferrell	BOS	Al Lopez		BRO
	Mel Harder	CLE	Pepper Martin		SLN
	Mike Higgins	PHA	Van Mungo		BRO
	Red Ruffing	NYA	Mel Ott		NY
	Jack Russell	WAS	Arky Vaughan		PIT
	Sam West	SLA	Paul Waner		PIT
			Lon Warneke		CHN

+ player replaced on roster

American League	000	261	000-	9				
National League	103	030	000-	7				

AMERICAN LEAGUE

	ab	r	h	bi	bb	so	po	a
C.Gehringer, 2b	3	0	2	0	3	0	2	1
H.Manush, lf	2	0	0	0	1	0	0	0
R.Ruffing, p	1	0	1	2	0	0	0	0
M.Harder, p	2	0	0	0	0	1	1	0
B.Ruth, rf	2	1	0	0	2	1	0	0
B.Chapman, rf	2	0	1	0	0	0	0	1
L.Gehrig, 1b	4	1	0	0	1	3	11	1
J.Foxx, 3b	5	1	2	1	0	2	1	2
A.Simmons, cf-lf	5	3	3	1	0	1	3	0
J.Cronin, ss	5	1	2	2	0	1	2	8
B.Dickey, c	2	1	1	0	2	1	4	0
M.Cochrane, c	1	0	0	0	0	0	1	1
L.Gomez, p	1	0	0	0	0	1	0	0
E.Averill, ph-cf	4	1	2	3	0	1	1	0
S.West, cf	0	0	0	0	0	0	1	0
Totals	39	9	14	9	9	12	27	14

NATIONAL LEAGUE

	ab	r	h	bi	bb	so	po	a
F.Frisch, 2b	3	3	2	1	1	0	1	1
B.Herman, ph-2b	2	0	1	0	0	0	0	1
P.Traynor, 3b	5	2	2	1	0	0	1	0
J.Medwick, lf	2	1	1	3	0	1	0	0
C.Klein, ph-lf	3	0	1	1	0	0	1	0
K.Cuyler, rf	2	0	0	0	0	0	2	0
M.Ott, ph-rf	2	0	0	0	0	0	1	0
W.Berger, cf	2	0	0	0	0	1	0	0
P.Waner, ph-rf-cf	2	0	0	0	0	1	1	0
B.Terry, 1b	3	0	1	0	1	0	4	0
T.Jackson, ss	2	0	0	0	0	1	0	1
A.Vaughan, ph-ss	2	0	0	0	0	0	2	1
G.Hartnett, c	2	0	0	0	0	0	9	0
A.Lopez, c	2	0	0	0	0	1	5	1
C.Hubbell, p	0	0	0	0	0	0	0	0
B.Herman, ph-2b	2	0	1	0	0	0	0	1
L.Warneke, p	0	0	0	0	0	0	0	0
V.Mungo, p	0	0	0	0	0	0	0	0
P.Martin, ph	0	1	0	0	1	0	0	0
D.Dean, p	1	0	0	0	0	0	0	0
F.Frankhouse, p	1	0	0	0	0	0	0	0
Totals	38	7	9	6	3	5	27	6

PITCHING	ip	h	r	er	bb	so
American League						
L.Gomez	3.0	3	4	4	1	3
R.Ruffing	*1.0	4	3	3	1	0
M.Harder (w)	5.0	1	0	0	1	2
National League						
C.Hubbell	3.0	2	0	0	2	6
L.Warneke	+1.0	3	4	4	3	1
V.Mungo (L)	1.0	4	4	4	2	1
D.Dean	3.0	5	1	1	1	4
F.Frankhouse	1.0	0	0	0	1	0

* Pitched to 4 batters in 5th
+ Pitched to 2 batters in 5th

BATTING

2B: A.Simmons 2 (off L.Warneke; off D.Dean); E.Averill (off V.Mungo); J.Cronin (off D.Dean); J.Foxx (off D.Dean).

3B: E.Averill (off L.Warneke); B.Chapman (off D.Dean).

2-out RBI: E.Averill.

RBI, scoring position, less than 2 outs: R.Ruffing 2–2; B.Ruth 0–2; L.Gehrig 0–1; J.Foxx 1–1; A.Simmons 1–2; J.Cronin 2–4; E.Averill 2–3.

BASERUNNING

SB: C.Gehringer (Double SB 3rd base off C.Hubbell/G.Hartnett); H.Manush (Double SB 2nd base off C.Hubbell/G.Hartnett).

CS: J.Cronin (3rd base by D.Dean/A.Lopez).

Team LOB: 12

FIELDING

E: L.Gehrig (throw).

Outfield assist: B.Chapman (C.Klein at 2B).

BATTING

2B: B.Herman (off M.Harder).

HR: F.Frisch (1st inning off L.Gomez, 0 on, 0 out); J.Medwick (3rd inning off L.Gomez, 2 on, 2 out).

2-out RBI: J.Medwick 3.

RBI, scoring position, less than 2 outs: P.Traynor 1–2; C.Klein 1–1; M.Ott 0–1; P.Waner 0–1.

BASERUNNING

SB: P.Traynor (Double SB HP off M.Harder/B.Dickey); M.Ott (Double SB 2nd base off M.Harder/B.Dickey).

Team LOB: 5

FIELDING

E: W.Berger.

DP: (1). A.Lopez-A.Vaughan-F.Frisch.

Inherited Runners—Scored:
R.Ruffing 0–0; M.Harder 2–1; L.Warneke 0–0; V.Mungo 2–2; D.Dean 0–0; F.Frankhouse 0–0.

IBB: C.Gehringer by V.Mungo.

GAME DATA—T: 2:44; A: 48368; Temp: Unknown; Wind: Unknown direction, Speed: Unknown

UMPIRES—HP: Cy Pfirman (NL), 1B: Brick Owens (AL), 2B: Dolly Stark (NL), 3B: George Moriarty (AL)

STARTING LINEUPS

	American League	National League
1.	C.Gehringer 2b	F.Frisch 2b
2.	H.Manush lf	P.Traynor 3b
3.	B.Ruth rf	J.Medwick lf
4.	L.Gehrig 1b	K.Cuyler rf
5.	J.Foxx 3b	W.Berger cf
6.	A.Simmons cf	B.Terry 1b
7.	J.Cronin ss	T.Jackson ss
8.	B.Dickey c	G.Hartnett c
9.	L.Gomez p	C.Hubbell p

AL 1ST: C.Gehringer singled to center field [C.Gehringer to second (error by W.Berger-cf)]; H.Manush walked; B.Ruth struck out; L.Gehrig struck out while C.Gehringer stole third and H.Manush stole second; J.Foxx struck out; 0 R, 1 H, 1 E, 2 LOB. AL 0, NL 0.

NL 1ST: F.Frisch homered to deep rightfield; P.Traynor grounded out (C.Gehringer-2b to L.Gehrig-1b); J.Medwick struck out; K.Cuyler grounded out (J.Cronin-ss to L.Gehrig-1b); 1 R, 1 H, 0 E, 0 LOB. AL 0, NL 1.

AL 2ND: A.Simmons struck out; J.Cronin struck out; Hubbell struck out five Hall of Famers consecutively; B.Dickey singled; L.Gomez struck out; 0 R, 1 H, 0 E, 1 LOB. AL 0, NL 1.

NL 2ND: W.Berger struck out; B.Terry flied to A.Simmons-cf; T.Jackson struck out; 0 R, 0 H, 0 E, 0 LOB. AL 0, NL 1.

AL 3RD: C.Gehringer flied to K.Cuyler-rf; H.Manush grounded out (F.Frisch-2b to B.Terry-1b); B.Ruth walked; L.Gehrig flied to K.Cuyler-rf; 0 R, 0 H, 0 E, 1 LOB. AL 0, NL 1.

NL 3RD: G.Hartnett grounded out (J.Cronin-ss to L.Gehrig-1b); **B.Herman batted for C.Hubbell;** B.Herman popped to J.Cronin-ss; F.Frisch walked; P.Traynor singled to center field [F.Frisch to third]; J.Medwick homered to deep leftfield [F.Frisch scored, P.Traynor scored]; K.Cuyler lined to A.Simmons-cf; 3 R, 2 H, 0 E, 0 LOB. AL 0, NL 4.

AL 4TH: **L.Warneke replaced B.Herman (pitching);** J.Foxx grounded out (T.Jackson-ss to B.Terry-1b); A.Simmons doubled to left field; J.Cronin singled to left field [A.Simmons scored]; B.Dickey struck out; **E.Averill batted for L.Gomez;** E.Averill tripled to right field [J.Cronin scored]; C.Gehringer walked; H.Manush popped to P.Traynor-3b in foul territory; 2 R, 3 H, 0 E, 2 LOB. AL 2, NL 4.

NL 4TH: **R.Ruffing replaced H.Manush (pitching); E.Averill stayed in game (playing cf); A.Simmons changed positions (playing lf);** W.Berger popped to J.Foxx-3b in foul territory; B.Terry singled to left field; T.Jackson flied to E.Averill-cf; G.Hartnett grounded out (J.Foxx-3b to L.Gehrig-1b); 0 R, 1 H, 0 E, 1 LOB. AL 2, NL 4.

AL 5TH: B.Ruth walked; L.Gehrig walked [B.Ruth to second]; **V.Mungo replaced L.Warneke (pitching);** J.Foxx singled to center field [B.Ruth scored, L.Gehrig to third]; A.Simmons singled to shortstop [L.Gehrig scored, J.Foxx to second]; On a bunt J.Cronin popped to G.Hartnett-c; B.Dickey walked [J.Foxx to third, A.Simmons to second]; E.Averill doubled to right field [J.Foxx scored, A.Simmons scored, B.Dickey to third]; C.Gehringer was walked intentionally; R.Ruffing singled to left field [B.Dickey scored, E.Averill scored, C.Gehringer to second]; B.Ruth grounded out (B.Terry-1b unassisted) [C.Gehringer to third, R.Ruffing to second]; L.Gehrig struck out; 6 R, 4 H, 0 E, 2 LOB. AL 8, NL 4.

NL 5TH: Umpires move: Owens (hp), Stark (1b), Moriarty (2b), Pfirma; **B.Chapman replaced B.Ruth (playing rf); P.Martin batted for V.Mungo;** P.Martin walked; F.Frisch singled to left-center [P.Martin to third]; P.Traynor singled to deep second base [P.Martin scored, F.Frisch to third]; **C.Klein batted for J.Medwick;** C.Klein singled to right field [F.Frisch scored, P.Traynor to second]; **M.Harder replaced R.Ruffing (pitching); M.Ott batted for K.Cuyler;** M.Ott lined to B.Chapman-rf (B.Chapman-rf to J.Cronin-ss) [P.Traynor to third, M.Ott to first]; **P.Waner batted for W.Berger;** P.Waner struck out; P.Traynor stole home and M.Ott stole second; B.Terry walked; **A.Vaughan batted for T.Jackson;** A.Vaughan forced B.Terry (J.Cronin-ss to C.Gehringer-2b) [A.Vaughan to first]; 3 R, 3 H, 0 E, 2 LOB. AL 8, NL 7.

AL 6TH: **C.Klein stayed in game (playing lf); P.Waner stayed in game (playing rf); P.Waner changed positions (playing cf); M.Ott stayed in game (playing rf); A.Vaughan stayed in game (playing ss); A.Lopez replaced G.Hartnett (playing c); D.Dean replaced P.Martin (pitching);** J.Foxx struck out; A.Simmons doubled to center field; J.Cronin doubled to left field [A.Simmons scored]; B.Dickey walked; E.Averill struck out while (A.Lopez-c to A.Vaughan-ss to F.Frisch-2b); 1 R, 2 H, 0 E, 1 LOB. AL 9, NL 7.

NL 6TH: **M.Cochrane replaced B.Dickey (playing c);** A.Lopez struck out; D.Dean lined to A.Simmons-lf; F.Frisch grounded out (J.Cronin-ss to L.Gehrig-1b); 0 R, 0 H, 0 E, 0 LOB. AL 9, NL 7.

AL 7TH: **B.Herman replaced F.Frisch (playing 2b);** Frisch had sprained his right foot in the fifth; Herman had previously pinch hit in the third and was allowed to play by manager Joe Cronin; C.Gehringer singled to right field (M.Ott-rf unassisted) [C.Gehringer out at second]; M.Harder struck out; B.Chapman tripled to left field; L.Gehrig struck out; 0 R, 2 H, 0 E, 1 LOB. AL 9, NL 7.

NL 7TH: P.Traynor grounded out (J.Cronin-ss to L.Gehrig-1b); C.Klein reached on an error by L.Gehrig-1b [C.Klein to first]; M.Ott forced C.Klein (J.Cronin-ss to C.Gehringer-2b) [M.Ott to first]; P.Waner popped to L.Gehrig-1b; 0 R, 0 H, 1 E, 1 LOB. AL 9, NL 7.

AL 8TH: J.Foxx doubled; A.Simmons popped to A.Vaughan-ss; J.Cronin flied to P.Waner-cf; M.Cochrane grounded out (B.Herman-2b to B.Terry-1b); 0 R, 1 H, 0 E, 1 LOB. AL 9, NL 7.

NL 8TH: B.Terry grounded out (J.Cronin-ss to L.Gehrig-1b); A.Vaughan grounded out (J.Cronin-ss to L.Gehrig-1b); A.Lopez grounded out (J.Foxx-3b to L.Gehrig-1b); 0 R, 0 H, 0 E, 0 LOB. AL 9, NL 7.

AL 9TH: **F.Frankhouse replaced D.Dean (pitching);** E.Averill popped to A.Vaughan-ss; C.Gehringer walked; On a bunt M.Harder popped to A.Lopez-c in foul territory; B.Chapman flied to C.Klein-lf; 0 R, 0 H, 0 E, 1 LOB. AL 9, NL 7.

NL 9TH: **S.West replaced E.Averill (playing cf);** F.Frankhouse grounded out (M.Cochrane-c to L.Gehrig-1b); B.Herman doubled; P.Traynor flied to S.West-cf; C.Klein grounded out (L.Gehrig-1b to M.Harder-p); 0 R, 1 H, 0 E, 1 LOB. AL 9, NL 7.

Final Totals	R	H	E	LOB
American League	9	14	1	12
National League	7	8	1	5

GAME **3**

Monday, July 8, 1935

Municipal Stadium, Cleveland

American League 4, National League 1

SERIES RESULTS: AL 3, NL 0

The NL Remains Winless

The American League used the combined four-hit pitching of Lefty Gomez of the Yankees and Mel Harder of the Indians to notch its third consecutive All-Star victory. The AL's 4–1 triumph was played before a crowd of 69,812, then the third-largest crowd ever to see a baseball game. Only the Indians' July 31, 1932, game against Philadelphia, the first game played at Municipal Stadium, and the September 9, 1928, doubleheader between the A's and the Yankees at Yankee Stadium had drawn more fans. The Indians had actually expected even more of a crowd, but the less-than-full bleacher seats kept it from being a complete sellout. Approximately $60,000 of the close to $94,000 in gate receipts would be donated to the Association of Professional Baseball Players of America, a charity that provided for baseball's needy.

Although they enjoyed the game, many fans complained about being "gouged" for food at the event. Peanuts, popcorn, ice cream, hot dogs, and soda, normally ten cents for regular season and World Series games, cost fifteen cents the day of the All-Star Game. The Indians denied responsibility for the increase, claiming the fault lay with the new sellers they had hired for this one game.

The arrival of the recently retired Babe Ruth, accompanied by Mrs. Ruth, highlighted the pre-game activities. Not only did all the photographers run toward the Babe, but many of the players did too. A less noticed spectator was another Babe, Cincinnati Reds slugger Babe Herman. Although not picked to play in this year's game, Herman had paid his own railroad fare from St. Louis, where the Reds had played Sunday, and he had even stood in line to buy a ticket.

For Gomez, this was his third consecutive All-Star start, an achievement no other American League pitcher has accomplished since. (National Leaguer Robin Roberts of the Phillies started three straight from 1953 to 1955.) Gomez had pitched the first three innings in both 1933 and 1934, but he stayed out there for a record six innings in this game. This still-unbroken record, along with Harder's five-inning stint the year before, led the National League to force a rules change. Beginning in 1936, pitchers would be limited to three innings unless the game went into extra innings.

American League manager Mickey Cochrane's decision to start Gomez may have caught the National League by surprise. Cochrane, manager of the defending AL champion Tigers, had previously announced that he intended to start Harder. The Cleveland right-hander had even begun warming up when Cochrane called him back and told Gomez to get ready. Gomez was having a below-average season, but he sparkled this afternoon, allowing just one run and three hits in his six innings.

Perhaps even more surprising than Cochrane's switch to Gomez was the pitching choice of National League manager Frankie Frisch. Everyone had assumed that Frisch would open with the Giants' Hal Schumacher, a twelve-game winner who was in the midst of a ten-game winning streak. Frisch's decision to bypass Schumacher in favor of left-hander Bill Walker was quite controversial. Walker had been named to the team only a few days earlier as a substitute for injured Brooklyn pitcher Van Mungo.

"I thought it was the best strategy at the moment," Frisch later said. Frisch, who was Walker's manager with the Cardinals, claimed that Walker was not effective in relief, and that if he were going to use him, it would best be as a starter. But Walker would also prove ineffective as a starter, at least for today. He gave up a two-run homer to Jimmie Foxx in the very first inning, which turned out to be all the American League would need. Foxx's drive, deep into the seats in left, came on a 3-2 curve ball. "They will try to hook that three-and-two ball, these National Leaguers," said the A's slugger.

The American Leaguers added a third run against Walker in the second inning on a triple off the left-field wall by catcher Rollie Hemsley and a scoring fly by shortstop Joe Cronin. Hemsley, the first member of the St. Louis Browns to start an All-Star Game, was playing because of an injury to the Yanks' Bill Dickey. He would catch the entire game despite having been under observation for a possible case of appendicitis.

Schumacher relieved Walker in the third and pitched four innings, giving up the AL's final run. In the fifth, with two out and nobody on, singles by Joe Vosmik (Cleveland's first All-Star starter) and Detroit's Charlie Gehringer and a walk to Lou Gehrig loaded the bases. Foxx then got his third run batted in with a single on a sharp grounder that bounced off Schumacher's leg and rolled to shortstop. Only Vosmik could score on the hit, and the bases were left loaded for the Athletics' Bob Johnson. With a .359 average, Johnson was the American League's leading hitter, but this would be a terrible afternoon for him. He left the three runners stranded by striking out, one of his three strikeouts in an 0-4 day. Johnson's three strikeouts tied the All-Star mark set by Gehrig a year earlier.

Johnson was one of five players on the twenty-man AL squad who had been chosen for the first time. This group did not include Tigers first baseman Hank Greenberg, whom Cochrane omitted despite the fact that Greenberg was leading the league with 25 home runs and an amazing 101 runs batted in. Unlike in the previous two games, the managers were making their selections without the benefit of input from the fans, although Frisch had asked for recommendations from other National League managers and owners. The fans' poll had been only advisory anyway, and a binding vote by the fans wouldn't come until 1947. Besides leaving Greenberg off the team, Cochrane had raised some eyebrows by choosing Cronin as his shortstop when both Eric McNair, Cronin's Red Sox teammate, and Cleveland's Bill Knickerbocker had batting averages more than thirty points higher than Cronin's.

Neither Cochrane nor Frisch played in the game, and while Frisch used eighteen players, Cochrane made only four changes to his starting lineup. In addition to replacing Gomez with Harder, he substituted Ossie Bluege of Washington for Foxx at third base, Ben Chapman of the Yankees for Johnson in left field, and Doc Cramer of the A's for Al Simmons in center field. These three player substitutions were all made in the ninth inning.

The National Leaguers scored their only run off Gomez in the fourth. Pittsburgh's Arky Vaughan, batting a Major League–leading .398, led off with a double to right. Gomez got Mel Ott to pop to Hemsley but walked the Cardinals' Joe Medwick. Giants first baseman Bill Terry then ripped a single to center, scoring Vaughan. The tying runs were on base, but Gomez settled down to throw a third strike past Boston's Wally Berger and get Chicago's Billy Herman on a fly to Johnson. Over the next two innings, the only runner to reach base against Gomez was Vaughan, who drew a lead-off walk in the sixth.

Harder came on in the seventh to the cheers of the hometown fans and proved as effective as he had been a year earlier. He allowed only one hit in his three innings, a two-out bloop double by Phillies catcher Jimmy Wilson in the seventh. Wilson was the first National Leaguer to have been an All-Star starter for two different teams, having been a member of the Cardinals in the 1933 game. Boston's Cronin, the former Senator, was setting the same precedent for the American League.

Harder had now pitched eight innings against the National League's best hitters and had allowed only two runs. Meanwhile, the Reds' Paul Derringer, who had thrown a complete game the day before, pitched a scoreless seventh, and the Cardinals' Dizzy Dean, who had gone 5.2 innings in relief the previous Sunday, tossed a scoreless eighth.

Dean, as he often was, had been a center of controversy earlier in the week after refusing to take part in an exhibition game in St. Paul. Frisch had told reporters that, as punishment, he would not use Dean in the All-Star Game. "Boys, you can rest assured that Dizzy Dean will not be among those present," he said.

Nevertheless, Dean was present and heading out to the mound. His appearance electrified the fans, who responded with equal amounts of booing and cheering. Waiting to face him was Foxx, the batting star of the game. The great slugger and the great pitcher battled to a full count before Foxx let a high fastball go by for ball four. The fans loved it, viewing the walk to Foxx as a defeat for the often loudmouthed Dean. After Johnson struck out, Simmons sliced a double into the right-field corner, sending Foxx to third. For Simmons, benched recently by the White Sox for weak hitting, this was his second hit of the day and his sixth in All-Star competition, more than any other player to date.

Hemsley hit a ground ball to shortstop Vaughan, who threw home attempting to prevent Foxx from scoring. Foxx stopped halfway down the line and then retreated with catcher Gabby Hartnett in pursuit. When they arrived back at third base, they found Simmons also there. While Foxx reclaimed third base, Hartnett put the tag on Simmons for the second out. Cronin's pop to Vaughan ended the inning.

Harder easily set down Medwick, Rip Collins, and Joe Moore in the ninth, and the American League had won again. League president Will Harridge, recuperating in a Chicago hospital from a kidney problem that had prevented him from attending the game, listened and naturally was overjoyed at the result.

"I am delighted," he said. "I want to extend my congratulations to Mickey Cochrane and his All-Stars for another splendid American League victory."

	AL		NL	
P	Lefty Gomez	NYA	Bill Walker	SLN
C	Rollie Hemsley	SLA	Jimmy Wilson	PHI
1B	Lou Gehrig	NYA	Bill Terry	NY
2B	Charlie Gehringer	DET	Billy Herman	CHN
3B	Jimmie Foxx	PHA	Pepper Martin	SLN
SS	Joe Cronin	BOS	Arky Vaughan	PIT
OF	Bob Johnson	PHA	Wally Berger	BSN
OF	Al Simmons	CHA	Joe Medwick	SLN
OF	Joe Vosmik	CLE	Mel Ott	NY
	Earl Averill +	CLE	Ripper Collins	SLN
	Ossie Bluege	WAS	Dizzy Dean	SLN
	Tommy Bridges	DET	Paul Derringer	CIN
	Ben Chapman	NYA	Frankie Frisch	SLN
	Mickey Cochrane	DET	Gabby Hartnett	CHN
	Doc Cramer	PHA	Carl Hubbell	NY
	Rick Ferrell	BOS	Gus Mancuso	NY
	Lefty Grove	BOS	Jo-Jo Moore	NY
	Mel Harder	CLE	Van Mungo +	BRO
	Buddy Myer	WAS	Hal Schumacher	NY
	Schoolboy Rowe	DET	Paul Waner	PIT
	Sam West	SLA	Burgess Whitehead	SLN

+ player replaced on roster

National League	000	100	000-	1			
American League	210	010	00X-	4			

NATIONAL LEAGUE

	ab	r	h	bi	bb	so	po	a
P.Martin, 3b	4	0	1	0	0	2	0	1
A.Vaughan, ss	3	1	1	0	1	0	2	2
M.Ott, rf	4	0	0	0	0	1	1	0
J.Medwick, lf	3	0	0	0	1	1	0	0
B.Terry, 1b	3	0	1	1	0	0	5	1
R.Collins, 1b	1	0	0	0	0	0	2	0
W.Berger, cf	2	0	0	0	0	1	1	0
J.Moore, ph-cf	2	0	0	0	0	0	1	0
B.Herman, 2b	3	0	0	0	0	0	1	3
J.Wilson, c	3	0	1	0	0	0	8	0
B.Whitehead, pr	0	0	0	0	0	0	0	0
G.Hartnett, c	0	0	0	0	0	0	3	0
B.Walker, p	0	0	0	0	0	0	0	0
G.Mancuso, ph	1	0	0	0	0	0	0	0
H.Schumacher, p	1	0	0	0	0	0	0	1
P.Waner, ph	1	0	0	0	0	0	0	0
P.Derringer, p	0	0	0	0	0	0	0	0
D.Dean, p	0	0	0	0	0	0	0	0
Totals	31	1	4	1	2	5	24	8

BATTING
2B: A.Vaughan (off L.Gomez); J.Wilson (off M.Harder).
RBI, scoring position, less than 2 outs: M.Ott 0–2; B.Terry 1–1; W.Berger 0–1.

BASERUNNING
SB: P.Martin (2nd base off L.Gomez / R.Hemsley).
Team LOB: 5

FIELDING
E: P.Martin (throw).

AMERICAN LEAGUE

	ab	r	h	bi	bb	so	po	a
J.Vosmik, rf	4	1	1	0	0	0	1	0
C.Gehringer, 2b	3	0	2	0	1	0	1	3
L.Gehrig, 1b	3	1	0	0	1	0	13	0
J.Foxx, 3b	3	1	2	3	1	1	0	0
O.Bluege, 3b	0	0	0	0	0	0	0	0
B.Johnson, lf	4	0	0	0	0	3	4	0
B.Chapman, lf	0	0	0	0	0	0	0	0
A.Simmons, cf	4	0	2	0	0	2	2	0
D.Cramer, cf	0	0	0	0	0	0	0	0
R.Hemsley, c	4	1	1	0	0	0	6	0
J.Cronin, ss	4	0	0	1	0	1	0	5
L.Gomez, p	2	0	0	0	0	1	0	2
M.Harder, p	1	0	0	0	0	1	0	1
Totals	32	4	8	4	3	9	27	11

BATTING
2B: C.Gehringer (off P.Derringer); A.Simmons (off D.Dean).
3B: R.Hemsley (off B.Walker).
2HR: J.Foxx (1st inning off B.Walker, 1 on, 2 out).
2-out RBI: J.Foxx 3.
RBI, scoring position, less than 2 outs: R.Hemsley 0–2; J.Cronin 1–1.

BASERUNNING
Team LOB: 7

FIELDING

PITCHING	ip	h	r	er	bb	so
National League						
B.Walker (L)	2.0	2	3	3	1	2
H.Schumacher	4.0	4	1	1	1	5
P.Derringer	1.0	1	0	0	0	1
D.Dean	1.0	1	0	0	1	1
American League						
L.Gomez (W)	6.0	3	1	1	2	4
M.Harder (S)	3.0	1	0	0	0	1

Inherited Runners—Scored:
H.Schumacher 0–0; P.Derringer 0–0; D.Dean 0–0; M.Harder 0–0.

GAME DATA—T: 2:06; A: 69812; Temp: Unknown; Wind: Unknown direction, Speed: Unknown

UMPIRES—HP: Red Ormsby (AL), 1B: George Magerkurth (NL), 2B: Harry Geisel (AL), 3B: Ziggy Sears (NL)

STARTING LINEUPS

	National League	American League
1.	P.Martin 3b	J.Vosmik rf
2.	A.Vaughan ss	C.Gehringer 2b
3.	M.Ott rf	L.Gehrig 1b
4.	J.Medwick lf	J.Foxx 3b
5.	B.Terry 1b	B.Johnson lf
6.	W.Berger cf	A.Simmons cf
7.	B.Herman 2b	R.Hemsley c
8.	J.Wilson c	J.Cronin ss
9.	B.Walker p	L.Gomez p

NL 1ST: P.Martin singled; Texas League single; A.Vaughan flied to B.Johnson-lf; P.Martin stole second; M.Ott grounded out (J.Cronin-ss to L.Gehrig-1b) [P.Martin to third]; J.Medwick struck out; 0 R, 1 H, 0 E, 1 LOB. NL 0, AL 0.

AL 1ST: J.Vosmik grounded out (B.Herman-2b to B.Terry-1b); C.Gehringer walked; L.Gehrig forced C.Gehringer (B.Terry-1b to A.Vaughan-ss) [L.Gehrig to first]; J.Foxx homered to leftfield [L.Gehrig scored]; B.Johnson popped to B.Herman-2b; 2 R, 1 H, 0 E, 0 LOB. NL 0, AL 2.

NL 2ND: B.Terry lined to B.Johnson-lf; W.Berger popped to L.Gehrig-1b in foul territory; B.Herman grounded out (L.Gomez-p to L.Gehrig-1b); 0 R, 0 H, 0 E, 0 LOB. NL 0, AL 2.

AL 2ND: A.Simmons struck out; R.Hemsley tripled to left field; J.Cronin flied to W.Berger-cf [R.Hemsley scored]; L.Gomez struck out; 1 R, 1 H, 0 E, 0 LOB. NL 0, AL 3.

NL 3RD: J.Wilson grounded out (C.Gehringer-2b to L.Gehrig-1b); **G.Mancuso batted for B.Walker;** G.Mancuso grounded out (J.Cronin-ss to L.Gehrig-1b); P.Martin struck out; 0 R, 0 H, 0 E, 0 LOB. NL 0, AL 3.

AL 3RD: **H.Schumacher replaced G.Mancuso (pitching);** J.Vosmik grounded out (H.Schumacher-p to B.Terry-1b); C.Gehringer grounded out (B.Herman-2b to B.Terry-1b); L.Gehrig grounded out (B.Herman-2b to B.Terry-1b); 0 R, 0 H, 0 E, 0 LOB. NL 0, AL 3.

NL 4TH: A.Vaughan doubled to right field; M.Ott popped to R.Hemsley-c; J.Medwick walked; B.Terry singled [A.Vaughan scored, J.Medwick to second]; W.Berger struck out; B.Herman flied to B.Johnson-lf; 1 R, 2 H, 0 E, 2 LOB. NL 1, AL 3.

AL 4TH: J.Foxx struck out; B.Johnson struck out; A.Simmons singled to third base [A.Simmons to second (error by P.Martin-3b)]; R.Hemsley grounded out (J.Wilson-c unassisted); 0 R, 1 H, 1 E, 1 LOB. NL 1, AL 3.

NL 5TH: J.Wilson flied to B.Johnson-lf; H.Schumacher grounded out (J.Cronin-ss to L.Gehrig-1b); P.Martin struck out; 0 R, 0 H, 0 E, 0 LOB. NL 1, AL 3.

AL 5TH: Umpires moved: Magerkurth (hp), Geisel (1b), Sears (2b), Orsmby (3b); J.Cronin struck out; L.Gomez grounded out (A.Vaughan-ss to B.Terry-1b); J.Vosmik singled to right field; C.Gehringer singled to right field [J.Vosmik to third]; L.Gehrig walked [C.Gehringer to second]; J.Foxx singled to center field [J.Vosmik scored, C.Gehringer to third, L.Gehrig to second]; B.Johnson struck out; 1 R, 3 H, 0 E, 3 LOB. NL 1, AL 4.

NL 6TH: A.Vaughan walked; M.Ott flied to A.Simmons-cf; J.Medwick flied to J.Vosmik-rf; B.Terry forced A.Vaughan (L.Gomez-p to C.Gehringer-2b) [B.Terry to first]; 0 R, 0 H, 0 E, 1 LOB. NL 1, AL 4.

AL 6TH: **R.Collins replaced B.Terry (playing 1b);** A.Simmons struck out; R.Hemsley popped to R.Collins-1b; J.Cronin flied to M.Ott-rf; 0 R, 0 H, 0 E, 0 LOB. NL 1, AL 4.

NL 7TH: **M.Harder replaced L.Gomez (pitching); J.Moore batted for W.Berger;** J.Moore flied to A.Simmons-cf; B.Herman grounded out (M.Harder-p to L.Gehrig-1b); J.Wilson doubled to right field; **P.Waner batted for H.Schumacher; B.Whitehead ran for J.Wilson;** P.Waner grounded out (C.Gehringer-2b to L.Gehrig-1b); 0 R, 1 H, 0 E, 1 LOB. NL 1, AL 4.

AL 7TH: **J.Moore stayed in game (playing cf); G.Hartnett replaced B.Whitehead (playing c); P.Derringer replaced P.Waner (pitching);** M.Harder struck out; J.Vosmik grounded out (P.Martin-3b to R.Collins-1b); C.Gehringer doubled to right field; off Collin's mitt; L.Gehrig flied to J.Moore-cf; 0 R, 1 H, 0 E, 1 LOB. NL 1, AL 4.

NL 8TH: P.Martin grounded out (J.Cronin-ss to L.Gehrig-1b); A.Vaughan grounded out (J.Cronin-ss to L.Gehrig-1b); M.Ott struck out; 0 R, 0 H, 0 E, 0 LOB. NL 1, AL 4.

AL 8TH: **D.Dean replaced P.Derringer (pitching);** J.Foxx walked; B.Johnson struck out; A.Simmons doubled to right field [J.Foxx to third]; R.Hemsley reached on a fielder's choice (A.Vaughan-ss to G.Hartnett-c) [A.Simmons out at third]; both runners ended up at 3b; J.Cronin popped to A.Vaughan-ss; 0 R, 1 H, 0 E, 2 LOB. NL 1, AL 4.

NL 9TH: **O.Bluege replaced J.Foxx (playing 3b); B.Chapman replaced B.Johnson (playing lf); D.Cramer replaced A.Simmons (playing cf);** J.Medwick popped to L.Gehrig-1b in foul territory; R.Collins grounded out (L.Gehrig-1b unassisted); J.Moore grounded out (C.Gehringer-2b to L.Gehrig-1b); 0 R, 0 H, 0 E, 0 LOB. NL 1, AL 4.

Final Totals	R	H	E	LOB
National League	1	4	1	5
American League	4	8	0	7

GAME 4

Tuesday, July 7, 1936

National League Park, Boston

National League 4, American League 3

SERIES RESULTS: AL 3, NL 1

DiMaggio's Disappointing Debut

Brilliant pitching by Dizzy Dean, Carl Hubbell, and Lon Warneke led the National League to its first All-Star win. The 4–3 triumph, which followed NL losses in each of the first three games, was played in 89-degree weather, Boston's hottest July 7 since 1883. However, while thousands of Bostonians chose to spend the day at nearby beaches, it was not the weather that was responsible for the disappointingly small crowd of 25,534. Nor was it, as some said, that because baseball players and management had treated the last two games as meaningless exhibitions the fans just weren't interested.

The reason for the poor turnout—it remains the lowest-ever attendance at an All-Star Game—was poor planning, explainable, perhaps, because this was Boston's first "showcase game" since the Red Sox had played in the 1918 World Series. The Bees had announced that they had sold seventeen thousand reserved seats and would put the remaining twenty-five thousand unreserved seats on sale the morning of the game. (During the winter, the Braves had changed their name to the Bees. Braves Field was now officially called National League Park, although informally it was known as Bees Field or just the Bee Hive.) Club president Bob Quinn had issued this statement: "We expect that the crowd will number about forty-two thousand. We could probably get more than that into the park if we desired. But I believe in providing comfort for all those who attend and I don't propose to swell the gate by squeezing in a few extra thousands."

Boston club officials also notified the public that to reduce congestion on game day, the Babcock Street entrances to the park would be open for the first time. Nevertheless, fans purchased fewer than nine thousand of those unreserved seats. Evidently, Bostonians had decided they didn't want to wait in what they assumed would be long ticket lines on such a hot day. Of course those lines never

materialized, and large portions of the left- and right-field bleachers remained unoccupied. The real victim of the low turnout was the Association of Professional Baseball Players of America, which received 83½ percent of the proceeds from the game.

Although Boston was then a two-team city, the crowd was decidedly rooting for the National Leaguers, maybe because they were, as usual, the underdogs. "We admit the American League power at bat, but we're going to combat it by great pitching, by speed, and by generally tight defense," said National League manager Charlie Grimm. "And we are not sparing our horses in our effort to win this game," he added. That last sentiment was in line with National League president Ford Frick's position. Frick, stung by three straight losses, felt that in the last two games his league had not always put its best players on the field.

Grimm named two starters strictly because of their superior defensive abilities. He started St. Louis's Leo Durocher at shortstop, ahead of Pittsburgh's Arky Vaughan, the league's defending batting champion and fans' choice, and his own Augie Galan in center, over many other outfielders who had received more votes. Although the leagues had increased the size of the rosters from twenty to twenty-one, the National League had some surprising omissions. Neither Philadelphia's Dolph Camilli nor Boston's Buck Jordan, co-leaders at .348 in the National League batting race, made the team; nor did the eventual batting champion, Pittsburgh's Paul Waner. True to his word not to "spare the horses," Grimm made only two nonpitching substitutions in the game. Both were in the eighth inning: Mel Ott batted for right fielder Frank Demaree, and Lew Riggs batted for third baseman Pinky Whitney.

American League manager Joe McCarthy took a different approach. He said he would try to start the lineup that the fans favored and to play as many men as possible. While Grimm's strategy worked, it left many Bees fans disgruntled. Wally

22

Berger, the Bees' only representative and the starting center fielder in the three previous All-Star Games, didn't get to play. In addition to Galan, Grimm had three other of his Cubs in the starting lineup: second baseman Billy Herman, right fielder Demaree, and catcher Gabby Hartnett. The starters also included four players from the Cardinals and one from the Phillies.

Not surprising for a team that had entered the break with a ten-game lead, McCarthy had seven of his Yankees on the squad and easily could have had nine. Red Rolfe, generally considered the league's best third baseman, wasn't chosen, and Washington outfielder Ben Chapman had been a Yankee before he had been traded to the Senators for Jake Powell three weeks earlier. McCarthy chose to put just two of his Yankees in the starting lineup: first baseman Lou Gehrig, the league's leading hitter, who had also started the previous three games, and twenty-one-year-old Joe DiMaggio, the first rookie ever to start an All-Star Game. In fact, DiMaggio was the first rookie ever named by either league to its All-Star squad. McCarthy's selection of Lefty Grove of Boston, the fans' choice, as his starting pitcher ended the run of three consecutive starts by his own ace Lefty Gomez.

Detroit had repeated as American League pennant winners in 1935, a victory that would have given their manager, Mickey Cochrane, winner of the 1935 game, the privilege of again managing his league's entry. However, Cochrane was in Wyoming recuperating from a nervous breakdown, and because the Yanks were in first place and had finished second to the Tigers in 1935, the league named McCarthy to take Cochrane's place. It was the first All-Star appearance for both McCarthy and Grimm, although each had each led his team to a pennant in 1932. Had it not been for the sentimental choices of Connie Mack and John McGraw, McCarthy and Grimm might have been the managers in the first All-Star Game.

Grimm picked Dean, the Majors' winningest pitcher at 14-4, to start. Dean responded with an overpowering performance, pitching three hitless innings and not allowing a ball out of the infield. He did walk two batters but faced just the minimum nine batters because both runners were erased on the base paths.

Dean got two quick strikes on Luke Appling, the game's first batter, before walking him after Appling wasted half a dozen good pitches by fouling them off. In the second inning, Gehrig walked on four pitches, several of which Hartnett disputed. Dean picked Gehrig off with a quick throw to his teammate Rip Collins, while Appling was retired as DiMaggio bounced into a double play. The crowd had given DiMaggio a big hand when

he stepped in, but it would be a very disappointing day for the Yankees' rookie sensation. DiMaggio had excited the baseball world with a .358 average since making his big league debut in May, but he would bat five times in this game, each time with one or more runners on base, and fail to get a hit or drive in a run. He also had his problems in the field. He erred on a Herman single in the fifth, which allowed Herman to go to second, drawing some boos from the crowd. Three innings earlier, he'd misplayed into a triple Hartnett's low line drive, one that most observers felt he should have caught or at worst held to a single. Red Sox manager Joe Cronin, a spectator at the game, said afterward that DiMaggio had played the ball "a trifle nonchalantly," while a Boston writer said it would have been "a routine catch for a good outfielder." DiMaggio made no excuses, saying the ball just sunk on him. He also, no doubt, never forgot the criticism.

Hartnett's second-inning triple, following a lead-off single by Demaree and preceding Whitney's scoring fly ball, gave the National League an early two-run lead against Grove. The Nationals added two more in the fifth against Detroit's Schoolboy Rowe, who had replaced Grove an inning earlier. With one out, Galan, now turned around to bat left-handed, homered off the flagpole in right field. After hitting the pole, which served to separate fair and foul territory, the ball caromed into foul ground. The American Leaguers protested, claiming it should be a ground-rule double, the ruling for such hits in many AL parks. The umpires (three of whom—Bill Stewart, Beans Reardon, and Bill Summers—were Massachusetts natives) correctly stayed with their ruling of a home run. Herman's single and his advancement to second on DiMaggio's error followed, and after Collins walked, Joe Medwick scored Herman with a single to left.

Meanwhile, Hubbell, the Giants' great left-hander, replaced Dean in the fourth and continued the same mastery over the American Leaguers that he'd shown at the Polo Grounds in 1934. He pitched three more scoreless innings, allowing just two hits (singles by Charlie Gehringer and Rip Radcliff) and a walk (to Gehringer). In the seventh, still leading 4–0, Grimm called on right-hander Curt Davis, whom he'd acquired in a May 21 trade with the Phillies, to wind it up. Before the game, some National Leaguers had felt that Grimm would start Davis because his unusual delivery might baffle the American League hitters. Davis, however, proved no mystery to the Americans. Gehrig, hitless in ten previous All-Star at bats, greeted him with a long home run to right. Then, after Davis got Earl Averill and pinch hitter

Bill Dickey on ground balls, the Americans loaded the bases on singles by Goose Goslin and pinch hitter Jimmie Foxx and a walk to pinch hitter George Selkirk. Appling's single to right scored Goslin and Foxx, making the score 4–3 and finishing Davis.

Grimm brought in Warneke, another of his Cubs' pitchers, who immediately walked Gehringer to reload the bases. That brought DiMaggio to the plate with a chance to redeem himself. He didn't, but only because Durocher was standing in the right place and managed to hold on to a scorching line drive that appeared to be headed safely to left field. The American Leaguers mounted another rally in the eighth. They had runners at first and third with two out and Foxx at the plate. But Foxx, already immensely popular in his first season in Boston, struck out, dashing the hopes of the American League fans. A final chance came in the ninth when Gehringer doubled with two outs. Once again, DiMaggio came up with a chance to tie the score, but Joe popped weakly to Herman to end the game.

Commissioner Kenesaw Mountain Landis, who had attended the game, later said "it was a bully game," and it "maintained the standard of the All-Star Games. I hope we shall see many more like it. . . . These games are good for baseball."

Former National League star Johnny Evers, who had come from his home in Troy, New York, to see the game, called it "a splendid contest between two great ball teams."

American League president Will Harridge was gracious in defeat. "We cannot reasonably expect to win all these games," he said. "We already had won our share, and a defeat under these circumstances is nothing to cause despondency." McCarthy was less gracious, attributing the American League's loss to its getting "the worst of the breaks," citing as examples Durocher's grab of DiMaggio's liner and Galan's contested home run.

Frick and Grimm praised their league's efforts, with Grimm singling out Dean for his great pitching. However, Dean, almost never gracious in victory or defeat, said he could have done better. He complained about his two walks and his own failure to get a base hit.

	AL		NL	
P	Lefty Grove	BOS	Dizzy Dean	SLN
C	Rick Ferrell	BOS	Gabby Hartnett	CHN
1B	Lou Gehrig	NYA	Ripper Collins	SLN
2B	Charlie Gehringer	DET	Billy Herman	CHN
3B	Mike Higgins	PHA	Pinky Whitney	PHI
SS	Luke Appling	CHA	Leo Durocher	SLN
OF	Earl Averill	CLE	Frank Demaree	CHN
OF	Joe DiMaggio	NYA	Augie Galan	CHN
OF	Rip Radcliff	CHA	Joe Medwick	SLN
	Tommy Bridges +	DET	Wally Berger	BSN
	Ben Chapman	WAS	Curt Davis	CHN
	Frankie Crosetti	NYA	Carl Hubbell	NY
	Bill Dickey	NYA	Ernie Lombardi	CIN
	Jimmie Foxx	BOS	Stu Martin	SLN
	Lefty Gomez	NYA	Jo-Jo Moore	NY
	Goose Goslin	DET	Van Mungo	BRO
	Mel Harder	CLE	Mel Ott	NY
	Rollie Hemsley	SLA	Lew Riggs	CIN
	Vern Kennedy	CHA	Gus Suhr	PIT
	Monte Pearson	NYA	Arky Vaughan	PIT
	Schoolboy Rowe	DET	Lon Warneke	CHN
	George Selkirk	NYA		

+ player replaced on roster

| American League | 000 000 300- | 3 |
| National League | 020 020 00x- | 4 |

AMERICAN LEAGUE

	ab	r	h	bi	bb	so	po	a
L.Appling, ss	4	0	1	2	1	0	2	2
C.Gehringer, 2b	3	0	2	0	2	0	2	1
J.DiMaggio, rf	5	0	0	0	0	0	1	0
L.Gehrig, 1b	2	1	1	1	2	0	7	0
E.Averill, cf	3	0	0	0	0	0	3	1
B.Chapman, cf	1	0	0	0	0	0	0	0
R.Ferrell, c	2	0	0	0	0	2	4	0
B.Dickey, ph-c	2	0	0	0	0	0	2	0
R.Radcliff, lf	2	0	1	0	0	0	2	0
G.Goslin, lf	1	1	1	0	1	0	1	0
M.Higgins, 3b	2	0	0	0	0	2	0	1
J.Foxx, ph-3b	2	1	1	0	0	1	0	1
L.Grove, p	1	0	0	0	0	1	0	0
S.Rowe, p	1	0	0	0	0	0	0	0
G.Selkirk, ph	0	0	0	0	1	0	0	0
M.Harder, p	0	0	0	0	0	0	0	1
F.Crosetti, ph	1	0	0	0	0	1	0	0
Totals	32	3	7	3	7	7	24	7

BATTING
2B: C.Gehringer (off L.Warneke).
HR: L.Gehrig (7th inning off C.Davis, 0 on, 0 out).
2-out RBI: L.Appling 2.
RBI, scoring position, less than 2 outs: B.Dickey 0–1.
GDP: J.DiMaggio.

BASERUNNING
Team LOB: 9

FIELDING
E: J.DiMaggio.
Outfield assist: E.Averill (L.Durocher at 2B).
DP: (1). M.Higgins-C.Gehringer-L.Gehrig.

NATIONAL LEAGUE

	ab	r	h	bi	bb	so	po	a
A.Galan, cf	4	1	1	1	0	2	1	0
B.Herman, 2b	3	1	2	0	1	0	4	4
R.Collins, 1b	2	0	0	0	2	0	9	1
J.Medwick, lf	4	0	1	1	0	0	0	0
F.Demaree, rf	3	1	1	0	0	0	1	0
M.Ott, ph-rf	1	0	1	0	0	0	0	0
G.Hartnett, c	4	1	1	1	0	0	7	0
P.Whitney, 3b	3	0	1	1	0	1	0	2
L.Riggs, ph-3b	1	0	0	0	0	1	0	0
L.Durocher, ss	3	0	1	0	0	1	3	0
D.Dean, p	1	0	0	0	0	1	0	2
C.Hubbell, p	1	0	0	0	0	0	2	1
C.Davis, p	0	0	0	0	0	0	0	1
L.Warneke, p	1	0	0	0	0	0	0	0
Totals	31	4	9	4	3	6	27	11

BATTING
3B: G.Hartnett (off L.Grove).
HR: A.Galan (5th inning off S.Rowe, 0 on, 1 out).
RBI, scoring position, less than 2 outs: J.Medwick 1–1;
   F.Demaree 0–1; P.Whitney 1–1.
GDP: F.Demaree.

BASERUNNING
Team LOB: 6

FIELDING
PB: G.Hartnett.
DP: (1). P.Whitney-B.Herman-R.Collins.

PITCHING	ip	h	r	er	bb	so
American League						
L.Grove (L)	3.0	3	2	2	2	2
S.Rowe	3.0	4	2	2	1	2
M.Harder	2.0	2	0	0	0	2
National League						
D.Dean (W)	3.0	0	0	0	2	3
C.Hubbell	3.0	2	0	0	1	2
C.Davis	0.2	4	3	3	1	0
L.Warneke (S)	2.1	1	0	0	3	2

Inherited Runners—Scored:
   S.Rowe 0–0; M.Harder 0–0; C.Hubbell 0–0; C.Davis
   0–0; L.Warneke 2–0.

GAME DATA—T: 2:00; A: 25556; Temp: Unknown; Wind: Unknown direction, Speed: Unknown

UMPIRES—HP: Beans Reardon (NL), 1B: Bill Summers (AL), 2B: Bill Stewart (NL), 3B: Lou Kolls (AL)

STARTING LINEUPS

American League	*National League*
1. L.Appling ss	A.Galan cf
2. C.Gehringer 2b	B.Herman 2b
3. J.DiMaggio rf	R.Collins 1b
4. L.Gehrig 1b	J.Medwick lf
5. E.Averill cf	F.Demaree rf
6. R.Ferrell c	G.Hartnett c
7. R.Radcliff lf	P.Whitney 3b
8. M.Higgins 3b	L.Durocher ss
9. L.Grove p	D.Dean p

AL 1ST: L.Appling walked; C.Gehringer popped to L.Durocher-ss; J.DiMaggio grounded into a double play (P.Whitney-3b to B.Herman-2b to R.Collins-1b) [L.Appling out at second]; 0 R, 0 H, 0 E, 0 LOB. AL 0, NL 0.

NL 1ST: A.Galan was called out on strikes; B.Herman flied to J.DiMaggio-rf; R.Collins walked; J.Medwick flied to E.Averill-cf; 0 R, 0 H, 0 E, 1 LOB. AL 0, NL 0.

AL 2ND: L.Gehrig walked; E.Averill popped to B.Herman-2b; R.Ferrell was called out on strikes; L.Gehrig was picked off first (D.Dean-p to R.Collins-1b); 0 R, 0 H, 0 E, 0 LOB. AL 0, NL 0.

NL 2ND: F.Demaree singled to left field (it was the 0–1 pitch); G.Hartnett tripled to right field (it was the 3–1 pitch) [F.Demaree scored]; P.Whitney lined to E.Averill-cf [G.Hartnett scored]; L.Durocher singled to center field (E.Averill-cf to L.Appling-ss) [L.Durocher out at second]; D.Dean struck out; 2 R, 3 H, 0 E, 0 LOB. AL 0, NL 2.

AL 3RD: R.Radcliff grounded out (D.Dean-p to R.Collins-1b); M.Higgins struck out; L.Grove struck out; 0 R, 0 H, 0 E, 0 LOB. AL 0, NL 2.

NL 3RD: A.Galan flied to E.Averill-cf; B.Herman walked; R.Collins flied to R.Radcliff-lf; J.Medwick lined to R.Radcliff-lf; 0 R, 0 H, 0 E, 1 LOB. AL 0, NL 2.

AL 4TH: **C.Hubbell replaced D.Dean (pitching);** L.Appling flied to F.Demaree-rf in foul territory; C.Gehringer singled to right field (it was the first pitch); J.DiMaggio popped to L.Durocher-ss; G.Hartnett allowed a passed ball [C.Gehringer to second]; L.Gehrig grounded out (R.Collins-1b to C.Hubbell-p); 0 R, 1 H, 0 E, 1 LOB. AL 0, NL 2.

NL 4TH: **S.Rowe replaced L.Grove (pitching);** F.Demaree popped to L.Gehrig-1b in foul territory; G.Hartnett grounded out (L.Appling-ss to L.Gehrig-1b); P.Whitney singled to center field (it was the 2–2 pitch); L.Durocher struck out; 0 R, 1 H, 0 E, 1 LOB. AL 0, NL 2.

AL 5TH: E.Averill popped to B.Herman-2b; R.Ferrell struck out; R.Radcliff singled to center field (it

was the 0–2 pitch); M.Higgins was called out on strikes; 0 R, 1 H, 0 E, 1 LOB. AL 0, NL 2.

NL 5TH: Umpires move: Summers (hp), Stewart (1b), Kolls (2b), Reard; C.Hubbell popped to C.Gehringer-2b; A.Galan homered to deep rightfield; Umpire Stewart called it foul, overruled by Reardon; B.Herman singled to right field [B.Herman to second (error by J.DiMaggio-rf)]; R.Collins walked; J.Medwick singled to left field [B.Herman scored, R.Collins to third]; F.Demaree grounded into a double play (M.Higgins-3b to C.Gehringer-2b to L.Gehrig-1b) [J.Medwick out at second]; 2 R, 3 H, 1 E, 1 LOB. AL 0, NL 4.

AL 6TH: S.Rowe popped to C.Hubbell-p; L.Appling flied to A.Galan-cf; C.Gehringer walked; J.DiMaggio grounded out (C.Hubbell-p to R.Collins-1b); 0 R, 0 H, 0 E, 1 LOB. AL 0, NL 4.

NL 6TH: **G.Goslin replaced R.Radcliff (playing lf);** G.Hartnett grounded out (L.Appling-ss to L.Gehrig-1b); P.Whitney was called out on strikes; L.Durocher popped to L.Gehrig-1b; 0 R, 0 H, 0 E, 0 LOB. AL 0, NL 4.

AL 7TH: **C.Davis replaced C.Hubbell (pitching);** L.Gehrig homered to deep rightfield (it was the 1–1 pitch); Gehrig's first All-Star hit, landed halfway up the rf stand; E.Averill grounded out (B.Herman-2b to R.Collins-1b); **B.Dickey batted for R.Ferrell;** B.Dickey grounded out (C.Davis-p to R.Collins-1b); G.Goslin singled to second base; **J.Foxx batted for M.Higgins;** J.Foxx singled to shortstop (it was the 1–2 pitch) [G.Goslin to second]; **G.Selkirk batted for S.Rowe;** G.Selkirk walked [G.Goslin to third, J.Foxx to second]; L.Appling singled to right field (it was the 2–2 pitch) [G.Goslin scored, J.Foxx scored, G.Selkirk to second]; **L.Warneke replaced C.Davis (pitching);** C.Gehringer walked [G.Selkirk to third, L.Appling to second]; J.DiMaggio lined to L.Durocher-ss; 3 R, 4 H, 0 E, 3 LOB. AL 3, NL 4.

NL 7TH: **J.Foxx stayed in game (playing 3b); B.Dickey stayed in game (playing c); M.Harder replaced G.Selkirk (pitching); B.Chapman replaced E.Averill (playing cf);** L.Warneke grounded out (M.Harder-p to L.Gehrig-1b); A.Galan struck out; B.Herman singled to center field; R.Collins flied to G.Goslin-lf; 0 R, 1 H, 0 E, 1 LOB. AL 3, NL 4.

AL 8TH: L.Gehrig walked; B.Chapman grounded out (P.Whitney-3b to R.Collins-1b) [L.Gehrig to second]; B.Dickey grounded out (B.Herman-2b to R.Collins-1b) [L.Gehrig to third]; G.Goslin walked; J.Foxx struck out; 0 R, 0 H, 0 E, 2 LOB. AL 3, NL 4.

NL 8TH: J.Medwick grounded out (J.Foxx-3b to L.Gehrig-1b); **M.Ott batted for F.Demaree;** M.Ott singled to center field (it was the 3–2 pitch); G.Hartnett lined to L.Appling-ss; **L.Riggs batted for P.Whitney;** L.Riggs was called out on strikes; 0 R, 1 H, 0 E, 1 LOB. AL 3, NL 4.

AL 9TH: **M.Ott stayed in game (playing rf);** **L.Riggs stayed in game (playing 3b);** **F.Crosetti batted for M.Harder;** F.Crosetti struck out; L.Appling grounded out (B.Herman-2b to R.Collins-1b); C.Gehringer doubled to left field (it was the 2–2 pitch); J.DiMaggio popped to B.Herman-2b; 0 R, 1 H, 0 E, 1 LOB. AL 3, NL 4.

Final Totals	R	H	E	LOB
American League	3	7	1	9
National League	4	9	0	6

Wednesday, July 7, 1937

Griffith Stadium, Washington DC

American League 8, National League 3

SERIES RESULTS: AL 4, NL 1

FDR Sees Yanks Bomb the NL

Rumors had circulated earlier in the week that this year's All-Star Game at Washington might be the last because the novelty of this midsummer battle between the stars of the two leagues had worn off. Evidently, Franklin D. Roosevelt, the president of the United States, didn't agree. After making his pregame entrance in an open car, the president threw out the first ball. He then sat in his unprotected box seat while cheering the American Leaguers to an easy 8–3 victory. Despite the scorching heat, typical of the nation's capital in July, the president, his entourage, and the 31,391 other fans that filled Griffith Stadium had a thoroughly enjoyable afternoon. Among those seated with FDR were Senators owner Clark Griffith, Postmaster General James Farley, and WPA administrator Harry Hopkins.

After having their three-game winning streak stopped the year before, the American League rang up its easiest victory to date. And although it was officially a league victory, most of the damage was done by members of the defending world champion New York Yankees. So dominant were the Yankees — they had entered the break with a five-and-a-half-game lead — some observers suggested that there were now three Major Leagues: the American, the National, and the Yankees.

Five of manager Joe McCarthy's Yanks were in the starting lineup; the only one he would replace would be pitcher Lefty Gomez — and he had no choice about that. Gomez had allowed just one base runner, a two-out, first-inning single by Arky Vaughan, but the All-Star rules allowed him to pitch no more than three innings. It wasn't only Yankee starters that McCarthy kept in for the entire game; he didn't replace any of his starting position players, which was the first time that had happened — and undoubtedly the last.

Earlier, the Yankee manager had generated some ill feeling in Washington when he chose Sam West of the Browns to replace injured Tigers out-fielder Gee Walker on the American League team. The *Washington Post* had telegraphed league president Will Harridge, asking him to replace Walker with the Senators' best outfielder, John Stone. Harridge didn't receive the message until McCarthy had already made his selection, and while Stone, at .326, was outhitting three of the outfielders chosen, West, at .358, wasn't one of these three. McCarthy did have three Senators on his squad but didn't use any of them. It was the second consecutive game in which a manager had failed to use a hometown player.

Beyond this disappointment to the local populace, there was also a feeling of dissatisfaction in all big league cities over the inability of the fans to have a voice in the teams' selections. Commissioner Kenesaw Mountain Landis and the league presidents, claiming that they wanted a test of the baseball ability of the two leagues rather than an exhibition of stars, had eliminated all fan participation. The 1937 selections were made by the two managers, although each based his choices on recommendations from the league's seven other managers.

Gomez had now started four of the five games played, missing only the 1936 game, the one year the AL lost. His opponent was Dizzy Dean, who was making his second consecutive All-Star start and the third in a row and fourth in five years by a Cardinal. Dean, as he always tried to do, had made himself the pregame center of attention. The Cardinals had been playing in Chicago, and after their last game there, Dean had announced that — rather than go to Washington — he was heading home.

"I'd like to do something for myself for a change," he proclaimed. "All I've been doing is running here and there for somebody else, and I'm sick and tired of it all. Not only that, I've got a sore arm."

But of course Dean, a shameless self-promoter who wouldn't miss a chance to be in the national spotlight, shrugged off his earlier statement. "I never said I wouldn't play," he said. "I can't imagine where that story originated."

Yankee players drove in seven of the American League's eight runs, beginning with Lou Gehrig's two-run homer in the third. Gehrig's blast came with two down as Dean was just one out away from completing three scoreless innings. However, Dean couldn't get past the Yankees' Joe DiMaggio, who lined a single to center. Dean had struck Gehrig out in a similar situation in the first inning: two men out and DiMaggio (via a walk) on first. Gehrig went down swinging while chasing a curve ball, and Dean left the mound grinning.

On this inning's at bat, however, the grin would belong to Gehrig. After hitting one ball over the right-field wall that went foul, the count went to 3-2. Catcher Gabby Hartnett called for another curve ball, but Dean shook him off, intent on throwing his fastball by Gehrig. He failed to do so. The Yankee slugger drove Dean's fastball over that same wall, and this time it was in fair territory. As he crossed the plate behind DiMaggio, Gehrig, with a big smile on his face, waved his cap to the president. The next batter was Cleveland center fielder Earl Averill. (McCarthy was playing his own center fielder, DiMaggio, in right.) Averill ripped a line drive through the middle that caromed off Dean's foot to second baseman Billy Herman, who threw Averill out.

In the fourth, Herman's single and Joe Medwick's double off Detroit's Tommy Bridges cut the lead to 2–1. Medwick, in the midst of a triple crown season, would have an outstanding day despite the NL's loss. He became the first player to get four hits in an All-Star Game, two of which were doubles, tying Al Simmons's 1934 mark.

The Americans roared back against Carl Hubbell in the home fourth to score three runs and increase their lead to 5–1. Hubbell had held the American Leaguers scoreless over eight innings in three previous games but was unable to exhibit that command this afternoon. Two runs scored when Yankee third baseman Red Rolfe tripled to right-center, driving in Bill Dickey, who had walked, and West, who had singled. Charlie Gehringer of the Tigers brought Rolfe home with one of his three singles, the American League's only RBI not delivered by a Yankee. NL manager Bill Terry removed Hubbell for Pittsburgh's Cy Blanton, who got the third out by fanning DiMaggio.

The Nationals again picked up single runs against Bridges in both the fifth and the sixth. Mel Ott batted for Blanton in the fifth and doubled, sending Hartnett, who had opened the inning with a single, to third. Hartnett scored on a fly ball by Paul Waner. Singles by Medwick and Chicago's Frank Demaree and a scoring fly by Cardinals first

baseman Johnny Mize produced the run in the sixth. They might have had more that inning were it not for a great throw by DiMaggio. With two out and Burgess Whitehead at first, Dick Bartell reached on an error by Rolfe. It was the second error for Rolfe, who committed the only two made in the game. With the two Giants, Whitehead and Bartell, aboard, Rip Collins of the Cubs, batting for pitcher Lee Grissom of the Reds, singled to right. Whitehead tried to score, but DiMaggio's perfect toss from deep right field nailed him at the plate.

In all, Bridges allowed all three runs the Nationals would get and seven of their thirteen hits. Mel Harder of the Indians replaced Bridges in the seventh, and although he allowed five hits, he kept the NL from scoring. Harder's three scoreless innings ran his remarkable All-Star consecutive-inning scoreless streak to thirteen.

Meanwhile, the Americans had added a run off Grissom in the sixth. After Gehrig and Averill had struck out, Grissom had yielded back-to-back doubles to Joe Cronin and Dickey. The AL scored its final two runs in the sixth when Rolfe and Gehringer rode home on Gehrig's long double to center field. As with their six previous runs, the Americans had scored these two runs after two batters were out. The runs came against Brooklyn's Van Mungo, who had boasted before the game: "I can pitch against American Leaguers with a case of paralysis."

The AL had two on with two out again in the eighth, but Cincinnati's Bucky Walters ended that threat by getting DiMaggio to foul out to third baseman Vaughan. Despite his leaving the two runners on, it had been a most satisfying day for DiMaggio, following his poor performance as a rookie in the 1936 game.

Although Vaughan was still Pittsburgh's regular shortstop, Terry had his own man, Bartell, playing there this afternoon. Terry had asked Vaughan beforehand if he would be willing to play third. When Vaughan said yes, Terry bypassed all the other third basemen in the league and used him there for the entire game. In accepting the switch to third, Vaughan became the first All-Star to start at two different positions.

Gomez was the winner, giving him three All-Star victories, which is still the record. In fact, to this day no other American League pitcher has even won twice. Unduly impressed, Gomez said after the game that he would trade those three All-Star wins for three victories in regular season competition. Nevertheless, Gomez and the rest of the Yankee players may have taken particular pleasure in this victory. The National Leaguers had upset them by having only ten of their All-Stars as contributors to the Association of Professional Baseball Players of America, the charity that paid the medical bills for old-time players and that was the beneficiary of this game. Every player on both the Yankees and the host Washington Senators was a member, as was every other AL All-Star with the exception of Bridges.

Over in the losers' clubhouse, the National Leaguers were still insisting that their league had the better players. Many of them (the gentlemanly Hubbell was an exception) claimed they had been victims of bad breaks. Surprisingly, while also claiming NL superiority, Dean (usually ready with an alibi) nevertheless took responsibility for the Gehrig home run that had started the rout.

"I shook Hartnett off twice and was belted each time," Dean said. "He wanted a curve with Gehrig up there in the third and I shook him off, sending up a fast one instead, and Gehrig hit a homer."

The American Leaguers were particularly happy to defeat the loudmouthed Dean, the man who had beaten them in 1936. Dean had pitched in each of the last four All-Star Games, but though he was only twenty-seven years old, this would be his last. The ball Averill had hit off his left foot for the final out of the third inning had broken his big toe. When Dean tried to pitch again before the toe had fully healed, he injured his right shoulder and was never again as effective. Coincidentally, Harder, who like Dean had pitched in the last four games, would also never make another All-Star appearance. He would pitch for Cleveland for ten more seasons but would never get another chance to add to that thirteen-inning scoreless streak.

	AL		NL	
P	Lefty Gomez	NYA	Dizzy Dean	SLN
C	Bill Dickey	NYA	Gabby Hartnett	CHN
1B	Lou Gehrig	NYA	Johnny Mize	SLN
2B	Charlie Gehringer	DET	Billy Herman	CHN
3B	Red Rolfe	NYA	Arky Vaughan	PIT
SS	Joe Cronin	BOS	Dick Bartell	NY
OF	Earl Averill	CLE	Frank Demaree	CHN
OF	Joe DiMaggio	NYA	Joe Medwick	SLN
OF	Gee Walker +	DET	Paul Waner	PIT
	Beau Bell	SLA	Cy Blanton	PIT
	Tommy Bridges	DET	Ripper Collins	CHN
	Harlond Clift	SLA	Lee Grissom	CIN
	Doc Cramer	BOS	Carl Hubbell	NY
	Rick Ferrell	WAS	Billy Jurges	CHN
	Wes Ferrell	WAS	Ernie Lombardi	CIN
	Jimmie Foxx	BOS	Gus Mancuso	NY
	Hank Greenberg	DET	Pepper Martin	SLN
	Lefty Grove	BOS	Gene Moore	BSN
	Mel Harder	CLE	Jo-Jo Moore	NY
	Wally Moses	PHA	Van Mungo	BRO
	Johnny Murphy	NYA	Mel Ott	NY
	Buddy Myer	WAS	Bucky Walters	PHI
	Luke Sewell	CHA	Burgess Whitehead	NY
	Monty Stratton +	CHA		
	Sam West	SLA		

+ player replaced on roster

```
National League    000  111  000-  3
American League    002  312  00x-  8
```

NATIONAL LEAGUE

	ab	r	h	bi	bb	so	po	a
P.Waner, rf	5	0	0	1	0	0	1	0
B.Herman, 2b	5	1	2	0	0	0	1	3
A.Vaughan, 3b	5	0	2	0	0	0	3	0
J.Medwick, lf	5	1	4	1	0	0	1	0
F.Demaree, cf	5	0	1	0	0	0	2	1
J.Mize, 1b	4	0	0	1	0	0	7	0
G.Hartnett, c	3	1	1	0	0	0	6	0
B.Whitehead, pr	0	0	0	0	0	0	0	0
G.Mancuso, c	1	0	0	0	0	0	1	0
D.Bartell, ss	4	0	1	0	0	0	2	3
D.Dean, p	1	0	0	0	0	0	0	1
C.Hubbell, p	0	0	0	0	0	0	0	0
C.Blanton, p	0	0	0	0	0	0	0	0
M.Ott, ph	1	0	1	0	0	0	0	0
L.Grissom, p	0	0	0	0	0	0	0	0
R.Collins, ph	1	0	1	0	0	0	0	0
V.Mungo, p	0	0	0	0	0	0	0	1
J.Moore, ph	1	0	0	0	0	0	0	0
B.Walters, p	0	0	0	0	0	0	0	0
Totals	41	3	13	3	0	0	24	9

BATTING
2B: J.Medwick 2 (off T.Bridges; off M.Harder); M.Ott (off T.Bridges).
RBI, scoring position, less than 2 outs: P.Waner 1–2; J.Medwick 1–1; F.Demaree 0–1; J.Mize 1–1.

BASERUNNING
Team LOB: 11

FIELDING
Outfield assist: F.Demaree (L.Gehrig at 3B).
DP: (1). D.Bartell-J.Mize.

AMERICAN LEAGUE

	ab	r	h	bi	bb	so	po	a
R.Rolfe, 3b	4	2	2	2	1	0	0	2
C.Gehringer, 2b	5	1	3	1	0	0	2	5
J.DiMaggio, rf	4	1	1	0	1	2	1	1
L.Gehrig, 1b	4	1	2	4	0	2	11	1
E.Averill, cf	3	0	1	0	1	1	2	0
J.Cronin, ss	4	1	1	0	0	0	3	4
B.Dickey, c	3	1	2	1	1	0	2	0
S.West, lf	4	1	1	0	0	0	5	0
L.Gomez, p	1	0	0	0	0	1	0	0
T.Bridges, p	1	0	0	0	0	1	0	1
J.Foxx, ph	1	0	0	0	0	0	0	0
M.Harder, p	1	0	0	0	0	0	1	1
Totals	35	8	13	8	4	7	27	15

BATTING
2B: J.Cronin (off L.Grissom); B.Dickey (off L.Grissom); L.Gehrig (off V.Mungo).
3B: R.Rolfe (off C.Hubbell).
HR: L.Gehrig (3rd inning off D.Dean, 1 on, 2 out).
2-out RBI: R.Rolfe 2; C.Gehringer; L.Gehrig 4; B.Dickey.
RBI, scoring position, less than 2 outs: J.DiMaggio 0–1; S.West 0–1; T.Bridges 0–1.

BASERUNNING
Team LOB: 7

FIELDING
E: R.Rolfe (dropped liner); R.Rolfe (fumble).
Outfield assist: J.DiMaggio (B.Whitehead at HP).

PITCHING	ip	h	r	er	bb	so
National League						
D.Dean (L)	3.0	4	2	2	1	2
C.Hubbell	0.2	3	3	3	1	1
C.Blanton	0.1	0	0	0	0	1
L.Grissom	1.0	2	1	1	0	2
V.Mungo	2.0	2	2	2	2	1
B.Walters	1.0	2	0	0	0	0
American League						
L.Gomez (w)	3.0	1	0	0	0	0
T.Bridges	3.0	7	3	3	0	0
M.Harder (s)	3.0	5	0	0	0	0

Inherited Runners—Scored:
C.Hubbell 0–0; C.Blanton 1–0; L.Grissom 0–0; V.Mungo 0–0; B.Walters 0–0; T.Bridges 0–0; M.Harder 0–0.

GAME DATA—T: 2:30; A: 31391; Temp: Unknown; Wind: Unknown direction, Speed: Unknown

UMPIRES—HP: Bill McGowan (AL), 1B: Babe Pinelli (NL), 2B: John Quinn (AL), 3B: George Barr (NL)

STARTING LINEUPS

National League	*American League*
1. P.Waner rf	R.Rolfe 3b
2. B.Herman 2b	C.Gehringer 2b
3. A.Vaughan 3b	J.DiMaggio rf
4. J.Medwick lf	L.Gehrig 1b
5. F.Demaree cf	E.Averill cf
6. J.Mize 1b	J.Cronin ss
7. G.Hartnett c	B.Dickey c
8. D.Bartell ss	S.West lf
9. D.Dean p	L.Gomez p

NL 1ST: P.Waner grounded out (R.Rolfe-3b to L.Gehrig-1b); B.Herman popped to B.Dickey-c in foul territory; A.Vaughan singled to center field; J.Medwick forced A.Vaughan (J.Cronin-ss to C.Gehringer-2b) [J.Medwick to first]; 0 R, 1 H, 0 E, 1 LOB. NL 0, AL 0.

AL 1ST: R.Rolfe grounded out (J.Mize-1b unassisted); C.Gehringer lined to D.Bartell-ss; J.DiMaggio walked; L.Gehrig struck out; 0 R, 0 H, 0 E, 1 LOB. NL 0, AL 0.

NL 2ND: F.Demaree flied to E.Averill-cf; J.Mize flied to S.West-lf; G.Hartnett grounded out (C.Gehringer-2b to L.Gehrig-1b); 0 R, 0 H, 0 E, 0 LOB. NL 0, AL 0.

AL 2ND: E.Averill singled to right field; J.Cronin flied to P.Waner-rf; B.Dickey singled to the shortstop side of second [E.Averill to second]; S.West flied to F.Demaree-cf; L.Gomez struck out; 0 R, 2 H, 0 E, 2 LOB. NL 0, AL 0.

NL 3RD: D.Bartell grounded out (J.Cronin-ss to L.Gehrig-1b); D.Dean flied to J.DiMaggio-rf; P.Waner flied to S.West-lf; 0 R, 0 H, 0 E, 0 LOB. NL 0, AL 0.

AL 3RD: R.Rolfe grounded out (D.Bartell-ss to J.Mize-1b); C.Gehringer grounded out (B.Herman-2b to J.Mize-1b); J.DiMaggio singled to center field; L.Gehrig homered to deep rightfield [J.DiMaggio scored]; E.Averill grounded out (D.Dean-p to B.Herman-2b to J.Mize-1b); 2 R, 2 H, 0 E, 0 LOB. NL 0, AL 2.

NL 4TH: Dean suffered broken toe on line drive; **T.Bridges replaced L.Gomez (pitching);** B.Herman singled to left field; A.Vaughan grounded out (T.Bridges-p to L.Gehrig-1b) [B.Herman to second]; J.Medwick doubled to short leftfield down the line [B.Herman scored]; F.Demaree popped to C.Gehringer-2b; J.Mize grounded out (J.Cronin-ss to L.Gehrig-1b); 1 R, 2 H, 0 E, 1 LOB. NL 1, AL 2.

AL 4TH: **C.Hubbell replaced D.Dean (pitching);** J.Cronin flied to J.Medwick-lf; B.Dickey walked; S.West singled [B.Dickey to third]; T.Bridges struck out; R.Rolfe tripled to right field

[B.Dickey scored, S.West scored]; C.Gehringer singled to deep between first and second [R.Rolfe scored]; **C.Blanton replaced C.Hubbell (pitching);** J.DiMaggio struck out; 3 R, 3 H, 0 E, 1 LOB. NL 1, AL 5.

NL 5TH: G.Hartnett singled to center field; D.Bartell flied to S.West-lf; **M.Ott batted for C.Blanton;** M.Ott doubled to right field [G.Hartnett to third]; P.Waner flied to S.West-lf [G.Hartnett scored]; B.Herman reached on an error by R.Rolfe-3b [M.Ott to third, B.Herman to first]; A.Vaughan popped to L.Gehrig-1b in foul territory; 1 R, 2 H, 1 E, 2 LOB. NL 2, AL 5.

AL 5TH: Umpires moved: Barr (hp), Quinn (1b), Pinelli (2b), McGowan; **L.Grissom replaced M.Ott (pitching);** L.Gehrig struck out; E.Averill struck out; J.Cronin doubled to right field; B.Dickey doubled to center field [J.Cronin scored]; S.West popped to A.Vaughan-3b; 1 R, 2 H, 0 E, 1 LOB. NL 2, AL 6.

NL 6TH: J.Medwick singled to right field; F.Demaree singled to left field [J.Medwick to third]; J.Mize flied to E.Averill-cf [J.Medwick scored]; G.Hartnett forced F.Demaree (C.Gehringer-2b to J.Cronin-ss) [G.Hartnett to first]; **B.Whitehead ran for G.Hartnett;** D.Bartell reached on an error by R.Rolfe-3b [B.Whitehead to second, D.Bartell to first]; **R.Collins batted for L.Grissom;** R.Collins singled to right field (J.DiMaggio-rf to B.Dickey-c) [B.Whitehead out at home, D.Bartell to third (on throw home)]; 1 R, 3 H, 1 E, 2 LOB. NL 3, AL 6.

AL 6TH: **G.Mancuso replaced B.Whitehead (playing c); V.Mungo replaced R.Collins (pitching); J.Foxx batted for T.Bridges;** J.Foxx grounded out (V.Mungo-p to J.Mize-1b); R.Rolfe walked; C.Gehringer singled to left-center [R.Rolfe to second]; J.DiMaggio struck out; L.Gehrig doubled to center field (F.Demaree-cf to D.Bartell-ss to A.Vaughan-3b) [R.Rolfe scored, C.Gehringer scored, L.Gehrig out at third]; 2 R, 2 H, 0 E, 0 LOB. NL 3, AL 8.

NL 7TH: **M.Harder replaced J.Foxx (pitching);** P.Waner grounded out (C.Gehringer-2b to L.Gehrig-1b); B.Herman singled to left field; A.Vaughan forced B.Herman (C.Gehringer-2b to J.Cronin-ss) [A.Vaughan to first]; J.Medwick doubled [A.Vaughan to third]; F.Demaree grounded out (J.Cronin-ss to L.Gehrig-1b); 0 R, 2 H, 0 E, 2 LOB. NL 3, AL 8.

AL 7TH: E.Averill walked; J.Cronin lined into a double play (D.Bartell-ss to J.Mize-1b) [E.Averill out at first]; B.Dickey flied to F.Demaree-cf; 0 R, 0 H, 0 E, 0 LOB. NL 3, AL 8.

NL 8TH: J.Mize flied to S.West-lf; G.Mancuso

grounded out (R.Rolfe-3b to L.Gehrig-1b); D.Bartell singled; **J.Moore batted for V.Mungo;** J.Moore forced D.Bartell (J.Cronin-ss unassisted) [J.Moore to first]; 0 R, 1 H, 0 E, 1 LOB. NL 3, AL 8.

AL 8TH: **B.Walters replaced J.Moore (pitching);** S.West popped to B.Herman-2b; M.Harder grounded out (B.Herman-2b to J.Mize-1b); R.Rolfe singled; C.Gehringer singled [R.Rolfe to third]; J.DiMaggio popped to A.Vaughan-3b in foul territory; 0 R, 2 H, 0 E, 2 LOB. NL 3, AL 8.

NL 9TH: P.Waner grounded out (M.Harder-p to L.Gehrig-1b); B.Herman grounded out (L.Gehrig-1b to M.Harder-p); A.Vaughan singled; J.Medwick singled [A.Vaughan to third]; F.Demaree grounded out (C.Gehringer-2b to L.Gehrig-1b); 0 R, 2 H, 0 E, 2 LOB. NL 3, AL 8.

Final Totals	R	H	E	LOB
National League	3	13	0	11
American League	8	13	2	7

A Scant Sum of Stars

Bill Terry had used as many players as he could when he had managed the National League to losses in 1934 and 1937. But this year he used the same strategy that American League manager Joe McCarthy had employed in 1937; Terry played his starting lineup the entire game, using just twelve players in the NL's 4–1 triumph. The Americans used just fifteen players, and the combined twenty-seven players used by both leagues remains the smallest total ever for an All-Star Game.

Crosley Field, the Major Leagues' smallest park, was completely filled. A crowd of 27,607 had turned out on an exceptionally hot afternoon to see the biggest game played here since the 1919 World Series. Interest in baseball was running extremely high in Cincinnati that year. The Reds were the surprise team of the 1938 season, and their fans were hoping to host another World Series that fall. They had finished last in 1937, but under their new manager, Bill McKechnie, Cincinnati had come into the All-Star Game still in pennant contention.

Befitting their new status as a league power, the Reds had a National League–high five men on the team. Four were in the starting lineup, including pitcher Johnny Vander Meer. The twenty-three-year-old Vander Meer had electrified the baseball world in June by pitching consecutive no-hitters against Boston and Brooklyn, the one against the Dodgers in the first-ever night game at Ebbets Field. Before losing to the Cubs in his last start, Vander Meer had run up a nine-game winning streak. The young left-hander was in only his second big league season and was understandably thrilled to be starting an All-Star Game.

"It's a wonderful honor for me to be on the team, not to mention the distinction of being the starting pitcher," he said.

The fastballing Vander Meer repaid the faith Terry showed in him by pitching three scoreless innings and allowing just one hit, Joe Cronin's lead-off single in the third. Following that hit, Vander Meer retired Washington's Buddy Lewis, the Yankees' Lefty Gomez, and Chicago's Mike Kreevich and left to a roaring ovation.

Bill Lee of the Cubs worked the middle three innings, and he too yielded just one hit, a double by Bill Dickey, while also walking one. Actually, Dickey's hit was a routine pop fly that shortstop Leo Durocher and third baseman Stan Hack couldn't locate in the bright sun. Pittsburgh's Mace Brown pitched the final three innings, surrendering the American League's only run. By that time, the Nationals already had four runs, although only one was earned. The American League pitching trio of Gomez, Cleveland's Johnny Allen, and Boston's Lefty Grove was almost as effective as its NL counterpart, but their teammates' defense betrayed them. The Americans committed four errors, three of which led to the Nationals' three unearned runs.

Gomez, the AL starter in five of the six All-Star Games played, was victimized in the very first inning. With Hack, who had led off with a single, on first, Billy Herman, Hack's Cubs teammate, hit a ground ball that went through the legs of shortstop Cronin. Hack went all the way to third. Reds favorite Ival Goodman couldn't bring him home (Gomez struck him out looking), but Joe Medwick did the job with a fly ball to center fielder Earl Averill. The run would make Gomez the losing pitcher, his first loss to the National League after eight consecutive wins, three in the All-Star Game and five in the World Series.

Allen gave the Nationals just two hits in his three innings; however, these hits came back to back in the fourth and produced the NL's only earned run. Mel Ott smashed a one-out triple off the center-field fence and came home on Ernie Lombardi's sharp single to left. Lombardi, Cincinnati's slow-footed catcher, was leading the league with a .360 batting average and would go on to win both the 1938 NL batting title and the Most Valuable Player Award. By catching the entire game (and losing fourteen pounds in the process),

Lombardi kept Gabby Hartnett from playing; this was the first All-Star Game the Cubs catcher had missed.

Grove was the victim of the National League's two runs in the seventh, the result of the most bizarre play in All-Star history. Reds first baseman Frank McCormick opened the inning with a single to center. Despite having just ninety-nine Major League at bats prior to this season, McCormick was the only first baseman selected for the National League squad. Because of the dissatisfaction shown with the selections made by Terry and McCarthy the previous year, the teams had been picked this year by a vote of all the league managers. Each manager named twenty-three players, and the twenty-three with the most votes were chosen.

Later, Indians first baseman Hal Trosky said he was glad the AL had lost. While complaining about not being picked for the team, Trosky specifically cited the managers' choice of a slumping Lou Gehrig ahead of him. Trosky may have had good reason to be bitter. Between 1934 and 1940, Trosky would average .324, with twenty-nine home runs and 121 RBI, yet he would never make an American League All-Star team. Still, his omissions were easily explained. Trosky was playing first base in the American League at the same time as Gehrig, Jimmie Foxx, and Hank Greenberg.

Durocher, a surprise selection over the Giants' Dick Bartell and the Cubs' Billy Jurges, came to bat with McCormick at first and nobody out. Everyone in the park knew that Durocher, the first Dodger to start an All-Star Game, was up there to move McCormick to second. First baseman Gehrig and third baseman Foxx moved up in anticipation of a bunt. Back in the fifth inning, Gehrig had batted for third baseman Lewis and had replaced him in the lineup. Gehrig, in his sixth and final All-Star Game, took over at first, while Foxx, the starting first baseman, moved over to third.

Durocher's bunt was to the left side, where Foxx fielded it and threw in the direction of first base. With Gehrig charging, it was second baseman Charlie Gehringer's job to cover first. But Gehringer, who was the only player to have started all six games and who had a .529 average for the first five, committed a mental error. He was not where Foxx threw the ball. As the ball headed down the right-field line, with various American Leaguers in pursuit, McCormick and Durocher continued to circle the bases. McCormick scored, and when right fielder Joe DiMaggio's throw sailed over the head of catcher Dickey, Durocher also scored.

Thanks to the throwing errors charged to Foxx and DiMaggio, Durocher's attempted sacrifice bunt had turned into a two-run "home run" and a 4–0 National League lead. The official scorers gave Durocher a hit on the play, while the error they charged to Foxx was in reality caused by Gehringer's failure to cover first base. Grove, looking extremely unhappy, then took matters into his own hands by striking out the next three batters, Brown, Hack, and Herman.

The American League's disastrous seventh inning was made even worse because it came after the team had failed to score in the top of the inning after mounting its first serious threat. Carl Hubbell had been warming up during Lee's stint on the mound, but Terry called instead on Brown. The AL loaded the bases against Brown with two out, and McCarthy, again the AL manager, sent right-handed-hitting Rudy York of the Tigers up to bat for Allen. Hubbell was warming up, but Terry stayed with the right-hander Brown.

The count went to three and two, and with all three runners moving, Brown got York on a swinging third strike. It had been the first suspenseful moment of the game, and the strikeout drew a deafening roar from the fans. York had fanned on a low fastball. Had he let it go, Lombardi said later, it would have been ball four.

A single by DiMaggio and a double by Cronin pushed across a run in the ninth and prevented the normally heavy-hitting American Leaguers from suffering the first All-Star Game shutout. Medwick's outstanding tumbling catch of a long drive to left-center by Dickey, batting between Di-Maggio and Cronin, prevented a possible big inning. Left-hander Hubbell, now joined by Boston right-hander Jim Turner, was throwing more seriously in the bullpen. Nevertheless, Terry stayed with Brown, who got Gehrig to hit a fly ball that Goodman caught against the bleacher wall in right. Brown then got the final out by striking out pinch hitter Bob Johnson.

"I wasn't worried a bit all day," Mel Ott said in a raucous NL clubhouse after the game. "Anytime you've a four-run lead and old Hubbell warming up in the bullpen, the game is as safe as the Federal Reserve Bank."

The National Leaguers still trailed the Americans four All-Star victories to two; however, they pointed out that they had now won two of the last three. Players and executives of the older league had been unhappy at their recent lack of success in All-Star and World Series games. They had set about to play this game with winning, rather than having fun, as their objective, and they had accomplished their goal.

	AL		NL	
P	Lefty Gomez	NYA	Johnny Vander Meer	CIN
C	Bill Dickey	NYA	Ernie Lombardi	CIN
1B	Jimmie Foxx	BOS	Frank McCormick	CIN
2B	Charlie Gehringer	DET	Billy Herman	CHN
3B	Buddy Lewis	WAS	Stan Hack	CHN
SS	Joe Cronin	BOS	Leo Durocher	BRO
OF	Earl Averill	CLE	Ival Goodman	CIN
OF	Joe DiMaggio	NYA	Joe Medwick	SLN
OF	Mike Kreevich	CHA	Mel Ott	NY
	Johnny Allen	CLE	Mace Brown	PIT
	Doc Cramer	BOS	Tony Cuccinello	BSN
	Bob Feller	CLE	Harry Danning	NY
	Rick Ferrell	WAS	Paul Derringer	CIN
	Lou Gehrig	NYA	Gabby Hartnett	CHN
	Hank Greenberg +	DET	Carl Hubbell	NY
	Lefty Grove	BOS	Cookie Lavagetto	BRO
	Bob Johnson	PHA	Bill Lee	CHN
	Vern Kennedy	DET	Hank Leiber	NY
	Johnny Murphy	NYA	Hersh Martin	PHI
	Bobo Newsom	SLA	Jo-Jo Moore	NY
	Red Rolfe	NYA	Babe Phelps +	BRO
	Red Ruffing	NYA	Jim Turner	BSN
	Cecil Travis	WAS	Arky Vaughan	PIT
	Rudy York	DET	Lloyd Waner	PIT

+ player replaced on roster

American League   000 000 001- 1
National League   100 100 20X- 4

AMERICAN LEAGUE

	ab	r	h	bi	bb	so	po	a
M.Kreevich, lf	2	0	0	0	0	0	1	0
D.Cramer, ph-lf	2	0	0	0	0	0	0	0
C.Gehringer, 2b	3	0	1	0	1	0	2	2
E.Averill, cf	4	0	0	0	0	1	5	1
J.Foxx, 1b-3b	4	0	1	0	0	1	5	1
J.DiMaggio, rf	4	1	1	0	0	1	2	0
B.Dickey, c	4	0	1	0	0	0	8	0
J.Cronin, ss	3	0	2	1	1	0	0	2
B.Lewis, 3b	1	0	0	0	0	0	0	1
L.Gehrig, ph-1b	3	0	1	0	0	0	1	0
L.Gomez, p	1	0	0	0	0	0	0	0
J.Allen, p	1	0	0	0	0	0	0	0
R.York, ph	1	0	0	0	0	1	0	0
L.Grove, p	0	0	0	0	0	0	0	0
B.Johnson, ph	1	0	0	0	0	1	0	0
Totals	34	1	7	1	2	5	24	7

NATIONAL LEAGUE

	ab	r	h	bi	bb	so	po	a
S.Hack, 3b	4	1	1	0	0	1	1	2
B.Herman, 2b	4	0	1	0	0	2	3	4
I.Goodman, rf	3	0	0	0	0	1	2	0
J.Medwick, lf	4	0	1	1	0	0	2	0
M.Ott, cf	4	1	1	0	0	1	3	0
E.Lombardi, c	4	0	2	1	0	0	5	0
F.McCormick, 1b	4	1	1	0	0	0	11	0
L.Durocher, ss	3	1	1	0	0	1	0	2
J.Vander Meer, p	0	0	0	0	0	0	0	3
H.Leiber, ph	1	0	0	0	0	0	0	0
B.Lee, p	1	0	0	0	0	0	0	0
M.Brown, p	1	0	0	0	0	1	0	1
Totals	33	4	8	2	0	7	27	12

PITCHING	ip	h	r	er	bb	so
American League						
L.Gomez (L)	3.0	2	1	0	0	1
J.Allen	3.0	2	1	1	0	3
L.Grove	2.0	3	2	0	0	3
National League						
J.Vander Meer (W)	3.0	1	0	0	0	1
B.Lee	3.0	1	0	0	1	2
M.Brown (S)	3.0	5	1	1	1	2

BATTING
2B: B.Dickey (off B.Lee); J.Cronin (off M.Brown).
RBI, scoring position, less than 2 outs: J.Cronin 0–1;
   L.Gehrig 0–2.

BASERUNNING
SB: J.DiMaggio (2nd base off M.Brown/E.Lombardi).
Team LOB: 8

FIELDING
E: J.Cronin (fumble); B.Dickey (throw); J.Foxx (fumble
   bunt); J.DiMaggio (throw).
Outfield assist: E.Averill (J.Medwick at 1B).

BATTING
3B: M.Ott (off J.Allen).
RBI, scoring position, less than 2 outs: I.Goodman 0–1;
   J.Medwick 1–1; M.Ott 0–1; E.Lombardi 1–1.
S: L.Durocher.

BASERUNNING
SB: I.Goodman (2nd base off J.Allen/B.Dickey).
Team LOB: 6

Inherited Runners—Scored:
   J.Allen 0–0; L.Grove 0–0; B.Lee 0–0; M.Brown 0–0.
HBP: I.Goodman by J.Allen.

GAME DATA—T: 1:58; A: 27067; Temp: Unknown; Wind:
Unknown direction, Speed: Unknown

UMPIRES—HP: Bill Klem (NL), 1B: Harry Geisel (AL), 2B:
Lee Ballanfant (NL), 3B: Steve Basil (AL)

STARTING LINEUPS

	American League	*National League*
1.	M.Kreevich lf	S.Hack 3b
2.	C.Gehringer 2b	B.Herman 2b
3.	E.Averill cf	I.Goodman rf
4.	J.Foxx 1b	J.Medwick lf
5.	J.DiMaggio rf	M.Ott cf
6.	B.Dickey c	E.Lombardi c
7.	J.Cronin ss	F.McCormick 1b
8.	B.Lewis 3b	L.Durocher ss
9.	L.Gomez p	J.Vander Meer p

AL 1ST: M.Kreevich flied to M.Ott-cf; C.Gehringer grounded out (J.Vander Meer-p to F.McCormick-1b); E.Averill grounded out (B.Herman-2b to F.McCormick-1b); 0 R, 0 H, 0 E, 0 LOB. AL 0, NL 0.

NL 1ST: S.Hack singled to left field; B.Herman reached on an error by J.Cronin-ss [S.Hack to third, B.Herman to first]; I.Goodman was called out on strikes; J.Medwick flied to E.Averill-cf [S.Hack scored (unearned)]; M.Ott flied to E.Averill-cf; 1 R (0 ER), 1 H, 1 E, 1 LOB. AL 0, NL 1.

AL 2ND: J.Foxx struck out; J.DiMaggio grounded out (J.Vander Meer-p to F.McCormick-1b); B.Dickey grounded out (B.Herman-2b to F.McCormick-1b); 0 R, 0 H, 0 E, 0 LOB. AL 0, NL 1.

NL 2ND: E.Lombardi grounded out (B.Lewis-3b to J.Foxx-1b); F.McCormick popped to C.Gehringer-2b; L.Durocher grounded out (J.Cronin-ss to J.Foxx-1b); 0 R, 0 H, 0 E, 0 LOB. AL 0, NL 1.

AL 3RD: J.Cronin singled; B.Lewis flied to M.Ott-cf; L.Gomez grounded out (J.Vander Meer-p to F.McCormick-1b) [J.Cronin to second]; M.Kreevich popped to B.Herman-2b; 0 R, 1 H, 0 E, 1 LOB. AL 0, NL 1.

NL 3RD: **H.Leiber batted for J.Vander Meer;** H.Leiber lined to M.Kreevich-lf; S.Hack grounded out (C.Gehringer-2b to J.Foxx-1b); B.Herman singled; I.Goodman popped to B.Dickey-c in foul territory; 0 R, 1 H, 0 E, 1 LOB. AL 0, NL 1.

AL 4TH: **B.Lee replaced H.Leiber (pitching);** C.Gehringer walked; E.Averill flied to J.Medwick-lf; J.Foxx forced C.Gehringer (L.Durocher-ss to B.Herman-2b) [J.Foxx to first]; J.DiMaggio struck out; 0 R, 0 H, 0 E, 1 LOB. AL 0, NL 1.

NL 4TH: **J.Allen replaced L.Gomez (pitching);** J.Medwick popped to J.Foxx-1b; M.Ott tripled; E.Lombardi singled to left field [M.Ott scored]; F.McCormick grounded out (C.Gehringer-2b to J.Foxx-1b) [E.Lombardi to second]; L.Durocher struck out; 1 R, 2 H, 0 E, 1 LOB. AL 0, NL 2.

AL 5TH: B.Dickey doubled; J.Cronin flied to M.Ott-cf; **L.Gehrig batted for B.Lewis;** L.Gehrig grounded out (B.Herman-2b to F.McCormick-1b) [B.Dickey to third]; J.Allen grounded

out (S.Hack-3b to F.McCormick-1b); 0 R, 1 H, 0 E, 1 LOB. AL 0, NL 2.

NL 5TH: **L.Gehrig stayed in game (playing 1b); J.Foxx changed positions (playing 3b);** B.Lee flied to E.Averill-cf; S.Hack flied to E.Averill-cf; B.Herman struck out; 0 R, 0 H, 0 E, 0 LOB. AL 0, NL 2.

AL 6TH: **D.Cramer batted for M.Kreevich;** D.Cramer grounded out (B.Herman-2b to F.McCormick-1b); C.Gehringer grounded out (L.Durocher-ss to F.McCormick-1b); E.Averill struck out; 0 R, 0 H, 0 E, 0 LOB. AL 0, NL 2.

NL 6TH: **D.Cramer stayed in game (playing lf);** I.Goodman was hit by a pitch; J.Medwick flied to E.Averill-cf (E.Averill-cf to J.DiMaggio-rf); I.Goodman stole second [I.Goodman to third (error by B.Dickey-c)]; M.Ott struck out; E.Lombardi grounded out (J.Cronin-ss to L.Gehrig-1b); 0 R, 0 H, 1 E, 1 LOB. AL 0, NL 2.

AL 7TH: **M.Brown replaced B.Lee (pitching);** J.Foxx singled; J.DiMaggio forced J.Foxx (B.Herman-2b unassisted) [J.DiMaggio to first]; B.Dickey popped to S.Hack-3b; J.DiMaggio stole second; J.Cronin walked; L.Gehrig singled [J.DiMaggio to third, J.Cronin to second]; **R.York batted for J.Allen;** R.York struck out; 0 R, 2 H, 0 E, 3 LOB. AL 0, NL 2.

NL 7TH: **L.Grove replaced R.York (pitching);** F.McCormick singled to center field; on a bunt L.Durocher singled to third base [F.McCormick scored (unearned) (no RBI) (error by J.Foxx-3b), L.Durocher scored (unearned) (error by J.DiMaggio-rf)]; M.Brown struck out; S.Hack struck out; B.Herman struck out; 1 R (-1 ER), 2 H, 2 E, 0 LOB. AL 0, NL 4.

AL 8TH: D.Cramer grounded out (S.Hack-3b to F.McCormick-1b); C.Gehringer singled to right field; E.Averill flied to I.Goodman-rf; J.Foxx grounded out (M.Brown-p to F.McCormick-1b); 0 R, 1 H, 0 E, 1 LOB. AL 0, NL 4.

NL 8TH: I.Goodman lined to J.DiMaggio-rf; J.Medwick singled to left field; M.Ott flied to E.Averill-cf; E.Lombardi singled to right-center [J.Medwick to third]; F.McCormick forced E.Lombardi (J.Foxx-3b to C.Gehringer-2b) [F.McCormick to first]; 0 R, 2 H, 0 E, 2 LOB. AL 0, NL 4.

AL 9TH: J.DiMaggio singled to left field; B.Dickey flied to J.Medwick-lf; J.Cronin doubled to left field [J.DiMaggio scored]; L.Gehrig lined to I.Goodman-rf [J.Cronin to third]; **B.Johnson batted for L.Grove;** B.Johnson struck out; 1 R, 2 H, 0 E, 1 LOB. AL 1, NL 4.

Final Totals	R	H	E	LOB
American League	1	7	3	8
National League	4	7	0	6

7

Tuesday, July 11, 1939

Yankee Stadium, New York City

American League 3, National League 1

SERIES RESULTS: AL 5, NL 2

Fledgling Feller Rescues the AL

Six players from the New York Yankees and five from the Cincinnati Reds were in the starting lineup at the 1939 All-Star Game, accurately reflecting the league-leading positions of the two teams. Although members of both the Yanks and Reds contributed to their respective league's efforts, the hero of the American League's 3–1 victory was Cleveland pitcher Bob Feller. The twenty-year-old "boy wonder" came on in the sixth inning to rescue his team from a dangerous situation and then completely dominated the National League batters over the final three innings.

Baseball had awarded this seventh All-Star Game to New York in conjunction with the city's hosting of the World's Fair. The game was played on a perfect midsummer afternoon, and the 62,892 fans in attendance constituted what was then the second-largest crowd to see an All-Star Game. Only the crowd of 69,812 at Cleveland's Municipal Stadium in 1935 had been larger.

Roster size had been raised to twenty-five this season, with a slight change in the method of team selection. Each manager in each league continued to select his team. Now, however, the manager had to include at least one player from every one of the eight teams, and the final squad also had to consist of at least one player from every team. Previously, such clubs as the 1934 Phillies and Reds and the 1935 Dodgers had gone unrepresented. That would never happen again.

Missing from the American League lineup in 1939 were two men who had played in each of the first six games: Charlie Gehringer of the Tigers was injured and hadn't been chosen, and Lou Gehrig of the Yankees, who had once seemed indestructible, had retired earlier in the season after being diagnosed with amyotrophic lateral sclerosis, now commonly known as Lou Gehrig's disease. Although no longer a player, Gehrig was serving as the American League's honorary captain and was at the game in uniform. A week earlier, on July 4,

the Yankees had honored their longtime first baseman by holding an emotion-filled day for him here at Yankee Stadium.

Because baseball was celebrating its centennial, American League president Will Harridge had bypassed precedent and asked the game's grand old man, Connie Mack, to manage the AL squad. Mack agreed, but when he later fell ill with a stomach ailment, Joe McCarthy, manager of the world champion Yankees, replaced him to manage for his fourth consecutive year. As he'd done two years earlier, in 1937, McCarthy made no substitutions among his position players. The Yankee skipper had a total of nine of his own players on the squad, while National League manager Gabby Hartnett of Chicago had seven Cincinnati Reds.

New York and Cincinnati were on their way to meeting in the World Series, and the day's starting pitchers, Red Ruffing of the Yanks and Paul Derringer of the Reds, both of whom had 11-3 records, would meet again in the World Series opener. Ruffing would outpitch Derringer in that game, and the Yanks would sweep the Series, but this afternoon the edge went to Derringer. He allowed just two hits in his three innings, singles by Doc Cramer and Joe Cronin, both of the Red Sox, and left with a 1–0 lead.

The Nationals scored what would be their only run of the game in the third inning, an inning in which Ruffing might easily have retired the side in order. Arky Vaughan led off with an infield hit and, one out later, took second on Stan Hack's bloop single to left. Reds second baseman Lonny Frey, a journeyman having the season of his life, followed with a double down the right-field line that scored Vaughan and sent Hack to third.

Frey was the first of four consecutive Cincinnati batters in Hartnett's lineup. Next was right fielder Ival Goodman, and although Frank McCormick and Ernie Lombardi, two of the league's best hitters, were due to follow, Ruffing gave Goodman an intentional walk to load the bases. Nevertheless, with the National League partisans in the crowd

39

calling for a big inning, Ruffing set down both Reds sluggers, McCormick on a called third strike and Lombardi on a pop to second baseman Joe Gordon.

With three big league clubs in New York, there were naturally fans of both leagues in the stands. The cheers that greeted Ruffing's clutch pitching seemed about equal to those that followed Frey's run-scoring double.

The heavily favored American Leaguers took the lead in the fourth with two runs off Chicago's Bill Lee. The first run scored on a two-out single by Canadian-born George Selkirk, who in 1936 became the first foreign-born player to appear in an All-Star Game. Selkirk's hit scored his Yankee teammate Bill Dickey, who had walked, and sent Detroit's Hank Greenberg, who had singled, to third. Lee had blanked the AL for three innings in 1938 and should have been out of this inning with just the one run; however, when shortstop Vaughan mishandled Gordon's ground ball, Greenberg came home with run number two.

Lee had come close to escaping with no runs scoring. Right fielder Goodman had dived for and almost come up with Selkirk's hit, a sinking line drive. Unfortunately, in doing so Goodman injured his left (nonthrowing) shoulder. He finished the inning but was in great pain and had to leave the game. His manager, Bill McKechnie, who was a spectator, feared a broken collar bone. X-rays taken at St. Elizabeth's Hospital later revealed that Goodman hadn't broken anything but had dislocated his shoulder.

The game's final run came in the fifth when, with two out and the bases empty, Joe DiMaggio connected for a long home run to left. DiMaggio, now in his fourth season, entered the game batting a league-leading .435 and was having what many consider his finest season ever.

The leading hitter in the National League was Philadelphia outfielder Morrie Arnovich, at .383. Despite that lofty average and despite his being one of five National Leaguers named on the ballots of all eight managers (Hack, Derringer, McCormick, and Joe Medwick were the others), Arnovich didn't get into the game. The Nationals started the same outfield as they did in 1938 — Medwick in left, Mel Ott in center, and Goodman in right — which was the first time that an outfield trio had started nonconsecutive All-Star Games. Later, when he needed a replacement for Goodman, Hartnett used the Cardinals' Terry Moore, who took over in center while Ott moved to right. For the traditionally more powerful American League, Red Sox rookie Ted Williams was leading the league with sixty-seven runs batted in, and he hadn't even made the team.

DiMaggio's home run put the AL ahead, 3–1, and ended the scoring, although the game's most dramatic moment followed soon after. Tommy Bridges of the Tigers had set the Nationals down in order in the fourth and fifth and had retired McCormick leading off the sixth. Lombardi broke the spell with a single to left, and then Medwick reached when shortstop Cronin booted his ground ball. Following Cronin's error, Gordon turned in a sensational play by preventing Ott's sharp ground ball from going into right field. Lombardi was forced to hold at third, but the bases were loaded with just one out and Vaughan at the plate.

Feller had been warming up in anticipation of relieving Bridges in the seventh inning, but McCarthy decided to bring him in now. It proved to be a brilliant move. If the blister on Feller's thumb that had bothered him in his past two starts bothered him today, it wasn't apparent. He made just one pitch, and the inning was over. Vaughan hit the pitch on the ground to Gordon, who threw to Cronin for the force on Ott, and then Cronin sent it on to Greenberg to complete the double play. It was the second time in the game that the National League had failed to take advantage of a bases-loaded, one-out situation.

Hartnett had planned to use Brooklyn's Whit Wyatt to pitch the last three innings, but Wyatt had injured a leg. Instead, Hartnett used Boston's Lou Fette, who did an excellent job by holding the Americans scoreless in the seventh and eighth. Still, Fette's effort was in vain because the Nationals could do nothing against Feller. The young Indians fireballer, who had a 14-3 record at the break, allowed just two base runners over the final three innings. Hack walked with one out in the seventh, and Ott singled to lead off the ninth. In both instances a home run would have tied the game, but Feller got Frey and Moore following the walk to Hack, and Vaughan, Johnny Mize, and Hack following the single by Ott. He finished with a flourish by striking out both Mize and Hack.

Mize, the NL home run leader who was batting for Fette, went down on three pitches, while Hack was caught looking at a full-count pitch that National League plate umpire George Magerkurth ruled was strike three. Hack slammed his bat down complaining that the pitch was a ball, but of course that didn't change anything. Hack, who fanned a record-tying three times that afternoon, later admitted that the third strike was indeed a strike, and that he was actually protesting some of Magerkurth's earlier calls.

Technically, neither Mize nor Hack should have faced Feller. When Vaughan lined out to DiMaggio for the first out of the ninth inning, it gave

Feller three full innings pitched, the All-Star limit. The Nationals chose not to protest this fact, perhaps embarrassed by their pregame claims of how they would have no trouble hitting the young prodigy.

Feller likely had those boasts in mind when he said after it was over: "The fellows in our league are tougher. I didn't expect to be called into the game so soon, so I wasn't quite loosened up. I didn't begin to throw them real fast until the ninth inning. My best pitches were made to Johnny Mize and Hack."

	AL		NL		
P	Red Ruffing	NYA	Paul Derringer	CIN	
C	Bill Dickey	NYA	Ernie Lombardi	CIN	
1B	Hank Greenberg	DET	Frank McCormick	CIN	
2B	Joe Gordon	NYA	Lonny Frey	CIN	
3B	Red Rolfe	NYA	Stan Hack	CHN	
SS	Joe Cronin	BOS	Arky Vaughan	PIT	
OF	Doc Cramer	BOS	Ival Goodman	CIN	
OF	Joe DiMaggio	NYA	Joe Medwick	SLN	
OF	George Selkirk	NYA	Mel Ott	NY	
	Luke Appling	CHA	Morrie Arnovich	PHI	
	Tommy Bridges	DET	Dolph Camilli	BRO	
	George Case	WAS	Harry Danning	NY	
	Frankie Crosetti	NYA	Curt Davis	SLN	
	Bob Feller	CLE	Lou Fette	BSN	
	Jimmie Foxx	BOS	Billy Herman	CHN	
	Lou Gehrig	NYA	Billy Jurges	NY	
	Lefty Gomez	NYA	Cookie Lavagetto +	BRO	
	Lefty Grove	BOS	Bill Lee	CHN	
	Frankie Hayes	PHA	Eddie Miller	BSN	
	Rollie Hemsley	CLE	Johnny Mize	SLN	
	Myril Hoag	SLA	Terry Moore	SLN	
	Bob Johnson	PHA	Babe Phelps	BRO	
	Ted Lyons	CHA	Johnny Vander Meer	CIN	
	George McQuinn	SLA	Bucky Walters	CIN	
	Johnny Murphy	NYA	Lon Warneke	SLN	
	Bobo Newsom	DET	Whit Wyatt	BRO	+ player replaced on roster

```
National League    001 000 000- 1
American League    000 210 00x- 3
```

NATIONAL LEAGUE

	ab	r	h	bi	bb	so	po	a
S.Hack, 3b	4	0	1	0	1	3	1	1
L.Frey, 2b	4	0	1	1	0	0	0	4
I.Goodman, rf	1	0	0	0	1	0	0	0
B.Herman, ph	1	0	0	0	0	1	0	0
T.Moore, cf	1	0	0	0	0	0	0	0
F.McCormick, 1b	4	0	0	0	0	1	7	1
E.Lombardi, c	4	0	2	0	0	0	6	0
J.Medwick, lf	4	0	0	0	0	1	1	0
M.Ott, cf-rf	4	0	2	0	0	0	4	0
A.Vaughan, ss	3	1	1	0	1	0	4	1
P.Derringer, p	1	0	0	0	0	1	0	0
D.Camilli, ph	1	0	0	0	0	1	0	0
B.Lee, p	0	0	0	0	0	0	0	0
B.Phelps, ph	1	0	0	0	0	0	0	0
L.Fette, p	0	0	0	0	0	0	1	0
J.Mize, ph	1	0	0	0	0	1	0	0
Totals	34	1	7	1	3	9	24	7

BATTING
2B: L.Frey (off R.Ruffing).
RBI, scoring position, less than 2 outs: L.Frey 1–1; F.McCormick 0–2; A.Vaughan 0–2.
GDP: A.Vaughan.

BASERUNNING
Team LOB: 9

FIELDING
E: A.Vaughan (fumble).

AMERICAN LEAGUE

	ab	r	h	bi	bb	so	po	a
D.Cramer, rf	4	0	1	0	0	1	3	0
R.Rolfe, 3b	4	0	1	0	0	0	1	0
J.DiMaggio, cf	4	1	1	1	0	0	1	0
B.Dickey, c	3	1	0	0	1	0	10	0
H.Greenberg, 1b	3	1	1	0	1	0	7	1
J.Cronin, ss	4	0	1	0	0	1	2	4
G.Selkirk, lf	2	0	1	1	2	0	0	0
J.Gordon, 2b	4	0	0	0	0	1	2	4
R.Ruffing, p	0	0	0	0	0	0	0	0
M.Hoag, ph	1	0	0	0	0	1	0	0
T.Bridges, p	1	0	0	0	0	1	1	0
B.Feller, p	1	0	0	0	0	1	0	0
Totals	31	3	6	2	4	6	27	9

BATTING
HR: J.DiMaggio (5th inning off B.Lee, 0 on, 2 out).
2-out RBI: J.DiMaggio; G.Selkirk.
RBI, scoring position, less than 2 outs: J.Cronin 0–1; J.Gordon 0–1.

BASERUNNING
Team LOB: 8

FIELDING
E: J.Cronin (fumble).
DP: (1). J.Gordon-J.Cronin-H.Greenberg.

PITCHING	ip	h	r	er	bb	so
National League						
P.Derringer	3.0	2	0	0	0	1
B.Lee (L)	3.0	3	3	2	3	4
L.Fette	2.0	1	0	0	1	1
American League						
R.Ruffing	3.0	4	1	1	1	4
T.Bridges (w)	2.1	2	0	0	1	3
B.Feller (s)	3.2	1	0	0	1	2

Inherited Runners—Scored:
B.Lee 0–0; L.Fette 0–0; T.Bridges 0–0; B.Feller 3–0.
IBB: I.Goodman by R.Ruffing; G.Selkirk by B.Lee.

GAME DATA—T: 1:55; A: 62892; Temp: Unknown; Wind: Unknown direction, Speed: Unknown

UMPIRES—HP: Cal Hubbard (AL), 1B: George Magerkurth (NL), 2B: Eddie Rommel (AL), 3B: Larry Goetz (NL)

STARTING LINEUPS

	National League	*American League*
1.	S.Hack 3b	D.Cramer rf
2.	L.Frey 2b	R.Rolfe 3b
3.	I.Goodman rf	J.DiMaggio cf
4.	F.McCormick 1b	B.Dickey c
5.	E.Lombardi c	H.Greenberg 1b
6.	J.Medwick lf	J.Cronin ss
7.	M.Ott cf	G.Selkirk lf
8.	A.Vaughan ss	J.Gordon 2b
9.	P.Derringer p	R.Ruffing p

NL 1ST: S.Hack struck out; L.Frey grounded out (J.Gordon-2b to H.Greenberg-1b); I.Goodman flied to D.Cramer-rf; 0 R, 0 H, 0 E, 0 LOB. NL 0, AL 0.

AL 1ST: D.Cramer singled to left field; R.Rolfe flied to M.Ott-cf; J.DiMaggio flied to M.Ott-cf; B.Dickey popped to A.Vaughan-ss; 0 R, 1 H, 0 E, 1 LOB. NL 0, AL 0.

NL 2ND: F.McCormick grounded out (J.Cronin-ss to H.Greenberg-1b); E.Lombardi singled to left field; J.Medwick was called out on strikes; M.Ott flied to D.Cramer-rf; 0 R, 1 H, 0 E, 1 LOB. NL 0, AL 0.

AL 2ND: H.Greenberg popped to A.Vaughan-ss; J.Cronin singled to right field; G.Selkirk flied to M.Ott-cf; J.Gordon flied to M.Ott-cf; 0 R, 1 H, 0 E, 1 LOB. NL 0, AL 0.

NL 3RD: A.Vaughan singled to shortstop; P.Derringer struck out; S.Hack singled to left field [A.Vaughan to second]; L.Frey doubled to right field [A.Vaughan scored, S.Hack to third]; I.Goodman was walked intentionally; F.McCormick was called out on strikes; E.Lombardi popped to J.Gordon-2b; 1 R, 3 H, 0 E, 3 LOB. NL 1, AL 0.

AL 3RD: **M.Hoag batted for R.Ruffing;** M.Hoag struck out; D.Cramer grounded out (L.Frey-2b to F.McCormick-1b); R.Rolfe lined to A.Vaughan-ss; 0 R, 0 H, 0 E, 0 LOB. NL 1, AL 0.

NL 4TH: **T.Bridges replaced M.Hoag (pitching);** J.Medwick grounded out (J.Cronin-ss to H.Greenberg-1b); M.Ott popped to B.Dickey-c; A.Vaughan walked; **D.Camilli batted for P.Derringer;** D.Camilli struck out; 0 R, 0 H, 0 E, 1 LOB. NL 1, AL 0.

AL 4TH: **B.Lee replaced D.Camilli (pitching);** J.DiMaggio grounded out (S.Hack-3b to F.McCormick-1b); B.Dickey walked; H.Greenberg singled to left field [B.Dickey to second]; J.Cronin struck out; G.Selkirk singled to right field [B.Dickey scored, H.Greenberg to third]; J.Gordon reached on an error by A.Vaughan-ss [H.Greenberg scored (unearned) (no RBI), G.Selkirk to second, J.Gordon to first]; T.Bridges struck out; 2 R (1 ER), 2 H, 1 E, 2 LOB. NL 1, AL 2.

NL 5TH: S.Hack was called out on strikes; L.Frey grounded out (H.Greenberg-1b to T.Bridges-p); **B.Herman batted for I.Goodman;** B.Herman struck out; 0 R, 0 H, 0 E, 0 LOB. NL 1, AL 2.

AL 5TH: Umpires move: Magerkurth (hp), Rommel (1b), Goetz (2b) Hubbard (3b); **M.Ott changed positions (playing rf); T.Moore replaced B.Herman (playing cf);** D.Cramer struck out; R.Rolfe grounded out (L.Frey-2b to F.McCormick-1b); J.DiMaggio homered to deep leftfield; B.Dickey grounded out (F.McCormick-1b unassisted); 1 R, 1 H, 0 E, 0 LOB. NL 1, AL 3.

NL 6TH: F.McCormick grounded out (J.Cronin-ss to H.Greenberg-1b); E.Lombardi singled to left field; J.Medwick reached on an error by J.Cronin-ss [E.Lombardi to second, J.Medwick to first]; M.Ott singled to second base [E.Lombardi to third, J.Medwick to second]; **B.Feller replaced T.Bridges (pitching);** A.Vaughan grounded into a double play (J.Gordon-2b to J.Cronin-ss to H.Greenberg-1b) [M.Ott out at second]; 0 R, 2 H, 1 E, 2 LOB. NL 1, AL 3.

AL 6TH: H.Greenberg walked; J.Cronin grounded out (L.Frey-2b to F.McCormick-1b) [H.Greenberg to second]; G.Selkirk was walked intentionally; J.Gordon flied to J.Medwick-lf; B.Feller struck out; 0 R, 0 H, 0 E, 2 LOB. NL 1, AL 3.

NL 7TH: **B.Phelps batted for B.Lee;** B.Phelps grounded out (J.Gordon-2b to H.Greenberg-1b); S.Hack walked; L.Frey flied to D.Cramer-rf; T.Moore popped to R.Rolfe-3b; 0 R, 0 H, 0 E, 1 LOB. NL 1, AL 3.

AL 7TH: **L.Fette replaced B.Phelps (pitching);** D.Cramer grounded out (L.Frey-2b to F.McCormick-1b); R.Rolfe singled to center field; J.DiMaggio popped to S.Hack-3b in foul territory; B.Dickey grounded out (F.McCormick-1b to L.Fette-p); 0 R, 1 H, 0 E, 1 LOB. NL 1, AL 3.

NL 8TH: F.McCormick popped to J.Cronin-ss; E.Lombardi grounded out (J.Gordon-2b to H.Greenberg-1b); J.Medwick lined to J.Gordon-2b; 0 R, 0 H, 0 E, 0 LOB. NL 1, AL 3.

AL 8TH: H.Greenberg grounded out (A.Vaughan-ss to F.McCormick-1b); J.Cronin lined to A.Vaughan-ss; G.Selkirk walked; J.Gordon struck out; 0 R, 0 H, 0 E, 1 LOB. NL 1, AL 3.

NL 9TH: M.Ott singled to center field; A.Vaughan lined to J.DiMaggio-cf; **J.Mize batted for L.Fette;** J.Mize struck out; S.Hack was called out on strikes; 0 R, 1 H, 0 E, 1 LOB. NL 1, AL 3.

Final Totals	R	H	E	LOB
National League	1	7	1	9
American League	3	6	1	8

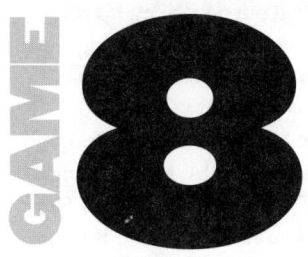

8

Tuesday, July 9, 1940

Sportsman's Park, St. Louis

National League 4, American League 0

SERIES RESULTS: AL 5, NL 3

The NL Closes the Gap with First All-Star Shutout

On a typically torrid St. Louis afternoon, five National League pitchers combined to throw the first shutout in All-Star history. With their 4–0 victory, the Nationals, losers of the first three games, had now won three of the last five. A crowd of 32,373, made up mostly of National League adherents, looked on as Paul Derringer, Bucky Walters, Whit Wyatt, Larry French, and Carl Hubbell limited the heavily favored American Leaguers to just three hits. Among the spectators broiling in the mid-summer sun were Commissioner Kenesaw Mountain Landis, AL president Will Harridge, NL president Ford Frick, and representatives of fifteen of the sixteen Major League teams. The Philadelphia Athletics were the lone team without representation, although their manager, Connie Mack, made news from Philadelphia by protesting the awarding of the 1941 game to Detroit. Mack claimed that because this year's game was in St. Louis, a western city, next year's game should be in an eastern city, such as Philadelphia.

Each member of the NL pitching quintet was effective, combining to allow just five base runners. Only one American Leaguer, Luke Appling, who doubled in the second inning, got as far as third base. The scarcity of base runners led to the shortest game in All-Star history — one hour and fifty-three minutes. Despite the game's brevity and the oppressive heat, the fans had a wonderful afternoon. Although the American League Browns and National League Cardinals shared Sportsman's Park, this was an NL home game; moreover, the successes of the Cardinals over the past fifteen years had made them by far St. Louis's more popular team.

An early indication that the crowd was made up of predominantly Cardinals fans came with the boos that greeted Dodgers outfielder Joe Medwick. A longtime Cardinals favorite, Medwick was making his first appearance in St. Louis since his recent trade to Brooklyn. Meanwhile, the Browns had only one player on the AL squad, first baseman George McQuinn, who was in uniform but recovering from a thigh injury, never getting into the game.

Boston Bees outfielder Max West's first-inning, three-run homer off the Yankees' Red Ruffing provided all the offense the Nationals would need, although they would add a final run against Bob Feller in the eighth. Ruffing and Derringer had also started the 1939 game in New York, making this the first time that two pitchers had opened against each other in consecutive games. (They had also been the opposing pitchers in game one of the 1939 World Series.)

Cincinnati pitchers had now started the last three games — Johnny Vander Meer started in 1938 — while Yankee pitchers had started every game except the 1934 one, when the assignment went to Boston's Lefty Grove. In addition to Ruffing, Lefty Gomez had been the starter in five games, but this year marked the end of both Gomez and Grove as members of the American League team.

The only negative aspect of the game for the Nationals came in the top of the second inning when West injured himself while attempting to catch Appling's double. In jumping for the ball, a high arcing fly that hit against the pavilion wall in right field, West banged his left hip against the wall and he fell to the ground. With Appling settled in at second base, time was called as West's teammates rushed to see how badly he was hurt. National League team trainer Dr. Richard Rohde administered first aid, and after a few minutes, West was able to walk off the field on his own power.

West, the object of the crowd's applause for the second time this day, was not seriously injured, but he did have a severely bruised hip. Bill Nicholson, a late addition to the NL squad when he replaced Cubs teammate Hank Leiber (out with an infected throat), took West's place in right field.

Ruffing, with a mediocre 7-6 record this season, found himself trailing 3–0 after pitching to just three batters. Pittsburgh's Arky Vaughan led off the home first with a ground ball that took a bad hop over second baseman Joe Gordon's head and went for a hit. Billy Herman, who had three of the Nationals' seven safeties, followed with a hit-and-run single that put runners at first and third with no one out. That brought up West, a third-year man playing in his first (and what would be his only) All-Star Game. National League manager Bill McKechnie had planned originally to use the Giants' Mel Ott, a member of every NL squad since 1934, in right field but made an overnight decision to start West. With the count at no balls and one strike, West, a native Missourian, smashed a long home run to the covered pavilion in right-center field. It was the first All-Star home run by a Boston National Leaguer and the first ever by a batter in his first All-Star at bat.

Later, West confessed that he wasn't sure what he had hit; however, Ruffing said, "It was a low fast ball, but it seemed to be faster after he swung."

That one pitch was enough to make the Yankee right-hander the losing pitcher on a very poor day overall for the four-time defending champions. Despite the fourth-place position of the Yankees, seven games behind the league-leading Tigers, four other Yanks joined Ruffing in the starting lineup. Another, Red Rolfe, was selected but missed the game with an injury. Washington's Cecil Travis replaced him. None of the Yankees had been having particularly good seasons (Joe DiMaggio was batting below .300), and none distinguished himself this afternoon. Center fielder DiMaggio (0-4), second baseman Gordon (0-2, two strikeouts), right fielder Charlie Keller (0-2, one strikeout), catcher Bill Dickey (0-1), and Ruffing (0-1) batted a combined zero for ten against National League pitching.

No one else on the AL squad did much better. Appling's double was the only one of the three AL hits that was for extra bases. The other two hits were Appling's single in the eighth and a sixth-inning single by Tigers pitcher Bobo Newsom.

None of their critics could blame this year's usual large complement of Yankees on the fact that the team was managed by their own Joe McCarthy. McCarthy, the American League manager for the previous four games, had asked to be excused for this one, and Joe Cronin of the Red Sox was handling the team.

Derringer pitched the first two innings, allowing a walk to Boston left fielder Ted Williams (playing in his first All-Star Game) in the first inning and Appling's double in the second. Both came with only one out, but both times the next two

batters, Yankees in both cases, couldn't take advantage. Derringer got Keller and DiMaggio following the Williams walk and Dickey and Gordon following the Appling double.

Derringer, who had now pitched seven scoreless innings in his three All-Star appearances, was replaced in the third by Walters, his Cincinnati teammate. Walters set the Americans down in order in both the third and fourth and then turned it over to Wyatt, whose Dodgers trailed the league-leading Reds by just half a game. Wyatt retired the Americans in order again in the fifth and then yielded Newsom's single to lead off the sixth. McKechnie had replaced his entire infield to start the inning, so when Travis followed Newsom's hit by bouncing into a double play, it went from Brooklyn second baseman Pete Coscarat to Boston shortstop Eddie Miller to Cincinnati first baseman Frank McCormick. (Miller was a replacement for Billy Jurges, the Giants shortstop who had been beaned by Walters on June 24.)

In all, McKechnie used twenty-two of his allotted twenty-five players, leaving out only Philadelphia pitchers Kirby Higbe and Hugh Mulcahy and Dodgers shortstop (and rival manager) Leo Durocher. Cronin used eighteen players. Only three men played the entire game: DiMaggio, American League home run leader Jimmie Foxx, and Cardinals center fielder Terry Moore. Foxx's selection this year made him the only player in either league to have been picked for each of the eight All-Star Games.

Cubs left-hander French came on in the seventh, and like Wyatt, he too set the side down one-two-three in his first inning and gave up a lead-off single in his second. That single was to Appling, but French retired the next three batters without Appling's ever advancing. The last two batters, pinch hitter Ray Mack and his Cleveland teammate Feller, batting for himself, went down on strikes. Mack was one of four Indians and nine American Leaguers chosen for their first All-Star Game.

The National Leaguers hadn't done much either following their first-inning outburst. Ruffing held them scoreless in the second and third, as did Newsom through the middle innings and as did Feller in the seventh. Feller, the pitching star of the 1939 game, gave up the Nationals' final run in the eighth. Mel Ott led off with a walk, moved to second on a sacrifice bunt by McCormick, and scored on Harry Danning's single to right. The Giants' Danning was the National League's leading hitter (.343) and RBI man (58), but he hadn't entered the game until the seventh inning. Because Derringer was his starting pitcher, McKechnie had chosen to start Ernie Lombardi, Derringer's regular season battery mate behind the plate. In the middle three innings, McKechnie used Brooklyn's Babe Phelps, a move that enabled Wyatt to pitch to his regular season battery mate.

Red Sox outfielder Lou Finney, the AL's leading hitter at .359, didn't appear until the sixth inning. Neither did Detroit's Hank Greenberg, the Major Leagues RBI leader, with 71. Greenberg, the starter at first base in 1939, replaced Keller in left. Of the ten leading hitters, five from each league, going into this game, only White Sox shortstop Appling was in the starting lineup. Five of the hitters didn't even make the team: the Browns' Rip Radcliffe, the White Sox's Taft Wright, and the Tigers' Barney McCosky — the numbers two, four, and five hitters in the AL — and the Dodgers' Dixie Walker and the Cubs' Jimmy Gleeson — the numbers two and four hitters in the NL.

Hubbell, Danning's Giants battery mate, came on in the ninth and, after striking out Cleveland's Ken Keltner, issued a walk to Finney. Hubbell then ended it by getting Greenberg on a foul out to Danning and getting DiMaggio on a fly to Giants left fielder Joe Moore.

	AL			NL		
P	Red Ruffing		NYA	Paul Derringer		CIN
C	Bill Dickey		NYA	Ernie Lombardi		CIN
1B	Jimmie Foxx		BOS	Johnny Mize		SLN
2B	Joe Gordon		NYA	Billy Herman		CHN
3B	Red Rolfe	+	NYA	Cookie Lavagetto		BRO
SS	Luke Appling		CHA	Arky Vaughan		PIT
OF	Joe DiMaggio		NYA	Joe Medwick		BRO
OF	Charlie Keller		NYA	Terry Moore		SLN
OF	Ted Williams		BOS	Max West		BSN
	Lou Boudreau		CLE	Pete Coscarart		BRO
	Tommy Bridges		DET	Harry Danning		NY
	Doc Cramer		BOS	Leo Durocher		BRO
	Dom DiMaggio		BOS	Larry French		CHN
	Bob Feller		CLE	Kirby Higbe		PHI
	Lou Finney		BOS	Carl Hubbell		NY
	Hank Greenberg		DET	Billy Jurges	+	NY
	Frankie Hayes		PHA	Hank Leiber	+	CHN
	Rollie Hemsley		CLE	Pinky May		PHI
	Bob Johnson		PHA	Frank McCormick		CIN
	Ken Keltner		CLE	Eddie Miller		BSN
	Dutch Leonard		WAS	Jo-Jo Moore		NY
	Ray Mack		CLE	Hugh Mulcahy		PHI
	George McQuinn		SLA	Bill Nicholson		CHN
	Al Milnar		CLE	Mel Ott		NY
	Bobo Newsom		DET	Babe Phelps		BRO
	Monte Pearson		NYA	Bucky Walters		CIN
	Cecil Travis		WAS	Whit Wyatt		BRO

+ player replaced on roster

American League   ooo ooo ooo- o
National League   3oo ooo o1x- 4

AMERICAN LEAGUE

	ab	r	h	bi	bb	so	po	a
C.Travis, 3b	3	o	o	o	o	o	o	o
K.Keltner, 3b	1	o	o	o	o	1	2	1
T.Williams, lf	2	o	o	o	1	o	3	o
L.Finney, rf	o	o	o	o	1	o	o	o
C.Keller, rf	2	o	o	o	o	1	4	o
H.Greenberg, lf	2	o	o	o	o	o	o	o
J.DiMaggio, cf	4	o	o	o	o	o	1	o
J.Foxx, 1b	3	o	o	o	o	1	4	2
L.Appling, ss	3	o	2	o	o	o	o	o
L.Boudreau, ss	o	o	o	o	o	o	o	o
B.Dickey, c	1	o	o	o	o	o	2	o
F.Hayes, c	1	o	o	o	o	o	1	o
R.Hemsley, c	1	o	o	o	o	o	3	o
J.Gordon, 2b	2	o	o	o	o	2	3	1
R.Mack, ph-2b	1	o	o	o	o	1	o	o
R.Ruffing, p	1	o	o	o	o	o	o	o
B.Newsom, p	1	o	1	o	o	o	o	o
B.Feller, p	1	o	o	o	o	1	1	o
Totals	29	o	3	o	2	7	24	4

BATTING
2B: L.Appling (off P.Derringer).
RBI, scoring position, less than 2 outs: B.Dickey o–1.
GDP: C.Travis.

BASERUNNING
Team LOB: 4

FIELDING
E: R.Hemsley.

NATIONAL LEAGUE

	ab	r	h	bi	bb	so	po	a
A.Vaughan, ss	3	1	1	o	o	1	o	1
E.Miller, ss	1	o	o	o	o	1	2	1
B.Herman, 2b	3	1	3	o	o	o	o	3
P.Coscarart, 2b	1	o	o	o	o	1	o	2
M.West, rf	1	1	1	3	o	o	o	o
B.Nicholson, rf	2	o	o	o	o	o	1	o
M.Ott, rf	o	1	o	o	1	o	o	o
J.Mize, 1b	2	o	o	o	o	o	8	o
F.McCormick, 1b	1	o	o	o	o	o	2	o
E.Lombardi, c	2	o	1	o	o	o	3	o
B.Phelps, c	o	o	o	o	1	o	1	o
H.Danning, c	1	o	1	1	o	o	6	o
J.Medwick, lf	2	o	o	o	o	o	1	o
J.Moore, lf	2	o	o	o	o	o	1	o
C.Lavagetto, 3b	2	o	o	o	o	o	o	1
P.May, 3b	1	o	o	o	o	o	o	o
T.Moore, cf	3	o	o	o	1	1	2	o
P.Derringer, p	1	o	o	o	o	1	o	1
B.Walters, p	o	o	o	o	o	o	o	1
W.Wyatt, p	1	o	o	o	o	1	o	o
L.French, p	o	o	o	o	o	o	o	o
C.Hubbell, p	o	o	o	o	o	o	o	o
Totals	29	4	7	4	3	6	27	10

BATTING
HR: M.West (1st inning off R.Ruffing, 2 on, o out).
RBI, scoring position, less than 2 outs: E.Miller o–1;
M.West 1–1; J.Mize o–1; H.Danning 1–1; J.Moore o–1.
S: F.McCormick; L.French.

BASERUNNING
Team LOB: 7

FIELDING
DP: (1). P.Coscarart-E.Miller-F.McCormick.

PITCHING	ip	h	r	er	bb	so
American League						
R.Ruffing (L)	3.0	5	3	3	o	2
B.Newsom	3.0	1	o	o	1	1
B.Feller	2.0	1	1	1	2	3
National League						
P.Derringer (W)	2.0	1	o	o	1	3
B.Walters	2.0	o	o	o	o	o
W.Wyatt	2.0	1	o	o	o	1
L.French	2.0	1	o	o	o	2
C.Hubbell (s)	1.0	o	o	o	1	1

Inherited Runners—Scored:
B.Newsom o–o; B.Feller o–o; B.Walters o–o;
W.Wyatt o–o; L.French o–o; C.Hubbell o–o.
HBP: P.May by B.Feller.

GAME DATA—T: 1:53; A: 32373; Temp: Unknown; Wind:
Unknown direction, Speed: Unknown

UMPIRES—HP: Beans Reardon (NL), 1B: George Pipgras
(AL), 2B: Bill Stewart (NL), 3B: Steve Basil (AL)

STARTING LINEUPS

	American League	National League
1.	C.Travis 3b	A.Vaughan ss
2.	T.Williams lf	B.Herman 2b
3.	C.Keller rf	M.West rf
4.	J.DiMaggio cf	J.Mize 1b
5.	J.Foxx 1b	E.Lombardi c
6.	L.Appling ss	J.Medwick lf
7.	B.Dickey c	C.Lavagetto 3b
8.	J.Gordon 2b	T.Moore cf
9.	R.Ruffing p	P.Derringer p

AL 1ST: C.Travis flied to T.Moore-cf; T.Williams walked; C.Keller struck out; J.DiMaggio grounded out (P.Derringer-p to J.Mize-1b); 0 R, 0 H, 0 E, 1 LOB. AL 0, NL 0.

NL 1ST: A.Vaughan singled; B.Herman singled [A.Vaughan to third]; M.West homered to very deep right-center [A.Vaughan scored, B.Herman scored]; J.Mize flied to T.Williams-lf; E.Lombardi singled to center field; J.Medwick popped to J.Foxx-1b in foul territory; C.Lavagetto popped to J.Gordon-2b; 3 R, 4 H, 0 E, 1 LOB. AL 0, NL 3.

AL 2ND: J.Foxx was called out on strikes; L.Appling doubled to right field; West injured himself leaping for the ball; **B.Nicholson replaced M.West (playing rf)**; B.Dickey grounded out (B.Herman-2b to J.Mize-1b) [L.Appling to third]; J.Gordon struck out; 0 R, 1 H, 0 E, 1 LOB. AL 0, NL 3.

NL 2ND: T.Moore popped to J.Foxx-1b in foul territory; P.Derringer struck out; A.Vaughan struck out; 0 R, 0 H, 0 E, 0 LOB. AL 0, NL 3.

AL 3RD: **B.Walters replaced P.Derringer (pitching)**; R.Ruffing grounded out (B.Walters-p to J.Mize-1b); C.Travis flied to J.Medwick-lf; T.Williams grounded out (B.Herman-2b to J.Mize-1b); 0 R, 0 H, 0 E, 0 LOB. AL 0, NL 3.

NL 3RD: B.Herman singled to center field; B.Nicholson flied to C.Keller-rf in foul territory [B.Herman to second]; J.Mize grounded out (J.Gordon-2b to J.Foxx-1b) [B.Herman to third]; E.Lombardi flied to C.Keller-rf; 0 R, 1 H, 0 E, 1 LOB. AL 0, NL 3.

AL 4TH: **B.Phelps replaced E.Lombardi (playing c)**; C.Keller grounded out (B.Herman-2b to J.Mize-1b); J.DiMaggio flied to B.Nicholson-rf; J.Foxx grounded out (A.Vaughan-ss to J.Mize-1b); 0 R, 0 H, 0 E, 0 LOB. AL 0, NL 3.

NL 4TH: **B.Newsom replaced R.Ruffing (pitching)**; **F.Hayes replaced B.Dickey (playing c)**; J.Medwick lined to J.Gordon-2b; C.Lavagetto flied to C.Keller-rf; T.Moore flied to T.Williams-lf; 0 R, 0 H, 0 E, 0 LOB. AL 0, NL 3.

AL 5TH: **W.Wyatt replaced B.Walters (pitching)**; L.Appling grounded out (J.Mize-1b unassisted); F.Hayes grounded out (C.Lavagetto-3b to J.Mize-1b); J.Gordon struck out; 0 R, 0 H, 0 E, 0 LOB. AL 0, NL 3.

NL 5TH: W.Wyatt was called out on strikes; A.Vaughan flied to T.Williams-lf; B.Herman singled to right field; B.Nicholson flied to C.Keller-rf; 0 R, 1 H, 0 E, 1 LOB. AL 0, NL 3.

AL 6TH: **E.Miller replaced A.Vaughan (playing ss)**; **P.May replaced C.Lavagetto (playing 3b)**; **P.Coscarart replaced B.Herman (playing 2b)**; **F.McCormick replaced J.Mize (playing 1b)**; **M.Ott replaced B.Nicholson (playing rf)**; **J.Moore replaced J.Medwick (playing lf)**; B.Newsom singled to right field; C.Travis grounded into a double play (P.Coscarart-2b to E.Miller-ss to F.McCormick-1b) [B.Newsom out at second]; T.Williams grounded out (P.Coscarart-2b to F.McCormick-1b); 0 R, 1 H, 0 E, 0 LOB. AL 0, NL 3.

NL 6TH: **K.Keltner replaced C.Travis (playing 3b)**; **H.Greenberg replaced C.Keller (playing lf)**; **L.Finney replaced T.Williams (playing rf)**; F.McCormick popped to K.Keltner-3b in foul territory; B.Phelps walked; J.Moore popped to K.Keltner-3b in foul territory; P.May flied to J.DiMaggio-cf; 0 R, 0 H, 0 E, 1 LOB. AL 0, NL 3.

AL 7TH: **L.French replaced W.Wyatt (pitching)**; **H.Danning replaced B.Phelps (playing c)**; H.Greenberg popped to H.Danning-c in foul territory; J.DiMaggio popped to E.Miller-ss; J.Foxx lined to T.Moore-cf; 0 R, 0 H, 0 E, 0 LOB. AL 0, NL 3.

NL 7TH: **B.Feller replaced B.Newsom (pitching)**; **R.Hemsley replaced F.Hayes (playing c)**; T.Moore walked; L.French out on a sacrifice bunt (J.Foxx-1b to J.Gordon-2b) [T.Moore to second]; E.Miller struck out; P.Coscarart was called out on strikes; 0 R, 0 H, 0 E, 1 LOB. AL 0, NL 3.

AL 8TH: L.Appling singled to right field; R.Hemsley popped to H.Danning-c in foul territory; **R.Mack batted for J.Gordon**; R.Mack struck out; B.Feller struck out; 0 R, 1 H, 0 E, 1 LOB. AL 0, NL 3.

NL 8TH: **R.Mack stayed in game (playing 2b)**; **L.Boudreau replaced L.Appling (playing ss)**; M.Ott walked; F.McCormick out on a sacrifice bunt (K.Keltner-3b to J.Foxx-1b) [M.Ott to second]; H.Danning singled to right field [M.Ott scored, H.Danning to second (error by R.Hemsley-c)]; J.Moore grounded out (J.Foxx-1b to B.Feller-p) [H.Danning to third]; P.May was hit by a pitch; T.Moore struck out; 1 R, 1 H, 1 E, 2 LOB. AL 0, NL 4.

AL 9TH: **C.Hubbell replaced L.French (pitching)**; K.Keltner struck out; L.Finney walked; H.Green-

berg popped to H.Danning-c in foul territory;
J.DiMaggio flied to J.Moore-lf; 0 R, 0 H, 0 E,
1 LOB. AL 0, NL 4.

Final Totals	R	H	E	LOB
American League	0	3	1	4
National League	4	7	0	7

The Kid Climaxes a Ninth-Inning Explosion

In 1941, the National League was only one out away from attaining two All-Star goals that had thus far eluded it: winning in an American League park and winning consecutive games. But it was unable to realize either one and would have to wait until 1950 to achieve the first milestone and 1951 to accomplish the second. The NL's near victory was lost as a result of Ted Williams's stunningly dramatic two-on, two-out home run in the ninth inning. Williams's blast, off Chicago's Claude Passeau, crashed against the facing of the right-field upper deck and capped a four-run rally that turned the Americans' 5–3 deficit into a stirring 7–5 victory. The AL's thrilling come-from-behind win delighted the 54,674 fans in freshly repainted and resodded Briggs Stadium. America was still at peace in the summer of 1941 but was hurriedly building up its armed forces. For that reason, the net proceeds for this game ($53,226) would not go to the Association of Professional Baseball Players of America, as it had for previous All-Star Games, but to the United Service Organization's (USO's) Army-Navy Recreation Fund.

This was a well-pitched, low-scoring game for the first six innings. The Americans broke through with a run in the fourth, and both teams scored single runs in the sixth. Then the Nationals used the long ball, previously an American League weapon, to forge ahead. Veteran Pirates shortstop Arky Vaughan smashed consecutive-inning, two-run home runs in the seventh and eighth to give the NL a 5–2 lead. A single run by the AL in the eighth made it 5–3 and set the stage for the spectacular ninth-inning finish. Coincidentally, Vaughan's home runs were the first All-Star Game homers by a Pirate, while Williams's home run was the first by a member of the Red Sox.

The starting pitchers were also the first of their respective teams to start an All-Star Game. The Nationals started Whit Wyatt, who had a 13-4 rec-

ord for the league-leading Dodgers. The Americans opened with twenty-two-year-old Bob Feller, who joined Boston's Lefty Grove (1934) as the only non-Yankee to start on the mound for the American League. Feller, the AL's leading winner the previous two seasons, had been a sensational 16-4 in the first half of 1941 and proved just as effective against the National Leaguers. He struck out four of the nine men he faced and allowed just one base runner, Cincinnati second baseman Lonny Frey, who singled to lead off the third and then was picked off. Wyatt also faced the minimum number of batters in his two innings. He did walk Williams leading off the second but got the next batter, Cleveland's Jeff Heath, to bounce into a double play.

Heath, batting .371, was one of six outfielders on the American League squad, a group that entered the game batting a combined .348. The others were Williams, the DiMaggio brothers (Joe of the Yanks and Dom of the Red Sox), the Browns' Roy Cullenbine, and the Yanks' Charlie Keller. Both Cullenbine and Keller (leading the league in RBI and tied with teammate Joe DiMaggio for the lead in home runs) appeared as pinch hitters. The seven National League outfielders were at .306, led by Brooklyn's sensational youngster Pete Reiser's league-leading .360.

Paul Derringer replaced Wyatt in the third and retired the side in order before yielding the game's first run in the fourth. After getting Boston second baseman Bobby Doerr for the first out, he gave up a double to Washington third baseman Cecil Travis. Joe DiMaggio followed with a long fly to center, which Reiser ran down, but Travis easily moved to third after the catch. Williams then lashed a line drive to right that seemed to be heading directly to Pittsburgh's Bob Elliott, who had replaced NL RBI leader Bill Nicholson in right field. Elliott started in on the ball, then tried to reverse direction; his spikes caught in the soggy turf, however, and he fell to the ground as the ball sailed over him for a run-scoring double.

In the fourth, American League manager Del Baker of Detroit replaced Feller with White Sox left-hander Thornton Lee. Lee gave up a single to the Cubs' Stan Hack, the first man he faced, and two-out, fifth-inning singles to Vaughan and Billy Herman (who was pinch-hitting for Frey) but kept the Nationals scoreless. The National Leaguers finally pushed their first run across in the sixth. Reds' pitcher Bucky Walters, a former third baseman, led off with a double to left, moved to third on a sacrifice bunt by Hack, and scored on Terry Moore's fly ball to Williams. All three batters had gone after Lee's first pitch.

Facing Walters in the home sixth, the Americans quickly regained the lead. Walks to Joe DiMaggio and Heath put runners at first and second with two out. Next, Indians shortstop Lou Boudreau, who had replaced starter Joe Cronin in the top of the inning, lashed a single to center field that scored DiMaggio and sent Heath to third. Boudreau took second when Reiser failed to handle the ball cleanly, but Walters got Detroit's Rudy York on a fly ball to end the inning.

Although the Tigers were the defending American League champions and Detroit was hosting the game, York was one of only three Tigers on the AL squad. Pitcher Al Benton and catcher Birdie Tebbetts were the others, and only York got to play. Of course, the Tigers' best player, Hank Greenberg, was unavailable. Greenberg was currently in the U.S. Army, where his salary had dropped from $55,000 a year to $21 a month. He had gotten a forty-eight-hour pass from Fort Custer and was at the game, choosing to sit in the upper deck and out of the limelight. The Tigers had asked permission to present Greenberg with his 1940 Most Valuable Player trophy this afternoon, but Commissioner Landis had turned them down. No presentations, no matter how meritorious, could be made as part of the All-Star program, said Landis.

In the seventh, the Nationals needed just two batters to take the lead against the new AL pitcher, Washington right-hander Sid Hudson. Enos Slaughter opened the inning with a single to left, continuing to second when Williams stumbled and had trouble coming up with the ball. The error was one of five committed in this game, an All-Star record at the time. This error was meaningless because Slaughter soon rode home on Vaughan's blast into the right-field upper deck. The Nationals threatened to increase their lead when Herman followed Vaughan's home run with a double down the left-field line. Pirates catcher Al Lopez bunted Herman to third, but there he stayed. With the AL infield playing in, Hudson got Joe Medwick on a bouncer to Boudreau and, after walking Hack, fanned Moore.

The fans had greeted Medwick with a chorus of boos when NL manager Bill McKechnie had sent him up as a pinch hitter for Walters. Medwick was now a Dodger, and the 1934 World Series was seven years in the past, but the people in Detroit obviously hadn't forgotten the unpleasantness that had occurred between Medwick and Tiger third baseman Marv Owen in the seventh game of that series.

Vaughan became the first player to homer twice in an All-Star Game when he connected again in the eighth. It was another two-run blast because the Cardinals Johnny Mize, who had doubled (Mize's first hit in his eleventh All-Star at bat), was aboard. The second home run came off Chicago left-hander Edgar Smith and increased the Nationals' lead to 5–2. Vaughan, who had singled earlier, set an All-Star record with four runs batted in for the game, a record that Williams would tie an inning later.

Passeau, who like Wyatt had once belonged to the Tigers, came on in the seventh. He had a one-two-three inning but was touched for a run in the eighth. The run came on a one-out double by Joe DiMaggio and a two-out single by brother Dom DiMaggio, and it cut the NL's lead to 5–3. The DiMaggios were the first brothers to play together in an All-Star Game but not the first chosen to participate. Wes and Rick Ferrell, both of Washington, had been members of the American League squad in 1937; however, neither got into the game.

Boudreau followed Dom's hit with another single, and when Reiser bobbled the ball for his second error of the game, Boudreau took second. The tying runs were in scoring position, and Boston's Jimmie Foxx, who had replaced York at first base, was the batter. This was the final appearance for Foxx, the only player in either league who had been chosen for each of the first nine All-Star Games, and it ended ingloriously. Passeau struck him out on three consecutive pitches, all of which he swung at futilely. Although Foxx had been chosen for the previous nine games, he'd appeared in only seven, missing the 1933 and 1939 games. Medwick, Herman, and the Giants' Mel Ott (the NL's home run leader with eighteen, but a pinch hitter today) had appeared in the most games. None had been chosen for the first game in 1933, but all three had played in every game since. Herman, traded from the Cubs to the Dodgers early in May, had two hits this afternoon. He now had a total of eleven (eleven for twenty-four), which allowed him to pass Detroit's Charlie Gehringer as the reigning All-Star hit leader.

McKechnie had used five pitchers to shut out the American Leaguers in St. Louis in 1940, and he seemed on his way to using five pitchers this afternoon. However, he allowed Passeau to bat for himself in the top of the ninth and then sent him to the mound in the home half to nail down the victory. Passeau got the lead man, A's catcher Frankie Hayes, on a pop to Herman but then yielded an infield single to Cleveland's Ken Keltner, batting for pitcher Smith. Joe Gordon's single moved Keltner to second, and when Travis walked, the bases were loaded.

The tying runs were again in scoring position, and Joe DiMaggio was the batter. DiMaggio had entered the game with a .357 batting average and was in the midst of a record-breaking hitting streak that had reached forty-eight games. He had already had one hit this day, although that eighth-inning double would not, of course, count as part of his streak. Working very carefully, Passeau got DiMaggio to bounce sharply to shortstop for what looked to be a game-ending double play. Boston's Eddie Miller, who had replaced Vaughan to start the home ninth, fielded the ball cleanly and tossed it to Herman for the force on Travis. However, Travis slid hard into Herman, causing an off-the-mark relay that pulled first baseman Frank McCormick off the bag. DiMaggio was safe as Keltner scored, making it a 5–4 game, and Gordon, the tying run, went to third.

That set the stage for Williams, batting .405 and on his way to the Major Leagues last .400 season. If McKechnie chose to walk him, it would move DiMaggio, the potential winning run, to second. McKechnie decided to have Passeau pitch to Williams — as carefully as possible. Passeau's first pitch was a ball. Williams fouled off the second and then took another ball. Passeau's 2-1 pitch was a letter-high fastball that Williams connected with, and suddenly the game was over.

The twenty-two-year-old Boston slugger, affectionately known as The Kid, clapped his hands as he skipped joyously around the bases. Gordon and DiMaggio and coach Merv Shea happily greeted him at home plate, while Baker and the rest of the American Leaguers, as well as the capacity crowd, celebrated. The celebrations continued in the winners' locker room as players and American League executives congratulated their youthful hero. "What a way to win a ball game like that. What a finish!" Baker screamed.

The National Leaguers were visibly upset at having what seemed a certain victory taken from them. "You can't give a club like that four outs in an inning and expect to win," said McKechnie, alluding to the missed double play in the ninth inning. "It was a grand game," he said, and that it was.

AL			NL		
P	Bob Feller	CLE	Whit Wyatt		BRO
C	Bill Dickey	NYA	Mickey Owen		BRO
1B	Rudy York	DET	Johnny Mize		SLN
2B	Bobby Doerr	BOS	Lonny Frey		CIN
3B	Cecil Travis	WAS	Stan Hack		CHN
SS	Joe Cronin	BOS	Arky Vaughan		PIT
OF	Joe DiMaggio	NYA	Terry Moore		SLN
OF	Jeff Heath	CLE	Bill Nicholson		CHN
OF	Ted Williams	BOS	Pete Reiser		BRO
	Luke Appling	CHA	Cy Blanton		PHI
	Al Benton	DET	Dolph Camilli	+	BRO
	Lou Boudreau	CLE	Harry Danning		NY
	Roy Cullenbine	SLA	Paul Derringer		CIN
	Dom DiMaggio	BOS	Bob Elliott		PIT
	Jimmie Foxx	BOS	Billy Herman		BRO
	Joe Gordon	NYA	Carl Hubbell		NY
	Frankie Hayes	PHA	Cookie Lavagetto		BRO
	Sid Hudson	WAS	Hank Leiber	+	CHN
	Charlie Keller	NYA	Al Lopez		PIT
	Ken Keltner	CLE	Frank McCormick		CIN
	Thornton Lee	CHA	Joe Medwick		BRO
	Red Ruffing	NYA	Eddie Miller		BSN
	Marius Russo	NYA	Mel Ott		NY
	Eddie Smith	CHA	Claude Passeau		CHN
	Birdie Tebbetts	DET	Enos Slaughter		SLN
			Bucky Walters		CIN
			Lon Warneke		SLN

+ player replaced on roster

RETROSHEET EXPANDED BOX SCORE Tuesday, 7/8/1941 National League at American League (D)

```
National League    000  001  220-  5
American League    000  101  014-  7
   2 outs when winning run was scored.
```

NATIONAL LEAGUE

	ab	r	h	bi	bb	so	po	a
S.Hack, 3b	2	0	1	0	1	1	3	0
C.Lavagetto, ph-3b	1	0	0	0	0	0	0	0
T.Moore, lf	5	0	0	1	0	1	0	0
P.Reiser, cf	4	0	0	0	0	2	6	0
J.Mize, 1b	4	1	1	0	0	0	5	0
F.McCormick, 1b	0	0	0	0	0	0	0	0
B.Nicholson, rf	1	0	0	0	0	1	1	0
B.Elliott, rf	1	0	0	0	0	0	0	0
E.Slaughter, rf	2	1	1	0	0	1	0	0
A.Vaughan, ss	4	2	3	4	0	0	1	2
E.Miller, ss	0	0	0	0	0	0	0	1
L.Frey, 2b	1	0	1	0	0	0	1	3
B.Herman, ph-2b	3	0	2	0	0	0	3	0
M.Owen, c	1	0	0	0	0	0	0	0
A.Lopez, c	1	0	0	0	0	0	3	0
H.Danning, c	1	0	0	0	0	0	3	0
W.Wyatt, p	0	0	0	0	0	0	0	0
M.Ott, ph	1	0	0	0	0	1	0	0
P.Derringer, p	0	0	0	0	0	0	0	1
B.Walters, p	1	1	1	0	0	0	0	0
J.Medwick, ph	1	0	0	0	0	0	0	0
C.Passeau, p	1	0	0	0	0	0	0	0
Totals	35	5	10	5	1	7	26	7

BATTING
2B: B.Walters (off T.Lee); B.Herman (off S.Hudson); J.Mize (off E.Smith).
HR: A.Vaughan 2 (7th inning off S.Hudson, 1 on, 0 out; 8th inning off E.Smith, 1 on, 2 out).
2-out RBI: A.Vaughan 2.
RBI, scoring position, less than 2 outs: T.Moore 1–1; E.Slaughter 0–1; A.Vaughan 1–1; J.Medwick 0–1.
S: S.Hack; A.Lopez.
GDP: P.Reiser.

BASERUNNING
CS: L.Frey (2nd base by B.Feller/B.Dickey).
Team LOB: 6

FIELDING
E: P.Reiser 2.
DP: (1). L.Frey-A.Vaughan-J.Mize.

AMERICAN LEAGUE

	ab	r	h	bi	bb	so	po	a
B.Doerr, 2b	3	0	0	0	0	1	0	0
J.Gordon, 2b	2	1	1	0	0	0	2	0
C.Travis, 3b	4	1	1	0	0	1	1	2
J.DiMaggio, cf	4	3	1	1	1	0	1	0
T.Williams, lf	4	1	2	4	1	1	3	0
J.Heath, rf	2	0	0	0	1	1	1	0
D.DiMaggio, rf	1	0	1	1	0	0	1	0
J.Cronin, ss	2	0	0	0	0	1	3	0
L.Boudreau, ss	2	0	2	1	0	0	0	1
R.York, 1b	3	0	1	0	0	0	6	2
J.Foxx, 1b	1	0	0	0	0	1	2	1
B.Dickey, c	3	0	1	0	0	0	4	2
F.Hayes, c	1	0	0	0	0	0	2	0
B.Feller, p	0	0	0	0	0	0	0	1
R.Cullenbine, ph	1	0	0	0	0	0	0	0
T.Lee, p	1	0	0	0	0	0	0	1
S.Hudson, p	0	0	0	0	0	0	0	0
C.Keller, ph	1	0	0	0	0	1	0	0
E.Smith, p	0	0	0	0	0	0	1	0
K.Keltner, ph	1	1	1	0	0	0	0	0
Totals	36	7	11	7	4	6	27	10

BATTING
2B: C.Travis (off P.Derringer); T.Williams (off P.Derringer); J.DiMaggio (off C.Passeau).
HR: T.Williams (9th inning off C.Passeau, 2 on, 2 out).
2-out RBI: T.Williams 4; D.DiMaggio; L.Boudreau.
RBI, scoring position, less than 2 outs: J.DiMaggio 1–3; T.Williams 0–1; T.Lee 0–1.
GDP: J.Heath.

BASERUNNING
Team LOB: 7

FIELDING
E: J.Heath (dropped fly); T.Williams; E.Smith (dropped throw).
DP: (1). R.York-J.Cronin.

PITCHING

National League	ip	h	r	er	bb	so
W.Wyatt	2.0	0	0	0	1	0
P.Derringer	2.0	2	1	1	0	1
B.Walters	2.0	3	1	1	2	2
C.Passeau (L, BS)	2.2	6	5	5	1	3
American League						
B.Feller	3.0	1	0	0	0	4
T.Lee	3.0	4	1	1	0	0
S.Hudson (BS)	1.0	3	2	2	1	1
E.Smith (w)	2.0	2	2	2	0	2

Inherited Runners—Scored:
P.Derringer 0–0; B.Walters 0–0; C.Passeau 0–0; T.Lee 0–0; S.Hudson 0–0; E.Smith 0–0.

GAME DATA—T: 2:23; A: 54674; Temp: Unknown; Wind: Unknown direction, Speed: Unknown

UMPIRES—HP: Bill Summers (AL), 1B: Lou Jorda (NL), 2B: Bill Grieve (AL), 3B: Babe Pinelli (NL)

STARTING LINEUPS

National League	*American League*
1. S.Hack 3b	B.Doerr 2b
2. T.Moore lf	C.Travis 3b
3. P.Reiser cf	J.DiMaggio cf
4. J.Mize 1b	T.Williams lf
5. B.Nicholson rf	J.Heath rf
6. A.Vaughan ss	J.Cronin ss
7. L.Frey 2b	R.York 1b
8. M.Owen c	B.Dickey c
9. W.Wyatt p	B.Feller p

NL 1ST: S.Hack struck out; T.Moore popped to J.Cronin-ss; P.Reiser struck out; 0 R, 0 H, 0 E, 0 LOB. NL 0, AL 0.

AL 1ST: B.Doerr popped to L.Frey-2b; C.Travis flied to P.Reiser-cf; J.DiMaggio popped to S.Hack-3b in foul territory; 0 R, 0 H, 0 E, 0 LOB. NL 0, AL 0.

NL 2ND: J.Mize lined to J.DiMaggio-cf; B.Nicholson was called out on strikes; A.Vaughan flied to T.Williams-lf in foul territory; 0 R, 0 H, 0 E, 0 LOB. NL 0, AL 0.

AL 2ND: T.Williams walked; J.Heath grounded into a double play (L.Frey-2b to A.Vaughan-ss to J.Mize-1b) [T.Williams out at second]; J.Cronin flied to B.Nicholson-rf; 0 R, 0 H, 0 E, 0 LOB. NL 0, AL 0.

NL 3RD: L.Frey singled to right field (it was the 2–2 pitch); L.Frey was picked off and caught stealing second (it was the 1–1 pitch) (B.Feller-p to R.York-1b to J.Cronin-ss); M.Owen flied to T.Williams-lf; **M.Ott batted for W.Wyatt**; M.Ott struck out (B.Dickey-c to R.York-1b); 0 R, 1 H, 0 E, 0 LOB. NL 0, AL 0.

AL 3RD: **P.Derringer replaced M.Ott (pitching); A.Lopez replaced M.Owen (playing c);** R.York flied to P.Reiser-cf; B.Dickey grounded out (L.Frey-2b to J.Mize-1b); **R.Cullenbine batted for B.Feller;** R.Cullenbine grounded out (P.Derringer-p to J.Mize-1b); 0 R, 0 H, 0 E, 0 LOB. NL 0, AL 0.

NL 4TH: **T.Lee replaced R.Cullenbine (pitching);** S.Hack singled to the shortstop side of second (it was the 3–1 pitch); T.Moore flied to J.Heath-rf; P.Reiser grounded into a double play (R.York-1b to J.Cronin-ss) [S.Hack out at second]; 0 R, 1 H, 0 E, 0 LOB. NL 0, AL 0.

AL 4TH: **B.Elliott replaced B.Nicholson (playing rf);** B.Doerr grounded out (L.Frey-2b to J.Mize-1b); C.Travis doubled to left field; J.DiMaggio flied to P.Reiser-cf [C.Travis to third]; T.Williams doubled to right field [C.Travis scored]; Elliott momentarily misjudged the ball, rushed in a few steps and caught his spikes in the turf; J.Heath was called out on strikes; 1 R, 2 H, 0 E, 1 LOB. NL 0, AL 1.

NL 5TH: J.Mize grounded out (R.York-1b unassisted); B.Elliott grounded out (C.Travis-3b to R.York-1b); Travis dropped to his knees to field sharp grounder; A.Vaughan singled to second base (it was the 3–2 pitch); **B.Herman batted for L.Frey;** B.Herman singled to center field (it was the 0–2 pitch) [A.Vaughan to second]; A.Lopez forced A.Vaughan (C.Travis-3b unassisted) [A.Lopez to first]; 0 R, 2 H, 0 E, 2 LOB. NL 0, AL 1.

AL 5TH: **B.Walters replaced P.Derringer (pitching); B.Herman stayed in game (playing 2b);** Umpires moved: Pinelli (hp), Grieve (1b), Jorda (2b), Summe; J.Cronin was called out on strikes; R.York singled to left field; B.Dickey singled to left field [R.York to second]; T.Lee lined to P.Reiser-cf [R.York to third]; B.Doerr struck out; 0 R, 2 H, 0 E, 2 LOB. NL 0, AL 1.

NL 6TH: **J.Gordon replaced B.Doerr (playing 2b); L.Boudreau replaced J.Cronin (playing ss);** B.Walters doubled to left field; S.Hack out on a sacrifice bunt (T.Lee-p to R.York-1b) [B.Walters to third]; T.Moore flied to T.Williams-lf [B.Walters scored]; P.Reiser reached on an error by J.Heath-rf [P.Reiser to second]; J.Mize grounded out (C.Travis-3b to R.York-1b); 1 R, 1 H, 1 E, 1 LOB. NL 1, AL 1.

AL 6TH: **E.Slaughter replaced B.Elliott (playing rf);** C.Travis lined to B.Herman-2b; J.DiMaggio walked; T.Williams flied to P.Reiser-cf; J.Heath walked [J.DiMaggio to second]; L.Boudreau singled to center field [J.DiMaggio scored (RBI), J.Heath to third, L.Boudreau to second (error by P.Reiser-cf)]; R.York flied to P.Reiser-cf; 1 R, 1 H, 1 E, 2 LOB. NL 1, AL 2.

NL 7TH: **S.Hudson replaced T.Lee (pitching); J.Foxx replaced R.York (playing 1b); D.DiMaggio replaced J.Heath (playing rf);** E.Slaughter singled to left field [E.Slaughter to second (error by T.Williams-lf)]; Williams fumbled the ball then half fell; A.Vaughan homered to rightfield [E.Slaughter scored]; upper deck; B.Herman hit a ground rule double to leftfield down the line; fan inteference; A.Lopez out on a sacrifice bunt (B.Dickey-c to J.Gordon-2b) [B.Herman to third]; **J.Medwick batted for B.Walters;** J.Medwick grounded out (L.Boudreau-ss to J.Foxx-1b); S.Hack walked; T.Moore struck out; 2 R, 3 H, 1 E, 2 LOB. NL 3, AL 2.

AL 7TH: **C.Passeau replaced J.Medwick (pitching); H.Danning replaced A.Lopez (playing c);** B.Dickey lined to S.Hack-3b; **C.Keller batted for S.Hudson;** C.Keller struck out; J.Gordon grounded out (A.Vaughan-ss to J.Mize-1b); 0 R, 0 H, 0 E, 0 LOB. NL 3, AL 2.

NL 8TH: **E.Smith replaced C.Keller (pitching);**

F.Hayes replaced B.Dickey (playing c); P.Reiser was called out on strikes; J.Mize doubled to right field; 325′ liner off the wall; E.Slaughter was called out on strikes; A.Vaughan homered to rightfield [J.Mize scored]; 350′ into upper deck; B.Herman reached on an error [B.Herman to first (error by E.Smith-p; assist by J.Foxx-1b)]; Smith failed to touch 1b; H.Danning popped to J.Gordon-2b; 2 R, 2 H, 1 E, 1 LOB. NL 5, AL 2.

AL 8TH: **F.McCormick replaced J.Mize (playing 1b);** C.Travis popped to S.Hack-3b in foul territory; J.DiMaggio doubled to left-center; T.Williams was called out on strikes; D.DiMaggio singled to center field [J.DiMaggio scored]; L.Boudreau singled to center field [D.DiMaggio to third (error by P.Reiser-cf), L.Boudreau to second]; J.Foxx struck out; 1 R, 3 H, 1 E, 2 LOB. NL 5, AL 3.

NL 9TH: C.Passeau flied to D.DiMaggio-rf; **C.Lavagetto batted for S.Hack;** C.Lavagetto grounded out (J.Foxx-1b to E.Smith-p); T.Moore popped to J.Foxx-1b in foul territory; 0 R, 0 H, 0 E, 0 LOB. NL 5, AL 3.

AL 9TH: **C.Lavagetto stayed in game (playing 3b); E.Miller replaced A.Vaughan (playing ss);** F.Hayes popped to B.Herman-2b; **K.Keltner batted for E.Smith;** K.Keltner singled to shortstop; off Miller's chest; J.Gordon singled to right field [K.Keltner to second]; C.Travis walked [K.Keltner to third, J.Gordon to second]; J.DiMaggio forced C.Travis (E.Miller-ss to B.Herman-2b) [K.Keltner scored, J.Gordon to third, J.DiMaggio to first]; T.Williams homered to rightfield [J.Gordon scored, J.DiMaggio scored]; 4 R, 3 H, 0 E, 0 LOB. NL 5, AL 7.

Final Totals	R	H	E	LOB
National League	5	10	2	6
American League	7	11	3	7

10

Monday, July 6, 1942 (TL)

The Polo Grounds, New York City

American League 3, National League 1

SERIES RESULTS: AL 7, NL 3

The Stars Play under the Stars

A lead-off home run by Lou Boudreau and a two-run homer by Rudy York gave the American League three first-inning runs, all they would need to win this tenth All-Star Game. The 3–1 victory was the AL's third in four years and upped its overall lead to seven games to three.

As it had done to everything else, America's entry into the war the previous December had affected baseball. This year's game had been scheduled originally for Ebbets Field in Brooklyn but had been moved across the East River because of the Polo Grounds's larger seating capacity. Brooklyn would have to wait seven more years before hosting an All-Star Game, the last of the Major League locations in existence in 1933 to do so.

Ticket prices, which in previous years had been the same as for regular season games, had been doubled for this game. Box seats were $4.40, reserved seats $3.30, unreserved grandstand $2.20, and bleachers $1.10. Additionally, the starting time had been moved back to 6:30 P.M. to allow working people to attend. Baseball had made these changes to raise as much money as possible for the two beneficiaries of this year's contest, the Bat and Ball Fund, which supplied baseball equipment to servicemen, and the Army and Navy Relief Fund.

Unfortunately, rain fell in New York, limiting attendance to 33,694, just about the capacity of Ebbets Field and considerably below the 50,000 plus expected and the 48,000 that had attended the 1934 game here. Yet, because of the higher ticket prices, the two charities were able to split $95,000, almost twice the amount raised for the Association of Professional Baseball Players of America in 1934.

Only a few Major Leaguers were in the military in 1942, but among them were some of the game's brightest stars, including Hank Greenberg, Bob Feller, Cecil Travis, and Buddy Lewis. Conversely, sixteen players were making their first All-Star

appearances, including Giants outfielder Willard Marshall and Red Sox pitcher Tex Hughson, neither of whom had yet played a full season in the big leagues. Significantly absent this year was Jimmie Foxx, now a National Leaguer. A month earlier, the Red Sox had sold Foxx, the only man selected for each of the previous nine games, on waivers to the Chicago Cubs.

The two first-place teams, the Yankees and the Dodgers, had the most representatives. The Yanks, leading Boston by four games, had nine, while the Dodgers, eight and a half ahead of St. Louis, had seven. Four Yankees (pitcher Spud Chandler, second baseman Joe Gordon, center fielder Joe DiMaggio, and right fielder Tommy Henrich) and three Dodgers (third baseman Arky Vaughan, left fielder Joe Medwick, and center fielder Pete Reiser) were in the starting lineups.

The two managers, Joe McCarthy of the Yankees and Leo Durocher of the Dodgers, made directly opposite use of their twenty-five-man rosters. McCarthy set a still-existing All-Star record by using just eleven players, while Durocher used twenty-two. The entire AL starting lineup played all nine innings, but the only National Leaguer to play all nine was hometown favorite Mel Ott of the Giants.

A thunderstorm delayed the start of the game for nearly an hour. By the time pitcher Mort Cooper (11-4) took the sign from catcher Walker Cooper, his brother and Cardinals teammate, it was 7:23 P.M. and the lights were on for the first time in an All-Star Game. Boudreau took the first pitch for a ball before driving the next offering into the left-field upper deck. The home run for Boudreau, who was not yet twenty-five and was in his first season as manager of the Cleveland Indians, was the first in All-Star competition by a Cleveland player. Similarly, the game's two other home runs, one by York of Detroit and one by Mickey Owen of Brooklyn, were the first hit by members of those teams.

Henrich, making his All-Star debut, followed by lashing a full-count pitch on a line to right-center.

The ball hit a puddle and stopped, and before Ott could retrieve it, Henrich had hustled into second with a double. Cooper now had to face Ted Williams, the hero of the 1941 game in Detroit, who was following his .406 season with another sensational year. Williams was currently atop the AL in batting (.348), home runs (18), and RBI (80). He would finish the season leading in all three departments to win his first triple crown (but not the MVP Award, which would go to Gordon).

Cooper got Williams on a fly to Medwick and then retired the equally dangerous DiMaggio on a ground ball to Vaughan. Henrich took third on the play, but Cooper had only to retire York to finish the inning having allowed just the one run. With a 1-1 count on him, York poked a high fly that landed in the lower deck in right just inside the foul line. Although it was the kind of hit that would be a home run in only one Major League park, the Polo Grounds, it was enough to give the American League a 3–0 lead.

The Nationals got their first batter on in the home first when Chandler (9-2) hit second baseman Jimmy Brown, the third member of the Cardinals in the starting lineup. Chandler got the next hitter, Vaughan, to hit into a double play and then allowed only two more runners over his four-inning stint, singles by Walker Cooper in the third and Reiser in the fourth. Johnny Mize, leading the NL in home runs and RBI in his first season as a Giant, followed Reiser's hit with a long drive to right-center, more than one hundred feet longer than York's home run. But again, this was the Polo Grounds, and Henrich was able to catch up with it in front of the bullpen.

Chandler's start was the eighth by a Yankee pitcher in the ten All-Star Games. He had been permitted to pitch beyond the three-inning limit because the winner of this game would go to Cleveland the next day to play a servicemen's all-star team. Both clubs had agreed to the lifting of the three-inning limit in order to hold back some pitchers for the next day. They agreed that a pitcher could go as long as five innings today, and that is what Detroit's Al Benton, who relieved Chandler, did. Over those last five innings, Benton walked two and gave up four hits, but the only run he allowed was Owen's eighth-inning home run.

The scheduling of the game for a Monday, one day after the usual Sunday doubleheaders and two days after the traditional Fourth of July doubleheaders, had made pitching selections more difficult for McCarthy and Durocher. Managers in both leagues had promised to keep the All-Star Game in mind when making their holiday weekend pitching selections. Still, Durocher had to replace one of his chosen pitchers, Paul Derringer,

Collision of three players at second base, 1942
*Bob Johnson of the Athletics is tangled up with Cardinals second baseman Jimmy Brown after being forced at second on pitcher Johnny Vander Meer's throw to Braves shortstop Eddie Miller. © Bettmann/*CORBIS.

after the Cincinnati right-hander took a line drive above the knee off the bat of Pittsburgh's Bob Elliott on Sunday. Derringer's teammate, Ray Starr, 12-3 on the season, replaced him. The Americans also were forced to make a last-minute substitution, replacing the injured Bill Dickey with Red Sox catcher Hal Wagner.

The Nationals mounted a threat in the seventh, the inning Durocher put in an almost entirely new team, but the threat started after two were already out. Enos Slaughter singled and Boston's Ernie Lombardi walked, bringing Brooklyn shortstop Pee Wee Reese to the plate. Reese, a .230 hitter, got a big hand from the crowd when he stepped in as the potential tying run. He hit the ball hard, but it was a low liner that shortstop Boudreau dived to his left for and caught.

Owen's home run, which crashed against the facing of the upper deck in right, came while he was pinch-hitting for Cubs pitcher Claude Passeau. Before hitting the home run, the first pinch homer in an All-Star Game, Owen had tried unsuccessfully to bunt his way on. Ironically, he would play in 133 games for Brooklyn in 1942, but this would be his only home run.

Following their first-inning power display, the Americans managed just four singles against Cooper, Passeau, and the Reds duo of Johnny Vander Meer and Bucky Walters. DiMaggio, who had now played the full game in each of his seven All-Star appearances, had two of the hits, Williams one, and the A's Bob Johnson, who had pinch-hit for Chandler, the other. The late start, caused by the rain, had posed a potential problem. The military authorities had decided that the lights would have to be turned out by 9:10 P.M., but then, shortly before the first pitch, they had agreed to allow play to continue until 9:30, the time for Mayor Fiorello LaGuardia's regularly scheduled total blackout of the city. The deadline turned out to be no problem because the quick pace of the game allowed it to end two minutes before 9:30. Despite the darkness, the crowd made its way to cars, buses, and subways without incident, pleasing everybody involved because this was the first major sports event to take place during a blackout.

The following night, the victorious American Leaguers traveled to Cleveland to take on Lt. Mickey Cochrane's Service All-Stars. More than sixty-two thousand fans showed up to see the AL knock Feller out in the second inning on its way to a 5–0 victory. Jim Bagby of the Indians, Sid Hudson of the Senators, and Hughson combined for the shutout.

	AL		NL	
P	Spud Chandler	NYA	Mort Cooper	SLN
C	Birdie Tebbetts	DET	Walker Cooper	SLN
1B	Rudy York	DET	Johnny Mize	NY
2B	Joe Gordon	NYA	Jimmy Brown	SLN
3B	Ken Keltner	CLE	Arky Vaughan	BRO
SS	Lou Boudreau	CLE	Eddie Miller	BSN
OF	Joe DiMaggio	NYA	Joe Medwick	BRO
OF	Tommy Henrich	NYA	Mel Ott	NY
OF	Ted Williams	BOS	Pete Reiser	BRO
	Jim Bagby	CLE	Paul Derringer +	CIN
	Al Benton	DET	Bob Elliott	PIT
	Tiny Bonham	NYA	Billy Herman	BRO
	Bill Dickey +	NYA	Danny Litwhiler	PHI
	Dom DiMaggio	BOS	Ernie Lombardi	BSN
	Bobby Doerr	BOS	Willard Marshall	NY
	Sid Hudson	WAS	Frank McCormick	CIN
	Tex Hughson	BOS	Cliff Melton	NY
	Bob Johnson	PHA	Terry Moore	SLN
	George McQuinn	SLA	Mickey Owen	BRO
	Hal Newhouser	DET	Claude Passeau	CHN
	Phil Rizzuto	NYA	Pee Wee Reese	BRO
	Buddy Rosar	NYA	Enos Slaughter	SLN
	Red Ruffing	NYA	Ray Starr	CIN
	Eddie Smith	CHA	Johnny Vander Meer	CIN
	Stan Spence	WAS	Bucky Walters	CIN
	Hal Wagner	PHA	Whit Wyatt	BRO

+ player replaced on roster

```
American League    300 000 000- 3
National League    000 000 010- 1
```

AMERICAN LEAGUE

	ab	r	h	bi	bb	so	po	a
L.Boudreau, ss	4	1	1	1	0	0	4	5
T.Henrich, rf	4	1	1	0	0	1	2	0
T.Williams, lf	4	0	1	0	0	0	0	0
J.DiMaggio, cf	4	0	2	0	0	0	2	0
R.York, 1b	4	1	1	2	0	1	11	3
J.Gordon, 2b	4	0	0	0	0	3	1	4
K.Keltner, 3b	4	0	0	0	0	1	0	1
B.Tebbetts, c	4	0	0	0	0	2	4	1
S.Chandler, p	1	0	0	0	0	0	3	1
B.Johnson, ph	1	0	1	0	0	0	0	0
A.Benton, p	1	0	0	0	0	0	0	1
Totals	35	3	7	3	0	8	27	16

NATIONAL LEAGUE

	ab	r	h	bi	bb	so	po	a
J.Brown, 2b	2	0	0	0	0	0	1	0
B.Herman, 2b	1	0	0	0	0	0	0	0
A.Vaughan, 3b	2	0	0	0	1	0	1	2
B.Elliott, 3b	1	0	1	0	0	0	1	2
P.Reiser, cf	3	0	1	0	0	0	3	0
T.Moore, cf	1	0	0	0	0	0	1	0
J.Mize, 1b	2	0	0	0	0	0	2	0
F.McCormick, 1b	2	0	0	0	0	0	3	0
M.Ott, rf	4	0	0	0	0	2	1	0
J.Medwick, lf	2	0	0	0	0	0	1	0
E.Slaughter, lf	2	0	1	0	0	0	1	0
W.Cooper, c	2	0	1	0	0	0	8	0
E.Lombardi, c	1	0	0	0	1	0	2	0
E.Miller, ss	2	0	0	0	0	1	2	1
P.Reese, ss	1	0	0	0	0	0	0	1
M.Cooper, p	0	0	0	0	0	0	0	0
W.Marshall, ph	1	0	0	0	0	0	0	0
J.Vander Meer, p	0	0	0	0	0	0	0	1
D.Litwhiler, ph	1	0	1	0	0	0	0	0
C.Passeau, p	0	0	0	0	0	0	0	0
M.Owen, ph	1	1	1	1	0	0	0	0
B.Walters, p	0	0	0	0	0	0	0	0
Totals	31	1	6	1	2	3	27	7

PITCHING	ip	h	r	er	bb	so
American League						
S.Chandler (w)	4.0	2	0	0	0	2
A.Benton (s)	5.0	4	1	1	2	1
National League						
M.Cooper (L)	3.0	4	3	3	0	2
J.Vander Meer	3.0	2	0	0	0	4
C.Passeau	2.0	1	0	0	0	1
B.Walters	1.0	0	0	0	0	1

BATTING
2B: T.Henrich (off M.Cooper).
HR: L.Boudreau (1st inning off M.Cooper, 0 on, 0 out);
R.York (1st inning off M.Cooper, 1 on, 2 out).
2-out RBI: R.York 2.
RBI, scoring position, less than 2 outs: T.Williams 0–1;
J.DiMaggio 0–1; J.Gordon 0–1.

BASERUNNING
Team LOB: 5

FIELDING
PB: B.Tebbetts.
DP: (2). J.Gordon-L.Boudreau-R.York; L.Boudreau-
R.York.

BATTING
HR: M.Owen (8th inning off A.Benton, 0 on, 0 out).
GDP: J.Brown; A.Vaughan.

BASERUNNING
Team LOB: 6

FIELDING
E: J.Brown (dropped throw).

Inherited Runners—Scored:
A.Benton 0–0; J.Vander Meer 0–0; C.Passeau 0–0;
B.Walters 0–0.
HBP: J.Brown by S.Chandler.

GAME DATA—T: 2:07; A: 34178; Temp: Unknown;
Wind: Unknown direction, Speed: Unknown

UMPIRES—HP: Lee Ballanfant (NL), 1B: Ernest Stewart
(AL), 2B: Al Barlick (NL), 3B: Bill McGowan (AL)

STARTING LINEUPS

American League	National League
1. L.Boudreau ss	J.Brown 2b
2. T.Henrich rf	A.Vaughan 3b
3. T.Williams lf	P.Reiser cf
4. J.DiMaggio cf	J.Mize 1b
5. R.York 1b	M.Ott rf
6. J.Gordon 2b	J.Medwick lf
7. K.Keltner 3b	W.Cooper c
8. B.Tebbetts c	E.Miller ss
9. S.Chandler p	M.Cooper p

AL 1ST: L.Boudreau homered to deep leftfield (it was the 1–0 pitch); T.Henrich doubled to right field (it was the 3–2 pitch); T.Williams flied to J.Medwick-lf; J.DiMaggio grounded out (A.Vaughan-3b to J.Mize-1b) [T.Henrich to third]; R.York homered to deep rightfield (it was the 1–1 pitch) [T.Henrich scored]; J.Gordon struck out; 3 R, 3 H, 0 E, 0 LOB. AL 3, NL 0.

NL 1ST: J.Brown was hit by a pitch; A.Vaughan grounded into a double play (J.Gordon-2b to L.Boudreau-ss to R.York-1b) [J.Brown out at second]; P.Reiser grounded out (J.Gordon-2b to R.York-1b); 0 R, 0 H, 0 E, 0 LOB. AL 3, NL 0.

AL 2ND: K.Keltner grounded out (E.Miller-ss to J.Mize-1b); B.Tebbetts struck out; S.Chandler flied to P.Reiser-cf; 0 R, 0 H, 0 E, 0 LOB. AL 3, NL 0.

NL 2ND: J.Mize grounded out (R.York-1b to S.Chandler-p); M.Ott was called out on strikes; J.Medwick grounded out (R.York-1b to S.Chandler-p); 0 R, 0 H, 0 E, 0 LOB. AL 3, NL 0.

AL 3RD: L.Boudreau flied to P.Reiser-cf; T.Henrich popped to J.Brown-2b; T.Williams singled to right field; J.DiMaggio popped to W.Cooper-c in foul territory; 0 R, 1 H, 0 E, 1 LOB. AL 3, NL 0.

NL 3RD: W.Cooper singled to right field; E.Miller struck out; **W.Marshall batted for M.Cooper;** W.Marshall forced W.Cooper (S.Chandler-p to L.Boudreau-ss) [W.Marshall to first]; J.Brown grounded out (J.Gordon-2b to R.York-1b); 0 R, 1 H, 0 E, 1 LOB. AL 3, NL 0.

AL 4TH: **J.Vander Meer replaced W.Marshall (pitching);** R.York struck out; J.Gordon was called out on strikes; K.Keltner popped to E.Miller-ss; 0 R, 0 H, 0 E, 0 LOB. AL 3, NL 0.

NL 4TH: A.Vaughan grounded out (R.York-1b to S.Chandler-p); P.Reiser singled to second base; J.Mize lined to T.Henrich-rf; B.Tebbetts allowed a passed ball [P.Reiser to second]; M.Ott grounded out (J.Gordon-2b to R.York-1b); 0 R, 1 H, 0 E, 1 LOB. AL 3, NL 0.

AL 5TH: B.Tebbetts popped to W.Cooper-c in foul territory; **B.Johnson batted for S.Chandler;** B.Johnson singled to left field; L.Boudreau forced B.Johnson (J.Vander Meer-p to E.Miller-ss) [L.Boudreau to first]; T.Henrich struck out; 0 R, 1 H, 0 E, 1 LOB. AL 3, NL 0.

NL 5TH: Umpires moved: McGowan (hp), Ballanfant (1b), Stewart (2b), Barlick (3b); **A.Benton replaced B.Johnson (pitching);** J.Medwick grounded out (K.Keltner-3b to R.York-1b); On a bunt W.Cooper grounded out (B.Tebbetts-c to R.York-1b); E.Miller grounded out (L.Boudreau-ss to R.York-1b); 0 R, 0 H, 0 E, 0 LOB. AL 3, NL 0.

AL 6TH: T.Williams flied to P.Reiser-cf; J.DiMaggio singled to first base; R.York reached on an error [J.DiMaggio to second, R.York to first (error by J.Brown-2b; assist by A.Vaughan-3b)]; J.Gordon struck out; K.Keltner popped to A.Vaughan-3b; 0 R, 1 H, 1 E, 2 LOB. AL 3, NL 0.

NL 6TH: **D.Litwhiler batted for J.Vander Meer;** D.Litwhiler singled to deep second base; J.Brown grounded into a double play (L.Boudreau-ss to R.York-1b) [D.Litwhiler out at second]; A.Vaughan walked; P.Reiser flied to J.DiMaggio-cf; 0 R, 1 H, 0 E, 1 LOB. AL 3, NL 0.

AL 7TH: **C.Passeau replaced D.Litwhiler (pitching); E.Lombardi replaced W.Cooper (playing c); F.McCormick replaced J.Mize (playing 1b); P.Reese replaced E.Miller (playing ss); B.Herman replaced J.Brown (playing 2b); B.Elliott replaced A.Vaughan (playing 3b); E.Slaughter replaced J.Medwick (playing lf); T.Moore replaced P.Reiser (playing cf);** B.Tebbetts struck out; A.Benton grounded out (B.Elliott-3b to F.McCormick-1b); L.Boudreau flied to E.Slaughter-lf; 0 R, 0 H, 0 E, 0 LOB. AL 3, NL 0.

NL 7TH: F.McCormick grounded out (L.Boudreau-ss to R.York-1b); M.Ott struck out; E.Slaughter singled to second base; E.Lombardi walked [E.Slaughter to second]; P.Reese lined to L.Boudreau-ss; 0 R, 1 H, 0 E, 2 LOB. AL 3, NL 0.

AL 8TH: T.Henrich lined to M.Ott-rf; T.Williams flied to T.Moore-cf; J.DiMaggio singled to left field; R.York grounded out (B.Elliott-3b to F.McCormick-1b); 0 R, 1 H, 0 E, 1 LOB. AL 3, NL 0.

NL 8TH: **M.Owen batted for C.Passeau;** M.Owen homered to deep leftfield (it was the 0–1 pitch); Owen bunted the first pitch foul; B.Herman grounded out (A.Benton-p to R.York-1b); B.Elliott singled to right field; T.Moore popped to R.York-1b in foul territory; F.McCormick forced B.Elliott (L.Boudreau-ss to J.Gordon-2b) [F.McCormick to first]; 1 R, 2 H, 0 E, 1 LOB. AL 3, NL 1.

AL 9TH: **B.Walters replaced M.Owen (pitching);** J.Gordon grounded out (P.Reese-ss to F.McCormick-1b); K.Keltner struck out; B.Tebbetts popped to B.Elliott-3b; 0 R, 0 H, 0 E, 0 LOB. AL 3, NL 1.

NL 9TH: M.Ott popped to B.Tebbetts-c in foul territory; E.Slaughter flied to J.DiMaggio-cf; E.Lom-
bardi flied to T.Henrich-rf; 0 R, 0 H, 0 E, 0 LOB.
AL 3, NL 1.

Final Totals	R	H	E	LOB
American League	3	7	0	5
National League	1	6	1	6

11

No Yankees Needed

By 1943, the American League had won seven of the first ten All-Star Games, an imbalance the National Leaguers attributed mainly to the many players from the New York Yankees, baseball's predominant team, on the AL squad. The Yanks were in first place again this year, but in an attempt to demonstrate his league's overall superiority, manager Joe McCarthy kept all his Yankee players on the bench for this game. McCarthy's gimmick succeeded when Bobby Doerr's three-run home run, along with the pitching of Dutch Leonard, Hal Newhouser, and Tex Hughson, led the AL to yet another victory. The final score was 5–3 in this first scheduled night game in All-Star history. (Although the 1942 game at the Polo Grounds had been played under the lights, it had been scheduled to start at twilight and was delayed by rain.)

The game raised $115,174 for the Bat and Ball Fund of the U.S. Army and U.S. Navy, while each of the selected players received a $50 war bond. In addition to the $65,174 realized in gate receipts from a crowd of 31,938, radio rights brought an additional $25,000, Commissioner Kenesaw Mountain Landis's office contributed $20,000, and each league contributed $2,500.

The 1943 season—including the All-Star Game—was the first to be greatly affected by World War II. Fourteen of the fifty players on the 1942 All-Star rosters were currently serving in the military, including Joe and Dom DiMaggio, Ted Williams, Tommy Henrich, Phil Rizzuto, Pee Wee Reese, Johnny Mize, Pete Reiser, Terry Moore, and Enos Slaughter. In all likelihood, some of them listened to the game courtesy of the British Broadcasting Company, which beamed it to servicemen around the world via shortwave radio.

Despite the loss of Moore and Slaughter, the defending world champion St. Louis Cardinals were atop the National League, entering the break with a five-and-a-half-game lead over Brooklyn. Eight Cardinals were chosen for the NL squad,

which was managed by St. Louis's Billy Southworth, and five were in the starting lineup. Among them were Mort Cooper, the starting pitcher, and Stan Musial, the league's batting leader at .331. Musial was playing in the first of what would be a record twenty-four consecutive games. Only seven Cardinals players would be at the game, however, because left-hander Howie Pollet had to report for Army duty. Giants right-hander Ace Adams, originally slated to be the NL's batting practice pitcher, replaced Pollet on the roster.

Scheduled to start at 8:45 P.M., Leonard didn't make his first pitch until 9:00 to satisfy the BBC's request for a delay. The Nationals scored a quick run against the Washington knuckleballer, who was starting despite an unimpressive 5-8 record. Cubs third baseman Stan Hack went after the first pitch and beat out a ground ball behind second. Hack went to third on a hit-and-run single by Billy Herman—a master at that maneuver—and scored on Musial's fly ball to Browns center fielder Chet Laabs.

Cooper, 11-5, also allowed the first man he faced to reach base. He hit Senators right fielder George Case, the game's speediest runner, but then retired the next three batters. Cooper, who had been touched for two first-inning home runs in the 1942 game, had his downfall in the second inning this time. After getting Dick Siebert of the A's on a fly out to open the inning, he walked both Washington catcher Jake Early and Laabs. Red Sox second baseman Doerr, the number eight hitter, was next. On the 1-1 pitch, a letter-high curve ball, Doerr launched a high fly ball that just made it into the lower left-field seats. It gave the Americans a 3–1 lead, one they would never surrender. Leonard then slapped a single to right, before Cooper got Case to bounce into an around-the-horn, inning-ending double play.

The Americans made it 4–1 in the third on doubles by the first two batters, Cleveland's Ken Keltner and rookie sensation Dick Wakefield of Detroit. Wakefield, the first rookie to start an All-Star

Game since Joe DiMaggio in 1936, was playing in place of the injured Charlie Keller. The next batter was Vern Stephens, the American League's leading batter and home run hitter. The Browns shortstop was also just one RBI behind leader Nick Etten; nevertheless, McCarthy ordered him to lay down a sacrifice bunt. Stephens put down an excellently placed bunt that moved Wakefield to third. At that point, Southworth removed Cooper and brought in Cincinnati left-hander Johnny Vander Meer to face the left-handed-hitting Siebert. McCarthy countered by sending right-handed slugger Rudy York of Detroit up to bat for Siebert. The fans booed the early exit of the only Philadelphia player in the American League lineup and then cheered when Vander Meer fanned York. (Shibe Park was home to both the American League Athletics and the National League Phillies, but although this was the AL's turn to play host, the crowd was mainly rooting for the National Leaguers.)

Vander Meer left Wakefield stranded by also fanning Laabs. In all, he struck out six batters in his 2.2 innings, tying the mark set by Carl Hubbell in the 1934 game. Furthermore, Vander Meer had now struck out eleven American Leaguers in his 8.2 innings spread over three All-Star Games, the same amount as Hubbell, whose eleven strikeouts came in 9.2 innings over five games.

Vander Meer struck out the side in the fifth, although the Americans did get a run against him, an unearned one. Case, who had walked to lead off the inning, was on third, and Stephens, who had singled with two out, was on first, with York at the plate. On the 3-1 pitch, the runners attempted a delayed double steal. Catcher Walker Cooper, Mort's brother and Cardinals battery mate, threw down to second, seemingly in time to get Stephens. But Herman, seeing Case breaking for the plate, threw home rather than attempting to make the tag. It was a poor throw that bounced in front of Cooper and skidded past him as Case slid in safely. It was now a 5–1 game, and although the AL was unable to score against Pittsburgh's Rip Sewell and Boston's Al Javery over the final three innings, the team had already tallied enough runs to win.

Newhouser, the young left-hander who would go 8-17 for the Tigers this season, made his first All-Star appearance in relief of Leonard in the fourth. He retired Bill Nicholson and Elbie Fletcher but then gave up a single to Walker Cooper and a pinch-hit single to Pittsburgh's Vince DiMaggio, batting for Harry Walker. Newhouser ended the threat by getting Cardinals shortstop Marty Marion on a force out, and then he set the side down in order in the fifth.

The Nationals mounted a strong threat in the sixth but failed to capitalize. A lead-off double by

Musial and a walk to Brooklyn's Augie Galan, batting for Nicholson, put runners at first and second with nobody out. Fletcher was the due batter, but Southworth chose Babe Dahlgren, the lone member of the Phillies on the team, to pinch-hit for the Pittsburgh first baseman. The crowd cheered this substitution but quickly quieted down when Dahlgren grounded into a snappy Stephens-to-Doerr-to-York double play. Musial moved to third, but he stayed there as Ernie Lombardi of the Giants, batting for Walker Cooper, flied out. Lombardi's appearance made him the first player to represent three different teams in the All-Star Game. He had previously appeared as a member of the Reds and the Braves.

In the seventh, Newhouser yielded to Boston's Hughson, whose twenty-two wins had led the AL in 1942, but who was having a so-so season this year. Vince DiMaggio, playing in his first All-Star Game, greeted Hughson with a triple off the left-field wall. After pinch hitter Mel Ott fanned, DiMaggio came home on pinch hitter Dixie Walker's long fly to Wakefield. Dixie and Harry Walker, the NL's starting center fielder, were brothers, but unlike the other pair of brothers on the NL squad (the Coopers), they played for different teams. Dixie was with Brooklyn, while Harry was a Cardinals teammate of the Coopers.

With two out and no one on, Hack and Herman singled, the second hit of the game for each, but Musial ended the inning with a pop to Keltner. Herman and Ott had now played for the NL in every game since 1934; however, missing from the NL squad for the first time since that year was Joe Medwick. Ott would play again in 1944, but this was Herman's final appearance. Herman had been a most effective player for the National League, and his total of thirteen hits (in thirty at bats) was then the All-Star record.

The Nationals scored their final run in the ninth when DiMaggio led off with a long home run to the bleachers in left. It was the third hit in three at bats for Vince, the eldest of the three Major League DiMaggios. Two outs later, Hack singled for his third hit of the game and the NL's tenth, but Hughson ended it by getting Herman on a liner to left fielder Bob Johnson. The crowd that had booed in the third inning when McCarthy used York to pinch-hit for Siebert had cheered in the eighth when he sent Johnson in to replace Wakefield. Johnson had starred for the A's from 1933 to 1942 and was now in his first season with Washington.

In the home team clubhouse, McCarthy had a simple explanation for not using any Yankee players in the game. "We didn't need them," he said. "We got out there in front early enough. Besides, these other boys deserved a chance to shine. The Yankees have had enough of the limelight. Let some of the other guys get some of it."

The usual gloom pervaded the losing clubhouse. Mort Cooper, the National League's Most Valuable Player in 1942, had now made four starts against the American League, two in the All-Star Game and two in the 1942 World Series against the Yankees. He had lost both All-Star Games (Cardinals pitchers now had a 1-5 record in All-Star competition), and though he was charged with only one World Series defeat, he was hit soundly in both starts. The Yanks reached him for seventeen hits and eight earned runs in thirteen innings. Nevertheless, Southworth, claiming after the game that Cooper was "a better pitcher than that," said that if the Cardinals should win the pennant in 1943, Cooper would be his pitcher in game one of the World Series. The Cards did win the pennant in 1943, but Southworth chose left-hander Max Lanier to pitch the Series opener.

	AL			NL		
P	Dutch Leonard	WAS		Mort Cooper	SLN	
C	Jake Early	WAS		Walker Cooper	SLN	
1B	Dick Siebert	PHA		Frank McCormick	+	CIN
2B	Bobby Doerr	BOS		Billy Herman	BRO	
3B	Ken Keltner	CLE		Stan Hack	CHN	
SS	Vern Stephens	SLA		Marty Marion	SLN	
OF	George Case	WAS		Stan Musial	SLN	
OF	Charlie Keller	+	NYA	Bill Nicholson	CHN	
OF	Chet Laabs	SLA		Harry Walker	SLN	
	Luke Appling	CHA		Ace Adams	NY	
	Jim Bagby	CLE		Babe Dahlgren	PHI	
	Tiny Bonham	NYA		Vince DiMaggio	PIT	
	Lou Boudreau	CLE		Elbie Fletcher	PIT	
	Spud Chandler	NYA		Lonny Frey	CIN	
	Bill Dickey	NYA		Augie Galan	BRO	
	Joe Gordon	NYA		Al Javery	BSN	
	Jeff Heath	CLE		Whitey Kurowski	SLN	
	Tex Hughson	BOS		Max Lanier	SLN	
	Bob Johnson	WAS		Ernie Lombardi	NY	
	Oscar Judd	BOS		Eddie Miller	CIN	
	Johnny Lindell	NYA		Mel Ott	NY	
	Hal Newhouser	DET		Mickey Owen	BRO	
	Buddy Rosar	CLE		Claude Passeau	CHN	
	Al Smith	CLE		Howie Pollet	+	SLN
	Dick Wakefield	DET		Rip Sewell	PIT	
	Rudy York	DET		Johnny Vander Meer	CIN	
				Dixie Walker	BRO	

+ player replaced on roster

National League	100 000 101-	3
American League	031 010 00x-	5

NATIONAL LEAGUE

	ab	r	h	bi	bb	so	po	a
S.Hack, 3b	5	1	3	0	0	0	0	2
B.Herman, 2b	5	0	2	0	0	0	3	2
S.Musial, lf-rf	4	0	1	1	0	0	0	0
B.Nicholson, rf	2	0	0	0	0	0	0	0
A.Galan, ph-lf	1	0	0	0	1	0	1	0
E.Fletcher, 1b	2	0	0	0	0	0	4	0
B.Dahlgren, ph-1b	2	0	0	0	0	0	2	0
W.Cooper, c	2	0	1	0	0	0	7	1
E.Lombardi, ph-c	2	0	0	0	0	0	3	0
H.Walker, cf	1	0	0	0	0	0	1	0
V.DiMaggio, ph-cf	3	2	3	1	0	0	1	0
M.Marion, ss	2	0	0	0	0	0	2	2
M.Ott, ph	1	0	0	0	0	1	0	0
E.Miller, ss	1	0	0	0	0	1	0	1
M.Cooper, p	1	0	0	0	0	0	0	1
J.Vander Meer, p	1	0	0	0	0	1	0	1
R.Sewell, p	0	0	0	0	0	0	0	1
D.Walker, ph	1	0	0	1	0	0	0	0
A.Javery, p	0	0	0	0	0	0	0	0
L.Frey, ph	1	0	0	0	0	0	0	0
Totals	37	3	10	3	1	3	24	11

BATTING
2B: S.Musial (off H.Newhouser).
3B: V.DiMaggio (off T.Hughson).
HR: V.DiMaggio (9th inning off T.Hughson, 0 on, 0 out).
RBI, scoring position, less than 2 outs: S.Musial 1-1;
 B.Dahlgren 0-1; M.Ott 0-1; D.Walker 1-1.
GDP: B.Dahlgren.

BASERUNNING
Team LOB: 8

FIELDING
E: B.Herman (dropped throw); S.Hack (fumble);
 B.Herman (fumble).
DP: (3). S.Hack-B.Herman-E.Fletcher; J.Vander Meer-
 M.Marion-E.Fletcher; E.Miller-B.Herman.

AMERICAN LEAGUE

	ab	r	h	bi	bb	so	po	a
G.Case, rf	2	1	0	0	1	1	0	0
K.Keltner, 3b	4	1	1	0	0	3	2	2
D.Wakefield, lf	4	0	2	1	0	1	3	0
B.Johnson, lf	0	0	0	0	0	0	1	0
V.Stephens, ss	3	0	1	0	0	1	1	3
D.Siebert, 1b	1	0	0	0	0	0	3	1
R.York, ph-1b	3	0	1	0	0	2	4	0
C.Laabs, cf	3	1	0	0	1	1	7	0
J.Early, c	2	1	0	0	1	1	3	0
B.Doerr, 2b	4	1	2	3	0	3	3	3
D.Leonard, p	1	0	1	0	0	0	0	1
H.Newhouser, p	1	0	0	0	0	0	0	0
J.Heath, ph	1	0	0	0	0	0	0	0
T.Hughson, p	0	0	0	0	0	0	0	0
Totals	29	5	8	4	3	10	27	10

BATTING
2B: K.Keltner (off M.Cooper); D.Wakefield (off
 M.Cooper).
HR: B.Doerr (2nd inning off M.Cooper, 2 on, 1 out).
RBI, scoring position, less than 2 outs: D.Wakefield 1-
 1; R.York 0-1; B.Doerr 1-2.
S: V.Stephens; J.Early.
GDP: G.Case; C.Laabs.

BASERUNNING
Team LOB: 6

FIELDING
E: V.Stephens (fumble).
DP: (1). V.Stephens-B.Doerr-R.York.

PITCHING	ip	h	r	er	bb	so
National League						
M.Cooper (L)	2.1	4	4	4	2	1
J.Vander Meer	2.2	2	1	0	1	6
R.Sewell	1.0	0	0	0	0	0
A.Javery	2.0	2	0	0	0	3
American League						
D.Leonard (w)	3.0	2	1	1	0	0
H.Newhouser	3.0	3	0	0	1	1
T.Hughson (s)	3.0	5	2	2	0	2

Inherited Runners—Scored:
 J.Vander Meer 1-0; R.Sewell 0-0; A.Javery 0-0;
 H.Newhouser 0-0; T.Hughson 0-0.
HBP: G.Case by M.Cooper.

GAME DATA—T: 2:07; A: 31938; Temp: Unknown;
Wind: Unknown direction, Speed: Unknown

UMPIRES—HP: Eddie Rommel (AL), 1B: Jocko Conlan
(NL), 2B: Joe Rue (AL), 3B: Tom Dunn (NL)

STARTING LINEUPS

	National League	American League
1.	S.Hack 3b	G.Case rf
2.	B.Herman 2b	K.Keltner 3b
3.	S.Musial lf	D.Wakefield lf
4.	B.Nicholson rf	V.Stephens ss
5.	E.Fletcher 1b	D.Siebert 1b
6.	W.Cooper c	C.Laabs cf
7.	H.Walker cf	J.Early c
8.	M.Marion ss	B.Doerr 2b
9.	M.Cooper p	D.Leonard p

NL 1ST: first night game (broadcast to GIs via short-wave radio); S.Hack singled to deep second base; B.Herman singled [S.Hack to third]; S.Musial flied to C.Laabs-cf [S.Hack scored]; B.Nicholson forced B.Herman (D.Siebert-1b to V.Stephens-ss) [B.Nicholson to first]; E.Fletcher grounded out (B.Doerr-2b to D.Siebert-1b); 1 R, 2 H, 0 E, 1 LOB. NL 1, AL 0.

AL 1ST: G.Case was hit by a pitch; K.Keltner struck out; D.Wakefield forced G.Case (B.Herman-2b to M.Marion-ss) [D.Wakefield to first]; V.Stephens grounded out (M.Marion-ss to E.Fletcher-1b); 0 R, 0 H, 0 E, 1 LOB. NL 1, AL 0.

NL 2ND: W.Cooper popped to B.Doerr-2b; H.Walker grounded out (D.Leonard-p to D.Siebert-1b); M.Marion reached on an error by V.Stephens-ss [M.Marion to first]; M.Cooper flied to C.Laabs-cf; 0 R, 0 H, 1 E, 1 LOB. NL 1, AL 0.

AL 2ND: D.Siebert flied to H.Walker-cf; C.Laabs walked; J.Early walked [C.Laabs to second]; B.Doerr homered to deep leftfield [C.Laabs scored, J.Early scored]; D.Leonard singled to right field; G.Case grounded into a double play (S.Hack-3b to B.Herman-2b to E.Fletcher-1b) [D.Leonard out at second]; 3 R, 2 H, 0 E, 0 LOB. NL 1, AL 3.

NL 3RD: S.Hack flied to D.Wakefield-lf; B.Herman popped to K.Keltner-3b; S.Musial grounded out (B.Doerr-2b to D.Siebert-1b); 0 R, 0 H, 0 E, 0 LOB. NL 1, AL 3.

AL 3RD: K.Keltner doubled to center field; D.Wakefield doubled to left field [K.Keltner scored]; V.Stephens out on a sacrifice bunt (M.Cooper-p to E.Fletcher-1b) [D.Wakefield to third]; **J.Vander Meer replaced M.Cooper (pitching); R.York batted for D.Siebert;** R.York struck out; C.Laabs struck out; 1 R, 2 H, 0 E, 1 LOB. NL 1, AL 4.

NL 4TH: **H.Newhouser replaced D.Leonard (pitching); R.York stayed in game (playing 1b);** B.Nicholson flied to C.Laabs-cf; E.Fletcher flied to D.Wakefield-lf; W.Cooper singled to center field; **V.DiMaggio batted for H.Walker;** V.DiMag-gio singled to left field [W.Cooper to second]; M.Marion forced V.DiMaggio (K.Keltner-3b to B.Doerr-2b) [M.Marion to first]; 0 R, 2 H, 0 E, 2 LOB. NL 1, AL 4.

AL 4TH: **V.DiMaggio stayed in game (playing cf);** J.Early struck out; B.Doerr singled to left field; On a bunt H.Newhouser hit into a double play (J.Vander Meer-p to M.Marion-ss to E.Fletcher-1b) [B.Doerr out at second]; 0 R, 1 H, 0 E, 0 LOB. NL 1, AL 4.

NL 5TH: J.Vander Meer struck out; S.Hack grounded out (K.Keltner-3b to R.York-1b); B.Herman grounded out (V.Stephens-ss to R.York-1b); 0 R, 0 H, 0 E, 0 LOB. NL 1, AL 4.

AL 5TH: Umpires moved: Dunn (hp), Rue (1b), Conlan (2b), Rommel (3b; G.Case walked; K.Keltner struck out; D.Wakefield struck out; V.Stephens singled to left field [G.Case to third]; G.Case advanced to home (error by B.Her-man-2b; assist by W.Cooper-c) and V.Stephens advanced to second; Stephens broke for second; as W. Cooper threw to Herman, Case made a dash for the plate and scored when Herman's return throw bounced in front of Cooper; R.York struck out; 0 R, 1 H, 1 E, 1 LOB. NL 1, AL 5.

NL 6TH: S.Musial doubled to left field; **A.Galan batted for B.Nicholson;** A.Galan walked; **B.Dahlgren batted for E.Fletcher;** B.Dahlgren grounded into a double play (V.Stephens-ss to B.Doerr-2b to R.York-1b) [S.Musial to third, A.Galan out at second]; **E.Lombardi batted for W.Cooper;** E.Lombardi flied to C.Laabs-cf; 0 R, 1 H, 0 E, 1 LOB. NL 1, AL 5.

AL 6TH: **A.Galan stayed in game (playing lf); S.Musial changed positions (playing rf); E.Lombardi stayed in game (playing c); B.Dahlgren stayed in game (playing 1b); R.Sewell replaced J.Vander Meer (pitching);** C.Laabs reached on an error by S.Hack-3b [C.Laabs to first]; J.Early out on a sacrifice bunt (R.Sewell-p to B.Dahlgren-1b) [C.Laabs to second]; B.Doerr grounded out (S.Hack-3b to B.Dahlgren-1b) [C.Laabs to third]; **J.Heath batted for H.Newhouser;** J.Heath flied to V.DiMaggio-cf; 0 R, 0 H, 1 E, 1 LOB. NL 1, AL 5.

NL 7TH: **T.Hughson replaced J.Heath (pitching);** V.DiMaggio tripled to left field; **M.Ott batted for M.Marion;** M.Ott struck out; **D.Walker batted for R.Sewell;** D.Walker flied to D.Wakefield-lf [V.Di-Maggio scored]; S.Hack singled to third base; B.Herman singled [S.Hack to third]; S.Musial popped to K.Keltner-3b; 1 R, 3 H, 0 E, 2 LOB. NL 2, AL 5.

AL 7TH: **E.Miller replaced M.Ott (playing ss); A.Jav-ery replaced D.Walker (pitching);** G.Case struck out; K.Keltner struck out; D.Wakefield singled to center field; V.Stephens struck out; 0 R, 1 H, 0 E, 1 LOB. NL 2, AL 5.

NL 8TH: **B.Johnson replaced D.Wakefield (playing lf);** A.Galan flied to C.Laabs-cf; B.Dahlgren grounded out (V.Stephens-ss to R.York-1b); E.Lombardi flied to C.Laabs-cf; 0 R, 0 H, 0 E, 0 LOB. NL 2, AL 5.

AL 8TH: R.York singled to center field; C.Laabs grounded into a double play (E.Miller-ss to B.Herman-2b) [R.York out at second]; J.Early reached on an error by B.Herman-2b [J.Early to

first]; B.Doerr flied to A.Galan-lf; 0 R, 1 H, 1 E, 1 LOB. NL 2, AL 5.

NL 9TH: V.DiMaggio homered to deep leftfield; E.Miller struck out; **L.Frey batted for A.Javery;** L.Frey flied to C.Laabs-cf; S.Hack singled to first base; B.Herman flied to B.Johnson-lf; 1 R, 2 H, 0 E, 1 LOB. NL 3, AL 5.

Final Totals	R	H	E	LOB
National League	3	10	3	8
American League	5	8	1	6

12

A Perfect Cavaretta Helps the NL to a Rare Victory

Held scoreless for four innings, the National League exploded for four runs in the fifth on their way to a 7–1 triumph in the Major Leagues' twelfth All-Star Game. The win was just the fourth for the Nationals, although their six-run margin of victory did set a new standard, exceeding the five-run edge the Americans had in their 8–3 win at Washington in 1937. The fifth-inning assault on Boston's Tex Hughson, the NL's most productive inning to date, erased a 1–0 American League lead and delighted the overwhelmingly pro–National League crowd on this sweltering night. Cardinals manager Billy Southworth, whose team was again leading the National League, used four pitchers, who combined to hold the Americans to six hits — none after the fifth inning — and one unearned run. This victory would be the only one the Nationals would have in the ten-year span between their 4–0 win in 1940 and their 4–3 win in 1950.

Attendance for the 9:00 P.M. contest was 29,589, well below the Forbes Field capacity of 40,000. Pirate officials had expected a much larger crowd for Pittsburgh's biggest baseball event since the 1927 World Series. Still, the Bat and Ball Fund of the U.S. Army and U.S. Navy received $81,275 from the gate receipts, plus $25,000 from the Gillette Safety Razor Company for the radio rights and a donation from Sportservice, the concessionaire. Even sportswriters and club officials were asked to pay the admission price, which, as it had been for all the wartime All-Star Games, was double the usual price.

A year earlier, Joe McCarthy had kept all his Yankee players on the bench in the AL's 5–3 win at Philadelphia. But for this game, McCarthy, the AL manager for the seventh and final time, started two of the three Yanks on the team, including the all-Yankee battery of right-hander Hank Borowy and veteran catcher Rollie Hemsley. Borowy, the ninth Yankee pitcher to start in the twelve games

played, was one of seven American Leaguers chosen as All-Stars for the first time. By contrast, the Yanks were the third team Hemsley had represented in the game. He had been selected five times and had appeared previously for the Browns in 1935 and the Indians in 1940. Two of his American League teammates, Bobo Newsom and Bob Johnson, and Joe Medwick of the National League were also representing their third team.

National League managers had been using regular season teammates to form their starting batteries ever since the 1938 game. Southworth changed that practice this year, choosing Cincinnati's Bucky Walters as his pitcher and St. Louis's Walker Cooper to catch him. In doing so, Southworth bypassed Walters's regular catcher, Ray Mueller, who on Sunday had caught his 137th straight game, an NL record. Walters, with a 14-3 record, including an 8-1 mark in night games, was clearly the league's best pitcher and the logical choice to start.

Two of Southworth's Cardinals pitchers had also been selected, but both had to miss the game. Bill Voiselle of the Giants replaced Max Lanier, who had injured his arm four days earlier, and Jim Tobin of the Braves replaced George Munger, who was scheduled for his army induction at Missouri's Jefferson Barracks on the day of the game. (Munger pitched that night and beat the Lambert Field Navy Wings, 2–1.)

Southworth also lost his backup shortstop when Cincinnati's Eddie Miller withdrew the day before the game because of a sore shoulder. Pirates infielder Pete Coscarat was Southworth's first choice to replace Miller; however, when no one could locate Coscarat, who was off on a fishing trip, Southworth selected Pittsburgh shortstop Frankie Zak, a rookie batting .296.

Two members of the league-leading St. Louis Browns, first baseman George McQuinn and shortstop Vern Stephens, had base hits in the first inning, although both came with two outs, and Walters ended the threat by striking out Johnson.

Borowy, 11-4 this season, also ran into first-inning trouble. Stan Musial followed a one-out walk to the Cubs' Phil Cavaretta with a ground ball between McQuinn and second baseman Bobby Doerr. Doerr fielded it, but his throw to Borowy, covering first, was wide. Musial was safe, and Cavaretta went all the way to third. The official scorers ruled the play a hit for Musial and an error for Doerr. Cooper then lined out to right, and when Cavaretta tried to score after the catch, right fielder Stan Spence of Washington nailed him with a perfect throw to Hemsley. Although highly partisan, the Pittsburgh fans acknowledged Spence's excellent toss with a big round of applause.

Cleveland third baseman Ken Keltner's lead-off single in the second led to the American League's lone run. Keltner moved to second as Doerr bounced out to second baseman Connie Ryan and to third as Hemsley grounded to shortstop Marty Marion. Keltner scored on Borowy's single up the middle, a bounder to Ryan, who made a fine back-hand stop but whose throw to first was too late.

The Nationals got a lead-off single by Brooklyn's Dixie Walker in the second and a two-out triple by Cavaretta in the third; neither player could score, and when Borowy turned the game over to Hughson, the AL's 1–0 lead was intact. At 13-3, Hughson had the best win-loss record on the American League staff. He had pitched a few innings late in a game against Cleveland on Sunday; nevertheless, the "two-day rule," which said a pitcher couldn't pitch two days before the All-Star Game, was being waived this year.

Hughson retired the Nationals in order in the fourth but was routed in the fifth. Ryan had a lead-off single and then stole second as Marion was striking out. He scored the tying run on pinch hitter Bill Nicholson's double, which landed just fair down the right-field line. Nicholson, the Cubs slugger, had batted for Ken Raffensberger. The Philadelphia left-hander, who had pitched two scoreless innings, would be the winning pitcher.

Nicholson scored the go-ahead run when Augie Galan's ground ball took a bad hop off Stephens's glove for a single. A walk to Cavaretta and an error by McQuinn, who dropped Doerr's throw of Musial's ground ball, loaded the bases. Cooper then ripped a single between short and third that scored Galan, but Cavaretta was out at the plate on the throw from left fielder Johnson to catcher Frankie Hayes. It was the second time that Cavaretta had been cut down at the plate, but this time the National Leaguers vociferously protested the call by Cal Hubbard, the American League umpire who had taken over at home plate in this half inning.

When play resumed, Walker singled to right,

scoring Musial with the fourth run of the inning and finishing Hughson. Bob Muncrief of the Browns ended the inning by getting hometown favorite Bob Elliott of the Pirates on a foul fly to left fielder Johnson.

The Nationals added two more runs in the seventh against Detroit's Hal Newhouser, who would follow his 13-5 record in the season's first half with a 16-4 mark in the second. Cavaretta greeted Newhouser with a single to center and went to second on Musial's sacrifice bunt, an odd strategy with a three-run lead and the game's best hitter at the plate. (Musial was batting a Major League–leading .366.)

Cooper had an infield hit, sending Cavaretta to third. Then, after Stephens made an excellent catch on Walker's little looper to short left, Cardinals third baseman Whitey Kurowski, the NL's RBI leader, lashed a double to left. Both Cavaretta and Cooper scored, making it 6–1, although a better throw from relay man Stephens might have gotten Cooper.

Newhouser was touched for a final run, albeit an unearned one, in the eighth. He struck out Marion to open the inning, but when Hayes mishandled the third strike, the Cardinals shortstop reached first base. Evidently Southworth felt a five-run lead with one inning to go wasn't enough and had pinch hitter Joe Medwick sacrifice Marion to second. This was the final All-Star appearance for both Medwick, who had been selected in ten of the twelve games, and Mel Ott, who had pinch-hit earlier and had been selected in eleven of the twelve games. Walks to Galan and Cavaretta loaded the bases, and Musial's long fly ball scored Marion before McCarthy brought Newsom in to get the final out.

Playing in his first All-Star Game, Cavaretta had quite an evening. He finished with three walks, a single, and a triple, although having been twice thrown out at the plate, he scored only one run. He was the first National Leaguer to reach base five times in one game — Charlie Gehringer did it for the AL in 1934 — and he and Gehringer are to this day the only batters to draw three walks in an All-Star Game.

While the National League was adding to its lead, Pittsburgh's Rip Sewell and Boston's Jim Tobin were completely shutting down the American League batters. Sewell faced only nine men in his three innings, as Johnson, whom he walked, was erased when Keltner hit into a double play. Tobin, a knuckleballer who had no-hit Brooklyn back in April, pitched a perfect ninth. Sewell further entertained the home crowd by throwing three of his famous blooper pitches. Hubbard called one a ball and one a strike, while on the third, McQuinn, who was attempting to bunt for a hit, was thrown out on a fine play by catcher Cooper.

Afterward, Southworth lauded Sewell's pitching, while reminding everyone of Nicholson's contribution. "I think Nicholson should get a lot of credit for it. That pinch double just started something the American League couldn't stop," he said.

American League coach Joe Cronin spoke for the losing side. "You can't beat that kind of pitching and hitting," Cronin said. "We just couldn't get to those slow ball pitchers. They had us nailed down right."

	AL		NL	
P	Hank Borowy	NYA	Bucky Walters	CIN
C	Rollie Hemsley	NYA	Walker Cooper	SLN
1B	George McQuinn	SLA	Phil Cavarretta	CHN
2B	Bobby Doerr	BOS	Connie Ryan	BSN
3B	Ken Keltner	CLE	Bob Elliott	PIT
SS	Vern Stephens	SLA	Marty Marion	SLN
OF	Bob Johnson	BOS	Augie Galan	BRO
OF	Stan Spence	WAS	Stan Musial	SLN
OF	Thurman Tucker	CHA	Dixie Walker	BRO
	Lou Boudreau	CLE	Nate Andrews	BSN
	George Case +	WAS	Vince DiMaggio	PIT
	Roy Cullenbine	CLE	Al Javery	BSN
	Rick Ferrell	WAS	Don Johnson	CHN
	Pete Fox	BOS	Whitey Kurowski	SLN
	Orval Grove	CHA	Max Lanier +	SLN
	Frankie Hayes	PHA	Frank McCormick	CIN
	Mike Higgins	DET	Joe Medwick	NY
	Oris Hockett	CLE	Eddie Miller +	CIN
	Tex Hughson	BOS	Ray Mueller	CIN
	Dutch Leonard	WAS	Red Munger +	SLN
	Bob Muncrief	SLA	Bill Nicholson	CHN
	Hal Newhouser	DET	Mel Ott	NY
	Bobo Newsom	PHA	Mickey Owen	BRO
	Joe Page	NYA	Ken Raffensberger	PHI
	Dizzy Trout	DET	Rip Sewell	PIT
	Rudy York	DET	Jim Tobin	BSN
			Bill Voiselle	NY
			Frankie Zak	PIT

+ player replaced on roster

American League	010 000 000-	1
National League	000 040 21x-	7

AMERICAN LEAGUE

	ab	r	h	bi	bb	so	po	a
T.Tucker, cf	4	0	0	0	0	0	4	0
S.Spence, rf	4	0	2	0	0	0	2	1
G.McQuinn, 1b	4	0	1	0	0	1	5	1
V.Stephens, ss	4	0	1	0	0	1	1	0
B.Johnson, lf	3	0	0	0	1	1	2	1
K.Keltner, 3b	4	1	1	0	0	0	0	4
B.Doerr, 2b	3	0	0	0	0	1	4	0
R.Hemsley, c	2	0	0	0	0	0	1	0
F.Hayes, c	1	0	0	0	0	1	4	0
H.Borowy, p	1	0	1	1	0	0	0	0
T.Hughson, p	1	0	0	0	0	0	0	0
B.Muncrief, p	0	0	0	0	0	0	1	0
M.Higgins, ph	1	0	0	0	0	0	0	0
H.Newhouser, p	0	0	0	0	0	0	0	1
B.Newsom, p	0	0	0	0	0	0	0	0
Totals	32	1	6	1	1	5	24	8

BATTING
2-out RBI: H.Borowy.
RBI, scoring position, less than 2 outs: R.Hemsley 0–1.
GDP: K.Keltner.

BASERUNNING
Team LOB: 5

FIELDING
E: B.Doerr (throw); G.McQuinn (dropped throw); F.Hayes.
Outfield assist: S.Spence (P.Cavarretta at 3B); B.Johnson (P.Cavarretta at HP).
DP: (1). S.Spence-R.Hemsley.

NATIONAL LEAGUE

	ab	r	h	bi	bb	so	po	a
A.Galan, lf	4	1	1	1	1	0	2	0
P.Cavarretta, 1b	2	1	2	0	3	0	12	0
S.Musial, cf-rf	4	1	1	1	0	0	2	1
W.Cooper, c	5	1	2	1	0	1	5	2
R.Mueller, c	0	0	0	0	0	0	0	0
D.Walker, rf	4	0	2	1	0	0	0	0
V.DiMaggio, cf	0	0	0	0	0	0	0	0
B.Elliott, 3b	3	0	0	0	0	0	0	3
W.Kurowski, 3b	1	0	1	2	0	0	0	0
C.Ryan, 2b	4	1	2	0	0	0	4	4
M.Marion, ss	3	1	0	0	0	2	2	3
B.Walters, p	0	0	0	0	0	0	0	1
M.Ott, ph	1	0	0	0	0	0	0	0
K.Raffensberger, p	0	0	0	0	0	0	0	0
B.Nicholson, ph	1	1	1	1	0	0	0	0
R.Sewell, p	1	0	0	0	0	1	0	0
J.Medwick, ph	0	0	0	0	0	0	0	0
J.Tobin, p	0	0	0	0	0	0	0	0
Totals	33	7	12	7	4	4	27	15

BATTING
2B: B.Nicholson (off T.Hughson); W.Kurowski (off H.Newhouser).
3B: P.Cavarretta (off H.Borowy).
2-out RBI: D.Walker; W.Kurowski 2.
RBI, scoring position, less than 2 outs: A.Galan 1–1; S.Musial 1–2; W.Cooper 1–2; D.Walker 0–1; B.Nicholson 1–1; R.Sewell 0–1.
S: S.Musial; M.Marion; J.Medwick.

BASERUNNING
SB: C.Ryan (2nd base off T.Hughson/F.Hayes).
Team LOB: 9

FIELDING
E: C.Ryan (fumble).
Outfield assist: S.Musial (S.Spence at 2B).
DP: (1). M.Marion-C.Ryan-P.Cavarretta.

PITCHING	ip	h	r	er	bb	so
American League						
H.Borowy	3.0	3	0	0	1	0
T.Hughson (L)	1.2	5	4	3	1	2
B.Muncrief	1.1	1	0	0	0	1
H.Newhouser	1.2	3	3	3	2	1
B.Newsom	0.1	0	0	0	0	0
National League						
B.Walters	3.0	5	1	1	0	1
K.Raffensberger (W)	2.0	1	0	0	0	2
R.Sewell	3.0	0	0	0	1	2
J.Tobin (S)	1.0	0	0	0	0	0

Inherited Runners—Scored:
T.Hughson 0–0; B.Muncrief 2–0; H.Newhouser 0–0; B.Newsom 2–0; K.Raffensberger 0–0; R.Sewell 0–0; J.Tobin 0–0.
WP: B.Muncrief

GAME DATA—T: 2:11; A: 29589; Temp: Unknown; Wind: Unknown direction, Speed: Unknown

UMPIRES—HP: George Barr (NL), 1B: Charlie Berry (AL), 2B: Ziggy Sears (NL), 3B: Cal Hubbard (AL)

STARTING LINEUPS

American League	National League
1. T.Tucker cf	A.Galan lf
2. S.Spence rf	P.Cavarretta 1b
3. G.McQuinn 1b	S.Musial cf
4. V.Stephens ss	W.Cooper c
5. B.Johnson lf	D.Walker rf
6. K.Keltner 3b	B.Elliott 3b
7. B.Doerr 2b	C.Ryan 2b
8. R.Hemsley c	M.Marion ss
9. H.Borowy p	B.Walters p

AL 1ST: T.Tucker grounded out (M.Marion-ss to P.Cavarretta-1b); S.Spence grounded out (P.Cavarretta-1b unassisted); G.McQuinn singled to right field; V.Stephens singled to left-center [G.McQuinn to second]; B.Johnson struck out; 0 R, 2 H, 0 E, 2 LOB. AL 0, NL 0.

NL 1ST: A.Galan grounded out (K.Keltner-3b to G.McQuinn-1b); P.Cavarretta walked; S.Musial singled to second base [P.Cavarretta to third (error by B.Doerr-2b)]; W.Cooper flied into a double play (S.Spence-rf to R.Hemsley-c) [P.Cavarretta out at third]; 0 R, 1 H, 1 E, 1 LOB. AL 0, NL 0.

AL 2ND: K.Keltner singled to left field; B.Doerr grounded out (C.Ryan-2b to P.Cavarretta-1b) [K.Keltner to second]; R.Hemsley grounded out (M.Marion-ss to P.Cavarretta-1b) [K.Keltner to third]; H.Borowy singled to center field [K.Keltner scored]; T.Tucker grounded out (C.Ryan-2b to P.Cavarretta-1b); 1 R, 2 H, 0 E, 1 LOB. AL 1, NL 0.

NL 2ND: D.Walker singled to center field; B.Elliott forced D.Walker (K.Keltner-3b to B.Doerr-2b) [B.Elliott to first]; C.Ryan flied to T.Tucker-cf; M.Marion lined to B.Doerr-2b; 0 R, 1 H, 0 E, 1 LOB. AL 1, NL 0.

AL 3RD: S.Spence singled to right field; G.McQuinn forced S.Spence (B.Walters-p to M.Marion-ss) [G.McQuinn to first]; V.Stephens grounded out (W.Cooper-c to P.Cavarretta-1b) [G.McQuinn to second]; B.Johnson grounded out (B.Elliott-3b to P.Cavarretta-1b) [G.McQuinn to third]; 0 R, 1 H, 0 E, 1 LOB. AL 1, NL 0.

NL 3RD: **M.Ott batted for B.Walters;** M.Ott flied to T.Tucker-cf; A.Galan flied to T.Tucker-cf; P.Cavarretta tripled to left-center; S.Musial grounded out (K.Keltner-3b to G.McQuinn-1b); 0 R, 1 H, 0 E, 1 LOB. AL 1, NL 0.

AL 4TH: **K.Raffensberger replaced M.Ott (pitching);** K.Keltner popped to P.Cavarretta-1b; B.Doerr struck out; R.Hemsley lined to C.Ryan-2b; 0 R, 0 H, 0 E, 0 LOB. AL 1, NL 0.

NL 4TH: **T.Hughson replaced H.Borowy (pitching); F.Hayes replaced R.Hemsley (playing c);**

W.Cooper struck out; D.Walker flied to S.Spence-rf; B.Elliott flied to T.Tucker-cf; 0 R, 0 H, 0 E, 0 LOB. AL 1, NL 0.

AL 5TH: T.Hughson reached on an error by C.Ryan-2b [T.Hughson to first]; On a bunt T.Tucker forced T.Hughson (B.Elliott-3b to M.Marion-ss) [T.Tucker to first]; S.Spence singled to center field (S.Musial-cf to B.Elliott-3b to C.Ryan-2b) [T.Tucker to third, S.Spence out at second]; G.McQuinn was called out on strikes; 0 R, 1 H, 1 E, 1 LOB. AL 1, NL 0.

NL 5TH: Umpires moved: Hubbard (hp), Sears (1b), Berry (2b), Barr (; C.Ryan singled to center field; M.Marion struck out while C.Ryan stole second; **B.Nicholson batted for K.Raffensberger;** B.Nicholson doubled to right field [C.Ryan scored]; A.Galan singled to shortstop [B.Nicholson scored]; P.Cavarretta walked [A.Galan to second]; S.Musial reached on an error [A.Galan to third, P.Cavarretta to second, S.Musial to first (error by G.McQuinn-1b; assist by B.Doerr-2b)]; W.Cooper singled to left field (B.Johnson-lf to F.Hayes-c) [A.Galan scored, P.Cavarretta out at home, S.Musial to third]; D.Walker singled to right field [S.Musial scored (unearned), W.Cooper to second]; **B.Muncrief replaced T.Hughson (pitching);** B.Elliott flied to B.Johnson-lf in foul territory; 4 R (3 ER), 5 H, 1 E, 2 LOB. AL 1, NL 4.

AL 6TH: **R.Sewell replaced B.Nicholson (pitching); W.Kurowski replaced B.Elliott (playing 3b);** V.Stephens struck out; B.Johnson walked; K.Keltner grounded into a double play (M.Marion-ss to C.Ryan-2b to P.Cavarretta-1b) [B.Johnson out at second]; 0 R, 0 H, 0 E, 0 LOB. AL 1, NL 4.

NL 6TH: C.Ryan singled to third base; M.Marion out on a sacrifice bunt (G.McQuinn-1b unassisted) [C.Ryan to second]; B.Muncrief threw a wild pitch [C.Ryan to third]; R.Sewell struck out; A.Galan grounded out (G.McQuinn-1b to B.Muncrief-p); 0 R, 1 H, 0 E, 1 LOB. AL 1, NL 4.

AL 7TH: B.Doerr flied to A.Galan-lf; F.Hayes struck out; **M.Higgins batted for B.Muncrief;** M.Higgins grounded out (W.Kurowski-3b to P.Cavarretta-1b); 0 R, 0 H, 0 E, 0 LOB. AL 1, NL 4.

NL 7TH: **H.Newhouser replaced M.Higgins (pitching);** P.Cavarretta singled to center field; S.Musial out on a sacrifice bunt (K.Keltner-3b to G.McQuinn-1b) [P.Cavarretta to second]; W.Cooper singled to second base [P.Cavarretta to third]; D.Walker popped to V.Stephens-ss; W.Kurowski doubled to left-center [P.Cavarretta scored, W.Cooper scored]; C.Ryan popped to B.Doerr-2b; 2 R, 3 H, 0 E, 1 LOB. AL 1, NL 6.

AL 8TH: T.Tucker flied to S.Musial-cf; S.Spence

grounded out (C.Ryan-2b to P.Cavarretta-1b); On a bunt G.McQuinn grounded out (W.Cooper-c to P.Cavarretta-1b); 0 R, 0 H, 0 E, 0 LOB. AL 1, NL 6.

NL 8TH: M.Marion struck out [M.Marion to first (error by F.Hayes-c)]; **J.Medwick batted for R.Sewell;** J.Medwick out on a sacrifice bunt (H.Newhouser-p to G.McQuinn-1b) [M.Marion to second]; A.Galan walked; P.Cavarretta walked [M.Marion to third, A.Galan to second]; S.Musial flied to B.Johnson-lf [M.Marion scored]; **B.Newsom replaced H.Newhouser (pitching);** W.Cooper popped to B.Doerr-2b; 1 R, 0 H, 1 E, 2 LOB. AL 1, NL 7.

AL 9TH: **J.Tobin replaced J.Medwick (pitching); R.Mueller replaced W.Cooper (playing c); S.Musial changed positions (playing rf); V.DiMaggio replaced D.Walker (playing cf);** V.Stephens flied to S.Musial-rf; B.Johnson flied to A.Galan-lf; K.Keltner popped to C.Ryan-2b; 0 R, 0 H, 0 E, 0 LOB. AL 1, NL 7.

Final Totals	R	H	E	LOB
American League	1	6	3	5
National League	7	12	1	9

A Casualty of War

On February 21, 1945, World War II was clearly nearing its end. American troops under General George S. Patton were advancing on Berlin along a fifty-mile front from the west, while Soviet troops were nearing the German capital from the east. In the Pacific, U.S. Marines were fighting on Iwo Jima and getting ever closer to the Japanese mainland.

Nevertheless, it was on that date that Monroe Johnson, director of the Office of Defense Transportation (ODT), made a "request" that would force cancellation of the 1945 All-Star Game. Calling it part of the war effort, Johnson asked that all athletic teams, including Major League Baseball, cut their travel for the upcoming season by 25 percent of their 1944 levels.

Looking for ways to keep their full-season schedules intact, the owners decided to cancel the All-Star Game, which had been set for July 10 at Boston's Fenway Park. According to calculations made by National League president Ford Frick, travel by players, press, and various league and club officials to Boston would have totaled approximately five hundred thousand passenger miles. Canceling the game would allow the teams to apply those miles to regular-season travel.

The decision generated disappointment among the fans, who believed the 25-percent travel cut was an unnecessary limitation. In its twelve-year history, the All-Star Game had become a fixture. For the fans, it was now one of the components that made up a baseball season. Only the unthinkable — canceling the World Series — would have been worse. (Johnson suggested that the 1945 Series would be held only if transportation and war conditions at the time permitted.)

Although the managers in both leagues made no official selection of All-Star players in 1945, the Associated Press conducted a poll in which some managers did choose twenty-five-man unofficial teams. Thirteen of the sixteen managers partici-

pated, with Joe McCarthy of the Yankees, Luke Sewell of the Browns, and Billy Southworth of the Cardinals declining. (By virtue of their leading the 1944 pennant winners, Sewell and Southworth would have been the opposing managers in the All-Star Game.)

The Chicago Cubs, with seven, had the most players chosen, while the Cleveland Indians, with five, had the most chosen in the American League. (*The Sporting News* also made hypothetical selections, which differed slightly from those selected by the managers.) Following are the managers' choices.

THE NATIONAL LEAGUE

First Base	Phil Cavaretta (CHI); Frank McCormick (CIN)
Second Base	Don Johnson (CHI); Emil Verban (STL)
Third Base	Bob Elliott (PIT); Whitey Kurowski (STL); Stan Hack (CHI)
Shortstop	Marty Marion (STL)
Outfield	Tommy Holmes (BOS; Bill Nicholson (CHI); Mel Ott (NY); Goody Rosen (BKL); Andy Pafko (CHI); Dixie Walker (BKL)
Catcher	Ernie Lombardi (NY); Phil Masi (BOS); Ken O'Dea (STL)
Pitcher	Red Barrett (BOS); Mort Cooper (STL); Hal Gregg (BKL); Claude Passeau (CHI); Preacher Roe (PIT); Van Mungo (NY); Rip Sewell (PIT); Hank Wyse (CHI)

THE AMERICAN LEAGUE

First Base	Nick Etten (NY); George McQuinn (STL)
Second Base	Eddie Mayo (DET); George Stirnweiss (NY)
Third Base	Tony Cuccinello (CHI); Oscar Grimes (NY)
Shortstop	Lou Boudreau (CLE); Vern Stephens (STL)

Outfield	George Case (WAS); Doc Cramer (DET); Bob Johnson (BOS); Hank Greenberg (DET); Jeff Heath (CLE); Wally Moses (CHI)
Catcher	Rick Ferrell (WAS); Frankie Hayes (CLE); Mike Tresh (CHI)
Pitcher	Hank Borowy (NY); Russ Christopher (PHI); Dave Ferris (BOS); Steve Gromek (CLE); Dutch Leonard (WAS); Hal Newhouser (DET); Thornton Lee (CHI); Allie Reynolds (CLE)

A week after Johnson's "request," *Boston Post* baseball writer Jack Malaney proposed that baseball use the All-Star open dates for a series of exhibition games. (The two leagues had left the traditional three-day All-Star break in the schedule, hoping that an improvement in the war situation might allow the game to be played.) All sixteen teams would participate in the exhibition games, which would be between the closest geographical rivals from the two leagues.

The owners adopted the plan on April 24 at a meeting in Cleveland, the major purpose of which was the selection of former Kentucky governor and senator A. B. "Happy" Chandler to succeed Kenesaw Mountain Landis as the new commissioner. The games, scheduled for July 9 and 10, would be between the Boston Braves and Boston Red Sox, Chicago Cubs and Chicago White Sox, New York Giants and New York Yankees, Philadelphia Blue Jays and Philadelphia Athletics, St. Louis Cardinals and St. Louis Browns, Cincinnati Reds and Cleveland Indians, Brooklyn Dodgers and Washington Senators, and Pittsburgh Pirates and Detroit Tigers. However, the ODT refused to allow the Detroit team to detour the necessary sixty-two miles to get to Pittsburgh, so the Tigers-Pirates game was canceled.

The seven games played raised more than $240,000, which was split between the National War Fund and the American Red Cross. Neither players nor fans considered the exhibition games a very satisfying replacement for the All-Star Game. For Tresh, O'Dea, Etten, Mayo, Grimes, Rosen, Christopher, Gromek, Barrett, Gregg, and Wyse, the 1945 All-Star Game would have been their one chance to play in the midsummer classic. None had been chosen previously, nor would any be chosen in the future.

13

The Thumper Leads a Boston Massacre

Normalcy returned to baseball in 1946, America's first peacetime summer in five years, and with it came the return of the All-Star Game. The site was Boston's Fenway Park, where the game was to have been played a year earlier but was canceled because of wartime restrictions on travel. Fenway Park was one of the three big league parks that didn't have lights (Briggs Stadium in Detroit and Wrigley Field in Chicago were the others); lights wouldn't be installed until the following season. Lights weren't necessary, however, because unlike the three wartime games, which were played at night, the All-Star Game was again an afternoon affair. Regularly scheduled nighttime All-Star Games wouldn't return until 1968.

The return of peace also signaled a change in the designated All-Star charity, shifting from the Bat and Ball Fund of the U.S. Army and U.S. Navy to the Baseball Welfare Fund. This season, a portion of that fund was going to the families of the nine players from the Spokane Indians team of the Western International League who had died in a June 24 bus accident.

With most of baseball's biggest names serving in the military in 1945, Bostonians would have seen a watered-down version if the All-Star Game had been played that year. Now all the stars were back, and the capacity crowd of 34,908 was treated to an awesome display of offense, particularly by hometown hero Ted Williams. Williams's two home runs and record five RBI helped crush the National Leaguers, 12–0, in what remains the most one-sided victory in All-Star history. Williams also had two singles and a walk, giving him a still-standing All-Star record ten total bases. In addition, he scored an All-Star record four runs and tied Joe Medwick's 1937 mark of four hits in one game. And while the American Leaguers were battering four National League pitchers for fourteen hits, Cleveland's Bob Feller, Detroit's Hal Newhouser,

and St. Louis's Jack Kramer combined to toss the AL's first shutout. Between them, they had ten strikeouts and limited the NL to just three hits, two of which never left the infield.

The decisiveness of the victory may have surprised some, although the Americans had been the overwhelming favorite to win. Besides having never lost to the NL in an American League park, they appeared to have a vastly superior team, especially in their pitching. Despite all the offense, the flurry of home runs into and over the nets atop the close-in left-field wall that had been much anticipated by both media and fans never materialized. Only Joe Gordon, with a double, and Kramer, with a single, even reached the wall in left.

Only one National League base runner got as far as third base; in the first inning, Stan Musial got aboard on a one-out throwing error by shortstop Johnny Pesky. Musial moved up on Johnny Hopp's infield single and a ground out by Dixie Walker, who at .368 was the Major Leagues' leading batter. Feller ended what would be the NL's only serious threat of the day by striking out the Cardinals' Whitey Kurowski.

National League manager Charlie Grimm of the Cubs chose his ace Claude Passeau to oppose Feller. Passeau and right fielder Walker of the Dodgers were the only two players in the NL's starting lineup who were not current or former members of the St. Louis Cardinals. Left fielder Musial, third baseman Kurowski, second baseman Red Schoendienst, and shortstop Marty Marion were current Cardinals, while Braves center fielder Hopp, first baseman Johnny Mize, and catcher Walker Cooper (Mize and Cooper both of the Giants) had begun their big league careers with St. Louis. The second-place Cardinals were currently five games behind Brooklyn, but the two teams would eventually tie, necessitating the Major Leagues' first-ever playoff.

St. Louis would win that playoff and go on to defeat the Red Sox in the Sox's first Series appearance since 1918. In most seasons, hosting an

All-Star Game would be the highlight of the baseball summer in New England. But this year the big news was the pennant race. The Sox, with a seven-and-a-half-game lead on the second-place Yankees, were running away with the American League race. Their sizzling start helped to heighten the excitement surrounding this game. Manager Steve O'Neill of Detroit chose eight Red Sox players for the AL team, and four—Williams, Pesky, second basemen Bobby Doerr, and center fielder Dom Di-Maggio—were in the starting lineup. O'Neill did say that if Cardinals left-hander Howie Pollet had started for the Nationals, he would have used Boston's Rudy York rather than Washington's Mickey Vernon, the league's batting leader, at first base. He also would have substituted the Browns' Vern Stephens for Pesky at shortstop.

The American Leaguers were unusually strong at shortstop, with Pesky, Stephens, and Chicago's Luke Appling—so strong that three-time All-Star Lou Boudreau didn't even make the team, an omission strongly objected to by new Indians owner Bill Veeck. Along with the bypassing of Boudreau, several other exclusions rankled the fans. Among these were Detroit's Hank Greenberg, second in the league in home runs, Vic Lombardi and Eddie Stanky of the league-leading Dodgers, and Tex Hughson of the Red Sox.

Bill DeWitt, vice president of the St. Louis Browns, had gone so far as to write a note of protest to American League president Will Harridge concerning the passing over of Browns second baseman Johnny Berardino, the AL's fifth-leading hitter. While the fans had often expressed discontent in the past with the selections made by the leagues' managers, their objections were particularly heated this year. The public was clamoring to have the vote returned to them, and baseball would yield to that request in 1947.

O'Neill caused some further controversy, at least in Boston, when he bypassed Red Sox manager Joe Cronin in selecting his coaches. O'Neill picked Art Mills, one of his coaches in Detroit, and Luke Sewell, the Browns manager who would have piloted the AL squad had there been a game in 1945.

Among the players chosen, a difference of opinion had surfaced concerning which DiMaggio, Joe or Dom, would start in center field for the American League. Dom was hitting .349, about seventy-five points higher than Joe, but some argued that an All-Star Game wouldn't be complete without Joe DiMaggio in the starting lineup. The problem was solved on the Sunday before the game. Joe injured an ankle sliding into second base in the first game of a doubleheader in Philadelphia and was expected to be out for ten days. The NL also lost a probable starter that Sunday when Brooklyn shortstop Pee Wee Reese, batting .308, chipped a vertebra in his neck at Braves Field. Reese remained in Boston and was at the game wearing a special neck brace.

Passeau had been the pitcher at Detroit in 1941 when Williams hit the dramatic two-out, ninth-inning home run that won that year's game for the American League. So, after retiring DiMaggio and Pesky in the bottom of the first, Passeau pitched very carefully to Williams and ended up walking him. The walk cost Passeau, because Charlie Keller followed by blasting a 3-1 pitch into the National League bullpen in right-center to get the AL off to a 2–0 lead. (Keller was third in the AL with thirteen home runs, while league leader Williams had twenty-three and Greenberg had twenty-two.) Passeau later said that he'd wanted to pitch Keller high but had pitched him low on the advice of his teammate Hank Borowy, a former Yankee.

Passeau allowed only one more hit and one more walk over the next two innings, and when Grimm replaced him with Kirby Higbe in the fourth, it was still a 2–0 game. But Williams, the first batter to face the Brooklyn right-hander, quickly made it 3–0 by driving a 2-1 pitch more than four hundred feet into the center-field bleachers.

The AL scored three more in the fifth, making it 6–0 and finishing Higbe. Athletics catcher Buddy Rosar, who had singled, was on first with one out when Newhouser, who had taken over the pitching duties from Feller in the fourth, came to the plate. Newhouser, the only member of the defending champion Tigers on the AL squad, dumped a hit into short right-center that fell between Walker and Hopp. Rosar took third, and when Hopp foolishly threw to third baseman Kurowski trying to get Rosar, Newhouser continued to second. Faced with runners at second and third, Grimm ordered an intentional pass for Washington's Stan Spence, who had replaced DiMaggio in center. He would try for a double play on Stephens, who had replaced Pesky at short.

Stephens foiled the NL strategy by doubling just inside the right-field foul line, sending Rosar and Newhouser home and Spence to third. Williams followed with a single to left, scoring Spence and moving Stephens to third. Grimm had seen enough of Higbe and replaced him with side-arming right-hander Ewell Blackwell of Cincinnati. Keller grounded to Philadelphia first baseman Frank McCormick (chosen to replace the injured Reese), whose throw home to catcher Phil Masi caught Stephens in a rundown that ended when Kurowski tagged him out. Williams moved to third and Keller to second on a wild pitch, but Marion made an excellent play on Gordon's slowly hit ground ball to end the inning.

Blackwell got the Americans in order in the sixth, the third out coming when he threw a third strike past pinch hitter Bill Dickey, the recently named manager of the Yankees, who was making his final All-Star appearance. Blackwell also got the first two batters in the seventh, before Williams singled, Keller walked, and both scored on Gordon's double off the left-field wall. Blackwell and twenty-one-year-old Phillies outfielder Del Ennis were the first rookies ever selected for an NL team, a team that this year featured fourteen returning servicemen and only eight players who had been on the 1944 team.

Facing Pittsburgh's Rip Sewell in the eighth, the Americans added their final four runs while creating one of the more memorable moments in All-Star history. Sewell had previously worked four scoreless and hitless innings against the American League (one inning in 1943 and three innings in 1944), but, of course, he would be facing a much different American League team today. Yankee third baseman George Stirnweiss led off the inning with a single. Sewell retired Red Sox catcher Hal Wagner, but Kramer's single off the wall in left and a scoring fly by the A's Sam Chapman made it 9–0.

With the game hopelessly lost, Sewell decided to entertain the fans by throwing a blooper pitch (named the "eephus" pitch by teammate Maurice Van Robays) to Stephens. The result was a bouncing single that just eluded the grasp of second baseman Frank Gustine and sent Kramer to second. Then, with Williams at the plate, Sewell threw another blooper. Williams connected and sent it soaring into the right-field bleachers for a three-run homer. The crowd, which had been up and cheering most of the afternoon, came to their feet with the biggest ovation of the game. "I was never so embarrassed in my life," Sewell said afterward.

Williams's second home run of the game tied a record set by Pittsburgh's Arky Vaughan in 1941. It was Williams's home run that won that game, and his two today made him the first man to hit three All-Star home runs.

O'Neill had said that, despite their having pitched Sunday, Feller, who had defeated the Browns for his fifteenth victory, and Newhouser, who had topped the White Sox for his sixteenth, would be his first two pitchers. He seemed to be leaning toward the Yankees' Spud Chandler, who had also worked Sunday, for the final three innings. However, when Chandler informed him before the game that his arm felt stiff, O'Neill chose Kramer instead. The Browns right-hander handily completed the shutout, and while Feller had allowed hits to Hopp and Cooper (both infield singles), and Newhouser had allowed a clean single to Cubs outfielder Peanuts Lowrey, Kramer's three innings were hitless. He struck out three and allowed only one base runner, an eighth-inning walk to Pittsburgh's Gustine.

Not surprisingly, most of the postgame interviews centered around Williams. "That Williams is the greatest hitter of all time," said O'Neill. Grimm echoed him, saying "Ted is the best slugger of them all." Sewell remembered that the longest previous hit off his "eephus" pitch was a Stan Musial triple and said that he didn't think anyone could hit it for a home run. Sewell added, "I've never seen Williams before today, but I know now he's the greatest of all hitters."

Feller, whose three strikeouts raised his All-Star total to a record-high twelve, also came in for his share of praise. "I think that Feller has more stuff than Walter Johnson," said Grimm. "Bob is certainly much harder to hit against."

To add insult to injury in this most ignominious of National League defeats, league president Ford Frick had $85 stolen from his hotel room earlier in the day.

	AL		NL	
P	Bob Feller	CLE	Claude Passeau	CHN
C	Frankie Hayes	CHA	Walker Cooper	NY
1B	Mickey Vernon	WAS	Johnny Mize	NY
2B	Bobby Doerr	BOS	Red Schoendienst	SLN
3B	Ken Keltner	CLE	Whitey Kurowski	SLN
SS	Johnny Pesky	BOS	Marty Marion	SLN
OF	Dom DiMaggio	BOS	Johnny Hopp	BSN
OF	Charlie Keller	NYA	Stan Musial	SLN
OF	Ted Williams	BOS	Dixie Walker	BRO
	Luke Appling	CHA	Ewell Blackwell	CIN
	Spud Chandler	NYA	Phil Cavarretta	CHN
	Sam Chapman	PHA	Mort Cooper	BSN
	Bill Dickey	NYA	Del Ennis	PHI
	Joe DiMaggio	NYA	Frankie Gustine	PIT
	Dave Ferriss	BOS	Kirby Higbe	BRO
	Joe Gordon	NYA	Ray Lamanno	CIN
	Mickey Harris	BOS	Peanuts Lowrey	CHN
	Jack Kramer	SLA	Phil Masi	BSN
	Hal Newhouser	DET	Frank McCormick	PHI
	Buddy Rosar	PHA	Eddie Miller +	CIN
	Stan Spence	WAS	Howie Pollet	SLN
	Vern Stephens	SLA	Pee Wee Reese +	BRO
	Snuffy Stirnweiss	NYA	Pete Reiser	BRO
	Hal Wagner	BOS	Johnny Schmitz	CHN
	Rudy York	BOS	Rip Sewell	PIT
			Enos Slaughter	SLN
			Emil Verban	PHI

+ player replaced on roster

```
National League    000 000 000-  0
American League    200 130 24X- 12
```

NATIONAL LEAGUE

	ab	r	h	bi	bb	so	po	a
R.Schoendienst, 2b	2	0	0	0	0	0	0	2
F.Gustine, ph-2b	1	0	0	0	1	1	1	1
S.Musial, lf	2	0	0	0	0	0	0	0
D.Ennis, ph-lf	2	0	0	0	0	2	0	0
J.Hopp, cf	2	0	1	0	0	0	0	0
P.Lowrey, ph-cf	2	0	1	0	0	0	3	0
D.Walker, rf	3	0	0	0	0	0	1	0
E.Slaughter, rf	1	0	0	0	0	0	0	0
W.Kurowski, 3b	3	0	0	0	0	2	2	1
E.Verban, ph	1	0	0	0	0	0	0	0
J.Mize, 1b	1	0	0	0	0	0	7	0
F.McCormick, ph-1b	1	0	0	0	0	0	1	1
P.Cavarretta, ph-1b	1	0	0	0	0	1	1	0
W.Cooper, c	1	0	1	0	0	0	0	0
P.Masi, c	2	0	0	0	0	0	4	1
M.Marion, ss	3	0	0	0	0	2	4	6
C.Passeau, p	1	0	0	0	0	1	0	1
K.Higbe, p	1	0	0	0	0	1	0	0
E.Blackwell, p	0	0	0	0	0	0	0	0
R.Lamanno, ph	1	0	0	0	0	0	0	0
R.Sewell, p	0	0	0	0	0	0	0	0
Totals	31	0	3	0	1	10	24	13

BATTING

RBI, scoring position, less than 2 outs: D.Walker 0–1.

BASERUNNING

Team LOB: 5

FIELDING

DP: (2). M.Marion-J.Mize; R.Schoendienst-M.Marion-J.Mize.

AMERICAN LEAGUE

	ab	r	h	bi	bb	so	po	a
D.DiMaggio, cf	2	0	1	0	0	0	1	0
S.Spence, cf	0	1	0	0	1	0	1	0
S.Chapman, cf	2	0	0	1	0	0	1	0
J.Pesky, ss	2	0	0	0	0	0	1	0
V.Stephens, ss	3	1	2	2	0	0	0	4
T.Williams, lf	4	4	4	5	1	0	1	0
C.Keller, rf	4	2	1	2	1	1	1	0
B.Doerr, 2b	2	0	0	0	0	1	1	1
J.Gordon, 2b	2	0	1	2	0	0	0	1
M.Vernon, 1b	2	0	0	0	0	0	2	1
R.York, 1b	2	0	1	0	0	0	5	0
K.Keltner, 3b	0	0	0	0	1	0	0	0
S.Stirnweiss, 3b	3	1	1	0	0	1	0	0
F.Hayes, c	1	0	0	0	0	0	3	0
B.Rosar, c	2	1	1	0	0	0	5	0
H.Wagner, c	1	0	0	0	0	0	4	0
B.Feller, p	0	0	0	0	0	0	0	0
L.Appling, ph	1	0	0	0	0	0	0	0
H.Newhouser, p	1	1	1	0	0	0	1	0
B.Dickey, ph	1	0	0	0	0	1	0	0
J.Kramer, p	1	1	1	0	0	0	0	0
Totals	36	12	14	12	4	3	27	7

BATTING

2B: V.Stephens (off K.Higbe); J.Gordon (off E.Blackwell).

HR: T.Williams 2 (4th inning off K.Higbe, 0 on, 0 out; 8th inning off R.Sewell, 2 on, 2 out); C.Keller (1st inning off C.Passeau, 1 on, 2 out).

2-out RBI: T.Williams 3; C.Keller 2; J.Gordon 2.

RBI, scoring position, less than 2 outs: S.Chapman 1–1; V.Stephens 2–2; T.Williams 1–1; C.Keller 0–1.

GDP: J.Pesky.

BASERUNNING

Team LOB: 4

FIELDING

E: J.Pesky (throw).

PITCHING

National League	ip	h	r	er	bb	so
C.Passeau (L)	3.0	2	2	2	2	0
K.Higbe	1.1	5	4	4	1	2
E.Blackwell	2.2	3	2	2	1	1
R.Sewell	1.0	4	4	4	0	0

American League	ip	h	r	er	bb	so
B.Feller (w)	3.0	2	0	0	0	3
H.Newhouser	3.0	1	0	0	0	4
J.Kramer (s)	3.0	0	0	0	1	3

Inherited Runners—Scored:
K.Higbe 0–0; E.Blackwell 2–0; R.Sewell 0–0; H.Newhouser 0–0; J.Kramer 0–0.

IBB: S.Spence by K.Higbe.

WP: E.Blackwell

GAME DATA—T: 2:19; A: 34906; Temp: Unknown; Wind: Unknown direction, Speed: Unknown

UMPIRES—HP: Bill Summers (AL), 1B: Dusty Boggess (NL), 2B: Eddie Rommel (AL), 3B: Larry Goetz (NL)

STARTING LINEUPS

National League	American League
1. R.Schoendienst 2b	D.DiMaggio cf
2. S.Musial lf	J.Pesky ss
3. J.Hopp cf	T.Williams lf
4. D.Walker rf	C.Keller rf
5. W.Kurowski 3b	B.Doerr 2b
6. J.Mize 1b	M.Vernon 1b
7. W.Cooper c	K.Keltner 3b
8. M.Marion ss	F.Hayes c
9. C.Passeau p	B.Feller p

NL 1ST: Schoendienst fouled off 5 pitches; R.Schoendienst grounded out (M.Vernon-1b unassisted); S.Musial reached on an error by J.Pesky-ss [S.Musial to first]; J.Hopp singled to third base [S.Musial to second]; D.Walker grounded out (B.Doerr-2b to M.Vernon-1b) [S.Musial to third, J.Hopp to second]; W.Kurowski struck out; 0 R, 1 H, 1 E, 2 LOB. NL 0, AL 0.

AL 1ST: D.DiMaggio grounded out (J.Mize-1b unassisted); J.Pesky grounded out (R.Schoendienst-2b to J.Mize-1b); T.Williams walked; C.Keller homered to rightfield [T.Williams scored]; B.Doerr grounded out (M.Marion-ss to J.Mize-1b); 2 R, 1 H, 0 E, 0 LOB. NL 0, AL 2.

NL 2ND: J.Mize popped to J.Pesky-ss; W.Cooper singled to shortstop; M.Marion struck out; C.Passeau was called out on strikes; 0 R, 1 H, 0 E, 1 LOB. NL 0, AL 2.

AL 2ND: M.Vernon grounded out (M.Marion-ss to J.Mize-1b); K.Keltner walked; F.Hayes lined into a double play (M.Marion-ss to J.Mize-1b) [K.Keltner out at first]; 0 R, 0 H, 0 E, 0 LOB. NL 0, AL 2.

NL 3RD: R.Schoendienst flied to T.Williams-lf; S.Musial popped to B.Doerr-2b; J.Hopp flied to D.DiMaggio-cf; 0 R, 0 H, 0 E, 0 LOB. NL 0, AL 2.

AL 3RD: **L.Appling batted for B.Feller;** L.Appling grounded out (C.Passeau-p to J.Mize-1b); D.DiMaggio singled to center field; J.Pesky grounded into a double play (R.Schoendienst-2b to M.Marion-ss to J.Mize-1b) [D.DiMaggio out at second]; 0 R, 1 H, 0 E, 0 LOB. NL 0, AL 2.

NL 4TH: **H.Newhouser replaced L.Appling (pitching); B.Rosar replaced F.Hayes (playing c); S.Spence replaced D.DiMaggio (playing cf);** D.Walker grounded out (M.Vernon-1b to H.Newhouser-p); W.Kurowski struck out; **F.McCormick batted for J.Mize;** F.McCormick flied to S.Spence-cf; 0 R, 0 H, 0 E, 0 LOB. NL 0, AL 2.

AL 4TH: **K.Higbe replaced C.Passeau (pitching); P.Masi replaced W.Cooper (playing c); F.McCormick stayed in game (playing 1b);** T.Williams homered to centerfield (it was the 2–1 pitch); C.Keller was called out on strikes; B.Doerr

popped to W.Kurowski-3b in foul territory; M.Vernon flied to D.Walker-rf; 1 R, 1 H, 0 E, 0 LOB. NL 0, AL 3.

NL 5TH: **V.Stephens replaced J.Pesky (playing ss); J.Gordon replaced B.Doerr (playing 2b); S.Stirnweiss replaced K.Keltner (playing 3b); R.York replaced M.Vernon (playing 1b);** P.Masi grounded out (V.Stephens-ss to R.York-1b); M.Marion flied to C.Keller-rf; K.Higbe struck out; 0 R, 0 H, 0 E, 0 LOB. NL 0, AL 3.

AL 5TH: Umpires moved: Goetz (hp) Rommel (1b) Boggess (2b) Summers ; S.Stirnweiss struck out; B.Rosar singled to left field; H.Newhouser singled to center field [B.Rosar to third, H.Newhouser to second (on throw)]; S.Spence was walked intentionally; V.Stephens doubled to right field [B.Rosar scored, H.Newhouser scored, S.Spence to third]; T.Williams singled to left field [S.Spence scored, V.Stephens to third]; **E.Blackwell replaced K.Higbe (pitching);** C.Keller reached on a fielder's choice (F.McCormick-1b to P.Masi-c to W.Kurowski-3b) [V.Stephens out at home, T.Williams to second]; E.Blackwell threw a wild pitch [T.Williams to third, C.Keller to second]; J.Gordon grounded out (M.Marion-ss to F.McCormick-1b); 3 R, 4 H, 0 E, 2 LOB. NL 0, AL 6.

NL 6TH: **F.Gustine batted for R.Schoendienst;** F.Gustine struck out; **D.Ennis batted for S.Musial;** D.Ennis struck out; **P.Lowrey batted for J.Hopp;** P.Lowrey singled to center field; D.Walker popped to B.Rosar-c in foul territory; 0 R, 1 H, 0 E, 1 LOB. NL 0, AL 6.

AL 6TH: **F.Gustine stayed in game (playing 2b); D.Ennis stayed in game (playing lf); P.Lowrey stayed in game (playing cf); E.Slaughter replaced D.Walker (playing rf);** R.York singled to right field; S.Stirnweiss forced R.York (F.Gustine-2b to M.Marion-ss) [S.Stirnweiss to first]; B.Rosar forced S.Stirnweiss (W.Kurowski-3b to F.Gustine-2b) [B.Rosar to first]; **B.Dickey batted for H.Newhouser;** B.Dickey was called out on strikes; 0 R, 1 H, 0 E, 1 LOB. NL 0, AL 6.

NL 7TH: **J.Kramer replaced B.Dickey (pitching); H.Wagner replaced B.Rosar (playing c); S.Chapman replaced S.Spence (playing cf);** W.Kurowski flied to S.Chapman-cf; **P.Cavarretta batted for F.McCormick;** P.Cavarretta struck out; P.Masi grounded out (V.Stephens-ss to R.York-1b); 0 R, 0 H, 0 E, 0 LOB. NL 0, AL 6.

AL 7TH: **P.Cavarretta stayed in game (playing 1b);** S.Chapman flied to P.Lowrey-cf; V.Stephens grounded out (M.Marion-ss to P.Cavarretta-1b); T.Williams singled to first base; C.Keller walked [T.Williams to second]; J.Gordon doubled to left field [T.Williams scored, C.Keller scored]; R.York popped to M.Marion-ss; 2 R, 2 H, 0 E, 1 LOB. NL 0, AL 8.

NL 8TH: M.Marion struck out; **R.Lamanno batted for E.Blackwell;** R.Lamanno grounded out (J.Gordon-2b to R.York-1b); F.Gustine walked; D.Ennis struck out; 0 R, 0 H, 0 E, 1 LOB. NL 0, AL 8.

AL 8TH: **R.Sewell replaced R.Lamanno (pitching);** S.Stirnweiss singled to left field; H.Wagner flied to P.Lowrey-cf; J.Kramer singled to left field [S.Stirnweiss to third]; S.Chapman flied to P.Lowrey-cf [S.Stirnweiss scored]; V.Stephens singled to second base [J.Kramer to second]; T.Williams homered to rightfield [J.Kramer

scored, V.Stephens scored]; into the bullpen off Sewell's "Eephus Pitch'; C.Keller popped to P.Masi-c in foul territory; 4 R, 4 H, 0 E, 0 LOB. NL 0, AL 12.

NL 9TH: P.Lowrey grounded out (V.Stephens-ss to R.York-1b); E.Slaughter grounded out (V.Stephens-ss to R.York-1b); **E.Verban batted for W.Kurowski;** E.Verban popped to H.Wagner-c in foul territory; 0 R, 0 H, 0 E, 0 LOB. NL 0, AL 12.

Final Totals	R	H	E	LOB
National League	0	3	0	5
American League	12	14	1	4

Fans Pick the Teams, but Results Are the Same

In a decision driven by past complaints about managerial All-Star selections, complaints that were particularly bitter in 1946, baseball returned the vote to the fans in 1947. However, in the years immediately after World War II, it seemed to make little difference who picked the teams; whatever it took, the American Leaguers were going to win. By contrast to the previous season's 12–0 blowout in Boston, the 41,123 fans at Chicago's Wrigley Field on this perfect summer afternoon saw a close, hard-fought battle. Still the AL, with single runs in the sixth and seventh innings, had managed to eke out a 2–1 victory, its tenth All-Star triumph against only four defeats.

National League fans had hoped for a different outcome this year because of their league's overall superiority in number of home runs hit. The NL, led by the Giants trio of Johnny Mize, Walker Cooper, and Willard Marshall, had become the power league, a role traditionally held by the American League. It didn't work out to NL fans' satisfaction, because pitching and defense dominated the game. Mize's fourth-inning home run was the NL's lone run, and the combined three runs scored by the two teams was a new All-Star low. The American League, outhit eight to five, scored their first run as Joe DiMaggio was grounding into a double play. The second came on pinch hitter Stan Spence's single following a stolen base and a muffed pick-off.

Had the fans been given the option of voting for the starting pitchers, rather than just the eight position players, they likely would have chosen a match-up of Cleveland ace Bob Feller, generally acknowledged as the game's best pitcher, and Cincinnati's Ewell Blackwell, the pitching sensation of the 1947 season. The Cardinals' Eddie Dyer, manager of the NL squad, did choose Blackwell, but Blackwell wouldn't be facing Feller, who had withdrawn from the game a week earlier. In four previous All-Star appearances, Feller had allowed the National League just one run and five hits in 11.2 innings, but he had been forced to leave in the second inning of a July 2 game against the Browns. Indians manager Lou Boudreau accurately predicted that the torn muscles in Feller's back would prevent him from pitching until after the All-Star Game. Two days later, when regular season play resumed on July 10, Feller went 8.1 innings in a 3–1 win over the Athletics. (In the second game of that twinighter at Cleveland, Don Black pitched a 3–0 no-hitter.)

American League manager Joe Cronin of Boston named Washington right-hander Early Wynn to take Feller's place on the team but planned to use the Yanks' Spud Chandler as his starting pitcher. However, after Chandler told him that he had a slightly sore arm, Cronin made the switch to Detroit left-hander Hal Newhouser. It was the second consecutive year that Chandler had been scheduled to pitch and had withdrawn with arm problems.

Another Chandler, Baseball Commissioner A. B. ("Happy") Chandler, threw out the first ball, after which Blackwell (14-2) and Newhouser (9-8) took over. Both men turned in three outstanding innings apiece, and both left the mound to enthusiastic cheers from the partisan National League crowd. Blackwell had electrified the baseball world in June by no-hitting Boston and, in his next start, coming within two outs of no-hitting Brooklyn. The six-foot-six side-armer had been dominating National League hitters all season, and the American League's best could do no better. Blackwell allowed them one hit, a single to center field by DiMaggio, and struck out four, including Ted Williams looking. DiMaggio eventually reached third on a passed ball by Cooper and a wild pitch, but two were out, and after fouling off four two-strike pitches, the Indians' Joe Gordon fanned.

Newhouser, meanwhile, had no problems with the feared National League lineup. He retired the first eight men he faced before giving up his only hit, a pinch single to Cincinnati's Bert Haas, and ending his stint by striking out Harry Walker of the Phillies. With Walker, traded from the Cardinals in May, starting in center field, and Emil Verban starting at second base, the Phillies had their first starters since Pinky May in 1936. This was also the first time the perennial last-place finishers had two men in the starting lineup since Dick Bartell and Chuck Klein had started in the first All-Star Game back in 1933.

Verban almost hadn't made it. He, pitcher Schoolboy Rowe, and Phillies manager Ben Chapman, chosen as a coach, had all been injured in a train accident coming from Philadelphia to Chicago. Rowe was knocked unconscious and Verban lost feeling in his legs for a short time, but both recovered and both participated, while Chapman shared the coaching duties with Giants manager Mel Ott.

Harry Brecheen, the stylish Cardinals left-hander who had won three games against the Red Sox in the 1946 World Series, came on for the Nationals in the fourth. The pennant-winning Sox had placed eight men on the 1946 All-Star team but had only two representatives this year: Williams and Bobby Doerr. Williams had complained after batting practice about the background for hitters at Wrigley, saying, "You can't see the ball." Despite his alleged trouble seeing the ball and despite having had just one single against Brecheen in the Series, Williams laced a one-out double down the line in right. He stayed put as DiMaggio grounded out to third baseman Frank Gustine but moved to third on Boudreau's infield hit to that area. Working very carefully, Brecheen struck out George McQuinn, one of eight Yankees on the AL team, for the final out. Many thought that McQuinn, at age thirty-seven, was finished as a big leaguer, but he'd been having an excellent year in New York and the fans had voted him to be the starting first baseman.

In the home fourth, Cronin replaced Newhouser with Frank Shea, a Yankee rookie. Shea was the first rookie to make an American League All-Star team since his teammate DiMaggio did it in 1936. He was also, of course, the first rookie pitcher to do so, earning his spot with ten wins (10-2), which tied him with Feller for the league high. Shea got the first two batters he faced, Brooklyn's Dixie Walker and Cooper, before NL home run leader Mize lifted a 1-1 fastball well back into the seats in right. The home run, hit into a fairly stiff breeze, was the first ever by a member of the Giants. The crowd cheered lustily at Mize's blast, little suspecting that he would be the last National Leaguer to cross the plate. Shea, for the next two innings, and Washington's Walt Master-

son and the Yankees' Joe Page, over the final three, held the Nationals scoreless. The American League had taken a 2–1 lead during Shea's stay on the mound, making him the first rookie to get an All-Star win.

Masterson had retired the side in order in the seventh and had two out and a man on first — a walk to Marshall — in the eighth when Cronin chose to remove him. With the left-handed-hitting Mize at the plate, Cronin brought in left-hander Page to pitch to the big slugger. Cronin didn't want to see another Mize home run, something he thought less likely against Page. Mize didn't homer, but he did hit a sharp single to right that sent Marshall around to third. The next batter was the Cardinals' Enos Slaughter, the NL's leading vote getter and second-leading hitter. But Page had been having a magical season in the role of a relief pitcher, and the magic continued in Wrigley Field. Slaughter hit one up the middle that looked destined to produce the tying run before shortstop Boudreau ranged to the other side of second base to snare it and throw Slaughter out.

The Americans had tied the score against Brecheen in the sixth. Responding to cheers rarely heard for a White Sox player in Wrigley Field, Luke Appling opened the inning with a single to left. Appling was batting for Washington's Buddy Lewis, appearing in his first All-Star Game since 1938. Lewis was batting just .278, but because the fans were forced to vote for outfielders by individual position rather than choose any three, he'd finished on top among right fielders.

Williams had his second hit off Brecheen, a single to right, that moved Appling to third. Appling scored when DiMaggio bounced into a double play that went from Dodger shortstop Pee Wee Reese to his regular season double play partner, second baseman Eddie Stanky, to first baseman Mize. After a relatively poor year in 1946, DiMaggio had returned to his prewar form. He was batting .339 and leading the league in runs batted in, and the fans had responded by giving him more All-Star votes (782,194) than any other player. Close to two million votes had been cast in the poll conducted by 193 newspapers across the country. This was DiMaggio's eighth All-Star appearance and his ninth selection, more than any player on either side in this game.

The Nationals had a new battery in the seventh inning. Boston's Johnny Sain was the pitcher, and Brooklyn's Bruce Edwards took over for Cooper behind the plate. For Cooper, leading the majors with sixty-six RBI, this was his fifth consecutive start at catcher, tying Bill Dickey's mark set between 1937 and 1941.

Sain got the lead-off batter, McQuinn, on a

ground ball to Reese, but then Doerr ripped a single to left. Edwards had recently recovered from a hand injury, and word around the National League was that he still was not throwing well. Because there are very few secrets in baseball, Cronin was also aware of Edwards's problem. He ordered a steal, which Doerr accomplished successfully. Aware that Doerr represented the go-ahead run, Sain wanted to keep him close to the bag. However, in attempting to do so, one of his throws hit Doerr and rolled into center field, putting the lead run just ninety feet away.

After Sain settled down to fan Buddy Rosar for the second out, Cronin called on the left-handed-hitting Spence to pinch-hit for Shea. Sain, with the best curve ball in the league — he'd used it to whiff Rosar — quickly sent two over for strikes. But when he tried to throw a fastball by Spence, the Washington outfielder lined the 0-2 pitch into right-center. Doerr trotted home easily with what would be the winning run. Detroit's George Kell forced Spence, and lefty Warren Spahn, Sain's Braves teammate, pitched a scoreless, hitless eighth and ninth, but the damage was already done.

The NL had a final shot in the ninth, getting the tying run on when Page issued a one-out walk to Reese. Dyer had picked Reese as the roster replacement for Cincinnati's Eddie Miller, whom the fans had voted to start at shortstop, and he had named the fans' second choice, Marty Marion, as the starter. Similarly, at third base he'd replaced Boston's Bob Elliott, the fans' choice, with Cardinal Whitey Kurowski on the roster and Pittsburgh's Gustine in the starting lineup.

Stanky followed the walk with a sharp grounder to the right side, but Doerr snagged it and threw to Boudreau for the force on Reese. The Nationals were down to their last out, and the next sched-uled hitter was Spahn. With no nonpitchers left on his bench, Dyer chose pitcher Rowe to bat for Spahn. Rowe, formerly of the Tigers, had been a member of the American League teams in 1935 and 1936, pitching three innings in the 1936 game. His appearance today made him not only the first player selected in both leagues but the first player to play for both leagues.

Rowe, who had always been a good hitter, lifted a high twisting fly ball to right that got caught up in the wind. It appeared that it might drop safely, but right fielder Tommy Henrich, named to the team as a replacement for injured Yankee teammate Charlie Keller, stayed with the ball and caught it for the final out.

"It was a swell game and a great victory," said Cronin, crediting the fielding of Henrich, Doerr, and Boudreau, along with the outstanding pitching, for the AL win. A disappointed Dyer agreed. "They played a great defensive game, and their pitching was strong."

Boudreau, meanwhile, was praising Blackwell. "He was fast and deceptive; he's as good as any pitcher in our league. That's the highest compliment I can pay him," said the man who managed Bob Feller.

Sain, the losing pitcher, blamed himself for Spence's hit. "I pitched to Spence backward and threw just the kind of pitch Dyer had warned me against," he confessed.

Everyone agreed that the fans had done an excellent job in picking the two teams. And while one team had won and one had lost, all Major League players profited from the game. For the first time, the players' pension fund was a beneficiary of the All-Star contest and received 75 percent of the $105,315 in net receipts.

	AL		NL		
P	Hal Newhouser	DET	Ewell Blackwell		CIN
C	Buddy Rosar	PHA	Walker Cooper		NY
1B	George McQuinn	NYA	Johnny Mize		NY
2B	Joe Gordon	CLE	Emil Verban		PHI
3B	George Kell	DET	Bob Elliott	+	BSN
SS	Lou Boudreau	CLE	Eddie Miller	+	CIN
OF	Joe DiMaggio	NYA	Enos Slaughter		SLN
OF	Buddy Lewis	WAS	Dixie Walker		BRO
OF	Ted Williams	BOS	Harry Walker		PHI
	Luke Appling	CHA	Ralph Branca		BRO
	Spud Chandler	NYA	Harry Brecheen		SLN
	Bobby Doerr	BOS	Phil Cavarretta		CHN
	Bob Feller	+ CLE	Bruce Edwards		BRO
	Jim Hegan	CLE	Frankie Gustine		PIT
	Tommy Henrich	NYA	Bert Haas		CIN
	Billy Johnson	NYA	Whitey Kurowski		SLN
	Charlie Keller	+ NYA	Marty Marion		SLN
	Jack Kramer	SLA	Willard Marshall		NY
	Walt Masterson	WAS	Phil Masi		BSN
	Pat Mullin	DET	Red Munger		SLN
	Joe Page	NYA	Stan Musial		SLN
	Aaron Robinson	NYA	Andy Pafko		CHN
	Spec Shea	NYA	Pee Wee Reese		BRO
	Stan Spence	WAS	Schoolboy Rowe		PHI
	Dizzy Trout	DET	Johnny Sain		BSN
	Early Wynn	WAS	Warren Spahn		BSN
	Rudy York	CHA	Eddie Stanky		BRO

+ player replaced on roster

American League   000 001 100- 2
National League   000 100 000- 1

AMERICAN LEAGUE

	ab	r	h	bi	bb	so	po	a
G.Kell, 3b	4	0	0	0	0	2	0	0
B.Johnson, 3b	0	0	0	0	0	0	0	0
B.Lewis, rf	2	0	0	0	0	0	1	0
L.Appling, ph	1	1	1	0	0	0	0	0
T.Henrich, rf	1	0	0	0	0	1	3	0
T.Williams, lf	4	0	2	0	0	1	3	0
J.DiMaggio, cf	3	0	1	0	1	0	1	0
L.Boudreau, ss	4	0	1	0	0	1	4	4
G.McQuinn, 1b	4	0	0	0	0	1	9	1
J.Gordon, 2b	2	0	1	0	0	1	0	4
B.Doerr, 2b	2	1	1	0	0	0	0	2
B.Rosar, c	4	0	0	0	0	1	6	0
H.Newhouser, p	1	0	0	0	0	0	0	0
S.Shea, p	1	0	0	0	0	0	0	0
S.Spence, ph	1	0	1	1	0	0	0	0
W.Masterson, p	0	0	0	0	0	0	0	0
J.Page, p	0	0	0	0	0	0	0	0
Totals	34	2	8	1	1	8	27	11

BATTING
2B: T.Williams (off H.Brecheen); J.Gordon (off
  H.Brecheen).
2-out RBI: S.Spence.
RBI, scoring position, less than 2 outs: J.DiMaggio 0–1;
  L.Boudreau 0–1; G.McQuinn 0–1; B.Rosar 0–2;
  S.Shea 0–1.
GDP: J.DiMaggio.

BASERUNNING
SB: B.Doerr (2nd base off J.Sain/B.Edwards).
Team LOB: 6

FIELDING

NATIONAL LEAGUE

	ab	r	h	bi	bb	so	po	a
H.Walker, cf	2	0	0	0	0	1	1	0
A.Pafko, cf	2	0	1	0	0	0	2	0
D.Walker, rf	2	0	0	0	0	0	1	0
W.Marshall, rf	1	0	0	0	1	1	3	0
W.Cooper, c	3	0	0	0	0	1	6	0
B.Edwards, c	0	0	0	0	0	0	2	0
P.Cavarretta, ph-1b	1	0	0	0	0	1	1	0
J.Mize, 1b	3	1	2	1	1	0	8	0
P.Masi, pr-c	0	0	0	0	0	0	0	0
E.Slaughter, lf	3	0	0	0	1	0	1	0
F.Gustine, 3b	2	0	0	0	0	0	0	2
W.Kurowski, 3b	2	0	0	0	0	1	0	1
M.Marion, ss	2	0	1	0	0	0	0	1
P.Reese, ss	1	0	0	0	1	1	0	2
E.Verban, 2b	2	0	0	0	0	0	0	0
E.Stanky, 2b	2	0	0	0	0	0	2	2
E.Blackwell, p	0	0	0	0	0	0	0	0
B.Haas, ph	1	0	1	0	0	0	0	0
H.Brecheen, p	1	0	0	0	0	0	0	1
J.Sain, p	0	0	0	0	0	0	0	0
S.Musial, ph	1	0	0	0	0	0	0	0
W.Spahn, p	0	0	0	0	0	0	0	0
S.Rowe, ph	1	0	0	0	0	0	0	0
Totals	32	1	5	1	4	6	27	9

BATTING
HR: J.Mize (4th inning off S.Shea, 0 on, 2 out).
2-out RBI: J.Mize.

BASERUNNING
Team LOB: 8

FIELDING
E: J.Sain (dropped throw).
PB: W.Cooper.
DP: (1). P.Reese-E.Stanky-J.Mize.

PITCHING	ip	h	r	er	bb	so
American League						
H.Newhouser	3.0	1	0	0	0	2
S.Shea (w)	3.0	3	1	1	2	2
W.Masterson	1.2	0	0	0	1	2
J.Page (s)	1.1	1	0	0	1	0
National League						
E.Blackwell	3.0	1	0	0	0	4
H.Brecheen	3.0	5	1	1	0	2
J.Sain (L)	1.0	2	1	1	0	1
W.Spahn	2.0	0	0	0	1	1

Inherited Runners—Scored:
  S.Shea 0–0; W.Masterson 0–0; J.Page 1–0;
  H.Brecheen 0–0; J.Sain 0–0; W.Spahn 0–0.
WP: E.Blackwell

GAME DATA—T: 2:19; A: 41123; Temp: Unknown; Wind:
Unknown direction, Speed: Unknown

UMPIRES—HP: Jocko Conlan (NL), 1B: Jim Boyer (AL), 2B:
Butch Henline (NL), 3B: Art Passarella (AL)

STARTING LINEUPS

	American League	National League
1.	G.Kell 3b	H.Walker cf
2.	B.Lewis rf	D.Walker rf
3.	T.Williams lf	W.Cooper c
4.	J.DiMaggio cf	J.Mize 1b
5.	L.Boudreau ss	E.Slaughter lf
6.	G.McQuinn 1b	F.Gustine 3b
7.	J.Gordon 2b	M.Marion ss
8.	B.Rosar c	E.Verban 2b
9.	H.Newhouser p	E.Blackwell p

AL 1ST: G.Kell struck out; B.Lewis grounded out (J.Mize-1b unassisted); T.Williams was called out on strikes; 0 R, 0 H, 0 E, 0 LOB. AL 0, NL 0.

NL 1ST: H.Walker grounded out (J.Gordon-2b to G.McQuinn-1b); D.Walker grounded out (J.Gordon-2b to G.McQuinn-1b); W.Cooper struck out; 0 R, 0 H, 0 E, 0 LOB. AL 0, NL 0.

AL 2ND: J.DiMaggio singled to center field; W.Cooper allowed a passed ball [J.DiMaggio to second]; L.Boudreau was called out on strikes; G.McQuinn flied to E.Slaughter-lf; E.Blackwell threw a wild pitch [J.DiMaggio to third]; Gordon fouled four balls into the stands; J.Gordon struck out; 0 R, 1 H, 0 E, 1 LOB. AL 0, NL 0.

NL 2ND: J.Mize flied to T.Williams-lf; E.Slaughter flied to T.Williams-lf; F.Gustine grounded out (L.Boudreau-ss to G.McQuinn-1b); 0 R, 0 H, 0 E, 0 LOB. AL 0, NL 0.

AL 3RD: B.Rosar flied to D.Walker-rf; H.Newhouser grounded out (M.Marion-ss to J.Mize-1b); G.Kell grounded out (F.Gustine-3b to J.Mize-1b); 0 R, 0 H, 0 E, 0 LOB. AL 0, NL 0.

NL 3RD: M.Marion flied to J.DiMaggio-cf; E.Verban grounded out (J.Gordon-2b to G.McQuinn-1b); **B.Haas batted for E.Blackwell;** B.Haas singled to left field (it was the first pitch); H.Walker was called out on strikes; 0 R, 1 H, 0 E, 1 LOB. AL 0, NL 0.

AL 4TH: **H.Brecheen replaced B.Haas (pitching);** B.Lewis flied to H.Walker-cf; T.Williams doubled to right field; J.DiMaggio grounded out (F.Gustine-3b to J.Mize-1b); L.Boudreau singled to third base [T.Williams to third]; G.McQuinn struck out; 0 R, 2 H, 0 E, 2 LOB. AL 0, NL 0.

NL 4TH: **S.Shea replaced H.Newhouser (pitching);** D.Walker flied to T.Williams-lf; W.Cooper popped to G.McQuinn-1b in foul territory; J.Mize homered to deep rightfield (it was the 1−1 pitch); E.Slaughter walked; F.Gustine forced E.Slaughter (J.Gordon-2b to L.Boudreau-ss) [F.Gustine to first]; 1 R, 1 H, 0 E, 1 LOB. AL 0, NL 1.

AL 5TH: **A.Pafko replaced H.Walker (playing cf);** **W.Marshall replaced D.Walker (playing rf);** J.Gor-

don doubled to left field; B.Rosar flied to W.Marshall-rf; S.Shea grounded out (H.Brecheen-p to J.Mize-1b); G.Kell was called out on strikes; 0 R, 1 H, 0 E, 1 LOB. AL 0, NL 1.

NL 5TH: Umpires moved: Passarella (hp), Henline (1b), Boyer (2b), C; M.Marion singled to left field; E.Verban flied to B.Lewis-rf; H.Brecheen forced M.Marion (G.McQuinn-1b to L.Boudreau-ss) [H.Brecheen to first]; A.Pafko singled to center field (it was the first pitch) [H.Brecheen to second]; W.Marshall struck out; 0 R, 2 H, 0 E, 2 LOB. AL 0, NL 1.

AL 6TH: **P.Reese replaced M.Marion (playing ss);** **E.Stanky replaced E.Verban (playing 2b);** **W.Kurowski replaced F.Gustine (playing 3b);** **L.Appling batted for B.Lewis;** L.Appling singled to left field; T.Williams singled to right field [L.Appling to third]; J.DiMaggio grounded into a double play (P.Reese-ss to E.Stanky-2b to J.Mize-1b) [L.Appling scored (no RBI), T.Williams out at second]; L.Boudreau flied to W.Marshall-rf; 1 R, 2 H, 0 E, 0 LOB. AL 1, NL 1.

NL 6TH: **B.Doerr replaced J.Gordon (playing 2b);** **T.Henrich replaced L.Appling (playing rf);** W.Cooper flied to T.Henrich-rf; J.Mize walked; E.Slaughter popped to L.Boudreau-ss; W.Kurowski struck out; 0 R, 0 H, 0 E, 1 LOB. AL 1, NL 1.

AL 7TH: **J.Sain replaced H.Brecheen (pitching);** **B.Edwards replaced W.Cooper (playing c);** G.McQuinn grounded out (P.Reese-ss to J.Mize-1b); B.Doerr singled to left field; B.Doerr stole second; B.Doerr was picked off second, but was safe on an error by J.Sain-p [B.Doerr to third]; Sain's throw went into cf; B.Rosar struck out; **S.Spence batted for S.Shea;** S.Spence singled to right-center [B.Doerr scored]; G.Kell forced S.Spence (W.Kurowski-3b to E.Stanky-2b) [G.Kell to first]; 1 R, 2 H, 1 E, 1 LOB. AL 2, NL 1.

NL 7TH: **W.Masterson replaced S.Spence (pitching);** **B.Johnson replaced G.Kell (playing 3b);** P.Reese was called out on strikes; E.Stanky lined to T.Henrich-rf; **S.Musial batted for J.Sain;** S.Musial grounded out (L.Boudreau-ss to G.McQuinn-1b); 0 R, 0 H, 0 E, 0 LOB. AL 2, NL 1.

AL 8TH: **W.Spahn replaced S.Musial (pitching);** T.Henrich struck out; T.Williams grounded out (E.Stanky-2b to J.Mize-1b); J.DiMaggio walked; L.Boudreau flied to A.Pafko-cf; 0 R, 0 H, 0 E, 1 LOB. AL 2, NL 1.

NL 8TH: A.Pafko grounded out (L.Boudreau-ss to G.McQuinn-1b); W.Marshall walked; **P.Cavarretta batted for B.Edwards;** P.Cavarretta struck out; **J.Page replaced W.Masterson (pitching);** J.Mize singled to right field [W.Marshall to third]; **P.Masi ran for J.Mize;** E.Slaughter grounded out

(L.Boudreau-ss to G.McQuinn-1b); 0 R, 1 H, 0 E, 2 LOB. AL 2, NL 1.

AL 9TH: **P.Cavarretta stayed in game (playing 1b); P.Masi stayed in game (playing c);** G.McQuinn grounded out (P.Cavarretta-1b unassisted); B.Doerr flied to W.Marshall-rf; B.Rosar flied to A.Pafko-cf; 0 R, 0 H, 0 E, 0 LOB. AL 2, NL 1.

NL 9TH: W.Kurowski grounded out (B.Doerr-2b to G.McQuinn-1b); P.Reese walked; E.Stanky forced P.Reese (B.Doerr-2b to L.Boudreau-ss) [E.Stanky to first]; **S.Rowe batted for W.Spahn;** S.Rowe flied to T.Henrich-rf; 0 R, 0 H, 0 E, 1 LOB. AL 2, NL 1.

Final Totals	R	H	E	LOB
American League	2	8	0	6
National League	1	5	1	8

Tuesday, July 13, 1948

Sportsman's Park, St. Louis

American League 5, National League 2

SERIES RESULTS: AL 11, NL 4

Despite Assorted Adversities, the Americans Win Again

Exasperated by his league's ten losses in the fourteen previous All-Star Games, National League president Ford Frick had exhorted his troops to put forth their best effort to win this year's game. The league cooperated to the extent that the pitchers selected by manager Leo Durocher were well-rested, and the twenty-five-man team was mostly healthy. Meanwhile, four of the top stars in the American League were injured, and a feud had erupted between AL manager Bucky Harris and the duo of owner Bill Veeck and manager Lou Boudreau of Cleveland over the withdrawal by Bob Feller. Everything seemed to point to a National League victory in 1948. Even history was on the NL's side because it had won all three of the games played in previous presidential election years.

The Nationals even got off to an excellent start. They jumped out to a first-inning, two-run lead on a home run by Stan Musial, the NL's leading vote getter. Musial's blast thrilled the Cardinals fans, predominant among the 34,009 at Sportsman's Park, but those two runs would be all the National Leaguers would get. The Americans tied the game with single runs in the third and fourth, then pushed across three more in the fifth to come away with a 5–2 win, their third straight victory and their sixth in the last seven games.

Musial's home run came against Washington's Walt Masterson, named to start by Harris after left-hander Hal Newhouser of Detroit had asked not to be used. In contrast to the more well-rested NL staff, Newhouser was one of six AL pitchers who had pitched Sunday. He had also pitched the Sunday before the previous year's All-Star Game, when he was the starter, and had set the NL down on one hit in his three innings.

The Sunday before this game, however, rain had twice held up play, and Newhouser reported that his pitching arm was lame. Diagnosed with bursitis in his left shoulder, he appeared dejected at not being able to be the starter again, but he was with the team on the bench. So too were his teammate third baseman George Kell (sore ankle) and outfielders Joe DiMaggio (sore heels and a swollen knee) and Ted Williams (torn rib cartilage). The fans had selected them to start, but all three had to forego that honor due to injury, although they were available to pinch-hit.

Feller's absence was very much a different story. He had missed the 1947 game with torn muscles in his back, although he had recovered sufficiently to pitch two days after the game. His withdrawal this year was rumored to have been at the urging of Veeck and Boudreau. Harris was furious. He replaced Feller with Boston right-hander Joe Dobson while claiming that if he should ever again be the All-Star manager, he would not under any circumstances invite Feller to be on the team. Veeck and Boudreau countered by saying they believed that no more than one pitcher should be selected from any club. Because Harris had also chosen pitcher Bob Lemon, they believed Lemon, named for the first time, should be the one to go. That the first-place Indians were in a heated pennant race with Harris's Yankees, the A's, and the Red Sox made the disagreement even more acrimonious.

Without specifically mentioning names, the Cincinnati Reds players had gone so far as to send a letter to Pirates outfielder Dixie Walker, the National League's player representative, concerning players who bypassed the All-Star Game. The letter, signed by pitcher Bucky Walters, suggested a fine, equivalent to three days' pay, for players who skipped the game. Walker said that other NL clubs endorsed the Reds' plan, and so did those in the American League, as Walker learned after he discussed the letter with Tigers pitcher Freddie Hutchinson, the AL's player representative.

Cincinnati players were also vocal in their criticism of the last-minute withdrawal of Cardinals shortstop Marty Marion. The Reds claimed that Marion looked perfectly healthy against them Sunday when he got St. Louis's only hit to spoil

Ken Raffensberger's potential no-hitter. Following a meeting of baseball's Executive Council, Commissioner Happy Chandler, while neither endorsing the plan nor naming names, issued the following statement: "I am very much concerned over the failure of club owners and players to take seriously the All-Star Game. We have had some straight talk. I assume that in the future every player who is voted on the All-Star team will show up. We have no plan to punish anybody, but we will take whatever steps are necessary."

The injuries to his stars had forced Harris to revamp the American League lineup selected by the record four million fans who cast All-Star ballots that summer. In the three-week poll, conducted by 453 newspapers and radio stations, the fans had chosen an outfield that included Williams, who was leading the AL with a .388 batting average and was the overall vote leader (more than 1.5 million), in left, and DiMaggio, second in total votes in the AL, in center. But because both Williams and DiMaggio were unavailable to start, Harris replaced them with Detroit's Hoot Evers in center and the Yanks' Tommy Henrich in left. Evers and Henrich joined Detroit's Pat Mullin, who had won the voting among right fielders. Evers had finished second behind DiMaggio, but Henrich had actually finished second in the voting for *right fielders*. However, Harris had failed to select both Henrich's teammate Johnny Lindell and Philadelphia's Barney McCosky, who had finished second and third behind Williams. Instead, he'd chosen three right fielders, the third being the Browns' Al Zarilla, a move that had allowed him to fulfill the charge of selecting at least one player from every team.

The Browns were the host team in this second game played at Sportsman's Park, and it was a former Brownie, Burt Shotton, who had the honor of throwing out the first ball. The honor was not, however, for Shotton's service as a Browns outfielder from 1909 to 1917; it was for his having led Brooklyn to the 1947 National League pennant. Dodger president Branch Rickey, his old Browns manager, had asked Shotton to step in after Chandler had imposed a one-year ban on Durocher for his alleged ties to gamblers. Durocher was back to lead the Dodgers this season, and as manager of the defending champions, he was named to manage the league's All-Stars. Throwing out the first ball was baseball's sop to Shotton. Ironically, three days later, Shotton and Durocher would be central players in one of the biggest stories in New York baseball history. The Giants would fire their manager, Mel Ott, and hire Durocher, and Brooklyn would again replace Durocher with Shotton.

With the opening ceremonies completed, Phil-lies center fielder Richie Ashburn went after Masterson's first pitch and hit it up the middle. Second baseman Joe Gordon caught up with the ball, but his throw pulled first baseman George McQuinn off the bag. The official scorers called it a hit for the speedy Ashburn, whose .350 average was second only to Musial's .403 in the NL batting race. Ashburn then stole second and, after moving to third on a ground out by Red Schoendienst, rode home as Musial blasted an 0-2 pitch onto the roof of the pavilion in right-center field.

Along with Musial and right fielder Enos Slaughter, Schoendienst was one of three Cardinals in the starting lineup. He was himself recovering from a sore shoulder but was playing in place of the Braves' Eddie Stanky, the one National Leaguer voted to the team who was unavailable. Stanky had fractured an ankle bone in a game against Brooklyn five days earlier. The Dodgers had traded Stanky to Boston during spring training to make room at second base for Jackie Robinson, and Stanky blamed the move on Durocher, claiming his former manager had "stabbed him in the back."

Because of those charges, many neutral observers were disappointed at Stanky's absence. They had looked forward to this game to see how these two fiery personalities would handle the alleged treachery. In 1950, Durocher would bring Stanky to the Giants, where the two would get along just fine.

Giants slugger Johnny Mize followed the Musial home run with a single and went to second on a wild pitch. Masterson then walked Slaughter but avoided further trouble by getting both Andy Pafko of the Cubs and Walker Cooper of the Giants to bounce into force outs.

Ever the gambler (at least on the ballfield), Durocher had upset the conventional All-Star roster makeup by selecting six pitchers instead of the traditional eight. (Of the six, only Pittsburgh's Elmer Riddle had no previous All-Star experience.) Durocher used the two extra spots to add a pair of power-hitting third basemen: Sid Gordon of the Giants with 18eighteen home runs and Bob Elliott of Boston with ten. He did, however, omit from the team Chicago slugger Hank Sauer, who had finished behind Musial and Ralph Kiner in the voting for a left fielder. Sauer was the NL home run leader with twenty-four and was tied with Musial for the RBI lead with sixty-four.

Durocher chose as his starter Ralph Branca, the ace of his Brooklyn staff, whom he'd rested during the Dodgers' weekend series with the Giants. Branca breezed through the first inning, striking out the first two American League hitters, Mullin and Henrich, and retiring Boudreau on a grounder to Pee Wee Reese. Then, after cleanup hitter Joe Gordon flied out to lead off the second, Evers lined a home run into the seats in left. In cutting the NL lead in half, Evers duplicated Max West's feat of hitting a home run in his first All-Star at bat. West, of the Boston Bees, had smashed a first-inning, three-run homer off the Yankees' Red Ruffing in this park in 1940.

In the third, Branca suffered a temporary loss of control that allowed the AL to tie the game. He walked the first two batters, lead-off hitter Mickey Vernon (batting for Masterson) and Mullin. Henrich struck out for the second time, but as he took the called third strike, Vernon and Mullin executed a double steal. Cooper, making his sixth consecutive start behind the plate, made a good throw to third, but third baseman Pafko had been playing back and had to take it on the run. Vernon slid in safely and then scored as Boudreau flied deep to Slaughter in right.

The Yanks' Vic Raschi and the Cubs' Johnny Schmitz took over the pitching duties in the fourth. Raschi set the National Leaguers down one-two-three, but Schmitz failed to survive the inning. After Evers went out on a pop to Reese, the Americans loaded the bases on singles by Ken Keltner and McQuinn and a walk to Birdie Tebbetts. (Boston's Tebbetts, who had finished second to the A's Buddy Rosar by thirty-five thousand votes — the closest voting in either league — had replaced Rosar at catcher in the fourth inning.)

Raschi was next, and Harris, his regular season manager, aware that he was a decent-hitting pitcher, allowed him to bat. (Five years later, on August 4, 1953, Raschi would set an American League record for most RBI in a game with seven.) With the NL hoping for an inning-ending double play, Raschi came through with a sharp single into left field. Keltner scored easily, while McQuinn slid in just ahead of Musial's strong throw and Tebbetts took third. Durocher had seen enough of the left-hander Schmitz and called Boston right-hander Johnny Sain out of the bullpen. The left-handed-hitting Mullin was due up; nevertheless, Harris sent DiMaggio in to pinch-hit. DiMaggio lined Sain's first pitch to deep left, where Musial caught up with it, but Tebbetts scored after the catch, making it a 5–2 game. Sain got Henrich on

a pop to Reese for the third out and then struck out the side in the fifth, getting Vern Stephens, Bobby Doerr, and Evers.

Ewell Blackwell pitched the sixth, seventh, and eighth, allowing singles to McQuinn and Stephens and a walk to Williams. McQuinn's single and the walk to Williams, batting for Raschi, were in the sixth and put two on with two out. Newhouser, running for Williams, became the third out on a force-play grounder by Zarilla.

Raschi had also gotten out of a tight spot in the sixth. Two members of the pennant-bound Braves, Elliott and catcher Phil Masi, had singled and were on first and second with one out. They moved up a base as the Giants' Buddy Kerr (Marion's replacement) grounded to third. Raschi then walked Eddie Waitkus of the Cubs to load the bases. The batter was Ashburn, who already had two hits in the game, including a single off Raschi in the fifth. But what would be the NL's final threat ended when the Yankee ace threw a third strike past the Phillies' rookie sensation. The Athletics' Joe Coleman pitched a hitless and scoreless final three innings to end the game, which had begun under a blistering sun but which ended with rain falling. Dark clouds and thunder had moved in early in the afternoon, and rain had also fallen in the sixth and seventh innings.

"We had our chances," said Blackwell in the subdued National League locker room afterward. "We had men on bases, but we just couldn't get any base hits when they counted."

Manager Durocher had no excuses. "We just got beat," he said. Mize was one of many National Leaguers who mentioned Raschi's game-winning hit. "How are you going to figure on a thing like a pitcher getting the big hit of the ball game?" he asked.

Raschi was not only the hitting star of the game, he was also the winning pitcher, giving Yankee pitchers six of the American League's eleven wins, along with three of their four losses. Oddly, no Yankee pitcher has won an All-Star Game in the more than fifty years since Raschi's 1948 triumph.

The loser was Schmitz, who joined previous Chicago losers Bill Lee (1939) and Claude Passeau (1941 and 1946) to give Cubs pitchers an 0-4 record in All-Star competition.

	AL			NL	
P	Walt Masterson	WAS		Ralph Branca	BRO
C	Buddy Rosar	PHA		Walker Cooper	NY
1B	George McQuinn	NYA		Johnny Mize	NY
2B	Joe Gordon	CLE		Eddie Stanky +	BSN
3B	Ken Keltner	CLE		Andy Pafko	CHN
SS	Lou Boudreau	CLE		Pee Wee Reese	BRO
OF	Hoot Evers	DET		Richie Ashburn	PHI
OF	Tommy Henrich	NYA		Stan Musial	SLN
OF	Pat Mullin	DET		Enos Slaughter	SLN
	Yogi Berra	NYA		Ewell Blackwell	CIN
	Joe Coleman	PHA		Harry Brecheen	SLN
	Joe DiMaggio	NYA		Bob Elliott	BSN
	Joe Dobson	BOS		Sid Gordon	NY
	Bobby Doerr	BOS		Frankie Gustine	PIT
	Bob Feller +	CLE		Tommy Holmes	BSN
	Joe Haynes	CHA		Buddy Kerr	NY
	George Kell	DET		Ralph Kiner	PIT
	Bob Lemon	CLE		Marty Marion +	SLN
	Hal Newhouser	DET		Phil Masi	BSN
	Joe Page	NYA		Clyde McCullough	CHN
	Vic Raschi	NYA		Elmer Riddle	PIT
	Vern Stephens	BOS		Bill Rigney	NY
	Birdie Tebbetts	BOS		Johnny Sain	BSN
	Mickey Vernon	WAS		Johnny Schmitz	CHN
	Ted Williams	BOS		Red Schoendienst	SLN
	Al Zarilla	SLA		Bobby Thomson	NY
				Eddie Waitkus	CHN

+ player replaced on roster

National League	200 000 000- 2							
American League	011 300 00X- 5							

NATIONAL LEAGUE

	ab	r	h	bi	bb	so	po	a
R.Ashburn, cf	4	1	2	0	0	1	1	0
R.Kiner, lf	1	0	0	0	0	0	1	0
R.Schoendienst, 2b	4	0	0	0	0	0	0	1
B.Rigney, 2b	0	0	0	0	1	0	2	0
S.Musial, lf-cf	4	1	2	2	1	1	3	0
J.Mize, 1b	4	0	1	0	0	1	4	1
E.Slaughter, rf	2	0	1	0	1	0	2	0
T.Holmes, rf	1	0	0	0	0	0	1	0
A.Pafko, 3b	2	0	0	0	0	0	0	0
B.Elliott, 3b	2	0	1	0	0	0	0	0
W.Cooper, c	2	0	0	0	0	0	3	0
P.Masi, c	2	0	1	0	0	0	4	0
P.Reese, ss	2	0	0	0	0	1	2	2
B.Kerr, ss	2	0	0	0	0	1	1	0
R.Branca, p	1	0	0	0	0	0	0	0
F.Gustine, ph	1	0	0	0	0	1	0	0
J.Schmitz, p	0	0	0	0	0	0	0	0
J.Sain, p	0	0	0	0	0	0	0	0
E.Waitkus, ph	0	0	0	0	1	0	0	0
E.Blackwell, p	0	0	0	0	0	0	0	0
B.Thomson, ph	1	0	0	0	0	1	0	0
Totals	35	2	8	2	4	7	24	4

AMERICAN LEAGUE

	ab	r	h	bi	bb	so	po	a
P.Mullin, rf	1	0	0	0	1	1	0	0
J.DiMaggio, ph	1	0	0	1	0	0	0	0
A.Zarilla, rf	2	0	0	0	0	0	2	0
T.Henrich, lf	3	0	0	0	1	2	1	0
L.Boudreau, ss	2	0	0	1	0	0	2	0
V.Stephens, ss	2	0	1	0	0	1	0	0
J.Gordon, 2b	2	0	0	0	0	0	1	2
B.Doerr, 2b	2	0	0	0	0	1	0	3
H.Evers, cf	4	1	1	1	0	1	0	0
K.Keltner, 3b	3	1	1	0	1	0	1	6
G.McQuinn, 1b	4	1	2	0	0	0	14	0
B.Rosar, c	1	0	0	0	0	0	1	0
B.Tebbetts, c	1	1	0	0	2	1	5	1
W.Masterson, p	0	0	0	0	0	0	0	0
M.Vernon, ph	0	1	0	0	1	0	0	0
V.Raschi, p	1	0	1	2	0	0	0	1
T.Williams, ph	0	0	0	0	1	0	0	0
H.Newhouser, pr	0	0	0	0	0	0	0	0
J.Coleman, p	0	0	0	0	0	0	0	1
Totals	29	5	6	5	7	7	27	14

PITCHING	ip	h	r	er	bb	so
National League						
R.Branca	3.0	1	2	2	3	3
J.Schmitz (L)	0.1	3	3	3	1	0
J.Sain	1.2	0	0	0	0	3
E.Blackwell	3.0	2	0	0	3	1
American League						
W.Masterson	3.0	5	2	2	1	1
V.Raschi (w)	3.0	3	0	0	1	3
J.Coleman (s)	3.0	0	0	0	2	3

BATTING

HR: S.Musial (1st inning off W.Masterson, 1 on, 1 out).
RBI, scoring position, less than 2 outs: R.Schoendienst 0–1; S.Musial 1–1; A.Pafko 0–1; B.Kerr 0–1.

BASERUNNING

SB: R.Ashburn (2nd base off W.Masterson/B.Rosar).
Team LOB: 10

BATTING

HR: H.Evers (2nd inning off R.Branca, 0 on, 1 out).
RBI, scoring position, less than 2 outs: J.DiMaggio 1–1; T.Henrich 0–1; L.Boudreau 1–2; B.Doerr 0–1; H.Evers 0–1; B.Tebbetts 0–1; V.Raschi 2–2.
S: J.Coleman.

BASERUNNING

SB: P.Mullin (Double SB 2nd base off R.Branca/ W.Cooper); G.McQuinn (2nd base off E.Blackwell/ P.Masi); M.Vernon (Double SB 3rd base off R.Branca/W.Cooper).
Team LOB: 8

Inherited Runners—Scored:
J.Schmitz 0–0; J.Sain 2–1; E.Blackwell 0–0; V.Raschi 0–0; J.Coleman 0–0.
WP: W.Masterson

GAME DATA—T: 2:27; A: 34009; Temp: Unknown; Wind: Unknown direction, Speed: Unknown

UMPIRES—HP: Charlie Berry (AL), 1B: Bill Stewart (NL), 2B: Joe Paparella (AL), 3B: Beans Reardon (NL)

STARTING LINEUPS

	National League	*American League*
1.	R.Ashburn cf	P.Mullin rf
2.	R.Schoendienst 2b	T.Henrich lf
3.	S.Musial lf	L.Boudreau ss
4.	J.Mize 1b	J.Gordon 2b
5.	E.Slaughter rf	H.Evers cf
6.	A.Pafko 3b	K.Keltner 3b
7.	W.Cooper c	G.McQuinn 1b
8.	P.Reese ss	B.Rosar c
9.	R.Branca p	W.Masterson p

NL 1ST: R.Ashburn singled to second base; R.Ashburn stole second; R.Schoendienst grounded out (G.McQuinn-1b unassisted) [R.Ashburn to third]; S.Musial homered to deep rightfield [R.Ashburn scored]; J.Mize singled to center field; W.Masterson threw a wild pitch [J.Mize to second]; E.Slaughter walked; A.Pafko forced J.Mize (K.Keltner-3b unassisted) [E.Slaughter to second, A.Pafko to first]; W.Cooper forced A.Pafko (K.Keltner-3b to J.Gordon-2b) [W.Cooper to first]; 2 R, 3 H, 0 E, 2 LOB. NL 2, AL 0.

AL 1ST: P.Mullin struck out; T.Henrich struck out; L.Boudreau grounded out (P.Reese-ss to J.Mize-1b); 0 R, 0 H, 0 E, 0 LOB. NL 2, AL 0.

NL 2ND: P.Reese struck out; R.Branca grounded out (K.Keltner-3b to G.McQuinn-1b); R.Ashburn flied to T.Henrich-lf; 0 R, 0 H, 0 E, 0 LOB. NL 2, AL 0.

AL 2ND: J.Gordon flied to S.Musial-lf; H.Evers homered to deep leftfield; K.Keltner walked; G.McQuinn flied to R.Ashburn-cf; B.Rosar flied to E.Slaughter-rf; 1 R, 1 H, 0 E, 1 LOB. NL 2, AL 1.

NL 3RD: R.Schoendienst popped to G.McQuinn-1b in foul territory; S.Musial singled to center field; J.Mize forced S.Musial (J.Gordon-2b to L.Boudreau-ss) [J.Mize to first]; E.Slaughter singled to third base [J.Mize to second]; A.Pafko forced E.Slaughter (J.Gordon-2b to L.Boudreau-ss) [A.Pafko to first]; 0 R, 2 H, 0 E, 2 LOB. NL 2, AL 1.

AL 3RD: **M.Vernon batted for W.Masterson;** M.Vernon walked; P.Mullin walked [M.Vernon to second]; T.Henrich struck out while M.Vernon stole third and P.Mullin stole second; L.Boudreau flied to E.Slaughter-rf [M.Vernon scored]; J.Gordon grounded out (P.Reese-ss to J.Mize-1b); 1 R, 0 H, 0 E, 1 LOB. NL 2, AL 2.

NL 4TH: **B.Tebbetts replaced B.Rosar (playing c); V.Raschi replaced M.Vernon (pitching);** W.Cooper grounded out (K.Keltner-3b to G.McQuinn-1b); P.Reese grounded out (K.Keltner-3b to G.McQuinn-1b); **F.Gustine batted for R.Branca;** F.Gustine struck out (B.Tebbetts-c to G.McQuinn-1b); 0 R, 0 H, 0 E, 0 LOB. NL 2, AL 2.

AL 4TH: **J.Schmitz replaced F.Gustine (pitching);** H.Evers popped to P.Reese-ss; K.Keltner singled to left field; G.McQuinn singled to center field [K.Keltner to second]; B.Tebbetts walked [K.Keltner to third, G.McQuinn to second]; V.Raschi singled to left field [K.Keltner scored, G.McQuinn scored, B.Tebbetts to third]; **J.Sain replaced J.Schmitz (pitching); J.DiMaggio batted for P.Mullin;** J.DiMaggio lined to S.Musial-lf [B.Tebbetts scored]; T.Henrich popped to P.Reese-ss; 3 R, 3 H, 0 E, 1 LOB. NL 2, AL 5.

NL 5TH: **A.Zarilla replaced J.DiMaggio (playing rf); B.Doerr replaced J.Gordon (playing 2b); V.Stephens replaced L.Boudreau (playing ss);** R.Ashburn singled to center field; R.Schoendienst flied to A.Zarilla-rf; S.Musial struck out; J.Mize grounded out (B.Doerr-2b to G.McQuinn-1b); 0 R, 1 H, 0 E, 1 LOB. NL 2, AL 5.

AL 5TH: Umpires moved: Reardon (hp), Paparella (1b), Stewart (2b), Berry (3b); **P.Masi replaced W.Cooper (playing c); B.Elliott replaced A.Pafko (playing 3b); B.Kerr replaced P.Reese (playing ss);** V.Stephens was called out on strikes; B.Doerr struck out; H.Evers struck out; 0 R, 0 H, 0 E, 0 LOB. NL 2, AL 5.

NL 6TH: E.Slaughter grounded out (V.Raschi-p to G.McQuinn-1b); B.Elliott singled to left field; P.Masi singled to center field [B.Elliott to second]; B.Kerr grounded out (K.Keltner-3b to G.McQuinn-1b) [B.Elliott to third, P.Masi to second]; **E.Waitkus batted for J.Sain;** E.Waitkus walked; R.Ashburn was called out on strikes; 0 R, 2 H, 0 E, 3 LOB. NL 2, AL 5.

AL 6TH: **E.Blackwell replaced E.Waitkus (pitching); T.Holmes replaced E.Slaughter (playing rf);** K.Keltner lined to T.Holmes-rf; G.McQuinn singled to left field; G.McQuinn stole second; B.Tebbetts was called out on strikes; **T.Williams batted for V.Raschi;** T.Williams walked; **H.Newhouser ran for T.Williams;** A.Zarilla forced H.Newhouser (R.Schoendienst-2b to B.Kerr-ss) [A.Zarilla to first]; 0 R, 1 H, 0 E, 2 LOB. NL 2, AL 5.

NL 7TH: **J.Coleman replaced H.Newhouser (pitching);** R.Schoendienst grounded out (B.Doerr-2b to G.McQuinn-1b); S.Musial walked; J.Mize struck out; T.Holmes grounded out (J.Coleman-p to G.McQuinn-1b); 0 R, 0 H, 0 E, 1 LOB. NL 2, AL 5.

AL 7TH: **S.Musial changed positions (playing cf); R.Kiner replaced R.Ashburn (playing lf); B.Rigney replaced R.Schoendienst (playing 2b);** T.Henrich walked; V.Stephens singled to left field [T.Henrich to second]; On a bunt B.Doerr popped to J.Mize-1b; H.Evers popped to B.Rigney-2b; K.Keltner lined to R.Kiner-lf; 0 R, 1 H, 0 E, 2 LOB. NL 2, AL 5.

NL 8TH: B.Elliott lined to A.Zarilla-rf; P.Masi popped to G.McQuinn-1b in foul territory; B.Kerr was called out on strikes; 0 R, 0 H, 0 E, 0 LOB. NL 2, AL 5.

AL 8TH: G.McQuinn grounded out (J.Mize-1b unassisted); B.Tebbetts walked; J.Coleman out on a sacrifice bunt (J.Mize-1b to B.Rigney-2b) [B.Tebbetts to second]; A.Zarilla flied to S.Musial-cf; 0 R, 0 H, 0 E, 1 LOB. NL 2, AL 5.

NL 9TH: **B.Thomson batted for E.Blackwell;** B.Thomson struck out; R.Kiner grounded out (K.Keltner-3b to G.McQuinn-1b); B.Rigney walked; S.Musial grounded out (B.Doerr-2b to G.McQuinn-1b); 0 R, 0 H, 0 E, 1 LOB. NL 2, AL 5.

Final Totals	R	H	E	LOB
National League	2	8	0	10
American League	5	6	0	8

16

Tuesday, July 12, 1949

Ebbets Field, Brooklyn

American League 11, National League 7

SERIES RESULTS: AL 12, NL 4

Democracy Comes to the All-Star Game

With their 11–7 victory at Ebbets Field in Brooklyn, the American League reached its high-water mark in All-Star competition. The win, its fourth in a row and seventh in the last eight games, gave it an overwhelming 12–4 lead in the series. Yet the pattern of this AL triumph was very different from the wins of the previous two years. In both its 2–1 win in 1947 and their 5–2 win in 1948, the National League had taken the lead on an early home run: Johnny Mize in the second inning in 1947, and Stan Musial in the first inning in 1948. And in both games, the American League had come back to tie and eventually win. In fact, Mize's solo blast and Musial's two-run homer were the only runs the Nationals scored in the two games. Counting their shutout in 1946, the Nationals scored a total of just three runs in the last three games.

In 1949, Ebbets Field was hosting the All-Star contest for the first time, the last of the current Major League locations in existence in 1933 to have the honor. Brooklyn was to have hosted the 1942 game, but baseball shifted the contest to the Polo Grounds. The thinking was that the Polo Grounds's larger seating capacity would produce greater attendance and thus more revenue for the two charitable beneficiaries—the Bat and Ball Fund, which supplied baseball equipment to servicemen, and the Army and Navy Relief Fund. Fifty thousand fans were expected that evening in 1942, but rain limited the crowd to just 33,694, which was about one thousand more than the 32,577 that saw this afternoon's game at Ebbets Field.

Dodger broadcaster Red Barber had often proclaimed that "anything can happen at Ebbets Field, and usually does." This contest, played through an intermittent drizzle, did its best to verify that claim. It was a sloppily played slugfest that featured twenty-five hits, a record eighteen runs,

and a record six errors, five by the Nationals. Two of those errors came in the first inning and allowed the AL to score four unearned runs. The NL fought back, and despite squandering several scoring opportunities, actually went ahead 5–4 in the third, only to surrender the lead permanently an inning later. Vic Raschi of the Yankees, the winning pitcher a year earlier, entered the game in the seventh inning and pitched three scoreless innings to preserve the victory.

For the first time in All-Star play, six umpires were used, with one stationed down the left-field line and one down the right-field line. Yet, oddly, when the umpires made the traditional switch after four and a half innings, NL ump Al Barlick, who had been behind the plate, departed, resulting in the right-field line's being uncovered for the remainder of the game.

National League manager Billy Southworth of the Boston Braves was managing his third All-Star Game. As the leader of the pennant-winning Cardinals, he'd been the losing manager of the All-Star Game in 1943 and its winning manager in 1944, the last time the NL had won. He chose as his starting pitcher lefty Warren Spahn, who along with Johnny Sain had helped pitch Boston to its first pennant in thirty-four years in 1948. But Spahn was mainly ineffective today, giving up four runs, six hits, and two walks in one and a third innings. Yet, in all fairness, the four runs were unearned, and with better luck, he might have retired the Americans in order in the first.

Spahn struck out lead-off hitter Dom DiMaggio and number three batter Ted Williams and should have had the number two man George Kell. The Tiger third baseman had bounced a routine grounder to his opposite number, Eddie Kazak of the Cardinals, but the rookie's throw handcuffed first baseman Mize, and Kell was safe. The official scorers charged Mize with the error, later decided the error should go to Kazak, and several days afterward changed it back to Mize. Sportswriter Roscoe McGowen, the chief scorer, said that the three-man scoring panel had determined that Kazak's throw was not in the dirt and that Mize should have handled it.

Kell stole second as Williams was striking out, but even there, a better throw by Phillies catcher Andy Seminick might have gotten him. Joe DiMaggio, playing in his tenth All-Star Game, singled to left, and the AL had its first run. Then, after walking A's shortstop Eddie Joost, Spahn gave up a single to Senators first baseman Eddie Robinson. DiMaggio scored and Joost went to third.

When Cass Michaels of the White Sox followed with a bouncer to Pee Wee Reese, Spahn appeared to have escaped with just the two runs allowed. But the Dodger shortstop failed to handle the routine ground ball. Joost scored run number three, and Red Sox catcher Birdie Tebbetts's single to left brought Robinson home with the fourth run. American League starter Mel Parnell of Boston fanned to finally end the NL's disastrous first inning. Spahn had struck out the side (all three victims were members of the crosstown Red Sox) but, in between, had been the victim of four unearned runs.

Parnell was the first Red Sox pitcher to start an All-Star Game since Lefty Grove in 1936, and his match-up with Spahn was the first time two pitchers from the same city had squared off since the Giants' Carl Hubbell and the Yankees' Lefty Gomez had done so in 1934.

After taking the mound, Parnell quickly surrendered half the lead. He retired Reese, but then Jackie Robinson slashed a double to left and Musial, in what was a familiar sight to Brooklyn fans, drove a home run over the wall in right and onto Bedford Avenue.

Robinson, playing in his third big league season, was the first African American to participate in an All-Star Game. Currently leading the National League with a .362 average, he'd been the league's leading vote getter (1,891,212) and second overall to Williams (2,087,466). The *Chicago Tribune*, conductor of the poll, announced that the fans had cast 4,637,743 votes, more than half a million higher than in 1948.

Southworth and AL manager Lou Boudreau of Cleveland had selected three additional black players: Southworth chose pitcher Don Newcombe and catcher Roy Campanella, both of the Dodgers, for the NL team, and Boudreau chose Indians outfielder Larry Doby for the AL squad. (Doby was one of five Cleveland players on the AL team, although none of the defending world champions had been elected to start.)

With one out in the AL second, Kell singled and Williams walked. Joe DiMaggio was the due batter,

prompting Southworth to bring Newcombe in to replace Spahn. Newcombe had made his big league debut on May 20, less than two months earlier, making the fifty-three days between his debut and his appearance in an All-Star Game the shortest span ever. If the rookie was nervous, however, he didn't show it. He retired DiMaggio on a fly to Ralph Kiner in left and then got Joost on a pop-up to Robinson to end the threat.

In the home second, a walk to Willard Marshall, a single by Kazak, and a pitch that hit Seminick loaded the bases with no outs and finished Parnell. Boudreau called on Tigers right-hander Virgil Trucks to pitch to Newcombe, a pitcher who hit exceptionally well. Newcombe, a left-handed batter, drove a ball deep to left field that the overwhelmingly National League crowd thought for a moment might be the first All-Star grand slam home run. However, the ball got held up in the wind just enough to allow Williams, playing despite a fractured rib, to make an outstanding one-handed catch while crashing into the wall. The blow scored Marshall, but when Reese followed by grounding into a 4-6-3 double play, the NL was forced to settle for just the one run.

Another double play prevented the Nationals from a possible big inning in the third, although the two they did push across put them ahead, 5–4. Jackie Robinson, on his way to a batting championship and a Most Valuable Player Award, opened the inning with a walk. He went to third on Musial's single and scored the tying run as Kiner was bouncing into a double play. However, the Nationals weren't through. Mize singled to right and moved to second on a walk to Marshall. Brooklyn's Gil Hodges went in to run for Mize and scored when Kazak followed with a single. Hodges had finished third in the voting for first basemen, behind Mize and Philadelphia's Eddie Waitkus, but Waitkus had been incapacitated since suffering a gunshot wound on June 15. (Waitkus was listed as an honorary member of the team, but for the first time since 1933, neither side had had to replace anyone because of last-minute injuries.)

When the National Leaguers took the field in the top of the fourth, Hodges was at first base while Campanella had replaced Seminick behind the plate. The new NL configuration had five of the hometown Dodgers in the field, three of whom were black, including an all-black battery.

After Newcombe began the inning by getting Dom DiMaggio to ground out to third baseman Sid Gordon of the Giants, Kell singled and Williams walked. Newcombe got the big second out by again getting Joe DiMaggio, who also grounded out to Gordon, but he couldn't get by Joost. The eleven-year veteran, playing in his first All-Star Game, hit a twisting grounder off the end of his bat between first baseman Hodges and second baseman Robinson. Hodges made a barehanded attempt to grab it, but the ball bounced off his hand and into right field as Kell and Williams raced home. The "fluke" hit put the AL back ahead, 6–5, and would serve to make Newcombe the losing pitcher and Trucks the winner.

George Munger of the Cardinals worked a scoreless fifth, but in the sixth the Americans scored two more off Boston's Vern Bickford to stretch their lead to 8–5. Again the Nationals came back, scoring two in the home half to once more make it a one-run game. The AL's runs came on Joe DiMaggio's double that scored brother Dom and the Browns' Bob Dillinger, running for Kell. DiMaggio, with three RBI for the day, left for pinch runner Doby, making the Cleveland outfielder the first African American to play for the American League in All-Star competition.

Because an injured heel had sidelined DiMaggio for the first sixty-five games of the season, his name had not been on the AL ballot. Nevertheless, he'd batted .331 since returning to the Yankee lineup, and Boudreau had named him to start in place of his teammate Tommy Henrich. Unlike in 1947 and 1948, the first two years of fan balloting, the outfielders were chosen as a group rather than by individual position. Henrich had finished second behind Williams but had missed the last week with a knee injury, and though he was on the bench and in uniform, he was unavailable to play.

Following an eleven-minute rain delay in the home sixth, Kiner blasted a two-run homer off A's left-hander Lou Brissie, who had replaced Trucks in the fourth. These would be the NL's final runs because any hopes for a National League victory ended with the new pitchers chosen to work the seventh inning. The Americans jumped on Howie Pollet for a quick three runs, while Raschi would hold the Nationals scoreless the rest of the way.

Cleveland's Joe Gordon greeted Pollet with a double to right, but the Cardinals lefty settled down to get the next two batters. Reese threw out Yogi Berra, and Andy Pafko made a sliding catch in center to rob Vic Wertz of a hit. But singles by Dom DiMaggio and Dillinger and a double by Indians outfielder Dale Mitchell netted three more runs and made the score 11–7.

Cincinnati's Ewell Blackwell and Brooklyn's Preacher Roe were the sixth and seventh National League pitchers used and, like the three before them, worked just one inning apiece. Both pitchers were highly effective; Blackwell set the Americans down in order in the eighth, and Roe did the

Musial sliding into second base, 1949
Pitcher Vic Raschi and his Yankee teammate, catcher Yogi Berra, watch the eighth-inning action as Red Sox shortstop Vern Stephens puts the tag on Stan Musial sliding into second base. Associated Press Photo.

same in the ninth. Unfortunately for the NL, those fine performances came too late. For although Raschi, a thirteen-game winner at the break, was far from invincible — the Nationals had runners on in each of the final three innings — he duplicated his three scoreless innings of the previous year. Two men were on via walks in the seventh, but neither Reese nor Robinson could deliver them. Nor could the Nationals take advantage of Musial's lead-off walk in the eighth or Pafko's two-out single in the ninth. Pafko had taken second when Mitchell mishandled the ball, the AL's only error of the day, but Reese, having an awful day, made the final out. In addition to his costly error, the popular Dodger captain's pop-out to second baseman Gordon was his fifth hitless at bat.

The less than crisply played game lasted three hours and four minutes, the first All-Star Game to exceed the three-hour mark. Records were also set for the most pitchers used by one team (7 by the NL) and by both teams (11), and for the most players used by both teams (42).

"DiMaggio's hitting stood out, particularly his double in the sixth," said winning manager Boudreau. "Those were two big runs, but the break of the game came in the fourth on Joost's hit," he added.

Southworth, while agreeing that Joost's hit was a

"break" for the AL, was nevertheless proud of the pitching job turned in by Newcombe and Blackwell. He had been criticized for both selections: Newcombe because of his lack of experience, and Blackwell because his sore arm had limited him to just one victory in the season's first half. Critics had claimed that either Robin Roberts, Ken Heintzleman of the Phillies, or the Reds' Ken Raffensberger would have been better choices.

	AL		NL	
P	Mel Parnell	BOS	Warren Spahn	BSN
C	Birdie Tebbetts	BOS	Andy Seminick	PHI
1B	Eddie Robinson	WAS	Johnny Mize	NY
2B	Cass Michaels	CHA	Jackie Robinson	BRO
3B	George Kell	DET	Eddie Kazak	SLN
SS	Eddie Joost	PHA	Pee Wee Reese	BRO
OF	Dom DiMaggio	BOS	Ralph Kiner	PIT
OF	Joe DiMaggio	NYA	Willard Marshall	NY
OF	Ted Williams	BOS	Stan Musial	SLN
	Yogi Berra	NYA	Vern Bickford	BSN
	Lou Brissie	PHA	Ewell Blackwell	CIN
	Bob Dillinger	SLA	Ralph Branca	BRO
	Larry Doby	CLE	Roy Campanella	BRO
	Billy Goodman	BOS	Walker Cooper	CIN
	Joe Gordon	CLE	Sid Gordon	NY
	Jim Hegan	CLE	Gil Hodges	BRO
	Tommy Henrich	NYA	Marty Marion	SLN
	Alex Kellner	PHA	Red Munger	SLN
	Bob Lemon	CLE	Don Newcombe	BRO
	Dale Mitchell	CLE	Andy Pafko	CHN
	Vic Raschi	NYA	Howie Pollet	SLN
	Allie Reynolds	NYA	Preacher Roe	BRO
	Vern Stephens	BOS	Red Schoendienst	SLN
	Virgil Trucks	DET	Enos Slaughter	SLN
	Vic Wertz	DET	Bobby Thomson	NY

American League	400 202 300- 11							
National League	212 002 000- 7							

AMERICAN LEAGUE

	ab	r	h	bi	bb	so	po	a
D.DiMaggio, rf-cf	5	2	2	1	0	1	2	0
V.Raschi, p	1	0	0	0	0	0	0	1
G.Kell, 3b	3	2	2	0	1	0	0	1
B.Dillinger, pr-3b	1	2	1	1	0	0	0	2
T.Williams, lf	2	1	0	0	2	1	1	0
D.Mitchell, lf	1	0	1	1	0	0	1	0
J.DiMaggio, cf	4	1	2	3	0	0	0	0
L.Doby, pr-rf-cf	1	0	0	0	0	0	2	0
E.Joost, ss	2	1	1	2	1	0	2	2
V.Stephens, ss	2	0	0	0	0	1	3	0
E.Robinson, 1b	5	1	1	1	0	0	8	0
B.Goodman, 1b	0	0	0	0	0	0	1	1
C.Michaels, 2b	2	0	0	0	1	0	1	3
J.Gordon, 2b	2	1	1	0	0	1	2	3
B.Tebbetts, c	2	0	2	1	0	0	2	0
Y.Berra, c	3	0	0	0	0	0	2	1
M.Parnell, p	1	0	0	0	0	1	0	1
V.Trucks, p	1	0	0	0	0	0	0	0
L.Brissie, p	1	0	0	0	0	0	0	0
V.Wertz, ph-rf	2	0	0	0	0	0	0	0
Totals	41	11	13	10	5	5	27	15

BATTING
2B: B.Tebbetts (off D.Newcombe); D.DiMaggio (off V.Bickford); J.DiMaggio (off V.Bickford); J.Gordon (off H.Pollet); D.Mitchell (off H.Pollet).
2-out RBI: D.DiMaggio; B.Dillinger; D.Mitchell; J.DiMaggio; E.Joost 2; E.Robinson; B.Tebbetts.
RBI, scoring position, less than 2 outs: T.Williams 0–1; J.DiMaggio 2–3; V.Stephens 0–1; Y.Berra 0–1; V.Wertz 0–1.
GDP: L.Brissie.

BASERUNNING
SB: G.Kell (2nd base off W.Spahn / A.Seminick).
Team LOB: 8

FIELDING
E: D.Mitchell.
DP: (2). C.Michaels-E.Joost-E.Robinson; E.Joost-C.Michaels-E.Robinson.

NATIONAL LEAGUE

	ab	r	h	bi	bb	so	po	a
P.Reese, ss	5	0	0	0	1	0	3	3
J.Robinson, 2b	4	3	1	0	1	0	1	1
S.Musial, cf-rf	4	1	3	2	1	0	2	0
R.Kiner, lf	5	1	1	2	0	0	3	0
J.Mize, 1b	2	0	1	0	0	1	1	0
G.Hodges, pr-1b	3	1	1	0	0	0	8	2
W.Marshall, rf	1	1	0	0	2	0	1	0
V.Bickford, p	0	0	0	0	0	0	0	0
B.Thomson, ph	1	0	0	0	0	0	0	0
H.Pollet, p	0	0	0	0	0	0	1	0
E.Blackwell, p	0	0	0	0	0	0	0	0
E.Slaughter, ph	1	0	0	0	0	0	0	0
P.Roe, p	0	0	0	0	0	0	0	0
E.Kazak, 3b	2	0	2	1	0	0	0	1
S.Gordon, 3b	2	0	1	0	1	0	0	4
A.Seminick, c	1	0	0	0	0	0	3	0
R.Campanella, c	2	0	0	0	1	1	2	0
W.Spahn, p	0	0	0	0	0	0	0	0
D.Newcombe, p	1	0	0	1	0	0	0	0
R.Schoendienst, ph	1	0	1	0	0	0	0	0
R.Munger, p	0	0	0	0	0	0	0	0
A.Pafko, ph-cf	2	0	1	0	1	1	2	0
Totals	37	7	12	6	8	3	27	11

BATTING
2B: J.Robinson (off M.Parnell); S.Gordon (off L.Brissie).
HR: S.Musial (1st inning off M.Parnell, 1 on, 1 out); R.Kiner (6th inning off L.Brissie, 1 on, 2 out).
2-out RBI: R.Kiner 2; E.Kazak.
RBI, scoring position, less than 2 outs: P.Reese 0–2; S.Musial 1–1; D.Newcombe 1–2.
GDP: P.Reese; R.Kiner.

BASERUNNING
Team LOB: 12

FIELDING
E: J.Mize (dropped throw); P.Reese (fumble); A.Seminick (dropped foul ball); W.Marshall; R.Campanella.
DP: (1). J.Robinson-P.Reese-G.Hodges.

PITCHING	ip	h	r	er	bb	so
American League						
M.Parnell (L)	* 1.0	3	3	3	1	1
V.Trucks (w)	2.0	3	2	2	2	0
L.Brissie	3.0	5	2	2	2	1
V.Raschi (s)	3.0	1	0	0	3	1

Inherited Runners—Scored:
V.Trucks 3–1; L.Brissie 0–0; V.Raschi 0–0; D.Newcombe 2–0; R.Munger 0–0; V.Bickford 0–0; H.Pollet 0–0; E.Blackwell 0–0; P.Roe 0–0.
IBB: R.Campanella by L.Brissie.
HBP: A.Seminick by M.Parnell.

PITCHING	ip	h	r	er	bb	so
National League						
W.Spahn	1.1	4	4	0	2	3
D.Newcombe (L)	2.2	3	2	2	1	0
R.Munger	1.0	0	0	0	1	0
V.Bickford	1.0	2	2	2	1	0
H.Pollet	1.0	4	3	3	0	0
E.Blackwell	1.0	0	0	0	0	2
P.Roe	1.0	0	0	0	0	0

* Pitched to 3 batters in 2nd

GAME DATA—T: 3:04; A: 32577; Temp: Unknown; Wind: Unknown direction, Speed: Unknown

UMPIRES—HP: Al Barlick (NL), 1B: Cal Hubbard (AL), 2B: Artie Gore (NL), 3B: Bill Summers (AL), LF: Bill Grieve (AL), RF: Lee Ballanfant (NL)

STARTING LINEUPS

	American League	*National League*
1.	D.DiMaggio rf	P.Reese ss
2.	G.Kell 3b	J.Robinson 2b
3.	T.Williams lf	S.Musial cf
4.	J.DiMaggio cf	R.Kiner lf
5.	E.Joost ss	J.Mize 1b
6.	E.Robinson 1b	W.Marshall rf
7.	C.Michaels 2b	E.Kazak 3b
8.	B.Tebbetts c	A.Seminick c
9.	M.Parnell p	W.Spahn p

AL 1ST: D.DiMaggio struck out; G.Kell reached on an error [G.Kell to first (error by J.Mize-1b; assist by E.Kazak-3b)]; error first charged to Mize, then to Kazak, then (several days later) changed back to Mize; T.Williams struck out while G.Kell stole second; J.DiMaggio singled to left field [G.Kell scored (unearned)]; E.Joost walked [J.DiMaggio to second]; E.Robinson singled to right field [J.DiMaggio scored (unearned), E.Joost to third]; C.Michaels reached on an error by P.Reese-ss [E.Joost scored (unearned) (no RBI), E.Robinson to second, C.Michaels to first]; B.Tebbetts singled to left field [E.Robinson scored (unearned), C.Michaels to third]; Michaels got to 3b when bag was left unprotected; M.Parnell struck out; 4 R (0 ER), 3 H, 2 E, 2 LOB. AL 4, NL 0.

NL 1ST: P.Reese grounded out (M.Parnell-p to E.Robinson-1b); First at-bat by a black player in all-star history; J.Robinson doubled to left field; S.Musial homered to deep rightfield [J.Robinson scored]; R.Kiner popped to B.Tebbetts-c in foul territory; J.Mize struck out; 2 R, 2 H, 0 E, 0 LOB. AL 4, NL 2.

AL 2ND: D.DiMaggio popped to J.Mize-1b in foul territory; G.Kell singled to center field; T.Williams walked [G.Kell to second]; **D.Newcombe replaced W.Spahn (pitching);** First black pitcher in all-star history; J.DiMaggio flied to R.Kiner-lf; E.Joost popped to J.Robinson-2b; 0 R, 1 H, 0 E, 2 LOB. AL 4, NL 2.

NL 2ND: W.Marshall walked; E.Kazak singled to left field [W.Marshall to second]; A.Seminick was hit by a pitch [W.Marshall to third, E.Kazak to second]; **V.Trucks replaced M.Parnell (pitching);** D.Newcombe lined to T.Williams-lf [W.Marshall scored]; P.Reese grounded into a double play (C.Michaels-2b to E.Joost-ss to E.Robinson-1b) [A.Seminick out at second]; 1 R, 1 H, 0 E, 1 LOB. AL 4, NL 3.

AL 3RD: E.Robinson flied to W.Marshall-rf; C.Michaels flied to R.Kiner-lf; A.Seminick-c dropped a foul fly hit by B.Tebbetts; B.Tebbetts doubled to right-center [B.Tebbetts to third (error by W.Marshall-rf)]; V.Trucks flied to R.Kiner-lf; 0 R, 1 H, 2 E, 1 LOB. AL 4, NL 3.

NL 3RD: J.Robinson walked; S.Musial singled to left field [J.Robinson to third]; R.Kiner grounded into a double play (E.Joost-ss to C.Michaels-2b to E.Robinson-1b) [J.Robinson scored (no RBI), S.Musial out at second]; J.Mize singled to right field; W.Marshall walked [J.Mize to second]; **G.Hodges ran for J.Mize;** E.Kazak singled to left field [G.Hodges scored, W.Marshall to second]; A.Seminick grounded out (G.Kell-3b to E.Robinson-1b); 2 R, 3 H, 0 E, 2 LOB. AL 4, NL 5.

AL 4TH: **G.Hodges stayed in game (playing 1b); S.Gordon replaced E.Kazak (playing 3b); R.Campanella replaced A.Seminick (playing c);** D.DiMaggio grounded out (S.Gordon-3b to G.Hodges-1b); G.Kell singled to left field; T.Williams walked [G.Kell to second]; J.DiMaggio grounded out (S.Gordon-3b to G.Hodges-1b) [G.Kell to third, T.Williams to second]; E.Joost singled to first base [G.Kell scored, T.Williams scored]; E.Robinson flied to S.Musial-cf; 2 R, 2 H, 0 E, 1 LOB. AL 6, NL 5.

NL 4TH: **L.Brissie replaced V.Trucks (pitching); Y.Berra replaced B.Tebbetts (playing c); R.Schoendienst batted for D.Newcombe;** R.Schoendienst singled to center field; P.Reese forced R.Schoendienst (C.Michaels-2b to E.Joost-ss) [P.Reese to first]; J.Robinson flied to D.DiMaggio-rf; S.Musial singled to first base [P.Reese to second]; R.Kiner flied to D.DiMaggio-rf; 0 R, 2 H, 0 E, 2 LOB. AL 6, NL 5.

AL 5TH: **R.Munger replaced R.Schoendienst (pitching);** C.Michaels walked; Y.Berra forced C.Michaels (G.Hodges-1b to P.Reese-ss) [Y.Berra to first]; L.Brissie grounded into a double play (J.Robinson-2b to P.Reese-ss to G.Hodges-1b) [Y.Berra out at second]; 0 R, 0 H, 0 E, 0 LOB. AL 6, NL 5.

NL 5TH: Umpires moved: Summers (hp), Gore (1b), Hubbard (2B), Ballanfant (3b), Grieve (lf), Barlick (rf); **J.Gordon replaced C.Michaels (playing 2b); V.Stephens replaced E.Joost (playing ss);** G.Hodges grounded out (J.Gordon-2b to E.Robinson-1b); W.Marshall grounded out (J.Gordon-2b to E.Robinson-1b); S.Gordon doubled to deep left-center; R.Campanella was walked intentionally; **A.Pafko batted for R.Munger;** A.Pafko struck out; 0 R, 1 H, 0 E, 2 LOB. AL 6, NL 5.

AL 6TH: **A.Pafko stayed in game (playing cf); S.Musial changed positions (playing rf); V.Bickford replaced W.Marshall (pitching);** D.DiMaggio doubled to left field; G.Kell walked; T.Williams flied to A.Pafko-cf [D.DiMaggio to third]; **B.Dil-linger ran for G.Kell;** J.DiMaggio doubled to left field [D.DiMaggio scored (RBI), B.Dillinger scored (error by R.Campanella-c), J.DiMaggio to third (error by R.Campanella-c)]; **L.Doby ran for J.DiMaggio;** V.Stephens grounded out (S.Gordon-3b to G.Hodges-1b); E.Robinson grounded out (G.Hodges-1b unassisted); 2 R, 2 H, 1 E, 1 LOB. AL 8, NL 5.

NL 6TH: **B.Dillinger stayed in game (playing 3b); L.Doby stayed in game (playing rf); D.DiMaggio changed positions (playing cf); D.Mitchell replaced T.Williams (playing lf);** P.Reese walked; J.Robinson forced P.Reese (B.Dillinger-3b to J.Gordon-2b) [J.Robinson to first]; 11 minute rain delay; S.Musial grounded out (Y.Berra-c to E.Robinson-1b) [J.Robinson to second]; R.Kiner homered to deep leftfield [J.Robinson scored]; G.Hodges singled to third base; **B.Thomson batted for V.Bickford;** B.Thomson flied to D.Mitchell-lf; 2 R, 2 H, 0 E, 1 LOB. AL 8, NL 7.

AL 7TH: **H.Pollet replaced B.Thomson (pitching);** J.Gordon doubled to right field; Y.Berra grounded out (P.Reese-ss to G.Hodges-1b); **V.Wertz batted for L.Brissie;** V.Wertz flied to A.Pafko-cf; D.DiMaggio singled to left field [J.Gordon scored, D.DiMaggio to second (on throw home)]; B.Dillinger singled to left field [D.DiMaggio scored]; D.Mitchell doubled to left field [B.Dillinger scored]; L.Doby grounded out (G.Hodges-1b to H.Pollet-p); 3 R, 4 H, 0 E, 1 LOB. AL 11, NL 7.

NL 7TH: **V.Wertz stayed in game (playing rf); L.Doby changed positions (playing cf); V.Raschi replaced**

D.DiMaggio (pitching); S.Gordon walked; R.Campanella popped to V.Stephens-ss; A.Pafko walked [S.Gordon to second]; P.Reese popped to V.Stephens-ss; J.Robinson grounded out (V.Raschi-p to E.Robinson-1b); 0 R, 0 H, 0 E, 2 LOB. AL 11, NL 7.

AL 8TH: **E.Blackwell replaced H.Pollet (pitching);** V.Stephens struck out; E.Robinson popped to P.Reese-ss; J.Gordon struck out; 0 R, 0 H, 0 E, 0 LOB. AL 11, NL 7.

NL 8TH: **B.Goodman replaced E.Robinson (playing 1b);** S.Musial walked; R.Kiner lined to L.Doby-cf; G.Hodges popped to J.Gordon-2b (J.Gordon-2b to B.Goodman-1b to V.Stephens-ss) [G.Hodges to first]; Gordon trapped the popup, then forced Musial; **E.Slaughter batted for E.Blackwell;** E.Slaughter flied to L.Doby-cf; 0 R, 0 H, 0 E, 1 LOB. AL 11, NL 7.

AL 9TH: **P.Roe replaced E.Slaughter (pitching);** Y.Berra flied to S.Musial-rf; V.Wertz grounded out (P.Reese-ss to G.Hodges-1b); V.Raschi grounded out (S.Gordon-3b to G.Hodges-1b); 0 R, 0 H, 0 E, 0 LOB. AL 11, NL 7.

NL 9TH: S.Gordon grounded out (B.Dillinger-3b to B.Goodman-1b); R.Campanella struck out; A.Pafko singled to left field [A.Pafko to second (error by D.Mitchell-lf)]; P.Reese popped to J.Gordon-2b; 0 R, 1 H, 1 E, 1 LOB. AL 11, NL 7.

Final Totals	R	H	E	LOB
American League	11	13	1	8
National League	7	12	5	12

Tuesday, July 11, 1950

Comiskey Park, Chicago

National League 4, American League 3

(14 innings)

SERIES RESULTS: AL 12, NL 5

The Tide Begins to Turn

Dramatic blasts by Ralph Kiner, whose home run tied the game in the ninth, and Red Schoendienst, whose home run won it in the fourteenth, gave the National Leaguers an exciting 4–3 victory in the first All-Star Game to go into extra innings. The home runs, both off pitchers from the league-leading Detroit Tigers, helped the Nationals to their first win since 1944 and their first ever in American League territory. A crowd of 46,127 at Comiskey Park witnessed the most well-played and suspenseful All-Star Game to date. It was also the most widely seen because it was the first one to be nationally televised.

Six months later, in January 1951, Commissioner Happy Chandler would sign a six-year, $6 million contract granting television rights to both the All-Star Game and the World Series. Many in baseball criticized the deal, arguing, correctly as it turned out, that the growth of television would make the rights to these events worth much more than $1 million per year.

Comiskey Park had been the site of the first All-Star Game back in 1933, a fact celebrated in two pregame ceremonies at this year's game. A's manager Connie Mack, the AL manager for the 1933 game, was the honorary manager for this game and threw out the first ball. Moments earlier, the crowd stood for a minute of silence to honor the late Babe Ruth, whose homer in the 1933 game was the first in All-Star play.

Pitchers Larry Jansen of the Giants, with five scoreless innings in relief, and Ewell Blackwell of the Reds, with three, shared the heroes' laurels with Kiner and Schoendienst. Pitching from the seventh inning to the eleventh, Jansen allowed just one hit, a tenth-inning single by Cleveland's Larry Doby, and struck out six. The six strikeouts tied the All-Star record set by Carl Hubbell of the Giants in 1934 and equaled by Cincinnati's Johnny Vander Meer in 1943. Jansen was allowed to exceed the normal three-inning limit imposed on pitchers because the game had gone past nine innings. Only Lefty Gomez, who pitched six innings in 1935, before the implementation of the three-inning rule, had ever gone longer.

Blackwell, the winning pitcher, also allowed just one hit, while fanning two. The hit was a one-out single in the fourteenth by the Athletics' Ferris Fain, but Blackwell then got Joe DiMaggio, in what would be his final All-Star at bat, to bounce into a game-ending double play. DiMaggio had replaced starter Hoot Evers in right field in the ninth inning, the same position he'd played in his first All-Star Game in 1936.

Managers Casey Stengel of the Yankees and Burt Shotton of the Dodgers chose as their starting pitchers a pair of ten-game winners: Vic Raschi (10-6) of the Yanks and Robin Roberts (10-3) of the Phillies. Raschi's start was the tenth by a Yankee pitcher in the seventeen games, while Roberts was the first Phillies pitcher so honored.

Raschi had been the winning pitcher in 1948 and had helped save the AL's win in 1949. He carried a six-inning All-Star scoreless streak into the contest, which he extended to seven before the Nationals broke the drought with two runs in the second. Jackie Robinson, for the second consecutive year the National League's leading vote getter, led off with a single. Enos Slaughter scored him with a triple to deep left-center and then rode home on Hank Sauer's fly ball to Evers.

Sauer had been at the center of a heated dispute in the days before the game. The fans had voted for a National League outfield consisting of Sauer, Slaughter, and Ralph Kiner, none of whom was a legitimate center fielder. Shotton expressed a desire to replace the Cubs' Sauer with his own Duke Snider, the best center fielder in the league. National League president Ford Frick okayed the plan, but Chandler said no, forcing Shotton to use Slaughter, the most mobile of the three, in center. Upset at Shotton's intention to bypass the local player, the fans in Chicago were unforgiving. The booing he received during the pregame introduc-

105

tions for the managers and starting lineups was probably the fiercest ever given to anyone at an All-Star Game. Conversely, the cheers were especially loud for Sauer, a sound not often heard for a Cubs player on the city's south side. (Only one White Sox player, pitcher Ray Scarborough, was on the AL squad, and Stengel never did use him.)

The cheers were also generous for Cass Michaels, formerly of the White Sox, when he pinch-hit for Raschi leading off the third. Michaels, traded to Washington six weeks earlier as part of the Scarborough deal, hit a long drive to left-center and was awarded a ground-rule double when the ball bounced into the bullpen. Yankees shortstop Phil Rizzuto, playing in his first All-Star Game after a long and distinguished career, then laid down a perfect bunt along the third-base line. Third baseman Willie Jones of the Phillies had no choice but to let it roll, hoping it would go foul; however, it stayed fair and Michaels moved to third. He remained there while Roberts was throwing a wild pitch that advanced Rizzuto to second and while Doby was striking out, but he scored on George Kell's fly to Slaughter.

The AL went ahead, 3–2, in the fifth, scoring two runs against Brooklyn's Don Newcombe. An inning earlier, Red Sox rookie first baseman Walt Dropo had greeted Newcombe's entrance into the game with a long triple to center field. But after holding while Evers grounded out to shortstop Marty Marion, Dropo got caught on Yogi Berra's come-backer to the mound and was tagged out by Jones.

Then in the fifth, Cleveland pitcher Bob Lemon, who had replaced Raschi in the fourth, drew a lead-off walk. After Rizzuto struck out, Doby hit a ball up the middle that Robinson got a glove on but couldn't hold. As the ball trickled into short center field, Lemon went to third and the speedy Doby reached second with a most unusual double. After Kell's second scoring fly ball to center, this one to Andy Pafko, brought Lemon home, Ted Williams singled to right to score Doby. (Shotton had replaced Sauer with Pafko, another Cub, instead of Snider and had moved Slaughter to right.)

Earlier, Williams had made the fielding play of the game when he crashed into the scoreboard in the first inning to take away an extra-base hit from Kiner. The Boston slugger took some time rubbing his left elbow but eventually signaled that he was okay. He played through the eighth inning, but x-rays taken later revealed a bone fracture in the left elbow, and Williams would miss Boston's next sixty-six games.

Lemon protected the 3–2 lead through the sixth, allowing just one hit, a pinch single by Phila-delphia's Dick Sisler. Detroit's Art Houtteman, who like Lemon had pitched Sunday, much to Stengel's dismay, was next. Houtteman added two more shutout innings, but just when it appeared that the Nationals had lost another one, Kiner led off the ninth by blasting his second pitch into the left-field seats. The crowd, which seemed stunned by Kiner's blow, was about to be treated to a continuation of the best sustained All-Star pitching effort to date.

Phillies relief ace Jim Konstanty had relieved Newcombe in the sixth and retired the AL in order, including strikeouts of Evers and Jim Hegan. Then came the heroic efforts from Jansen and Blackwell. The three right-handers limited the powerful American League hitters to just two singles over the final nine innings. On the American League side, Allie Reynolds of New York allowed the Nationals just one hit between the tenth and the twelfth, and Detroit's Ted Gray, the only left-hander among the eleven pitchers who appeared, blanked them in the thirteenth.

The only serious scoring threat by either team came against Reynolds in the eleventh. A double by Kiner and an intentional walk to Stan Musial (playing first base today after five starts and six appearances as an outfielder) gave the NL runners at first and second with only one out. Reynolds retired Cincinnati's Johnny Wyrostek, batting for Robinson, and then got Slaughter to hit a routine ground ball to Jerry Coleman. But the Yankees second baseman booted the ball, and the bases were loaded. Reynolds got his teammate off the hook by getting Pafko on a long fly ball that left fielder Dom DiMaggio caught with his back against the wall.

Red Schoendienst of the Cardinals, who had replaced Robinson at second base after Wyrostek hit for him, had his first at bat as the lead-off man in the fourteenth inning. On leaving the dugout, Schoendienst, not normally a home run hitter (he had only three this season), predicted to his teammates that he would hit one in this at bat. "I'm going up there and park one in the left-field stands," he said. And he did. Batting right-handed against left-hander Gray, Schoendienst smacked a 2-2 pitch into the upper deck in left to put the Nationals ahead 4–3.

Pafko followed the home run with a single to left and moved to second when the pitch that struck out Roy Campanella got away from catcher Hegan for a passed ball. Anxious to keep it a one-run game, Stengel replaced Gray with Bob Feller. Shotton had three pitchers left: Warren Spahn of Boston, Bob Rush of Chicago, and his own Preacher Roe. Nevertheless, he allowed Blackwell to hit for himself. Not surprisingly, Feller struck him out and then, after walking Pee Wee Reese, got Jones on a fly to Doby.

In the home fourteenth, Dom DiMaggio opened by attempting to bunt his way on, but Blackwell pounced on the ball and threw him out. Fain followed with a single to left, putting the tying run aboard and bringing the potential winning run, in the person of Joe DiMaggio, to the plate. DiMaggio hit the ball sharply, but it was right at third baseman Jones, who converted it into the game-ending double play.

Jones had set a record for most at bats in a game (seven), an extra-inning record that still stands. Despite the length of the game in innings and time (three hours and nineteen minutes), Jones was one of seven players who played all fourteen innings. Oddly, the seven players included the one-two-three batters for each side: Rizzuto, Doby, and Kell (the overall high vote getter) for the American League, and Jones, Kiner, and Musial, plus Campanella, for the National League.

Blackwell was the winning pitcher, giving Cincinnati hurlers three of the NL's five wins; oddly, despite the Nationals' many subsequent successes, no Reds pitcher has won since 1950. Gray was the loser, becoming the first Tiger pitcher charged with an All-Star loss. Shotton, who had stood stoically in front of the NL dugout throughout the pregame booing, felt vindicated.

"I wonder if those forty-six thousand people who booed me aren't ashamed of themselves for the way they acted," he said in the jubilant National League dressing room.

Everyone agreed that it had been a splendid game and that there was no disgrace in losing. "They have to win one once in a while and this is it," said one American Leaguer, who obviously had no way of knowing that the Nationals would also win the next three and five of the next six.

	AL		NL	
P	Vic Raschi	NYA	Robin Roberts	PHI
C	Yogi Berra	NYA	Roy Campanella	BRO
1B	Walt Dropo	BOS	Stan Musial	SLN
2B	Bobby Doerr	BOS	Jackie Robinson	BRO
3B	George Kell	DET	Willie Jones	PHI
SS	Phil Rizzuto	NYA	Marty Marion	SLN
OF	Larry Doby	CLE	Ralph Kiner	PIT
OF	Hoot Evers	DET	Hank Sauer	CHN
OF	Ted Williams	BOS	Enos Slaughter	SLN
	Tommy Byrne	NYA	Ewell Blackwell	CIN
	Jerry Coleman	NYA	Walker Cooper	BSN
	Dom DiMaggio	BOS	Gil Hodges	BRO
	Joe DiMaggio	NYA	Larry Jansen	NY
	Ferris Fain	PHA	Jim Konstanty	PHI
	Bob Feller	CLE	Don Newcombe	BRO
	Ted Gray	DET	Andy Pafko	CHN
	Jim Hegan	CLE	Pee Wee Reese	BRO
	Tommy Henrich	NYA	Preacher Roe	BRO
	Art Houtteman	DET	Bob Rush	CHN
	Bob Lemon	CLE	Red Schoendienst	SLN
	Sherm Lollar	SLA	Dick Sisler	PHI
	Cass Michaels	WAS	Duke Snider	BRO
	Allie Reynolds	NYA	Warren Spahn	BSN
	Rae Scarborough	CHA	Eddie Stanky	NY
	Vern Stephens	BOS	Johnny Wyrostek	CIN

National League	020	000	001	000	01-	4
American League	001	020	000	000	00-	3 (14)

NATIONAL LEAGUE

	ab	r	h	bi	bb	so	po	a
W.Jones, 3b	7	0	1	0	0	0	2	3
R.Kiner, lf	6	1	2	1	0	1	1	0
S.Musial, 1b	5	0	0	0	1	0	11	0
J.Robinson, 2b	4	1	1	0	0	0	3	2
J.Wyrostek, ph-rf	2	0	0	0	0	0	0	0
E.Slaughter, cf-rf	4	1	2	1	1	0	3	0
R.Schoendienst, 2b	1	1	1	1	0	0	1	1
H.Sauer, rf	2	0	0	1	0	0	1	0
A.Pafko, cf	4	0	2	0	0	0	4	0
R.Campanella, c	6	0	0	0	0	2	13	2
M.Marion, ss	2	0	0	0	0	0	0	2
J.Konstanty, p	0	0	0	0	0	0	0	0
L.Jansen, p	2	0	0	0	0	1	1	0
D.Snider, ph	1	0	0	0	0	0	0	0
E.Blackwell, p	1	0	0	0	0	1	0	1
R.Roberts, p	1	0	0	0	0	1	0	0
D.Newcombe, p	0	0	0	0	0	0	0	1
D.Sisler, ph	1	0	1	0	0	0	0	0
P.Reese, pr-ss	3	0	0	0	1	1	2	4
Totals	52	4	10	4	3	7	42	17

BATTING
2B: R.Kiner (off A.Reynolds).
3B: E.Slaughter (off V.Raschi).
HR: R.Kiner (9th inning off A.Houtteman, 0 on, 0 out); R.Schoendienst (14th inning off T.Gray, 0 on, 0 out).
RBI, scoring position, less than 2 outs: J.Wyrostek 0–1; H.Sauer 1–1; E.Blackwell 0–1.
GDP: W.Jones.

BASERUNNING
Team LOB: 9

FIELDING
DP: (1). W.Jones-R.Schoendienst-S.Musial.

AMERICAN LEAGUE

	ab	r	h	bi	bb	so	po	a
P.Rizzuto, ss	6	0	2	0	0	1	2	2
L.Doby, cf	6	1	2	0	0	2	9	0
G.Kell, 3b	6	0	0	2	0	1	2	4
T.Williams, lf	4	0	1	1	0	1	2	0
D.DiMaggio, lf	2	0	0	0	0	0	1	0
W.Dropo, 1b	3	0	1	0	0	0	8	1
F.Fain, ph-1b	3	0	1	0	0	0	2	1
H.Evers, rf	2	0	0	0	1	1	1	0
J.DiMaggio, rf	3	0	0	0	0	0	3	0
Y.Berra, c	2	0	0	0	0	0	2	0
J.Hegan, pr-c	3	0	0	0	0	3	7	1
B.Doerr, 2b	3	0	0	0	0	0	1	4
J.Coleman, 2b	2	0	0	0	0	2	0	0
V.Raschi, p	0	0	0	0	0	0	0	0
C.Michaels, ph	1	1	1	0	0	0	0	0
B.Lemon, p	0	1	0	0	1	0	1	0
A.Houtteman, p	1	0	0	0	0	1	1	0
A.Reynolds, p	1	0	0	0	0	0	0	0
T.Henrich, ph	1	0	0	0	0	0	0	0
T.Gray, p	0	0	0	0	0	0	0	0
B.Feller, p	0	0	0	0	0	0	0	0
Totals	49	3	8	3	2	12	42	13

BATTING
2B: C.Michaels (off R.Roberts); L.Doby (off D.Newcombe).
3B: W.Dropo (off D.Newcombe).
2-out RBI: T.Williams.
RBI, scoring position, less than 2 outs: L.Doby 0–2; G.Kell 2–5; H.Evers 0–1; Y.Berra 0–1.
GDP: J.DiMaggio.

BASERUNNING
Team LOB: 6

FIELDING
E: J.Coleman (fumble).
PB: J.Hegan.
DP: (1). P.Rizzuto-B.Doerr-W.Dropo.

PITCHING	ip	h	r	er	bb	so
National League						
R.Roberts	3.0	3	1	1	1	1
D.Newcombe	2.0	3	2	2	1	1
J.Konstanty	1.0	0	0	0	0	2
L.Jansen	5.0	1	0	0	0	6
E.Blackwell (w)	3.0	1	0	0	0	2
American League						
V.Raschi	3.0	2	2	2	0	1
B.Lemon	3.0	1	0	0	0	2
A.Houtteman (BS)	3.0	3	1	1	1	0
A.Reynolds	3.0	1	0	0	1	2
T.Gray (L)	1.1	3	1	1	0	1
B.Feller	0.2	0	0	0	1	1

Inherited Runners—Scored:
D.Newcombe 0–0; J.Konstanty 0–0; L.Jansen 0–0; E.Blackwell 0–0; B.Lemon 0–0; A.Houtteman 0–0; A.Reynolds 0–0; T.Gray 0–0; B.Feller 1–0.
IBB: S.Musial by A.Reynolds.
WP: R.Roberts

GAME DATA—T: 3:19; A: 46127; Temp: Unknown;
Wind: Unknown direction, Speed: Unknown

UMPIRES—HP: Bill McGowan (AL), 1B: Babe Pinelli (NL),
2B: Eddie Rommel (AL), 3B: Jocko Conlan (NL),
LF: Scotty Robb (NL), RF: Johnny Stevens (AL)

STARTING LINEUPS

	National League	*American League*
1.	W.Jones 3b	P.Rizzuto ss
2.	R.Kiner lf	L.Doby cf
3.	S.Musial 1b	G.Kell 3b
4.	J.Robinson 2b	T.Williams lf
5.	E.Slaughter cf	W.Dropo 1b
6.	H.Sauer rf	H.Evers rf
7.	R.Campanella c	Y.Berra c
8.	M.Marion ss	B.Doerr 2b
9.	R.Roberts p	V.Raschi p

NL 1ST: W.Jones lined to L.Doby-cf; R.Kiner flied to T.Williams-lf; Williams bumped into wall as he made the catch; x-rays the next day revealed a fracture of the left elbow; surgery removed 7 bone fragments on 7–13; S.Musial flied to L.Doby-cf; 0 R, 0 H, 0 E, 0 LOB. NL 0, AL 0.

AL 1ST: P.Rizzuto singled to left field; L.Doby grounded out (J.Robinson-2b to S.Musial-1b) [P.Rizzuto to second]; G.Kell flied to E.Slaughter-cf; T.Williams grounded out (J.Robinson-2b to S.Musial-1b); 0 R, 1 H, 0 E, 1 LOB. NL 0, AL 0.

NL 2ND: J.Robinson singled to right field; E.Slaughter tripled to very deep left-center [J.Robinson scored]; H.Sauer flied to H.Evers-rf [E.Slaughter scored]; R.Campanella grounded out (B.Doerr-2b to W.Dropo-1b); M.Marion popped to Y.Berra-c in foul territory; 2 R, 2 H, 0 E, 0 LOB. NL 2, AL 0.

AL 2ND: W.Dropo flied to E.Slaughter-cf; H.Evers walked; Y.Berra forced H.Evers (W.Jones-3b to J.Robinson-2b) [Y.Berra to first]; B.Doerr lined to H.Sauer-rf; 0 R, 0 H, 0 E, 1 LOB. NL 2, AL 0.

NL 3RD: R.Roberts was called out on strikes; W.Jones popped to G.Kell-3b in foul territory; R.Kiner lined to T.Williams-lf; 0 R, 0 H, 0 E, 0 LOB. NL 2, AL 0.

AL 3RD: **C.Michaels batted for V.Raschi;** C.Michaels hit a ground rule double to centerfield; On a bunt P.Rizzuto singled to third base [C.Michaels to third]; R.Roberts threw a wild pitch [P.Rizzuto to second]; L.Doby struck out (R.Campanella-c to S.Musial-1b); G.Kell flied to E.Slaughter-cf [C.Michaels scored, P.Rizzuto to third]; T.Williams flied to R.Kiner-lf; 1 R, 2 H, 0 E, 1 LOB. NL 2, AL 1.

NL 4TH: **B.Lemon replaced C.Michaels (pitching);** S.Musial flied to L.Doby-cf; J.Robinson flied to L.Doby-cf; E.Slaughter grounded out (W.Dropo-1b to B.Lemon-p); 0 R, 0 H, 0 E, 0 LOB. NL 2, AL 1.

AL 4TH: **D.Newcombe replaced R.Roberts (pitching);** W.Dropo tripled to center field; H.Evers grounded out (M.Marion-ss to S.Musial-1b);

Y.Berra reached on a fielder's choice (D.Newcombe-p to R.Campanella-c to W.Jones-3b) [W.Dropo out at home]; **J.Hegan ran for Y.Berra;** B.Doerr forced J.Hegan (M.Marion-ss to J.Robinson-2b) [B.Doerr to first]; 0 R, 1 H, 0 E, 1 LOB. NL 2, AL 1.

NL 5TH: **J.Hegan stayed in game (playing c);** H.Sauer grounded out (G.Kell-3b to W.Dropo-1b); R.Campanella struck out (J.Hegan-c to W.Dropo-1b); M.Marion grounded out (G.Kell-3b to W.Dropo-1b); 0 R, 0 H, 0 E, 0 LOB. NL 2, AL 1.

AL 5TH: **E.Slaughter changed positions (playing rf); A.Pafko replaced H.Sauer (playing cf);** Umpires moved: Pinelli (hp), Rommel (1b), Conlan (2b) McGowan (3b), Robb (lf), Stevens (rf); B.Lemon walked; P.Rizzuto struck out; L.Doby doubled to the second base side of the bag [B.Lemon to third]; G.Kell flied to A.Pafko-cf [B.Lemon scored, L.Doby to third]; T.Williams singled to right field [L.Doby scored]; W.Dropo popped to W.Jones-3b in foul territory; 2 R, 2 H, 0 E, 1 LOB. NL 2, AL 3.

NL 6TH: **D.Sisler batted for D.Newcombe;** D.Sisler singled to right field; **P.Reese ran for D.Sisler;** W.Jones grounded into a double play (P.Rizzuto-ss to B.Doerr-2b to W.Dropo-1b) [P.Reese out at second]; R.Kiner struck out; 0 R, 1 H, 0 E, 0 LOB. NL 2, AL 3.

AL 6TH: **P.Reese stayed in game (playing ss); J.Konstanty replaced M.Marion (pitching);** H.Evers struck out; J.Hegan struck out; B.Doerr grounded out (P.Reese-ss to S.Musial-1b); 0 R, 0 H, 0 E, 0 LOB. NL 2, AL 3.

NL 7TH: **A.Houtteman replaced B.Lemon (pitching);** S.Musial grounded out (B.Doerr-2b to W.Dropo-1b); J.Robinson flied to L.Doby-cf; E.Slaughter walked; A.Pafko singled to shortstop [E.Slaughter to second]; R.Campanella flied to L.Doby-cf; 0 R, 1 H, 0 E, 2 LOB. NL 2, AL 3.

AL 7TH: **L.Jansen replaced J.Konstanty (pitching);** A.Houtteman was called out on strikes; P.Rizzuto popped to R.Campanella-c in foul territory; L.Doby struck out; 0 R, 0 H, 0 E, 0 LOB. NL 2, AL 3.

NL 8TH: L.Jansen grounded out (B.Doerr-2b to W.Dropo-1b); P.Reese popped to J.Hegan-c in foul territory; W.Jones grounded out (P.Rizzuto-ss to W.Dropo-1b); 0 R, 0 H, 0 E, 0 LOB. NL 2, AL 3.

AL 8TH: G.Kell struck out; T.Williams was called out on strikes; **F.Fain batted for W.Dropo;** F.Fain popped to P.Reese-ss; 0 R, 0 H, 0 E, 0 LOB. NL 2, AL 3.

NL 9TH: **F.Fain stayed in game (playing 1b); D.DiMaggio replaced T.Williams (playing lf); J.DiMaggio replaced H.Evers (playing rf); J.Coleman** replaced **B.Doerr (playing 2b)**; R.Kiner homered to leftfield; S.Musial grounded out (F.Fain-1b to A.Houtteman-p); J.Robinson popped to P.Rizzuto-ss; E.Slaughter singled to center field; A.Pafko grounded out (G.Kell-3b to F.Fain-1b); 1 R, 2 H, 0 E, 1 LOB. NL 3, AL 3.

AL 9TH: J.DiMaggio flied to A.Pafko-cf; J.Hegan struck out; J.Coleman struck out; 0 R, 0 H, 0 E, 0 LOB. NL 3, AL 3.

NL 10TH: first extra-innings all-star game; **A.Reynolds replaced A.Houtteman (pitching)**; R.Campanella popped to P.Rizzuto-ss; L.Jansen struck out; P.Reese popped to G.Kell-3b in foul territory; 0 R, 0 H, 0 E, 0 LOB. NL 3, AL 3.

AL 10TH: A.Reynolds grounded out (W.Jones-3b to S.Musial-1b); P.Rizzuto popped to P.Reese-ss; L.Doby singled to center field; G.Kell forced L.Doby (P.Reese-ss to J.Robinson-2b) [G.Kell to first]; 0 R, 1 H, 0 E, 1 LOB. NL 3, AL 3.

NL 11TH: W.Jones grounded out (G.Kell-3b to F.Fain-1b); R.Kiner doubled to right-center; S.Musial was walked intentionally; **J.Wyrostek batted for J.Robinson;** J.Wyrostek flied to L.Doby-cf; E.Slaughter reached on an error by J.Coleman-2b [R.Kiner to third, S.Musial to second, E.Slaughter to first]; A.Pafko flied to D.DiMaggio-lf; 0 R, 1 H, 1 E, 3 LOB. NL 3, AL 3.

AL 11TH: **J.Wyrostek stayed in game (playing rf); R.Schoendienst replaced E.Slaughter (playing 2b);** D.DiMaggio grounded out (P.Reese-ss to S.Musial-1b); F.Fain grounded out (S.Musial-1b to L.Jansen-p); J.DiMaggio popped to R.Campanella-c in foul territory; 0 R, 0 H, 0 E, 0 LOB. NL 3, AL 3.

NL 12TH: R.Campanella popped to J.Hegan-c in foul territory; **D.Snider batted for L.Jansen;** D.Snider flied to J.DiMaggio-rf; P.Reese was called out on strikes; 0 R, 0 H, 0 E, 0 LOB. NL 3, AL 3.

AL 12TH: **E.Blackwell replaced D.Snider (pitching);** J.Hegan struck out; J.Coleman struck out; **T.Henrich batted for A.Reynolds;** T.Henrich lined to A.Pafko-cf; 0 R, 0 H, 0 E, 0 LOB. NL 3, AL 3.

NL 13TH: **T.Gray replaced T.Henrich (pitching);** W.Jones singled to left field; R.Kiner flied to J.DiMaggio-rf; S.Musial flied to L.Doby-cf; J.Wyrostek flied to J.DiMaggio-rf; 0 R, 1 H, 0 E, 1 LOB. NL 3, AL 3.

AL 13TH: P.Rizzuto flied to A.Pafko-cf; L.Doby grounded out (S.Musial-1b unassisted); G.Kell grounded out (P.Reese-ss to S.Musial-1b); 0 R, 0 H, 0 E, 0 LOB. NL 3, AL 3.

NL 14TH: R.Schoendienst homered to leftfield (it was the 2–2 pitch); A.Pafko singled to left field; R.Campanella struck out while A.Pafko advanced to second on a passed ball; **B.Feller replaced T.Gray (pitching);** E.Blackwell struck out; P.Reese walked; W.Jones flied to L.Doby-cf; 1 R, 2 H, 0 E, 2 LOB. NL 4, AL 3.

AL 14TH: On a bunt D.DiMaggio grounded out (E.Blackwell-p to S.Musial-1b); F.Fain singled to left field; J.DiMaggio grounded into a double play (W.Jones-3b to R.Schoendienst-2b to S.Musial-1b) [F.Fain out at second]; 0 R, 1 H, 0 E, 0 LOB. NL 4, AL 3.

Final Totals	R	H	E	LOB
National League	4	10	0	9
American League	3	8	1	6

GAME 18

Tuesday, July 10, 1951

Briggs Stadium, Detroit

National League 8, American League 3

SERIES RESULTS: AL 12, NL 6

An Explosion of Power

For the second consecutive year, the National League used the long ball to subdue its American League rivals. Home runs from Stan Musial of St. Louis, Bob Elliott of Boston, Gil Hodges of Brooklyn, and Ralph Kiner of Pittsburgh powered the Nationals to an 8–3 victory, marking the first time they had won successive games. The four NL homers set a one-team All-Star record, and even had the AL not hit any, a new two-team record would have been established. As it was, Vic Wertz and George Kell of the hometown Tigers also reached the inviting Briggs Stadium seats, making for a combined six home runs by the two clubs. The National Leaguers left no doubt among the sun-baked crowd of 52,075 that they were the superior team. They not only outhit the Americans, they also outpitched, outfielded, and outran them.

According to the alternate-year schedule in place since 1933, this year's game was supposed to be in a National League park. The leagues had agreed to switch it from Shibe Park in Philadelphia, where the Phillies were to be the host, to Detroit, a city that was celebrating its 250th birthday. This was also a significant birthday year in the history of the two leagues: the NL was celebrating its 75th and the AL its 50th.

The American League owners had instituted a new rule regarding pitching selections for this year's game. In what they obviously thought was a good idea, they had decreed that one pitcher had to be picked from each team, and that no team could furnish more than one. The ruling forced manager Casey Stengel to choose such unlikely All-Stars as Randy Gumpert of Chicago and Connie Marrero of Washington, while he had to bypass other worthy possibilities from the pitching-rich Yankees and Indians. Stengel selected Eddie Lopat from the Yanks and Bob Lemon from Cleveland, but among those unavailable to him were Bob Feller, Allie Reynolds, and Vic Raschi, all of whom were having outstanding seasons. News-

papermen, who were openly critical of the AL's scheme, gained new ammunition when Feller pitched a no-hitter on the day Stengel announced his choices and Reynolds pitched one two days after the All-Star Game. The AL's one-sided defeat doomed the one-pitcher-per-team rule, and the AL owners repealed it the next winter.

Just before game time, players from both teams lined up along the foul lines for the (then) typically brief pregame ceremonies. This year, the ceremonies included a moment of silence for former Tiger great Harry Heilmann, who had died a day earlier. The greatest of all Tigers, Ty Cobb, who was attending his first All-Star Game, threw out the first ball. Stengel chose as his starter Ned Garver of the last-place St. Louis Browns. The Browns were already twenty-five games behind the first-place Chicago White Sox, but Garver, at 11-4, had half their twenty-two wins.

Philadelphia center fielder Richie Ashburn opened the game by stroking Garver's first pitch down the left-field line for a double. (Perhaps because of the Burt Shotton–Hank Sauer controversy of the previous year, voting for outfielders this year was again by individual position.) After Ashburn went to third on Alvin Dark's fly ball, Musial, batting a league-leading .369, drew a walk. Jackie Robinson popped out, and then with Gil Hodges at the plate, Musial attempted to steal second. Yogi Berra's throw to second baseman Nellie Fox of the White Sox was in time, but Fox dropped the ball. Musial was safe, and Ashburn raced home. The official scorers charged Fox with an error, awarded no stolen bases, and ruled that the run was unearned.

A year before, for the game at Comiskey Park, the White Sox had had only one player on the team, pitcher Ray Scarborough, and he didn't play. This year, the Sox were leading the league, and six of their players were on the AL squad, including two starters: Fox and his double play partner, Venezuelan-born shortstop Chico Carrasquel. The Dodgers, with what seemed like a comfortable

111

eight-and-a-half-game lead in the NL, had seven players chosen.

Fox had received more votes than any other American League player, while Musial was this year's overall top vote getter. Fans submitted more than 4.7 million ballots (up from 3.1 million in 1950); still, several positions had remained undecided until the final count. After leading most of the way, Eddie Robinson, also of the White Sox, lost the AL's first base start to Philadelphia's Ferris Fain; in the race at shortstop in the NL, Brooklyn's Pee Wee Reese was edged out by Alvin Dark, of the Giants.

Expected to open with Brooklyn's ace right-hander Don Newcombe, Phillies manager Eddie Sawyer chose his own ace Robin Roberts, instead. Roberts was the first pitcher to start back-to-back games since Mort Cooper had started for the Nationals in 1942 and 1943. (Cooper was the loser in both.) Roberts, who had allowed one run in three innings in 1950, wasn't as effective this year, yielding a run on four hits and a walk in two innings.

The run scored when Fain, the AL's leading hitter at .347, tripled home Berra, who had opened the second inning with a single. While better fielding by Phillies right fielder Del Ennis might have kept Fain at second, he was at third when Carrasquel followed with a bloop single to center. Fain, thinking the ball would be caught, got a late jump and was out on Ashburn's throw to catcher Roy Campanella. Ashburn also contributed the fielding play of the game. In the sixth, he made a sensational one-handed catch against the screen in right-center that robbed Wertz of possibly another home run or at least an extra-base hit.

Garver, who had pitched extremely well, worked three innings, retiring the side in order in both the second and the third. He left with the score tied at 1–1, but the tie was quickly broken against Lopat. Musial drove the Yankee left-hander's first pitch of the fourth inning into the upper deck in right field. One out later, with Hodges at first via an infield single, Elliott hit the second homer of the inning, putting the NL ahead, 4–1. Elliott's blow marked the first time an American League pitcher had allowed two home runs in one inning. (Lou Boudreau and Rudy York had victimized Cooper in the first inning of the 1942 game at the Polo Grounds.)

When Phillies third baseman Willie Jones replaced Elliott in the home fourth, it brought an end to active participation in All-Star competition by members of the Boston Braves. Warren Spahn was the only other Braves player on the NL squad this year and the only one chosen for the 1952 game, but he didn't get to pitch in either contest.

By the time of the 1953 game, the Braves had moved to Milwaukee.

Sal Maglie, who had replaced Roberts in the third, was the beneficiary of the home runs and would be the first (and only) New York Giant to win an All-Star Game. Ironically, Maglie was the least effective of the four National League pitchers, having yielded the home runs by Wertz in the fourth and Kell in the fifth. (Before this game, Kell had hit only one home run all season, and that was on the road.)

The two American League home runs cut the lead to 4–3, but the Nationals got both runs back after just two men had batted in the sixth. Detroit's Fred Hutchinson, another pitcher likely chosen because of the "one pitcher per team" edict, had come on in the fifth after losing pitcher Lopat's one disastrous inning.

Hutchinson walked the lead-off batter, Jackie Robinson, a walk that Hodges, the Major Leagues' leading home run hitter with twenty-eight, followed by lashing a fastball on a line to the seats in left.

Newcombe entered the game in the sixth and, aided by Ashburn's catch on Wertz, blanked the AL over the next three innings. He gave up just two hits, while fanning three. One of the hits was Ted Williams's lead-off triple in the eighth, a long drive to right-center that Duke Snider got his glove on but couldn't hold. Although Williams was at third base with nobody out, he had to remain there as Berra popped out to Robinson, Phil Rizzuto fouled out to third baseman Jones, and Eddie Robinson, batting for Fain, tapped back to the mound. It was the only hit in three at bats for Williams, and it lowered his lifetime All-Star batting average to .407. Joe DiMaggio, Williams's longtime rival and contemporary, had been picked for the thirteenth time, despite a .261 average this year. DiMaggio, who would retire at season's end, had an injured leg and spent the afternoon on the bench.

After Newcombe's fine effort, Sawyer called on Cincinnati's Ewell Blackwell to pitch the ninth. Blackwell had now pitched in six consecutive All-Star Games, a record later tied by Early Wynn between 1955 and 1959 (Wynn pitched in both games in 1959). The AL reached Blackwell for a hit and a walk but no runs. In 13.2 innings, Blackwell had allowed just two runs and eight hits, while striking out twelve. He was only twenty-eight years old, but because of arm problems, this would be his last big season. After 1951, he would win only six more Major League games.

The National League scored another run against Hutchinson in the seventh and then a final one on Kiner's home run against Boston's Mel Par-

Berra sliding home, 1951

Yogi Berra slides home with the game's first run in the second inning run as the ball sails past Dodgers catcher Roy Campanella. Berra, who had singled, scored on Ferris Fain's triple. National Baseball Hall of Fame Library and Archive, Cooperstown, New York. Associated Press Photo.

nell in the eighth. In the seventh, Ashburn, who had led off the inning with a walk, was on third with two out and Robinson at the plate. Kell was playing deep, and when Robinson placed a perfect bunt down the third-base line, Kell could do nothing but watch as Ashburn scored. Kiner's blast, into the upper deck in left, was the third consecutive All-Star Game in which he'd homered, something no other player has done.

"We just weren't a good ball club today," said a disappointed Stengel in the losers' clubhouse. Stengel had now won two consecutive World Series while losing two consecutive All-Star Games.

Sawyer mused that "this sort of makes up for the licking the Yanks gave us in the last World Series."

Sawyer had particular praise for Newcombe, who himself felt that this was the best he'd done in his three All-Star appearances.

By the time of the 1952 game, Ford Frick had succeeded Happy Chandler as commissioner and would have to profess neutrality in All-Star competition. But after today's contest, Frick, who was still president of the National League and who had suffered through many defeats, said, "I hate to recall how long I've waited for these two straight victories."

	AL		NL	
P	Ned Garver	SLA	Robin Roberts	PHI
C	Yogi Berra	NYA	Roy Campanella	BRO
1B	Ferris Fain	PHA	Gil Hodges	BRO
2B	Nellie Fox	CHA	Jackie Robinson	BRO
3B	George Kell	DET	Bob Elliott	BSN
SS	Chico Carrasquel	CHA	Al Dark	NY
OF	Dom DiMaggio	BOS	Richie Ashburn	PHI
OF	Vic Wertz	DET	Del Ennis	PHI
OF	Ted Williams	BOS	Stan Musial	SLN
	Jim Busby	CHA	Ewell Blackwell	CIN
	Joe DiMaggio	NYA	Bruce Edwards	CHN
	Larry Doby	CLE	Larry Jansen	NY
	Bobby Doerr	BOS	Willie Jones	PHI
	Randy Gumpert	CHA	Ralph Kiner	PIT
	Jim Hegan	CLE	Dutch Leonard	CHN
	Fred Hutchinson	DET	Sal Maglie	NY
	Bob Lemon	CLE	Don Newcombe	BRO
	Eddie Lopat	NYA	Pee Wee Reese	BRO
	Connie Marrero	WAS	Preacher Roe	BRO
	Minnie Minoso	CHA	Red Schoendienst	SLN
	Mel Parnell	BOS	Enos Slaughter	SLN
	Phil Rizzuto	NYA	Duke Snider	BRO
	Eddie Robinson	CHA	Warren Spahn	BSN
	Bobby Shantz	PHA	Wally Westlake	SLN
	Vern Stephens	BOS	Johnny Wyrostek	CIN

```
National League    100  302  110-  8
American League    010  110  000-  3
```

NATIONAL LEAGUE

	ab	r	h	bi	bb	so	po	a
R.Ashburn, cf	4	2	2	0	1	0	4	1
D.Snider, cf	0	0	0	0	0	0	0	0
A.Dark, ss	5	0	1	0	0	0	0	3
P.Reese, ss	0	0	0	0	0	0	0	1
S.Musial, lf-rf	4	1	2	1	1	0	0	0
W.Westlake, lf	0	0	0	0	0	0	0	0
J.Robinson, 2b	4	1	2	1	1	0	3	1
R.Schoendienst, 2b	0	0	0	0	0	0	0	0
G.Hodges, 1b	5	2	2	2	0	1	6	0
B.Elliott, 3b	2	1	1	2	0	0	1	1
W.Jones, 3b	2	0	0	0	1	1	3	0
D.Ennis, rf	2	0	0	0	0	1	0	0
R.Kiner, lf	2	1	1	1	0	0	1	0
J.Wyrostek, rf	1	0	0	0	0	0	0	0
R.Campanella, c	4	0	0	0	0	0	9	1
R.Roberts, p	0	0	0	0	0	0	0	0
E.Slaughter, ph	1	0	0	0	0	0	0	0
S.Maglie, p	1	0	0	0	0	0	0	0
D.Newcombe, p	2	0	1	0	0	0	0	1
E.Blackwell, p	0	0	0	0	0	0	0	0
Totals	39	8	12	7	4	3	27	9

BATTING
2B: R.Ashburn (off N.Garver).
HR: S.Musial (4th inning off E.Lopat, o on, o out); G.Hodges (6th inning off F.Hutchinson, 1 on, o out); B.Elliott (4th inning off E.Lopat, 1 on, 1 out); R.Kiner (8th inning off M.Parnell, o on, 1 out).
2-out RBI: J.Robinson.
RBI, scoring position, less than 2 outs: R.Ashburn 0-1; A.Dark 0-2; S.Musial 0-1; J.Robinson 0-1; G.Hodges 0-1.

BASERUNNING
CS: S.Musial (2nd base by N.Garver/Y.Berra); J.Robinson (2nd base by B.Lemon/Y.Berra).
Team LOB: 8

FIELDING
E: J.Robinson (fumble).
PB: R.Campanella.
Outfield assist: R.Ashburn (F.Fain at HP).

AMERICAN LEAGUE

	ab	r	h	bi	bb	so	po	a
D.DiMaggio, cf	5	0	1	0	0	2	1	0
N.Fox, 2b	3	0	1	0	0	0	3	1
B.Doerr, ph-2b	1	0	1	0	1	0	1	0
G.Kell, 3b	4	1	1	1	0	1	4	2
T.Williams, lf	3	0	1	0	1	1	3	0
J.Busby, lf	0	0	0	0	0	0	0	0
Y.Berra, c	4	1	1	0	0	0	4	2
V.Wertz, rf	3	1	1	1	0	0	2	0
P.Rizzuto, ss	1	0	0	0	0	0	1	2
F.Fain, 1b	3	0	1	1	0	1	5	0
E.Robinson, ph-1b	1	0	0	0	0	0	0	1
C.Carrasquel, ss	2	0	1	0	0	0	0	3
M.Minoso, ph-rf	2	0	0	0	0	0	2	0
N.Garver, p	1	0	0	0	0	1	0	0
E.Lopat, p	0	0	0	0	0	0	0	0
L.Doby, ph	1	0	0	0	0	0	0	0
F.Hutchinson, p	0	0	0	0	0	0	0	0
V.Stephens, ph	1	0	0	0	0	1	0	0
M.Parnell, p	0	0	0	0	0	0	0	0
B.Lemon, p	0	0	0	0	0	0	1	0
J.Hegan, ph	1	0	1	0	0	0	0	0
Totals	36	3	10	3	2	7	27	11

BATTING
2B: J.Hegan (off E.Blackwell).
3B: F.Fain (off R.Roberts); T.Williams (off D.Newcombe).
HR: G.Kell (5th inning off S.Maglie, o on, 2 out); V.Wertz (4th inning off S.Maglie, o on, 1 out).
2-out RBI: G.Kell.
RBI, scoring position, less than 2 outs: D.DiMaggio 0-1; Y.Berra 0-1; P.Rizzuto 0-1; C.Carrasquel 0-1.
S: G.Kell.

BASERUNNING
Team LOB: 9

FIELDING
E: N.Fox (dropped throw); Y.Berra (throw).
DP: (1). Y.Berra-G.Kell.

PITCHING	ip	h	r	er	bb	so
National League						
R.Roberts	2.0	4	1	1	0	1
S.Maglie (w)	3.0	3	2	2	1	1
D.Newcombe	3.0	2	0	0	0	3
E.Blackwell (s)	1.0	1	0	0	1	2
American League						
N.Garver	3.0	1	1	0	1	1
E.Lopat (L)	1.0	3	3	3	0	0
F.Hutchinson	3.0	3	3	3	2	0
M.Parnell	1.0	3	1	1	0	1
B.Lemon	1.0	2	0	0	1	1

Inherited Runners—Scored:
S.Maglie 0-0; D.Newcombe 0-0; E.Blackwell 0-0; E.Lopat 0-0; F.Hutchinson 0-0; M.Parnell 0-0; B.Lemon 0-0.

GAME DATA—T: 2:41; A: 52075; Temp: Unknown; Wind: Unknown direction, Speed: Unknown

UMPIRES—HP: Art Passarella (AL), 1B: Scotty Robb (NL), 2B: Eddie Hurley (AL), 3B: Lou Jorda (NL), LF: Frank Dascoli (NL), RF: Jim Honochick (AL)

STARTING LINEUPS

National League	*American League*
1. R.Ashburn cf	D.DiMaggio cf
2. A.Dark ss	N.Fox 2b
3. S.Musial lf	G.Kell 3b
4. J.Robinson 2b	T.Williams lf
5. G.Hodges 1b	Y.Berra c
6. B.Elliott 3b	V.Wertz rf
7. D.Ennis rf	F.Fain 1b
8. R.Campanella c	C.Carrasquel ss
9. R.Roberts p	N.Garver p

NL 1ST: R.Ashburn doubled to left field; A.Dark flied to V.Wertz-rf [R.Ashburn to third]; S.Musial walked; J.Robinson popped to Y.Berra-c; S.Musial was caught stealing second [R.Ashburn scored (unearned), S.Musial to second (error by N.Fox-2b; assist by Y.Berra-c)]; G.Hodges grounded out (C.Carrasquel-ss to F.Fain-1b); 1 R (0 ER), 1 H, 1 E, 1 LOB. NL 1, AL 0.

AL 1ST: On a bunt D.DiMaggio singled to third base; N.Fox popped to R.Campanella-c; G.Kell forced D.DiMaggio (R.Campanella-c to J.Robinson-2b) [G.Kell to first]; failed hit and run; T.Williams popped to B.Elliott-3b; 0 R, 1 H, 0 E, 1 LOB. NL 1, AL 0.

NL 2ND: B.Elliott flied to T.Williams-lf; D.Ennis struck out; R.Campanella grounded out (C.Carrasquel-ss to F.Fain-1b); 0 R, 0 H, 0 E, 0 LOB. NL 1, AL 0.

AL 2ND: Y.Berra singled to left-center; V.Wertz flied to R.Ashburn-cf; F.Fain tripled to right field [Y.Berra scored]; C.Carrasquel singled to center field (R.Ashburn-cf to R.Campanella-c) [F.Fain out at home, C.Carrasquel to second]; Fain held up at third, thinking Texas Leaguer might be caug; N.Garver struck out; 1 R, 3 H, 0 E, 1 LOB. NL 1, AL 1.

NL 3RD: **E.Slaughter batted for R.Roberts;** E.Slaughter lined to T.Williams-lf; R.Ashburn flied to V.Wertz-rf; A.Dark grounded out (G.Kell-3b to F.Fain-1b); 0 R, 0 H, 0 E, 0 LOB. NL 1, AL 1.

AL 3RD: **S.Maglie replaced E.Slaughter (pitching);** D.DiMaggio grounded out (A.Dark-ss to G.Hodges-1b); N.Fox singled to right field; G.Kell out on a sacrifice bunt (B.Elliott-3b to G.Hodges-1b) [N.Fox to second]; T.Williams struck out; 0 R, 1 H, 0 E, 1 LOB. NL 1, AL 1.

NL 4TH: **E.Lopat replaced N.Garver (pitching);** S.Musial homered to deep rightfield; J.Robinson lined to D.DiMaggio-cf; G.Hodges singled to third base; ball hit 3b bag, then umpire Jorda; B.Elliott homered to deep leftfield [G.Hodges scored]; D.Ennis flied to T.Williams-lf; R.Campanella lined to F.Fain-1b; 3 R, 3 H, 0 E, 0 LOB. NL 4, AL 1.

AL 4TH: **W.Jones replaced B.Elliott (playing 3b); R.Kiner replaced D.Ennis (playing lf); S.Musial changed positions (playing rf);** Y.Berra popped to W.Jones-3b; V.Wertz homered to deep rightfield; F.Fain reached on an error by J.Robinson-2b [F.Fain to first]; C.Carrasquel forced F.Fain (A.Dark-ss to J.Robinson-2b) [C.Carrasquel to first]; **L.Doby batted for E.Lopat;** L.Doby popped to W.Jones-3b; 1 R, 1 H, 1 E, 1 LOB. NL 4, AL 2.

NL 5TH: **F.Hutchinson replaced L.Doby (pitching);** S.Maglie reached on an error by Y.Berra-c [S.Maglie to second]; R.Ashburn popped to N.Fox-2b; A.Dark reached on a fielder's choice (C.Carrasquel-ss to G.Kell-3b) [S.Maglie out at third]; S.Musial popped to N.Fox-2b; 0 R, 0 H, 1 E, 1 LOB. NL 4, AL 2.

AL 5TH: Umpires moved: Robb (hp), Hurley (1b), Jorda (2b), Passarella (3b), Dascoli (lf), Honochick (rf); D.DiMaggio flied to R.Kiner-lf; N.Fox flied to R.Ashburn-cf; G.Kell homered to deep leftfield; T.Williams walked; Y.Berra grounded out (J.Robinson-2b to G.Hodges-1b); 1 R, 1 H, 0 E, 1 LOB. NL 4, AL 3.

NL 6TH: J.Robinson walked; G.Hodges homered to deep leftfield [J.Robinson scored]; W.Jones popped to G.Kell-3b in foul territory; R.Kiner grounded out (G.Kell-3b to F.Fain-1b); R.Campanella popped to G.Kell-3b; 2 R, 1 H, 0 E, 0 LOB. NL 6, AL 3.

AL 6TH: **D.Newcombe replaced S.Maglie (pitching);** V.Wertz lined to R.Ashburn-cf; F.Fain struck out; **M.Minoso batted for C.Carrasquel;** M.Minoso grounded out (A.Dark-ss to G.Hodges-1b); 0 R, 0 H, 0 E, 0 LOB. NL 6, AL 3.

NL 7TH: **M.Minoso stayed in game (playing rf); P.Rizzuto replaced V.Wertz (playing ss);** D.Newcombe lined to M.Minoso-rf; R.Ashburn walked; A.Dark singled to center field [R.Ashburn to second]; S.Musial forced A.Dark (N.Fox-2b to P.Rizzuto-ss) [R.Ashburn to third, S.Musial to first]; On a bunt J.Robinson singled to third base [R.Ashburn scored, S.Musial to second]; G.Hodges forced J.Robinson (P.Rizzuto-ss to N.Fox-2b) [G.Hodges to first]; 1 R, 2 H, 0 E, 2 LOB. NL 7, AL 3.

AL 7TH: **V.Stephens batted for F.Hutchinson;** V.Stephens struck out; D.DiMaggio struck out; **B.Doerr batted for N.Fox;** B.Doerr singled to center field; G.Kell flied to R.Ashburn-cf; 0 R, 1 H, 0 E, 1 LOB. NL 7, AL 3.

NL 8TH: **B.Doerr stayed in game (playing 2b); M.Parnell replaced V.Stephens (pitching);** W.Jones struck out; R.Kiner homered to deep leftfield; R.Campanella flied to M.Minoso-rf in foul territory; D.Newcombe singled to right field; R.Ashburn singled to right field [D.Newcombe to second]; A.Dark forced R.Ashburn (P.Rizzuto-ss to B.Doerr-2b) [A.Dark to first]; 1 R, 3 H, 0 E, 2 LOB. NL 8, AL 3.

AL 8TH: **S.Musial changed positions (playing lf); P.Reese replaced A.Dark (playing ss); D.Snider replaced R.Ashburn (playing cf); J.Wyrostek replaced R.Kiner (playing rf);** T.Williams tripled to very deep right-center; Y.Berra popped to J.Robinson-2b; P.Rizzuto popped to W.Jones-3b in foul territory; **E.Robinson batted for F.Fain;** E.Robinson grounded out (D.Newcombe-p to G.Hodges-1b); 0 R, 1 H, 0 E, 1 LOB. NL 8, AL 3.

NL 9TH: **E.Robinson stayed in game (playing 1b); J.Busby replaced T.Williams (playing lf); B.Lemon replaced M.Parnell (pitching);** S.Musial singled to right field; J.Robinson singled to pitcher [S.Musial to second]; G.Hodges struck

out while J.Robinson was caught stealing second (Y.Berra-c to G.Kell-3b); W.Jones walked; J.Wyrostek grounded out (E.Robinson-1b to B.Lemon-p); 0 R, 2 H, 0 E, 2 LOB. NL 8, AL 3.

AL 9TH: **E.Blackwell replaced D.Newcombe (pitching); R.Schoendienst replaced J.Robinson (playing 2b); W.Westlake replaced S.Musial (playing lf);** M.Minoso grounded out (P.Reese-ss to G.Hodges-1b); **J.Hegan batted for B.Lemon;** J.Hegan doubled to left-center; the ball fell between three fielders; D.DiMaggio was called out on strikes; R.Campanella allowed a passed ball [J.Hegan to third]; B.Doerr walked; G.Kell struck out; 0 R, 1 H, 0 E, 2 LOB. NL 8, AL 3.

Final Totals	R	H	E	LOB
National League	8	12	1	8
American League	3	10	2	9

GAME **19**

Tuesday, July 8, 1952

Shibe Park, Philadelphia

National League 3, American League 2

(5 innings)

SERIES RESULTS: AL 12, NL 7

Shantz Revives Memories of Hubbell

With the Phillies doing the honors for the 1952 game, all sixteen of the original teams had now hosted an All-Star Game. The game had been held at Shibe Park once before, in 1943, but the Athletics had been the host team. The American League had won that game, 5–3, for its third straight victory. But the balance of power had since shifted, and what the 32,285 fans saw this rain-soaked afternoon was a third straight victory for the National League. Like in the previous two wins, the NL had used the home run ball to defeat its rivals. Four-baggers by Jackie Robinson and Hank Sauer had given the National League a 3–2 lead when rain forced the umpires to halt play at the end of the fifth inning. Although a tarpaulin had covered the infield before the start of action—a start delayed for twenty minutes—the tarp had gotten so waterlogged it couldn't be used again. After waiting close to an hour, the umpires called the game.

Casey Stengel of the Yankees and Leo Durocher of the Giants, who had faced each other in the 1951 World Series, were, by custom, the opposing managers. While they were the two most famous managers of the time as well as two of the all-time greats, they had a combined All-Star record of no wins and four losses. Stengel had lost the 1950 and 1951 games, while Durocher, as manager of the Dodgers, had lost in 1942 and 1948.

Local favorites Robin Roberts of the Phillies, the NL starter the past two years, and Bobby Shantz of the A's, the Major Leagues' leading winner at 14-3, seemed the logical choices to open on the mound. However, both had pitched the previous Sunday, and so both were bypassed. Durocher selected another member of the Phillies, left-hander Curt Simmons, who was still serving in the National Guard when the season began. Stengel chose his own ace Vic Raschi.

Because rain had fallen intermittently all morn-

ing, it appeared for a while that the All-Star Game would suffer its first postponement. Ford Frick, presiding over his first All-Star Game as commissioner, gave the go-ahead to play, but because the tarp had remained on the field, neither team took batting or fielding practice. A light drizzle was still falling when the National Leaguers finally took the field. The crowd gave Simmons a big round of applause as he began to throw his warmup pitches. A year earlier, then-Corporal Simmons had used part of a three-day pass to pitch batting practice for the National Leaguers in the game at Detroit.

The first batter Simmons faced was Dom DiMaggio, playing in his sixth All-Star Game. With his Red Sox teammate Ted Williams serving in Korea, DiMaggio had the most All-Star experience on the AL squad. He drew a walk but remained at first as Simmons used an overpowering fastball to strike out Hank Bauer of the Yankees and Dale Mitchell of the Indians and to get Al Rosen, also of Cleveland, to bounce into a force out.

Rosen and Mitchell were two of the four Indians in Stengel's starting lineup, which also had three Yankees. Rosen had actually finished second, barely behind Boston's George Kell, but Kell was injured and had to miss the game. The Yanks were in first place, slightly ahead of second-place Chicago and third-place Cleveland; yet, while the Yanks and Indians were well represented, the White Sox had only one starter, first baseman Eddie Robinson. The White Sox had come very near to having more; Nellie Fox and Chico Carrasquel, Chicago's double play combination, had both lost out in extremely close votes. Cleveland second baseman Bobby Avila edged Fox, while Yankee shortstop Phil Rizzuto squeezed past Carrasquel. The closest voting in the National League had also been at shortstop, where the Phillies' Granny Hamner edged the Giants' Alvin Dark.

The Nationals took a 1–0 lead in the home first when, with one out, Jackie Robinson lined Raschi's first-pitch curve ball into the upper deck in left.

118

Raschi then righted himself by fanning Sauer and Stan Musial, the NL's leading hitter (.333) and the season's top vote getter.

The strong pitching continued through the next two innings. In the second, Simmons set down Yogi Berra, Eddie Robinson, and Avila in order, while Raschi did the same to Roy Campanella, Enos Slaughter, and Bobby Thomson. DiMaggio broke the spell in the third with a two-out double, but Simmons concluded his very impressive outing by getting Bauer to foul out to Campanella.

Cleveland's Bob Lemon replaced Raschi in the third and continued the strong pitching by retiring the Nationals in order. When the inning began, Stengel had also sent Minnie Minoso of the White Sox out to play left field in place of Mitchell. Home plate umpire Al Barlick, citing the rule that All-Star starters must play three innings, told Stengel that Mitchell would have to play at least one more inning. Stengel later confirmed that he knew the rule but was hoping to remove Mitchell because he had an injured right knee.

Minoso got his chance in the top of the fourth when, pinch-hitting for Mitchell, he ripped a lead-off double to right off the Cubs' Bob Rush. After Rosen walked and Berra popped out, Eddie Robinson grounded a single to right that Jackie Robinson couldn't reach because of the muddy track. The hit scored Minoso and sent Rosen to third. Avila drove a scorcher back through the box that Robinson was able to knock down but had no play to make. Rosen scored, and the Americans had a 2–1 lead.

With runners at first and second and a chance for more, Stengel allowed Rizzuto, a .258 hitter this year, to bat for himself. Rush got him to bounce a routine grounder to short, where Hamner fielded it and flipped to second baseman Robinson for the force on Avila. But Robinson's hurried relay to first was wild and pulled Giants first baseman Whitey Lockman off the bag. He beat Rizzuto to first to complete the inning-ending double play only because Rizzuto had slipped at the plate after hitting the ball and wasn't going at full speed. A few minutes earlier, the always vociferous Philadelphia fans had booed Jackie Robinson for allowing Eddie Robinson's grounder to scoot through. Now they turned their wrath on Rizzuto for a perceived lack of hustle.

Robinson led off the National League fourth by popping to Rosen, making nine National Leaguers in a row who had gone out. The streak ended when Lemon hit the next batter, Musial. That brought up Sauer, the Major League home run leader with twenty-three. Going after Lemon's first pitch, the big Cubs slugger smashed it over the

left-field roof. The blow was among the longest home runs in All-Star history and allowed the Nationals to regain the lead at 3–2. They seemed ready to add to that lead when Lemon followed the Sauer home run by walking Campanella and issuing a double to Enos Slaughter.

Shantz was warming up in the bullpen, but Stengel chose to stay with Lemon. The Indians ace got Thomson for the second out and then intentionally walked Hamner, the number eight hitter, to load the bases. The due batter was Rush, who hadn't fared very well in his one inning. Among the players Durocher had available to pinch-hit were the Cardinals' Red Schoendienst and a trio of Dodgers: Gil Hodges, Carl Furillo, and Duke Snider. He also had on his bench Ralph Kiner, who had homered in each of the last three All-Star contests. Yet, Durocher opted to let Rush bat for himself. The result was a ground out to Rosen that stranded the three runners.

"I'm not going to hit for him when I'm one run ahead," Durocher later explained. "The boy was pitching all right. He just had to settle down."

Stengel did much the same in the top of the fifth. Despite Lemon's poor inning, Stengel allowed him to lead off the fifth. Lemon was an above-average hitter for a pitcher. However, he was not the equal of those who remained on the AL bench. (After the game, Stengel said he was saving those players to use in the later innings.) Rush got Lemon on a grounder to second and then threw a third strike past DiMaggio. Bauer followed with an infield single but was out trying to steal second, Campanella to Hamner.

That Stengel had allowed Lemon to bat for himself because of his hitting and not because he wanted him to continue on the mound became obvious when the NL batted in the home fifth. Lemon was gone, and the Nationals were now facing Shantz, the Athletics' five-foot-six left-hander. Shantz would win twenty-four games and the American League's Most Valuable Player Award this season and would have a decent, if injury-marred, big league career. Yet he would always be remembered for his performance in this one inning.

The Yankees had knocked Shantz around for four innings on Sunday, but he was magnificent this day. Facing the top of the National League order, he struck out Lockman, Robinson, and Musial in succession, getting both Lockman and Musial to look at called third strikes. Musial, who almost never argued ball and strike calls, did question plate umpire Bill Summers's call on strike three.

Just as they had earlier in the day for Sim-

Robinson scoring on his home run, 1952
Brooklyn's Jackie Robinson is greeted by the Phillies batboy following his first inning home run off Vic Raschi. Stan Musial waits to greet Robinson as American League catcher Yogi Berra and National League umpire Al Barlick look on.
© *Bettmann/*CORBIS.

mons, the Philadelphia fans, seemingly both A's and Phillies fans, had cheered their local hero when he took the mound. The ovation was deafening after the three strikeouts, and comparisons with Carl Hubbell began immediately. From a pitching standpoint, the most memorable moment in the brief twenty-year history of the All-Star Game had been Hubbell's fanning five consecutive American Leaguers at the Polo Grounds in 1934. Baseball fans across the country now wondered whether Shantz could match, or even exceed, Hubbell's feat while pitching against Sauer, Campanella, and Slaughter, the NL's scheduled batters in the sixth. Unfortunately, they never found out. Rush had a 1-1 count on Minoso, leading off the top of the sixth, when the drizzle turned

to a downpour and play was stopped. Fifty-six minutes later, at 4:13 P.M., the umpires called it off.

"We were gonna beat those guys," said Berra, voicing the American Leaguers' disappointment with the premature ending. Several others said they were certain that had it gone the distance, they would have won. But it didn't, and the National League's victory in the first All-Star Game to go less than nine innings cut the AL's margin to 12-7. Though not particularly effective, Rush was the winner, the first Cub to win, following losses by Bill Lee in 1939, Claude Passeau in 1941 and 1946, and Johnny Schmitz in 1948. Lemon became the first Cleveland pitcher to lose an All-Star Game.

	AL			NL	
P	Vic Raschi	NYA		Curt Simmons	PHI
C	Yogi Berra	NYA		Roy Campanella	BRO
1B	Eddie Robinson	CHA		Whitey Lockman	NY
2B	Bobby Avila	CLE		Jackie Robinson	BRO
3B	Al Rosen	CLE		Bobby Thomson	NY
SS	Phil Rizzuto	NYA		Granny Hamner	PHI
OF	Hank Bauer	NYA		Stan Musial	SLN
OF	Dom DiMaggio	BOS		Hank Sauer	CHN
OF	Dale Mitchell	CLE		Enos Slaughter	SLN
	Larry Doby	CLE		Toby Atwell	CHN
	Ferris Fain	PHA		Al Dark	NY
	Nellie Fox	CHA		Carl Furillo	BRO
	Mike Garcia	CLE		Grady Hatton	CIN
	Jim Hegan	CLE		Jim Hearn	NY
	Jackie Jensen	WAS		Gil Hodges	BRO
	Eddie Joost	PHA		Monte Irvin	NY
	George Kell +	BOS		Ralph Kiner	PIT
	Bob Lemon	CLE		Sal Maglie	NY
	Mickey Mantle	NYA		Pee Wee Reese	BRO
	Gil McDougald	NYA		Robin Roberts	PHI
	Minnie Minoso	CHA		Preacher Roe +	BRO
	Satchel Paige	SLA		Bob Rush	CHN
	Allie Reynolds	NYA		Red Schoendienst	SLN
	Bobby Shantz	PHA		Duke Snider	BRO
	Vic Wertz	DET		Warren Spahn	BSN
	Eddie Yost	WAS		Gerry Staley	SLN
				Wes Westrum	NY

+ player replaced on roster

RETROSHEET EXPANDED BOX SCORE Tuesday, 7/8/1952 American League at National League (D)

```
American League    000 20-   2
National League    100 20-   3   (5)
```

AMERICAN LEAGUE

	ab	r	h	bi	bb	so	po	a
D.DiMaggio, cf	2	0	1	0	1	1	1	0
L.Doby, cf	0	0	0	0	0	0	0	0
H.Bauer, rf	3	0	1	0	0	1	2	0
J.Jensen, rf	0	0	0	0	0	0	0	0
D.Mitchell, lf	1	0	0	0	0	1	1	0
M.Minoso, ph-lf	1	1	1	0	0	0	0	0
A.Rosen, 3b	1	1	0	0	1	0	3	1
Y.Berra, c	2	0	0	0	0	0	6	0
E.Robinson, 1b	2	0	1	1	0	1	1	0
B.Avila, 2b	2	0	1	1	0	0	0	0
P.Rizzuto, ss	2	0	0	0	0	0	1	0
V.Raschi, p	0	0	0	0	0	0	0	0
G.McDougald, ph	1	0	0	0	0	0	0	0
B.Lemon, p	1	0	0	0	0	0	0	0
B.Shantz, p	0	0	0	0	0	0	0	0
Totals	18	2	5	2	2	4	15	1

NATIONAL LEAGUE

	ab	r	h	bi	bb	so	po	a
W.Lockman, 1b	3	0	0	0	0	1	5	0
J.Robinson, 2b	3	1	1	1	0	1	2	2
S.Musial, cf	2	1	0	0	0	2	1	0
H.Sauer, lf	2	1	1	2	0	1	0	0
R.Campanella, c	1	0	0	0	1	0	5	1
E.Slaughter, rf	2	0	1	0	0	1	0	0
B.Thomson, 3b	2	0	0	0	0	0	1	1
G.Hamner, ss	1	0	0	0	1	0	1	3
C.Simmons, p	0	0	0	0	0	0	0	0
P.Reese, ph	1	0	0	0	0	0	0	0
B.Rush, p	1	0	0	0	0	0	0	0
Totals	18	3	3	3	2	6	15	7

PITCHING	ip	h	r	er	bb	so
American League						
V.Raschi	2.0	1	1	1	0	3
B.Lemon (L)	2.0	2	2	2	2	0
B.Shantz	1.0	0	0	0	0	3
National League						
C.Simmons	3.0	1	0	0	1	3
B.Rush (W)	2.0	4	2	2	1	1

BATTING

2B: D.DiMaggio (off C.Simmons); M.Minoso (off B.Rush).

RBI, scoring position, less than 2 outs: Y.Berra 0–1; E.Robinson 1–1; B.Avila 1–1; P.Rizzuto 0–1.

GDP: P.Rizzuto.

BASERUNNING

CS: H.Bauer (2nd base by B.Rush/R.Campanella).
Team LOB: 3

BATTING

2B: E.Slaughter (off B.Lemon).

HR: J.Robinson (1st inning off V.Raschi, 0 on, 1 out); H.Sauer (4th inning off B.Lemon, 1 on, 1 out).

RBI, scoring position, less than 2 outs: B.Thomson 0–2.

BASERUNNING

Team LOB: 3

FIELDING

DP: (1). G.Hamner-J.Robinson-W.Lockman.

Inherited Runners—Scored:
B.Lemon 0–0; B.Shantz 0–0; B.Rush 0–0.

IBB: G.Hamner by B.Lemon.

HBP: S.Musial by B.Lemon.

GAME DATA—T: 1:29; A: 32785; Temp: Unknown; Wind: Unknown direction, Speed: Unknown

UMPIRES—HP: Al Barlick (NL), 1B: Charlie Berry (AL), 2B: Dusty Boggess (NL), 3B: Bill Summers (AL), LF: Hank Soar (AL), RF: Lon Warneke (NL)

STARTING LINEUPS

	American League	*National League*
1.	D.DiMaggio cf	W.Lockman 1b
2.	H.Bauer rf	J.Robinson 2b
3.	D.Mitchell lf	S.Musial cf
4.	A.Rosen 3b	H.Sauer lf
5.	Y.Berra c	R.Campanella c
6.	E.Robinson 1b	E.Slaughter rf
7.	B.Avila 2b	B.Thomson 3b
8.	P.Rizzuto ss	G.Hamner ss
9.	V.Raschi p	C.Simmons p

AL 1ST: Start delayed 20 minutes by rain; D.DiMaggio walked; H.Bauer struck out; D.Mitchell struck out; A.Rosen forced D.DiMaggio (G.Hamner-ss to J.Robinson-2b) [A.Rosen to first]; 0 R, 0 H, 0 E, 1 LOB. AL 0, NL 0.

NL 1ST: W.Lockman popped to P.Rizzuto-ss; J.Robinson homered to deep leftfield; S.Musial was called out on strikes; H.Sauer struck out; 1 R, 1 H, 0 E, 0 LOB. AL 0, NL 1.

AL 2ND: Y.Berra lined to S.Musial-cf; E.Robinson struck out; B.Avila grounded out (G.Hamner-ss to W.Lockman-1b); 0 R, 0 H, 0 E, 0 LOB. AL 0, NL 1.

NL 2ND: R.Campanella popped to A.Rosen-3b in foul territory; E.Slaughter struck out; B.Thomson flied to H.Bauer-rf; 0 R, 0 H, 0 E, 0 LOB. AL 0, NL 1.

AL 3RD: P.Rizzuto popped to B.Thomson-3b in foul territory; **G.McDougald batted for V.Raschi;** G.McDougald grounded out (B.Thomson-3b to W.Lockman-1b); D.DiMaggio doubled to deep rightfield down the line; H.Bauer popped to R.Campanella-c in foul territory; 0 R, 1 H, 0 E, 1 LOB. AL 0, NL 1.

NL 3RD: **B.Lemon replaced G.McDougald (pitching);** Stengel attempted to put Minoso in lf here, but Frick ordered him to let starters play the required three innings; G.Hamner flied to H.Bauer-rf; **P.Reese batted for C.Simmons;** P.Reese flied to D.Mitchell-lf; W.Lockman flied to D.DiMaggio-cf; 0 R, 0 H, 0 E, 0 LOB. AL 0, NL 1.

AL 4TH: **B.Rush replaced P.Reese (pitching);** **M.Minoso batted for D.Mitchell;** M.Minoso doubled to right field; A.Rosen walked; Y.Berra popped to W.Lockman-1b in foul territory; E.Robinson singled to right field [M.Minoso scored, A.Rosen to third]; B.Avila singled to second base [A.Rosen scored, E.Robinson to second]; P.Rizzuto grounded into a double play (G.Hamner-ss to J.Robinson-2b to W.Lockman-1b) [B.Avila out at second]; 2 R, 3 H, 0 E, 1 LOB. AL 2, NL 1.

NL 4TH: **M.Minoso stayed in game (playing lf);** J.Robinson popped to A.Rosen-3b; S.Musial was hit by a pitch; H.Sauer homered to very deep left-center [S.Musial scored]; R.Campanella walked; E.Slaughter doubled to right field [R.Campanella to third]; B.Thomson popped to A.Rosen-3b in foul territory; G.Hamner was walked intentionally; B.Rush grounded out (A.Rosen-3b to E.Robinson-1b); 2 R, 2 H, 0 E, 3 LOB. AL 2, NL 3.

AL 5TH: B.Lemon grounded out (J.Robinson-2b to W.Lockman-1b); D.DiMaggio was called out on strikes; H.Bauer singled to pitcher; H.Bauer was caught stealing second (R.Campanella-c to G.Hamner-ss); 0 R, 1 H, 0 E, 0 LOB. AL 2, NL 3.

NL 5TH: Umpires moved: Summers (hp), Boggess (1b) Berry (2b), Barlick (3b), Soar (lf), Warneke (rf); **B.Shantz replaced B.Lemon (pitching);** **L.Doby replaced D.DiMaggio (playing cf);** **J.Jensen replaced H.Bauer (playing rf);** W.Lockman was called out on strikes; J.Robinson struck out; S.Musial was called out on strikes; 0 R, 0 H, 0 E, 0 LOB. AL 2, NL 3.

Final Totals	R	H	E	LOB
American League	2	5	0	3
National League	3	3	0	3

20

The Newly Dominant Nationals

The balance of power between the two leagues had done a complete turnaround over the previous few years. This year's 5–1 victory by the Nationals was the NL's fourth straight, matching the Americans' four consecutive wins between 1946 and 1949. The crowd of 30,846 for this return visit to Crosley Field raised the total attendance for the twenty All-Star Games played to more than 800,000. In all, the fans had paid more than $1.5 million to watch these midsummer classics, with most of the revenue going to the players' pension fund.

The Nationals had been expected to win this game because of their superior home run power; NL starters had combined to hit 124 home runs to the AL's 78 in the season's first half. However, a strong cross wind blowing in from left field negated that advantage and helped prevent any home runs from being hit, the first time this had happened since the NL's 7–1 win at Pittsburgh in 1944. Instead, the Nationals prevailed, thanks to the outstanding pitching of Robin Roberts, Warren Spahn, Curt Simmons, and Murry Dickson. The four veterans kept the Americans scoreless until two were out in the ninth inning.

For the second consecutive season, the war in Korea had kept Ted Williams, baseball's biggest star, out of the American League lineup. Williams, a Marine captain who had served as a jet pilot, had recently returned to the United States and was at Crosley Field. Before he threw out the first ball, players and officials from both sides gathered around the Red Sox slugger to welcome him home. Even the fans greeted his presence more warmly than they ever had in his playing days. Chosen as an honorary member of the AL team, Williams watched the game from the AL dugout. "I'm glad you're here, and I'm glad you're not playing," said NL president Warren Giles, remembering Williams's past All-Star heroics.

On the other hand, National League pitching

was so dominating that even the addition of Williams might not have helped. The Americans managed only two hits over the first eight innings, before getting three against Pittsburgh's Dickson in the ninth. All five hits were singles, as were nine of the ten NL safeties. Brooklyn's Pee Wee Reese had the only extra-base hit, a run-scoring double in the seventh. This blow, which extended the NL's lead to 3–0, was a solid single that Reese made a two-bagger with hustle. Two innings earlier, Reese had driven in the Nationals' second run when the NL scored two to break what had been a scoreless tie. Overall, it was a most gratifying day for the long-time Dodger shortstop. Reese had entered the game hitless in thirteen previous All-Star at bats and had twice grounded out to Cleveland third baseman Al Rosen this afternoon before ending his drought. He later revealed that the hits had come with a bat he borrowed from the Reds' Gus Bell, a Louisville neighbor.

AL manager Casey Stengel chose Chicago's Billy Pierce to start, the first White Sox pitcher ever given that assignment. The Dodgers' Charlie Dressen went with Roberts, even though the Phillies ace had pitched nine innings the Sunday before. Roberts had started two previous games (1950 and 1951), making him the first National League pitcher to start three All-Star Games. And because Roberts's teammate Curt Simmons had started the 1952 game in Philadelphia, Phillies pitchers had now started the last four.

Both Roberts and Pierce were highly effective, each allowing one hit in three innings. Roberts allowed a two-out single by Gus Zernial of the Athletics in the second inning, and Pierce gave up a single, also with two down, to Stan Musial in the first. Pierce's success had revived the pregame criticism leveled at Stengel's pitching selections. To oppose the predominantly left-handed-hitting National League team, the Yankee manager had chosen only one left-hander, Pierce, for his six-man staff. Stengel's omission of Boston's Mel Parnell (12-5) seemed particularly baffling.

Spahn followed Roberts with two hitless innings, although, like his predecessor, he did walk one batter. Roberts walked Boston's Billy Goodman in the first (he was out stealing), and Spahn walked Mickey Mantle, the AL's leading vote getter, in the fourth.

Allie Reynolds of the Yankees replaced Pierce in the fourth and retired the side in order. Then, after getting Roy Campanella leading off the fifth, Reynolds hit Eddie Mathews on the foot. Reynolds and Stengel protested the call, but veteran American League umpire Bill McKinley refused to change it, claiming the ball had hit Mathews's toe.

Reynolds got Bell on a pop to second baseman Goodman, but he walked Enos Slaughter to put runners at first and second. Spahn had pitched two strong innings and was ready to pitch another; however, Dressen saw a chance to break the deadlock and pulled him in favor of Richie Ashburn. It proved to be an excellent move. Ashburn came through with a single to center, scoring Mathews, the first man to appear in an All-Star Game wearing the uniform of the "Milwaukee" Braves. Ashburn had fallen behind in the count, no balls and two strikes, but when Reynolds came in high and tight with his next one, Ashburn somehow was able to stroke it up the middle. Reese's single to right scored Slaughter, and the Nationals had all the runs they would need.

Simmons replaced Spahn in the sixth and reeled off two more scoreless innings, though he was not as dominant as his predecessors. Detroit's Harvey Kuenn, the first batter he faced, hit a sinking liner to right that Slaughter grabbed with a sliding catch. In the seventh, Simmons walked the lead-off batter, Hank Bauer. After Mantle forced his Yankee teammate and Rosen popped out, Chicago's Minnie Minoso singled to right. That sent Billy Hunter (running for Mantle) to third. The tying runs were on, but Simmons stranded them by getting Yogi Berra to fly out to center fielder Bell.

Having escaped the Americans' first serious threat, the Nationals came back to add a run against Cleveland's Mike Garcia in the home seventh. Garcia had come on in the sixth and gotten into immediate trouble. Back-to-back singles by Musial and Cincinnati favorite Ted Kluszewski put runners at first and third with nobody out. This was the first All-Star appearance for Kluszewski, the muscular Reds first baseman, who had received the most votes in this year's balloting. Around 4.4 million fans had voted this year, an amount second only to the 4.6 million who had cast ballots in 1949.

After Dressen displeased the crowd by inserting Brooklyn's Gil Hodges to run for Kluszewski, Garcia came through with some excellent clutch pitching. He struck out Campanella and then got

Mathews, the NL leader in home runs and RBI, to bounce into a double play.

With one out in the NL seventh, Slaughter, playing in his tenth and final All-Star Game, beat out a grounder to short. Slaughter, who even at age thirty-seven played all out in every game, then stole second, using a fadeaway slide to avoid shortstop Chico Carrasquel's tag. One out later, Slaughter scored the NL's third run on Reese's double to left-center. Davey Williams of the Giants kept the inning alive by drawing a walk, but Garcia ended it by fanning Musial.

In the eighth, the National Leaguers extended their lead to 5–0, scoring twice against Satchel Paige of the Browns. Paige and Billy Hunter, who had run for Mantle in the seventh, would be the final players to represent the St. Louis Browns in All-Star competition. The Browns would become the Baltimore Orioles in 1954. Similarly, Zernial and Eddie Robinson, who had hit for Garcia in the eighth, would be the last players to appear in the game wearing the uniform of the Philadelphia Athletics. The A's wouldn't move to Kansas City until 1955, but their 1954 representative, Jim Finigan, didn't appear in that year's game.

Paige, a legendary figure, received an ovation when he took the mound. He got Hodges, the first batter he faced, although Larry Doby had his back against the scoreboard when he caught up with Hodges's long drive. Campanella, who was familiar with Paige from when both were in the Negro Leagues, followed with a single to center. Campy was second in the league in RBI and third in home runs. He was having another outstanding season, one that would earn him his second Most Valuable Player Award. However, like his teammate Reese, Campanella had never hit safely in an All-Star Game. His single off Paige ended a streak of sixteen hitless at bats, including three earlier in this game.

After Mathews popped to shortstop Phil Rizzuto for the second out, Paige walked Duke Snider, batting for Bell. Slaughter followed with a single to center that scored Campanella and sent Snider to third. Dickson, the lone member of the last-place Pirates on the NL squad (Pittsburgh had traded Ralph Kiner to the Cubs in June), poked a single to left, bringing Snider home with the Nationals' fifth and final run; however, when Dickson tried to stretch his hit into a double, he was out at second on a relay that went from center fielder Doby to third baseman Rosen to second baseman Nellie Fox.

Perhaps tired after his adventures on the base paths, Dickson yielded singles to the first two batters in the ninth: Chicago's Ferris Fain and the Yanks' Johnny Mize, batting for teammate Bauer.

Like Slaughter, this was Mize's tenth and final All-Star appearance, although his first as an American Leaguer. He and fellow Yankee Johnny Sain, who saw no action today, were the first former National League All-Stars to appear on the American League team.

Dickson got the next two batters: Doby flied to Snider, with Fain going to third, and Rosen popped to Hodges. Now, only Minoso stood in the way of the Nationals getting their first shutout since 1940, and he spoiled it. Minoso's second hit of the day scored Fain and saved the AL the added embarrassment of being blanked. Berra's pop to second baseman Davey Williams ended the Americans' long afternoon.

Williams's selection to the NL squad had generated its own controversy. The fans had voted overwhelmingly for St. Louis's Red Schoendienst, the National League's leading hitter, as the starter at second base. Jack Dittmer of the Braves finished second and Connie Ryan of the Phillies, third. However, Dressen decided to bypass Dittmer and Ryan and choose Williams as Schoendienst's backup, a move that had been roundly criticized. Not only had Williams finished fourth in the voting, the critics argued, but Giants manager Leo Durocher had recently benched him for weak hitting. Dressen was unmoved. "Williams is a damn good ballplayer," he said in an attempt to justify his choice.

Jackie Robinson had started the previous four games at second base for the NL, but Dressen had moved Robinson to third this season to make room for rookie Jim Gilliam. Robinson made the team nevertheless, finishing second to Mathews in the voting. Robinson was one of six Dodgers on the squad, a number one fewer than they had placed on the team for each of the last four All-Star Games.

The victory went to Spahn and the loss to Reynolds. The win was the first for a Braves pitcher, while Yankee pitchers had now been involved in eleven of the twenty All-Star decisions, winning six and losing five.

Mathews scoring a run, 1953
Eddie Mathews scores the National League's first run on Richie Ashburn's fifth-inning pinch-hit single. Associated Press Photo.

Stengel apologized to league president Will Harridge for the AL's loss. "I'm sorry I couldn't do it for you, Will, because I know you like to win," he said. The Yankee manager, the winner of the last four World Series against the National League, was now the loser to the NL in four consecutive All-Star Games. The overall American League lead, which had once stood at 12-4, was now down to 12-8.

	AL		NL	
P	Billy Pierce	CHA	Robin Roberts	PHI
C	Yogi Berra	NYA	Roy Campanella	BRO
1B	Mickey Vernon	WAS	Ted Kluszewski	CIN
2B	Billy Goodman	BOS	Red Schoendienst	SLN
3B	Al Rosen	CLE	Eddie Mathews	MIL
SS	Chico Carrasquel	CHA	Pee Wee Reese	BRO
OF	Hank Bauer	NYA	Gus Bell	CIN
OF	Mickey Mantle	NYA	Stan Musial	SLN
OF	Gus Zernial	PHA	Enos Slaughter	SLN
	Larry Doby	CLE	Richie Ashburn	PHI
	Ferris Fain	CHA	Del Crandall +	MIL
	Nellie Fox	CHA	Murry Dickson	PIT
	Mike Garcia	CLE	Carl Furillo	BRO
	Billy Hunter	SLA	Harvey Haddix	SLN
	George Kell	BOS	Granny Hamner	PHI
	Harvey Kuenn	DET	Gil Hodges	BRO
	Bob Lemon	CLE	Ralph Kiner	CHN
	Minnie Minoso	CHA	Clyde McCullough	CHN
	Johnny Mize	NYA	Del Rice +	SLN
	Satchel Paige	SLA	Jackie Robinson	BRO
	Allie Reynolds	NYA	Curt Simmons	PHI
	Phil Rizzuto	NYA	Duke Snider	BRO
	Eddie Robinson	PHA	Warren Spahn	MIL
	Johnny Sain	NYA	Gerry Staley	SLN
	Sammy White	BOS	Wes Westrum	NY
	*Ted Williams	BOS	Hoyt Wilhelm	NY
			Davey Williams	NY

+ player replaced on roster
*named as honorary member of team

American League   000 000 001- 1
National League   000 020 12x- 5

AMERICAN LEAGUE

	ab	r	h	bi	bb	so	po	a
B.Goodman, 2b	2	0	0	0	1	0	1	1
N.Fox, 2b	1	0	0	0	0	0	1	0
M.Vernon, 1b	3	0	0	0	0	2	6	0
F.Fain, 1b	1	1	1	0	0	0	1	1
H.Bauer, rf	2	0	0	0	1	1	3	0
J.Mize, ph	1	0	1	0	0	0	0	0
M.Mantle, cf	2	0	0	0	1	0	0	0
B.Hunter, pr	0	0	0	0	0	0	0	0
L.Doby, cf	1	0	0	0	0	0	1	1
A.Rosen, 3b	4	0	0	0	0	0	2	4
G.Zernial, lf	2	0	1	0	0	1	1	0
M.Minoso, lf	2	0	2	1	0	0	0	0
Y.Berra, c	4	0	0	0	0	0	4	0
C.Carrasquel, ss	2	0	0	0	0	0	2	1
G.Kell, ph	1	0	0	0	0	0	0	0
P.Rizzuto, ss	0	0	0	0	0	0	1	0
B.Pierce, p	1	0	0	0	0	1	0	0
A.Reynolds, p	0	0	0	0	0	0	0	0
H.Kuenn, ph	1	0	0	0	0	0	0	0
M.Garcia, p	0	0	0	0	0	0	1	0
E.Robinson, ph	1	0	0	0	0	0	0	0
S.Paige, p	0	0	0	0	0	0	0	0
Totals	31	1	5	1	3	5	24	8

NATIONAL LEAGUE

	ab	r	h	bi	bb	so	po	a
P.Reese, ss	4	0	2	2	0	0	1	1
G.Hamner, ss	0	0	0	0	0	0	0	0
R.Schoendienst, 2b	3	0	0	0	0	0	0	3
D.Williams, 2b	0	0	0	0	1	0	2	0
S.Musial, lf	4	0	2	0	0	1	3	0
T.Kluszewski, 1b	3	0	1	0	0	0	5	0
G.Hodges, pr-1b	1	0	0	0	0	0	1	0
R.Campanella, c	4	1	1	0	0	1	6	2
E.Mathews, 3b	3	1	0	0	0	0	0	0
G.Bell, cf	3	0	0	0	0	0	4	0
D.Snider, ph-cf	0	1	0	0	1	0	1	0
E.Slaughter, rf	3	2	2	1	1	0	4	0
R.Roberts, p	0	0	0	0	0	0	0	1
R.Kiner, ph	1	0	0	0	0	1	0	0
W.Spahn, p	0	0	0	0	0	0	0	0
R.Ashburn, ph	1	0	1	1	0	0	0	0
C.Simmons, p	0	0	0	0	0	0	0	0
J.Robinson, ph	1	0	0	0	0	0	0	0
M.Dickson, p	1	0	1	1	0	0	0	0
Totals	32	5	10	5	3	3	27	7

PITCHING	ip	h	r	er	bb	so
American League						
B.Pierce	3.0	1	0	0	0	1
A.Reynolds (L)	2.0	2	2	2	1	0
M.Garcia	2.0	4	1	1	1	2
S.Paige	1.0	3	2	2	1	0
National League						
R.Roberts	3.0	1	0	0	1	2
W.Spahn (w)	2.0	0	0	0	1	2
C.Simmons	2.0	1	0	0	1	1
M.Dickson (s)	2.0	3	1	1	0	0

BATTING
2-out RBI: M.Minoso.
RBI, scoring position, less than 2 outs: L.Doby 0–1; A.Rosen 0–1.

BASERUNNING
CS: B.Goodman (2nd base by R.Roberts/ R.Campanella).
Team LOB: 6

FIELDING
Outfield assist: L.Doby (M.Dickson at 2B).
DP: (1). C.Carrasquel-M.Vernon.

BATTING
2B: P.Reese (off M.Garcia).
2-out RBI: P.Reese 2; E.Slaughter; R.Ashburn; M.Dickson.
RBI, scoring position, less than 2 outs: R.Campanella 0–1; E.Mathews 0–1; J.Robinson 0–1.
GDP: E.Mathews.

BASERUNNING
SB: E.Slaughter (2nd base off M.Garcia/Y.Berra).
Team LOB: 7

FIELDING

Inherited Runners—Scored:
A.Reynolds 0–0; M.Garcia 0–0; S.Paige 0–0; W.Spahn 0–0; C.Simmons 0–0; M.Dickson 0–0.
HBP: E.Mathews by A.Reynolds.

GAME DATA—T: 2:19; A: 30846; Temp: Unknown; Wind: Right to left, Speed: Unknown

UMPIRES—HP: Jocko Conlan (NL), 1B: Johnny Stevens (AL), 2B: Augie Donatelli (NL), 3B: Bill McKinley (AL), LF: Larry Napp (AL), RF: Bill Engeln (NL)

STARTING LINEUPS

	American League	National League
1.	B.Goodman 2b	P.Reese ss
2.	M.Vernon 1b	R.Schoendienst 2b
3.	H.Bauer rf	S.Musial lf
4.	M.Mantle cf	T.Kluszewski 1b
5.	A.Rosen 3b	R.Campanella c
6.	G.Zernial lf	E.Mathews 3b
7.	Y.Berra c	G.Bell cf
8.	C.Carrasquel ss	E.Slaughter rf
9.	B.Pierce p	R.Roberts p

AL 1ST: 3.5 for standing room, $1.5 for bleachers; the first two levels were up from $5.5 and $4 in 1952 Ted Williams was AL captain, just back from Korea; he threw out first pitch; B.Goodman walked; M.Vernon flied to E.Slaughter-rf; H.Bauer struck out; B.Goodman was caught stealing second (R.Campanella-c to P.Reese-ss); 0 R, 0 H, 0 E, 0 LOB. AL 0, NL 0.

NL 1ST: P.Reese grounded out (A.Rosen-3b to M.Vernon-1b); R.Schoendienst flied to H.Bauer-rf; S.Musial singled to center field; T.Kluszewski popped to Y.Berra-c in foul territory; 0 R, 1 H, 0 E, 1 LOB. AL 0, NL 0.

AL 2ND: M.Mantle grounded out (R.Roberts-p to T.Kluszewski-1b); A.Rosen flied to S.Musial-lf; G.Zernial singled to left field; Y.Berra flied to G.Bell-cf; 0 R, 1 H, 0 E, 1 LOB. AL 0, NL 0.

NL 2ND: R.Campanella grounded out (A.Rosen-3b to M.Vernon-1b); E.Mathews grounded out (B.Goodman-2b to M.Vernon-1b); G.Bell flied to G.Zernial-lf; 0 R, 0 H, 0 E, 0 LOB. AL 0, NL 0.

AL 3RD: C.Carrasquel popped to R.Campanella-c in foul territory; B.Pierce struck out (R.Campanella-c to T.Kluszewski-1b); B.Goodman flied to G.Bell-cf; 0 R, 0 H, 0 E, 0 LOB. AL 0, NL 0.

NL 3RD: E.Slaughter popped to A.Rosen-3b; **R.Kiner batted for R.Roberts;** R.Kiner struck out; P.Reese grounded out (A.Rosen-3b to M.Vernon-1b); 0 R, 0 H, 0 E, 0 LOB. AL 0, NL 0.

AL 4TH: **W.Spahn replaced R.Kiner (pitching);** M.Vernon was called out on strikes; H.Bauer flied to S.Musial-lf in foul territory; M.Mantle walked; A.Rosen flied to G.Bell-cf; 0 R, 0 H, 0 E, 1 LOB. AL 0, NL 0.

NL 4TH: **A.Reynolds replaced B.Pierce (pitching);** R.Schoendienst flied to H.Bauer-rf; S.Musial lined to C.Carrasquel-ss; T.Kluszewski grounded out (M.Vernon-1b unassisted); 0 R, 0 H, 0 E, 0 LOB. AL 0, NL 0.

AL 5TH: G.Zernial was called out on strikes; Y.Berra grounded out (R.Schoendienst-2b to T.Kluszewski-1b); C.Carrasquel grounded out (R.Schoendienst-2b to T.Kluszewski-1b); 0 R, 0 H, 0 E, 0 LOB. AL 0, NL 0.

NL 5TH: Umpires moved: McKinley (hp), Dona (1b), Stevens (2b) Conlan (3b), Napp (lf), Engeln (rf); **M.Minoso replaced G.Zernial (playing lf);** R.Campanella popped to A.Rosen-3b in foul territory; E.Mathews was hit by a pitch; G.Bell popped to B.Goodman-2b; E.Slaughter walked [E.Mathews to second]; **R.Ashburn batted for W.Spahn;** R.Ashburn singled to center field [E.Mathews scored, E.Slaughter to second]; P.Reese singled to right field [E.Slaughter scored, R.Ashburn to second]; R.Schoendienst flied to H.Bauer-rf; 2 R, 2 H, 0 E, 2 LOB. AL 0, NL 2.

AL 6TH: **C.Simmons replaced R.Ashburn (pitching);** **H.Kuenn batted for A.Reynolds;** H.Kuenn lined to E.Slaughter-rf; diving catch by Slaughter; B.Goodman grounded out (R.Schoendienst-2b to T.Kluszewski-1b); M.Vernon was called out on strikes; 0 R, 0 H, 0 E, 0 LOB. AL 0, NL 2.

NL 6TH: **N.Fox replaced B.Goodman (playing 2b);** **M.Garcia replaced H.Kuenn (pitching);** S.Musial singled to shortstop; T.Kluszewski singled to center field [S.Musial to third]; **G.Hodges ran for T.Kluszewski;** R.Campanella struck out; E.Mathews grounded into a double play (C.Carrasquel-ss to M.Vernon-1b) [G.Hodges out at second]; 0 R, 2 H, 0 E, 1 LOB. AL 0, NL 2.

AL 7TH: **G.Hodges stayed in game (playing 1b);** **D.Williams replaced R.Schoendienst (playing 2b);** H.Bauer walked; M.Mantle forced H.Bauer (P.Reese-ss to D.Williams-2b) [M.Mantle to first]; **B.Hunter ran for M.Mantle;** A.Rosen popped to R.Campanella-c in foul territory; M.Minoso singled to right field [B.Hunter to third]; Y.Berra flied to G.Bell-cf; 0 R, 1 H, 0 E, 2 LOB. AL 0, NL 2.

NL 7TH: **L.Doby replaced B.Hunter (playing cf);** **F.Fain replaced M.Vernon (playing 1b);** G.Bell grounded out (F.Fain-1b to M.Garcia-p); E.Slaughter singled to shortstop; **J.Robinson batted for C.Simmons;** E.Slaughter stole second; J.Robinson popped to F.Fain-1b; P.Reese doubled to left-center [E.Slaughter scored]; D.Williams walked; S.Musial struck out; 1 R, 2 H, 0 E, 2 LOB. AL 0, NL 3.

AL 8TH: **M.Dickson replaced J.Robinson (pitching);** **G.Kell batted for C.Carrasquel;** G.Kell flied to S.Musial-lf; **E.Robinson batted for M.Garcia;** Robinson flew out to rf but the play was waved off by McKinley who had called time; E.Robinson flied to E.Slaughter-rf; N.Fox flied to E.Slaughter-rf; 0 R, 0 H, 0 E, 0 LOB. AL 0, NL 3.

NL 8TH: **S.Paige replaced E.Robinson (pitching);** **P.Rizzuto replaced G.Kell (playing ss);** G.Hodges lined to L.Doby-cf; R.Campanella singled to center field; E.Mathews popped to P.Rizzuto-ss; **D.Snider batted for G.Bell;** D.Snider walked [R.Campanella to second]; E.Slaughter singled to center field [R.Campanella scored, D.Snider to third]; M.Dickson singled to short left-center (L.Doby-cf to A.Rosen-3b to N.Fox-2b) [D.Snider scored, E.Slaughter to third, M.Dickson out at second]; 2 R, 3 H, 0 E, 1 LOB. AL 0, NL 5.

AL 9TH: **G.Hamner replaced P.Reese (playing ss); D.Snider stayed in game (playing cf);** F.Fain singled to left field; **J.Mize batted for H.Bauer;**

J.Mize singled to center field [F.Fain to second]; L.Doby flied to D.Snider-cf [F.Fain to third]; A.Rosen popped to G.Hodges-1b; M.Minoso singled to shortstop [F.Fain scored, J.Mize to second]; Y.Berra popped to D.Williams-2b; 1 R, 3 H, 0 E, 2 LOB. AL 1, NL 5.

Final Totals	R	H	E	LOB
American League	1	5	0	6
National League	5	10	0	7

21

A Record-Setting Slugfest

Baseball had dominated the news in Cleveland all spring and summer in 1954. Despite losing a Sunday doubleheader that cut the Indians' lead over the Yankees to half a game, Clevelanders remained confident that this was the year their Indians would break the Yanks' five-year stranglehold on the American League pennant. Hosting the All-Star Game only added to the baseball fever. Excitement over the game had even driven the sensational July 4 murder of Marilyn Sheppard, allegedly by her husband, Dr. Sam Sheppard, from the front pages. On game day, 68,751 fans turned out, making the crowd the second largest ever to watch an All-Star Game. Only the 1935 contest, which had been played in this same stadium and had attracted an additional 1,061 fans, exceeded the total of this gathering. However, the gross gate receipts of $292,678 collected this afternoon set a record, eclipsing by more than $100,000 the previous high, set at Cincinnati in 1953.

The hometown gathering was delighted with the American League's winning an 11–7 slugfest, a game that All-Star Game founder Arch Ward called the best ever. To make the event even more enjoyable, Al Rosen and other Cleveland players led the AL's offense. Rosen had two home runs and five runs batted in, and he combined with Indians teammates Larry Doby and Bobby Avila to drive in eight runs. The game saw seven All-Star records broken and four tied, and it ended both the AL's and manager Casey Stengel's four-game losing streak.

A seesaw battle that featured several stirring comebacks, the game was in many ways the most entertaining of any All-Star contest yet played. Ironically, it had started as a pitchers' duel between the Phillies' Robin Roberts and the Yankees' Whitey Ford. Roberts, who had also started in 1950, 1951, and 1953, was the first National League pitcher to make four All-Star starts. Stengel's naming of Ford, however, had come as a surprise. Stengel had used him for three innings of relief at Washington on Sunday, while Chicago right-hander Bob Keegan hadn't pitched since Friday and seemed the better choice.

Still, Ford was effective. He worked three scoreless innings, holding the Nationals to one hit, a second-inning single by Stan Musial. Meanwhile, Roberts, who had blanked the Americans for the first two innings, gave up a walk to Minnie Minoso and a single to Avila, leading off the third. He recovered to strike out Mickey Mantle and get Yogi Berra on a ground out, and he seemed on the verge of escaping. But Roberts, who had already been touched for nineteen home runs this season, gave up another one. He'd fanned Rosen to strand two runners in the first inning—but not this time. Rosen connected on an 0-1 pitch, and suddenly the American League was ahead, 3–0.

Rosen, the league's MVP in 1953, had gathered more All-Star votes than any other American Leaguer, finishing second overall to Stan Musial. And he'd done this at a new position, first base. Despite having been the All-Star starter at third base the past two seasons, he'd moved to first so Indians manager Al Lopez could find a place for promising rookie third baseman Rudy Regalado. By June, Regalado was back in the minors, and Rosen was back at third.

Still, Rosen had been slumping recently, partially because of a fractured index finger suffered on May 25, and had approached Stengel before the game with an offer to withdraw. Stengel conferred with Commissioner Ford Frick, and they decided to leave the decision to Rosen, who after thinking it over chose to play.

"With the bum finger and being in a slump, I was scared to death about being the All-Star Game goat," he said later. "But that strikeout made me mad, and maybe I forgot about the finger."

The roar after the home run was understandably deafening, but shortly after the fans had settled back in their seats, they were up again. Detroit's Ray Boone, a former Indian, followed Rosen's blast with another home run to almost to the same spot, just to the left of straightaway center. The blows by Rosen and Boone allowed Roberts to join Mort Cooper (1942) and Ed Lopat (1951) as pitchers who had surrendered two home runs in one inning. However, he was the first to allow the home runs back to back.

Sandy Consuegra of the White Sox took the mound in the fourth and quickly squandered the Americans' four-run lead. Consuegra, named the day before the game as a replacement for injured Cleveland pitcher Mike Garcia, retired only one man. He got Giants shortstop Alvin Dark on a fly to Mantle before yielding hits to the next five batters. Consecutive sharply hit singles by Duke Snider, Musial, Ted Kluszewski, and Ray Jablonski, along with a double by Jackie Robinson, produced four runs and finished Consuegra.

Snider, Musial, and Robinson, elected as the left fielder this year, composed the NL's starting outfield. Willie Mays, back from the military, finished second in the center-field race to Snider, despite his thirty-one home runs, which had him on a pace to break Babe Ruth's record. Yet many voters obviously believed that Snider, currently leading the league with a .367 average, was even more deserving.

Cleveland's Bob Lemon replaced Consuegra and ended the barrage of hits by getting Roy Campanella on a pop to third baseman Boone for the second out. But before Lemon could get the third, Don Mueller of the Giants, batting for Roberts, singled Robinson home with the go-ahead fifth run.

After singles by Chico Carrasquel and Minoso and a sacrifice fly by Avila against the Giants' Johnny Antonelli tied it in the home fourth, each team got a two-run homer in the fifth. Kluszewski connected off Washington's Bob Porterfield following a Snider single, and Rosen followed a lead-off base hit by Berra with his second of the game, this one off Antonelli. Rosen was the third player to hit two home runs in one All-Star Game. Pittsburgh's Arky Vaughan did it at Detroit in 1941, and Boston's Ted Williams did it at Fenway Park in 1946. Rosen's five RBI tied the mark Williams set in 1946.

Porterfield shut down the Nationals in the sixth, allowing the Americans to again take the lead in the home half. Williams, who had missed the last two games serving in Korea, led off by drawing a walk from Warren Spahn. The Boston slugger had finished second to Minoso in the voting for left field but had pinch-hit for Lemon and stayed in the game. Minoso, who had moved from left field to right, got his second hit, sending Williams to

third. Avila followed with a single to left that scored Williams, but when Minoso tried to go to third, he was out on a throw from Musial to Cubs third baseman Randy Jackson.

Minoso's failed gamble proved to be a big play. Later in the inning, the AL got infield singles from Mantle and Rosen to load the bases with two outs. Following Rosen's hit, Walter Alston of the Dodgers replaced Spahn with relief specialist Marv Grissom of the Giants. Grissom retired Boone on a fly to Mays, ending what might have been another big inning.

NL manager Alston was in his first season with Brooklyn. Charlie Dressen had managed the Dodgers to the 1953 pennant and as a result had earned the right to manage the NL in this game. But during the winter, Dodgers owner Walter O'Malley had fired Dressen after a contract dispute and replaced him with Alston. In March, at O'Malley's urging, NL president Warren Giles had appointed Alston as the All-Star manager, making him the first rookie manager so honored. O'Malley further showed his loyalty to his team and fans on game day by denying emphatically that the Dodgers would be moving to Dallas.

The Nationals failed to score against Porterfield in the seventh, as did the Americans against Grissom. That left the American Leaguers ahead, 8–7, and set up the dramatic eighth inning, one of the more interesting innings in All-Star history. In the top half, Mays, playing in the first of what would be a record-tying twenty-four games, had a one-out single against Keegan. Campanella fanned for the second out, but this would be the last out Keegan would get. Cincinnati's Gus Bell, batting for Grissom, smashed a tremendous home run to deep right-center to put the Nationals ahead, 9–8. Bell's homer and the earlier one by Kluszewski were the first ever in All-Star competition by Reds players.

Following Bell's home run, Red Schoendienst got aboard on a two-base error by Minoso, who, after a long run, dropped his fly ball near the right-field line. Dark had an infield single that sent Schoendienst to third, Snider to the plate, and Keegan to the showers.

Stengel brought in Senators left-hander Dean Stone, a twenty-three-year-old rookie, to pitch to the left-handed-hitting Snider. The count went to one ball and one strike, and as Stone prepared to deliver the next pitch, Schoendienst broke for home. Stone's throw to Berra was in time, and plate umpire Bill Stewart of the National League called Schoendienst out. His call ignited a heated protest from the National Leaguers, led by third base coach Leo Durocher and first base coach

Fox's single, 1954
Nellie Fox's eighth-inning bases-loaded single puts the American League ahead to stay. National Baseball Hall of Fame Library and Archive, Cooperstown, New York.

Charlie Grimm. They didn't dispute the out call but claimed that, in making the throw home, Stone had balked; not surprisingly, Stewart stayed with his call.

Leading 9–8, Alston called on Milwaukee right-hander Gene Conley to preserve the lead. However, this was the American League's day and — more specifically — Cleveland's day. Conley got the first batter, Minoso, on a ground ball, but Doby, batting for Stone, followed with a game-tying home run. Doby's was the second pinch-hit home run of the game and the first ever by an American Leaguer. After singles by Mantle and Berra and a walk to Rosen loaded the bases, Alston replaced Conley with Brooklyn's Carl Erskine. Stengel countered by sending Washington's Mickey Vernon up to bat for Boone. Stengel had wanted to use the Yanks' Irv Noren as a pinch hitter because of the familiarity Noren had gained with Erskine when both were Dodger farm hands. However, Noren had an injured hand and couldn't handle the bat. Erskine fanned Vernon for the second out, which brought Nellie Fox to the plate. Fox came through with a blooper into short center that scored two runs and put the AL back on top, 11–9.

In the ninth, it was Virgil Trucks of the White Sox, the seventh pitcher Stengel had used, who was being asked to protect a lead. His walk to the lead-off batter, Snider, meant that sluggers Stan Musial, Gil Hodges, and Randy Jackson might each be coming to the plate as the potential tying run. Musial was first, and twice he came close to tying the score. Before bouncing out to Vernon, he lashed two long drives that were barely foul into the right-field seats. Trucks then retired Hodges and Jackson on pop flies, giving the Americans their thirteenth victory in twenty-one games. Stone, who retired no batters, was the winner, and Conley was the loser.

Doby's eighth-inning home run had tied two records. It was the AL's fourth home run, tying the record for the most home runs by one team in a game (first set by the NL in 1951), and the game's sixth, tying the record for the most home runs by two teams combined in one game (1951). Records were also set for the most hits by both clubs (31); the most hits by one club (the AL had 17); the most runs by both clubs (20); the most runs by a losing club (the NL had 9); the most pitchers used by both clubs (13); and the most pitchers used by one club (the AL used seven).

Fox's bloop single and Stone's alleged balk were the major topics of conversation among the losers. "In spite of all the homers out there today, that was the blow that beat us," said Alston of Fox's hit.

Speaking of Stewart's call on Stone, Durocher said, "It was a disgrace. The pitcher has got to come to a stop position, and he didn't stop. That call was a disgrace. Every person in the ballpark saw the play except the one man who should have.

He just missed it and cost us one run for sure and no telling how many more."

Stengel had been optimistic before the game. "I got a good ball club," he said. "There ain't any of these fellas going for waivers. You gotta get good pitchin' though. That's the big thing."

While it wasn't the pitching that clinched it, after four consecutive losses, Stengel was nevertheless happy to have his first All-Star win.

	AL			NL	
P	Whitey Ford	NYA		Robin Roberts	PHI
C	Yogi Berra	NYA		Roy Campanella	BRO
1B	Al Rosen	CLE		Ted Kluszewski	CIN
2B	Bobby Avila	CLE		Granny Hamner	PHI
3B	Ray Boone	DET		Ray Jablonski	SLN
SS	Chico Carrasquel	CHA		Al Dark	NY
OF	Hank Bauer	NYA		Stan Musial	SLN
OF	Mickey Mantle	NYA		Jackie Robinson	BRO
OF	Minnie Minoso	CHA		Duke Snider	BRO
	Sandy Consuegra	CHA		Johnny Antonelli	NY
	Larry Doby	CLE		Gus Bell	CIN
	Ferris Fain	+ CHA		Smoky Burgess	PHI
	Jim Finigan	PHA		Gene Conley	MIL
	Nellie Fox	CHA		Del Crandall	MIL
	Mike Garcia	+ CLE		Carl Erskine	BRO
	Bob Keegan	CHA		Marv Grissom	NY
	George Kell	+ CHA		Harvey Haddix	+ SLN
	Harvey Kuenn	DET		Gil Hodges	BRO
	Bob Lemon	CLE		Randy Jackson	CHN
	Sherm Lollar	CHA		Willie Mays	NY
	Irv Noren	NYA		Don Mueller	NY
	Jim Piersall	BOS		Pee Wee Reese	BRO
	Bob Porterfield	WAS		Red Schoendienst	SLN
	Allie Reynolds	+ NYA		Warren Spahn	MIL
	Dean Stone	WAS		Frank Thomas	PIT
	Virgil Trucks	CHA		Jim Wilson	MIL
	Bob Turley	BAL			
	Mickey Vernon	WAS			
	Ted Williams	BOS			

+ player replaced on roster

National League	000	520	020-	9			
American League	004	121	03X-	11			

NATIONAL LEAGUE

	ab	r	h	bi	bb	so	po	a
G.Hamner, 2b	3	0	0	0	0	0	0	0
R.Schoendienst, 2b	2	0	0	0	0	0	1	0
A.Dark, ss	5	0	1	0	0	0	1	2
D.Snider, cf-rf	4	2	3	0	1	0	2	0
S.Musial, rf-lf	5	1	2	0	0	0	2	1
T.Kluszewski, 1b	4	2	2	3	0	0	5	0
G.Hodges, 1b	1	0	0	0	0	0	1	0
R.Jablonski, 3b	3	1	1	1	0	0	0	1
R.Jackson, 3b	2	0	0	0	0	0	1	1
J.Robinson, lf	2	1	1	2	0	0	0	0
W.Mays, cf	2	1	1	0	0	0	1	0
R.Campanella, c	3	0	1	0	1	1	9	0
S.Burgess, c	0	0	0	0	0	0	1	0
R.Roberts, p	1	0	0	0	0	0	0	0
D.Mueller, ph	1	0	1	1	0	0	0	0
J.Antonelli, p	0	0	0	0	0	0	0	0
F.Thomas, ph	1	0	0	0	0	1	0	0
W.Spahn, p	0	0	0	0	0	0	0	0
M.Grissom, p	0	0	0	0	0	0	0	0
G.Bell, ph	1	1	1	2	0	0	0	0
G.Conley, p	0	0	0	0	0	0	0	0
C.Erskine, p	0	0	0	0	0	0	0	0
Totals	40	9	14	9	2	2	24	5

BATTING
2B: J.Robinson (off S.Consuegra); D.Mueller (off B.Lemon); D.Snider (off B.Porterfield).
HR: T.Kluszewski (5th inning off B.Porterfield, 1 on, 2 out); G.Bell (8th inning off B.Keegan, 1 on, 2 out).
2-out RBI: T.Kluszewski 2; D.Mueller; G.Bell 2.
RBI, scoring position, less than 2 outs: S.Musial 0–1; T.Kluszewski 1–1; G.Hodges 0–1; R.Jablonski 1–1; J.Robinson 2–1; R.Campanella 0–1.
GDP: T.Kluszewski.

BASERUNNING
CS: R.Schoendienst (HP by D.Stone/Y.Berra).
Team LOB: 6

FIELDING
Outfield assist: S.Musial (M.Minoso at 3B).
DP: (1). J.Antonelli-G.Conley-W.Spahn.

AMERICAN LEAGUE

	ab	r	h	bi	bb	so	po	a
M.Minoso, lf-rf	4	1	2	0	1	0	1	0
J.Piersall, rf	0	0	0	0	0	0	0	0
B.Avila, 2b	3	1	3	2	0	0	1	1
B.Keegan, p	0	0	0	0	0	0	0	0
D.Stone, p	0	0	0	0	0	0	0	1
L.Doby, ph-cf	1	1	1	1	0	0	0	0
M.Mantle, cf	5	1	2	0	0	1	2	0
V.Trucks, p	0	0	0	0	0	0	0	0
Y.Berra, c	4	2	2	0	1	0	5	0
A.Rosen, 1b-3b	4	2	3	5	1	1	7	0
R.Boone, 3b	4	1	1	1	0	0	1	3
M.Vernon, ph-1b	1	0	0	0	0	1	1	0
H.Bauer, rf	2	0	1	0	0	1	1	0
B.Porterfield, p	1	0	0	0	0	0	0	0
N.Fox, ph-2b	2	0	1	2	0	1	1	0
C.Carrasquel, ss	5	1	1	0	0	2	5	4
W.Ford, p	1	0	0	0	0	1	0	0
S.Consuegra, p	0	0	0	0	0	0	0	0
B.Lemon, p	0	0	0	0	0	0	0	0
T.Williams, ph-lf	2	1	0	0	1	2	2	0
I.Noren, lf	0	0	0	0	0	0	0	0
Totals	39	11	17	11	4	10	27	9

BATTING
HR: L.Doby (8th inning off G.Conley, 0 on, 1 out); A.Rosen 2 (3rd inning off R.Roberts, 2 on, 2 out; (5th inning off J.Antonelli, 1 on, 0 out); R.Boone (3rd inning off R.Roberts, 0 on, 2 out).
2-out RBI: A.Rosen 3; R.Boone; N.Fox 2.
RBI, scoring position, less than 2 outs: B.Avila 2–2; M.Mantle 0–2; Y.Berra 0–2; M.Vernon 0–2.
SF: B.Avila.

BASERUNNING
Team LOB: 9

FIELDING
E: M.Minoso (dropped fly).
DP: (1) B.Avila-C.Carrasquel-A.Rosen

PITCHING	ip	h	r	er	bb	so
National League						
R.Roberts	3.0	5	4	4	2	5
J.Antonelli	2.0	4	3	3	0	2
W.Spahn	0.2	4	1	1	1	0
M.Grissom	1.1	0	0	0	0	2
G.Conley (L, BS)	0.1	3	3	3	1	0
C.Erskine	0.2	1	0	0	0	1

Inherited Runners—Scored:
J.Antonelli 0–0; W.Spahn 0–0; M.Grissom 3–0; G.Conley 0–0; C.Erskine 3–2; S.Consuegra 0–0; B.Lemon 1–1; B.Porterfield 0–0; B.Keegan 0–0; D.Stone 2–0; V.Trucks 0–0.

GAME DATA—T: 3:10; A: 69751; Temp: Unknown; Wind: Unknown direction, Speed: Unknown

PITCHING	ip	h	r	er	bb	so
American League						
W.Ford	3.0	1	0	0	1	0
S.Consuegra	0.1	5	5	5	0	0
B.Lemon	0.2	1	0	0	0	0
B.Porterfield	3.0	4	2	2	0	1
B.Keegan (BS)	0.2	3	2	2	0	1
D.Stone (W)	0.1	0	0	0	0	0
V.Trucks (S)	1.0	0	0	0	1	0

UMPIRES—HP: Eddie Rommel (AL), 1B: Lee Ballanfant (NL), 2B: Jim Honochick (AL), 3B: Bill Stewart (NL), LF: Tom Gorman (NL), RF: Joe Paparella (AL)

STARTING LINEUPS

National League	*American League*
1. G.Hamner 2b	M.Minoso lf
2. A.Dark ss	B.Avila 2b
3. D.Snider cf	M.Mantle cf
4. S.Musial rf	Y.Berra c
5. T.Kluszewski 1b	A.Rosen 1b
6. R.Jablonski 3b	R.Boone 3b
7. J.Robinson lf	H.Bauer rf
8. R.Campanella c	C.Carrasquel ss
9. R.Roberts p	W.Ford p

NL 1ST: G.Hamner flied to H.Bauer-rf; A.Dark popped to C.Carrasquel-ss in foul territory; D.Snider flied to M.Minoso-lf; 0 R, 0 H, 0 E, 0 LOB. NL 0, AL 0.

AL 1ST: M.Minoso flied to D.Snider-cf; B.Avila singled to left field; M.Mantle flied to D.Snider-cf; Y.Berra walked [B.Avila to second]; A.Rosen struck out; 0 R, 1 H, 0 E, 2 LOB. NL 0, AL 0.

NL 2ND: S.Musial singled to right field; T.Kluszewski grounded into a double play (B.Avila-2b to C.Carrasquel-ss to A.Rosen-1b) [S.Musial out at second]; R.Jablonski grounded out (C.Carrasquel-ss to A.Rosen-1b); 0 R, 1 H, 0 E, 0 LOB. NL 0, AL 0.

AL 2ND: R.Boone popped to T.Kluszewski-1b in foul territory; H.Bauer singled to left field; C.Carrasquel struck out; W.Ford was called out on strikes; 0 R, 1 H, 0 E, 1 LOB. NL 0, AL 0.

NL 3RD: J.Robinson grounded out (C.Carrasquel-ss to A.Rosen-1b); R.Campanella walked; On a bunt R.Roberts forced R.Campanella (R.Boone-3b to C.Carrasquel-ss) [R.Roberts to first]; G.Hamner popped to C.Carrasquel-ss; 0 R, 0 H, 0 E, 1 LOB. NL 0, AL 0.

AL 3RD: M.Minoso walked; B.Avila singled to left field [M.Minoso to second]; M.Mantle struck out; Y.Berra grounded out (T.Kluszewski-1b unassisted) [M.Minoso to third, B.Avila to second]; A.Rosen homered to very deep left-center [M.Minoso scored, B.Avila scored]; R.Boone homered to very deep left-center; H.Bauer struck out; 4 R, 3 H, 0 E, 0 LOB. NL 0, AL 4.

NL 4TH: **S.Consuegra replaced W.Ford (pitching);** A.Dark flied to M.Mantle-cf; D.Snider singled to center field; S.Musial singled to right field [D.Snider to third]; T.Kluszewski singled to pitcher [D.Snider scored, S.Musial to third]; R.Jablonski singled to center field [S.Musial scored, T.Kluszewski to second]; J.Robinson doubled to right-center [T.Kluszewski scored, R.Jablonski scored]; **B.Lemon replaced S.Consuegra (pitching);** R.Campanella popped to R.Boone-3b; **D.Mueller batted for R.Roberts;** D.Mueller doubled to right-center [J.Robinson scored];

G.Hamner grounded out (R.Boone-3b to A.Rosen-1b); 5 R, 6 H, 0 E, 1 LOB. NL 5, AL 4.

AL 4TH: **J.Antonelli replaced D.Mueller (pitching); D.Snider changed positions (playing rf); S.Musial changed positions (playing lf); W.Mays replaced J.Robinson (playing cf);** C.Carrasquel singled to left field; **T.Williams batted for B.Lemon;** T.Williams struck out; M.Minoso singled to right-center [C.Carrasquel to third]; B.Avila out on a sacrifice fly to S.Musial-lf [C.Carrasquel scored]; M.Mantle grounded out (R.Jablonski-3b to T.Kluszewski-1b); 1 R, 2 H, 0 E, 1 LOB. NL 5, AL 5.

NL 5TH: **T.Williams stayed in game (playing lf); M.Minoso changed positions (playing rf); B.Porterfield replaced H.Bauer (pitching);** A.Dark flied to M.Mantle-cf; D.Snider singled to right field; S.Musial popped to C.Carrasquel-ss; T.Kluszewski homered to deep rightfield [D.Snider scored]; R.Jablonski grounded out (R.Boone-3b to A.Rosen-1b); 2 R, 2 H, 0 E, 0 LOB. NL 7, AL 5.

AL 5TH: Umpires moved: Stewart (hp), Honochick (1b), Ballanfant (2b), Rommel (3b), Gorman (lf), Paparella (rf); **R.Schoendienst replaced G.Hamner (playing 2b); R.Jackson replaced R.Jablonski (playing 3b);** Y.Berra singled to left field; A.Rosen homered to deep leftfield [Y.Berra scored]; R.Boone grounded out (R.Jackson-3b to T.Kluszewski-1b); B.Porterfield flied to S.Musial-lf; C.Carrasquel struck out; 2 R, 2 H, 0 E, 0 LOB. NL 7, AL 7.

NL 6TH: W.Mays flied to T.Williams-lf; R.Campanella singled to right-center; **F.Thomas batted for J.Antonelli;** F.Thomas was called out on strikes; R.Schoendienst flied to T.Williams-lf; 0 R, 1 H, 0 E, 1 LOB. NL 7, AL 7.

AL 6TH: **W.Spahn replaced F.Thomas (pitching);** T.Williams walked; M.Minoso singled to right field [T.Williams to third]; B.Avila singled to left field (S.Musial-lf to R.Jackson-3b) [T.Williams scored, M.Minoso out at third, B.Avila to second (on throw)]; M.Mantle singled to shortstop; Y.Berra popped to R.Schoendienst-2b; A.Rosen singled to third base [B.Avila to third, M.Mantle to second]; **M.Grissom replaced W.Spahn (pitching);** R.Boone flied to W.Mays-cf; 1 R, 4 H, 0 E, 3 LOB. NL 7, AL 8.

NL 7TH: A.Dark popped to Y.Berra-c in foul territory; D.Snider doubled to left field; S.Musial popped to B.Avila-2b; T.Kluszewski grounded out (A.Rosen-1b unassisted); 0 R, 1 H, 0 E, 1 LOB. NL 7, AL 8.

AL 7TH: **N.Fox batted for B.Porterfield;** N.Fox struck out; C.Carrasquel grounded out (A.Dark-ss to T.Kluszewski-1b); T.Williams struck out; 0 R, 0 H, 0 E, 0 LOB. NL 7, AL 8.

NL 8TH: **N.Fox stayed in game (playing 2b); B.Keegan replaced B.Avila (pitching);** R.Jackson grounded out (C.Carrasquel-ss to A.Rosen-1b); W.Mays singled to center field; R.Campanella struck out; **G.Bell batted for M.Grissom;** G.Bell homered to very deep right-center [W.Mays scored]; R.Schoendienst reached on an error by M.Minoso-rf [R.Schoendienst to second]; A.Dark singled to third base [R.Schoendienst to third]; **D.Stone replaced B.Keegan (pitching);** R.Schoendienst was caught stealing home (D.Stone-p to Y.Berra-c); 2 R, 3 H, 1 E, 1 LOB. NL 9, AL 8.

AL 8TH: NL insisted that Stone balked which caused huge argument; **S.Burgess replaced R.Campanella (playing c); G.Conley replaced G.Bell (pitching); G.Hodges replaced T.Kluszewski (playing 1b);** M.Minoso grounded out (A.Dark-ss to G.Hodges-1b); **L.Doby batted for D.Stone;** L.Doby homered to deep leftfield; M.Mantle singled to center field; Y.Berra singled to left field [M.Mantle to second]; A.Rosen walked [M.Man-tle to third, Y.Berra to second]; **M.Vernon batted for R.Boone; C.Erskine replaced G.Conley (pitching);** M.Vernon was called out on strikes; N.Fox singled to center field [M.Mantle scored, Y.Berra scored, A.Rosen to second]; C.Carrasquel popped to A.Dark-ss; 3 R, 4 H, 0 E, 2 LOB. NL 9, AL 11.

NL 9TH: **A.Rosen changed positions (playing 3b); M.Vernon stayed in game (playing 1b); L.Doby stayed in game (playing cf); I.Noren replaced T.Williams (playing lf); J.Piersall replaced M.Minoso (playing rf); V.Trucks replaced M.Man-tle (pitching);** D.Snider walked; S.Musial grounded out (M.Vernon-1b unassisted) [D.Snider to second]; G.Hodges popped to N.Fox-2b; R.Jackson popped to Y.Berra-c in foul territory; 0 R, 0 H, 0 E, 1 LOB. NL 9, AL 11.

Final Totals	R	H	E	LOB
National League	9	14	0	6
American League	11	17	1	9

22

Tuesday, July 12, 1955

County Stadium, Milwaukee

National League 6, American League 5

(12 innings)

SERIES RESULTS: AL 13, NL 9

Stan's The Man in Brewtown

The 1955 All-Star Game started late and ended late. There was a thirty-minute delay from the scheduled 1:30 P.M. first pitch because several of the game's dignitaries had attended the funeral of sportswriter Arch Ward in Chicago that morning and were late returning to Milwaukee. Arch, of course, was the *Chicago Tribune* writer who had conceived the midsummer classic in 1933. Three days before the 1955 game, he died from heart problems in Chicago at age fifty-eight. The game's late ending came because the National Leaguers scored two runs in the seventh and three in the eighth to force overtime, allowing Stan Musial of the Cardinals to hit a dramatic game-winning homer leading off the bottom of the twelfth, winning the game 6–5.

It was fitting that the game should end with a blast into the bleachers; Leo Durocher, the manager of the Giants and the skipper of the NL squad, had gotten all of the sluggers he could onto the roster. His efforts met with criticism when he snubbed the Phillies' Richie Ashburn, the NL leader in batting average with .327 (he eventually led the league with a .338 mark). The slap-hitting Ashburn, a fine defensive center fielder, didn't have enough power to suit Leo, who at least was evenhanded in his decision. Durocher had also passed over the singles-hitting Whitey Lockman, a member of his own Giants. Both Ashburn and Lockman were left-handed batters, and Durocher said that he needed right-handers to balance the heavily left-handed starting group chosen by the poll of over six and a half million fans. Durocher's determination was reinforced by a late roster change made necessary when Roy Campanella of the Dodgers, the leading vote getter in the fan poll with over two million votes, withdrew due to an injured knee. Rather than console the critics and pick Ashburn, Durocher took his Phillies teammate Stan Lopata, a catcher with home run ability; Stan had hit twenty-two round-trippers in 303 at

bats that year. Of course, replacing an injured catcher with another catcher was certainly a reasonable thing to do, but Durocher emphasized that power hitting was the more important factor in his decision.

As a result of Durocher's decision, the NL squad had five members with more home runs than the 21 hit by Mickey Mantle of the Yankees, the AL leader at the time of the game: Ted Kluszewski of the Reds (29), Duke Snider of the Dodgers (28), Willie Mays of the Giants (27), Ernie Banks of the Cubs (23), and Eddie Mathews of the hometown Braves (22). Just behind in the totals and awaiting his starring role was reserve Stan Musial, who had 19 homers. In fact the NL squad greatly outdistanced the AL sluggers with 269 homers to 163 going into the game, not counting the five that pitcher Don Newcombe of the Dodgers had to his credit.

There was some roster controversy on the other side as well. Al Lopez, skipper of the AL, chose six players from his own Indians while bypassing other likely players, such as Bill Skowron of the Yankees, who was batting .358. No Indians had been chosen by the fans to start for the American League.

Despite the pregame focus on homers and the game-ending blow, which deservedly commanded the lion's share of media attention, the game had only four extra-base hits among its total of twenty-three hits. Musial's homer was accompanied by doubles by Kluszewski and Al Kaline of the Tigers, and a long three-run home run to center field by Mickey Mantle in the first, a ball that traveled an estimated 430 feet. Mantle's shot gave the AL a four-run advantage before the NL got to bat, and it came at the expense of Robin Roberts of the Phillies, who was shelled for the second straight year. Nonetheless, with his fifth starting appearance, Robin did tie the All-Star Game record of the Yankees' Lefty Gomez. Roberts had started each season from 1950 to 1955, except for 1952, when the honor went to his Phillies teammate Curt Simmons. While the AL batters were jumping out to this fast start, their pitchers were shutting down the NL as Billy Pierce of the White Sox and Early Wynn of the Indians combined to allow only four hits and no walks in hurling the first six innings. There was one other potential long ball, this one launched by Ted Williams of the Red Sox with two outs in the seventh inning. However, Willie Mays made a great leaping catch well above the fence in right-center, denying the Boston slugger two RBI that would have advanced the AL lead to 7–0.

Given this reprieve, the National Leaguers began their comeback with the five runs they scored in the seventh and eighth, all coming at the expense of Yankee ace Whitey Ford. However, two of these runs were unearned due to a throwing error by shortstop Chico Carrasquel of the White Sox in the seventh and a misplay by third baseman Al Rosen of the Indians in the eighth, when he missed a throw coming from right field after a hit by Henry Aaron. Rosen contended that the ball hit Randy Jackson of the Cubs, who was sliding into third base.

The 1955 season is remembered by many primarily as the year that Brooklyn won its only World Series, but the All-Star Game showed that the rest of the National League also had some excellent talent. Although Musial's homer off Frank Sullivan of the Red Sox grabbed the headlines by ending the game, The Man's teammates collected twelve hits of their own off four AL pitchers. Joe Nuxhall of the Reds allowed only two hits in 3.1 scoreless innings, helped out by a fine play far to the right by Cardinals second baseman Red Schoendienst to retire Yogi Berra of the Yankees in the eleventh on a close play that drew strenuous objections from Yogi. Winning pitcher Gene Conley, of the Braves, the sixth hurler used by NL manager Leo Durocher, earned the win by pitching the twelfth inning and striking out the side (Kaline, Mickey Vernon of the Senators, and Rosen). He received a standing ovation for this feat from his hometown crowd, cheers that were still ringing as Musial ended the game on Sullivan's only pitch in the bottom of the twelfth.

This was a record-setting day for Musial in three ways: the homer was his fourth in All-Star competition, breaking a tie with Ralph Kiner and Ted Williams; he played in his twelfth classic, passing the mark he had shared with Mel Ott and Joe DiMaggio; and his four at bats ran his total to forty-three, eclipsing the forty of The Yankee Clipper. Stan accomplished all this even though he didn't start the game; Durocher did get him in at the earliest opportunity, using him to pinch-hit for Del Ennis of the Phillies in the fourth, after Del had completed the three innings mandated for starters. Durocher raised some eyebrows by his decision to bat slugger Ennis second, but Durocher had said in advance that he was going to remove Del for Stan as soon as the rules permitted, and that he wanted Stan to get as many at bats as possible. Hence, Ennis batted near the top of the order. Prior to his heroics at the end, Musial had struck out, grounded into a double play, grounded out, and walked.

There was one injury scare, when Al Kaline smashed a double off the wrist of Eddie Mathews in the sixth inning. The Braves slugger left the game at the end of the inning and was taken to the hospital for x-rays, which revealed that there was no fracture. This play led to the AL's last run, as Berra scooted to third on the double and scored when Mickey Vernon grounded to Ted Kluszewksi, who tagged him short of the bag for the second out, Kaline moving to third. This rally ended when Jim Finigan of the Athletics struck out against Harvey Haddix of the Cardinals.

With this exciting come-from-behind victory, the National League continued its dominance in the decade with its fifth win in six years, reducing the overall American League advantage to 13–9. Manager Durocher accomplished his task even though he used everyone on his roster except pitcher Luis Arroyo of the Cardinals. AL manager Al Lopez, of the Indians, who was denied his revenge for the sweep his charges suffered in the 1954 World Series at the hands of the Giants, kept seven men on the bench: five pitchers plus catcher Sherm Lollar of the White Sox and outfielder Larry Doby of his own team. Yogi Berra caught the entire game as one of four American Leaguers to go the route (Mantle, Kaline, and Vernon were the others). Berra's effort set a record; he became the first man to catch five complete All-Star Games (Roy Campanella had shared the record with him at four). The NL had only two such "iron men": Schoendienst and Kluszewski.

	AL		NL	
P	Billy Pierce	CHA	Robin Roberts	PHI
C	Yogi Berra	NYA	Roy Campanella +	BRO
1B	Mickey Vernon	WAS	Ted Kluszewski	CIN
2B	Nellie Fox	CHA	Red Schoendienst	SLN
3B	Jim Finigan	KC	Eddie Mathews	MIL
SS	Harvey Kuenn	DET	Ernie Banks	CHN
OF	Al Kaline	DET	Del Ennis	PHI
OF	Mickey Mantle	NYA	Don Mueller	NY
OF	Ted Williams	BOS	Duke Snider	BRO
	Bobby Avila	CLE	Hank Aaron	MIL
	Chico Carrasquel	CHA	Luis Arroyo	SLN
	Larry Doby	CLE	Gene Baker	CHN
	Dick Donovan	CHA	Smoky Burgess	CIN
	Whitey Ford	NYA	Gene Conley	MIL
	Billy Hoeft	DET	Del Crandall	MIL
	Jackie Jensen	BOS	Harvey Haddix	SLN
	Sherm Lollar	CHA	Gil Hodges	BRO
	Vic Power	KC	Randy Jackson	CHN
	Al Rosen	CLE	Sam Jones	CHN
	Herb Score	CLE	Johnny Logan	MIL
	Al Smith	CLE	Stan Lopata	PHI
	Frank Sullivan	BOS	Willie Mays	NY
	Bob Turley	NYA	Stan Musial	SLN
	Jim Wilson	AL	Don Newcombe	BRO
	Early Wynn	CLE	Joe Nuxhall	CIN
			Frank Thomas	PIT

+ player replaced on roster

American League   400 001 000 000- 5
National League   000 000 230 001- 6   (12)
    0 outs when winning run was scored.

AMERICAN LEAGUE

	ab	r	h	bi	bb	so	po	a
H.Kuenn, ss	3	1	1	0	0	0	1	0
C.Carrasquel, ss	3	0	2	0	0	0	1	3
N.Fox, 2b	3	1	1	0	0	0	2	0
B.Avila, 2b	1	0	0	0	1	1	1	2
T.Williams, lf	3	1	1	0	1	0	1	0
A.Smith, lf	1	0	0	0	1	1	0	0
M.Mantle, cf	6	1	2	3	0	1	3	0
Y.Berra, c	6	1	1	0	0	0	8	2
A.Kaline, rf	4	0	1	0	1	2	6	0
M.Vernon, 1b	5	0	1	1	1	2	8	0
J.Finigan, 3b	3	0	0	0	0	1	2	0
A.Rosen, 3b	2	0	0	0	1	2	0	0
B.Pierce, p	0	0	0	0	0	0	0	0
J.Jensen, ph	1	0	0	0	0	0	0	0
E.Wynn, p	0	0	0	0	0	0	0	1
V.Power, ph	1	0	0	0	0	0	0	0
W.Ford, p	1	0	0	0	0	1	0	1
F.Sullivan, p	1	0	0	0	0	1	0	0
Totals	44	5	10	4	6	12	33	9

BATTING
2B: A.Kaline (off H.Haddix).
HR: M.Mantle (1st inning off R.Roberts, 2 on, 0 out).
RBI, scoring position, less than 2 outs: H.Kuenn 0–1; M.Mantle 1–2; M.Vernon 1–2; J.Finigan 0–1.
S: B.Avila; B.Pierce.
GDP: Y.Berra.

BASERUNNING
Team LOB: 12

FIELDING
E: C.Carrasquel (throw); A.Rosen.
DP: (1). E.Wynn-C.Carrasquel-M.Vernon.

NATIONAL LEAGUE

	ab	r	h	bi	bb	so	po	a
R.Schoendienst, 2b	6	0	2	0	0	0	3	2
D.Ennis, lf	1	0	0	0	0	1	1	0
S.Musial, ph-lf	4	1	1	1	1	1	0	0
D.Snider, cf	2	0	0	0	0	1	3	0
W.Mays, cf	3	2	2	0	0	1	3	0
T.Kluszewski, 1b	5	1	2	0	0	0	9	1
E.Mathews, 3b	2	0	0	0	0	0	0	3
R.Jackson, 3b	3	1	1	1	0	1	0	0
D.Mueller, rf	2	0	1	0	0	0	0	0
H.Aaron, pr-rf	2	1	2	1	1	0	0	0
E.Banks, ss	2	0	0	0	0	1	2	1
J.Logan, ss	3	0	1	1	0	1	1	1
D.Crandall, c	1	0	0	0	0	0	1	0
S.Burgess, ph-c	1	0	0	0	0	0	2	0
S.Lopata, ph-c	3	0	0	0	0	1	10	0
R.Roberts, p	0	0	0	0	0	0	1	1
F.Thomas, ph	1	0	0	0	0	0	0	0
H.Haddix, p	0	0	0	0	0	0	0	2
G.Hodges, ph	1	0	1	0	0	0	0	0
D.Newcombe, p	0	0	0	0	0	0	0	0
G.Baker, ph	1	0	0	0	0	0	0	0
S.Jones, p	0	0	0	0	0	0	0	0
J.Nuxhall, p	2	0	0	0	0	0	0	1
G.Conley, p	0	0	0	0	0	0	0	0
Totals	45	6	13	4	2	8	36	12

BATTING
2B: T.Kluszewski (off E.Wynn).
HR: S.Musial (12th inning off F.Sullivan, 0 on, 0 out).
2-out RBI: R.Jackson; H.Aaron; J.Logan.
RBI, scoring position, less than 2 outs: E.Mathews 0–1; E.Banks 0–1.
GDP: S.Musial.

BASERUNNING
Team LOB: 8

FIELDING
E: E.Mathews (fumble).
PB: D.Crandall.
DP: (1). T.Kluszewski-E.Banks-R.Roberts.

PITCHING	ip	h	r	er	bb	so
American League						
B.Pierce	3.0	1	0	0	0	3
E.Wynn	3.0	3	0	0	0	1
W.Ford	1.2	5	5	4	1	0
F.Sullivan (L, BS)	3.1	4	1	1	1	4

Inherited Runners—Scored:
    E.Wynn 0–0; W.Ford 0–0; F.Sullivan 2–2; H.Haddix 0–0; D.Newcombe 0–0; S.Jones 0–0; J.Nuxhall 3–0; G.Conley 0–0.
HBP: A.Kaline by S.Jones.
WP: R.Roberts

PITCHING	ip	h	r	er	bb	so
National League						
R.Roberts	3.0	4	4	4	1	0
H.Haddix	3.0	3	1	1	0	2
D.Newcombe	1.0	1	0	0	0	1
S.Jones	0.2	0	0	0	2	1
J.Nuxhall	3.1	2	0	0	3	5
G.Conley (w)	1.0	0	0	0	0	3

GAME DATA—T: 3:17; A: 45643; Temp: Unknown; Wind: Unknown direction, Speed: Unknown

UMPIRES—HP: Al Barlick (NL), 1B: Hank Soar (AL), 2B: Dusty Boggess (NL), 3B: Bill Summers (AL), LF: Frank Secory (NL), RF: Ed Runge (AL)

STARTING LINEUPS

	American League	*National League*
1.	H.Kuenn ss	R.Schoendienst 2b
2.	N.Fox 2b	D.Ennis lf
3.	T.Williams lf	D.Snider cf
4.	M.Mantle cf	T.Kluszewski 1b
5.	Y.Berra c	E.Mathews 3b
6.	A.Kaline rf	D.Mueller rf
7.	M.Vernon 1b	E.Banks ss
8.	J.Finigan 3b	D.Crandall c
9.	B.Pierce p	R.Roberts p

AL 1ST: H.Kuenn singled to left field; N.Fox singled to right-center [H.Kuenn to third]; R.Roberts threw a wild pitch [H.Kuenn scored, N.Fox to second]; T.Williams walked; M.Mantle homered to deep centerfield [N.Fox scored, T.Williams scored]; Y.Berra lined to D.Ennis-lf; A.Kaline grounded out (E.Mathews-3b to T.Kluszewski-1b); M.Vernon flied to D.Snider-cf; 4 R, 3 H, 0 E, 0 LOB. AL 4, NL 0.

NL 1ST: R.Schoendienst singled to right-center; R.Schoendienst was out trying to advance to second (Y.Berra-c to N.Fox-2b); the pitch got away from Berra, but he recovered in time; D.Ennis struck out (Y.Berra-c to M.Vernon-1b); D.Snider was called out on strikes; 0 R, 1 H, 0 E, 0 LOB. AL 4, NL 0.

AL 2ND: J.Finigan reached on an error by E.Mathews-3b [J.Finigan to first]; B.Pierce out on a sacrifice bunt (R.Roberts-p to R.Schoendienst-2b) [J.Finigan to second]; H.Kuenn lined to D.Snider-cf; N.Fox lined to R.Schoendienst-2b; 0 R, 0 H, 1 E, 1 LOB. AL 4, NL 0.

NL 2ND: T.Kluszewski popped to H.Kuenn-ss; E.Mathews popped to J.Finigan-3b in foul territory; D.Mueller popped to J.Finigan-3b in foul territory; 0 R, 0 H, 0 E, 0 LOB. AL 4, NL 0.

AL 3RD: T.Williams singled to right-center; M.Mantle flied to D.Snider-cf; Y.Berra grounded into a double play (T.Kluszewski-1b to E.Banks-ss to R.Roberts-p) [T.Williams out at second]; 0 R, 1 H, 0 E, 0 LOB. AL 4, NL 0.

NL 3RD: E.Banks struck out; D.Crandall flied to A.Kaline-rf; **F.Thomas batted for R.Roberts;** F.Thomas popped to M.Vernon-1b; 0 R, 0 H, 0 E, 0 LOB. AL 4, NL 0.

AL 4TH: **H.Haddix replaced F.Thomas (pitching);** A.Kaline struck out; M.Vernon singled to center field; D.Crandall allowed a passed ball [M.Vernon to second]; J.Finigan grounded out (E.Mathews-3b to T.Kluszewski-1b); **J.Jensen batted for B.Pierce;** J.Jensen popped to E.Banks-ss; 0 R, 1 H, 0 E, 1 LOB. AL 4, NL 0.

NL 4TH: **E.Wynn replaced J.Jensen (pitching);**

R.Schoendienst flied to T.Williams-lf; **S.Musial batted for D.Ennis;** S.Musial struck out; D.Snider flied to A.Kaline-rf; 0 R, 0 H, 0 E, 0 LOB. AL 4, NL 0.

AL 5TH: **S.Musial stayed in game (playing lf);** H.Kuenn grounded out (E.Mathews-3b to T.Kluszewski-1b); N.Fox grounded out (H.Haddix-p to R.Schoendienst-2b to T.Kluszewski-1b); T.Williams grounded out (H.Haddix-p to T.Kluszewski-1b); 0 R, 0 H, 0 E, 0 LOB. AL 4, NL 0.

NL 5TH: Umpires moved: Summers (hp), Bogg (1b), Soar (2b), Barlick (3b), Runge (lf), Napp (rf); T.Kluszewski doubled to rightfield down the line; E.Mathews flied to A.Kaline-rf; D.Mueller singled to left field [T.Kluszewski to third]; **H.Aaron ran for D.Mueller;** E.Banks popped to Y.Berra-c in foul territory; **S.Burgess batted for D.Crandall;** S.Burgess forced H.Aaron (N.Fox-2b unassisted) [S.Burgess to first]; 0 R, 2 H, 0 E, 2 LOB. AL 4, NL 0.

AL 6TH: **H.Aaron stayed in game (playing rf); S.Burgess stayed in game (playing c); W.Mays replaced D.Snider (playing cf); J.Logan replaced E.Banks (playing ss);** M.Mantle grounded out (J.Logan-ss to T.Kluszewski-1b); Y.Berra singled to right field; A.Kaline doubled to third base [Y.Berra to third]; M.Vernon grounded out (T.Kluszewski-1b unassisted) [Y.Berra scored, A.Kaline to third]; J.Finigan struck out; 1 R, 2 H, 0 E, 1 LOB. AL 5, NL 0.

NL 6TH: **A.Rosen replaced J.Finigan (playing 3b); C.Carrasquel replaced H.Kuenn (playing ss); B.Avila replaced N.Fox (playing 2b); G.Hodges batted for H.Haddix;** G.Hodges singled to center field; R.Schoendienst flied to A.Kaline-rf; S.Musial grounded into a double play (E.Wynn-p to C.Carrasquel-ss to M.Vernon-1b) [G.Hodges out at second]; 0 R, 1 H, 0 E, 0 LOB. AL 5, NL 0.

AL 7TH: **D.Newcombe replaced G.Hodges (pitching); R.Jackson replaced E.Mathews (playing 3b); V.Power batted for E.Wynn;** V.Power popped to T.Kluszewski-1b; C.Carrasquel singled to third base; B.Avila was called out on strikes; T.Williams flied to W.Mays-cf; 0 R, 1 H, 0 E, 1 LOB. AL 5, NL 0.

NL 7TH: **W.Ford replaced V.Power (pitching); A.Smith replaced T.Williams (playing lf);** W.Mays singled to left field; T.Kluszewski lined to M.Mantle-cf; R.Jackson lined to M.Mantle-cf; H.Aaron walked [W.Mays to second]; J.Logan singled to right field [W.Mays scored, H.Aaron to third]; **S.Lopata batted for S.Burgess;** S.Lopata reached on an error by C.Carrasquel-ss [H.Aaron scored (unearned) (no RBI), J.Logan to second, S.Lopata to first]; **G.Baker batted for D.New-**

combe; G.Baker flied to M.Mantle-cf; 2 R (1 ER), 2 H, 1 E, 2 LOB. AL 5, NL 2.

AL 8TH: **S.Lopata stayed in game (playing c); S.Jones replaced G.Baker (pitching);** M.Mantle struck out; Y.Berra popped to S.Lopata-c in foul territory; A.Kaline was hit by a pitch; M.Vernon walked [A.Kaline to second]; A.Rosen walked [A.Kaline to third, M.Vernon to second]; **J.Nuxhall replaced S.Jones (pitching);** W.Ford struck out; 0 R, 0 H, 0 E, 3 LOB. AL 5, NL 2.

NL 8TH: R.Schoendienst grounded out (W.Ford-p to M.Vernon-1b); S.Musial grounded out (B.Avila-2b to M.Vernon-1b); W.Mays singled to right field; T.Kluszewski singled to right field [W.Mays to third]; R.Jackson singled to right field [W.Mays scored, T.Kluszewski to second]; **F.Sullivan replaced W.Ford (pitching);** H.Aaron singled to right field [T.Kluszewski scored (RBI), R.Jackson scored (no RBI) (error by A.Rosen-3b), H.Aaron to second (error by A.Rosen-3b)]; J.Logan grounded out (C.Carrasquel-ss to M.Vernon-1b); 3 R, 4 H, 1 E, 1 LOB. AL 5, NL 5.

AL 9TH: C.Carrasquel singled to left field; B.Avila out on a sacrifice bunt (J.Nuxhall-p to R.Schoendienst-2b) [C.Carrasquel to second]; A.Smith walked; M.Mantle flied to W.Mays-cf [C.Carrasquel to third]; Y.Berra popped to J.Logan-ss; 0 R, 1 H, 0 E, 2 LOB. AL 5, NL 5.

NL 9TH: S.Lopata popped to B.Avila-2b; J.Nuxhall flied to A.Kaline-rf; R.Schoendienst singled to center field; S.Musial walked [R.Schoendienst to second]; W.Mays was called out on strikes; 0 R, 1 H, 0 E, 2 LOB. AL 5, NL 5.

AL 10TH: A.Kaline walked; M.Vernon struck out; A.Rosen was called out on strikes; F.Sullivan was called out on strikes; 0 R, 0 H, 0 E, 1 LOB. AL 5, NL 5.

NL 10TH: T.Kluszewski flied to A.Kaline-rf; R.Jackson struck out; H.Aaron singled to center field; J.Logan was called out on strikes; 0 R, 1 H, 0 E, 1 LOB. AL 5, NL 5.

AL 11TH: C.Carrasquel flied to W.Mays-cf; B.Avila walked; A.Smith was called out on strikes; M.Mantle singled to left field [B.Avila to second]; Y.Berra grounded out (R.Schoendienst-2b to T.Kluszewski-1b); 0 R, 1 H, 0 E, 2 LOB. AL 5, NL 5.

NL 11TH: S.Lopata struck out; J.Nuxhall grounded out (C.Carrasquel-ss to M.Vernon-1b); R.Schoendienst grounded out (B.Avila-2b to M.Vernon-1b); 0 R, 0 H, 0 E, 0 LOB. AL 5, NL 5.

AL 12TH: **G.Conley replaced J.Nuxhall (pitching);** A.Kaline struck out; M.Vernon struck out; A.Rosen struck out; 0 R, 0 H, 0 E, 0 LOB. AL 5, NL 5.

NL 12TH: S.Musial homered to deep rightfield; 1 R, 1 H, 0 E, 0 LOB. AL 5, NL 6.

Final Totals	R	H	E	LOB
American League	5	10	2	12
National League	6	13	1	8

23

Tuesday, July 10, 1956

Griffith Stadium, Washington DC

National League 7, American League 3

SERIES RESULTS: AL 13, NL 10

The AL Sees Reds Too Many Times

Venerable Griffith Stadium hosted the All-Star Game for the second and final time in 1956; the first time had been in 1937. The game was designated as a memorial to the late Clark Griffith, the president of the Washington team since 1920 and the man for whom the stadium was named. Griffith had died the previous October. His grand-nephew, Clark Griffith II, had the honor of throwing out the ceremonial first ball.

The biggest story before the game was the fan balloting by which the starting lineups had been chosen for several years. Ballots were distributed nationally in newspapers, magazines, and annual baseball books, but this year Bob Firestone of the *Cincinnati Enquirer* had mounted a campaign to elect as many players from the local Redlegs (as they were known for several years in response to political machinations in the nation) as possible. This effort eventually provided an estimated one-third of the total ballots cast. From the *Enquirer*'s point of view, the effort was successful because five of the eight starting nonpitchers were from Cincinnati; Stan Musial and Ken Boyer of the Cardinals and Dale Long of the Pirates were the other three. The Cincinnati ballots came in to the commissioner's office at the end of the voting period, June 22. The preliminary totals released the next day had no members of the Redlegs leading at any position. The closest NL race was between Rip Repulski of the Cardinals and Frank Thomas of the Pirates for left field. When the final tabulation was announced on June 29, the Redlegs' Frank Robinson, who would be the National League's Rookie of the Year in 1956, had come from a distant third place to win the left-field starting spot, and four of his teammates joined him. Two players who had been named to the twenty-five-man rosters were forced to withdraw before the game. They were pitcher Ray Narleski of Cleveland, who had a sore arm, and catcher Del Crandall of the Milwaukee Braves, who had an elbow problem. They were re-

placed by Herb Score of the Indians and Stan Lopata of the Phillies.

Judging by performance, the choices weren't so bad either; players from the league-leading Cincinnati team collected six of the NL's eleven hits, including the game's only two doubles by big Ted Kluszewksi, who entered as a pinch hitter for Long in the sixth. The Reds' double play duo, shortstop Roy McMillan and second baseman Johnny Temple, collected four of the six safeties, each had a walk, both were excellent in the field, and Temple had the game's only stolen base. Among other feats, they turned the game's only double play in conjunction with their teammate Kluszewski. The AL also managed eleven hits and matched the NL with two home runs. However, the NL collected four walks while the AL amazingly had none. All four home runs in the game were hit by future Hall of Famers: Willie Mays of the Giants, Stan Musial of the Cardinals, Ted Williams of the Red Sox, and Mickey Mantle of the Yankees. The crowd expected fireworks from Mantle, who hit fifty-two that year in his great triple crown season and had twenty-nine of these homers at the time of the All-Star Game. Mickey's other at bats were all strikeouts as he struggled with a lame knee that had been injured a week earlier in Boston. The homers by Williams and Mantle came back to back in the sixth inning off future Hall of Famer Warren Spahn after Nellie Fox of the White Sox, yet another future immortal, had singled; the other eight of the AL hits were scattered singles, two of which stayed in the infield. The balanced and powerful performance by the National Leaguers gave them their sixth win in the past seven games, a streak begun with a fourteenth-inning home run by the Cardinals' Red Schoendienst in Comiskey Park, Chicago, in 1950.

By the time the AL had its sixth-inning burst, the NL had built a 5–0 lead on nine hits and three walks. Billy Pierce of the White Sox started the game on the mound for AL manager Casey Stengel of the Yankees and allowed only one run in his three innings, striking out five, but that was enough to be charged with the loss. The run against Pierce was a Cincinnati affair in the third, put together from a walk to McMillan, a sacrifice by starting pitcher Bob Friend of the Pirates, and a single by Temple. Whitey Ford came on next and was quite ineffective, giving up two earned runs on three hits and a walk, while also striking out two in his one inning of work. Whitey allowed the runs on a single by Boyer and a long home run to left field by Mays, who was pinch-hitting for the Reds' Gus Bell. Jim Wilson of the White Sox allowed one run in his inning on a bunt single by Temple, two outs, and a single by Boyer. Tom Brewer of the Red Sox was roughed up for three runs on four hits and a walk in two innings. He also threw two wild pitches, advancing Kluszewski each time, the wide one in the sixth inning allowing him to score. The NL completed the game's scoring in the seventh when Musial homered to left-center and Mays walked and then scored on a hit-and-run play as Kluszewski doubled into the right-field corner. Herb Score and Early Wynn, teammates on the Indians, pitched an inning apiece very effectively: the only base runner was Temple, who walked and then stole second in the eighth inning.

The American League was victimized by three excellent defensive plays by Ken Boyer, beginning with their lead-off batter in the first inning. Harvey Kuenn of the Tigers hit a rope that was destined for left field, but Boyer made a spectacular diving stop to his left. Kuenn had similar bad luck in the fifth inning, when Boyer made a diving, backhand stop and threw Harvey out. Kuenn did get one past Boyer in the third for a single to left. The last gem by Boyer came in the seventh at the expense of pinch hitter Ray Boone of Detroit, who hit a liner that the Cardinals star snagged with a great leap. Stan Musial also made a fine defensive play in left field in the eighth inning, diving to catch a fly ball hit by Ted Williams. Unfortunately, while making the catch, Musial twisted his knee as he got his feet tangled with those of Boyer; he was replaced by Henry Aaron of the Braves. The injury proved minor, and Stan did not miss any playing time when the regular schedule resumed.

Aside from the brief explosion against Spahn in the sixth, the NL had three innings of scoreless pitching from Friend, who earned the win, two innings from Spahn, and four from Johnny Antonelli of the Giants, who closed out the game and earned a save. NL manager Walt Alston's decision to use Antonelli for four innings was greeted with some challenges because it appeared to go against the rule limiting pitching appearances to three innings. It was finally decided that, because the All-Star Game rules permitted a reliever to pitch three innings beyond the one in which he entered, no violation had occurred. Since Johnny came on with no outs in the sixth, the count on his limit of three innings began with the seventh. The record for innings pitched in a single game is six, by Lefty Gomez in 1935. Including Antonelli's appearance, there have been fifteen occasions on which a pitcher was used for more than three innings. In fact, before Antonelli's stint in 1956, it had happened twice in the 1955 game. Bob Friend ended a streak of six straight starts by pitchers from the Philadelphia Phillies, five by Robin Roberts and one by lefty Curt Simmons. Roberts was on the roster for 1956 but did not see action. There were eight NL players who were not used, and four from the AL also had great seats in the dugout for the festivities. Friend's fine pitching was all the more remarkable since he had had an abscess in his infected throat lanced two days before the game by the Giants' team physician.

The only member of the hometown Senators chosen for the American League team was first baseman Roy Sievers. He made his appearance in the bottom of the ninth inning as a pinch hitter and popped out to Boyer. Catcher Sherm Lollar of the White Sox, playing in his first All-Star Game, entered in the seventh inning, although this was the fourth time he had been named to the AL team. Lollar caught the last three innings and collected a single in two trips to the plate. However, this appearance occurred only because of an injury to Yankee star catcher Yogi Berra. In the top of the sixth inning, Kluszewski had fouled a pitch off Berra's bare hand, causing discoloration and swelling of the ring and little fingers. Berra's hand became numb, and Stengel used Lollar to bat for Yogi in the bottom of the sixth.

	AL		NL	
P	Billy Pierce	CHA	Bob Friend	PIT
C	Yogi Berra	NYA	Ed Bailey	CIN
1B	Mickey Vernon	BOS	Dale Long	PIT
2B	Nellie Fox	CHA	Johnny Temple	CIN
3B	George Kell	BAL	Ken Boyer	SLN
SS	Harvey Kuenn	DET	Roy McMillan	CIN
OF	Al Kaline	DET	Gus Bell	CIN
OF	Mickey Mantle	NYA	Stan Musial	SLN
OF	Ted Williams	BOS	Frank Robinson	CIN
	Ray Boone	DET	Hank Aaron	MIL
	Tom Brewer	BOS	Johnny Antonelli	NY
	Whitey Ford	NYA	Ernie Banks	CHN
	Johnny Kucks	NYA	Roy Campanella	BRO
	Sherm Lollar	CHA	Del Crandall +	MIL
	Billy Martin	NYA	Jim Gilliam	BRO
	Charlie Maxwell	DET	Ted Kluszewski	CIN
	Gil McDougald	NYA	Clem Labine	BRO
	Ray Narleski +	CLE	Brooks Lawrence	CIN
	Jim Piersall	BOS	Stan Lopata	PHI
	Vic Power	KC	Eddie Mathews	MIL
	Herb Score	CLE	Willie Mays	NY
	Roy Sievers	WAS	Joe Nuxhall	CIN
	Harry Simpson	KC	Rip Repulski	SLN
	Frank Sullivan	BOS	Robin Roberts	PHI
	Jim Wilson	CHA	Duke Snider	BRO
	Early Wynn	CLE	Warren Spahn	MIL

+ player replaced on roster

National League   001 211 200- 7
American League   000 003 000- 3

NATIONAL LEAGUE

	ab	r	h	bi	bb	so	po	a
J.Temple, 2b	4	1	2	1	1	2	2	3
F.Robinson, lf	2	0	0	0	0	2	1	0
D.Snider, ph-cf	3	0	0	0	0	1	1	0
S.Musial, rf-lf	4	1	1	1	0	1	2	0
H.Aaron, lf	1	0	0	0	0	0	0	0
K.Boyer, 3b	5	1	3	1	0	0	3	1
G.Bell, cf	1	0	0	0	0	1	2	0
W.Mays, ph-cf-rf	3	2	1	2	1	2	2	0
D.Long, 1b	2	0	0	0	0	2	6	0
T.Kluszewski, ph-1b	2	1	2	1	0	0	2	0
E.Bailey, c	3	0	0	0	1	0	3	1
R.Campanella, c	0	0	0	0	0	0	1	0
R.McMillan, ss	3	1	2	0	1	0	1	5
B.Friend, p	0	0	0	0	0	0	0	0
R.Repulski, ph	1	0	0	0	0	0	0	0
W.Spahn, p	1	0	0	0	0	0	0	0
J.Antonelli, p	1	0	0	0	0	1	1	0
Totals	36	7	11	6	4	12	27	10

BATTING

2B: T.Kluszewski 2 (off T.Brewer; off T.Brewer).
HR: S.Musial (7th inning off T.Brewer, 0 on, 1 out);
   W.Mays (4th inning off W.Ford, 1 on, 1 out).
2-out RBI: J.Temple; K.Boyer; T.Kluszewski.
RBI, scoring position, less than 2 outs: E.Bailey 0–1;
   W.Spahn 0–1.
S: B.Friend.

BASERUNNING

SB: J.Temple (2nd base off H.Score / S.Lollar).
CS: K.Boyer (2nd base by B.Pierce / Y.Berra).
Team LOB: 7

FIELDING

DP: (1). R.McMillan-J.Temple-T.Kluszewski.

AMERICAN LEAGUE

	ab	r	h	bi	bb	so	po	a
H.Kuenn, ss	5	0	1	0	0	0	2	3
N.Fox, 2b	4	1	2	0	0	0	1	0
T.Williams, lf	4	1	1	2	0	1	2	0
M.Mantle, cf	4	1	1	1	0	3	0	0
Y.Berra, c	2	0	2	0	0	0	10	1
S.Lollar, ph-c	2	0	1	0	0	0	4	0
A.Kaline, rf	3	0	1	0	0	0	0	0
J.Piersall, rf	1	0	0	0	0	0	1	0
M.Vernon, 1b	2	0	0	0	0	0	4	0
V.Power, ph-1b	2	0	1	0	0	0	3	0
G.Kell, 3b	4	0	1	0	0	0	0	1
B.Pierce, p	0	0	0	0	0	0	0	1
H.Simpson, ph	1	0	0	0	0	1	0	0
W.Ford, p	0	0	0	0	0	0	0	0
J.Wilson, p	0	0	0	0	0	0	0	1
B.Martin, ph	1	0	0	0	0	0	0	0
T.Brewer, p	0	0	0	0	0	0	0	0
R.Boone, ph	1	0	0	0	0	0	0	0
H.Score, p	0	0	0	0	0	0	0	0
E.Wynn, p	0	0	0	0	0	0	0	0
R.Sievers, ph	1	0	0	0	0	0	0	0
Totals	37	3	11	3	0	5	27	7

BATTING

HR: T.Williams (6th inning off W.Spahn, 1 on, 0 out);
   M.Mantle (6th inning off W.Spahn, 0 on, 0 out).
RBI, scoring position, less than 2 outs: V.Power 0–1;
   G.Kell 0–1; R.Sievers 0–1.
GDP: G.Kell.

BASERUNNING

Team LOB: 7

PITCHING	ip	h	r	er	bb	so
National League						
B.Friend (w)	3.0	3	0	0	0	3
W.Spahn	* 2.0	4	3	3	0	1
J.Antonelli (s)	4.0	4	0	0	0	1
American League						
B.Pierce (L)	3.0	2	1	1	1	5
W.Ford	1.0	3	2	2	1	2
J.Wilson	1.0	2	1	1	0	1
T.Brewer	2.0	4	3	3	1	2
H.Score	1.0	0	0	0	1	1
E.Wynn	1.0	0	0	0	0	1

* Pitched to 3 batters in 6th

Inherited Runners—Scored:
   W.Spahn 0–0; J.Antonelli 0–0; W.Ford 0–0; J.Wilson
   0–0; T.Brewer 0–0; H.Score 0–0; E.Wynn 0–0.
WP: T.Brewer 2

GAME DATA—T: 2:45; A: 28843; Temp: Unknown;
Wind: Unknown direction, Speed: Unknown

UMPIRES—HP: Charlie Berry (AL), 1B: Babe Pinelli (NL),
2B: Eddie Hurley (AL), 3B: Artie Gore (NL), LF: Bill
Jackowski (NL), RF: Red Flaherty (AL)

STARTING LINEUPS

	National League	American League
1.	J.Temple 2b	H.Kuenn ss
2.	F.Robinson lf	N.Fox 2b
3.	S.Musial rf	T.Williams lf
4.	K.Boyer 3b	M.Mantle cf
5.	G.Bell cf	Y.Berra c
6.	D.Long 1b	A.Kaline rf
7.	E.Bailey c	M.Vernon 1b
8.	R.McMillan ss	G.Kell 3b
9.	B.Friend p	B.Pierce p

NL 1ST: J.Temple struck out; F.Robinson struck out; S.Musial grounded out (H.Kuenn-ss to M.Vernon-1b); 0 R, 0 H, 0 E, 0 LOB. NL 0, AL 0.

AL 1ST: H.Kuenn lined to K.Boyer-3b; N.Fox grounded out (J.Temple-2b to D.Long-1b); T.Williams struck out; 0 R, 0 H, 0 E, 0 LOB. NL 0, AL 0.

NL 2ND: K.Boyer singled to center field; G.Bell struck out; D.Long was called out on strikes; K.Boyer was caught stealing second (Y.Berra-c to H.Kuenn-ss); 0 R, 1 H, 0 E, 0 LOB. NL 0, AL 0.

AL 2ND: M.Mantle was called out on strikes; Y.Berra singled to left field; A.Kaline flied to G.Bell-cf; M.Vernon flied to G.Bell-cf; 0 R, 1 H, 0 E, 1 LOB. NL 0, AL 0.

NL 3RD: E.Bailey popped to M.Vernon-1b in foul territory; R.McMillan walked; B.Friend out on a sacrifice bunt (B.Pierce-p to N.Fox-2b) [R.McMillan to second]; J.Temple singled to center field [R.McMillan scored]; F.Robinson struck out; 1 R, 1 H, 0 E, 1 LOB. NL 1, AL 0.

AL 3RD: G.Kell flied to F.Robinson-lf; **H.Simpson batted for B.Pierce;** H.Simpson struck out (E.Bailey-c to D.Long-1b); H.Kuenn singled to left field; N.Fox singled to left field [H.Kuenn to second]; T.Williams grounded out (D.Long-1b unassisted); 0 R, 2 H, 0 E, 2 LOB. NL 1, AL 0.

NL 4TH: **W.Ford replaced H.Simpson (pitching);** S.Musial was called out on strikes; K.Boyer singled to left field; **W.Mays batted for G.Bell;** W.Mays homered to left-center [K.Boyer scored]; D.Long struck out; E.Bailey walked; R.McMillan singled to left field [E.Bailey to second]; **R.Repulski batted for B.Friend;** R.Repulski popped to Y.Berra-c in foul territory; 2 R, 3 H, 0 E, 2 LOB. NL 3, AL 0.

AL 4TH: **W.Mays stayed in game (playing cf);** **W.Spahn replaced R.Repulski (pitching);** M.Mantle struck out; Y.Berra singled to second base; A.Kaline flied to W.Mays-cf; M.Vernon forced Y.Berra (J.Temple-2b to R.McMillan-ss) [M.Vernon to first]; 0 R, 1 H, 0 E, 1 LOB. NL 3, AL 0.

NL 5TH: **J.Wilson replaced W.Ford (pitching);** On a

bunt J.Temple singled to third base; **D.Snider batted for F.Robinson;** D.Snider flied to T.Williams-lf; S.Musial grounded out (J.Wilson-p to M.Vernon-1b) [J.Temple to second]; K.Boyer singled to center field [J.Temple scored]; W.Mays was called out on strikes; 1 R, 2 H, 0 E, 1 LOB. NL 4, AL 0.

AL 5TH: Umpires moved: Pinelli (hp), Hurley (1b) Gore (2b), Berry (3b), Jackowski (lf), Flaherty (rf); **D.Snider stayed in game (playing cf);** **W.Mays changed positions (playing rf); S.Musial changed positions (playing lf);** G.Kell grounded out (R.McMillan-ss to D.Long-1b); **B.Martin batted for J.Wilson;** B.Martin grounded out (R.McMillan-ss to D.Long-1b); H.Kuenn grounded out (K.Boyer-3b to D.Long-1b); 0 R, 0 H, 0 E, 0 LOB. NL 4, AL 0.

NL 6TH: **T.Brewer replaced B.Martin (pitching);** **T.Kluszewski batted for D.Long;** T.Kluszewski doubled to left field; E.Bailey flied to T.Williams-lf; R.McMillan singled to right field [T.Kluszewski to third]; T.Brewer threw a wild pitch [T.Kluszewski scored, R.McMillan to second]; W.Spahn grounded out (G.Kell-3b to M.Vernon-1b); J.Temple struck out; 1 R, 2 H, 0 E, 1 LOB. NL 5, AL 0.

AL 6TH: **T.Kluszewski stayed in game (playing 1b);** N.Fox singled to left-center; T.Williams homered to deep rightfield [N.Fox scored]; M.Mantle homered to deep leftfield; **J.Antonelli replaced W.Spahn (pitching);** **S.Lollar batted for Y.Berra;** S.Lollar singled to center field; A.Kaline singled to left field [S.Lollar to second]; **V.Power batted for M.Vernon;** V.Power flied to S.Musial-lf; G.Kell grounded into a double play (R.McMillan-ss to J.Temple-2b to T.Kluszewski-1b) [A.Kaline out at second]; 3 R, 5 H, 0 E, 1 LOB. NL 5, AL 3.

NL 7TH: **V.Power stayed in game (playing 1b); S.Lollar stayed in game (playing c);** D.Snider struck out; S.Musial homered to very deep left-center; K.Boyer grounded out (H.Kuenn-ss to V.Power-1b); W.Mays walked; T.Kluszewski doubled to right field [W.Mays scored]; T.Brewer threw a wild pitch [T.Kluszewski to third]; E.Bailey grounded out (H.Kuenn-ss to V.Power-1b); 2 R, 2 H, 0 E, 1 LOB. NL 7, AL 3.

AL 7TH: **R.Campanella replaced E.Bailey (playing c);** **R.Boone batted for T.Brewer;** R.Boone lined to K.Boyer-3b; H.Kuenn flied to W.Mays-rf; N.Fox popped to J.Antonelli-p; 0 R, 0 H, 0 E, 0 LOB. NL 7, AL 3.

NL 8TH: **H.Score replaced R.Boone (pitching);** **J.Piersall replaced A.Kaline (playing rf);** R.McMillan popped to V.Power-1b in foul territory; J.Antonelli struck out; J.Temple walked;

J.Temple stole second; D.Snider popped to S.Lollar-c; 0 R, 0 H, 0 E, 1 LOB. NL 7, AL 3.

AL 8TH: T.Williams flied to S.Musial-lf; Musial hurt making play; **H.Aaron replaced S.Musial (playing lf)**; M.Mantle struck out; S.Lollar flied to D.Snider-cf; 0 R, 0 H, 0 E, 0 LOB. NL 7, AL 3.

NL 9TH: **E.Wynn replaced H.Score (pitching)**; H.Aaron flied to J.Piersall-rf; K.Boyer popped to H.Kuenn-ss; W.Mays struck out; 0 R, 0 H, 0 E, 0 LOB. NL 7, AL 3.

AL 9TH: J.Piersall grounded out (R.McMillan-ss to T.Kluszewski-1b); V.Power singled to second base; G.Kell singled to right field [V.Power to second]; **R.Sievers batted for E.Wynn**; R.Sievers popped to K.Boyer-3b; H.Kuenn forced G.Kell (R.McMillan-ss to J.Temple-2b) [H.Kuenn to first]; 0 R, 2 H, 0 E, 2 LOB. NL 7, AL 3.

Final Totals	R	H	E	LOB
National League	7	11	0	7
American League	3	11	0	7

24

A Wild Ninth on the Banks of the Mississippi

The American League got back on track in 1957, winning only its second game in the last eight years. The game was an exciting 6–5 contest with each team scoring three runs in a wild ninth inning. The two teams combined for nineteen hits, and although they hit no home runs, they did pound out four doubles and a triple. It was only the fourth game out of the twenty-four that were played through 1957 to have no homers. For the second straight year, there was a controversy over fan voting for the starting nonpitchers, and once again the trouble came from Cincinnati. In the late stages of the balloting, five hundred thousand ballots arrived from the Queen City, with the result that seven of the Reds' eight regulars received the most votes at their positions; first baseman George Crowe was the only one left out. Commissioner Ford Frick cited an "overbalance of Cincinnati votes" and ordered outfielders Gus Bell and Wally Post dropped from the list of starters. The managers, the Dodgers' Walter Alston for the NL and the Yankees' Casey Stengel for the AL, chose the remaining players and all the pitchers to complete the twenty-five-man rosters. Alston included Bell in his selections, which in the seventh inning proved to be a very wise choice.

The American League dominated the early going as starting pitcher Jim Bunning of the Tigers pitched three perfect innings. Bunning was followed by Billy Loes of the Orioles, who also held the National League off the scoreboard for three innings but had a much more adventuresome time than Bunning in doing so. Loes allowed three hits, beginning in the fourth with a one-out single to the Braves' Henry Aaron, who received credit for the hit when Nellie Fox of the White Sox couldn't get the ball out of his glove after fielding it behind second base. Aaron went to third when Stan Musial of the Cardinals doubled off the right-field screen, much to the delight of the St. Louis crowd. How-

ever, Loes toughened and retired Willie Mays of the Giants on a pop-up and got a ground ball to first from Cincinnati catcher Ed Bailey. In the fifth inning, Frank Robinson of the Reds opened with a single to right-center, then was forced at second in a very unusual way when right fielder Al Kaline of the Tigers trapped a low liner off the bat of Milwaukee's Eddie Mathews, who was pinch-hitting for Don Hoak of the Reds; Kaline's throw to shortstop Gil McDougald of the Yankees retired Robinson. The inning was then ended when Ernie Banks of the Cubs pinch-hit for the Reds' Roy McMillan and grounded into a double play. The NL put no one on base against Loes in the sixth, Loes's last inning of work, thanks in part to Kaline's excellent leaping catch of a ball hit by the Braves' Red Schoendienst, who was pinch-hitting for the Reds' Johnny Temple.

In the meantime, the AL was having its way with starter Curt Simmons of the Phillies and Lew Burdette of the Braves, who relieved in the second inning. The start by Simmons for the NL was the seventh in the last eight years by a Philadelphia pitcher; Curt had one, and Robin Roberts had the other five. Simmons retired the side in order in the first but no one in the second, yielding two singles and two walks before departing. Burdette came in with the bases loaded, one run in, and no one out and retired the first two batters he faced. However, Harvey Kuenn of the Tigers drew a walk on a 3-2 pitch to force in Ted Williams of the Red Sox with the second run. Fox ended the threat by hitting a soft fly to left field. Burdette stayed to pitch three more innings, giving up harmless singles in the third and fourth. Burdette's replacement, Jack Sanford of the Phillies, allowed the third AL run in the fifth, his only inning. With one out, Bill Skowron of the Yankees doubled off the right-field screen, and Sanford sent him to third with a wild pitch, where he scored on a single by Yankee teammate Yogi Berra.

Larry Jackson of the Cardinals replaced Sanford, who had departed for a pinch hitter in the bottom of the sixth. Jackson was quite effective in his two rounds, retiring the side in order in the seventh and stranding two runners in the eighth after allowing a walk and a single. Center fielder Mays helped a great deal by catching a drive from Williams in deep left-center after a long run. The NL finally broke through in the seventh and scored its first two runs, both coming at the expense of Cleveland's Early Wynn, who did not have a good day. After retiring Musial on a line drive to Yankee center fielder Mickey Mantle, Wynn was reached for a single by Mays, a single by Bailey that advanced Willie two bases, and a pinch-hit double by Gus Bell, batting for his Reds teammate Frank Robinson, that scored both runners and must have brought a smile to the face of manager Alston, who had restored Gus to the roster. Billy Pierce of the White Sox then relieved and retired the next two batters: Mathews on a ground out and Banks on a strikeout.

The well-played 3–2 game was about to change dramatically as the teams traded three-run salvos in the ninth. In the top half, pitcher Pierce led off against new NL pitcher Clem Labine of the Dodgers with a slow roller to second base that Red Schoendienst knocked down but not could not retrieve to make a play; Pierce was credited with a hit. McDougald hit a similar ball and this time Schoendienst fumbled it as he tried for a force at second, hoping to start a double play. Fox sacrificed the runners along, and Kaline scored them both with a single to left-center. Labine fanned Mantle, but Minnie Minoso of the White Sox hit a hard shot to right-center for a double that scored Kaline with the AL's sixth run. Labine retired Skowron to end the bleeding. As the bottom of the ninth began, the game appeared to be well in hand for Stengel's crew, but the eventual victory

turned out to be a lot harder to claim than expected. Musial opened the inning with a walk, the first one allowed by an AL pitcher on the day. Mays promptly scored The Man with a triple into the right-field corner, and Pierce plated Willie with a wild pitch. The Pirates' Hank Foiles batted for Bailey, singling over second base, and Bell drew the NL's second walk of the inning and game.

The Indians' Don Mossi relieved a somewhat startled Pierce at this point, who left as the second pitcher on the day to let four straight men reach base at the start of an inning. Mathews was called out on strikes for the first out, and Banks hit a very hard ground ball off the glove of Boston third baseman Frank Malzone, scoring Foiles; the play was scored as a single. However, Bell was a little too eager and undid some of his earlier good work when he tried for third on the play and was retired easily from Minoso to Malzone, with Banks moving to second on the throw. Both managers spun their wheels again and called on players from their own teams, with Alston sending up Brooklyn's Gil Hodges as a pinch hitter for Labine and Stengel countering with his relief ace Bob Grim. Hodges hit Grim's second pitch on a line to left field, but it was right at Minoso, who hauled it in to end the game at 6–5.

The game saw an unusual mixture of good and bad pitching. Interestingly, although most of the action was in the last inning, the winning and losing pitchers were the starters since the lead never changed hands. It was Bunning's only All-Star win and Simmons's only All-Star loss. This game also marked the end of direct voting by the fans for the starting nonpitchers, as a result of the problems in Cincinnati in 1956 and 1957. It would be 1970 before the vote was returned to the fans.

	AL		NL	
P	Jim Bunning	DET	Curt Simmons	PHI
C	Yogi Berra	NYA	Ed Bailey	CIN
1B	Vic Wertz	CLE	Stan Musial	SLN
2B	Nellie Fox	CHA	Johnny Temple	CIN
3B	George Kell	BAL	Don Hoak	CIN
SS	Harvey Kuenn	DET	Roy McMillan	CIN
OF	Al Kaline	DET	Hank Aaron	MIL
OF	Mickey Mantle	NYA	Willie Mays	NY
OF	Ted Williams	BOS	Frank Robinson	CIN
	Joe DeMaestri	KC	Johnny Antonelli	NY
	Bob Grim	NYA	Ernie Banks	CHN
	Elston Howard	NYA	Gus Bell	CIN
	Billy Loes	BAL	Lew Burdette	MIL
	Frank Malzone	BOS	Gino Cimoli	BRO
	Charlie Maxwell	DET	Hank Foiles	PIT
	Gil McDougald	NYA	Gil Hodges	BRO
	Minnie Minoso	CHA	Larry Jackson	SLN
	Don Mossi	CLE	Clem Labine	BRO
	Billy Pierce	CHA	Johnny Logan	MIL
	Bobby Richardson	NYA	Eddie Mathews	MIL
	Bobby Shantz	NYA	Wally Moon	SLN
	Roy Sievers	WAS	Jack Sanford	PHI
	Bill Skowron	NYA	Red Schoendienst	MIL
	Gus Triandos	BAL	Hal Smith	SLN
	Early Wynn	CLE	Warren Spahn	MIL

American League   020   001   003-   6
National League   000   000   203-   5

AMERICAN LEAGUE

	ab	r	h	bi	bb	so	po	a
H.Kuenn, ss	2	0	0	1	1	0	0	1
G.McDougald, ss	2	1	0	0	0	0	1	0
N.Fox, 2b	4	0	0	0	0	0	2	4
A.Kaline, rf	5	1	2	2	0	0	1	1
M.Mantle, cf	4	1	1	0	1	1	4	0
T.Williams, lf	3	1	0	0	1	0	2	0
M.Minoso, lf	1	0	1	1	0	0	1	1
V.Wertz, 1b	2	0	1	1	0	0	3	0
B.Skowron, 1b	3	1	2	0	0	1	5	1
Y.Berra, c	3	0	1	1	1	0	6	0
G.Kell, 3b	2	0	0	0	0	0	0	1
F.Malzone, 3b	2	0	0	0	0	0	1	1
J.Bunning, p	1	0	0	0	0	0	0	0
C.Maxwell, ph	1	0	1	0	0	0	0	0
B.Loes, p	1	0	0	0	0	0	0	1
E.Wynn, p	0	0	0	0	0	0	0	0
B.Pierce, p	1	1	1	0	0	0	1	0
D.Mossi, p	0	0	0	0	0	0	0	0
B.Grim, p	0	0	0	0	0	0	0	0
Totals	37	6	10	6	4	2	27	11

BATTING
2B: B.Skowron (off J.Sanford); M.Minoso (off C.Labine).
2-out RBI: H.Kuenn; M.Minoso.
RBI, scoring position, less than 2 outs: A.Kaline 2–2;
   V.Wertz 1–1; Y.Berra 1–2; G.Kell 0–2; J.Bunning 0–2.
S: N.Fox.

BASERUNNING
Team LOB: 9

FIELDING
Outfield assist: A.Kaline (F.Robinson at 2B); M.Minoso
   (G.Bell at 3B).
DP: (1). F.Malzone-N.Fox-B.Skowron.

NATIONAL LEAGUE

	ab	r	h	bi	bb	so	po	a
J.Temple, 2b	2	0	0	0	0	1	3	0
R.Schoendienst, ph-2b	2	0	0	0	0	0	0	0
H.Aaron, rf	4	0	1	0	0	1	2	0
S.Musial, 1b	3	1	1	0	1	0	8	0
W.Mays, cf	4	2	2	1	0	1	2	0
E.Bailey, c	3	1	1	0	0	0	3	0
H.Foiles, ph	1	1	1	0	0	0	0	0
F.Robinson, lf	2	0	1	0	0	0	5	0
G.Bell, ph-lf	1	0	1	2	1	0	0	0
D.Hoak, 3b	1	0	0	0	0	0	1	0
E.Mathews, ph-3b	3	0	0	0	0	1	1	0
R.McMillan, ss	1	0	0	0	0	0	2	0
E.Banks, ph-ss	3	0	1	1	0	1	0	2
C.Simmons, p	0	0	0	0	0	0	0	0
L.Burdette, p	1	0	0	0	0	0	0	0
J.Sanford, p	0	0	0	0	0	0	0	0
W.Moon, ph	1	0	0	0	0	0	0	0
L.Jackson, p	0	0	0	0	0	0	0	1
G.Cimoli, ph	1	0	0	0	0	1	0	0
C.Labine, p	0	0	0	0	0	0	0	1
G.Hodges, ph	1	0	0	0	0	0	0	0
Totals	34	5	9	4	2	6	27	4

BATTING
2B: S.Musial (off B.Loes); G.Bell (off E.Wynn).
3B: W.Mays (off B.Pierce).
RBI, scoring position, less than 2 outs: W.Mays 0–2;
   G.Bell 2–1; E.Mathews 0–2; E.Banks 1–1.
GDP: E.Banks.

BASERUNNING
Team LOB: 4

FIELDING
E: R.Schoendienst (fumble).

PITCHING	ip	h	r	er	bb	so
American League						
J.Bunning (w)	3.0	0	0	0	0	1
B.Loes	3.0	3	0	0	0	1
E.Wynn	0.1	3	2	2	0	0
B.Pierce	*1.2	2	3	3	2	3
D.Mossi	0.2	1	0	0	0	1
B.Grim (s)	0.1	0	0	0	0	0

Inherited Runners—Scored:
   B.Loes 0–0; E.Wynn 0–0; B.Pierce 1–0; D.Mossi 2–1;
   B.Grim 1–0; L.Burdette 3–1; J.Sanford 0–0; L.Jackson
   0–0; C.Labine 0–0.
WP: J.Sanford; B.Pierce

GAME DATA—T: 2:43; A: 30693; Temp: Unknown; Wind:
Unknown direction, Speed: Unknown

PITCHING	ip	h	r	er	bb	so
National League						
C.Simmons (L)	+ 1.0	2	2	2	2	0
L.Burdette	4.0	2	0	0	1	0
J.Sanford	1.0	2	1	1	0	0
L.Jackson	2.0	1	0	0	1	0
C.Labine	1.0	3	3	1	0	2

* Pitched to 4 batters in 9th
+ Pitched to 4 batters in 2nd

UMPIRES—HP: Frank Dascoli (NL), 1B: Larry Napp (AL), 2B: Hal Dixon (NL), 3B: Johnny Stevens (AL), LF: Stan Landes (NL), RF: Nestor Chylak (AL)

STARTING LINEUPS

	American League	National League
1.	H.Kuenn ss	J.Temple 2b
2.	N.Fox 2b	H.Aaron rf
3.	A.Kaline rf	S.Musial 1b
4.	M.Mantle cf	W.Mays cf
5.	T.Williams lf	E.Bailey c
6.	V.Wertz 1b	F.Robinson lf
7.	Y.Berra c	D.Hoak 3b
8.	G.Kell 3b	R.McMillan ss
9.	J.Bunning p	C.Simmons p

AL 1ST: H.Kuenn flied to F.Robinson-lf; N.Fox popped to J.Temple-2b; A.Kaline flied to W.Mays-cf; 0 R, 0 H, 0 E, 0 LOB. AL 0, NL 0.

NL 1ST: J.Temple flied to M.Mantle-cf; H.Aaron lined to T.Williams-lf; S.Musial popped to T.Williams-lf; 0 R, 0 H, 0 E, 0 LOB. AL 0, NL 0.

AL 2ND: M.Mantle singled to third base; T.Williams walked [M.Mantle to second]; V.Wertz singled to left field [M.Mantle scored, T.Williams to second]; Y.Berra walked [T.Williams to third, V.Wertz to second]; **L.Burdette replaced C.Simmons (pitching);** G.Kell popped to S.Musial-1b in foul territory; J.Bunning popped to R.McMillan-ss; H.Kuenn walked [T.Williams scored, V.Wertz to third, Y.Berra to second]; N.Fox flied to F.Robinson-lf; 2 R, 2 H, 0 E, 3 LOB. AL 2, NL 0.

NL 2ND: W.Mays was called out on strikes; E.Bailey grounded out (N.Fox-2b to V.Wertz-1b); F.Robinson grounded out (G.Kell-3b to V.Wertz-1b); 0 R, 0 H, 0 E, 0 LOB. AL 2, NL 0.

AL 3RD: A.Kaline singled to third base; M.Mantle popped to R.McMillan-ss; T.Williams grounded out (S.Musial-1b unassisted) [A.Kaline to second]; V.Wertz popped to J.Temple-2b; 0 R, 1 H, 0 E, 1 LOB. AL 2, NL 0.

NL 3RD: D.Hoak grounded out (H.Kuenn-ss to V.Wertz-1b); R.McMillan flied to M.Mantle-cf; L.Burdette flied to M.Mantle-cf; 0 R, 0 H, 0 E, 0 LOB. AL 2, NL 0.

AL 4TH: Y.Berra popped to E.Bailey-c in foul territory; G.Kell flied to F.Robinson-lf; **C.Maxwell batted for J.Bunning;** C.Maxwell singled to right field; H.Kuenn popped to D.Hoak-3b; 0 R, 1 H, 0 E, 1 LOB. AL 2, NL 0.

NL 4TH: **B.Loes replaced C.Maxwell (pitching); B.Skowron replaced V.Wertz (playing 1b); G.McDougald replaced H.Kuenn (playing ss); F.Malzone replaced G.Kell (playing 3b);** J.Temple was called out on strikes; H.Aaron singled to second base; S.Musial doubled to deep rightfield [H.Aaron to third]; W.Mays popped to N.Fox-2b; E.Bailey grounded out (B.Skowron-1b unassisted); 0 R, 2 H, 0 E, 2 LOB. AL 2, NL 0.

AL 5TH: N.Fox grounded out (S.Musial-1b unassisted); A.Kaline flied to H.Aaron-rf; M.Mantle flied to F.Robinson-lf; 0 R, 0 H, 0 E, 0 LOB. AL 2, NL 0.

NL 5TH: Umpires moved: Stevens (hp), Dixon (1b), Napp (2b), Dascoli (3b), Landes (lf), Chylak (rf); F.Robinson singled to right-center; **E.Mathews batted for D.Hoak;** E.Mathews forced F.Robinson (A.Kaline-rf to G.McDougald-ss) [E.Mathews to first]; Kaline trapped ball; **E.Banks batted for R.McMillan;** E.Banks grounded into a double play (F.Malzone-3b to N.Fox-2b to B.Skowron-1b) [E.Mathews out at second]; 0 R, 1 H, 0 E, 0 LOB. AL 2, NL 0.

AL 6TH: **E.Mathews stayed in game (playing 3b); E.Banks stayed in game (playing ss); J.Sanford replaced L.Burdette (pitching);** T.Williams flied to F.Robinson-lf; B.Skowron doubled to right field; J.Sanford threw a wild pitch [B.Skowron to third]; Y.Berra singled to left field [B.Skowron scored]; F.Malzone forced Y.Berra (E.Banks-ss to J.Temple-2b) [F.Malzone to first]; B.Loes grounded out (E.Banks-ss to S.Musial-1b); 1 R, 2 H, 0 E, 1 LOB. AL 3, NL 0.

NL 6TH: **W.Moon batted for J.Sanford;** W.Moon grounded out (N.Fox-2b to B.Skowron-1b); **R.Schoendienst batted for J.Temple;** R.Schoendienst flied to A.Kaline-rf; H.Aaron grounded out (B.Loes-p to B.Skowron-1b); 0 R, 0 H, 0 E, 0 LOB. AL 3, NL 0.

AL 7TH: **R.Schoendienst stayed in game (playing 2b); L.Jackson replaced W.Moon (pitching);** G.McDougald grounded out (L.Jackson-p to S.Musial-1b); N.Fox grounded out (S.Musial-1b unassisted); A.Kaline lined to S.Musial-1b; 0 R, 0 H, 0 E, 0 LOB. AL 3, NL 0.

NL 7TH: **E.Wynn replaced B.Loes (pitching);** S.Musial lined to M.Mantle-cf; W.Mays singled to left field; E.Bailey singled to right field [W.Mays to third]; **G.Bell batted for F.Robinson;** G.Bell doubled to left field [W.Mays scored, E.Bailey scored]; **B.Pierce replaced E.Wynn (pitching);** E.Mathews grounded out (B.Skowron-1b to B.Pierce-p) [G.Bell to third]; E.Banks struck out; 2 R, 3 H, 0 E, 1 LOB. AL 3, NL 2.

AL 8TH: **G.Bell stayed in game (playing lf);** M.Mantle walked; T.Williams flied to W.Mays-cf; B.Skowron singled to center field [M.Mantle to second]; Y.Berra flied to H.Aaron-rf; F.Malzone lined to E.Mathews-3b; 0 R, 1 H, 0 E, 2 LOB. AL 3, NL 2.

NL 8TH: **M.Minoso replaced T.Williams (playing lf); G.Cimoli batted for L.Jackson;** G.Cimoli was called out on strikes; R.Schoendienst grounded out (N.Fox-2b to B.Skowron-1b); H.Aaron struck out; 0 R, 0 H, 0 E, 0 LOB. AL 3, NL 2.

AL 9TH: **C.Labine replaced G.Cimoli (pitching);** B.Pierce singled to second base; G.McDougald reached on an error by R.Schoendienst-2b [B.Pierce to second, G.McDougald to first]; N.Fox out on a sacrifice bunt (C.Labine-p to S.Musial-1b) [B.Pierce to third, G.McDougald to second]; A.Kaline singled to left-center [B.Pierce scored, G.McDougald scored (unearned)]; M.Mantle struck out; M.Minoso doubled to right-center [A.Kaline scored (unearned)]; B.Skowron struck out; 3 R (1 ER), 3 H, 1 E, 1 LOB. AL 6, NL 2.

NL 9TH: S.Musial walked; W.Mays tripled to right-field down the line [S.Musial scored]; **H.Foiles batted for E.Bailey;** B.Pierce threw a wild pitch [W.Mays scored]; H.Foiles singled to center field; G.Bell walked [H.Foiles to second]; **D.Mossi replaced B.Pierce (pitching);** E.Mathews was called out on strikes; E.Banks singled to third base (M.Minoso-lf to F.Malzone-3b) [H.Foiles scored, G.Bell out at third, E.Banks to second (on throw)]; **G.Hodges batted for C.Labine; B.Grim replaced D.Mossi (pitching);** G.Hodges lined to M.Minoso-lf; 3 R, 3 H, 0 E, 1 LOB. AL 6, NL 5.

Final Totals	R	H	E	LOB
American League	6	10	0	9
National League	5	9	1	4

25

A Singular Offense and Local Relief

The American League made it two wins in a row in 1958, winning 4–3 in the only All-Star Game ever played in Baltimore's Memorial Stadium. The city was eager to welcome the game's greatest players, and the pregame publicity was extensive. On the day of the game, the players traveled in a motorcade from their downtown hotels to the stadium. The route was described in the *Baltimore Sun* that morning, with good vantage points carefully noted. Before the day was over, there would be reason for the local fans to celebrate not only the AL victory but also the perfect three innings pitched by Billy O'Dell of the Orioles to end the game and earn a save. Many dignitaries from nearby Washington DC attended the game, including Vice President Richard Nixon, who threw out the first ball, just as he had done at the stadium's inaugural game in 1954. The 1958 All-Star Game's attendance of 48,829 was the largest to date in Memorial Stadium.

There were some off-field items of note as well for 1958. The game marked the first time in several years that the starting players were not chosen by vote of the fans. After the difficulties with votes from Cincinnati the previous two years, all starting players except pitchers were chosen by votes of players, managers, and coaches. The leagues voted separately, and no one could vote for a player on his own team. Those receiving the most votes were Frank Malzone of the Red Sox for the AL, with 186 of a possible 205, and Stan Musial of the Cardinals for the NL, with 201 of a possible 202. Musial was batting .354 at the time, second in the league to the .373 mark of the Giants' Willie Mays.

An issue that attracted even more attention was the announcement by Calvin Griffith, owner of the Washington Senators, that he would use the annual gathering of owners at the game to seek permission to move his team to Minnesota. This permission was not forthcoming, and there were assurances that the team was in Washington to stay. Of course, this stay lasted only two years; the team departed for Minneapolis following the 1960 season and was replaced by an expansion team with the same name.

Although seven runs were scored in the game, there were only seven hits. The only strikeouts were recorded by the final pitcher for each side: two for O'Dell and four for Dick Farrell of the Phillies. The game was a mixture of good and bad play, in both fielding and pitching. There were four errors, two by each side, but also four double plays, three turned by the losing National League. For the second consecutive year, there were no home runs and, even more remarkably, there were no extra-base hits for either team. The 1958 contest remains the only All-Star Game with no extra-base hits; there have been three games with only one safety greater than a single.

The offense came early, with the last AL hit a single by the Yankees' Gil McDougald in the sixth. The NL had only one base runner (on an error) after Frank Thomas of the Pirates lined a hit to right field in the third, with twenty of the last twenty-one National Leaguers to bat retired. The game started on a more promising note for the NL as Mays drilled the first pitch from AL starter Bob Turley of the Yankees off the third base bag and into left field for a hit. With one out, Musial worked the hit and run with Mays, sending Mays to third on a ground ball single into the hole on the right side. The Braves' Henry Aaron then hit a sacrifice fly to score Mays with the first run. Bullet Bob, who would go on to win the Cy Young Award at the end of the season, then lost his control, hitting the Cubs' Ernie Banks with a pitch and walking Thomas to load the bases. The first pitch to Pittsburgh's Bill Mazeroski was off the glove of Baltimore catcher Gus Triandos, being scored as a wild pitch that allowed the second run of the inning to score and the other two runners to advance. The inning nearly turned disastrous when Mazeroski hit a line drive to left field, where Bob

Cerv of the Athletics slipped as he started in for the ball. However, he recovered and made the play to end the inning.

In the second, the NL continued its assault with one out as Spahn walked on four straight pitches after one strike. He was forced at second by Mays, who then stole second and continued to third as the throw from Triandos sailed into center field. The Pirates' Bob Skinner singled Mays home, and that was it for Turley, who left with a very disappointing record of three runs (all earned) allowed on three hits, two walks, and a wild pitch in 1.2 innings. Ray Narleski of the Indians relieved, and he retired Musial on a pop-up to end the threat.

The AL was also active at the plate in the first two stanzas, taking advantage of NL starter Spahn for two runs and five hits, with Nellie Fox of the White Sox figuring prominently. The fielding problems began when lead-off batter Fox reached base on a high throw from Banks. Mickey Mantle of the Yankees sent him to third with a single that was hit farther than any other in the game, and Jackie Jensen of the Red Sox brought Fox home with an unearned run as he grounded into a double play. In the second inning, the AL scored an untainted run on three singles, including one by pitcher Narleski, who normally would not have batted but found himself at the plate when Turley's early departure forced AL manager Stengel to alter his plans. Triandos got the first of the three hits with one out. He was forced at second by Luis Aparicio of the White Sox, who went to second on Narleski's single to center and scored on a hit by his Chicago teammate Fox.

Narleski pitched a very effective 3.1 innings and left for a pinch hitter in the bottom of the fifth as the AL tied the game. The NL victim was the Pirates' Bob Friend, who succeeded Spahn and also ran into trouble. Once again, the amount of offensive activity was not reflected in the run total; the American Leaguers collected two hits and two walks but only one run, thanks to the second double play turned by the National League. Mickey Vernon of the Indians, pinch-hitting for Narleski, opened the inning with a single and moved up one station on Fox's second hit. Mantle was walked semi-intentionally on four pitches, and the only run of the inning then scored on a ground out by Jensen. The bases were refilled on an intentional pass to Cerv, and Bill Skowron ended the charge by grounding into a double play. Early Wynn of the White Sox entered to pitch the sixth and retired the only three batters he faced. The last of these outs was a line drive by Milwaukee's Del Crandall that Cerv caught while crashing into the left-field wall. Cerv reinjured his broken toe on the play and left the game, although he did not miss any regular season games as a result. Wynn received credit for the win when his teammates scored the final run of the game in the bottom of the inning, an unearned tally off Friend that saddled Bob with the loss. Malzone singled to left and, with one out, Boston's Ted Williams was safe when Thomas couldn't play his ground ball. McDougald pinch-hit for Wynn and got the game-winning hit, the last safe blow of the game, scoring Malzone. The Cardinals' Larry Jackson replaced Friend and induced Fox to hit into yet another double play, sparing the NL even more runs.

From here on, the game belonged to relievers Farrell and O'Dell. Farrell walked Mantle, the first batter he faced, then retired the next six, four of them on strikes, as the crowd expressed its admiration for his blazing fastball. The last of the six batters was Williams, who fanned. The perfect three innings by O'Dell capped off a complete stifling of the NL as the last fifteen batters went out in order.

	AL		NL	
P	Bob Turley	NYA	Warren Spahn	MIL
C	Gus Triandos	BAL	Del Crandall	MIL
1B	Bill Skowron	NYA	Stan Musial	SLN
2B	Nellie Fox	CHA	Bill Mazeroski	PIT
3B	Frank Malzone	BOS	Frank Thomas	PIT
SS	Luis Aparicio	CHA	Ernie Banks	CHN
OF	Bob Cerv	KC	Hank Aaron	MIL
OF	Jackie Jensen	BOS	Willie Mays	SFN
OF	Mickey Mantle	NYA	Bob Skinner	PIT
	Yogi Berra	NYA	Johnny Antonelli	SFN
	Rocky Bridges	WAS	Richie Ashburn	PHI
	Ryne Duren	NYA	Don Blasingame	SLN
	Whitey Ford	NYA	George Crowe	CIN
	Elston Howard	NYA	Turk Farrell	PHI
	Al Kaline	DET	Bob Friend	PIT
	Tony Kubek	NYA	Larry Jackson	SLN
	Harvey Kuenn	DET	Johnny Logan	MIL
	Sherm Lollar	CHA	Eddie Mathews	MIL
	Gil McDougald	NYA	Don McMahon	MIL
	Ray Narleski	CLE	Walt Moryn	CHN
	Billy O'Dell	BAL	Johnny Podres	LAN
	Billy Pierce	CHA	Bob Purkey	CIN
	Mickey Vernon	CLE	John Roseboro	LAN
	Ted Williams	BOS	Bob Schmidt	SFN
	Early Wynn	CHA	Lee Walls	CHN

```
National League    210  000  000- 3
American League    110  011  00X- 4
```

NATIONAL LEAGUE

	ab	r	h	bi	bb	so	po	a
W.Mays, cf	4	2	1	0	0	0	1	0
B.Skinner, lf	3	0	1	1	0	0	2	0
L.Walls, ph-lf	1	0	0	0	0	0	0	0
S.Musial, 1b	4	1	1	0	0	0	7	0
H.Aaron, rf	2	0	0	1	1	0	2	0
E.Banks, ss	3	0	0	0	0	1	2	3
F.Thomas, 3b	3	0	1	0	1	0	1	3
B.Mazeroski, 2b	4	0	0	0	0	1	4	5
D.Crandall, c	4	0	0	0	0	0	5	0
W.Spahn, p	0	0	0	0	1	0	0	1
D.Blasingame, ph	1	0	0	0	0	0	0	0
B.Friend, p	0	0	0	0	0	0	0	0
L.Jackson, p	0	0	0	0	0	0	0	0
J.Logan, ph	1	0	0	0	0	0	0	0
T.Farrell, p	0	0	0	0	0	0	0	0
Totals	30	3	4	2	3	2	24	12

BATTING
2-out RBI: B.Skinner.
RBI, scoring position, less than 2 outs: H.Aaron 1–1;
   B.Mazeroski 0–1.
SF: H.Aaron.
GDP: B.Mazeroski.

BASERUNNING
SB: W.Mays (2nd base off B.Turley/G.Triandos).
Team LOB: 5

FIELDING
E: E.Banks (throw); F.Thomas (fumble).
DP: (3). F.Thomas-B.Mazeroski-S.Musial; E.Banks-
   B.Mazeroski-S.Musial [2].

AMERICAN LEAGUE

	ab	r	h	bi	bb	so	po	a
N.Fox, 2b	4	1	2	1	0	0	5	3
M.Mantle, cf	2	0	1	0	2	0	3	0
J.Jensen, rf	4	0	0	1	0	1	1	0
B.Cerv, lf	2	0	1	0	1	0	4	0
B.O'Dell, p	0	0	0	0	0	0	0	0
B.Skowron, 1b	4	0	0	0	0	1	8	0
F.Malzone, 3b	4	1	1	0	0	1	0	2
G.Triandos, c	2	0	1	0	0	0	1	0
Y.Berra, ph-c	2	0	0	0	0	0	3	0
L.Aparicio, ss	2	1	0	0	0	0	1	1
T.Williams, ph-lf	2	0	0	0	0	1	1	0
A.Kaline, lf	0	0	0	0	0	0	0	0
B.Turley, p	0	0	0	0	0	0	0	0
R.Narleski, p	1	0	1	0	0	0	0	0
M.Vernon, ph	1	1	1	0	0	0	0	0
E.Wynn, p	0	0	0	0	0	0	0	0
G.McDougald, ph-ss	1	0	1	1	0	0	0	3
Totals	31	4	9	3	3	4	27	9

BATTING
2-out RBI: N.Fox.
RBI, scoring position, less than 2 outs: N.Fox 0–1;
   J.Jensen 1–2; B.Skowron 0–2; G.McDougald 1–1.
S: B.O'Dell.
GDP: N.Fox; J.Jensen; B.Skowron.

BASERUNNING
Team LOB: 7

FIELDING
E: G.Triandos (throw); N.Fox (fumble).
DP: (1). F.Malzone-N.Fox-B.Skowron.

PITCHING	ip	h	r	er	bb	so
National League						
W.Spahn	3.0	5	2	1	0	0
B.Friend (L)	2.1	4	2	1	2	0
L.Jackson	0.2	0	0	0	0	0
T.Farrell	2.0	0	0	0	1	4
American League						
B.Turley	1.2	3	3	3	2	0
R.Narleski	3.1	1	0	0	1	0
E.Wynn (W)	1.0	0	0	0	0	0
B.O'Dell (S)	3.0	0	0	0	0	2

Inherited Runners—Scored:
   B.Friend 0–0; L.Jackson 2–0; T.Farrell 0–0;
   R.Narleski 1–0; E.Wynn 0–0; B.O'Dell 0–0.
IBB: B.Cerv by B.Friend.
HBP: E.Banks by B.Turley.
WP: B.Turley

GAME DATA—T: 2:13; A: 48829; Temp: Unknown;
Wind: Unknown direction, Speed: Unknown

UMPIRES—HP: Eddie Rommel (AL), 1B: Tom Gorman
(NL), 2B: Bill McKinley (AL), 3B: Jocko Conlan (NL),
LF: Frank Umont (AL), RF: Frank Secory (NL)

STARTING LINEUPS

	National League	*American League*
1.	W.Mays cf	N.Fox 2b
2.	B.Skinner lf	M.Mantle cf
3.	S.Musial 1b	J.Jensen rf
4.	H.Aaron rf	B.Cerv lf
5.	E.Banks ss	B.Skowron 1b
6.	F.Thomas 3b	F.Malzone 3b
7.	B.Mazeroski 2b	G.Triandos c
8.	D.Crandall c	L.Aparicio ss
9.	W.Spahn p	B.Turley p

NL 1ST: W.Mays singled to third base; B.Skinner lined to J.Jensen-rf; S.Musial singled to right field [W.Mays to third]; H.Aaron out on a sacrifice fly to M.Mantle-cf [W.Mays scored]; E.Banks was hit by a pitch [S.Musial to second]; F.Thomas walked [S.Musial to third, E.Banks to second]; B.Turley threw a wild pitch [S.Musial scored, E.Banks to third, F.Thomas to second]; B.Mazeroski lined to B.Cerv-lf; 2 R, 2 H, 0 E, 2 LOB. NL 2, AL 0.

AL 1ST: N.Fox reached on an error by E.Banks-ss [N.Fox to first]; M.Mantle singled to left-center [N.Fox to third]; J.Jensen grounded into a double play (F.Thomas-3b to B.Mazeroski-2b to S.Musial-1b) [N.Fox scored (unearned) (no RBI), M.Mantle out at second]; B.Cerv singled to center field; B.Skowron flied to H.Aaron-rf; 1 R (0 ER), 2 H, 1 E, 1 LOB. NL 2, AL 1.

NL 2ND: D.Crandall flied to B.Cerv-lf; W.Spahn walked; W.Mays forced W.Spahn (F.Malzone-3b to N.Fox-2b) [W.Mays to first]; W.Mays stole second [W.Mays to third (error by G.Triandos-c)]; B.Skinner singled to left field [W.Mays scored]; **R.Narleski replaced B.Turley (pitching)**; S.Musial popped to N.Fox-2b; 1 R, 1 H, 1 E, 1 LOB. NL 3, AL 1.

AL 2ND: F.Malzone flied to B.Skinner-lf; G.Triandos singled to center field; L.Aparicio forced G.Triandos (B.Mazeroski-2b to E.Banks-ss) [L.Aparicio to first]; R.Narleski singled to center field [L.Aparicio to second]; N.Fox singled to left field [L.Aparicio scored, R.Narleski to second]; M.Mantle flied to W.Mays-cf; 1 R, 3 H, 0 E, 2 LOB. NL 3, AL 2.

NL 3RD: H.Aaron walked; E.Banks popped to N.Fox-2b; F.Thomas singled to right field [H.Aaron to second]; B.Mazeroski grounded into a double play (F.Malzone-3b to N.Fox-2b to B.Skowron-1b) [F.Thomas out at second]; 0 R, 1 H, 0 E, 1 LOB. NL 3, AL 2.

AL 3RD: J.Jensen flied to B.Skinner-lf; B.Cerv flied to H.Aaron-rf; B.Skowron grounded out (W.Spahn-p to S.Musial-1b); 0 R, 0 H, 0 E, 0 LOB. NL 3, AL 2.

NL 4TH: D.Crandall flied to B.Cerv-lf; **D.Blasingame batted for W.Spahn**; D.Blasingame flied to M.Mantle-cf; W.Mays popped to B.Skowron-1b in foul territory; 0 R, 0 H, 0 E, 0 LOB. NL 3, AL 2.

AL 4TH: **B.Friend replaced D.Blasingame (pitching)**; F.Malzone popped to E.Banks-ss; G.Triandos popped to D.Crandall-c in foul territory; L.Aparicio grounded out (F.Thomas-3b to S.Musial-1b); 0 R, 0 H, 0 E, 0 LOB. NL 3, AL 2.

NL 5TH: B.Skinner reached on an error by N.Fox-2b [B.Skinner to first]; S.Musial popped to L.Aparicio-ss; H.Aaron flied to M.Mantle-cf; E.Banks grounded out (L.Aparicio-ss to B.Skowron-1b); 0 R, 0 H, 1 E, 1 LOB. NL 3, AL 2.

AL 5TH: Umpires moved: Conlan (hp), McKinley (1b), Gorman (2b), Rommel (3B); the outfield umpires did not move; **M.Vernon batted for R.Narleski**; M.Vernon singled to right field; N.Fox singled to right field [M.Vernon to second]; M.Mantle walked [M.Vernon to third, N.Fox to second]; J.Jensen grounded out (B.Mazeroski-2b to S.Musial-1b) [M.Vernon scored, N.Fox to third, M.Mantle to second]; B.Cerv was walked intentionally; B.Skowron grounded into a double play (E.Banks-ss to B.Mazeroski-2b to S.Musial-1b) [B.Cerv out at second]; 1 R, 2 H, 0 E, 2 LOB. NL 3, AL 3.

NL 6TH: **E.Wynn replaced M.Vernon (pitching)**; F.Thomas popped to G.Triandos-c in foul territory; B.Mazeroski grounded out (N.Fox-2b to B.Skowron-1b); D.Crandall lined to B.Cerv-lf; 0 R, 0 H, 0 E, 0 LOB. NL 3, AL 3.

AL 6TH: F.Malzone singled to left field; **Y.Berra batted for G.Triandos**; Y.Berra popped to F.Thomas-3b; **T.Williams batted for L.Aparicio**; T.Williams reached on an error by F.Thomas-3b [F.Malzone to second, T.Williams to first]; **G.McDougald batted for E.Wynn**; G.McDougald singled to left-center [F.Malzone scored (unearned), T.Williams to second]; **L.Jackson replaced B.Friend (pitching)**; N.Fox grounded into a double play (E.Banks-ss to B.Mazeroski-2b to S.Musial-1b) [G.McDougald out at second]; 1 R (0 ER), 2 H, 1 E, 1 LOB. NL 3, AL 4.

NL 7TH: **G.McDougald stayed in game (playing ss)**; **T.Williams stayed in game (playing lf)**; **Y.Berra stayed in game (playing c)**; **B.O'Dell replaced B.Cerv (pitching)**; **J.Logan batted for L.Jackson**; J.Logan lined to T.Williams-lf; W.Mays grounded out (G.McDougald-ss to B.Skowron-1b); **L.Walls batted for B.Skinner**; L.Walls grounded out (N.Fox-2b to B.Skowron-1b); 0 R, 0 H, 0 E, 0 LOB. NL 3, AL 4.

AL 7TH: **L.Walls stayed in game (playing lf)**; **T.Farrell replaced J.Logan (pitching)**; M.Mantle walked; J.Jensen was called out on strikes; B.O'Dell out on a sacrifice bunt (F.Thomas-3b to B.Mazer-oski-2b) [M.Mantle to second]; B.Skowron struck out; 0 R, 0 H, 0 E, 1 LOB. NL 3, AL 4.

NL 8TH: S.Musial grounded out (G.McDougald-ss to B.Skowron-1b); H.Aaron grounded out (G.McDougald-ss to B.Skowron-1b); E.Banks struck out; 0 R, 0 H, 0 E, 0 LOB. NL 3, AL 4.

AL 8TH: F.Malzone was called out on strikes; Y.Berra grounded out (E.Banks-ss to S.Musial-1b); T.Williams struck out; 0 R, 0 H, 0 E, 0 LOB. NL 3, AL 4.

NL 9TH: **A.Kaline replaced T.Williams (playing lf);** F.Thomas popped to Y.Berra-c in foul territory; B.Mazeroski struck out; D.Crandall popped to N.Fox-2b; 0 R, 0 H, 0 E, 0 LOB. NL 3, AL 4.

Final Totals	R	H	E	LOB
National League	3	4	2	5
American League	4	9	2	7

GAME 26

Late NL Rally Saves Face

The biggest story for the All-Star Game in 1959 was that two contests were played for the first time. Breaking from tradition has never been easy for Major League Baseball, and there was plenty of criticism when the decision to play a second game was announced early in the season. Veteran sportswriters denounced the plan as a move that would cheapen the image of the game. The reason for doubling the All-Star pleasure was simple: money. The three recipients of the additional income were to be the players' pension fund, youth baseball, and old-timers who had played before the start of the pension plan in 1947. The players received 60 percent of the broadcast revenue for each game and the same amount of the gate receipts for the second game. In all, the pension fund gained a bit over $300,000 in additional funds. This money was applied to the fund's back-service obligations.

For the second straight year, the starting lineups were chosen by a poll of players, managers, and coaches, with the restriction that no one could vote for a player on his own team. Henry Aaron of the Braves was the first player to be a unanimous choice, receiving votes on all 208 ballots from the seven other NL clubs. Managers Casey Stengel of the Yankees and Fred Haney of the Braves made the selections to complete the rosters.

The first contest was the regularly scheduled one in Pittsburgh on July 7, which was held as part of the Smokey City's bicentennial celebration; for the second consecutive year, Vice President Richard Nixon threw out the first ball. The game began as a pitching duel, with starters Don Drysdale of the Dodgers and Early Wynn of the White Sox leading the way. Big D, making his first All-Star appearance, retired all nine batters he faced, striking out four of them. Wynn yielded a homer to Eddie Mathews of the Braves in the first and a double to Ernie Banks of the Cubs and a walk to Wally Moon of the Dodgers in the second, but he

handled everyone else. The Braves' Lew Burdette and the Yanks' Ryne Duren continued the pitching mastery through the sixth inning, with the only scoring coming in the fourth as the AL tied the game at 1–1 on a homer by Detroit's Al Kaline. Burdette got into some two-out trouble in the sixth when Kaline hit a grounder through the legs of Mathews for an error. Bill Skowron of the Yankees moved the Detroit star to third with his second single of the day, but the fidgety Milwaukee right-hander ended the threat by getting Cleveland's Rocky Colavito to hit into a force play.

The offenses came to life in the seventh and eighth innings as the NL scored twice in each frame and the AL plated three in the eighth to make the final score 5–4 in favor of the National League. The victims on the AL side were Jim Bunning of the Tigers and Whitey Ford of the Yankees. Ernie Banks greeted Bunning with his second double of the game, scoring on a single by the Braves' Del Crandall. Ford was battered in the eighth as he retired only one batter on a sacrifice while yielding two singles and a game-winning triple (to Willie Mays of the Giants) in one-third of an inning; Whitey was charged with the loss. With that triple, which short-hopped the right-center-field wall some 435 feet away, Mays collected his fourth straight All-Star hit against Ford, who never retired him. The other three hits were a pair of singles in 1955 and a home run in 1956.

The three runs for the AL in the eighth came at the expense of Roy Face, the Pirates' ace reliever, who came into the game with a remarkable 12-0 record on the way to a mark of 18-1 for the season, all in relief. After retiring the side on two strikeouts and a ground ball in the seventh and getting the first two batters on pop-ups in the eighth, Face disappointed the hometown crowd as he was touched for two walks, two singles, and a two-run double down the third-base line by the Orioles' Gus Triandos. Johnny Antonelli of the Giants relieved Face, gave up a walk to reload the bases, then ended the inning on a force out by Sherm

Lollar of the White Sox. This brief appearance (he threw only six pitches) was enough to earn Antonelli the win because he was the pitcher of record when the NL scored the decisive runs in the eighth. In the ninth inning, Nellie Fox of the White Sox got to second on a single and a wild pitch after just missing a home run on a long foul. However, the Cubs' Don Elston allowed nothing else while he earned a save.

Stengel used all but three of his players, while Haney kept eight NL stars on the bench, including Frank Robinson and Vada Pinson of the Reds, Bill White and Joe Cunningham of the Cardinals, and catchers Smoky Burgess of the Pirates and Hal Smith of the Cardinals. In the meantime, Crandall caught the entire game and Aaron went the distance in right field. Stengel received some criticism about the timing of his pitching changes and some of his pinch-hitting selections, but he defended himself vigorously after the game. As he noted, using six-time batting champ Ted Williams of the Red Sox as a pinch hitter seems pretty reasonable, even if Williams did replace slugger Colavito. The Kid walked as Rocky's replacement, loading the bases before the double by Triandos.

	AL		NL	
P	Early Wynn	CHA	Don Drysdale	LAN
C	Gus Triandos	BAL	Del Crandall	MIL
1B	Bill Skowron	NYA	Orlando Cepeda	SFN
2B	Nellie Fox	CHA	Johnny Temple	CIN
3B	Harmon Killebrew	WAS	Eddie Mathews	MIL
SS	Luis Aparicio	CHA	Ernie Banks	CHN
OF	Rocky Colavito	CLE	Hank Aaron	MIL
OF	Al Kaline	DET	Willie Mays	SFN
OF	Minnie Minoso	CLE	Wally Moon	LAN
	Yogi Berra	NYA	Johnny Antonelli	SFN
	Jim Bunning	DET	Ken Boyer	SLN
	Bud Daley	KC	Lew Burdette	MIL
	Ryne Duren	NYA	Smoky Burgess	PIT
	Whitey Ford	NYA	Gene Conley	PHI
	Harvey Kuenn	DET	Joe Cunningham	SLN
	Sherm Lollar	CHA	Don Elston	CHN
	Frank Malzone	BOS	Roy Face	PIT
	Mickey Mantle	NYA	Dick Groat	PIT
	Gil McDougald	NYA	Bill Mazeroski	PIT
	Billy Pierce	CHA	Wilmer Mizell +	SLN
	Vic Power	CLE	Stan Musial	SLN
	Pete Runnels	BOS	Vada Pinson	CIN
	Roy Sievers	WAS	Frank Robinson	CIN
	Hoyt Wilhelm	BAL	Hal Smith	SLN
	Ted Williams	BOS	Warren Spahn	MIL
			Bill White	SLN

+ player replaced on roster

American League   000 100 030- 4
National League   100 000 22x- 5

AMERICAN LEAGUE

	ab	r	h	bi	bb	so	po	a
M.Minoso, lf	5	0	0	0	0	2	0	1
N.Fox, 2b	5	1	2	0	0	1	2	0
A.Kaline, cf	3	1	1	1	0	1	1	0
H.Kuenn, cf	1	1	0	0	1	0	0	0
B.Skowron, 1b	3	0	2	0	0	0	3	0
V.Power, 1b	1	1	1	1	0	0	3	0
R.Colavito, rf	3	0	1	0	0	1	1	0
T.Williams, ph	0	0	0	0	1	0	0	0
G.McDougald, pr-ss	0	0	0	0	0	0	0	0
G.Triandos, c	4	0	1	2	0	0	8	0
M.Mantle, pr-rf	0	0	0	0	0	0	0	0
H.Killebrew, 3b	3	0	0	0	0	1	0	1
J.Bunning, p	0	0	0	0	0	0	0	0
P.Runnels, ph	0	0	0	0	0	0	0	0
R.Sievers, ph	0	0	0	0	1	0	0	0
W.Ford, p	0	0	0	0	0	0	0	1
B.Daley, p	0	0	0	0	0	0	0	0
L.Aparicio, ss	3	0	0	0	0	1	4	2
S.Lollar, ph-c	1	0	0	0	0	0	1	0
E.Wynn, p	1	0	0	0	0	1	1	0
R.Duren, p	1	0	0	0	0	1	0	0
F.Malzone, 3b	2	0	0	0	0	0	0	0
Totals	36	4	8	4	3	9	24	5

BATTING
2B: G.Triandos (off R.Face).
HR: A.Kaline (4th inning off L.Burdette, 0 on, 2 out).
2-out RBI: A.Kaline; V.Power; G.Triandos 2.

BASERUNNING
Team LOB: 8

FIELDING
Outfield assist: M.Minoso (B.Mazeroski at 2B).
DP: (1). L.Aparicio-B.Skowron.

NATIONAL LEAGUE

	ab	r	h	bi	bb	so	po	a
J.Temple, 2b	2	0	0	0	0	0	1	3
S.Musial, ph	1	0	0	0	0	0	0	0
R.Face, p	0	0	0	0	0	0	0	0
J.Antonelli, p	0	0	0	0	0	0	0	0
K.Boyer, ph-3b	1	1	1	0	0	0	1	0
E.Mathews, 3b	3	1	1	1	0	1	2	1
D.Groat, ph	0	0	0	0	0	0	0	0
D.Elston, p	0	0	0	0	0	0	0	0
H.Aaron, rf	4	1	2	1	0	1	2	0
W.Mays, cf	4	0	1	1	0	1	2	0
E.Banks, ss	3	1	2	0	1	1	1	2
O.Cepeda, 1b	4	0	0	0	0	0	6	0
W.Moon, lf	2	0	0	0	1	2	1	0
D.Crandall, c	3	1	1	1	0	1	10	0
D.Drysdale, p	1	0	0	0	0	1	0	0
L.Burdette, p	1	0	0	0	0	1	0	0
B.Mazeroski, 2b	1	0	1	1	0	0	1	0
Totals	30	5	9	5	2	9	27	6

BATTING
2B: E.Banks 2 (off E.Wynn; off J.Bunning).
3B: W.Mays (off W.Ford).
HR: E.Mathews (1st inning off E.Wynn, 0 on, 1 out).
2-out RBI: D.Crandall; B.Mazeroski.
RBI, scoring position, less than 2 outs: H.Aaron 1-1;
    E.Banks 0-1; O.Cepeda 0-2; W.Moon 0-1;
    D.Crandall 0-1.
S: D.Groat.
GDP: O.Cepeda.

BASERUNNING
Team LOB: 4

FIELDING
E: E.Mathews (fumble).

PITCHING	ip	h	r	er	bb	so
American League						
E.Wynn	3.0	2	1	1	1	3
R.Duren	3.0	1	0	0	1	4
J.Bunning	1.0	3	2	2	0	1
W.Ford (L, BS)	0.1	3	2	2	0	0
B.Daley	0.2	0	0	0	0	1
National League						
D.Drysdale	3.0	0	0	0	0	4
L.Burdette	3.0	4	1	1	0	2
R.Face	1.2	3	3	3	2	2
J.Antonelli (w)	0.1	0	0	0	1	0
D.Elston (s)	1.0	1	0	0	0	1

Inherited Runners—Scored:
    R.Duren 0-0; J.Bunning 0-0; W.Ford 0-0;
    B.Daley 1-0; L.Burdette 0-0; R.Face 0-0;
    J.Antonelli 2-0; D.Elston 0-0.
WP: D.Elston

GAME DATA—T: 2:33; A: 35277; Temp: Unknown;
Wind: Unknown direction, Speed: Unknown

UMPIRES—HP: Al Barlick (NL), 1B: Ed Runge (AL),
2B: Augie Donateli (NL), 3B: Joe Paparella (AL), LF: Shag
Crawford (NL), RF: John Rice (AL)

STARTING LINEUPS

American League	National League
1. M.Minoso lf	J.Temple 2b
2. N.Fox 2b	E.Mathews 3b
3. A.Kaline cf	H.Aaron rf
4. B.Skowron 1b	W.Mays cf
5. R.Colavito rf	E.Banks ss
6. G.Triandos c	O.Cepeda 1b
7. H.Killebrew 3b	W.Moon lf
8. L.Aparicio ss	D.Crandall c
9. E.Wynn p	D.Drysdale p

AL 1ST: M.Minoso flied to W.Mays-cf; N.Fox struck out; A.Kaline struck out; 0 R, 0 H, 0 E, 0 LOB. AL 0, NL 0.

NL 1ST: J.Temple flied to A.Kaline-cf; E.Mathews homered to deep rightfield; H.Aaron struck out; W.Mays lined to E.Wynn-p; 1 R, 1 H, 0 E, 0 LOB. AL 0, NL 1.

AL 2ND: B.Skowron grounded out (J.Temple-2b to O.Cepeda-1b); R.Colavito struck out; G.Triandos popped to O.Cepeda-1b; 0 R, 0 H, 0 E, 0 LOB. AL 0, NL 1.

NL 2ND: E.Banks doubled to left-center; O.Cepeda popped to L.Aparicio-ss; W.Moon walked; D.Crandall was called out on strikes; D.Drysdale struck out; 0 R, 1 H, 0 E, 2 LOB. AL 0, NL 1.

AL 3RD: H.Killebrew flied to W.Mays-cf; L.Aparicio flied to H.Aaron-rf; Drysdale pitched 3 perfect innings; E.Wynn struck out; 0 R, 0 H, 0 E, 0 LOB. AL 0, NL 1.

NL 3RD: J.Temple flied to R.Colavito-rf; E.Mathews popped to B.Skowron-1b in foul territory; H.Aaron lined to L.Aparicio-ss; 0 R, 0 H, 0 E, 0 LOB. AL 0, NL 1.

AL 4TH: **L.Burdette replaced D.Drysdale (pitching);** M.Minoso grounded out (J.Temple-2b to O.Cepeda-1b); N.Fox popped to E.Mathews-3b in foul territory; A.Kaline homered to deep left-field; B.Skowron singled to left field; R.Colavito singled to center field [B.Skowron to second]; G.Triandos flied to H.Aaron-rf; 1 R, 3 H, 0 E, 2 LOB. AL 1, NL 1.

NL 4TH: **R.Duren replaced E.Wynn (pitching);** W.Mays struck out; E.Banks walked; O.Cepeda grounded into a double play (L.Aparicio-ss to B.Skowron-1b) [E.Banks out at second]; 0 R, 0 H, 0 E, 0 LOB. AL 1, NL 1.

AL 5TH: H.Killebrew grounded out (E.Banks-ss to O.Cepeda-1b); L.Aparicio flied to W.Moon-lf; R.Duren struck out; 0 R, 0 H, 0 E, 0 LOB. AL 1, NL 1.

NL 5TH: Umpires moved: Paparella (hp), Donatelli (1b), Runge (2b), Barlick (3b), Crawford (lf), Rice (rf); W.Moon struck out; D.Crandall

grounded out (H.Killebrew-3b to B.Skowron-1b); L.Burdette struck out; 0 R, 0 H, 0 E, 0 LOB. AL 1, NL 1.

AL 6TH: M.Minoso was called out on strikes; N.Fox grounded out (J.Temple-2b to O.Cepeda-1b); A.Kaline reached on an error by E.Mathews-3b [A.Kaline to first]; B.Skowron singled to right-center [A.Kaline to third]; R.Colavito forced B.Skowron (E.Banks-ss to J.Temple-2b) [R.Colavito to first]; 0 R, 1 H, 1 E, 2 LOB. AL 1, NL 1.

NL 6TH: **H.Kuenn replaced A.Kaline (playing cf); V.Power replaced B.Skowron (playing 1b); S.Musial batted for J.Temple;** S.Musial popped to V.Power-1b; E.Mathews struck out; H.Aaron singled to left-center; W.Mays forced H.Aaron (L.Aparicio-ss to N.Fox-2b) [W.Mays to first]; 0 R, 1 H, 0 E, 1 LOB. AL 1, NL 1.

AL 7TH: **R.Face replaced S.Musial (pitching); B.Mazeroski replaced L.Burdette (playing 2b);** G.Triandos grounded out (E.Mathews-3b to O.Cepeda-1b); H.Killebrew struck out; L.Aparicio was called out on strikes; 0 R, 0 H, 0 E, 0 LOB. AL 1, NL 1.

NL 7TH: **J.Bunning replaced H.Killebrew (pitching); F.Malzone replaced R.Duren (playing 3b);** E.Banks doubled to left field; O.Cepeda popped to L.Aparicio-ss; W.Moon was called out on strikes; D.Crandall singled to center field [E.Banks scored, D.Crandall to second (on throw home)]; B.Mazeroski singled to left field (M.Minoso-lf to N.Fox-2b) [D.Crandall scored, B.Mazeroski out at second]; 2 R, 3 H, 0 E, 0 LOB. AL 1, NL 3.

AL 8TH: F.Malzone popped to B.Mazeroski-2b; M.Minoso popped to D.Crandall-c in foul territory; N.Fox singled to center field; H.Kuenn walked [N.Fox to second]; V.Power singled to center field [N.Fox scored, H.Kuenn to second]; **T.Williams batted for R.Colavito;** T.Williams walked [H.Kuenn to third, V.Power to second]; **G.McDougald ran for T.Williams;** G.Triandos doubled to left field [H.Kuenn scored, V.Power scored, G.McDougald to third]; **P.Runnels batted for J.Bunning; J.Antonelli replaced R.Face (pitching); M.Mantle ran for G.Triandos; R.Sievers batted for P.Runnels;** R.Sievers walked; **S.Lollar batted for L.Aparicio;** S.Lollar forced M.Mantle (E.Mathews-3b unassisted) [S.Lollar to first]; 3 R, 3 H, 0 E, 3 LOB. AL 4, NL 3.

NL 8TH: **S.Lollar stayed in game (playing c); G.McDougald stayed in game (playing ss); M.Mantle stayed in game (playing rf); W.Ford replaced R.Sievers (pitching); K.Boyer batted for J.Antonelli;** K.Boyer singled to left-center; **D.Groat batted for E.Mathews;** D.Groat out on a sacrifice bunt (W.Ford-p to V.Power-1b) [K.Boyer to second]; H.Aaron singled to center field [K.Boyer scored]; W.Mays tripled to very deep right-center [H.Aaron scored]; **B.Daley replaced W.Ford (pitching);** E.Banks struck out; O.Cepeda popped to V.Power-1b in foul territory; 2 R, 3 H, 0 E, 1 LOB. AL 4, NL 5.

AL 9TH: **K.Boyer stayed in game (playing 3b); D.Elston replaced D.Groat (pitching);** F.Malzone popped to E.Banks-ss; M.Minoso struck out; N.Fox singled to left field; D.Elston threw a wild pitch [N.Fox to second]; H.Kuenn popped to K.Boyer-3b in foul territory; 0 R, 1 H, 0 E, 1 LOB. AL 4, NL 5.

Final Totals	R	H	E	LOB
American League	4	8	0	8
National League	5	9	1	4

27

The AL Has Fun in the California Sun

The second game of 1959 was played in Los Angeles on August 3 with some modifications to the rosters and lineups. All nonpitchers from the Pittsburgh game were invited to return, and the managers were allowed to change their pitching staffs. In addition, each side was allowed to add three players, bringing the rosters to twenty-eight players. As it worked out, there were several changes, especially to the AL squad. Bill Skowron and Gil McDougald of the Yankees, Harvey Kuenn of the Tigers, and Gus Triandos of the Orioles were injured and replaced by the Orioles' Jerry Walker and the Yankees' Elston Howard, Bobby Richardson, and Tony Kubek. In addition, three pitchers from the first game — Billy Pierce of the White Sox, Jim Bunning of the Tigers, and Whitey Ford of the Yankees — were left off and replaced by Baltimore's Billy O'Dell, Cleveland's Cal McLish, and Washington's Camilo Pascual. Pascual withdrew from the game and was replaced by his teammate Pedro Ramos. The three "bonus" players for the American League were Bob Allison of the Senators, Gene Woodling of the Orioles, and Roger Maris of the A's. The National League contingent was much more stable, with Haney deciding to keep all the pitchers from the first game. He chose Sam Jones of the Giants, Jim Gilliam of the Dodgers, and Johnny Logan of the Braves as his three additions, while the Dodgers' Charlie Neal replaced injured Cardinal Bill White. The managers were not bound by the starting lineup choices from the first game, and many changes were indeed made.

The game started at the unusual hour of 4 P.M., partly to increase the potential TV audience in the East and partly to avoid the anticipated high temperatures of a summer day in southern California. It was very hot when the game started, over 90 degrees in fact, although none of the players complained about the weather. Of much greater concern was the scheduling. All teams had played the day before, many of them in doubleheaders, and all but two teams were scheduled to play the following day as well. This was the first time that regular season games had been played the day before an All-Star Game. Given the western location of the game, some players spent a lot of late hours on airplanes getting both to Los Angeles and then back to their teams. Many felt that if there were going to be two All-Star Games in the future, they should be scheduled in a block of four or five days to avoid the fatigue.

The left-field fence at Memorial Coliseum, though topped by a 42-foot screen, was only 251 feet from home plate, and the game's star sluggers were expected to benefit accordingly. In fact, there were five home runs in the game, but three of them were hit so far that they would clearly have been out of any park. Only the circuit hits by Boston's Frank Malzone in the second and Gilliam in the seventh were fly balls that just cleared the screen. The Dodgers' Don Drysdale, voted Player of the Game in the Pittsburgh contest in July, once again got the starting nod from manager Haney. However, the results couldn't have been more different this time. Casey Stengel had been criticized for his decisions during the first game, but this time, with complete freedom in his choice of starters, he put six left-handed batters at the top of the order. Casey's strategy paid off as Drysdale was pounded before the home folks, giving up four hits, three walks, two homers, and three earned runs in his three-inning stint. Although he did record five strikeouts among the nine outs he collected, Drysdale was the losing pitcher in the 5–3 game. The player of the game was Yankee catcher Yogi Berra, who belted a Drysdale fastball over the right-field fence with Nellie Fox of the White Sox on first base after a single. Winning pitcher Walker, a twenty-year old who was added to the roster only one night before the game, pitched the first three innings and earned the win, allowing one walk and two hits. The only run the NL managed off the youngster came in the first when the

Mantle's drag bunt, 1959, game 2
Slugger Mickey Mantle drags a bunt past Don Drysdale for a hit in the second inning. © *Bettmann/*CORBIS.

Reds' Johnny Temple led off with a line drive to left field that became a double when it took an unusual bounce and eluded Boston's Ted Williams. Temple scored on a sacrifice fly by Henry Aaron after advancing on an infield out.

The National League got closer in the fifth inning when Frank Robinson of the Reds hit a long home run to left field off Chicago's Early Wynn, who was appearing in his sixth consecutive game, tying the mark of Ewell Blackwell, who had turned the trick from 1946 to 1951. Before the inning ended, Wynn lost his control and loaded the bases with three walks. However, the NL lost a golden opportunity when Aaron hit a weak grounder to first to end the threat. Gene Conley of the Phillies pitched hitless ball in the fourth and fifth, and Jones did the same in the sixth. However, poor fielding for the NL caught up with Jones in the seventh. Jones, who would lead the league with an ERA of 2.82 and would tie for the lead in wins with twenty-one, contributed to his problems by walking pinch hitter Tony Kubek of the Yankees and then making a wild throw on a pick-off attempt. Pete Runnels of the Red Sox hit a ground ball to Ernie Banks of the Cubs, who fumbled it for an error, allowing Kubek to reach third, where he

scored on a single by Fox. The third error of the inning was charged to first baseman Robinson, who missed a pick-off throw from catcher Hal Smith of the Cardinals, allowing Runnels to take third, although he did not score.

The final two runs of the game came on homers, a short one for the NL by Gilliam in the seventh off O'Dell and a 430-foot blast by the Indians' Rocky Colavito for the AL in the eighth on the first pitch thrown by the Pirates' Roy Face. McLish pitched a scoreless eighth and ninth to earn a save, although there was excitement for the NL at the end. Robinson singled, and Wally Moon of the Dodgers walked; both advanced on a ground out by Smoky Burgess of the Pirates. McLish sent the NL crowd home unhappy by retiring Gilliam on a hard grounder to first baseman Vic Power of the Indians.

The biggest disappointment of the two games combined was Face, who had a tremendous regular season but was extremely ineffective in both his All-Star appearances, compiling an ERA of 9.81 over three and two-thirds innings for the two games. On the positive side, Fox garnered four hits in nine at bats along with a walk and two runs scored.

	AL		NL	
P	Jerry Walker	BAL	Don Drysdale	LAN
C	Yogi Berra	NYA	Del Crandall	MIL
1B	Pete Runnels	BOS	Stan Musial	SLN
2B	Nellie Fox	CHA	Johnny Temple	CIN
3B	Frank Malzone	BOS	Ken Boyer	SLN
SS	Luis Aparicio	CHA	Ernie Banks	CHN
OF	Mickey Mantle	NYA	Hank Aaron	MIL
OF	Roger Maris	KC	Willie Mays	SFN
OF	Ted Williams	BOS	Wally Moon	LAN
	Bob Allison	WAS	Johnny Antonelli	SFN
	Rocky Colavito	CLE	Lew Burdette	MIL
	Bud Daley	KC	Smoky Burgess	PIT
	Ryne Duren	NYA	Orlando Cepeda	SFN
	Elston Howard	NYA	Gene Conley	PHI
	Al Kaline	DET	Joe Cunningham	SLN
	Harmon Killebrew	WAS	Don Elston	CHN
	Tony Kubek	NYA	Roy Face	PIT
	Harvey Kuenn	DET	Jim Gilliam	LAN
	Sherm Lollar	CHA	Dick Groat	PIT
	Gil McDougald	NYA	Sam Jones	SFN
	Cal McLish	CLE	Johnny Logan	MIL
	Minnie Minoso	CLE	Eddie Mathews	MIL
	Billy O'Dell	BAL	Bill Mazeroski	PIT
	Camilo Pascual +	WAS	Charlie Neal	LAN
	Vic Power	CLE	Vada Pinson	CIN
	Pedro Ramos	WAS	Frank Robinson	CIN
	Bobby Richardson	NYA	Hal Smith	SLN
	Roy Sievers	WAS	Warren Spahn	MIL
	Bill Skowron	NYA	Bill White	SLN
	Gus Triandos	BAL		
	Hoyt Wilhelm	BAL		
	Gene Woodling	BAL		
	Early Wynn	CHA		

+ player replaced on roster

American League	012	000	110-	5			
National League	100	010	100-	3			

AMERICAN LEAGUE

	ab	r	h	bi	bb	so	po	a
P.Runnels, 1b	3	0	0	0	1	2	9	0
V.Power, 1b	1	0	0	0	0	0	4	0
N.Fox, 2b	4	1	2	1	1	0	3	1
T.Williams, lf	3	0	0	0	0	1	0	0
A.Kaline, lf-cf	2	0	0	0	0	1	0	0
Y.Berra, c	3	1	1	2	0	2	2	0
S.Lollar, c	0	0	0	0	1	0	2	0
M.Mantle, cf	3	0	1	0	1	1	3	0
B.O'Dell, p	0	0	0	0	0	0	0	0
C.McLish, p	0	0	0	0	0	0	0	0
R.Maris, rf	2	0	0	0	0	1	1	0
R.Colavito, rf	2	1	1	1	0	1	0	0
F.Malzone, 3b	4	1	1	1	0	0	1	6
L.Aparicio, ss	3	0	0	0	1	1	1	2
J.Walker, p	1	0	0	0	0	1	0	0
G.Woodling, ph	1	0	0	0	0	0	0	0
E.Wynn, p	0	0	0	0	0	0	1	0
H.Wilhelm, p	0	0	0	0	0	0	0	0
T.Kubek, ph-lf	1	1	0	0	1	1	0	0
Totals	33	5	6	5	6	12	27	9

BATTING
HR: Y.Berra (3rd inning off D.Drysdale, 1 on, 2 out);
  R.Colavito (8th inning off R.Face, 0 on, 0 out);
  F.Malzone (2nd inning off D.Drysdale, 0 on, 2 out).
2-out RBI: Y.Berra 2; F.Malzone.
RBI, scoring position, less than 2 outs: N.Fox 1–1;
  A.Kaline 0–1.

BASERUNNING
SB: L.Aparicio (2nd base off D.Drysdale / D.Crandall).
CS: M.Mantle (2nd base by D.Drysdale / D.Crandall).
Team LOB: 7

FIELDING
DP: (1). P.Runnels, unassisted.

NATIONAL LEAGUE

	ab	r	h	bi	bb	so	po	a
J.Temple, 2b	2	1	1	0	0	0	1	1
J.Gilliam, ph-3b	2	1	1	1	1	0	0	0
K.Boyer, 3b	2	0	0	0	1	0	0	1
C.Neal, 2b	1	0	0	0	0	0	0	2
H.Aaron, rf	3	0	0	1	0	0	2	0
W.Mays, cf	4	0	0	0	0	0	3	0
E.Banks, ss	4	0	0	0	0	2	2	0
S.Musial, 1b	0	0	0	0	1	0	3	1
F.Robinson, 1b	3	1	3	1	0	0	3	0
W.Moon, lf	2	0	0	0	2	0	1	0
D.Crandall, c	2	0	1	0	0	0	7	1
H.Smith, c	2	0	0	0	0	1	5	0
D.Drysdale, p	0	0	0	0	0	0	0	0
E.Mathews, ph	1	0	0	0	0	1	0	0
G.Conley, p	0	0	0	0	0	0	0	1
J.Cunningham, ph	1	0	0	0	0	0	0	0
V.Pinson, pr	0	0	0	0	0	0	0	0
S.Jones, p	0	0	0	0	0	0	0	0
D.Groat, ph	1	0	0	0	0	0	0	0
R.Face, p	0	0	0	0	0	0	0	0
S.Burgess, ph	1	0	0	0	0	0	0	0
Totals	31	3	6	3	5	4	27	7

BATTING
2B: J.Temple (off J.Walker).
HR: J.Gilliam (7th inning off B.O'Dell, 0 on, 2 out);
  F.Robinson (5th inning off E.Wynn, 0 on, 0 out).
2-out RBI: J.Gilliam.
RBI, scoring position, less than 2 outs: K.Boyer 0–1;
  H.Aaron 1–1; H.Smith 0–1; S.Burgess 0–1.
SF: H.Aaron.

BASERUNNING
Team LOB: 7

FIELDING
E: S.Jones (dropped throw); E.Banks (fumble);
  F.Robinson (dropped throw).

PITCHING

	ip	h	r	er	bb	so
American League						
J.Walker (w)	3.0	2	1	1	1	1
E.Wynn	2.0	1	1	1	3	1
H.Wilhelm	1.0	1	0	0	0	0
B.O'Dell	1.0	1	1	1	0	0
C.McLish (s)	2.0	1	0	0	1	2
National League						
D.Drysdale (L)	3.0	4	3	3	3	5
G.Conley	2.0	0	0	0	1	2
S.Jones	2.0	1	1	0	2	3
R.Face	2.0	1	1	1	0	2

Inherited Runners—Scored:
  E.Wynn 0–0; H.Wilhelm 0–0; B.O'Dell 0–0;
  C.McLish 0–0; G.Conley 0–0; S.Jones 0–0;
  R.Face 0–0.

GAME DATA—T: 2:24; A: 55105; Temp: Unknown;
Wind: Unknown direction, Speed: Unknown

UMPIRES—HP: Bill Jackowski (NL), 1B: Charlie Berry
(AL), 2B: Tony Venzon (NL), 3B: Bill Summers (AL),
LF: Ken Burkhart (NL), RF: Hank Soar (AL)

STARTING LINEUPS

	American League	*National League*
1.	P.Runnels 1b	J.Temple 2b
2.	N.Fox 2b	K.Boyer 3b
3.	T.Williams lf	H.Aaron rf
4.	Y.Berra c	W.Mays cf
5.	M.Mantle cf	E.Banks ss
6.	R.Maris rf	S.Musial 1b
7.	F.Malzone 3b	W.Moon lf
8.	L.Aparicio ss	D.Crandall c
9.	J.Walker p	D.Drysdale p

AL 1ST: P.Runnels struck out; N.Fox walked; T.Williams grounded out (S.Musial-1b to J.Temple-2b) [N.Fox to second]; Y.Berra struck out; 0 R, 0 H, 0 E, 1 LOB. AL 0, NL 0.

NL 1ST: J.Temple doubled to left field; K.Boyer grounded out (N.Fox-2b to P.Runnels-1b) [J.Temple to third]; H.Aaron out on a sacrifice fly to R.Maris-rf [J.Temple scored]; W.Mays grounded out (F.Malzone-3b to P.Runnels-1b); 1 R, 1 H, 0 E, 0 LOB. AL 0, NL 1.

AL 2ND: On a bunt M.Mantle singled; M.Mantle was caught stealing second (D.Crandall-c to E.Banks-ss); R.Maris struck out; F.Malzone homered to deep leftfield; L.Aparicio walked; L.Aparicio stole second; J.Walker struck out; 1 R, 2 H, 0 E, 1 LOB. AL 1, NL 1.

NL 2ND: E.Banks grounded out (F.Malzone-3b to P.Runnels-1b); S.Musial walked; W.Moon lined into a double play (P.Runnels-1b unassisted) [S.Musial out at first]; 0 R, 0 H, 0 E, 0 LOB. AL 1, NL 1.

AL 3RD: P.Runnels was called out on strikes; N.Fox singled to right field; T.Williams flied to W.Moon-lf; Y.Berra homered to deep rightfield [N.Fox scored]; M.Mantle walked; R.Maris lined to H.Aaron-rf; 2 R, 2 H, 0 E, 1 LOB. AL 3, NL 1.

NL 3RD: D.Crandall singled to center field; **E.Mathews batted for D.Drysdale;** E.Mathews struck out; J.Temple flied to M.Mantle-cf; K.Boyer popped to L.Aparicio-ss; 0 R, 1 H, 0 E, 1 LOB. AL 3, NL 1.

AL 4TH: **G.Conley replaced E.Mathews (pitching);** F.Malzone grounded out (G.Conley-p to S.Musial-1b); L.Aparicio grounded out (K.Boyer-3b to S.Musial-1b); **G.Woodling batted for J.Walker;** G.Woodling grounded out (S.Musial-1b unassisted); 0 R, 0 H, 0 E, 0 LOB. AL 3, NL 1.

NL 4TH: **E.Wynn replaced G.Woodling (pitching);** H.Aaron popped to F.Malzone-3b; W.Mays popped to N.Fox-2b; E.Banks struck out; 0 R, 0 H, 0 E, 0 LOB. AL 3, NL 1.

AL 5TH: **F.Robinson replaced S.Musial (playing 1b);** P.Runnels walked; N.Fox forced P.Runnels (J.Temple-2b to E.Banks-ss) [N.Fox to first]; T.Williams struck out; Y.Berra struck out; 0 R, 0 H, 0 E, 1 LOB. AL 3, NL 1.

NL 5TH: Umpires moved: Summers (hp), Venzon (1b), Berry (2b), Jackowski (3b), Burkhart (lf), Soar (rf); **A.Kaline replaced T.Williams (playing lf); R.Colavito replaced R.Maris (playing rf);** F.Robinson homered to very deep left-center; W.Moon walked; On a bunt D.Crandall popped to E.Wynn-p; **J.Cunningham batted for G.Conley;** J.Cunningham forced W.Moon (L.Aparicio-ss to N.Fox-2b) [J.Cunningham to first]; **V.Pinson ran for J.Cunningham; J.Gilliam batted for J.Temple;** J.Gilliam walked [V.Pinson to second]; K.Boyer walked [V.Pinson to third, J.Gilliam to second]; H.Aaron grounded out (P.Runnels-1b unassisted); 1 R, 1 H, 0 E, 3 LOB. AL 3, NL 2.

AL 6TH: **J.Gilliam stayed in game (playing 3b); S.Jones replaced V.Pinson (pitching); C.Neal replaced K.Boyer (playing 2b); H.Smith replaced D.Crandall (playing c);** M.Mantle flied to W.Mays-cf; R.Colavito was called out on strikes; F.Malzone lined to W.Mays-cf; 0 R, 0 H, 0 E, 0 LOB. AL 3, NL 2.

NL 6TH: **H.Wilhelm replaced E.Wynn (pitching); S.Lollar replaced Y.Berra (playing c);** W.Mays popped to P.Runnels-1b in foul territory; E.Banks lined to M.Mantle-cf; F.Robinson singled to center field; W.Moon flied to M.Mantle-cf; 0 R, 1 H, 0 E, 1 LOB. AL 3, NL 2.

AL 7TH: L.Aparicio struck out; **T.Kubek batted for H.Wilhelm;** T.Kubek walked; T.Kubek was picked off first, but was safe on an error by S.Jones-p [T.Kubek to second]; P.Runnels reached on an error by E.Banks-ss [T.Kubek to third, P.Runnels to first]; N.Fox singled to center field [T.Kubek scored (unearned), P.Runnels to second]; A.Kaline flied to W.Mays-cf; N.Fox was picked off first, but was safe on an error by F.Robinson-1b [P.Runnels to third]; S.Lollar walked [N.Fox to second]; M.Mantle struck out; 1 R (0 ER), 1 H, 3 E, 3 LOB. AL 4, NL 2.

NL 7TH: **T.Kubek stayed in game (playing lf); A.Kaline changed positions (playing cf); B.O'Dell replaced M.Mantle (pitching);** H.Smith popped to N.Fox-2b; **D.Groat batted for S.Jones;** D.Groat grounded out (L.Aparicio-ss to P.Runnels-1b); J.Gilliam homered to very deep left-center; C.Neal grounded out (F.Malzone-3b to P.Runnels-1b); 1 R, 1 H, 0 E, 0 LOB. AL 4, NL 3.

AL 8TH: **R.Face replaced D.Groat (pitching);** R.Colavito homered to deep leftfield; F.Malzone grounded out (C.Neal-2b to F.Robinson-1b); L.Aparicio flied to H.Aaron-rf; T.Kubek struck out; 1 R, 1 H, 0 E, 0 LOB. AL 5, NL 3.

NL 8TH: **V.Power replaced P.Runnels (playing 1b);**

C.McLish replaced B.O'Dell (pitching); H.Aaron grounded out (F.Malzone-3b to V.Power-1b); W.Mays grounded out (F.Malzone-3b to V.Power-1b); E.Banks struck out; 0 R, 0 H, 0 E, 0 LOB. AL 5, NL 3.

AL 9TH: V.Power grounded out (F.Robinson-1b unassisted); N.Fox grounded out (C.Neal-2b to F.Robinson-1b); A.Kaline struck out; 0 R, 0 H, 0 E, 0 LOB. AL 5, NL 3.

NL 9TH: F.Robinson singled to center field; W.Moon walked [F.Robinson to second]; H.Smith struck out; **S.Burgess batted for R.Face;** S.Burgess grounded out (F.Malzone-3b to V.Power-1b) [F.Robinson to third, W.Moon to second]; J.Gilliam grounded out (V.Power-1b unassisted); 0 R, 1 H, 0 E, 2 LOB. AL 5, NL 3.

Final Totals	R	H	E	LOB
American League	5	6	0	7
National League	3	6	3	7

Monday, July 11, 1960

Municipal Stadium, Kansas City

National League 5, American League 3

SERIES RESULTS: AL 16, NL 12

The NL Warms to the Task in KC

In 1960, the National League continued its surge and closed the overall gap to 16-13 by winning both games in the second year of two All-Star meetings. Since both games had been played in NL cities the year before, in 1960 the hosts were the AL's Kansas City Athletics and the New York Yankees. Several changes were implemented, with the most important being the decision to play the two games during a single four-day break rather than a month apart as in 1959. For the second straight time, however, the game was held on a day following regular championship season play. Players arrived Sunday evening on very late planes from all around the country. The rosters were expanded from twenty-five to thirty players so that there would be enough pitchers to share the load over the two games. There was a proposal to allow pitchers to pitch in only one of the games, but that plan was dropped. As it developed, Gary Bell of the Indians, Frank Lary of the Tigers, and Vern Law of the Pirates were the only ones to pitch in both games.

Starting lineups were again selected by a poll of players, managers, and coaches. Roger Maris of the Yankees was the leading vote getter, with 198 of a possible 208. At the time of the game, Maris had twenty-seven home runs and had generated a lot of media attention in his first year in pinstripes, foreshadowing what would become nearly unbearable pressure in 1961. In the NL, the Giants' Willie Mays had the most support, with 193 of a possible 205. Willie was batting .353 with eighteen home runs at the time of the break, although he would fall off sharply in the second half to finish the year at .319 with twenty-nine homers. Four of the nine NL starters came from Milwaukee and three from the Pirates; only Mays and Ernie Banks of the Cubs broke through for another team. Managers Walt Alston of the Dodgers and Al Lopez of the White Sox, leaders of the 1959 World Series opponents, selected players to complete the rosters and also

chose the starting pitchers. Pitcher Camilo Pascual of the Senators withdrew for the second straight year, once again for arm trouble. He was replaced by outfielder Jim Lemon, his teammate. During the course of the two games, the NL used all thirty players on the roster, twenty-six in the second game. For the AL, only pitcher Dick Stigman of the Indians did not appear in either contest.

The game was played in scorching 101-degree heat. Nevertheless, the contest was sold out, with an enthusiastic crowd happy to see the only All-Star Game ever played in Kansas City's Municipal Stadium. National League starter Bob Friend of the Pirates was the winner because he pitched three scoreless innings, allowing only one hit and one walk, although he did have a lapse in the second inning. While pitching to pinch hitter Ted Williams of the Red Sox with two outs, Friend committed a balk and threw a wild pitch, advancing the Orioles' Ron Hansen to third; Hansen had singled. However, Williams grounded out to end the threat. In the meantime, the NL jumped out to a 5–0 lead in the first three innings, beginning with a three-spot in the first against Bill Monbouquette of the Red Sox. Mays opened the game with a triple, and the Pirates' Bob Skinner followed with a single for the first run. After Braves teammates Eddie Mathews and Henry Aaron went out, Banks homered to left, and Joe Adcock completed an interesting trifecta when he flied out and combined with Mathews and Aaron to have all of the outs in the inning made by Braves. Del Crandall, the other starter from Milwaukee, homered in the second inning, and the NL got its final run in the third against Oriole Chuck Estrada. Third baseman Frank Malzone of the Red Sox hit second base umpire Nestor Chylak in the stomach with a throw while trying for a force out, which worked to the AL's advantage because otherwise the throw would have gone into right field and scored at least one more run. After gathering nine hits in the first three innings, the National Leaguers were held to three more safeties the rest of the way by

Jim Coates of the Yankees, Gary Bell of the Indians, Frank Lary of the Tigers, and Bud Daley of the hometown Athletics.

The Giants' Mike McCormick replaced Friend to start the fourth and got through the inning with two walks, two strikeouts, and a pop-up. He was perfect in the fifth but had major problems in the sixth, retiring only Harvey Kuenn, who led off the inning with a pop fly to short right field that fell between Aaron and Bill Mazeroski of the Pirates. Harvey tried for two, but Aaron gunned him out at second. The Tigers' Al Kaline hit a grounder to third, which Eddie Mathews booted for his second error of the game. Bill Skowron of the Yankees singled, and his teammate Elston Howard walked to load the bases. A single by Nellie Fox of the White Sox plated the only run of the inning, a meager result for all the action. At this point, the Pirates' Roy Face of the Pirates came in and put out the fire, inducing Luis Aparicio of the White Sox to ground one to Banks for an inning-ending double play. Face pitched a perfect seventh inning as well, recording two strikeouts and a grounder to short and compiling one and two-thirds innings pitched while facing only four batters. This performance had to be extremely satisfying after his disasters in 1959.

The last of the scoring came in the eighth when Al Kaline homered after Kuenn reached base on an error by Dodger second baseman Charlie Neal. The Braves' Bob Buhl was the victim of this blast, having come on to relieve Face to start the eighth. The AL had one more threat in the ninth when catcher Smokey Burgess of the Pirates dropped a foul ball for an error, giving Oriole Jim Gentile another chance, which he used to single to right field. When Lemon walked, Alston brought in Pittsburgh's ace Vern Law, who retired Brooks Robinson of the Orioles and Kuenn on fly balls, earning a save as he became the third member of the league-leading Pirates to pitch very effectively this day.

In many ways, the game was not as close as the 5–3 final score would indicate. Not only did the NL build an early 5–0 lead, at one point it had twenty-three total bases to the AL's one. Mays and Banks combined on the day for more total bases than the entire AL squad had. The resurgence of the Americans in the late innings occurred after most starters had departed in a game that saw a record forty-eight players take part. This turnabout didn't impress Arthur Daley, who wrote rather cynically in the *New York Times* the next day: "All it proved was that the American League junior varsity was more potent than the National jayvees."

There was a sour note on the day, when first baseman Vic Power of the Indians was unable to answer manager Lopez's call to battle in the sixth inning. The AL skipper replaced all the other starters with the second-place vote getters at each position. Power had arrived at the park late and had retired to the clubhouse in the third inning, complaining of illness. Lopez and Power had "had words" several years earlier, but both insisted that dispute was behind them. This was round one in a situation that grew more prominent and alarming at the year's second All-Star Game two days later in New York.

Although the Pittsburgh pitching trio certainly deserved compliments too, the star of the game was Mays, who gathered a single, double, and triple, coming closer to hitting for the cycle than anyone else ever has in an All-Star Game.

	AL			NL	
P	Bill Monbouquette	BOS		Bob Friend	PIT
C	Yogi Berra	NYA		Del Crandall	MIL
1B	Bill Skowron	NYA		Joe Adcock	MIL
2B	Pete Runnels	BOS		Bill Mazeroski	PIT
3B	Frank Malzone	BOS		Eddie Mathews	MIL
SS	Ron Hansen	BAL		Ernie Banks	CHN
OF	Mickey Mantle	NYA		Hank Aaron	MIL
OF	Roger Maris	NYA		Willie Mays	SFN
OF	Minnie Minoso	CHA		Bob Skinner	PIT
	Luis Aparicio	CHA		Ed Bailey	CIN
	Gary Bell	CLE		Ken Boyer	SLN
	Jim Coates	NYA		Bob Buhl	MIL
	Bud Daley	KC		Smoky Burgess	PIT
	Chuck Estrada	BAL		Orlando Cepeda	SFN
	Whitey Ford	NYA		Roberto Clemente	PIT
	Nellie Fox	CHA		Roy Face	PIT
	Jim Gentile	BAL		Dick Groat	PIT
	Elston Howard	NYA		Bill Henry	CIN
	Al Kaline	DET		Larry Jackson	SLN
	Harvey Kuenn	CLE		Norm Larker	LAN
	Frank Lary	DET		Vern Law	PIT
	Jim Lemon	WAS		Mike McCormick	SFN
	Sherm Lollar	CHA		Lindy McDaniel	SLN
	Camilo Pascual +	WAS		Stan Musial	SLN
	Vic Power	CLE		Charlie Neal	LAN
	Brooks Robinson	BAL		Vada Pinson	CIN
	Al Smith	CHA		Johnny Podres	LAN
	Gerry Staley	CHA		Tony Taylor	PHI
	Dick Stigman	CLE		Bill White	SLN
	Ted Williams	BOS		Stan Williams	LAN
	Early Wynn	CHA			

+ player replaced on roster

RETROSHEET EXPANDED BOX SCORE Monday, 7/11/1960 National League at American League (D)

```
National League    311 000 000- 5
American League     000 001 020- 3
```

NATIONAL LEAGUE

	ab	r	h	bi	bb	so	po	a
W.Mays, cf	4	1	3	0	0	0	4	0
V.Pinson, cf	1	0	0	0	0	1	1	0
B.Skinner, lf	4	1	1	1	0	1	1	0
O.Cepeda, lf	1	0	0	0	0	1	0	0
E.Mathews, 3b	4	0	0	0	0	0	1	0
K.Boyer, 3b	0	0	0	0	1	0	0	2
H.Aaron, rf	4	0	0	0	0	0	0	1
R.Clemente, rf	1	0	0	0	0	0	2	0
E.Banks, ss	4	2	2	2	0	0	3	2
D.Groat, ss	0	0	0	0	0	0	0	1
J.Adcock, 1b	3	0	2	0	0	0	3	0
B.White, pr-1b	1	0	0	0	0	1	4	0
B.Mazeroski, 2b	2	0	1	1	0	0	1	2
S.Musial, ph	1	0	1	0	0	0	0	0
T.Taylor, pr	0	0	0	0	0	0	0	0
C.Neal, 2b	0	0	0	0	0	0	0	0
D.Crandall, c	3	1	2	1	0	0	4	0
S.Burgess, c	1	0	0	0	0	0	3	0
B.Friend, p	2	0	0	0	0	2	0	0
M.McCormick, p	1	0	0	0	0	0	0	0
R.Face, p	0	0	0	0	0	0	0	0
N.Larker, ph	1	0	0	0	0	0	0	0
B.Buhl, p	0	0	0	0	0	0	0	0
V.Law, p	0	0	0	0	0	0	0	0
Totals	38	5	12	5	1	6	27	8

BATTING
2B: E.Banks (off C.Estrada); W.Mays (off J.Coates); J.Adcock (off J.Coates).
3B: W.Mays (off B.Monbouquette).
HR: E.Banks (1st inning off B.Monbouquette, 1 on, 2 out); D.Crandall (2nd inning off B.Monbouquette, 0 on, 1 out).
2-out RBI: E.Banks 2; B.Mazeroski.
RBI, scoring position, less than 2 outs: B.Skinner 1–2; E.Mathews 0–1; H.Aaron 0–1; D.Crandall 0–1.
GDP: D.Crandall.

BASERUNNING
SB: B.Skinner (2nd base off B.Monbouquette/Y.Berra).
Team LOB: 8

FIELDING
E: E.Mathews 2 (fumble); C.Neal (throw); S.Burgess (dropped foul ball).
Outfield assist: H.Aaron (H.Kuenn at 2B).
DP: (1). E.Banks-B.Mazeroski-B.White.

AMERICAN LEAGUE

	ab	r	h	bi	bb	so	po	a
M.Minoso, lf	3	0	0	0	0	0	0	0
J.Lemon, lf	1	0	0	0	1	1	1	0
F.Malzone, 3b	3	0	0	0	0	0	1	1
B.Robinson, 3b	2	0	0	0	0	0	0	0
R.Maris, rf	2	0	0	0	0	1	1	0
H.Kuenn, rf	3	1	1	0	0	0	1	0
M.Mantle, cf	0	0	0	0	2	0	2	0
A.Kaline, cf	2	2	1	2	0	0	1	0
B.Skowron, 1b	3	0	1	0	0	2	9	0
F.Lary, p	0	0	0	0	0	0	0	0
S.Lollar, ph	1	0	0	0	0	0	0	0
B.Daley, p	0	0	0	0	0	0	0	0
Y.Berra, c	2	0	0	0	0	0	5	0
E.Howard, c	1	0	0	0	1	1	4	0
P.Runnels, 2b	1	0	0	0	1	0	0	1
N.Fox, 2b	2	0	1	1	0	0	1	3
R.Hansen, ss	2	0	1	0	0	1	0	0
L.Aparicio, ss	2	0	0	0	0	0	1	1
B.Monbouquette, p	0	0	0	0	0	0	0	0
T.Williams, ph	1	0	0	0	0	0	0	0
C.Estrada, p	0	0	0	0	0	0	0	0
J.Coates, p	0	0	0	0	0	0	0	1
A.Smith, ph	1	0	0	0	0	0	0	0
G.Bell, p	0	0	0	0	0	0	0	1
J.Gentile, ph-1b	2	0	1	0	0	1	0	0
Totals	34	3	6	3	5	7	27	8

BATTING
HR: A.Kaline (8th inning off B.Buhl, 1 on, 0 out).
RBI, scoring position, less than 2 outs: B.Robinson 0–1; N.Fox 1–1; L.Aparicio 0–2.
GDP: L.Aparicio.

BASERUNNING
Team LOB: 9

FIELDING
E: B.Daley (dropped throw).
DP: (1). F.Malzone-B.Skowron.

PITCHING	ip	h	r	er	bb	so
National League						
B.Friend (w)	3.0	1	0	0	1	2
M.McCormick	2.1	3	1	1	3	2
R.Face	1.2	0	0	0	0	2
B.Buhl	1.1	2	2	1	1	1
V.Law (s)	0.2	0	0	0	0	0
American League						
B.Monbouquette (L)	2.0	5	4	4	0	2
C.Estrada	1.0	4	1	1	0	1
J.Coates	2.0	2	0	0	0	0
G.Bell	2.0	0	0	0	0	0
F.Lary	1.0	1	0	0	0	1
B.Daley	1.0	0	0	0	1	2

Inherited Runners—Scored:
M.McCormick 0–0; R.Face 3–0; B.Buhl 0–0; V.Law 2–0; C.Estrada 0–0; J.Coates 0–0; G.Bell 0–0; F.Lary 0–0; B.Daley 0–0.

HBP: B.Mazeroski by J.Coates.

WP: B.Friend

BK: B.Friend

GAME DATA—T: 2:39; A: 30619; Temp: Unknown; Wind: Unknown direction, Speed: Unknown

UMPIRES—HP: Jim Honochick (AL), 1B: Tom Gorman (NL), 2B: Nestor Chylak (AL), 3B: Dusty Boggess (NL), LF: Johnny Stevens (AL), RF: Vinnie Smith (NL)

STARTING LINEUPS

	National League	*American League*
1.	W.Mays cf	M.Minoso lf
2.	B.Skinner lf	F.Malzone 3b
3.	E.Mathews 3b	R.Maris rf
4.	H.Aaron rf	M.Mantle cf
5.	E.Banks ss	B.Skowron 1b
6.	J.Adcock 1b	Y.Berra c
7.	B.Mazeroski 2b	P.Runnels 2b
8.	D.Crandall c	R.Hansen ss
9.	B.Friend p	B.Monbouquette p

NL 1ST: W.Mays tripled to right field; B.Skinner singled to left-center [W.Mays scored]; E.Mathews popped to B.Skowron-1b in foul territory; B.Skinner stole second; H.Aaron flied to M.Mantle-cf; E.Banks homered to deep leftfield [B.Skinner scored]; J.Adcock flied to R.Maris-rf; 3 R, 3 H, 0 E, 0 LOB. NL 3, AL 0.

AL 1ST: M.Minoso flied to W.Mays-cf; F.Malzone reached on an error by E.Mathews-3b [F.Malzone to first]; R.Maris struck out; M.Mantle walked [F.Malzone to second]; B.Skowron struck out; 0 R, 0 H, 1 E, 2 LOB. NL 3, AL 0.

NL 2ND: B.Mazeroski popped to B.Skowron-1b in foul territory; D.Crandall homered to deep leftfield; B.Friend struck out; W.Mays singled to left field; B.Skinner struck out; 1 R, 2 H, 0 E, 1 LOB. NL 4, AL 0.

AL 2ND: Y.Berra popped to E.Mathews-3b in foul territory; P.Runnels lined to B.Skinner-lf; R.Hansen singled to center field; **T.Williams batted for B.Monbouquette;** B.Friend balked [R.Hansen to second]; B.Friend threw a wild pitch [R.Hansen to third]; T.Williams grounded out (B.Mazeroski-2b to J.Adcock-1b); 0 R, 1 H, 0 E, 1 LOB. NL 4, AL 0.

NL 3RD: **C.Estrada replaced T.Williams (pitching);** E.Mathews popped to Y.Berra-c in foul territory; H.Aaron popped to B.Skowron-1b; E.Banks doubled to deep leftfield; J.Adcock singled to third base [E.Banks to third]; B.Mazeroski singled to left field [E.Banks scored, J.Adcock to second]; D.Crandall singled to third base [J.Adcock to third, B.Mazeroski to second]; B.Friend struck out; 1 R, 4 H, 0 E, 3 LOB. NL 5, AL 0.

AL 3RD: M.Minoso grounded out (E.Banks-ss to J.Adcock-1b); F.Malzone flied to W.Mays-cf; R.Maris grounded out (J.Adcock-1b unassisted); 0 R, 0 H, 0 E, 0 LOB. NL 5, AL 0.

NL 4TH: **J.Coates replaced C.Estrada (pitching);** W.Mays doubled to center field; B.Skinner grounded out (J.Coates-p to B.Skowron-1b); E.Mathews grounded out (P.Runnels-2b to B.Skowron-1b) [W.Mays to third]; H.Aaron flied to M.Mantle-cf; 0 R, 1 H, 0 E, 1 LOB. NL 5, AL 0.

AL 4TH: **M.McCormick replaced B.Friend (pitching);** M.Mantle walked; B.Skowron struck out; Y.Berra popped to E.Banks-ss; P.Runnels walked [M.Mantle to second]; R.Hansen struck out; 0 R, 0 H, 0 E, 2 LOB. NL 5, AL 0.

NL 5TH: E.Banks popped to Y.Berra-c in foul territory; J.Adcock doubled to very deep right-center; **B.White ran for J.Adcock;** B.Mazeroski was hit by a pitch; D.Crandall grounded into a double play (F.Malzone-3b to B.Skowron-1b) [B.White out at third]; 0 R, 1 H, 0 E, 1 LOB. NL 5, AL 0.

AL 5TH: **B.White stayed in game (playing 1b);** Umpires moved: Boggess (hp), Chylak (1b), Gorman (2b), Honochick (3b), Stevens (lf), Smith (rf); **A.Smith batted for J.Coates;** A.Smith flied to W.Mays-cf; M.Minoso popped to E.Banks-ss; F.Malzone flied to W.Mays-cf; 0 R, 0 H, 0 E, 0 LOB. NL 5, AL 0.

NL 6TH: **G.Bell replaced A.Smith (pitching); E.Howard replaced Y.Berra (playing c); N.Fox replaced P.Runnels (playing 2b); L.Aparicio replaced R.Hansen (playing ss); B.Robinson replaced F.Malzone (playing 3b); A.Kaline replaced M.Mantle (playing cf); J.Lemon replaced M.Minoso (playing lf); H.Kuenn replaced R.Maris (playing rf);** On a bunt M.McCormick grounded out (G.Bell-p to B.Skowron-1b); W.Mays flied to H.Kuenn-rf; B.Skinner popped to E.Howard-c in foul territory; 0 R, 0 H, 0 E, 0 LOB. NL 5, AL 0.

AL 6TH: **O.Cepeda replaced B.Skinner (playing lf); V.Pinson replaced W.Mays (playing cf);** H.Kuenn singled to right field (H.Aaron-rf to E.Banks-ss) [H.Kuenn out at second]; Mazeroski and Aaron let pop drop, but Aaron recovered; A.Kaline reached on an error by E.Mathews-3b [A.Kaline to first]; B.Skowron singled to right field [A.Kaline to third]; E.Howard walked [B.Skowron to second]; N.Fox singled to left field [A.Kaline scored, B.Skowron to third, E.Howard to second]; **R.Face replaced M.McCormick (pitching);** L.Aparicio grounded into a double play (E.Banks-ss to B.Mazeroski-2b to B.White-1b) [N.Fox out at second]; 1 R, 3 H, 1 E, 2 LOB. NL 5, AL 1.

NL 7TH: E.Mathews grounded out (N.Fox-2b to B.Skowron-1b); H.Aaron flied to A.Kaline-cf; E.Banks grounded out (N.Fox-2b to B.Skowron-1b); 0 R, 0 H, 0 E, 0 LOB. NL 5, AL 1.

AL 7TH: **R.Clemente replaced H.Aaron (playing rf); D.Groat replaced E.Banks (playing ss); K.Boyer replaced E.Mathews (playing 3b); S.Burgess replaced D.Crandall (playing c); J.Gentile batted for G.Bell;** J.Gentile struck out; J.Lemon was called out on strikes; B.Robinson grounded out

(D.Groat-ss to B.White-1b); 0 R, 0 H, 0 E, 0 LOB. NL 5, AL 1.

NL 8TH: **J.Gentile stayed in game (playing 1b); F.Lary replaced B.Skowron (pitching);** B.White struck out; **S.Musial batted for B.Mazeroski;** S.Musial singled to second base; **T.Taylor ran for S.Musial;** S.Burgess forced T.Taylor (N.Fox-2b to L.Aparicio-ss) [S.Burgess to first]; **N.Larker batted for R.Face;** N.Larker forced S.Burgess (L.Aparicio-ss to N.Fox-2b) [N.Larker to first]; 0 R, 1 H, 0 E, 1 LOB. NL 5, AL 1.

AL 8TH: **B.Buhl replaced N.Larker (pitching); C.Neal replaced T.Taylor (playing 2b);** H.Kuenn reached on an error by C.Neal-2b [H.Kuenn to first]; A.Kaline homered to deep leftfield [H.Kuenn scored (unearned)]; **S.Lollar batted for F.Lary;** S.Lollar grounded out (K.Boyer-3b to B.White-1b); E.Howard struck out; N.Fox flied to R.Clemente-rf; 2 R (1 ER), 1 H, 1 E, 0 LOB. NL 5, AL 3.

NL 9TH: **B.Daley replaced S.Lollar (pitching);** V.Pinson struck out; O.Cepeda struck out; K.Boyer walked; K.Boyer was picked off first, but was safe on an error by B.Daley-p [K.Boyer to second]; Boyer got to 3b but was returned to 2b because of fan inter; R.Clemente lined to J.Lemon-lf; 0 R, 0 H, 1 E, 1 LOB. NL 5, AL 3.

AL 9TH: L.Aparicio grounded out (K.Boyer-3b to B.White-1b); S.Burgess-c dropped a foul fly hit by J.Gentile; J.Gentile singled to right-center; J.Lemon walked [J.Gentile to second]; **V.Law replaced B.Buhl (pitching);** B.Robinson flied to V.Pinson-cf; H.Kuenn lined to R.Clemente-rf; 0 R, 1 H, 1 E, 2 LOB. NL 5, AL 3.

Final Totals	R	H	E	LOB
National League	5	12	4	8
American League	3	6	1	9

GAME 29

Wednesday, July 13, 1960

Yankee Stadium, New York City

National League 6, American League 0

SERIES RESULTS: AL 16, NL 13

A Clean Sweep Completed in the Big Apple

The second 1960 game, played in Yankee Stadium two days after the first, drew a very disappointing crowd of 38,362, reflecting the lukewarm enthusiasm many fans had for the two-games-a-year format. Maybe the New Yorkers had a premonition about what was coming, because the NL scored an easy 6–0 victory to sweep the season series. Leading the charge against holding two All-Star Games in a season was Arthur Daley of the *New York Times,* who was very critical and attributed the situation entirely to player greed. Using such language as "watering down" and "deglamorization," Daley sniffed: "A single game made for a delightful reunion of the stars. . . . Two games smack of work and dilute the pleasure." Nonetheless, he concluded his column on a positive note, a view likely shared by most: "Now this traveling circus hits the big town. Though it has some flaws, it still ranks as a worthwhile show. It usually is."

The flap involving the Indians' Vic Power that had arisen in the Kansas City game two days earlier had gathered steam while everyone was in transit to the East Coast. Power conceded that he had said to Cleveland announcer Bob Neal: "I'll bet you $100 he (Lopez) doesn't play me in the All-Star Game." Before the game, the first baseman was visited in the clubhouse by Commissioner Ford Frick, underscoring Major League Baseball's extreme sensitivity to any implications of wagering by players. Power explained that his remark had been meant as a joke, an answer that apparently satisfied Frick, because no further action was ever taken.

Another off-field matter of much interest was expansion. The American League owners and president had held their summer meeting the day before the New York game. Although a scheduled thirty-minute meeting with "no agenda" (according to AL prexy Joe Cronin) ran to four and a half hours, everyone insisted the topic "never came up." National League president Warren Giles said, "It has never been discussed at a league meeting, either formally or informally and it is not on the agenda for our July 18 meeting." Robert Cannon, counsel to the player representatives, also said the topic "never came up." Of course, despite all of these protestations, the National League owners announced on October 17, 1960, that the league would expand to ten teams for the 1962 season. Nine days later, the American League trumped that by declaring that it would field ten teams in 1961, leaving a scant five months for implementation.

There was much pregame hype for the "return to New York" by Willie Mays, who had been a huge fan favorite for the Giants before they left town for the Golden Gate after the 1957 season. Willie didn't disappoint as he gathered three more hits, including a home run, giving him six hits (three singles, a double, a triple, and a home run) for the two games. He also stole a base and had five putouts in center field for an all-around fine day. Mays wasn't the only bomber for the NL; the Braves' Eddie Mathews and Ken Boyer and the Cardinals' Stan Musial also went deep. Musial's circuit clout was his sixth in an All-Star Game, which is still the record.

The National League's pitching was steady if not spectacular as six men were used for the shutout. NL manager Walter Alston of the Dodgers called Vern Law of the Pirates to start the game. Law continued his mastery from Monday by pitching the first two innings, allowing only a single to Bill Skowron. Law was followed by Johnny Podres and Stan Williams, both Dodgers, who turned in two scoreless frames each despite giving up three hits and four walks between them. Larry Jackson of the Cardinals, Bill Henry of the Reds, and Lindy McDaniel of the Cardinals blanked the AL for one inning each, giving up two more walks and four more hits in the process. The AL wasn't exactly dominated at the plate; it ended up with eight hits, seven of them singles, and six walks. The Nationals also grounded into two double plays and left twelve men on base, being retired in order only in the first inning.

The AL pitchers allowed ten hits and three walks, but the four home runs were too much to overcome. Whitey Ford of the Yankees continued his All-Star woes as he was touched for a pair of home runs: a two-run shot by Mathews in the second with his Milwaukee teammate Joe Adcock on base and a solo job by Mays in the third. Ford, a future Hall of Famer, took the loss this day and increased his ERA to 11.00 over nine innings. His final career All-Star numbers would be a 9.00 ERA in twelve innings. In the seventh inning, Musial pinch-hit for Williams and homered into the third deck in right field off Gerry Staley of the White Sox. Early Wynn of the White Sox and Frank Lary of the Tigers combined for three scoreless innings before and after the seventh. The scoring was completed in the ninth when Boyer touched Gary Bell of the Indians for a homer to left field with the Dodgers' Norm Larker aboard after the Dodger first sacker walked as a pinch hitter for Bill White.

The homers by Musial and Boyer had some interesting features as well. The blast from Stan The Man was his sixth in All-Star competition, a record that still stands. It was widely believed that this would be the final All-Star contest for Musial and Ted Williams of the Red Sox; Williams collected a pinch-hit single this day. Arthur Daley noted that this game had "ended the all-star appearances of those two ancient gladiators on happy notes." Although this was the last season for Williams, Musial went on to play in five more All-Star Games in his last three seasons before retiring, running his total to twenty-four, putting him in a tie with Mays and Henry Aaron for the most appearances. Boyer's homer was a triumph of willpower because he had arrived in New York with a seriously strained muscle in his side. "I'd like to get in for an inning or two, but only in the field," he said. "I don't want to get to bat because I'm in such bad shape that I can't swing properly." Perhaps it was the warm day (88 degrees and humid), but the Cardinals' slugging third baseman strode to the plate in the ninth inning and drove one into the left-field stands.

No errors were committed in the game, in contrast to the four charged to the NL two days earlier. The only base-running gaffe came in the first inning when Mays was caught off third base after a swing and miss by Adcock on a broken hit-and-run play. Willie was charged with a caught stealing because Yogi Berra and Frank Malzone ran him down. Mays had teased Berra about stealing before the game and had in fact reached third base on a steal. The caught stealing on the rundown brought a big smile to Yogi's face.

There were no changes in the rosters of players or coaches between the two games, but there was a switch in announcers. The first game was covered by Curt Gowdy and Russ Hodges (TV) and Merle Harmon and Jack Quinlan (radio), while Mel Allen and Vin Scully handled the TV and Bob Elson and Waite Hoyt the radio for the second game. The telecast of the second game was the first one ever broadcast in color.

	AL		NL	
P	Whitey Ford	NYA	Vern Law	PIT
C	Yogi Berra	NYA	Del Crandall	MIL
1 B	Bill Skowron	NYA	Joe Adcock	MIL
2 B	Pete Runnels	BOS	Bill Mazeroski	PIT
3 B	Frank Malzone	BOS	Eddie Mathews	MIL
SS	Ron Hansen	BAL	Ernie Banks	CHN
OF	Mickey Mantle	NYA	Hank Aaron	MIL
OF	Roger Maris	NYA	Willie Mays	SFN
OF	Minnie Minoso	CHA	Bob Skinner	PIT
	Luis Aparicio	CHA	Ed Bailey	CIN
	Gary Bell	CLE	Ken Boyer	SLN
	Jim Coates	NYA	Bob Buhl	MIL
	Bud Daley	KC	Smoky Burgess	PIT
	Chuck Estrada	BAL	Orlando Cepeda	SFN
	Nellie Fox	CHA	Roberto Clemente	PIT
	Jim Gentile	BAL	Roy Face	PIT
	Elston Howard	NYA	Bob Friend	PIT
	Al Kaline	DET	Dick Groat	PIT
	Harvey Kuenn	CLE	Bill Henry	CIN
	Frank Lary	DET	Larry Jackson	SLN
	Jim Lemon	WAS	Norm Larker	LAN
	Sherm Lollar	CHA	Mike McCormick	SFN
	Bill Monbouquette	BOS	Lindy McDaniel	SLN
	Camilo Pascual	WAS	Stan Musial	SLN
	Vic Power	CLE	Charlie Neal	LAN
	Brooks Robinson	BAL	Vada Pinson	CIN
	Al Smith	CHA	Johnny Podres	LAN
	Gerry Staley	CHA	Tony Taylor	PHI
	Dick Stigman	CLE	Bill White	SLN
	Ted Williams	BOS	Stan Williams	LAN
	Early Wynn	CHA		

```
National League    021 000 102- 6
American League    000 000 000- 0
```

NATIONAL LEAGUE

	ab	r	h	bi	bb	so	po	a
W.Mays, cf	4	1	3	1	0	0	5	0
V.Pinson, cf	0	0	0	0	1	0	0	0
B.Skinner, lf	3	0	1	0	0	1	2	0
O.Cepeda, lf	2	0	0	0	0	0	0	0
H.Aaron, rf	3	0	0	0	0	0	1	0
R.Clemente, ph-rf	0	0	0	0	1	0	0	0
E.Banks, ss	3	0	1	0	0	0	2	3
D.Groat, ph-ss	1	0	0	0	0	0	0	1
J.Adcock, 1b	2	1	1	0	0	1	3	0
B.White, 1b	1	0	0	0	0	0	2	0
N.Larker, ph-1b	0	1	0	0	1	0	3	0
E.Mathews, 3b	3	1	1	2	0	0	0	1
K.Boyer, 3b	1	1	1	2	0	0	1	0
B.Mazeroski, 2b	2	0	0	0	0	0	0	0
C.Neal, 2b	1	0	0	0	0	0	1	2
T.Taylor, 2b	1	0	1	0	0	0	2	1
D.Crandall, c	2	0	0	0	0	0	3	0
S.Williams, p	0	0	0	0	0	0	0	0
S.Musial, ph	1	1	1	1	0	0	0	0
E.Bailey, c	1	0	0	0	0	0	0	0
V.Law, p	1	0	0	0	0	0	0	1
J.Podres, p	0	0	0	0	0	0	0	1
S.Burgess, ph-c	2	0	0	0	0	1	2	0
L.Jackson, p	0	0	0	0	0	0	0	0
B.Henry, p	0	0	0	0	0	0	0	0
L.McDaniel, p	0	0	0	0	0	0	0	0
Totals	34	6	10	6	3	3	27	10

BATTING

HR: W.Mays (3rd inning off W.Ford, 0 on, 0 out);
E.Mathews (2nd inning off W.Ford, 1 on, 0 out);
K.Boyer (9th inning off G.Bell, 1 on, 0 out); S.Musial
(7th inning off G.Staley, 0 on, 2 out).

2-out RBI: S.Musial.

RBI, scoring position, less than 2 outs: H.Aaron 0–1;
E.Banks 0–1; D.Groat 0–1.

S: B.Henry.

GDP: D.Groat.

BASERUNNING

SB: W.Mays (3rd base off W.Ford/Y.Berra).

CS: W.Mays (HP by W.Ford/Y.Berra).

Team LOB: 5

FIELDING

DP: (2). V.Law-E.Banks-J.Adcock; E.Banks-C.Neal-
B.White.

AMERICAN LEAGUE

	ab	r	h	bi	bb	so	po	a
M.Minoso, lf	2	0	0	0	1	1	1	0
T.Williams, ph	1	0	1	0	0	0	0	0
B.Robinson, pr-3b	1	0	0	0	0	0	0	0
P.Runnels, 2b	2	0	0	0	1	1	0	1
G.Staley, p	0	0	0	0	0	0	1	1
A.Kaline, ph-lf	1	0	1	0	1	0	3	0
R.Maris, rf	4	0	0	0	1	0	0	0
M.Mantle, cf	4	0	1	0	0	1	3	0
B.Skowron, 1b	1	0	1	0	1	0	6	0
V.Power, 1b	2	0	0	0	0	0	5	1
Y.Berra, c	2	0	0	0	0	1	4	1
S.Lollar, c	2	0	1	0	0	0	0	0
F.Malzone, 3b	2	0	0	0	1	0	2	2
F.Lary, p	0	0	0	0	0	0	0	0
A.Smith, ph	1	0	0	0	0	0	0	0
G.Bell, p	0	0	0	0	0	0	0	1
R.Hansen, ss	4	0	2	0	0	0	2	4
W.Ford, p	0	0	0	0	0	0	0	0
H.Kuenn, ph	1	0	0	0	0	0	0	0
E.Wynn, p	0	0	0	0	0	0	0	0
N.Fox, ph-2b	3	0	1	0	0	0	0	1
Totals	33	0	8	0	6	4	27	12

BATTING

2B: S.Lollar (off B.Henry).

RBI, scoring position, less than 2 outs: M.Minoso 0–1;
A.Smith 0–2.

GDP: M.Minoso; Y.Berra.

BASERUNNING

Team LOB: 12

FIELDING

DP: (1). N.Fox-R.Hansen-V.Power.

PITCHING	ip	h	r	er	bb	so
National League						
V.Law (w)	2.0	1	0	0	0	1
J.Podres	2.0	1	0	0	3	1
S.Williams	2.0	2	0	0	1	2
L.Jackson	1.0	1	0	0	2	0
B.Henry	1.0	2	0	0	0	0
L.McDaniel (s)	1.0	1	0	0	0	0
American League						
W.Ford (l)	3.0	5	3	3	0	1
E.Wynn	2.0	0	0	0	0	2
G.Staley	2.0	2	1	1	0	0
F.Lary	1.0	1	0	0	1	0
G.Bell	1.0	2	2	2	2	0

Inherited Runners—Scored:
   J.Podres 0–0; S.Williams 0–0; L.Jackson 0–0;
   B.Henry 0–0; L.McDaniel 0–0; E.Wynn 0–0;
   G.Staley 0–0; F.Lary 0–0; G.Bell 0–0.

GAME DATA—T: 2:42; A: 38362; Temp: 88;
Wind: Unknown direction, Speed: Unknown

UMPIRES—HP: Nestor Chylak (AL), 1B: Dusty Boggess
(NL), 2B: Jim Honochick (AL), 3B: Tom Gorman (NL),
LF: Johnny Stevens (AL), RF: Vinnie Smith (NL)

STARTING LINEUPS

	National League	*American League*
1.	W.Mays cf	M.Minoso lf
2.	B.Skinner lf	P.Runnels 2b
3.	H.Aaron rf	R.Maris rf
4.	E.Banks ss	M.Mantle cf
5.	J.Adcock 1b	B.Skowron 1b
6.	E.Mathews 3b	Y.Berra c
7.	B.Mazeroski 2b	F.Malzone 3b
8.	D.Crandall c	R.Hansen ss
9.	V.Law p	W.Ford p

NL 1ST: W.Mays singled to left field; B.Skinner singled [W.Mays to second]; H.Aaron popped to R.Hansen-ss; W.Mays stole third; E.Banks popped to B.Skowron-1b; W.Mays was picked off and caught stealing home (Y.Berra-c to F.Malzone-3b to Y.Berra-c to F.Malzone-3b); 0 R, 2 H, 0 E, 1 LOB. NL 0, AL 0.

AL 1ST: M.Minoso struck out; P.Runnels flied to B.Skinner-lf; R.Maris flied to W.Mays-cf; 0 R, 0 H, 0 E, 0 LOB. NL 0, AL 0.

NL 2ND: J.Adcock singled to center field; E.Mathews homered to deep leftfield [J.Adcock scored]; B.Mazeroski popped to Y.Berra-c in foul territory; D.Crandall grounded out (R.Hansen-ss to B.Skowron-1b); V.Law grounded out (P.Runnels-2b to B.Skowron-1b); 2 R, 2 H, 0 E, 0 LOB. NL 2, AL 0.

AL 2ND: M.Mantle popped to J.Adcock-1b; B.Skowron singled to center field; Y.Berra grounded into a double play (V.Law-p to E.Banks-ss to J.Adcock-1b) [B.Skowron out at second]; 0 R, 1 H, 0 E, 0 LOB. NL 2, AL 0.

NL 3RD: W.Mays homered to deep leftfield; B.Skinner was called out on strikes; H.Aaron flied to M.Mantle-cf; E.Banks popped to F.Malzone-3b in foul territory; 1 R, 1 H, 0 E, 0 LOB. NL 3, AL 0.

AL 3RD: **J.Podres replaced V.Law (pitching);** F.Malzone grounded out (E.Mathews-3b to J.Adcock-1b); R.Hansen singled to center field; **H.Kuenn batted for W.Ford;** H.Kuenn flied to B.Skinner-lf; M.Minoso walked [R.Hansen to second]; P.Runnels walked [R.Hansen to third, M.Minoso to second]; R.Maris popped to D.Crandall-c; 0 R, 1 H, 0 E, 3 LOB. NL 3, AL 0.

NL 4TH: **E.Wynn replaced H.Kuenn (pitching);** J.Adcock struck out; E.Mathews lined to M.Mantle-cf; B.Mazeroski grounded out (R.Hansen-ss to B.Skowron-1b); 0 R, 0 H, 0 E, 0 LOB. NL 3, AL 0.

AL 4TH: **B.White replaced J.Adcock (playing 1b); C.Neal replaced B.Mazeroski (playing 2b);** M.Mantle flied to W.Mays-cf; B.Skowron walked; Y.Berra struck out; F.Malzone forced B.Skowron (J.Podres-p to C.Neal-2b to E.Banks-ss) [F.Malzone to first]; 0 R, 0 H, 0 E, 1 LOB. NL 3, AL 0.

NL 5TH: D.Crandall popped to B.Skowron-1b in foul territory; **S.Burgess batted for J.Podres;** S.Burgess struck out; W.Mays popped to B.Skowron-1b in foul territory; 0 R, 0 H, 0 E, 0 LOB. NL 3, AL 0.

AL 5TH: Umpires moved: Gorman (hp), Honochick (1b) Boggess (2b), Chylak (3b), Stevens (lf), Smith (rf); **S.Burgess stayed in game (playing c); S.Williams replaced D.Crandall (pitching);** R.Hansen singled to right field; **N.Fox batted for E.Wynn;** On a bunt N.Fox singled to third base [R.Hansen to second]; M.Minoso grounded into a double play (E.Banks-ss to C.Neal-2b to B.White-1b) [R.Hansen to third, N.Fox out at second]; P.Runnels struck out; 0 R, 2 H, 0 E, 1 LOB. NL 3, AL 0.

NL 6TH: **N.Fox stayed in game (playing 2b); S.Lollar replaced Y.Berra (playing c); G.Staley replaced P.Runnels (pitching); V.Power replaced B.Skowron (playing 1b);** B.Skinner grounded out (R.Hansen-ss to V.Power-1b); H.Aaron grounded out (F.Malzone-3b to V.Power-1b); E.Banks singled to third base; B.White flied to M.Mantle-cf; 0 R, 1 H, 0 E, 1 LOB. NL 3, AL 0.

AL 6TH: R.Maris walked; M.Mantle was called out on strikes; V.Power flied to W.Mays-cf; S.Lollar grounded out (E.Banks-ss to B.White-1b); 0 R, 0 H, 0 E, 1 LOB. NL 3, AL 0.

NL 7TH: E.Mathews grounded out (G.Staley-p to V.Power-1b); C.Neal flied to M.Minoso-lf; **S.Musial batted for S.Williams;** S.Musial homered to deep rightfield; S.Burgess grounded out (V.Power-1b to G.Staley-p); 1 R, 1 H, 0 E, 0 LOB. NL 4, AL 0.

AL 7TH: **L.Jackson replaced S.Burgess (pitching); E.Bailey replaced S.Musial (playing c); K.Boyer replaced E.Mathews (playing 3b); O.Cepeda replaced B.Skinner (playing lf);** F.Malzone walked; R.Hansen flied to W.Mays-cf; N.Fox flied to H.Aaron-rf; **T.Williams batted for M.Minoso;** T.Williams singled to right field [F.Malzone to third]; **B.Robinson ran for T.Williams; A.Kaline batted for G.Staley;** A.Kaline walked [B.Robinson to second]; R.Maris flied to W.Mays-cf; 0 R, 1 H, 0 E, 3 LOB. NL 4, AL 0.

NL 8TH: **B.Robinson stayed in game (playing 3b); A.Kaline stayed in game (playing lf); F.Lary replaced F.Malzone (pitching);** W.Mays singled to center field; O.Cepeda flied to A.Kaline-lf; **R.Clemente batted for H.Aaron;** R.Clemente walked [W.Mays to second]; **D.Groat batted for E.Banks;** D.Groat grounded into a double play (N.Fox-2b to R.Hansen-ss to V.Power-1b) [R.Clemente out at second]; 0 R, 1 H, 0 E, 1 LOB. NL 4, AL 0.

AL 8TH: **D.Groat stayed in game (playing ss); V.Pinson replaced W.Mays (playing cf); R.Clemente stayed in game (playing rf); T.Taylor replaced C.Neal (playing 2b); B.Henry replaced L.Jackson (pitching);** M.Mantle singled to center field; V.Power popped to T.Taylor-2b; S.Lollar hit a ground rule double to rightfield down the line [M.Mantle to third]; **A.Smith batted for F.Lary;** A.Smith popped to K.Boyer-3b; R.Hansen popped to T.Taylor-2b; 0 R, 2 H, 0 E, 2 LOB. NL 4, AL 0.

NL 9TH: **G.Bell replaced A.Smith (pitching); N.Larker batted for B.White;** N.Larker walked; K.Boyer homered to deep leftfield [N.Larker scored]; T.Taylor singled to center field; E.Bailey flied to A.Kaline-lf; B.Henry out on a sacrifice bunt (G.Bell-p to V.Power-1b) [T.Taylor to second]; V.Pinson walked; O.Cepeda flied to A.Kaline-lf; 2 R, 2 H, 0 E, 2 LOB. NL 6, AL 0.

AL 9TH: **N.Larker stayed in game (playing 1b); L.McDaniel replaced B.Henry (pitching);** N.Fox grounded out (T.Taylor-2b to N.Larker-1b); B.Robinson grounded out (D.Groat-ss to N.Larker-1b); A.Kaline singled to second base; R.Maris grounded out (N.Larker-1b unassisted); 0 R, 1 H, 0 E, 1 LOB. NL 6, AL 0.

Final Totals	R	H	E	LOB
National League	6	10	0	5
American League	0	8	0	12

30

The NL Jumps over the Candlestick

The pair of games played in 1961 will go down as the "weather contests." The game in San Francisco's Candlestick Park on July 11 was plagued by high winds, which set the stage for one of the classic images in All-Star folklore: Stu Miller was blown off the mound for a balk in the ninth inning. In 1960, the two games had been played during a four-day break, and the rosters remained stable. For 1961, the decision was made not to disrupt the regular schedule to such an extent, and the games were therefore separated by almost three weeks. Although the wind played some havoc with the players, it was welcome as a public health measure because 95 people were treated for heat prostration during the 81-degree afternoon. First-aid officials said that the wind prevented the setting of a new record in this unpleasant category; there had been 104 victims of the heat the previous Sunday.

Starting lineups (except for the pitcher) were again chosen by players, coaches, and managers. The top vote getters for the AL were Norm Cash of the Tigers with 235 and Roger Maris with 233. For the NL, the leader was Frank Bolling of the Braves with 183. The rosters were filled out by the managers, with a limit of twenty-five players. For the second game, the roster was increased to twenty-eight, and changes to the pitching staffs were permitted. The managers were Danny Murtaugh of the Pirates and Paul Richards of the Orioles. Casey Stengel, the manager of the pennant-winning Yankees in 1960, had been fired after the World Series, so the AL honor went to Richards, who had guided the 1960 Orioles to a second-place finish, eight games behind New York. Stengel did have the honor of throwing out the ceremonial first ball.

The Pirates' Roberto Clemente had an excellent day at the plate. He scored the game's first run in the second inning after hitting a triple against the Yankees' Whitey Ford, the AL starter; the Cardinals' Bill White brought him in with a sacrifice fly. Clemente hit his own sacrifice fly in the fourth inning to score the Giants' Willie Mays, who had reached second when his rocket to shortstop Tony Kubek cracked the Yankee in the knee and rolled into left field. Mays was the only batter faced by Detroit's Frank Lary, who left with an inflamed tendon in his pitching shoulder. Dick Donovan of the Senators came on and retired the Giants' Orlando Cepeda on a ground ball, sending Mays to third before the sacrifice fly scored him. After White singled, the inning ended when Bolling hit a line drive up the middle that second baseman Johnny Temple of the Indians caught with a spectacular leap. This play was possible only because White was going on the pitch and Temple was covering the base. In the fifth, the NL loaded the bases against Donovan on three singles, but Cepeda popped up to end the inning.

Most of the offense came in the ninth and tenth innings, when five of the game's nine runs were scored. These last two innings also saw five of the game's record seven errors, five of them by the winning NL. However, only one of the errors, a dropped foul pop by Smokey Burgess, was related to the wind, which was howling by that time. Burgess had made a similar error the year before in Kansas City. Through the first eight innings, the AL was limited to one run and one hit, both coming on a sixth-inning pinch-hit home run by Harmon Killebrew of the Twins against Mike McCormick of the host Giants. Warren Spahn of the Braves started the game with three hitless innings and was succeeded by Bob Purkey of the Reds, who retired six straight batters in his two-inning stint after the first batter he faced, the Indians' Johnny Temple, reached second when left fielder Cepeda dropped his line drive. The trouble for the NL began against the Pirates' Roy Face in the ninth. Face, who had turned in an excellent performance in 1960 after taking his lumps in 1959, once again was ineffective. He faced three batters, striking out Jim Gentile of the Orioles and allowing a double to Norm Cash and a single to Al

Kaline, both of the Tigers. Left-handed Dodger Sandy Koufax came on but was touched for a single by Yankee Roger Maris, scoring Nellie Fox of the White Sox, who had run for Cash. Stu Miller was then brought in to face slugger Rocky Colavito, also of the Tigers. At this point the already strong wind really picked up, and Miller committed his famous balk. Colavito hit a ground ball to third baseman Ken Boyer of the Cardinals, who had made three brilliant fielding plays in the 1956 game. This time, Boyer's performance was different as he booted the ball, allowing Kaline to score the tying run while Maris remained at second. The AL did not score again that inning, but there were two more errors, the dropped foul by Burgess and a bad throw by second baseman Don Zimmer of the Cubs. The Yankees' Yogi Berra pinch-hit a grounder to Zimmer, whose throw pulled first baseman White off the bag and loaded the bases. Miller hung in and got Dick Howser of the Athletics to fly out and end the nightmare.

Although Miller and his windblown balk are common conversation topics, Miller actually pitched very well before his hometown fans and very deservedly received credit for the win. Over his 1.2 innings, he allowed no hits and one walk. However, his All-Star mates committed four errors while he was on the mound, three of which put runners on base (Kubek hit the foul pop that Burgess dropped and then struck out). The one run charged to Miller was unearned and came in the tenth. After striking out the first two batters, Miller walked Fox, and then Boyer made his second error in as many innings, this one a very wild throw past first base after he fielded a grounder from Kaline. Fox scored the go-ahead run all the way from first as Kaline came around to third. Miller fanned Maris to strike out the side; of the five outs he got, four were on whiffs.

The final pitcher of the day for the American League was knuckle-balling Hoyt Wilhelm of the Orioles, who did not fare nearly as well. The knuckle ball is always a treacherous pitch; on a day with a near gale blowing, it was a cruel thing to do to the AL catchers, but AL manager Richards, Wilhelm's skipper at the time in Baltimore, wanted his ace reliever in the game. In fact, in his 1.2 innings, Wilhelm pitched to three different catchers. John Romano of the Indians was the starter and still in the game when Hoyt entered in the eighth, replacing Mike Fornieles of the Red Sox, who had allowed a first-pitch, pinch-hit home run to George Altman of the Cubs, giving the NL a 3–1 lead. The Reds' Frank Robinson had singled and immediately taken advantage of the slow and unpredictable delivery as he stole second. After Berra batted for Romano, he went in to catch in the ninth, but as soon as there was a base runner (Boyer walked), Yogi was removed in favor of his teammate Elston Howard, a disrespectful action at any time but even more so in the bright publicity of the All-Star Game. As it developed, Wilhelm hurt his own cause by making a wild throw trying to pick Boyer off first, but he retired Maury Wills of the Dodgers on a pop-up to end the inning.

In the fateful tenth, Wilhelm and the AL lost the game when the NL rallied to score two runs without making an out. Henry Aaron of the Braves led off with a single, went to second on a passed ball by Howard, and scored on a double down the third base line by Mays. Frank Robinson was hit by a pitch, and the game ended when Clemente singled to right to score Mays, running the National League's record in extra-inning games to a perfect 3-0. Maris fielded the ball and threw it in to second base instead of toward the plate, unaware that Mays was scoring the winning run.

	AL		NL	
P	Whitey Ford	NYA	Bob Purkey	CIN
C	John Romano	CLE	Smoky Burgess	PIT
1B	Norm Cash	DET	Bill White	SLN
2B	Johnny Temple	CLE	Frank Bolling	MIL
3B	Brooks Robinson	BAL	Eddie Mathews	MIL
SS	Tony Kubek	NYA	Maury Wills	LAN
OF	Rocky Colavito	DET	Orlando Cepeda	SFN
OF	Mickey Mantle	NYA	Roberto Clemente	PIT
OF	Roger Maris	NYA	Willie Mays	SFN
	Yogi Berra	NYA	Hank Aaron	MIL
	Jackie Brandt	BAL	George Altman	CHN
	Jim Bunning	DET	Ken Boyer	SLN
	Dick Donovan	WAS	Roy Face	PIT
	Ryne Duren	LAA	Joey Jay	CIN
	Mike Fornieles	BOS	Eddie Kasko	CIN
	Nellie Fox	CHA	Sandy Koufax	LAN
	Jim Gentile	BAL	Art Mahaffey	PHI
	Elston Howard	NYA	Mike McCormick	SFN
	Dick Howser	KC	Stu Miller	SFN
	Al Kaline	DET	Stan Musial	SLN
	Harmon Killebrew	MIN	Frank Robinson	CIN
	Frank Lary	DET	John Roseboro	LAN
	Jim Perry	CLE	Dick Stuart	PIT
	Billy Pierce	CHA	Don Zimmer	CHN
	Hoyt Wilhelm	BAL		

American League   000 001 002 1- 4
National League   010 100 010 2- 5 (10)
   0 outs when winning run was scored.

AMERICAN LEAGUE

	ab	r	h	bi	bb	so	po	a
J.Temple, 2b	3	0	0	0	0	0	1	2
J.Gentile, ph-1b	2	0	0	0	0	2	2	0
N.Cash, 1b	4	0	1	0	0	2	6	1
N.Fox, pr-2b	0	2	0	0	1	0	1	0
M.Mantle, cf	3	0	0	0	0	2	3	0
A.Kaline, cf	2	1	1	1	0	0	1	0
R.Maris, rf	4	0	1	0	1	2	3	0
R.Colavito, lf	4	0	0	1	0	0	1	0
T.Kubek, ss	4	0	0	0	0	1	1	2
J.Romano, c	3	0	0	0	0	1	7	0
Y.Berra, ph-c	1	0	0	0	0	0	0	0
E.Howard, c	0	0	0	0	0	0	0	0
B.Robinson, 3b	2	0	0	0	0	0	0	2
J.Bunning, p	0	0	0	0	0	0	1	0
J.Brandt, ph	1	0	0	0	0	1	0	0
M.Fornieles, p	0	0	0	0	0	0	0	0
H.Wilhelm, p	1	0	0	0	0	0	0	1
W.Ford, p	1	0	0	0	0	0	0	1
F.Lary, p	0	0	0	0	0	0	0	0
D.Donovan, p	0	0	0	0	0	0	0	0
H.Killebrew, ph-3b	2	1	1	1	0	0	0	0
D.Howser, 3b	1	0	0	0	0	1	0	1
Totals	38	4	4	3	2	12	27	10

BATTING
2B: N.Cash (off R.Face).
HR: H.Killebrew (6th inning off M.McCormick, 0 on, 1 out).
RBI, scoring position, less than 2 outs: N.Cash 0–1; M.Mantle 0–1; A.Kaline 1–1; R.Colavito 1–1; T.Kubek 0–1.

BASERUNNING
Team LOB: 6

FIELDING
E: T.Kubek (fumble); J.Gentile (dropped throw).
PB: E.Howard.

NATIONAL LEAGUE

	ab	r	h	bi	bb	so	po	a
M.Wills, ss	5	0	1	0	0	0	0	2
E.Mathews, 3b	2	0	0	0	0	0	0	0
B.Purkey, p	0	0	0	0	0	0	1	0
S.Musial, ph	1	0	0	0	0	0	0	0
M.McCormick, p	0	0	0	0	0	0	0	0
G.Altman, ph	1	1	1	1	0	0	0	0
R.Face, p	0	0	0	0	0	0	0	0
S.Koufax, p	0	0	0	0	0	0	0	0
S.Miller, p	0	0	0	0	0	0	0	0
H.Aaron, ph	1	1	1	0	0	0	0	0
W.Mays, cf	5	2	2	1	0	1	3	0
O.Cepeda, lf	3	0	0	0	0	0	1	0
F.Robinson, lf	1	0	1	0	0	0	2	0
R.Clemente, rf	4	1	2	2	0	1	2	0
B.White, 1b	3	0	1	1	0	1	7	1
F.Bolling, 2b	3	0	0	0	0	1	1	3
D.Zimmer, 2b	1	0	0	0	0	0	0	0
S.Burgess, c	4	0	1	0	0	0	13	0
W.Spahn, p	0	0	0	0	0	0	0	1
D.Stuart, ph	1	0	1	0	0	0	0	0
K.Boyer, 3b	2	0	0	0	1	2	0	1
Totals	37	5	11	5	1	6	30	8

BATTING
2B: D.Stuart (off W.Ford); W.Mays (off H.Wilhelm).
3B: R.Clemente (off W.Ford).
HR: G.Altman (8th inning off M.Fornieles, 0 on, 0 out).
RBI, scoring position, less than 2 outs: M.Wills 0–1; S.Musial 0–1; W.Mays 1–1; O.Cepeda 0–1; R.Clemente 2–3; B.White 1–1.
SF: R.Clemente; B.White.

BASERUNNING
SB: F.Robinson (2nd base off H.Wilhelm/J.Romano).
Team LOB: 9

FIELDING
E: O.Cepeda (dropped liner); K.Boyer (fumble); S.Burgess (dropped foul ball); D.Zimmer (throw); K.Boyer (throw).

PITCHING	ip	h	r	er	bb	so
American League						
W.Ford	3.0	2	1	1	0	2
F.Lary	* 0.0	0	1	0	0	0
D.Donovan	2.0	4	0	0	0	1
J.Bunning	2.0	0	0	0	0	2

Inherited Runners—Scored:
F.Lary 0–0; D.Donovan 1–1; J.Bunning 0–0; M.Fornieles 0–0; H.Wilhelm 1–0; B.Purkey 0–0; M.McCormick 0–0; R.Face 0–0; S.Koufax 1–1; S.Miller 2–1.

PITCHING	ip	h	r	er	bb	so
American League *continued*						
M.Fornieles	0.1	2	1	1	0	0
H.Wilhelm (L)	1.2	3	2	2	1	1
National League						
W.Spahn	3.0	0	0	0	0	3
B.Purkey	2.0	0	0	0	0	1
M.McCormick	3.0	1	1	1	1	3
R.Face	0.1	2	2	2	0	1
S.Koufax +	0.0	1	0	0	0	0
S.Miller (W, BS)	1.2	0	1	0	1	4

* Pitched to 1 batter in 4th
+ Pitched to 1 batter in 9th

HBP: F.Robinson by H.Wilhelm.
BK: S.Miller

GAME DATA—T: 2:53; A: 44115; Temp: 81;
Wind: Unknown direction, Speed: Unknown

UMPIRES—HP: Stan Landes (NL), 1B: Frank Umont (AL),
2B: Shag Crawford (NL), 3B: Ed Runge (AL), LF: Ed Vargo
(NL), RF: Cal Drummond (AL)

STARTING LINEUPS

American League	National League
1. J.Temple 2b	M.Wills ss
2. N.Cash 1b	E.Mathews 3b
3. M.Mantle cf	W.Mays cf
4. R.Maris rf	O.Cepeda lf
5. R.Colavito lf	R.Clemente rf
6. T.Kubek ss	B.White 1b
7. J.Romano c	F.Bolling 2b
8. B.Robinson 3b	S.Burgess c
9. W.Ford p	W.Spahn p

AL 1ST: J.Temple flied to R.Clemente-rf; N.Cash struck out; M.Mantle struck out; 0 R, 0 H, 0 E, 0 LOB. AL 0, NL 0.

NL 1ST: M.Wills grounded out (T.Kubek-ss to N.Cash-1b); E.Mathews grounded out (B.Robin-son-3b to N.Cash-1b); W.Mays was called out on strikes; 0 R, 0 H, 0 E, 0 LOB. AL 0, NL 0.

AL 2ND: R.Maris was called out on strikes; R.Colavito popped to F.Bolling-2b; T.Kubek grounded out (F.Bolling-2b to B.White-1b); 0 R, 0 H, 0 E, 0 LOB. AL 0, NL 0.

NL 2ND: O.Cepeda flied to M.Mantle-cf; R.Clemente tripled to right field; B.White out on a sacrifice fly to M.Mantle-cf [R.Clemente scored]; F.Bolling struck out; 1 R, 1 H, 0 E, 0 LOB. AL 0, NL 1.

AL 3RD: J.Romano grounded out (M.Wills-ss to B.White-1b); B.Robinson grounded out (M.Wills-ss to B.White-1b); W.Ford grounded out (W.Spahn-p to B.White-1b); 0 R, 0 H, 0 E, 0 LOB. AL 0, NL 1.

NL 3RD: S.Burgess flied to R.Maris-rf; **D.Stuart batted for W.Spahn;** D.Stuart doubled to left-center; M.Wills grounded out (W.Ford-p to J.Temple-2b to N.Cash-1b) [D.Stuart to third]; E.Mathews popped to J.Romano-c in foul territory; 0 R, 1 H, 0 E, 1 LOB. AL 0, NL 1.

AL 4TH: **B.Purkey replaced E.Mathews (pitching); K.Boyer replaced D.Stuart (playing 3b);** J.Temple reached on an error by O.Cepeda-lf [J.Temple to second]; N.Cash grounded out (F.Bolling-2b to B.White-1b); M.Mantle grounded out (F.Boll-ing-2b to B.White-1b) [J.Temple to third]; R.Maris grounded out (B.White-1b to B.Purkey-p); 0 R, 0 H, 1 E, 1 LOB. AL 0, NL 1.

NL 4TH: **F.Lary replaced W.Ford (pitching);** W.Mays reached on an error by T.Kubek-ss [W.Mays to second]; off Kubek's knee into short lf; **D.Dono-van replaced F.Lary (pitching);** Lary complained of sore shoulder; O.Cepeda grounded out (B.Robinson-3b to N.Cash-1b) [W.Mays to third]; R.Clemente out on a sacrifice fly to R.Maris-rf [W.Mays scored (unearned)]; B.White singled to

center field; F.Bolling lined to J.Temple-2b; 1 R (0 ER), 1 H, 1 E, 1 LOB. AL 0, NL 2.

AL 5TH: Temple went to cover 2b because White was running; R.Colavito flied to W.Mays-cf; T.Kubek flied to W.Mays-cf; J.Romano struck out; 0 R, 0 H, 0 E, 0 LOB. AL 0, NL 2.

NL 5TH: Umpires moved: Runge (hp), Crawford (1b), Umont (2b), Lande Varge (lf), Drummond (rf); S.Burgess singled to right field; K.Boyer struck out; M.Wills singled to center field [S.Bur-gess to second]; **S.Musial batted for B.Purkey;** S.Musial flied to R.Colavito-lf; W.Mays singled to third base [S.Burgess to third, M.Wills to sec-ond]; O.Cepeda popped to T.Kubek-ss; 0 R, 3 H, 0 E, 3 LOB. AL 0, NL 2.

AL 6TH: **M.McCormick replaced S.Musial (pitching);** B.Robinson flied to O.Cepeda-lf; **H.Killebrew batted for D.Donovan;** H.Killebrew homered to leftfield; On a bunt J.Temple grounded out (K.Boyer-3b to B.White-1b); N.Cash was called out on strikes; 1 R, 1 H, 0 E, 0 LOB. AL 1, NL 2.

NL 6TH: **H.Killebrew stayed in game (playing 3b); J.Bunning replaced B.Robinson (pitching);** R.Clemente flied to M.Mantle-cf; B.White struck out; F.Bolling grounded out (N.Cash-1b unas-sisted); 0 R, 0 H, 0 E, 0 LOB. AL 1, NL 2.

AL 7TH: **F.Robinson replaced O.Cepeda (playing lf);** M.Mantle was called out on strikes; R.Maris walked; R.Colavito flied to F.Robinson-lf; T.Kubek flied to W.Mays-cf; 0 R, 0 H, 0 E, 1 LOB. AL 1, NL 2.

NL 7TH: **A.Kaline replaced M.Mantle (playing cf);** S.Burgess grounded out (N.Cash-1b to J.Bunning-p); K.Boyer struck out; M.Wills grounded out (J.Temple-2b to N.Cash-1b); 0 R, 0 H, 0 E, 0 LOB. AL 1, NL 2.

AL 8TH: J.Romano flied to R.Clemente-rf; **J.Brandt batted for J.Bunning;** J.Brandt struck out; H.Kil-lebrew popped to S.Burgess-c in foul territory; 0 R, 0 H, 0 E, 0 LOB. AL 1, NL 2.

NL 8TH: **M.Fornieles replaced J.Brandt (pitching); D.Howser replaced H.Killebrew (playing 3b); G.Altman batted for M.McCormick;** G.Altman homered to rightfield; W.Mays flied to A.Kaline-cf; F.Robinson singled to left field; **H.Wilhelm re-placed M.Fornieles (pitching);** F.Robinson stole second; R.Clemente struck out; B.White flied to R.Maris-rf; 1 R, 2 H, 0 E, 1 LOB. AL 1, NL 3.

AL 9TH: **R.Face replaced G.Altman (pitching); D.Zimmer replaced F.Bolling (playing 2b); J.Gen-tile batted for J.Temple;** wind starts to blow; J.Gentile struck out; N.Cash doubled to right-center; **N.Fox ran for N.Cash;** A.Kaline singled to center field [N.Fox scored]; **S.Koufax replaced R.Face (pitching);** R.Maris singled to right field

[A.Kaline to second]; **S.Miller replaced S.Koufax (pitching);** S.Miller balked [A.Kaline to third, R.Maris to second]; the famous wind-blown balk; R.Colavito reached on an error by K.Boyer-3b [A.Kaline scored, R.Colavito to first]; S.Burgess-c dropped a foul fly hit by T.Kubek; wind-blown popup; T.Kubek struck out; **Y.Berra batted for J.Romano;** Y.Berra reached on an error by D.Zimmer-2b [R.Maris to third, R.Colavito to second, Y.Berra to first]; H.Wilhelm flied to F.Robinson-lf; 2 R, 3 H, 3 E, 3 LOB. AL 3, NL 3.

NL 9TH: **J.Gentile stayed in game (playing 1b); N.Fox stayed in game (playing 2b); Y.Berra stayed in game (playing c);** D.Zimmer grounded out (T.Kubek-ss to J.Gentile-1b); S.Burgess grounded out (D.Howser-3b to J.Gentile-1b); K.Boyer walked; **E.Howard replaced Y.Berra (playing c);** K.Boyer was picked off first, but was safe on an error by J.Gentile-1b [K.Boyer to second];

M.Wills popped to N.Fox-2b; 0 R, 0 H, 1 E, 1 LOB. AL 3, NL 3.

AL 10TH: D.Howser was called out on strikes; J.Gentile struck out; N.Fox walked; A.Kaline reached on an error by K.Boyer-3b [N.Fox scored (unearned) (no RBI), A.Kaline to third]; R.Maris struck out; 1 R (0 ER), 0 H, 1 E, 1 LOB. AL 4, NL 3.

NL 10TH: **H.Aaron batted for S.Miller;** H.Aaron singled to center field; E.Howard allowed a passed ball [H.Aaron to second]; W.Mays doubled to left field [H.Aaron scored]; F.Robinson was hit by a pitch; R.Clemente singled to right field [W.Mays scored, F.Robinson to second]; 2 R, 3 H, 0 E, 2 LOB. AL 4, NL 5.

Final Totals	R	H	E	LOB
American League	4	4	2	6
National League	5	11	5	9

31

Rain Leaves All-Stars Fit to Be Tied

The second game of 1961, played in Fenway Park in Boston on July 31, became the only contest in the series to end in a tie, as heavy rain stopped play with the score tied 1–1 after nine innings. It was only the second All-Star Game ever stopped for rain; the 1952 game in Shibe Park, Philadelphia, had been terminated after five innings. Interestingly, the day began with bright sunshine in a cloudless sky, but by the seventh inning the drizzle began. Two innings later, it was a steady rain, and the game was called as a 1–1 draw after a mere twenty-one-minute wait.

The game was dominated by the pitchers on both sides. The AL scored in the first on a home run over the Green Monster by Rocky Colavito of the Tigers off NL starter Bob Purkey of the Reds. For the rest of the game, the Americans could manage only three singles against the Cincinnati right-hander's successors, getting no one past second base. Art Mahaffey of the Phillies followed Purkey to start the third and pitched two scoreless innings, allowing no hits, one walk, and one batter to reach base on second baseman Frank Bolling's error. Sandy Koufax of the Dodgers took the mound in the fifth and allowed one single in each of his innings, the first to Baltimore's Brooks Robinson and the second an infield safety to Detroit's Al Kaline. Stu Miller of the Giants once again was very effective, this time allowing no runs and only one single. He was perfect in the seventh and eighth, but he allowed a single in the ninth inning to Kaline, who stole second. However, he struck out Mickey Mantle and Elston Howard of the Yankees and Roy Sievers of the White Sox to end the ninth as the rains came. This gave the diminutive relief ace of the Giants five strikeouts, all swinging, for his three innings of work. After the game, Mantle and Sievers granted grudging admiration to Miller, whose slow breaking stuff caused these two sluggers to miss the ball by wide margins. Whitey Ford of the Yankees noted the shoulder twitch and

head fakes that Miller employed, techniques Ford considered important to Miller's success.

On the other side, the National League gathered only five hits, and the game would have been a 1–0 AL victory if not for some indecision by shortstop Luis Aparicio of the White Sox in the sixth inning. The Tigers' Jim Bunning started the game and pitched three perfect innings, striking out one. Bunning had also turned in two perfect rounds in San Francisco for a remarkable 1961 All-Star performance. Camilo Pascual of the Twins pitched the final three innings, with the lights on against the gathering darkness, allowing no hits and one walk. However, in the middle three innings Don Schwall of the host Red Sox, who would become the AL Rookie of the Year for 1961, had all kinds of trouble, some of which might be seen as bad luck. Schwall hit a batter and allowed a walk and all five NL hits. Two of the hits were singles in the scoreless fourth, and the Cardinals' Bill White doubled to no effect in the fifth. In the sixth, however, Schwall walked the Braves' Eddie Mathews on four pitches after retiring Henry Aaron of the Braves on a ground ball. Willie Mays of the Giants flied out, and Schwall got the count to 0-2 on San Francisco's Orlando Cepeda before hitting him with a pitch. The next batter was Eddie Kasko of the Reds, and the count also went to two strikes before Kasko hit a slow roller toward Aparicio. Aparicio inexplicably did not charge the ball, got a tricky hop, and ultimately had no play as Kasko received credit for a single to load the bases. White then hit a grounder that Schwall deflected and Aparicio fielded behind second base with an excellent effort. Mathews scored on the play, but Cepeda had to hold third, and the inning then ended when Bolling flied out. It was an unusual rally, consisting of a walk, a hit batter, and two infield singles. One of the hits resulted from a poor play by shortstop Aparicio, but the other was despite a fine play by the same man. As Joe Garagiola wrote: "Baseball is a funny game." In fact, Garagiola had a good vantage point to observe the game as he and Curt Gowdy announced the game on television for NBC.

Before the game, there was speculation that the assembled sluggers would take dead aim at the fabled left-field wall, and many predicted a high-scoring game. Colavito's first-inning homer over the wall was the only ball hit near it, however, because the pitchers on both sides were generally dominant. The only other extra-base hit was a double to center field by White in the fifth inning. There was a bit of pregame nostalgia, as often at-tends All-Star Games. Ted Williams, recently re-tired superstar of the Red Sox, threw out the cere-monial first pitch from a box beside the American League's dugout. Warren Spahn, forty-year-old southpaw of the Braves, received the loudest ova-tion of all as the Boston fans recalled his many fine years pitching in Boston. The crowd knew this would be their only chance to cheer Spahn that day because he had pitched a ten-inning complete game against the Cardinals the day before in Mil-waukee for his 298th career victory.

	AL		NL	
P	Warren Spahn	MIL	Jim Bunning	DET
C	John Romano	CLE	Smoky Burgess	PIT
1B	Norm Cash	DET	Bill White	SLN
2B	Johnny Temple	CLE	Frank Bolling	MIL
3B	Brooks Robinson	BAL	Eddie Mathews	MIL
SS	Luis Aparicio	CHA	Maury Wills	LAN
OF	Rocky Colavito	DET	Orlando Cepeda	SFN
OF	Al Kaline	DET	Roberto Clemente	PIT
OF	Mickey Mantle	NYA	Willie Mays	SFN
	Luis Arroyo	NYA	Hank Aaron	MIL
	Yogi Berra	NYA	George Altman	CHN
	Jackie Brandt	BAL	Ed Bailey	SFN
	Dick Donovan	WAS	Ernie Banks	CHN
	Whitey Ford	NYA	Ken Boyer	SLN
	Nellie Fox	CHA	Don Drysdale	LAN
	Tito Francona	CLE	Roy Face	PIT
	Jim Gentile	BAL	Joey Jay	CIN
	Elston Howard	NYA	Eddie Kasko	CIN
	Dick Howser	KC	Sandy Koufax	LAN
	Harmon Killebrew	MIN	Art Mahaffey	PHI
	Tony Kubek	NYA	Mike McCormick	SFN
	Barry Latman	CLE	Stu Miller	SFN
	Roger Maris	NYA	Stan Musial	SLN
	Ken McBride	LAA	Bob Purkey	CIN
	Camilo Pascual	MIN	Frank Robinson	CIN
	Don Schwall	BOS	John Roseboro	LAN
	Roy Sievers	CHA	Warren Spahn	MIL
	Bill Skowron	NYA	Dick Stuart	PIT
	Hoyt Wilhelm	BAL	Don Zimmer	CHN

```
National League    000  001  000- 1
American League    100  000  000- 1
```

NATIONAL LEAGUE

	ab	r	h	bi	bb	so	po	a
M.Wills, ss	2	0	1	0	0	0	1	1
H.Aaron, rf	2	0	0	0	0	0	1	0
S.Miller, p	0	0	0	0	0	0	0	0
E.Mathews, 3b	3	1	0	0	1	1	0	2
W.Mays, cf	3	0	1	0	1	0	1	0
O.Cepeda, lf	3	0	0	0	0	0	0	0
R.Clemente, rf	2	0	0	0	0	0	0	0
E.Kasko, ss	1	0	1	0	0	0	2	4
E.Banks, ph-ss	1	0	0	0	0	1	0	0
B.White, 1b	4	0	2	1	0	0	11	1
F.Bolling, 2b	4	0	0	0	0	0	3	2
S.Burgess, c	1	0	0	0	0	1	2	0
J.Roseboro, c	3	0	0	0	0	3	6	0
B.Purkey, p	0	0	0	0	0	0	0	1
D.Stuart, ph	1	0	0	0	0	0	0	0
A.Mahaffey, p	0	0	0	0	0	0	0	0
S.Musial, ph	1	0	0	0	0	1	0	0
S.Koufax, p	0	0	0	0	0	0	0	0
G.Altman, ph-rf	1	0	0	0	0	0	0	0
Totals	32	1	5	1	2	7	27	11

BATTING
2B: B.White (off D.Schwall).
2-out RBI: B.White.
RBI, scoring position, less than 2 outs: O.Cepeda 0–1;
F.Bolling 0–1; J.Roseboro 0–1.

BASERUNNING
Team LOB: 7

FIELDING
E: F.Bolling (fumble).
PB: S.Burgess.
DP: (2). F.Bolling-E.Kasko-B.White; B.White-E.Kasko-
F.Bolling.

AMERICAN LEAGUE

	ab	r	h	bi	bb	so	po	a
N.Cash, 1b	4	0	0	0	0	1	11	0
R.Colavito, lf	4	1	1	1	0	0	3	0
A.Kaline, rf	4	0	2	0	0	0	1	0
M.Mantle, cf	3	0	0	0	1	2	2	0
J.Romano, c	1	0	0	0	0	0	1	0
R.Maris, ph	1	0	0	0	0	0	0	0
E.Howard, c	2	0	0	0	0	1	6	0
L.Aparicio, ss	2	0	0	0	1	1	1	3
R.Sievers, ph	1	0	0	0	0	1	0	0
J.Temple, 2b	2	0	0	0	1	1	2	3
B.Robinson, 3b	3	0	1	0	0	1	0	3
J.Bunning, p	1	0	0	0	0	0	0	0
D.Schwall, p	1	0	0	0	0	0	0	0
C.Pascual, p	1	0	0	0	0	0	0	0
Totals	30	1	4	1	3	8	27	9

BATTING
HR: R.Colavito (1st inning off B.Purkey, 0 on, 1 out).
RBI, scoring position, less than 2 outs: E.Howard 0–1;
J.Temple 0–1; B.Robinson 0–1.
GDP: J.Temple; D.Schwall.

BASERUNNING
SB: A.Kaline (2nd base off S.Miller/J.Roseboro).
Team LOB: 5

PITCHING	ip	h	r	er	bb	so
National League						
B.Purkey	2.0	1	1	1	2	2
A.Mahaffey	2.0	0	0	0	1	0
S.Koufax	2.0	2	0	0	0	1
S.Miller	3.0	1	0	0	0	5
American League						
J.Bunning	3.0	0	0	0	0	1
D.Schwall	3.0	5	1	1	1	2
C.Pascual	3.0	0	0	0	1	4

Inherited Runners—Scored:
A.Mahaffey 0–0; S.Koufax 0–0; S.Miller 0–0;
D.Schwall 0–0; C.Pascual 0–0.
HBP: O.Cepeda by D.Schwall.

GAME DATA—T: 2:27; A: 31851; Temp: Unknown;
Wind: Unknown direction, Speed: Unknown

UMPIRES—HP: Larry Napp (AL), 1B: Frank Secory (NL),
2B: Red Flaherty (AL), 3B: Ed Sudol (NL), LF: Al Smith
(AL), RF: Chris Pelekoudas (NL)

STARTING LINEUPS

National League	*American League*
1. M.Wills ss	N.Cash 1b
2. E.Mathews 3b	R.Colavito lf
3. W.Mays cf	A.Kaline rf
4. O.Cepeda lf	M.Mantle cf
5. R.Clemente rf	J.Romano c
6. B.White 1b	L.Aparicio ss
7. F.Bolling 2b	J.Temple 2b
8. S.Burgess c	B.Robinson 3b
9. B.Purkey p	J.Bunning p

NL 1ST: M.Wills lined to N.Cash-1b; E.Mathews popped to J.Temple-2b in foul territory; W.Mays grounded out (B.Robinson-3b to N.Cash-1b); 0 R, 0 H, 0 E, 0 LOB. NL 0, AL 0.

AL 1ST: N.Cash was called out on strikes; R.Colavito homered to leftfield; A.Kaline grounded out (B.Purkey-p to B.White-1b); M.Mantle flied to W.Mays-cf; 1 R, 1 H, 0 E, 0 LOB. NL 0, AL 1.

NL 2ND: O.Cepeda lined to L.Aparicio-ss; R.Clemente flied to M.Mantle-cf; B.White grounded out (J.Temple-2b to N.Cash-1b); 0 R, 0 H, 0 E, 0 LOB. NL 0, AL 1.

AL 2ND: J.Romano popped to F.Bolling-2b; L.Aparicio walked; S.Burgess allowed a passed ball [L.Aparicio to second]; J.Temple walked; B.Robinson struck out; J.Bunning popped to B.White-1b; 0 R, 0 H, 0 E, 2 LOB. NL 0, AL 1.

NL 3RD: F.Bolling grounded out (B.Robinson-3b to N.Cash-1b); S.Burgess struck out; **D.Stuart batted for B.Purkey;** D.Stuart grounded out (L.Aparicio-ss to N.Cash-1b); 0 R, 0 H, 0 E, 0 LOB. NL 0, AL 1.

AL 3RD: **A.Mahaffey replaced D.Stuart (pitching);** N.Cash popped to B.White-1b in foul territory; R.Colavito popped to M.Wills-ss; A.Kaline grounded out (M.Wills-ss to B.White-1b); 0 R, 0 H, 0 E, 0 LOB. NL 0, AL 1.

NL 4TH: **D.Schwall replaced J.Bunning (pitching);** M.Wills singled to center field; E.Mathews flied to R.Colavito-lf; W.Mays singled to left field [M.Wills to second]; O.Cepeda popped to J.Temple-2b; R.Clemente grounded out (L.Aparicio-ss to N.Cash-1b); 0 R, 2 H, 0 E, 2 LOB. NL 0, AL 1.

AL 4TH: mild protest because Cash appeared to juggle throw in dirt; **J.Roseboro replaced S.Burgess (playing c); E.Kasko replaced R.Clemente (playing ss); H.Aaron replaced M.Wills (playing rf);** M.Mantle walked; **R.Maris batted for J.Romano;** R.Maris popped to F.Bolling-2b; L.Aparicio reached on an error by F.Bolling-2b [M.Mantle to second, L.Aparicio to first]; J.Temple grounded into a double play (F.Bolling-2b to E.Kasko-ss to B.White-1b) [L.Aparicio out at second]; 0 R, 0 H, 1 E, 1 LOB. NL 0, AL 1.

NL 5TH: **E.Howard replaced R.Maris (playing c);** B.White doubled to center field; F.Bolling grounded out (J.Temple-2b to N.Cash-1b) [B.White to third]; J.Roseboro struck out; **S.Musial batted for A.Mahaffey;** S.Musial struck out; 0 R, 1 H, 0 E, 1 LOB. NL 0, AL 1.

AL 5TH: **S.Koufax replaced S.Musial (pitching);** B.Robinson singled to left field; On a bunt D.Schwall grounded into a double play (B.White-1b to E.Kasko-ss to F.Bolling-2b) [B.Robinson out at second]; N.Cash grounded out (E.Kasko-ss to B.White-1b); 0 R, 1 H, 0 E, 0 LOB. NL 0, AL 1.

NL 6TH: H.Aaron grounded out (L.Aparicio-ss to N.Cash-1b); E.Mathews walked; W.Mays flied to A.Kaline-rf; O.Cepeda was hit by a pitch (it was the 0–2 pitch) [E.Mathews to second]; E.Kasko singled to shortstop (it was the 0–2 pitch) [E.Mathews to third, O.Cepeda to second]; B.White singled to shortstop [E.Mathews scored, O.Cepeda to third, E.Kasko to second]; F.Bolling flied to R.Colavito-lf; 1 R, 2 H, 0 E, 3 LOB. NL 1, AL 1.

AL 6TH: R.Colavito flied to H.Aaron-rf; A.Kaline singled to second base; M.Mantle struck out; E.Howard grounded out (E.Mathews-3b to B.White-1b); 0 R, 1 H, 0 E, 1 LOB. NL 1, AL 1.

NL 7TH: lights turned on; **C.Pascual replaced D.Schwall (pitching);** J.Roseboro was called out on strikes; **G.Altman batted for S.Koufax;** G.Altman flied to M.Mantle-cf; H.Aaron lined to R.Colavito-lf; 0 R, 0 H, 0 E, 0 LOB. NL 1, AL 1.

AL 7TH: **G.Altman stayed in game (playing rf); S.Miller replaced H.Aaron (pitching);** L.Aparicio struck out; J.Temple struck out; B.Robinson grounded out (E.Kasko-ss to B.White-1b); 0 R, 0 H, 0 E, 0 LOB. NL 1, AL 1.

NL 8TH: E.Mathews was called out on strikes; W.Mays walked; O.Cepeda grounded out (J.Temple-2b to N.Cash-1b) [W.Mays to second]; **E.Banks batted for E.Kasko;** E.Banks struck out; 0 R, 0 H, 0 E, 1 LOB. NL 1, AL 1.

AL 8TH: **E.Banks stayed in game (playing ss);** C.Pascual popped to B.White-1b in foul territory; N.Cash grounded out (F.Bolling-2b to B.White-1b); rain starts; R.Colavito grounded out (E.Mathews-3b to B.White-1b); 0 R, 0 H, 0 E, 0 LOB. NL 1, AL 1.

NL 9TH: B.White grounded out (N.Cash-1b unassisted); F.Bolling grounded out (B.Robinson-3b to N.Cash-1b); J.Roseboro was called out on strikes; 0 R, 0 H, 0 E, 0 LOB. NL 1, AL 1.

AL 9TH: A.Kaline singled to right-center; M.Mantle struck out; A.Kaline stole second; E.Howard struck out; **R.Sievers batted for L.Aparicio;**

R.Sievers struck out; 0 R, 1 H, 0 E, 1 LOB.
NL 1, AL 1.

Final Totals	R	H	E	LOB
National League	1	5	1	7
American League	1	4	0	5

32

Local Boy Does Very Well

For the first time since the second game of the series in 1934, the National League was in a position to tie the All-Star standings with a sweep of the two games set for 1962. The National Leaguers came within one by winning the first contest, played in the new District of Columbia Stadium, but were moved back to trailing by a pair as the AL trounced them in Wrigley Field, Chicago, in the second game twenty days later. This was the last year of the double-feature format, which was never very popular. A major factor in the decision to return to playing once a year was a concession by Major League owners to turn over 95 percent of the net revenue from the game to the players' pension fund. Previously, the players had received 60 percent, with this lower amount serving as a prime motivator for playing two games a year.

Once again, the starting nonpitchers were chosen by vote of players, managers, and coaches. The largest totals in the NL were received by San Francisco teammates Orlando Cepeda and Willie Mays, with 229 and 213, respectively, while Rich Rollins of the Minnesota Twins led the AL players with 183 votes. The managers were Ralph Houk of the Yankees and Fred Hutchinson of the Reds, leaders of the 1961 World Series opponents. The twenty-five-man rosters for the first game were completed by the managers with the provisions that they could add three players and make any changes they desired to the pitching staff for the second game. Pitcher Warren Spahn of the Braves was added to the roster at the last moment to replace his teammate Henry Aaron, who had an injured leg.

The first game attracted many Washington political figures, including President John Kennedy and Vice President Lyndon Johnson. Kennedy threw out the first ball before a capacity crowd of 45,000 fans, some 3,300 more than had attended on opening day. It was fitting that the star of the game was a native of Washington DC, Dodger shortstop Maury Wills. Even though Wills did not

enter the game until the sixth inning, it was his daring base running that led directly to two of the NL's three runs. The day started on a sour note for the Dodger speedster, who would go on to steal 104 bases in 1962, breaking the record set by Ty Cobb of the Tigers in 1915. Wills, who had forty-six steals at the time of the Washington game, was denied entrance to the stadium for a time by a security guard who did not recognize the star from the other league and did not think he looked like a Major Leaguer. The guard was eventually convinced of the identity of Wills, who went on to be the MVP of the game.

The first five innings were scoreless for both sides as Jim Bunning of the Tigers and Camilo Pascual of the Twins limited the National Leaguers to two hits, both by Roberto Clemente of the Pirates, who delivered a first-inning double and a fourth-inning single. For the National League, starter Don Drysdale of the Dodgers and Juan Marichal of the Giants combined to yield only one hit over the first five frames, but the American Leaguers came closer to scoring. In fact, Drysdale was in a bit of trouble in each of his three innings, allowing the first batter to reach base on each occasion. He hit Rich Rollins of the Twins to lead off the game, then retired the Angels' Billy Moran on a fly ball and struck out the Yankees' Roger Maris and Mickey Mantle. In the second, he walked the Orioles' Jim Gentile to start the inning but was bailed out when the Twins' Earl Battey hit into a double play with one out. In the third, Drysdale really had to work after Luis Aparicio of the White Sox led off with a triple to right-center. He proceeded to retire Angels pinch hitter Lee Thomas and Rollins on pop-ups, then fanned Moran to get out of the jam. Marichal had a much easier time; the only runner he allowed was a fourth-inning walk to Mantle. Juan would also end up as the winning pitcher.

The sixth inning was Pascual's third and last time to the mound, and he was batted around a bit as the NL scored two runs that would saddle him with the loss. Cardinal Stan Musial pinch-hit for Marichal and singled to right on an 0-2 pitch, and then the Maury Wills show began as he ran for Musial. Wills immediately stole second on the Twins' battery (Battey was still catching), and his jump on Pascual was so good that no throw was made. Dick Groat of the Pirates hit a ground ball single up the middle, and Wills scored easily. Clemente followed with his third straight hit, advancing his teammate to second. Mays hit a fly ball to center fielder Maris that allowed both runners to move up. The second run scored as Cepeda grounded out to third, and the inning ended when Tommy Davis of the Dodgers also grounded to Twins third baseman Rich Rollins, who made a nice play on the hard-hit ball. The American League came right back in its half of the sixth against Bob Purkey of the Reds, scoring one run and being kept from more thanks to an excellent play by Mays. Rollins and Moran singled to put runners at the corners, and Maris hit a ball that appeared destined for the right-center-field wall. However, Mays flashed his usual defensive brilliance and caught it against the wall with a leap, turning it into a sacrifice fly as Rollins tagged and scored easily. The Tigers' Rocky Colavito hit a smash up the middle that Purkey knocked down and turned into the second out, and Oriole Jim Gentile took strike three to end the threat.

Dick Donovan of the Indians took over the mound duties for the next two innings, allowing the third and final NL run in the eighth, a run that was almost entirely attributable to Wills. Wills led off with a soft fly ball single to left and took off when Jim Davenport of the Giants singled in the same direction. Wills rounded second, paused briefly, and then headed for third when left fielder Colavito threw behind him. The play was very close, and Wills made a fine slide to elude the tag of Brooks Robinson, the mild-mannered Oriole, who complained loudly over umpire Tony Venzon's safe call. Wills scored when the next batter, San Francisco's Felipe Alou, hit a sacrifice fly to foul ground in medium-depth right field that was caught by the Angels' Leon Wagner, whose wide throw to the plate made it easy for Wills. Johnny Callison of the Phillies also singled before the inning was over, but Donovan clamped down and there was no more scoring. Oriole Milt Pappas pitched a perfect ninth. Bob Shaw of the Braves pitched the last two innings to earn a save as the AL made a small challenge to tie in the ninth, beginning with a lead-off walk to Colavito. After two outs were made, John Romano of the Indians singled to bring up Aparicio, who hit a long drive to right-center that appeared at first to have a chance to be a game-tying triple. However, the fleet-footed Mays made a nice running catch in the gap to end the game.

Both managers used nineteen of their twenty-five players. Warren Spahn of the Braves had been a last-minute replacement for his teammate Henry Aaron, who had an injured hamstring. Spahn had teased Aaron about the disruption of his plans to spend time with his family during the break, so the fact that he did not see action in Washington had to have caused some wry smiles. Ironically, Aaron was added to the roster for the second game while Spahn was retained. Aaron played in Chicago, but once again Spahn did not, joining Ralph Terry of the Yankees in the dubious distinction of warming the bench for both contests.

	AL		NL	
P	Jim Bunning	DET	Don Drysdale	LAN
C	Earl Battey	MIN	Del Crandall	MIL
1B	Jim Gentile	BAL	Orlando Cepeda	SFN
2B	Billy Moran	LAA	Bill Mazeroski	PIT
3B	Rich Rollins	MIN	Ken Boyer	SLN
SS	Luis Aparicio	CHA	Dick Groat	PIT
OF	Mickey Mantle	NYA	Roberto Clemente	PIT
OF	Roger Maris	NYA	Tommy Davis	LAN
OF	Leon Wagner	LAA	Willie Mays	SFN
	Hank Aguirre	DET	Hank Aaron +	MIL
	Rocky Colavito	DET	Felipe Alou	SFN
	Dick Donovan	CLE	Richie Ashburn	NYN
	Frank Howard	LAN	Ernie Banks	CHN
	Jim Landis	CHA	Frank Bolling	MIL
	Bill Monbouquette	BOS	Johnny Callison	PHI
	Milt Pappas	BAL	Jim Davenport	SFN
	Camilo Pascual	MIN	Turk Farrell	HOU
	Bobby Richardson	NYA	Bob Gibson	SLN
	Brooks Robinson	BAL	Sandy Koufax	LAN
	John Romano	CLE	Juan Marichal	SFN
	Norm Siebern	KC	Stan Musial	SLN
	Dave Stenhouse	WAS	Bob Purkey	CIN
	Ralph Terry	NYA	John Roseboro	LAN
	Lee Thomas	LAA	Bob Shaw	MIL
	Tom Tresh	NYA	Warren Spahn	MIL
	Hoyt Wilhelm +	BAL	Maury Wills	LAN

+ player replaced on roster

204 : THE GAMES

RETROSHEET EXPANDED BOX SCORE Tuesday, 7/10/1962 National League at American League (D)

```
National League    000 002 010- 3
American League    000 001 000- 1
```

NATIONAL LEAGUE

	ab	r	h	bi	bb	so	po	a
D.Groat, ss	3	1	1	1	0	0	3	3
J.Davenport, 3b	1	0	1	0	0	0	0	1
R.Clemente, rf	3	0	3	0	0	0	2	0
F.Alou, rf	0	0	0	1	0	0	0	0
W.Mays, cf	3	0	0	0	1	0	3	0
O.Cepeda, 1b	3	0	0	1	0	1	2	2
B.Purkey, p	0	0	0	0	0	0	0	1
J.Callison, ph	1	0	1	0	0	0	0	0
B.Shaw, p	0	0	0	0	0	0	1	0
T.Davis, lf	4	0	0	0	0	0	2	0
K.Boyer, 3b	2	0	0	0	0	1	1	0
E.Banks, 1b	2	0	0	0	0	0	4	1
D.Crandall, c	4	0	0	0	0	0	5	0
B.Mazeroski, 2b	2	0	0	0	0	0	1	0
F.Bolling, 2b	2	0	0	0	0	0	1	3
D.Drysdale, p	1	0	0	0	0	1	1	0
J.Marichal, p	0	0	0	0	0	0	0	0
S.Musial, ph	1	0	1	0	0	0	0	0
M.Wills, pr-ss	1	2	1	0	0	0	1	1
Totals	33	3	8	3	1	3	27	12

BATTING
2B: R.Clemente (off J.Bunning).
RBI, scoring position, less than 2 outs: D.Groat 1–1;
    F.Alou 1–1; W.Mays 0–2; O.Cepeda 1–3.
SF: F.Alou.

BASERUNNING
SB: W.Mays (3rd base off C.Pascual / E.Battey); M.Wills
    (2nd base off C.Pascual / E.Battey).
CS: R.Clemente (3rd base by C.Pascual / E.Battey).
Team LOB: 5

FIELDING
DP: (1). O.Cepeda-D.Groat-D.Drysdale.

AMERICAN LEAGUE

	ab	r	h	bi	bb	so	po	a
R.Rollins, 3b	2	1	1	0	0	0	1	3
B.Robinson, 3b	0	0	0	0	0	0	0	1
B.Moran, 2b	3	0	1	0	0	1	0	0
B.Richardson, 2b	1	0	0	0	0	0	1	0
R.Maris, cf	2	0	0	1	0	1	2	0
J.Landis, cf	1	0	0	0	0	1	2	0
M.Mantle, rf	1	0	0	0	1	1	0	0
R.Colavito, pr-lf	1	0	0	0	1	0	1	0
J.Gentile, 1b	3	0	0	0	1	1	8	0
L.Wagner, lf-rf	4	0	0	0	0	0	4	0
E.Battey, c	2	0	0	0	0	0	4	1
J.Romano, c	2	0	1	0	0	0	1	0
L.Aparicio, ss	4	0	1	0	0	0	3	2
J.Bunning, p	0	0	0	0	0	0	0	0
L.Thomas, ph	1	0	0	0	0	0	0	0
C.Pascual, p	1	0	0	0	0	0	0	1
D.Donovan, p	0	0	0	0	0	0	0	0
N.Siebern, ph	1	0	0	0	0	0	0	0
M.Pappas, p	0	0	0	0	0	0	0	0
Totals	29	1	4	1	3	5	27	8

BATTING
3B: L.Aparicio (off D.Drysdale).
RBI, scoring position, less than 2 outs: R.Rollins 0–1;
    R.Maris 1–1; L.Thomas 0–1.
SF: R.Maris.
GDP: E.Battey.

BASERUNNING
Team LOB: 7

FIELDING
DP: (1). E.Battey-R.Rollins.

PITCHING	ip	h	r	er	bb	so
National League						
D.Drysdale	3.0	1	0	0	1	3
J.Marichal (w)	2.0	0	0	0	1	0
B.Purkey	2.0	2	1	1	0	1
B.Shaw (s)	2.0	1	0	0	1	1
American League						
J.Bunning	3.0	1	0	0	0	2
C.Pascual (L)	3.0	4	2	2	1	1
D.Donovan	2.0	3	1	1	0	0
M.Pappas	1.0	0	0	0	0	0

Inherited Runners—Scored:
    J.Marichal 0–0; B.Purkey 0–0; B.Shaw 0–0;
    C.Pascual 0–0; D.Donovan 0–0; M.Pappas 0–0.
HBP: R.Rollins by D.Drysdale; B.Robinson by B.Shaw.

GAME DATA—T: 2:23; A: 45480; Temp: Unknown;
Wind: Unknown direction, Speed: Unknown

UMPIRES—HP: Eddie Hurley (AL), 1B: Augie Donatelli
(NL), 2B: Bob Stewart (AL), 3B: Tony Venzon (NL),
LF: Mel Steiner (NL), RF: Harry Schwarts (AL)

TUESDAY, JULY 10, 1962 : 205

STARTING LINEUPS

	National League	*American League*
1.	D.Groat ss	R.Rollins 3b
2.	R.Clemente rf	B.Moran 2b
3.	W.Mays cf	R.Maris cf
4.	O.Cepeda 1b	M.Mantle rf
5.	T.Davis lf	J.Gentile 1b
6.	K.Boyer 3b	L.Wagner lf
7.	D.Crandall c	E.Battey c
8.	B.Mazeroski 2b	L.Aparicio ss
9.	D.Drysdale p	J.Bunning p

NL 1ST: D.Groat grounded out (L.Aparicio-ss to J.Gentile-1b); R.Clemente doubled to right field; W.Mays popped to J.Gentile-1b in foul territory; O.Cepeda popped to E.Battey-c in foul territory; O R, 1 H, O E, 1 LOB. NL O, AL O.

AL 1ST: R.Rollins was hit by a pitch; B.Moran flied to R.Clemente-rf; R.Maris struck out; M.Mantle struck out; O R, O H, O E, 1 LOB. NL O, AL O.

NL 2ND: T.Davis lined to R.Maris-cf; K.Boyer struck out; D.Crandall flied to L.Wagner-lf; O R, O H, O E, O LOB. NL O, AL O.

AL 2ND: J.Gentile walked; L.Wagner forced J.Gentile (O.Cepeda-1b to D.Groat-ss) [L.Wagner to first]; E.Battey grounded into a double play (O.Cepeda-1b to D.Groat-ss to D.Drysdale-p) [L.Wagner out at second]; O R, O H, O E, O LOB. NL O, AL O.

NL 3RD: B.Mazeroski flied to L.Wagner-lf; D.Drysdale struck out; D.Groat grounded out (R.Rollins-3b to J.Gentile-1b); O R, O H, O E, O LOB. NL O, AL O.

AL 3RD: L.Aparicio tripled to very deep right-center; **L.Thomas batted for J.Bunning;** L.Thomas popped to D.Groat-ss; R.Rollins popped to B.Mazeroski-2b; B.Moran struck out; O R, 1 H, O E, 1 LOB. NL O, AL O.

NL 4TH: **C.Pascual replaced L.Thomas (pitching);** R.Clemente singled to left field; W.Mays walked [R.Clemente to second]; O.Cepeda struck out while R.Clemente was caught stealing third (E.Battey-c to R.Rollins-3b); W.Mays stole third; T.Davis popped to L.Aparicio-ss; O R, 1 H, O E, 1 LOB. NL O, AL O.

AL 4TH: **J.Marichal replaced D.Drysdale (pitching);** R.Maris flied to W.Mays-cf; M.Mantle walked; **R.Colavito ran for M.Mantle;** J.Gentile flied to T.Davis-lf; L.Wagner popped to K.Boyer-3b in foul territory; O R, O H, O E, 1 LOB. NL O, AL O.

NL 5TH: **R.Colavito stayed in game (playing lf);** **L.Wagner changed positions (playing rf);** K.Boyer grounded out (L.Aparicio-ss to J.Gentile-1b); D.Crandall grounded out (C.Pascual-p to J.Gentile-1b); B.Mazeroski popped to L.Aparicio-ss; O R, O H, O E, O LOB. NL O, AL O.

AL 5TH: E.Battey lined to R.Clemente-rf; L.Aparicio grounded out (D.Groat-ss to O.Cepeda-1b); C.Pascual grounded out (D.Groat-ss to O.Cepeda-1b); O R, O H, O E, O LOB. NL O, AL O.

NL 6TH: **S.Musial batted for J.Marichal;** S.Musial singled to right field; **M.Wills ran for S.Musial;** M.Wills stole second; D.Groat singled to center field [M.Wills scored]; R.Clemente singled to between third and short [D.Groat to second]; W.Mays flied to R.Maris-cf [D.Groat to third, R.Clemente to second]; O.Cepeda grounded out (R.Rollins-3b to J.Gentile-1b) [D.Groat scored, R.Clemente to third]; T.Davis grounded out (R.Rollins-3b to J.Gentile-1b); 2 R, 3 H, O E, 1 LOB. NL 2, AL O.

AL 6TH: **M.Wills stayed in game (playing ss); E.Banks replaced K.Boyer (playing 1b); F.Alou replaced R.Clemente (playing rf); F.Bolling replaced B.Mazeroski (playing 2b); J.Davenport replaced D.Groat (playing 3b); B.Purkey replaced O.Cepeda (pitching);** R.Rollins singled to right field; B.Moran singled to left-center [R.Rollins to third]; R.Maris lined out on a sacrifice fly to W.Mays-cf [R.Rollins scored]; R.Colavito grounded out (B.Purkey-p to E.Banks-1b) [B.Moran to second]; J.Gentile was called out on strikes; 1 R, 2 H, O E, 1 LOB. NL 2, AL 1.

NL 7TH: **B.Robinson replaced R.Rollins (playing 3b); B.Richardson replaced B.Moran (playing 2b); J.Landis replaced R.Maris (playing cf); J.Romano replaced E.Battey (playing c); D.Donovan replaced C.Pascual (pitching);** E.Banks grounded out (B.Robinson-3b to J.Gentile-1b); D.Crandall lined to L.Wagner-rf; F.Bolling popped to L.Aparicio-ss; O R, O H, O E, O LOB. NL 2, AL 1.

AL 7TH: L.Wagner grounded out (F.Bolling-2b to E.Banks-1b); J.Romano grounded out (J.Davenport-3b to E.Banks-1b); L.Aparicio grounded out (F.Bolling-2b to E.Banks-1b); O R, O H, O E, O LOB. NL 2, AL 1.

NL 8TH: M.Wills singled to left field; J.Davenport singled to left field [M.Wills to third]; F.Alou out on a sacrifice fly to L.Wagner-rf in foul territory [M.Wills scored]; W.Mays popped to J.Romano-c in foul territory; **J.Callison batted for B.Purkey;** J.Callison singled to right field [J.Davenport to third]; T.Davis flied to J.Landis-cf; 1 R, 3 H, O E, 2 LOB. NL 3, AL 1.

AL 8TH: **B.Shaw replaced J.Callison (pitching); N.Siebern batted for D.Donovan;** N.Siebern grounded out (E.Banks-1b to B.Shaw-p); B.Robinson was hit by a pitch; B.Richardson forced B.Robinson (M.Wills-ss to F.Bolling-2b) [B.Richardson to first]; J.Landis struck out; O R, O H, O E, 1 LOB. NL 3, AL 1.

NL 9TH: **M.Pappas replaced N.Siebern (pitching);** E.Banks flied to R.Colavito-lf; D.Crandall popped to B.Richardson-2b; F.Bolling flied to J.Landis-cf; 0 R, 0 H, 0 E, 0 LOB. NL 3, AL 1.

AL 9TH: R.Colavito walked; J.Gentile forced R.Colavito (F.Bolling-2b to M.Wills-ss) [J.Gentile to first]; L.Wagner flied to T.Davis-lf in foul terri-tory; J.Romano singled to left field [J.Gentile to second]; L.Aparicio flied to W.Mays-cf; 0 R, 1 H, 0 E, 2 LOB. NL 3, AL 1.

Final Totals	R	H	E	LOB
National League	3	8	0	5
American League	1	4	0	7

American League Power Reappears

The hot topic before the second 1962 game was that the NL finally had a chance to tie the series. Things looked good for the National Leaguers as they drew first blood in the second inning when their starting pitcher, Johnny Podres of the Dodgers, doubled with two outs and the bases empty. Dick Groat of the Pirates promptly singled him home. AL starter Dave Stenhouse struck out the Pirates' Roberto Clemente to end the inning. Stenhouse was fortunate to allow only the single run in his two innings, because the NL loaded the bases with one out to no avail in the first as Dave stiffened to record a pop-up and a line drive. The batting success of pitcher Podres was surprising enough, but a further surprise came when NL manager Fred Hutchinson of the Reds did not let Podres return to the mound, replacing him instead with Philadelphia's Art Mahaffey, although Podres had been effective, allowing no runs and only one single in each of his two innings of work.

The first batter to face Mahaffey in the top of the third was veteran Pete Runnels of the Red Sox, who was a roster addition when the squads expanded for the second game. Runnels was a good hitter for average and in fact led the AL in 1962 with a mark of .326. However, Runnels was not a power hitter (his season high for homers was ten, coincidentally also in 1962), so it was surprising when the left-handed Runnels took a Mahaffey pitch over the wall to left-center field to tie the game. The AL settled for the one run, but it could have been more as the NL made two of its four errors on the day. Shortstop Groat fumbled the grounder of the Angels' Billy Moran, and Rocky Colavito of the Tigers hit a line drive to left fielder Tommy Davis of the Dodgers, which Davis dropped for an error. However, the NL dodged the bullet when Moran tried to score on the play and was gunned down at the plate, Davis to Cardinals third baseman Ken Boyer to Braves catcher Del Crandall. Mahaffey also pitched the fourth inning, but his luck ran out

when Earl Battey of the Twins walked with two outs and Leon Wagner of the Angels homered to right field. Mahaffey would ultimately be charged with the loss.

The second AL pitcher, Ray Herbert of the White Sox, fared much better in his three innings, allowing one single in each and getting good support with immediate double plays following the hits in the third and fourth innings. Herbert would be rewarded with the win. Bob Gibson of the Cardinals, the third NL pitcher, helped the AL widen the margin when he allowed a run in the sixth inning, a rally that could easily have led to more runs. The run was scored by Al Kaline of the Tigers, running for Battey, who had walked. Yankee Tom Tresh drove Kaline in with a double to left but got too aggressive and was tagged out in a rundown when left fielder Stan Musial of the Cardinals got the ball back in quickly.

The AL blew the game open in the seventh with three runs off new pitcher Dick Farrell of the Houston Colts. The fireballing Farrell allowed three hits and a walk, accompanied by some controversy. The second hit of the inning was a liner by Moran to center fielder Henry Aaron of the Braves, who claimed he caught the ball. However, umpire Ken Burkhart said Aaron had trapped the ball, a decision that did not sit well with the NL players. After a force out, Colavito hit a three-run home run to expand the lead to 7–1. The National League did score single runs in the seventh, eighth, and ninth innings, the first two off Hank Aguirre of the Tigers and the last one off Milt Pappas of the Orioles. The big hit for the NL in the eighth was a double to right-center by Milwaukee's Frank Bolling, scoring the Mets' Richie Ashburn, who had reached base on a bloop single to left. The last run came on a ninth-inning homer by John Roseboro of the Dodgers against Pappas. The American Leaguers didn't let the game get too close, however, as they added two more runs in the ninth inning against the Giants' Juan Marichal, who was let down a bit by the Braves' Eddie

Mathews, who had entered to play third base in the seventh. Mathews was charged with two errors when he fumbled the grounder from lead-off pinch hitter Yogi Berra of the Yankees and then made a wild throw to first, allowing Yogi to stroll into second. However, Juan was not sharp, allowing a double to Maris and also throwing two wild pitches in the inning, setting up a sacrifice fly by Colavito. Amazingly, these two runs would prove to be the only ones ever allowed by Marichal in his record-tying eight All-Star Games, during which he pitched eighteen innings and allowed only one earned run for a career All-Star ERA of 0.50.

Fans were disappointed that Mickey Mantle was not able to play. Mantle had strained his left knee the day before in the second game of a doubleheader against the White Sox in Yankee Stadium. He did take batting practice and put on a fine show, driving two balls over the bleachers in left-center field and into the street. However, Mantle was unable to run, and AL manager Ralph Houk of the Yankees scratched him from the lineup in favor of Rocky Colavito, who contributed four RBI to the AL cause. Mantle's injury was not too serious, although he did miss the Yankees' first three games when play resumed the day after the All-Star Game. This was the last of the four years in which two All-Star Games were played. One factor that had influenced the change back to one game was the interference of two games with the scheduling of regular season games. Once again, almost all teams were scheduled to play the day before and the day after the interleague clash, some with doubleheaders. As a result, many of the star players spent two consecutive evenings making late flights.

AL			NL	
P	Dave Stenhouse	WAS	Johnny Podres	LAN
C	Earl Battey	MIN	Del Crandall	MIL
1B	Jim Gentile	BAL	Orlando Cepeda	SFN
2B	Billy Moran	LAA	Bill Mazeroski	PIT
3B	Rich Rollins	MIN	Ken Boyer	SLN
SS	Luis Aparicio	CHA	Dick Groat	PIT
OF	Rocky Colavito	DET	Roberto Clemente	PIT
OF	Roger Maris	NYA	Tommy Davis	LAN
OF	Leon Wagner	LAA	Willie Mays	SFN
	Hank Aguirre	DET	Hank Aaron	MIL
	Yogi Berra	NYA	George Altman	CHN
	Jim Bunning	DET	Richie Ashburn	NYN
	Dick Donovan	CLE	Ernie Banks	CHN
	Ray Herbert	CHA	Frank Bolling	MIL
	Elston Howard	NYA	Johnny Callison	PHI
	Jim Kaat	MIN	Jim Davenport	SFN
	Al Kaline	DET	Turk Farrell	HOU
	Jim Landis	CHA	Bob Gibson	SLN
	Mickey Mantle	NYA	Art Mahaffey	PHI
	Ken McBride +	LAA	Juan Marichal	SFN
	Milt Pappas	BAL	Eddie Mathews	MIL
	Camilo Pascual	MIN	Stan Musial	SLN
	Bobby Richardson	NYA	Bob Purkey	CIN
	Brooks Robinson	BAL	Frank Robinson	CIN
	John Romano	CLE	John Roseboro	LAN
	Pete Runnels	BOS	Warren Spahn	MIL
	Norm Siebern	KC	Billy Williams	CHN
	Ralph Terry	NYA	Maury Wills	LAN
	Lee Thomas	LAA		
	Tom Tresh	NYA		
	Hoyt Wilhelm	BAL		

+ player replaced on roster

American League	001	201	302- 9
National League	010	000	111- 4

AMERICAN LEAGUE

	ab	r	h	bi	bb	so	po	a
R.Rollins, 3b	3	0	1	0	0	0	0	1
B.Robinson, 3b	1	1	0	0	1	0	0	1
B.Moran, 2b	4	0	1	0	0	0	1	3
Y.Berra, ph	1	0	0	0	0	0	0	0
B.Richardson, pr-2b	0	1	0	0	0	0	2	0
R.Maris, cf	4	2	1	1	1	0	4	0
R.Colavito, rf	4	1	1	4	0	1	2	0
J.Gentile, 1b	4	0	1	0	1	1	10	0
E.Battey, c	2	1	0	0	1	0	2	0
A.Kaline, pr	0	1	0	0	0	0	0	0
E.Howard, c	2	0	0	0	0	2	2	0
L.Wagner, lf	4	1	3	2	0	0	1	0
L.Thomas, lf	0	0	0	0	0	0	1	0
L.Aparicio, ss	2	0	0	0	0	1	2	3
T.Tresh, ss	2	0	1	1	0	0	0	5
D.Stenhouse, p	0	0	0	0	0	0	0	0
P.Runnels, ph	1	1	1	1	0	0	0	0
R.Herbert, p	1	0	0	0	0	1	0	0
H.Aguirre, p	2	0	0	0	0	2	0	0
M.Pappas, p	0	0	0	0	0	0	0	0
Totals	37	9	10	9	4	8	27	13

BATTING
2B: T.Tresh (off B.Gibson); R.Maris (off J.Marichal).
HR: R.Colavito (7th inning off T.Farrell, 2 on, 2 out);
L.Wagner (4th inning off A.Mahaffey, 1 on, 1 out);
P.Runnels (3rd inning off A.Mahaffey, 0 on, 0 out).
2-out RBI: R.Colavito 3; T.Tresh.
RBI, scoring position, less than 2 outs: R.Maris 1–2;
R.Colavito 1–1.
SF: R.Colavito.

BASERUNNING
Team LOB: 6

FIELDING
DP: (2). L.Aparicio-B.Moran-J.Gentile; B.Moran-
L.Aparicio-J.Gentile.

NATIONAL LEAGUE

	ab	r	h	bi	bb	so	po	a
D.Groat, ss	3	0	2	2	0	0	3	3
M.Wills, ss	1	0	0	0	0	0	0	1
R.Clemente, rf	2	0	0	0	0	1	2	0
F.Robinson, rf	3	0	0	0	0	0	1	0
W.Mays, cf	2	0	2	0	0	0	2	0
H.Aaron, cf	2	0	0	0	0	0	1	0
O.Cepeda, 1b	1	0	0	0	1	0	2	0
E.Banks, 1b	2	1	1	0	0	0	1	1
T.Davis, lf	1	0	0	0	0	0	0	1
S.Musial, ph-lf	2	0	0	0	0	0	0	1
B.Williams, lf	1	0	0	1	0	0	2	0
K.Boyer, 3b	3	0	1	0	0	0	1	2
E.Mathews, 3b	1	0	0	0	0	1	0	0
D.Crandall, c	1	0	0	0	0	0	3	0
J.Roseboro, c	3	1	1	1	0	1	6	0
B.Mazeroski, 2b	1	0	0	0	0	0	0	0
G.Altman, ph	1	0	0	0	0	0	0	0
B.Gibson, p	0	0	0	0	0	0	0	0
T.Farrell, p	0	0	0	0	0	0	0	0
R.Ashburn, ph	1	1	1	0	0	0	0	0
J.Marichal, p	0	0	0	0	0	0	0	0
J.Callison, ph	0	0	0	0	1	0	0	0
J.Podres, p	1	1	1	0	0	0	0	0
A.Mahaffey, p	0	0	0	0	0	0	0	0
F.Bolling, 2b	3	0	1	0	0	0	3	1
Totals	35	4	10	4	2	3	27	10

BATTING
2B: J.Podres (off D.Stenhouse); F.Bolling (off
H.Aguirre).
3B: E.Banks (off H.Aguirre).
HR: J.Roseboro (9th inning off M.Pappas, 0 on, 0 out).
2-out RBI: D.Groat.
RBI, scoring position, less than 2 outs: D.Groat 1–2;
T.Davis 0–2; B.Williams 1–1.
GDP: O.Cepeda; J.Roseboro.

BASERUNNING
Team LOB: 7

FIELDING
E: D.Groat (fumble); T.Davis (dropped liner);
E.Mathews (fumble); E.Mathews (throw).
Outfield assist: T.Davis (B.Moran at HP); S.Musial
(T.Tresh at 2B).

PITCHING	ip	h	r	er	bb	so
American League						
D.Stenhouse	2.0	3	1	1	1	1
R.Herbert (w)	3.0	3	0	0	0	0

Inherited Runners—Scored:
R.Herbert 0–0; H.Aguirre 0–0; M.Pappas 0–0;
A.Mahaffey 0–0; B.Gibson 0–0; T.Farrell 0–0;
J.Marichal 0–0.

PITCHING	ip	h	r	er	bb	so
American League (*continued*)						
H.Aguirre	3.0	3	2	2	0	2
M.Pappas (s)	1.0	1	1	1	1	0
National League						
J.Podres	2.0	2	0	0	0	2
A.Mahaffey (L)	2.0	2	3	3	1	1
B.Gibson	2.0	1	1	1	2	1
T.Farrell	1.0	3	3	3	1	2
J.Marichal	2.0	2	2	1	0	2

HBP: D.Groat by D.Stenhouse.
WP: J.Marichal 2

GAME DATA—T: 2:28; A: 38359; Temp: Unknown;
Wind: Unknown direction, Speed: Unknown

UMPIRES—HP: Jocko Conlan (NL), 1B: Bill McKinley (AL),
2B: Ken Burkhart (NL), 3B: John Rice (AL), LF: Al Forman
(NL), RF: Bill Kinnamon (AL)

STARTING LINEUPS

	American League	National League
1.	R.Rollins 3b	D.Groat ss
2.	B.Moran 2b	R.Clemente rf
3.	R.Maris cf	W.Mays cf
4.	R.Colavito rf	O.Cepeda 1b
5.	J.Gentile 1b	T.Davis lf
6.	E.Battey c	K.Boyer 3b
7.	L.Wagner lf	D.Crandall c
8.	L.Aparicio ss	B.Mazeroski 2b
9.	D.Stenhouse p	J.Podres p

AL 1ST: R.Rollins singled to left field; B.Moran flied to W.Mays-cf; R.Maris flied to R.Clemente-rf; R.Colavito lined to K.Boyer-3b; 0 R, 1 H, 0 E, 1 LOB. AL 0, NL 0.

NL 1ST: D.Groat was hit by a pitch; R.Clemente flied to R.Colavito-rf; W.Mays singled to left field [D.Groat to second]; O.Cepeda walked [D.Groat to third, W.Mays to second]; T.Davis popped to E.Battey-c in foul territory; K.Boyer lined to L.Aparicio-ss; 0 R, 1 H, 0 E, 3 LOB. AL 0, NL 0.

AL 2ND: J.Gentile struck out; E.Battey grounded out (D.Groat-ss to O.Cepeda-1b); L.Wagner singled to shortstop; L.Aparicio was called out on strikes; 0 R, 1 H, 0 E, 1 LOB. AL 0, NL 0.

NL 2ND: D.Crandall flied to R.Maris-cf; B.Mazeroski grounded out (R.Rollins-3b to J.Gentile-1b); J.Podres doubled to right-center; D.Groat singled to right-center [J.Podres scored]; R.Clemente struck out; 1 R, 2 H, 0 E, 1 LOB. AL 0, NL 1.

AL 3RD: **A.Mahaffey replaced J.Podres (pitching); P.Runnels batted for D.Stenhouse;** P.Runnels homered to deep leftfield; R.Rollins flied to R.Clemente-rf in foul territory; B.Moran reached on an error by D.Groat-ss [B.Moran to first]; R.Maris flied to W.Mays-cf; R.Colavito reached on an error by T.Davis-lf (T.Davis-lf to K.Boyer-3b to D.Crandall-c) [B.Moran out at home, R.Colavito to first]; 1 R, 1 H, 2 E, 1 LOB. AL 1, NL 1.

NL 3RD: **R.Herbert replaced P.Runnels (pitching);** W.Mays singled to shortstop; O.Cepeda grounded into a double play (L.Aparicio-ss to B.Moran-2b to J.Gentile-1b) [W.Mays out at second]; **S.Musial batted for T.Davis;** S.Musial grounded out (L.Aparicio-ss to J.Gentile-1b); 0 R, 1 H, 0 E, 0 LOB. AL 1, NL 1.

AL 4TH: **S.Musial stayed in game (playing lf); H.Aaron replaced W.Mays (playing cf); F.Robinson replaced R.Clemente (playing rf); J.Roseboro replaced D.Crandall (playing c);** J.Gentile grounded out (O.Cepeda-1b unassisted); E.Battey walked; L.Wagner homered to deep rightfield [E.Battey scored]; L.Aparicio lined to D.Groat-ss; R.Herbert struck out; 2 R, 1 H, 0 E, 0 LOB. AL 3, NL 1.

NL 4TH: K.Boyer singled to left field; J.Roseboro grounded into a double play (B.Moran-2b to L.Aparicio-ss to J.Gentile-1b) [K.Boyer out at second]; **G.Altman batted for B.Mazeroski;** G.Altman flied to L.Wagner-lf; 0 R, 1 H, 0 E, 0 LOB. AL 3, NL 1.

AL 5TH: **E.Banks replaced O.Cepeda (playing 1b); F.Bolling replaced A.Mahaffey (playing 2b); B.Gibson replaced G.Altman (pitching);** R.Rollins grounded out (D.Groat-ss to E.Banks-1b); B.Moran flied to F.Robinson-rf; R.Maris walked; R.Colavito struck out; 0 R, 0 H, 0 E, 1 LOB. AL 3, NL 1.

NL 5TH: **B.Robinson replaced R.Rollins (playing 3b); T.Tresh replaced L.Aparicio (playing ss);** F.Bolling flied to R.Maris-cf; D.Groat singled to shortstop; F.Robinson flied to R.Maris-cf; H.Aaron grounded out (T.Tresh-ss to J.Gentile-1b); 0 R, 1 H, 0 E, 1 LOB. AL 3, NL 1.

AL 6TH: J.Gentile walked; E.Battey forced J.Gentile (K.Boyer-3b to F.Bolling-2b) [E.Battey to first]; **A.Kaline ran for E.Battey;** L.Wagner popped to D.Groat-ss; T.Tresh doubled to left field (S.Musial-lf to D.Groat-ss to E.Banks-1b to F.Bolling-2b) [A.Kaline scored (RBI), T.Tresh out at second]; 1 R, 1 H, 0 E, 0 LOB. AL 4, NL 1.

NL 6TH: **H.Aguirre replaced R.Herbert (pitching); E.Howard replaced A.Kaline (playing c);** E.Banks grounded out (J.Gentile-1b unassisted); S.Musial flied to R.Maris-cf; K.Boyer flied to R.Colavito-rf; 0 R, 0 H, 0 E, 0 LOB. AL 4, NL 1.

AL 7TH: **T.Farrell replaced B.Gibson (pitching); E.Mathews replaced K.Boyer (playing 3b); B.Williams replaced S.Musial (playing lf);** H.Aguirre struck out; B.Robinson walked; B.Moran singled to center field [B.Robinson to second]; argument as Aaron claimed a catch and Burkhart ruled a trap; R.Maris forced B.Moran (F.Bolling-2b to D.Groat-ss) [B.Robinson to third, R.Maris to first]; R.Colavito homered to deep leftfield [B.Robinson scored, R.Maris scored]; J.Gentile singled to center field; E.Howard struck out; 3 R, 3 H, 0 E, 1 LOB. AL 7, NL 1.

NL 7TH: J.Roseboro struck out; **R.Ashburn batted for T.Farrell;** R.Ashburn singled to left field; F.Bolling doubled to right-center [R.Ashburn to third]; D.Groat grounded out (T.Tresh-ss to J.Gentile-1b) [R.Ashburn scored, F.Bolling to third]; F.Robinson grounded out (B.Robinson-3b to J.Gentile-1b); 1 R, 2 H, 0 E, 1 LOB. AL 7, NL 2.

AL 8TH: **M.Wills replaced D.Groat (playing ss); J.Marichal replaced R.Ashburn (pitching);** L.Wagner singled to center field; T.Tresh forced L.Wagner (M.Wills-ss to F.Bolling-2b) [T.Tresh to first]; H.Aguirre struck out; B.Robinson flied to B.Williams-lf; 0 R, 1 H, 0 E, 1 LOB. AL 7, NL 2.

NL 8TH: **L.Thomas replaced L.Wagner (playing lf);** H.Aaron grounded out (B.Moran-2b to J.Gentile-1b); E.Banks tripled to deep centerfield; B.Williams grounded out (T.Tresh-ss to J.Gentile-1b) [E.Banks scored]; E.Mathews struck out; 1 R, 1 H, 0 E, 0 LOB. AL 7, NL 3.

AL 9TH: **Y.Berra batted for B.Moran;** Y.Berra reached on an error by E.Mathews-3b [Y.Berra to second (error by E.Mathews-3b)]; **B.Richardson ran for Y.Berra;** J.Marichal threw a wild pitch [B.Richardson to third]; R.Maris doubled to right field [B.Richardson scored (unearned)]; J.Marichal threw a wild pitch [R.Maris to third]; R.Colavito out on a sacrifice fly to H.Aaron-cf [R.Maris scored]; J.Gentile flied to B.Williams-lf;

E.Howard struck out; 2 R (1 ER), 1 H, 2 E, 0 LOB. AL 9, NL 3.

NL 9TH: **B.Richardson stayed in game (playing 2b); M.Pappas replaced H.Aguirre (pitching);** J.Roseboro homered to deep rightfield; **J.Callison batted for J.Marichal;** J.Callison walked; F.Bolling forced J.Callison (T.Tresh-ss to B.Richardson-2b) [F.Bolling to first]; M.Wills forced F.Bolling (T.Tresh-ss to B.Richardson-2b) [M.Wills to first]; F.Robinson flied to L.Thomas-lf; 1 R, 1 H, 0 E, 1 LOB. AL 9, NL 4.

Final Totals	R	H	E	LOB
American League	9	10	0	6
National League	4	10	4	7

Back to One per Year

The All-Star Game returned to its format as a single contest in 1963 as the game's greats migrated to the shores of Lake Erie for the thirty-fourth meeting. The attendance was a healthy 44,160, but that was a disappointing turnout in a park that seated nearly 74,000. Nonetheless, the players and their pension fund received nearly $250,000 from their 95-percent cut of the money from ticket sales.

Starting lineups once again were selected by a poll of players, coaches, and managers. The most surprising selection was that of Mickey Mantle, who was injured and had not played since June 5 because of a broken foot. He would not return until August 4 and even then was exclusively a pinch hitter until September 2. This impressive compliment from Mantle's peers was supported by his performance before the injury. He had a batting average of .310, an on-base average of .441, and a slugging percentage of .647, which would have led the league by nearly ten points if he had played enough to qualify for the title. In Mantle's absence, the starting center fielder for the AL became Albie Pearson of the Angels, who had finished second to Mantle in the voting. On the National League side, Bill Mazeroski of the Pirates withdrew from the game with a pulled leg muscle and was replaced by Julian Javier of the Cardinals. As a result, the starting infielders for the NL were all from the Cardinals; first baseman Bill White, shortstop Dick Groat, and third baseman Ken Boyer rounded out the inner defense. Groat was tops in votes for the NL with 238, and Al Kaline of the Tigers led the AL with 226.

The star of the game was the Giants' Willie Mays, although he had only one hit, a single. He stole two bases, scored two runs, and drove in two more while also making the most spectacular catch of the day. The victim of Willie's great play was Joe Pepitone of the Yankees, who drove Mays to the fence to end the eighth inning. Mays was

slightly hurt on the play when he caught his toe under the chain-link fence. Although he left the field under his own power and was not seriously injured, Roberto Clemente of the Pirates replaced him for the ninth inning. Although eight runs were scored in the game, there was rather surprisingly only one extra-base hit among the seventeen safeties, a double by Albie Pearson to greet Larry Jackson leading off the third inning. It was only the second time an All-Star Game had a single extra-base blow (the first had been in 1953).

The teams posted matching totals through the first three innings, scoring zero, one, and two runs, respectively, to create a 3–3 tie. Even though the first frame was scoreless, it had one of the most exciting plays of the game. After the NL went out in order, Nellie Fox and Pearson singled against the Reds' Jim O'Toole to put runners at the corners with no one out. Al Kaline of the Tigers hit a fly ball to left field, where Dodger Tommy Davis caught it and fired a strike on the fly to Giants catcher Ed Bailey to complete the double play on Fox. Mays and Groat combined for the first run of the game in the second inning on a walk, steal, and single. The AL responded promptly with a single by Leon Wagner of the Angels, a two-out hit batter (Zoilo Versalles of the Twins), and a single by pitcher Ken McBride of the Angels off the glove of third baseman Ken Boyer. It may seem surprising by today's standards to let a pitcher bat in an All-Star Game, but it was only the second inning and McBride had some pop (he hit six doubles and a triple in 1963).

The two runs for the NL in the third came via classic "little ball": single, force out, infield out, single for a run, steal of second, single for a run. Mays was in the middle of all this with the second single in the string for the first RBI, the steal, and the second run on the last single. The two-run response by the AL was a little more powerful because it began with Pearson's double off the wall in left-center, but the scoring came on a one-out single, an infield out, and another single. The Cardinals' Larry Jackson was the victim as he allowed two runs on four hits in his two innings. Despite this ineffectiveness, Jackson ended up the winning pitcher. NL manager Alvin Dark of the Giants inserted the Reds' Johnny Edwards to catch as the third inning began, but home plate umpire Hank Soar of the AL pointed out that starters other than pitchers were required to play three innings, so Ed Bailey came back behind the plate. Edwards got into the game in the fifth. Neither starting pitcher had a very good day on the mound, with O'Toole allowing five runners but only one run in his two innings, while McBride put six men on, three of whom scored. However, neither pitcher figured in the decision.

The rest of the scoring for the day belonged to the National Leaguers as they tallied single runs in the fifth and the eighth. Jim Bunning of the Tigers took the loss because he allowed an unearned run, but he clearly deserved a better fate. Bunning pitched two innings, allowing only a walk and no hits, but gave up an unearned run due to the combination of an error by Yankee Bobby Richardson and a very poor decision by Pepitone. Tommy Davis walked to open the inning, and Bill White hit a dribbler to third baseman Frank Malzone of the Red Sox, who tried to force Davis at second. However, Richardson was playing in the hole for the left-handed-batting White and had to race a long way to second base for Malzone's throw. The ball bounced off his glove into left-center field, letting Davis move to third. Mays then hit a grounder to first baseman Pepitone, who apparently had too many choices. He looked toward second, where he may have been able to start a double play on White. Then he looked home, where he had a good chance to get Tommy Davis. He finally decided to go to the bag as the ultimate winning run came across. The inning ended as Stan Musial of the Cardinals made his twenty-fourth and last All-Star appearance as a pinch hitter for Bailey, lining out to Kaline. The final run scored in the eighth against Dick Radatz of the Red Sox on a single by White, who then stole second and scored on a hit by Ron Santo of the Cubs. Even though he allowed this run, Radatz was overpowering, striking out five in his two innings of work.

In the meantime, the AL was shut out for the last five innings by Ray Culp of the Phillies, Hal Woodeshick of the Colts, and Don Drysdale of the Dodgers, who was credited with a save. While these three combined to allow three singles and a walk, there were two scoring chances, both of which were ended by double plays in the sixth and ninth, the latter ending the game after Oriole Brooks Robinson had gathered his second hit. The hapless Bobby Richardson was the batter for both double plays as he completed a forgettable game. The Cleveland crowd was very hostile to every Yankee on the field, starting with the pregame introductions, which made the fielding mishaps in the fifth inning even more grating for the Cleveland fans.

	AL		NL	
P	Ken McBride	LAA	Jim O'Toole	CIN
C	Earl Battey	MIN	Ed Bailey	SFN
1B	Joe Pepitone	NYA	Bill White	SLN
2B	Nellie Fox	CHA	Bill Mazeroski +	PIT
3B	Frank Malzone	BOS	Ken Boyer	SLN
SS	Zoilo Versalles	MIN	Dick Groat	SLN
OF	Al Kaline	DET	Hank Aaron	MIL
OF	Albie Pearson	LAA	Tommy Davis	LAN
OF	Leon Wagner	LAA	Willie Mays	SFN
	Bob Allison	MIN	Orlando Cepeda	SFN
	Luis Aparicio	BAL	Roberto Clemente	PIT
	Steve Barber +	BAL	Ray Culp	PHI
	Jim Bouton	NYA	Don Drysdale	LAN
	Jim Bunning	DET	Johnny Edwards	CIN
	Jim Grant	CLE	Larry Jackson	CHN
	Elston Howard	NYA	Julian Javier	SLN
	Harmon Killebrew	MIN	Sandy Koufax	LAN
	Don Leppert	WAS	Juan Marichal	SFN
	Mickey Mantle	NYA	Willie McCovey	SFN
	Bill Monbouquette	BOS	Stan Musial	SLN
	Juan Pizarro	CHA	Ron Santo	CHN
	Dick Radatz	BOS	Duke Snider	NYN
	Bobby Richardson	NYA	Warren Spahn	MIL
	Brooks Robinson	BAL	Joe Torre	MIL
	Norm Siebern	KC	Maury Wills	LAN
	Tom Tresh	NYA	Hal Woodeshick	HOU
	Carl Yastrzemski	BOS		

+ player replaced on roster

```
National League    012 010 010- 5
American League    012 000 000- 3
```

NATIONAL LEAGUE

	ab	r	h	bi	bb	so	po	a
T.Davis, lf	3	1	1	0	1	0	2	1
D.Snider, ph-lf	1	0	0	0	0	1	0	0
H.Aaron, rf	4	1	0	0	0	0	3	0
B.White, 1b	4	1	1	0	0	0	5	3
W.Mays, cf	3	2	1	2	1	1	1	0
R.Clemente, cf	0	0	0	0	0	0	0	0
E.Bailey, c	1	0	1	1	1	0	4	1
S.Musial, ph	1	0	0	0	0	0	0	0
R.Culp, p	0	0	0	0	0	0	0	1
R.Santo, 3b	1	0	1	1	0	0	0	0
K.Boyer, 3b	3	0	0	0	1	0	0	0
H.Woodeshick, p	0	0	0	0	0	0	0	1
W.McCovey, ph	1	0	0	0	0	1	0	0
D.Drysdale, p	0	0	0	0	0	0	0	0
D.Groat, ss	4	0	1	1	0	1	2	2
J.Javier, 2b	4	0	0	0	0	2	4	1
J.O'Toole, p	1	0	0	0	0	0	0	0
L.Jackson, p	1	0	0	0	0	0	1	0
J.Edwards, c	2	0	0	0	0	0	5	0
Totals	34	5	6	5	3	6	27	10

BATTING
2-out RBI: W.Mays; E.Bailey.
RBI, scoring position, less than 2 outs: W.Mays 1–1;
R.Santo 1–1; K.Boyer 0–1; D.Groat 1–1; J.Javier 0–1.

BASERUNNING
SB: B.White (2nd base off D.Radatz / E.Howard);
W.Mays 2 (2nd base off K.McBride / E.Battey; 2nd
base off K.McBride / E.Battey).
Team LOB: 5

FIELDING
Outfield assist: T.Davis (N.Fox at 3B).
DP: (3). T.Davis-E.Bailey; D.Groat-J.Javier-B.White;
B.White-D.Groat-B.White.

AMERICAN LEAGUE

	ab	r	h	bi	bb	so	po	a
N.Fox, 2b	3	0	1	0	0	1	3	1
B.Richardson, 2b	2	0	0	0	0	0	0	1
A.Pearson, cf	4	1	2	0	0	1	4	0
T.Tresh, cf	0	0	0	0	0	0	0	0
A.Kaline, rf	3	0	0	0	0	1	2	0
B.Allison, rf	1	0	0	0	0	1	0	0
F.Malzone, 3b	3	1	1	1	0	0	1	3
J.Bouton, p	0	0	0	0	0	0	0	0
J.Pizarro, p	0	0	0	0	0	0	0	0
H.Killebrew, ph	1	0	0	0	0	1	0	0
D.Radatz, p	0	0	0	0	0	0	0	0
L.Wagner, lf	3	1	2	0	0	0	1	0
E.Howard, c	1	0	0	0	0	1	5	0
E.Battey, c	2	0	1	1	0	0	1	0
C.Yastrzemski, ph-lf	2	0	0	0	0	1	1	0
J.Pepitone, 1b	4	0	0	0	0	2	8	0
Z.Versalles, ss	1	0	1	0	1	0	0	2
L.Aparicio, ss	1	0	0	0	0	0	0	0
K.McBride, p	1	0	1	1	0	0	0	0
J.Bunning, p	0	0	0	0	0	0	0	0
B.Robinson, 3b	2	0	2	0	0	0	1	1
Totals	34	3	11	3	1	9	27	8

BATTING
2B: A.Pearson (off L.Jackson).
2-out RBI: E.Battey; K.McBride.
RBI, scoring position, less than 2 outs: N.Fox 0–1;
B.Richardson 0–1; A.Kaline 0–2; F.Malzone 1–1.
S: J.Bunning.
GDP: B.Richardson 2.

BASERUNNING
Team LOB: 7

FIELDING
E: B.Richardson (dropped throw).

PITCHING	ip	h	r	er	bb	so
National League						
J.O'Toole	2.0	4	1	1	0	1
L.Jackson (w)	2.0	4	2	2	0	3
R.Culp	1.0	1	0	0	0	0
H.Woodeshick	2.0	1	0	0	1	3
D.Drysdale (s)	2.0	1	0	0	0	2
American League						
K.McBride	3.0	4	3	3	2	1
J.Bunning (L)	2.0	0	1	0	1	0
J.Bouton	1.0	0	0	0	0	0
J.Pizarro	1.0	0	0	0	0	0
D.Radatz	2.0	2	1	1	0	5

Inherited Runners—Scored:
L.Jackson 0–0; R.Culp 0–0; H.Woodeshick 0–0;
D.Drysdale 0–0; J.Bunning 0–0; J.Bouton 0–0;
J.Pizarro 0–0; D.Radatz 0–0.
HBP: Z.Versalles by J.O'Toole.

GAME DATA—T: 2:20; A: 44160; Temp: Unknown;
Wind: Unknown direction, Speed: Unknown

UMPIRES—HP: Hank Soar (AL), 1B: Bill Jackowski (NL),
2B: Al Smith (AL), 3B: Paul Pryor (NL), LF: Bill Haller
(AL), RF: Doug Harvey (NL)

STARTING LINEUPS

National League	*American League*
1. T.Davis lf	N.Fox 2b
2. H.Aaron rf	A.Pearson cf
3. B.White 1b	A.Kaline rf
4. W.Mays cf	F.Malzone 3b
5. E.Bailey c	L.Wagner lf
6. K.Boyer 3b	E.Battey c
7. D.Groat ss	J.Pepitone 1b
8. J.Javier 2b	Z.Versalles ss
9. J.O'Toole p	K.McBride p

NL 1ST: T.Davis grounded out (F.Malzone-3b to J.Pepitone-1b); H.Aaron grounded out (F.Malzone-3b to J.Pepitone-1b); B.White grounded out (N.Fox-2b to J.Pepitone-1b); O R, O H, O E, O LOB. NL O, AL O.

AL 1ST: N.Fox singled to center field; A.Pearson singled to right field [N.Fox to third]; A.Kaline flied into a double play (T.Davis-lf to E.Bailey-c) [N.Fox out at third, A.Pearson to second (on throw)]; F.Malzone popped to D.Groat-ss; O R, 2 H, O E, 1 LOB. NL O, AL O.

NL 2ND: W.Mays walked; W.Mays stole second; E.Bailey walked; K.Boyer popped to N.Fox-2b; D.Groat singled to left field [W.Mays scored, E.Bailey to second]; J.Javier was called out on strikes; J.O'Toole forced D.Groat (Z.Versalles-ss to N.Fox-2b) [J.O'Toole to first]; 1 R, 1 H, O E, 2 LOB. NL 1, AL O.

AL 2ND: L.Wagner singled to left field; E.Battey flied to H.Aaron-rf; J.Pepitone struck out; Z.Versalles was hit by a pitch [L.Wagner to second]; K.McBride singled to left field [L.Wagner scored, Z.Versalles to third, K.McBride to second (on throw home)]; N.Fox flied to T.Davis-lf; 1 R, 2 H, O E, 2 LOB. NL 1, AL 1.

NL 3RD: T.Davis singled to center field; H.Aaron forced T.Davis (F.Malzone-3b to N.Fox-2b) [H.Aaron to first]; B.White grounded out (J.Pepitone-1b unassisted) [H.Aaron to second]; W.Mays singled to center field [H.Aaron scored]; W.Mays stole second; E.Bailey singled to center field [W.Mays scored]; K.Boyer flied to L.Wagner-lf; 2 R, 3 H, O E, 1 LOB. NL 3, AL 1.

AL 3RD: **L.Jackson replaced J.O'Toole (pitching);** Dark attempted to put Edwards at catcher for NL, but Soar pointed out that starters had to play three innings; A.Pearson doubled to very deep left-center; A.Kaline was called out on strikes; F.Malzone singled to center field [A.Pearson scored]; L.Wagner grounded out (B.White-1b to L.Jackson-p) [F.Malzone to second]; E.Battey singled to center field [F.Malzone scored]; J.Pepi-

tone lined to H.Aaron-rf; 2 R, 3 H, O E, 1 LOB. NL 3, AL 3.

NL 4TH: **J.Bunning replaced K.McBride (pitching);** D.Groat flied to A.Kaline-rf; J.Javier popped to F.Malzone-3b; L.Jackson flied to A.Pearson-cf; O R, O H, O E, O LOB. NL 3, AL 3.

AL 4TH: Z.Versalles singled to left field; J.Bunning out on a sacrifice bunt (B.White-1b to J.Javier-2b) [Z.Versalles to second]; N.Fox struck out (E.Bailey-c to B.White-1b); A.Pearson struck out; O R, 1 H, O E, 1 LOB. NL 3, AL 3.

NL 5TH: **B.Richardson replaced N.Fox (playing 2b);** T.Davis walked; H.Aaron flied to A.Pearson-cf; B.White reached on an error [T.Davis to third, B.White to first (error by B.Richardson-2b; assist by F.Malzone-3b)]; W.Mays grounded out (J.Pepitone-1b unassisted) [T.Davis scored (unearned), B.White to second]; **S.Musial batted for E.Bailey;** S.Musial lined to A.Kaline-rf; 1 R (O ER), O H, 1 E, 1 LOB. NL 4, AL 3.

AL 5TH: **J.Edwards replaced L.Jackson (playing c); R.Culp replaced S.Musial (pitching);** A.Kaline grounded out (R.Culp-p to B.White-1b); F.Malzone flied to H.Aaron-rf; L.Wagner singled to right field; **C.Yastrzemski batted for E.Battey;** C.Yastrzemski popped to J.Javier-2b in foul territory; O R, 1 H, O E, 1 LOB. NL 4, AL 3.

NL 6TH: **C.Yastrzemski stayed in game (playing lf); B.Robinson replaced J.Bunning (playing 3b); B.Allison replaced A.Kaline (playing rf); E.Howard replaced L.Wagner (playing c); J.Bouton replaced F.Malzone (pitching);** K.Boyer popped to B.Robinson-3b in foul territory; D.Groat grounded out (B.Robinson-3b to J.Pepitone-1b); J.Javier grounded out (Z.Versalles-ss to J.Pepitone-1b); O R, O H, O E, O LOB. NL 4, AL 3.

AL 6TH: **R.Santo replaced R.Culp (playing 3b); H.Woodeshick replaced K.Boyer (pitching);** J.Pepitone struck out; Z.Versalles walked; B.Robinson singled to center field [Z.Versalles to third]; B.Richardson grounded into a double play (D.Groat-ss to J.Javier-2b to B.White-1b) [B.Robinson out at second]; O R, 1 H, O E, 1 LOB. NL 4, AL 3.

NL 7TH: **J.Pizarro replaced J.Bouton (pitching); L.Aparicio replaced Z.Versalles (playing ss);** J.Edwards grounded out (B.Richardson-2b to J.Pepitone-1b); T.Davis flied to A.Pearson-cf; H.Aaron popped to A.Pearson-cf; O R, O H, O E, O LOB. NL 4, AL 3.

AL 7TH: A.Pearson grounded out (H.Woodeshick-p to B.White-1b); B.Allison struck out; **H.Killebrew batted for J.Pizarro;** H.Killebrew was called out on strikes; O R, O H, O E, O LOB. NL 4, AL 3.

NL 8TH: **T.Tresh replaced A.Pearson (playing cf);** **D.Radatz replaced H.Killebrew (pitching);** B.White singled to center field; W.Mays struck out while B.White stole second; R.Santo singled to center field [B.White scored]; **W.McCovey batted for H.Woodeshick;** W.McCovey struck out; D.Groat was called out on strikes; 1 R, 2 H, 0 E, 1 LOB. NL 5, AL 3.

AL 8TH: **D.Drysdale replaced W.McCovey (pitching);** E.Howard struck out; C.Yastrzemski struck out; J.Pepitone flied to W.Mays-cf; 0 R, 0 H, 0 E, 0 LOB. NL 5, AL 3.

NL 9TH: great catch by Mays; J.Javier struck out; J.Edwards flied to C.Yastrzemski-lf; **D.Snider batted** for T.Davis; D.Snider was called out on strikes; 0 R, 0 H, 0 E, 0 LOB. NL 5, AL 3.

AL 9TH: **D.Snider stayed in game (playing lf);** **R.Clemente replaced W.Mays (playing cf);** L.Aparicio popped to J.Javier-2b; B.Robinson singled to center field; B.Richardson grounded into a double play (B.White-1b to D.Groat-ss to B.White-1b) [B.Robinson out at second]; 0 R, 1 H, 0 E, 0 LOB. NL 5, AL 3.

Final Totals	R	H	E	LOB
National League	5	6	0	5
American League	3	11	1	7

35

The NL Ties the Series

The 1964 contest at Shea Stadium, which brought the National League even after thirty-two years of trying, was the third one to end on a home run. The games of 1941 and 1955 also ended with circuit clouts by Ted Williams and Stan Musial, respectively. This game's blast by Philadelphia's Johnny Callison brought the standing in the series to seventeen wins apiece, with one game ending in a tie. This result met with great approval from the more than fifty thousand fans in attendance, helping to celebrate the first year of operation for the permanent home of the Mets as they ended their temporary occupancy of the Polo Grounds, where they had played in 1962 and 1963.

The practice of choosing starters by vote of players, managers, and coaches continued for the seventh straight year. The managers, Walter Alston of the Dodgers for the NL and Al Lopez of the White Sox for the AL, completed the rosters. Lopez got the reins for the day because the manager of the 1963 AL champion Yankees, Ralph Houk, had left the field to become the general manager of the Bronx team. Lopez led Chicago to a second-place finish in 1963, ten and a half games behind the Yankees. The top vote getter in the AL was Bobby Richardson of the Yankees, with 253 votes, while for the NL it was Willie Mays of the Giants, with 240.

Don Drysdale of the Dodgers made his fourth All-Star start and was touched for an unearned first-inning run. The Angels' Jim Fregosi led off the game with a single to left and moved to second on a passed ball by the Braves' Joe Torre. After Tony Oliva of the Twins grounded out and Mickey Mantle of the Yankees struck out, the Twins' Harmon Killebrew brought Fregosi home with a single to left, the first of The Killer's three hits for the day. After a wild pitch, the inning ended as Minnesota's Bob Allison struck out. Drysdale allowed no one else to reach base in the second and third innings and gave way to Jim Bunning of the Phillies, who pitched scoreless ball for the fourth and

fifth, allowing two singles and striking out four batters. One of the hits was an unlikely infield single by Killebrew; as the ball hit his bat while he was ducking from a pitch up and in. In the meantime, the NL was producing three runs during the first five innings. Dean Chance of the Angels, who would win the Cy Young Award for 1964 (there was still only a single, combined award in 1964), was the starting pitcher and allowed only two singles in his three innings after starting the game with a flourish by striking out Roberto Clemente and Dick Groat, both of the Pirates. This was the third time that the two starting pitchers came from the same city, as the Angels were in their third season of sharing Dodger Stadium. John Wyatt of the Athletics relieved to start the fourth and had a rough time for his one inning as he was greeted by the Cubs' Billy Williams with a home run to right-center. With two outs, the Cardinals' Ken Boyer gave the NL the lead with a homer to left. Ken would go on to have a great season and win the National League's Most Valuable Player Award; the American League award would go to his third-base counterpart from Baltimore, Brooks Robinson, who also had a fine All-Star Game. Camilo Pascual of the Twins came on to pitch the fifth and, with two out, allowed Clemente and Groat to avenge their first-inning problems with a single and double for the NL's third run.

Chris Short of the Phillies and Dick Farrell of the Colts combined to pitch the sixth through eighth innings for the NL and allowed the AL back in the lead with three runs on five hits, a walk, and a hit batter. The big blow for the AL was a two-run triple by Robinson, whose liner to right-center was just missed by Mays, scoring Mantle and Killebrew, who had both singled. It was Killebrew's third hit of the game. The final AL run came against Farrell in the eighth. Elston Howard of the Yankees started off by getting hit by a pitch; then the Athletics' Rocky Colavito, pinch-hitting for Pascual, ripped a double to left-center, just past the diving Mays. Despite missing this ball and Robinson's triple in the sixth, Mays had a great game defensively and led all NL players with seven put-outs, one more than first baseman Orlando Cepeda of the Giants. Fregosi got Howard home from third with a sacrifice fly to Mays, whose throw home was just late. Juan Marichal of the Giants pitched a perfect ninth and would become the winning pitcher as the beneficiary of the NL comeback.

The loser for the AL was hard-throwing Dick Radatz of the Red Sox, who had entered to begin the seventh. Radatz pitched the final 2.2 innings and struck five batters. He also gave up two hits and two walks and was victimized by an error by Yankee Joe Pepitone, who had gone to play first base in the eighth after pinch-running for Bob Allison. Mays opened the inning with a hard-earned walk that took eleven pitches to complete, including five straight foul balls. Radatz tried to hold Mays close to first, but Mays stole on the second pitch. Cepeda then hit a pop fly single to short right field that was retrieved by Pepitone. When Joe threw wildly to the plate, Mays, who had been content to stop at third, scored the tying run, and Cepeda advanced to second. This was the second straight year that Pepitone's poor fielding proved costly; in 1963, his indecision had allowed what proved to be the winning run to score. Mays had

an indirect effect on Cepeda's hit as well. Richardson was convinced that Mays would try to steal third, so he played closer to the bag to hold him on. As a result, Richardson was unable to make a play in short right field that he might normally have done with ease. Radatz then got Boyer to pop up, intentionally walked catcher Johnny Edwards of the Reds, and appeared to be out of the woods when he struck out Henry Aaron, who was batting for Ron Hunt of the hometown Mets. Callison then hit his homer to send everyone home.

As expected, Callison was named the game's Most Valuable Player and thus the winner of the Arch Ward Memorial Trophy, named in honor of the man credited with starting the midsummer meetings in 1933. This decision required a second ballot, since the vote had been taken earlier in the ninth inning in anticipation of an American League win, and Robinson had been the initial pick to get the trophy. Although he had no hits, Mays was second in the balloting (39–28), due largely to his indispensable role in tying the game in the last inning. The ninth inning comeback fit in well with the surge the NL had put in since the AL won in Baltimore in 1958. In the ten games from 1959 to 1964, the NL won seven and tied one, outscoring the AL by a margin of 44–34 in the process.

	AL		NL	
P	Dean Chance	LAA	Don Drysdale	LAN
C	Elston Howard	NYA	Joe Torre	MIL
1B	Bob Allison	MIN	Orlando Cepeda	SFN
2B	Bobby Richardson	NYA	Ron Hunt	NYN
3B	Brooks Robinson	BAL	Ken Boyer	SLN
SS	Jim Fregosi	LAA	Dick Groat	SLN
OF	Harmon Killebrew	MIN	Roberto Clemente	PIT
OF	Mickey Mantle	NYA	Willie Mays	SFN
OF	Tony Oliva	MIN	Billy Williams	CHN
	Luis Aparicio +	BAL	Hank Aaron	MIL
	Eddie Bressoud	BOS	Jim Bunning	PHI
	Rocky Colavito	KC	Smoky Burgess	PIT
	Whitey Ford	NYA	Johnny Callison	PHI
	Bill Freehan	DET	Leo Cardenas	CIN
	Jimmie Hall	MIN	Johnny Edwards	CIN
	Chuck Hinton	WAS	Dick Ellsworth	CHN
	Al Kaline +	DET	Turk Farrell	HOU
	Jack Kralick	CLE	Curt Flood	SLN
	Jerry Lumpe	DET	Sandy Koufax	LAN
	Frank Malzone	BOS	Juan Marichal	SFN
	Camilo Pascual	MIN	Bill Mazeroski	PIT
	Joe Pepitone	NYA	Ron Santo	CHN
	Gary Peters	CHA	Chris Short	PHI
	Juan Pizarro	CHA	Willie Stargell	PIT
	Dick Radatz	BOS	Bill White	SLN
	Norm Siebern	BAL		
	John Wyatt	KC		

+ player replaced on roster

American League   100 002 100- 4
National League   000 210 004- 7
  2 outs when winning run was scored.

AMERICAN LEAGUE

	ab	r	h	bi	bb	so	po	a
J.Fregosi, ss	4	1	1	1	0	1	4	1
T.Oliva, rf	4	0	0	0	0	1	0	0
D.Radatz, p	1	0	0	0	0	1	0	0
M.Mantle, cf	4	1	1	0	0	2	2	0
J.Hall, cf	0	0	0	0	0	0	0	0
H.Killebrew, lf	4	1	3	1	0	0	0	0
C.Hinton, lf	0	0	0	0	0	0	0	0
B.Allison, 1b	3	0	0	0	1	2	9	0
J.Pepitone, pr-1b	0	0	0	0	0	0	1	0
B.Robinson, 3b	4	0	2	2	0	0	1	2
B.Richardson, 2b	4	0	1	0	0	1	0	4
E.Howard, c	3	1	0	0	0	2	9	0
D.Chance, p	1	0	0	0	0	0	0	1
J.Wyatt, p	0	0	0	0	0	0	0	1
N.Siebern, ph	1	0	0	0	0	0	0	0
C.Pascual, p	0	0	0	0	0	0	0	1
R.Colavito, ph-rf	2	0	1	0	0	0	0	0
Totals	35	4	9	4	1	10	26	10

BATTING
2B: R.Colavito (off T.Farrell).
3B: Robinson (off C.Short).
2-out RBI: H.Killebrew; B.Robinson 2.
RBI, scoring position, less than 2 outs: J.Fregosi 1–2;
  T.Oliva 0–2; M.Mantle 0–1; B.Allison 0–1.
SF: J.Fregosi.

BASERUNNING
Team LOB: 7

FIELDING
E: J.Pepitone (throw).

NATIONAL LEAGUE

	ab	r	h	bi	bb	so	po	a
R.Clemente, rf	3	1	1	0	0	1	1	0
C.Short, p	0	0	0	0	0	0	0	1
T.Farrell, p	0	0	0	0	0	0	0	0
B.White, ph	1	0	0	0	0	1	0	0
J.Marichal, p	0	0	0	0	0	0	0	0
D.Groat, ss	3	0	1	1	0	1	0	0
L.Cardenas, pr-ss	1	0	0	0	0	1	1	0
B.Williams, lf	4	1	1	1	0	0	1	0
W.Mays, cf	3	1	0	0	1	0	7	0
O.Cepeda, 1b	4	0	1	0	0	0	5	1
C.Flood, pr	0	1	0	0	0	0	0	0
K.Boyer, 3b	4	1	2	1	0	1	0	2
J.Torre, c	2	0	0	0	0	0	5	0
J.Edwards, c	1	1	0	0	1	1	5	0
R.Hunt, 2b	3	0	1	0	0	1	1	0
H.Aaron, ph	1	0	0	0	0	1	0	0
D.Drysdale, p	0	0	0	0	0	0	1	2
W.Stargell, ph	1	0	0	0	0	0	0	0
J.Bunning, p	0	0	0	0	0	0	0	0
J.Callison, ph-rf	3	1	1	3	0	0	0	0
Totals	34	7	8	6	2	8	27	6

BATTING
2B: D.Groat (off C.Pascual).
HR: B.Williams (4th inning off J.Wyatt, 0 on, 0 out);
  K.Boyer (4th inning off J.Wyatt, 0 on, 2 out);
  J.Callison (9th inning off D.Radatz, 2 on, 2 out).
2-out RBI: D.Groat; K.Boyer; J.Callison 3.
RBI, scoring position, less than 2 outs: R.Clemente 0–1;
  K.Boyer 0–1; H.Aaron 0–1.

BASERUNNING
SB: W.Mays (2nd base off D.Radatz/E.Howard).
Team LOB: 3

FIELDING
PB: J.Torre.

PITCHING	ip	h	r	er	bb	so
American League						
D.Chance	3.0	2	0	0	0	2
J.Wyatt	1.0	2	2	2	0	0
C.Pascual	2.0	2	1	1	0	1
D.Radatz (L, BS)	2.2	2	4	4	2	5
National League						
D.Drysdale	3.0	2	1	0	0	3
J.Bunning	2.0	2	0	0	0	4
C.Short (BS)	1.0	3	2	2	0	1
T.Farrell	2.0	2	1	1	1	1
J.Marichal (W)	1.0	0	0	0	0	1

Inherited Runners—Scored:
  J.Wyatt 0–0; C.Pascual 0–0; D.Radatz 0–0;
  J.Bunning 0–0; C.Short 0–0; T.Farrell 0–0;
  J.Marichal 0–0.
IBB: J.Edwards by D.Radatz.
HBP: E.Howard by T.Farrell.
WP: D.Drysdale

GAME DATA—T: 2:37; A: 50850; Temp: Unknown;
Wind: Unknown direction, Speed: Unknown

UMPIRES—HP: Ed Sudol (NL), 1B: Joe Paparella (AL),
2B: Frank Secory (NL), 3B: Nestor Chylak (AL), LF: Doug
Harvey (NL), RF: Al Salerno (AL)

STARTING LINEUPS

	American League	National League
1.	J.Fregosi ss	R.Clemente rf
2.	T.Oliva rf	D.Groat ss
3.	M.Mantle cf	B.Williams lf
4.	H.Killebrew lf	W.Mays cf
5.	B.Allison 1b	O.Cepeda 1b
6.	B.Robinson 3b	K.Boyer 3b
7.	B.Richardson 2b	J.Torre c
8.	E.Howard c	R.Hunt 2b
9.	D.Chance p	D.Drysdale p

AL 1ST: J.Fregosi singled to left field; J.Torre allowed a passed ball [J.Fregosi to second]; T.Oliva grounded out (D.Drysdale-p to O.Cepeda-1b); M.Mantle struck out; H.Killebrew singled to left field [J.Fregosi scored (unearned)]; D.Drysdale threw a wild pitch [H.Killebrew to second]; B.Allison struck out; 1 R (0 ER), 2 H, 0 E, 1 LOB. AL 1, NL 0.

NL 1ST: R.Clemente struck out; D.Groat struck out; B.Williams popped to J.Fregosi-ss; 0 R, 0 H, 0 E, 0 LOB. AL 1, NL 0.

AL 2ND: B.Robinson lined to W.Mays-cf; B.Richardson grounded out (K.Boyer-3b to O.Cepeda-1b); E.Howard was called out on strikes; 0 R, 0 H, 0 E, 0 LOB. AL 1, NL 0.

NL 2ND: W.Mays grounded out (B.Robinson-3b to B.Allison-1b); O.Cepeda flied to M.Mantle-cf; K.Boyer singled to shortstop; J.Torre forced K.Boyer (J.Fregosi-ss unassisted) [J.Torre to first]; 0 R, 1 H, 0 E, 1 LOB. AL 1, NL 0.

AL 3RD: On a bunt D.Chance grounded out (D.Drysdale-p to O.Cepeda-1b); J.Fregosi flied to R.Clemente-rf; T.Oliva grounded out (O.Cepeda-1b to D.Drysdale-p); 0 R, 0 H, 0 E, 0 LOB. AL 1, NL 0.

NL 3RD: R.Hunt singled to left field; **W.Stargell batted for D.Drysdale;** W.Stargell grounded out (D.Chance-p to B.Allison-1b) [R.Hunt to second]; R.Clemente grounded out (J.Fregosi-ss to B.Allison-1b); D.Groat grounded out (B.Richardson-2b to B.Allison-1b); 0 R, 1 H, 0 E, 1 LOB. AL 1, NL 0.

AL 4TH: **J.Bunning replaced W.Stargell (pitching);** On a bunt M.Mantle popped to R.Hunt-2b; H.Killebrew singled to third base; Killebrew ducked out of the way, ball hit bat and dribbled down the 3rd base line; B.Allison struck out; B.Robinson singled to right field [H.Killebrew to second]; B.Richardson struck out; 0 R, 2 H, 0 E, 2 LOB. AL 1, NL 0.

NL 4TH: **J.Wyatt replaced D.Chance (pitching);** B.Williams homered to very deep right-center; W.Mays popped to E.Howard-c in foul territory; O.Cepeda grounded out (J.Wyatt-p to B.Allison-1b); K.Boyer homered to deep leftfield; J.Torre grounded out (B.Richardson-2b to B.Allison-1b); 2 R, 2 H, 0 E, 0 LOB. AL 1, NL 2.

AL 5TH: **J.Edwards replaced J.Torre (playing c);** E.Howard struck out; **N.Siebern batted for J.Wyatt;** N.Siebern flied to W.Mays-cf; J.Fregosi was called out on strikes; 0 R, 0 H, 0 E, 0 LOB. AL 1, NL 2.

NL 5TH: **C.Pascual replaced N.Siebern (pitching);** R.Hunt grounded out (C.Pascual-p to B.Allison-1b); **J.Callison batted for J.Bunning;** J.Callison popped to J.Fregosi-ss; R.Clemente singled to center field; D.Groat doubled to left-center [R.Clemente scored]; **L.Cardenas ran for D.Groat;** B.Williams grounded out (B.Richardson-2b to B.Allison-1b); 1 R, 2 H, 0 E, 1 LOB. AL 1, NL 3.

AL 6TH: **J.Callison stayed in game (playing rf);** **C.Short replaced R.Clemente (pitching); L.Cardenas stayed in game (playing ss);** T.Oliva struck out; M.Mantle singled to center field; H.Killebrew singled to left-center [M.Mantle to second]; B.Allison flied to W.Mays-cf; B.Robinson tripled to right-center [M.Mantle scored, H.Killebrew scored]; Mays just missed a diving catch; B.Richardson grounded out (C.Short-p to O.Cepeda-1b); 2 R, 3 H, 0 E, 1 LOB. AL 3, NL 3.

NL 6TH: W.Mays lined to J.Fregosi-ss; O.Cepeda grounded out (B.Robinson-3b to B.Allison-1b); K.Boyer struck out; 0 R, 0 H, 0 E, 0 LOB. AL 3, NL 3.

AL 7TH: **T.Farrell replaced C.Short (pitching);** E.Howard was hit by a pitch; **R.Colavito batted for C.Pascual;** R.Colavito doubled to left-center [E.Howard to third]; J.Fregosi out on a sacrifice fly to W.Mays-cf [E.Howard scored]; T.Oliva popped to L.Cardenas-ss; M.Mantle struck out; 1 R, 1 H, 0 E, 1 LOB. AL 4, NL 3.

NL 7TH: **R.Colavito stayed in game (playing rf); D.Radatz replaced T.Oliva (pitching);** J.Edwards was called out on strikes; R.Hunt was called out on strikes; J.Callison flied to M.Mantle-cf; 0 R, 0 H, 0 E, 0 LOB. AL 4, NL 3.

AL 8TH: H.Killebrew grounded out (K.Boyer-3b to O.Cepeda-1b); B.Allison walked; **J.Pepitone ran for B.Allison;** B.Robinson flied to W.Mays-cf; B.Richardson singled to center field [J.Pepitone to second]; E.Howard flied to W.Mays-cf; 0 R, 1 H, 0 E, 2 LOB. AL 4, NL 3.

NL 8TH: **J.Pepitone stayed in game (playing 1b); C.Hinton replaced H.Killebrew (playing lf); B.White batted for T.Farrell;** B.White struck out; L.Cardenas struck out; B.Williams grounded out (B.Richardson-2b to J.Pepitone-1b); 0 R, 0 H, 0 E, 0 LOB. AL 4, NL 3.

AL 9TH: **J.Marichal replaced B.White (pitching);** R.Colavito flied to B.Williams-lf; J.Fregosi lined to W.Mays-cf; D.Radatz struck out; 0 R, 0 H, 0 E, 0 LOB. AL 4, NL 3.

NL 9TH: **J.Hall replaced M.Mantle (playing cf);** W.Mays walked; W.Mays stole second; O.Cepeda singled to first base [W.Mays scored (no RBI) (error by J.Pepitone-1b), O.Cepeda to second (error by J.Pepitone-1b)]; **C.Flood ran for O.Cepeda;** K.Boyer popped to B.Robinson-3b; J.Edwards was walked intentionally; **H.Aaron batted for R.Hunt;** H.Aaron struck out; J.Callison homered to deep rightfield [C.Flood scored, J.Edwards scored]; 4 R, 2 H, 1 E, 0 LOB. AL 4, NL 7.

Final Totals	R	H	E	LOB
American League	4	9	1	7
National League	7	8	0	3

GAME 36

Tuesday, July 13, 1965

Metropolitan Stadium, Minneapolis

National League 6, American League 5

SERIES RESULTS: NL 18, AL 17, 1 TIE

The NL Moves Ahead in Twin Cities Power Show

Minneapolis had a banner baseball year in 1965 as the city hosted the All-Star Game in July and the Twins played in the World Series, taking the Dodgers to seven games before losing to Sandy Koufax in a dramatic 2–0 finale. Although the NL finally pulled ahead of the AL with its eighteenth All-Star win, the 6–5 outcome was anything but certain as the teams compiled eleven runs on nineteen hits and nine walks. The hometown crowd of nearly forty-seven thousand was ultimately disappointed as it watched the NL mount a comeback while the two offenses pounded out a double and five home runs, one short of the All-Star record for the two teams combined in a single game. Each team had a two-inning streak in which it scored five unanswered runs, but the deciding tally scored, ironically enough, on an infield single.

Once again, the starting nonpitchers were chosen by poll of players, managers, and coaches, with the restriction that no one could vote for a member of his own team. Pete Rose got the starting nod at second base, making the first of his sixteen All-Star appearances. The top vote getters were Earl Battey of the Twins for the AL and Willie Mays of the Giants for the NL. Mays was the only center fielder named by the opposing National League teams; Vada Pinson of the Reds received seventeen votes from members of the Giants. For the first time since 1944, no member of the Yankees was chosen as a starter. The twenty-five-man rosters, including all pitchers, were selected by the two managers. Since 1934, the practice has been for the managers of the previous year's World Series teams to lead the All-Star squads. On six previous occasions (1936, 1940, 1948, 1954, 1961, and 1964), this pattern had been broken, due to retirement or dismissal. For the canceled game of 1945, the 1944 World Series managers had no teams to lead. The 1965 All-Star Game was the first one in which both managers were replacements for the previous year's World Series leaders. Yogi Berra, leader of the 1964 AL champion Yankees, had been fired after the World Series, and Johnny Keane, skipper of the world champion Cardinals, had resigned to become the new Yankee boss. In place of Keane, the 1965 NL All-Star team was managed by Gene Mauch of the Phillies, whose team had finished in a second-place tie with the Reds in 1964, one game behind St. Louis. The AL manager was Al Lopez of Chicago, whose White Sox had won ninety-eight games in 1964 but had come in one game behind New York. By interesting coincidence, this was the second straight year that Lopez was the substitute AL manager, having replaced Ralph Houk for the 1964 game.

The scoring burst for the NL came right at the start as Mays homered to left field on the second pitch of the game from Baltimore's Milt Pappas. For Mays, who would lead the majors with fifty-two homers in 1965, this was his third All-Star homer and his twenty-first hit, making him the all-time leader in the latter category as he broke a tie with Cardinal great Stan Musial. Henry Aaron of Milwaukee flied out, Willie Stargell of the Pirates singled, and Joe Torre of the Braves homered to left. Ernie Banks of the Cubs singled and Rose walked, but Maury Wills of the Dodgers ended the threat by bouncing back to Pappas. The Twins' Jim "Mudcat" Grant relieved Pappas to begin the second inning and did only a little better than Pappas had done. Pitcher Juan Marichal of the Giants singled up the middle to start the inning, and Mays walked. Aaron grounded to Baltimore's Brooks Robinson at third, and the AL turned the double play. However, Stargell didn't let Mudcat off the hook as he blasted a homer into the bullpen in right-center. Grant did retire the side in order in the third but left with the NL enjoying a five-run lead. In the meantime, the American League was almost completely baffled by Marichal as the Dominican Dandy allowed only a single by Vic Davalillo of the Indians to lead off the third. However, he was immediately erased when Battey hit a grounder to Wills, who started a double play.

The fortunes of the American League changed dramatically when Jim Maloney of the Reds came on to pitch as Marichal reached his limit of three innings pitched. Singles by Dick McAuliffe of the Tigers and Rocky Colavito of the Indians combined with a walk to the Twins' Harmon Killebrew to produce a run in the fourth. A wild pitch increased the threat, but Maloney stiffened to get the last two outs with no further damage. However, in the fifth inning, the roof fell in as big Jim suffered through one of the worst outings any All-Star pitcher has endured. Pitching in his only All-Star Game (it was the only time he was named to the team), Maloney retired the first two batters and then allowed a walk, homer, single, and homer. Dick McAuliffe hit the first one out, with a shot to the deepest part of the ballpark, but the greatest joy for the Minnesota crowd came on the second circuit clout, which was hit by Killebrew. Maloney departed with credit for 1.2 innings pitched as he yielded five hits, two walks, five runs (all earned), and a wild pitch to compile a game and career All-Star ERA of 27.00. Don Drysdale of the Dodgers replaced Maloney and retired Colavito on a ground ball to end the inning. Meanwhile, the Senators' Pete Richert was holding the NL to a fifth-inning single by the Phillies' Dick Allen while striking out a pair in his two innings of relief, leaving the game with the score tied, 5–5.

The last four innings of the game were comparatively quiet as a trio of National League pitchers held the AL scoreless while allowing two hits and four walks, and two of their American League counterparts gave up one run on four hits and a walk. Sandy Koufax pitched the sixth inning and was effective if not impressive as he began by walking Willie Horton of the Tigers on four pitches. The AL gathered two walks and had a long fly ball to left-center off the bat of the Yankees' Bobby Richardson, which was caught by Mays. Dick Farrell of the Astros gave up one walk in the seventh, and Bob Gibson of the Cardinals closed out the game by allowing two hits and a walk in the last two innings, both of which saw AL threats. In the eighth, the American League had runners on second and third with two outs when Jimmie Hall of the Twins hit a fly ball to center that was gathered in by Mays on a leaping catch after he had slipped and nearly fallen. In the ninth, Tony Oliva led off with a double, but a failed sacrifice try and two strikeouts (Killebrew and Joe Pepitone of the Yankees) ended it. Koufax was credited with the win because the NL scored its sixth run while he was the pitcher of record, and Gibson recorded a save. The NL run in the seventh was scored against Sam McDowell of the Indians. Mays led off with a walk, went to third on a single by Aaron, and scored on an infield single by the Cubs' Ron Santo. The Braves' Joe Torre ended the rally by grounding back to McDowell, who started a double play. Eddie Fisher of the White Sox pitched the last two frames for the AL, allowing only one hit, although he was in some trouble in the eighth. After Ernie Banks of the Cubs singled, Rose sacrificed, and everyone was safe when Indians third baseman Max Alvis threw late to second base in an attempt to force Banks. Scoring was averted when Wills fouled out on a bunt attempt, and Billy Williams of the Cubs and Mays grounded out.

The two biggest stars for the winning National League were San Francisco teammates Mays and Marichal. The voting for the game's Most Valuable Player was very close, but the members of the media who made the decision gave the award to Marichal by a narrow margin. Both managers made ample use of their reserves, with four from the American League being merely spectators while five from the NL also only watched.

	AL		NL	
P	Milt Pappas	BAL	Juan Marichal	SFN
C	Earl Battey	MIN	Joe Torre	MIL
1B	Bill Skowron +	CHA	Ernie Banks	CHN
2B	Felix Mantilla	BOS	Pete Rose	CIN
3B	Brooks Robinson	BAL	Dick Allen	PHI
SS	Dick McAuliffe	DET	Maury Wills	LAN
OF	Rocky Colavito	CLE	Hank Aaron	MIL
OF	Vic Davalillo	CLE	Willie Mays	SFN
OF	Willie Horton	DET	Willie Stargell	PIT
	Max Alvis	CLE	Johnny Callison	PHI
	Eddie Fisher	CHA	Leo Cardenas	CIN
	Bill Freehan	DET	Roberto Clemente	PIT
	Jim Grant	MIN	Don Drysdale	LAN
	Jimmie Hall	MIN	Johnny Edwards	CIN
	Elston Howard	NYA	Sammy Ellis	CIN
	Al Kaline	DET	Turk Farrell	HOU
	Harmon Killebrew	MIN	Bob Gibson	SLN
	Bob Lee	CAL	Sandy Koufax	LAN
	Mickey Mantle +	NYA	Ed Kranepool	NYN
	Sam McDowell	CLE	Jim Maloney	CIN
	John O'Donoghue	KC	Frank Robinson	CIN
	Tony Oliva	MIN	Cookie Rojas	PHI
	Joe Pepitone	NYA	Ron Santo	CHN
	Bobby Richardson	NYA	Bob Veale	PIT
	Pete Richert	WAS	Billy Williams	CHN
	Mel Stottlemyre	NYA		
	Zoilo Versalles	MIN		
	Carl Yastrzemski +	BOS		

+ player replaced on roster

```
National League    320  000  100-  6
American League    000  140  000-  5
```

NATIONAL LEAGUE

	ab	r	h	bi	bb	so	po	a
W.Mays, cf	3	2	1	1	2	1	4	0
H.Aaron, rf	5	0	1	0	0	0	0	0
W.Stargell, lf	3	2	2	2	0	1	1	0
R.Clemente, ph-lf	2	0	0	0	0	0	0	0
D.Allen, 3b	3	0	1	0	0	1	0	1
R.Santo, 3b	2	0	1	1	0	0	2	0
J.Torre, c	4	1	1	2	0	0	5	1
E.Banks, 1b	4	0	2	0	0	1	11	0
P.Rose, 2b	2	0	0	0	1	2	1	5
M.Wills, ss	4	0	1	0	0	0	2	3
L.Cardenas, ss	0	0	0	0	0	0	0	0
J.Marichal, p	1	1	1	0	0	0	0	0
C.Rojas, ph	1	0	0	0	0	0	0	0
J.Maloney, p	0	0	0	0	0	0	0	0
D.Drysdale, p	0	0	0	0	0	0	0	0
F.Robinson, ph	1	0	0	0	0	1	0	0
S.Koufax, p	0	0	0	0	0	0	0	0
T.Farrell, p	0	0	0	0	0	0	0	0
B.Williams, ph	1	0	0	0	0	0	0	0
B.Gibson, p	0	0	0	0	0	0	1	0
Totals	36	6	11	6	3	7	27	10

BATTING

HR: W.Mays (1st inning off M.Pappas, 0 on, 0 out); W.Stargell (2nd inning off J.Grant, 1 on, 2 out); J.Torre (1st inning off M.Pappas, 1 on, 2 out).

2-out RBI: W.Stargell 2; J.Torre 2.

RBI, scoring position, less than 2 outs: H.Aaron 0–1; R.Clemente 0–1; R.Santo 1–1; J.Torre 0–1; M.Wills 0–1; B.Williams 0–1.

S: P.Rose.

GDP: H.Aaron; J.Torre.

BASERUNNING

Team LOB: 7

FIELDING

DP: (1). M.Wills-P.Rose-E.Banks.

AMERICAN LEAGUE

	ab	r	h	bi	bb	so	po	a
D.McAuliffe, ss	3	2	2	2	0	0	3	0
S.McDowell, p	0	0	0	0	0	0	0	1
T.Oliva, ph-rf	2	0	1	0	0	0	0	0
B.Robinson, 3b	4	1	1	0	0	1	1	2
M.Alvis, 3b	1	0	0	0	0	0	0	0
H.Killebrew, 1b	3	1	1	2	2	1	7	1
R.Colavito, rf	4	0	1	1	0	0	1	0
E.Fisher, p	0	0	0	0	0	0	1	1
J.Pepitone, ph	1	0	0	0	0	1	0	0
W.Horton, lf	3	0	0	0	1	1	2	0
F.Mantilla, 2b	2	0	0	0	0	0	1	1
B.Richardson, 2b	2	0	0	0	0	0	2	1
V.Davalillo, cf	2	0	1	0	0	0	1	0
Z.Versalles, ss	1	0	0	0	1	0	0	2
E.Battey, c	2	0	0	0	0	0	4	1
B.Freehan, c	1	0	0	0	1	0	4	0
M.Pappas, p	0	0	0	0	0	0	0	1
J.Grant, p	0	0	0	0	0	0	0	0
A.Kaline, ph	1	0	0	0	0	0	0	0
P.Richert, p	0	0	0	0	0	0	0	0
J.Hall, ph-cf	2	1	0	0	1	1	0	0
Totals	34	5	8	5	6	5	27	11

BATTING

2B: T.Oliva (off B.Gibson).

HR: D.McAuliffe (5th inning off J.Maloney, 1 on, 2 out); H.Killebrew (5th inning off J.Maloney, 1 on, 2 out).

2-out RBI: D.McAuliffe 2; H.Killebrew 2.

RBI, scoring position, less than 2 outs: M.Alvis 0–1; H.Killebrew 0–1; R.Colavito 1–1; W.Horton 0–2.

GDP: E.Battey.

BASERUNNING

Team LOB: 8

FIELDING

DP: (2). B.Robinson-F.Mantilla-H.Killebrew; S.McDowell-B.Richardson-H.Killebrew.

PITCHING	ip	h	r	er	bb	so
National League						
J.Marichal	3.0	1	0	0	0	0
J.Maloney	1.2	5	5	5	2	1
D.Drysdale	0.1	0	0	0	0	0
S.Koufax (w)	1.0	0	0	0	2	1

Inherited Runners—Scored:
J.Maloney 0–0; D.Drysdale 0–0; S.Koufax 0–0; T.Farrell 0–0; B.Gibson 0–0; J.Grant 0–0; P.Richert 0–0; S.McDowell 0–0; E.Fisher 0–0.

WP: J.Maloney

PITCHING	ip	h	r	er	bb	so
National League *(continued)*						
T.Farrell	1.0	0	0	0	1	0
B.Gibson (s)	2.0	2	0	0	1	3
American League						
M.Pappas	1.0	4	3	3	1	0
J.Grant	2.0	2	2	2	1	3
P.Richert	2.0	1	0	0	0	2
S.McDowell (L)	2.0	3	1	1	1	2
E.Fisher	2.0	1	0	0	0	0

GAME DATA—T: 2:45; A: 46706; Temp: Unknown; Wind: Unknown direction, Speed: Unknown

UMPIRES—HP: Johnny Stevens (AL), 1B: Lee Weyer (NL), 2B: Lou DiMuro (AL), 3B: Bill Williams (NL), LF: Bill Valentine (AL), RF: John Kibler (NL)

STARTING LINEUPS

	National League	American League
1.	W.Mays cf	D.McAuliffe ss
2.	H.Aaron rf	B.Robinson 3b
3.	W.Stargell lf	H.Killebrew 1b
4.	D.Allen 3b	R.Colavito rf
5.	J.Torre c	W.Horton lf
6.	E.Banks 1b	F.Mantilla 2b
7.	P.Rose 2b	V.Davalillo cf
8.	M.Wills ss	E.Battey c
9.	J.Marichal p	M.Pappas p

NL 1ST: Bill Skowron chosen at first, withdrew due to injury; plus, Mantle and Yaz had to withdraw, replaced by Oliva and Pepitone MVP: Juan Marichal (San Francisco NL); W.Mays homered to deep leftfield; H.Aaron flied to W.Horton-lf; W.Stargell singled to center field; D.Allen popped to D.McAuliffe-ss; J.Torre homered to deep leftfield down the line [W.Stargell scored]; E.Banks singled to left field; P.Rose walked [E.Banks to second]; M.Wills grounded out (M.Pappas-p to H.Killebrew-1b); 3 R, 4 H, 0 E, 2 LOB. NL 3, AL 0.

AL 1ST: D.McAuliffe popped to M.Wills-ss in foul territory; B.Robinson flied to W.Stargell-lf; H.Killebrew flied to W.Mays-cf; 0 R, 0 H, 0 E, 0 LOB. NL 3, AL 0.

NL 2ND: **J.Grant replaced M.Pappas (pitching);** J.Marichal singled to center field; W.Mays walked [J.Marichal to second]; H.Aaron grounded into a double play (B.Robinson-3b to F.Mantilla-2b to H.Killebrew-1b) [J.Marichal to third, W.Mays out at second]; W.Stargell homered to very deep right-center [J.Marichal scored]; D.Allen struck out; 2 R, 2 H, 0 E, 0 LOB. NL 5, AL 0.

AL 2ND: R.Colavito grounded out (M.Wills-ss to E.Banks-1b); W.Horton grounded out (M.Wills-ss to E.Banks-1b); F.Mantilla grounded out (J.Torre-c to E.Banks-1b); 0 R, 0 H, 0 E, 0 LOB. NL 5, AL 0.

NL 3RD: J.Torre lined to B.Robinson-3b; E.Banks struck out; P.Rose struck out (E.Battey-c to H.Killebrew-1b); 0 R, 0 H, 0 E, 0 LOB. NL 5, AL 0.

AL 3RD: V.Davalillo singled to center field; E.Battey grounded into a double play (M.Wills-ss to P.Rose-2b to E.Banks-1b) [V.Davalillo out at second]; **A.Kaline batted for J.Grant;** A.Kaline grounded out (D.Allen-3b to E.Banks-1b); 0 R, 1 H, 0 E, 0 LOB. NL 5, AL 0.

NL 4TH: **P.Richert replaced A.Kaline (pitching);** M.Wills flied to R.Colavito-rf; **C.Rojas batted for J.Marichal;** C.Rojas flied to V.Davalillo-cf; W.Mays struck out; 0 R, 0 H, 0 E, 0 LOB. NL 5, AL 0.

AL 4TH: **J.Maloney replaced C.Rojas (pitching);** D.McAuliffe singled to right-center; B.Robinson struck out; H.Killebrew walked [D.McAuliffe to second]; R.Colavito singled to center field [D.McAuliffe scored, H.Killebrew to second]; J.Maloney threw a wild pitch [H.Killebrew to third, R.Colavito to second]; W.Horton grounded out (E.Banks-1b unassisted); F.Mantilla flied to W.Mays-cf; 1 R, 2 H, 0 E, 2 LOB. NL 5, AL 1.

NL 5TH: H.Aaron popped to D.McAuliffe-ss; W.Stargell struck out; D.Allen singled to center field; J.Torre lined to D.McAuliffe-ss; 0 R, 1 H, 0 E, 1 LOB. NL 5, AL 1.

AL 5TH: **R.Santo replaced D.Allen (playing 3b);** V.Davalillo popped to R.Santo-3b; E.Battey grounded out (P.Rose-2b to E.Banks-1b); **J.Hall batted for P.Richert;** J.Hall walked; D.McAuliffe homered to deep centerfield [J.Hall scored]; B.Robinson singled to third base; H.Killebrew homered to very deep left-center [B.Robinson scored]; **D.Drysdale replaced J.Maloney (pitching);** R.Colavito grounded out (P.Rose-2b to E.Banks-1b); 4 R, 3 H, 0 E, 0 LOB. NL 5, AL 5.

NL 6TH: **J.Hall stayed in game (playing cf); B.Freehan replaced E.Battey (playing c); S.McDowell replaced D.McAuliffe (pitching); B.Richardson replaced F.Mantilla (playing 2b); Z.Versalles replaced V.Davalillo (playing ss);** E.Banks popped to B.Freehan-c in foul territory; P.Rose struck out; M.Wills singled to short right-center; **F.Robinson batted for D.Drysdale;** F.Robinson struck out; 0 R, 1 H, 0 E, 1 LOB. NL 5, AL 5.

AL 6TH: **S.Koufax replaced F.Robinson (pitching);** W.Horton walked; B.Richardson flied to W.Mays-cf; Z.Versalles popped to M.Wills-ss; B.Freehan walked [W.Horton to second]; J.Hall was called out on strikes; 0 R, 0 H, 0 E, 2 LOB. NL 5, AL 5.

NL 7TH: W.Mays walked; H.Aaron singled to right-center [W.Mays to third]; **R.Clemente batted for W.Stargell;** R.Clemente forced H.Aaron (B.Robinson-3b to B.Richardson-2b) [R.Clemente to first]; R.Santo singled to shortstop [W.Mays scored, R.Clemente to second]; J.Torre grounded into a double play (S.McDowell-p to B.Richardson-2b to H.Killebrew-1b) [R.Santo out at second]; 1 R, 2 H, 0 E, 1 LOB. NL 6, AL 5.

AL 7TH: **R.Clemente stayed in game (playing lf); T.Farrell replaced S.Koufax (pitching); T.Oliva batted for S.McDowell;** T.Oliva grounded out (P.Rose-2b to E.Banks-1b); B.Robinson popped to E.Banks-1b in foul territory; H.Killebrew walked; R.Colavito popped to R.Santo-3b in foul territory; 0 R, 0 H, 0 E, 1 LOB. NL 6, AL 5.

NL 8TH: **T.Oliva stayed in game (playing rf); E.Fisher replaced R.Colavito (pitching); M.Alvis replaced B.Robinson (playing 3b);** E.Banks singled to left-center; P.Rose reached on a fielder's choice on a sacrifice bunt [E.Banks to second]; On a bunt M.Wills popped to B.Freehan-c in foul territory; **B.Williams batted for T.Farrell;** B.Williams grounded out (H.Killebrew-1b to E.Fisher-p) [E.Banks to third, P.Rose to second]; W.Mays grounded out (E.Fisher-p to H.Killebrew-1b); 0 R, 1 H, 0 E, 2 LOB. NL 6, AL 5.

AL 8TH: **B.Gibson replaced B.Williams (pitching); L.Cardenas replaced M.Wills (playing ss);** W.Horton struck out; B.Richardson grounded out (P.Rose-2b to E.Banks-1b); Z.Versalles walked; B.Freehan singled to center field [Z.Versalles to third, B.Freehan to second (on throw)]; Mays slipped, recovered and made a leaping back-handed catch; J.Hall flied to W.Mays-cf; 0 R, 1 H, 0 E, 2 LOB. NL 6, AL 5.

NL 9TH: H.Aaron flied to W.Horton-lf; R.Clemente grounded out (Z.Versalles-ss to H.Killebrew-1b); R.Santo grounded out (Z.Versalles-ss to H.Killebrew-1b); 0 R, 0 H, 0 E, 0 LOB. NL 6, AL 5.

AL 9TH: T.Oliva doubled to left-center; On a bunt M.Alvis popped to B.Gibson-p; H.Killebrew struck out; **J.Pepitone batted for E.Fisher;** J.Pepitone struck out; 0 R, 1 H, 0 E, 1 LOB. NL 6, AL 5.

Final Totals	R	H	E	LOB
National League	6	11	0	7
American League	5	8	0	8

GAME

37

Tuesday, July 12, 1966

Busch Stadium, St. Louis

National League 2, American League 1

(10 innings)

SERIES RESULTS: NL 19, AL 17, 1 TIE

New Park, Same Result

The previous All-Star Game played in Missouri had been in 1960, and the players had sweltered in 101-degree heat in Kansas City during the first of two games played that year. In 1966, that mark was topped at the eastern end of the state as the mercury topped out at 105 degrees in St. Louis in the new Busch Stadium, which had opened only two months earlier. To make matters worse, the game went into overtime, although it took a surprisingly short two hours and nineteen minutes to complete the ten innings. Over one hundred fans were treated for effects of the heat, and many people abandoned their expensive box seats in the early innings until things cooled off a bit. Amazingly enough, eight men played the entire game, including the first five players in the NL lineup. However, the winning run was manufactured by three substitutes, who may have been a little fresher.

Selection of the starting nonpitchers continued to be made by poll of players, managers, and coaches, but there was a new wrinkle this year ordered by Commissioner William Eckert. For the first time, outfielders were considered as a single group, rather than by individual positions as had been done previously. There had been concern in earlier years that the best outfielders had been competing for the same spots. The new policy did just what it was supposed to. All three starting AL gardeners were normally right fielders as were two of those selected for the NL. The remaining outfield star was center fielder Willie Mays of the Giants. Managers Sam Mele of the Twins and Walter Alston of the Dodgers made the choices to fill out the twenty-five-man squads, including all of the pitchers. The Astros' Joe Morgan was selected to start at second base but suffered a broken kneecap after the voting was announced. Jim Lefebvre of the Dodgers was Alston's choice to start in Morgan's spot. Two replacement pitchers were also needed after the initial rosters were announced, both due to arm ailments. Bob Gibson of the Car-

dinals was replaced by Phil Regan of the Dodgers, and Sam McDowell of the Indians was replaced by his teammate Sonny Siebert. Siebert pitched two effective innings for the AL, while Regan did not get in the game. Ted Williams and Casey Stengel were honorary coaches one month before their inductions into the Hall of Fame.

The first three innings were dominated by starting pitchers Denny McLain of the Tigers and Sandy Koufax of the Dodgers. Only one runner reached base in this time, and he scored a tainted run due to a fielding mistake by the Braves' Henry Aaron. With one out in the second, Brooks Robinson of the Orioles hit a fly ball toward Aaron, who was playing the unfamiliar position of left field because of the new method of choosing the starters. Aaron had trouble picking the ball up against the white-shirted background and made a late break, eventually missing a shoestring try as the ball skipped past him, and Robinson made it to third, receiving credit for a triple. George Scott of the Red Sox fouled out, and Koufax threw a wild pitch that allowed Robinson to trot home with the only run the AL would score in the game. The second game in 1961, a rain-terminated tie at 1–1, would have been the classic's first 1–0 finish except for a questionable fielding play, and the same could be said for the 1966 game and Aaron's difficulty.

The succeeding pitchers were also effective but not quite as overpowering. Jim Bunning of the Phillies followed Koufax to the hill for the NL and allowed only a harmless two-out single to the Tigers' Bill Freehan in the fifth as he struck out two in his pair of innings. Bunning's appearance, his eighth in an All-Star Game, set the record, since tied three times, for pitching appearances. Juan Marichal of the Giants was the next NL twirler; he turned in three scoreless innings, meeting his only challenge in the first three batters he faced. Pinch hitter Harmon Killebrew of the Twins and Al Kaline of the Tigers reached the Giants' ace for singles, sandwiched around a strikeout of Detroit's Dick McAuliffe. However, Frank Robinson of the

Orioles popped up, and Tony Oliva of the Twins grounded out to end the threat. Brooks Robinson gathered his second hit in the seventh but was immediately erased as the Tigers' Norm Cash grounded into a double play. Gaylord Perry of the Giants pitched the last two innings for the NL, allowing a tenth-inning walk and a hit, Brooks Robinson's third of the day, plus a wild pitch, but he kept the AL off the board, thanks in part to an excellent catch by his San Francisco teammate Willie McCovey, who reached into the stands for a foul ball. Perry was thus in position to be credited with the win when the NL scored in the bottom of the tenth.

In the meantime, the AL mound corps also did a good job after McLain departed, at least through the ninth. Jim Kaat of the Twins entered to pitch the fourth and was greeted by back-to-back singles off the bats of Mays and Pittsburgh's Roberto Clemente. After a foul out and a force play that moved Mays to third, Ron Santo of the Cubs got Willie home with a slow roller to third base that went for an infield single. Mel Stottlemyre of the Yankees came in to begin the sixth and had a bit of difficulty when Clemente lined a double down the right-field line with one out. After a ground out, McCovey was intentionally walked, and this time

Santo's bouncer to Brooks Robinson became a force out to end the inning. Late addition Siebert took over for the eighth and ninth, retiring all six batters he faced, with the last one, Santo, being thrown out after a fine play by Brooks Robinson down the line. Pete Richert of the Senators came on to pitch the fateful tenth and was charged with the defeat. Tim McCarver of the hometown Cardinals opened the inning with a ground ball to single to right and was sacrificed to second by Ron Hunt of the Mets. The Dodgers' Maury Wills singled to short right field, and McCarver easily beat Oliva's throw to end the game.

The heroes of the game were an interesting group. Wills not only got the game-winning hit, but he also made an excellent defensive play on a pop fly in short center field to retire Frank Robinson. Before the game, Wills had been openly annoyed that he had not been chosen as the starting shortstop, an honor that went to the Reds' Leo Cardenas by a vote of 149 to 88, so his late-inning performance was especially satisfying to the highly competitive Wills. However, the Most Valuable Player of the game came from the losing side. Brooks Robinson had half the AL's six hits, scored the only AL run, and set an All-Star record with eight chances at third base, four of them put-outs.

	AL		NL	
P	Denny McLain	DET	Sandy Koufax	LAN
C	Bill Freehan	DET	Joe Torre	ATL
1B	George Scott	BOS	Willie McCovey	SFN
2B	Bobby Knoop	CAL	Joe Morgan +	HOU
3B	Brooks Robinson	BAL	Ron Santo	CHN
SS	Dick McAuliffe	DET	Leo Cardenas	CIN
OF	Al Kaline	DET	Hank Aaron	ATL
OF	Tony Oliva	MIN	Roberto Clemente	PIT
OF	Frank Robinson	BAL	Willie Mays	SFN
	Tommie Agee	CHA	Dick Allen	PHI
	Steve Barber	BAL	Felipe Alou	ATL
	Earl Battey	MIN	Jim Bunning	PHI
	Gary Bell	CLE	Curt Flood	SLN
	Norm Cash	DET	Bob Gibson +	SLN
	Rocky Colavito	CLE	Tom Haller	SFN
	Andy Etchebarren	BAL	Jim Ray Hart	SFN
	Jim Fregosi	CAL	Ron Hunt	NYN
	Catfish Hunter	KC	Jim Lefebvre	LAN
	Jim Kaat	MIN	Juan Marichal	SFN
	Harmon Killebrew	MIN	Tim McCarver	SLN
	Sam McDowell +	CLE	Billy McCool	CIN
	Bobby Richardson	NYA	Gaylord Perry	SFN
	Pete Richert	WAS	Claude Raymond	HOU
	Sonny Siebert	CLE	Phil Regan	LAN
	Mel Stottlemyre	NYA	Willie Stargell	PIT
	Carl Yastrzemski	BOS	Bob Veale	PIT
			Maury Wills	LAN

+ player replaced on roster

```
American League     010 000 000 0- 1
National League     000 100 000 1- 2 (10)
    1 out when winning run was scored.
```

AMERICAN LEAGUE

	ab	r	h	bi	bb	so	po	a
D.McAuliffe, ss	3	0	0	0	0	1	1	1
M.Stottlemyre, p	0	0	0	0	0	0	0	0
R.Colavito, ph	1	0	0	0	0	0	0	0
S.Siebert, p	0	0	0	0	0	0	0	0
P.Richert, p	0	0	0	0	0	0	0	1
A.Kaline, cf	4	0	1	0	0	0	3	0
T.Agee, cf	0	0	0	0	0	0	1	0
F.Robinson, lf	4	0	0	0	0	1	2	0
T.Oliva, rf	4	0	0	0	0	0	0	0
B.Robinson, 3b	4	1	3	0	0	0	4	4
G.Scott, 1b	2	0	0	0	0	0	4	1
N.Cash, ph-1b	2	0	0	0	0	0	4	0
B.Freehan, c	2	0	1	0	0	0	4	0
E.Battey, c	1	0	0	0	1	1	1	0
B.Knoop, 2b	2	0	0	0	0	1	3	1
B.Richardson, ph-2b	2	0	0	0	0	0	1	1
D.McLain, p	1	0	0	0	0	1	0	1
J.Kaat, p	0	0	0	0	0	0	0	0
H.Killebrew, ph	1	0	1	0	0	0	0	0
J.Fregosi, pr-ss	2	0	0	0	0	1	0	1
Totals	35	1	6	0	1	6	28	11

BATTING
3B: B.Robinson (off S.Koufax).
RBI, scoring position, less than 2 outs: F.Robinson 0–1; G.Scott 0–1; N.Cash 0–1; B.Richardson 0–1.
GDP: N.Cash.

BASERUNNING
Team LOB: 5

NATIONAL LEAGUE

	ab	r	h	bi	bb	so	po	a
W.Mays, cf	4	1	1	0	0	1	3	0
R.Clemente, rf	4	0	2	0	0	0	2	0
H.Aaron, lf	4	0	0	0	0	1	2	0
W.McCovey, 1b	3	0	0	0	1	0	10	1
R.Santo, 3b	4	0	1	1	0	0	2	2
J.Torre, c	3	0	0	0	0	1	5	0
T.McCarver, c	1	1	1	0	0	0	1	0
J.Lefebvre, 2b	2	0	0	0	0	0	2	0
R.Hunt, 2b	1	0	0	0	0	0	0	1
L.Cardenas, ss	2	0	0	0	0	0	2	2
W.Stargell, ph	1	0	0	0	0	0	0	0
M.Wills, ss	1	0	1	1	0	0	1	1
S.Koufax, p	0	0	0	0	0	0	0	0
C.Flood, ph	1	0	0	0	0	0	0	0
J.Bunning, p	0	0	0	0	0	0	0	0
D.Allen, ph	1	0	0	0	0	1	0	0
J.Marichal, p	0	0	0	0	0	0	0	0
J.Hart, ph	1	0	0	0	0	1	0	0
G.Perry, p	0	0	0	0	0	0	0	0
Totals	33	2	6	2	1	5	30	7

BATTING
2B: R.Clemente (off M.Stottlemyre).
2-out RBI: R.Santo.
RBI, scoring position, less than 2 outs: H.Aaron 0–2; W.McCovey 0–1; M.Wills 1–1.
S: R.Hunt.

BASERUNNING
Team LOB: 5

FIELDING
DP: (1). W.McCovey-L.Cardenas-W.McCovey.

PITCHING	ip	h	r	er	bb	so
American League						
D.McLain	3.0	0	0	0	0	3
J.Kaat	2.0	3	1	1	0	1
M.Stottlemyre	2.0	1	0	0	1	0
S.Siebert	2.0	0	0	0	0	1
P.Richert (L)	0.1	2	1	1	0	0
National League						
S.Koufax	3.0	1	1	1	0	1
J.Bunning	2.0	1	0	0	0	2
J.Marichal	3.0	3	0	0	0	2
G.Perry (W)	2.0	1	0	0	1	1

Inherited Runners—Scored:
J.Kaat 0–0; M.Stottlemyre 0–0; S.Siebert 0–0; P.Richert 0–0; J.Bunning 0–0; J.Marichal 0–0; G.Perry 0–0.
IBB: W.McCovey by M.Stottlemyre.
WP: S.Koufax; G.Perry

GAME DATA—T: 2:19; A: 49936; Temp: 105; Wind: Unknown direction, Speed: Unknown

UMPIRES—HP: Al Barlick (NL), 1B: Frank Umont (AL), 2B: Ed Vargo (NL), 3B: Jim Honochick (AL), LF: Jerry Neudecker (AL), RF: Bob Engel (NL)

STARTING LINEUPS

	American League	National League
1.	D.McAuliffe ss	W.Mays cf
2.	A.Kaline cf	R.Clemente rf
3.	F.Robinson lf	H.Aaron lf
4.	T.Oliva rf	W.McCovey 1b
5.	B.Robinson 3b	R.Santo 3b
6.	G.Scott 1b	J.Torre c
7.	B.Freehan c	J.Lefebvre 2b
8.	B.Knoop 2b	L.Cardenas ss
9.	D.McLain p	S.Koufax p

AL 1ST: Injuries: Joe Morgan was to start, hurt knee Bob Gibson hurt before game, Phil Regan replaced him Sam McDowell hurt, replaced by Sonny Siebert MVP: Brooks Robinson (Baltimore AL); D.McAuliffe popped to R.Santo-3b in foul territory; A.Kaline popped to W.McCovey-1b in foul territory; F.Robinson flied to H.Aaron-lf; 0 R, 0 H, 0 E, 0 LOB. AL 0, NL 0.

NL 1ST: W.Mays was called out on strikes; R.Clemente flied to A.Kaline-cf; H.Aaron was called out on strikes; 0 R, 0 H, 0 E, 0 LOB. AL 0, NL 0.

AL 2ND: T.Oliva lined to W.Mays-cf; B.Robinson tripled to left field; Aaron lost the ball in the background of white shirts; G.Scott popped to W.McCovey-1b in foul territory; S.Koufax threw a wild pitch [B.Robinson scored]; B.Freehan flied to R.Clemente-rf; 1 R, 1 H, 0 E, 0 LOB. AL 1, NL 0.

NL 2ND: W.McCovey popped to B.Robinson-3b; R.Santo lined to B.Robinson-3b; J.Torre struck out; 0 R, 0 H, 0 E, 0 LOB. AL 1, NL 0.

AL 3RD: B.Knoop grounded out (R.Santo-3b to W.McCovey-1b); D.McLain struck out; D.McAuliffe popped to R.Santo-3b in foul territory; 0 R, 0 H, 0 E, 0 LOB. AL 1, NL 0.

NL 3RD: J.Lefebvre flied to F.Robinson-lf; L.Cardenas lined to B.Knoop-2b; **C.Flood batted for S.Koufax;** McLain pitched 3 perfect innings; C.Flood grounded out (D.McLain-p to B.Knoop-2b to G.Scott-1b); 0 R, 0 H, 0 E, 0 LOB. AL 1, NL 0.

AL 4TH: **J.Bunning replaced C.Flood (pitching);** A.Kaline popped to J.Lefebvre-2b; F.Robinson was called out on strikes; T.Oliva popped to L.Cardenas-ss; 0 R, 0 H, 0 E, 0 LOB. AL 1, NL 0.

NL 4TH: **J.Kaat replaced D.McLain (pitching);** W.Mays singled to left field; R.Clemente singled to center field [W.Mays to second]; H.Aaron popped to G.Scott-1b in foul territory; W.Mc-Covey forced R.Clemente (G.Scott-1b to D.McAuliffe-ss) [W.Mays to third, W.McCovey to first]; R.Santo singled to third base [W.Mays scored, W.McCovey to second]; J.Torre forced R.Santo (D.McAuliffe-ss to B.Knoop-2b) [J.Torre to first]; 1 R, 3 H, 0 E, 2 LOB. AL 1, NL 1.

AL 5TH: B.Robinson grounded out (L.Cardenas-ss to W.McCovey-1b); G.Scott popped to J.Lefebvre-2b; B.Freehan singled to left-center; B.Knoop struck out; 0 R, 1 H, 0 E, 1 LOB. AL 1, NL 1.

NL 5TH: J.Lefebvre flied to F.Robinson-lf; L.Cardenas popped to G.Scott-1b in foul territory; **D.Allen batted for J.Bunning;** D.Allen struck out; 0 R, 0 H, 0 E, 0 LOB. AL 1, NL 1.

AL 6TH: **J.Marichal replaced D.Allen (pitching); R.Hunt replaced J.Lefebvre (playing 2b);** Umpires moved: Honochick (hp), Vargo (1b), Umont (2b) Barlick (3b), Neudecker (lf), Engel (rf); **H.Killebrew batted for J.Kaat;** H.Killebrew singled to center field; D.McAuliffe struck out; A.Kaline singled to center field [H.Killebrew to second]; **J.Fregosi ran for H.Killebrew;** F.Robinson popped to W.McCovey-1b in foul territory; T.Oliva grounded out (R.Hunt-2b to W.Mc-Covey-1b); 0 R, 2 H, 0 E, 2 LOB. AL 1, NL 1.

NL 6TH: **J.Fregosi stayed in game (playing ss); E.Battey replaced B.Freehan (playing c); M.Stottlemyre replaced D.McAuliffe (pitching);** W.Mays flied to A.Kaline-cf; R.Clemente doubled to right field; H.Aaron grounded out (B.Robinson-3b to G.Scott-1b); W.McCovey was walked intentionally; R.Santo forced W.McCovey (B.Robinson-3b to B.Knoop-2b) [R.Santo to first]; 0 R, 1 H, 0 E, 2 LOB. AL 1, NL 1.

AL 7TH: B.Robinson singled to left field; **N.Cash batted for G.Scott;** N.Cash grounded into a double play (W.McCovey-1b to L.Cardenas-ss to W.Mc-Covey-1b) [B.Robinson out at second]; E.Battey struck out; 0 R, 1 H, 0 E, 0 LOB. AL 1, NL 1.

NL 7TH: **N.Cash stayed in game (playing 1b);** J.Torre grounded out (B.Robinson-3b to N.Cash-1b); R.Hunt grounded out (J.Fregosi-ss to N.Cash-1b); **W.Stargell batted for L.Cardenas;** W.Stargell popped to B.Robinson-3b in foul territory; 0 R, 0 H, 0 E, 0 LOB. AL 1, NL 1.

AL 8TH: **M.Wills replaced W.Stargell (playing ss); T.McCarver replaced J.Torre (playing c); B.Richardson batted for B.Knoop;** B.Richardson grounded out (M.Wills-ss to W.McCovey-1b); J.Fregosi flied to R.Clemente-rf; **R.Colavito batted for M.Stottlemyre;** R.Colavito flied to H.Aaron-lf; 0 R, 0 H, 0 E, 0 LOB. AL 1, NL 1.

NL 8TH: **B.Richardson stayed in game (playing 2b); S.Siebert replaced R.Colavito (pitching); J.Hart batted for J.Marichal;** J.Hart was called out on strikes; W.Mays flied to A.Kaline-cf; R.Clemente grounded out (B.Richardson-2b to N.Cash-1b); 0 R, 0 H, 0 E, 0 LOB. AL 1, NL 1.

AL 9TH: **G.Perry replaced J.Hart (pitching);** A.Kaline grounded out (R.Santo-3b to W.McCovey-1b);

F.Robinson popped to M.Wills-ss; T.Oliva flied to W.Mays-cf; 0 R, 0 H, 0 E, 0 LOB. AL 1, NL 1.

NL 9TH: **T.Agee replaced A.Kaline (playing cf);** H.Aaron flied to T.Agee-cf; W.McCovey popped to B.Robinson-3b; R.Santo grounded out (B.Robinson-3b to N.Cash-1b); 0 R, 0 H, 0 E, 0 LOB. AL 1, NL 1.

AL 10TH: B.Robinson singled to short left-center; G.Perry threw a wild pitch [B.Robinson to second]; N.Cash flied to W.Mays-cf; E.Battey walked; B.Richardson popped to W.McCovey-1b in foul territory; J.Fregosi struck out; 0 R, 1 H, 0 E, 2 LOB. AL 1, NL 1.

NL 10TH: **P.Richert replaced S.Siebert (pitching);** T.McCarver singled to right field; R.Hunt out on a sacrifice bunt (P.Richert-p to B.Richardson-2b) [T.McCarver to second]; M.Wills singled to right field [T.McCarver scored]; 1 R, 2 H, 0 E, 1 LOB. AL 1, NL 2.

Final Totals	R	H	E	LOB
American League	1	6	0	5
National League	2	6	0	5

Tuesday, July 12, 1967

Anaheim Stadium, Anaheim

National League 2, American League 1

(15 innings)

SERIES RESULTS: NL 20, AL 17, 1 TIE

Thirty Strikeouts and Three Home Runs

Anaheim Stadium hosted the longest game in All-Star history in 1967, a fifteen-inning affair that the NL won 2–1, the second straight year it won by the same score. This was also the second consecutive extra-inning game, and it ran the NL's record to a perfect 5-0 in overtime contests. The game began at 4:15 P.M. in California, which made it prime time on the East Coast, and it was a great success in the TV ratings, with an estimated fifty-five million people tuned in, the most ever for a baseball game other than a game in the World Series. However, the late local starting time was not well received by some players, most vocally Roberto Clemente. The Pittsburgh star, who would lead the NL with a .357 batting average in 1967, expressed the feelings of many when he complained that the late afternoon shadows made it difficult to pick up breaking pitches.

Whether the shadows were to blame or the pitching was simply that good, the game set a number of marks for pitching dominance that are unlikely to be matched. A total of thirty batters struck out, ten more than the previous record of twenty, which came in the twelve-inning contest of 1955. The figure works out to an average of exactly one strikeout per team each half inning. Twelve different pitchers appeared in the game, and each one had at least one strikeout, with Ferguson Jenkins of the Cubs leading the way with six. Fergie's half-dozen matched the All-Star Game mark for one game, tying him with the Giants' Carl Hubbell (1934) and Larry Jansen (1950) along with the Reds' Johnny Vander Meer (1943). Only two walks were issued to the 105 batters who tried their luck at the plate, both by the victorious NL hurlers. Interestingly enough, there were five extra-base hits among the seventeen safeties for the day, and all three runs scored on solo homers, again showing how difficult it was to generate a conventional rally against the strong pitching.

The starting lineups, except for pitchers, were once again chosen by players, managers, and coaches with AL manager Hank Bauer of the Orioles and NL manager Walter Alston of the Dodgers completing the squads and choosing all the moundsmen. Two of those voted to start, outfielders Frank Robinson of the Orioles and Al Kaline of the Tigers, were injured and were replaced by Tony Oliva of the Twins and Tony Conigliaro of the Red Sox. One interesting off-field note is that Sandy Koufax, starting NL pitcher the previous year, worked this game as a television announcer for NBC along with Curt Gowdy and former Dodger Pee Wee Reese.

The game-winning blow came in the fifteenth off the bat of third baseman Tony Perez of Cincinnati against Catfish Hunter of the A's, who thereby was charged with the loss. Hunter, the fifth AL pitcher, was working his fifth inning of relief, the most for any pitcher in an All-Star Game since Larry Jansen's five-inning stint for the NL in 1950 and one short of the record six innings pitched by Lefty Gomez as the AL starter in 1935. Manager Bauer explained his leaving Hunter in so long by saying that he wanted to avoid using pitchers who had worked on Sunday and therefore had had only one day's rest (the game was played on Tuesday). Don Drysdale of the Dodgers was the beneficiary as the pitcher of record and received credit for the win. Rookie Tom Seaver of the Mets pitched a scoreless bottom of the fifteenth to record the save. The first NL run came on a homer in the second inning by the starting third baseman, the Phillies' Dick Allen, against starter Dean Chance, formerly the ace of the hometown Angels but now a member of the Twins. The AL tied the score on a circuit clout by Baltimore's Brooks Robinson in the sixth against Jenkins, who pitched three innings after relieving Juan Marichal of the Giants. Marichal had opened the game with three scoreless innings, allowing only a single to Jim Fregosi of the Angels. From that point until the shot by Perez in the fifteenth, most of the highlights involved the routine mowing down of batters on both sides. The performance by Gary Peters of the White Sox was noteworthy as he pitched three perfect innings, striking out four.

There were some offensive achievements besides the home runs, most notably by Carl Yastrzemski of the Red Sox, who would go on to complete a marvelous triple crown season that year. Yaz struck out against Marichal to end the second inning but then reached base five straight times with two singles, a double, and the only two walks of the game, the first of which came in the tenth inning against Chris Short of the Phillies. His double came in the fifth inning off Jenkins when center fielder Henry Aaron of the Braves missed a shoestring try for a line drive with one out. That potential rally died when the Cubs star got a pop-up and a strikeout to end the inning. Tony Oliva played the entire game in center field for the AL and collected two singles, one off Jenkins in the fourth and the other off Drysdale in the fourteenth, but both times he was caught stealing, becoming the only All-Star to earn that dubious distinction. For the NL, the Cardinals' Tim McCarver gathered two hits after entering in the tenth inning. The first was a double down the left-field line against Hunter in the thirteenth. McCarver was then sacrificed to third by Bill Mazeroski of the Pirates but stayed there as Hunter struck out Pittsburgh's Gene Alley and got the Reds' Pete Rose of the Reds on a fly ball. Tim's other hit was a single, which came immediately after the Perez home run, but he was doubled off first base on a line drive hit by Tommy Helms, batting for Drysdale.

The pitching was so stifling that only one noteworthy defensive play occurred. Tony Conigliaro made a fine running, backhanded catch in right-center of a line drive hit by Orlando Cepeda of the Cardinals to lead off the tenth. Cepeda would go on to be the unanimous choice for the National League MVP that year. Two batters later, the Cubs' Ernie Banks pinch-hit a soft single into right-center that would likely have scored Cepeda and ended the contest five innings earlier. The Most Valuable Player Award went to Perez for his game-winning homer. Although there were many good pitching performances this day, none stood out enough to beat this dramatic home run for the honor.

	AL			NL	
P	Dean Chance	MIN		Juan Marichal	SFN
C	Bill Freehan	DET		Joe Torre	ATL
1B	Harmon Killebrew	MIN		Orlando Cepeda	SLN
2B	Rod Carew	MIN		Bill Mazeroski	PIT
3B	Brooks Robinson	BAL		Dick Allen	PHI
SS	Rico Petrocelli	BOS		Gene Alley	PIT
OF	Al Kaline	+ DET		Hank Aaron	ATL
OF	Frank Robinson	+ BAL		Lou Brock	SLN
OF	Carl Yastrzemski	BOS		Roberto Clemente	PIT
	Tommie Agee	CHA		Ernie Banks	CHN
	Max Alvis	CLE		Mike Cuellar	HOU
	Ken Berry	CHA		Don Drysdale	LAN
	Paul Casanova	WAS		Bob Gibson	SLN
	Tony Conigliaro	BOS		Tom Haller	SFN
	Al Downing	NYA		Tommy Helms	CIN
	Andy Etchebarren	BAL		Ferguson Jenkins	CHN
	Jim Fregosi	CAL		Denny Lemaster +	ATL
	Steve Hargan	CLE		Willie Mays	SFN
	Joe Horlen	CHA		Tim McCarver	SLN
	Catfish Hunter	KC		Darrell Osteen	CIN
	Jim Lonborg	BOS		Tony Perez	CIN
	Mickey Mantle	NYA		Pete Rose	CIN
	Dick McAuliffe	DET		Tom Seaver	NYN
	Jim McGlothlin	CAL		Chris Short	PHI
	Don Mincher	CAL		Rusty Staub	HOU
	Tony Oliva	MIN		Jim Wynn	HOU
	Gary Peters	CHA			

+ player replaced on roster

National League	010	000	000	000	001-	2		
American League	000	001	000	000	000-	1	(15)	

NATIONAL LEAGUE

	ab	r	h	bi	bb	so	po	a
L.Brock, lf	2	0	0	0	0	0	1	0
W.Mays, ph-cf	4	0	0	0	0	1	3	0
R.Clemente, rf	6	0	1	0	0	4	6	0
H.Aaron, cf-lf	6	0	1	0	0	0	2	0
O.Cepeda, 1b	6	0	0	0	0	1	6	0
D.Allen, 3b	4	1	1	1	0	3	1	2
T.Perez, 3b	2	1	1	1	0	1	0	3
J.Torre, c	2	0	0	0	0	0	4	1
T.Haller, c	1	0	0	0	0	0	7	0
E.Banks, ph	1	0	1	0	0	0	0	0
T.McCarver, c	2	0	2	0	0	0	7	1
B.Mazeroski, 2b	4	0	0	0	0	0	7	0
D.Drysdale, p	0	0	0	0	0	0	0	0
T.Helms, ph	1	0	0	0	0	0	0	0
T.Seaver, p	0	0	0	0	0	0	0	0
G.Alley, ss	5	0	0	0	0	3	0	3
J.Marichal, p	1	0	0	0	0	0	0	0
F.Jenkins, p	1	0	0	0	0	0	0	0
B.Gibson, p	0	0	0	0	0	0	0	1
J.Wynn, ph	1	0	1	0	0	0	0	0
C.Short, p	0	0	0	0	0	0	0	1
R.Staub, ph	1	0	1	0	0	0	0	0
M.Cuellar, p	0	0	0	0	0	0	0	0
P.Rose, ph-2b	1	0	0	0	0	0	1	0
Totals	51	2	9	2	0	13	45	12

BATTING
2B: T.McCarver (off J.Hunter).
HR: D.Allen (2nd inning off D.Chance, 0 on, 0 out);
    T.Perez (15th inning off J.Hunter, 0 on, 1 out).
RBI, scoring position, less than 2 outs: R.Clemente 0–1;
    G.Alley 0–1.
S: B.Mazeroski.
GDP: O.Cepeda.

BASERUNNING
SB: H.Aaron (2nd base off D.Chance / B.Freehan).
Team LOB: 5

AMERICAN LEAGUE

	ab	r	h	bi	bb	so	po	a
B.Robinson, 3b	6	1	1	1	0	1	0	6
R.Carew, 2b	3	0	0	0	0	1	2	3
D.McAuliffe, 2b	3	0	0	0	0	0	3	2
T.Oliva, cf	6	0	2	0	0	3	4	0
H.Killebrew, 1b	6	0	0	0	0	2	14	1
T.Conigliaro, rf	6	0	0	0	0	2	4	0
C.Yastrzemski, lf	4	0	3	0	2	1	2	0
B.Freehan, c	5	0	0	0	0	2	13	0
R.Petrocelli, ss	1	0	0	0	0	0	0	1
J.McGlothlin, p	0	0	0	0	0	0	0	0
M.Mantle, ph	1	0	0	0	0	1	0	0
G.Peters, p	0	0	0	0	0	0	0	1
D.Mincher, ph	1	0	1	0	0	0	0	0
T.Agee, pr	0	0	0	0	0	0	0	0
A.Downing, p	0	0	0	0	0	0	0	0
M.Alvis, ph	1	0	0	0	0	0	0	0
J.Hunter, p	1	0	0	0	0	1	1	0
K.Berry, ph	1	0	0	0	0	1	0	0
D.Chance, p	0	0	0	0	0	0	0	0
J.Fregosi, ph-ss	4	0	1	0	0	2	2	3
Totals	49	1	8	1	2	17	45	17

BATTING
2B: C.Yastrzemski (off F.Jenkins).
HR: B.Robinson (6th inning off F.Jenkins, 0 on, 1 out).
RBI, scoring position, less than 2 outs: B.Robinson 0–1;
    B.Freehan 0–1; M.Alvis 0–1.
S: B.Freehan; J.Fregosi.

BASERUNNING
CS: T.Oliva 2 (2nd base by F.Jenkins / J.Torre; 2nd base
    by D.Drysdale / T.McCarver).
Team LOB: 7

FIELDING
DP: (2). B.Robinson-R.Carew-H.Killebrew; D.McAuliffe-
    J.Hunter.

PITCHING	ip	h	r	er	bb	so
National League						
J.Marichal	3.0	1	0	0	0	3
F.Jenkins	3.0	3	1	1	0	6
B.Gibson	2.0	2	0	0	0	2
C.Short	2.0	0	0	0	1	1

Inherited Runners—Scored:
    F.Jenkins 0–0; B.Gibson 0–0; C.Short 0–0;
    M.Cuellar 0–0; D.Drysdale 0–0; T.Seaver 0–0;
    J.McGlothlin 0–0; G.Peters 0–0; A.Downing 0–0;
    J.Hunter 0–0.

PITCHING	ip	h	r	er	bb	so
National League *(continued)*						
M.Cuellar	2.0	1	0	0	0	2
D.Drysdale (w)	2.0	1	0	0	0	2
T.Seaver (s)	1.0	0	0	0	1	1
American League						
D.Chance	3.0	2	1	1	0	1
J.McGlothlin	2.0	1	0	0	0	2
G.Peters	3.0	0	0	0	0	4
A.Downing	2.0	2	0	0	0	2
J.Hunter (L)	5.0	4	1	1	0	4

GAME DATA—T: 3:41; A: 46309; Temp: Unknown; Wind: Unknown direction, Speed: Unknown

UMPIRES—HP: Ed Runge (AL), 1B: Frank Secory (NL), 2B: Lou DiMuro (AL), 3B: Ken Burkhart (NL), LF: Emmett Ashford (AL), RF: Chris Pelekoudas (NL)

STARTING LINEUPS

	National League	*American League*
1.	L.Brock lf	B.Robinson 3b
2.	R.Clemente rf	R.Carew 2b
3.	H.Aaron cf	T.Oliva cf
4.	O.Cepeda 1b	H.Killebrew 1b
5.	D.Allen 3b	T.Conigliaro rf
6.	J.Torre c	C.Yastrzemski lf
7.	B.Mazeroski 2b	B.Freehan c
8.	G.Alley ss	R.Petrocelli ss
9.	J.Marichal p	D.Chance p

NL 1ST: Starters chosen by players; two injury re-placements: Frank Robinson and Al Kaline were replaced by Tony Oliva and Tony Conigliaro Alston and Bauer chose all pitchers and reserves MVP: Tony Perez (Cincinnati NL); L.Brock grounded out (B.Robinson-3b to H.Kille-brew-1b); R.Clemente singled to first base; H.Aaron forced R.Clemente (B.Robinson-3b to R.Carew-2b) [H.Aaron to first]; H.Aaron stole second; O.Cepeda grounded out (H.Killebrew-1b unassisted); O R, 1 H, O E, 1 LOB. NL O, AL O.

AL 1ST: B.Robinson popped to O.Cepeda-1b; R.Carew flied to L.Brock-lf; T.Oliva was called out on strikes; O R, O H, O E, O LOB. NL O, AL O.

NL 2ND: D.Allen homered to deep centerfield; J.Torre grounded out (R.Carew-2b to H.Kille-brew-1b); B.Mazeroski grounded out (R.Petro-celli-ss to H.Killebrew-1b); G.Alley flied to T.Conigliaro-rf; 1 R, 1 H, O E, O LOB. NL 1, AL O.

AL 2ND: H.Killebrew grounded out (D.Allen-3b to O.Cepeda-1b); T.Conigliaro flied to R.Clemente-rf; C.Yastrzemski struck out; O R, O H, O E, O LOB. NL 1, AL O.

NL 3RD: J.Marichal grounded out (B.Robinson-3b to H.Killebrew-1b); L.Brock grounded out (R.Carew-2b to H.Killebrew-1b); R.Clemente struck out; O R, O H, O E, O LOB. NL 1, AL O.

AL 3RD: B.Freehan was called out on strikes; R.Petro-celli popped to B.Mazeroski-2b; **J.Fregosi batted for D.Chance**; J.Fregosi singled to center field; B.Robinson grounded out (D.Allen-3b to O.Cepeda-1b); O R, 1 H, O E, 1 LOB. NL 1, AL O.

NL 4TH: **J.Fregosi stayed in game (playing ss)**; **J.McGlothlin replaced R.Petrocelli (pitching)**; H.Aaron singled to shortstop; O.Cepeda grounded into a double play (B.Robinson-3b to R.Carew-2b to H.Killebrew-1b) [H.Aaron out at second]; D.Allen struck out; O R, 1 H, O E, O LOB. NL 1, AL O.

AL 4TH: **F.Jenkins replaced J.Marichal (pitching)**; R.Carew flied to H.Aaron-cf; T.Oliva singled to center field; H.Killebrew was called out on strikes; T.Oliva was caught stealing second (J.Torre-c to B.Mazeroski-2b); O R, 1 H, O E, O LOB. NL 1, AL O.

NL 5TH: J.Torre grounded out (J.Fregosi-ss to H.Kil-lebrew-1b); B.Mazeroski grounded out (J.Fre-gosi-ss to H.Killebrew-1b); G.Alley was called out on strikes; O R, O H, O E, O LOB. NL 1, AL O.

AL 5TH: **T.Haller replaced J.Torre (playing c)**; T.Co-nigliaro struck out; C.Yastrzemski doubled to short centerfield; Aaron missed a shoestring catch; B.Freehan popped to D.Allen-3b; **M.Man-tle batted for J.McGlothlin**; M.Mantle was called out on strikes; O R, 1 H, O E, 1 LOB. NL 1, AL O.

NL 6TH: **G.Peters replaced M.Mantle (pitching)**; F.Jenkins flied to T.Conigliaro-rf; **W.Mays batted for L.Brock**; W.Mays was called out on strikes; R.Clemente was called out on strikes; O R, O H, O E, O LOB. NL 1, AL O.

AL 6TH: **W.Mays stayed in game (playing cf)**; **H.Aaron changed positions (playing lf)**; J.Fregosi struck out; B.Robinson homered to deep left-field; R.Carew struck out; T.Oliva struck out; 1 R, 1 H, O E, O LOB. NL 1, AL 1.

NL 7TH: Jenkins tied record with six strikeouts; **D.McAuliffe replaced R.Carew (playing 2b)**; H.Aaron grounded out (B.Robinson-3b to H.Kil-lebrew-1b); O.Cepeda was called out on strikes; D.Allen struck out; O R, O H, O E, O LOB. NL 1, AL 1.

AL 7TH: **B.Gibson replaced F.Jenkins (pitching)**; H.Killebrew flied to W.Mays-cf; T.Conigliaro struck out; C.Yastrzemski singled to center field; B.Freehan struck out; O R, 1 H, O E, 1 LOB. NL 1, AL 1.

NL 8TH: T.Haller popped to J.Fregosi-ss; B.Mazeroski lined to C.Yastrzemski-lf; G.Alley grounded out (G.Peters-p to H.Killebrew-1b); O R, O H, O E, O LOB. NL 1, AL 1.

AL 8TH: **D.Mincher batted for G.Peters**; D.Mincher singled to center field; **T.Agee ran for D.Mincher**; J.Fregosi out on a sacrifice bunt (B.Gibson-p to B.Mazeroski-2b) [T.Agee to second]; B.Robinson flied to R.Clemente-rf; D.McAuliffe flied to R.Clemente-rf; O R, 1 H, O E, 1 LOB. NL 1, AL 1.

NL 9TH: **A.Downing replaced T.Agee (pitching)**; **J.Wynn batted for B.Gibson**; J.Wynn singled to right field; W.Mays flied to T.Oliva-cf [J.Wynn to second]; R.Clemente struck out; H.Aaron grounded out (B.Robinson-3b to H.Kille-brew-1b); O R, 1 H, O E, 1 LOB. NL 1, AL 1.

AL 9TH: **C.Short replaced J.Wynn (pitching)**; T.Oliva grounded out (G.Alley-ss to O.Cepeda-1b); H.Kil-lebrew popped to B.Mazeroski-2b; T.Conigliaro flied to R.Clemente-rf; O R, O H, O E, O LOB. NL 1, AL 1.

NL 10TH: O.Cepeda lined to T.Conigliaro-rf; D.Allen struck out; **E.Banks batted for T.Haller**; E.Banks singled to right-center; B.Mazeroski flied to C.Yastrzemski-lf; O R, 1 H, O E, 1 LOB. NL 1, AL 1.

AL 10TH: **T.McCarver replaced E.Banks (playing c); T.Perez replaced D.Allen (playing 3b);** C.Yastrzemski walked; B.Freehan out on a sacrifice bunt (C.Short-p to B.Mazeroski-2b) [C.Yastrzemski to second]; **M.Alvis batted for A.Downing;** M.Alvis reached on a fielder's choice (G.Alley-ss to T.Perez-3b to B.Mazeroski-2b) [C.Yastrzemski out at third]; J.Fregosi struck out; O R, O H, O E, 1 LOB. NL 1, AL 1.

NL 11TH: **J.Hunter replaced M.Alvis (pitching);** G.Alley was called out on strikes; **R.Staub batted for C.Short;** R.Staub singled to center field; W.Mays grounded out (J.Fregosi-ss to H.Killebrew-1b) [R.Staub to second]; R.Clemente struck out; O R, 1 H, O E, 1 LOB. NL 1, AL 1.

AL 11TH: **M.Cuellar replaced R.Staub (pitching);** B.Robinson was called out on strikes; D.McAuliffe flied to R.Clemente-rf; T.Oliva struck out; O R, O H, O E, O LOB. NL 1, AL 1.

NL 12TH: H.Aaron popped to J.Fregosi-ss; O.Cepeda popped to D.McAuliffe-2b; T.Perez struck out; O R, O H, O E, O LOB. NL 1, AL 1.

AL 12TH: H.Killebrew grounded out (G.Alley-ss to O.Cepeda-1b); T.Conigliaro popped to T.McCarver-c in foul territory; C.Yastrzemski singled to right-center; B.Freehan forced C.Yastrzemski (T.Perez-3b to B.Mazeroski-2b) [B.Freehan to first]; O R, 1 H, O E, 1 LOB. NL 1, AL 1.

NL 13TH: T.McCarver doubled to left field; B.Mazeroski out on a sacrifice bunt (H.Kille-

brew-1b to D.McAuliffe-2b) [T.McCarver to third]; G.Alley struck out; **P.Rose batted for M.Cuellar;** P.Rose flied to T.Oliva-cf; O R, 1 H, O E, 1 LOB. NL 1, AL 1.

AL 13TH: **P.Rose stayed in game (playing 2b); D.Drysdale replaced B.Mazeroski (pitching);** J.Hunter struck out; J.Fregosi grounded out (T.Perez-3b to O.Cepeda-1b); B.Robinson flied to W.Mays-cf; O R, O H, O E, O LOB. NL 1, AL 1.

NL 14TH: W.Mays flied to T.Oliva-cf; R.Clemente grounded out (D.McAuliffe-2b to H.Killebrew-1b); H.Aaron flied to T.Oliva-cf; O R, O H, O E, O LOB. NL 1, AL 1.

AL 14TH: D.McAuliffe flied to R.Clemente-rf; T.Oliva singled to center field; H.Killebrew was called out on strikes; T.Oliva was caught stealing second (T.McCarver-c to P.Rose-2b); O R, 1 H, O E, O LOB. NL 1, AL 1.

NL 15TH: O.Cepeda flied to T.Conigliaro-rf; T.Perez homered to deep leftfield; T.McCarver singled to right field; **T.Helms batted for D.Drysdale;** T.Helms lined into a double play (D.McAuliffe-2b to J.Hunter-p) [T.McCarver out at first]; 1 R, 2 H, O E, O LOB. NL 2, AL 1.

AL 15TH: **T.Seaver replaced T.Helms (pitching);** T.Conigliaro flied to H.Aaron-lf; C.Yastrzemski walked; B.Freehan flied to W.Mays-cf; **K.Berry batted for J.Hunter;** K.Berry struck out; O R, O H, O E, 1 LOB. NL 2, AL 1.

Final Totals	R	H	E	LOB
National League	2	9	0	5
American League	1	8	0	7

39

Tuesday, July 9, 1968

Astrodome, Houston

National League 1, American League 0

SERIES RESULTS: NL 21, AL 17, 1 TIE

A Minimum of Offense

The 1968 season was known as the "year of the pitcher," so it was only fitting that it saw the only 1–0 game in All-Star history. In some ways, this game was just a logical extension of the previous two years, which were both decided by a 2–1 margin. The win was also the National League's sixth consecutive victory. The game at the Houston Astrodome was also the first midsummer classic played indoors. An effort to attract a large prime-time TV audience, the evening starting time paid off; the NBC viewership estimate was some sixty million people.

However, there were still some clouds on the horizon regarding the sport's position in society. The summer of 1968 was one of tremendous upheaval, mostly under the shadow of the Vietnam War, with riots in many large cities and protests at the Democratic convention in Chicago and at the Olympics in Mexico City. Against this backdrop, baseball was criticized in many circles as slow, antiquated, and out of touch with the pace of the modern world. The nadir of offense that was reached that summer was taken as more evidence that the sport was inherently dull, and a highly visible 1–0 All-Star Game didn't help the image, especially since the only run that scored came in during a double play. Football was seen as a better match for a future America that was expected to be ever more frenetic and violent. These political overtones were quite real, but the predicted demise of the game was far off base. It might have helped if the James Earl Jones speech from the end of *Field of Dreams* had been available then; even in the rough times, baseball has marked the passage of time in America.

The starting lineups, except for the pitchers, were again chosen by vote of players, managers, and coaches. Due to injuries, three players were replaced after the rosters were chosen. The Reds' Pete Rose had been selected to start, but his roster spot went to Billy Williams of the Cubs and his starting position to Willie Mays of the Giants. Gene Alley of the Pirates gave way to Leo Cardenas of the Reds, and shoulder problems for Jose Santiago of the Red Sox led to the addition of Gary Bell of Cleveland in his place. There was also a coaching change when Cubs manager Leo Durocher became ill and was replaced by Dave Bristol, manager of the Reds. The remainder of the rosters and all of the pitchers were chosen by the managers, Dick Williams of the Red Sox and Red Schoendienst of the Cardinals.

The game's only run came in the bottom of the first on a very unusual series of plays. Mays led off with a single to left and went to second when a pick-off throw from AL starting pitcher Luis Tiant of the Indians got past first baseman Harmon Killebrew of the Twins for an error. The error was charged to Killebrew although Mays said that the ball "glanced off my back," so perhaps the error should have been on the pitcher. Tiant walked the next batter, the Cardinals' Curt Flood, with ball four a wild pitch that moved Mays to third base. Willie McCovey of the Giants then hit a hard grounder to the Twins' Rod Carew at second base, and the AL turned a double play as Mays scored. Henry Aaron of the Braves walked, but Tiant got out of further trouble by getting the Cubs' Ron Santo to ground out. The popular Cleveland right-hander pitched only one more inning and yielded a double to Tommy Helms of the Reds but nothing else. Although this was not a great performance by Tiant and he was charged with the loss, it must be noted that he had pitched 6.1 innings for the Indians only two days before, making many wonder why he was pitching in the All-Star Game at all. There were five more pitchers for the AL, and none allowed more than a single hit, although two of them did walk a pair of batters apiece for a game total of six. The only other scoring threat from the NL came in the sixth when Denny McLain of the Tigers, who would win thirty-one games that season, allowed a single to Aaron, who then stole second. After a walk to Santo, Helms hit into a force play to place runners at the corners with one out. However, the Detroit ace stiffened and got a pop-up and a fly ball to end the danger. Cleveland's Sam McDowell pitched one inning and struck out three men while allowing an infield single.

On the other side, Dodger Don Drysdale started his fifth All-Star Game, tying the record held by Robin Roberts of the Phillies and Lefty Gomez of the Yankees. Big D tied another record and set yet another as well. The game was his eighth and last in the midsummer competition, tying him with Jim Bunning (two more have joined them at eight since then), and by the time Drysdale was done for the day, he had 19.1 innings pitched. Although he recorded no strikeouts in the 1968 game, Drysdale's All-Star career total of nineteen strikeouts still stands along with the innings pitched mark. Although it is not a record, he also received credit for the win, his second in All-Star competition. Of course, Drysdale was used to setting records in 1968; in the spring, he had pitched six straight shutouts, tying the Major League record on his way to 58.2 consecutive scoreless innings, surpassing Walter Johnson's mark of 56. The AL managed only one base runner against Drysdale, a double by Jim Fregosi of the Angels to lead off the game. Fregosi advanced to third on a ground out but got no farther. The Giants' Juan Marichal pitched perfect ball for his two innings, the fourth and fifth, striking out three. Tommy Helms, second baseman of the Reds, helped out in the fourth with an excellent play in the hole between first and second to retire Carl Yastrzemski of the Red Sox.

NL manager Schoendienst used four pitchers after Marichal to navigate the last four innings. Only Tom Seaver of the Mets allowed anyone to reach base, yielding doubles to the Twins' Tony Oliva in the seventh and the Tigers' Don Wert in the eighth. Oliva's ball, which hit high off the wall in left-center field, just missed tying the game when it hit below the home run stripe. The AL had only three base runners, all coming on doubles. From Fregosi's two-bagger in the first to Oliva's in the seventh, the AL had twenty consecutive men retired. Although Seaver allowed two hits, he also struck out five in his two innings, although he had a little help from the umpires getting the third one. Boog Powell of the Orioles led off the eighth inning with a ground out to Helms, but right-field umpire Harry Wendelstedt of the NL ruled that he had called time before the pitch due to a bullpen ball rolling into fair territory. The Baltimore strongman did not take advantage of this reprieve and proceeded to strike out.

The most negative feature of the game was a serious injury suffered by Harmon Killebrew in the third inning. While making a long stretch for a throw in the third inning, he ruptured his right hamstring. Said the big first baseman, "I heard it snap like a rubber band." Unfortunately and unfairly, some used this injury as an opportunity to attack the sport, commenting that baseball players weren't very athletic and weren't in very good shape. The Killer was sidelined until September 1, when he returned with a flair, hitting a pinch-hit home run in his first at bat. However, it was mostly a lost second half of the season for Harmon because he was able to start only ten games in September, collecting a total of four home runs.

The two teams managed a total of only eight hits between them, the lowest number for any regulation-length All-Star Game. The rain-shortened 1952 contest also had had only eight hits. One other pitcher who had a spectacular season in 1968 was the Cardinals' Bob Gibson, who set the modern record with an ERA of 1.12, but the NL didn't need his services in Houston. Mays, who was voted Most Valuable Player of the game, also extended two of his own All-Star records, scoring his twentieth run and collecting his twenty-third hit. (Cardinals great Stan Musial is second in each category with eleven runs and twenty hits.)

	AL			NL	
P	Luis Tiant	CLE		Don Drysdale	LAN
C	Bill Freehan	DET		Jerry Grote	NYN
1B	Harmon Killebrew	MIN		Willie McCovey	SFN
2B	Rod Carew	MIN		Tommy Helms	CIN
3B	Brooks Robinson	BAL		Ron Santo	CHN
SS	Jim Fregosi	CAL		Don Kessinger	CHN
OF	Willie Horton	DET		Hank Aaron	ATL
OF	Frank Howard	WAS		Willie Mays	SFN
OF	Carl Yastrzemski	BOS		Pete Rose +	CIN
	Joe Azcue	CLE		Gene Alley +	PIT
	Gary Bell	BOS		Felipe Alou	ATL
	Bert Campaneris	OAK		Matty Alou	PIT
	Ken Harrelson	BOS		Johnny Bench	CIN
	Dave Johnson	BAL		Leo Cardenas	CIN
	Tommy John	CHA		Steve Carlton	SLN
	Duane Josephson	CHA		Curt Flood	SLN
	Mickey Mantle	NYA		Woodie Fryman	PHI
	Sam McDowell	CLE		Bob Gibson	SLN
	Denny McLain	DET		Tom Haller	LAN
	Rick Monday	OAK		Julian Javier	SLN
	Johnny Odom	OAK		Jerry Koosman	NYN
	Tony Oliva	MIN		Juan Marichal	SFN
	Boog Powell	BAL		Tony Perez	CIN
	Jose Santiago +	BOS		Ron Reed	ATL
	Mel Stottlemyre	NYA		Tom Seaver	NYN
	Don Wert	DET		Rusty Staub	HOU
				Billy Williams	CHN

+ player replaced on roster

American League   000 000 000- 0
National League   100 000 00x- 1

AMERICAN LEAGUE

	ab	r	h	bi	bb	so	po	a
J.Fregosi, ss	3	0	1	0	0	1	1	6
B.Campaneris, ss	1	0	0	0	0	0	1	0
R.Carew, 2b	3	0	0	0	0	0	2	2
D.Johnson, 2b	1	0	0	0	0	1	1	1
C.Yastrzemski, cf-lf	4	0	0	0	0	2	0	0
F.Howard, rf	2	0	0	0	0	1	0	0
T.Oliva, rf	1	0	1	0	0	0	2	0
W.Horton, lf	2	0	0	0	0	0	1	0
J.Azcue, c	1	0	0	0	0	1	5	0
D.Josephson, c	0	0	0	0	0	0	0	0
H.Killebrew, 1b	1	0	0	0	0	0	4	0
B.Powell, 1b	2	0	0	0	0	2	2	0
B.Freehan, c	2	0	0	0	0	1	4	0
D.McLain, p	0	0	0	0	0	0	0	0
S.McDowell, p	0	0	0	0	0	0	0	0
M.Mantle, ph	1	0	0	0	0	1	0	0
M.Stottlemyre, p	0	0	0	0	0	0	0	0
T.John, p	0	0	0	0	0	0	0	0
B.Robinson, 3b	2	0	0	0	0	0	0	1
D.Wert, 3b	1	0	1	0	0	0	1	0
L.Tiant, p	0	0	0	0	0	0	0	0
K.Harrelson, ph	1	0	0	0	0	0	0	0
J.Odom, p	0	0	0	0	0	0	0	0
R.Monday, cf	2	0	0	0	0	1	0	0
Totals	30	0	3	0	0	11	24	10

BATTING
2B: J.Fregosi (off D.Drysdale); T.Oliva (off T.Seaver); D.Wert (off T.Seaver).
RBI, scoring position, less than 2 outs: R.Carew 0–1; C.Yastrzemski 0–1.

BASERUNNING
Team LOB: 3

FIELDING
E: L.Tiant (dropped throw).
DP: (2). R.Carew-J.Fregosi-H.Killebrew; D.Johnson-B.Powell.

NATIONAL LEAGUE

	ab	r	h	bi	bb	so	po	a
W.Mays, cf	4	1	1	0	0	1	0	0
C.Flood, lf	1	0	0	0	2	0	1	0
M.Alou, lf	1	0	1	0	0	0	1	0
J.Javier, 2b	0	0	0	0	0	0	0	0
W.McCovey, 1b	4	0	0	0	0	3	10	0
H.Aaron, rf	3	0	1	0	1	2	1	0
R.Santo, 3b	2	0	1	0	2	0	1	1
T.Perez, 3b	0	0	0	0	0	0	0	1
T.Helms, 2b	3	0	1	0	1	0	1	2
R.Reed, p	0	0	0	0	0	0	0	0
J.Koosman, p	0	0	0	0	0	0	0	0
J.Grote, c	2	0	0	0	0	1	3	0
S.Carlton, p	0	0	0	0	0	0	0	1
R.Staub, ph	1	0	0	0	0	0	0	0
T.Seaver, p	0	0	0	0	0	0	0	0
F.Alou, lf	0	0	0	0	0	0	0	0
D.Kessinger, ss	2	0	0	0	0	1	1	2
B.Williams, ph	1	0	0	0	0	0	0	0
L.Cardenas, ss	0	0	0	0	0	0	0	1
D.Drysdale, p	1	0	0	0	0	0	0	1
J.Marichal, p	0	0	0	0	0	0	0	0
T.Haller, ph-c	2	0	0	0	0	1	6	0
J.Bench, c	0	0	0	0	0	0	2	0
Totals	27	1	5	0	6	9	27	9

BATTING
2B: T.Helms (off L.Tiant).
RBI, scoring position, less than 2 outs: T.Helms 0–1; J.Grote 0–2; R.Staub 0–1; D.Kessinger 0–1.
GDP: W.McCovey; T.Helms.

BASERUNNING
SB: H.Aaron (2nd base off D.McLain / J.Azcue).
Team LOB: 8

PITCHING	ip	h	r	er	bb	so
American League						
L.Tiant (L)	2.0	2	1	0	2	2
J.Odom	2.0	0	0	0	2	2
D.McLain	2.0	1	0	0	2	1
S.McDowell	1.0	1	0	0	0	3
M.Stottlemyre	0.1	0	0	0	0	1
T.John	0.2	1	0	0	0	0
National League						
D.Drysdale (w)	3.0	1	0	0	0	0
J.Marichal	2.0	0	0	0	0	3
S.Carlton	1.0	0	0	0	0	1
T.Seaver	2.0	2	0	0	0	5
R.Reed	0.2	0	0	0	0	1
J.Koosman (s)	0.1	0	0	0	0	1

Inherited Runners—Scored:
J.Odom 0–0; D.McLain 0–0; S.McDowell 0–0; M.Stottlemyre 0–0; T.John 0–0; J.Marichal 0–0; S.Carlton 0–0; T.Seaver 0–0; R.Reed 0–0; J.Koosman 0–0.
WP: L.Tiant

GAME DATA—T: 2:10; A: 48321; Temp: 72; Wind: Unknown direction, Speed: Unknown

UMPIRES—HP: Shag Crawford (NL), 1B: Larry Napp (AL), 2B: Mel Steiner (NL), 3B: Bill Kinnamon (AL), LF: Jim Odom (AL), RF: Harry Wendelstedt (NL)

STARTING LINEUPS

American League	National League
1. J.Fregosi ss	W.Mays cf
2. R.Carew 2b	C.Flood lf
3. C.Yastrzemski cf	W.McCovey 1b
4. F.Howard rf	H.Aaron rf
5. W.Horton lf	R.Santo 3b
6. H.Killebrew 1b	T.Helms 2b
7. B.Freehan c	J.Grote c
8. B.Robinson 3b	D.Kessinger ss
9. L.Tiant p	D.Drysdale p

AL 1ST: Injuries: Pete Rose and Gene Alley (replaced by Williams and Cardenas), Jose Santiago (replaced by Bell) MVP: Willie Mays (San Francisco NL); J.Fregosi doubled to left field; R.Carew grounded out (W.McCovey-1b unassisted) [J.Fregosi to third]; C.Yastrzemski popped to R.Santo-3b in foul territory; F.Howard lined to D.Kessinger-ss; 0 R, 1 H, 0 E, 1 LOB. AL 0, NL 0.

NL 1ST: W.Mays singled to left field; W.Mays was picked off first, but was safe on an error by L.Tiant-p [W.Mays to second]; C.Flood walked while W.Mays advanced to third on a wild pitch; W.McCovey grounded into a double play (R.Carew-2b to J.Fregosi-ss to H.Killebrew-1b) [W.Mays scored (unearned) (no RBI), C.Flood out at second]; H.Aaron walked; R.Santo grounded out (J.Fregosi-ss to H.Killebrew-1b); 1 R (0 ER), 1 H, 1 E, 1 LOB. AL 0, NL 1.

AL 2ND: W.Horton flied to H.Aaron-rf; H.Killebrew popped to T.Helms-2b; B.Freehan grounded out (R.Santo-3b to W.McCovey-1b); 0 R, 0 H, 0 E, 0 LOB. AL 0, NL 1.

NL 2ND: T.Helms doubled to right field; J.Grote struck out; D.Kessinger struck out; D.Drysdale flied to W.Horton-lf; 0 R, 1 H, 0 E, 1 LOB. AL 0, NL 1.

AL 3RD: B.Robinson grounded out (D.Kessinger-ss to W.McCovey-1b); **K.Harrelson batted for L.Tiant;** K.Harrelson flied to C.Flood-lf; J.Fregosi grounded out (D.Drysdale-p to W.McCovey-1b); 0 R, 0 H, 0 E, 0 LOB. AL 0, NL 1.

NL 3RD: **J.Odom replaced K.Harrelson (pitching);** W.Mays grounded out (J.Fregosi-ss to H.Killebrew-1b); C.Flood grounded out (J.Fregosi-ss to H.Killebrew-1b); Killebrew hurt stretching for ball, replaced by Powell; **B.Powell replaced H.Killebrew (playing 1b);** W.McCovey struck out; 0 R, 0 H, 0 E, 0 LOB. AL 0, NL 1.

AL 4TH: **J.Marichal replaced D.Drysdale (pitching);** R.Carew grounded out (D.Kessinger-ss to W.McCovey-1b); C.Yastrzemski grounded out (T.Helms-2b to W.McCovey-1b); F.Howard struck out; 0 R, 0 H, 0 E, 0 LOB. AL 0, NL 1.

NL 4TH: **T.Oliva replaced F.Howard (playing rf);** H.Aaron struck out; R.Santo walked; T.Helms walked [R.Santo to second]; J.Grote forced T.Helms (J.Fregosi-ss to R.Carew-2b) [R.Santo to third, J.Grote to first]; D.Kessinger forced J.Grote (J.Fregosi-ss to R.Carew-2b) [D.Kessinger to first]; 0 R, 0 H, 0 E, 2 LOB. AL 0, NL 1.

AL 5TH: W.Horton grounded out (T.Helms-2b to W.McCovey-1b); B.Powell struck out; B.Freehan struck out; 0 R, 0 H, 0 E, 0 LOB. AL 0, NL 1.

NL 5TH: **D.McLain replaced B.Freehan (pitching); R.Monday replaced J.Odom (playing cf); C.Yastrzemski changed positions (playing lf); J.Azcue replaced W.Horton (playing c); T.Haller batted for J.Marichal;** T.Haller flied to T.Oliva-rf; W.Mays grounded out (B.Robinson-3b to B.Powell-1b); C.Flood walked; W.McCovey struck out; 0 R, 0 H, 0 E, 1 LOB. AL 0, NL 1.

AL 6TH: **T.Haller stayed in game (playing c); M.Alou replaced C.Flood (playing lf); S.Carlton replaced J.Grote (pitching);** B.Robinson flied to M.Alou-lf; R.Monday grounded out (S.Carlton-p to W.McCovey-1b); J.Fregosi struck out; 0 R, 0 H, 0 E, 0 LOB. AL 0, NL 1.

NL 6TH: **D.Wert replaced B.Robinson (playing 3b); B.Campaneris replaced J.Fregosi (playing ss);** H.Aaron singled to left field; H.Aaron stole second; R.Santo walked; T.Helms forced R.Santo (R.Carew-2b to B.Campaneris-ss) [H.Aaron to third, T.Helms to first]; **R.Staub batted for S.Carlton;** R.Staub popped to D.Wert-3b; **B.Williams batted for D.Kessinger;** B.Williams flied to T.Oliva-rf; 0 R, 1 H, 0 E, 2 LOB. AL 0, NL 1.

AL 7TH: **T.Seaver replaced R.Staub (pitching); L.Cardenas replaced B.Williams (playing ss);** R.Carew grounded out (L.Cardenas-ss to W.McCovey-1b); C.Yastrzemski struck out; T.Oliva doubled to very deep left-center; J.Azcue struck out; 0 R, 1 H, 0 E, 1 LOB. AL 0, NL 1.

NL 7TH: **D.Johnson replaced R.Carew (playing 2b); S.McDowell replaced D.McLain (pitching);** T.Haller struck out; W.Mays struck out; M.Alou singled to shortstop; W.McCovey was called out on strikes; 0 R, 1 H, 0 E, 1 LOB. AL 0, NL 1.

AL 8TH: Powell grounded out 43, but rf umpire called time as pitch was delivered; B.Powell struck out; **M.Mantle batted for S.McDowell;** M.Mantle struck out; D.Wert doubled to right field; R.Monday struck out; 0 R, 1 H, 0 E, 1 LOB. AL 0, NL 1.

NL 8TH: **M.Stottlemyre replaced M.Mantle (pitching);** H.Aaron struck out; **T.John replaced M.Stottlemyre (pitching); D.Josephson replaced J.Azcue (playing c);** R.Santo singled to left-center; T.Helms grounded into a double play (D.Johnson-2b to B.Powell-1b) [R.Santo out at second]; O R, 1 H, O E, O LOB. AL 0, NL 1.

AL 9TH: **J.Javier replaced M.Alou (playing 2b); F.Alou replaced T.Seaver (playing lf); T.Perez replaced R.Santo (playing 3b); J.Bench replaced T.Haller (playing c); R.Reed replaced T.Helms (pitching)**; B.Campaneris grounded out (T.Perez-3b to W.McCovey-1b); D.Johnson struck out; **J.Koosman replaced R.Reed (pitching)**; C.Yastrzemski struck out; O R, O H, O E, O LOB. AL 0, NL 1.

Final Totals	R	H	E	LOB
American League	0	3	1	3
National League	1	5	0	8

40

Big Mac Attack

Washington hosted the All-Star Game for the fourth and final time in 1969, only seven years after it did so for the first game of 1962. The rapid repeat came about as part of the celebration of professional baseball's centennial; the nation's capital was a logical place to focus midseason attention. Ironically, the Washington team would move to Texas after only two more seasons, leaving a symbolic gap that still rankles for many fans. As part of the festivities, there was a formal black-tie dinner, on the evening before the game was scheduled, to honor the "Greatest Team Ever" and a reception at the White House. As it turned out, the game was delayed by a day because of two days of heavy rains and flooding in the DC area, making this the only All-Star Game ever to be postponed. As a result, many people who had tickets could not make the new date, and the attendance was the lowest for an All-Star Game since the 1963 contest in Cleveland. The field was soggy but playable as Vice President Spiro Agnew, acting as a substitute for President Richard Nixon, threw out the first ball. President Nixon, an ardent baseball fan, had participated in the celebrations and would have attended the game, but he had a previous engagement in the Pacific Ocean to welcome the Apollo 11 astronauts back to earth following their historic first walk on the moon.

This was the last year that starting lineups were chosen by vote of the players, managers, and coaches. No team had more than two players among the starters. The balance of the rosters and all of the pitchers were picked by the managers, Mayo Smith of Detroit for the American League and Red Schoendienst of the Cardinals for the National League. There were no replacements after the rosters were picked.

The game itself continued the recent National League dominance but in a way quite different from the low-scoring affairs of recent years. The final score was 9–3, and there were seventeen hits,

with three doubles and five home runs among them, two by Willie McCovey of the Giants. There were also five walks and two runners who reached base on errors, for a total of twenty-four base runners. The NL began bombing away from the start and had its nine runs by the end of the fourth inning, five of them coming in the third. AL manager Smith had to make a last-minute change in his plans when scheduled starting pitcher Denny McLain of his own Tigers missed the start of the game for a previously scheduled dental appointment in Detroit on what had been expected to be an off day. Mel Stottlemyre of the Yankees took McLain's place on the mound and did not have a good time. The Pirates' Matty Alou led off with a single and advanced to second on a ground out and to third on a wild pitch. He scored from there as left fielder Frank Howard of the hometown Senators misjudged a high fly off the bat of Atlanta's Henry Aaron, playing it into a two-base error. Two ground balls ended the trouble, but the NL continued its attack in the second inning. Cleon Jones of the Mets beat out an infield hit to shortstop, and Cincinnati's Johnny Bench homered to left field. Alou got his second hit of the game in as many innings, but Stottlemyre allowed no more runs, although he was saddled with the loss.

The roof fell in for the AL in the third when John "Blue Moon" Odom of the A's took the mound. The flamboyant right-hander faced seven batters but was able to retire only one of them as he allowed five hits and was victimized on an error by Boston shortstop Rico Petrocelli. Aaron opened with a single, and McCovey belted his first homer, a monster shot off the scoreboard in right-center. After Ron Santo of the Cubs grounded to Petrocelli, Jones rolled another to short and Rico drew the error when he couldn't pick it up. Bench singled to right, and Felix Millan of the Braves doubled down the third base line to score Jones and Bench. The final and perhaps cruelest blow came next when pitcher Steve Carlton of St. Louis scored Millan with his own double to left-center. Darold

Knowles came in to pitch for the AL and retired the side on two ground balls. The savaging of Odom tied an All-Star Game record for runs allowed, although the mark has since been surpassed by Atlee Hammaker (1983). NL scoring was completed in the fourth against McLain on McCovey's second home run.

The American League's scoring was accomplished with single runs in the second, third, and fourth. The first run was on a homer by Howard, and the second on a circuit clout by Detroit catcher Bill Freehan, both against National League starter Carlton, who would end up with the win for the game. Freehan also drove in the run in the fourth with a single off the Cardinals' Bob Gibson following a walk to Howard and a single by Sal Bando of Oakland. Four NL pitchers combined to pitch the final five innings, allowing no walks and only two hits along the way. Petrocelli doubled in the seventh against Jerry Koosman of the Mets, and Boog Powell singled in the eighth off Larry Dierker of the Astros. Phil Niekro of the Braves pitched a perfect ninth inning for the save, striking out two. The NL actually had less offense for these last five innings as it managed only one walk and one single against the offerings of three AL hurlers. However, there were nearly two more runs when Bench hit a ball over the left-field fence in the sixth with two out and one man on, but Boston's Carl Yastrzemski leaped high to bring it back in the park. The three final AL pitchers struck out seven batters, with Sam McDowell of the Indians recording four of them in his two perfect innings of work. However, the lethal damage was already done, and the AL went down to its seventh straight defeat, running the series record to 22-17 in favor of the NL, with one tie.

Willie McCovey was named the Most Valuable Player on the strength of his two homers. This was a foreshadowing of the larger season because Willie had his best year ever, leading the National League in homers (45) and RBI (126), on-base average (.458), and slugging average (.656). He also had his career-high batting average at .320 and received the amazing total of forty-five intentional walks, which still stands as the Major League record. Major League Baseball made many changes in 1969, including the institution of divisions and a conscious attempt to increase offense by lowering the mound from fifteen inches back to ten. The very visible and exuberant celebrations before the game brought the nation's attention back to the sport in a positive way. The All-Star Game was an important part of the resurgence of the public's interest in baseball.

	AL			NL	
P	Mel Stottlemyre	NYA		Steve Carlton	SLN
C	Bill Freehan	DET		Johnny Bench	CIN
1B	Boog Powell	BAL		Willie McCovey	SFN
2B	Rod Carew	MIN		Felix Millan	ATL
3B	Sal Bando	OAK		Ron Santo	CHN
SS	Rico Petrocelli	BOS		Don Kessinger	CHN
OF	Frank Howard	WAS		Hank Aaron	ATL
OF	Reggie Jackson	OAK		Matty Alou	PIT
OF	Frank Robinson	BAL		Cleon Jones	NYN
	Mike Andrews	BOS		Ernie Banks	CHN
	Paul Blair	BAL		Glenn Beckert	CHN
	Ray Culp	BOS		Chris Cannizzaro	SDN
	Jim Fregosi	CAL		Roberto Clemente	PIT
	Mike Hegan	+ SEA		Larry Dierker	HOU
	Dave Johnson	+ BAL		Bob Gibson	SLN
	Harmon Killebrew	MIN		Randy Hundley	CHN
	Darold Knowles	WAS		Grant Jackson	PHI
	Mickey Lolich	DET		Jerry Koosman	NYN
	Carlos May	CHA		Juan Marichal	SFN
	Sam McDowell	CLE		Lee May	CIN
	Denny McLain	DET		Willie Mays	SFN
	Dave McNally	BAL		Denis Menke	HOU
	Don Mincher	SEA		Phil Niekro	ATL
	Johnny Odom	OAK		Tony Perez	CIN
	Tony Oliva	+ MIN		Pete Rose	CIN
	Brooks Robinson	BAL		Tom Seaver	NYN
	Ellie Rodriguez	KCA		Bill Singer	LAN
	John Roseboro	MIN		Rusty Staub	MON
	Reggie Smith	BOS			
	Roy White	NYA			
	Carl Yastrzemski	BOS			

+ player replaced on roster

RETROSHEET EXPANDED BOX SCORE Wednesday, 7/23/1969 National League at American League (N)

```
National League    125  100  000-  9
American League    011  100  000-  3
```

NATIONAL LEAGUE

	ab	r	h	bi	bb	so	po	a
M.Alou, cf	4	1	2	0	1	1	5	0
D.Kessinger, ss	3	0	0	0	0	0	0	0
W.Mays, ph	1	0	0	0	0	0	0	0
D.Menke, ss	1	0	0	0	0	1	1	0
H.Aaron, rf	4	1	1	0	0	1	0	0
B.Singer, p	0	0	0	0	0	0	0	0
G.Beckert, 2b	1	0	0	0	0	0	0	0
W.McCovey, 1b	4	2	2	3	0	1	2	0
L.May, 1b	1	0	0	0	0	1	3	0
R.Santo, 3b	3	0	0	0	1	0	2	1
T.Perez, 3b	1	0	0	0	0	1	1	1
C.Jones, lf	4	2	2	0	0	0	3	0
P.Rose, lf	1	0	0	0	0	0	2	0
J.Bench, c	3	2	2	2	1	0	4	0
R.Hundley, c	1	0	0	0	0	1	3	0
F.Millan, 2b	4	1	1	2	0	1	1	1
J.Koosman, p	0	0	0	0	0	0	0	0
L.Dierker, p	0	0	0	0	0	0	0	0
P.Niekro, p	0	0	0	0	0	0	0	1
S.Carlton, p	2	0	1	1	0	1	0	1
B.Gibson, p	0	0	0	0	0	0	0	0
E.Banks, ph	1	0	0	0	0	0	0	0
R.Clemente, rf	1	0	0	0	0	1	0	0
Totals	40	9	11	8	3	10	27	5

BATTING
2B: F.Millan (off J.Odom); S.Carlton (off J.Odom).
HR: W.McCovey 2 (3rd inning off J.Odom, 1 on, 0 out; 4th inning off D.McLain, 0 on, 1 out); J.Bench (2nd inning off M.Stottlemyre, 1 on, 0 out).
RBI, scoring position, less than 2 outs: M.Alou 0–1; W.McCovey 0–1; F.Millan 2–1; S.Carlton 1–1.

BASERUNNING
Team LOB: 7

AMERICAN LEAGUE

	ab	r	h	bi	bb	so	po	a
R.Carew, 2b	3	0	0	0	0	0	0	2
M.Andrews, 2b	1	0	0	0	0	0	0	0
R.Jackson, cf-rf	2	0	0	0	1	0	2	0
C.Yastrzemski, lf	1	0	0	0	0	0	1	0
F.Robinson, rf	2	0	0	0	0	1	0	0
P.Blair, cf	2	0	0	0	0	0	2	0
B.Powell, 1b	4	0	1	0	0	1	9	1
F.Howard, lf	1	1	1	1	1	0	0	0
R.Smith, pr-lf-rf	2	1	0	0	0	0	0	0
S.Bando, 3b	3	0	1	0	0	0	0	1
S.McDowell, p	0	0	0	0	0	0	0	0
R.Culp, p	0	0	0	0	0	0	0	0
R.White, ph	1	0	0	0	0	1	0	0
R.Petrocelli, ss	3	0	1	0	0	1	1	3
J.Fregosi, ss	1	0	0	0	0	0	0	0
B.Freehan, c	2	1	2	2	0	0	4	0
J.Roseboro, c	1	0	0	0	0	0	6	0
C.May, ph	1	0	0	0	0	1	0	0
M.Stottlemyre, p	0	0	0	0	0	0	1	0
J.Odom, p	0	0	0	0	0	0	0	0
D.Knowles, p	0	0	0	0	0	0	0	0
H.Killebrew, ph	1	0	0	0	0	0	0	0
D.McLain, p	0	0	0	0	0	0	0	0
D.Mincher, ph	1	0	0	0	0	1	0	0
D.McNally, p	0	0	0	0	0	0	0	0
B.Robinson, 3b	1	0	0	0	0	1	1	1
Totals	33	3	6	3	2	7	27	8

BATTING
2B: R.Petrocelli (off J.Koosman).
HR: F.Howard (2nd inning off S.Carlton, 0 on, 1 out); B.Freehan (3rd inning off S.Carlton, 0 on, 0 out).
2-out RBI: B.Freehan.
RBI, scoring position, less than 2 outs: R.Petrocelli 0–1; J.Roseboro 0–1; B.Robinson 0–1.

BASERUNNING
Team LOB: 5

FIELDING
E: F.Howard (dropped fly); R.Petrocelli (fumble).

PITCHING	ip	h	r	er	bb	so
National League						
S.Carlton (w)	3.0	2	2	2	1	2
B.Gibson	1.0	2	1	1	1	2
B.Singer	2.0	0	0	0	0	0
J.Koosman	1.2	1	0	0	0	1
L.Dierker	0.1	1	0	0	0	0
P.Niekro (s)	1.0	0	0	0	0	2
American League						
M.Stottlemyre (l)	2.0	4	3	2	0	1
J.Odom	0.1	5	5	4	0	0
D.Knowles	0.2	0	0	0	0	0
D.McLain	1.0	1	1	1	2	2
D.McNally	2.0	1	0	0	1	1
S.McDowell	2.0	0	0	0	0	4
R.Culp	1.0	0	0	0	0	2

Inherited Runners—Scored:
B.Gibson 0–0; B.Singer 0–0; J.Koosman 0–0;
L.Dierker 0–0; P.Niekro 0–0; J.Odom 0–0;
D.Knowles 1–0; D.McLain 0–0; D.McNally 0–0;
S.McDowell 0–0; R.Culp 0–0.
wp: M.Stottlemyre

GAME DATA—T: 2:38; A: 45259; Temp: Unknown;
Wind: Unknown direction, Speed: Unknown

UMPIRES—HP: Red Flaherty (AL), 1B: Augie Donatelli
(NL), 2B: Bob Stewart (AL), 3B: Tom Gorman (NL),
LF: Marty Springstead (AL), RF: Tony Venzon (NL)

STARTING LINEUPS

	National League	*American League*
1.	M.Alou cf	R.Carew 2b
2.	D.Kessinger ss	R.Jackson cf
3.	H.Aaron rf	F.Robinson rf
4.	W.McCovey 1b	B.Powell 1b
5.	R.Santo 3b	F.Howard lf
6.	C.Jones lf	S.Bando 3b
7.	J.Bench c	R.Petrocelli ss
8.	F.Millan 2b	B.Freehan c
9.	S.Carlton p	M.Stottlemyre p

NL 1ST: M.Alou singled to left-center; D.Kessinger grounded out (B.Powell-1b to M.Stottlemyre-p) [M.Alou to second]; M.Stottlemyre threw a wild pitch [M.Alou to third]; H.Aaron reached on an error by F.Howard-lf [M.Alou scored (unearned) (no RBI), H.Aaron to second]; W.McCovey grounded out (R.Carew-2b to B.Powell-1b) [H.Aaron to third]; R.Santo grounded out (S.Bando-3b to B.Powell-1b); 1 R (0 ER), 1 H, 1 E, 1 LOB. NL 1, AL 0.

AL 1ST: R.Carew flied to C.Jones-lf; R.Jackson popped to R.Santo-3b in foul territory; F.Robinson was called out on strikes; 0 R, 0 H, 0 E, 0 LOB. NL 1, AL 0.

NL 2ND: C.Jones singled to shortstop; J.Bench homered to deep leftfield [C.Jones scored]; F.Millan grounded out (B.Powell-1b unassisted); S.Carlton struck out; M.Alou singled to center field; D.Kessinger grounded out (B.Powell-1b unassisted); 2 R, 3 H, 0 E, 1 LOB. NL 3, AL 0.

AL 2ND: B.Powell flied to M.Alou-cf; F.Howard homered to deep centerfield; S.Bando grounded out (S.Carlton-p to W.McCovey-1b); R.Petrocelli struck out; 1 R, 1 H, 0 E, 0 LOB. NL 3, AL 1.

NL 3RD: **J.Odom replaced M.Stottlemyre (pitching);** H.Aaron singled to left field; W.McCovey homered to very deep right-center [H.Aaron scored]; R.Santo grounded out (R.Petrocelli-ss to B.Powell-1b); C.Jones reached on an error by R.Petrocelli-ss [C.Jones to first]; J.Bench singled to right field [C.Jones to third]; F.Millan doubled to left field [C.Jones scored (unearned), J.Bench scored]; S.Carlton doubled to left-center [F.Millan scored]; **D.Knowles replaced J.Odom (pitching);** M.Alou grounded out (R.Carew-2b to B.Powell-1b) [S.Carlton to third]; D.Kessinger grounded out (R.Petrocelli-ss to B.Powell-1b); 5 R (4 ER), 5 H, 1 E, 1 LOB. NL 8, AL 1.

AL 3RD: B.Freehan homered to deep leftfield; **H.Killebrew batted for D.Knowles;** H.Killebrew flied to C.Jones-lf; R.Carew flied to M.Alou-cf; R.Jackson walked; F.Robinson forced R.Jackson (R.Santo-3b to F.Millan-2b) [F.Robinson to first]; 1 R, 1 H, 0 E, 1 LOB. NL 8, AL 2.

NL 4TH: **D.McLain replaced H.Killebrew (pitching);** H.Aaron struck out; W.McCovey homered to deep rightfield; R.Santo walked; C.Jones flied to R.Jackson-cf; J.Bench walked [R.Santo to second]; F.Millan struck out; 1 R, 1 H, 0 E, 2 LOB. NL 9, AL 2.

AL 4TH: **B.Gibson replaced S.Carlton (pitching);** B.Powell struck out; F.Howard walked; **R.Smith ran for F.Howard;** S.Bando singled to shortstop [R.Smith to second]; R.Petrocelli flied to M.Alou-cf; B.Freehan singled to center field [R.Smith scored, S.Bando to third]; **D.Mincher batted for D.McLain;** D.Mincher struck out; 1 R, 2 H, 0 E, 2 LOB. NL 9, AL 3.

NL 5TH: **R.Smith stayed in game (playing lf); R.Jackson changed positions (playing rf); D.McNally replaced D.Mincher (pitching); P.Blair replaced F.Robinson (playing cf); E.Banks batted for B.Gibson;** E.Banks lined to R.Petrocelli-ss; M.Alou walked; **W.Mays batted for D.Kessinger;** W.Mays flied to R.Jackson-rf; H.Aaron flied to P.Blair-cf; 0 R, 0 H, 0 E, 1 LOB. NL 9, AL 3.

AL 5TH: **D.Menke replaced W.Mays (playing ss); R.Clemente replaced E.Banks (playing rf); B.Singer replaced H.Aaron (pitching);** R.Carew grounded out (W.McCovey-1b unassisted); R.Jackson popped to R.Santo-3b; P.Blair popped to D.Menke-ss; 0 R, 0 H, 0 E, 0 LOB. NL 9, AL 3.

NL 6TH: **R.Smith changed positions (playing rf); M.Andrews replaced R.Carew (playing 2b); C.Yastrzemski replaced R.Jackson (playing lf);** W.McCovey struck out; R.Santo grounded out (R.Petrocelli-ss to B.Powell-1b); C.Jones singled to center field; J.Bench lined to C.Yastrzemski-lf; 0 R, 1 H, 0 E, 1 LOB. NL 9, AL 3.

AL 6TH: **L.May replaced W.McCovey (playing 1b); T.Perez replaced R.Santo (playing 3b); R.Hundley replaced J.Bench (playing c);** B.Powell flied to C.Jones-lf; R.Smith grounded out (F.Millan-2b to L.May-1b); S.Bando flied to M.Alou-cf; 0 R, 0 H, 0 E, 0 LOB. NL 9, AL 3.

NL 7TH: **B.Robinson replaced D.McNally (playing 3b); S.McDowell replaced S.Bando (pitching); J.Roseboro replaced B.Freehan (playing c);** F.Millan grounded out (B.Robinson-3b to B.Powell-1b); R.Clemente struck out; M.Alou struck out; 0 R, 0 H, 0 E, 0 LOB. NL 9, AL 3.

AL 7TH: **G.Beckert replaced B.Singer (playing 2b); J.Koosman replaced F.Millan (pitching);** R.Petrocelli doubled to left field; J.Roseboro flied to M.Alou-cf; B.Robinson struck out; M.Andrews grounded out (T.Perez-3b to L.May-1b); 0 R, 1 H, 0 E, 1 LOB. NL 9, AL 3.

NL 8TH: **J.Fregosi replaced R.Petrocelli (playing ss);** D.Menke struck out; G.Beckert flied to P.Blair-cf; L.May struck out; 0 R, 0 H, 0 E, 0 LOB. NL 9, AL 3.

AL 8TH: **P.Rose replaced C.Jones (playing lf);** C.Yastrzemski flied to P.Rose-lf; P.Blair flied to P.Rose-lf; **L.Dierker replaced J.Koosman (pitching);** B.Powell singled to right field; R.Smith popped to T.Perez-3b; 0 R, 1 H, 0 E, 1 LOB. NL 9, AL 3.

NL 9TH: **R.Culp replaced S.McDowell (pitching);** T.Perez struck out; P.Rose popped to B.Robinson-3b in foul territory; R.Hundley struck out; 0 R, 0 H, 0 E, 0 LOB. NL 9, AL 3.

AL 9TH: **P.Niekro replaced L.Dierker (pitching);** **R.White batted for R.Culp;** R.White struck out; J.Fregosi grounded out (P.Niekro-p to L.May-1b); **C.May batted for J.Roseboro;** C.May struck out; 0 R, 0 H, 0 E, 0 LOB. NL 9, AL 3.

Final Totals	R	H	E	LOB
National League	9	11	0	7
American League	3	6	2	5

Tuesday, July 14, 1970

Riverfront Stadium, Cincinnati

National League 5, American League 4

(12 innings)

SERIES RESULTS: NL 23, AL 17, 1 TIE

Pete Meets Ray

Of all the plays in all the All-Star Games in all the sports, the one that is almost certainly the best remembered is the collision at home plate between Pete Rose and Ray Fosse that ended the 1970 game. However, much more happened that night as the two leagues played one of the most exciting games in several years. The site was Cincinnati's Riverfront Stadium, which had opened two weeks earlier and had seen only eleven regular season games. This was the first year since 1957 that the fans had chosen the starting lineups, a fact that carried with it a bit of irony since it was problems with ballot-box stuffing in Cincinnati that had previously ended fan participation. The new voting system was a computer-based procedure funded by a longtime baseball sponsor, the Gillette Company. There were some problems, most stemming from the February deadline for printing the ballots, even before spring training began. As a result, some controversy brewed over omitted players. The ballot had a write-in provision, which worked as it was intended. Rico Carty of the Braves, who was leading both leagues in batting when the voting took place, was named to the starting lineup through this route. There was one replacement from the fans' choices: Rod Carew of the Twins was selected to start at second base, but a knee injury took him out of the game. He was replaced by Davey Johnson of the Orioles, who was a distant fifth in the fan voting. President Richard Nixon was on hand, at least partly to make up for his absence the previous year, when he was greeting the Apollo 11 astronauts in the Pacific Ocean. He threw out the first ball twice — once to each starting catcher: Bill Freehan of the Tigers and Johnny Bench of the Reds.

The twenty-eight-man rosters, including all pitchers, were completed by managers Gil Hodges of the Mets and Earl Weaver of the Orioles, opponents in the 1969 World Series. One replacement

was made on the final day. Jim Hickman of the Cubs was picked by Hodges as a utility outfielder and barely made it to the game, arriving in Cincinnati at 5 P.M.. This choice would become quite significant in the final inning.

The National League had won seven straight going into the 1970 game and eleven out of the last thirteen (one of those was a tie), so there was much anticipation as the American League built a 4–1 lead through eight innings. Up to that point, the AL collected nine hits and three walks, while the NL was held to three singles but managed five bases on balls and a hit batter. Jim Palmer of the Orioles, the choice of his manager to start the game, pitched three scoreless innings while striking out three and yielding only a walk to Rico Carty of the Braves and a single to Don Kessinger of the Cubs, both in the second inning. Sam McDowell of the Indians covered frames four through six and did only a little worse. Sudden Sam also allowed no runs and fanned three on one hit but did have some control problems and walked three. Minnesota's Jim Perry, the 1970 AL Cy Young Award winner, pitched the next two innings and was nicked for the first NL run in the seventh. He was actually lucky to get away so cheaply. Bud Harrelson of the Mets singled to right, Cito Gaston of the Padres walked, and Denis Menke of the Astros was hit by a pitch to load the bases with no outs. However, the Giants' Willie McCovey of the Giants then grounded into a double play, which scored Harrelson as the AL gladly traded the run for two outs. Big Mac had also hit into a double play that scored a run in 1968, but that time it was the only run of the game. Dick Allen of the Cardinals was called out on strikes to end the rally, which left the score 2–1 in favor of the Americans.

The AL started its offense slowly, gathering only two singles in the first five innings. Manager Hodges did the same as Weaver and chose his ace Tom Seaver to start the game. Seaver repaid that confidence with three fine innings, allowing a hit to Carl Yastrzemski of the Red Sox in the first while striking out four. The next two innings were handled by Jim Merritt of the hometown Reds, who allowed a single to Harmon Killebrew and nothing else. Merritt was in the midst of his best season, one that saw him win twenty and lose twelve while compiling an unimpressive ERA of 4.08. Sadly, he began to have elbow problems the last month of 1970, and in 1971 he lost his first eleven decisions, ending that campaign 1-11. Gaylord Perry of the Giants, Jim's younger brother, pitched the sixth and seventh innings for the NL and was roughed up for two runs on four hits and a walk. Gaylord would go on to have a fine 1970 season with a record of 23-12 and an ERA of 3.20, while turning in a remarkable 328.2 innings, one of six seasons in which he would top the 300-inning mark. However, the determined American Leaguers collected two hits in each of Perry's innings, with Yastrzemski driving in Ray Fosse of the Indians with a single and Fosse scoring Brooks Robinson of the Orioles with a sacrifice fly. The final two AL runs came in the eighth inning at the expense of the Cardinals' Bob Gibson, who would win the NL Cy Young Award in 1970. With one out, Yastrzemski singled to right for his third hit of the night, and the Tigers' Willie Horton advanced Yaz to second with another single. After a fly out, Robinson tripled over Gaston's head, scoring two runs. This was Robinson's third All-Star triple, making him an unlikely career co-leader in this category with the fleet Willie Mays.

The American Leaguers needed just three more outs to get back on the winning track, and they sent Catfish Hunter of the A's to the mound in the ninth to get them. The Giants' Dick Dietz greeted him with a home run to center field, and Harrelson followed with his second single of the game. Gaston popped out, but Joe Morgan of the Astros singled to move Harrelson to second. That was all for Hunter, and Fritz Peterson of the Yankees replaced him, only to be greeted by a single up the middle off the bat of McCovey, scoring Harrelson and sending the speedy Morgan to third. Claude Osteen of the Dodgers, an unexpected pinch runner, replaced McCovey at first base. Mel Stottlemyre of the Yankees took over for Peterson, and Pittsburgh's Roberto Clemente batted for Gibson. Clemente brought Morgan in with a line drive sacrifice fly to Kansas City's Amos Otis in center field, and the game was tied. All three runs were charged to Hunter.

Claude Osteen, who had stayed in to pitch, held off AL charges in each of the next three innings with some fine support from his fielders. In the tenth, Horton hit a ball off the right-field wall but was held to a single by the quick play and strong arm of Clemente. Otis grounded into a double play to end the inning. The threat in the eleventh came on a double into the right-field corner by Minnesota's Tony Oliva, but Osteen got two ground balls to end that problem. In the twelfth, Yastrzemski, who would be named Most Valuable Player of the game even though he played for the losing team, doubled for his fourth hit of the game when Gaston missed a try for a shoestring catch with two outs. An intentional walk to Horton brought up Otis, who lined out to Clemente. The four hits by Yastrzemski tied the All-Star Game record, set originally by Joe Medwick of the Cardinals in his triple crown year of 1937 and matched by Ted Williams of the Red Sox in 1946.

In the meantime, the NL made no progress against Stottlemyre, who retired all four batters he faced, and the Angels' Clyde Wright, who came in to start the eleventh inning. Wright retired the first five batters, but unfortunately for the American League, he would get no one else out. Rose, who had struck out in his other two at bats after replacing Atlanta's Henry Aaron, singled to center. Billy Grabarkewitz of the Dodgers moved him up one station with a line drive to left, setting the stage for Jim Hickman, the late roster addition. Hickman singled to center, and Rose was off with the crack of the bat, getting to the plate just as the throw from center fielder Otis arrived. It appeared that Rose would be out, but he didn't slide, choosing instead to bowl Fosse over with a left forearm and lowered shoulder as though he were plunging off right tackle for the NFL's Cincinnati Bengals. Both players went down in a heap, the ball came loose as Fosse's glove was knocked off his hand, and the NL had its eighth straight win.

This violent game-ending play has become an enduring part of the story of Pete Rose. It is often written that Rose severely injured Fosse and ended the catcher's career as an effective player. Although one can certainly argue that Rose was wrong to smash into Fosse the way he did, the claim that Fosse's career was ruined is simply not supported by the evidence and may best be seen as a myth or a legend. In the short run, Rose suffered much more than Fosse. The collision was on July 14, and Rose did not play again until July 19, when he pinch-hit in Pittsburgh, having missed the inaugural game in Three Rivers Stadium on July 16. His next start was on July 20 in St. Louis. On the other hand, Fosse started in Cleveland's next scheduled game on July 16 and played every game for the next nine days, including a doubleheader on the 24th, in which he caught both games! At

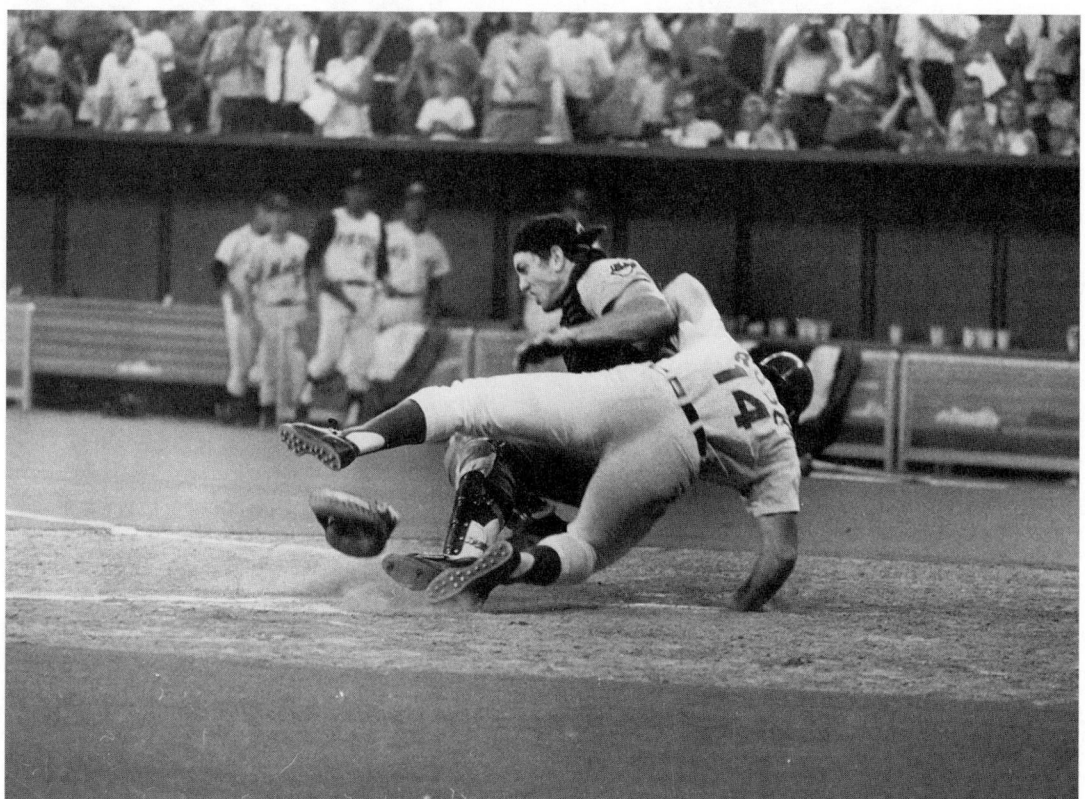

Rose colliding with Fosse, 1970
Pete Rose flattens Ray Fosse to score the game-winning run in the twelfth inning. UPI / CORBIS-*Bettmann.*

the time of the All-Star Game, Fosse was batting .309 in 291 at bats. He finished the season at .307 in 450 at bats. His season was cut short by a broken finger on September 3. Rose was batting .323 in 356 at bats on July 14 and finished the year at .316 in 649 at bats. As for Fosse's career, 1970 was clearly his best season, but in the following three years he played over 130 games each season, catching from 124 to 141 games. It is not possible to know what might have been, but conjecture on the topic should have objective support.

	AL		NL	
P	Jim Palmer	BAL	Tom Seaver	NYN
C	Bill Freehan	DET	Johnny Bench	CIN
1B	Boog Powell	BAL	Dick Allen	SLN
2B	Rod Carew +	MIN	Glenn Beckert	CHN
3B	Harmon Killebrew	MIN	Tony Perez	CIN
SS	Luis Aparicio	CHA	Don Kessinger	CHN
OF	Frank Howard	WAS	Hank Aaron	ATL
OF	Frank Robinson	BAL	Rico Carty	ATL
OF	Carl Yastrzemski	BOS	Willie Mays	SFN
	Sandy Alomar	CAL	Roberto Clemente	PIT
	Mike Cuellar	BAL	Dick Dietz	SFN
	Ray Fosse	CLE	Cito Gaston	SDN
	Jim Fregosi	CAL	Bob Gibson	SLN
	Tommy Harper	MIL	Billy Grabarkewitz	LAN
	Willie Horton	DET	Bud Harrelson	NYN
	Catfish Hunter	OAK	Jim Hickman	CHN
	Alex Johnson	CAL	Joe Hoerner	PHI
	Dave Johnson	BAL	Willie McCovey	SFN
	Sam McDowell	CLE	Denis Menke	HOU
	Dave McNally	BAL	Jim Merritt	CIN
	Jerry Moses	BOS	Felix Millan +	ATL
	Tony Oliva	MIN	Joe Morgan	HOU
	Amos Otis	KCA	Claude Osteen	LAN
	Jim Perry	MIN	Gaylord Perry	SFN
	Fritz Peterson	NYA	Pete Rose	CIN
	Brooks Robinson	BAL	Wayne Simpson	CIN
	Mel Stottlemyre	NYA	Rusty Staub	MON
	Roy White	NYA	Joe Torre	SLN
	Clyde Wright	CAL	Hoyt Wilhelm	ATL

+ player replaced on roster

American League   000 001 120 000- 4
National League   000 000 103 001- 5 (12)
   2 outs when winning run was scored.

AMERICAN LEAGUE

	ab	r	h	bi	bb	so	po	a
L.Aparicio, ss	6	0	0	0	0	2	0	3
C.Yastrzemski, cf-1b	6	1	4	1	0	0	8	0
F.Robinson, rf-lf	3	0	0	0	0	2	1	0
W.Horton, lf	2	1	2	0	1	0	1	0
B.Powell, 1b	3	0	0	0	0	0	5	0
A.Otis, cf	3	0	0	0	0	0	2	0
H.Killebrew, 3b	2	0	1	0	0	1	0	0
T.Harper, pr	0	0	0	0	0	0	0	0
B.Robinson, 3b	3	1	2	2	0	0	1	1
F.Howard, lf	2	0	0	0	0	1	0	0
T.Oliva, rf	2	0	1	0	1	0	0	0
D.Johnson, 2b	5	0	1	0	0	1	6	2
C.Wright, p	0	0	0	0	0	0	0	0
B.Freehan, c	1	0	0	0	0	0	4	0
R.Fosse, c	2	1	1	1	1	0	7	0
J.Palmer, p	1	0	0	0	0	0	0	0
S.McDowell, p	0	0	0	0	0	0	0	3
A.Johnson, ph	1	0	0	0	0	0	0	0
J.Perry, p	0	0	0	0	0	0	0	0
J.Fregosi, ph	1	0	0	0	0	0	0	0
J.Hunter, p	0	0	0	0	0	0	0	0
F.Peterson, p	0	0	0	0	0	0	0	0
M.Stottlemyre, p	0	0	0	0	0	0	0	0
S.Alomar, 2b	1	0	0	0	0	0	0	2
Totals	44	4	12	4	3	7	35	11

BATTING
2B: T.Oliva (off C.Osteen); C.Yastrzemski (off C.Osteen).
3B: B.Robinson (off B.Gibson).
2-out RBI: C.Yastrzemski; B.Robinson 2.
RBI, scoring position, less than 2 outs: L.Aparicio 0–1;
   A.Otis 0–1; D.Johnson 0–1; R.Fosse 1–2.
S: S.McDowell.
SF: R.Fosse.
GDP: A.Otis.

BASERUNNING
CS: T.Harper (2nd base by J.Merritt / J.Bench).
Team LOB: 9

FIELDING
DP: (1). D.Johnson-C.Yastrzemski.

NATIONAL LEAGUE

	ab	r	h	bi	bb	so	po	a
W.Mays, cf	3	0	0	0	0	1	3	0
G.Perry, p	0	0	0	0	0	0	0	2
W.McCovey, ph-1b	2	0	1	1	0	0	1	0
C.Osteen, pr-p	0	0	0	0	0	0	1	0
J.Torre, ph	1	0	0	0	0	0	0	0
D.Allen, 1b	3	0	0	0	1	1	4	0
B.Gibson, p	0	0	0	0	0	0	0	0
R.Clemente, ph-rf	1	0	0	1	0	0	2	0
H.Aaron, rf	2	0	0	0	0	0	1	0
P.Rose, rf-lf	3	1	1	0	1	2	3	0
T.Perez, 3b	3	0	0	0	0	2	1	1
B.Grabarkewitz, 3b	3	0	1	0	0	0	0	1
R.Carty, lf	1	0	0	0	1	0	0	0
J.Hickman, lf-1b	4	0	1	1	0	2	6	1
J.Bench, c	3	0	0	0	0	3	5	1
D.Dietz, c	2	1	1	1	0	0	2	0
D.Kessinger, ss	2	0	2	0	0	0	0	0
B.Harrelson, ss	3	2	2	0	0	0	0	4
G.Beckert, 2b	2	0	0	0	0	0	2	1
C.Gaston, cf	2	0	0	0	1	0	2	0
T.Seaver, p	0	0	0	0	0	0	0	0
R.Staub, ph	1	0	0	0	0	0	0	0
J.Merritt, p	0	0	0	0	0	0	0	0
D.Menke, ph-2b	0	0	0	0	1	0	2	1
J.Morgan, 2b	2	1	1	0	0	0	1	2
Totals	43	5	10	4	5	11	36	14

BATTING
HR: D.Dietz (9th inning off J.Hunter, 0 on, 0 out).
2-out RBI: J.Hickman.
RBI, scoring position, less than 2 outs: W.McCovey 1–2;
   R.Clemente 1–1; T.Perez 0–1; J.Hickman 0–1.
SF: R.Clemente.
GDP: W.McCovey.

BASERUNNING
Team LOB: 10

FIELDING
DP: (1). B.Harrelson-J.Morgan-J.Hickman.

PITCHING	ip	h	r	er	bb	so
American League						
J.Palmer	3.0	1	0	0	1	3
S.McDowell	3.0	1	0	0	3	3
J.Perry	2.0	1	1	1	1	3
J.Hunter	0.1	3	3	3	0	0
F.Peterson	* 0.0	1	0	0	0	0
M.Stottlemyre (BS)	1.2	0	0	0	0	2
C.Wright (L)	1.2	3	1	1	0	0
National League						
T.Seaver	3.0	1	0	0	0	4
J.Merritt	2.0	1	0	0	0	1
G.Perry	2.0	4	2	2	1	0
B.Gibson	2.0	3	2	2	1	2
C.Osteen (W)	3.0	3	0	0	1	0

* Pitched to 1 batter in 9th

Inherited Runners—Scored:
   S.McDowell 0–0; J.Perry 0–0; J.Hunter 0–0;
   F.Peterson 2–2; M.Stottlemyre 2–1; C.Wright 0–0;
   J.Merritt 0–0; G.Perry 0–0; B.Gibson 0–0;
   C.Osteen 0–0.
IBB: W.Horton by C.Osteen.
HBP: D.Menke by J.Perry.

GAME DATA—T: 3:19; A: 51838; Temp: 80;
Wind: Unknown direction, Speed: Unknown

UMPIRES—HP: Al Barlick (NL), 1B: John Rice (AL),
2B: Frank Secory (NL), 3B: Bill Haller (AL), LF: Frank
Dezelan (NL), RF: Russ Goetz (AL)

STARTING LINEUPS

	American League	National League
1.	L.Aparicio ss	W.Mays cf
2.	C.Yastrzemski cf	D.Allen 1b
3.	F.Robinson rf	H.Aaron rf
4.	B.Powell 1b	T.Perez 3b
5.	H.Killebrew 3b	R.Carty lf
6.	F.Howard lf	J.Bench c
7.	D.Johnson 2b	D.Kessinger ss
8.	B.Freehan c	G.Beckert 2b
9.	J.Palmer p	T.Seaver p

AL 1ST: L.Aparicio struck out; C.Yastrzemski singled to center field; F.Robinson struck out; B.Powell popped to T.Perez-3b; 0 R, 1 H, 0 E, 1 LOB. AL 0, NL 0.

NL 1ST: W.Mays struck out; D.Allen flied to F.Robinson-rf; H.Aaron grounded out (L.Aparicio-ss to B.Powell-1b); 0 R, 0 H, 0 E, 0 LOB. AL 0, NL 0.

AL 2ND: H.Killebrew struck out; F.Howard struck out; D.Johnson flied to H.Aaron-rf; 0 R, 0 H, 0 E, 0 LOB. AL 0, NL 0.

NL 2ND: T.Perez struck out; R.Carty walked; J.Bench struck out; D.Kessinger singled to center field [R.Carty to second]; G.Beckert grounded out (D.Johnson-2b to B.Powell-1b); 0 R, 1 H, 0 E, 2 LOB. AL 0, NL 0.

AL 3RD: B.Freehan lined to W.Mays-cf; On a bunt J.Palmer grounded out (T.Perez-3b to D.Allen-1b); L.Aparicio grounded out (G.Beckert-2b to D.Allen-1b); 0 R, 0 H, 0 E, 0 LOB. AL 0, NL 0.

NL 3RD: R.Staub batted for T.Seaver; R.Staub flied to C.Yastrzemski-cf; W.Mays popped to B.Powell-1b in foul territory; D.Allen lined to D.Johnson-2b; 0 R, 0 H, 0 E, 0 LOB. AL 0, NL 0.

AL 4TH: **J.Merritt replaced R.Staub (pitching);** C.Yastrzemski flied to W.Mays-cf; F.Robinson was called out on strikes; B.Powell flied to W.Mays-cf; 0 R, 0 H, 0 E, 0 LOB. AL 0, NL 0.

NL 4TH: **S.McDowell replaced J.Palmer (pitching);** H.Aaron grounded out (S.McDowell-p to B.Powell-1b); T.Perez struck out; R.Carty grounded out (S.McDowell-p to B.Powell-1b); 0 R, 0 H, 0 E, 0 LOB. AL 0, NL 0.

AL 5TH: **P.Rose replaced H.Aaron (playing rf); J.Hickman replaced R.Carty (playing lf);** H.Killebrew singled to left field; **T.Harper ran for H.Killebrew;** F.Howard flied to J.Hickman-lf; D.Johnson popped to G.Beckert-2b in foul territory; T.Harper was caught stealing second (J.Bench-c to G.Beckert-2b); 0 R, 1 H, 0 E, 0 LOB. AL 0, NL 0.

NL 5TH: **F.Robinson changed positions (playing lf);**

replaced B.Freehan (playing c); B.Robinson replaced T.Harper (playing 3b); J.Bench struck out; D.Kessinger singled to center field; G.Beckert forced D.Kessinger (S.McDowell-p to D.Johnson-2b) [G.Beckert to first]; **D.Menke batted for J.Merritt;** D.Menke walked [G.Beckert to second]; W.Mays popped to B.Robinson-3b in foul territory; 0 R, 1 H, 0 E, 2 LOB. AL 0, NL 0.

AL 6TH: **D.Menke stayed in game (playing 2b); G.Perry replaced W.Mays (pitching); C.Gaston replaced G.Beckert (playing cf);** R.Fosse singled to right field; S.McDowell out on a sacrifice bunt (G.Perry-p to D.Menke-2b) [R.Fosse to second]; L.Aparicio flied to P.Rose-rf; C.Yastrzemski singled to right-center [R.Fosse scored]; F.Robinson grounded out (D.Menke-2b to D.Allen-1b); 1 R, 2 H, 0 E, 1 LOB. AL 1, NL 0.

NL 6TH: **W.Horton replaced F.Robinson (playing lf);** D.Allen walked; P.Rose walked [D.Allen to second]; T.Perez popped to D.Johnson-2b; J.Hickman popped to D.Johnson-2b; J.Bench struck out; 0 R, 0 H, 0 E, 2 LOB. AL 1, NL 0.

AL 7TH: **B.Grabarkewitz replaced T.Perez (playing 3b); B.Harrelson replaced D.Kessinger (playing ss); D.Dietz replaced J.Bench (playing c);** B.Powell grounded out (G.Perry-p to D.Allen-1b); B.Robinson singled to center field; T.Oliva walked [B.Robinson to second]; D.Johnson singled to shortstop [B.Robinson to third, T.Oliva to second]; R.Fosse lined out on a sacrifice fly to C.Gaston-cf [B.Robinson scored, T.Oliva to third]; **A.Johnson batted for S.McDowell;** A.Johnson forced D.Johnson (B.Harrelson-ss to D.Menke-2b) [A.Johnson to first]; 1 R, 2 H, 0 E, 2 LOB. AL 2, NL 0.

NL 7TH: **C.Yastrzemski changed positions (playing 1b); J.Perry replaced A.Johnson (pitching); A.Otis replaced B.Powell (playing cf);** B.Harrelson singled to right field; C.Gaston walked [B.Harrelson to second]; D.Menke was hit by a pitch [B.Harrelson to third, C.Gaston to second]; **W.McCovey batted for G.Perry;** W.McCovey grounded into a double play (D.Johnson-2b to C.Yastrzemski-1b) [B.Harrelson scored (no RBI), C.Gaston to third, D.Menke out at second]; D.Allen was called out on strikes; 1 R, 1 H, 0 E, 1 LOB. AL 2, NL 1.

AL 8TH: **W.McCovey stayed in game (playing 1b); J.Morgan replaced D.Menke (playing 2b); B.Gibson replaced D.Allen (pitching);** L.Aparicio grounded out (J.Morgan-2b to W.McCovey-1b); C.Yastrzemski singled to right field; W.Horton singled to center field [C.Yastrzemski to second]; A.Otis flied to P.Rose-rf [C.Yastrzemski to third];

B.Robinson tripled to center field [C.Yastrzemski scored, W.Horton scored]; T.Oliva flied to P.Rose-rf; 2 R, 3 H, O E, 1 LOB. AL 4, NL 1.

NL 8TH: P.Rose struck out; B.Grabarkewitz flied to W.Horton-lf; J.Hickman struck out; O R, O H, O E, O LOB. AL 4, NL 1.

AL 9TH: D.Johnson struck out; R.Fosse walked; **J.Fregosi batted for J.Perry**; J.Fregosi flied to J.Hickman-lf; L.Aparicio struck out; O R, O H, O E, 1 LOB. AL 4, NL 1.

NL 9TH: **J.Hunter replaced J.Fregosi (pitching)**; D.Dietz homered to deep centerfield; B.Harrelson singled to left field; C.Gaston popped to C.Yastrzemski-1b; J.Morgan singled to right field [B.Harrelson to second]; **F.Peterson replaced J.Hunter (pitching)**; W.McCovey singled to center field [B.Harrelson scored, J.Morgan to third]; **C.Osteen ran for W.McCovey; R.Clemente batted for B.Gibson; M.Stottlemyre replaced F.Peterson (pitching)**; R.Clemente lined out on a sacrifice fly to A.Otis-cf [J.Morgan scored]; P.Rose struck out; 3 R, 4 H, O E, 1 LOB. AL 4, NL 4.

AL 10TH: **R.Clemente stayed in game (playing rf); P.Rose changed positions (playing lf); J.Hickman changed positions (playing 1b); C.Osteen stayed in game (pitching)**; C.Yastrzemski grounded out (J.Hickman-1b to C.Osteen-p); W.Horton singled to right field; A.Otis grounded into a double play (B.Harrelson-ss to J.Morgan-2b to J.Hickman-1b) [W.Horton out at second]; O R, 1 H, O E, O LOB. AL 4, NL 4.

NL 10TH: B.Grabarkewitz grounded out (L.Aparicio-ss to C.Yastrzemski-1b); J.Hickman struck out;

D.Dietz lined to D.Johnson-2b; O R, O H, O E, O LOB. AL 4, NL 4.

AL 11TH: B.Robinson grounded out (B.Harrelson-ss to J.Hickman-1b); T.Oliva doubled to right field; D.Johnson grounded out (B.Grabarkewitz-3b to J.Hickman-1b); R.Fosse grounded out (B.Harrelson-ss to J.Hickman-1b); O R, 1 H, O E, 1 LOB. AL 4, NL 4.

NL 11TH: **S.Alomar replaced M.Stottlemyre (playing 2b); C.Wright replaced D.Johnson (pitching)**; B.Harrelson flied to A.Otis-cf; C.Gaston grounded out (S.Alomar-2b to C.Yastrzemski-1b); J.Morgan grounded out (L.Aparicio-ss to C.Yastrzemski-1b); O R, O H, O E, O LOB. AL 4, NL 4.

AL 12TH: S.Alomar flied to R.Clemente-rf; L.Aparicio lined to C.Gaston-cf; C.Yastrzemski doubled to center field; Gaston missed a shoestring catch here; W.Horton was walked intentionally; A.Otis lined to R.Clemente-rf; O R, 1 H, O E, 2 LOB. AL 4, NL 4.

NL 12TH: **J.Torre batted for C.Osteen**; J.Torre grounded out (B.Robinson-3b to C.Yastrzemski-1b); R.Clemente grounded out (S.Alomar-2b to C.Yastrzemski-1b); P.Rose singled to center field; B.Grabarkewitz singled to left field [P.Rose to second]; J.Hickman singled to center field [P.Rose scored, B.Grabarkewitz to second]; 1 R, 3 H, O E, 2 LOB. AL 4, NL 5.

Final Totals	R	H	E	LOB
American League	4	12	0	9
National League	5	10	0	10

Tuesday, July 13, 1971

Tiger Stadium, Detroit

American League 6, National League 4

SERIES RESULTS: NL 23, AL 18, 1 TIE

Reggie Is Mr. July for One Night

When the All-Star Game was held in Briggs Stadium in 1951, the teams combined for a record six home runs as the National League won, 8–3. The game didn't return to the Motor City for twenty years, and by 1971, the grand old park was known as Tiger Stadium. Once again, there were six homers, but this time the American League prevailed by a 6–4 margin, winning for the first time since 1962 as it broke an eight-game NL winning streak. American League manager Earl Weaver of the Orioles had his league's recent woes firmly in mind when he commented that he always hated to lose but that he especially wanted to avoid the unpleasant mail he received after leading the AL to its twelfth-inning loss in 1970. Detroit legend Charlie Gehringer was on hand to throw out the first ball, and perhaps it brought good luck for the AL. Gehringer played in the first six All-Star Games, of which the AL won four, and garnered ten hits in twenty at bats. This .500 average is still the highest for players with more than ten at bats.

This was the third All-Star Game with six round-trippers; the 1954 game in Cleveland was the other homer bonanza. There was a substantial wind blowing out to right field this night in Detroit, reaching gusts of thirty-one miles per hour. As a result, there were plenty of suggestions that the home run barrage was a little tainted. However, the blast by Oakland's Reggie Jackson in the third inning had nothing to do with the wind. The ball hit a light tower on top of the roof in right-center field, traveling an estimated 520 to 540 feet and becoming the consensus choice for the longest homer in All-Star history. The young A's slugger deemed it the farthest he had ever hit a ball, and many opined that it was also the number one home run of all they had seen. The only disagreement came from Billy Martin, the Detroit manager who served as one of the AL coaches. Deadpanned Billy the Kid: "It didn't knock the light tower down, did it?"

All ten runs scored in the game came on the six circuit clouts, which represented exactly half of the contest's twelve hits; all of the others were singles. Each team hit three over the fence, but the AL hit each of its homers with a mate aboard, while two of the NL shots were solo, accounting for the run differential. Frank Robinson of the Orioles, who won the game's Most Valuable Player Award, became the first All-Star to homer for each league; he had hit his NL homer in 1959 while a member of the Reds. Robinson is also the first player to win the Most Valuable Player Award for the season in each league, capturing the honor for the 1961 Reds and the 1966 Orioles.

For the second consecutive year, the starting lineups, except for the pitchers, were chosen by computerized ballot of the fans, and for the second straight year Henry Aaron of the Braves drew the most votes. There were some unexpected choices, notably Luis Aparicio of the Red Sox, who was selected to start at shortstop despite a batting average of .209 at game time (he would end the season at .232). As it turned out, the fans didn't really get their wish for the AL because three players named to start were sidelined by injuries. Tony Oliva of the Twins, Boog Powell of the Orioles, and Ray Fosse of the Indians were replaced in the lineup by Bobby Murcer of the Yankees, Norm Cash of the Tigers, and Cash's teammate Bill Freehan, respectively. The starting pitcher for the American League was the sensational rookie from Oakland, Vida Blue. The fireballing left-hander, who was two weeks and a day short of his twenty-second birthday, had seventeen wins coming into the All-Star Game. The previous record was held by Bob Feller, who had sixteen triumphs at the time of the break in 1941. Feller went on to compile a record of 25-13 in 1941 before joining the Navy in 1942 and missing three and a half seasons during World War II. Blue turned in a record of 24-8 for 1971, twirling eight shutouts and leading the league with an ERA of 1.82; he was also selected as the winner of the AL Cy Young and Most Valuable Player Awards.

Although the game was ultimately an American League success, the Americans had to make it a come-from-behind effort because the National League squad built up a 3–0 lead against Blue. Blue started out with a dominant first-inning performance in which he threw seven pitches (all for strikes) to retire the side in order on two ground balls and a pop-up. However, in the second inning, he hit Willie Stargell of the Pirates to start things off, and the Reds' Johnny Bench hit a wind-aided homer into the upper-right-field stands. In the third inning, Aaron hit a line drive to the upper deck in right for his first All-Star home run, which came in his fifty-ninth All-Star at bat (sixty-fifth plate appearance). In the bottom of the third, the American League forged ahead with four runs off NL starter and eventual losing pitcher Dock Ellis of the Pirates. After Jackson's monstrous homer as a pinch hitter for Blue, Frank Robinson completed the AL's burst by hitting into the lower-right-field seats following a walk to Minnesota's Rod Carew and two pop-ups. Since Blue was the pitcher of record when Robinson's homer put the AL into the lead, he became the youngest man to win an All-Star Game, despite not pitching especially well.

Innings four through seven saw the NL manage only two singles and a walk against the Baltimore duo of Jim Palmer and Mike Cuellar, each of whom struck out two in his two innings. Brooks Robinson, their Orioles teammate, made two good plays at third base in support. He executed a fine stop of a ball smashed toward the hole by Bench in the fourth, and he started a double play on a sharp grounder by Joe Torre of the Cardinals in the sixth. Robinson had tormented the Reds with his great plays at the hot corner in the 1970 World Series, so it was appropriate that he rob Bench in the succeeding All-Star Game. Although it was not a well-hit ball, the last out of the game was a pop-up by Bench that Robinson caught near the mound. However, the night was not a complete loss for the hard-hitting catcher; he was the only batter in the game to collect two hits.

Juan Marichal of the Giants followed Ellis to the mound and continued his All-Star excellence with two scoreless and hitless innings, allowing a walk

to Carew in the fifth as his only base runner. The next NL hurler, Ferguson Jenkins of the Cubs, did not fare as well in his one inning, the sixth. The Tigers' Al Kaline led off with a single, the Twins' Harmon Killebrew hit a line drive home run into the left-field stands, and Brooks Robinson singled before Jenkins settled down to retire the side on a fly ball and a double play. Killebrew's homer was an impressive hit that was actually hindered by the strong wind. Don Wilson of the Astros pitched the last two rounds for the NL and allowed only one base runner, who reached on a walk and was then erased by a double play. The final pitcher of the game was Detroit's Mickey Lolich, whom manager Earl Weaver said he selected because "he knows the kind of pitches you have to make here." As it turned out, one of those pitches wasn't the best because Pittsburgh's Roberto Clemente hit it over the right-center-field fence for his first and only All-Star home run.

Even great players can have rough times in spectacles such as the All-Star Game, and three of the greatest stars broke out of All-Star doldrums in 1971. Frank Robinson's homer broke a personal 0-14 streak since the 1961 game in San Francisco. Aaron's woes in the midsummer contest were even worse; he came into the game with a composite .175 batting average with no extra-base hits. Clemente had done better than that, with a .310 batting mark, including two doubles and a triple, but he had not homered before. He did have a great World Series against Baltimore in the fall of 1971, but this was his last All-Star appearance because he tragically lost his life in late 1972 in an airplane crash while on a humanitarian mission to help Nicaraguan earthquake victims. One odd occurrence was that NL manager Sparky Anderson of the Reds removed Aaron along with Willie Mays and Willie McCovey of the Giants at the end of the third inning. Sparky noted that Aaron and McCovey had been suffering from knee problems while Mays was "in the middle of a pennant race and I didn't want him to get hurt here." Only three members of the winning team had been members of the 1962 AL team, which was the last to win: Brooks Robinson, Kaline, and Aparicio.

	AL			NL	
P	Vida Blue		OAK	Dock Ellis	PIT
C	Ray Fosse	+	CLE	Johnny Bench	CIN
1B	Boog Powell		BAL	Willie McCovey	SFN
2B	Rod Carew		MIN	Glenn Beckert	CHN
3B	Brooks Robinson		BAL	Joe Torre	SLN
SS	Luis Aparicio		BOS	Bud Harrelson	NYN
OF	Tony Oliva	+	MIN	Hank Aaron	ATL
OF	Frank Robinson		BAL	Willie Mays	SFN
OF	Carl Yastrzemski		BOS	Willie Stargell	PIT
	Don Buford		BAL	Bobby Bonds	SFN
	Leo Cardenas		MIN	Lou Brock	SLN
	Norm Cash		DET	Steve Carlton	SLN
	Mike Cuellar		BAL	Clay Carroll	CIN
	Dave Duncan		OAK	Roberto Clemente	PIT
	Bill Freehan		DET	Nate Colbert	SDN
	Frank Howard		WAS	Willie Davis	LAN
	Reggie Jackson		OAK	Larry Dierker +	HOU
	Al Kaline		DET	Ferguson Jenkins	CHN
	Harmon Killebrew		MIN	Don Kessinger	CHN
	Mickey Lolich		DET	Juan Marichal	SFN
	Sam McDowell	+	CLE	Lee May	CIN
	Bill Melton		CHA	Felix Millan	ATL
	Andy Messersmith		CAL	Pete Rose	CIN
	Thurman Munson		NYA	Manny Sanguillen	PIT
	Bobby Murcer		NYA	Ron Santo	CHN
	Amos Otis		KCA	Tom Seaver	NYN
	Jim Palmer		BAL	Rusty Staub	MON
	Marty Pattin		MIL	Don Wilson	HOU
	Jim Perry		MIN	Rick Wise	PHI
	Cookie Rojas		KCA		
	Sonny Siebert		BOS		
	Wilbur Wood		CHA		

+ player replaced on roster

National League   021 000 010- 4
American League   004 002 00x- 6

NATIONAL LEAGUE

	ab	r	h	bi	bb	so	po	a
W.Mays, cf	2	0	0	0	0	0	0	0
R.Clemente, rf	2	1	1	1	0	1	1	0
F.Millan, 2b	0	0	0	0	0	0	1	1
H.Aaron, rf	2	1	1	1	0	0	0	0
L.May, 1b	1	0	0	0	1	0	6	0
J.Torre, 3b	3	0	0	0	0	1	1	0
R.Santo, ph-3b	1	0	0	0	0	0	0	1
W.Stargell, lf	2	1	0	0	0	2	2	0
L.Brock, ph	1	0	0	0	0	0	0	0
W.McCovey, 1b	2	0	0	0	0	1	4	0
J.Marichal, p	0	0	0	0	0	0	0	1
D.Kessinger, ss	2	0	0	0	0	0	1	1
J.Bench, c	4	1	2	2	0	0	5	0
G.Beckert, 2b	3	0	0	0	0	0	0	5
P.Rose, rf	0	0	0	0	0	0	0	0
B.Harrelson, ss	2	0	0	0	0	0	1	2
F.Jenkins, p	0	0	0	0	0	0	0	0
N.Colbert, ph	1	0	0	0	0	1	0	0
D.Wilson, p	0	0	0	0	0	0	0	0
D.Ellis, p	1	0	0	0	0	1	0	0
W.Davis, cf	1	0	1	0	0	0	2	0
B.Bonds, ph-cf	1	0	0	0	0	1	0	0
Totals	31	4	5	4	1	8	24	11

BATTING
HR: R.Clemente (8th inning off M.Lolich, 0 on, 1 out);
    H.Aaron (3rd inning off V.Blue, 0 on, 2 out); J.Bench
    (2nd inning off V.Blue, 1 on, 1 out).
2-out RBI: H.Aaron.
GDP: J.Torre.

BASERUNNING
Team LOB: 2

FIELDING
DP: (2). G.Beckert-D.Kessinger-L.May; R.Santo-
    F.Millan-L.May.

AMERICAN LEAGUE

	ab	r	h	bi	bb	so	po	a
R.Carew, 2b	1	1	0	0	2	0	1	2
C.Rojas, 2b	1	0	0	0	0	0	1	1
B.Murcer, cf	3	0	1	0	0	1	0	0
M.Cuellar, p	0	0	0	0	0	0	0	0
D.Buford, ph	1	0	0	0	0	1	0	0
M.Lolich, p	0	0	0	0	0	0	0	3
C.Yastrzemski, lf	3	0	0	0	1	0	0	0
F.Robinson, rf	2	1	1	2	0	0	3	0
A.Kaline, rf	2	1	1	0	0	1	2	0
N.Cash, 1b	2	0	0	0	0	2	7	0
H.Killebrew, 1b	2	1	1	2	0	0	4	0
B.Robinson, 3b	3	0	1	0	0	0	1	3
B.Freehan, c	3	0	0	0	0	0	6	1
T.Munson, c	0	0	0	0	0	0	1	0
L.Aparicio, ss	3	1	1	0	0	0	1	2
V.Blue, p	0	0	0	0	0	0	0	0
R.Jackson, ph	1	1	1	2	0	0	0	0
J.Palmer, p	0	0	0	0	0	0	0	0
F.Howard, ph	1	0	0	0	0	0	0	0
A.Otis, cf	1	0	0	0	0	0	0	0
Totals	29	6	7	6	3	5	27	12

BATTING
HR: F.Robinson (3rd inning off D.Ellis, 1 on, 2 out);
    H.Killebrew (6th inning off F.Jenkins, 1 on, 0 out);
    R.Jackson (3rd inning off D.Ellis, 1 on, 0 out).
2-out RBI: F.Robinson 2.
GDP: H.Killebrew; L.Aparicio.

BASERUNNING
Team LOB: 2

FIELDING
DP: (1). B.Robinson-C.Rojas-H.Killebrew.

PITCHING	ip	h	r	er	bb	so
National League						
D.Ellis (L)	3.0	4	4	4	1	2
J.Marichal	2.0	0	0	0	1	1
F.Jenkins	1.0	3	2	2	0	0
D.Wilson	2.0	0	0	0	1	2
American League						
V.Blue (W)	3.0	2	3	3	0	3
J.Palmer	2.0	1	0	0	0	2
M.Cuellar	2.0	1	0	0	1	2
M.Lolich (S)	2.0	1	1	1	0	1

Inherited Runners—Scored:
    J.Marichal 0-0; F.Jenkins 0-0; D.Wilson 0-0;
    J.Palmer 0-0; M.Cuellar 0-0; M.Lolich 0-0.
HBP: W.Stargell by V.Blue.

GAME DATA—T: 2:05; A: 53559; Temp: Unknown;
Wind: To right, Speed: 25 mph

UMPIRES—HP: Frank Umont (AL), 1B: Paul Pryor (NL),
2B: Jake O'Donnell (AL), 3B: Doug Harvey (NL), LF: Don
Denkinger (AL), RF: Nick Colosi (NL)

STARTING LINEUPS

	National League	*American League*
1.	W.Mays cf	R.Carew 2b
2.	H.Aaron rf	B.Murcer cf
3.	J.Torre 3b	C.Yastrzemski lf
4.	W.Stargell lf	F.Robinson rf
5.	W.McCovey 1b	N.Cash 1b
6.	J.Bench c	B.Robinson 3b
7.	G.Beckert 2b	B.Freehan c
8.	B.Harrelson ss	L.Aparicio ss
9.	D.Ellis p	V.Blue p

NL 1ST: W.Mays grounded out (L.Aparicio-ss to N.Cash-1b); H.Aaron grounded out (B.Robinson-3b to N.Cash-1b); J.Torre popped to R.Carew-2b; 0 R, 0 H, 0 E, 0 LOB. NL 0, AL 0.

AL 1ST: R.Carew grounded out (G.Beckert-2b to W.McCovey-1b); B.Murcer singled to center field; C.Yastrzemski grounded out (G.Beckert-2b to W.McCovey-1b) [B.Murcer to second]; F.Robinson grounded out (B.Harrelson-ss to W.McCovey-1b); 0 R, 1 H, 0 E, 1 LOB. NL 0, AL 0.

NL 2ND: W.Stargell was hit by a pitch; W.McCovey was called out on strikes; J.Bench homered to very deep right-center [W.Stargell scored]; G.Beckert flied to F.Robinson-rf; B.Harrelson flied to F.Robinson-rf; 2 R, 1 H, 0 E, 0 LOB. NL 2, AL 0.

AL 2ND: N.Cash struck out; B.Robinson grounded out (B.Harrelson-ss to W.McCovey-1b); B.Freehan flied to W.Stargell-lf; 0 R, 0 H, 0 E, 0 LOB. NL 2, AL 0.

NL 3RD: D.Ellis struck out; W.Mays flied to F.Robinson-rf; H.Aaron homered to deep rightfield; Aaron's first All-Star homer; J.Torre struck out; 1 R, 1 H, 0 E, 0 LOB. NL 3, AL 0.

AL 3RD: L.Aparicio singled to center field; **R.Jackson batted for V.Blue;** R.Jackson homered to very deep right-center [L.Aparicio scored]; ball hit light tower, circa 540'; R.Carew walked; B.Murcer popped to J.Torre-3b; C.Yastrzemski popped to B.Harrelson-ss; F.Robinson homered to deep rightfield [R.Carew scored]; Robinson the first to homer for both sides in the All-Star; N.Cash was called out on strikes; 4 R, 3 H, 0 E, 0 LOB. NL 3, AL 4.

NL 4TH: **J.Palmer replaced R.Jackson (pitching);** W.Stargell struck out (B.Freehan-c to N.Cash-1b); Stargell did not run to 1b; W.McCovey grounded out (R.Carew-2b to N.Cash-1b); J.Bench grounded out (B.Robinson-3b to N.Cash-1b); 0 R, 0 H, 0 E, 0 LOB. NL 3, AL 4.

AL 4TH: **W.Davis replaced D.Ellis (playing cf);** **R.Clemente replaced W.Mays (playing rf); L.May replaced H.Aaron (playing 1b); J.Marichal re-**

placed W.McCovey (pitching); B.Robinson flied to W.Davis-cf; B.Freehan popped to L.May-1b in foul territory; L.Aparicio grounded out (J.Marichal-p to L.May-1b); 0 R, 0 H, 0 E, 0 LOB. NL 3, AL 4.

NL 5TH: G.Beckert grounded out (R.Carew-2b to N.Cash-1b); B.Harrelson grounded out (L.Aparicio-ss to N.Cash-1b); W.Davis singled to center field; R.Clemente was called out on strikes; 0 R, 1 H, 0 E, 1 LOB. NL 3, AL 4.

AL 5TH: **F.Howard batted for J.Palmer;** F.Howard grounded out (G.Beckert-2b to L.May-1b); R.Carew walked; B.Murcer struck out; C.Yastrzemski grounded out (G.Beckert-2b to L.May-1b); 0 R, 0 H, 0 E, 1 LOB. NL 3, AL 4.

NL 6TH: **H.Killebrew replaced N.Cash (playing 1b); C.Rojas replaced R.Carew (playing 2b); A.Otis replaced F.Howard (playing cf); A.Kaline replaced F.Robinson (playing rf); M.Cuellar replaced B.Murcer (pitching);** L.May walked; J.Torre grounded into a double play (B.Robinson-3b to C.Rojas-2b to H.Killebrew-1b) [L.May out at second]; W.Stargell struck out; 0 R, 0 H, 0 E, 0 LOB. NL 3, AL 4.

AL 6TH: **D.Kessinger replaced J.Marichal (playing ss); F.Jenkins replaced B.Harrelson (pitching);** A.Kaline singled to center field; H.Killebrew homered to deep leftfield [A.Kaline scored]; B.Robinson singled to center field; B.Freehan flied to W.Davis-cf; L.Aparicio grounded into a double play (G.Beckert-2b to D.Kessinger-ss to L.May-1b) [B.Robinson out at second]; 2 R, 3 H, 0 E, 0 LOB. NL 3, AL 6.

NL 7TH: D.Kessinger flied to A.Kaline-rf; J.Bench singled to left field; G.Beckert popped to L.Aparicio-ss; **N.Colbert batted for F.Jenkins;** N.Colbert struck out; 0 R, 1 H, 0 E, 1 LOB. NL 3, AL 6.

AL 7TH: **D.Wilson replaced N.Colbert (pitching);** A.Otis flied to W.Stargell-lf; C.Rojas flied to R.Clemente-rf; **D.Buford batted for M.Cuellar;** D.Buford struck out; 0 R, 0 H, 0 E, 0 LOB. NL 3, AL 6.

NL 8TH: **M.Lolich replaced D.Buford (pitching); T.Munson replaced B.Freehan (playing c); B.Bonds batted for W.Davis;** B.Bonds struck out; R.Clemente homered to very deep right-center; L.May grounded out (M.Lolich-p to H.Killebrew-1b); **R.Santo batted for J.Torre;** R.Santo grounded out (M.Lolich-p to H.Killebrew-1b); 1 R, 1 H, 0 E, 0 LOB. NL 4, AL 6.

AL 8TH: **B.Bonds stayed in game (playing cf); R.Santo stayed in game (playing 3b); P.Rose replaced G.Beckert (playing rf); F.Millan replaced R.Clemente (playing 2b);** C.Yastrzemski walked; A.Kaline struck out; H.Killebrew grounded into a double play (R.Santo-3b to F.Millan-2b to L.May-1b) [C.Yastrzemski out at second]; 0 R, 0 H, 0 E, 0 LOB. NL 4, AL 6.

NL 9TH: **L.Brock batted for W.Stargell;** On a bunt L.Brock grounded out (M.Lolich-p to H.Killebrew-1b); D.Kessinger flied to A.Kaline-rf;

J.Bench popped to B.Robinson-3b; 0 R, 0 H, 0 E, 0 LOB. NL 4, AL 6.

Final Totals	R	H	E	LOB
National League	4	5	0	2
American League	6	7	0	2

GAME **43**

Tuesday, July 25, 1972

Atlanta Stadium, Atlanta

National League 4, American League 3

(10 innings)

SERIES RESULTS: NL 24, AL 18, 1 TIE

Another Overtime Win for the NL

In the days leading up to the 1972 All-Star Game in Atlanta, there was a great deal of speculation about the chance of a new home run record being set in the contest. Atlanta Stadium, as it was still known then before later becoming Atlanta–Fulton County Stadium, had gained the nickname of "The Launching Pad" since it opened in 1966, and everyone was ready for at least seven homers to be hit, surpassing the record of six, which has been accomplished three times, including in 1971 in Detroit. However, only two balls went over the wall, and the expected Battle of Atlanta was instead a relatively tame 4–3 National League win in ten innings. Perhaps the threatening weather contributed to the low offense because storm clouds forced the cancellation of batting practice.

One of the home runs came from Henry Aaron of the host Braves, who hit his second All-Star home run in as many years, setting off tumultuous cheering from his home fans. The press box denizens were rewarded with "Oh, Henry" candy bars, distributed after each Aaron home run by the Ward Candy Company. At the time, Aaron was fifty-five homers behind Babe Ruth's career record. The other homer came from a very unlikely source: second baseman Cookie Rojas of the Royals, who was pinch-hitting for Minnesota's Rod Carew. Rojas, who had thirty-nine career homers at the time, did not expect to play, since AL manager Earl Weaver of the Orioles was concerned about running out of players and planned to keep Cookie in reserve. However, Carew's sore rib cage acted up, and Rojas got his chance.

Once again, the starting lineups were selected by vote of the fans, with Johnny Bench of the Reds leading all players with more than 1.2 million votes. Dick Allen of the White Sox was the top vote getter in the AL by a small margin over Brooks Robinson of the Orioles. *The Sporting News* conducted its own poll of players, managers, and coaches, following the procedure that was in place from 1958 to 1969. The results differed from the fan poll in five of the sixteen starting positions (pitchers were not included in either procedure), but there was clear sentiment that the fans' view should prevail. The biggest difference was in the votes received by Boston's Carl Yastrzemski. Yaz placed second in the fan poll, trailing only Reggie Jackson of Oakland among outfielders, but tenth in the player/manager/coach voting, gathering only 8 of a possible 233 votes. At the time of the game, he was batting .304 but had hit no home runs, easily the lowest power production of his career. He would end the season with twelve round-trippers and a .264 batting average.

There was a last-minute change in the NL starting lineup because Roberto Clemente of the Pirates informed manager Danny Murtaugh, formerly of the Pirates, that his nagging knee and ankle injuries were bad enough that he could not play that night. As a result, Willie Mays of the Mets started for the eighteenth time in All-Star competition, a record that still stands. Murtaugh, who led the Pirates to their World Series victory over the Orioles in 1971, had retired during the winter due to poor health but came out of retirement for the game in Atlanta.

There was an interesting controversy involving the starting pitchers for the contest. Bob Gibson of the Cardinals expressed his preference for starting his team's next regular season game in Montreal, scheduled for two days later, rather than pitch in Atlanta. Gibson, who had a record of 11-5 and was seventh in the NL with an ERA of 2.49, did start the Atlanta game at Murtaugh's request. His scheduled start in Montreal was pushed back one day, and he pitched a complete game in a 3–1 loss. For the American League, Mickey Lolich of the Tigers was compiling a fine season, with a mark of 17-6 and an ERA of 2.35, also good for seventh in his league. This was the second straight year that a pitcher came to the All-Star break with seventeen wins, Vida Blue of Oakland having turned the trick the year before. Lolich was upset when manager Weaver announced that his choice to start for the AL was his own Jim Palmer, who was at 13-4 with an ERA of 1.92, second best in the league. Mickey said he would not appear if he did not start, but he later relented and in fact followed Palmer as the second pitcher for the AL.

The offense was minimal at the start of the game, and the two teams combined for a total of five hits through the first five innings. Reggie Jackson had a double and a single, but the other AL hit, a single by Carew in the third, drove in the lone tally of these five frames. That hit scored Bill Freehan of the Tigers, who had walked and been sacrificed to second by Palmer as the AL scored a run in a very atypical manner for an Earl Weaver–managed team. The pitchers who were throwing this blanket over the hitters were Palmer and Lolich for the AL and Gibson, Steve Blass of the Pirates, and Don Sutton of the Dodgers for the NL. Blass, who had pitched 8.2 innings two days earlier, yielded the third-inning run.

The NL got on the board in the sixth after the Phillies' Steve Carlton pitched a scoreless top of the inning. Gaylord Perry of the Indians, who was having an excellent first season in the AL, leading the league in ERA at 1.73 and holding a 16-8 win-loss record, was treated badly by his former NL mates. With two outs, Cesar Cedeno of the Astros, the leading batter in the majors at .355, singled to left field, setting the stage for Aaron's dramatic homer on Perry's first pitch. After the game, Aaron insisted that he had hit a spitter, but Perry issued his usual denial of having added any foreign substance to the ball. Neither team scored in the seventh as Perry allowed a single in his final inning, and the Expos' Bill Stoneman retired the AL in order. Stoneman's second inning was the eighth, and he allowed a single to Carlton Fisk of the Red Sox and, with two outs, was reached by Rojas for a two-run homer that gave the Americans a one-run lead. Wilbur Wood of the White Sox came on for the bottom of the eighth and allowed only a walk and a stolen base, to Joe Morgan of the Reds.

Tug McGraw of the Mets took over on the mound for the NL in the ninth and notched three strikeouts, sandwiched around a double by Joe Rudi of the A's. In the bottom of the ninth, the NL tied the score on two singles and a force out. The Cubs' Billy Williams led off with a single, and the Pirates' Manny Sanguillen bounced a hit into center field, sending Williams to third. With no outs, Weaver ordered the AL infield to play back and try for the double play. The Astros' Lee May hit a

Freehan sliding into Bench at home, 1972
Bill Freehan scores on Rod Carew's hit in the third inning. Johnny Bench is the catcher, and pitcher Steve Blass backs up the play. Associated Press Photo.

ground ball to Orioles shortstop Bobby Grich, but the AL was able to get only the force on Sanguillen as Williams scored to tie the game. Ron Santo of the Cubs followed with a grounder to Oakland third baseman Sal Bando, who started an inning-ending double play. After the game, Weaver defended his decision by saying that giving up a run while getting a double play would have given his team the best chance of staying tied. As it turned out, the damage was limited to one run. Said Earl, "We got out of it pretty good."

McGraw, who would become the winning pitcher, turned in a perfect tenth, recording his fourth strikeout in the two innings he pitched. Dave McNally of the Orioles pitched the bottom of the tenth and took the loss. Batting for McGraw, Nate Colbert of the Padres walked on a full count. Chris Speier of the Giants sacrificed him to second, and Morgan lined a 2-2 slider into right-center field, easily scoring Colbert for the win. This was the seventh extra-inning game in the series, all of which the NL rather amazingly had won. Morgan was voted the Most Valuable Player of the game, although Aaron received serious consideration as well.

The victory was the second for Murtaugh, who piloted the NL in both of the 1961 games. His charges won the first game that year, also in ten innings, and the second contest was the only tie. One other interesting feature of the game was the different philosophies about pitching staffs shown by the two managers, who as usual made all of the selections for the mound corps. Weaver was very traditional, choosing only starting pitchers, while Murtaugh picked two relievers, McGraw and the Reds' Clay Carroll, who did not see action.

	AL			NL	
P	Jim Palmer		BAL	Bob Gibson	SLN
C	Bill Freehan		DET	Johnny Bench	CIN
1B	Dick Allen		CHA	Lee May	HOU
2B	Rod Carew		MIN	Joe Morgan	CIN
3B	Brooks Robinson		BAL	Joe Torre	SLN
SS	Luis Aparicio	+	BOS	Don Kessinger	CHN
OF	Reggie Jackson		OAK	Hank Aaron	ATL
OF	Bobby Murcer		NYA	Roberto Clemente	PIT
OF	Carl Yastrzemski		BOS	Willie Stargell	PIT
	Sal Bando		OAK	Glenn Beckert	CHN
	Bert Campaneris		OAK	Steve Blass	PIT
	Norm Cash		DET	Lou Brock	SLN
	Joe Coleman	+	DET	Steve Carlton	PHI
	Pat Dobson		BAL	Clay Carroll	CIN
	Carlton Fisk		BOS	Cesar Cedeno	HOU
	Bobby Grich		BAL	Nate Colbert	SDN
	Toby Harrah	+	TEX	Ferguson Jenkins	CHN
	Ken Holtzman		OAK	Willie Mays	NYN
	Catfish Hunter		OAK	Tug McGraw	NYN
	Mickey Lolich		DET	Gary Nolan +	CIN
	Carlos May		CHA	Al Oliver	PIT
	Dave McNally		BAL	Manny Sanguillen	PIT
	Amos Otis		KCA	Ron Santo	CHN
	Freddie Patek	+	KCA	Tom Seaver	NYN
	Gaylord Perry		CLE	Ted Simmons	SLN
	Lou Piniella		KCA	Chris Speier	SFN
	Ellie Rodriguez		MIL	Bill Stoneman	MON
	Cookie Rojas		KCA	Don Sutton	LAN
	Joe Rudi		OAK	Billy Williams	CHN
	Nolan Ryan		CAL		
	Richie Scheinblum		KCA		
	Reggie Smith		BOS		
	Wilbur Wood		CHA		

+ player replaced on roster

American League   001 000 020 0- 3
National League   000 002 001 1- 4 (10)
  1 out when winning run was scored.

AMERICAN LEAGUE

	ab	r	h	bi	bb	so	po	a
R.Carew, 2b	2	0	1	1	1	0	2	3
C.Rojas, ph-2b	1	1	1	2	0	0	3	1
B.Murcer, cf	3	0	0	0	0	0	1	0
R.Scheinblum, rf	1	0	0	0	0	0	1	0
R.Jackson, rf-cf	4	0	2	0	0	1	5	0
D.Allen, 1b	3	0	0	0	0	0	4	0
N.Cash, 1b	1	0	0	0	0	1	3	0
C.Yastrzemski, lf	3	0	0	0	0	1	3	0
J.Rudi, lf	1	0	1	0	0	0	0	0
B.Grich, ss	4	0	0	0	0	2	0	3
B.Robinson, 3b	2	0	0	0	0	0	0	1
S.Bando, 3b	2	0	0	0	0	0	1	1
B.Freehan, c	1	1	0	0	1	0	3	0
C.Fisk, c	2	1	1	0	0	1	2	0
J.Palmer, p	0	0	0	0	0	0	0	0
M.Lolich, p	1	0	0	0	0	1	0	0
G.Perry, p	0	0	0	0	0	0	0	0
R.Smith, ph	1	0	0	0	0	1	0	0
W.Wood, p	0	0	0	0	0	0	0	0
L.Piniella, ph	1	0	0	0	0	0	0	0
D.McNally, p	0	0	0	0	0	0	0	1
Totals	33	3	6	3	2	8	28	10

BATTING
2B: R.Jackson (off B.Gibson); J.Rudi (off T.McGraw).
HR: C.Rojas (8th inning off B.Stoneman, 1 on, 2 out).
2-out RBI: C.Rojas 2.
RBI, scoring position, less than 2 outs: R.Carew 1–1.
S: J.Palmer.
GDP: B.Murcer.

BASERUNNING
Team LOB: 3

FIELDING
DP: (2). R.Carew-D.Allen; S.Bando-C.Rojas-N.Cash.

NATIONAL LEAGUE

	ab	r	h	bi	bb	so	po	a
J.Morgan, 2b	4	0	1	1	1	0	3	5
W.Mays, cf	2	0	0	0	0	1	2	0
C.Cedeno, cf	2	1	1	0	0	1	0	0
H.Aaron, rf	3	1	1	2	0	1	0	0
A.Oliver, rf	1	0	0	0	0	0	0	0
W.Stargell, lf	1	0	0	0	1	0	0	0
B.Williams, lf	2	1	1	0	0	0	0	0
J.Bench, c	2	0	1	0	0	0	3	0
M.Sanguillen, c	2	0	1	0	0	0	6	0
L.May, 1b	4	0	1	1	0	0	13	2
J.Torre, 3b	3	0	1	0	0	1	1	2
R.Santo, 3b	1	0	0	0	0	0	0	0
D.Kessinger, ss	2	0	0	0	0	0	0	0
S.Carlton, p	0	0	0	0	0	0	0	0
B.Stoneman, p	1	0	0	0	0	1	0	0
T.McGraw, p	0	0	0	0	0	0	0	0
N.Colbert, ph	0	1	0	0	1	0	0	0
B.Gibson, p	0	0	0	0	0	0	1	0
S.Blass, p	0	0	0	0	0	0	0	0
G.Beckert, ph	1	0	0	0	0	0	0	0
D.Sutton, p	0	0	0	0	0	0	0	0
C.Speier, ss	2	0	0	0	0	0	1	5
Totals	33	4	8	4	3	5	30	14

BATTING
HR: H.Aaron (6th inning off G.Perry, 1 on, 2 out).
2-out RBI: H.Aaron 2.
RBI, scoring position, less than 2 outs: J.Morgan 1–1;
  C.Cedeno 0–1; L.May 1–1.
S: C.Speier.
GDP: J.Bench; R.Santo.

BASERUNNING
SB: J.Morgan (2nd base off W.Wood/C.Fisk).
Team LOB: 5

FIELDING
DP: (2). L.May, unassisted; L.May-C.Speier-L.May.

PITCHING	ip	h	r	er	bb	so
American League						
J.Palmer	3.0	1	0	0	1	2
M.Lolich	2.0	1	0	0	0	1
G.Perry (BS)	2.0	3	2	2	0	1

Inherited Runners—Scored:
  M.Lolich 0–0; G.Perry 0–0; W.Wood 0–0; D.McNally
  0–0; S.Blass 0–0; D.Sutton 0–0; S.Carlton 0–0;
  B.Stoneman 0–0; T.McGraw 0–0.

PITCHING	ip	h	r	er	bb	so
American League *(continued)*						
W.Wood (BS)	2.0	2	1	1	1	1
D.McNally (L)	0.1	1	1	1	1	0
National League						
B.Gibson	2.0	1	0	0	0	0
S.Blass	1.0	1	1	1	1	0
D.Sutton	2.0	1	0	0	0	2
S.Carlton	1.0	0	0	0	1	0
B.Stoneman (BS)	2.0	2	2	2	0	2
T.McGraw (W)	2.0	1	0	0	0	4

GAME DATA—T: 2:26; A: 53107; Temp: Unknown; Wind: Unknown direction, Speed: Unknown

UMPIRES—HP: Stan Landes (NL), 1B: Lou DiMuro (AL), 2B: Lee Weyer (NL), 3B: Jerry Neudecker (AL), LF: Jerry Dale (NL), RF: Bill Kunkel (AL)

STARTING LINEUPS

	American League	National League
1.	R.Carew 2b	J.Morgan 2b
2.	B.Murcer cf	W.Mays cf
3.	R.Jackson rf	H.Aaron rf
4.	D.Allen 1b	W.Stargell lf
5.	C.Yastrzemski lf	J.Bench c
6.	B.Grich ss	L.May 1b
7.	B.Robinson 3b	J.Torre 3b
8.	B.Freehan c	D.Kessinger ss
9.	J.Palmer p	B.Gibson p

AL 1ST: R.Carew grounded out (J.Morgan-2b to B.Gibson-p); B.Murcer popped to J.Bench-c in foul territory; R.Jackson doubled to very deep right-center; D.Allen grounded out (J.Morgan-2b to L.May-1b); 0 R, 1 H, 0 E, 1 LOB. AL 0, NL 0.

NL 1ST: J.Morgan flied to B.Murcer-cf; W.Mays grounded out (B.Robinson-3b to D.Allen-1b); H.Aaron was called out on strikes; 0 R, 0 H, 0 E, 0 LOB. AL 0, NL 0.

AL 2ND: C.Yastrzemski grounded out (J.Morgan-2b to L.May-1b); B.Grich popped to J.Torre-3b in foul territory; B.Robinson grounded out (J.Torre-3b to L.May-1b); 0 R, 0 H, 0 E, 0 LOB. AL 0, NL 0.

NL 2ND: W.Stargell walked; J.Bench grounded into a double play (R.Carew-2b to D.Allen-1b) [W.Stargell out at second]; L.May singled to left field; J.Torre struck out; 0 R, 1 H, 0 E, 1 LOB. AL 0, NL 0.

AL 3RD: **S.Blass replaced B.Gibson (pitching);** B.Freehan walked; J.Palmer out on a sacrifice bunt (L.May-1b to J.Morgan-2b) [B.Freehan to second]; R.Carew singled to center field [B.Freehan scored]; B.Murcer lined into a double play (L.May-1b unassisted) [R.Carew out at first]; 1 R, 1 H, 0 E, 0 LOB. AL 1, NL 0.

NL 3RD: D.Kessinger flied to C.Yastrzemski-lf; **G.Beckert batted for S.Blass;** G.Beckert flied to R.Jackson-rf; J.Morgan flied to C.Yastrzemski-lf; 0 R, 0 H, 0 E, 0 LOB. AL 1, NL 0.

AL 4TH: **D.Sutton replaced G.Beckert (pitching);** R.Jackson singled to right field; D.Allen forced R.Jackson (J.Torre-3b to J.Morgan-2b) [D.Allen to first]; C.Yastrzemski flied to W.Mays-cf; B.Grich struck out; 0 R, 1 H, 0 E, 1 LOB. AL 1, NL 0.

NL 4TH: **M.Lolich replaced J.Palmer (pitching);** W.Mays was called out on strikes; H.Aaron flied to R.Jackson-rf; W.Stargell popped to R.Jackson-rf; 0 R, 0 H, 0 E, 0 LOB. AL 1, NL 0.

AL 5TH: B.Robinson popped to J.Morgan-2b; B.Freehan flied to W.Mays-cf; M.Lolich was called out on strikes; 0 R, 0 H, 0 E, 0 LOB. AL 1, NL 0.

NL 5TH: **S.Bando replaced B.Robinson (playing 3b);** J.Bench singled to left field; L.May flied to

C.Yastrzemski-lf; J.Torre popped to D.Allen-1b in foul territory; D.Kessinger forced J.Bench (B.Grich-ss to R.Carew-2b) [D.Kessinger to first]; 0 R, 1 H, 0 E, 1 LOB. AL 1, NL 0.

AL 6TH: **C.Cedeno replaced W.Mays (playing cf); B.Williams replaced W.Stargell (playing lf); C.Speier replaced D.Sutton (playing ss); M.Sanguillen replaced J.Bench (playing c); S.Carlton replaced D.Kessinger (pitching);** R.Carew walked; B.Murcer grounded into a double play (L.May-1b to C.Speier-ss to L.May-1b) [R.Carew out at second]; R.Jackson grounded out (J.Morgan-2b to L.May-1b); 0 R, 0 H, 0 E, 0 LOB. AL 1, NL 0.

NL 6TH: **R.Jackson changed positions (playing cf); R.Scheinblum replaced B.Murcer (playing rf); C.Fisk replaced B.Freehan (playing c); G.Perry replaced M.Lolich (pitching);** C.Speier flied to R.Scheinblum-rf; J.Morgan grounded out (R.Carew-2b to D.Allen-1b); C.Cedeno singled to left field; H.Aaron homered to very deep left-center [C.Cedeno scored]; B.Williams flied to R.Jackson-cf; 2 R, 2 H, 0 E, 0 LOB. AL 1, NL 2.

AL 7TH: **B.Stoneman replaced S.Carlton (pitching);** D.Allen grounded out (C.Speier-ss to L.May-1b); C.Yastrzemski struck out; B.Grich grounded out (C.Speier-ss to L.May-1b); 0 R, 0 H, 0 E, 0 LOB. AL 1, NL 2.

NL 7TH: **N.Cash replaced D.Allen (playing 1b); J.Rudi replaced C.Yastrzemski (playing lf);** M.Sanguillen grounded out (R.Carew-2b to N.Cash-1b); L.May flied to R.Jackson-cf; J.Torre singled to left field; B.Stoneman was called out on strikes; 0 R, 1 H, 0 E, 1 LOB. AL 1, NL 2.

AL 8TH: **R.Santo replaced J.Torre (playing 3b); A.Oliver replaced H.Aaron (playing rf);** S.Bando grounded out (J.Morgan-2b to L.May-1b); C.Fisk singled to left field; **R.Smith batted for G.Perry;** R.Smith struck out; **C.Rojas batted for R.Carew;** C.Rojas homered to deep leftfield [C.Fisk scored]; R.Scheinblum grounded out (L.May-1b unassisted); 2 R, 2 H, 0 E, 0 LOB. AL 3, NL 2.

NL 8TH: **C.Rojas stayed in game (playing 2b); W.Wood replaced R.Smith (pitching);** C.Speier grounded out (B.Grich-ss to N.Cash-1b); J.Morgan walked; J.Morgan stole second; C.Cedeno struck out; A.Oliver popped to S.Bando-3b; 0 R, 0 H, 0 E, 1 LOB. AL 3, NL 2.

AL 9TH: **T.McGraw replaced B.Stoneman (pitching);** R.Jackson struck out; N.Cash was called out on strikes; J.Rudi doubled to right field; B.Grich struck out; 0 R, 1 H, 0 E, 1 LOB. AL 3, NL 2.

NL 9TH: B.Williams singled to center field; M.Sanguillen singled to center field [B.Williams to third]; L.May forced M.Sanguillen (B.Grich-ss to C.Rojas-2b) [B.Williams scored, L.May to first]; R.Santo grounded into a double play (S.Bando-3b to C.Rojas-2b to N.Cash-1b) [L.May out at second]; 1 R, 2 H, 0 E, 0 LOB. AL 3, NL 3.

AL 10TH: S.Bando grounded out (C.Speier-ss to L.May-1b); C.Fisk struck out; **L.Piniella batted for W.Wood;** L.Piniella grounded out (C.Speier-ss to L.May-1b); 0 R, 0 H, 0 E, 0 LOB. AL 3, NL 3.

NL 10TH: **D.McNally replaced L.Piniella (pitching); N.Colbert batted for T.McGraw;** N.Colbert walked; C.Speier out on a sacrifice bunt (D.McNally-p to C.Rojas-2b) [N.Colbert to second]; J.Morgan singled to right-center [N.Colbert scored]; 1 R, 1 H, 0 E, 1 LOB. AL 3, NL 4.

Final Totals	R	H	E	LOB
American League	3	6	0	3
National League	4	8	0	5

44

NL Power Does the Job

The 1973 All-Star Game, held in brand-new Royals Stadium, marked the fortieth anniversary of the first meeting between the elite of the two leagues in Chicago in 1933. As part of the celebration, all of the surviving members of that first game were invited to the festivities, and twenty of them attended. The ceremonial first balls were tossed out by three men simultaneously: Lefty Gomez and Bill Hallahan, the AL and NL starting pitchers in 1933, respectively, and Ewing Kauffman, owner of the 1973 host team. The new park was a great enjoyment to the fans with its huge animated scoreboard and fountains putting on a colorful show. However, the action on the field wasn't so much fun for the home crowd as the NL won handily 7–1.

There was some disagreement with the starting lineups chosen by the fans, especially the fact that Bobby Bonds of the Giants came in fourth in the balloting for NL outfielders behind the Reds' Pete Rose, the Cubs' Billy Williams, and the Astros' Cesar Cedeno. Bonds was having an excellent season, including twenty-five homers, twenty-eight stolen bases, and an average of .308 at the time of the break. He would finish the year with thirty-nine homers and forty-three steals, leaving him just short of the 40-40 mark, which was finally reached by Jose Canseco of the A's in 1988. Sparky Anderson, the Cincinnati manager who was in charge of the NL team, said simply, "He's the best player in baseball today." Sparky got Bonds into the game in the fourth inning as a replacement for Williams, as soon as the starters had played their mandatory three innings. This turned out to be an excellent move because Bonds would end up winning the Most Valuable Player Award for the game. American League manager Dick Williams of the A's didn't have lineup controversies, but he did have some personal concerns because he had undergone surgery for an emergency appendectomy only five days earlier.

Unfortunately, another health concern marred the game. AL starter Catfish Hunter of the A's was struck by a line drive off the bat of Williams in the second inning. The ball went for a single, but more importantly the Oakland ace suffered a hairline fracture of the thumb on his right (pitching) hand. The first four National Leaguers had gone down in order before the injury. Ken Holtzman, Hunter's Oakland teammate, finished the inning, allowing another single but no runs. Hunter, who came into the game with a record of 15-3, did not play again until August 19, missing five or six starts. He was effective upon his return, finishing at 21-5 with an ERA of 3.34, good enough for third in the AL Cy Young Award voting behind Baltimore's Jim Palmer and California's Nolan Ryan.

The American League offense was meager and got even weaker as the game went on. It collected five hits for the night, but four of them came in the first four innings. However, two of these were back-to-back hits leading off the second inning against NL starter Rick Wise of the Cardinals. Reggie Jackson of the A's opened with a booming double off the center-field fence and scored when Amos Otis of the hometown Royals hit a ball off the glove of second baseman Joe Morgan of the Reds. The ball rolled into short center field, and Jackson scored the first run of the game, which was the only one the AL would get. Wise then retired the side on three fly balls and ended up as the winning pitcher when the NL took the lead in the third and never gave it up. Dodger Claude Osteen yielded a single to Otis and a triple to Buddy Bell of the Indians in his pair of innings following Wise. Bell's triple led off the third, but Osteen bore down, striking out Bert Campaneris of the A's and then coaxing two ground balls, wrapped around a walk, to get out of trouble. Five subsequent NL hurlers allowed only one more safety, a double by John Mayberry of the Royals in the sixth inning off Wayne Twitchell of the Phillies. By this time, the score had reached 7–1, the advantage that ultimately became the final margin.

The American League also used seven pitchers,

Bench swinging, 1973

Johnny Bench follows through on his third inning home run off Bill Singer. Carlton Fisk is the catcher.
© *Bettmann*/CORBIS.

with the combined total of fourteen setting the All-Star mark. Of the fourteen, none worked more than two innings, the first time in All-Star history that no pitcher had at least three innings pitched. The NL put the game away with a methodical attack from the third through the sixth, scoring in each inning to reach its total of seven runs. The pitching victims for the AL were Bert Blyleven of the Twins and Angels teammates Bill Singer and Nolan Ryan. This trio allowed the seven runs in four innings on six hits and five walks, although Singer and Ryan did record two strikeouts apiece in their two innings. The hard-throwing right-handers came into the game with solid first-half accomplishments. Singer had fifteen wins, and Ryan had already thrown two no-hitters on his way to a 21-16 mark and the all-time single-season record of 383 strikeouts.

Blyleven pitched only the third but was touched for two runs on two walks and two singles. There could have been even more scoring, but Cedeno was out when he overslid third while trying to advance from corner to corner on a run-scoring single by Atlanta's Henry Aaron. Singer pitched the

fourth and fifth, allowing three runs, including a home run by Johnny Bench of the Reds, the first batter he faced. In the fifth, Morgan doubled into the left-field corner to start the inning. With two outs, Bonds got his first at bat and homered to left-center to bring the score to 5–1. Ryan gave up the last two runs on a sixth-inning, pinch-hit home run from the Dodgers' Willie Davis, who was wearing Aaron's batting helmet because none of the Dodgers remembered to bring his to the game. Davis planned to keep the headgear as a souvenir. The NL gathered two more hits, a seventh-inning double by Bonds and an eighth-inning line drive single by Davis, the latter coming at the expense of Sparky Lyle of the Yankees. The double by Bonds was a routine single to left-center that the fleet Giant stretched into a two-bagger, just beating the throw from Bobby Murcer of the Yankees. This hustling play brought an appreciative cheer from the Kansas City crowd, even though the outcome of the game was no longer in doubt.

A hot topic of discussion after the game in both clubhouses was Singer's pitching. Although he did not have an effective night, both teams were convinced that he was throwing a lot of doctored pitches. Pete Rose claimed that he saw four straight spitballs in the fourth inning before grounding out. One of the pitches got past catcher Carlton Fisk of the Red Sox for a passed ball. Said Fisk, "He really loaded one, and the ball went all the way back to the screen. Rose looked at me and I said to him, 'He surprised me more than he did you.' " No response from Singer was reported.

A number of records were set and tied in the 1973 game. Willie Mays of the Mets played in his twenty-fourth and final game, tying the mark set by Stan Musial. Mays also played on the winning side for the seventeenth time, and the Orioles' Brooks Robinson set the dubious mark of appearing for the losing side for the fourteenth time. The teams combined to use a record fifty-four players,

twenty-eight by the National League. The only stars who simply watched the entire proceedings were Jack Billingham of the Reds, Bill Lee of the Red Sox, Jim Colborn of the Brewers, and Bill Freehan of the Tigers. Singer and the Braves' Davey Johnson became the twelfth and thirteenth players to appear for both leagues in the All-Star Game. Singer had played for the NL in 1969, when he was a Dodger, and Johnson had played for the AL in 1968 and 1970, while a member of the Orioles. Although it did not set a record, the win made NL manager Sparky Anderson one of the happiest men in Kansas City that day. Anderson had been the losing skipper in the World Series in 1970 and 1972 as well as in the 1971 All-Star Game. He called the win "the biggest thrill I've had in baseball."

	AL		NL	
P	Catfish Hunter	OAK	Rick Wise	SLN
C	Carlton Fisk	BOS	Johnny Bench	CIN
1B	Dick Allen	+ CHA	Hank Aaron	ATL
2B	Rod Carew	MIN	Joe Morgan	CIN
3B	Brooks Robinson	BAL	Ron Santo	CHN
SS	Bert Campaneris	OAK	Chris Speier	SFN
OF	Reggie Jackson	OAK	Cesar Cedeno	HOU
OF	Bobby Murcer	NYA	Pete Rose	CIN
OF	Amos Otis	KCA	Billy Williams	CHN
	Sal Bando	OAK	Jack Billingham	CIN
	Buddy Bell	CLE	Bobby Bonds	SFN
	Paul Blair	BAL	Jim Brewer	LAN
	Bert Blyleven	MIN	Nate Colbert	SDN
	Ed Brinkman	DET	Dave Concepcion +	CIN
	Jim Colborn	MIL	Willie Davis	LAN
	Rollie Fingers	OAK	Darrell Evans	ATL
	Bill Freehan	DET	Ron Fairly	MON
	Ken Holtzman	OAK	Dave Giusti	PIT
	Willie Horton	DET	Dave Johnson	ATL
	Pat Kelly	CHA	Willie Mays	NYN
	Bill Lee	BOS	Manny Mota	LAN
	Sparky Lyle	NYA	Claude Osteen	LAN
	Dave May	MIL	Bill Russell	LAN
	John Mayberry	KCA	Tom Seaver	NYN
	Thurman Munson	NYA	Ted Simmons	SLN
	Dave Nelson	TEX	Willie Stargell	PIT
	Cookie Rojas	KCA	Don Sutton	LAN
	Nolan Ryan	CAL	Joe Torre	SLN
	Bill Singer	CAL	Wayne Twitchell	PHI
	Jim Spencer	TEX	Bob Watson	HOU
	Carl Yastrzemski +	BOS		

+ player replaced on roster

RETROSHEET EXPANDED BOX SCORE Tuesday, 7/24/1973 National League at American League (N)

National League	002	122	000-	7			
American League	010	000	000-	1			

NATIONAL LEAGUE

	ab	r	h	bi	bb	so	po	a
P.Rose, lf	3	1	0	0	1	0	1	0
W.Twitchell, p	0	0	0	0	0	0	0	0
D.Giusti, p	0	0	0	0	0	0	0	0
M.Mota, ph-lf	1	0	0	0	0	0	0	0
J.Brewer, p	0	0	0	0	0	0	0	0
J.Morgan, 2b	3	2	1	0	1	0	2	2
D.Johnson, 2b	1	0	0	0	0	0	1	1
C.Cedeno, cf	3	0	1	1	0	2	3	0
B.Russell, ss	2	0	0	0	0	0	0	2
H.Aaron, 1b	2	0	1	1	0	0	3	1
J.Torre, 1b-3b	3	0	0	0	0	0	5	0
B.Williams, rf	2	0	1	0	0	0	0	0
B.Bonds, rf	2	1	2	2	0	0	0	0
J.Bench, c	3	1	1	1	0	0	3	0
T.Simmons, ph-c	1	0	0	0	0	1	1	1
R.Santo, 3b	1	1	1	0	2	0	0	1
N.Colbert, ph	1	0	0	0	0	0	0	0
R.Fairly, 1b	0	0	0	0	0	0	4	0
C.Speier, ss	2	0	0	0	0	1	1	1
W.Stargell, ph-lf	1	0	0	0	0	1	1	0
W.Mays, ph	1	0	0	0	0	1	0	0
T.Seaver, p	0	0	0	0	0	0	0	1
B.Watson, lf	0	0	0	0	0	0	0	0
R.Wise, p	0	0	0	0	0	0	1	0
D.Evans, ph	0	0	0	0	1	0	0	0
C.Osteen, p	0	0	0	0	0	0	0	1
D.Sutton, p	0	0	0	0	0	0	0	1
W.Davis, ph-cf	2	1	2	2	0	0	1	0
Totals	34	7	10	7	5	6	27	12

BATTING
2B: J.Morgan (off B.Singer); B.Bonds (off N.Ryan).
HR: B.Bonds (5th inning off B.Singer, 1 on, 2 out);
J.Bench (4th inning off B.Singer, 0 on, 0 out);
W.Davis (6th inning off N.Ryan, 1 on, 1 out).
2-out RBI: B.Bonds 2.
RBI, scoring position, less than 2 outs: C.Cedeno 1–2;
H.Aaron 1–1; J.Torre 0–1.
S: C.Osteen.
GDP: J.Morgan.

BASERUNNING
Team LOB: 6

AMERICAN LEAGUE

	ab	r	h	bi	bb	so	po	a
B.Campaneris, ss	3	0	0	0	0	2	1	2
E.Brinkman, ss	1	0	0	0	0	0	1	1
R.Carew, 2b	3	0	0	0	0	0	5	1
C.Rojas, 2b	0	0	0	0	1	0	1	1
J.Mayberry, 1b	3	0	1	0	1	0	8	0
R.Jackson, rf	4	1	1	0	0	1	0	0
P.Blair, cf	0	0	0	0	0	0	1	0
A.Otis, cf	2	0	2	1	0	0	0	0
D.May, cf-rf	2	0	0	0	0	0	0	0
B.Murcer, lf	3	0	0	0	1	0	0	1
C.Fisk, c	2	0	0	0	0	0	3	0
T.Munson, c	2	0	0	0	0	1	5	1
B.Robinson, 3b	2	0	0	0	0	0	1	3
S.Bando, 3b	1	0	0	0	0	0	0	1
D.Nelson, 3b	0	0	0	0	0	0	1	0
W.Horton, ph	1	0	0	0	0	1	0	0
J.Hunter, p	0	0	0	0	0	0	0	0
K.Holtzman, p	0	0	0	0	0	0	0	0
B.Blyleven, p	0	0	0	0	0	0	0	0
B.Bell, ph	1	0	1	0	0	0	0	0
B.Singer, p	0	0	0	0	0	0	0	1
P.Kelly, ph	1	0	0	0	0	0	0	0
N.Ryan, p	0	0	0	0	0	0	0	0
J.Spencer, ph	1	0	0	0	0	0	0	0
S.Lyle, p	0	0	0	0	0	0	0	0
R.Fingers, p	0	0	0	0	0	0	0	0
Totals	32	1	5	1	3	5	27	12

BATTING
2B: R.Jackson (off R.Wise); J.Mayberry (off W.Twitchell).
3B: B.Bell (off C.Osteen).
RBI, scoring position, less than 2 outs: B.Campaneris
0–1; R.Carew 0–1; R.Jackson 0–1; A.Otis 1–1; D.May
0–1; C.Fisk 0–1.

BASERUNNING
SB: A.Otis (2nd base off C.Osteen/J.Bench).
Team LOB: 7

FIELDING
PB: C.Fisk.
Outfield assist: B.Murcer (C.Cedeno at 3B).
DP: (1). C.Rojas-E.Brinkman-J.Mayberry.

PITCHING	ip	h	r	er	bb	so
National League						
R.Wise (w)	2.0	2	1	1	0	1
C.Osteen	2.0	2	0	0	1	1
D.Sutton	1.0	0	0	0	0	0
W.Twitchell	1.0	1	0	0	0	1
D.Giusti	1.0	0	0	0	0	0
T.Seaver	1.0	0	0	0	1	0
J.Brewer (s)	1.0	0	0	0	1	2
American League						
J.Hunter	1.1	1	0	0	0	1
K.Holtzman	0.2	1	0	0	0	0
B.Blyleven (L)	1.0	2	2	2	2	0
B.Singer	2.0	3	3	3	1	2
N.Ryan	2.0	2	2	2	2	2
S.Lyle	1.0	1	0	0	0	1
R.Fingers	1.0	0	0	0	0	0

Inherited Runners—Scored:
C.Osteen 0–0; D.Sutton 0–0; W.Twitchell 0–0; D.Giusti 0–0; T.Seaver 0–0; J.Brewer 0–0; K.Holtzman 1–0; B.Blyleven 0–0; B.Singer 0–0; N.Ryan 0–0; S.Lyle 0–0; R.Fingers 0–0.

GAME DATA—T: 2:45; A: 40849; Temp: Unknown; Wind: Unknown direction, Speed: Unknown

UMPIRES—HP: Nestor Chylak (AL), 1B: Ken Burkhart (NL), 2B: Larry Barnett (AL), 3B: Bill Williams (NL), LF: Ron Luciano (AL), RF: Bob Engel (NL)

STARTING LINEUPS

	National League	*American League*
1.	P.Rose lf	B.Campaneris ss
2.	J.Morgan 2b	R.Carew 2b
3.	C.Cedeno cf	J.Mayberry 1b
4.	H.Aaron 1b	R.Jackson rf
5.	B.Williams rf	A.Otis cf
6.	J.Bench c	B.Murcer lf
7.	R.Santo 3b	C.Fisk c
8.	C.Speier ss	B.Robinson 3b
9.	R.Wise p	J.Hunter p
	R.Wise p	J.Hunter p

NL 1ST: P.Rose grounded out (R.Carew-2b to J.Mayberry-1b); J.Morgan popped to R.Carew-2b; C.Cedeno struck out; 0 R, 0 H, 0 E, 0 LOB. NL 0, AL 0.

AL 1ST: B.Campaneris was called out on strikes; R.Carew grounded out (C.Speier-ss to H.Aaron-1b); J.Mayberry grounded out (H.Aaron-1b to R.Wise-p); 0 R, 0 H, 0 E, 0 LOB. NL 0, AL 0.

NL 2ND: H.Aaron popped to B.Campaneris-ss; B.Williams singled to pitcher; ball hit Hunter's hand; **K.Holtzman replaced J.Hunter (pitching)**; J.Bench forced B.Williams (B.Robinson-3b to R.Carew-2b) [J.Bench to first]; R.Santo singled to left field [J.Bench to second]; C.Speier forced R.Santo (B.Robinson-3b to R.Carew-2b) [C.Speier to first]; 0 R, 2 H, 0 E, 2 LOB. NL 0, AL 0.

AL 2ND: R.Jackson doubled to center field; A.Otis singled to second base [R.Jackson scored]; B.Murcer lined to C.Cedeno-cf; C.Fisk flied to P.Rose-lf; B.Robinson flied to C.Cedeno-cf; 1 R, 2 H, 0 E, 1 LOB. NL 0, AL 1.

NL 3RD: **B.Blyleven replaced K.Holtzman (pitching)**; **D.Evans batted for R.Wise**; D.Evans walked; P.Rose forced D.Evans (B.Campaneris-ss to R.Carew-2b) [P.Rose to first]; J.Morgan walked [P.Rose to second]; C.Cedeno singled to center field [P.Rose scored, J.Morgan to third]; H.Aaron singled to left field (B.Murcer-lf to B.Robinson-3b) [J.Morgan scored, C.Cedeno out at third]; B.Williams grounded out (J.Mayberry-1b unassisted); 2 R, 2 H, 0 E, 1 LOB. NL 2, AL 1.

AL 3RD: **C.Osteen replaced D.Evans (pitching)**; **B.Bell batted for B.Blyleven**; B.Bell tripled to very deep right-center; B.Campaneris struck out; R.Carew grounded out (J.Morgan-2b to H.Aaron-1b); J.Mayberry walked; R.Jackson grounded out (J.Morgan-2b to H.Aaron-1b); 0 R, 1 H, 0 E, 2 LOB. NL 2, AL 1.

NL 4TH: **B.Singer replaced B.Bell (pitching)**; J.Bench homered to deep leftfield; R.Santo walked; C.Speier was called out on strikes; C.Osteen out on a sacrifice bunt (B.Singer-p to R.Carew-2b)

[R.Santo to second]; C.Fisk allowed a passed ball [R.Santo to third]; P.Rose grounded out (B.Robinson-3b to J.Mayberry-1b); 1 R, 1 H, 0 E, 1 LOB. NL 3, AL 1.

AL 4TH: **J.Torre replaced H.Aaron (playing 1b)**; **B.Bonds replaced B.Williams (playing rf)**; A.Otis singled to left field; B.Murcer popped to J.Morgan-2b; A.Otis stole second; C.Fisk lined to C.Cedeno-cf; B.Robinson grounded out (C.Osteen-p to J.Torre-1b); 0 R, 1 H, 0 E, 1 LOB. NL 3, AL 1.

NL 5TH: **D.May replaced A.Otis (playing cf)**; **S.Bando replaced B.Robinson (playing 3b)**; J.Morgan doubled to left field; C.Cedeno struck out; J.Torre popped to J.Mayberry-1b; B.Bonds homered to very deep left-center [J.Morgan scored]; J.Bench grounded out (B.Campaneris-ss to J.Mayberry-1b); 2 R, 2 H, 0 E, 0 LOB. NL 5, AL 1.

AL 5TH: **D.Sutton replaced C.Osteen (pitching)**; **P.Kelly batted for B.Singer**; P.Kelly popped to C.Speier-ss; B.Campaneris grounded out (R.Santo-3b to J.Torre-1b); R.Carew grounded out (D.Sutton-p to J.Torre-1b); 0 R, 0 H, 0 E, 0 LOB. NL 5, AL 1.

NL 6TH: **E.Brinkman replaced B.Campaneris (playing ss)**; **T.Munson replaced C.Fisk (playing c)**; **C.Rojas replaced R.Carew (playing 2b)**; **N.Ryan replaced P.Kelly (pitching)**; R.Santo walked; **W.Stargell batted for C.Speier**; W.Stargell struck out; **W.Davis batted for D.Sutton**; W.Davis homered to deep rightfield [R.Santo scored]; P.Rose walked; J.Morgan grounded into a double play (C.Rojas-2b to E.Brinkman-ss to J.Mayberry-1b) [P.Rose out at second]; 2 R, 1 H, 0 E, 0 LOB. NL 7, AL 1.

AL 6TH: **W.Davis stayed in game (playing cf)**; **W.Stargell stayed in game (playing lf)**; **W.Twitchell replaced P.Rose (pitching)**; **B.Russell replaced C.Cedeno (playing ss)**; J.Mayberry doubled to right-center; R.Jackson struck out; D.May popped to J.Morgan-2b; B.Murcer grounded out (B.Russell-ss to J.Torre-1b); 0 R, 1 H, 0 E, 1 LOB. NL 7, AL 1.

NL 7TH: B.Russell grounded out (S.Bando-3b to J.Mayberry-1b); J.Torre grounded out (T.Munson-c to J.Mayberry-1b); checked swing; B.Bonds doubled to left-center; **T.Simmons batted for J.Bench**; T.Simmons was called out on strikes; 0 R, 1 H, 0 E, 1 LOB. NL 7, AL 1.

AL 7TH: **T.Simmons stayed in game (playing c)**; **D.Giusti replaced W.Twitchell (pitching)**; T.Munson popped to J.Torre-1b; S.Bando lined to W.Davis-cf; **J.Spencer batted for N.Ryan**; J.Spencer flied to W.Stargell-lf; 0 R, 0 H, 0 E, 0 LOB. NL 7, AL 1.

NL 8TH: **D.Nelson replaced S.Bando (playing 3b); S.Lyle replaced J.Spencer (pitching); N.Colbert batted for R.Santo;** N.Colbert popped to D.Nelson-3b in foul territory; **W.Mays batted for W.Stargell;** W.Mays struck out; W.Davis singled to right field; **M.Mota batted for D.Giusti;** M.Mota forced W.Davis (C.Rojas-2b unassisted) [M.Mota to first]; 0 R, 1 H, 0 E, 1 LOB. NL 7, AL 1.

AL 8TH: **M.Mota stayed in game (playing lf); J.Torre changed positions (playing 3b); D.Johnson replaced J.Morgan (playing 2b); R.Fairly replaced N.Colbert (playing 1b); T.Seaver replaced W.Mays (pitching);** E.Brinkman grounded out (B.Russell-ss to R.Fairly-1b); C.Rojas walked; J.Mayberry grounded out (D.Johnson-2b to R.Fairly-1b) [C.Rojas to second]; R.Jackson grounded out (T.Seaver-p to R.Fairly-1b); 0 R, 0 H, 0 E, 1 LOB. NL 7, AL 1.

NL 9TH: **D.May changed positions (playing rf); R.Fingers replaced S.Lyle (pitching); P.Blair replaced R.Jackson (playing cf);** D.Johnson popped to T.Munson-c in foul territory; B.Russell lined to P.Blair-cf; J.Torre popped to T.Munson-c; 0 R, 0 H, 0 E, 0 LOB. NL 7, AL 1.

AL 9TH: **B.Watson replaced T.Seaver (playing lf); J.Brewer replaced M.Mota (pitching);** D.May popped to D.Johnson-2b; B.Murcer walked; T.Munson struck out; **W.Horton batted for D.Nelson;** W.Horton struck out (T.Simmons-c to R.Fairly-1b); 0 R, 0 H, 0 E, 1 LOB. NL 7, AL 1.

Final Totals	R	H	E	LOB
National League	7	10	0	6
American League	1	5	0	7

45

Tuesday, July 23, 1974

Three Rivers Stadium, Pittsburgh

National League 7, American League 2

SERIES RESULTS: NL 26, AL 18, 1 TIE

AL Bats Muffled Again

Lee MacPhail, the new president of the American League in 1974, was embarrassed that his league had won only six of the previous twenty-eight All-Star Games. He very much wanted to bring home a win and so took some unusual steps to reverse the AL's fortunes for the contest played in Pittsburgh's Three Rivers Stadium. He instructed each team to have its All-Star pitchers rested before the game and urged manager Dick Williams to use the best players available, regardless of possible hurt feelings on the part of those who did not see action. The AL managers responded to these recommendations from on high, with the result that only three of the selected pitchers had been used on the previous Saturday (the All-Star Game was played on its usual Tuesday) and none (except relievers) had pitched on Sunday. Despite these extraordinary measures, which could conceivably have had an effect on the pennant races, the American Leaguers were soundly beaten once again. They managed only three singles and a double, although they did collect six walks, and could put only two men across the plate. On the other side of the equation, the four AL pitchers, including three well-rested starters, were each scored upon as the National Leaguers collected ten hits, with half of them going for extra bases (three doubles, a triple, and a home run), as they won 7–2.

The fan voting for the starting lineups was an interesting part of the story. First baseman Steve Garvey of the Dodgers was not on the ballot, which was prepared in spring training, because of his limited service in 1973 (only seventy-six games at first base). The Dodger representative at that position on the ballot was Bill Buckner, who had played nearly all of 1974 in left field. However, Garvey was having a solid season as the cleanup hitter for the West Division leaders, ranking among the league leaders in hits, RBI, and home runs, and would win the NL MVP Award at the end of the year. A large public relations campaign mounted in Los An-

geles to get Garvey into the game as a write-in was ultimately successful in the last stages of the voting; Garvey passed Tony Perez of the Reds by a mere twenty-three thousand votes out of the nearly 4 million that were cast. Garvey thereby became the second player named to start via the write-in route; Rico Carty of the Braves was the other in 1970, the first year of the current system. Henry Aaron of the Braves led NL players with 2.6 million votes, while Reggie Jackson of Oakland was the overall top vote getter as the choice on nearly 3.5 million ballots.

The managers were Yogi Berra of the Mets and Dick Williams of the Angels, and therein lie some tales. Berra, who led the Mets to the 1973 World Series, was also the skipper of the 1964 Yankees. However, he had been fired that fall and had become employed as a coach for the Mets by the time of the 1965 game. He was replaced at the AL helm by Al Lopez, manager of the White Sox. The saga of Dick Williams was even more unusual. Manager of the world champion A's in 1973, Williams had a string of disputes with Oakland owner Charlie Finley throughout the season and very publicly during the World Series. Although in midseason he had signed a contract extension running through the 1975 season, following the World Series Williams resigned in a very acrimonious debate that left him in limbo. On July 1, 1974, he replaced Bobby Winkles as manager of the Angels (Whitey Herzog handled the halos for four games while the arrangements were being finalized with Williams). Finley, who still had contractual rights to the services of Williams, gave the necessary permission for his signing by the Angels out of his friendship for California owner Gene Autry. The AL had made plans for Baltimore's Earl Weaver to manage the All-Star team, since his Orioles had won the East Division title in 1973, but the return of Williams as an AL field boss, even though it was barely three weeks before the clash with the NL, made Williams eligible to assume the reins and Weaver became a coach for the game instead.

There was also a bit of melodrama, which had to

do with early replacements made by Williams. The AL manager came under criticism when he removed Rod Carew of the Twins and Dick Allen of the White Sox after two and a half innings, in apparent violation of the requirement that starters play at least three innings, barring injury. Williams's explanation was that Carew had injured himself sliding into second base, and Allen had fouled a pitch off his foot. "I didn't want to mess with anybody else's players. I had one hurt last year," Williams said. That reference was to Catfish Hunter, who had suffered a broken hand in the game at Kansas City. The situations for the two players were quite different. Carew wasn't buying the injury argument, saying that if he couldn't get the playing time he thought he deserved, he would prefer to stay home in the future. Everyone assumed that the real reason for removing Allen was the manager's displeasure that the Chicago slugger did not appear until forty-five minutes before game time, missing the pregame workout. Williams was in the process of revamping his lineup when Allen arrived. When questioned about his tardy arrival, the enigmatic Allen replied: "It's an 8:30 game, isn't it? On time is game time."

After all of these considerations, the game itself was something of an anticlimax. With two outs in the second, the NL drew first blood against Gaylord Perry of the Indians when Garvey singled for the game's initial hit and came around to score on a double to left-center by his Dodger teammate Ron Cey. The lead was short-lived because the AL mounted its only offensive threat of the game in the top of the third against NL starter Andy Messersmith of the Dodgers. Yankee Thurman Munson led off with a double and was sacrificed to third by Perry. Carew walked and stole second as Bert Campaneris of the A's struck out on a 3-2 pitch. Catcher Johnny Bench of the Reds then made a wild throw into center field, allowing Munson to score and sending Campaneris to third. Allen singled Campaneris home, and the inning ended when Garvey made a great stop to his right on a ball hit by Bobby Murcer of the Yankees, Messersmith covering first to record the out.

Hometown Pirate Ken Brett, the new NL pitcher in the fourth, turned in two scoreless innings. He also became the winning pitcher when the National League took the lead for good in the bottom of the fourth against Luis Tiant of the Red Sox. Tiant, who pitched poorly, was deservedly charged with the loss. After Bench opened with a single, Jim Wynn of the Dodgers singled to send the Reds catcher to third. Garvey then tied the game with a double down the left-field line, and Cey plated what proved to be the game winner with a ground ball to Orioles second baseman

Carew stealing second, 1974
Rod Carew slides under Joe Morgan for a steal in the third inning. © Bettmann/CORBIS.

Bobby Grich, who had replaced Carew. Grich singled to start the fifth, but the AL was thwarted when Cesar Cedeno of the Astros made a fine running catch in deep right-center against Campaneris. The inning ended on another fine defensive play, this one in the hole on the right side by Joe Morgan of the Reds against Carl Yastrzemski of the Red Sox. In the bottom of the fifth, the Cardinals' Lou Brock put on a display that led to another run. The St. Louis speedster came into the game with 60 steals on his way to stealing 118, breaking the single-season mark of Maury Wills. He batted for Brett and singled to right field. On the first two pitches to Morgan, Brock faked steal attempts, but on the third pitch he took off. He stole the bag and continued to third when the throw by Munson sailed into center field, reprising Bench's play in the third. Morgan scored Brock with a sacrifice fly.

From here on out, it was all National League as the American League managed only one more hit, a sixth-inning single by Cleveland's George Hendrick against the Mets' Jon Matlack. Lynn McGlothen of the Cardinals and Mike Marshall of the Dodgers finished up the last three innings, with Marshall pitching the last two frames. This was a typical closing performance for Iron Mike, who won the NL Cy Young Award that season, setting records for relief appearances (106) and innings pitched (208) while winning fifteen games. As he turned out the lights on MacPhail's warriors, Marshall had appeared in sixty-six of the ninety-seven games played by the Dodgers. The National League rolled up its last three runs at the expense of a pair of Oakland pitchers, Hunter and Rollie

Fingers. Reggie Smith of the Cardinals homered off Hunter in the seventh, and Fingers allowed the last two tallies in the eighth as the Phillies' Mike Schmidt walked and the Cubs' Don Kessinger tripled. Kessinger scored when Fingers uncorked a wild pitch.

A human interest note came in the seventh when Reggie Smith fouled a pitch and the bat slipped from his hands, striking a woman in the stands behind the NL dugout on the first-base line. Reggie went over to be sure the woman was not seriously hurt, gave her the bat as an apology, then picked a new war club and, with the count at 0-2,

hit the next pitch over the fence for his first All-Star hit.

Many players contributed to the NL win, a balanced effort resulting in several possible choices for the game's Most Valuable Player, but Garvey was selected for the honor. The emotional nature of his election to the team was likely a factor in the choice, including the fact that he nearly did not make it to the game because he had been very ill the previous week. As one press-box wag noted, perhaps what MacPhail had really needed to do to help his team was hide the antibiotics that had cured Garvey.

	AL			NL	
P	Gaylord Perry		CLE	Andy Messersmith	LAN
C	Carlton Fisk	+	BOS	Johnny Bench	CIN
1B	Dick Allen		CHA	Steve Garvey	LAN
2B	Rod Carew		MIN	Joe Morgan	CIN
3B	Brooks Robinson		BAL	Ron Cey	LAN
SS	Bert Campaneris		OAK	Larry Bowa	PHI
OF	Jeff Burroughs		TEX	Hank Aaron	ATL
OF	Reggie Jackson		OAK	Pete Rose	CIN
OF	Bobby Murcer		NYA	Jim Wynn	LAN
	Sal Bando	+	OAK	Ken Brett	PIT
	Steve Busby		KCA	Lou Brock	SLN
	Dave Chalk		CAL	Buzz Capra	ATL
	Mike Cuellar		BAL	Steve Carlton	PHI
	Rollie Fingers		OAK	Dave Cash	PHI
	Bobby Grich		BAL	Cesar Cedeno	HOU
	George Hendrick		CLE	Ralph Garr	ATL
	Ed Herrmann	+	CHA	Jerry Grote	NYN
	John Hiller		DET	John Grubb	SDN
	Catfish Hunter		OAK	Don Kessinger	CHN
	Al Kaline		DET	Mike Marshall	LAN
	John Mayberry		KCA	Jon Matlack	NYN
	Don Money		MIL	Lynn McGlothen	SLN
	Thurman Munson		NYA	Tony Perez	CIN
	Darrell Porter		MIL	Steve Rogers	MON
	Frank Robinson		CAL	Mike Schmidt	PHI
	Cookie Rojas		KCA	Ted Simmons	SLN
	Joe Rudi		OAK	Reggie Smith	SLN
	Jim Sundberg		TEX	Chris Speier	SFN
	Luis Tiant		BOS		
	Wilbur Wood		CHA		
	Carl Yastrzemski		BOS		

+ player replaced on roster

American League	002	000	000-	2
National League	010	210	12X-	7

AMERICAN LEAGUE

	ab	r	h	bi	bb	so	po	a
R.Carew, 2b	1	1	0	0	1	0	0	1
B.Grich, 2b	3	0	1	0	0	0	0	2
B.Campaneris, ss	4	0	0	0	0	2	2	3
R.Jackson, rf	3	0	0	0	1	2	3	0
D.Allen, 1b	2	0	1	1	0	1	2	0
C.Yastrzemski, 1b	1	0	0	0	1	0	5	0
B.Murcer, cf	2	0	0	0	0	0	0	0
G.Hendrick, cf	2	0	1	0	0	0	3	0
J.Burroughs, lf	0	0	0	0	2	0	1	0
J.Rudi, lf	2	0	0	0	0	1	1	0
B.Robinson, 3b	3	0	0	0	0	0	0	0
J.Mayberry, ph	1	0	0	0	0	0	0	0
R.Fingers, p	0	0	0	0	0	0	0	0
T.Munson, c	3	1	1	0	1	0	7	0
G.Perry, p	0	0	0	0	0	0	0	0
A.Kaline, ph	1	0	0	0	0	0	0	0
L.Tiant, p	0	0	0	0	0	0	0	0
F.Robinson, ph	1	0	0	0	0	0	0	0
J.Hunter, p	0	0	0	0	0	0	0	0
D.Chalk, 3b	1	0	0	0	0	1	0	0
Totals	30	2	4	1	6	7	24	6

BATTING
2B: T.Munson (off A.Messersmith).
2-out RBI: D.Allen.
s G.Perry.

BASERUNNING
SB: R.Carew (2nd base off A.Messersmith/J.Bench).
Team LOB: 8

FIELDING
E: T.Munson (throw).

NATIONAL LEAGUE

	ab	r	h	bi	bb	so	po	a
P.Rose, lf	2	0	0	0	0	1	1	0
K.Brett, p	0	0	0	0	0	0	0	0
L.Brock, ph	1	1	1	0	0	0	0	0
R.Smith, rf	2	1	1	1	0	0	2	0
J.Morgan, 2b	2	0	1	1	0	1	3	4
D.Cash, ph-2b	1	0	0	0	0	0	0	1
H.Aaron, rf	2	0	0	0	0	0	0	0
C.Cedeno, cf	2	0	0	0	0	1	2	0
J.Bench, c	3	1	2	0	1	1	7	0
J.Grote, c	0	0	0	0	0	0	1	0
J.Wynn, cf-rf	3	1	1	0	0	0	0	0
J.Matlack, p	0	0	0	0	0	0	0	0
J.Grubb, lf	1	0	0	0	0	0	0	0
S.Garvey, 1b	4	1	2	1	0	1	6	3
R.Cey, 3b	2	0	1	2	0	0	0	0
M.Schmidt, ph-3b	0	1	0	0	2	0	0	1
L.Bowa, ss	2	0	0	0	0	0	2	0
T.Perez, ph	1	0	0	0	0	1	0	0
D.Kessinger, ss	1	1	1	1	0	0	1	0
A.Messersmith, p	0	0	0	0	0	0	2	1
R.Garr, ph-lf	3	0	0	0	0	1	0	0
L.McGlothen, p	0	0	0	0	0	0	0	0
M.Marshall, p	1	0	0	0	0	0	0	0
Totals	33	7	10	6	3	7	27	10

BATTING
2B: R.Cey (off G.Perry); J.Morgan (off G.Perry); S.Garvey (off L.Tiant).
3B: D.Kessinger (off R.Fingers).
HR: R.Smith (7th inning off J.Hunter, 0 on, 0 out).
2-out RBI: R.Cey.
RBI, scoring position, less than 2 outs: J.Morgan 1–1; S.Garvey 1–1; R.Cey 1–2; L.Bowa 0–1.
SF: J.Morgan.

BASERUNNING
SB: L.Brock (2nd base off L.Tiant/T.Munson).
Team LOB: 6

FIELDING
E: J.Bench (throw).

PITCHING	ip	h	r	er	bb	so
American League						
G.Perry	3.0	3	1	1	0	4
L.Tiant (L)	2.0	4	3	2	1	0
J.Hunter	2.0	2	1	1	1	3
R.Fingers	1.0	1	2	2	1	0
National League						
A.Messersmith	3.0	2	2	2	3	4
K.Brett (W)	2.0	1	0	0	1	0
J.Matlac	1.0	1	0	0	1	0
L.McGlothen	1.0	0	0	0	0	1
M.Marshall	2.0	0	0	0	1	2

Inherited Runners—Scored:
L.Tiant 0–0; J.Hunter 0–0; R.Fingers 0–0;
K.Brett 0–0; J.Matlack 0–0; L.McGlothen 0–0;
M.Marshall 0–0.
WP: R.Fingers

GAME DATA—T: 2:37; A: 50706; Temp: Unknown;
Wind: Unknown direction, Speed: Unknown

UMPIRES—HP: Ed Sudol (NL), 1B: Art Frantz (AL), 2B: Ed
Vargo (NL), 3B: Merlyn Anthony (AL), LF: John Kibler
(NL), RF: George Maloney (AL)

STARTING LINEUPS

	American League	*National League*
1.	R.Carew 2b	P.Rose lf
2.	B.Campaneris ss	J.Morgan 2b
3.	R.Jackson rf	H.Aaron rf
4.	D.Allen 1b	J.Bench c
5.	B.Murcer cf	J.Wynn cf
6.	J.Burroughs lf	S.Garvey 1b
7.	B.Robinson 3b	R.Cey 3b
8.	T.Munson c	L.Bowa ss
9.	G.Perry p	A.Messersmith p

AL 1ST: R.Carew grounded out (J.Morgan-2b to S.Garvey-1b); B.Campaneris struck out; R.Jackson struck out; 0 R, 0 H, 0 E, 0 LOB. AL 0, NL 0.

NL 1ST: P.Rose struck out; J.Morgan struck out; H.Aaron flied to J.Burroughs-lf; 0 R, 0 H, 0 E, 0 LOB. AL 0, NL 0.

AL 2ND: D.Allen struck out; B.Murcer grounded out (S.Garvey-1b to A.Messersmith-p); J.Burroughs walked; B.Robinson lined to P.Rose-lf; 0 R, 0 H, 0 E, 1 LOB. AL 0, NL 0.

NL 2ND: J.Bench struck out; J.Wynn grounded out (B.Campaneris-ss to D.Allen-1b); S.Garvey singled to center field; R.Cey doubled to left-center [S.Garvey scored]; L.Bowa grounded out (R.Carew-2b to D.Allen-1b); 1 R, 2 H, 0 E, 1 LOB. AL 0, NL 1.

AL 3RD: T.Munson doubled to left field; G.Perry out on a sacrifice bunt (A.Messersmith-p to J.Morgan-2b) [T.Munson to third]; R.Carew walked; B.Campaneris struck out while R.Carew stole second [R.Carew to third (error by J.Bench-c)]; R.Jackson walked; D.Allen singled to left field [R.Carew scored, R.Jackson to second]; B.Murcer grounded out (S.Garvey-1b to A.Messersmith-p); 1 R, 2 H, 1 E, 2 LOB. AL 2, NL 1.

NL 3RD: **C.Yastrzemski replaced D.Allen (playing 1b); B.Grich replaced R.Carew (playing 2b);** Controversial substitutions: Williams claimed that Carew had hurt himself sliding into second; denied by Carew; **R.Garr batted for A.Messersmith;** R.Garr struck out; P.Rose grounded out (B.Grich-2b to C.Yastrzemski-1b); J.Morgan doubled to right field; ball hit umpire Art Frantz; H.Aaron grounded out (B.Campaneris-ss to C.Yastrzemski-1b); 0 R, 1 H, 0 E, 1 LOB. AL 2, NL 1.

AL 4TH: **R.Garr stayed in game (playing lf); J.Wynn changed positions (playing rf); K.Brett replaced P.Rose (pitching); C.Cedeno replaced H.Aaron (playing cf);** J.Burroughs walked; B.Robinson popped to J.Morgan-2b; T.Munson popped to J.Morgan-2b; **A.Kaline batted for G.Perry;** A.Kaline popped to J.Bench-c in foul territory; 0 R, 0 H, 0 E, 1 LOB. AL 2, NL 1.

NL 4TH: **L.Tiant replaced A.Kaline (pitching); J.Rudi replaced J.Burroughs (playing lf);** J.Bench singled to left field; J.Wynn singled to center field [J.Bench to third]; S.Garvey doubled to left field [J.Bench scored, J.Wynn to third]; R.Cey grounded out (B.Grich-2b to C.Yastrzemski-1b) [J.Wynn scored, S.Garvey to third]; L.Bowa grounded out (B.Campaneris-ss to C.Yastrzemski-1b); R.Garr popped to B.Campaneris-ss in foul territory; 2 R, 3 H, 0 E, 1 LOB. AL 2, NL 3.

AL 5TH: B.Grich singled to right field; B.Campaneris flied to C.Cedeno-cf; R.Jackson forced B.Grich (J.Morgan-2b to L.Bowa-ss) [R.Jackson to first]; C.Yastrzemski grounded out (J.Morgan-2b to S.Garvey-1b); 0 R, 1 H, 0 E, 1 LOB. AL 2, NL 3.

NL 5TH: **G.Hendrick replaced B.Murcer (playing cf); L.Brock batted for K.Brett;** L.Brock singled to right field; L.Brock stole second [L.Brock to third (error by T.Munson-c)]; J.Morgan lined out on a sacrifice fly to G.Hendrick-cf [L.Brock scored (unearned)]; C.Cedeno flied to G.Hendrick-cf; J.Bench walked; J.Wynn lined to R.Jackson-rf; 1 R (0 ER), 1 H, 1 E, 1 LOB. AL 2, NL 4.

AL 6TH: **J.Matlack replaced J.Wynn (pitching); R.Smith replaced L.Brock (playing rf);** G.Hendrick singled to center field; J.Rudi flied to R.Smith-rf; B.Robinson flied to C.Cedeno-cf; T.Munson walked [G.Hendrick to second]; **F.Robinson batted for L.Tiant;** F.Robinson forced T.Munson (J.Morgan-2b to L.Bowa-ss) [F.Robinson to first]; 0 R, 1 H, 0 E, 2 LOB. AL 2, NL 4.

NL 6TH: **J.Hunter replaced F.Robinson (pitching);** S.Garvey struck out; **M.Schmidt batted for R.Cey;** M.Schmidt walked; **T.Perez batted for L.Bowa;** T.Perez struck out; R.Garr grounded out (C.Yastrzemski-1b unassisted); 0 R, 0 H, 0 E, 1 LOB. AL 2, NL 4.

AL 7TH: **M.Schmidt stayed in game (playing 3b); D.Kessinger replaced T.Perez (playing ss); J.Grubb replaced J.Matlack (playing lf); L.McGlothen replaced R.Garr (pitching);** B.Grich grounded out (M.Schmidt-3b to S.Garvey-1b); B.Campaneris flied to R.Smith-rf; R.Jackson was called out on strikes; 0 R, 0 H, 0 E, 0 LOB. AL 2, NL 4.

NL 7TH: R.Smith homered to deep rightfield; **D.Cash batted for J.Morgan;** D.Cash flied to G.Hendrick-cf; C.Cedeno struck out; J.Bench singled to left field; J.Grubb popped to B.Campaneris-ss; 1 R, 2 H, 0 E, 1 LOB. AL 2, NL 5.

AL 8TH: **D.Cash stayed in game (playing 2b); M.Marshall replaced L.McGlothen (pitching);** C.Yastrzemski walked; G.Hendrick forced C.Yastrzemski (S.Garvey-1b to D.Kessinger-ss) [G.Hendrick to first]; J.Rudi struck out; **J.May-**

berry batted for B.Robinson; J.Mayberry grounded out (S.Garvey-1b unassisted); 0 R, 0 H, 0 E, 1 LOB. AL 2, NL 5.

NL 8TH: **R.Fingers replaced J.Mayberry (pitching); D.Chalk replaced J.Hunter (playing 3b);** S.Garvey flied to J.Rudi-lf in foul territory; M.Schmidt walked; D.Kessinger tripled to very deep right-center [M.Schmidt scored]; R.Fingers threw a wild pitch [D.Kessinger scored]; M.Marshall lined to R.Jackson-rf; R.Smith flied to R.Jackson-rf; 2 R, 1 H, 0 E, 0 LOB. AL 2, NL 7.

AL 9TH: **J.Grote replaced J.Bench (playing c);** T.Munson grounded out (D.Cash-2b to S.Garvey-1b); D.Chalk struck out; B.Grich grounded out (S.Garvey-1b unassisted); 0 R, 0 H, 0 E, 0 LOB. AL 2, NL 7.

Final Totals	R	H	E	LOB
American League	2	4	1	8
National League	7	10	1	6

46

Tuesday, July 15, 1975

County Stadium, Milwaukee

National League 6, American League 3

SERIES RESULTS: NL 27, AL 18, 1 TIE

Late Rally Gives the NL Another Win

In 1975, the All-Star Game returned to County Stadium in Milwaukee, where it had been played twenty years earlier. In the previous contest, the stadium had been the home of the National League's Braves, but now it was the venue of the American League's Brewers. Major League Baseball made a connection to the earlier days by naming Hall of Famers Mickey Mantle of the Yankees and Stan Musial of the Cardinals as honorary captains. For Musial, it was an especially nice return, since he had homered in the twelfth inning to win the game for the NL in 1955.

During the buildup to the game, much discussion prevailed about the recent dominance of the NL, which had won eleven of the previous twelve games. The word *embarrassment* was heard frequently, and the AL teams were encouraged to have their best pitchers rested and ready for All-Star duty, although no team was expected to compromise its regular season pitching rotations just to achieve that goal. The embarrassment concern was reversed from the early years of the series, when the American League had overwhelming success, jumping to a 12-4 lead following the 1949 slugfest in Brooklyn's Ebbets Field. However, 1975 was not to be the year the AL would right the ship, as the NL won an exciting 6–3 contest with three runs in the top of the ninth.

The biggest ovation of the night came during pregame introductions, going to Henry Aaron of the Brewers, who had returned to his first Major League city that season following his long career with the Milwaukee and Atlanta Braves. Aaron made his twenty-fourth and final All-Star appearance, tying him with Willie Mays and Stan Musial for the all-time record for games played. He lined out to short as a pinch hitter in the second inning. There was one other dignitary at the game as well: Secretary of State Henry Kissinger, who was the guest of Baseball Commissioner Bowie Kuhn. Kis-

singer threw out the ceremonial first ball and also confessed to being a Yankees fan.

The game had lots of action, with twenty-three base hits (including a double and three home runs), four stolen bases, two caught stealings, two batters hit by pitches, two errors, a balk, and a passed ball. There was only one base on balls, and no double plays were turned. Although they ended up on the short end of the score, the American Leaguers attacked consistently throughout the game. The only inning in which they had no one reach base was the ninth.

Oakland manager Alvin Dark, skipper of the AL by virtue of the Athletics' 1974 AL championship, chose his own ace Vida Blue to start the game. Vida would compile a mark of 22-11 in 1975 with an ERA of 3.01, and his record at the time of the game in Milwaukee was 12-7 with an ERA of 3.15. However, the NL treated the hard-throwing left-hander roughly, touching him for five hits and two runs in the two innings he pitched. Pete Rose of the Reds led off for the NL with a single and, with one out, was thrown out trying to go from first to third on the single of his teammate Joe Morgan. In the second, a trio of Dodgers started the inning with hits, the first two of which were home runs by Steve Garvey and Jim Wynn; Ron Cey followed with a single. Steve Busby of the Royals took the mound for the AL to start the third and gave up a single to Lou Brock, the only NL starter (except for the pitcher) who was not a member of either the Reds or the Dodgers. Brock's presence at first base upset Busby, who balked him to second. From there, Brock stole third base and scored on a single by the Reds' Johnny Bench.

Jim Kaat of the White Sox relieved to begin the fifth and turned in two perfect innings, retiring the number two through number seven batters with little trouble. The Yankees' Catfish Hunter came on to pitch the seventh and allowed only a harmless single to Rose in his first two innings. However, in the ninth inning, the NL mounted its winning rally. Reggie Smith of the Cardinals was credited with a single on a ball that Claudell Washington of the A's could not reach in left-center. Pinch hitter Al Oliver of the Pirates doubled into the left-field corner, sending Smith to third and ending the evening for Hunter. Rich Gossage of the White Sox, the replacement hurler, promptly hit Larry Bowa of the Phillies to load the bases. The Cubs' Bill Madlock grounded a single down the third base line, scoring Smith and Oliver. Bowa went to third on the play, and Madlock took second when the throw home from left fielder Washington got past Oakland catcher Gene Tenace for an error on the receiver. Rose scored Bowa with a sacrifice fly, but the NL was stopped when the side was retired on two ground balls.

The American Leaguers had a frustrating start as they collected six hits, had one batter hit by a pitch, and saw another reach base on an error in the first five innings. However, they could move none of their eight runners across the plate, leaving seven stranded and watching the fourth inning end when Bert Campaneris of the A's was picked off first on a strong throw from catcher Bench with runners at the corners. The escape artists on the mound for the NL during this time were starter Jerry Reuss of the Pirates and Don Sutton of the Dodgers. The American League broke through to score all of its runs on one swing of the bat in the sixth inning against Mets ace Tom Seaver. Tom Terrific would compile a record of 22-9 with a 2.38 ERA in 1975 (he had a 13-5 mark and a 1.93 ERA at the time of the All-Star meeting), but this was not his night. Joe Rudi of the A's singled, and Tenace walked. With one out, Carl Yastrzemski of the Red Sox pinch-hit for Kaat and hit the first pitch into the right-field bullpen to tie the score. Seaver was replaced on the mound by his New York teammate Jon Matlack to start the following inning. Matlack had much more success in his two rounds, allowing one single in each, one of them an infield hit by George Hendrick of the Indians that second baseman Dave Cash of the Phillies could not get out of his glove. Matlack struck out four batters and helped his own cause in the seventh inning by picking Washington off first base on a play that went as a caught stealing. In the ninth, Randy Jones earned a save as he dispatched the AL in order on a ground ball, strikeout, and fly ball; Matlack received credit for the win.

For the only time in All-Star history, the Most Valuable Player Award for the game was divided between two players: Bill Madlock and Jon Matlack. Both made significant contributions to the NL win, but at least one wag noted that the similarity of their names may have contributed to the tie vote.

	AL		NL	
P	Vida Blue	OAK	Jerry Reuss	PIT
C	Thurman Munson	NYA	Johnny Bench	CIN
1B	Gene Tenace	OAK	Steve Garvey	LAN
2B	Rod Carew	MIN	Joe Morgan	CIN
3B	Graig Nettles	NYA	Ron Cey	LAN
SS	Bert Campaneris	OAK	Dave Concepcion	CIN
OF	Bobby Bonds	NYA	Lou Brock	SLN
OF	Reggie Jackson	OAK	Pete Rose	CIN
OF	Joe Rudi	OAK	Jim Wynn	LAN
	Hank Aaron	MIL	Larry Bowa	PHI
	Steve Busby	KCA	Gary Carter	MON
	Dave Chalk	CAL	Dave Cash	PHI
	Bucky Dent	CHA	Randy Jones	SDN
	Rollie Fingers	OAK	Greg Luzinski	PHI
	Bill Freehan	DET	Bill Madlock	CHN
	Rich Gossage	CHA	Mike Marshall	LAN
	Mike Hargrove	TEX	Jon Matlack	NYN
	Toby Harrah	TEX	Tug McGraw	PHI
	George Hendrick	CLE	Andy Messersmith	LAN
	Catfish Hunter	NYA	Bobby Murcer	SFN
	Jim Kaat	CHA	Phil Niekro	ATL
	Fred Lynn	BOS	Al Oliver	PIT
	Hal McRae	KCA	Tony Perez	CIN
	Jorge Orta +	CHA	Manny Sanguillen	PIT
	Jim Palmer	BAL	Tom Seaver	NYN
	Nolan Ryan	CAL	Reggie Smith	SLN
	George Scott	MIL	Don Sutton	LAN
	Claudell Washington	OAK	Bob Watson	HOU
	Carl Yastrzemski	BOS		

+ player replaced on roster

National League   021 000 003- 6
American League   000 003 000- 3

NATIONAL LEAGUE

	ab	r	h	bi	bb	so	po	a
P.Rose, rf-lf	4	0	2	1	0	0	4	0
G.Carter, lf	0	0	0	0	0	0	1	0
L.Brock, lf	3	1	1	0	0	0	2	0
B.Murcer, rf	2	0	0	0	0	0	1	0
R.Jones, p	0	0	0	0	0	0	0	1
J.Morgan, 2b	4	0	1	0	0	0	0	1
D.Cash, 2b	1	0	0	0	0	0	0	0
J.Bench, c	4	0	1	1	0	0	10	1
S.Garvey, 1b	3	1	2	1	0	0	4	1
T.Perez, ph-1b	1	0	0	0	0	1	1	0
J.Wynn, cf	2	1	1	1	0	0	1	0
R.Smith, cf-rf	2	1	1	0	0	0	0	0
R.Cey, 3b	3	0	1	0	0	0	0	1
T.Seaver, p	0	0	0	0	0	0	0	0
J.Matlack, p	0	0	0	0	0	0	0	2
A.Oliver, ph-cf	1	1	1	0	0	0	0	0
D.Concepcion, ss	2	0	1	0	0	1	1	1
G.Luzinski, ph	1	0	0	0	0	1	0	0
L.Bowa, ss	0	1	0	0	0	0	2	0
J.Reuss, p	1	0	0	0	0	0	0	0
B.Watson, ph	1	0	0	0	0	0	0	0
D.Sutton, p	0	0	0	0	0	0	0	0
B.Madlock, 3b	2	0	1	2	0	0	0	0
Totals	37	6	13	6	0	3	27	8

BATTING
2B: A.Oliver (off J.Hunter).
HR: S.Garvey (2nd inning off V.Blue, 0 on, 0 out);
J.Wynn (2nd inning off V.Blue, 0 on, 0 out).
RBI, scoring position, less than 2 outs: P.Rose 1–2;
B.Murcer 0–1; J.Morgan 0–1; J.Bench 1–1; J.Wynn
0–1; B.Madlock 2–2.
SF: P.Rose.

BASERUNNING
SB: L.Brock (3rd base off S.Busby/T.Munson).
CS: D.Concepcion (2nd base by S.Busby/T.Munson).
Team LOB: 6

FIELDING
E: D.Concepcion (fumble).
PB: J.Bench.

AMERICAN LEAGUE

	ab	r	h	bi	bb	so	po	a
B.Bonds, cf	3	0	0	0	0	1	0	1
G.Scott, 1b	2	0	0	0	0	2	5	0
R.Carew, 2b	5	0	1	0	0	1	3	1
T.Munson, c	2	0	1	0	0	0	1	1
C.Washington, pr-cf-lf	1	0	1	0	0	0	1	0
R.Jackson, rf	3	0	1	0	0	2	2	0
B.Dent, ss	1	0	0	0	0	1	0	1
J.Rudi, lf	3	0	1	0	0	0	5	0
G.Hendrick, pr-rf	1	1	1	0	0	0	0	0
G.Nettles, 3b	4	0	1	0	0	1	2	2
G.Tenace, 1b-c	3	1	0	0	1	1	4	0
B.Campaneris, ss	2	0	2	0	0	0	3	2
F.Lynn, ph-cf	2	0	0	0	0	1	1	0
V.Blue, p	0	0	0	0	0	0	0	1
H.Aaron, ph	1	0	0	0	0	0	0	0
S.Busby, p	0	0	0	0	0	0	0	0
M.Hargrove, ph	1	0	0	0	0	0	0	0
J.Kaat, p	0	0	0	0	0	0	0	0
C.Yastrzemski, ph	1	1	1	3	0	0	0	0
J.Hunter, p	0	0	0	0	0	0	0	0
R.Gossage, p	0	0	0	0	0	0	0	0
H.McRae, ph	1	0	0	0	0	0	0	0
Totals	36	3	10	3	1	10	27	9

BATTING
HR: C.Yastrzemski (6th inning off T.Seaver, 2 on, 2 out).
2-out RBI: C.Yastrzemski 3.
RBI, scoring position, less than 2 outs: G.Nettles 0–1;
F.Lynn 0–1; M.Hargrove 0–1.

BASERUNNING
SB: C.Washington (2nd base off D.Sutton/J.Bench);
G.Hendrick (2nd base off T.Seaver/J.Bench);
G.Nettles (2nd base off J.Matlack/J.Bench).
CS: C.Washington (2nd base by J.Matlack/J.Bench).
Team LOB: 8

FIELDING
E: G.Tenace.
Outfield assist: B.Bonds (P.Rose at 3B).

PITCHING	ip	h	r	er	bb	so
National League						
J.Reuss	3.0	3	0	0	0	2
D.Sutton	2.0	3	0	0	0	1
T.Seaver	1.0	2	3	3	1	2

Inherited Runners—Scored:
D.Sutton 0–0; T.Seaver 0–0; J.Matlack 0–0;
R.Jones 0–0; S.Busby 0–0; J.Kaat 0–0; J.Hunter 0–0;
R.Gossage 2–2.

PITCHING	ip	h	r	er	bb	so
National League *(continued)*						
J.Matlack (w)	2.0	2	0	0	0	4
R.Jones (s)	1.0	0	0	0	0	1
American League						
V.Blue	2.0	5	2	2	0	1
S.Busby	2.0	4	1	1	0	0
J.Kaat	2.0	0	0	0	0	0
J.Hunter (L) *	2.0	3	2	2	0	2
R.Gossage	1.0	1	1	1	0	0

* Pitched to 2 batters in 9th

HBP: T.Munson by J.Reuss; L.Bowa by R.Gossage.
BK: S.Busby

GAME DATA—T: 3:35; A: 51480; Temp: Unknown;
Wind: Unknown direction, Speed: Unknown

UMPIRES—HP: Bill Haller (AL), 1B: Chris Pelekoudas
(NL), 2B: Marty Springstead (AL), 3B: Bruce Froemming
(NL), LF: Russ Goetz (AL), RF: John McSherry (NL)

STARTING LINEUPS

	National League	American League
1.	P.Rose rf	B.Bonds cf
2.	L.Brock lf	R.Carew 2b
3.	J.Morgan 2b	T.Munson c
4.	J.Bench c	R.Jackson rf
5.	S.Garvey 1b	J.Rudi lf
6.	J.Wynn cf	G.Nettles 3b
7.	R.Cey 3b	G.Tenace 1b
8.	D.Concepcion ss	B.Campaneris ss
9.	J.Reuss p	V.Blue p
	J.Reuss p	V.Blue p

NL 1ST: P.Rose singled to center field; L.Brock lined to J.Rudi-lf; J.Morgan singled to center field (B.Bonds-cf to G.Nettles-3b) [P.Rose out at third, J.Morgan to second (on throw)]; J.Bench popped to B.Campaneris-ss in foul territory; 0 R, 2 H, 0 E, 1 LOB. NL 0, AL 0.

AL 1ST: B.Bonds lined to P.Rose-rf; R.Carew lined to L.Brock-lf; T.Munson was hit by a pitch; R.Jackson was called out on strikes; 0 R, 0 H, 0 E, 1 LOB. NL 0, AL 0.

NL 2ND: S.Garvey homered to deep leftfield; J.Wynn homered to deep leftfield; R.Cey singled to left field; D.Concepcion was called out on strikes; On a bunt J.Reuss forced R.Cey (V.Blue-p to B.Campaneris-ss) [J.Reuss to first]; P.Rose flied to R.Jackson-rf; 2 R, 3 H, 0 E, 1 LOB. NL 2, AL 0.

AL 2ND: J.Rudi grounded out (R.Cey-3b to S.Garvey-1b); G.Nettles flied to P.Rose-rf; G.Tenace reached on an error by D.Concepcion-ss [G.Tenace to first]; B.Campaneris singled to right field [G.Tenace to second]; **H.Aaron batted for V.Blue;** Aaron's 24th AS Game, tying Mays/Musial record; H.Aaron lined to D.Concepcion-ss; 0 R, 1 H, 1 E, 2 LOB. NL 2, AL 0.

NL 3RD: **S.Busby replaced H.Aaron (pitching);** L.Brock singled to left-center; S.Busby balked [L.Brock to second]; J.Morgan popped to G.Tenace-1b in foul territory; L.Brock stole third; J.Bench singled to right field [L.Brock scored]; S.Garvey singled to left field [J.Bench to second]; J.Wynn forced S.Garvey (B.Campaneris-ss to R.Carew-2b) [J.Bench to third, J.Wynn to first]; R.Cey lined to J.Rudi-lf; 1 R, 3 H, 0 E, 2 LOB. NL 3, AL 0.

AL 3RD: B.Bonds struck out; R.Carew singled to center field; T.Munson flied to J.Wynn-cf; R.Jackson singled to shortstop [R.Carew to second]; J.Rudi grounded out (D.Concepcion-ss to S.Garvey-1b); 0 R, 2 H, 0 E, 2 LOB. NL 3, AL 0.

NL 4TH: D.Concepcion singled to left field; **B.Watson batted for J.Reuss;** D.Concepcion was caught stealing second (T.Munson-c to R.Carew-2b);

B.Watson flied to J.Rudi-lf; P.Rose lined to B.Campaneris-ss; 0 R, 1 H, 0 E, 0 LOB. NL 3, AL 0.

AL 4TH: **D.Sutton replaced B.Watson (pitching);** G.Nettles singled to right field; G.Tenace flied to L.Brock-lf; B.Campaneris singled to pitcher [G.Nettles to second]; **M.Hargrove batted for S.Busby;** M.Hargrove flied to P.Rose-rf [G.Nettles to third]; B.Campaneris was picked off first (J.Bench-c to S.Garvey-1b); 0 R, 2 H, 0 E, 1 LOB. NL 3, AL 0.

NL 5TH: **J.Kaat replaced M.Hargrove (pitching);** L.Brock grounded out (B.Campaneris-ss to G.Tenace-1b); J.Morgan popped to G.Nettles-3b in foul territory; J.Bench lined to J.Rudi-lf; 0 H, 0 E, 0 LOB. NL 3, AL 0.

AL 5TH: **P.Rose changed positions (playing lf); B.Murcer replaced L.Brock (playing rf); R.Smith replaced J.Wynn (playing cf);** B.Bonds lined to P.Rose-lf; R.Carew grounded out (J.Morgan-2b to S.Garvey-1b); T.Munson singled to left field; **C.Washington ran for T.Munson;** C.Washington stole second; R.Jackson was called out on strikes; 0 R, 1 H, 0 E, 1 LOB. NL 3, AL 0.

NL 6TH: **C.Washington stayed in game (playing cf); G.Tenace changed positions (playing c); G.Scott replaced B.Bonds (playing 1b);** S.Garvey flied to R.Jackson-rf; R.Smith flied to J.Rudi-lf; R.Cey grounded out (G.Nettles-3b to G.Scott-1b); 0 R, 0 H, 0 E, 0 LOB. NL 3, AL 0.

AL 6TH: **B.Madlock replaced D.Sutton (playing 3b); T.Seaver replaced R.Cey (pitching);** J.Rudi singled to left field; **G.Hendrick ran for J.Rudi;** G.Hendrick stole second; G.Nettles struck out; G.Tenace walked; **F.Lynn batted for B.Campaneris;** F.Lynn flied to B.Murcer-rf; **C.Yastrzemski batted for J.Kaat;** C.Yastrzemski homered to very deep right-center [G.Hendrick scored, G.Tenace scored]; G.Scott struck out; 3 R, 2 H, 0 E, 0 LOB. NL 3, AL 3.

NL 7TH: **F.Lynn stayed in game (playing cf); G.Hendrick stayed in game (playing rf); C.Washington changed positions (playing lf); J.Hunter replaced C.Yastrzemski (pitching); B.Dent replaced R.Jackson (playing ss); G.Luzinski batted for D.Concepcion;** G.Luzinski struck out; B.Madlock flied to F.Lynn-cf; P.Rose singled to center field; B.Murcer grounded out (G.Nettles-3b to G.Scott-1b); 0 R, 1 H, 0 E, 1 LOB. NL 3, AL 3.

AL 7TH: **L.Bowa replaced G.Luzinski (playing ss); J.Matlack replaced T.Seaver (pitching);** R.Carew struck out; C.Washington singled to center field; C.Washington was picked off and caught stealing second (J.Matlack-p to S.Garvey-1b to L.Bowa-ss); B.Dent struck out; 0 R, 1 H, 0 E, 0 LOB. NL 3, AL 3.

NL 8TH: J.Morgan popped to R.Carew-2b; J.Bench popped to G.Scott-1b; **T.Perez batted for S.Garvey;** T.Perez was called out on strikes; 0 R, 0 H, 0 E, 0 LOB. NL 3, AL 3.

AL 8TH: **T.Perez stayed in game (playing 1b); D.Cash replaced J.Morgan (playing 2b);** G.Hendrick singled to second base; G.Nettles forced G.Hendrick (J.Matlack-p to L.Bowa-ss) [G.Nettles to first]; G.Tenace struck out; G.Nettles stole second [G.Nettles to third (on passed ball by J.Bench)]; F.Lynn struck out; 0 R, 1 H, 0 E, 1 LOB. NL 3, AL 3.

NL 9TH: R.Smith singled to left field; **A.Oliver batted for J.Matlack;** A.Oliver doubled to left field [R.Smith to third]; **R.Gossage replaced J.Hunter (pitching);** L.Bowa was hit by a pitch; B.Madlock singled to left field [R.Smith scored, A.Oliver scored, L.Bowa to third, B.Madlock to second (error by G.Tenace-c)]; P.Rose out on a sacrifice fly to C.Washington-lf [L.Bowa scored, B.Madlock to third]; B.Murcer grounded out (R.Carew-2b to G.Scott-1b); D.Cash grounded out (B.Dent-ss to G.Scott-1b); 3 R, 3 H, 1 E, 1 LOB. NL 6, AL 3.

AL 9TH: **A.Oliver stayed in game (playing cf); R.Smith changed positions (playing rf); G.Carter replaced P.Rose (playing lf); R.Jones replaced B.Murcer (pitching); H.McRae batted for R.Gossage;** H.McRae grounded out (R.Jones-p to T.Perez-1b); G.Scott struck out; R.Carew flied to G.Carter-lf; 0 R, 0 H, 0 E, 0 LOB. NL 6, AL 3.

Final Totals	R	H	E	LOB
National League	6	13	1	6
American League	3	10	1	8

47

The Big Red Machine Leads the Way

The 1976 All-Star Game was played in Philadelphia as a logical part of the nation's bicentennial celebration. President Gerald Ford attended and threw out the first ball, then retired to the pressbox level in the second inning. Baseball dignitaries at the game included Robin Roberts and Bob Lemon, two great right-handed pitchers who were inducted into the Hall of Fame the following month. They served as honorary captains, accompanying the managers to the pregame meeting at home plate and staying on the bench in uniform for the duration of the contest.

The last time the game had been held in the city of Brotherly Love was 1952, when rain shortened the contest at Shibe Park to five innings in a 3–2 NL win. By strange coincidence, Connie Mack Stadium (the name to which Shibe Park had been changed) was undergoing demolition at the time of the 1976 All-Star Game, and the pregame special supplement in the *Philadelphia Inquirer* had a photo feature on the work. The game at Veterans Stadium was a great financial success, with an attendance of almost sixty-four thousand fans, the third-largest crowd ever for an All-Star Game, trailing only the two games in Cleveland in 1935 and 1954. Estimated TV viewership was sixty million people on ABC, which far surpassed the Democratic National Convention, airing at the same time on CBS and NBC.

The starting lineups were again chosen by the fans with the reserves and pitchers picked by the managers, Darrell Johnson of the Red Sox for the AL and Sparky Anderson of the Reds for the NL. There were some complaints about the roster selections, as there usually are, but there were also a couple of interesting features this year. Baltimore's Jim Palmer, the AL Cy Young Award winner in 1975 who would repeat with that honor in 1976, was not picked for the AL team, and he was steamed, expressing his anger in the press. Jim's biggest complaint was not about his absence so much as about the presence of the Yankees' Catfish Hunter on the team, since Palmer was convinced he was having a much better year than Hunter was. At the time of the game, Palmer had a record of 11-8 and an ERA of 3.00, whereas Hunter's marks were 10-8 and 3.34. Palmer finished the year at 22-13 with an ERA of 2.51 while Hunter's final numbers for the eventual world champions were 17-15 and 3.52. The Red Sox front office apparently had some questions about Johnson's managerial choices as well, with the manager losing his job four days after the game in Philadelphia.

On the National League side, Anderson expressed regrets about leaving Willie Montanez of the Braves off the team, saying, "If he's not an All-Star, there aren't any." However, he named Tony Perez from his own team as the backup first sacker to the Dodgers' Steve Garvey, instead of the flamboyant Montanez. Said Sparky, "I feel you owe the players on your own club. These are the guys who got you there." There was one injury replacement: Willie Randolph of the Yankees gave up his roster spot to Phil Garner of the A's. Phillies fans were unhappy that their own Bob Boone had finished second to Cincinnati's Johnny Bench in the national voting, and they booed Bench's every move. In the fourth inning, Bench was rattled by a nasty foul tip off his shoulder, awakening the boo birds and bringing out the ire of Joe Morgan, Bench's Cincinnati teammate, who denounced the crowd for booing an injury. Boone entered the game the following inning.

On the field, the only celebrating was done by the National Leaguers as they defeated the American League squad with ease, the 7–1 victory marking their thirteenth win in the last fourteen tries and increasing their advantage in the series to a ten-game margin. It was clear that the AL felt the recent losses keenly going into this game. In fact, league president Lee MacPhail sent a letter to each player, reminding him how important it was to win and noting rather pointedly that the manager should not feel an obligation to get every player into the game. Randy Jones of the Padres, who would win the NL Cy Young Award in 1976, was the NL starter. He yielded a lead-off single to Ron LeFlore of the Tigers, who was erased on a double play hit into by the Twins' Rod Carew. George Brett of the Royals walked on four pitches, but the threat ended as Thurman Munson of the Yankees grounded out. Jones allowed only one other runner in his three innings: a single to the Tigers' Rusty Staub in the second. Jones was the eventual winning pitcher. The AL scored its only run off Randy's successor, Tom Seaver of the Mets, who allowed a solo homer to Fred Lynn of the Red Sox in the fourth inning. Anderson used three more pitchers to cover the final four innings, and they turned out to be excellent choices because the AL collected only one hit, an infield single by Yankees speedster Mickey Rivers in the eighth. Rivers was erased by one of three double plays turned by the NL infield.

The National League got out to an early lead and was never in trouble. The Reds' Pete Rose singled to center off AL starter Mark Fidrych of the Tigers and scored when Steve Garvey of the Dodgers followed with a triple to right field. Garvey scored on a one-out ground out by George Foster of the Reds. Fidrych was a national sensation in 1976, due not only to his effective pitching but also to his eccentric habits, which included smoothing the dirt on the mound with his hands and talking to the ball. Known as The Bird, the free-spirited rookie did not get his first start until May 15. He was immediately successful and, at the time of the All-Star Game, had a 9-2 mark with an ERA of 1.78. However, his results against the NL were not so good; he allowed the two first-inning runs and a total of four hits in his two innings. Hunter succeeded The Bird and was reached for two runs when Morgan singled with one out and Foster followed with a home run to right-center, a turn of events that probably drew a wry smile from Palmer. The scoring for the night was completed in the eighth when the NL tallied three times against the Angels' Frank Tanana. Dave Cash of the Phillies led off with a single, the only hit among the five members of the local team in the game. After Perez walked, Bill Russell of the Dodgers grounded into a double play, and it looked as

Rivers sliding into second, 1976
Shortstop Bill Russell eludes Mickey Rivers and completes a double play in the eighth inning. Associated Press Photo.

if the California left-hander might escape. But Ken Griffey of the Reds singled Cash home, and Cesar Cedeno of the Astros put one over the wall for the last two runs.

In one sense, the one-sided game was a preview of what was to come in the fall, because there were so many Cincinnati players involved. Five of the starters came from the Queen City team as did two of the substitutes. Sparky Anderson was very proud because this portion of the Big Red Machine scored four of the NL's seven runs, drove in four, and collected seven of the team's ten hits. In the postseason that year, the Reds became the first team to win all of their games since the inception of divisions as they swept the Phillies in the best-of-five National League Championship Series and then took four straight from the Yankees in the World Series.

	AL			NL	
P	Mark Fidrych	DET		Randy Jones	SDN
C	Thurman Munson	NYA		Johnny Bench	CIN
1B	Rod Carew	MIN		Steve Garvey	LAN
2B	Bobby Grich	BAL		Joe Morgan	CIN
3B	George Brett	KCA		Pete Rose	CIN
SS	Toby Harrah	TEX		Dave Concepcion	CIN
OF	Ron LeFlore	DET		George Foster	CIN
OF	Fred Lynn	BOS		Dave Kingman	NYN
OF	Rusty Staub	DET		Greg Luzinski	PHI
	Mark Belanger	BAL		Bob Boone	PHI
	Chris Chambliss	NYA		Larry Bowa	PHI
	Rollie Fingers	OAK		Dave Cash	PHI
	Carlton Fisk	BOS		Cesar Cedeno	HOU
	Phil Garner	OAK		Ron Cey	LAN
	Rich Gossage	CHA		Ken Forsch	HOU
	Catfish Hunter	NYA		Woodie Fryman	MON
	Dave LaRoche	CLE		Ken Griffey	CIN
	Sparky Lyle	NYA		Jon Matlack	NYN
	Hal McRae	KCA		Bake McBride	SLN
	Don Money	MIL		Andy Messersmith	ATL
	Amos Otis	KCA		John Montefusco	SFN
	Freddie Patek	KCA		Al Oliver	PIT
	Willie Randolph +	NYA		Tony Perez	CIN
	Mickey Rivers	NYA		Rick Rhoden	LAN
	Frank Tanana	CAL		Bill Russell	LAN
	Luis Tiant	BOS		Dick Ruthven	ATL
	Bill Travers	MIL		Mike Schmidt	PHI
	Butch Wynegar	MIN		Tom Seaver	NYN
	Carl Yastrzemski	BOS		Steve Swisher	CHN

+ player replaced on roster

```
American League    000  100  000-  1
National League    202  000  03X-  7
```

AMERICAN LEAGUE

	ab	r	h	bi	bb	so	po	a
R.LeFlore, lf	2	0	1	0	0	1	2	0
C.Yastrzemski, lf	2	0	0	0	0	0	0	0
R.Carew, 1b	3	0	0	0	1	0	9	1
G.Brett, 3b	2	0	0	0	1	0	0	1
D.Money, 3b	1	0	0	0	0	0	0	1
T.Munson, c	2	0	0	0	0	0	4	0
C.Fisk, c	1	0	0	0	0	0	1	0
C.Chambliss, ph	1	0	0	0	0	0	0	0
F.Lynn, cf	3	1	1	1	0	1	0	0
A.Otis, ph	1	0	0	0	0	1	0	0
T.Harrah, ss	2	0	0	0	0	0	0	0
M.Belanger, ss	1	0	0	0	0	0	1	1
F.Patek, ss	0	0	0	0	0	0	0	1
R.Staub, rf	2	0	2	0	0	0	1	0
L.Tiant, p	0	0	0	0	0	0	0	0
B.Wynegar, ph	0	0	0	0	1	0	0	0
F.Tanana, p	0	0	0	0	0	0	1	0
B.Grich, 2b	2	0	0	0	0	0	1	1
P.Garner, 2b	1	0	0	0	0	1	1	2
M.Fidrych, p	0	0	0	0	0	0	1	0
H.McRae, ph	1	0	0	0	0	0	0	0
J.Hunter, p	0	0	0	0	0	0	0	0
M.Rivers, ph-rf	2	0	1	0	0	1	2	0
Totals	29	1	5	1	3	5	24	8

BATTING
HR: F.Lynn (4th inning off T.Seaver, 0 on, 2 out).
2-out RBI: F.Lynn.
GDP: C.Yastrzemski; R.Carew; B.Grich.

BASERUNNING
SB: R.Carew (2nd base off J.Montefusco / B.Boone).
Team LOB: 4

FIELDING
PB: T.Munson.
DP: (1). D.Money-P.Garner-R.Carew.

NATIONAL LEAGUE

	ab	r	h	bi	bb	so	po	a
P.Rose, 3b	3	1	2	0	0	0	0	1
A.Oliver, rf-lf	1	0	0	0	0	0	1	0
S.Garvey, 1b	3	1	1	1	0	0	6	0
D.Cash, 2b	1	1	1	0	0	0	1	1
J.Morgan, 2b	3	1	1	0	0	0	2	3
T.Perez, 1b	0	0	0	0	1	0	2	0
G.Foster, cf-rf	3	1	1	3	0	0	0	0
J.Montefusco, p	0	0	0	0	0	0	0	0
B.Russell, ss	1	0	0	0	0	0	1	2
G.Luzinski, lf	3	0	0	0	0	0	0	0
K.Griffey, rf	1	1	1	1	0	0	1	0
J.Bench, c	2	0	1	0	0	1	1	0
C.Cedeno, cf	2	1	1	2	0	1	1	0
D.Kingman, rf	2	0	0	0	0	1	1	0
B.Boone, c	2	0	0	0	0	0	5	0
D.Concepcion, ss	2	0	1	0	0	0	2	3
L.Bowa, ss	1	0	0	0	0	0	2	1
R.Rhoden, p	0	0	0	0	0	0	0	0
R.Cey, 3b	0	0	0	0	0	0	0	0
R.Jones, p	1	0	0	0	0	1	1	1
T.Seaver, p	1	0	0	0	0	1	0	0
M.Schmidt, 3b	1	0	0	0	0	0	0	0
K.Forsch, p	0	0	0	0	0	0	0	0
Totals	33	7	10	7	1	5	27	12

BATTING
3B: S.Garvey (off M.Fidrych); P.Rose (off L.Tiant).
HR: G.Foster (3rd inning off J.Hunter, 1 on, 1 out);
C.Cedeno (8th inning off F.Tanana, 1 on, 2 out).
2-out RBI: K.Griffey; C.Cedeno 2.
RBI, scoring position, less than 2 outs: S.Garvey 0–1;
J.Morgan 0–2; G.Foster 1–1; B.Russell 0–1; R.Jones
0–2.
GDP: B.Russell.

BASERUNNING
Team LOB: 3

FIELDING
DP: (3). J.Morgan-D.Concepcion-S.Garvey; J.Morgan-
L.Bowa-S.Garvey; D.Cash-B.Russell-T.Perez.

PITCHING	ip	h	r	er	bb	so
American League						
M.Fidrych (L)	2.0	4	2	2	0	1
J.Hunter	2.0	2	2	2	0	3

Inherited Runners—Scored:
J.Hunter 0–0; L.Tiant 0–0; F.Tanana 0–0;
T.Seaver 0–0; J.Montefusco 0–0; R.Rhoden 0–0;
K.Forsch 0–0.

PITCHING	ip	h	r	er	bb	so
American League *(continued)*						
L.Tiant	2.0	1	0	0	0	1
F.Tanana	2.0	3	3	3	1	0
National League						
R.Jones (w)	3.0	2	0	0	1	1
T.Seaver	2.0	2	1	1	0	1
J.Montefusco	2.0	0	0	0	2	2
R.Rhoden	1.0	1	0	0	0	0
K.Forsch	1.0	0	0	0	0	1

GAME DATA—T: 2:12; A: 63974; Temp: Unknown; Wind: Unknown direction, Speed: Unknown

UMPIRES—HP: Harry Wendelstedt (NL), 1B: Jerry Neudecker (AL), 2B: Andy Olsen (NL), 3B: Don Denkinger (AL), LF: Satch Davidson (NL), RF: Jim Evans (AL)

STARTING LINEUPS

	American League	National League
1.	R.LeFlore lf	P.Rose 3b
2.	R.Carew 1b	S.Garvey 1b
3.	G.Brett 3b	J.Morgan 2b
4.	T.Munson c	G.Foster cf
5.	F.Lynn cf	G.Luzinski lf
6.	T.Harrah ss	J.Bench c
7.	R.Staub rf	D.Kingman rf
8.	B.Grich 2b	D.Concepcion ss
9.	M.Fidrych p	R.Jones p

AL 1ST: R.LeFlore singled to left field; R.Carew grounded into a double play (J.Morgan-2b to D.Concepcion-ss to S.Garvey-1b) [R.LeFlore out at second]; G.Brett walked; T.Munson forced G.Brett (D.Concepcion-ss to J.Morgan-2b) [T.Munson to first]; 0 R, 1 H, 0 E, 1 LOB. AL 0, NL 0.

NL 1ST: P.Rose singled to center field; S.Garvey tripled to right field [P.Rose scored]; ball fell in front of Staub, then rolled past him; J.Morgan flied to R.Staub-rf; G.Foster grounded out (B.Grich-2b to R.Carew-1b) [S.Garvey scored]; G.Luzinski popped to R.Carew-1b in foul territory; 2 R, 2 H, 0 E, 0 LOB. AL 0, NL 2.

AL 2ND: F.Lynn popped to S.Garvey-1b in foul territory; T.Harrah grounded out (P.Rose-3b to S.Garvey-1b); R.Staub singled to right field; B.Grich grounded out (D.Concepcion-ss to S.Garvey-1b); 0 R, 1 H, 0 E, 1 LOB. AL 0, NL 2.

NL 2ND: J.Bench singled to left field; D.Kingman popped to R.Carew-1b in foul territory; D.Concepcion singled to center field [J.Bench to third]; T.Munson allowed a passed ball [D.Concepcion to second]; R.Jones struck out; P.Rose grounded out (R.Carew-1b to M.Fidrych-p); 0 R, 2 H, 0 E, 2 LOB. AL 0, NL 2.

AL 3RD: **H.McRae batted for M.Fidrych;** H.McRae grounded out (R.Jones-p to S.Garvey-1b); R.LeFlore struck out; R.Carew grounded out (J.Morgan-2b to R.Jones-p); 0 R, 0 H, 0 E, 0 LOB. AL 0, NL 2.

NL 3RD: **J.Hunter replaced H.McRae (pitching);** S.Garvey popped to R.Carew-1b in foul territory; J.Morgan singled to center field; G.Foster homered to very deep left-center [J.Morgan scored]; G.Luzinski flied to R.LeFlore-lf; J.Bench struck out; 2 R, 2 H, 0 E, 0 LOB. AL 0, NL 4.

AL 4TH: **T.Seaver replaced R.Jones (pitching);** G.Brett flied to D.Kingman-rf; T.Munson popped to D.Concepcion-ss; F.Lynn homered to deep rightfield down the line; T.Harrah popped to J.Morgan-2b; 1 R, 1 H, 0 E, 0 LOB. AL 1, NL 4.

NL 4TH: D.Kingman struck out; D.Concepcion flied to R.LeFlore-lf; T.Seaver struck out; 0 R, 0 H, 0 E, 0 LOB. AL 1, NL 4.

AL 5TH: **G.Foster changed positions (playing rf); C.Cedeno replaced J.Bench (playing cf); L.Bowa replaced D.Concepcion (playing ss); B.Boone replaced D.Kingman (playing c);** R.Staub singled to right field; B.Grich grounded into a double play (J.Morgan-2b to L.Bowa-ss to S.Garvey-1b) [R.Staub out at second]; **M.Rivers batted for J.Hunter;** M.Rivers struck out; 0 R, 1 H, 0 E, 0 LOB. AL 1, NL 4.

NL 5TH: **M.Rivers stayed in game (playing rf); C.Yastrzemski replaced R.Leflore (playing lf); C.Fisk replaced T.Munson (playing c); M.Belanger replaced T.Harrah (playing ss); L.Tiant replaced R.Staub (pitching);** P.Rose tripled to very deep right-center; S.Garvey grounded out (G.Brett-3b to R.Carew-1b); J.Morgan popped to B.Grich-2b; G.Foster grounded out (M.Belanger-ss to R.Carew-1b); 0 R, 1 H, 0 E, 1 LOB. AL 1, NL 4.

AL 6TH: **A.Oliver replaced P.Rose (playing rf); D.Cash replaced S.Garvey (playing 2b); T.Perez replaced J.Morgan (playing 1b); M.Schmidt replaced T.Seaver (playing 3b); J.Montefusco replaced G.Foster (pitching);** C.Yastrzemski popped to L.Bowa-ss; R.Carew walked; G.Brett flied to C.Cedeno-cf; R.Carew stole second; C.Fisk popped to B.Boone-c in foul territory; 0 R, 0 H, 0 E, 1 LOB. AL 1, NL 4.

NL 6TH: **D.Money replaced G.Brett (playing 3b); P.Garner replaced B.Grich (playing 2b);** G.Luzinski popped to R.Carew-1b in foul territory; C.Cedeno struck out; B.Boone popped to M.Belanger-ss; 0 R, 0 H, 0 E, 0 LOB. AL 1, NL 4.

AL 7TH: **K.Griffey replaced G.Luzinski (playing rf); A.Oliver changed positions (playing lf);** F.Lynn struck out; M.Belanger flied to K.Griffey-rf; **B.Wynegar batted for L.Tiant;** B.Wynegar walked; P.Garner struck out; 0 R, 0 H, 0 E, 1 LOB. AL 1, NL 4.

NL 7TH: **F.Tanana replaced B.Wynegar (pitching); F.Patek replaced M.Belanger (playing ss);** L.Bowa flied to M.Rivers-rf; M.Schmidt grounded out (F.Patek-ss to R.Carew-1b); A.Oliver grounded out (P.Garner-2b to F.Tanana-p); 0 R, 0 H, 0 E, 0 LOB. AL 1, NL 4.

AL 8TH: **B.Russell replaced J.Montefusco (playing ss); R.Rhoden replaced L.Bowa (pitching);** M.Rivers singled to pitcher; C.Yastrzemski grounded into a double play (D.Cash-2b to B.Russell-ss to T.Perez-1b) [M.Rivers out at second]; R.Carew lined to A.Oliver-lf; 0 R, 1 H, 0 E, 0 LOB. AL 1, NL 4.

NL 8TH: D.Cash singled to left field; T.Perez walked [D.Cash to second]; B.Russell grounded into a double play (D.Money-3b to P.Garner-2b to R.Carew-1b) [D.Cash to third, T.Perez out at second]; K.Griffey singled to center field [D.Cash scored]; C.Cedeno homered to deep leftfield [K.Griffey scored]; B.Boone flied to M.Rivers-rf; 3 R, 3 H, 0 E, 0 LOB. AL 1, NL 7.

AL 9TH: **R.Cey replaced R.Rhoden (playing 3b); K.Forsch replaced M.Schmidt (pitching);** D.Money popped to D.Cash-2b; **C.Chambliss bat-** **ted for C.Fisk;** C.Chambliss grounded out (B.Russell-ss to T.Perez-1b); **A.Otis batted for F.Lynn;** A.Otis struck out; 0 R, 0 H, 0 E, 0 LOB. AL 1, NL 7.

Final Totals	R	H	E	LOB
American League	1	5	0	4
National League	7	10	0	3

48

The NL Turns on the Heat

The first All-Star Game in New York since 1964 at Shea Stadium and the first one in Yankee Stadium since 1960 was played on one of the hottest days of the year in the metropolitan area, where temperatures had been hovering near 100 degrees. The NL came into the contest having won five consecutive games and thirteen of the last fourteen, and it continued to turn on the heat for the AL pitchers in this contest.

This game featured two starting pitchers who had previously pitched in three All-Star Games without surrendering a run. Jim Palmer of the Orioles, who had eleven wins at the break, faced Don Sutton of the Dodgers, who had won ten games.

The AL squad was hampered because many of its top stars were suffering from various injuries. Some of those players did not attend, and some played even though they were at less than top form. Vida Blue, Frank Tanana, Mark Fidrych, and Don Money stayed home, while Thurman Munson, Richie Zisk, Rod Carew, Fred Lynn, and Carl Yastrzemski were hurt but at the game.

The remaining representatives of the Junior Circuit could hardly be called stars. A comparison of the statistics of the two teams showed a heavily one-sided advantage for the NL to continue its winning streak, and this with the AL minus a center fielder on its team. NL manager Sparky Anderson of Cincinnati called his squad "the best overall [NL] team in at least ten years."

Indeed, the fans picked none of the top four home run hitters in the AL. George Scott, leading the AL with twenty-five dingers, was not happy about the starting lineup. "All of our statistics are on the bench. There are ninety darn taters on the pine," he complained.

The results met the expectations as the NL beat the AL with power early in the game; and the AL was never in the contest. Jim Palmer appeared to be a little stiff as he started the game because he had had to wait through a thirty-minute pregame cere-

mony after warming up in the bullpen. He threw three balls and two strikes to the first batter of the game, Cincinnati second baseman Joe Morgan, before Morgan, the reigning two-time NL MVP, homered into the right-field seats. After Palmer struck out Steve Garvey, Dave Parker, playing on the first of his seven All-Star teams, singled to left field and then scored when the 1977 NL MVP, George Foster, doubled to left-center. Foster moved to third on a wild pitch; and then Greg Luzinski of the Phillies homered to right on a 3-2 count for a 4–0 NL lead.

The two homers surrendered by Palmer, who had won the AL Cy Young Award three of the last four years, hardly came as a surprise to Orioles watchers. Palmer had given up twenty homers at the break to lead the Major Leagues in this dubious distinction.

The NL had never before scored four runs in the first inning, but its early lead was nothing new. Since 1965, the NL had scored thirty-three runs to the AL's mere eleven in the first three innings. In fact, this was the third consecutive All-Star Game in which the AL failed to score in the first three frames.

The dispirited AL team went out weakly in the first and second, with only the Yankees' Reggie Jackson reaching on a single to center field. In the top of the third inning, Garvey, the Dodgers' first baseman, homered to left-center field, ending Palmer's night. When AL manager Billy Martin came out to get him, Palmer looked at Martin and said, "What took you so long?" Jim Kern of Cleveland replaced Palmer and quieted the NL bats by striking out both Parker and Foster and retiring Luzinski on a grounder to second base.

The pitchers took over until the bottom of the sixth inning, but there were also two outstanding defensive plays in center field during this time. In the third inning, Foster, normally a left fielder, snagged a line drive by Rod Carew near the top of the fence. Then, in the fifth inning, Fred Lynn tracked down a Joe Morgan fly ball and crashed into the wall.

Tom Seaver, who had been traded to the Reds on June 15 by the Mets, received an ovation from the New York fans during the pregame ceremonies. His reception was louder than that received by the two former New York stars serving as honorary captains, Joe DiMaggio and Willie Mays. Seaver was again greeted enthusiastically as he entered the game in the sixth inning. The crowd reaction turned out to be the highlight of his night, however.

Carew, the 1977 AL MVP, started Seaver off with a single to center field and moved to second on a ground out. That ball, a line drive by Willie Randolph, struck Seaver, but he recovered in time to make the play. One out later, Fred Lynn walked and Richie Zisk of the White Sox, fifth in the AL in both homers and RBI, doubled to right-center to score both runners, and the AL was finally on the scoreboard.

In the seventh inning, Minnesota catcher Butch Wynegar singled to right field and, one out later, moved to second when Graig Nettles reached on an error by Cardinals shortstop Garry Templeton. After George Scott flew out, Yankees second baseman Willie Randolph singled to center field to drive Wynegar across the plate with an unearned run. Randolph was the only starter on either side to play the entire game, because the AL had no backup second baseman.

Pinch hitter Ron Fairly of the Toronto Blue Jays followed Randolph. He had hit quite a few balls into the short-right-field stands during batting practice, and a repeat now would have put the AL ahead. Fairly pulled one pitch into the third deck in right field that landed foul. He then ended the inning by striking out.

Pete Rose, Seaver's teammate in Cincinnati, commented on Seaver's night: "It never fails. The guy that gets the biggest hand gives up the runs." Seaver had now given up all seven runs scored by the AL since the 1975 game.

In the eighth inning, the NL scored two more runs off new pitcher Sparky Lyle, the Yankees' relief specialist and 1977 AL Cy Young Award winner. Garry Templeton doubled to left field, and Jerry Morales was hit by a pitch. Both runners advanced a base on a wild pitch, and Dave Winfield, the San Diego outfielder playing on his first of twelve All-Star teams, singled to left field to plate both runners. Although Reggie Smith of the Dodgers followed with a single to left field, no further damage was done. Smith was representing his third team in All-Star play, having been a member of the AL squad with the Red Sox and the NL contingent with the Cardinals.

The American Leaguers scored two more runs

in the ninth but could not catch their opponents. Bert Campaneris walked to lead off the inning. Campy, representing the Rangers, was at the last of his five All-Star Games. After Nettles struck out, George Scott hit one of his "taters" into the right-center-field stands, scoring Campaneris ahead of him.

The NL collected nine hits in the game, with Dave Winfield the only player having two. The AL had eight hits, and Richie Zisk gathered two. Both Winfield and Zisk had a single and a double.

Don Sutton, who had won at least fifteen games each of the last eight years for the Dodgers, was credited with the win and was named the game's MVP. Sutton, who grew up pitching "mental shutouts" for the Yankees, said, "I was on the mound in the middle of Yankee Stadium, where all the guys I've idolized played. I don't even remember the guys I faced in the first inning."

Gary Lavelle of the Giants and Rick Reuschel of the Cubs each pitched well for the NL. For the AL, Jim Kern and Dennis Eckersley did not allow a base runner in three innings. This was the first of six All-Star appearances by the Eck. Bill Campbell of Boston allowed only one walk in an inning of work.

Nolan Ryan, who had won thirteen games with 222 strikeouts at the break, refused to go to the game when picked to replace his injured teammate Frank Tanana. Ryan explained a few years later: "I was having a good year, and I was planning on going to New York for the game at Yankee Stadium and seeing some old friends. But then I wasn't picked, and I made plans to take my family away during the All-Star break. Then, when I was picked as a replacement for Tanana, I decided to take my family away anyway. Some people thought I was mad but I wasn't. I just made other plans and stuck to my guns. I have no regrets."

Jim Palmer talked about the missing Ryan before the game: "Something is wrong with a system that leaves a pitcher like Nolan Ryan off an All-Star team. I would like to see Nolan here because it would add considerable strength to the team. But it's a bad system when you have to pick a player from each team."

Manager Billy Martin, who was less sympathetic, said, "[Ryan] should be suspended and not receive his salary for a week. I think baseball should dictate policy to the players and not let the players dictate policy to baseball." Martin insisted that he had not intentionally snubbed Ryan, but that he had chosen Tanana because he was having a better year. The next season, Martin announced that he would not pick Ryan if he was 40-0 at the break.

Rachel Robinson, widow of Jackie Robinson,

threw the ceremonial pitch before the game. Thirty years before, Jackie Robinson had become the first black player in the Major Leagues in the twentieth century.

During the pregame workout, Pete Rose had his son, seven-year-old Pete Jr., working out in left field. "The kid's got to learn how to play the sun field sometime," said the elder Rose.

	AL		NL	
P	Jim Palmer	BAL	Don Sutton	LAN
C	Carlton Fisk	BOS	Johnny Bench	CIN
1B	Rod Carew	MIN	Steve Garvey	LAN
2B	Willie Randolph	NYA	Joe Morgan	CIN
3B	George Brett	KCA	Ron Cey	LAN
SS	Rick Burleson	BOS	Dave Concepcion	CIN
OF	Reggie Jackson	NYA	George Foster	CIN
OF	Carl Yastrzemski	BOS	Greg Luzinski	PHI
OF	Richie Zisk	CHA	Dave Parker	PIT
	Vida Blue +	OAK	Joaquin Andujar	HOU
	Bill Campbell	BOS	John Candelaria	PIT
	Bert Campaneris	TEX	Steve Carlton	PHI
	Dennis Eckersley	CLE	Rich Gossage	PIT
	Ron Fairly	TOR	Ken Griffey	CIN
	Mark Fidrych +	DET	Gary Lavelle	SFN
	Wayne Gross	OAK	Willie Montanez	ATL
	Larry Hisle	MIN	Jerry Morales	CHN
	Ruppert Jones	SEA	Rick Reuschel	CHN
	Jim Kern	CLE	Pete Rose	CIN
	Dave LaRoche	CAL	Mike Schmidt	PHI
	Sparky Lyle	NYA	Tom Seaver	CIN
	Fred Lynn	BOS	Ted Simmons	SLN
	Don Money +	MIL	Reggie Smith	LAN
	Thurman Munson	NYA	John Stearns	NYN
	Graig Nettles	NYA	Bruce Sutter +	CHN
	Jim Rice	BOS	Garry Templeton	SLN
	Nolan Ryan +	CAL	Manny Trillo	CHN
	George Scott	BOS	Ellis Valentine	MON
	Ken Singleton	BAL	Dave Winfield	SDN
	Jim Slaton	MIL		
	Frank Tanana +	CAL		
	Jason Thompson	DET		
	Butch Wynegar	MIN		

+ player replaced on roster

National League   401 000 020- 7
American League   000 002 102- 5

NATIONAL LEAGUE

	ab	r	h	bi	bb	so	po	a
J.Morgan, 2b	4	1	1	1	0	1	1	0
M.Trillo, 2b	1	0	0	0	0	1	0	1
S.Garvey, 1b	3	1	1	1	0	2	1	0
W.Montanez, 1b	2	0	0	0	0	1	6	1
D.Parker, rf	3	1	1	0	0	1	2	0
G.Templeton, ss	1	1	1	0	0	0	1	2
G.Foster, cf	3	1	1	1	0	1	2	0
J.Morales, cf	0	1	0	0	0	0	1	0
G.Luzinski, lf	2	1	1	2	0	0	0	0
D.Winfield, lf	2	0	2	2	0	0	1	0
R.Cey, 3b	2	0	0	0	1	1	0	0
T.Seaver, p	0	0	0	0	0	0	0	1
R.Smith, ph	1	0	1	0	0	0	0	0
M.Schmidt, pr	0	0	0	0	0	0	0	0
R.Reuschel, p	0	0	0	0	0	0	0	0
J.Stearns, c	0	0	0	0	0	0	2	0
J.Bench, c	2	0	0	0	0	1	4	0
G.Lavelle, p	0	0	0	0	0	0	0	0
P.Rose, ph-3b	2	0	0	0	0	0	0	1
D.Concepcion, ss	1	0	0	0	1	0	1	1
E.Valentine, rf	1	0	0	0	1	0	0	0
D.Sutton, p	0	0	0	0	0	0	0	1
T.Simmons, c	3	0	0	0	0	0	5	0
R.Gossage, p	0	0	0	0	0	0	0	0
Totals	33	7	9	7	3	9	27	8

BATTING
2B: G.Foster (off J.Palmer); D.Winfield (off D.LaRoche); G.Templeton (off S.Lyle).
HR: J.Morgan (1st inning off J.Palmer, 0 on, 0 out); S.Garvey (3rd inning off J.Palmer, 0 on, 0 out); G.Luzinski (1st inning off J.Palmer, 1 on, 1 out).
RBI, scoring position, less than 2 outs: J.Morgan 0–1; G.Luzinski 1–1; D.Winfield 2–2; P.Rose 0–1.
S: D.Sutton.
GDP: P.Rose.

BASERUNNING
CS: D.Concepcion (3rd base by J.Palmer/C.Fisk).
Team LOB: 4

FIELDING
E: G.Templeton (fumble).
DP: (1). W.Montanez-G.Templeton-W.Montanez.

AMERICAN LEAGUE

	ab	r	h	bi	bb	so	po	a
R.Carew, 1b	3	1	1	0	0	0	7	0
G.Scott, 1b	2	1	1	2	0	0	4	0
W.Randolph, 2b	5	0	1	1	0	2	2	6
G.Brett, 3b	2	0	0	0	1	0	2	1
B.Campbell, p	0	0	0	0	0	0	0	0
R.Fairly, ph	1	0	0	0	0	1	0	0
S.Lyle, p	0	0	0	0	0	0	0	0
T.Munson, ph	1	0	0	0	0	1	0	0
C.Yastrzemski, cf	2	0	0	0	0	1	0	0
F.Lynn, cf	1	1	0	0	1	0	2	0
R.Zisk, lf	3	0	2	2	0	1	0	0
K.Singleton, rf	0	0	0	0	0	0	0	0
R.Jackson, rf	2	0	1	0	0	1	0	0
J.Rice, rf-lf	2	0	1	0	0	0	1	0
C.Fisk, c	2	0	0	0	0	1	6	1
B.Wynegar, c	2	1	1	0	0	0	3	0
R.Burleson, ss	2	0	0	0	0	0	0	0
B.Campaneris, ss	1	1	0	0	1	1	0	1
J.Palmer, p	0	0	0	0	0	0	0	0
J.Kern, p	0	0	0	0	0	0	0	0
R.Jones, ph	1	0	0	0	0	0	0	0
D.Eckersley, p	0	0	0	0	0	0	0	1
L.Hisle, ph	1	0	0	0	0	0	0	0
D.LaRoche, p	0	0	0	0	0	0	0	0
G.Nettles, 3b	2	0	0	0	0	1	0	1
Totals	35	5	8	5	3	10	27	11

BATTING
2B: R.Zisk (off T.Seaver).
HR: G.Scott (9th inning off R.Gossage, 1 on, 1 out).
2-out RBI: W.Randolph; R.Zisk 2.
RBI, scoring position, less than 2 outs: G.Scott 0–1; G.Brett 0–1; B.Wynegar 0–1.
GDP: B.Wynegar.

BASERUNNING
Team LOB: 7

FIELDING
DP: (1). W.Randolph-G.Scott.

PITCHING	ip	h	r	er	bb	so
National League						
D.Sutton (w)	3.0	1	0	0	1	4
G.Lavelle	2.0	1	0	0	0	2
T.Seaver	2.0	4	3	2	1	2
R.Reuschel	1.0	1	0	0	0	0
R.Gossage	1.0	1	2	2	1	2
American League						
J.Palmer (L)	* 2.0	5	5	5	1	3
J.Kern	1.0	0	0	0	0	2
D.Eckersley	2.0	0	0	0	0	1
D.LaRoche	1.0	1	0	0	1	0
B.Campbell	1.0	0	0	0	1	2
S.Lyle	2.0	3	2	2	0	1

* Pitched to 1 batter in 3rd

Inherited Runners—Scored:
G.Lavelle 0–0; T.Seaver 0–0; R.Reuschel 0–0; R.Gossage 0–0; J.Kern 0–0; D.Eckersley 0–0; D.LaRoche 0–0; B.Campbell 0–0; S.Lyle 0–0.

HBP: J.Morales by S.Lyle; K.Singleton by R.Reuschel.

WP: J.Palmer; S.Lyle

GAME DATA—T: 2:34; A: 56683; Temp: Unknown; Wind: Unknown direction, Speed: Unknown

UMPIRES—HP: Bill Kunkel (AL), 1B: Doug Harvey (NL), 2B: Dave Phillips (AL), 3B: Dick Stello (NL), LF: Frank Pulli (NL), RF: Joe Brinkman (AL)

STARTING LINEUPS

National League	*American League*
1. J.Morgan 2b	R.Carew 1b
2. S.Garvey 1b	W.Randolph 2b
3. D.Parker rf	G.Brett 3b
4. G.Foster cf	C.Yastrzemski cf
5. G.Luzinski lf	R.Zisk lf
6. R.Cey 3b	R.Jackson rf
7. J.Bench c	C.Fisk c
8. D.Concepcion ss	R.Burleson ss
9. D.Sutton p	J.Palmer p
D.Sutton p	J.Palmer p

NL 1ST: Plenty of injuries: Bruce Sutter did not come, and John Candelaria and Joaquin Andujar dressed but couldn't play for For AL, Frank Tanana and Mark Fidrych could not play, and Nolan Ryan, chosen as replacement, refused to come because he was not originally chosen Game dedicated to Jackie Robinson First pitch: Rachel Robinson AL captain: Joe DiMaggio; NL captain: Willie Mays Terrence Cardinal Cooke gave invocation, Pearl Bailey sang 'America the Beautiful' and baritone Robert Merrill sang the National Anthem MVP: Don Sutton (Los Angeles); J.Morgan homered to deep rightfield (it was the 3–2 pitch); S.Garvey was called out on strikes; D.Parker singled to left field; G.Foster doubled to left-center [D.Parker scored]; J.Palmer threw a wild pitch [G.Foster to third]; G.Luzinski homered to deep rightfield (it was the 3–2 pitch) [G.Foster scored]; R.Cey struck out; J.Bench struck out; 4 R, 4 H, 0 E, 0 LOB. NL 4, AL 0.

AL 1ST: R.Carew grounded out (D.Sutton-p to S.Garvey-1b); W.Randolph was called out on strikes; G.Brett walked; C.Yastrzemski popped to J.Morgan-2b; 0 R, 0 H, 0 E, 1 LOB. NL 4, AL 0.

NL 2ND: D.Concepcion walked; D.Sutton out on a sacrifice bunt (R.Carew-1b unassisted) [D.Concepcion to second]; D.Concepcion was caught stealing third (C.Fisk-c to G.Brett-3b); J.Morgan lined to W.Randolph-2b; 0 R, 0 H, 0 E, 0 LOB. NL 4, AL 0.

AL 2ND: R.Zisk struck out; R.Jackson singled to center field; C.Fisk was called out on strikes; R.Burleson lined to G.Foster-cf; 0 R, 1 H, 0 E, 1 LOB. NL 4, AL 0.

NL 3RD: S.Garvey homered to very deep left-center; **J.Kern replaced J.Palmer (pitching);** D.Parker struck out; G.Foster struck out; G.Luzinski grounded out (W.Randolph-2b to R.Carew-1b); 1 R, 1 H, 0 E, 0 LOB. NL 5, AL 0.

AL 3RD: **R.Jones batted for J.Kern;** R.Jones flied to D.Parker-rf; R.Carew lined to G.Foster-cf; W.Randolph struck out; 0 R, 0 H, 0 E, 0 LOB. NL 5, AL 0.

NL 4TH: **D.Eckersley replaced R.Jones (pitching);** R.Cey grounded out (W.Randolph-2b to R.Carew-1b); J.Bench popped to G.Brett-3b; D.Concepcion grounded out (D.Eckersley-p to R.Carew-1b); 0 R, 0 H, 0 E, 0 LOB. NL 5, AL 0.

AL 4TH: **D.Winfield replaced G.Luzinski (playing lf); T.Simmons replaced D.Sutton (playing c); G.Lavelle replaced J.Bench (pitching);** G.Brett flied to D.Winfield-lf; C.Yastrzemski struck out; R.Zisk singled to center field; R.Jackson struck out; 0 R, 1 H, 0 E, 1 LOB. NL 5, AL 0.

NL 5TH: **J.Rice replaced R.Jackson (playing rf); F.Lynn replaced C.Yastrzemski (playing cf);** T.Simmons grounded out (W.Randolph-2b to R.Carew-1b); J.Morgan flied to F.Lynn-cf; S.Garvey struck out; 0 R, 0 H, 0 E, 0 LOB. NL 5, AL 0.

AL 5TH: **W.Montanez replaced S.Garvey (playing 1b);** C.Fisk popped to D.Concepcion-ss; R.Burleson grounded out (D.Concepcion-ss to W.Montanez-1b); **L.Hisle batted for D.Eckersley;** L.Hisle flied to D.Parker-rf; 0 R, 0 H, 0 E, 0 LOB. NL 5, AL 0.

NL 6TH: **B.Campaneris replaced R.Burleson (playing ss); B.Wynegar replaced C.Fisk (playing c); D.Laroche replaced L.Hisle (pitching);** D.Parker grounded out (B.Campaneris-ss to R.Carew-1b); G.Foster grounded out (G.Brett-3b to R.Carew-1b); D.Winfield doubled to right field; Rice dropped ball; R.Cey walked; **P.Rose batted for G.Lavelle;** P.Rose flied to J.Rice-rf; 0 R, 1 H, 0 E, 2 LOB. NL 5, AL 0.

AL 6TH: **P.Rose stayed in game (playing 3b); G.Templeton replaced D.Parker (playing ss); J.Morales replaced G.Foster (playing cf); E.Valentine replaced D.Concepcion (playing rf); T.Seaver replaced R.Cey (pitching);** Seaver, recently traded from Mets, received a huge ovation; R.Carew singled to center field; W.Randolph grounded out (T.Seaver-p to W.Montanez-1b) [R.Carew to second]; G.Brett grounded out (P.Rose-3b to W.Montanez-1b); F.Lynn walked; R.Zisk doubled to right-center [R.Carew scored, F.Lynn scored]; J.Rice popped to T.Simmons-c in foul territory; 2 R, 2 H, 0 E, 1 LOB. NL 5, AL 2.

NL 7TH: **J.Rice changed positions (playing lf); G.Scott replaced R.Carew (playing 1b); G.Nettles replaced D.Laroche (playing 3b); K.Singleton replaced R.Zisk (playing rf); B.Campbell replaced G.Brett (pitching);** E.Valentine walked; T.Simmons grounded out (W.Randolph-2b to G.Scott-1b) [E.Valentine to second]; J.Morgan struck out; W.Montanez struck out; 0 R, 0 H, 0 E, 1 LOB. NL 5, AL 2.

AL 7TH: **M.Trillo replaced J.Morgan (playing 2b);**

B.Wynegar singled to right field; B.Campaneris struck out; G.Nettles reached on an error by G.Templeton-ss [B.Wynegar to second, G.Nettles to first]; G.Scott flied to J.Morales-cf; W.Randolph singled to center field [B.Wynegar scored (unearned), G.Nettles to second]; **R.Fairly batted for B.Campbell;** R.Fairly struck out; 1 R (0 ER), 2 H, 1 E, 2 LOB. NL 5, AL 3.

NL 8TH: **S.Lyle replaced R.Fairly (pitching);** G.Templeton doubled to left field; J.Morales was hit by a pitch; S.Lyle threw a wild pitch [G.Templeton to third, J.Morales to second]; D.Winfield singled to left field [G.Templeton scored, J.Morales scored]; **R.Smith batted for T.Seaver;** R.Smith singled to left field [D.Winfield to second]; **M.Schmidt ran for R.Smith;** P.Rose grounded into a double play (W.Randolph-2b to G.Scott-1b) [D.Winfield to third, M.Schmidt out at second]; E.Valentine flied to F.Lynn-cf; 2 R, 3 H, 0 E, 1 LOB. NL 7, AL 3.

AL 8TH: **R.Reuschel replaced M.Schmidt (pitching);** F.Lynn grounded out (M.Trillo-2b to W.Montanez-1b); K.Singleton was hit by a pitch; J.Rice singled to center field [K.Singleton to second]; B.Wynegar grounded into a double play (W.Montanez-1b to G.Templeton-ss to W.Montanez-1b) [J.Rice out at second]; 0 R, 1 H, 0 E, 1 LOB. NL 7, AL 3.

NL 9TH: T.Simmons grounded out (G.Nettles-3b to G.Scott-1b); M.Trillo struck out; W.Montanez grounded out (W.Randolph-2b to G.Scott-1b); 0 R, 0 H, 0 E, 0 LOB. NL 7, AL 3.

AL 9TH: **R.Gossage replaced T.Simmons (pitching); J.Stearns replaced R.Reuschel (playing c);** B.Campaneris walked; G.Nettles struck out; G.Scott homered to very deep right-center [B.Campaneris scored]; W.Randolph grounded out (G.Templeton-ss to W.Montanez-1b); **T.Munson batted for S.Lyle;** T.Munson struck out; 2 R, 1 H, 0 E, 0 LOB. NL 7, AL 5.

Final Totals	R	H	E	LOB
National League	7	9	1	4
American League	5	8	0	7

GAME 49

Tuesday, July 11, 1978

San Diego Stadium, San Diego

National League 7, American League 3

SERIES RESULTS: NL 30, AL 18, 1 TIE

Replacements Galore

The first All-Star Game in San Diego featured many of baseball's finest players but also was the subject of many critical statements regarding the rosters. In a seemingly annual rite, pundits derided many of the fans' choices for starters and many of the managers' choices for alternates. The worst case in the NL saw Johnny Bench elected for the tenth consecutive year as the catcher even though he had missed five weeks of the season with back trouble. In the AL, Don Money was elected as the AL second baseman even though he had played only ten games at that spot all season.

Cincinnati manager Sparky Anderson commented on the fan voting: "The whole thing hands me a laugh." Bench seemed embarrassed by the vote, saying, "Two years after I'm dead, I'll still be getting All-Star votes."

The *New York Times* polled players in early July for their starting lineups. Not surprisingly, the players disagreed with half of the sixteen elected starters, including five in the AL. Many of the top players in the fan ballot were well down in the players' vote. Chief among them were Dodgers outfielder Rick Monday, who placed tenth in the player vote, and Yankees outfielder Reggie Jackson, who placed sixth and received only two of ten votes from his New York teammates.

AL President Lee MacPhail was dismayed that none of the starting outfielders for his league was a center fielder and also complained that "not one of them is a particularly good fielder, which is not the way to run an All-Star Game." MacPhail suggested a different manner of selecting players, with the manager picking the starters but ensuring that the fans' choices played at least three innings sometime during the game.

Many of the pregame announcements sounded like hospital press releases instead of ones from a baseball team. Six replacements were made for various reasons, including ankle and back injuries and fevers. There was even one controversial re-

placement; Yankees third baseman Graig Nettles was replaced against his wishes due to a toe injury.

"I didn't want to miss this game due to a silly little injury," said the San Diego native. He claimed that Yankees officials made the decision without his knowledge after not letting him play the final two games of the first half of the season. "They must know more about my injury than I do. I know it wasn't Billy Martin's decision, and I put up a thousand good reasons to play. A lot of guys may want to skip this game, but I want to play, especially in my hometown."

Larry Hisle, who had been overlooked in the original selection process, replaced Nettles. However, when Reggie Jackson received permission to miss the game due to a fever, Nettles was reinstated to the squad. He was delighted.

Once the game started, it seemed the AL would break its recent pattern, in which it had lost six consecutive games and fourteen of the last fifteen. The American Leaguers started out by taking an early lead against Vida Blue of the Giants, who became the first pitcher to start for both leagues in All-Star competition. Blue, who had started both the 1971 and 1975 games as a member of the Athletics, led the NL in wins at the 1978 break with his 12-4 record to accompany his 2.42 ERA.

The Twins' perennial batting champion, Rod Carew, led off the game with a triple to left-center on the game's third pitch and scored on George Brett's double to the same field. Brett moved to third on a ground out, and the AL appeared poised for a big inning when Texas outfielder Richie Zisk walked. Boston catcher Carlton Fisk hit a pop-up to shallow right field that Cincinnati second baseman Joe Morgan tracked down, running away from the infield. Brett scored on the unusual sacrifice fly, but Zisk was then thrown out trying to steal second base to end the inning.

In the top of the third inning, Carew, the 1977 AL MVP, again led off with a hit deep into the outfield, this time to center. Cincinnati left fielder George Foster, the 1977 NL MVP, who was out of position in center, misplayed the ball slightly, allowing Carew his second triple of the game. Carew was the first player to have two triples in one All-Star contest. In fact, the two hits tied the record for most triples by a team in one game. The double triple had been accomplished previously in 1934 and 1951 by the AL and in 1976 by the NL. Brett drove Carew home again, this time with a sacrifice fly to Foster in center, and Zisk singled later in the inning but was stranded.

AL starter Jim Palmer of the Orioles, who was starting his second consecutive All-Star Game, seemed to be in control as he faced only seven batters in the first two innings. He allowed one hit and one walk but forced Rick Monday to ground into a double play to end the second. In the third inning, Palmer allowed a lead-off single to Larry Bowa of the Phillies. Bowa was at third base with two out when Palmer lost control of the situation by walking Joe Morgan, George Foster, and Greg Luzinski of the Phillies in succession, thus forcing in a run.

"I had pine tar all over my hands after batting in the second inning," said Palmer. "I couldn't control the ball as well as I wanted to, and I had trouble holding on to it."

It got worse for Palmer as the next hitter, Dodgers first baseman Steve Garvey, knocked in two runs with a single to left field. "I knew Palmer would give me a breaking ball," said Garvey, while Palmer, who left the game after the hit, commented that "it was a slider that didn't break as much as I wanted.". This was the second consecutive bad outing for the three-time AL Cy Young Award winner. In the 1977 game, Palmer gave up five runs on five hits in two innings.

With the game now tied at three runs apiece, the pitchers took over. For the Junior Circuit, Matt Keough of Oakland, Lary Sorensen of Milwaukee, Jim Kern of Texas, and Ron Guidry of the Yankees allowed just three hits and a walk in the next four and one-third innings. Sorensen was especially effective in his three innings of work. For the NL, Steve Rogers of the Expos, Rollie Fingers of the Padres, Bruce Sutter of the Cubs, and Phil Niekro of the Braves shut down the AL with only three hits through the rest of the game.

In the bottom of the eighth, AL manager Billy Martin brought in his Yankee closer, Rich Gossage. Steve Garvey, already sporting a two-run single and a walk in three trips to the plate, led off with a triple to right-center field on the 1-2 pitch. The ball hit high off the wall, just missing a homer. "I thought the ball was out. Earlier in the evening, when the air was lighter, it would have been," said Garvey.

Gossage then threw a pitch to the backstop, and Garvey scored the eventual winning run. Cincinnati shortstop Dave Concepcion walked, and San Diego favorite Dave Winfield sent Concepcion to third when he singled to left. When Chet Lemon misplayed the ball in left, Winfield advanced to second base. Phillies catcher Bob Boone then drove both runners across the plate with a single to center and later scored from second when Dodgers infielder Dave Lopes singled to right field.

Garvey's triple, in combination with the two by Carew, set a record for most by both clubs, breaking the previous record of two triples, which had been accomplished three times. Garvey had now hit in five consecutive All-Star Games, with eight hits in sixteen at bats, and was the unanimous choice for the game's MVP. Garvey had previously won the honor in 1974 and was only the second player to win the award twice, following Willie Mays, who won in 1963 and 1968.

"I played in 1974 right after getting over the mumps," Garvey reminisced. He played with twenty stitches in his chin in this game. "When I went into third base on the triple, I think I popped a stitch. But I'll take a popped stitch for a triple any time."

Gossage, the losing pitcher, was the first player to play for the AL, then for the NL, then for the AL again. "I was very disappointed," said Gossage. "With Garvey, I got the ball up and over the plate and he just hit it. On that wild pitch, I just started muscling the ball and tried to throw it too hard. That's what happens when you overthrow the ball. This hurts."

Brett and Carew, with two hits apiece, accounted for half the AL total. Carew came into the game with three singles in twenty-seven All-Star at bats. Garvey and Bowa each had two hits for the NL.

Pete Rose, who had reached three thousand career hits in May, had one hit in the game, a double off Kern in the seventh. He had a twenty-five-game hitting streak at the break and would tie Willie Keeler's NL record for most consecutive games with a hit, in forty-four straight games, at the end of the month.

Earlier in the year, Billy Martin had said that Nolan Ryan, who had refused to go to the 1977 game, "won't be on my team if he's 40-0." Martin needn't have worried because Ryan was in the middle of a subpar year with the Angels.

Former President Gerald Ford attended the game and toured the clubhouses before the start. At one point, he compared golf games with Billy Martin.

Martin refused a request from the commissioner to wear a microphone during the game for the television audience. "I'll do it for $20,000 and then donate the money to a fund for indigent minor league players," he said. He did not get an answer to his proposal.

NL manager Tommy Lasorda of the Dodgers decided to apologize to four players — Garry Maddox of the Phillies, Ken Griffey and Dan Driessen of the Reds, and Bill Madlock of the Giants — for leaving them off the roster. Both Lasorda and Martin talked about the twenty-eight-player limit, each knowing there are always many more players that should be chosen. "I've got a solution," said Martin. "Extend the All-Star Game to sixty-eight innings, and we'll play everybody."

	AL			NL		
P	Jim Palmer		BAL	Vida Blue		SFN
C	Carlton Fisk		BOS	Johnny Bench	+	CIN
1B	Rod Carew		MIN	Steve Garvey		LAN
2B	Don Money		MIL	Joe Morgan		CIN
3B	George Brett		KCA	Pete Rose		CIN
SS	Freddie Patek		KCA	Larry Bowa		PHI
OF	Reggie Jackson	+	NYA	George Foster		CIN
OF	Jim Rice		BOS	Greg Luzinski		PHI
OF	Richie Zisk		TEX	Rick Monday		LAN
	Rick Burleson	+	BOS	Bob Boone		PHI
	Dwight Evans		BOS	Jeff Burroughs		ATL
	Mike Flanagan		BAL	Ron Cey		LAN
	Rich Gossage		NYA	Jack Clark		SFN
	Ron Guidry		NYA	Dave Concepcion		CIN
	Larry Hisle		MIL	Rollie Fingers		SDN
	Roy Howell		TOR	Ross Grimsley		MON
	Matt Keough		OAK	Tommy John		LAN
	Jim Kern		CLE	Davey Lopes		LAN
	Chet Lemon		CHA	Phil Niekro		ATL
	Fred Lynn		BOS	Biff Pocoroba		ATL
	Thurman Munson	+	NYA	Terry Puhl		HOU
	Eddie Murray		BAL	Steve Rogers		MON
	Graig Nettles	+	NYA	Tom Seaver		CIN
	Darrell Porter		KCA	Ted Simmons		SLN
	Jerry Remy		BOS	Reggie Smith		LAN
	Craig Reynolds		SEA	Willie Stargell		PIT
	Lary Sorensen		MIL	Bruce Sutter		CHN
	Jim Sundberg		TEX	Dave Winfield		SDN
	Frank Tanana		CAL	Pat Zachry		NYN
	Jason Thompson		DET			
	Frank White		KCA			
	Carl Yastrzemski	+	BOS			

+ player replaced on roster

American League   201 000 000- 3
National League   003 000 04x- 7

AMERICAN LEAGUE

	ab	r	h	bi	bb	so	po	a
R.Carew, 1b	4	2	2	0	0	0	6	1
G.Brett, 3b	3	1	2	2	0	0	0	2
R.Gossage, p	0	0	0	0	0	0	0	0
J.Rice, lf	4	0	0	0	0	2	2	0
C.Lemon, lf	0	0	0	0	0	0	0	0
R.Zisk, rf	2	0	1	0	1	1	0	0
D.Evans, rf	1	0	0	0	0	1	3	0
C.Fisk, c	2	0	0	1	0	0	4	0
J.Sundberg, c	0	0	0	0	0	0	2	1
J.Thompson, ph	1	0	0	0	0	0	0	0
F.Lynn, cf	4	0	1	0	0	1	3	0
D.Money, 2b	2	0	0	0	0	1	1	1
F.White, 2b	1	0	0	0	0	0	1	2
D.Porter, ph	1	0	0	0	0	0	0	0
F.Patek, ss	3	0	1	0	0	1	1	1
J.Palmer, p	1	0	0	0	0	0	1	0
M.Keough, p	0	0	0	0	0	0	0	0
R.Howell, ph	1	0	0	0	0	0	0	0
L.Sorensen, p	0	0	0	0	0	0	0	1
L.Hisle, ph	1	0	1	0	0	0	0	0
J.Kern, p	0	0	0	0	0	0	0	0
R.Guidry, p	0	0	0	0	0	0	0	0
G.Nettles, 3b	0	0	0	0	0	0	0	1
Totals	31	3	8	3	1	7	24	10

BATTING
2B: G.Brett (off V.Blue).
3B: R.Carew 2 (off V.Blue; off V.Blue).
RBI, scoring position, less than 2 outs: G.Brett 2–2;
    J.Rice 0–2; C.Fisk 1–1; D.Money 0–1; F.Patek 0–1.
SF: G.Brett; C.Fisk.

BASERUNNING
SB: G.Brett (2nd base off S.Rogers/T.Simmons).
CS: R.Carew (2nd base by R.Fingers/B.Boone); R.Zisk
    (2nd base by V.Blue/T.Simmons).
Team LOB: 4

FIELDING
E: C.Lemon.
PB: J.Sundberg.
DP: (1). G.Brett-D.Money-R.Carew.

NATIONAL LEAGUE

	ab	r	h	bi	bb	so	po	a
P.Rose, 3b	4	0	1	0	0	0	1	0
D.Lopes, pr-2b	1	0	1	1	0	0	0	1
J.Morgan, 2b	3	1	0	0	1	1	2	1
J.Clark, rf	1	0	0	0	0	1	0	0
G.Foster, cf	2	1	0	0	2	1	2	0
G.Luzinski, lf	2	0	1	1	1	0	0	0
R.Fingers, p	0	0	0	0	0	0	0	2
W.Stargell, ph	1	0	0	0	0	0	0	0
B.Sutter, p	0	0	0	0	0	0	0	0
P.Niekro, p	0	0	0	0	0	0	0	0
S.Garvey, 1b	3	1	2	2	1	0	7	0
T.Simmons, c	3	0	1	0	0	1	4	1
D.Concepcion, ss	0	1	0	0	1	0	2	0
R.Monday, rf	2	0	0	0	0	0	1	0
S.Rogers, p	0	0	0	0	0	0	0	0
D.Winfield, lf	2	1	1	0	0	0	1	0
L.Bowa, ss	3	1	2	0	0	0	2	4
B.Boone, c	1	1	1	2	0	0	3	1
B.Pocoroba, c	0	0	0	0	0	0	0	0
V.Blue, p	0	0	0	0	0	0	0	1
R.Smith, ph-rf	3	0	0	0	0	2	1	0
R.Cey, 3b	1	0	0	0	0	0	1	0
Totals	32	7	10	6	6	6	27	11

BATTING
2B: P.Rose (off J.Kern).
3B: S.Garvey (off R.Gossage).
2-out RBI: G.Luzinski; S.Garvey 2.
RBI, scoring position, less than 2 outs: P.Rose 0–1;
    D.Lopes 1–1; J.Morgan 0–1; T.Simmons 0–1;
    R.Monday 0–1; B.Boone 2–2.
GDP: R.Monday.

BASERUNNING
SB: L.Bowa (2nd base off J.Palmer/C.Fisk).
CS: D.Lopes (2nd base by R.Gossage/J.Sundberg).
Team LOB: 7

PITCHING	ip	h	r	er	bb	so
American League						
J.Palmer	2.2	3	3	3	4	4
M.Keough	0.1	1	0	0	0	0
L.Sorensen	3.0	1	0	0	0	0

Inherited Runners—Scored:
    M.Keough 2–0; L.Sorensen 0–0; J.Kern 0–0;
    R.Guidry 2–0; R.Gossage 0–0; S.Rogers 0–0;
    R.Fingers 0–0; B.Sutter 0–0; P.Niekro 0–0.

PITCHING	ip	h	r	er	bb	so
American League *(continued)*						
J.Kern	0.2	1	0	0	1	1
R.Guidry	0.1	0	0	0	0	0
R.Gossage (L)	1.0	4	4	4	1	1
National League						
V.Blue	3.0	5	3	3	1	2
S.Rogers	2.0	2	0	0	0	2
R.Fingers	2.0	1	0	0	0	1
B.Sutter (W)	1.2	0	0	0	0	2
P.Niekro	0.1	0	0	0	0	0

IBB: G.Foster by J.Kern.
WP: S.Rogers; R.Gossage

GAME DATA—T: 2:32; A: 51549; Temp: Unknown; Wind: Unknown direction, Speed: Unknown

UMPIRES—HP: Paul Pryor (NL), 1B: Nestor Chylak (AL), 2B: Terry Tata (NL), 3B: Bill Deegan (AL), LF: Paul Runge (NL), RF: Larry McCoy (AL)

STARTING LINEUPS

American League	National League
1. R.Carew 1b	P.Rose 3b
2. G.Brett 3b	J.Morgan 2b
3. J.Rice lf	G.Foster cf
4. R.Zisk rf	G.Luzinski lf
5. C.Fisk c	S.Garvey 1b
6. F.Lynn cf	T.Simmons c
7. D.Money 2b	R.Monday rf
8. F.Patek ss	L.Bowa ss
9. J.Palmer p	V.Blue p

AL 1ST: R.Carew tripled to left field (it was the 0–2 pitch); G.Brett doubled to left-center [R.Carew scored]; J.Rice grounded out (J.Morgan-2b to S.Garvey-1b) [G.Brett to third]; R.Zisk walked; C.Fisk popped out on a sacrifice fly to J.Morgan-2b [G.Brett scored]; R.Zisk was caught stealing second (T.Simmons-c to L.Bowa-ss); 2 R, 2 H, 0 E, 0 LOB. AL 2, NL 0.

NL 1ST: P.Rose flied to F.Lynn-cf; J.Morgan was called out on strikes; G.Foster struck out; 0 R, 0 H, 0 E, 0 LOB. AL 2, NL 0.

AL 2ND: F.Lynn struck out; D.Money struck out; F.Patek singled to center field; On a bunt J.Palmer grounded out (V.Blue-p to S.Garvey-1b); 0 R, 1 H, 0 E, 1 LOB. AL 2, NL 0.

NL 2ND: G.Luzinski singled to left field; S.Garvey walked [G.Luzinski to second]; T.Simmons struck out; R.Monday grounded into a double play (G.Brett-3b to D.Money-2b to R.Carew-1b) [S.Garvey out at second]; 0 R, 1 H, 0 E, 1 LOB. AL 2, NL 0.

AL 3RD: R.Carew tripled to center field; Foster, not normally a center fielder, misplayed the ball; G.Brett out on a sacrifice fly to G.Foster-cf [R.Carew scored]; J.Rice flied to R.Monday-rf; R.Zisk singled to left field; C.Fisk forced R.Zisk (L.Bowa-ss to J.Morgan-2b) [C.Fisk to first]; 1 R, 2 H, 0 E, 1 LOB. AL 3, NL 0.

NL 3RD: L.Bowa singled to right field; **R.Smith batted for V.Blue;** R.Smith struck out while L.Bowa stole second; P.Rose grounded out (R.Carew-1b to J.Palmer-p) [L.Bowa to third]; J.Morgan walked; G.Foster walked [J.Morgan to second]; G.Luzinski walked [L.Bowa scored, J.Morgan to third, G.Foster to second]; S.Garvey singled to left field [J.Morgan scored, G.Foster scored, G.Luzinski to second]; **M.Keough replaced J.Palmer (pitching);** T.Simmons singled to third base [G.Luzinski to third, S.Garvey to second]; R.Monday flied to J.Rice-lf; 3 R, 3 H, 0 E, 3 LOB. AL 3, NL 3.

AL 4TH: **R.Smith stayed in game (playing rf); S.Rogers replaced R.Monday (pitching);** F.Lynn singled to center field; S.Rogers threw a wild pitch [F.Lynn to second]; D.Money lined to R.Smith-rf; F.Patek reached on a fielder's choice (L.Bowa-ss to P.Rose-3b) [F.Lynn out at third]; **R.Howell batted for M.Keough;** R.Howell grounded out (S.Garvey-1b unassisted); 0 R, 1 H, 0 E, 1 LOB. AL 3, NL 3.

NL 4TH: **L.Sorensen replaced R.Howell (pitching); F.White replaced D.Money (playing 2b);** L.Bowa singled to first base; R.Smith flied to F.Lynn-cf; P.Rose flied to J.Rice-lf; J.Morgan popped to F.Patek-ss; 0 R, 1 H, 0 E, 1 LOB. AL 3, NL 3.

AL 5TH: R.Carew grounded out (L.Bowa-ss to S.Garvey-1b); G.Brett singled to right field; G.Brett stole second; J.Rice struck out; R.Zisk struck out; 0 R, 1 H, 0 E, 1 LOB. AL 3, NL 3.

NL 5TH: **D.Evans replaced R.Zisk (playing rf);** G.Foster grounded out (F.White-2b to R.Carew-1b); G.Luzinski grounded out (L.Sorensen-p to F.White-2b to R.Carew-1b); S.Garvey grounded out (F.Patek-ss to R.Carew-1b); 0 R, 0 H, 0 E, 0 LOB. AL 3, NL 3.

AL 6TH: **R.Fingers replaced G.Luzinski (pitching); D.Winfield replaced S.Rogers (playing lf);** C.Fisk popped to L.Bowa-ss; F.Lynn grounded out (R.Fingers-p to L.Bowa-ss to S.Garvey-1b); F.White popped to S.Garvey-1b in foul territory; 0 R, 0 H, 0 E, 0 LOB. AL 3, NL 3.

NL 6TH: **J.Sundberg replaced C.Fisk (playing c);** T.Simmons flied to D.Evans-rf; D.Winfield grounded out (G.Brett-3b to R.Carew-1b); L.Bowa lined to D.Evans-rf; 0 R, 0 H, 0 E, 0 LOB. AL 3, NL 3.

AL 7TH: **D.Concepcion replaced T.Simmons (playing ss); B.Boone replaced L.Bowa (playing c);** F.Patek struck out; **L.Hisle batted for L.Sorensen;** L.Hisle singled to shortstop; R.Carew forced L.Hisle (R.Fingers-p to D.Concepcion-ss) [R.Carew to first]; R.Carew was caught stealing second (B.Boone-c to D.Concepcion-ss); 0 R, 1 H, 0 E, 0 LOB. AL 3, NL 3.

NL 7TH: **J.Kern replaced L.Hisle (pitching);** R.Smith struck out; P.Rose doubled to left field; **D.Lopes ran for P.Rose;** J.Morgan flied to D.Evans-rf; G.Foster was walked intentionally; **W.Stargell batted for R.Fingers; R.Guidry replaced J.Kern (pitching);** J.Sundberg allowed a passed ball [D.Lopes to third, G.Foster to second]; W.Stargell flied to F.Lynn-cf; 0 R, 1 H, 0 E, 2 LOB. AL 3, NL 3.

AL 8TH: **D.Lopes stayed in game (playing 2b); R.Cey replaced R.Smith (playing 3b); B.Sutter replaced W.Stargell (pitching); J.Clark replaced J.Morgan (playing rf);** G.Brett grounded out (D.Lopes-2b to S.Garvey-1b); J.Rice struck out; D.Evans struck out; 0 R, 0 H, 0 E, 0 LOB. AL 3, NL 3.

NL 8TH: **R.Gossage replaced G.Brett (pitching);** **G.Nettles replaced R.Guidry (playing 3b);** **C.Lemon replaced J.Rice (playing lf);** S.Garvey tripled to very deep right-center at the wall (it was the 1–2 pitch); R.Gossage threw a wild pitch [S.Garvey scored]; D.Concepcion walked; D.Winfield singled to left field [D.Concepcion to third, D.Winfield to second (error by C.Lemon-lf)]; B.Boone singled to center field [D.Concepcion scored, D.Winfield scored]; R.Cey grounded out (G.Nettles-3b to R.Carew-1b) [B.Boone to second]; D.Lopes singled to right field [B.Boone scored]; J.Clark was called out on strikes; D.Lopes was caught stealing second (J.Sundberg-c to F.White-2b); 4 R, 4 H, 1 E, 0 LOB. AL 3, NL 7.

AL 9TH: **B.Pocoroba replaced B.Boone (playing c);** **J.Thompson batted for J.Sundberg;** J.Thompson flied to G.Foster-cf; F.Lynn flied to D.Winfield-lf; **P.Niekro replaced B.Sutter (pitching); D.Porter batted for F.White;** D.Porter popped to R.Cey-3b in foul territory; 0 R, 0 H, 0 E, 0 LOB. AL 3, NL 7.

Final Totals	R	H	E	LOB
American League	3	8	1	4
National League	7	10	0	7

A Walk in the Park

Expectations were high for an offensive explosion in the AL's only indoor stadium. At the All-Star break, more homers had been hit in the Kingdome than in any other Major League park, and the two lineups were built with that in mind. The middle of each lineup featured most of the leading power hitters in the game; these six hitters accounted for 141 homers at the break.

During batting practice the day before the game, ten thousand fans (who were allowed in at no charge) sat in awe as the players hit one blast after another. Indeed, even participants enjoyed the show. "Put the big boys in there together," said NL coach Chuck Tanner of the Pirates. "Give the folks a thrill." He grouped Mike Schmidt of the Phillies (31 homers), Dave Winfield of the Padres (22), George Foster of the Reds (20), and Dave Parker of the Pirates (16) together for their turn in the batting cage.

Cardinals outfielder Lou Brock, at his sixth and last All-Star Game, stood at the cage open-mouthed. "Is there a normal bat in here? I can't even lift these," he said, looking at the large clubs being used by the sluggers. The NL carried this concept to its extreme when pitcher Gaylord Perry of the Padres got in for a few swings. Perry, the 1978 NL Cy Young Award winner, hit two pitches into the left-field seats, which were only 316 feet down the line.

The game featured nine extra-base hits, including two homers and a triple, but was decided on a bases-loaded walk in the ninth inning by the 1978 AL Cy Young Award winner, Ron Guidry. The inning started with the game tied at six runs apiece, but Jim Kern of the Rangers walked Cincinnati's Joe Morgan with one out. After balking Morgan to second base, Kern walked 1978 NL MVP Dave Parker intentionally. After a pop-out, Ron Cey of the Dodgers also walked to load the bases. AL manager Bob Lemon, who had led the Yankees to the 1978 World Series championship but had been fired in June, brought in his Yankee ace Guidry.

Guidry had pitched two days before and had also warmed up several times in the bullpen. When he came into the game, his arm was tired and not ready to pitch. He threw two balls to Lee Mazzilli of the Mets, the third pitch was hit foul down the third base line, and then Guidry threw two more balls to force Morgan, playing in the last of his ten All-Star Games, across with the lead run.

Guidry was disgusted with the outcome: "I didn't have nothing when I came in. I'm still recuperating from pitching Sunday. I'm both tired and disappointed but disappointed first. You hate to walk a guy with the bases loaded, but I hated to get up even more as many times as I did because I only had so many pitches in me. After pitching nine innings Sunday and being tight, it's hard to come in and throw strikes."

In the first inning, the NL took an early lead off starter Nolan Ryan of the Angels. Fred Lynn of the Red Sox had talked about Ryan before the game: "He is the perfect pitcher for this park. The ball flies out of here if you hit it. But the lights are bad in here so the ball looks fuzzy. It's hard to make contact. Nolan pitching in the Kingdome should be almost invisible." Slugger Schmidt echoed that feeling: "We're putting on a batting practice show, but when Ryan gets on the mound, I'll settle for a couple of balls hit anywhere."

This was a realistic viewpoint because Ryan had entered the All-Star break with 160 strikeouts, far more than anyone else in the AL, and he sported a 12-6 record with a 2.54 ERA and only 62 walks in 145 innings. However, Ryan told a different story before the game. "Knowing the Kingdome, I think this will be a high-scoring game. I've given up eight home runs this season—four here. These measurements [of the fences] make for good power alleys in left- and right-center. Good for the hitters, not the pitchers."

However, after the first two batters of the game

struck out, Dodger first baseman Steve Garvey walked, and Mike Schmidt, the Majors' leading homer hitter at the break, tripled to center field to score Garvey. George Foster then followed with a double down the right-field line to plate Schmidt.

The lead was short-lived, however. Steve Carlton of the Phillies, 11-8 at the break, started for the NL, partly because the AL lineup was loaded with lefties. With one out, Kansas City's George Brett walked, and California's Don Baylor, playing in his only All-Star Game, doubled down the left-field line to score Brett. One out later, Lynn, the AL home run leader at the break with twenty-four, drove a ball deep into the right-center-field seats to put the Junior Circuit ahead, 3–2. Lynn, who was playing with a groin pull, immediately left the game.

Bob Boone continued the offense by leading off the second with a single. One out later, pinch hitter Brock singled to right, and Dave Lopes of the Dodgers beat out an infield single to load the bases. Parker then tied the score with a sacrifice fly.

In the top of the third inning, Bob Stanley replaced Ryan on the mound. Schmidt greeted Stanley with his second extra-base hit of the game, doubling to right-center. Gary Matthews of the Braves reached on a fielder's choice as Schmidt moved to third, and Winfield forced Matthews at second as Schmidt scored.

In its half of the inning, the AL reclaimed the lead. With one out, Baylor singled to left and advanced to second on Joaquin Andujar's wild pitch. Baylor moved to third base on an infield out, and Andujar hit Chet Lemon with a pitch. Boston's Carl Yastrzemski, playing in his fifteenth consecutive All-Star contest, singled to center field to score Baylor as Lemon moved to second. Darrell Porter hit a ground ball to Schmidt at third base, but Schmidt threw the ball away, scoring Lemon with an unearned run.

The pitchers took over until the top of the sixth, when the NL struck for another run to even up the score. With one out, Winfield doubled to right-center and scored when Expos catcher Gary Carter singled to left field.

Pete Rose, who had pinch-hit in the top of the inning, stayed in the game at first base for the NL in the bottom of the sixth. Rose set an All-Star record by appearing at his fifth different position in an All-Star Game, having already played second and third base and left and right field.

Yaz led off the inning with a single to right, and his Red Sox teammate Rick Burleson ran for him. Darrell Porter doubled to right-center, moving Burleson to third, and pinch hitter Bruce Bochte of the hometown Mariners beat out a single in the hole at shortstop, scoring Burleson. Houston hurler Joe Sambito replaced Perry on the hill for the NL, and Reggie Jackson hit for Mark Clear. Jackson hit a grounder to second baseman Lopes, who threw home to nail Porter while Bochte and Jackson each advanced two bases in the rundown.

After Sambito walked Roy Smalley intentionally to load the bases, George Brett flew out, and Baylor forced Smalley at second. Thus, three of the AL's most potent hitters left a total of eight runners on base without scoring a run.

In the top of the eighth inning, the NL tied the score once again. Mazzilli, a switch hitter batting left-handed against Kern, hit a short fly ball to left field that just cleared the fence near the pole and landed in the first row of seats. It was the thirteenth pinch homer in All-Star history (the seventh by the NL) and the seventh time a player had homered on his first All-Star at bat. Mazzilli was also the second player to hit a pinch homer in his first All-Star at bat. The only previous hitter to perform the feat was George Altman of the Cubs in the first game of 1961. (Jeff Conine would join the group in 1995.) Mazzilli, who had nine homers at the break, was the first New York Met to homer in All-Star competition.

Although Mazzilli was the batter when the NL tied and won the game, the real hero for the visitors was right-fielder Dave Parker, who played the entire game. Parker threw out two runners late in the game and was named the MVP of the contest.

Jim Rice, the reigning AL MVP, led off the seventh inning for the AL by blooping a ball into short right field. Second baseman Joe Morgan and Parker lost sight of the ball against the concrete roof, and it dropped in for a double. However, Rice tried for a triple, and Parker recovered in time to throw him out. "I saw the ball go up, but after it got in the vicinity of the lights I lost it," said Parker. "I was fortunate to get the ball on the first bounce and turn and make a good throw."

In the eighth inning, Brian Downing of the Angels singled to left-center field and was sacrificed to second by Bochte. Jackson was walked intentionally, and Bobby Grich struck out. After Graig Nettles singled to right, Downing was waved home. Parker charged the ball, fielding it on one hop, and made a perfect throw to Gary Carter. Downing tried to slide around Carter, but Carter blocked the plate and tagged him out.

"I got a good grip on the ball and wanted to throw it low on a bounce," said Parker. "But it carried all the way in, and Gary Carter blocked the plate and made a sensational tag." NL manager Tommy Lasorda enjoyed the throw to the plate: "It looked like it was shot out of a cannon."

The nine extra-base hits in the game were one

Winfield sliding home, 1979
Dave Winfield scores on Gary Carter's sixth-inning single. Darrell Porter of Kansas City is the American League catcher. © Bettmann/CORBIS.

World Series is team against team where depth and finesse are more important. The All-Star Game is power hitting and power pitching."

AL president Lee MacPhail, who had not seen his league win an All-Star Game since he had become president in 1974, talked about the losses. "Managers go through losing streaks that last maybe a week or ten days, but when a losing streak lasts seven years, it's pretty miserable."

For the first time in All-Star history, three outfielders from one team were voted to the starting lineup; Rice, Lynn, and Carl Yastrzemski of the Red Sox led the fan ballot in the AL. However, Yaz was moved to first base to replace the injured Rod Carew, and Baylor, the 1979 AL MVP, started in left field. Carew, who received the most votes in the fan ballot, was recovering from torn ligaments in his right thumb.

Cardinals shortstop Garry Templeton refused to come to Seattle because he had not been voted as a starter by the fans. His refusal seemed to have something to do with the position; Reds shortstop Dave Concepcion backed out at the last minute because Larry Bowa was chosen over him. Concepcion claimed a leg injury.

Schmidt's attitude was much different. "I'm psyched as heck just to be here, let alone getting to bat cleanup. As for Garry, if you'd asked him ten years ago when he was a kid if he'd like to be here, he'd have been tickled to death."

Reggie Jackson left his Yankee uniform in Oakland when he flew to Seattle. It arrived just in time for the game, but Jackson wore a Mariners uniform for the team photo. One of his teammates quipped: "I knew Reggie wanted to be traded, but I didn't know he'd actually go get another uniform."

short of the record set in 1951, when each team had five. In that game, the NL had four homers and a double, while the AL had two homers, two triples, and a double. The record would be tied in 1993.

Cubs relief pitcher Bruce Sutter pitched the last two innings and earned the win. At the end of the season, Sutter was named the NL Cy Young Award winner. Lasorda talked about Sutter: "There's no man on earth I'd rather have in that situation."

The loss was the eighth consecutive for the AL and the sixteenth in the last seventeen All-Star Games. Fred Lynn remarked that he was "pretty sick of hearing about it." He continued, "The

	AL		NL	
P	Nolan Ryan	CAL	Steve Carlton	PHI
C	Darrell Porter	KCA	Ted Simmons +	SLN
1B	Rod Carew +	CAL	Steve Garvey	LAN
2B	Frank White	KCA	Davey Lopes	LAN
3B	George Brett	KCA	Mike Schmidt	PHI
SS	Roy Smalley	MIN	Larry Bowa	PHI
OF	Fred Lynn	BOS	George Foster	CIN
OF	Jim Rice	BOS	Dave Parker	PIT
OF	Carl Yastrzemski	BOS	Dave Winfield	SDN
	Don Baylor	CAL	Joaquin Andujar	HOU
	Bruce Bochte	SEA	Johnny Bench +	CIN
	Rick Burleson	BOS	Bob Boone	PHI
	Mark Clear	CAL	Lou Brock	SLN
	Cecil Cooper	MIL	Gary Carter	MON
	Brian Downing	CAL	Ron Cey	LAN
	Bobby Grich	CAL	Jack Clark	SFN
	Ron Guidry	NYA	Dave Concepcion +	CIN
	Reggie Jackson	NYA	Keith Hernandez	SLN
	Tommy John	NYA	Dave Kingman +	CHN
	Steve Kemp	DET	Mike LaCoss	CIN
	Jim Kern	TEX	Gary Matthews	ATL
	Dave Lemanczyk	TOR	Lee Mazzilli	NYN
	Chet Lemon	CHA	Joe Morgan	CIN
	Sid Monge	CLE	Joe Niekro	HOU
	Graig Nettles	NYA	Larry Parrish	MON
	Jeff Newman	OAK	Gaylord Perry	SDN
	Ken Singleton	BAL	Craig Reynolds	HOU
	Bob Stanley	BOS	Steve Rogers	MON
	Don Stanhouse	BAL	Pete Rose	PHI
			Joe Sambito	HOU
			John Stearns	NYN
			Bruce Sutter	CHN
			Garry Templeton +	SLN

+ player replaced on roster

RETROSHEET EXPANDED BOX SCORE Tuesday, 7/17/1979 National League at American League (N)

National League   211 001 011- 7
American League   302 001 000- 6

NATIONAL LEAGUE

	ab	r	h	bi	bb	so	po	a
D.Lopes, 2b	3	0	1	0	0	1	4	1
J.Morgan, ph-2b	1	1	0	0	1	1	1	1
D.Parker, rf	3	0	1	1	1	1	0	2
S.Garvey, 1b	2	1	0	0	1	0	5	0
G.Perry, p	0	0	0	0	0	0	0	0
J.Sambito, p	0	0	0	0	0	0	0	0
C.Reynolds, ss	2	0	0	0	0	0	0	1
M.Schmidt, 3b	3	2	2	1	0	0	1	1
R.Cey, 3b	1	0	0	0	1	0	1	1
L.Parrish, 3b	0	0	0	0	0	0	0	0
G.Foster, lf	1	0	1	1	0	0	0	0
G.Matthews, lf	2	0	0	0	0	0	2	0
L.Mazzilli, ph-cf	1	1	1	2	1	0	0	0
D.Winfield, cf-lf	5	1	1	1	0	1	3	0
B.Boone, c	2	1	1	0	0	0	0	0
G.Carter, c	2	0	1	1	0	0	6	1
L.Bowa, ss	2	0	0	0	1	0	1	3
M.LaCoss, p	0	0	0	0	0	0	0	0
K.Hernandez, ph	1	0	0	0	0	1	0	0
B.Sutter, p	0	0	0	0	0	0	0	1
S.Carlton, p	0	0	0	0	0	0	0	0
L.Brock, ph	1	0	1	0	0	0	0	0
J.Andujar, p	0	0	0	0	0	0	0	0
J.Clark, ph	1	0	0	0	0	0	0	0
S.Rogers, p	0	0	0	0	0	0	0	0
P.Rose, ph-1b	2	0	0	0	0	0	3	0
Totals	35	7	10	7	6	5	27	12

BATTING
2B: G.Foster (off N.Ryan); M.Schmidt (off B.Stanley); D.Winfield (off M.Clear).
3B: M.Schmidt (off N.Ryan).
HR: L.Mazzilli (8th inning off J.Kern, o on, o out).
2-out RBI: M.Schmidt; G.Foster; L.Mazzilli.
RBI, scoring position, less than 2 outs: D.Parker 1-2; C.Reynolds 0-1; G.Matthews 0-1; D.Winfield 1-1; G.Carter 1-1; P.Rose 0-1.
SF: D.Parker.
GDP: B.Boone; P.Rose.

BASERUNNING
Team LOB: 8

FIELDING
E: M.Schmidt (throw).
Outfield assist: D.Parker 2 (J.Rice at 3B; B.Downing at HP).

AMERICAN LEAGUE

	ab	r	h	bi	bb	so	po	a
R.Smalley, ss	3	0	0	0	1	0	2	2
B.Grich, 2b	1	0	0	0	0	1	2	0
G.Brett, 3b	3	1	0	0	1	0	1	2
G.Nettles, 3b	1	0	1	0	0	0	1	2
D.Baylor, lf	4	2	2	1	0	0	1	0
J.Kern, p	0	0	0	0	0	0	0	0
R.Guidry, p	0	0	0	0	0	0	0	0
K.Singleton, ph	1	0	0	0	0	0	0	0
J.Rice, rf-lf	5	0	1	0	0	2	3	0
F.Lynn, cf	1	1	1	2	0	0	0	0
C.Lemon, cf	2	1	0	0	1	1	2	0
C.Yastrzemski, 1b	3	0	2	1	0	0	5	1
R.Burleson, pr-ss	2	1	0	0	0	1	0	1
D.Porter, c	3	0	1	0	0	0	2	0
B.Downing, c 1	0	1	0	0	0	3	0	
F.White, 2b	2	0	0	0	0	0	2	2
B.Bochte, ph-1b	1	0	1	1	0	0	2	0
N.Ryan, p	0	0	0	0	0	0	0	0
C.Cooper, ph	0	0	0	0	1	0	0	0
B.Stanley, p	0	0	0	0	0	0	1	0
S.Kemp, ph	1	0	0	0	0	0	0	0
M.Clear, p	0	0	0	0	0	0	0	0
R.Jackson, ph-rf	1	0	0	0	1	0	0	0
Totals	35	6	10	5	5	5	27	10

BATTING
2B: D.Baylor (off S.Carlton); D.Porter (off G.Perry); J.Rice (off M.LaCoss).
HR: F.Lynn (1st inning off S.Carlton, 1 on, 2 out).
2-out RBI: F.Lynn 2; C.Yastrzemski.
RBI, scoring position, less than 2 outs: B.Grich 0-1; G.Brett 0-2; J.Rice 0-2; B.Bochte 1-1; R.Jackson 0-1.
S: B.Bochte.

BASERUNNING
Team LOB: 9

FIELDING
DP: (2). G.Brett-F.White-C.Yastrzemski; F.White-R.Smalley-C.Yastrzemski.

PITCHING		ip	h	r	er	bb	so
National League							
S.Carlton		1.0	2	3	3	1	0
J.Andujar		2.0	2	2	1	1	0
S.Rogers		2.0	0	0	0	0	2
G.Perry	*	0.0	3	1	1	0	0
J.Sambito		0.2	0	0	0	1	0
M.LaCoss		1.1	1	0	0	0	0
B.Sutter (w)		2.0	2	0	0	2	3
American League							
N.Ryan		2.0	5	3	3	1	2
B.Stanley		2.0	1	1	1	0	0
M.Clear		2.0	2	1	1	1	0
J.Kern (L, BS)		2.2	2	2	2	3	3
R.Guidry		0.1	0	0	0	1	0

* Pitched to 3 batters in 6th

Inherited Runners—Scored:
J.Andujar 0–0; S.Rogers 0–0; G.Perry 0–0; J.Sambito 2–0; M.LaCoss 3–0; B.Sutter 0–0; B.Stanley 0–0; M.Clear 0–0; J.Kern 0–0; R.Guidry 3–1.
IBB: R.Smalley by J.Sambito; R.Jackson by B.Sutter; D.Parker by J.Kern.
HBP: C.Lemon by J.Andujar.
WP: J.Andujar
BK: J.Kern

GAME DATA—T: 3:11; A: 58905; Temp: Unknown; Wind: Unknown direction, Speed: Unknown

UMPIRES—HP: George Maloney (AL), 1B: Lee Weyer (NL), 2B: Nick Bremigan (AL), 3B: Bill Williams (NL), LF: Terry Cooney (AL), RF: Dutch Rennert (NL)

STARTING LINEUPS

National League	American League
1. D.Lopes 2b	R.Smalley ss
2. D.Parker rf	G.Brett 3b
3. S.Garvey 1b	D.Baylor lf
4. M.Schmidt 3b	J.Rice rf
5. G.Foster lf	F.Lynn cf
6. D.Winfield cf	C.Yastrzemski 1b
7. B.Boone c	D.Porter c
8. L.Bowa ss	F.White 2b
9. S.Carlton p	N.Ryan p

NL 1ST: D.Lopes was called out on strikes; D.Parker struck out; S.Garvey walked; M.Schmidt tripled to center field [S.Garvey scored]; G.Foster doubled to rightfield down the line [M.Schmidt scored]; D.Winfield lined to J.Rice-rf; 2 R, 2 H, 0 E, 1 LOB. NL 2, AL 0.

AL 1ST: R.Smalley popped to L.Bowa-ss; G.Brett walked; D.Baylor doubled to leftfield down the line [G.Brett scored]; J.Rice popped to D.Lopes-2b; F.Lynn homered to very deep right-center [D.Baylor scored]; C.Yastrzemski flied to D.Winfield-cf; 3 R, 2 H, 0 E, 0 LOB. NL 2, AL 3.

NL 2ND: **C.Lemon replaced F.Lynn (playing cf);** Lynn had pulled groin a few days earlier; B.Boone singled to center field; L.Bowa popped to G.Brett-3b in foul territory; **L.Brock batted for S.Carlton;** L.Brock singled to right field [B.Boone to second]; D.Lopes singled to the mound [B.Boone to third, L.Brock to second]; D.Parker out on a sacrifice fly to C.Lemon-cf [B.Boone scored]; S.Garvey popped to C.Yastrzemski-1b in foul territory; 1 R, 3 H, 0 E, 2 LOB. NL 3, AL 3.

AL 2ND: **G.Matthews replaced G.Foster (playing lf); J.Andujar replaced L.Brock (pitching);** D.Porter flied to G.Matthews-lf; F.White popped to S.Garvey-1b in foul territory; **C.Cooper batted for N.Ryan;** C.Cooper walked; R.Smalley flied to G.Matthews-lf; 0 R, 0 H, 0 E, 1 LOB. NL 3, AL 3.

NL 3RD: **B.Stanley replaced C.Cooper (pitching);** M.Schmidt doubled to right-center; G.Matthews reached on a fielder's choice [M.Schmidt to third]; D.Winfield forced G.Matthews (G.Brett-3b to F.White-2b) [M.Schmidt scored, D.Winfield to first]; B.Boone grounded into a double play (G.Brett-3b to F.White-2b to C.Yastrzemski-1b) [D.Winfield out at second]; 1 R, 1 H, 0 E, 0 LOB. NL 4, AL 3.

AL 3RD: G.Brett grounded out (S.Garvey-1b unassisted); D.Baylor singled to left field; J.Andujar threw a wild pitch [D.Baylor to second]; J.Rice grounded out (L.Bowa-ss to S.Garvey-1b) [D.Bay-

lor to third]; C.Lemon was hit by a pitch; C.Yastrzemski singled to center field [D.Baylor scored, C.Lemon to second]; D.Porter reached on an error by M.Schmidt-3b [C.Lemon scored (unearned) (no RBI), C.Yastrzemski to third, D.Porter to first]; F.White forced D.Porter (M.Schmidt-3b to D.Lopes-2b) [F.White to first]; 2 R (1 ER), 2 H, 1 E, 2 LOB. NL 4, AL 5.

NL 4TH: L.Bowa lined to R.Smalley-ss; **J.Clark batted for J.Andujar;** J.Clark grounded out (C.Yastrzemski-1b to B.Stanley-p); D.Lopes grounded out (R.Smalley-ss to C.Yastrzemski-1b); 0 R, 0 H, 0 E, 0 LOB. NL 4, AL 5.

AL 4TH: **S.Rogers replaced J.Clark (pitching); S.Kemp batted for B.Stanley;** S.Kemp lined to D.Lopes-2b; R.Smalley popped to M.Schmidt-3b in foul territory; G.Brett grounded out (L.Bowa-ss to S.Garvey-1b); 0 R, 0 H, 0 E, 0 LOB. NL 4, AL 5.

NL 5TH: **M.Clear replaced S.Kemp (pitching);** D.Parker flied to C.Lemon-cf; S.Garvey lined to J.Rice-rf; M.Schmidt flied to D.Baylor-lf; 0 R, 0 H, 0 E, 0 LOB. NL 4, AL 5.

AL 5TH: **G.Carter replaced B.Boone (playing c); R.Cey replaced M.Schmidt (playing 3b);** D.Baylor grounded out (L.Bowa-ss to S.Garvey-1b); J.Rice struck out; C.Lemon struck out; 0 R, 0 H, 0 E, 0 LOB. NL 4, AL 5.

NL 6TH: G.Matthews popped to C.Yastrzemski-1b; D.Winfield doubled to right-center; G.Carter singled to left field [D.Winfield scored, G.Carter to second (on throw home)]; L.Bowa walked; **P.Rose batted for S.Rogers;** P.Rose grounded into a double play (F.White-2b to R.Smalley-ss to C.Yastrzemski-1b) [L.Bowa out at second]; 1 R, 2 H, 0 E, 1 LOB. NL 5, AL 5.

AL 6TH: **P.Rose stayed in game (playing 1b); G.Perry replaced S.Garvey (pitching);** C.Yastrzemski singled to right field; **R.Burleson ran for C.Yastrzemski;** D.Porter doubled to right-center [R.Burleson to third]; **B.Bochte batted for F.White;** B.Bochte singled to deep shortstop [R.Burleson scored, D.Porter to third]; **R.Jackson batted for M.Clear; J.Sambito replaced G.Perry (pitching);** R.Jackson reached on a fielder's choice (D.Lopes-2b to G.Carter-c to R.Cey-3b) [D.Porter out at home, B.Bochte to third, R.Jackson to second]; R.Smalley was walked intentionally; G.Brett flied to D.Winfield-cf; **M.Lacoss replaced L.Bowa (pitching); C.Reynolds replaced J.Sambito (playing ss);** D.Baylor forced R.Smalley (C.Reynolds-ss to D.Lopes-2b) [D.Baylor to first]; 1 R, 3 H, 0 E, 3 LOB. NL 5, AL 6.

NL 7TH: **J.Rice changed positions (playing lf); R.Burleson stayed in game (playing ss); B.Bochte stayed in game (playing 1b); R.Jackson stayed in game** (playing rf); **B.Grich replaced R.Smalley (playing 2b); J.Kern replaced D.Baylor (pitching); G.Nettles replaced G.Brett (playing 3b); B.Downing replaced D.Porter (playing c); J.Morgan batted for D.Lopes;** J.Morgan struck out; D.Parker singled to pitcher; C.Reynolds grounded out (G.Nettles-3b to B.Bochte-1b) [D.Parker to second]; R.Cey grounded out (G.Nettles-3b to B.Bochte-1b); 0 R, 1 H, 0 E, 1 LOB. NL 5, AL 6.

NL 7TH: **J.Morgan stayed in game (playing 2b);** J.Rice doubled to rightfield down the line (D.Parker-rf to P.Rose-1b) [J.Rice out at third]; C.Lemon grounded out (R.Cey-3b to P.Rose-1b); R.Burleson flied to D.Winfield-cf; 0 R, 1 H, 0 E, 0 LOB. NL 5, AL 6.

NL 8TH: **L.Mazzilli batted for G.Matthews;** L.Mazzilli homered to deep leftfield down the line; Mazzilli's first All-Star at bat; D.Winfield struck out; G.Carter popped to B.Grich-2b; **K.Hernandez batted for M.Lacoss;** K.Hernandez struck out; 1 R, 1 H, 0 E, 0 LOB. NL 6, AL 6.

AL 8TH: **L.Mazzilli stayed in game (playing cf); D.Winfield changed positions (playing lf); B.Sutter replaced K.Hernandez (pitching);** B.Downing singled to left-center; B.Bochte out on a sacrifice bunt (B.Sutter-p to J.Morgan-2b) [B.Downing to second]; R.Jackson was walked intentionally; B.Grich struck out; G.Nettles singled to right field (D.Parker-rf to G.Carter-c) [B.Downing out at home, R.Jackson to second]; 0 R, 2 H, 0 E, 2 LOB. NL 6, AL 6.

NL 9TH: P.Rose lined to J.Rice-lf; J.Morgan walked; J.Kern balked [J.Morgan to second]; D.Parker was walked intentionally; C.Reynolds popped to G.Nettles-3b in foul territory; R.Cey walked [J.Morgan to third, D.Parker to second]; **R.Guidry replaced J.Kern (pitching);** L.Mazzilli walked [J.Morgan scored, D.Parker to third, R.Cey to second]; D.Winfield forced L.Mazzilli (R.Burleson-ss to B.Grich-2b) [D.Winfield to first]; 1 R, 0 H, 0 E, 3 LOB. NL 7, AL 6.

AL 9TH: **L.Parrish replaced R.Cey (playing 3b); K.Singleton batted for R.Guidry;** K.Singleton grounded out (J.Morgan-2b to P.Rose-1b); J.Rice struck out; C.Lemon walked; R.Burleson struck out; 0 R, 0 H, 0 E, 1 LOB. NL 7, AL 6.

Final Totals	R	H	E	LOB
National League	7	10	1	8
American League	6	10	0	9

Tuesday, July 8, 1980

Dodger Stadium, Los Angeles

National League 4, American League 2

SERIES RESULTS: NL 32, AL 18, 1 TIE

AL: Perfection Then Imperfection

The first All-Star Game at Dodger Stadium began differently from all previous contests but ended in the same way as the previous eight games. Two AL pitchers retired the first fourteen NL batters (no team had ever gone that long without a runner before), but the Senior Circuit eventually triumphed for the ninth consecutive time. This nine-game winning streak was unprecedented in All-Star competition. The NL had now won seventeen of the last eighteen All-Star contests.

AL manager Earl Weaver of Baltimore chose one of his own pitchers, Steve Stone, to start the game. Stone, who would be named the AL Cy Young Award winner at the end of the season, entered the game with a 12-3 record and a 3.10 ERA and was one of fourteen first-time selectees in the league. In 1976, Stone had suffered a torn rotator cuff in his pitching shoulder, but in a two-week period in 1980 he was named an AL player of the week, pitcher of the month, and starter for the All-Star Game.

Stone's reaction was humorous: "I've played the game twelve years and never received any honors. I haven't sold my soul to the devil, but I've had a hard time convincing my parents."

Stone pitched a perfect three innings against the NL, matching Denny McLain's performance in 1966. He retired the nine batters on fewer than thirty pitches, although there was some disagreement about the exact number. "I was always very tough in All-Star Games," said Stone. "In 1965 I pitched in the Ohio high school All-Star Game and I won that." This was Stone's only Major League All-Star Game.

The only tough play in the three innings came on the first batter, Dave Lopes, who hit a grounder to the left of Yankees third baseman Graig Nettles. Nettles dove for the ball and made a good throw to get the speedy Dodger infielder, a move by Nettles the Dodger Stadium crowd remembered well from his performance in the 1978 World Series.

Tommy John, another pitcher who had suffered severe arm damage, followed Stone to the mound and retired the first five batters he faced. Finally, with two out in the fifth inning, the NL got its first base runner, although Ken Griffey did not remain on the bases very long. Griffey hit a homer to the deepest spot in right-center field to cut the AL lead in half.

As he walked to the plate, Griffey turned to NL teammate Reggie Smith and predicted: "I'm going to hit one out of here." It was a prediction that seemed easy to make because Griffey had hit .422 in his six-year career against John while John played in the NL.

Griffey later said, "He tries to throw the slider inside to me, and I usually can adjust to it. The pitch I hit tonight was a fast ball, and I knew it was out as soon as I hit it." Griffey was named the game's MVP for his two-hit performance in a game in which no one player dominated.

While the AL pitchers shut down their opponents for almost five innings, the AL batters wasted many scoring chances. They faced Houston's fireballer J. R. Richard to start the game. Richard, also a first-time All-Star, came into the break with a 10-4 record and a 1.96 ERA. NL manager Chuck Tanner of Pittsburgh chose Richard over Steve Carlton of the Phillies (14-4 with a league-leading 153 strikeouts) because he would work on four days' rest while Carlton had pitched on Sunday.

With one out in the first, the Angels' Rod Carew walked and then stole second base. He moved to third on Fred Lynn's ground out but was stranded when Yankee Reggie Jackson struck out.

In the second inning, Milwaukee's Ben Oglivie, the AL home run leader at the break, walked and then moved to third base two outs later on Yankees shortstop Bucky Dent's single to right field. Once again, a strikeout ended the threat, this time when Steve Stone went down swinging. Stone had not hit since 1976, when he pitched for the Cubs.

In the third inning, Bob Welch of the Dodgers replaced Richard on the mound. Willie Randolph greeted him with a single to right field but was picked off by Welch. "No one told me he had a good move," Randolph complained later. Rod Carew then doubled to left field, and one out later, Jackson walked and Carew moved to third when ball four was wild. However, for the third time in three innings, the AL threat died as a batter struck out. This time it was Oglivie.

With two out in the top of the fifth, Carew singled to right field. Boston outfielder Fred Lynn then hit Welch's 3-2 pitch deep down the right-field line for a two-run homer, the first runs of the game.

It was Lynn's third All-Star homer. Only Stan Musial, with six, and Ted Williams, with four, had more, and at the time there were five other players with three (Johnny Bench, Rocky Colavito, Harmon Killebrew, Ralph Kiner, and Willie Mays). Lynn said, "I hadn't played in five days because of a hamstring. Welch struck me out on a fastball the first time. It seems like every time I get a hit in the All-Star Game, it's a home run."

After Griffey's homer in the fifth, the momentum of the game switched to the home team. "I think my hit pumped the team up. It gave us more enthusiasm, and we took advantage of their mistakes," said Griffey later.

Jerry Reuss of the Dodgers took the mound in the sixth inning and struck out Royals catcher Darrell Porter, Texas third baseman Buddy Bell, and Tommy John in succession. It was Reuss's only inning of work.

In their half of the inning, the National Leaguers scored two runs to take the lead. With one out, Ray Knight, Cincinnati's third baseman, singled to left field. Pittsburgh second sacker Phil Garner advanced Knight to second base with a single to center field, and Knight scored when Cardinals outfielder George Hendrick singled to right-center. Ed Farmer replaced Tommy John on the hill for the AL. Padres outfielder Dave Winfield hit a grounder to the left of second baseman Randolph that took a funny hop. Randolph failed to snag the short hop and was charged with an error on the play. Garner, who had raced to third base on Hendrick's hit, scored as Hendrick advanced to second.

Randolph talked about the play later: "I don't see they could give me an error on that play. The ball had a funny knuckleball spin." Weaver backed up Randolph: "The ball [he] handled on Winfield was a difficult play. If he makes it, it's the play of the game and may turn things around. As it turned out, we didn't make the big play tonight and that made the difference in the outcome."

Randolph had a bad night, also making a throwing error in the fifth inning. His two errors tied

the All-Star record for a single game. This, added to the pick-off in the third inning, negated what might have been a positive game for him with his two hits in four trips to the plate.

In the seventh inning, the NL scored an insurance run courtesy of Toronto's Dave Stieb. Ken Griffey led off with a single to right field but was forced at second base by his Cincinnati teammate Dave Concepcion. Concepcion moved to second on a wild pitch and to third on a passed ball on ball four to Ray Knight. After Knight stole second, Stieb threw another wild pitch to score Concepcion. The two wild pitches equaled the All-Star mark for a single game.

The key for the NL was its pitchers. Richard, Reuss, Pittsburgh's Jim Bibby, and the Cubs' Bruce Sutter allowed only two singles and five total base runners in six innings of work. Dodgers first baseman Steve Garvey said it best: "You start with J. R. Richard and finish with Bruce Sutter, with Jerry Reuss and Jim Bibby in between, and you've got something going."

Reuss was credited with the win and Sutter with the save. Sutter had won the previous two All-Star Games in relief.

After the game, the members of the NL squad talked about their dominance. Bibby, who had experience in both leagues, said, "It's easy now to draw lines between the leagues and say we're definitely better." Reggie Smith of the Dodgers, another player who had played in both leagues, echoed Bibby's remarks: "The National League has better individual players, more true superstars. And it's that talent that comes out in the end."

Stone countered those thoughts: "They've done better in this game, but the AL East is the strongest division in baseball. One game a year certainly doesn't make supremacy, and the World Series has shown that. We're a pretty strong league."

AL manager Weaver was also asked about the NL dominance. "I don't know the reason. All I know is that after the final out in the ninth inning, the other guys seem to have more runs," he responded.

Another topic among players after the game was the hitting conditions. This was the third consecutive All-Star Game played on the West Coast, although the previous year's contest had been held indoors at Seattle's Kingdome. The twilight start caused trouble for the hitters as they watched the ball approach.

"The light was very bad when I hit the first time in the sixth inning," said Keith Hernandez of the Cardinals. "By the time I batted in the eighth, the lighting had improved." Steve Garvey explained the concept: "You lose the ball halfway to the plate. Then you pick it up at the last second in the twilight."

Steve Carlton, who was named to the NL squad but did not play, had recently passed Mickey Lolich as the career leader for most strikeouts by a left-hander. Carlton entered the All-Star break with 2,836 punch-outs but still trailed the all-time leader, Walter Johnson, who ended his career with 3,509 strikeouts. Carlton would go on to win the 1980 NL Cy Young Award as he led his Phillies to the World Series championship.

Three of the eight elected AL starters could not play due to injury: George Brett of Kansas City, Paul Molitor of Milwaukee, and Jim Rice of Boston. For the NL, Mike Schmidt, the NL home run leader at the break, and Vida Blue sat out with injuries. Brett and Schmidt would each be named the MVP in his respective league at the end of the season.

For the third consecutive year, the *New York Times* polled Major League players for their All-Star starters. In this year's vote, taken in late June, the players disagreed with the choices of nine of the sixteen men voted to start the game by the fans. The players seemed to vote for currently hot players as opposed to the general fan trend that makes the vote a popularity contest.

Neither player who received the most votes in his league made the player-elected team. Dave Lopes of Los Angeles received more fan votes than any other player but ranked third in the player poll. Similarly, Carew led the AL in the fan ballot but lost to Oglivie when his peers voted.

The player who received the most votes in the player poll was Steve Carlton, whose name appeared on 87 percent of the votes cast even though pitcher names had to be written on the ballot. Molitor received the second-highest vote total.

	AL			NL	
P	Steve Stone		BAL	J.R. Richard	HOU
C	Carlton Fisk		BOS	Johnny Bench	CIN
1B	Rod Carew		CAL	Steve Garvey	LAN
2B	Paul Molitor	+	MIL	Davey Lopes	LAN
3B	George Brett	+	KCA	Mike Schmidt +	PHI
SS	Bucky Dent		NYA	Bill Russell	LAN
OF	Reggie Jackson		NYA	Dave Kingman	CHN
OF	Fred Lynn		BOS	Dave Parker	PIT
OF	Jim Rice	+	BOS	Reggie Smith	LAN
	Buddy Bell		TEX	Jim Bibby	PIT
	Al Bumbry		BAL	Vida Blue +	SFN
	Tom Burgmeier		BOS	Steve Carlton	PHI
	Cecil Cooper		MIL	Gary Carter	MON
	Ed Farmer		CHA	Dave Concepcion	CIN
	Rich Gossage		NYA	Jose Cruz	HOU
	Bobby Grich		CAL	Phil Garner	PIT
	Larry Gura		KCA	Ken Griffey	CIN
	Rickey Henderson		OAK	George Hendrick	SLN
	Rick Honeycutt		SEA	Keith Hernandez	SLN
	Tommy John		NYA	Ray Knight	CIN
	Ken Landreaux		MIN	Dale Murphy	ATL
	Graig Nettles		NYA	Ken Reitz	SLN
	Ben Oglivie		MIL	Jerry Reuss	LAN
	Al Oliver		TEX	Pete Rose	PHI
	Jorge Orta		CLE	John Stearns	NYN
	Lance Parrish		DET	Bruce Sutter	CHN
	Darrell Porter		KCA	Kent Tekulve	PIT
	Willie Randolph		NYA	Bob Welch	LAN
	Dave Stieb		TOR	Eddie Whitson	SFN
	Alan Trammell		DET	Dave Winfield	SDN
	Robin Yount		MIL		

+ player replaced on roster

```
American League     000 020 000- 2
National League     000 012 10X- 4
```

AMERICAN LEAGUE

	ab	r	h	bi	bb	so	po	a
W.Randolph, 2b	4	0	2	0	0	0	0	3
D.Stieb, p	0	0	0	0	0	0	0	0
A.Trammell, ss	0	0	0	0	0	0	0	0
R.Carew, 1b	2	1	2	0	1	0	4	0
C.Cooper, 1b	1	0	0	0	0	0	6	0
F.Lynn, cf	3	1	1	2	0	1	2	0
A.Bumbry, cf	1	0	0	0	0	0	2	0
R.Jackson, rf	2	0	1	0	1	1	0	0
K.Landreaux, pr-rf	1	0	0	0	0	0	1	0
B.Oglivie, lf	2	0	0	0	1	1	1	0
A.Oliver, lf	1	0	0	0	0	0	0	0
R.Gossage, p	0	0	0	0	0	0	0	0
C.Fisk, c	2	0	0	0	0	2	5	0
D.Porter, c	1	0	0	0	0	1	0	1
R.Henderson, lf	1	0	0	0	0	0	0	0
G.Nettles, 3b	2	0	0	0	0	0	0	1
B.Bell, 3b	2	0	0	0	0	1	0	2
B.Dent, ss	2	0	1	0	0	1	0	1
T.John, p	1	0	0	0	0	1	0	1
E.Farmer, p	0	0	0	0	0	0	0	0
B.Grich, 2b	0	0	0	0	1	0	0	1
S.Stone, p	1	0	0	0	0	1	0	0
R.Yount, ss	2	0	0	0	0	0	3	2
L.Parrish, c	1	0	0	0	0	1	0	0
Totals	32	2	7	2	4	11	24	12

BATTING
2B: R.Carew (off B.Welch).
HR: F.Lynn (5th inning off B.Welch, 1 on, 2 out).
2-out RBI: F.Lynn 2.
RBI, scoring position, less than 2 outs: F.Lynn 0–2.
GDP: C.Cooper.

BASERUNNING
SB: R.Carew (2nd base off J.Richard / J.Bench).
Team LOB: 7

FIELDING
E: W.Randolph (throw); W.Randolph (fumble).
PB: D.Porter.
DP: (1). W.Randolph-R.Yount-C.Cooper.

NATIONAL LEAGUE

	ab	r	h	bi	bb	so	po	a
D.Lopes, 2b	1	0	0	0	0	0	0	2
P.Garner, 2b	2	1	1	0	1	1	1	3
R.Smith, cf	2	0	0	0	0	0	0	0
G.Hendrick, cf	2	0	1	1	0	0	0	0
B.Sutter, p	0	0	0	0	0	0	0	0
D.Parker, rf	2	0	0	0	0	1	0	0
D.Winfield, rf	2	0	0	1	0	0	1	0
S.Garvey, 1b	2	0	0	0	0	0	7	0
K.Hernandez, ph-1b	2	0	2	0	0	0	5	0
J.Bench, c	1	0	0	0	0	0	5	0
J.Stearns, c	1	0	0	0	0	0	5	0
P.Rose, ph	1	0	0	0	0	0	0	0
J.Bibby, p	0	0	0	0	0	0	0	0
D.Murphy, cf	1	0	0	0	0	0	0	0
D.Kingman, lf	1	0	0	0	0	1	0	0
K.Griffey, lf	3	1	2	1	0	0	1	0
K.Reitz, 3b	2	0	0	0	0	0	1	0
J.Reuss, p	0	0	0	0	0	0	0	0
D.Concepcion, ss	1	1	0	0	0	0	0	2
B.Russell, ss	2	0	0	0	0	0	0	2
G.Carter, c	1	0	0	0	0	0	1	0
J.Richard, p	0	0	0	0	0	0	0	0
B.Welch, p	1	0	0	0	0	1	0	1
R.Knight, 3b	1	1	1	0	1	0	0	1
Totals	31	4	7	3	2	4	27	11

BATTING
HR: K.Griffey (5th inning off T.John, 0 on, 2 out).
2-out RBI: K.Griffey.
RBI, scoring position, less than 2 outs: G.Hendrick 1–1;
D.Winfield 1–1; P.Rose 0–2; G.Carter 0–1.
GDP: P.Rose.

BASERUNNING
SB: P.Garner (2nd base off D.Stieb / D.Porter); R.Knight
(2nd base off D.Stieb / D.Porter).
Team LOB: 5

FIELDING
DP: (1). D.Concepcion-P.Garner-K.Hernandez.

PITCHING	ip	h	r	er	bb	so
American League						
S.Stone	3.0	0	0	0	0	3
T.John (L)	2.1	4	3	3	0	1
E.Farmer	0.2	1	0	0	0	0
D.Stieb	1.0	1	1	0	2	0
R.Gossage	1.0	1	0	0	0	0
National League						
J.Richard	2.0	1	0	0	2	3
B.Welch	3.0	5	2	2	1	4
J.Reuss (w)	1.0	0	0	0	0	3
J.Bibby	1.0	1	0	0	0	0
B.Sutter (s)	2.0	0	0	0	1	1

Inherited Runners—Scored:
   T.John 0–0; E.Farmer 2–1; D.Stieb 0–0;
   R.Gossage 0–0; B.Welch 0–0; J.Reuss 0–0;
   J.Bibby 0–0; B.Sutter 0–0.
WP: B.Welch; D.Stieb 2

GAME DATA—T: 2:33; A: 56088; Temp: Unknown;
Wind: Unknown direction, Speed: Unknown

UMPIRES—HP: John Kibler (NL), 1B: Larry Barnett (AL),
2B: Nick Colosi (NL), 3B: Jim McKean (AL), LF: Jerry Dale
(NL), RF: Rich Garcia (AL)

STARTING LINEUPS

	American League	National League
1.	W.Randolph 2b	D.Lopes 2b
2.	R.Carew 1b	R.Smith cf
3.	F.Lynn cf	D.Parker rf
4.	R.Jackson rf	S.Garvey 1b
5.	B.Oglivie lf	J.Bench c
6.	C.Fisk c	D.Kingman lf
7.	G.Nettles 3b	K.Reitz 3b
8.	B.Dent ss	B.Russell ss
9.	S.Stone p	J.Richard p

AL 1ST: W.Randolph grounded out (D.Lopes-2b to S.Garvey-1b); R.Carew walked; R.Carew stole second; F.Lynn grounded out (D.Lopes-2b to S.Garvey-1b) [R.Carew to third]; R.Jackson struck out; 0 R, 0 H, 0 E, 1 LOB. AL 0, NL 0.

NL 1ST: D.Lopes grounded out (G.Nettles-3b to R.Carew-1b); R.Smith flied to F.Lynn-cf; D.Parker struck out; 0 R, 0 H, 0 E, 0 LOB. AL 0, NL 0.

AL 2ND: B.Oglivie walked; C.Fisk struck out; G.Nettles popped to K.Reitz-3b in foul territory; B.Dent singled to right field [B.Oglivie to third]; S.Stone struck out; 0 R, 1 H, 0 E, 2 LOB. AL 0, NL 0.

NL 2ND: S.Garvey popped to C.Fisk-c in foul territory; J.Bench grounded out (B.Dent-ss to R.Carew-1b); D.Kingman struck out; 0 R, 0 H, 0 E, 0 LOB. AL 0, NL 0.

AL 3RD: **B.Welch replaced J.Richard (pitching);** W.Randolph singled to right field; W.Randolph was picked off first (B.Welch-p to S.Garvey-1b); R.Carew doubled to left field; F.Lynn struck out; R.Jackson walked while R.Carew advanced to third on a wild pitch; B.Oglivie struck out; 0 R, 2 H, 0 E, 2 LOB. AL 0, NL 0.

NL 3RD: K.Reitz grounded out (W.Randolph-2b to R.Carew-1b); B.Russell flied to B.Oglivie-lf; B.Welch struck out; 0 R, 0 H, 0 E, 0 LOB. AL 0, NL 0.

AL 4TH: **P.Garner replaced D.Lopes (playing 2b); K.Griffey replaced D.Kingman (playing lf); J.Stearns replaced J.Bench (playing c);** C.Fisk struck out; G.Nettles grounded out (S.Garvey-1b unassisted); B.Dent struck out; 0 R, 0 H, 0 E, 0 LOB. AL 0, NL 0.

NL 4TH: **T.John replaced B.Dent (pitching); R.Yount replaced S.Stone (playing ss);** P.Garner struck out; R.Smith grounded out (R.Yount-ss to R.Carew-1b); D.Parker flied to F.Lynn-cf; 0 R, 0 H, 0 E, 0 LOB. AL 0, NL 0.

AL 5TH: **G.Hendrick replaced R.Smith (playing cf); D.Winfield replaced D.Parker (playing rf);** R.Yount grounded out (B.Russell-ss to S.Garvey-1b); W.Randolph grounded out (B.Russell-ss to S.Garvey-1b); R.Carew singled to right field; F.Lynn homered to deep rightfield down the line (it was the 3–2 pitch) [R.Carew scored]; R.Jackson singled to center field; **K.Landreaux ran for R.Jackson;** B.Oglivie grounded out (S.Garvey-1b unassisted); 2 R, 3 H, 0 E, 1 LOB. AL 2, NL 0.

NL 5TH: **K.Landreaux stayed in game (playing rf); C.Cooper replaced R.Carew (playing 1b); A.Bumbry replaced F.Lynn (playing cf); A.Oliver replaced B.Oglivie (playing lf); D.Porter replaced C.Fisk (playing c); B.Bell replaced G.Nettles (playing 3b);** S.Garvey grounded out (B.Bell-3b to C.Cooper-1b); J.Stearns grounded out (W.Randolph-2b to C.Cooper-1b); K.Griffey homered to very deep right-center; K.Reitz reached on an error by W.Randolph-2b (D.Porter-c to R.Yount-ss) [K.Reitz out at second]; 1 R, 1 H, 1 E, 0 LOB. AL 2, NL 1.

AL 6TH: **R.Knight replaced B.Welch (playing 3b); J.Reuss replaced K.Reitz (pitching);** D.Porter struck out; B.Bell struck out; T.John struck out; 0 R, 0 H, 0 E, 0 LOB. AL 2, NL 1.

NL 6TH: B.Russell grounded out (T.John-p to C.Cooper-1b); R.Knight singled to left field; P.Garner singled to center field [R.Knight to second]; G.Hendrick singled to right-center [R.Knight scored, P.Garner to third]; **E.Farmer replaced T.John (pitching);** D.Winfield reached on an error by W.Randolph-2b [P.Garner scored (RBI), G.Hendrick to second, D.Winfield to first]; **K.Hernandez batted for S.Garvey;** K.Hernandez singled to pitcher [G.Hendrick to third, D.Winfield to second]; **P.Rose batted for J.Stearns;** P.Rose grounded into a double play (W.Randolph-2b to R.Yount-ss to C.Cooper-1b) [K.Hernandez out at second]; 2 R, 4 H, 1 E, 2 LOB. AL 2, NL 3.

AL 7TH: **K.Hernandez stayed in game (playing 1b); J.Bibby replaced P.Rose (pitching); G.Carter replaced B.Russell (playing c); D.Concepcion replaced J.Reuss (playing ss);** R.Yount flied to D.Winfield-rf; W.Randolph singled to center field; C.Cooper grounded into a double play (D.Concepcion-ss to P.Garner-2b to K.Hernandez-1b) [W.Randolph out at second]; 0 R, 1 H, 0 E, 0 LOB. AL 2, NL 3.

NL 7TH: **D.Stieb replaced W.Randolph (pitching); B.Grich replaced E.Farmer (playing 2b);** K.Griffey singled to right field; D.Concepcion forced K.Griffey (B.Grich-2b to R.Yount-ss) [D.Concepcion to first]; D.Stieb threw a wild pitch [D.Concepcion to second]; G.Carter grounded out (B.Bell-3b to C.Cooper-1b); R.Knight walked while D.Concepcion advanced to third on a passed ball; R.Knight stole second; D.Stieb threw a wild pitch [D.Concepcion scored (unearned), R.Knight to third]; P.Garner walked; P.Garner stole second; G.Hendrick flied to A.Bumbry-cf; 1 R (0 ER), 1 H, 0 E, 2 LOB. AL 2, NL 4.

AL 8TH: **B.Sutter replaced G.Hendrick (pitching); D.Murphy replaced J.Bibby (playing cf);** A.Bumbry grounded out (P.Garner-2b to K.Hernandez-1b); K.Landreaux lined to K.Griffey-lf; A.Oliver grounded out (P.Garner-2b to K.Hernandez-1b); 0 R, 0 H, 0 E, 0 LOB. AL 2, NL 4.

NL 8TH: **R.Gossage replaced A.Oliver (pitching); L.Parrish replaced R.Yount (playing c); R.Henderson replaced D.Porter (playing lf); A.Trammell replaced D.Stieb (playing ss);** D.Winfield lined to K.Landreaux-rf; K.Hernandez singled to left field; D.Murphy grounded out (C.Cooper-1b unassisted) [K.Hernandez to second]; K.Griffey flied to A.Bumbry-cf; 0 R, 1 H, 0 E, 1 LOB. AL 2, NL 4.

AL 9TH: R.Henderson grounded out (R.Knight-3b to K.Hernandez-1b); B.Bell grounded out (D.Concepcion-ss to K.Hernandez-1b); B.Grich walked; L.Parrish struck out; 0 R, 0 H, 0 E, 1 LOB. AL 2, NL 4.

Final Totals	R	H	E	LOB
American League	2	7	2	7
National League	4	7	0	5

52

Business as Usual after the Strike

The 1981 season is chiefly remembered for the player strike that halted the season for fifty-nine days. There were no games played from June 12 through August 9, which is usually the heart of the season. Once the dispute was settled, baseball played the twice-postponed All-Star Game on Sunday for the only time in the history of the gala. This was the latest date ever for an All-Star Game; the only other August contest was the second game in 1959, which was played on August 3.

The players were thinking about the damage as they gathered in Cleveland. Mike Schmidt, the reigning NL MVP, said, "Whatever damage the game's suffered, it's been done and can't be undone. Now, we have to start the rehabilitation."

There were many problems getting the game played. It appeared that the umpires would not work the All-Star Game because of problems with the revised postseason schedule. Then it rained steadily in Cleveland on the two days prior to the game. On the night before the contest, an NFL exhibition game was played, which threatened to destroy the field because of the mud. The last concern was that the air traffic controllers were on strike, possibly delaying or preventing players from getting to Cleveland for the game. However, only Fernando Valenzuela, the NL starting pitcher, arrived too late to attend the press conference the day before the game.

Before the contest, the players seemed to be taking the game seriously. No player selected for either All-Star squad asked not to play. There were no excuses about phony injuries or personal problems. In fact, Rich Gossage of the Yankees, who had a stiff shoulder and was replaced on the AL roster, was at the game in uniform.

Kansas City's Jim Frey, the AL manager, was asked whether he would rather be supervising the workouts of his Royals team as they prepared to restart the season. "I don't mind telling you that

this is a pretty big kick to me," he replied. "I'm a guy who played fourteen years in the minors and never made the majors. Plenty of times I didn't even know what I'd be doing for a living, much less managing a Major League All-Star team."

Once the game started, it was business as usual as the NL won its tenth consecutive game before a record crowd of 72,086. Bill Madlock of the Pirates said, "From what I can see, the AL is just sitting over there waiting to get beat."

The game featured nine-game winners for each side. Detroit's Jack Morris, 9-3 with a 2.56 ERA, was chosen to start for the AL, and Dodger rookie Fernando Valenzuela, 9-4 with a 2.45 ERA, started for the NL.

The first batter, Pete Rose of the Phillies, singled. Rose, playing in his fifteenth All-Star Game, set a record by starting at his fifth different position in All-Star competition. He had previously started at second base, left field, right field, and third base, and he started at first base in this game. In this inning, Rose was stranded as the next three batters all made outs.

In the bottom of the inning, Rod Carew of the Angels beat out an infield single but was out trying to steal second base. Yankee Willie Randolph then singled but was left stranded. The first run of the game came in the second inning as Tom Seaver replaced Valenzuela on the hill for the NL. Ken Singleton of the Orioles greeted Seaver with a homer to right field on a two-strike count. It was the only damage done, although both New York's Bucky Dent and Seattle's Tom Paciorek singled in the inning.

Pinch hitter Dwight Evans of the Red Sox walked in the bottom of the fourth, and Dent doubled down the left-field line, moving Evans to third base. However, pinch hitter Gorman Thomas of the Brewers popped out, and Carew struck out to end the inning, thus wasting another scoring opportunity. Ken Forsch of the Angels started the visitor's fifth by striding in from the bullpen and promptly surrendering a home run to Expos catcher Gary Carter on his first pitch of the game, tying the score, 1–1. One inning later, Pittsburgh outfielder Dave Parker homered off Mike Norris to put the NL ahead.

In the bottom of the sixth, the AL squad loaded the bases with no one out on successive singles by Singleton, Evans, and former Red Sox catcher Carlton Fisk, who was in his first year with the White Sox. Fred Lynn, another Red Sox refugee, who was in his first year with the Angels, pinch-hit for Dent and singled home Singleton, tying the game again. Rangers third baseman Buddy Bell hit a sacrifice fly to score Evans, and one out later pinch hitter Ted Simmons from Milwaukee singled home Fisk. The AL might have scored more runs if not for the spectacular catch made by Dusty Baker on Al Oliver's fly ball. Baker pulled a groin muscle making the catch on the rain- and football-damaged field.

In the top of the seventh, Gary Carter greeted a new pitcher with a homer on the first pitch for the second time in the game. The victim this time was Ron Davis of the Yankees, who had replaced teammate Rich Gossage on the roster. Carter was the fifth player to hit two homers in an All-Star Game, following Arky Vaughan (1941), Ted Williams (1946), Al Rosen (1954), and Willie McCovey (1969). All except Williams hit their blasts in consecutive at bats.

Carter commented on his feat after the game: "When you're in an All-Star Game like this, you just go up there hacking. I will have to say that I was looking for fastballs, and that's what I got both times." This marked the first time that a Montreal player had homered in an All-Star Game.

The NL struck for two more runs in the eighth to win the game. San Diego shortstop Ozzie Smith, in his first of fourteen All-Star Games, walked and stole second base. Bo Diaz's throw went into center field, and Smith rounded the bag too far and was eventually caught in a rundown, with the pitcher, Rollie Fingers, recording the out. The Pirates' Mike Easler then walked and scored when Mike Schmidt homered to center field. Schmidt said later, "It was as good as I ever felt running around the bases, as good as the World Series."

The blast was the fourth for the NL, tying the record for one team in All-Star competition held by the NL in 1951 and 1960 (game two) and the AL in 1954. It also meant that all five NL runs scored on homers.

The AL went out quietly in the last two innings as all six batters were retired easily. In the ninth, Toronto pitcher Dave Stieb had to bat for himself because Frey had run out of players when Fred Lynn left the game after hurting his knee sliding into second base.

"When I went to bat, I had Rick Burleson's bat, Buddy Bell's glove, and Tom Paciorek's helmet. I'd have been extremely surprised if I had touched the ball." He didn't, striking out instead.

Frey's reaction after the game was predictable: "I suppose we'll win one sometime. We played well, got hits, scored runs. We had plenty of chances to win, but they just kept hitting home runs. The players were disappointed they didn't win, but now it's on to the rest of the season." Ken Singleton echoed his skipper: "I really thought we had them. I really thought we were going to win this game."

Mike Schmidt, with a double and a home run, and Gary Carter, with his two homers, were the only NL players with multiple-hit games. Carter was named the game's MVP. On the other side, Ken Singleton collected a homer and a single, and Bucky Dent had a double and a single.

Vida Blue of San Francisco, Nolan Ryan of Houston, and Bruce Sutter of the Cardinals each pitched one perfect inning for the winners. Sutter collected a save, and Blue was the winner, becoming the first pitcher to win an All-Star Game for each league. Sutter had won or saved the last four All-Star contests. "Maybe sometime they'll get me," he remarked.

For the AL, Len Barker pitched two perfect innings, and Jack Morris allowed three runners in two innings but shut out the visitors. Rollie Fingers, who gave up Schmidt's homer, was charged with the loss. "Right now, I feel like I'm one or two weeks into spring training," said Fingers. That was a common feeling among the players, many of whom showed signs of not having played for two months.

A record fifty-six players were used by both teams, with only four selectees not seeing action. The NL used twenty-nine different players, a record for one team. The AL set a record by using eight pitchers, and the fifteen pitchers used by both teams was also a record. Valenzuela and Tim Raines were the only rookies named to the squad, both in the NL.

Vice President George Bush threw out the ceremonial pitch before the game. Half an hour before the event, Bush told reporters, "I'm going with a slider. I know there's a lot of risk there, but if I keep it low and outside, I think I'll be all right."

In a touching story, Britt Burns, the White Sox hurler playing on his first and only All-Star team, talked about his father. Burns had spent the previous three weeks at the hospital where his dad was in a coma. At one point, Burns said to his dad, "I made the All-Star team." Upon hearing that, the elder Burns opened his eyes in response to the comment.

The player strike cost a lot more than lost revenue and jobs. Pete Rose, who led the NL with seventy-three hits when the strike occurred, needed one more to break Stan Musial's league record of 3,630 hits. The strike made him wait eight and a half weeks, but he finally collected the record hit in his fourth at bat in the second half's first game.

	AL		NL	
P	Jack Morris	DET	Fernando Valenzuela	LAN
C	Carlton Fisk	CHA	Gary Carter	MON
1B	Rod Carew	CAL	Pete Rose	PHI
2B	Willie Randolph	NYA	Davey Lopes	LAN
3B	George Brett	KCA	Mike Schmidt	PHI
SS	Bucky Dent	NYA	Dave Concepcion	CIN
OF	Reggie Jackson	NYA	Andre Dawson	MON
OF	Ken Singleton	BAL	George Foster	CIN
OF	Dave Winfield	NYA	Dave Parker	PIT
	Tony Armas	OAK	Dusty Baker	LAN
	Len Barker	CLE	Bruce Benedict	ATL
	Buddy Bell	TEX	Vida Blue	SFN
	Rick Burleson	CAL	Bill Buckner	CHN
	Britt Burns	CHA	Steve Carlton	PHI
	Doug Corbett	MIN	Mike Easler	PIT
	Ron Davis	NYA	Phil Garner	PIT
	Bo Diaz	CLE	Steve Garvey	LAN
	Dwight Evans	BOS	Pedro Guerrero	LAN
	Rollie Fingers	MIL	Burt Hooton	LAN
	Ken Forsch	CAL	Terry Kennedy	SDN
	Rich Gossage +	NYA	Bob Knepper	HOU
	Fred Lynn	CAL	Bill Madlock	PIT
	Scott McGregor	BAL	Tim Raines	MON
	Eddie Murray	BAL	Dick Ruthven	PHI
	Mike Norris	OAK	Nolan Ryan	HOU
	Al Oliver	TEX	Tom Seaver	CIN
	Tom Paciorek	SEA	Ozzie Smith	SDN
	Ted Simmons	MIL	Bruce Sutter	SLN
	Dave Stieb	TOR	Manny Trillo	PHI
	Gorman Thomas	MIL	Joel Youngblood	NYN
	Frank White	KCA		

+ player replaced on roster

RETROSHEET EXPANDED BOX SCORE Sunday, 8/9/1981 National League at American League (N)

National League	000	011	120- 5
American League	010	003	000- 4

NATIONAL LEAGUE

	ab	r	h	bi	bb	so	po	a
P.Rose, 1b	3	0	1	0	0	0	5	0
B.Hooton, p	0	0	0	0	0	0	0	0
D.Ruthven, p	0	0	0	0	0	0	0	0
P.Guerrero, ph	1	0	0	0	0	1	0	0
V.Blue, p	0	0	0	0	0	0	0	0
B.Madlock, 3b	1	0	0	0	0	0	0	1
D.Concepcion, ss	3	0	0	0	0	1	0	0
O.Smith, ss	0	0	0	0	2	0	1	0
D.Parker, rf	3	1	1	1	0	1	1	0
M.Easler, rf	1	1	0	0	1	0	0	0
M.Schmidt, 3b	4	1	2	2	0	1	0	2
N.Ryan, p	0	0	0	0	0	0	0	0
P.Garner, 2b	0	0	0	0	0	0	0	0
G.Foster, lf	2	0	0	0	0	0	0	0
D.Baker, lf	2	0	1	0	0	0	2	0
T.Raines, pr-lf	0	0	0	0	0	0	1	0
A.Dawson, cf	4	0	1	0	0	1	4	0
G.Carter, c	3	2	2	2	0	0	5	1
B.Benedict, c	1	0	0	0	0	1	3	0
D.Lopes, 2b	0	0	0	0	1	0	1	0
M.Trillo, 2b	2	0	0	0	0	0	1	1
B.Buckner, ph	1	0	0	0	0	0	0	0
B.Sutter, p	0	0	0	0	0	0	0	0
F.Valenzuela, p	0	0	0	0	0	0	0	1
J.Youngblood, ph	1	0	0	0	0	0	0	0
T.Seaver, p	0	0	0	0	0	0	0	2
B.Knepper, p	0	0	0	0	0	0	0	1
T.Kennedy, ph	1	0	0	0	0	0	0	0
S.Garvey, 1b	2	0	1	0	0	0	3	1
Totals	35	5	9	5	4	6	27	10

BATTING
2B: M.Schmidt (off M.Norris); S.Garvey (off D.Stieb).
HR: D.Parker (6th inning off M.Norris, 0 on, 1 out); M.Schmidt (8th inning off R.Fingers, 1 on, 1 out); G.Carter 2 (5th inning off K.Forsch, 0 on, 0 out; 7th inning off R.Davis, 0 on, 0 out).
RBI, scoring position, less than 2 outs: B.Madlock 0–1; D.Baker 0–1; A.Dawson 0–1; G.Carter 0–1.

BASERUNNING
SB: O.Smith (2nd base off R.Fingers/B.Diaz); A.Dawson (2nd base off J.Morris/C.Fisk).
Team LOB: 7

FIELDING
E: M.Schmidt (fumble).

AMERICAN LEAGUE

	ab	r	h	bi	bb	so	po	a
R.Carew, 1b	3	0	1	0	0	1	12	0
E.Murray, ph-1b	2	0	0	0	0	0	2	1
W.Randolph, 2b	3	0	1	0	0	1	0	5
T.Simmons, ph	1	0	1	1	0	0	0	0
F.White, pr-2b	1	0	0	0	0	0	1	0
G.Brett, 3b	3	0	0	0	0	2	0	1
M.Norris, p	0	0	0	0	0	0	0	0
A.Oliver, ph	1	0	0	0	0	0	0	0
R.Davis, p	0	0	0	0	0	0	0	0
R.Fingers, p	0	0	0	0	0	0	1	0
D.Stieb, p	1	0	0	0	0	1	1	1
D.Winfield, cf	4	0	0	0	1	0	0	1
K.Singleton, lf	3	2	2	1	0	0	0	0
R.Burleson, ss	1	0	0	0	0	0	1	3
R.Jackson, rf	1	0	0	0	0	0	0	0
D.Evans, ph-rf	2	1	1	0	1	0	2	0
C.Fisk, c	3	1	1	0	0	1	4	0
B.Diaz, c	1	0	0	0	0	1	2	0
B.Dent, ss	2	0	2	0	0	0	0	2
F.Lynn, ph	1	0	1	1	0	0	0	0
T.Armas, lf	1	0	0	0	0	1	0	0
J.Morris, p	0	0	0	0	0	0	0	0
T.Paciorek, ph	1	0	1	0	0	0	0	0
L.Barker, p	0	0	0	0	0	0	0	0
G.Thomas, ph	1	0	0	0	0	1	0	0
K.Forsch, p	0	0	0	0	0	0	0	0
B.Bell, 3b	1	0	0	1	0	0	1	2
Totals	37	4	11	4	2	8	27	16

BATTING
2B: B.Dent (off B.Knepper).
HR: K.Singleton (2nd inning off T.Seaver, 0 on, 0 out).
2-out RBI: T.Simmons.
RBI, scoring position, less than 2 outs: E.Murray 0–1; D.Evans 0–1; F.Lynn 1–1; G.Thomas 0–2; B.Bell 1–2.
SF: B.Bell.

BASERUNNING
CS: R.Carew (2nd base by F.Valenzuela/G.Carter).
Team LOB: 9

FIELDING
E: R.Fingers (dropped throw).
Outfield assist: D.Winfield (O.Smith at 3B).

PITCHING	ip	h	r	er	bb	so
National League						
F.Valenzuela	1.0	2	0	0	0	0
T.Seaver	1.0	3	1	1	0	1
B.Knepper	2.0	1	0	0	2	3
B.Hooton	1.2	5	3	3	0	1
D.Ruthven	0.1	0	0	0	0	0
V.Blue (w)	1.0	0	0	0	0	1
N.Ryan	1.0	0	0	0	0	1
B.Sutter (s)	1.0	0	0	0	0	1
American League						
J.Morris	2.0	2	0	0	1	2
L.Barker	2.0	0	0	0	0	1
K.Forsch	1.0	1	1	1	0	0
M.Norris	1.0	2	1	1	0	1
R.Davis	1.0	1	1	1	0	1
R.Fingers (l, bs)	0.1	2	2	2	2	0
D.Stieb	1.2	1	0	0	1	1

Inherited Runners—Scored:
   T.Seaver 0–0; B.Knepper 0–0; B.Hooton 0–0;
   D.Ruthven 2–0; V.Blue 0–0; N.Ryan 0–0;
   B.Sutter 0–0; L.Barker 0–0; K.Forsch 0–0;
   M.Norris 0–0; R.Davis 0–0; R.Fingers 0–0;
   D.Stieb 1–0.
wp: V.Blue

GAME DATA—T: 2:59; A: 72086; Temp: Unknown;
Wind: Unknown direction, Speed: Unknown

UMPIRES—hp: Bill Haller (al), 1b: Ed Vargo (nl),
2b: Lou DiMuro (al), 3b: Bob Engel (nl), lf: Greg Kosc
(al), rf: Jim Quick (nl)

STARTING LINEUPS

	National League	*American League*
1.	P.Rose 1b	R.Carew 1b
2.	D.Concepcion ss	W.Randolph 2b
3.	D.Parker rf	G.Brett 3b
4.	M.Schmidt 3b	D.Winfield cf
5.	G.Foster lf	K.Singleton lf
6.	A.Dawson cf	R.Jackson rf
7.	G.Carter c	C.Fisk c
8.	D.Lopes 2b	B.Dent ss
9.	F.Valenzuela p	J.Morris p
	F.Valenzuela p	J.Morris p

NL 1ST: P.Rose singled to left field; D.Concepcion struck out; D.Parker grounded out (R.Carew-1b unassisted) [P.Rose to second]; M.Schmidt struck out; 0 R, 1 H, 0 E, 1 LOB. NL 0, AL 0.

AL 1ST: R.Carew singled to second base; R.Carew was caught stealing second (G.Carter-c to D.Lopes-2b); W.Randolph singled to left field; G.Brett grounded out (F.Valenzuela-p to P.Rose-1b) [W.Randolph to second]; D.Winfield grounded out (M.Schmidt-3b to P.Rose-1b); 0 R, 2 H, 0 E, 1 LOB. NL 0, AL 0.

NL 2ND: G.Foster grounded out (G.Brett-3b to R.Carew-1b); A.Dawson singled to first base; A.Dawson stole second; G.Carter popped to R.Carew-1b; D.Lopes walked; **J.Youngblood batted for F.Valenzuela;** J.Youngblood popped to R.Carew-1b in foul territory; 0 R, 1 H, 0 E, 2 LOB. NL 0, AL 0.

AL 2ND: **T.Seaver replaced J.Youngblood (pitching);** K.Singleton homered to deep rightfield (it was the 0–2 pitch); R.Jackson grounded out (T.Seaver-p to P.Rose-1b); C.Fisk was called out on strikes; B.Dent singled to right field; **T.Paciorek batted for J.Morris;** T.Paciorek singled to third base [B.Dent to third]; R.Carew grounded out (T.Seaver-p to P.Rose-1b); 1 R, 3 H, 0 E, 2 LOB. NL 0, AL 1.

NL 3RD: **L.Barker replaced T.Paciorek (pitching);** P.Rose grounded out (W.Randolph-2b to R.Carew-1b); D.Concepcion grounded out (W.Randolph-2b to R.Carew-1b); D.Parker struck out; 0 R, 0 H, 0 E, 0 LOB. NL 0, AL 1.

AL 3RD: **M.Trillo replaced D.Lopes (playing 2b); B.Knepper replaced T.Seaver (pitching);** W.Randolph was called out on strikes; G.Brett was called out on strikes; D.Winfield walked; K.Singleton grounded out (B.Knepper-p to P.Rose-1b); 0 R, 0 H, 0 E, 1 LOB. NL 0, AL 1.

NL 4TH: M.Schmidt grounded out (B.Dent-ss to R.Carew-1b); G.Foster grounded out (W.Randolph-2b to R.Carew-1b); A.Dawson grounded out (B.Dent-ss to R.Carew-1b); 0 R, 0 H, 0 E, 0 LOB. NL 0, AL 1.

AL 4TH: **D.Baker replaced G.Foster (playing lf); D.Evans batted for R.Jackson;** D.Evans walked; C.Fisk flied to D.Parker-rf; B.Dent doubled to left-field down the line [D.Evans to third]; **G.Thomas batted for L.Barker;** G.Thomas popped to M.Trillo-2b; R.Carew struck out; 0 R, 1 H, 0 E, 2 LOB. NL 0, AL 1.

NL 5TH: **D.Evans stayed in game (playing rf); K.Forsch replaced G.Thomas (pitching);** G.Carter homered to deep leftfield (it was the first pitch); M.Trillo flied to D.Evans-rf; **T.Kennedy batted for B.Knepper;** T.Kennedy grounded out (W.Randolph-2b to R.Carew-1b); P.Rose grounded out (W.Randolph-2b to R.Carew-1b); 1 R, 1 H, 0 E, 0 LOB. NL 1, AL 1.

AL 5TH: **S.Garvey replaced T.Kennedy (playing 1b); B.Hooton replaced P.Rose (pitching);** W.Randolph grounded out (M.Schmidt-3b to S.Garvey-1b); G.Brett struck out; D.Winfield flied to A.Dawson-cf; 0 R, 0 H, 0 E, 0 LOB. NL 1, AL 1.

NL 6TH: **M.Norris replaced G.Brett (pitching); B.Bell replaced K.Forsch (playing 3b);** D.Concepcion grounded out (B.Bell-3b to R.Carew-1b); D.Parker homered to deep rightfield; M.Schmidt doubled to rightfield down the line; D.Baker reached on a fielder's choice (B.Bell-3b unassisted) [M.Schmidt out at third]; A.Dawson struck out; 1 R, 2 H, 0 E, 1 LOB. NL 2, AL 1.

AL 6TH: **O.Smith replaced D.Concepcion (playing ss); M.Easler replaced D.Parker (playing rf);** K.Singleton singled to center field; D.Evans singled to right field [K.Singleton to second]; C.Fisk singled to right field [K.Singleton to third, D.Evans to second]; **F.Lynn batted for B.Dent;** F.Lynn singled to right field [K.Singleton scored, D.Evans to third, C.Fisk to second]; B.Bell out on a sacrifice fly to D.Baker-lf [D.Evans scored]; **E.Murray batted for R.Carew;** E.Murray forced F.Lynn (S.Garvey-1b to O.Smith-ss) [C.Fisk to third, E.Murray to first]; **T.Simmons batted for W.Randolph;** T.Simmons singled to right field [C.Fisk scored, E.Murray to second]; **D.Ruthven replaced B.Hooton (pitching); F.White ran for T.Simmons; A.Oliver batted for M.Norris;** A.Oliver flied to D.Baker-lf; 3 R, 5 H, 0 E, 2 LOB. NL 2, AL 4.

NL 7TH: **E.Murray stayed in game (playing 1b); F.White stayed in game (playing 2b); R.Burleson replaced K.Singleton (playing ss); B.Diaz replaced C.Fisk (playing c); T.Armas replaced F.Lynn (playing lf); R.Davis replaced A.Oliver (pitching);** Lynn may have been removed due to injury—there was a dispute between him and Manager Frey on this issue; G.Carter homered to deep centerfield (it was the first pitch); fifth player to hit two homers in one AS game; M.Trillo flied to D.Evans-rf; S.Garvey popped to R.Burleson-ss; **P.Guerrero batted for D.Ruthven;** P.Guerrero struck out; 1 R, 1 H, 0 E, 0 LOB. NL 3, AL 4.

AL 7TH: **V.Blue replaced P.Guerrero (pitching); B.Benedict replaced G.Carter (playing c);** D.Winfield flied to A.Dawson-cf; R.Burleson reached on an error by M.Schmidt-3b [R.Burleson to first]; V.Blue threw a wild pitch [R.Burleson to third]; D.Evans flied to A.Dawson-cf; B.Diaz struck out; 0 R, 0 H, 1 E, 1 LOB. NL 3, AL 4.

NL 8TH: **R.Fingers replaced R.Davis (pitching);** O.Smith walked; O.Smith stole second (D.Winfield-cf to B.Bell-3b to R.Burleson-ss to R.Fingers-p) [O.Smith out at third]; M.Easler walked; M.Schmidt homered to deep centerfield [M.Easler scored]; D.Baker singled to left field; **T.Raines ran for D.Baker;** T.Raines was picked off first, but was safe on an error by R.Fingers-p [T.Raines to second]; **D.Stieb replaced R.Fingers (pitching);** Fingers threw one pitch to Dawson before being replaced; A.Dawson grounded out (D.Stieb-p to E.Murray-1b) [T.Raines to third];

B.Benedict struck out; 2 R, 2 H, 1 E, 1 LOB. NL 5, AL 4.

AL 8TH: **N.Ryan replaced M.Schmidt (pitching); B.Madlock replaced V.Blue (playing 3b); T.Raines stayed in game (playing lf);** T.Armas struck out; B.Bell flied to A.Dawson-cf; E.Murray grounded out (M.Trillo-2b to S.Garvey-1b); 0 R, 0 H, 0 E, 0 LOB. NL 5, AL 4.

NL 9TH: **B.Buckner batted for M.Trillo;** B.Buckner grounded out (E.Murray-1b to D.Stieb-p); S.Garvey doubled to deep leftfield; B.Madlock grounded out (R.Burleson-ss to E.Murray-1b) [S.Garvey to third]; O.Smith walked; M.Easler forced O.Smith (R.Burleson-ss to F.White-2b) [M.Easler to first]; 0 R, 1 H, 0 E, 2 LOB. NL 5, AL 4.

AL 9TH: **P.Garner replaced N.Ryan (playing 2b); B.Sutter replaced B.Buckner (pitching);** F.White grounded out (B.Madlock-3b to S.Garvey-1b); D.Stieb struck out; Frey used up all his position players, but blamed this on Lynn leaving the game; D.Winfield flied to T.Raines-lf; 0 R, 0 H, 0 E, 0 LOB. NL 5, AL 4.

Final Totals	R	H	E	LOB
National League	5	9	1	7
American League	4	11	1	9

Tuesday, July 13, 1982

Olympic Stadium, Montreal

National League 4, American League 1

SERIES RESULTS: NL 34, AL 18, 1 TIE

Different Country, Same Result

The National League entered the first All-Star Game played outside the United States with a ten-game winning streak and having won eighteen of the last nineteen games. Representatives of the two leagues were telling different stories before the game. White Sox catcher Carlton Fisk, the leading vote getter on the AL squad, said, "I've never felt that winning or losing was the object of the All-Star Game, but maybe that's the problem. We don't put our game faces on for this one. It doesn't go on our record."

Pete Rose, the starting first baseman for the NL, disagreed with Fisk: "The whole thing in sports is to win. Why go out there for two and a half hours and waste your time? Losing stinks." This was the sixteenth All-Star Game for Rose, who became the oldest starter ever at forty-one years and two months.

Al Oliver, who played for both sides in All-Star competition, said, "There's just much more enthusiasm and determination to win on the NL side. No question about it."

Oakland Manager Billy Martin was named the AL manager because the Yankees had fired Bob Lemon early in the season. This was Martin's third and last time as the All-Star manager, and he was full of fire before the game: "We'll rip them. I don't think our guys took the All-Star Game seriously in the past few years. But they will this time."

The AL featured an outstanding lineup. Oakland's Rickey Henderson, called by many the best lead-off man in history, was followed in the batting order by three MVPs. Fred Lynn of the Angels had won in 1975 with Boston, George Brett of Kansas City had won in 1980, and Reggie Jackson of the Angels had won in 1973 with Oakland. They were followed by two of Milwaukee's finest, Cecil Cooper and Robin Yount. The latter would be named the 1982 AL Most Valuable Player as he led the Brewers to the AL flag at the end of the season.

However, even though the Junior Circuit talked

a good game, the result was the same as it had been since 1972, as the NL won behind good pitching and timely hitting. Three NL pitchers struck out ten AL batters during the first seven innings, often in critical situations with men on base.

Steve Rogers of the hometown Expos started for manager Tommy Lasorda's NL squad and surrendered the game's only AL run in the first inning. Henderson led off with a single to left field on the first pitch of the game and moved to second one out later on Brett's single to left. Both runners advanced a base on Rogers's wild pitch. Jackson, in his first year with the Angels, smashed a pitch into the left-field seats, but it was foul by about three feet. He then hit a sacrifice fly on a 3-2 count to score Henderson. After Cooper's single moved Brett to third, Rogers struck out Yount to end the threat. This was the fourth time in five years that the AL had scored the first run of the game.

With two out in the bottom of the second inning, starter Dennis Eckersley of the Red Sox walked the Braves' Dale Murphy, who would be named the NL Most Valuable Player at the end of the season for the first of two consecutive years. Cincinnati shortstop Dave Concepcion, who had one homer at the All-Star break, then drove the 1-1 pitch inside the left-field pole for the first two NL runs and his only All-Star home run. The ball was fair by less than the distance that Jackson's went foul.

Concepcion said later, "It was a slider, up and in. I don't think it broke, and I was able to get it pretty good." He was named the game's MVP in his ninth and last appearance as an All-Star.

In the top of the third, Brett collected his second hit but was left standing at first base when Jackson popped out to end the inning. The AL had eight hits in the game, with Brett's two and Henderson's three accounting for five of them.

Ruppert Jones of the Padres pinch-hit for Rogers to start the bottom of the third and tripled to right-center field. It should have been a routine out, but Jackson misplayed the ball into a triple. The Expos'

341

Tim Raines walked and stole second base before Pete Rose hit a sacrifice fly for the third NL run off Eckersley on just two hits, a homer and a triple.

Steve Carlton of the Phillies, in the last of his ten All-Star Games, replaced Rogers on the mound for the NL in the fourth inning. Lefty surrendered walks to Yount and Bobby Grich, who was playing on his sixth and last All-Star squad, in between striking out Cooper, Fisk, and pinch hitter Andre Thornton of the Indians. Carlton struck his fourth batter, pinch hitter Buddy Bell of the Indians, in the fifth.

In the top of the sixth, the Reds' Mario Soto made his All-Star debut by replacing Carlton. The AL got a runner to second base with two out on Dave Winfield's single and a force out by Yount. On the play, Dodger rookie second baseman Steve Sax, who would be named NL Rookie of the Year, threw the ball away trying to complete the double play, and Yount ran to second. However, Soto struck out pinch hitter Carl Yastrzemski of the Red Sox to end the inning.

The NL struck again in its half of the inning with a run created by the hometown team. Montreal's Al Oliver greeted new pitcher Dan Quisenberry with a double to left field and continued to third when Rickey Henderson misplayed the ball after tripping on a seam in the artificial turf. After two outs, Expos catcher Gary Carter, who had received more votes than any other player, singled to center, scoring teammate Oliver.

The AL wasted its best opportunity to score in the seventh. First, Detroit catcher Lance Parrish doubled to center field. After Frank White struck out, Henderson beat out an infield hit, moving Parrish to third, and then stole second base. Fireballer Soto, who came into the game leading the majors in strikeouts, did not rely on his ninety-seven-mile-an-hour fastball in this situation. Instead, he struck out both Willie Wilson of the Royals and Buddy Bell on change-ups that fooled the hitters.

Soto said later, "My change-up is my breaking ball. I am a fastball, change-up pitcher. My change is my second-best pitch. But every time I get in trouble, I go to the change." Wilson commented, "The bottom dropped out."

The AL threatened again in the eighth inning off the 1981 NL Rookie of the Year, Dodger pitcher Fernando Valenzuela. Baltimore's Eddie Murray walked with one out, and Yount forced him at second base. Pinch hitter Hal McRae of the Royals also walked, but Greg Minton of San Francisco, who replaced Valenzuela, ended the inning by getting Parrish to ground out.

The American Leaguers had eight hits and five walks but left eleven runners on base in the game. They had at least one base runner in eight of the nine innings. The seven NL hurlers held their opponents down when necessary, allowing only the first-inning run. For the AL, Jim Clancy pitched a perfect fourth inning, while Floyd Bannister of Seattle and Rollie Fingers of Milwaukee each pitched an inning without any major damage. This was the last of seven times that Fingers was named to an All-Star team.

For the NL, Oliver had two hits in two trips to the plate. He was the only member of the team with multiple hits in the game.

The theme of the game was "A Salute to International Baseball," so it was appropriate that a native of Venezuela, Concepcion, was named the game's outstanding player. Before the game, twelve former players who represented eleven countries participated in a mass ceremonial pitch as part of the international festivities.

As usual, there was a lot of talk about the fan balloting. Many of the players who were having fine years were ignored for other "more popular" players. Marvin Miller, executive director of the Players' Association, said, "You will find very few players who base incentive clauses on whether they make the All-Star team. They feel it's unreliable as a measure of the worth. They don't trust the voting system."

However, Hank Greenberg, who was an overlooked victim twice in the 1930s, said, "I don't see how any system could be fair. The fans are going to vote for the most popular players. If you asked me to name two players on the Seattle team today, I couldn't do it."

Johnny Callison, who won the 1964 game with a homer, remarked, "I still think it's good to involve the fans in the voting. You might leave out some hot players that way. But the players did it, too, when they did the voting."

Billy Martin had the typical manager's answer: "They should have thirty-five guys on the All-Star squads, not twenty-eight. But then I suppose forty guys would complain."

Lance Parrish set two All-Star records by throwing out three potential base stealers. In addition to the most runners caught stealing, Parrish set a new record for most assists in a game by a catcher. Walker Cooper (1944), Yogi Berra (1951), and Roy Campanella (1953) each had been credited with two assists by throwing out two would-be base stealers.

	AL			NL	
P	Dennis Eckersley	BOS		Steve Rogers	MON
C	Carlton Fisk	CHA		Gary Carter	MON
1B	Rod Carew	+ CAL		Pete Rose	PHI
2B	Bobby Grich	CAL		Manny Trillo	PHI
3B	George Brett	KCA		Mike Schmidt	PHI
SS	Robin Yount	MIL		Dave Concepcion	CIN
OF	Rickey Henderson	OAK		Andre Dawson	MON
OF	Reggie Jackson	CAL		Dale Murphy	ATL
OF	Fred Lynn	CAL		Tim Raines	MON
	Floyd Bannister	SEA		Dusty Baker	LAN
	Buddy Bell	TEX		Steve Carlton	PHI
	Jim Clancy	TOR		Leon Durham	CHN
	Mark Clear	BOS		Bob Horner	ATL
	Cecil Cooper	MIL		Steve Howe	LAN
	Rollie Fingers	MIL		Tom Hume	CIN
	Rich Gossage	NYA		Ruppert Jones	SDN
	Ron Guidry	NYA		Ray Knight	HOU
	Toby Harrah	CLE		Greg Minton	SFN
	Kent Hrbek	MIN		Phil Niekro	ATL
	Hal McRae	KCA		Al Oliver	MON
	Eddie Murray	BAL		Tony Pena	PIT
	Ben Oglivie	MIL		Steve Sax	LAN
	Lance Parrish	DET		Lonnie Smith	SLN
	Dan Quisenberry	KCA		Ozzie Smith	SLN
	Andre Thornton	CLE		Mario Soto	CIN
	Frank White	KCA		John Stearns	NYN
	Willie Wilson	KCA		Jason Thompson	PIT
	Dave Winfield	NYA		Fernando Valenzuela	LAN
	Carl Yastrzemski	BOS			

+ player replaced on roster

```
American League    100  000  000-  1
National League    021  001  00X-  4
```

AMERICAN LEAGUE

	ab	r	h	bi	bb	so	po	a
R.Henderson, lf	4	1	3	0	1	0	3	0
F.Lynn, cf	2	0	0	0	0	0	0	0
W.Wilson, cf	2	0	0	0	0	1	1	0
K.Hrbek, ph	1	0	0	0	0	0	0	0
G.Brett, 3b	2	0	2	0	0	0	0	0
B.Bell, ph-3b	3	0	0	0	0	2	0	1
R.Jackson, rf	1	0	0	1	0	0	3	0
D.Winfield, rf	2	0	1	0	0	0	0	0
C.Cooper, 1b	2	0	1	0	0	1	5	0
E.Murray, ph-1b	1	0	0	0	1	0	4	0
R.Yount, ss	3	0	0	0	1	1	0	2
B.Grich, 2b	1	0	0	0	1	1	2	2
C.Yastrzemski, ph	1	0	0	0	0	1	0	0
D.Quisenberry, p	0	0	0	0	0	0	0	0
H.McRae, ph	0	0	0	0	1	0	0	0
R.Fingers, p	0	0	0	0	0	0	0	0
C.Fisk, c	2	0	0	0	0	1	2	0
L.Parrish, c	2	0	1	0	0	0	2	3
D.Eckersley, p	1	0	0	0	0	0	0	0
A.Thornton, ph	1	0	0	0	0	1	0	0
J.Clancy, p	0	0	0	0	0	0	0	0
F.Bannister, p	0	0	0	0	0	0	0	0
F.White, 2b	1	0	0	0	0	1	2	1
B.Oglivie, ph	1	0	0	0	0	0	0	0
Totals	33	1	8	1	5	10	24	9

BATTING
2B: L.Parrish (off M.Soto).
RBI, scoring position, less than 2 outs: W.Wilson 0–2; R.Jackson 1–2; C.Fisk 0–1; F.White 0–1.
SF: R.Jackson.
GDP: W.Wilson.

BASERUNNING
SB: R.Henderson (2nd base off M.Soto/T.Pena).
Team LOB: 11

FIELDING
E: R.Henderson; B.Bell (fumble).

NATIONAL LEAGUE

	ab	r	h	bi	bb	so	po	a
T.Raines, lf	1	0	0	0	1	1	0	
S.Carlton, p	0	0	0	0	0	0	0	
B.Horner, ph	1	0	0	0	0	0	0	0
M.Soto, p	0	0	0	0	0	0	0	0
J.Thompson, ph	1	0	0	0	0	0	0	0
F.Valenzuela, p	0	0	0	0	0	0	0	0
G.Minton, p	0	0	0	0	0	0	0	0
S.Howe, p	0	0	0	0	0	0	0	0
T.Hume, p	0	0	0	0	0	0	0	0
P.Rose, 1b	1	0	0	1	0	0	4	0
A.Oliver, 1b	2	1	2	0	0	0	2	0
A.Dawson, cf	4	0	1	0	0	0	4	0
M.Schmidt, 3b	1	0	0	0	0	0	0	0
R.Knight, 3b	3	0	0	0	0	1	1	4
G.Carter, c	3	0	1	1	0	0	7	0
T.Pena, pr-c	1	0	0	0	0	0	3	0
J.Stearns, c	0	0	0	0	0	0	0	0
D.Murphy, rf	2	1	0	0	1	0	2	0
D.Concepcion, ss	3	1	1	2	0	0	1	1
O.Smith, pr-ss	0	0	0	0	0	0	0	1
M.Trillo, 2b	2	0	1	0	0	0	0	1
S.Sax, pr-2b	1	0	1	0	0	0	2	0
S.Rogers, p	0	0	0	0	0	0	0	0
R.Jones, ph	1	1	1	0	0	0	0	0
D.Baker, lf	2	0	0	0	0	0	0	0
L.Smith, lf	0	0	0	0	0	0	1	0
Totals	29	4	8	4	2	2	27	8

BATTING
2B: A.Oliver (off D.Quisenberry).
3B: R.Jones (off D.Eckersley).
HR: D.Concepcion (2nd inning off D.Eckersley, 1 on, 2 out).
2-out RBI: G.Carter; D.Concepcion 2.
RBI, scoring position, less than 2 outs: P.Rose 1–2; A.Dawson 0–2; R.Knight 0–1.
SF: P.Rose.

BASERUNNING
SB: T.Raines (2nd base off D.Eckersley/C.Fisk); T.Pena (2nd base off D.Quisenberry/L.Parrish).
CS: A.Oliver (2nd base by R.Fingers/L.Parrish); O.Smith (2nd base by D.Quisenberry/L.Parrish); S.Sax (2nd base by F.Bannister/L.Parrish).
Team LOB: 4

FIELDING
E: S.Sax (throw).
DP: (1). S.Carlton-D.Concepcion-P.Rose.

PITCHING	ip	h	r	er	bb	so
American League						
D.Eckersley (L)	3.0	2	3	3	2	1
J.Clancy	1.0	0	0	0	0	0
F.Bannister	1.0	1	0	0	0	0
D.Quisenberry	2.0	3	1	1	0	1
R.Fingers	1.0	2	0	0	0	0
National League						
S.Rogers (w)	3.0	4	1	1	0	2
S.Carlton	2.0	1	0	0	2	4
M.Soto	2.0	3	0	0	0	4
F.Valenzuela	0.2	0	0	0	2	0
G.Minton	0.2	0	0	0	1	0
S.Howe	0.1	0	0	0	0	0
T.Hume (s)	0.1	0	0	0	0	0

Inherited Runners—Scored:
  J.Clancy 0–0; F.Bannister 0–0; D.Quisenberry 0–0;
  R.Fingers 0–0; S.Carlton 0–0; M.Soto 0–0;
  F.Valenzuela 0–0; G.Minton 2–0; S.Howe 1–0;
  T.Hume 1–0.
WP: S.Rogers

GAME DATA—T: 2:53; A: 59057; Temp: Unknown;
Wind: Unknown direction, Speed: Unknown

UMPIRES—HP: Doug Harvey (NL), 1B: Marty Springstead
(AL), 2B: John McSherry (NL), 3B: Jim McKean (AL),
LF: Ed Montague (NL), RF: Mike Reilly (AL)

STARTING LINEUPS

	American League	National League
1.	R.Henderson lf	T.Raines lf
2.	F.Lynn cf	P.Rose 1b
3.	G.Brett 3b	A.Dawson cf
4.	R.Jackson rf	M.Schmidt 3b
5.	C.Cooper 1b	G.Carter c
6.	R.Yount ss	D.Murphy rf
7.	B.Grich 2b	D.Concepcion ss
8.	C.Fisk c	M.Trillo 2b
9.	D.Eckersley p	S.Rogers p

AL 1ST: R.Henderson singled to left field; F.Lynn flied to A.Dawson-cf; G.Brett singled to left field [R.Henderson to second]; S.Rogers threw a wild pitch [R.Henderson to third, G.Brett to second]; R.Jackson out on a sacrifice fly to A.Dawson-cf [R.Henderson scored]; C.Cooper singled [G.Brett to third]; R.Yount struck out; 1 R, 3 H, 0 E, 2 LOB. AL 1, NL 0.

NL 1ST: T.Raines struck out; P.Rose lined to R.Henderson-lf; A.Dawson flied to R.Jackson-rf; 0 R, 0 H, 0 E, 0 LOB. AL 1, NL 0.

AL 2ND: B.Grich was called out on strikes; C.Fisk flied to A.Dawson-cf; D.Eckersley grounded out (M.Trillo-2b to P.Rose-1b); 0 R, 0 H, 0 E, 0 LOB. AL 1, NL 0.

NL 2ND: M.Schmidt popped to C.Fisk-c in foul territory; G.Carter grounded out (B.Grich-2b to C.Cooper-1b); D.Murphy walked; D.Concepcion homered to deep leftfield down the line [D.Murphy scored]; M.Trillo grounded out (R.Yount-ss to C.Cooper-1b); 2 R, 1 H, 0 E, 0 LOB. AL 1, NL 2.

AL 3RD: **R.Knight replaced M.Schmidt (playing 3b);** R.Henderson grounded out (R.Knight-3b to P.Rose-1b); F.Lynn grounded out (P.Rose-1b unassisted); G.Brett singled to center field; R.Jackson popped to R.Knight-3b; 0 R, 1 H, 0 E, 1 LOB. AL 1, NL 2.

NL 3RD: **R.Jones batted for S.Rogers;** R.Jones tripled to very deep right-center; T.Raines walked; T.Raines stole second; P.Rose out on a sacrifice fly to R.Jackson-rf [R.Jones scored]; A.Dawson grounded out (B.Grich-2b to C.Cooper-1b) [T.Raines to third]; R.Knight popped to B.Grich-2b; 1 R, 1 H, 0 E, 1 LOB. AL 1, NL 3.

AL 4TH: **D.Baker replaced R.Jones (playing lf); S.Carlton replaced T.Raines (pitching);** C.Cooper struck out; R.Yount walked; B.Grich walked [R.Yount to second]; C.Fisk struck out; **A.Thornton batted for D.Eckersley;** A.Thornton struck out; 0 R, 0 H, 0 E, 2 LOB. AL 1, NL 3.

NL 4TH: **J.Clancy replaced A.Thornton (pitching); W.Wilson replaced F.Lynn (playing cf);** G.Carter grounded out (R.Yount-ss to C.Cooper-1b);

D.Murphy flied to R.Jackson-rf; D.Concepcion grounded out (C.Cooper-1b unassisted); 0 R, 0 H, 0 E, 0 LOB. AL 1, NL 3.

AL 5TH: R.Henderson singled to right field; W.Wilson grounded into a double play (S.Carlton-p to D.Concepcion-ss to P.Rose-1b) [R.Henderson out at second]; **B.Bell batted for G.Brett;** B.Bell struck out; 0 R, 1 H, 0 E, 0 LOB. AL 1, NL 3.

NL 5TH: **B.Bell stayed in game (playing 3b); F.Bannister replaced J.Clancy (pitching); L.Parrish replaced C.Fisk (playing c); D.Winfield replaced R.Jackson (playing rf);** M.Trillo singled to center field; **S.Sax ran for M.Trillo;** S.Sax was caught stealing second (L.Parrish-c to B.Grich-2b); D.Baker flied to R.Henderson-lf; **B.Horner batted for S.Carlton;** B.Horner flied to R.Henderson-lf; 0 R, 1 H, 0 E, 0 LOB. AL 1, NL 3.

AL 6TH: **S.Sax stayed in game (playing 2b); M.Soto replaced B.Horner (pitching); A.Oliver replaced P.Rose (playing 1b);** D.Winfield singled to center field; **E.Murray batted for C.Cooper;** E.Murray flied to D.Murphy-rf; R.Yount forced D.Winfield (R.Knight-3b to S.Sax-2b) [R.Yount to second (error by S.Sax-2b)]; **C.Yastrzemski batted for B.Grich;** C.Yastrzemski struck out; 0 R, 1 H, 1 E, 1 LOB. AL 1, NL 3.

NL 6TH: **E.Murray stayed in game (playing 1b); D.Quisenberry replaced C.Yastrzemski (pitching); F.White replaced F.Bannister (playing 2b);** A.Oliver doubled to left field [A.Oliver to third (error by R.Henderson-lf)]; A.Dawson grounded out (E.Murray-1b unassisted); R.Knight struck out; G.Carter singled to center field [A.Oliver scored]; **T.Pena ran for G.Carter;** T.Pena stole second; D.Murphy grounded out (B.Bell-3b to E.Murray-1b); 1 R, 2 H, 1 E, 1 LOB. AL 1, NL 4.

AL 7TH: **T.Pena stayed in game (playing c);** L.Parrish doubled to center field; F.White struck out; R.Henderson singled to pitcher [L.Parrish to third]; R.Henderson stole second; W.Wilson struck out; B.Bell struck out; 0 R, 2 H, 0 E, 2 LOB. AL 1, NL 4.

NL 7TH: D.Concepcion reached on an error by B.Bell-3b [D.Concepcion to first]; **O.Smith ran for D.Concepcion;** O.Smith was caught stealing second (L.Parrish-c to F.White-2b); pitchout; S.Sax singled to third base; D.Baker flied to W.Wilson-cf; **J.Thompson batted for M.Soto;** J.Thompson grounded out (F.White-2b to E.Murray-1b); 0 R, 1 H, 1 E, 1 LOB. AL 1, NL 4.

AL 8TH: **O.Smith stayed in game (playing ss); F.Valenzuela replaced J.Thompson (pitching);** D.Winfield grounded out (R.Knight-3b to A.Oliver-1b); E.Murray walked; R.Yount forced E.Murray (R.Knight-3b to S.Sax-2b) [R.Yount to first];

H.McRae batted for D.Quisenberry; H.McRae walked [R.Yount to second]; **G.Minton replaced F.Valenzuela (pitching);** L.Parrish grounded out (O.Smith-ss to A.Oliver-1b); 0 R, 0 H, 0 E, 2 LOB. AL 1, NL 4.

NL 8TH: **R.Fingers replaced H.McRae (pitching);** A.Oliver singled to right field; A.Oliver was caught stealing second (L.Parrish-c to F.White-2b); A.Dawson singled to center field; R.Knight grounded out (E.Murray-1b unassisted) [A.Dawson to second]; T.Pena popped to L.Parrish-c in foul territory; 0 R, 2 H, 0 E, 1 LOB. AL 1, NL 4.

AL 9TH: **L.Smith replaced D.Baker (playing lf); J.Stearns replaced T.Pena (playing c); B.Oglivie batted for F.White;** B.Oglivie flied to L.Smith-lf; R.Henderson walked; **K.Hrbek batted for W.Wilson; S.Howe replaced G.Minton (pitching);** K.Hrbek flied to A.Dawson-cf; **T.Hume replaced S.Howe (pitching);** B.Bell flied to D.Murphy-rf; 0 R, 0 H, 0 E, 1 LOB. AL 1, NL 4.

Final Totals	R	H	E	LOB
American League	1	8	2	11
National League	4	8	1	4

Lynn Slams the NL

The fiftieth anniversary of All-Star competition occurred exactly fifty years to the day after the first game. For this occasion, baseball returned to seventy-three-year-old Comiskey Park as the site of the first game hosted the gala for the third and last time. There were many special celebrations for the game that was originally conceived as a once-in-a-lifetime event.

As part of the festivities, ninety former players participated in an old-timers game on July 5. Among those present was Lefty Gomez, who started and won the 1933 game. Gomez threw out the ceremonial pitch for the 1983 All-Star contest while flanked by eleven survivors of the inaugural game. In another tribute, on game day the U.S. Postal Service issued a new twenty-cent stamp in Chicago honoring Babe Ruth, who had homered in that first game.

The hitting of the American Leaguers—who collected thirteen runs and fifteen hits (including seven for extra bases) off six of the seven NL hurlers—was the highlight of this game. The thirteen runs set a record for a team in one game, besting the 1946 AL squad that had scored twelve times. This total was duplicated by both the 1992 and the 1998 AL teams.

The ten-run winning margin was the largest in thirty-seven years, since the American Leaguers had pounded their NL brethren 12–0 in the 1946 game. The seven extra-base hits tied the record set in 1934 by the AL. After losing eleven straight games and nineteen of twenty, it was a sweet victory for the Junior Circuit.

Many of the National Leaguers in the game, including six of the pitchers, were first-time All-Stars. Only starter Mario Soto among the pitchers had been an All-Star previously. Of the members of both squads, only Rod Carew, Carl Yastrzemski, and Johnny Bench had played in the last game won by the American League, in 1971. All three had started that game. There were three rookies

named to the teams: Matt Young, Bill Dawley, and AL Rookie of the Year Ron Kittle.

The majority of the damage was done in the third inning as the AL sent ten batters to the plate. Atlee Hammaker came into the All-Star Game leading the National League in ERA at 1.70. He had compiled a record of 9-4 with the San Francisco Giants, who were in fifth place in the NL West with a 39-40 record. Hammaker was a natural choice for Whitey Herzog's NL pitching staff. However, the Giants hurler became the biggest casualty of the day.

Hammaker started the third inning and was greeted by a homer to left field by the first batter he faced, Jim Rice. Rice came into this game leading the AL in homers with twenty-two and RBI with fifty-eight. His homer off Hammaker was followed by a triple off the bat of George Brett. One out later, both Dave Winfield and Manny Trillo singled. Following another out, Rod Carew came to the plate. The Angels first baseman was leading the AL in hitting at .402 and showed how as he stroked a single to left and went to second on the throw in. He ended the day with two hits and a walk in four plate appearances. Following Carew, an intentional walk to Robin Yount (the leading vote getter at nearly two million) loaded the bases for Fred Lynn.

Lynn came into the game with fourteen homers for the season, including one grand slam. After working the count to 2-2, Lynn drove a hanging slider into the right-field seats for the first slam in the history of the All-Star Game. As he rounded first base, Lynn thrust his fist in the air in celebration. He was named the game's MVP.

The round-tripper was Lynn's fourth in All-Star competition, which placed him in a tie for second place on the career list with Ted Williams. (Stan Musial leads with six circuit clouts.) The blast ended Hammaker's night, who said afterward, "To put it bluntly, it's probably the worst exhibition of pitching you'll ever see."

The two-thirds of an inning was Hammaker's

only appearance in the All-Star spectacular. After that day, he was never the same quality pitcher again and was eventually relegated to the San Francisco bullpen. For the rest of 1983, he pitched in only eight more games (he had appeared in fifteen during the first half of the season) and ended with a 10-9 record.

The seven runs in the third inning set a record for All-Star competition, besting the 1934 AL squad, which scored six in the fifth inning. The game was never in doubt after those seven runs. On the other side of the field, the NL unit collected eight hits in the game with only Al Oliver knocking extra bases, with a double to lead off the fourth inning. The two homers by Rice and Lynn marked the eleventh time in the history of the game that a team hit two big flies in one inning. Surprisingly, on all eleven occasions, both homers had been surrendered by one pitcher.

Carl Yastrzemski pinch-hit in the game, his eighteenth and last time as a member of the American League squad. Cal Ripken Jr. played in his first game for the team. Ripken would have a great sec-

ond half and would end the season leading the AL in hits (211), doubles (47), and runs scored (121) and being named the league MVP. For the Senior Circuit, Johnny Bench also pinch-hit in his last appearance for the NL after being named to the squad fourteen times.

Before the game, one topic of conversation in the home clubhouse had been the fireworks that exploded over the scoreboard for White Sox home runs. "We knew about the fireworks. We wanted to see them and we did," said Dave Winfield. AL Manager Harvey Kuenn of the Brewers, in his only All-Star managing stint, told his team, "Go out and let's hit and have some fun. My game is hitting, not holding meetings." And hit they did.

Lee MacPhail planned to retire as AL president at the end of the 1983 season. Since he had become president, MacPhail had watched the opposition win nine straight games. After the game, he was asked whether he might reconsider staying on as president since his team had finally won. MacPhail laughed and said, "No, it makes it possible for me to leave."

	AL			NL	
P	Dave Stieb	TOR		Mario Soto	CIN
C	Ted Simmons	MIL		Gary Carter	MON
1B	Rod Carew	CAL		Al Oliver	MON
2B	Manny Trillo	CLE		Steve Sax	LAN
3B	George Brett	KCA		Mike Schmidt	PHI
SS	Robin Yount	MIL		Ozzie Smith	SLN
OF	Reggie Jackson	+ CAL		Andre Dawson	MON
OF	Fred Lynn	CAL		Dale Murphy	ATL
OF	Dave Winfield	NYA		Tim Raines	MON
	Bob Boone	CAL		Johnny Bench	CIN
	Cecil Cooper	MIL		Bruce Benedict	ATL
	Doug DeCinces	CAL		Bill Dawley	HOU
	Ron Guidry	+ NYA		Dave Dravecky	SDN
	Rickey Henderson	OAK		Leon Durham	CHN
	Rick Honeycutt	TEX		Darrell Evans	SFN
	Ron Kittle	CHA		Pedro Guerrero	LAN
	Aurelio Lopez	DET		Atlee Hammaker	SFN
	Tippy Martinez	BAL		George Hendrick	SLN
	Eddie Murray	BAL		Glenn Hubbard	ATL
	Ben Oglivie	MIL		Terry Kennedy	SDN
	Lance Parrish	DET		Gary Lavelle	SFN
	Dan Quisenberry	KCA		Bill Madlock	PIT
	Jim Rice	BOS		Willie McGee	SLN
	Cal Ripken	BAL		Jesse Orosco	NYN
	Bob Stanley	BOS		Pascual Perez	ATL
	Rick Sutcliffe	CLE		Steve Rogers	MON
	Gary Ward	MIN		Lee Smith	CHN
	Lou Whitaker	DET		Dickie Thon	HOU
	Willie Wilson	KCA		Fernando Valenzuela	LAN
	Carl Yastrzemski	BOS			
	Matt Young	SEA			

+ player replaced on roster

```
National League    100  110  000- 3
American League    117  000  22X-13
```

NATIONAL LEAGUE

	ab	r	h	bi	bb	so	po	a
S.Sax, 2b	3	1	1	1	0	0	2	0
G.Hubbard, 2b	1	0	1	0	0	0	0	0
T.Raines, lf	3	0	0	0	0	1	2	0
B.Madlock, ph-3b	1	0	0	0	0	0	0	0
A.Dawson, cf	3	0	0	0	0	1	3	0
D.Dravecky, p	0	0	0	0	0	0	0	1
P.Perez, p	0	0	0	0	0	0	0	0
J.Orosco, p	0	0	0	0	0	0	0	0
J.Bench, ph	1	0	0	0	0	0	0	0
L.Smith, p	0	0	0	0	0	0	1	0
A.Oliver, 1b	2	1	1	0	1	0	2	1
D.Evans, 1b	1	0	0	0	0	0	2	1
D.Murphy, rf	3	0	1	0	1	0		
P.Guerrero, 3b-lf	1	0	0	0	0	1	0	0
M.Schmidt, 3b	3	0	0	0	0	1	0	0
B.Benedict, c	1	0	1	0	0	0	5	0
G.Carter, c	2	0	0	0	0	0	3	0
L.Durham, rf	2	0	0	0	0	1	0	0
O.Smith, ss	2	1	1	0	0	0	0	0
W.McGee, cf	2	0	1	0	0	0	2	0
M.Soto, p	1	0	0	0	0	0	2	0
A.Hammaker, p	0	0	0	0	0	0	0	0
B.Dawley, p	0	0	0	0	0	0	0	0
D.Thon, ph-ss	3	0	1	0	0	0	0	2
Totals	35	3	8	2	1	6	24	5

BATTING
2B: A.Oliver (off R.Honeycutt).
RBI, scoring position, less than 2 outs: S.Sax 1–1; T.Raines 0–1; A.Dawson 0–1; D.Murphy 1–2.
GDP: M.Schmidt.

BASERUNNING
Team LOB: 6

FIELDING
E: M.Schmidt (fumble); S.Sax (throw); P.Guerrero (fumble).

AMERICAN LEAGUE

	ab	r	h	bi	bb	so	po	a
R.Carew, 1b	3	2	2	1	1	0	3	0
E.Murray, 1b	2	0	0	0	0	0	4	0
R.Yount, ss	2	1	0	1	1	1	0	1
C.Ripken, ss	0	0	0	0	1	0	1	0
F.Lynn, cf	3	1	1	4	1	2	1	0
W.Wilson, cf	1	0	1	1	0	0	2	0
J.Rice, lf	4	1	2	1	0	0	1	0
B.Oglivie, rf	1	0	0	0	0	1	0	0
M.Young, p	0	0	0	0	0	0	0	0
D.Quisenberry, p	0	0	0	0	0	0	0	0
G.Brett, 3b	4	2	2	1	0	1	1	5
T.Simmons, c	2	0	0	0	0	0	4	0
L.Parrish, c	2	0	0	0	0	1	1	0
C.Cooper, ph	1	1	1	0	0	0	0	0
B.Boone, c	0	0	0	0	0	0	1	0
D.Winfield, rf	3	2	3	1	0	0	3	0
R.Kittle, lf-rf	2	1	1	0	0	1	1	0
M.Trillo, 2b	3	1	1	0	0	0	3	1
L.Whitaker, ph-2b	1	1	1	2	0	0	1	0
D.Stieb, p	0	0	0	0	0	0	0	1
D.DeCinces, ph	1	0	0	0	0	0	0	0
R.Honeycutt, p	0	0	0	0	0	0	0	0
G.Ward, ph	1	0	0	0	0	0	0	0
B.Stanley, p	0	0	0	0	0	0	0	1
C.Yastrzemski, ph	1	0	0	0	0	1	0	0
R.Henderson, lf	1	0	0	1	0	0	0	0
Totals	38	13	15	13	4	8	27	9

BATTING
2B: D.Winfield (off M.Soto); W.Wilson (off P.Perez); G.Brett (off L.Smith).
3B: G.Brett (off A.Hammaker); L.Whitaker (off P.Perez).
HR: F.Lynn (3rd inning off A.Hammaker, 3 on, 2 out); J.Rice (3rd inning off A.Hammaker, 0 on, 0 out).
2-out RBI: R.Carew; F.Lynn 4; W.Wilson.
RBI, scoring position, less than 2 outs: E.Murray 0–1; R.Yount 1–2; G.Brett 1–2; T.Simmons 0–1; D.Winfield 1–1; R.Kittle 0–1; L.Whitaker 1–2; D.Stieb 0–1; D.DeCinces 0–1; C.Yastrzemski 0–1; R.Henderson 1–2.
S: D.Stieb.
SF: R.Yount; G.Brett; L.Whitaker.

BASERUNNING
Team LOB: 9

FIELDING
E: D.Stieb (throw); R.Carew (dropped throw).
DP: (2). R.Yount-M.Trillo-R.Carew; G.Brett-M.Trillo.

PITCHING	ip	h	r	er	bb	so
National League						
M.Soto (L)	2.0	2	2	0	2	2
A.Hammaker	0.2	6	7	7	1	0
B.Dawley	1.1	1	0	0	0	1
D.Dravecky	2.0	1	0	0	0	2
P.Perez	0.2	3	2	2	1	1
J.Orosco	0.1	0	0	0	0	1
L.Smith	1.0	2	2	1	0	1
American League						
D.Stieb (W)	3.0	0	1	0	1	4
R.Honeycutt	2.0	5	2	2	0	0
B.Stanley	2.0	2	0	0	0	0
M.Young	1.0	0	0	0	0	1
D.Quisenberry	1.0	1	0	0	0	1

Inherited Runners—Scored:
A.Hammaker 0–0; B.Dawley 0–0; D.Dravecky 0–0; P.Perez 0–0; J.Orosco 2–0; L.Smith 0–0; R.Honeycutt 0–0; B.Stanley 0–0; M.Young 0–0; D.Quisenberry 0–0.
IBB: R.Carew by M.Soto; R.Yount by A.Hammaker.

GAME DATA—T: 3:05; A: 43801; Temp: Unknown; Wind: Unknown direction, Speed: Unknown

UMPIRES—HP: George Maloney (AL), 1B: Harry Wendelstedt (NL), 2B: Ted Hendry (AL), 3B: Jim Quick (NL), LF: John Shulock (AL), RF: Dave Pallone (NL)

STARTING LINEUPS

	National League	American League
1.	S.Sax 2b	R.Carew 1b
2.	T.Raines lf	R.Yount ss
3.	A.Dawson cf	F.Lynn cf
4.	A.Oliver 1b	J.Rice lf
5.	D.Murphy rf	G.Brett 3b
6.	M.Schmidt 3b	T.Simmons c
7.	G.Carter c	D.Winfield rf
8.	O.Smith ss	M.Trillo 2b
9.	M.Soto p	D.Stieb p
	M.Soto p	D.Stieb p

NL 1ST: S.Sax reached on an error by D.Stieb-p [S.Sax to first]; T.Raines reached on an error [S.Sax scored (unearned) (no RBI), T.Raines to third (error by R.Carew-1b; assist by D.Stieb-p)]; A.Dawson struck out; A.Oliver walked; D.Murphy struck out; M.Schmidt struck out; 1 R (0 ER), 0 H, 2 E, 2 LOB. NL 1, AL 0.

AL 1ST: R.Carew singled to left-center; R.Yount struck out; F.Lynn walked [R.Carew to second]; J.Rice reached on an error by M.Schmidt-3b [R.Carew to third, F.Lynn to second, J.Rice to first]; G.Brett out on a sacrifice fly to A.Dawson-cf [R.Carew scored (unearned)]; T.Simmons grounded out (A.Oliver-1b to M.Soto-p); 1 R (0 ER), 1 H, 1 E, 2 LOB. NL 1, AL 1.

NL 2ND: G.Carter flied to D.Winfield-rf; O.Smith flied to J.Rice-lf; M.Soto grounded out (G.Brett-3b to R.Carew-1b); 0 R, 0 H, 0 E, 0 LOB. NL 1, AL 1.

AL 2ND: D.Winfield doubled to left field; M.Trillo reached on an error by S.Sax-2b [D.Winfield to third, M.Trillo to first]; D.Stieb out on a sacrifice bunt (M.Soto-p unassisted) [M.Trillo to second]; R.Carew was walked intentionally; R.Yount out on a sacrifice fly to A.Dawson-cf [D.Winfield scored (unearned)]; F.Lynn struck out; 1 R (0 ER), 1 H, 1 E, 2 LOB. NL 1, AL 2.

NL 3RD: S.Sax grounded out (D.Stieb-p to R.Carew-1b); T.Raines was called out on strikes; A.Dawson lined to D.Winfield-rf; 0 R, 0 H, 0 E, 0 LOB. NL 1, AL 2.

AL 3RD: **A.Hammaker replaced M.Soto (pitching);** J.Rice homered to deep leftfield; G.Brett tripled to center field; T.Simmons popped to S.Sax-2b; D.Winfield singled to center field [G.Brett scored]; M.Trillo singled to left field [D.Winfield to second]; **D.Decinces batted for D.Stieb;** D.DeCinces flied to A.Dawson-cf; R.Carew singled to left field [D.Winfield scored, M.Trillo to third, R.Carew to second (on throw)]; R.Yount was walked intentionally; F.Lynn homered (it was the 2–2 pitch) [M.Trillo scored, R.Carew scored,

R.Yount scored]; first grand slam in All-Star history; **B.Dawley replaced A.Hammaker (pitching);** J.Rice popped to S.Sax-2b; 7 R, 6 H, 0 E, 0 LOB. NL 1, AL 9.

NL 4TH: **R.Honeycutt replaced D.Decinces (pitching); L.Parrish replaced T.Simmons (playing c);** A.Oliver doubled to left field; D.Murphy singled to center field [A.Oliver scored]; M.Schmidt grounded into a double play (R.Yount-ss to M.Trillo-2b to R.Carew-1b) [D.Murphy out at second]; G.Carter flied to F.Lynn-cf; 1 R, 2 H, 0 E, 0 LOB. NL 2, AL 9.

AL 4TH: G.Brett flied to T.Raines-lf in foul territory; L.Parrish was called out on strikes; D.Winfield singled to left field; M.Trillo flied to T.Raines-lf; 0 R, 1 H, 0 E, 1 LOB. NL 2, AL 9.

NL 5TH: O.Smith singled to right field; **D.Thon batted for B.Dawley;** D.Thon singled to center field [O.Smith to second]; S.Sax singled to left field [O.Smith scored, D.Thon to second]; T.Raines hit into a double play (G.Brett-3b to M.Trillo-2b) [D.Thon out at third, S.Sax out at second, T.Raines to first]; Sax overslid the bag DV check if GDP; A.Dawson flied to D.Winfield-rf; 1 R, 3 H, 0 E, 1 LOB. NL 3, AL 9.

AL 5TH: **D.Thon stayed in game (playing ss); D.Dravecky replaced A.Dawson (pitching); G.Hubbard replaced S.Sax (playing 2b); W.McGee replaced O.Smith (playing cf); G.Ward batted for R.Honeycutt;** G.Ward flied to W.McGee-cf; R.Carew grounded out (D.Dravecky-p to A.Oliver-1b); R.Yount grounded out (D.Thon-ss to A.Oliver-1b); 0 R, 0 H, 0 E, 0 LOB. NL 3, AL 9.

NL 6TH: **B.Stanley replaced G.Ward (pitching); E.Murray replaced R.Carew (playing 1b); C.Ripken replaced R.Yount (playing ss);** A.Oliver grounded out (G.Brett-3b to E.Murray-1b); D.Murphy popped to E.Murray-1b in foul territory; M.Schmidt grounded out (E.Murray-1b unassisted); 0 R, 0 H, 0 E, 0 LOB. NL 3, AL 9.

AL 6TH: **D.Evans replaced A.Oliver (playing 1b); P.Guerrero replaced D.Murphy (playing 3b); B.Benedict replaced M.Schmidt (playing c); L.Durham replaced G.Carter (playing rf);** F.Lynn struck out; J.Rice singled to third base; G.Brett struck out; L.Parrish flied to W.McGee-cf; 0 R, 1 H, 0 E, 1 LOB. NL 3, AL 9.

NL 7TH: **R.Kittle replaced D.Winfield (playing lf); W.Wilson replaced F.Lynn (playing cf); B.Oglivie replaced J.Rice (playing rf);** L.Durham grounded out (B.Stanley-p to E.Murray-1b); W.McGee singled to shortstop; D.Thon forced W.McGee (G.Brett-3b to M.Trillo-2b) [D.Thon to first]; G.Hubbard singled to shortstop [D.Thon to second]; **B.Madlock batted for T.Raines;** B.Madlock flied to R.Kittle-lf; 0 R, 2 H, 0 E, 2 LOB. NL 3, AL 9.

AL 7TH: **B.Madlock stayed in game (playing 3b); P.Guerrero changed positions (playing lf); P.Perez replaced D.Dravecky (pitching);** R.Kittle singled to shortstop; **L.Whitaker batted for M.Trillo;** L.Whitaker tripled to center field [R.Kittle scored]; **C.Yastrzemski batted for B.Stanley;** C.Yastrzemski was called out on strikes; E.Murray grounded out (D.Evans-1b unassisted); C.Ripken walked; W.Wilson doubled to rightfield down the line [L.Whitaker scored, C.Ripken to third]; **J.Orosco replaced P.Perez (pitching);** B.Oglivie struck out; 2 R, 3 H, 0 E, 2 LOB. NL 3, AL 11.

NL 8TH: **L.Whitaker stayed in game (playing 2b); R.Kittle changed positions (playing rf); R.Henderson replaced C.Yastrzemski (playing lf); M.Young replaced B.Oglivie (pitching); J.Bench batted for J.Orosco;** J.Bench popped to C.Ripken-ss; D.Evans lined to W.Wilson-cf; P.Guerrero was called out on strikes; 0 R, 0 H, 0 E, 0 LOB. NL 3, AL 11.

AL 8TH: **L.Smith replaced J.Bench (pitching);** G.Brett doubled to second base; ball rolled off Hubbard's glove; **C.Cooper batted for L.Parrish;** C.Cooper singled to left field [G.Brett to third]; R.Kittle struck out; L.Whitaker reached on an error on a sacrifice fly by P.Guerrero-lf [G.Brett scored (RBI), C.Cooper to third, L.Whitaker to second]; R.Henderson grounded out (D.Thon-ss to D.Evans-1b) [C.Cooper scored (unearned)]; record 13 runs for one team, surpassing 12 (AL) in 1946; E.Murray grounded out (D.Evans-1b to L.Smith-p); 2 R (1 ER), 2 H, 1 E, 1 LOB. NL 3, AL 13.

NL 9TH: **D.Quisenberry replaced M.Young (pitching); B.Boone replaced C.Cooper (playing c);** B.Benedict singled to right field; L.Durham struck out; W.McGee flied to W.Wilson-cf; D.Thon forced B.Benedict (G.Brett-3b to L.Whitaker-2b) [D.Thon to first]; 0 R, 1 H, 0 E, 1 LOB. NL 3, AL 13.

Final Totals	R	H	E	LOB
National League	3	8	3	6
American League	13	15	2	9

55

NL Pitchers Strike Back

The All-Star Game returned to cold, windy Candlestick Park for the first time since 1961, when Stu Miller had balked due to a gust of wind. The weather conditions were typical for the ballpark by the bay, with a twenty-five-mile-an-hour wind. The weather was compounded by the 5:45 P.M. (local) starting time dictated by the television network broadcasting the game, which caused the contest to be played in the twilight, the worst time of day for batters to see the ball.

NL starting catcher Gary Carter of Montreal talked about the conditions at "The Stick" before the game: "Maybe the American Leaguers will experience some of the same frustrations we all experience here during the season. At least I hope so."

Atlanta's Dale Murphy, the two-time reigning NL MVP, later described the game conditions: "It was like three different games. The first three innings it was cold but sunny. The next three you had the shadows, and that made it almost impossible to hit. The last three it got darker, and you could see a little."

The NL won the low-scoring game as its pitchers dominated the AL hitters. It was the nineteenth victory in twenty-one years for the NL and came after an unusual win by the AL the previous year following eleven straight NL victories.

The game's most memorable feature was the strikeout; twenty-one batters went down via this route, a record for a nine-inning game. The NL recorded eleven of those punch-outs, six of which occurred consecutively. In the fourth inning, Fernando Valenzuela of the Dodgers struck out both the Yankees' Dave Winfield and the Angels' Reggie Jackson (playing in the last of his fourteen All-Star Games) and caught George Brett looking. In the fifth, Mets rookie Dwight Gooden, who came into the game leading all Major League pitchers with 133 strikeouts, set down Detroit's Lance Parrish and Chet Lemon and Seattle pinch hitter Alvin Davis.

The six consecutive strikeouts eclipsed the record of five set by Carl Hubbell fifty years ago to the day. The eighty-one-year-old Hubbell was at the game and threw out the ceremonial pitch as part of a celebration of his accomplishment, which is considered by many to be the most remarkable feat in All-Star history because he struck out five Hall of Famers. Valenzuela would match the record in 1986 by striking out five consecutive AL batters.

Bill Caudill, from across the bay in Oakland, pitched the seventh inning for the AL and struck out the only three batters he faced: Montreal's Tim Raines, the Cubs' Ryne Sandberg, and the Mets' Keith Hernandez.

The three pitchers joined four others who had struck out the side in previous All-Star Games. In 1948, Johnny Sain was the first to strike out all three batters he faced in an inning; he was joined by Bobby Shantz (1952), Gene Conley (1955), and Jerry Reuss (1980). Valenzuela repeated this feat in the 1986 game during his run of five.

Brett was not surprised by the strikeouts. "When you are facing the best pitchers in the world, a lot of guys are going to strike out," he said. Baltimore and AL manager Joe Altobelli agreed: "When you add a little twilight to those arms out there, you're going to get a lot of strikeouts."

The NL scored first in the initial inning. After two ground outs, San Diego first baseman Steve Garvey singled to right. Jackson, who had not played in the field since the previous August, booted the ball, and Garvey reached second. Dale Murphy singled to left, and Winfield fielded the ball, making a perfect throw home on one bounce. Parrish dropped the throw, however, and Garvey ran right through him to give the NL the early lead.

Garvey remarked later, "I've been in nine of these things, and the thing you learn is that you have to go out and be aggressive. I was trying to give the team a boost." Parrish needed two stitches after biting his tongue in the collision with Garvey. Parrish also struck out twice in the game and said later that it was "not my best night. I just dropped the ball, simple as that."

In the top of the second, Brett homered to center field on a 2-0 fastball. Expos pitcher Charlie Lea, playing in his only All-Star Game, commented, "He just crushed it. I was trying to throw a strike and, unfortunately, I did."

In the bottom of the inning, Carter gave the NL its winning margin by homering to left off Toronto's Dave Stieb. For his effort, Carter received his second All-Star MVP Award, having won it in 1981. This was Stieb's second consecutive starting assignment. Although he won the 1983 game, Stieb was tagged with the loss this year.

Valenzuela, who was named to the squad in place of Joaquin Andujar, replaced Lea in the third. Pinch hitter Andre Thornton of the Indians greeted the Dodger left-hander with a single to center field. Detroit's Lou Whitaker followed with another single, and Thornton raced to third, beating a strong throw by Mets right fielder Darryl Strawberry. Rod Carew of the Angels, playing in his eighteenth and last All-Star Game, hit a grounder right to Garvey, a step off the first base bag.

Garvey stepped on the base and threw home. Carter grabbed the wide throw and tagged Thornton, who was trying to score on the play. Thornton, not the swiftest runner in the game, commented on the play after the game: "Later in the game I might have held up, but that early I had to go. You have to take the chance."

Garvey's high throw caused Carter to stretch, exposing his body to Thornton. It could have been a replay of the Pete Rose–Ray Fosse collision in the 1970 game, but Thornton elected to slide into the plate, and the AL threat was over.

In the fourth inning, the Senior Circuit had runners on first and second on Ryne Sandberg's infield hit and Dale Murphy's walk, but Mike Schmidt grounded out to end the inning. In the fifth, Tony Gwynn singled and stole second base. He moved to third on a ground out but was stranded there.

The NL continued to get runners on in the sixth inning. Claudell Washington of Atlanta doubled to left field, and Carter walked. Washington advanced to third on a force out by Ozzie Smith, but once again no runs scored. The NL scored the final run of the game in the eighth on a home run to left field by Murphy.

After not scoring in the third inning, the AL saw eighteen of nineteen hitters retired from the end of the third to the beginning of the ninth innings. Mario Soto of Cincinnati recorded six of those

outs by retiring all of the batters he faced in the seventh and eighth innings. The one AL runner in that span, Orioles first baseman Eddie Murray, reached on a windblown pop-up in the sixth. With two out in the ninth, Winfield doubled to left field but was left at second when Oakland's Rickey Henderson was called out on strikes to end the game.

Steve Garvey best expressed the attitude in the NL clubhouse afterward: "We were a little embarrassed last year [in a 13-3 loss]. Tonight, you could tell on the bench, everyone wanted to get even."

Rookie Dwight Gooden, at nineteen years old, became the youngest player to appear in an All-Star Game. In addition to Gooden, the 1984 NL Rookie of the Year, two other rookies were named to the squads: the Phillies' Juan Samuel and Seattle's Alvin Davis, who was named the 1984 AL Rookie of the Year.

Once again, there was some controversy concerning the player selection process. The fans voted Rod Carew the starting first baseman in the AL, even though Baltimore's Eddie Murray and the Yankees' Don Mattingly deserved the honor more. Dave Kingman, the Oakland designated hitter, came into the All-Star break leading the majors in home runs with twenty-three and tied for second with seventy-one RBI. However, the three-time All-Star was not chosen as a member of the AL team.

Caudill, angry the last two years because he was not chosen, made the most of his opportunity this year with the three strikeouts. Before the game, he explained his feelings: "Whatever happens to me from now on, I sat in this room with these guys, and I played on an All-Star team. Anyone in this room who says that isn't special is crazy."

Phil Niekro didn't get into the game and was very unhappy, complaining, "It's old hat. Five All-Star Games and I've pitched to four batters. I'm just a wasted uniform, a wasted body." He indicated that he might not come to any more games, which proved prophetic because this was his last year to be named.

Each player is allowed to bring one guest to the All-Star Game, and Major League Baseball pays the bill for the player and the guest. That guest is usually a wife or girlfriend, but this year, Toronto second baseman Damaso Garcia had brought his double play partner, Alfredo Griffin. When shortstop Alan Trammel of the Tigers injured his arm two days before the All-Star Game, Griffin was named to replace him because, in addition to being a fine player, he was already in San Francisco. It was Griffin's only All-Star Game.

	AL		NL	
P	Dave Stieb	TOR	Charlie Lea	MON
C	Lance Parrish	DET	Gary Carter	MON
1B	Rod Carew	CAL	Steve Garvey	SDN
2B	Lou Whitaker	DET	Ryne Sandberg	CHN
3B	George Brett	KCA	Mike Schmidt	PHI
SS	Cal Ripken	BAL	Ozzie Smith	SLN
OF	Reggie Jackson	CAL	Tony Gwynn	SDN
OF	Chet Lemon	DET	Dale Murphy	ATL
OF	Dave Winfield	NYA	Darryl Strawberry	NYN
	Tony Armas	BOS	Joaquin Andujar +	SLN
	Buddy Bell	TEX	Bob Brenly	SFN
	Mike Boddicker	BAL	Chili Davis	SFN
	Bill Caudill	OAK	Jody Davis	CHN
	Alvin Davis	SEA	Dwight Gooden	NYN
	Richard Dotson	CHA	Rich Gossage	SDN
	Dave Engle	MIN	Keith Hernandez	NYN
	Damaso Garcia	TOR	Al Holland	PHI
	Alfredo Griffin	TOR	Mike Marshall	LAN
	Rickey Henderson	OAK	Jerry Mumphrey	HOU
	Guillermo Hernandez	DET	Jesse Orosco	NYN
	Don Mattingly	NYA	Tony Pena	PIT
	Jack Morris	DET	Tim Raines	MON
	Eddie Murray	BAL	Rafael Ramirez	ATL
	Phil Niekro	NYA	Juan Samuel	PHI
	Dan Quisenberry	KCA	Mario Soto	CIN
	Jim Rice	BOS	Bruce Sutter	SLN
	Jim Sundberg	MIL	Fernando Valenzuela	LAN
	Andre Thornton	CLE	Tim Wallach	MON
	Alan Trammell +	DET	Claudell Washington	ATL

+ player replaced on roster

RETROSHEET EXPANDED BOX SCORE Tuesday, 7/10/1984 American League at National League (N)

American League	010	000	000-	1			
National League	110	000	01X-	3			

AMERICAN LEAGUE

	ab	r	h	bi	bb	so	po	a
L.Whitaker, 2b	3	0	2	0	0	0	0	5
D.Garcia, 2b	1	0	0	0	0	0	1	0
R.Carew, 1b	2	0	0	0	0	1	5	0
E.Murray, 1b	2	0	1	0	0	1	3	0
C.Ripken, ss	3	0	0	0	0	0	0	0
A.Griffin, ss	0	0	0	0	0	0	0	1
D.Mattingly, ph	1	0	0	0	0	0	0	0
D.Winfield, lf-rf	4	0	1	0	0	1	2	1
R.Jackson, rf	2	0	0	0	0	1	0	0
R.Henderson, lf-cf	2	0	0	0	0	1	0	0
G.Brett, 3b	3	1	1	1	0	1	3	0
B.Caudill, p	0	0	0	0	0	0	0	0
W.Hernandez, p	0	0	0	0	0	0	0	0
L.Parrish, c	2	0	0	0	0	2	3	1
J.Sundberg, c	1	0	0	0	0	0	6	0
C.Lemon, cf	2	0	1	0	0	1	0	0
J.Rice, ph-lf	1	0	0	0	0	1	1	0
D.Stieb, p	0	0	0	0	0	0	0	0
A.Thornton, ph	1	0	1	0	0	0	0	0
J.Morris, p	0	0	0	0	0	0	0	1
A.Davis, ph	1	0	0	0	0	1	0	0
R.Dotson, p	0	0	0	0	0	0	0	0
B.Bell, 3b	1	0	0	0	0	0	0	1
Totals	32	1	7	1	0	11	24	10

BATTING
2B: L.Whitaker (off C.Lea); E.Murray (off D.Gooden); D.Winfield (off R.Gossage).
HR: G.Brett (2nd inning off C.Lea, 0 on, 1 out).
RBI, scoring position, less than 2 outs: R.Carew 0–2; C.Ripken 0–2.

BASERUNNING
Team LOB: 4

FIELDING
E: R.Jackson; L.Parrish (dropped throw).

NATIONAL LEAGUE

	ab	r	h	bi	bb	so	po	a
T.Gwynn, lf	3	0	1	0	0	1	0	0
T.Raines, lf	1	0	0	0	0	1	4	0
R.Sandberg, 2b	4	0	1	0	0	1	0	0
S.Garvey, 1b	3	1	1	0	0	0	5	1
K.Hernandez, 1b	1	0	0	0	0	1	1	0
D.Murphy, cf	3	1	2	1	1	0	0	0
M.Schmidt, 3b	3	0	0	0	0	2	0	4
T.Wallach, 3b	1	0	0	0	0	0	0	0
D.Strawberry, rf	2	0	1	0	0	1	0	0
C.Washington, rf	2	0	1	0	0	1	1	0
G.Carter, c	2	1	1	1	1	0	9	0
J.Davis, c	1	0	0	0	0	0	1	0
R.Gossage, p	0	0	0	0	0	0	0	0
O.Smith, ss	3	0	0	0	0	0	3	0
C.Lea, p	0	0	0	0	0	0	0	1
C.Davis, ph	1	0	0	0	0	0	0	0
F.Valenzuela, p	0	0	0	0	0	0	0	0
J.Mumphrey, ph	1	0	0	0	0	1	0	0
D.Gooden, p	0	0	0	0	0	0	1	0
B.Brenly, ph	1	0	0	0	0	1	0	0
M.Soto, p	0	0	0	0	0	0	0	0
T.Pena, c	0	0	0	0	0	0	2	0
Totals	32	3	8	2	2	10	27	6

BATTING
2B: C.Washington (off R.Dotson).
HR: D.Murphy (8th inning off W.Hernandez, 0 on, 0 out); G.Carter (2nd inning off D.Stieb, 0 on, 1 out).
RBI, scoring position, less than 2 outs: R.Sandberg 0–1; S.Garvey 0–2; O.Smith 0–1.

BASERUNNING
SB: T.Gwynn (2nd base off R.Dotson/J.Sundberg); R.Sandberg (2nd base off J.Morris/L.Parrish); D.Strawberry (2nd base off J.Morris/L.Parrish); O.Smith (2nd base off R.Dotson/J.Sundberg).
Team LOB: 7

FIELDING
DP: (1). S.Garvey-G.Carter.

PITCHING	ip	h	r	er	bb	so
American League						
D.Stieb (L)	2.0	3	2	1	0	2
J.Morris	2.0	2	0	0	1	2
R.Dotson	2.0	2	0	0	1	2

Inherited Runners—Scored:
J.Morris 0–0; R.Dotson 0–0; B.Caudill 0–0; W.Hernandez 0–0; F.Valenzuela 0–0; D.Gooden 0–0; M.Soto 0–0; R.Gossage 0–0.

PITCHING	ip	h	r	er	bb	so
American League (continued)						
B.Caudill	1.0	0	0	0	0	3
W.Hernandez	1.0	1	1	1	0	1
National League						
C.Lea (w)	2.0	3	1	1	0	2
F.Valenzuela	2.0	2	0	0	0	3
D.Gooden	2.0	1	0	0	0	3
M.Soto	2.0	0	0	0	0	1
R.Gossage (s)	1.0	1	0	0	0	2

GAME DATA—T: 2:29; A: 57756; Temp: Unknown; Wind: Unknown direction, Speed: Unknown

UMPIRES—HP: Lee Weyer (NL), 1B: Al Clark (AL), 2B: Dutch Rennert (NL), 3B: Durwood Merrill (AL), LF: Fred Brocklander (NL), RF: Rocky Roe (AL)

STARTING LINEUPS

	American League	National League
1.	L.Whitaker 2b	T.Gwynn lf
2.	R.Carew 1b	R.Sandberg 2b
3.	C.Ripken ss	S.Garvey 1b
4.	D.Winfield lf	D.Murphy cf
5.	R.Jackson rf	M.Schmidt 3b
6.	G.Brett 3b	D.Strawberry rf
7.	L.Parrish c	G.Carter c
8.	C.Lemon cf	O.Smith ss
9.	D.Stieb p	C.Lea p

AL 1ST: L.Whitaker doubled to right field; R.Carew was called out on strikes; C.Ripken grounded out (M.Schmidt-3b to S.Garvey-1b); D.Winfield grounded out (M.Schmidt-3b to S.Garvey-1b); 0 R, 1 H, 0 E, 1 LOB. AL 0, NL 0.

NL 1ST: T.Gwynn grounded out (L.Whitaker-2b to R.Carew-1b); R.Sandberg grounded out (L.Whitaker-2b to R.Carew-1b); S.Garvey singled to right field [S.Garvey to second (error by R.Jackson-rf)]; D.Murphy singled to left field [S.Garvey scored (unearned) (no RBI) (error by L.Parrish-c; assist by D.Winfield-lf), D.Murphy to second (on throw home)]; M.Schmidt struck out (L.Parrish-c to R.Carew-1b); 1 R (0 ER), 2 H, 2 E, 1 LOB. AL 0, NL 1.

AL 2ND: R.Jackson popped to O.Smith-ss; G.Brett homered to centerfield (it was the 2–0 pitch); L.Parrish struck out; C.Lemon singled to short right-center; C.Lemon was picked off first (C.Lea-p to S.Garvey-1b); 1 R, 2 H, 0 E, 0 LOB. AL 1, NL 1.

NL 2ND: D.Strawberry was called out on strikes; G.Carter homered to leftfield; O.Smith grounded out (L.Whitaker-2b to R.Carew-1b); C.Davis batted for C.Lea; C.Davis lined to G.Brett-3b; 1 R, 1 H, 0 E, 0 LOB. AL 1, NL 2.

AL 3RD: F.Valenzuela replaced C.Davis (pitching); A.Thornton batted for D.Stieb; A.Thornton singled to center field; L.Whitaker singled to right field [A.Thornton to third]; Thornton beat a strong throw by Strawberry; R.Carew hit into a double play (S.Garvey-1b to G.Carter-c) [A.Thornton out at home, L.Whitaker to second]; C.Ripken grounded out (M.Schmidt-3b to S.Garvey-1b); 0 R, 2 H, 0 E, 1 LOB. AL 1, NL 2.

NL 3RD: J.Morris replaced A.Thornton (pitching); T.Gwynn struck out; R.Sandberg singled to in front of the plate; R.Sandberg stole second; S.Garvey flied to D.Winfield-lf; D.Murphy walked; M.Schmidt grounded out (J.Morris-p to R.Carew-1b); 0 R, 1 H, 0 E, 2 LOB. AL 1, NL 2.

AL 4TH: D.Winfield struck out; R.Jackson struck out; G.Brett was called out on strikes; 0 R, 0 H, 0 E, 0 LOB. AL 1, NL 2.

NL 4TH: E.Murray replaced R.Carew (playing 1b); D.Winfield changed positions (playing rf); R.Henderson replaced R.Jackson (playing lf); D.Strawberry singled to right field; G.Carter popped to G.Brett-3b; O.Smith popped to G.Brett-3b in foul territory; Brett reached into the photographer's box to make the catch; J.Mumphrey batted for F.Valenzuela; D.Strawberry stole second; J.Mumphrey struck out; 0 R, 1 H, 0 E, 1 LOB. AL 1, NL 2.

AL 5TH: D.Gooden replaced J.Mumphrey (pitching); C.Washington replaced D.Strawberry (playing rf); L.Parrish struck out; C.Lemon struck out; A.Davis batted for J.Morris; A.Davis struck out; 0 R, 0 H, 0 E, 0 LOB. AL 1, NL 2.

NL 5TH: six consecutive strikeouts by NL hurlers; R.Dotson replaced A.Davis (pitching); J.Sundberg replaced L.Parrish (playing c); T.Gwynn singled to left field; T.Gwynn stole second; R.Sandberg grounded out (L.Whitaker-2b to E.Murray-1b) [T.Gwynn to third]; S.Garvey grounded out (L.Whitaker-2b to E.Murray-1b); D.Murphy flied to D.Winfield-rf; 0 R, 1 H, 0 E, 1 LOB. AL 1, NL 2.

AL 6TH: T.Raines replaced T.Gwynn (playing lf); K.Hernandez replaced S.Garvey (playing 1b); L.Whitaker grounded out (D.Gooden-p unassisted); E.Murray doubled to shortstop; C.Ripken grounded out (M.Schmidt-3b to K.Hernandez-1b); D.Winfield flied to T.Raines-lf; 0 R, 1 H, 0 E, 1 LOB. AL 1, NL 2.

NL 6TH: D.Garcia replaced L.Whitaker (playing 2b); A.Griffin replaced C.Ripken (playing ss); M.Schmidt struck out; C.Washington doubled to left field; G.Carter walked; O.Smith forced G.Carter (A.Griffin-ss to D.Garcia-2b) [C.Washington to third, O.Smith to first]; B.Brenly batted for D.Gooden; O.Smith stole second; B.Brenly struck out; 0 R, 1 H, 0 E, 2 LOB. AL 1, NL 2.

AL 7TH: T.Wallach replaced M.Schmidt (playing 3b); J.Davis replaced G.Carter (playing c); M.Soto replaced B.Brenly (pitching); R.Henderson flied to C.Washington-rf; G.Brett flied to T.Raines-lf; J.Sundberg flied to T.Raines-lf; 0 R, 0 H, 0 E, 0 LOB. AL 1, NL 2.

NL 7TH: B.Bell replaced R.Dotson (playing 3b); B.Caudill replaced G.Brett (pitching); T.Raines struck out; R.Sandberg struck out; K.Hernandez struck out; 0 R, 0 H, 0 E, 0 LOB. AL 1, NL 2.

AL 8TH: third inning with three consecutive strike-outs; J.Rice batted for C.Lemon; J.Rice struck out; B.Bell popped to O.Smith-ss; D.Garcia popped to O.Smith-ss in foul territory; 0 R, 0 H, 0 E, 0 LOB. AL 1, NL 2.

NL 8TH: J.Rice stayed in game (playing lf); R.Henderson changed positions (playing cf); W.Hernandez replaced B.Caudill (pitching); D.Murphy homered to leftfield (it was the 2–2 pitch); T.Wallach grounded out (B.Bell-3b to E.Murray-1b); C.Washington struck out; J.Davis flied to J.Rice-lf; 1 R, 1 H, 0 E, 0 LOB. AL 1, NL 3.

AL 9TH: **R.Gossage replaced J.Davis (pitching); T.Pena replaced M.Soto (playing c);** E.Murray

struck out; **D.Mattingly batted for A.Griffin;** D.Mattingly flied to T.Raines-lf; D.Winfield doubled to left field; R.Henderson was called out on strikes; 0 R, 1 H, 0 E, 1 LOB. AL 1, NL 3.

Final Totals	R	H	E	LOB
American League	1	7	2	4
National League	3	8	0	7

Homerless in the Dome

The 1985 game was billed as a display of the AL power hitters in a ballpark known for home runs. Minneapolis's Metrodome, which opened in 1982, had acquired the nickname "Homerdome" because of the way the ball traveled in the indoor atmosphere. All eight AL position starters had a minimum of eleven homers at the break, including thirty-eight-year-old catcher Carlton Fisk's league-leading twenty-three. For the first time, an official home run–hitting contest was held on the day before the game, and more than forty-six thousand fans paid $2 each to watch batting practice.

Earlier in the season, Yankees manager Billy Martin had protested a game at the Dome, claiming the park was not fit for Major League Baseball. Martin called the structure a "Little League park." AL Manager Sparky Anderson of the Tigers, when asked about the Metrodome, remarked, "Oh, it's going to be a treat for NL guys who haven't seen it before."

However, the game did not meet expectations. The NL beat its opponents behind the dazzling pitching of five men who allowed only five hits — all singles—and one unearned run. The NL batters also were held in the park; no home runs were hit in the game for the first time since 1978 in San Diego. It was the eleventh time in fifty-six games that no homers were hit in an All-Star contest.

Mets outfielder Darryl Strawberry put it best: "Everybody saw the home run–hitting contest Monday and thought the game would be like that. But the pitchers are no dummies; they saw the same thing."

San Diego's LaMarr Hoyt, in his only All-Star appearance, started and pitched three innings, getting the win and the MVP trophy. In the first inning, Hoyt allowed a lead-off single to the Yankees' Rickey Henderson. One out later, Henderson stole second base and continued to third on a throwing error by catcher Terry Kennedy, Hoyt's

San Diego teammate. George Brett's sacrifice fly scored the only AL run.

Hoyt pitched a perfect second inning but allowed pinch hitter Harold Baines, Hoyt's former teammate with the White Sox, to reach on a single to right field. Nolan Ryan, the fireballing hurler from Houston, replaced Hoyt in the fourth inning and pitched a perfect inning.

In the AL fifth, Dave Winfield of the Yankees singled to center and stole second as Jim Rice struck out. With two out, Cecil Cooper walked, and the AL had two runners on in the same inning for the first time in the game. Henderson strode to the plate and immediately hit the dirt as Ryan threw a fastball under his chin. Henderson struck out to end the threat.

Ryan repeated his performance in the sixth. Brett walked with one out and moved to third on Cal Ripken Jr.'s two-out single. With Winfield at the plate, Ryan threw another duster, and then Winfield grounded out to second base.

Ryan, who had topped four thousand career strikeouts a week before this contest, claimed that his control was a little off during his stint on the mound. "With an 0-2 count on Winfield, I was just trying to pitch him inside to set up an outside pitch. I know he likes to extend his arms. That was vintage Nolan Ryan. It showed I could still do it," Ryan said with a smile.

Fernando Valenzuela of the Dodgers, Jeff Reardon of Montreal, and Rich Gossage of the Padres pitched one inning each for the NL. Each allowed one base runner, Valenzuela and Gossage on walks and Reardon on a single by Toronto's Damaso Garcia.

In the eighth, the American Leaguers ran themselves out of a scoring threat. Garcia's single opened the inning, and he stole second while Seattle's Phil Bradley struck out in his only All-Star plate appearance. However, Pittsburgh catcher Tony Pena's low throw skipped away from Cubs second sacker Ryne Sandberg, but pitcher Jeff

Reardon, playing in his first All-Star Game, retrieved the ball and threw Garcia out at third base.

The five bases stolen by the two teams set a record for one game. The previous record of four in a game had been reached four times in 1934 (twice by each team), 1948 (three times by the AL), 1975 (three times by the AL), and 1984 (all by the NL).

The visitors scored their first run in the second off AL starter (and St. Paul native) Jack Morris of the Tigers, who did not pitch to his potential, bouncing several pitches in front of the plate. With one out, Strawberry singled to left and stole second. After a fly out, Terry Kennedy singled to center, scoring Strawberry.

The Straw was voted to the starting lineup even though he had missed much of the first half with torn ligaments in his right thumb. He was hitting .229 with eight homers and nineteen RBI at the break, but he reached base in all three plate appearances and scored two runs. He said, "I was a little embarrassed when I saw I was getting votes despite missing all that time. My first reaction was that I shouldn't play in the game because I didn't have the numbers, but I didn't want to do that because it would be an injustice for all the people who voted for me."

NL manager Dick Williams of San Diego said, "When he came out of the game, I said, 'Job well done.' I could see he was pleased with what he did. He did it all — with his glove, his bat, and his feet. He should be proud."

In the third, the NL went ahead to stay. With two out, Cardinals second baseman Tommy Herr, in his only All-Star appearance, doubled to left and scored on Steve Garvey's single to center. This was the San Diego first baseman's tenth and last All-Star Game; the first eight had been while Garvey played for the Dodgers.

Two-time NL MVP Dale Murphy of the Braves then hit a ball down the left-field line that bounced over the fence for a double, moving Garvey to third. Strawberry walked to load the bases, and Jimmy Key of Toronto made his first All-Star appearance, replacing Morris on the mound for the AL. Key ended the threat when Padres third baseman Graig Nettles, playing in his last of six All-Star Games, popped up in foul territory.

The NL got two more runners on in the fourth when Padre Garry Templeton singled with two out and Jose Cruz of the Astros walked. Both were stranded when Herr grounded out.

In the fifth, the NL scored twice. With two out, Strawberry was hit on the leg by a Bert Blyleven pitch, and Expos third baseman Tim Wallach bounced a double over the left-field fence. Phillies catcher Ozzie Virgil singled to left, scoring both runners.

The Senior Circuit scored two more in the ninth. Ryne Sandberg, Expos outfielder Tim Raines, and Cardinals first baseman Jack Clark all walked to load the bases with one out. Willie McGee, the Cardinals' fleet center fielder, hit a ball to center that might have been an inside-the-park homer had it not bounced over the wall. Two runs scored, and Clark was held at third base by the rules. After another out, Wallach was walked intentionally, bringing up the pitcher, Reardon. Glenn Wilson of the Phillies came in to hit for Reardon, but Willie Hernandez struck out Wilson to end the inning.

NL starter Hoyt, who had won the AL Cy Young Award in 1983 while with Chicago, was not surprised at the performance by the NL pitchers: "In this league, I've seen pitchers who can absolutely dominate a game. I don't think I saw quite the same kind of pitching in the AL. Our pitchers were pumped up to the max about pitching in this game. They have a lot of big swingers over there, big boppers who can go deep. But they all can be pitched to, and it tends to show up in All-Star Games."

The pitching performance was even more amazing because the two best NL hurlers did not even play in the game. Dwight Gooden of the Mets had thrown 140 pitches two days before the game, and the Cardinals' Joaquin Andujar refused to attend. Andujar had heard that manager Williams was going to give the starting job to Hoyt and had announced that he wouldn't be part of the team if he was not the starter. Williams replied, "I think the game will go on without him. We [San Diego] beat him in St. Louis the other day for our only win against them. I'm happy he showed up for that game."

In contrast to Andujar, Cardinals shortstop Ozzie Smith played the entire game for the NL for the second consecutive year. AL and Boston outfielder Jim Rice also played the full game.

Detroit's Lou Whitaker showed up, but his equipment did not. Whitaker had left his bag in the back seat of his car when he flew to Minneapolis and had to wear a replica hat and jersey from a souvenir stand in the park. Since the shirt had no number on the back, Whitaker's "1" was written on it with a marker pen. Whitaker borrowed a pair of blue stirrup socks from the Twins to replace his black ones and a spare glove from Orioles shortstop Ripken.

Rich Gossage made his last All-Star appearance in this game, which was the record-setting sixth time he finished an All-Star Game. His nine selections included representing the White Sox, Pirates, Yankees, and Padres, making him the third player and first pitcher to represent four different teams in the All-Star Game. Walker Cooper attended as a Brave, Red, Cardinal, and Giant, and Smoky Burgess represented the White Sox, Reds, Pirates, and Phillies. The record total of four teams would be topped by Lee Smith in 1995, when he was selected from his fifth different team.

The ceremonial pitches were made by two active players, one who had recently reached a milestone and one who was approaching one. Nolan Ryan had just topped 4,000 strikeouts, and Pete Rose had 4,157 career hits on his march to Ty Cobb's record, which he would reach later in the season.

Rose, appearing in his seventeenth and last All-Star Game, grounded out as a pinch hitter in the eighth inning. The forty-four-year-old Rose was playing in his second All-Star contest in Minnesota, having previously been elected a starter for the 1965 game in Metropolitan Stadium. He commented, "When you play two All-Star Games in the same city, that shows how old I am." In fact, Rose became the oldest nonpitcher to play in an All-Star Game, having already become the oldest starting player in a game in 1982.

In a telephone poll taken by the game's tele-caster, NBC, during the contest, 59 percent of the nearly 250,000 callers voted against the designated hitter rule in baseball. Pete Rose, talking about worthy players who were left off rosters for the game, said, "I don't know why they don't use the DH [in the All-Star Game]. The pitchers never hit anyway."

In another vote, this by the players' union on the day before the All-Star Game, the players had voted a strike date of August 6. They had been trying to come to terms with the owners concerning a new collective bargaining agreement without success. After the games of August 5, the players did strike, forcing the cancellation of games on August 6 and 7. It was the second strike in five years and the fourth overall.

The All-Star MVP Award was renamed this year in honor of Arch Ward, the man who started the game. Ward, a *Chicago Tribune* sports editor, had conceived the game as a one-time event to be part of the 1933 Chicago Century of Progress Exposition.

	AL			NL		
P	Jack Morris		DET	LaMarr Hoyt		SDN
C	Lance Parrish	+	DET	Gary Carter	+	NYN
1B	Eddie Murray		BAL	Steve Garvey		SDN
2B	Lou Whitaker		DET	Tom Herr		SLN
3B	George Brett		KCA	Graig Nettles		SDN
SS	Cal Ripken		BAL	Ozzie Smith		SLN
OF	Rickey Henderson		NYA	Tony Gwynn		SDN
OF	Jim Rice		BOS	Dale Murphy		ATL
OF	Dave Winfield		NYA	Darryl Strawberry		NYN
	Harold Baines		CHA	Joaquin Andujar	+	SLN
	Bert Blyleven		CLE	Jack Clark		SLN
	Wade Boggs		BOS	Jose Cruz		HOU
	Phil Bradley		SEA	Ron Darling		NYN
	Tom Brunansky		MIN	Scott Garrelts		SFN
	Cecil Cooper		MIL	Dwight Gooden		NYN
	Carlton Fisk		CHA	Rich Gossage		SDN
	Damaso Garcia		TOR	Pedro Guerrero	+	LAN
	Rich Gedman		BOS	Terry Kennedy		SDN
	Guillermo Hernandez		DET	Willie McGee		SLN
	Jack Howell		CAL	Dave Parker		CIN
	Jimmy Key		TOR	Tony Pena		PIT
	Don Mattingly		NYA	Tim Raines		MON
	Paul Molitor		MIL	Jeff Reardon		MON
	Donnie Moore		CAL	Pete Rose		CIN
	Dan Petry		DET	Nolan Ryan		HOU
	Dave Stieb		TOR	Ryne Sandberg		CHN
	Alan Trammell		DET	Garry Templeton		SDN
	Gary Ward		TEX	Fernando Valenzuela		LAN
	Ernie Whitt		TOR	Ozzie Virgil		PHI
				Tim Wallach		MON
				Glenn Wilson		PHI

+ player replaced on roster

```
National League      011  020  002-  6
American League      100  000  000-  1
```

NATIONAL LEAGUE

	ab	r	h	bi	bb	so	po	a
T.Gwynn, lf	1	0	0	0	0	0	1	0
J.Cruz, lf	1	0	0	0	2	0	2	0
T.Raines, ph-lf	0	1	0	0	1	0	0	0
T.Herr, 2b	3	1	1	0	0	0	0	1
N.Ryan, p	1	0	0	0	0	1	0	0
T.Pena, c	1	0	0	0	0	1	4	0
S.Garvey, 1b	3	0	1	1	0	0	5	0
J.Clark, 1b	1	0	0	0	1	0	4	0
D.Murphy, cf	3	0	1	0	0	1	1	0
W.McGee, cf	2	0	1	2	0	0	1	0
D.Strawberry, rf	1	2	1	0	1	0	3	0
D.Parker, rf	2	0	0	0	0	1	1	0
G.Nettles, 3b	2	0	0	0	0	0	0	1
T.Wallach, 3b	2	1	1	0	1	1	1	1
T.Kennedy, c	2	0	1	1	0	0	0	0
O.Virgil, c	1	0	1	2	0	0	3	0
F.Valenzuela, p	0	0	0	0	0	0	0	0
P.Rose, ph	1	0	0	0	0	0	0	0
J.Reardon, p	0	0	0	0	0	0	0	1
G.Wilson, ph	1	0	0	0	0	1	0	0
R.Gossage, p	0	0	0	0	0	0	0	0
O.Smith, ss	4	0	0	0	0	0	1	3
L.Hoyt, p	1	0	0	0	0	1	0	0
G.Templeton, ph	1	0	1	0	0	0	0	0
R.Sandberg, 2b	1	1	0	0	1	1	0	3
Totals	35	6	9	6	7	8	27	10

BATTING
2B: T.Herr (off J.Morris); D.Murphy (off J.Morris); T.Wallach (off B.Blyleven); W.McGee (off W.Hernandez).
2-out RBI: S.Garvey; T.Kennedy; O.Virgil 2.
RBI, scoring position, less than 2 outs: T.Pena 0–1; W.McGee 2–2; D.Parker 0–2; G.Nettles 0–1.

BASERUNNING
SB: J.Cruz (2nd base off D.Stieb/E.Whitt); D.Strawberry (2nd base off J.Morris/C.Fisk).
Team LOB: 10

FIELDING
E: T.Kennedy (throw).
DP: (1). T.Pena-R.Sandberg-J.Reardon-T.Wallach.

AMERICAN LEAGUE

	ab	r	h	bi	bb	so	po	a
R.Henderson, cf	3	1	1	0	0	1	1	0
P.Molitor, 3b-cf	1	0	0	0	0	1	0	0
L.Whitaker, 2b	2	0	0	0	0	0	1	1
D.Garcia, 2b	2	0	1	0	0	0	0	3
G.Brett, 3b	1	0	0	1	1	0	2	1
P.Bradley, cf	1	0	0	0	0	1	1	0
D.Petry, p	0	0	0	0	0	0	0	0
W.Hernandez, p	0	0	0	0	0	0	0	0
E.Murray, 1b	3	0	0	0	0	0	5	2
T.Brunansky, rf	1	0	0	0	0	0	0	0
C.Ripken, ss	3	0	1	0	0	0	2	1
A.Trammell, ss	1	0	0	0	0	0	0	0
D.Winfield, rf	3	0	1	0	0	0	0	0
D.Moore, p	0	0	0	0	0	0	0	1
W.Boggs, 3b	0	0	0	0	1	0	0	0
J.Rice, lf	3	0	0	0	1	2	1	0
C.Fisk, c	2	0	0	0	0	0	2	0
E.Whitt, c	0	0	0	0	0	0	2	0
G.Ward, ph	1	0	0	0	0	0	0	0
R.Gedman, c	1	0	0	0	0	1	4	0
J.Morris, p	0	0	0	0	0	0	1	0
J.Key, p	0	0	0	0	0	0	0	0
H.Baines, ph	1	0	1	0	0	0	0	0
B.Blyleven, p	0	0	0	0	0	0	1	2
C.Cooper, ph	0	0	0	0	1	0	0	0
D.Stieb, p	0	0	0	0	0	0	0	0
D.Mattingly, 1b	1	0	0	0	0	0	4	0
Totals	30	1	5	1	4	6	27	11

BATTING
RBI, scoring position, less than 2 outs: G.Brett 1–1; C.Fisk 0–1; G.Ward 0–1; D.Mattingly 0–1.
SF: G.Brett.

BASERUNNING
SB: R.Henderson (2nd base off L.Hoyt/T.Kennedy); D.Garcia (2nd base off J.Reardon/T.Pena); D.Winfield (2nd base off N.Ryan/O.Virgil).
Team LOB: 7

PITCHING	ip	h	r	er	bb	so
National League						
L.Hoyt (w)	3.0	2	1	0	0	0
N.Ryan	3.0	2	0	0	2	2
F.Valenzuela	1.0	0	0	0	1	1
J.Reardon	1.0	1	0	0	0	1
R.Gossage	1.0	0	0	0	1	2
American League						
J.Morris (L)	2.2	5	2	2	1	1
J.Key	0.1	0	0	0	0	0
B.Blyleven	2.0	3	2	2	1	1
D.Stieb	1.0	0	0	0	1	2
D.Moore	2.0	0	0	0	0	1
D.Petry	0.1	0	2	2	3	1
W.Hernandez	0.2	1	0	0	1	2

Inherited Runners—Scored:
N.Ryan 0–0; F.Valenzuela 0–0; J.Reardon 0–0;
R.Gossage 0–0; J.Key 3–0; B.Blyleven 0–0;
D.Stieb 0–0; D.Moore 0–0; D.Petry 0–0;
W.Hernandez 3–2.
IBB: T.Wallach by W.Hernandez.
HBP: D.Strawberry by B.Blyleven.
WP: F.Valenzuela

GAME DATA—T: 2:54; A: 54960; Temp: Unknown;
Wind: Unknown direction, Speed: Unknown

UMPIRES—P: Larry McCoy (AL), 1B: John Kibler (NL),
2B: Nick Bremigan (AL), 3B: Charlie Williams (NL), LF:
Drew Coble (AL), RF: Randy Marsh (NL)

STARTING LINEUPS

	National League	*American League*
1.	T.Gwynn lf	R.Henderson cf
2.	T.Herr 2b	L.Whitaker 2b
3.	S.Garvey 1b	G.Brett 3b
4.	D.Murphy cf	E.Murray 1b
5.	D.Strawberry rf	C.Ripken ss
6.	G.Nettles 3b	D.Winfield rf
7.	T.Kennedy c	J.Rice lf
8.	O.Smith ss	C.Fisk c
9.	L.Hoyt p	J.Morris p
	L.Hoyt p	J.Morris p

NL 1ST: T.Gwynn grounded out (L.Whitaker-2b to E.Murray-1b); T.Herr popped to C.Ripken-ss; S.Garvey grounded out (G.Brett-3b to E.Murray-1b); 0 R, 0 H, 0 E, 0 LOB. NL 0, AL 0.

AL 1ST: R.Henderson singled to center field; L.Whitaker flied to D.Strawberry-rf; R.Henderson stole second [R.Henderson to third (error by T.Kennedy-c)]; G.Brett lined out on a sacrifice fly to T.Gwynn-lf [R.Henderson scored (unearned)]; E.Murray popped to O.Smith-ss; 1 R (0 ER), 1 H, 1 E, 0 LOB. NL 0, AL 1.

NL 2ND: D.Murphy popped to C.Ripken-ss; D.Strawberry singled to left field; D.Strawberry stole second; G.Nettles flied to J.Rice-lf; T.Kennedy singled to center field [D.Strawberry scored]; O.Smith popped to G.Brett-3b; 1 R, 2 H, 0 E, 1 LOB. NL 1, AL 1.

AL 2ND: over the shoulder catch; **J.Cruz replaced T.Gwynn (playing lf)**; C.Ripken grounded out (O.Smith-ss to S.Garvey-1b); D.Winfield grounded out (T.Herr-2b to S.Garvey-1b); J.Rice flied to D.Strawberry-rf; 0 R, 0 H, 0 E, 0 LOB. NL 1, AL 1.

NL 3RD: L.Hoyt struck out; J.Cruz grounded out (E.Murray-1b to J.Morris-p); T.Herr doubled to left field; S.Garvey singled to center field [T.Herr scored]; D.Murphy hit a ground rule double to deep leftfield down the line [S.Garvey to third]; D.Strawberry walked; **J.Key replaced J.Morris (pitching)**; G.Nettles popped to G.Brett-3b in foul territory; 1 R, 3 H, 0 E, 3 LOB. NL 2, AL 1.

AL 3RD: C.Fisk flied to D.Murphy-cf; **H.Baines batted for J.Key**; H.Baines singled to right field; R.Henderson grounded out (G.Nettles-3b to S.Garvey-1b) [H.Baines to second]; L.Whitaker flied to D.Strawberry-rf; 0 R, 1 H, 0 E, 1 LOB. NL 2, AL 1.

NL 4TH: **B.Blyleven replaced H.Baines (pitching)**; T.Kennedy grounded out (E.Murray-1b unassisted); O.Smith grounded out (B.Blyleven-p to E.Murray-1b); **G.Templeton batted for L.Hoyt**; G.Templeton singled to center field; J.Cruz walked [G.Templeton to second]; T.Herr

grounded out (E.Murray-1b to B.Blyleven-p); 0 R, 1 H, 0 E, 2 LOB. NL 2, AL 1.

AL 4TH: **N.Ryan replaced T.Herr (pitching); O.Virgil replaced T.Kennedy (playing c); R.Sandberg replaced G.Templeton (playing 2b); T.Wallach replaced G.Nettles (playing 3b)**; G.Brett grounded out (R.Sandberg-2b to S.Garvey-1b); E.Murray popped to O.Virgil-c in foul territory; C.Ripken grounded out (O.Smith-ss to S.Garvey-1b); 0 R, 0 H, 0 E, 0 LOB. NL 2, AL 1.

NL 5TH: S.Garvey grounded out (C.Ripken-ss to E.Murray-1b); D.Murphy struck out; D.Strawberry was hit by a pitch; hit on the leg; T.Wallach hit a ground rule double to leftfield [D.Strawberry to third]; O.Virgil singled to left field (B.Blyleven-p to L.Whitaker-2b) [D.Strawberry scored, T.Wallach scored, O.Virgil out at second]; 2 R, 2 H, 0 E, 0 LOB. NL 4, AL 1.

AL 5TH: Rice's throw got past Fisk; **J.Clark replaced S.Garvey (playing 1b); W.McGee replaced D.Murphy (playing cf); D.Parker replaced D.Strawberry (playing rf)**; D.Winfield singled to center field; J.Rice struck out while D.Winfield stole second; C.Fisk flied to J.Cruz-lf; **C.Cooper batted for B.Blyleven**; C.Cooper walked; R.Henderson struck out; 0 R, 1 H, 0 E, 2 LOB. NL 4, AL 1.

NL 6TH: **D.Stieb replaced C.Cooper (pitching); E.Whitt replaced C.Fisk (playing c); D.Garcia replaced L.Whitaker (playing 2b)**; O.Smith flied to R.Henderson-cf; R.Sandberg was called out on strikes; J.Cruz walked; J.Cruz stole second; N.Ryan struck out; 0 R, 0 H, 0 E, 1 LOB. NL 4, AL 1.

AL 6TH: D.Garcia flied to D.Parker-rf; G.Brett walked; E.Murray lined to J.Cruz-lf; C.Ripken singled to third base [G.Brett to second]; D.Winfield grounded out (R.Sandberg-2b to J.Clark-1b); 0 R, 1 H, 0 E, 2 LOB. NL 4, AL 1.

NL 7TH: **P.Molitor replaced R.Henderson (playing 3b); P.Bradley replaced G.Brett (playing cf); T.Brunansky replaced E.Murray (playing rf); A.Trammell replaced C.Ripken (playing ss); D.Mattingly replaced D.Stieb (playing 1b); D.Moore replaced D.Winfield (pitching)**; J.Clark grounded out (D.Moore-p to D.Mattingly-1b); W.McGee grounded out (D.Garcia-2b to D.Mattingly-1b); D.Parker grounded out (D.Garcia-2b to D.Mattingly-1b); 0 R, 0 H, 0 E, 0 LOB. NL 4, AL 1.

AL 7TH: **F.Valenzuela replaced O.Virgil (pitching); T.Pena replaced N.Ryan (playing c)**; J.Rice walked; **G.Ward batted for E.Whitt**; F.Valenzuela threw a wild pitch [J.Rice to second]; G.Ward lined to J.Clark-1b; D.Mattingly flied to W.McGee-cf [J.Rice to third]; Smith's relay hit Rice on the back; P.Molitor struck out; 0 R, 0 H, 0 E, 1 LOB. NL 4, AL 1.

NL 8TH: **R.Gedman replaced G.Ward (playing c);** T.Wallach struck out; **P.Rose batted for F.Valenzuela;** P.Rose grounded out (D.Garcia-2b to D.Mattingly-1b); O.Smith flied to P.Bradley-cf; 0 R, 0 H, 0 E, 0 LOB. NL 4, AL 1.

AL 8TH: **J.Reardon replaced P.Rose (pitching);** D.Garcia singled to left field; P.Bradley struck out while D.Garcia stole second (T.Pena-c to R.Sandberg-2b to J.Reardon-p to T.Wallach-3b) [D.Garcia out at third]; Pena's low throw skipped away from Sandberg; T.Brunansky grounded out (O.Smith-ss to J.Clark-1b); 0 R, 1 H, 0 E, 0 LOB. NL 4, AL 1.

NL 9TH: **P.Molitor changed positions (playing cf); W.Boggs replaced D.Moore (playing 3b); D.Petry replaced P.Bradley (pitching);** R.Sandberg walked; **T.Raines batted for J.Cruz;** T.Raines walked [R.Sandberg to second]; T.Pena struck out; J.Clark walked [R.Sandberg to third, T.Raines to second]; **W.Hernandez replaced D.Petry (pitching);** W.McGee hit a ground rule double to centerfield [R.Sandberg scored, T.Raines scored, J.Clark to third]; D.Parker struck out; T.Wallach was walked intentionally; **G.Wilson batted for J.Reardon;** G.Wilson struck out; 2 R, 1 H, 0 E, 3 LOB. NL 6, AL 1.

AL 9TH: **T.Raines stayed in game (playing lf); R.Gossage replaced G.Wilson (pitching);** A.Trammell grounded out (T.Wallach-3b to J.Clark-1b); W.Boggs walked; J.Rice struck out; R.Gedman struck out; 0 R, 0 H, 0 E, 1 LOB. NL 6, AL 1.

Final Totals	R	H	E	LOB
National League	6	9	1	10
American League	1	5	0	7

57

Shootout in Texas

The second consecutive game played indoors — the previous year's contest had been held in Minneapolis's Metrodome — was billed as the duel of the ninety-five-mile-an-hour fastballs. Both teams featured young fireballing hurlers, Roger Clemens for the AL and Dwight Gooden for the NL, among their very young rosters. At ages twenty-three and twenty-one, respectively, Clemens and Gooden were the second-youngest pair of starters in All-Star history. The youngest pair was Jerry Walker (age twenty) and Don Drysdale (age twenty-three) in 1959.

There were twenty-five first-time All-Stars among the players, most notably rookie sluggers Wally Joyner of California and Jose Canseco of Oakland, in addition to Clemens. Joyner became the fifteenth rookie to start the All-Star Game and the first rookie to be elected by the fans. Kansas City's Frank White commented on Joyner's election: "I salute the fans for picking someone like Wally Joyner. It shows they're paying attention." Canseco would be named the AL Rookie of the Year.

Longtime All-Star George Brett, absent from this year's lineup with a sore shoulder, talked about the young talent on the AL roster: "I'll tell you it's exciting. It really is. Look around this clubhouse and what you see is indicative of the young talent coming into our league. It's not a fluke. The thing is, you look at the NL team, and it seems the same guys have been playing every year."

Clemens, the Red Sox third-year pitcher who would win the AL MVP Award and the first of two consecutive AL Cy Young Awards at the end of the season, had grown up near Houston and attended the University of Texas. He came into the game with a 15-2 record and a 2.48 ERA, having won fourteen consecutive games to start the season; he had struck out 146 batters in 145 innings on his way to a season total of 238 strikeouts. Clemens's

homecoming — during which he pitched three perfect innings with two strikeouts and received credit for the win — was a success. The NL batters got only three balls out of the infield, all of which were easy flies. Clemens threw only twenty-five pitches in his stint on the mound, and only four of them were balls. For his efforts, he was named the game's MVP. NL slugger Darryl Strawberry of the Mets commented on Clemens after the game: "He is going to be one of the greats of the game."

Clemens's opponent, Dwight Gooden, was also in his third big league season. Gooden had been named the NL Rookie of the Year in 1984 and the NL Cy Young Award winner in 1985. At the break, he was 10-4 with a 2.77 ERA but had a tougher time in Houston than Clemens. In his three innings, Gooden surrendered two runs on three hits and balked on an attempted pick-off at first base. He was tagged with the loss.

Pitchers dominated the game as each team collected only five hits. For the AL, Teddy Higuera of Milwaukee followed Clemens and continued the perfect game until Strawberry singled with one out in the fifth inning. This was the only hit allowed by Higuera, who also walked Mike Schmidt, the 1986 NL MVP, following The Straw's hit. However, Higuera got out of the inning by retiring Atlanta's Dale Murphy, a two-time NL MVP, on a fly ball and Montreal's Hubie Brooks on a grounder.

The AL started the game with a hit from Minnesota outfielder Kirby Puckett, who was making the first of ten consecutive appearances as an All-Star. Puckett singled to center on Gooden's first pitch of the game. Oakland speedster Rickey Henderson forced Puckett at second but then drew a lot of attention from Gooden because of his knack for stealing bases. As Gooden tried to throw to first, he slipped; a balk was called, moving Henderson to second base. Gooden escaped any further damage with two fly outs to end the inning.

Facing the NL proved easy for Clemens in the first as San Diego's Tony Gwynn flew out, Ryne

Sandberg of the Cubs (the 1984 NL Most Valuable Player) was called out on strikes, and Mets first baseman Keith Hernandez grounded out.

After two outs in the top of the second, Dave Winfield doubled to right for his eleventh career hit in All-Star competition. He tied with former Dodger Steve Garvey for the second-highest career batting average in the game, at .393, but they both trailed Billy Herman, at .433.

Following Winfield's hit, Lou Whitaker, the Tigers' second baseman, got behind in the count at 0-2 but hit Gooden's next pitch for a home run over the right-field wall and a 2-0 lead for the Junior Circuit. "It was a curve that didn't break, and I just managed to get it out," Whitaker said later. "I didn't have any illusions. I'm not a home run hitter." Gooden said, "One pitch cost me two runs, and that's been my problem."

Clemens continued his domination in the second by striking out Strawberry in between fly outs by Gary Carter and Mike Schmidt. In the third, three ground outs retired the NL.

The most dominating pitching performance of the night belonged to Dodger Fernando Valenzuela, who in 1981 won both the NL Rookie of the Year Award and the Cy Young Award. Valenzuela replaced Gooden in the fourth and struck out Don Mattingly, the 1985 AL MVP; Cal Ripken Jr., the 1982 AL Rookie of the Year and 1983 AL MVP; and pinch hitter Jesse Barfield. The latter two were both called out. Valenzuela continued his performance in the fifth when Whitaker was called out on strikes and Higuera, who had never batted in the Majors, missed the third strike.

Thus, Valenzuela struck out five consecutive batters, the first five he faced, tying the mark set by Carl Hubbell in the 1934 game when Hubbell struck out five Hall of Famers (Babe Ruth, Lou Gehrig, Jimmie Foxx, Al Simmons, and Joe Cronin). Valenzuela's string was broken when Puckett grounded out. Valenzuela allowed only one player to reach base in his three innings, when Wade Boggs singled to center in the sixth.

With two out in the seventh on Mike Scott's split-finger strikeouts, Kansas City's Frank White pinch-hit for Whitaker—who had homered in the second—and got behind in the count 0-2, as had Whitaker. However, White turned the next pitch around and homered to left-center field. White said of Scott, the 1986 NL Cy Young Award winner: "He threw a fastball in over the plate—just missed with it, I think."

Texas knuckleballer Charlie Hough, who was playing in what was to be his only All-Star Game, pitched a perfect seventh inning to continue the shutout of the NL. However, in the eighth, the Se-

nior Circuit finally scored. Chris Brown of the Giants, also appearing in his only All-Star contest, led off the inning with a double to left-center field. On the third strike to Brown's Giants teammate Chili Davis, Brown advanced to third on a knuckleball that got away from Red Sox catcher Rich Gedman for a wild pitch, forcing Gedman to throw Davis out at first base.

Hubie Brooks, the next batter, also had trouble connecting with Hough's flutter pitch. On the third strike, Gedman again failed to catch the ball, this time for a passed ball, and while Brooks reached first, Brown scored an unearned run. Hough then balked Brooks to second, and, after a strikeout of Montreal's Tim Raines, Dodger second baseman Steve Sax singled to left-center, scoring Brooks with the second unearned run of the inning. Dave Righetti of the Yankees, playing in his first All-Star Game, replaced Hough on the mound. After Sax stole second, pinch hitter Glenn Davis of Houston, another first-time All-Star, fouled out to end the inning.

Gedman, who had never caught a knuckleball before, talked about catching Hough after the game: "That was embarrassing. It's just a matter of getting used to the knuckleball, which I'm not." Hough had brought an oversized catcher's mitt with him and gave it to Gedman to use. Hough said, "The balls that he missed didn't really get away from him. He just missed them with his glove."

With Righetti still pitching, the NL threatened in the ninth. With one out, Cubs catcher Jody Davis singled to center field, and Pittsburgh catcher Tony Pena ran for him. Reds outfielder Dave Parker singled to right, and Pena raced to third base. With only one out and the winning run on first, AL manager Dick Howser of the Royals decided to bring Don Aase out of the bullpen to put out the fire. Aase, the Orioles closer, who would end the year with thirty-four saves, threw two pitches to Brown. Brown tried to check his swing on the second-pitch slider but hit an easy bouncer to second baseman White, who stepped on the bag and threw to first for a game-ending double play.

Cardinals manager Whitey Herzog, the 1985 NL Manager of the Year, said that the game was important to him because "I'm the only NL manager who has lost in the last thirteen or fourteen years." Indeed, the last NL skipper to lose an All-Star Game had been Sparky Anderson of the Reds, in 1971. Herzog also was having a tough time with his Cardinals; they ended the year under .500 and in third place in the NL East. Herzog said, "I went out to make lineup changes, and Bruce Froemming [the plate umpire] said 'Hey, you put the hex on these guys, too.' " To make matters worse for Herzog, this was the first time that the AL had won in a NL ballpark since the second game in 1962 at Chicago's Wrigley Field.

Traveling to the game had been difficult for many All-Stars. Tony Fernandez, the Blue Jays shortstop, and Cal Ripken Jr., the Orioles shortstop, each had luggage lost—for Fernandez, the loss was more crucial since the lost bag contained his equipment. He had to borrow a glove from Frank White and uniform parts from other players. The Mets contingent was delayed at the airport and did not arrive in Houston until 5 A.M. on workout day.

Boston pitcher Dennis "Oil Can" Boyd had expected to be picked for the AL squad. When he was not, he destroyed much of the Boston clubhouse and was suspended.

The two teams approached many All-Star records in this game. The combined total of nineteen strikeouts was two short of the record set in the 1984 game. The twelve strikeouts by the NL pitching staff tied the record for most by one team in a nine-inning game; the feat had been accomplished three times previously, by the NL in 1934 and in the second game in 1959 and by the AL in 1956.

Appropriately, all of the records were by pitchers in this hurler-dominated game. Valenzuela's five strikeouts were one short of the record for a game, which was held by Carl Hubbell (1934), Johnny Vander Meer (1943), Larry Jansen (1950), and Fergie Jenkins (1967). Hough, at thirty-eight years and six months, became the third-oldest pitcher to play in the All-Star Game. Satchel Paige had been forty-seven when he played in 1953, and Gerry Staley had been thirty-nine years and ten months while playing in 1960.

	AL			NL	
P	Roger Clemens		BOS	Dwight Gooden	NYN
C	Lance Parrish		DET	Gary Carter	NYN
1B	Wally Joyner		CAL	Keith Hernandez	NYN
2B	Lou Whitaker		DET	Ryne Sandberg	CHN
3B	George Brett	+	KCA	Mike Schmidt	PHI
SS	Cal Ripken		BAL	Ozzie Smith	SLN
OF	Rickey Henderson		NYA	Tony Gwynn	SDN
OF	Kirby Puckett		MIN	Dale Murphy	ATL
OF	Dave Winfield		NYA	Darryl Strawberry	NYN
	Don Aase		BAL	Kevin Bass	HOU
	Harold Baines		CHA	Hubie Brooks	MON
	Jesse Barfield		TOR	Chris Brown	SFN
	Wade Boggs		BOS	Chili Davis	SFN
	Jose Canseco		OAK	Glenn Davis	HOU
	Tony Fernandez		TOR	Jody Davis	CHN
	Rich Gedman		BOS	Sid Fernandez	NYN
	Guillermo Hernandez		DET	John Franco	CIN
	Teddy Higuera		MIL	Mike Krukow	SFN
	Charlie Hough		TEX	Dave Parker	CIN
	Brook Jacoby		CLE	Tony Pena	PIT
	Don Mattingly		NYA	Tim Raines	MON
	Lloyd Moseby		TOR	Shane Rawley	PHI
	Eddie Murray		BAL	Jeff Reardon	MON
	Jim Presley		SEA	Rick Rhoden	PIT
	Jim Rice		BOS	Steve Sax	LAN
	Dave Righetti		NYA	Mike Scott	HOU
	Ken Schrom		CLE	Dave Smith	HOU
	Frank White		KCA	Fernando Valenzuela	LAN
	Mike Witt		CAL		

+ player replaced on roster

American League   020 000 100- 3
National League   000 000 020- 2

AMERICAN LEAGUE

	ab	r	h	bi	bb	so	po	a
K.Puckett, cf	3	0	1	0	1	0	5	0
R.Henderson, lf	3	0	0	0	0	1	2	0
L.Moseby, lf	0	0	0	0	1	0	0	0
W.Boggs, 3b	3	0	1	0	0	0	0	1
B.Jacoby, ph-3b	1	0	0	0	0	1	1	1
L.Parrish, c	3	0	0	0	0	0	4	0
J.Rice, ph	1	0	0	0	0	1	0	0
R.Gedman, c	0	0	0	0	0	0	1	1
W.Joyner, 1b	1	0	0	0	0	0	3	1
D.Mattingly, ph-1b	3	0	0	0	0	2	7	0
C.Ripken, ss	4	0	0	0	0	2	0	1
T.Fernandez, ss	0	0	0	0	0	0	0	0
D.Winfield, rf	1	1	1	0	0	0	0	0
J.Barfield, ph-rf	3	0	0	0	0	2	2	0
L.Whitaker, 2b	2	1	1	2	0	1	0	3
F.White, ph-2b	2	1	1	1	0	0	1	1
R.Clemens, p	1	0	0	0	0	1	1	0
T.Higuera, p	1	0	0	0	0	1	0	0
H.Baines, ph	1	0	0	0	0	0	0	0
C.Hough, p	0	0	0	0	0	0	0	0
D.Righetti, p	0	0	0	0	0	0	0	0
D.Aase, p	0	0	0	0	0	0	0	0
Totals	33	3	5	3	2	12	27	9

BATTING
B: D.Winfield (off D.Gooden).
HR: L.Whitaker (2nd inning off D.Gooden, 1 on, 2 out);
F.White (7th inning off M.Scott, 0 on, 2 out).
2-out RBI: L.Whitaker 2; F.White.
RBI, scoring position, less than 2 outs: W.Boggs 0–1;
B.Jacoby 0–1; J.Rice 0–1.

BASERUNNING
SB: K.Puckett (Double SB 3rd base off S.Fernandez/
J.Davis); L.Moseby (Double SB 2nd base off
S.Fernandez/J.Davis).
Team LOB: 5

FIELDING
PB: R.Gedman.
DP: (1). F.White-D.Mattingly.

NATIONAL LEAGUE

	ab	r	h	bi	bb	so	po	a
T.Gwynn, lf	3	0	0	0	0	1	1	0
S.Sax, 2b	1	0	1	1	0	0	0	1
R.Sandberg, 2b	3	0	0	0	0	2	0	2
M.Scott, p	0	0	0	0	0	0	0	0
S.Fernandez, p	0	0	0	0	0	0	0	0
G.Davis, ph	1	0	0	0	0	0	0	0
M.Krukow, p	0	0	0	0	0	0	0	1
K.Hernandez, 1b	4	0	0	0	0	0	5	0
G.Carter, c	3	0	0	0	0	0	9	0
J.Davis, c	1	0	1	0	0	0	3	0
T.Pena, pr	0	0	0	0	0	0	0	0
D.Strawberry, rf	2	0	1	0	0	1	1	0
D.Parker, rf	2	0	1	0	0	0	0	0
M.Schmidt, 3b	1	0	0	0	1	0	0	0
C.Brown, 3b	2	1	1	0	0	0	1	0
D.Murphy, cf	2	0	0	0	0	0	2	0
C.Davis, cf	1	0	0	0	0	1	0	0
O.Smith, ss	1	0	0	0	0	0	3	2
H.Brooks, ph-ss	2	1	0	0	0	1	1	0
D.Gooden, p	0	0	0	0	0	0	0	0
K.Bass, ph	1	0	0	0	0	0	0	0
F.Valenzuela, p	0	0	0	0	0	0	0	0
T.Raines, ph-lf	2	0	0	0	0	1	1	0
Totals	32	2	5	1	1	7	27	6

BATTING
2B: C.Brown (off C.Hough).
2-out RBI: S.Sax.
RBI, scoring position, less than 2 outs: C.Brown 0–1;
D.Murphy 0–1; C.Davis 0–1; T.Raines 0–1.
GDP: C.Brown.

BASERUNNING
SB: S.Sax (2nd base off D.Righetti/R.Gedman).
Team LOB: 4

FIELDING
E: R.Sandberg (fumble).

PITCHING	ip	h	r	er	bb	so
American League						
R.Clemens (w)	3.0	0	0	0	0	2
T.Higuera	3.0	1	0	0	1	2
C.Hough	1.2	2	2	1	0	3

Inherited Runners—Scored:
T.Higuera 0–0; C.Hough 0–0; D.Righetti 1–0;
D.Aase 2–0; F.Valenzuela 0–0; M.Scott 0–0;
S.Fernandez 0–0; M.Krukow 0–0.

PITCHING	ip	h	r	er	bb	so
American League *(continued)*						
D.Righetti	0.2	2	0	0	0	0
D.Aase (s)	0.2	0	0	0	0	0
National League						
D.Gooden (L)	3.0	3	2	2	0	2
F.Valenzuela	3.0	1	0	0	0	5
M.Scott	1.0	1	1	1	0	2
S.Fernandez	1.0	0	0	0	2	3
M.Krukow	1.0	0	0	0	0	0

WP: C.Hough
BK: D.Gooden; C.Hough

GAME DATA—T: 2:28; A: 45774; Temp: Unknown; Wind: Unknown direction, Speed: Unknown

UMPIRES—HP: Bruce Froemming (NL), 1B: Steve Palermo (AL), 2B: Paul Runge (NL), 3B: Rick Reed (AL), LF: Eric Gregg (NL), RF: Tim McClelland (AL)

STARTING LINEUPS

	American League	*National League*
1.	K.Puckett cf	T.Gwynn lf
2.	R.Henderson lf	R.Sandberg 2b
3.	W.Boggs 3b	K.Hernandez 1b
4.	L.Parrish c	G.Carter c
5.	W.Joyner 1b	D.Strawberry rf
6.	C.Ripken ss	M.Schmidt 3b
7.	D.Winfield rf	D.Murphy cf
8.	L.Whitaker 2b	O.Smith ss
9.	R.Clemens p	D.Gooden p

AL 1ST: K.Puckett singled to center field (it was the first pitch); R.Henderson forced K.Puckett (R.Sandberg-2b to O.Smith-ss) [R.Henderson to first]; D.Gooden balked [R.Henderson to second]; Gooden slipped while trying a pickoff at 1b; W.Boggs flied to T.Gwynn-lf; L.Parrish popped to O.Smith-ss; 0 R, 1 H, 0 E, 1 LOB. AL 0, NL 0.

NL 1ST: T.Gwynn lined to R.Henderson-lf; R.Sandberg was called out on strikes; K.Hernandez grounded out (W.Joyner-1b to R.Clemens-p); 0 R, 0 H, 0 E, 0 LOB. AL 0, NL 0.

AL 2ND: W.Joyner popped to O.Smith-ss; C.Ripken grounded out (O.Smith-ss to K.Hernandez-1b); D.Winfield doubled to right field; L.Whitaker homered to rightfield (it was the 0–2 pitch) [D.Winfield scored]; R.Clemens was called out on strikes; 2 R, 2 H, 0 E, 0 LOB. AL 2, NL 0.

NL 2ND: G.Carter flied to K.Puckett-cf; D.Strawberry struck out; M.Schmidt flied to K.Puckett-cf; 0 R, 0 H, 0 E, 0 LOB. AL 2, NL 0.

AL 3RD: K.Puckett flied to D.Strawberry-rf; R.Henderson struck out; W.Boggs reached on an error by R.Sandberg-2b [W.Boggs to first]; L.Parrish flied to D.Murphy-cf; 0 R, 0 H, 1 E, 1 LOB. AL 2, NL 0.

NL 3RD: D.Murphy grounded out (C.Ripken-ss to W.Joyner-1b); O.Smith grounded out (L.Whitaker-2b to W.Joyner-1b); **K.Bass batted for D.Gooden;** K.Bass grounded out (L.Whitaker-2b to W.Joyner-1b); 0 R, 0 H, 0 E, 0 LOB. AL 2, NL 0.

AL 4TH: **F.Valenzuela replaced K.Bass (pitching); D.Mattingly batted for W.Joyner;** D.Mattingly struck out; C.Ripken was called out on strikes; **J.Barfield batted for D.Winfield;** J.Barfield was called out on strikes; 0 R, 0 H, 0 E, 0 LOB. AL 2, NL 0.

NL 4TH: **D.Mattingly stayed in game (playing 1b); J.Barfield stayed in game (playing rf); T.Higuera replaced R.Clemens (pitching);** T.Gwynn was called out on strikes; R.Sandberg flied to R.Henderson-lf; K.Hernandez flied to K.Puckett-cf; 0 R, 0 H, 0 E, 0 LOB. AL 2, NL 0.

AL 5TH: L.Whitaker was called out on strikes; T.Higuera struck out; Valenzuela struck out 5 consecutive batters tying Hubbell; K.Puckett grounded out (O.Smith-ss to K.Hernandez-1b); 0 R, 0 H, 0 E, 0 LOB. AL 2, NL 0.

NL 5TH: G.Carter grounded out (W.Boggs-3b to D.Mattingly-1b); D.Strawberry singled to right field; M.Schmidt walked [D.Strawberry to second]; D.Murphy flied to K.Puckett-cf; **H.Brooks batted for O.Smith;** H.Brooks grounded out (L.Whitaker-2b to D.Mattingly-1b); 0 R, 1 H, 0 E, 2 LOB. AL 2, NL 0.

AL 6TH: **H.Brooks stayed in game (playing ss); D.Parker replaced D.Strawberry (playing rf); C.Brown replaced M.Schmidt (playing 3b);** R.Henderson popped to H.Brooks-ss; W.Boggs singled to center field; L.Parrish flied to D.Murphy-cf; D.Mattingly grounded out (R.Sandberg-2b to K.Hernandez-1b); 0 R, 1 H, 0 E, 1 LOB. AL 2, NL 0.

NL 6TH: **L.Moseby replaced R.Henderson (playing lf); T.Raines batted for F.Valenzuela;** T.Raines flied to K.Puckett-cf; T.Gwynn grounded out (D.Mattingly-1b unassisted); R.Sandberg struck out; 0 R, 0 H, 0 E, 0 LOB. AL 2, NL 0.

AL 7TH: **T.Raines stayed in game (playing lf); M.Scott replaced R.Sandberg (pitching); S.Sax replaced T.Gwynn (playing 2b); C.Davis replaced D.Murphy (playing cf);** C.Ripken struck out; J.Barfield struck out; **F.White batted for L.Whitaker;** F.White homered to left-center (it was the 0–2 pitch); **H.Baines batted for T.Higuera;** H.Baines grounded out (S.Sax-2b to K.Hernandez-1b); 1 R, 1 H, 0 E, 0 LOB. AL 3, NL 0.

NL 7TH: **F.White stayed in game (playing 2b); C.Hough replaced H.Baines (pitching);** K.Hernandez flied to J.Barfield-rf; G.Carter flied to J.Barfield-rf; D.Parker grounded out (D.Mattingly-1b unassisted); 0 R, 0 H, 0 E, 0 LOB. AL 3, NL 0.

AL 8TH: **S.Fernandez replaced M.Scott (pitching); J.Davis replaced G.Carter (playing c);** K.Puckett walked; L.Moseby walked [K.Puckett to second]; **B.Jacoby batted for W.Boggs;** B.Jacoby struck out; **J.Rice batted for L.Parrish;** J.Rice struck out while K.Puckett stole third and L.Moseby stole second; D.Mattingly struck out; 0 R, 0 H, 0 E, 2 LOB. AL 3, NL 0.

NL 8TH: **B.Jacoby stayed in game (playing 3b); R.Gedman replaced J.Rice (playing c);** C.Brown doubled to very deep left-center at the wall; C.Davis struck out while C.Brown advanced to third on a wild pitch (R.Gedman-c to D.Mattingly-1b); H.Brooks struck out while C.Brown advanced to home on a passed ball [H.Brooks to first]; C.Hough balked [H.Brooks to second]; T.Raines struck out; S.Sax singled to left-center [H.Brooks scored (unearned)]; **D.Righetti replaced C.Hough (pitching); G.Davis batted for S.Fernandez;** S.Sax stole second; G.Davis popped to B.Jacoby-3b in foul territory; 1 R (0 ER), 2 H, 0 E, 1 LOB. AL 3, NL 2.

AL 9TH: **M.Krukow replaced G.Davis (pitching);** C.Ripken grounded out (M.Krukow-p to K.Hernandez-1b); J.Barfield popped to C.Brown-3b; F.White flied to T.Raines-lf; 0 R, 0 H, 0 E, 0 LOB. AL 3, NL 2.

NL 9TH: **T.Fernandez replaced C.Ripken (playing ss);** K.Hernandez grounded out (B.Jacoby-3b to D.Mattingly-1b); high chopper; J.Davis singled to center field; **T.Pena ran for J.Davis;** D.Parker singled to right field [T.Pena to third]; **D.Aase replaced D.Righetti (pitching);** C.Brown grounded into a double play (F.White-2b to D.Mattingly-1b) [D.Parker out at second]; 0 R, 2 H, 0 E, 1 LOB. AL 3, NL 2.

Final Totals	R	H	E	LOB
American League	3	5	0	5
National League	2	5	1	4

58

Tuesday, July 14, 1987

Oakland Coliseum, Oakland CA

National League 2, American League 0

(13 innings)

SERIES RESULTS: NL 37, AL 20, 1 TIE

Homer a No-Show

At the All-Star break in 1987, the biggest star of the season was the home run. Batters were hitting the long ball at a far faster rate than ever before in Major League history. At the close of the season, 4,458 homers had been smashed, a total that would not be topped until 1996. Throughout the 1987 season, batters hit a big fly once every thirty-two at bats, a ridiculous increase over 1986, when batters homered once every thirty-seven at bats.

When play stopped for the All-Star Game, rookie Mark McGwire of the Oakland Athletics led the majors with thirty-three home runs on his way to breaking the rookie homer record with forty-nine at the end of the year and thus winning the AL Rookie of the Year honors. McGwire was one of eighteen players with at least twenty homers in the first half of the season, topping the previous high of sixteen in 1969.

With all of the concentration on homers, the fans and media expected a high-scoring game featuring the long ball. However, this was not the case as the NL won a pitcher's duel in the thirteenth inning with the only runs of the game scoring on two singles and a triple. It was the longest scoreless game in All-Star history and the longest game since the teams had played fifteen innings in 1967.

The contest featured two starting pitchers who were recent Cy Young Award winners with reborn careers. Host AL manager John McNamara of the Red Sox chose the Royals' Bret Saberhagen, who had won the AL Cy Young Award in 1985. Saberhagen started in the Majors at age nineteen and led Kansas City to a World Series title when he was twenty-one years old, winning the award the same year. According to his own statements, he then spent too much time enjoying life and ended 1986 with a sore shoulder and a 7-12 record. However, during the off-season following that campaign, he realized that he needed to rededicate himself to pitching. This successful effort brought him into the 1987 All-Star Game with a 15-3 record and a 2.47 ERA to claim the starting berth.

Saberhagen's mound opponent was Mike Scott of the Astros, who was the reigning NL Cy Young Award winner. Scott had been a mediocre pitcher who turned his career around starting in 1985. He sported a 29-44 career record at the start of the 1985 season, but he went 18-8 in 1985 and 18-10 in 1986 and came into the break at 10-5 on the way to a 16-13 season. At the same time, his ERA dropped from 4.68 in 1984 to 3.29 in 1985, followed by a 2.22 mark in 1986, when he won the Cy Young Award.

Scott's rebirth occurred because he developed a biting forkball that many opponents declared an illegal scuff ball. One of Scott's loudest detractors was Mets manager Davey Johnson, who reportedly saved a box of baseballs that he claimed Scott scuffed in the 1986 National League Championship Series. Johnson, the NL manager for this All-Star Game, was asked about that verbal battle. "He's legal with me today. He's my man. As far as I'm concerned, he can't do anything wrong the next couple of days," said the skipper. Reporters asked Scott whether he was planning to take a piece of sandpaper to the mound with him. "I'll have the same tools I always take out there. We'll wait and see," Scott said, smiling.

This was only the second time that two Cy Young Award winners started the game. In 1978, three-time winner Jim Palmer of the Orioles opposed Vida Blue of the Giants. Blue had won the AL award while a member of the Athletics in 1971.

The game started in the late afternoon on the West Coast due to the television requirements. As the twilight fell, batters had difficulty seeing and hitting the ball. Seattle pitcher Mark Langston, who pitched two perfect innings with three strikeouts, said, "With all the home runs so far this year, I expected a slugfest. Maybe the shadows are even tougher than anyone realizes." Phillies second baseman Juan Samuel had similar thoughts. "Without making any alibis, it was awfully hard seeing the ball. You couldn't pick up the spin or the rotation. This is not the best time to start a game," he said.

Dodger pitcher Orel Hershiser, who would win the 1988 NL Cy Young Award, was asked about the low run total. "To me, it was a combination of three things: the hitters really don't know the pitchers that well, the twilight, and just plain old quality pitching."

Cubs second baseman Ryne Sandberg echoed Hershiser's feelings: "It wasn't the sun that was a problem for me, it was the pitching. The pitchers have a great advantage in an All-Star Game. You only see them once a year and they come in and throw hard for a couple of innings. It's really a pitcher's game most of the time."

In the top of the first inning, outfielder Andre Dawson of the Cubs doubled to left off Saberhagen with two out but was stranded there. In the bottom of the frame, Yankee first baseman Don Mattingly reached on a fielding error by Mike Scott, but the team could not drive him in.

The next batter to reach base was Dave Winfield of the Yankees, who doubled in the bottom of the second. He was put out immediately as Oriole Cal Ripken Jr. lined into a double play. One inning later, pinch hitter Alan Trammel of Detroit faced new pitcher Rick Sutcliffe of the Cubs and reached first on an error by Cardinals wizard Ozzie Smith. Mattingly then walked, but once again the runners were stranded.

In the fourth inning, Mike Schmidt singled but was out trying to steal second base. In the AL half of the frame, Ripken singled but was forced out by his Baltimore teammate Terry Kennedy. The AL had two runners on base again in the fifth as Yankees outfielder Rickey Henderson singled and Mattingly walked again. However, Boston's Wade Boggs forced Mattingly to end the inning. The pitchers dominated until the bottom of the seventh, when Red Sox outfielder Dwight Evans singled to left, but the next three batters all made outs, and one more runner was wasted.

The NL's best chance to score came in the ninth inning. With one out, Expos outfielder Tim Raines singled to center field and stole second base. He continued on to third as the AL first baseman, Mark McGwire, threw the ball into left field trying to put out Raines at second. Manager McNamara brought in Blue Jays closer Tom Henke, who induced Juan Samuel to hit a fly ball to shallow right field, and Raines decided not to test the strong arm of Dwight Evans. Raines said later, "I thought about it, but it just wasn't deep enough. I have followed Dwight's career, and he is known for having a great arm."

Evans replied, "I was surprised he didn't try it,

but I did get a good throw off. From my position it was the perfect ball for me to make a play with." Evans was being somewhat modest; he made a perfect one-hop throw to the plate, and Raines would have had no chance to score on the play.

In the bottom of the ninth, the AL had another excellent chance to score. Winfield led off with a walk, and Toronto's Tony Fernandez sacrificed him to second. Evans then walked, but Harold Reynolds of the Mariners grounded to the Mets' Keith Hernandez at first base. Hernandez threw to second base for the force out, but Hubie Brooks's return throw was wide. Phillies pitcher Steve Bedrosian, the 1987 NL Cy Young Award winner, was covering the bag and had to make two excellent plays. First, he made a diving catch of the throw, and then he recovered quickly to throw to the plate, where Winfield was trying to score from second base.

Winfield, the only starter to play the entire game, said later, "I hesitated at third, but when I saw him dive for the ball I went. You don't know if the ball will trickle loose or he won't anticipate me trying to score. I would do it again, but I wouldn't hesitate." Catcher Ozzie Virgil said, "Winfield's a big man. He ran into me hard. There was a lot of beef hitting me, but I had to stay in and take the hit." Winfield commented that he had one more chance to score: "I could still count on the impact jarring the ball loose." Unfortunately for the big man, Virgil hung on to the ball.

In their half of the eleventh inning, the American Leaguers had another chance to end the game. Texas outfielder Larry Parrish, pinch-hitting for Henke, led off with a single to right-center. He was moved to second by Detroit catcher Matt Nokes's sacrifice bunt and to third on Winfield's ground out to shortstop. However, Tony Fernandez was called out on strikes to end the frame.

So it came down to the thirteenth inning for the NL. Ozzie Virgil of the Braves singled to left-center, and one out later, Brooks singled to right, moving Virgil to second. After another out, Raines took two pitches for balls and then collected his third hit of the game by smashing a triple that rolled to the left-center-field wall, scoring both runners. Raines was named the game's MVP.

Raines said later, "I was looking for a fastball, and he got one over the middle of the plate. In that situation, I'm just trying to make contact. It felt great. When I made third, I started jumping up and down on the bag. That's how happy I was." Raines could feel especially joyful about his three-hit performance because he had been hitless in seven previous All-Star at bats. "I told my wife that I was going to get a hit for her tonight," he said.

That Raines played well in the game was not a surprise. After the 1986 season, he had filed for free agency and received no offers. According to the rules, he could not re-sign with Montreal until May 1, and he rejoined the club on May 6 with very little formal preparation. He picked up where he left off the previous year, was hitting .346 at the break, and was picked by Johnson as a reserve. Raines was not listed on the fan ballot because of his status at the start of the year.

NL manager Johnson used his last player in the bottom of the thirteenth inning when he put his own Mets pitcher Sid Fernandez in to close out the game. Although he walked the first batter he faced, Fernandez had little trouble setting the Junior Circuit down to end the fifth shutout in All-Star history and the first since 1968. This was the fourteenth win for the NL in sixteen games and the twenty-second in twenty-five games. This was also the eighth extra-inning game in All-Star history, and the NL had won them all.

There were fourteen first-time attendees at this All-Star Game as well as three rookies: McGwire, Nokes, and Kevin Seitzer. Seitzer had been chosen as a replacement for his injured teammate George Brett. Wade Boggs commented on Brett's absence: "I'm like a lost puppy without him being here."

This was the last appearance at the All-Star classic for some players. Dale Murphy made the last of his seven All-Star appearances in this game, Keith Hernandez and Lou Whitaker the last of five, Jack Clark and Terry Kennedy the last of four, and Dwight Evans the last of three. It was also the last of seven consecutive appearances for Tim Raines.

The fans voted for sixteen starting players, fifteen of whom were from East Division teams. The lone exception was Eric Davis, who was the NL's starting left-fielder representing the Cincinnati Reds of the NL West, even though Cincinnati is not a "western" city. There were many theories about this result. Dave Winfield said, "There's more of a concentration of media and population in the East." Ozzie Smith of the Cardinals received the most votes.

With the number of players who have refused to play through the years, special mention should be made of Willie Randolph. Yankees owner George Steinbrenner told Randolph, his second baseman, not to play the game because of a sore left knee. Randolph refused, saying, "My family is here and I've been playing for two weeks. I just played fifteen innings on Saturday. It's my decision. Who wants to just come out and tip their hat? The fans want you to play." Randolph played three innings and flew out in his one at bat. Randolph's stance was a big contrast to Detroit second baseman Lou Whitaker, who refused to even come to the game because he was tired.

NL manager Davey Johnson was the nineteenth man to both play and manage in the All-Star Game. He played for both leagues in four appearances from 1968 to 1973.

Much of the talk about the high rate of home runs concentrated on the ball itself, with many in the media saying that it was "juiced up." The league presidents disputed this allegation, ordering tests to prove it. Players reacted as expected.

"I hear so much about the juiced-up ball and all that, but what about giving the players some credit? They're stronger, they have better bats, and they're thinking home runs," said Boggs. "When Mark McGwire hits his sixty-second homer, is it just an asterisk record for the year of the juiced-up ball?" Ozzie Smith was upset about the talk: "I wish they'd throw me one of those juiced-up balls. I've hit some balls that I thought I got pretty good, and they didn't go out." For the second consecutive year, Smith hit no homers.

The futility of the offense was evident throughout. The NL pitchers allowed only two hits after the seventh inning, and their colleagues in the AL did not allow a hit from the fourth to the ninth. Of the fifteen pitchers who worked in the game, only Oakland's Jay Howell, the fourth pitcher to lose the game in his own ballpark, allowed a runner to cross the plate. Before the runs scored, only two runners had reached third base: Raines in the ninth and Parrish in the thirteenth.

The big bats evidently stayed home.

	AL			NL	
P	Bret Saberhagen	KCA		Mike Scott	HOU
C	Terry Kennedy	BAL		Gary Carter	NYN
1B	Don Mattingly	NYA		Jack Clark	SLN
2B	Willie Randolph	NYA		Ryne Sandberg	CHN
3B	Wade Boggs	BOS		Mike Schmidt	PHI
SS	Cal Ripken	BAL		Ozzie Smith	SLN
OF	George Bell	TOR		Eric Davis	CIN
OF	Rickey Henderson	NYA		Andre Dawson	CHN
OF	Dave Winfield	NYA		Darryl Strawberry	NYN
	Harold Baines	CHA		Steve Bedrosian	PHI
	George Brett +	KCA		Hubie Brooks	MON
	Dwight Evans	BOS		Bo Diaz	CIN
	Tony Fernandez	TOR		Sid Fernandez	NYN
	Tom Henke	TOR		John Franco	CIN
	Jay Howell	OAK		Pedro Guerrero	LAN
	Bruce Hurst	BOS		Tony Gwynn	SDN
	Mark Langston	SEA		Keith Hernandez	NYN
	Mark McGwire	OAK		Orel Hershiser	LAN
	Jack Morris	DET		Jeffrey Leonard	SFN
	Matt Nokes	DET		Willie McGee	SLN
	Larry Parrish	TEX		Dale Murphy	ATL
	Dan Plesac	MIL		Tim Raines	MON
	Kirby Puckett	MIN		Rick Reuschel	PIT
	Harold Reynolds	SEA		Juan Samuel	PHI
	Dave Righetti	NYA		Lee Smith	CHN
	Kevin Seitzer	KCA		Rick Sutcliffe	CHN
	Pat Tabler	CLE		Ozzie Virgil	ATL
	Alan Trammell	DET		Tim Wallach	MON
	Lou Whitaker +	DET			
	Mike Witt	CAL			

+ player replaced on roster

```
National League    000 000 000 000 2- 2
American League    000 000 000 000 0- 0  (13)
```

NATIONAL LEAGUE

	ab	r	h	bi	bb	so	po	a
E.Davis, lf	3	0	0	0	0	1	1	0
T.Raines, lf	3	0	3	2	0	0	1	0
R.Sandberg, 2b	2	0	0	0	0	0	0	2
J.Samuel, 2b	4	0	0	0	0	1	6	2
A.Dawson, cf-rf	3	0	1	0	0	1	3	0
R.Reuschel, p	0	0	0	0	0	0	0	0
J.Leonard, rf	2	0	0	0	0	0	0	0
M.Schmidt, 3b	2	0	1	0	0	0	0	1
T.Wallach, 3b	3	0	0	0	0	2	0	2
J.Clark, 1b	3	0	0	0	0	2	7	1
K.Hernandez, 1b	2	0	1	0	0	1	5	2
D.Strawberry, rf	2	0	0	0	0	0	0	0
B.Diaz, c	1	0	0	0	0	0	1	0
O.Virgil, c	2	1	1	0	0	0	7	0
G.Carter, c	1	0	0	0	1	0	1	0
O.Hershiser, p	0	0	0	0	0	0	0	0
D.Murphy, rf	1	0	0	0	0	0	1	0
J.Franco, p	0	0	0	0	0	0	0	0
S.Bedrosian, p	0	0	0	0	0	0	0	2
P.Guerrero, ph	1	0	0	0	0	0	0	0
L.Smith, p	1	0	0	0	0	1	0	2
S.Fernandez, p	0	0	0	0	0	0	0	0
O.Smith, ss	2	0	0	0	0	0	3	2
H.Brooks, ss	3	1	1	0	0	1	1	1
M.Scott, p	0	0	0	0	0	0	0	0
T.Gwynn, ph	1	0	0	0	0	0	0	0
R.Sutcliffe, p	0	0	0	0	0	0	0	0
W.McGee, cf	4	0	0	0	0	0	2	0
Totals	46	2	8	2	1	10	39	17

BATTING
2B: A.Dawson (off B.Saberhagen).
3B: T.Raines (off J.Howell).
2-out RBI: T.Raines 2.
RBI, scoring position, less than 2 outs: J.Samuel 0–1; W.McGee 0–1.

BASERUNNING
SB: T.Raines (2nd base off D.Righetti/M.Nokes).
CS: M.Schmidt (2nd base by J.Morris/T.Kennedy).
Team LOB: 6

FIELDING
E: M.Scott (fumble); O.Smith (fumble).
DP: (2). J.Clark-O.Smith; S.Bedrosian-O.Virgil-K.Hernandez-H.Brooks.

AMERICAN LEAGUE

	ab	r	h	bi	bb	so	po	a
R.Henderson, cf	3	0	1	0	0	0	0	0
M.McGwire, 1b	3	0	0	0	0	1	7	0
D.Mattingly, 1b	1	0	0	0	2	0	10	0
K.Seitzer, 3b	2	0	0	0	1	0	0	0
W.Boggs, 3b	3	0	0	0	0	0	0	3
M.Langston, p	0	0	0	0	0	0	0	0
D.Plesac, p	0	0	0	0	0	0	0	0
H.Baines, ph	1	0	0	0	0	0	0	0
D.Righetti, p	0	0	0	0	0	0	0	0
T.Henke, p	0	0	0	0	0	0	0	1
L.Parrish, ph	1	0	1	0	0	0	0	0
J.Howell, p	0	0	0	0	0	0	0	0
P.Tabler, ph	1	0	0	0	0	1	0	0
G.Bell, lf	3	0	0	0	0	0	1	0
M.Nokes, c	2	0	0	0	0	0	8	0
D.Winfield, rf-lf	5	0	1	0	1	0	2	0
C.Ripken, ss	2	0	1	0	0	0	0	5
T.Fernandez, ss	2	0	0	0	0	1	1	3
T.Kennedy, c	2	0	0	0	0	1	3	1
D.Evans, rf	2	0	2	0	1	0	2	0
W.Randolph, 2b	1	0	0	0	0	0	0	1
H.Reynolds, 2b	3	0	0	0	0	0	4	4
B.Saberhagen, p	0	0	0	0	0	0	0	0
A.Trammell, ph	1	0	0	0	0	0	0	0
J.Morris, p	0	0	0	0	0	0	0	0
K.Puckett, ph-cf	4	0	0	0	0	3	1	0
Totals	42	0	6	0	5	7	39	18

BATTING
2B: D.Winfield (off M.Scott).
RBI, scoring position, less than 2 outs: D.Winfield 0–1; C.Ripken 0–1; H.Reynolds 0–1; K.Puckett 0–1.
S: M.Nokes; T.Fernandez; H.Reynolds.

BASERUNNING
Team LOB: 11

FIELDING
E: M.McGwire (throw).

PITCHING	ip	h	r	er	bb	so
National League						
M.Scott	2.0	1	0	0	0	1
R.Sutcliffe	2.0	1	0	0	1	0
O.Hershiser	2.0	1	0	0	1	0
R.Reuschel	1.1	1	0	0	0	1
J.Franco	0.2	0	0	0	0	0
S.Bedrosian	1.0	0	0	0	2	0
L.Smith (w)	3.0	2	0	0	0	4
S.Fernandez (s)	1.0	0	0	0	1	1
American League						
B.Saberhagen	3.0	1	0	0	0	0
J.Morris	2.0	1	0	0	1	2
M.Langston	2.0	0	0	0	0	3
D.Plesac	1.0	0	0	0	0	1
D.Righetti	0.1	1	0	0	0	0
T.Henke	2.2	2	0	0	0	1
J.Howell (L)	2.0	3	2	2	0	3

Inherited Runners—Scored:
R.Sutcliffe 0–0; O.Hershiser 0–0; R.Reuschel 0–0; J.Franco 0–0; S.Bedrosian 0–0; L.Smith 0–0; S.Fernandez 0–0; J.Morris 0–0; M.Langston 0–0; D.Plesac 0–0; D.Righetti 0–0; T.Henke 1–0; J.Howell 0–0.

GAME DATA—T: 3:39; A: 49671; Temp: Unknown; Wind: Unknown direction, Speed: Unknown

UMPIRES—HP: Don Denkinger (AL), 1B: Dick Stello (NL), 2B: Vic Voltaggio (AL), 3B: Joe West (NL), LF: Derryl Cousins (AL), RF: Bob Davidson (NL)

STARTING LINEUPS

	National League	American League
1.	E.Davis lf	R.Henderson cf
2.	R.Sandberg 2b	D.Mattingly 1b
3.	A.Dawson cf	W.Boggs 3b
4.	M.Schmidt 3b	G.Bell lf
5.	J.Clark 1b	D.Winfield rf
6.	D.Strawberry rf	C.Ripken ss
7.	G.Carter c	T.Kennedy c
8.	O.Smith ss	W.Randolph 2b
9.	M.Scott p	B.Saberhagen p
	M.Scott p	B.Saberhagen p

NL 1ST: MVP: Tim Raines (NL Montreal); E.Davis grounded out (C.Ripken-ss to D.Mattingly-1b); R.Sandberg grounded out (W.Boggs-3b to D.Mattingly-1b); A.Dawson doubled to left field (it was the first pitch); M.Schmidt grounded out (W.Boggs-3b to D.Mattingly-1b); 0 R, 1 H, 0 E, 1 LOB. NL 0, AL 0.

AL 1ST: checked swing; R.Henderson grounded out (R.Sandberg-2b to J.Clark-1b); D.Mattingly reached on an error by M.Scott-p [D.Mattingly to first]; W.Boggs forced D.Mattingly (R.Sandberg-2b to O.Smith-ss) [W.Boggs to first]; G.Bell popped to O.Smith-ss; 0 R, 0 H, 1 E, 1 LOB. NL 0, AL 0.

NL 2ND: J.Clark popped to D.Mattingly-1b; Mattingly shielded his eyes from the sun; D.Strawberry grounded out (W.Randolph-2b to D.Mattingly-1b); G.Carter grounded out (C.Ripken-ss to D.Mattingly-1b); 0 R, 0 H, 0 E, 0 LOB. NL 0, AL 0.

AL 2ND: D.Winfield doubled to left field; C.Ripken lined into a double play (J.Clark-1b to O.Smith-ss) [D.Winfield out at second]; T.Kennedy struck out; 0 R, 1 H, 0 E, 0 LOB. NL 0, AL 0.

NL 3RD: O.Smith lined to G.Bell-lf; **T.Gwynn batted for M.Scott;** T.Gwynn grounded out (C.Ripken-ss to D.Mattingly-1b); E.Davis grounded out (W.Boggs-3b to D.Mattingly-1b); 0 R, 0 H, 0 E, 0 LOB. NL 0, AL 0.

AL 3RD: **R.Sutcliffe replaced T.Gwynn (pitching);** W.Randolph flied to E.Davis-lf; **A.Trammell batted for B.Saberhagen;** A.Trammell reached on an error by O.Smith-ss [A.Trammell to first]; R.Henderson flied to A.Dawson-cf; D.Mattingly walked [A.Trammell to second]; W.Boggs flied to A.Dawson-cf; 0 R, 0 H, 1 E, 2 LOB. NL 0, AL 0.

NL 4TH: **J.Morris replaced A.Trammell (pitching); H.Reynolds replaced W.Randolph (playing 2b);** R.Sandberg grounded out (C.Ripken-ss to D.Mattingly-1b); A.Dawson struck out; M.Schmidt singled to right field; M.Schmidt was caught stealing second (T.Kennedy-c to H.Reynolds-2b); 0 R, 1 H, 0 E, 0 LOB. NL 0, AL 0.

AL 4TH: **J.Samuel replaced R.Sandberg (playing 2b);** G.Bell grounded out (J.Clark-1b unassisted); Bell's grounder hit the bag and bounced to Clark; D.Winfield grounded out (J.Samuel-2b to J.Clark-1b); C.Ripken singled to left field; T.Kennedy forced C.Ripken (O.Smith-ss to J.Samuel-2b) [T.Kennedy to first]; 0 R, 1 H, 0 E, 1 LOB. NL 0, AL 0.

NL 5TH: J.Clark struck out; D.Strawberry grounded out (H.Reynolds-2b to D.Mattingly-1b); G.Carter walked; O.Smith forced G.Carter (C.Ripken-ss to H.Reynolds-2b) [O.Smith to first]; 0 R, 0 H, 0 E, 1 LOB. NL 0, AL 0.

AL 5TH: **O.Hershiser replaced G.Carter (pitching); W.McGee replaced R.Sutcliffe (playing cf); B.Diaz replaced D.Strawberry (playing c); A.Dawson changed positions (playing rf);** H.Reynolds grounded out (O.Smith-ss to J.Clark-1b); **K.Puckett batted for J.Morris;** K.Puckett grounded out (J.Samuel-2b to J.Clark-1b); R.Henderson singled to second base; D.Mattingly walked [R.Henderson to second]; W.Boggs forced D.Mattingly (M.Schmidt-3b to J.Samuel-2b) [W.Boggs to first]; 0 R, 1 H, 0 E, 2 LOB. NL 0, AL 0.

NL 6TH: **K.Puckett stayed in game (playing cf); M.Langston replaced W.Boggs (pitching); K.Seitzer replaced D.Mattingly (playing 3b); M.McGwire replaced R.Henderson (playing 1b); T.Fernandez replaced C.Ripken (playing ss);** W.McGee grounded out (H.Reynolds-2b to M.McGwire-1b); E.Davis was called out on strikes; J.Samuel grounded out (H.Reynolds-2b to M.McGwire-1b); 0 R, 0 H, 0 E, 0 LOB. NL 0, AL 0.

AL 6TH: **T.Raines replaced E.Davis (playing lf); T.Wallach replaced M.Schmidt (playing 3b);** G.Bell grounded out (T.Wallach-3b to J.Clark-1b); D.Winfield lined to A.Dawson-rf; T.Fernandez flied to W.McGee-cf; 0 R, 0 H, 0 E, 0 LOB. NL 0, AL 0.

NL 7TH: **M.Nokes replaced G.Bell (playing c); D.Evans replaced T.Kennedy (playing rf); D.Winfield changed positions (playing lf);** A.Dawson grounded out (T.Fernandez-ss to M.McGwire-1b); T.Wallach struck out; J.Clark was called out on strikes; 0 R, 0 H, 0 E, 0 LOB. NL 0, AL 0.

AL 7TH: **R.Reuschel replaced A.Dawson (pitching); K.Hernandez replaced J.Clark (playing 1b); D.Murphy rePlaced O.Hershiser (playing rf); H.Brooks replaced O.Smith (playing ss);** D.Evans singled to left field (it was the first pitch); H.Reynolds out on a sacrifice bunt (K.Hernandez-1b to J.Samuel-2b) [D.Evans to second]; K.Puckett struck out; M.McGwire flied to D.Murphy-rf; 0 R, 1 H, 0 E, 1 LOB. NL 0, AL 0.

NL 8TH: **D.Plesac replaced M.Langston (pitching);** B.Diaz flied to D.Evans-rf; D.Murphy popped to T.Fernandez-ss in foul territory; H.Brooks struck out; 0 R, 0 H, 0 E, 0 LOB. NL 0, AL 0.

AL 8TH: **O.Virgil replaced B.Diaz (playing c); K.Seitzer popped to J.Samuel-2b; H.Baines batted for D.Plesac; J.Franco replaced D.Murphy (pitching); J.Leonard replaced R.Reuschel (playing rf);** H.Baines popped to J.Samuel-2b; M.Nokes flied to T.Raines-lf; 0 R, 0 H, 0 E, 0 LOB. NL 0, AL 0.

NL 9TH: **D.Righetti replaced H.Baines (pitching);** W.McGee grounded out (H.Reynolds-2b to M.McGwire-1b); T.Raines singled to center field; T.Raines stole second (it was the 1–2 pitch) [T.Raines to third (error by M.McGwire-1b)]; **T.Henke replaced D.Righetti (pitching);** J.Samuel flied to D.Evans-rf; Evans made a perfect one-hop throw to the plate to hold Rai; J.Leonard popped to M.Nokes-c in foul territory; 0 R, 1 H, 1 E, 1 LOB. NL 0, AL 0.

AL 9TH: **S.Bedrosian replaced J.Franco (pitching);** D.Winfield walked; T.Fernandez out on a sacrifice bunt (S.Bedrosian-p to K.Hernandez-1b) [D.Winfield to second]; D.Evans walked; H.Reynolds hit into a double play (S.Bedrosian-p to O.Virgil-c to K.Hernandez-1b to H.Brooks-ss) [D.Winfield scored (no RBI), H.Reynolds to first]; 1 R, 0 H, 0 E, 1 LOB. NL 0, AL 0.

NL 10TH: T.Wallach grounded out (T.Henke-p to M.McGwire-1b); K.Hernandez singled to center field; O.Virgil flied to D.Winfield-lf; **P.Guerrero batted for S.Bedrosian;** P.Guerrero lined to H.Reynolds-2b; 0 R, 1 H, 0 E, 1 LOB. NL 0, AL 0.

AL 10TH: **L.Smith replaced P.Guerrero (pitching);** K.Puckett struck out; M.McGwire struck out; K.Seitzer flied to W.McGee-cf; 0 R, 0 H, 0 E, 0 LOB. NL 0, AL 0.

NL 11TH: H.Brooks flied to K.Puckett-cf; W.McGee grounded out (T.Fernandez-ss to M.McGwire-1b); T.Raines singled to left field; J.Samuel was called out on strikes; 0 R, 1 H, 0 E, 1 LOB. NL 0, AL 0.

AL 11TH: **L.Parrish batted for T.Henke;** L.Parrish singled to right-center; M.Nokes out on a sacrifice bunt (L.Smith-p to K.Hernandez-1b) [L.Parrish to second]; D.Winfield grounded out (H.Brooks-ss to K.Hernandez-1b) [L.Parrish to third]; T.Fernandez was called out on strikes; 0 R, 1 H, 0 E, 1 LOB. NL 0, AL 0.

NL 12TH: **J.Howell replaced L.Parrish (pitching);** J.Leonard grounded out (T.Fernandez-ss to M.McGwire-1b); T.Wallach struck out; K.Hernandez struck out; 0 R, 0 H, 0 E, 0 LOB. NL 0, AL 0.

AL 12TH: D.Evans singled to center field; On a bunt H.Reynolds popped to K.Hernandez-1b; K.Puckett struck out; M.McGwire grounded out (L.Smith-p to K.Hernandez-1b); 0 R, 1 H, 0 E, 1 LOB. NL 0, AL 0.

NL 13TH: O.Virgil singled to left-center (it was the 1–2 pitch); On a bunt L.Smith struck out; H.Brooks singled to right field (it was the 1–1 pitch) [O.Virgil to second]; W.McGee lined to D.Winfield-lf; T.Raines tripled to very deep left-center at the wall (it was the 2–0 pitch) [O.Virgil scored, H.Brooks scored]; J.Samuel lined to H.Reynolds-2b; 2 R, 3 H, 0 E, 1 LOB. NL 2, AL 0.

AL 13TH: **S.Fernandez replaced L.Smith (pitching);** Fernandez is the last NL player available; K.Seitzer walked; **P.Tabler batted for J.Howell;** P.Tabler struck out; M.Nokes popped to O.Virgil-c in foul territory; D.Winfield forced K.Seitzer (T.Wallach-3b to J.Samuel-2b) [D.Winfield to first]; 0 R, 0 H, 0 E, 1 LOB. NL 2, AL 0.

Final Totals	R	H	E	LOB
National League	2	8	2	6
American League	0	6	1	11

Tuesday, July 12, 1988

Riverfront Stadium, Cincinnati

American League 2, National League 1

SERIES RESULTS: NL 37, AL 21, 1 TIE

Steinbach Stuffs the NL

The 1988 game featured a record thirty-two players who enjoyed their first All-Star selection. One of these first-timers—Terry Steinbach—claimed most of the attention before the game. However, the attention directed at Steinbach, part-time catcher for Oakland and starter for the AL, was not positive. Indeed, the media had applied many names, including "worst All-Star starter ever" and "mystery guest," to Steinbach's election to the AL squad. His election was due to two factors, primarily ballot box stuffing by fans in the Oakland Coliseum, who also elected Mark McGwire at first base and Jose Canseco in the outfield.

In fact, the commissioner's office threw out thousands of Oakland ballots because they had been mass-produced by nail punching, which is against the rules. But even with the discarding of many ballots, Steinbach won election due to a second factor: a weak AL catching contingent in 1988.

Steinbach, in his second year, had been suffering physically and at the plate. In May, he had been hit by a throw in practice that fractured the orbital bone around his eye in five places, forcing him to miss many games. At the break, he was still wearing an extra piece on his batting helmet to protect the tender area. He was hitting .212, twenty-nine points lower than the next-lowest batting average among the starters (his NL counterpart, Gary Carter), with only four homers and eighteen RBI.

Once the game started, however, Steinbach proved he could play with the best. He led off the third, facing NL starter Dwight Gooden, who had limited the AL to a walk and a hit in the first two innings. After swinging and missing a fastball ("He threw it right past me," Steinbach said later), he hit a fly to right field that just cleared the fence after striking Darryl Strawberry's glove.

"I didn't crush the ball. I hit it well, and I hit it to an area of the park where it had a chance to go out," said Steinbach. Gooden remarked, "I was

ahead of him on the count and tried to get the ball away, but it wasn't away enough. I thought it was a good pitch, a pop-up when he hit it, but it just carried."

Steinbach became the eighth player to homer in his first All-Star at bat as well as the first to also homer in his first Major League at bat. The last All-Star to debut with a homer had been Lee Mazzilli in 1979.

Steinbach's next plate appearance came in the fourth inning against Bob Knepper. With one out, Dave Winfield doubled to left-center, a record seventh career All-Star double, which extended his consecutive All-Star Game hitting streak to seven games, tying the record held by Mickey Mantle and Joe Morgan. After Cal Ripken Jr. walked and Mark McGwire singled to left, Steinbach batted with the bases filled. He hit a fly to the warning track in left field, missing a grand slam and his second consecutive homer by a few feet. Winfield scored on the sacrifice fly to give the AL a 2–0 lead and all the runs the pitching staff would need as the Junior Circuit won for the third time in six years. Steinbach's heroics earned him the All-Star MVP Award.

Steinbach talked about his experience after the game: "In the on-deck circle, I was nervous. You don't want to strike out—you don't want to embarrass yourself. Then to hit a home run, it's a tough feeling to describe. I'm not going to thumb my nose at anyone now, but I was hoping to change people's minds. I didn't expect to hit a home run, but I wanted to show what I could do. I expect to turn it around in the second half." Steinbach did hit better after the break, ending the season at .265 with nine homers and fifty-one RBI.

There was little offense in the first two innings, which continued the trend of the previous two years, in which only seven runs had been scored by both teams. The Yankees' premier lead-off man, Rickey Henderson, started with a walk but was doubled up by the Braves' Paul Molitor. Wade Boggs of the Red Sox, the AL's leading batter at the break at .355, singled to left but was stranded when 1988 AL MVP Jose Canseco flew out to right field.

AL starting pitcher Frank Viola of the Twins threw two perfect innings with a strikeout, and Gooden matched him in the second inning as he set the middle of the AL lineup down in order. Steinbach's homer to start the third broke a seventeen-inning shutout streak by NL hurlers that dated back to the eighth inning of the 1986 game, including the thirteen-inning 1987 game. Gary Gaetti of the Twins then batted for his teammate Viola and grounded out. Henderson reached base again, this time with a single to right, but Molitor forced him at second base, and Boggs lined out.

Boston's Roger Clemens replaced Viola on the mound and repeated his predecessor's performance by throwing a perfect third inning with one strikeout. Houston's Bob Knepper replaced Gooden for the NL and surrendered the one run to Steinbach's sacrifice fly after loading the bases.

The NL scored its lone run in the bottom of the fourth inning off Kansas City's Mark Gubicza. Cardinals outfielder Vince Coleman singled to left field, stole second base, and continued to third on Steinbach's throwing error. With one out, Gubicza threw a wild pitch to score Coleman. Cubs outfielder Andre Dawson and the Mets' Darryl Strawberry each beat out an infield single, but Gubicza retired the next two batters to get out of the jam.

Oakland's Dennis Eckersley finished the game for the AL with a perfect inning to earn the first of his three career saves. Eckersley had been an All-Star twice before as a starter, and this was his first game as a relief pitcher. He followed Doug Jones of the Indians and Dan Plesac of the Brewers, who combined to throw a hitless eighth inning, striking out two of the three batters they faced. The NL's only runner came on a Don Mattingly error. Toronto's Dave Stieb and Texas's Jeff Russell each surrendered one hit in one inning of work, with Russell also walking a batter.

"The whole AL staff pitched well. I was impressed with them," said Cardinals and NL manager Whitey Herzog, who was managing for the third time in six years and became the first NL manager to lose three games. "I'd like to have won, don't get me wrong. You always want to win. But I don't think it's any big thing. I've managed three All-Star Games, and they've scored six runs in those three. It kind of reminds me of my present team." The NL champion Cardinals struggled all through the 1988 season offensively, finishing the season in fifth place, twenty-five games behind the Mets.

Only Al Lopez managed more All-Star Games than Herzog without a win, leading the AL squad

five times. Billy Martin skippered the AL three times without winning.

For the NL, David Cone of the Mets and Kevin Gross of the Phillies each pitched a perfect inning with one strikeout each. Orel Hershiser of the Dodgers, the 1988 NL Cy Young Award winner, and Todd Worrell of the Cardinals finished the game for the Senior Circuit, each throwing a perfect inning.

There were only twelve total hits in the game, and no batter collected more than one. In addition to Steinbach's homer and Winfield's double, only Tim Laudner of the Twins, Steinbach's replacement behind the plate, had an extra-base hit. Laudner doubled to right-center in the seventh inning off San Diego's Mark Davis.

Viola was named the starter for the AL based on his fourteen victories and 2.24 ERA, both league leaders at the break. He was the first Twins pitcher to start an All-Star contest since Dean Chance in 1967 and the first one to win. Viola was named the AL Cy Young Award winner at the end of the season. Gooden ended the first half with an 11-5 record and a 3.04 ERA. He had struck out 102 and had pitched three shutouts in the first half of the season.

This was the second start in three years for Gooden, who had missed the first two months of the 1987 season due to drug rehabilitation. "Last year at home, watching the game with my family, you feel like you're missing out on something. I'm probably more pleased and happy to be here than I was my first year," said Gooden. He had been named to the NL squad each of his first three seasons. "After my first two years, I was thinking that I'd like to have the three days off. But you think how much you feel about the game, how much the game means to you. It's definitely a thrill to be here."

Cal Ripken Jr. started at shortstop for the AL when the elected starter, Alan Trammell, could not play due to a stress fracture in his left forearm. This was Ripken's fifth straight start at short for the AL.

This was the last appearance for three longtime All-Stars. Both Dave Winfield and George Brett had been named to twelve squads, and this was Gary Carter's eleventh time on the NL team. Winfield's double in the fourth was his only hit in three plate appearances in his twelfth consecutive game. He had appeared four times for the Padres in the NL and the last eight times as an All-Star from the Yankees. Kansas City's Brett pinch-hit for Dan Plesac to start the ninth inning, popping out to first base. Carter had a single in three trips to the plate; he had represented both Montreal and the New York Mets in the game.

The thirty-two first-time All-Stars included ten players for whom this would be their only appearance in the midsummer classic and only eight who would be named to more than five teams. The only rookie on either squad was Chris Sabo from Cincinnati, who would be named the NL Rookie of the Year at the end of the season. He pinch-ran for Carter in the seventh inning and stole second base. The Cardinals' Ozzie Smith received the most fan votes for the second consecutive year.

Vice President George Bush, former first baseman for Yale University, threw out the ceremonial pitch before the game. Bush, who was campaigning for president at the time, would attend two more All-Star Games while president in 1991 and 1992.

	AL		NL	
P	Frank Viola	MIN	Dwight Gooden	NYN
C	Terry Steinbach	OAK	Gary Carter	NYN
1B	Mark McGwire	OAK	Will Clark	SFN
2B	Paul Molitor	MIL	Ryne Sandberg	CHN
3B	Wade Boggs	BOS	Bobby Bonilla	PIT
SS	Alan Trammell +	DET	Ozzie Smith	SLN
OF	Jose Canseco	OAK	Vince Coleman	SLN
OF	Rickey Henderson	NYA	Andre Dawson	CHN
OF	Dave Winfield	NYA	Darryl Strawberry	NYN
	Doyle Alexander	DET	David Cone	NYN
	George Brett	KCA	Mark Davis	SDN
	Roger Clemens	BOS	Shawon Dunston	CHN
	Dennis Eckersley	OAK	Andres Galarraga	MON
	Gary Gaetti	MIN	Kevin Gross	PHI
	Mike Greenwell	BOS	Orel Hershiser	LAN
	Mark Gubicza	KCA	Danny Jackson	CIN
	Ozzie Guillen +	CHA	Bob Knepper	HOU
	Doug Jones	CLE	Barry Larkin	CIN
	Carney Lansford	OAK	Vance Law	CHN
	Tim Laudner	MIN	Greg Maddux	CHN
	Don Mattingly	NYA	Willie McGee	SLN
	Dan Plesac	MIL	Rafael Palmeiro	CHN
	Kirby Puckett	MIN	Lance Parrish	PHI
	Johnny Ray	CAL	Gerald Perry	ATL
	Jeff Reardon	MIN	Chris Sabo	CIN
	Harold Reynolds	SEA	Robby Thompson +	SFN
	Cal Ripken	BAL	Andy Van Slyke	PIT
	Jeff Russell	TEX	Bob Walk	PIT
	Dave Stieb	TOR	Todd Worrell	SLN
	Kurt Stillwell	KCA		

+ player replaced on roster

American League	001	100	000-	2
National League	000	100	000-	1

AMERICAN LEAGUE

	ab	r	h	bi	bb	so	po	a
R.Henderson, cf	2	0	1	0	1	0	1	0
C.Lansford, 3b	1	0	0	0	0	0	0	1
P.Molitor, 2b	3	0	0	0	0	1	1	2
K.Puckett, cf	1	0	0	0	0	0	1	0
W.Boggs, 3b	3	0	1	0	0	0	0	1
H.Reynolds, 2b	1	0	0	0	0	0	1	1
J.Canseco, lf-rf	4	0	0	0	0	1	3	0
D.Winfield, rf	3	1	1	0	0	0	1	0
D.Stieb, p	0	0	0	0	0	0	0	0
J.Russell, p	0	0	0	0	0	0	0	0
D.Jones, p	0	0	0	0	0	0	0	0
D.Plesac, p	0	0	0	0	0	0	0	0
G.Brett, ph	1	0	0	0	0	0	0	0
K.Stillwell, ss	0	0	0	0	0	0	1	0
C.Ripken, ss	3	0	0	0	1	0	1	4
D.Eckersley, p	0	0	0	0	0	0	0	0
M.McGwire, 1b	2	0	1	0	0	1	8	0
D.Mattingly, 1b	2	0	0	0	0	0	2	1
T.Steinbach, c	1	1	1	2	0	0	3	1
M.Greenwell, lf	1	0	0	0	0	0	1	0
F.Viola, p	0	0	0	0	0	0	0	0
G.Gaetti, ph	1	0	0	0	0	0	0	0
R.Clemens, p	0	0	0	0	0	0	0	0
J.Ray, ph	1	0	0	0	0	0	0	0
M.Gubicza, p	0	0	0	0	0	0	0	0
T.Laudner, c	1	0	1	0	0	0	3	0
Totals	31	2	6	2	2	3	27	11

BATTING
2B: D.Winfield (off B.Knepper); T.Laudner (off M.Davis).
HR: T.Steinbach (3rd inning off D.Gooden, 0 on, 0 out).
RBI, scoring position, less than 2 outs: T.Steinbach 1-2.
SF: T.Steinbach.
GDP: P.Molitor.

BASERUNNING
Team LOB: 5

FIELDING
E: T.Steinbach (throw); D.Mattingly (fumble).

NATIONAL LEAGUE

	ab	r	h	bi	bb	so	po	a
V.Coleman, lf	2	1	1	0	0	0	3	0
A.Galarraga, 1b	2	0	0	0	0	1	6	0
R.Sandberg, 2b	4	0	1	0	0	2	2	2
T.Worrell, p	0	0	0	0	0	0	0	0
A.Dawson, cf	2	0	1	0	0	0	0	0
W.McGee, pr-cf	2	0	0	0	0	0	1	0
D.Strawberry, rf	4	0	1	0	0	1	4	0
B.Bonilla, 3b	4	0	0	0	0	0	0	2
W.Clark, 1b	2	0	0	0	0	0	4	1
D.Cone, p	0	0	0	0	0	0	0	0
B.Larkin, ss	2	0	0	0	0	1	0	1
G.Carter, c	3	0	1	0	0	1	3	0
C.Sabo, pr	0	0	0	0	0	0	0	0
L.Parrish, c	1	0	0	0	0	0	0	0
O.Smith, ss	2	0	0	0	0	1	1	4
K.Gross, p	0	0	0	0	0	0	0	0
M.Davis, p	0	0	0	0	0	0	0	0
B.Walk, p	0	0	0	0	0	0	0	0
R.Palmeiro, ph-lf	0	0	0	0	1	0	1	0
D.Gooden, p	0	0	0	0	0	0	0	1
G.Perry, ph	1	0	0	0	0	0	0	0
B.Knepper, p	0	0	0	0	0	0	0	0
A.Van Slyke, lf	2	0	0	0	0	0	2	0
O.Hershiser, p	0	0	0	0	0	0	0	0
V.Law, 2b	0	0	0	0	0	0	0	0
Totals	33	1	5	0	1	7	27	11

BATTING
RBI, scoring position, less than 2 outs: R.Sandberg 0-1; B.Bonilla 0-1.

BASERUNNING
SB: V.Coleman (2nd base off M.Gubicza/T.Steinbach); C.Sabo (2nd base off J.Russell/T.Laudner).
Team LOB: 6

FIELDING
DP: (1). W.Clark-O.Smith-W.Clark.

PITCHING	ip	h	r	er	bb	so
American League						
F.Viola (w)	2.0	0	0	0	0	1
R.Clemens	1.0	0	0	0	0	1
M.Gubicza	2.0	3	1	1	0	2
D.Stieb	1.0	1	0	0	0	0
J.Russell	1.0	1	0	0	1	0
D.Jones	0.2	0	0	0	0	1
D.Plesac	0.1	0	0	0	0	1
D.Eckersley (s)	1.0	0	0	0	0	1
National League						
D.Gooden (L)	3.0	3	1	1	1	1
B.Knepper	1.0	2	1	1	1	0
D.Cone	1.0	0	0	0	0	1
K.Gross	1.0	0	0	0	0	1
M.Davis	0.2	1	0	0	0	0
B.Walk	0.1	0	0	0	0	0
O.Hershiser	1.0	0	0	0	0	0
T.Worrell	1.0	0	0	0	0	0

Inherited Runners—Scored:
  R.Clemens 0–0; M.Gubicza 0–0; D.Stieb 0–0;
  J.Russell 0–0; D.Jones 0–0; D.Plesac 1–0;
  D.Eckersley 0–0; B.Knepper 0–0; D.Cone 0–0;
  K.Gross 0–0; M.Davis 0–0; B.Walk 1–0;
  O.Hershiser 0–0; T.Worrell 0–0.
WP: M.Gubicza
BK: D.Gooden

GAME DATA—T: 2:26; A: 55837; Temp: Unknown;
Wind: Unknown direction, Speed: Unknown

UMPIRES—HP: Frank Pulli (NL), 1B: Larry Barnett (AL),
2B: Terry Tata (NL), 3B: Dale Ford (AL), LF: Randy Marsh
(NL), RF: Dan Morrison (AL)

STARTING LINEUPS

	American League	National League
1.	R.Henderson cf	V.Coleman lf
2.	P.Molitor 2b	R.Sandberg 2b
3.	W.Boggs 3b	A.Dawson cf
4.	J.Canseco lf	D.Strawberry rf
5.	D.Winfield rf	B.Bonilla 3b
6.	C.Ripken ss	W.Clark 1b
7.	M.McGwire 1b	G.Carter c
8.	T.Steinbach c	O.Smith ss
9.	F.Viola p	D.Gooden p

AL 1ST: R.Henderson walked; P.Molitor grounded into a double play (W.Clark-1b to O.Smith-ss to W.Clark-1b) [R.Henderson out at second]; W.Boggs singled to left field; J.Canseco flied to D.Strawberry-rf; 0 R, 1 H, 0 E, 1 LOB. AL 0, NL 0.

NL 1ST: V.Coleman flied to R.Henderson-cf; R.Sandberg was called out on strikes; A.Dawson grounded out (W.Boggs-3b to M.McGwire-1b); 0 R, 0 H, 0 E, 0 LOB. AL 0, NL 0.

AL 2ND: D.Winfield grounded out (O.Smith-ss to W.Clark-1b); C.Ripken grounded out (O.Smith-ss to W.Clark-1b); M.McGwire struck out; 0 R, 0 H, 0 E, 0 LOB. AL 0, NL 0.

NL 2ND: D.Strawberry grounded out (P.Molitor-2b to M.McGwire-1b); B.Bonilla grounded out (C.Ripken-ss to M.McGwire-1b); W.Clark grounded out (C.Ripken-ss to M.McGwire-1b); 0 R, 0 H, 0 E, 0 LOB. AL 0, NL 0.

AL 3RD: T.Steinbach homered to rightfield (it was the 0–1 pitch); off the top of the wall and Strawberry's glove; first All-Star at bat for Steinbach; **G.Gaetti batted for F.Viola;** G.Gaetti grounded out (D.Gooden-p to W.Clark-1b); R.Henderson singled to right field; P.Molitor forced R.Henderson (B.Bonilla-3b to R.Sandberg-2b) [P.Molitor to first]; D.Gooden balked [P.Molitor to second]; W.Boggs lined to R.Sandberg-2b; 1 R, 2 H, 0 E, 1 LOB. AL 1, NL 0.

NL 3RD: **R.Clemens replaced G.Gaetti (pitching);** G.Carter popped to P.Molitor-2b; O.Smith struck out; **G.Perry batted for D.Gooden;** G.Perry flied to J.Canseco-lf; 0 R, 0 H, 0 E, 0 LOB. AL 1, NL 0.

AL 4TH: **B.Knepper replaced G.Perry (pitching);** J.Canseco flied to V.Coleman-lf; D.Winfield doubled to very deep left-center; C.Ripken walked; M.McGwire singled to left field [D.Winfield to third, C.Ripken to second]; T.Steinbach out on a sacrifice fly to V.Coleman-lf [D.Winfield scored]; **J.Ray batted for R.Clemens;** J.Ray lined to V.Coleman-lf; 1 R, 2 H, 0 E, 2 LOB. AL 2, NL 0.

NL 4TH: **M.Gubicza replaced J.Ray (pitching);** V.Coleman singled to left field; V.Coleman stole second (it was the 1–2 pitch) [V.Coleman to

third (error by T.Steinbach-c)]; R.Sandberg struck out; M.Gubicza threw a wild pitch [V.Coleman scored]; A.Dawson singled to pitcher; **W.McGee ran for A.Dawson;** D.Strawberry singled to second base [W.McGee to second]; diving stop by Molitor behind the bag; B.Bonilla lined to D.Winfield-rf; W.Clark grounded out (P.Molitor-2b to M.McGwire-1b); 1 R, 3 H, 1 E, 2 LOB. AL 2, NL 1.

AL 5TH: **W.McGee stayed in game (playing cf); D.Cone replaced W.Clark (pitching); A.Van Slyke replaced B.Knepper (playing lf); A.Galarraga replaced V.Coleman (playing 1b);** R.Henderson flied to W.McGee-cf; P.Molitor was called out on strikes; W.Boggs grounded out (O.Smith-ss to A.Galarraga-1b); 0 R, 0 H, 0 E, 0 LOB. AL 2, NL 1.

NL 5TH: **C.Lansford replaced R.Henderson (playing 3b); K.Puckett replaced P.Molitor (playing cf); H.Reynolds replaced W.Boggs (playing 2b);** G.Carter struck out (T.Steinbach-c to M.McGwire-1b); O.Smith grounded out (C.Ripken-ss to M.McGwire-1b); A.Van Slyke grounded out (H.Reynolds-2b to M.McGwire-1b); 0 R, 0 H, 0 E, 0 LOB. AL 2, NL 1.

AL 6TH: **K.Gross replaced O.Smith (pitching); B.Larkin replaced D.Cone (playing ss);** J.Canseco struck out; D.Winfield flied to A.Van Slyke-lf; C.Ripken flied to D.Strawberry-rf; 0 R, 0 H, 0 E, 0 LOB. AL 2, NL 1.

NL 6TH: fan interference on Ripken's ball; **D.Stieb replaced D.Winfield (pitching); M.Greenwell replaced T.Steinbach (playing lf); T.Laudner replaced M.Gubicza (playing c); D.Mattingly replaced M.McGwire (playing 1b); J.Canseco changed positions (playing rf);** A.Galarraga flied to J.Canseco-rf; R.Sandberg singled to right field; W.McGee grounded out (C.Ripken-ss to D.Mattingly-1b) [R.Sandberg to second]; D.Strawberry flied to J.Canseco-rf; 0 R, 1 H, 0 E, 1 LOB. AL 2, NL 1.

AL 7TH: **M.Davis replaced K.Gross (pitching);** D.Mattingly grounded out (R.Sandberg-2b to A.Galarraga-1b); M.Greenwell lined to A.Van Slyke-lf; diving catch by Van Slyke; T.Laudner doubled to very deep right-center; **B.Walk replaced M.Davis (pitching);** C.Lansford grounded out (R.Sandberg-2b to A.Galarraga-1b); 0 R, 1 H, 0 E, 1 LOB. AL 2, NL 1.

NL 7TH: **J.Russell replaced D.Stieb (pitching);** B.Bonilla lined to M.Greenwell-lf; B.Larkin grounded out (C.Lansford-3b to D.Mattingly-1b); G.Carter singled to right-center; **C.Sabo ran for G.Carter; R.Palmeiro batted for B.Walk;** C.Sabo stole second; R.Palmeiro walked; A.Van Slyke forced R.Palmeiro (D.Mattingly-1b to C.Ripken-ss) [A.Van Slyke to first]; 0 R, 1 H, 0 E, 2 LOB. AL 2, NL 1.

AL 8TH: **R.Palmeiro stayed in game (playing lf); O.Hershiser replaced A.Van Slyke (pitching); L.Parrish replaced C.Sabo (playing c);** K.Puckett flied to D.Strawberry-rf; H.Reynolds flied to R.Palmeiro-lf; J.Canseco grounded out (B.Larkin-ss to A.Galarraga-1b); 0 R, 0 H, 0 E, 0 LOB. AL 2, NL 1.

NL 8TH: **D.Jones replaced J.Russell (pitching);** A.Galarraga struck out; R.Sandberg popped to H.Reynolds-2b; over the shoulder catch; W.McGee reached on an error by D.Mattingly-1b [W.McGee to first]; **D.Plesac replaced D.Jones (pitching);** D.Strawberry struck out; 0 R, 0 H, 1 E, 1 LOB. AL 2, NL 1.

AL 9TH: **T.Worrell replaced R.Sandberg (pitching); V.Law replaced O.Hershiser (playing 2b); G.Brett batted for D.Plesac;** G.Brett popped to A.Galarraga-1b; C.Ripken grounded out (B.Bonilla-3b to A.Galarraga-1b); D.Mattingly lined to D.Strawberry-rf; 0 R, 0 H, 0 E, 0 LOB. AL 2, NL 1.

NL 9TH: **K.Stillwell replaced G.Brett (playing ss); D.Eckersley replaced C.Ripken (pitching);** B.Bonilla lined to K.Stillwell-ss; B.Larkin struck out; L.Parrish flied to K.Puckett-cf; 0 R, 0 H, 0 E, 0 LOB. AL 2, NL 1.

Final Totals	R	H	E	LOB
American League	2	6	2	5
National League	1	5	0	6

60

Bo Knows All-Stars

Kansas City outfielder Bo Jackson, also known as the NFL's Los Angeles Raiders running back and college football's Heisman Trophy winner, came into the 1989 All-Star Game among the AL leaders in home runs, total bases, slugging percentage, runs batted in, and runs scored. He dominated this game by homering in his first All-Star at bat (a 450-foot blast to center field to lead off the game), stealing a base, and making a spectacular catch in left-center to end the first inning, thus walking away with the MVP trophy in his only All-Star appearance. As if his on-field performance was not enough, Jackson also starred in a television commercial for a shoe company that became the first of a well-known series of advertisements.

Jackson, the leading vote getter in the AL, was the second All-Star to hit a home run and steal a base in the same game; Willie Mays performed the trick in 1960's second game. Jackson became the ninth player to homer on his first All-Star at bat and the fifth to lead off a game with a long ball. Jackson said of the drive, "It wasn't a strike. He kept it low, but I saw it well. He didn't come out of the [twilight] glare, and I picked it up."

This game produced the first back-to-back victories for the AL since 1957–1958. The Junior Circuit had lost nineteen of twenty games before winning three of the last six contests. AL Manager Tony La Russa, in his initial stint as skipper in the midsummer classic, said, "For a long time, one side treated it as a game and the other treated it as an exhibition. Frankly, I think the American League got embarrassed, and the attitude has changed." Yankee first baseman Don Mattingly commented further, "We're starting to dominate this game. That's the way it's going to be for a few years."

La Russa's naming of Jackson as the lead-off hitter surprised many observers. The skipper said, "Bo at the top gives us a chance to get started quickly. We can put some pressure on the other

team right away." La Russa's hunch that Jackson could provide instant offense paid off right away for the team. "Unfortunately, that's what I saw the last week of the first half. That's the way he has been playing—home runs, line drives, and stolen bases. He's exciting," La Russa said.

The NL jumped on AL starting pitcher Dave Stewart of Oakland, who was making his only appearance in the star gala, for two runs in the first inning. Stewart came into the contest leading the Junior Circuit in wins with thirteen and had only been tagged with four losses, but the visitors quickly drove him from the game. After Cardinals shortstop Ozzie Smith singled and was caught stealing, Tony Gwynn of San Diego walked and moved to second on a ground out by the leading vote getter, the Giants' first sacker Will Clark. Clark entered the break with a .332 average, fourteen home runs, and sixty-four runs batted in and was the defending NL RBI champ. Clark said, "I have had a fairly consistent season myself, but it has been nothing compared to what Kevin has done."

Kevin, Giants left fielder Kevin Mitchell, came into the game leading the NL in homers (31) and RBI (81) and would end the season by being named the NL MVP. His homer total at the break was the fourth highest ever, higher than his own previous best season total of twenty-two in 1987. Mitchell singled to center to score Gwynn with the game's first run. Eric Davis of Cincinnati walked, and Mets third baseman Howard Johnson singled, scoring Mitchell. Pedro Guerrero of the Cardinals then became the first designated hitter in the All-Star Game, but he flew out to Jackson to end the inning.

It took the AL only eight pitches to tie the score. On Rick Reuschel's second pitch, Jackson homered onto the tarp that served as the hitter's backdrop in center field. Red Sox third baseman Wade Boggs watched the homer from the on-deck circle. He said of that hit: "It was a blast. There aren't too many people who can hit that tarp. I felt like I'd be let down if I came up next and hit a dribbler up the middle."

Boggs didn't have to worry as he took Reuschel's 3-2 pitch out of the park to left-center field. It was the first time that the first two All-Star batters had each homered and the fourth time that batters had hit back-to-back dingers. The last duo to perform this feat was Steve Garvey and Jim Wynn for the NL in 1975.

San Francisco's Reuschel, at age forty, was the second-oldest pitcher to start an All-Star Game. He came into the break with a 12-3 record and won the start over Houston's Mike Scott, who strained a hamstring two days before this contest. (Warren Spahn started the first game in 1961 when a month older than Reuschel.) Reuschel said his pitch to Jackson was a good one: "He just went down and got it. I heard about his power and strength, and I saw it firsthand. After that one, I just wanted to put the ball in play and throw a strike. Boggs hit it a long way."

Both starting pitchers were removed after one inning, in which they each surrendered two runs on three hits. Stewart also gave two free passes in his inning. Nolan Ryan relieved Stewart and pitched two innings of shutout ball, surrendering only an infield hit to Gwynn. Ryan, a twenty-three-year veteran, struck out three batters, including Will Clark and Kevin Mitchell consecutively in the third inning, and was named the winning pitcher in the ballpark where he had his best years. At forty-two years, five months, and ten days, he was the oldest pitcher to win an All-Star Game; in the last of his eight All-Star appearances, he had represented three teams (the Angels, Astros, and Rangers). Ryan also was the second oldest to pitch in an All-Star contest, behind Satchel Paige, who pitched in the 1953 game when he was forty-seven. This was the first winning pitching decision for the Rangers franchise, including its years in Washington.

NL Manager Tommy Lasorda, the former pitcher who was making the last of his four appearances as manager in the gala, was obviously in awe of Ryan: "He's an amazing man. How he continues is unbelievable. When he was with the Astros, I said that when he retires they should send his arm to the Smithsonian."

Ryan talked about his night: "Of all the All-Star Games I've pitched in, this was the most meaningful. I'm thankful I did well. No one wants to have a bad outing. Coming back to Anaheim and with a good chance this will be my last one, it's special."

Atlanta's John Smoltz relieved Reuschel in the bottom of the second inning. Ruben Sierra of the Rangers greeted Smoltz with the first of his two hits, a single to right field. One out later, Oak-

land's Terry Steinbach singled to center field, moving Sierra to third. Jackson forced Steinbach while Sierra scored the go-ahead run, and the AL never lost the lead after that.

The Junior Circuit continued the damage in the third. Facing new pitcher Rick Sutcliffe of the Cubs, Twins center fielder Kirby Puckett singled on the first pitch and moved to second on a wild pitch. Harold Baines, designated hitter for the AL and the White Sox, singled to right to score Puckett. Baines moved to third on two ground outs and scored when Sierra singled for the second time in the game.

Sutcliffe had been named as the replacement for the injured Mike Scott. He spent the day prior to the game fishing and golfing in Kansas City but did not hesitate when asked to come to Anaheim. "I wanted to be here; there was no doubt about that," he said. He arrived at the hotel only thirty minutes before the team bus left for the ballpark. The wife of a Cubs team official carried Sutcliffe's uniform to Los Angeles for the game. Sutcliffe surrendered four hits, two runs, and a wild pitch in his one inning of work.

Neither team scored again until the top of the eighth, when Astros first baseman Glenn Davis walked with two outs, moved to second on Mitchell's single, and scored on Phillies outfielder Von Hayes's single to left field.

In addition to Jackson and Sierra, Mitchell and Bobby Bonilla of the Pirates each collected two hits in the contest. All nine of the hits by the NL were singles (a repeat of the previous year's performance by the league), while the AL swatted four for extra bases, with Cal Ripken Jr. and Don Mattingly each doubling in addition to the homers by Jackson and Boggs. Ripken was making his record-setting sixth straight start at shortstop for the AL, while this was Mattingly's last of six All-Star appearances. The double was Mattingly's first All-Star hit after eight previous at bats. All nine AL starters collected at least one hit in the game, a feat never before accomplished in an All-Star Game. A designated hitter replaced the starting hurler at the plate for the first time this year, and there have been four squads with the eight non-pitchers all collecting at least one hit in a game: the AL in 1937, 1951, and 1954 and the NL in 1975.

AL pitchers surrendered only one run on six hits after the first inning. Kansas City's Mark Gubicza and Oakland's Mike Moore each pitched a perfect inning with one strikeout. Cleveland's Greg Swindell surrendered two hits in one and two-thirds scoreless innings while striking out three batters. Doug Jones of the Indians picked up a save by pitching one and one-third innings of one-hit ball.

On the NL side, the Padres' Mark Davis, who would be named the league's Cy Young Award winner at the end of the season, struck out two in a perfect sixth inning. Cubs bullpen specialist Mitch Williams allowed only a walk in his one inning while striking out a batter.

As noted above, NL skipper Tommy Lasorda was making his last appearance at the reins of the Senior Circuit. Lasorda had had a perfect 3-0 record before losing this game. In a strange twist on last names, Lasorda's counterpart in the other dugout, Tony La Russa, was making his first appearance leading an All-Star contingent.

Jeff Russell was named to the AL squad because of his record coming out of the bullpen for the Rangers. The previous year, he had been named as a starting pitcher and thus, in this game, became the fifth player to be named as both a starter and a reliever. The others are Hoyt Wilhelm, Rich Gossage, Bob Stanley, and Dennis Eckersley.

Ruben Sierra was named to the AL squad as a replacement for the injured Jose Canseco of Oakland. Sierra was the first graduate of the Roberto Clemente Sports City in Puerto Rico to be named an All-Star.

The paid attendance of 64,036 was the fourth largest for the All-Star Game. The top three crowds had all been in Cleveland's Municipal Stadium: 72,086 (1981), 69,831 (1935), and 68,751 (1954).

This was the second game at Anaheim Stadium, but it wasn't the same park in which the first game had been held in 1967. The configuration of the stadium was changed in 1979 to accommodate the new tenants, the NFL's Rams. At that time, the stadium was completely enclosed, thus eliminating most of the twilight shadows that had plagued the hitters in the 1967 contest.

Former president Ronald Reagan appeared on the television broadcast during the first inning, talking about the game and his broadcast career. This was the sixth time a president had attended the All-Star contest.

In addition to other players making their last appearance in the All-Star classic, Mike Schmidt of the Phillies was voted the starting third baseman even though he had retired in May. He never considered playing in the game, although he was in uniform (his twelfth appearance at the game) and received a long standing ovation during the player introductions prior to the game. He noted that the subject of his playing never came up: "I guess they wouldn't have stopped me, but I just decided it wasn't an option. Can you see a guy wanting to play after retiring? That would be a little ridiculous."

Angels coach Jimmie Reese threw out the ceremonial pitch. The eighty-three-year-old Reese was in his seventy-second year in professional baseball, having started as a batboy for the Los Angeles Angels of the Pacific Coast League in 1917.

	AL			NL	
P	Dave Stewart	OAK		Rick Reuschel	SFN
C	Terry Steinbach	OAK		Benito Santiago	SDN
1B	Mark McGwire	OAK		Will Clark	SFN
2B	Julio Franco	TEX		Ryne Sandberg	CHN
3B	Wade Boggs	BOS		Mike Schmidt +	PHI
SS	Cal Ripken	BAL		Ozzie Smith	SLN
OF	Jose Canseco +	OAK		Tony Gwynn	SDN
OF	Bo Jackson	KCA		Kevin Mitchell	SFN
OF	Kirby Puckett	MIN		Darryl Strawberry +	NYN
DH	Harold Baines	CHA		Pedro Guerrero	SLN
	Tony Fernandez	TOR		Bobby Bonilla	PIT
	Chuck Finley	CAL		Tim Burke	MON
	Gary Gaetti	MIN		Vince Coleman	SLN
	Mike Greenwell	BOS		Eric Davis	CIN
	Kelly Gruber	TOR		Glenn Davis	HOU
	Mark Gubicza	KCA		Mark Davis	SDN
	Mike Henneman	DET		Andre Dawson	CHN
	Doug Jones	CLE		John Franco	CIN
	Jeffrey Leonard	SEA		Von Hayes	PHI
	Don Mattingly	NYA		Orel Hershiser	LAN
	Mike Moore	OAK		Jay Howell	LAN
	Dan Plesac	MIL		Howard Johnson	NYN
	Jeff Russell	TEX		Barry Larkin	CIN
	Nolan Ryan	TEX		Tony Pena	SLN
	Steve Sax	NYA		Willie Randolph	LAN
	Ruben Sierra	TEX		Mike Scioscia	LAN
	Greg Swindell	CLE		Mike Scott +	HOU
	Mickey Tettleton	BAL		John Smoltz	ATL
	Devon White	CAL		Rick Sutcliffe	CHN
				Tim Wallach	MON
				Mitch Williams	CHN

+ player replaced on roster

National League   200 000 010- 3
American League   212 000 00X- 5

NATIONAL LEAGUE

	ab	r	h	bi	bb	so	po	a
O.Smith, ss	4	0	1	0	0	0	1	3
T.Gwynn, rf	2	1	1	0	1	1	2	0
A.Dawson, rf	1	0	0	0	0	0	1	0
W.Clark, 1b	2	0	0	0	0	1	5	0
G.Davis, 1b	1	1	1	0	1	0	7	0
K.Mitchell, lf	4	1	2	1	0	2	0	0
V.Coleman, pr-lf	0	0	0	0	0	0	0	0
E.Davis, cf	2	0	0	0	1	0	1	0
V.Hayes, cf	1	0	1	1	0	0	0	0
H.Johnson, 3b	3	0	1	1	0	1	0	0
T.Wallach, 3b	1	0	0	0	0	0	0	0
P.Guerrero, dh	2	0	0	0	0	0	0	0
B.Bonilla, ph	2	0	2	0	0	0	0	0
R.Sandberg, 2b	3	0	0	0	0	2	2	4
W.Randolph, 2b	1	0	0	0	0	0	0	0
B.Santiago, c	1	0	0	0	0	1	0	0
M.Scioscia, c	1	0	0	0	0	0	3	0
T.Pena, ph-c	2	0	0	0	0	0	2	0
Totals	33	3	9	3	3	8	24	7

BATTING
2-out RBI: K.Mitchell; V.Hayes; H.Johnson.
RBI, scoring position, less than 2 outs: W.Clark 0–1; K.Mitchell 0–1.
GDP: E.Davis; T.Pena.

BASERUNNING
SB: T.Gwynn (2nd base off N.Ryan/T.Steinbach); E.Davis (Double SB 3rd base off D.Stewart/T.Steinbach); H.Johnson (Double SB 2nd base off D.Stewart/T.Steinbach).
CS: O.Smith (2nd base by D.Stewart/T.Steinbach).
Team LOB: 6

FIELDING
E: B.Santiago (throw).

AMERICAN LEAGUE

	ab	r	h	bi	bb	so	po	a
B.Jackson, lf	4	1	2	2	0	1	2	0
M.Greenwell, lf	0	0	0	0	0	0	1	0
W.Boggs, 3b	3	1	1	1	0	0	1	1
G.Gaetti, 3b	1	0	0	0	0	1	1	0
K.Puckett, cf	3	1	1	0	0	0	0	0
D.White, cf	1	0	0	0	0	0	0	0
H.Baines, dh	3	1	1	1	0	1	0	0
J.Leonard, ph	1	0	0	0	0	1	0	0
J.Franco, 2b	3	0	1	0	0	0	1	1
D.Mattingly, 1b	1	0	1	0	0	0	4	0
C.Ripken, ss	3	0	1	0	0	0	0	0
T.Fernandez, pr-ss	1	0	0	0	0	0	2	2
R.Sierra, rf	3	1	2	1	1	0	1	0
M.McGwire, 1b	3	0	1	0	0	0	5	0
S.Sax, 2b	1	0	0	0	0	0	1	3
T.Steinbach, c	3	0	1	0	0	0	6	1
M.Tettleton, c	1	0	0	0	0	1	2	0
Totals	35	5	12	5	1	5	27	8

BATTING
2B: C.Ripken (off T.Burke); D.Mattingly (off J.Howell).
HR: B.Jackson (1st inning off R.Reuschel, 0 on, 0 out); W.Boggs (1st inning off R.Reuschel, 0 on, 0 out).
2-out RBI: R.Sierra.
RBI, scoring position, less than 2 outs: B.Jackson 1–1; K.Puckett 0–1; H.Baines 1–1; C.Ripken 0–1; R.Sierra 0–1.

BASERUNNING
SB: B.Jackson (2nd base off J.Smoltz/B.Santiago).
Team LOB: 7

FIELDING
DP: (2). D.Jones-T.Fernandez-D.Mattingly; T.Fernandez-S.Sax-D.Mattingly.

PITCHING	ip	h	r	er	bb	so
National League						
R.Reuschel	1.0	3	2	2	0	0
J.Smoltz (L)	1.0	2	1	1	0	0
R.Sutcliffe	1.0	4	2	2	0	0
T.Burke	2.0	2	0	0	0	1
M.Davis	1.0	0	0	0	0	2
J.Howell	1.0	1	0	0	0	1
M.Williams	1.0	0	0	0	1	1
American League						
D.Stewart	1.0	3	2	2	2	0
N.Ryan (w)	2.0	1	0	0	0	3
M.Gubicza	1.0	0	0	0	0	1
M.Moore	1.0	0	0	0	0	1
G.Swindell	1.2	2	0	0	0	3
J.Russell	1.0	1	1	1	1	0
D.Plesac (L) *	0.0	1	0	0	0	0
D.Jones (s)	1.1	1	0	0	0	0

* Pitched to 1 batter in 8th

Inherited Runners—Scored:
J.Smoltz 0–0; R.Sutcliffe 0–0; T.Burke 0–0; M.Davis 0–0; J.Howell 0–0; M.Williams 0–0; N.Ryan 0–0; M.Gubicza 0–0; M.Moore 0–0; G.Swindell 0–0; J.Russell 1–0; D.Plesac 2–1; D.Jones 2–0.
WP: R.Sutcliffe

GAME DATA—T: 2:48; A: 64036; Temp: Unknown; Wind: Unknown direction, Speed: Unknown

UMPIRES—HP: Jim Evans (AL), 1B: Bob Engle (NL), 2B: Terry Cooney (AL), 3B: Jerry Crawford (NL), LF: John Hirschbeck (AL), RF: Gerry Davis (NL)

STARTING LINEUPS

	National League	*American League*
1.	O.Smith ss	B.Jackson lf
2.	T.Gwynn rf	W.Boggs 3b
3.	W.Clark 1b	K.Puckett cf
4.	K.Mitchell lf	H.Baines dh
5.	E.Davis cf	J.Franco 2b
6.	H.Johnson 3b	C.Ripken ss
7.	P.Guerrero dh	R.Sierra rf
8.	R.Sandberg 2b	M.McGwire 1b
9.	B.Santiago c	T.Steinbach c
	R.Reuschel p	D.Stewart p

NL 1ST: first All-Star game to use the designated hitter; O.Smith singled to center field; O.Smith was caught stealing second (T.Steinbach-c to J.Franco-2b); T.Gwynn walked; W.Clark grounded out (M.McGwire-1b unassisted) [T.Gwynn to second]; high chopper; K.Mitchell singled to center field [T.Gwynn scored]; checked swing; E.Davis walked [K.Mitchell to second]; H.Johnson singled to left field (it was the first pitch) [K.Mitchell scored, E.Davis to second]; E.Davis stole third and H.Johnson stole second (it was the 0–2 pitch); P.Guerrero flied to B.Jackson-lf; 2 R, 3 H, 0 E, 2 LOB. NL 2, AL 0.

AL 1ST: B.Jackson homered to centerfield (it was the 1–0 pitch); Jackson's first All-Star at bat; W.Boggs homered to left-center (it was the 3–2 pitch); first time that first two batters each homered; K.Puckett grounded out (R.Sandberg-2b to W.Clark-1b); H.Baines grounded out (R.Reuschel-p to W.Clark-1b); J.Franco singled to left field; C.Ripken forced J.Franco (O.Smith-ss to R.Sandberg-2b) [C.Ripken to first]; 2 R, 3 H, 0 E, 1 LOB. NL 2, AL 2.

NL 2ND: **N.Ryan replaced D.Stewart (pitching);** R.Sandberg popped to M.McGwire-1b in foul territory; B.Santiago struck out; O.Smith popped to W.Boggs-3b; 0 R, 0 H, 0 E, 0 LOB. NL 2, AL 2.

AL 2ND: **J.Smoltz replaced R.Reuschel (pitching);** R.Sierra singled to right field; M.McGwire flied to T.Gwynn-rf; T.Steinbach singled to center field [R.Sierra to third]; B.Jackson forced T.Steinbach (O.Smith-ss to R.Sandberg-2b) [R.Sierra scored, B.Jackson to first]; B.Jackson stole second (it was the 1–1 pitch) [B.Jackson to third (error by B.Santiago-c)]; W.Boggs popped to O.Smith-ss; 1 R, 2 H, 1 E, 1 LOB. NL 2, AL 3.

NL 3RD: T.Gwynn singled to pitcher; T.Gwynn stole second (it was the 1–1 pitch); W.Clark struck out; K.Mitchell was called out on strikes; E.Davis flied to R.Sierra-rf; 0 R, 1 H, 0 E, 1 LOB. NL 2, AL 3.

AL 3RD: **R.Sutcliffe replaced J.Smoltz (pitching);** K.Puckett singled to left field; R.Sutcliffe threw a wild pitch [K.Puckett to second]; H.Baines singled to right field [K.Puckett scored]; J.Franco grounded out (R.Sutcliffe-p to W.Clark-1b) [H.Baines to second]; C.Ripken grounded out (R.Sandberg-2b to W.Clark-1b) [H.Baines to third]; R.Sierra singled to first base [H.Baines scored]; M.McGwire singled to center field [R.Sierra to second]; T.Steinbach flied to T.Gwynn-rf; 2 R, 4 H, 0 E, 2 LOB. NL 2, AL 5.

NL 4TH: **M.Gubicza replaced N.Ryan (pitching);** H.Johnson grounded out (M.McGwire-1b unassisted); P.Guerrero grounded out (W.Boggs-3b to M.McGwire-1b); R.Sandberg was called out on strikes; 0 R, 0 H, 0 E, 0 LOB. NL 2, AL 5.

AL 4TH: **T.Burke changed positions (pitching); M.Scioscia replaced B.Santiago (playing c);** B.Jackson singled to center field; W.Boggs grounded out (R.Sandberg-2b to W.Clark-1b) [B.Jackson to second]; K.Puckett flied to E.Davis-cf [B.Jackson to third]; H.Baines struck out; 0 R, 1 H, 0 E, 1 LOB. NL 2, AL 5.

NL 5TH: **G.Gaetti replaced W.Boggs (playing 3b); M.Moore replaced M.Gubicza (pitching);** M.Scioscia flied to B.Jackson-lf; O.Smith grounded out (J.Franco-2b to M.McGwire-1b); T.Gwynn was called out on strikes; 0 R, 0 H, 0 E, 0 LOB. NL 2, AL 5.

AL 5TH: **G.Davis replaced W.Clark (playing 1b); A.Dawson replaced T.Gwynn (playing rf);** J.Franco flied to A.Dawson-rf; C.Ripken doubled to right field; **T.Fernandez ran for C.Ripken;** R.Sierra grounded out (G.Davis-1b unassisted) [T.Fernandez to third]; M.McGwire grounded out (O.Smith-ss to G.Davis-1b); 0 R, 1 H, 0 E, 1 LOB. NL 2, AL 5.

NL 6TH: **T.Fernandez stayed in game (playing ss); D.Mattingly replaced J.Franco (playing 1b); S.Sax replaced M.McGwire (playing 2b); G.Swindell replaced M.Moore (pitching);** G.Davis singled to center field; K.Mitchell struck out; E.Davis grounded into a double play (T.Fernandez-ss to S.Sax-2b to D.Mattingly-1b) [G.Davis out at second]; 0 R, 1 H, 0 E, 0 LOB. NL 2, AL 5.

AL 6TH: **M.Davis replaced T.Burke (pitching);** T.Steinbach grounded out (R.Sandberg-2b to G.Davis-1b); B.Jackson struck out; G.Gaetti was called out on strikes; 0 R, 0 H, 0 E, 0 LOB. NL 2, AL 5.

NL 7TH: **M.Tettleton replaced T.Steinbach (playing c); M.Greenwell replaced B.Jackson (playing lf); D.White replaced K.Puckett (playing cf);** H.Johnson struck out; **B.Bonilla batted for P.Guerrero;** B.Bonilla singled to left field; R.Sandberg struck out; **T.Pena batted for M.Scioscia; J.Russell replaced G.Swindell (pitching);**

Pena broke his bat on ground out; T.Pena grounded out (D.Mattingly-1b unassisted); 0 R, 1 H, 0 E, 1 LOB. NL 2, AL 5.

AL 7TH: **T.Pena stayed in game (playing c); W.Randolph replaced R.Sandberg (playing 2b); T.Wallach replaced H.Johnson (playing 3b); V.Hayes replaced E.Davis (playing cf); J.Howell replaced M.Davis (pitching);** D.White grounded out (G.Davis-1b unassisted); **J.Leonard batted for H.Baines;** J.Leonard was called out on strikes; D.Mattingly doubled to right field; T.Fernandez grounded out (G.Davis-1b unassisted); 0 R, 1 H, 0 E, 1 LOB. NL 2, AL 5.

NL 8TH: O.Smith grounded out (S.Sax-2b to D.Mattingly-1b); A.Dawson popped to G.Gaetti-3b in foul territory; G.Davis walked; K.Mitchell singled to left field [G.Davis to second]; **V.Coleman ran for K.Mitchell; D.Plesac replaced J.Russell (pitching);** V.Hayes singled to left field [G.Davis scored, V.Coleman to third]; **D.Jones replaced D.Plesac**

(pitching); T.Wallach lined to M.Greenwell-lf; 1 R, 2 H, 0 E, 2 LOB. NL 3, AL 5.

AL 8TH: **V.Coleman stayed in game (playing lf); M.Williams replaced J.Howell (pitching);** R.Sierra walked; R.Sierra was picked off first (M.Williams-p to G.Davis-1b); S.Sax popped to G.Davis-1b; M.Tettleton struck out; 0 R, 0 H, 0 E, 0 LOB. NL 3, AL 5.

NL 9TH: B.Bonilla singled to first base down the line; Bonilla was unable to take 2b when the ball struck umpire Engel behind the bag; W.Randolph forced B.Bonilla (S.Sax-2b to T.Fernandez-ss) [W.Randolph to first]; T.Pena grounded into a double play (D.Jones-p to T.Fernandez-ss to D.Mattingly-1b) [W.Randolph out at second]; 0 R, 1 H, 0 E, 0 LOB. NL 3, AL 5.

Final Totals	R	H	E	LOB
National League	3	9	1	6
American League	5	12	0	7

61

GAME

Tuesday, July 10, 1990

Wrigley Field, Chicago

American League 2, National League 0

SERIES RESULTS: NL 37, AL 23, 1 TIE

The AL Rains on the NL

In 1990, the All-Star Game returned to Wrigley Field for the first time since 1962, and the pregame talk centered around a possible offensive explosion in the "Friendly Confines." Major League Baseball had avoided Wrigley because until lights were installed there in 1988, only day games were possible. The weather did not cooperate with hopes for a slugfest, however, and the game ended as a low-scoring event. The start of the contest was delayed by rain for seventeen minutes, and there was a sixty-three-minute rain delay in the seventh inning to dampen the offense and the spirits of those in attendance. In addition, a sixteen-mile-an-hour wind blew in from left field at game time. As AL third baseman Wade Boggs of the Red Sox said: "Someone would have to hit the ball eight hundred feet tonight to hit it out of here." Boggs was correct in his assumption; no homers were hit in the game among the nine total hits. In fact, there was only one extra-base hit, a double by Julio Franco of the Rangers, which produced the only two runs of the contest. That hit earned Franco the game's MVP honors.

The offensive futility was very evident. The NL set a record by collecting only two hits in the game, besting the previous low of three hits accomplished most recently by the 1968 AL squad. The contest remained scoreless longer than any All-Star Game except that of 1987, in which the Senior Circuit finally scored two runs in the thirteenth inning. The NL also had a string of sixteen consecutive batters retired by the AL pitchers from the time Padre outfielder Tony Gwynn walked in the third until Pirate outfielder and 1990 NL MVP Barry Bonds walked in the eighth. The only National Leaguers to collect hits were Will Clark of the Giants, who singled to center in the first inning, and Lenny Dykstra, who also singled to center in the ninth inning. The AL hurlers almost tossed a no-hitter in a season when nine no-hitters were thrown during the regular season.

The lack of offense was not a surprise to one batter. "I definitely think the pitchers have an advantage in the game," said Giants left fielder Kevin Mitchell, the reigning NL MVP who started for the league and had two at bats without a hit. "Not only are you facing a guy who you've never seen before, but he knows that he's only going to have to be out there for an inning or two."

The AL collected a hit in the first inning when Boggs singled. Boggs and Sandy Alomar Jr. were the only players to collect two safeties in the game. After Clark's base hit in the bottom of the inning, both teams were hitless until Alomar, the Indians' catcher and 1990 AL Rookie of the Year, beat out an infield roller in the fifth. He was doubled up, however, when Yankee second baseman Steve Sax hit a grounder to his NL counterpart, Ryne Sandberg of the Cubs, the leading NL vote getter.

The AL threatened in the third inning. Right-hander Ramon Martinez of the Dodgers replaced starter Jack Armstrong on the mound for the NL. Martinez walked Sax, who stole second before pinch hitter Brook Jacoby of the Indians grounded out. After Rickey Henderson struck out, NL skipper Roger Craig of the Giants had Martinez walk Boggs intentionally. That brought up Oakland slugger Jose Canseco, who received more fan votes than any other player.

Canseco took a powerful swing at Martinez's first offering but missed. The second pitch was a fastball up and in on Canseco, forcing him to bail out of the batter's box. Canseco stared out at Martinez, and Dodger catcher Mike Scioscia went out to talk with his teammate on the mound. After fouling off two pitches, Canseco finally grounded out to end the inning.

The next threat came in the AL half of the sixth inning. With Dave Smith of the Astros pitching, Boggs singled to right field with one out. Kelly Gruber ran for Boggs, Canseco walked, and after pinch hitter George Bell struck out, Gruber and Canseco pulled a double steal. Craig then ordered his second intentional walk of the game, this time

397

to Ken Griffey Jr., and then brought Jeff Brantley in to face Canseco's "Bash Brother" Mark Mc-Gwire. AL manager Tony La Russa of Oakland countered with a pinch hitter, the league's home run leader at the break, Tiger first baseman Cecil Fielder. Fielder came into the game with 28 homers, on his way to a Major League–leading 51, and 75 RBI on his way to a Major League–leading 132. Fielder failed to drive in his teammate, however, because he flew out to center field.

In the top of the seventh, with rain falling, Sandy Alomar beat out a grounder in the short-stop hole. Lance Parrish pinch-hit and singled to right field, moving Alomar to third. The rain came down harder, and home plate umpire Ed Montague called time. After waiting one hour and eight minutes, Julio Franco batted against new pitcher Rob Dibble of the Reds and, with a two-strike count, doubled to right-center to score two runs. After Ozzie Guillen grounded out and Gruber walked and stole second, Canseco hit a fly ball to Darryl Strawberry in right field. The Straw's throw to the plate was perfect, and Scioscia tagged Franco, who was trying to score from third, for an inning-ending double play.

The AL threatened to score again in the eighth inning. With one out, pinch hitter Kirby Puckett singled to right and raced to third on an error by Strawberry. Fielder and Parrish walked to load the bases for Julio Franco, but this time Franco flew out to right field to end the inning.

Reigning AL Cy Young Award winner Bret Saberhagen of the Royals pitched two perfect innings and received credit for the win. He was the first Royals pitcher to get credit for a decision in an All-Star Game and had been the first Royals starter in 1987. Toronto's Dave Stieb, in his seventh and last All-Star Game, pitched two innings, allowing only the walk to Gwynn. Bobby Thigpen of the White Sox pitched a perfect seventh inning. The NL used nine pitchers, which broke the old record of eight reached most recently by the 1989 AL squad. This record would be eclipsed by the 1992 AL team, who used ten hurlers. Dennis Martinez of Montreal and John Franco of the Mets, each pitching one inning, were the only NL pitchers to set the AL down in order.

Oakland's Bob Welch started for the AL and allowed only one base runner—on Clark's first-inning hit—in two innings of work. Welch was making his second appearance in the All-Star Game, having represented the Dodgers ten years before. Welch came into the game with a 13-3 rec-ord and a 2.91 ERA. He would win the AL Cy Young Award after the season.

This was the Junior Circuit's third consecutive victory and its fifth win in the last eight games, a string of wins that came after the NL had won eleven straight and nineteen of twenty games. The three AL victories represented the league's longest consecutive streak since it had won four in a row from 1946 through 1949.

Ozzie Smith made his tenth consecutive All-Star appearance and his eighth consecutive start for the NL at shortstop. AL shortstop Cal Ripken Jr. also made his eighth consecutive start in his ninth consecutive appearance.

The rosters included eighteen first-time All-Stars (twelve in the NL). Among these first-timers were the Alomar brothers, Roberto and Sandy, who became the twelfth brother combination in All-Star history. Sandy Jr. became the first rookie to start the All-Star Game since Wally Joyner had started in 1986 for California. Padres coach Sandy Alomar Sr. served as a batting practice pitcher for the NL. The senior Alomar had also been an All-Star with the Angels in 1970, and he became the first All-Star to have two sons as All-Stars. The only other family with three All-Stars had been the Di-Maggios, with brothers Joe, Dom, and Vince.

Other first-time players included two sons of All-Stars: Barry Bonds, son of Bobby, and Ken Griffey Jr. The strangest quirk among the first-time All-Stars was that there were two players, one on each team, with nearly identical names. The AL representative was Greggory William Olson, a relief pitcher for the Orioles, while the NL player was Gregory William Olson, a catcher for the Braves.

This game marked the last All-Star appearance for many players. Lance Parrish had a single and a walk in two plate appearances in his seventh and last All-Star Game appearance. He had been a member of eight squads for the Tigers, Phillies, and Angels. Seven-time All-Star Dave Parker made his first trip to the game as an American Leaguer as a representative of the Brewers. His previous trips had been with Pittsburgh and Cincinnati. This was Parker's last All-Star selection, but he did not play in the game. Steve Sax of the Yankees, the AL's starting second baseman, played in his fifth and last game and his second as a Yankee. Sax had played as a Dodger three times. Alan Trammell of the Tigers played in his fourth game on his sixth and last time as an All-Star, and Montreal third baseman Tim Wallach played in his fifth and last contest.

	AL		NL		
P	Bob Welch	OAK	Jack Armstrong		CIN
C	Sandy Alomar	CLE	Benito Santiago	+	SDN
1B	Mark McGwire	OAK	Will Clark		SFN
2B	Steve Sax	NYA	Ryne Sandberg		CHN
3B	Wade Boggs	BOS	Chris Sabo		CIN
SS	Cal Ripken	BAL	Ozzie Smith		SLN
OF	Jose Canseco	OAK	Andre Dawson		CHN
OF	Ken Griffey	SEA	Lenny Dykstra		PHI
OF	Rickey Henderson	OAK	Kevin Mitchell		SFN
	George Bell	TOR	Roberto Alomar		SDN
	Ellis Burks	+ BOS	Barry Bonds		PIT
	Roger Clemens	BOS	Bobby Bonilla		PIT
	Dennis Eckersley	OAK	Jeff Brantley		SFN
	Cecil Fielder	DET	Rob Dibble		CIN
	Chuck Finley	CAL	Shawon Dunston		CHN
	Julio Franco	TEX	John Franco		NYN
	Kelly Gruber	TOR	Tony Gwynn		SDN
	Ozzie Guillen	CHA	Neal Heaton		PIT
	Brook Jacoby	CLE	Barry Larkin		CIN
	Randy Johnson	SEA	Dennis Martinez		MON
	Doug Jones	CLE	Ramon Martinez		LAN
	Gregg Olson	BAL	Randy Myers		CIN
	Dave Parker	MIL	Greg Olson		ATL
	Lance Parrish	CAL	Mike Scioscia		LAN
	Kirby Puckett	MIN	Dave Smith		HOU
	Bret Saberhagen	KCA	Darryl Strawberry		NYN
	Dave Stieb	TOR	Frank Viola		NYN
	Bobby Thigpen	CHA	Tim Wallach		MON
	Alan Trammell	DET	Matt Williams		SFN

+ player replaced on roster

American League   000 000 200- 2
National League   000 000 000- 0

AMERICAN LEAGUE

	ab	r	h	bi	bb	so	po	a
R.Henderson, lf	3	0	0	0	0	1	2	0
O.Guillen, ss	2	0	0	0	0	0	0	2
W.Boggs, 3b	2	0	2	0	1	0	0	4
K.Gruber, pr-3b	1	0	0	0	1	0	0	1
J.Canseco, rf	4	0	0	0	1	1	1	0
C.Ripken, ss	2	0	0	0	0	0	1	1
G.Bell, ph-lf	2	0	0	0	0	1	2	0
K.Griffey Jr., cf	2	0	0	0	1	0	2	0
K.Puckett, ph-cf	1	0	1	0	0	0	1	0
M.McGwire, 1b	2	0	0	0	0	2	7	0
C.Fielder, ph-1b	1	0	0	0	1	0	3	1
S.Alomar Jr., c	3	1	2	0	0	0	3	0
B.Thigpen, p	0	0	0	0	0	0	1	0
A.Trammell, ph	1	0	0	0	0	0	0	0
C.Finley, p	0	0	0	0	0	0	0	0
D.Eckersley, p	0	0	0	0	0	0	0	0
S.Sax, 2b	1	0	0	0	1	0	0	1
B.Saberhagen, p	0	0	0	0	0	0	0	0
L.Parrish, ph-c	1	1	1	0	1	0	3	0
B.Welch, p	0	0	0	0	0	0	0	1
B.Jacoby, ph	1	0	0	0	0	0	0	0
D.Stieb, p	0	0	0	0	0	0	0	0
J.Franco, ph-2b	3	0	1	2	0	0	1	0
Totals	32	2	7	2	7	5	27	11

BATTING
2B: J.Franco (off R.Dibble).
RBI, scoring position, less than 2 outs: R.Henderson 0-1; O.Guillen 0-1; J.Canseco 0-2; G.Bell 0-1; A.Trammell 0-1; B.Jacoby 0-1; J.Franco 2-1.
GDP: S.Sax.

BASERUNNING
SB: K.Gruber 2 (Double SB 3rd base off D.Smith/M.Scioscia; 2nd base off R.Dibble/M.Scioscia); J.Canseco (Double SB 2nd base off D.Smith/M.Scioscia); S.Sax (2nd base off R.Martinez/M.Scioscia).
Team LOB: 10

NATIONAL LEAGUE

	ab	r	h	bi	bb	so	po	a
L.Dykstra, cf	4	0	1	0	0	0	3	0
R.Sandberg, 2b	3	0	0	0	0	0	1	2
R.Alomar, 2b	1	0	0	0	0	0	1	2
W.Clark, 1b	3	0	1	0	0	0	6	0
R.Myers, p	0	0	0	0	0	0	0	0
J.Franco, p	0	0	0	0	0	0	0	0
M.Williams, ph	1	0	0	0	0	1	0	0
K.Mitchell, lf	2	0	0	0	0	1	1	0
F.Viola, p	0	0	0	0	0	0	0	0
T.Wallach, 3b	2	0	0	0	0	0	0	0
A.Dawson, rf	2	0	0	0	0	1	1	0
D.Strawberry, rf	1	0	0	0	0	1	3	1
C.Sabo, 3b	2	0	0	0	0	0	0	2
D.Smith, p	0	0	0	0	0	0	0	0
J.Brantley, p	0	0	0	0	0	0	0	0
R.Dibble, p	0	0	0	0	0	0	0	0
B.Bonilla, 1b	1	0	0	0	0	0	1	0
M.Scioscia, c	2	0	0	0	0	1	6	0
G.Olson, ph-c	1	0	0	0	0	1	0	0
O.Smith, ss	1	0	0	0	0	0	1	1
D.Martinez, p	0	0	0	0	0	0	0	0
B.Bonds, lf	1	0	0	0	1	0	2	0
J.Armstrong, p	0	0	0	0	0	0	0	0
R.Martinez, p	0	0	0	0	0	0	0	0
T.Gwynn, ph	0	0	0	0	1	0	0	0
B.Larkin, pr-ss	0	0	0	0	0	0	1	2
S.Dunston, ss	2	0	0	0	0	0	0	0
Totals	29	0	2	0	2	6	27	10

BATTING

BASERUNNING
SB: B.Larkin (2nd base off D.Stieb/S.Alomar Jr.).
Team LOB: 4

FIELDING
E: D.Strawberry.
Outfield assist: D.Strawberry (J.Franco at home).
DP: (2). D.Strawberry-M.Scioscia; R.Sandberg-B.Larkin-W.Clark.

PITCHING	ip	h	r	er	bb	so
American League						
B.Welch	2.0	1	0	0	0	1
D.Stieb	2.0	0	0	0	1	1
B.Saberhagen (w)	2.0	0	0	0	0	1
B.Thigpen	1.0	0	0	0	0	1
C.Finley	1.0	0	0	0	1	1
D.Eckersley (s)	1.0	1	0	0	0	1
National League						
J.Armstrong	2.0	1	0	0	0	2
R.Martinez	1.0	0	0	0	2	1
D.Martinez	1.0	0	0	0	0	1
F.Viola	1.0	1	0	0	0	0
D.Smith	0.2	1	0	0	2	1
J.Brantley (L) *	0.1	2	2	2	0	0
R.Dibble	1.0	1	0	0	1	0
R.Myers	1.0	1	0	0	2	0
J.Franco	1.0	0	0	0	0	0

* Pitched to 2 batters in 7th

Inherited Runners—Scored:
D.Stieb 0–0; B.Saberhagen 0–0; B.Thigpen 0–0; C.Finley 0–0; D.Eckersley 0–0; R.Martinez 0–0; D.Martinez 0–0; F.Viola 0–0; D.Smith 0–0; J.Brantley 3–0; R.Dibble 2–2; R.Myers 0–0; J.Franco 0–0.

IBB: W.Boggs by R.Martinez; K.Griffey Jr. by D.Smith.

GAME DATA—T: 2:52; A: 39071; Temp: 68; Wind: From left, Speed: 16 mph

UMPIRES—HP: Ed Montague (NL), 1B: Dave Phillips (AL), 2B: Steve Rippley (NL), 3B: Mark Johnson (AL), LF: Dana DeMuth (NL), RF: Tim Welke (AL)

STARTING LINEUPS

	American League	*National League*
1.	R.Henderson lf	L.Dykstra cf
2.	W.Boggs 3b	R.Sandberg 2b
3.	J.Canseco rf	W.Clark 1b
4.	C.Ripken ss	K.Mitchell lf
5.	K.Griffey Jr. cf	A.Dawson rf
6.	M.McGwire 1b	C.Sabo 3b
7.	S.Alomar Jr. c	M.Scioscia c
8.	S.Sax 2b	O.Smith ss
9.	B.Welch p	J.Armstrong p

AL 1ST: R.Henderson flied to A.Dawson-rf; W.Boggs singled to third base; J.Canseco struck out; C.Ripken forced W.Boggs (O.Smith-ss to R.Sandberg-2b) [C.Ripken to first]; 0 R, 1 H, 0 E, 1 LOB. AL 0, NL 0.

NL 1ST: L.Dykstra flied to R.Henderson-lf; R.Sandberg grounded out (W.Boggs-3b to M.McGwire-1b); W.Clark singled to center field; K.Mitchell struck out; 0 R, 1 H, 0 E, 1 LOB. AL 0, NL 0.

AL 2ND: K.Griffey Jr. flied to K.Mitchell-lf in foul territory; M.McGwire struck out; S.Alomar Jr. popped to W.Clark-1b in foul territory; 0 R, 0 H, 0 E, 0 LOB. AL 0, NL 0.

NL 2ND: A.Dawson grounded out (B.Welch-p to M.McGwire-1b); C.Sabo grounded out (C.Ripken-ss to M.McGwire-1b); M.Scioscia lined to R.Henderson-lf; 0 R, 0 H, 0 E, 0 LOB. AL 0, NL 0.

AL 3RD: **R.Martinez replaced J.Armstrong (pitching);** S.Sax walked; **B.Jacoby batted for B.Welch;** S.Sax stole second; B.Jacoby grounded out (C.Sabo-3b to W.Clark-1b); R.Henderson struck out; W.Boggs was walked intentionally; J.Canseco forced W.Boggs (R.Sandberg-2b to O.Smith-ss) [J.Canseco to first]; 0 R, 0 H, 0 E, 2 LOB. AL 0, NL 0.

NL 3RD: **D.Stieb replaced B.Jacoby (pitching);** O.Smith lined to C.Ripken-ss; **T.Gwynn batted for R.Martinez;** T.Gwynn walked; **B.Larkin ran for T.Gwynn;** L.Dykstra flied to K.Griffey Jr.-cf; B.Larkin stole second; R.Sandberg grounded out (W.Boggs-3b to M.McGwire-1b); 0 R, 0 H, 0 E, 1 LOB. AL 0, NL 0.

AL 4TH: **D.Martinez replaced O.Smith (pitching); B.Larkin stayed in game (playing ss);** C.Ripken grounded out (C.Sabo-3b to W.Clark-1b); K.Griffey Jr. flied to L.Dykstra-cf; M.McGwire struck out; 0 R, 0 H, 0 E, 0 LOB. AL 0, NL 0.

NL 4TH: W.Clark grounded out (S.Sax-2b to M.McGwire-1b); K.Mitchell grounded out (W.Boggs-3b to M.McGwire-1b); A.Dawson struck out; 0 R, 0 H, 0 E, 0 LOB. AL 0, NL 0.

AL 5TH: **F.Viola replaced K.Mitchell (pitching); B.Bonds replaced D.Martinez (playing lf);**
S.Alomar Jr. singled to pitcher; S.Sax grounded into a double play (R.Sandberg-2b to B.Larkin-ss to W.Clark-1b) [S.Alomar Jr. out at second]; **J.Franco batted for D.Stieb;** J.Franco grounded out (B.Larkin-ss to W.Clark-1b); 0 R, 1 H, 0 E, 0 LOB. AL 0, NL 0.

NL 5TH: **B.Saberhagen replaced S.Sax (pitching); J.Franco stayed in game (playing 2b);** C.Sabo grounded out (W.Boggs-3b to M.McGwire-1b); M.Scioscia struck out; B.Bonds flied to J.Canseco-rf; 0 R, 0 H, 0 E, 0 LOB. AL 0, NL 0.

AL 6TH: **T.Wallach replaced F.Viola (playing 3b); D.Smith replaced C.Sabo (pitching); S.Dunston replaced B.Larkin (playing ss);** R.Henderson flied to B.Bonds-lf; W.Boggs singled to right field; **K.Gruber ran for W.Boggs;** J.Canseco walked [K.Gruber to second]; **G.Bell batted for C.Ripken;** G.Bell struck out; K.Gruber stole third and J.Canseco stole second; K.Griffey Jr. was walked intentionally; **C.Fielder batted for M.McGwire; J.Brantley replaced D.Smith (pitching);** C.Fielder flied to L.Dykstra-cf; 0 R, 1 H, 0 E, 3 LOB. AL 0, NL 0.

NL 6TH: **O.Guillen replaced R.Henderson (playing ss); K.Gruber stayed in game (playing 3b); G.Bell stayed in game (playing lf); C.Fielder stayed in game (playing 1b);** S.Dunston flied to G.Bell-lf; L.Dykstra flied to G.Bell-lf; R.Sandberg flied to K.Griffey Jr.-cf; 0 R, 0 H, 0 E, 0 LOB. AL 0, NL 0.

AL 7TH: **R.Alomar replaced R.Sandberg (playing 2b); D.Strawberry replaced A.Dawson (playing rf);** S.Alomar Jr. singled to shortstop; **L.Parrish batted for B.Saberhagen;** L.Parrish singled to right field [S.Alomar Jr. to third]; 1:08 rain delay; **R.Dibble replaced J.Brantley (pitching);** J.Franco doubled to right field [S.Alomar Jr. scored, L.Parrish scored]; O.Guillen grounded out (R.Alomar-2b to W.Clark-1b) [J.Franco to third]; K.Gruber walked; K.Gruber stole second; J.Canseco hit into a double play (D.Strawberry-rf to M.Scioscia-c) [J.Franco out at home]; 2 R, 3 H, 0 E, 1 LOB. AL 2, NL 0.

NL 7TH: **B.Thigpen replaced S.Alomar Jr. (pitching); L.Parrish stayed in game (playing c);** W.Clark grounded out (O.Guillen-ss to C.Fielder-1b); T.Wallach grounded out (C.Fielder-1b to B.Thigpen-p); D.Strawberry struck out; 0 R, 0 H, 0 E, 0 LOB. AL 2, NL 0.

AL 8TH: **R.Myers replaced W.Clark (pitching); B.Bonilla replaced R.Dibble (playing 1b);** G.Bell flied to D.Strawberry-rf; **K.Puckett batted for K.Griffey Jr.;** K.Puckett singled to right field [K.Puckett to third (error by D.Strawberry-rf)]; C.Fielder walked; **A.Trammell batted for B.Thigpen;** A.Trammell popped to R.Alomar-2b;

L.Parrish walked [C.Fielder to second]; J.Franco flied to D.Strawberry-rf; 0 R, 1 H, 1 E, 3 LOB. AL 2, NL 0.

NL 8TH: **K.Puckett stayed in game (playing cf);**
C.Finley replaced A.Trammell (pitching);
B.Bonilla grounded out (K.Gruber-3b to C.Fielder-1b); **G.Olson batted for M.Scioscia;** G.Olson struck out; B.Bonds walked; S.Dunston forced B.Bonds (O.Guillen-ss to J.Franco-2b) [S.Dunston to first]; 0 R, 0 H, 0 E, 1 LOB. AL 2, NL 0.

AL 9TH: **J.Franco replaced R.Myers (pitching);**
G.Olson stayed in game (playing c); O.Guillen grounded out (R.Alomar-2b to B.Bonilla-1b); K.Gruber flied to L.Dykstra-cf; J.Canseco flied to B.Bonds-lf; 0 R, 0 H, 0 E, 0 LOB. AL 2, NL 0.

NL 9TH: **D.Eckersley replaced C.Finley (pitching);**
L.Dykstra singled to center field; R.Alomar flied to K.Puckett-cf; **M.Williams batted for J.Franco;** M.Williams struck out; T.Wallach popped to C.Fielder-1b; 0 R, 1 H, 0 E, 1 LOB. AL 2, NL 0.

Final Totals	R	H	E	LOB
American League	2	7	0	10
National League	0	2	1	4

62

The NL Gets Ripped

The second All-Star Game to be played in Canada featured good baseball, old heroes, and national pride for two countries. Orioles iron man Cal Ripken Jr. provided all the runs the Junior Circuit needed with a three-run homer off former teammate Dennis Martinez of Montreal in the third inning. The rip came on a 2-1 slider that stayed up for Cal to power into the second deck just to the left of center field. Ripken, playing in his ninth consecutive All-Star Game, had been ineffective in previous All-Star competition, with only three singles in twenty at bats, but this performance earned him MVP honors. This recognition would be repeated after the season, when Ripken was named the AL MVP for 1991.

"I've been swinging the bat very well lately and that's the key—coming into the game hot," said Ripken. The homer meant that Ripken won two home run–hitting "contests" in Toronto. Ripken also won the annual long ball–hitting contest the day before the game, driving twelve of twenty-two pitches out of SkyDome. "I was concerned about being in the Home Run Derby because ordinarily when you try to hit home runs in batting practice, you get into bad habits," Ripken said. "In hindsight, maybe the Home Run Derby helped me to relax for the game."

Ripken's homer was only the third by an AL shortstop in an All-Star Game; Cleveland's Lou Boudreau hit the first in 1942, and Detroit's Dick McAuliffe hit the other in 1965. The dinger helped AL manager Tony La Russa of Oakland become the first man to manage three consecutive winning All-Star squads.

The fourth consecutive AL win, played before the largest crowd to watch a game in SkyDome since it opened in June 1989, featured an odd twist. An all-Canadian-team pitching decision included a win by Jimmy Key of the host Blue Jays and a loss for Martinez from Montreal. There had

been an all-Canadian-team decision in the 1984 All-Star Game, when Charlie Lea of Montreal beat Dave Stieb of Toronto. In the other All-Star Game in Canada, which had been played in Montreal in 1982, hometown pitcher Steve Rogers had started and won the game. SkyDome was the fourth covered facility to host the game, even though the roof was open for the contest. Previous indoor parks used for All-Star Games included the Astrodome in Houston, the Kingdome in Seattle, and the Metrodome in Minneapolis.

The starting pitchers provided a contrast of experience and youth. Scott Erickson of Minnesota was the hottest pitcher in the Majors but had been placed on the disabled list due to a sore elbow. In Erickson's place, his teammate Jack Morris, selected for his fifth and last All-Star team, made his third start for the AL. He had previously started in 1981 and 1985 as a representative of the Tigers. Morris, the winningest pitcher of the 1980s, was 11-6 at the All-Star break and had won eight consecutive games in May and June.

Morris's mound opponent was Tom Glavine, who was the first Braves pitcher to start the All-Star Game since the team had moved to Atlanta in 1966 and the first Braves starter since Warren Spahn in 1961. Glavine was enjoying his first consistent season and had twelve victories at the break, tied with fellow All-Star Mark Langston of California for the Major League lead. Glavine's 1.98 ERA led the NL for the first half of the season. To add to the Canadian theme, the Los Angeles Kings of the National Hockey League had once drafted Glavine. In speaking of his other sport, Glavine said, "Hockey played a factor in my aggressiveness on the mound."

Glavine was also happy about his selection as starter, saying, "This makes your whole existence in the game worthwhile. This kind of thing might be old hat for Ryne Sandberg or Cal Ripken, but it's my first time here, and it's just like this unbelievable dream where things just keep getting better and better." The Braves right-hander pitched well in his two innings, surrendering just one hit and one walk while striking out three batters.

The six runs scored in this game marked a higher total than recent All-Star Games, which had produced only thirty runs in seven previous games. The total might have been a portent of things to come, since the next three games produced forty-three runs.

The NL jumped out to a quick lead in the first inning when singles by San Diego's Tony Gwynn, San Francisco's Will Clark, and Pittsburgh's Bobby Bonilla produced the first tally. The run was the first scored by the NL since the eighth inning of the 1989 game (a ten-inning scoreless streak.) Bonilla's line drive struck the right heel of Morris and deflected for an infield hit, scoring Gwynn. Morris pitched the second inning but was later taken to the hospital for x-rays, which showed only a bruise. Morris refused to come out of the game after being struck in the first inning. "You only get to play in an All-Star Game a few times, and it was my foot that hurt and not my arm," he said.

The Cubs' Ryne Sandberg doubled with one out in the top of the third inning for the first NL extra-base hit since Tim Raines's triple in the thirteenth inning of the 1987 game. The AL took the lead in the bottom of the inning when Oakland's Rickey Henderson, appearing in his tenth All-Star Game, and Boston's Wade Boggs singled with one out. Ripken followed with his blast, and the AL never surrendered the lead. Cubs outfielder Andre Dawson greeted 1991 AL Cy Young Award winner Roger Clemens in the top of the fourth inning with the first NL homer since Dale Murphy's round-tripper in 1984. This was Dawson's eighth and last All-Star Game.

The Senior Circuit threatened in the sixth when Clark walked and Bonilla singled, but White Sox hurler Jack McDowell shut down the offense. The AL also failed to score after having two runners reach in the bottom of the inning. With two out, Mariner Ken Griffey Jr. singled to right, and Chicago catcher Carlton Fisk moved Griffey to third with a single to centerfield. Fisk, serving on his twelfth and last All-Star squad, became the oldest player — at forty-three years, seven months, and thirteen days — to collect a hit in an All-Star Game. He was also the third-oldest man to ever play in an All-Star Game, behind Satchel Paige (age forty-seven in 1953) and Pete Rose (age forty-four in 1985).

In the top of the seventh, Boston's Jeff Reardon retired the first two batters he faced. Gwynn then singled for the second time, and NL Manager Lou Piniella of Cincinnati inserted Dodger Brett Butler as a pinch runner. La Russa countered with the Twins closer Rick Aguilera. "We had talked about how Aguilera was quicker to the plate. We said if it was a one-run game and they got a stolen base guy on, we could use Aguilera in that situation," La Russa said later. After surrendering a single to Juan Samuel, Aguilera struck out Dodger Eddie Murray to end the threat. It was Murray's first appearance as a National Leaguer after being named to seven AL squads, and it was also his last All-Star appearance.

In the bottom of the seventh, Blue Jay outfielder Joe Carter, playing in his first All-Star Game, singled in front of the home fans. Pinch hitter Paul Molitor of the Brewers reached on the first catcher's interference in All-Star history (by Craig Biggio, in his first All-Star Game), and pinch hitter Ozzie Guillen from Chicago sacrificed the runners along. Texas Ranger Rafael Palmeiro, the third consecutive pinch hitter employed by La Russa, was walked intentionally, and Oakland's designated hitter Harold Baines hit a sacrifice fly to right field to plate Carter with the final run.

Oakland's Dennis Eckersley pitched a perfect ninth inning to record his third All-Star save, thus passing Bruce Sutter for the record. The Eck had previously saved the 1988 and 1990 games; Sutter's came in 1980 and 1981.

This was the fourth straight victory by the AL, tying the longest streak ever by the Junior Circuit (from 1946 through 1949), and it followed a long run of NL domination. From 1960 to 1985, the Senior Circuit won twenty-five of twenty-nine All-Star Games. The NL had won eight in a row and eleven in a row during that time. Eckersley talked about the relative length of the AL streak: "It means something because the National League can't say anything. Even though it doesn't mean that we're better than they are, at least we can keep them quiet."

The AL had adopted the NL's manner of playing the game. AL coach Tom Kelly of the Twins said, "Let's play it like a baseball game and not an exhibition." Tony La Russa agreed: "I had watched the National League for a couple of years as a coach. I watched them tonight, and they're starting runners and things like that. I mean, they're not just standing there waiting for somebody to put a pretty swing on it. They're playing baseball, and I think that's the way this game should be played."

The other dugout expressed the same desire to win. The Mets' Howard Johnson left no doubt in anyone's mind by saying, "I want to win. I want to stick it to the American League." Gwynn added to the sentiment: "Back in 1984, at my first All-

Star Game, I remember Tom Lasorda standing in the middle of the clubhouse and saying, 'National League pride, gentlemen, National League pride — that's what it's all about.' Then, for a while in the past couple of years, there wasn't as much ramming it down our throats. With Lou [Piniella], that could definitely change."

Even with that attitude, many players expressed a desire to enjoy their All-Star experience. Brett Butler, one of eighteen first-timers, said, "The idea is to have fun. I want to win, but first I want to have a good time. When I got here, I said to Tony Gwynn, 'Can I carry your bags for you?' And I would have done it, because I'm so thrilled just to be here."

The NL's leading vote getter for the second year in a row was Sandberg. Ken Griffey Jr. paced all of the AL players.

Leading up to the game was the usual discussion about players not selected. This year, it was the fans who were the target as two of the starters were questioned. Strangely enough, the two elected players were the brothers Sandy Jr. and Roberto Alomar, who for the second year in a row played in the game; however, this year they were teammates and batted eighth and ninth in the AL order. The fans' choice of Sandy, the 1990 AL Rookie of the Year, was questioned because of his statistics at the All-Star break: no home runs and only four RBI. Detroit's Mickey Tettleton had fifteen homers and forty-four RBI at the break, and the Yankees' Matt Nokes had eleven and forty-three, including

six RBI just three days before the All-Star Game. However, neither was chosen as Alomar's backup because that honor went to Carlton Fisk, with seven homers and thirty-six RBI. The choice of Roberto Alomar was questioned primarily by Rangers second baseman Julio Franco, who believed he should have been the starter. Franco spoke out often about his feelings, and Alomar reacted by saying, "If he wants to talk, let him keep talking. I'm just here to play." Franco later apologized to Alomar, saying that his frustration was aimed at the fans' voting, not at Roberto.

U.S. president George Bush and Canadian prime minister Brian Mulroney attended the game. It was Bush's third All-Star contest, for he had attended two while vice president: Cleveland in 1981 and Cincinnati in 1988. Earlier in the day, Bush had honored two of the game's greatest living legends, Ted Williams and Joe DiMaggio, at a White House ceremony. The salute was in celebration of the fiftieth anniversary of their 1941 exploits, when Williams batted .406 and DiMaggio hit safely in fifty-six consecutive games. Bush then took the Hall of Famers, along with Commissioner Fay Vincent, to the game in Toronto aboard Air Force One, the president's official aircraft. Appropriately, these two old heroes watched Cal Ripken Jr. win the game with his three-run homer; DiMaggio had been a teammate of another iron man, Lou Gehrig, and Williams had won the 1941 All-Star Game with a three-run homer.

	AL		NL	
P	Jack Morris	MIN	Tom Glavine	ATL
C	Sandy Alomar	CLE	Benito Santiago	SDN
1B	Mark McGwire +	OAK	Will Clark	SFN
2B	Roberto Alomar	TOR	Ryne Sandberg	CHN
3B	Wade Boggs	BOS	Chris Sabo	CIN
SS	Cal Ripken	BAL	Ozzie Smith	SLN
OF	Ken Griffey	SEA	Andre Dawson	CHN
OF	Dave Henderson	OAK	Tony Gwynn	SDN
OF	Rickey Henderson	OAK	Darryl Strawberry +	LAN
DH	Danny Tartabull	KCA	Bobby Bonilla	PIT
	Rick Aguilera	MIN	George Bell	CHN
	Harold Baines	OAK	Craig Biggio	HOU
	Joe Carter	TOR	Tom Browning	CIN
	Roger Clemens	BOS	Brett Butler	LAN
	Dennis Eckersley	OAK	Ivan Calderon	MON
	Cecil Fielder	DET	Rob Dibble	CIN
	Carlton Fisk	CHA	Pete Harnisch	HOU
	Julio Franco	TEX	Howard Johnson	NYN
	Ozzie Guillen	CHA	Felix Jose	SLN
	Bryan Harvey	CAL	John Kruk	PHI
	Jimmy Key	TOR	Barry Larkin	CIN
	Mark Langston	CAL	Dennis Martinez	MON
	Jack McDowell	CHA	Ramon Martinez +	LAN
	Paul Molitor	MIL	Mike Morgan	LAN
	Rafael Palmeiro	TEX	Eddie Murray	LAN
	Kirby Puckett	MIN	Paul O'Neill	CIN
	Jeff Reardon	BOS	Juan Samuel	LAN
	Scott Sanderson	NYA	John Smiley	PIT
	Ruben Sierra	TEX	Lee Smith	SLN
			Frank Viola	NYN

+ player replaced on roster

```
National League    100  100  000-  2
American League    003  000  10X-  4
```

NATIONAL LEAGUE

	ab	r	h	bi	bb	so	po	a
T.Gwynn, cf	4	1	2	0	0	0	6	0
B.Butler, pr-cf	1	0	0	0	0	0	0	0
R.Sandberg, 2b	3	0	1	0	0	0	2	1
J.Samuel, 2b	1	0	1	0	0	0	2	1
W.Clark, 1b	2	0	1	0	1	0	2	0
E.Murray, 1b	1	0	0	0	0	1	3	0
B.Bonilla, dh	4	0	2	1	0	1	0	0
A.Dawson, rf	2	1	1	1	0	0	0	0
F.Jose, rf	2	0	1	0	0	0	1	0
I.Calderon, lf	2	0	1	0	0	0	1	0
P.O'Neill, ph-lf	2	0	0	0	0	1	0	0
C.Sabo, 3b	2	0	0	0	0	0	1	0
H.Johnson, ph-3b	2	0	0	0	0	1	0	0
B.Santiago, c	3	0	0	0	0	1	4	0
C.Biggio, c	1	0	0	0	0	0	2	0
O.Smith, ss	1	0	0	0	1	0	0	1
B.Larkin, ss	1	0	0	0	0	0	0	2
G.Bell, ph	1	0	0	0	0	1	0	0
Totals	35	2	10	2	2	6	24	5

AMERICAN LEAGUE

	ab	r	h	bi	bb	so	po	a
R.Henderson, lf	2	1	1	0	0	0	0	0
J.Carter, lf	1	1	1	0	1	0	1	0
W.Boggs, 3b	2	1	1	0	1	0	1	2
P.Molitor, ph-3b	0	0	0	0	0	0	0	0
C.Ripken, ss	3	1	2	3	0	0	2	1
O.Guillen, ph-ss	0	0	0	0	0	0	1	0
C.Fielder, 1b	3	0	0	0	0	1	6	3
R.Palmeiro, ph-1b	0	0	0	0	1	0	2	0
D.Tartabull, dh	2	0	0	0	0	1	0	0
H.Baines, ph	1	0	0	1	0	0	0	0
D.Henderson, rf	2	0	0	0	0	1	2	0
R.Sierra, ph-rf	2	0	0	0	0	2	0	0
K.Griffey Jr., cf	3	0	2	0	0	0	2	0
K.Puckett, cf	1	0	0	0	0	0	0	0
S.Alomar Jr., c	2	0	0	0	0	0	2	0
C.Fisk, c	2	0	1	0	0	1	5	0
R.Alomar, 2b	4	0	0	0	0	0	2	4
Totals	30	4	8	4	3	6	26	10

PITCHING	ip	h	r	er	bb	so
National League						
T.Glavine	2.0	1	0	0	1	3
D.Martinez (L)	2.0	4	3	3	0	0
F.Viola	1.0	0	0	0	1	0
P.Harnisch	1.0	2	0	0	0	1
J.Smiley	* 0.0	1	1	1	0	0
R.Dibble	1.0	0	0	0	1	1
M.Morgan	1.0	0	0	0	0	1
American League						
J.Morris	2.0	4	1	1	0	1
J.Key (w)	1.0	1	0	0	0	1
R.Clemens	1.0	1	1	1	0	0
J.McDowell	2.0	1	0	0	2	0
J.Reardon	0.2	1	0	0	0	0
R.Aguilera	1.1	2	0	0	0	3
D.Eckersley (s)	1.0	0	0	0	0	1

* Pitched to 2 batters in 7th

BATTING
2B: R.Sandberg (off J.Key).
HR: A.Dawson (4th inning off R.Clemens, 0 on, 0 out).
RBI, scoring position, less than 2 outs: W.Clark 0–1; B.Bonilla 1–1; A.Dawson 0–1; F.Jose 0–1; P.O'Neill 0–1; B.Santiago 0–1.
GDP: T.Gwynn; A.Dawson.

BASERUNNING
SB: I.Calderon (3rd base off J.Morris / S.Alomar Jr.).
Team LOB: 8

FIELDING
E: C.Biggio (interference).

BATTING
HR: C.Ripken (3rd inning off D.Martinez, 2 on, 1 out).
RBI, scoring position, less than 2 outs: C.Ripken 1–1; C.Fielder 0–1; H.Baines 1–2.
S: O.Guillen.
SF: H.Baines.

BASERUNNING
Team LOB: 8

FIELDING
DP: (2). W.Boggs-R.Alomar-C.Fielder [2].

Inherited Runners—Scored:
D.Martinez 0–0; F.Viola 0–0; P.Harnisch 0–0; J.Smiley 0–0; R.Dibble 2–1; M.Morgan 0–0; J.Key 0–0; R.Clemens 0–0; J.McDowell 0–0; J.Reardon 0–0; R.Aguilera 1–0; D.Eckersley 0–0.
IBB: R.Palmeiro by R.Dibble.

GAME DATA—T: 3:04; A: 52383; Temp: Unknown; Wind: Unknown direction, Speed: 0 mph

UMPIRES—HP: Joe Brinkman (AL), 1B: John McSherry (NL), 2B: Ken Kaiser (AL), 3B: Jim Quick (NL), LF: Larry Young (AL), RF: Greg Bonin (NL)

STARTING LINEUPS

	National League	*American League*
1.	T.Gwynn cf	R.Henderson lf
2.	R.Sandberg 2b	W.Boggs 3b
3.	W.Clark 1b	C.Ripken ss
4.	B.Bonilla dh	C.Fielder 1b
5.	A.Dawson rf	D.Tartabull dh
6.	I.Calderon lf	D.Henderson rf
7.	C.Sabo 3b	K.Griffey Jr. cf
8.	B.Santiago c	S.Alomar Jr. c
9.	O.Smith ss	R.Alomar 2b
	T.Glavine p	J.Morris p

NL 1ST: third consecutive win for LaRussa; T.Gwynn singled to left field; R.Sandberg flied to D.Henderson-rf; W.Clark singled to right field [T.Gwynn to third]; B.Bonilla singled to pitcher [T.Gwynn scored, W.Clark to second]; off Morris' right ankle (x-rays negative); A.Dawson grounded into a double play (W.Boggs-3b to R.Alomar-2b to C.Fielder-1b) [B.Bonilla out at second]; 1 R, 3 H, 0 E, 1 LOB. NL 1, AL 0.

AL 1ST: R.Henderson popped to W.Clark-1b in foul territory; W.Boggs walked; C.Ripken singled to center field [W.Boggs to second]; C.Fielder struck out; D.Tartabull struck out; 0 R, 1 H, 0 E, 2 LOB. NL 1, AL 0.

NL 2ND: I.Calderon singled to right field; C.Sabo grounded out (J.Morris-p to C.Fielder-1b) [I.Calderon to second]; B.Santiago struck out while I.Calderon stole third; O.Smith lined to C.Ripken-ss; 0 R, 1 H, 0 E, 1 LOB. NL 1, AL 0.

AL 2ND: D.Henderson struck out; K.Griffey Jr. flied to T.Gwynn-cf; S.Alomar Jr. flied to T.Gwynn-cf; 0 R, 0 H, 0 E, 0 LOB. NL 1, AL 0.

NL 3RD: **J.Key replaced J.Morris (pitching);** T.Gwynn lined to C.Fielder-1b; R.Sandberg doubled to left-center; first NL extra-base hit since 1987; W.Clark grounded out (C.Fielder-1b to J.Key-p) [R.Sandberg to third]; B.Bonilla struck out; 0 R, 1 H, 0 E, 1 LOB. NL 1, AL 0.

AL 3RD: **D.Martinez replaced T.Glavine (pitching);** R.Alomar flied to I.Calderon-lf; R.Henderson singled to center field; W.Boggs singled to second base [R.Henderson to second]; C.Ripken homered to centerfield [R.Henderson scored, W.Boggs scored]; C.Fielder grounded out (R.Sandberg-2b to W.Clark-1b); D.Tartabull lined to C.Sabo-3b; 3 R, 3 H, 0 E, 0 LOB. NL 1, AL 3.

NL 4TH: **R.Clemens replaced J.Key (pitching); J.Carter replaced R.Henderson (playing lf);** A.Dawson homered to centerfield; I.Calderon flied to K.Griffey Jr.-cf; C.Sabo flied to J.Carter-lf; B.Santiago flied to K.Griffey Jr.-cf; 1 R, 1 H, 0 E, 0 LOB. NL 2, AL 3.

AL 4TH: **F.Jose replaced A.Dawson (playing rf);** D.Henderson flied to T.Gwynn-cf; K.Griffey Jr. singled to center field; S.Alomar Jr. forced K.Griffey Jr. (O.Smith-ss to R.Sandberg-2b) [S.Alomar Jr. to first]; R.Alomar lined to R.Sandberg-2b; 0 R, 1 H, 0 E, 1 LOB. NL 2, AL 3.

NL 5TH: **J.McDowell replaced R.Clemens (pitching); C.Fisk replaced S.Alomar Jr. (playing c);** O.Smith walked; T.Gwynn grounded into a double play (W.Boggs-3b to R.Alomar-2b to C.Fielder-1b) [O.Smith out at second]; R.Sandberg flied to D.Henderson-rf; 0 R, 0 H, 0 E, 0 LOB. NL 2, AL 3.

AL 5TH: **F.Viola replaced D.Martinez (pitching); B.Larkin replaced O.Smith (playing ss); J.Samuel replaced R.Sandberg (playing 2b);** J.Carter walked; W.Boggs flied to T.Gwynn-cf; C.Ripken forced J.Carter (B.Larkin-ss to J.Samuel-2b) [C.Ripken to first]; C.Fielder flied to T.Gwynn-cf; 0 R, 0 H, 0 E, 1 LOB. NL 2, AL 3.

NL 6TH: W.Clark walked; B.Bonilla singled [W.Clark to second]; F.Jose forced B.Bonilla (C.Fielder-1b to C.Ripken-ss) [W.Clark to third, F.Jose to first]; **P.O'Neill batted for I.Calderon;** P.O'Neill reached on a fielder's choice (C.Fielder-1b to C.Fisk-c) [W.Clark out at home, F.Jose to second]; **H.Johnson batted for C.Sabo;** H.Johnson popped to W.Boggs-3b in foul territory; 0 R, 1 H, 0 E, 2 LOB. NL 2, AL 3.

AL 6TH: **P.Harnisch replaced F.Viola (pitching); E.Murray replaced W.Clark (playing 1b); H.Johnson stayed in game (playing 3b); P.O'Neill stayed in game (playing lf); H.Baines batted for D.Tartabull;** H.Baines grounded out (J.Samuel-2b to E.Murray-1b); **R.Sierra batted for D.Henderson;** R.Sierra struck out; K.Griffey Jr. singled to right field; C.Fisk singled to center field [K.Griffey Jr. to third]; R.Alomar flied to T.Gwynn-cf; 0 R, 2 H, 0 E, 2 LOB. NL 2, AL 3.

NL 7TH: **J.Reardon replaced J.McDowell (pitching); R.Sierra stayed in game (playing rf); K.Puckett replaced K.Griffey Jr. (playing cf);** B.Santiago grounded out (R.Alomar-2b to C.Fielder-1b); B.Larkin grounded out (C.Ripken-ss to C.Fielder-1b); T.Gwynn singled to left field; **B.Butler ran for T.Gwynn; R.Aguilera replaced J.Reardon (pitching);** J.Samuel singled to left field [B.Butler to second]; E.Murray struck out; 0 R, 2 H, 0 E, 2 LOB. NL 2, AL 3.

AL 7TH: **J.Smiley replaced P.Harnisch (pitching); B.Butler stayed in game (playing cf); C.Biggio replaced B.Santiago (playing c);** J.Carter singled to left field; **P.Molitor batted for W.Boggs;** P.Molitor reached on catcher's interference by C.Biggio [J.Carter to second]; **R.Dibble replaced J.Smiley (pitching); O.Guillen batted for C.Ripken;**

O.Guillen out on a sacrifice bunt (R.Dibble-p to J.Samuel-2b) [J.Carter to third, P.Molitor to second]; **R.Palmeiro batted for C.Fielder;** R.Palmeiro was walked intentionally; H.Baines out on a sacrifice fly to F.Jose-rf [J.Carter scored, P.Molitor to third]; R.Sierra struck out; 1 R, 1 H, 1 E, 2 LOB. NL 2, AL 4.

NL 8TH: **R.Palmeiro stayed in game (playing 1b); O.Guillen stayed in game (playing ss); P.Molitor stayed in game (playing 3b);** B.Bonilla popped to O.Guillen-ss; F.Jose singled to right field; P.O'Neill struck out; H.Johnson struck out; 0 R, 1 H, 0 E, 1 LOB. NL 2, AL 4.

AL 8TH: **M.Morgan replaced R.Dibble (pitching);**
K.Puckett grounded out (B.Larkin-ss to E.Murray-1b); C.Fisk struck out; R.Alomar grounded out (M.Morgan-p to E.Murray-1b); 0 R, 0 H, 0 E, 0 LOB. NL 2, AL 4.

NL 9TH: **D.Eckersley replaced R.Aguilera (pitching);** C.Biggio grounded out (R.Alomar-2b to R.Palmeiro-1b); **G.Bell batted for B.Larkin;** G.Bell struck out; B.Butler grounded out (D.Eckersley-p to R.Palmeiro-1b); 0 R, 0 H, 0 E, 0 LOB. NL 2, AL 4.

Final Totals	R	H	E	LOB
National League	2	10	1	8
American League	4	8	0	8

63

Offensive by the Sea

The second All-Star Game in San Diego featured an offensive explosion the likes of which had not been seen in the midsummer classic in years. The teams set or tied ten records during the one-sided affair. This was in direct opposition to the game's recent history; there had been thirty-seven total runs scored in the previous eight contests, and the winning club had scored three or fewer runs five times in those eight games. The AL scored six times by the third inning in this game. The players agreed before the game that the hitters have a difficult task in the All-Star Game because they face unfamiliar pitchers, usually for one plate appearance in the game. The supposed advantage for the pitchers was not in evidence at Jack Murphy Stadium this night, however, as the batters had the upper hand.

The game's nineteen runs represented the second-highest total ever, behind only the 1954 game, which the AL won 11–9. The AL's thirteen runs tied the 1983 AL squad for most runs in a game, and the seventeen hits for the Junior Circuit set a record by topping the 1954 AL's seventeen. The hit total by both teams (thirty-one) tied the 1954 game. In addition, the NL pitchers surrendered thirteen earned runs, topping the previous record of twelve set in 1946 by the NL. The AL batters also tied the 1977 NL team by scoring four times in the first inning. NL starter Tom Glavine set two records by surrendering nine total hits, two more than Tommy Bridges in 1937, and seven in one inning, topping Atlee Hammaker's six in the third inning of the 1983 contest. The AL's twenty-nine total bases tied the mark set by the 1954 AL club, and the American Leaguers knocked out seven consecutive hits in the first inning, setting another record.

The AL started early to win its fifth consecutive game. After Toronto's Roberto Alomar grounded out in the first inning, Red Sox third baseman Wade Boggs (serving on his eighth consecutive AL squad), the Twins' Kirby Puckett (on his seventh squad), and the Blue Jays' Joe Carter each singled to center field to load the bases. Oakland first baseman Mark McGwire, playing in his sixth consecutive game, sent a change-up to center to score Boggs and Puckett. Baltimore's Cal Ripken Jr. (in his tenth straight game) knocked in Carter with a single to right, and Ken Griffey Jr. scored Mc-Gwire with yet another single to center. Cleveland's catcher Sandy Alomar Jr. finished the string with the AL's seventh consecutive single.

After the Rangers' Kevin Brown, in his first All-Star appearance, set the NL down in order while throwing only nine pitches, the AL batters got back to work in the second inning. Roberto Alomar singled to center and stole second and third, while both Boggs and Puckett made outs. It was the first time in All-Star history that a player had stolen two bases in one inning. Carter again singled to center, scoring Roberto Alomar, and that was all for starter Tom Glavine.

The Braves pitcher was the first to start consecutive All-Star Games for the NL since Don Drysdale had started both games in 1959, but Glavine was pounded for nine hits and five runs in the one and one-third innings he worked. The defending NL Cy Young Award winner came into the contest having won thirteen NL games, and he led the league in most categories but could not best the AL sluggers.

"There's not much you can do about it," Glavine said after the game. "Things didn't go well tonight, but when they get seven hits in a row, what are you going to do?" Glavine perhaps was being modest since four of those hits came on broken bats. He went on to say, "I'd have almost rather given up a six-hundred-foot homer than be blooped to death. It's unfortunate the way things went because a lot of people were watching, but in two weeks nobody will remember this, and by Saturday when I pitch in Houston, I won't remember this."

San Diego's Tony Gwynn, who viewed Glavine's

outing from right field, said later, "They dropped some grenades on us there. Being behind second base, that was like being in a minefield there in the first inning. They weren't hitting the ball hard off him, but they were hitting it to the right spots. Andy Van Slyke and I were talking about putting in a rover."

NL skipper Bobby Cox, for whom Glavine was the number one starter in Atlanta, talked about the first inning after the game: "I'd say 90 percent of those hits were off the end of the bat. They weren't hit very hard. It wasn't a good performance, but it wasn't like he was ripped."

In the third inning, twenty-two-year-old Ken Griffey Jr. homered to left field to increase the AL lead to 6–0. The blast completed a family event as Griffey and his father, Ken Griffey Sr., became the first father-son pair to each homer in All-Star competition. The senior Griffey, an outfielder for the Reds, smashed his in the 1980 game. Junior, who had a single, a double, and the homer in three plate appearances and knocked in two runs, was named the game's MVP, becoming the youngest player ever to win the award. His dad was the MVP of the 1980 game, making them the first family to be so named. The family theme was quite evident for the Junior Circuit since the starting lineup featured three "juniors": Griffey, Cal Ripken Jr. (son of Orioles third base coach Cal Sr.), and Sandy Alomar Jr. (son of former Major Leaguer Sandy Sr.). Sandy's brother, Roberto, also started for the AL.

Griffey, at twenty-two years and eight months, became the second-youngest All-Star player to start three times (he was just two months older than Al Kaline was in 1955–58). Bobby Cox remembered watching Griffey play in high school and called him "the best prospect I ever saw."

The NL got its first two hits in the third as pinch hitter Larry Walker of the Expos beat out an infield single and Cardinals shortstop Ozzie Smith, on his twelfth consecutive NL squad, doubled Walker to third. After Gwynn walked to load the bases, the players were stranded when Pirate Barry Bonds popped out.

The visitors ran the lead to 10–0 in the sixth. Griffey doubled and, after two ground outs, so did Cleveland's Carlos Baerga and Robin Ventura. White Sox third baseman Ventura celebrated his twenty-fifth birthday as an All-Star. Ruben Sierra then lined a homer to right field; at the All-Star break, he was a Ranger, but he was traded later in the season to Oakland.

The NL finally scored in its half of the sixth when Bonds hit a grounder to first that took a bad hop over Brewer Paul Molitor's shoulder, and Fred

McGriff drove him in with a single to left. It was somewhat appropriate that a Padre knocked in the first run since twelve current and former Padres were members of the two All-Star contingents. The five current Padres represented the largest group of All-Stars for a host team since the Expos also had five All-Stars in 1982, but the number of current Padres seemed a bit large given the team's 47-42 record at the break. The former Padres included Joe Carter, Sandy Jr. and Roberto Alomar, Carlos Baerga, John Kruk, Ozzie Smith, and Bip Roberts.

Indians pitcher Charles Nagy had an infield single in the eighth inning. It was the first hit by an AL pitcher since Ken McBride had singled in the second inning of the 1963 game.

Hidden among all of the offense were a few good pitching performances. In addition to Kevin Brown in the first, the following AL hurlers threw perfect innings: Chicago's Jack McDowell (the second), the Orioles' Mike Mussina (the fifth), and Cleveland's Charles Nagy (the seventh). For the NL, the Mets' David Cone threw a perfect third inning, and Cincinnati's Norm Charlton a perfect ninth.

Brown became the first Ranger pitcher to start an All-Star Game and the first for the franchise since Washington Senators pitcher Dave Stenhouse started the second game in 1962. Brown came into the break with a Major League–leading fourteen wins, six of them complete games. Brown, a first-time All-Star, won nine of his last eleven starts before the break.

President George Bush attended the game with a foreign head of state for the second year in a row. The previous year, his guest had been Canadian prime minister Brian Mulroney, and this year he brought Mexican president Carlos Salinas de Gortari. Bush accompanied Hall of Famer Ted Williams onto the field while Williams threw out the ceremonial pitch.

The roster controversy of the year centered around the absence of Detroit slugger Cecil Fielder, whose eighteen homers and seventy-five RBIS were not enough for an invitation. His RBI total led the majors at the break. There were many veteran players on the two squads, but the teams also featured twenty-four first-time All-Stars. There were no rookies on either team, and Ivan "Pudge" Rodriguez became the first All-Star born in the 1970s. This was the last All-Star appearance by Dennis Eckersley. The Eck was an All-Star in 1977 with Cleveland, in 1982 with Boston, and in 1988, 1990, 1991, and 1992 with Oakland. He would win both the AL Cy Young Award and the MVP Award after the season.

The fans cast the most votes for Ripken, and Ryne Sandberg led the voting in the NL for the third consecutive year.

Doug Harvey, behind the plate in his sixth All-Star Game, announced his retirement effective at the end of the season. Harvey had spent thirty years in the NL.

A technical innovation for the CBS television broadcast was a camera in the first base bag. Dubbed the "base cam," it gave fans an unusual look at runners diving into the bag.

	AL		NL	
P	Kevin Brown	TEX	Tom Glavine	ATL
C	Sandy Alomar	CLE	Benito Santiago	SDN
1B	Mark McGwire	OAK	Fred McGriff	SDN
2B	Roberto Alomar	TOR	Ryne Sandberg	CHN
3B	Wade Boggs	BOS	Terry Pendleton	ATL
SS	Cal Ripken	BAL	Ozzie Smith	SLN
OF	Jose Canseco +	OAK	Barry Bonds	PIT
OF	Ken Griffey	SEA	Tony Gwynn	SDN
OF	Kirby Puckett	MIN	Andy Van Slyke	PIT
	Rick Aguilera	MIN	Craig Biggio	HOU
	Brady Anderson	BAL	Norm Charlton	CIN
	Carlos Baerga	CLE	Will Clark	SFN
	Joe Carter	TOR	David Cone	NYN
	Roger Clemens	BOS	Darren Daulton	PHI
	Dennis Eckersley	OAK	Tony Fernandez	SDN
	Travis Fryman	DET	Ron Gant	ATL
	Juan Guzman	TOR	Doug Jones	HOU
	Bobby Kelly	NYA	John Kruk	PHI
	Chuck Knoblauch	MIN	Greg Maddux	CHN
	Mark Langston	CAL	Dennis Martinez	MON
	Edgar Martinez	SEA	Tom Pagnozzi	SLN
	Jack McDowell	CHA	Bip Roberts	CIN
	Paul Molitor	MIL	Mike Sharperson	LAN
	Jeff Montgomery	KCA	Gary Sheffield	SDN
	Mike Mussina	BAL	Lee Smith	SLN
	Charles Nagy	CLE	John Smoltz	ATL
	Ivan Rodriguez	TEX	Bob Tewksbury	SLN
	Ruben Sierra	TEX	Larry Walker	MON
	Robin Ventura	CHA		

+ player replaced on roster

American League   411 004 030-13
National League   000 001 032- 6

AMERICAN LEAGUE

	ab	r	h	bi	bb	so	po	a
R.Alomar, 2b	3	1	1	0	0	0	0	1
C.Baerga, 2b	1	1	1	1	0	0	1	2
C.Nagy, p	1	1	1	0	0	0	0	0
J.Montgomery, p	0	0	0	0	0	0	0	0
R.Aguilera, p	1	0	0	0	0	1	0	0
D.Eckersley, p	0	0	0	0	0	0	0	0
W.Boggs, 3b	3	1	1	0	0	1	1	0
R.Ventura, 3b	2	1	2	1	0	0	1	1
K.Puckett, lf	3	1	1	0	0	1	2	0
R.Clemens, p	0	0	0	0	0	0	0	0
R.Sierra, rf	2	2	1	2	0	0	1	0
J.Carter, rf	3	1	2	1	0	0	1	0
T.Fryman, ss	1	1	1	1	1	0	0	3
M.McGwire, 1b	3	1	1	2	0	0	4	0
P.Molitor, ph-1b	2	0	1	0	0	1	5	0
C.Ripken, ss	3	0	1	1	0	0	1	1
M.Mussina, p	0	0	0	0	0	0	0	0
R.Kelly, cf	2	0	1	2	0	1	1	0
K.Griffey Jr., cf	3	2	3	2	0	0	1	0
I.Rodriguez, c	2	0	0	0	0	1	4	0
S.Alomar Jr., c	3	0	1	0	0	0	3	0
M.Langston, p	0	0	0	0	0	0	0	0
C.Knoblauch, ph-2b	1	0	0	0	1	0	0	0
K.Brown, p	1	0	0	0	0	1	0	0
J.McDowell, p	0	0	0	0	0	0	0	0
E.Martinez, ph	1	0	0	0	0	0	0	0
J.Guzman, p	0	0	0	0	0	0	0	0
B.Anderson, lf	3	0	0	0	0	0	1	0
Totals	44	13	19	13	2	7	27	8

BATTING

2B: K.Griffey Jr. (off B.Tewksbury); C.Baerga (off B.Tewksbury); R.Ventura (off B.Tewksbury); R.Kelly (off D.Jones).

HR: R.Sierra (6th inning off B.Tewksbury, 1 on, 2 out); K.Griffey Jr. (3rd inning off G.Maddux, 0 on, 1 out).

2-out RBI: C.Baerga; R.Ventura; R.Sierra 2; J.Carter; R.Kelly 2; K.Griffey Jr..

RBI, scoring position, less than 2 outs: K.Puckett 0–1; R.Sierra 0–1; T.Fryman 1–1; M.McGwire 2–2; P.Molitor 0–1; C.Ripken 1–1; S.Alomar Jr. 0–1; B.Anderson 0–1.

BASERUNNING

SB: R.Alomar 2 (2nd base off T.Glavine/B.Santiago; 3rd base off T.Glavine/B.Santiago).

Team LOB: 6

FIELDING

E: P.Molitor (fumble).

DP: (1). C.Baerga-C.Ripken-M.McGwire.

NATIONAL LEAGUE

	ab	r	h	bi	bb	so	po	a
O.Smith, ss	3	0	1	0	0	1	1	1
T.Fernandez, ss	2	1	1	0	0	0	3	0
T.Gwynn, rf	2	0	0	0	1	0	0	2
J.Kruk, rf	2	1	2	0	0	0	0	1
B.Bonds, lf	3	1	1	0	0	0	2	0
B.Roberts, lf	2	1	2	2	0	0	0	0
F.McGriff, 1b	3	0	2	1	0	0	7	1
D.Martinez, p	0	0	0	0	0	0	0	0
D.Jones, p	0	0	0	0	0	0	0	0
T.Pagnozzi, ph	1	0	0	0	0	0	0	0
N.Charlton, p	1	0	0	0	0	1	0	0
T.Pendleton, 3b	2	0	1	0	0	0	0	2
B.Tewksbury, p	0	0	0	0	0	0	0	0
J.Smoltz, p	0	0	0	0	0	0	0	0
W.Clark, ph-1b	2	1	1	3	0	1	1	0
A.VanSlyke, cf	2	0	0	0	0	0	0	0
R.Gant, ph-cf	2	0	0	0	0	0	1	0
R.Sandberg, 2b	2	0	0	0	0	1	2	3
C.Biggio, 2b	2	0	0	0	0	1	0	2
B.Santiago, c	1	0	0	0	0	1	3	0
D.Daulton, c	3	1	0	0	0	0	5	0
T.Glavine, p	0	0	0	0	0	0	0	0
G.Maddux, p	0	0	0	0	0	0	1	0
L.Walker, ph	1	0	1	0	0	0	0	0
D.Cone, p	0	0	0	0	0	0	0	0
G.Sheffield, 3b	2	0	0	0	0	0	1	0
M.Sharperson, 3b	1	0	0	0	0	1	0	0
Totals	39	6	12	6	1	7	27	12

BATTING

2B: O.Smith (off J.Guzman); B.Bonds (off M.Langston).

HR: W.Clark (8th inning off R.Aguilera, 2 on, 2 out).

2-out RBI: B.Roberts 2; W.Clark 3.

RBI, scoring position, less than 2 outs: F.McGriff 1–1; T.Pagnozzi 0–1; A.VanSlyke 0–1.

GDP: A.VanSlyke.

BASERUNNING

Team LOB: 7

FIELDING

E: J.Kruk (dropped fly).

Outfield assist: T.Gwynn 2 (C.Ripken at 2B; T.Fryman at 2B); J.Kruk (I.Rodriguez at 3B).

PITCHING	ip	h	r	er	bb	so
American League						
K.Brown (w)	1.0	0	0	0	0	1
J.McDowell	1.0	0	0	0	0	0
J.Guzman	1.0	2	0	0	1	2
R.Clemens	1.0	2	0	0	0	0
M.Mussina	1.0	0	0	0	0	0
M.Langston	1.0	2	1	1	0	1
C.Nagy	1.0	0	0	0	0	1
J.Montgomery	0.2	2	2	2	0	0
R.Aguilera	0.2	1	1	1	0	0
D.Eckersley	0.2	3	2	0	0	2
National League						
T.Glavine (L)	1.2	9	5	5	0	2
G.Maddux	1.1	1	1	1	0	0
D.Cone	1.0	0	0	0	0	1
B.Tewksbury	1.2	4	4	4	1	0
J.Smoltz	0.1	1	0	0	0	0
D.Martinez	1.0	0	0	0	1	1
D.Jones	1.0	4	3	3	0	2
N.Charlton	1.0	0	0	0	0	1

Inherited Runners—Scored:
  J.McDowell 0–0; J.Guzman 0–0; R.Clemens 0–0;
  M.Mussina 0–0; M.Langston 0–0; C.Nagy 0–0;
  J.Montgomery 0–0; R.Aguilera 2–2; D.Eckersley 0–0;
  G.Maddux 1–0; D.Cone 0–0; B.Tewksbury 0–0;
  J.Smoltz 1–0; D.Martinez 0–0; D.Jones 0–0;
  N.Charlton 0–0.

GAME DATA—T: 2:55; A: 59372; Temp: 79; Wind: To center, Speed: 3 mph

UMPIRES—HP: Doug Harvey (NL); 1B: Rich Garcia (AL), 2B: Harry Wendelstedt (NL), 3B: Greg Kosc (AL), LF: Tom Hallion (NL), RF: Tim Tschida (AL)

STARTING LINEUPS

American League	National League
1. R.Alomar 2b	O.Smith ss
2. W.Boggs 3b	T.Gwynn rf
3. K.Puckett lf	B.Bonds lf
4. J.Carter rf	F.McGriff 1b
5. M.McGwire 1b	T.Pendleton 3b
6. C.Ripken ss	A.VanSlyke cf
7. K.Griffey Jr. cf	R.Sandberg 2b
8. S.Alomar Jr. c	B.Santiago c
9. K.Brown p	T.Glavine p

AL 1ST: R.Alomar grounded out (R.Sandberg-2b to F.McGriff-1b); W.Boggs singled to center field; K.Puckett singled to center field [W.Boggs to second]; J.Carter singled to center field [W.Boggs to third, K.Puckett to second]; M.McGwire singled to center field [W.Boggs scored, K.Puckett scored, J.Carter to second]; C.Ripken singled to right field (T.Gwynn-rf to O.Smith-ss) [J.Carter scored, M.McGwire to third, C.Ripken out at second]; K.Griffey Jr. singled to center field [M.McGwire scored]; S.Alomar Jr. singled to left field [K.Griffey Jr. to second]; seven consecutive singles by AL; K.Brown struck out; 4 R, 7 H, 0 E, 2 LOB. AL 4, NL 0.

NL 1ST: O.Smith struck out; T.Gwynn flied to K.Puckett-lf; B.Bonds flied to K.Puckett-lf; 0 R, 0 H, 0 E, 0 LOB. AL 4, NL 0.

AL 2ND: R.Alomar singled to center field; W.Boggs lined to B.Bonds-lf; R.Alomar stole second; K.Puckett struck out; R.Alomar stole third; J.Carter singled to center field [R.Alomar scored]; **G.Maddux replaced T.Glavine (pitching);** M.McGwire grounded out (T.Pendleton-3b to F.McGriff-1b); 1 R, 2 H, 0 E, 1 LOB. AL 5, NL 0.

NL 2ND: **J.McDowell replaced K.Brown (pitching);** F.McGriff flied to J.Carter-rf; T.Pendleton grounded out (R.Alomar-2b to M.McGwire-1b); A.VanSlyke flied to K.Griffey Jr.-cf; 0 R, 0 H, 0 E, 0 LOB. AL 5, NL 0.

AL 3RD: C.Ripken flied to B.Bonds-lf; K.Griffey Jr. homered to leftfield; S.Alomar Jr. grounded out (F.McGriff-1b to G.Maddux-p); **E.Martinez batted for J.McDowell;** E.Martinez grounded out (R.Sandberg-2b to F.McGriff-1b); 1 R, 1 H, 0 E, 0 LOB. AL 6, NL 0.

NL 3RD: **J.Guzman replaced E.Martinez (pitching);** R.Sandberg struck out; B.Santiago struck out; **L.Walker batted for G.Maddux;** L.Walker singled to third base; O.Smith doubled to left field [L.Walker to third]; T.Gwynn walked; B.Bonds popped to W.Boggs-3b in foul territory; 0 R, 2 H, 0 E, 3 LOB. AL 6, NL 0.

AL 4TH: **D.Cone replaced L.Walker (pitching);** R.Alo-

mar grounded out (O.Smith-ss to F.McGriff-1b); W.Boggs struck out; K.Puckett grounded out (T.Pendleton-3b to F.McGriff-1b); 0 R, 0 H, 0 E, 0 LOB. AL 6, NL 0.

NL 4TH: **R.Clemens replaced K.Puckett (pitching); C.Baerga replaced R.Alomar (playing 2b); R.Ventura replaced W.Boggs (playing 3b); B.Anderson replaced J.Guzman (playing lf);** F.McGriff singled to center field; T.Pendleton singled to left field [F.McGriff to second]; A.VanSlyke grounded into a double play (C.Baerga-2b to C.Ripken-ss to M.McGwire-1b) [F.McGriff to third, T.Pendleton out at second]; R.Sandberg grounded out (C.Baerga-2b to M.McGwire-1b); 0 R, 2 H, 0 E, 1 LOB. AL 6, NL 0.

AL 5TH: **B.Tewksbury replaced T.Pendleton (pitching); D.Daulton replaced B.Santiago (playing c); G.Sheffield replaced D.Cone (playing 3b);** J.Carter popped to R.Sandberg-2b; M.McGwire popped to R.Sandberg-2b; Ripken ran into his own batted ball; C.Ripken grounded out (D.Daulton-c unassisted); 0 R, 0 H, 0 E, 0 LOB. AL 6, NL 0.

NL 5TH: **M.Mussina replaced C.Ripken (pitching); T.Fryman replaced J.Carter (playing ss); R.Sierra replaced R.Clemens (playing rf);** D.Daulton popped to C.Baerga-2b; G.Sheffield lined to B.Anderson-lf; O.Smith grounded out (T.Fryman-ss to M.McGwire-1b); 0 R, 0 H, 0 E, 0 LOB. AL 6, NL 0.

AL 6TH: **T.Fernandez replaced O.Smith (playing ss);** K.Griffey Jr. doubled to right field; S.Alomar Jr. grounded out (R.Sandberg-2b to F.McGriff-1b) [K.Griffey Jr. to third]; B.Anderson grounded out (F.McGriff-1b unassisted); C.Baerga doubled to left-center [K.Griffey Jr. scored]; R.Ventura doubled to first base [C.Baerga scored]; off McGriff's glove; R.Sierra homered to rightfield [R.Ventura scored]; T.Fryman walked; **J.Smoltz replaced B.Tewksbury (pitching); P.Molitor batted for M.McGwire;** P.Molitor singled to right field (T.Gwynn-rf to T.Fernandez-ss) [T.Fryman out at second]; 4 R, 5 H, 0 E, 1 LOB. AL 10, NL 0.

NL 6TH: **M.Langston replaced S.Alomar Jr. (pitching); I.Rodriguez replaced K.Griffey Jr. (playing c); P.Molitor stayed in game (playing 1b); R.Kelly replaced M.Mussina (playing cf);** T.Gwynn grounded out (T.Fryman-ss to P.Molitor-1b); B.Bonds doubled to right field; bad hop over Molitor's shoulder; F.McGriff singled to left field [B.Bonds scored]; **W.Clark batted for J.Smoltz;** W.Clark struck out; **R.Gant batted for A.VanSlyke;** R.Gant grounded out (R.Ventura-3b to P.Molitor-1b); 1 R, 2 H, 0 E, 1 LOB. AL 10, NL 1.

AL 7TH: **W.Clark stayed in game (playing 1b); D.Mar-**

tinez replaced F.McGriff (pitching); C.Biggio replaced R.Sandberg (playing 2b); B.Roberts replaced B.Bonds (playing lf); R.Gant stayed in game (playing cf); J.Kruk replaced T.Gwynn (playing rf); R.Kelly struck out; I.Rodriguez reached on an error by J.Kruk-rf (J.Kruk-rf to C.Biggio-2b to G.Sheffield-3b) [I.Rodriguez out at third]; **C.Knoblauch batted for M.Langston;** C.Knoblauch walked; B.Anderson forced C.Knoblauch (T.Fernandez-ss unassisted) [B.Anderson to first]; 0 R, 0 H, 1 E, 1 LOB. AL 10, NL 1.

NL 7TH: **C.Knoblauch stayed in game (playing 2b); C.Nagy replaced C.Baerga (pitching);** C.Biggio struck out; D.Daulton grounded out (P.Molitor-1b unassisted); G.Sheffield grounded out (T.Fryman-ss to P.Molitor-1b); 0 R, 0 H, 0 E, 0 LOB. AL 10, NL 1.

AL 8TH: **D.Jones replaced D.Martinez (pitching); M.Sharperson replaced G.Sheffield (playing 3b);** C.Nagy singled to the mound; R.Ventura singled to center field [C.Nagy to second]; R.Sierra forced R.Ventura (C.Biggio-2b to T.Fernandez-ss) [C.Nagy to third, R.Sierra to first]; T.Fryman singled to right field [C.Nagy scored, R.Sierra to third]; P.Molitor struck out; R.Kelly doubled to left field [R.Sierra scored, T.Fryman scored]; I.Rodriguez struck out; 3 R, 4 H, 0 E, 1 LOB. AL 13, NL 1.

NL 8TH: **J.Montgomery replaced C.Nagy (pitching);** T.Fernandez grounded out (P.Molitor-1b unassisted); J.Kruk singled to center field; B.Roberts singled to right field [J.Kruk to second]; **T.Pagnozzi batted for D.Jones;** T.Pagnozzi flied to R.Sierra-rf; **R.Aguilera replaced J.Montgomery (pitching);** W.Clark homered to leftfield [J.Kruk scored, B.Roberts scored]; R.Gant popped to R.Ventura-3b in foul territory; 3 R, 3 H, 0 E, 0 LOB. AL 13, NL 4.

AL 9TH: **N.Charlton replaced T.Pagnozzi (pitching);** C.Knoblauch popped to W.Clark-1b; B.Anderson flied to R.Gant-cf; R.Aguilera struck out; 0 R, 0 H, 0 E, 0 LOB. AL 13, NL 4.

NL 9TH: C.Biggio lined to R.Kelly-cf; **D.Eckersley replaced R.Aguilera (pitching);** D.Daulton reached on an error by P.Molitor-1b [D.Daulton to first]; M.Sharperson struck out; T.Fernandez singled to right field [D.Daulton to second]; J.Kruk singled to second base [D.Daulton to third, T.Fernandez to second]; B.Roberts singled to right-center [D.Daulton scored (unearned), T.Fernandez scored (unearned), J.Kruk to second]; N.Charlton struck out; 2 R (0 ER), 3 H, 1 E, 2 LOB. AL 13, NL 6.

Final Totals	R	H	E	LOB
American League	13	19	1	6
National League	6	12	1	7

64

Tuesday, July 13, 1993

Oriole Park at Camden Yards,

Baltimore

American League 9, National League 3

SERIES RESULTS: NL 37, AL 26, 1 TIE

Cito for Mayor

Coming into the first All-Star Game held in Baltimore in thirty-five years, most observers focused on two questions: just how much offense will there be? and why are there seven Blue Jays on the AL squad? More about the first question later. As for the second, the seven Blue Jays represented one-quarter of the AL contingent in a fourteen-team league, and the total was more All-Stars than any team had had since the early 1970s Oakland Athletics.

AL manager Cito Gaston of the Blue Jays upset fans in many AL cities with his choices. Fans of the host Baltimore Orioles were especially upset since only two of their favorites were on the AL squad. The seven Blue Jays represented a team that came into the break with a 49-40 record, having lost ten of its last eleven games. Toronto would end the 1993 season by successfully defending its World Series crown by beating the Phillies, but at least for this week in July, they were not playing well. The seven players chosen included three voted as starters: Roberto Alomar, Joe Carter, and John Olerud.

However, Gaston selected four more of his players. Outfielder Devon White, a defensive specialist, was chosen when most commentators would have picked Rickey Henderson of Oakland, who had had a wonderful first half. Since the Athletics had to have a representative, catcher Terry Steinbach was taken instead of local backstop Chris Hoiles. Steinbach entered the break with seven homers and a .301 average, while Hoiles had an almost identical .300 average but eighteen home runs. Duane Ward, the Toronto closer with twenty-two saves and a 2.17 ERA, was picked over Oriole closer Gregg Olson, whose numbers at the break were twenty-three saves and a 1.24 ERA. Finally, Paul Molitor was chosen as the starting designated hitter, and Detroit's Mickey Tettleton was given a three-day vacation. Tettleton, playing three positions in the field as well as DH, came into the break

with twenty-four home runs to lead both leagues in that statistic, while Molitor was a pure DH with relatively little power.

The partisan crowd booed every Blue Jay at every opportunity. Conversely, Cal Ripken Jr. was given a thunderous ovation by his hometown Baltimore fans during the player introductions before the game. He later called it the biggest thrill of his career.

The AL skipper reacted to the turmoil by saying, "I've been getting criticized for years. I'm used to it—especially in Toronto. It doesn't bother me. One thing about this job: you will be criticized. I took six world champions and one Hall of Famer. I don't think I have to apologize to anyone. Those are All-Star players." Gaston was sensitive to the criticism, however. "Next time I see him, I'll tell Mickey he's an All-Star player and certainly deserved to be on the team," he said.

Hoiles's reaction to the snub was "I can't wait to play the Blue Jays." Olson said, "With seven All-Stars, I guess they really better win the division now. If they didn't, that would be pretty hard to explain."

Orioles pitcher Mike Mussina was chosen and understood that the hometown team needed more than one representative (starter Ripken was the other): "I'm not sure I deserve it. I've got a 4.10 ERA. Olson has a 1.24."

Mussina created another stir among the Baltimore fans. In the ninth inning, Ward was sent in to close out the game. Mussina, who had been told before the game by Gaston that he would not be used except in extra innings, threw in the AL bullpen. He was doing his regular work between starts, but the Orioles fans in the crowd thought he would be coming into the game. When Ward threw a one-two-three inning to end the game, another chorus of boos arose from the stands.

Mussina said later, "It was the first time I have ever been cheered for not pitching. It was like Ward was the mortal enemy, but he was on our side. I felt bad for him." Gaston reacted by saying, "I have to save him in case of extra innings. I never thought about using him. I didn't use one of my own pitchers [Pat Hentgen]. I guess I should just get out of town. We don't have to come back until the last series of the year. As long as they don't take it any further than that, then it's OK."

That was not the end of it for Baltimore fans, however. Within days of the game, street vendors started selling T-shirts with the inscription "Cito Sucks" in big, bold letters. The shirts were obviously very popular around town. However, by the time the Blue Jays arrived to play the season-ending series, they had already clinched the division title and the Orioles were mired in fourth place, making it a moot issue.

Now back to the first question: just how much offense will there be? The answer was "a lot." The offense started the day before during the Home Run Derby. Seattle's Ken Griffey Jr. hit a ball that cleared the park in right field, flew over Eutaw Street (the walkway between the ballpark and the warehouse building that contains the Orioles offices), and struck the warehouse eight feet up the wall. Nobody had ever hit the warehouse on the fly with a fair ball before. But Griffey's shot was not the biggest blast of the exhibition.

Ranger Juan Gonzalez drove a ball into the bunting on the front of the third deck in left field. Before this, no one had ever hit a ball into the second deck at Camden Yards. Gonzalez also hit two off the second-deck facade, one into the second-deck seats, and another off the wall in center field. Orioles minor league pitching coach Tom Brown, who threw to both Griffey and Gonzalez, said he was shell-shocked by the experience.

The All-Star contest the next day certainly lived up to expectations when the teams combined for twelve runs and eighteen hits. The combined total of ten extra-base hits tied a record set in 1951, and the seven doubles for the two squads tied a record set in 1949. This was also the first time in All-Star history that there were homers in each of the first three innings.

In the top of the first inning, Giants left fielder Barry Bonds doubled into the right-field corner, and Gary Sheffield followed with a homer off a high fastball that left the yard just inside the left-field pole. In the bottom of the second, Kirby Puckett crushed a low fastball from Phillies pitcher Terry Mulholland over the center-field fence. Blue Jay second baseman Roberto Alomar greeted new pitcher Andy Benes of the Padres in the bottom of the third with a homer to tie the game, 2–2.

The game proceeded relatively quietly until the AL half of the fifth inning. Rangers catcher Ivan Rodriguez, at age twenty-one the youngest player on either team, led off the frame by hitting a liner over the head of left fielder Bonds. It struck the padded wall at a seam and stuck there. Gold-glover Bonds waited for the carom, which never came. He then ran out to get the ball, but the play was called a ground-rule double. Rodriguez moved to third on an infield out by Roberto Alomar, and then pinch hitter Albert Belle of the Indians singled to right field to score Rodriguez. Belle did not stop at first, however, and was safe at second when Braves outfielder David Justice fumbled the ball in right. Justice, who committed five errors in 157 regular season games in 1993, said later that the ball took a bad bounce at the last moment.

Griffey followed with another chance for Justice, a line drive single. Belle scored on the play, and Griffey went to second when Justice's throw went over the head of the cutoff man, Phillies first baseman John Kruk. No error was charged on that play, but the damage was done two batters later when Puckett doubled to left to score Griffey with the third run of the inning.

The Senior Circuit got one run back in the next inning. Bonds led off the inning with his second double to right, which tied the record for most doubles in one game, held by Al Simmons (1934), Joe Medwick (1937), Ted Kluszewski (1956), and Ernie Banks (1959). Sheffield singled to left for his second hit, moving Bonds to third. One out later, Bonds scored on a sacrifice fly to center by the Reds' Barry Larkin.

The AL came charging back with three unearned runs in the bottom of the frame. With the Braves' Steve Avery on the mound and two out, Braves shortstop Jeff Blauser booted Carlos Baerga's grounder. Belle walked, and Devon White doubled to right, scoring Cleveland's Baerga. John Smoltz then replaced his Atlanta teammate on the hill. Smoltz's first offering to Juan Gonzalez was a wild pitch that scored Belle and allowed White to go to third. Gonzalez walked, and Smoltz threw his second wild pitch of the inning, allowing White to score. The two wild ones in one inning tied a mark held by Juan Marichal (1962) and Dave Stieb (1980). It also tied the record for most wild pitches in a game, held by Marichal, Stieb, and Tom Brewer (1956). The troubles by the four Braves players provoked a sarcastic tomahawk chop from the crowd (a reference to the Braves fans' war chants in Atlanta), obviously happy to see the AL in front, 8–3.

White Sox pitcher Jack McDowell, who would be named the AL Cy Young Award winner that fall, got credit for the win after throwing eight pitches in a perfect fifth inning. He was the first Pale Hose winner since Ray Herbert in the second game of 1962. Jeff Montgomery of Kansas City threw a perfect seventh inning and Ward a perfect ninth inning, while Mariner Randy Johnson threw perfectly in the third and fourth.

This was the sixth straight win for the AL, its seventh in eight games, and its eighth in eleven games. The six-game streak was the third longest in All-Star history. The NL won eleven games in succession from 1972 through 1982 and won eight games from 1963 through 1970 for an impressive nineteen out of twenty games.

Baltimore previously hosted the All-Star Game at Memorial Stadium in 1958. The thirty-five years between games is the longest such stretch for any city.

Puckett became the first Minnesota Twin to be named the All-Star MVP. He had come into the game without an extra-base hit or RBI in his seven appearances in the midseason classic but this time had a double and homer and two runs driven in.

The top vote getters were Bonds and Griffey. It was the first time that Bonds led the NL in voting, and the second for Griffey in the AL. Bonds, in the midst of winning his second consecutive NL MVP, garnered more votes than Griffey for top overall honors. Only one rookie was named to the teams: the Dodgers' Mike Piazza, who went on to win the NL Rookie of the Year Award. Cubs second baseman Ryne Sandberg made his tenth and last appearance at an All-Star Game.

Gary Sheffield, who had been traded by the San Diego Padres to the Florida Marlins in June, became the first player from a first-year expansion club to be elected to the All-Star Game's starting lineup. It was a dubious honor, since Sheffield was with the Padres when balloting started. In fact, he only went to Florida on June 24 as part of a five-player deal.

The comedy act of the night occurred in the top of the third inning. Randy Johnson, the powerful lefty who stands six-foot-ten and overpowers left-handed hitters, relieved starter Mark Langston. With two outs and no one on base, Johnson faced lefty John Kruk. The first pitch sailed over Kruk's head and struck the backstop. Kruk stepped out and tugged at his shirt as if he were suffering a heart attack. He bailed out on each of the next three pitches, taking horrible-looking swings at each. The third strike was a curve ball, and Johnson left the mound smiling. After the game, Johnson said, "The ball just got away, but John has the type of personality that he didn't think anything of it."

There were three sad items to report during the break. Former Dodger All-Stars Roy Campanella and Don Drysdale died within a week of each other, just before the end of the first half of the season. Eight-time All-Star Campanella died on June 26, while Drysdale, who had been on seven All-Star teams, died on July 2.

The Blue Jays suffered a loss when third base coach Rich Hacker was seriously injured in an auto accident while returning home for the break on July 11. Hacker, one of the few Toronto coaches who did not go to the game, suffered severe injuries to his head, right ankle, and foot, and doctors at first thought he would lose the foot. He recovered enough to throw out the first pitch for a game during the American League Championship Series that fall, and he returned to work with Toronto the following season.

	AL		NL	
P	Mark Langston	CAL	Terry Mulholland	PHI
C	Ivan Rodriguez	TEX	Darren Daulton	PHI
1B	John Olerud	TOR	John Kruk	PHI
2B	Roberto Alomar	TOR	Ryne Sandberg	CHN
3B	Wade Boggs	NYA	Gary Sheffield	FLO
SS	Cal Ripken	BAL	Barry Larkin	CIN
OF	Joe Carter	TOR	Barry Bonds	SFN
OF	Ken Griffey	SEA	Dave Justice	ATL
OF	Kirby Puckett	MIN	Andy Van Slyke +	PIT
DH	Paul Molitor	TOR	Mark Grace	CHN
	Rick Aguilera	MIN	Steve Avery	ATL
	Carlos Baerga	CLE	Rod Beck	SFN
	Albert Belle	CLE	Jay Bell	PIT
	Scott Cooper	BOS	Andy Benes	SDN
	Cecil Fielder	DET	Jeff Blauser	ATL
	Travis Fryman	DET	Bobby Bonilla	NYN
	Juan Gonzalez	TEX	John Burkett	SFN
	Pat Hentgen	TOR	Andres Galarraga	COL
	Randy Johnson	SEA	Tom Glavine	ATL
	Jimmy Key	NYA	Marquis Grissom	MON
	Jack McDowell	CHA	Tony Gwynn	SDN
	Jeff Montgomery	KCA	Bryan Harvey	FLO
	Mike Mussina	BAL	Dave Hollins	PHI
	Terry Steinbach	OAK	Gregg Jefferies	SLN
	Frank Thomas	CHA	Bobby Kelly	CIN
	Greg Vaughn	MIL	Darryl Kile	HOU
	Duane Ward	TOR	Mike Piazza	LAN
	Devon White	TOR	Lee Smith	SLN
			John Smoltz	ATL
			Robby Thompson	SFN

+ player replaced on roster

National League	200	001	000-	3				
American League	011	033	10X-	9				

NATIONAL LEAGUE

	ab	r	h	bi	bb	so	po	a
M.Grissom, cf	3	0	0	0	0	1	0	0
R.Kelly, cf	1	0	0	0	0	1	0	1
B.Bonds, lf	3	2	2	0	0	0	2	0
B.Bonilla, lf	1	0	1	0	0	0	2	0
G.Sheffield, 3b	3	1	2	2	0	0	0	2
D.Hollins, 3b	1	0	1	0	0	0	1	0
J.Kruk, 1b	3	0	0	0	0	2	7	0
A.Galarraga, 1b	1	0	0	0	0	0	0	0
B.Larkin, ss	2	0	0	1	0	1	2	1
J.Blauser, ss	1	0	0	0	0	1	1	2
M.Grace, dh	3	0	0	0	0	0	0	0
G.Jefferies, ph	1	0	0	0	0	1	0	0
D.Justice, rf	3	0	1	0	0	0	1	0
T.Gwynn, rf	1	0	0	0	0	0	0	0
D.Daulton, c	3	0	0	0	0	1	4	0
M.Piazza, c	1	0	0	0	0	1	3	0
R.Sandberg, 2b	1	0	0	0	1	0	0	2
J.Bell, 2b	1	0	0	0	0	0	1	1
Totals	33	3	7	3	1	9	24	9

BATTING

2B: B.Bonds 2 (off M.Langston; off J.Key); D.Hollins (off R.Aguilera).

HR: G.Sheffield (1st inning off M.Langston, 1 on, 1 out).

RBI, scoring position, less than 2 outs: G.Sheffield 1–1; J.Kruk 0–1; A.Galarraga 0–2; B.Larkin 1–1.

SF: B.Larkin.

BASERUNNING

Team LOB: 5

FIELDING

E: D.Justice; J.Blauser (fumble).
Outfield assist: R.Kelly (T.Steinbach at 3B).

AMERICAN LEAGUE

	ab	r	h	bi	bb	so	po	a
R.Alomar, 2b	3	1	1	1	0	0	0	1
C.Baerga, 2b	2	1	0	0	0	1	0	0
P.Molitor, dh	1	0	0	0	1	0	0	0
A.Belle, ph	1	2	1	1	1	0	0	0
F.Thomas, ph	1	0	1	0	0	0	0	0
K.Griffey Jr., cf	3	1	1	1	0	1	2	0
D.White, cf	2	1	1	1	0	0	1	0
J.Carter, rf	3	0	1	0	0	1	1	0
J.Gonzalez, rf	1	0	0	0	1	1	1	0
J.Olerud, 1b	2	0	0	0	0	0	4	0
C.Fielder, 1b	1	0	0	0	0	0	4	0
K.Puckett, lf	3	1	2	2	0	0	1	0
G.Vaughn, lf	1	1	1	0	0	0	0	0
C.Ripken, ss	3	0	0	0	0	1	1	2
T.Fryman, ss	1	0	0	0	0	0	1	1
W.Boggs, 3b	1	0	0	0	1	0	1	0
S.Cooper, 3b	2	0	0	0	0	1	1	0
I.Rodriguez, c	2	1	1	0	0	0	3	0
T.Steinbach, c	2	0	1	1	0	1	6	0
Totals	35	9	11	7	4	7	27	4

BATTING

2B: I.Rodriguez (off J.Burkett); K.Puckett (off J.Burkett); D.White (off S.Avery); T.Steinbach (off R.Beck).

HR: R.Alomar (3rd inning off A.Benes, 0 on, 0 out); K.Puckett (2nd inning off T.Mulholland, 0 on, 1 out).

2-out RBI: D.White; K.Puckett; T.Steinbach.

RBI, scoring position, less than 2 outs: R.Alomar 0–1; A.Belle 1–1; K.Griffey Jr. 1–1; J.Carter 0–1.

BASERUNNING

SB: D.White (2nd base off B.Harvey/M.Piazza).
Team LOB: 7

PITCHING

	ip	h	r	er	bb	so
National League						
T.Mulholland	2.0	1	1	1	2	0
A.Benes	2.0	2	1	1	0	2
J.Burkett (L)	0.2	4	3	3	0	1
S.Avery	1.0	1	3	0	1	1
J.Smoltz	0.1	0	0	0	1	0
R.Beck	1.0	2	1	1	0	1
B.Harvey	1.0	1	0	0	0	2
American League						
M.Langston	2.0	3	2	2	1	2
R.Johnson	2.0	0	0	0	0	1
J.McDowell (w)	1.0	0	0	0	0	0
J.Key	1.0	2	1	1	0	1
J.Montgomery	1.0	0	0	0	0	1
R.Aguilera	1.0	2	0	0	0	2
D.Ward	1.0	0	0	0	0	2

Inherited Runners—Scored:
A.Benes 0–0; J.Burkett 0–0; S.Avery 2–0; J.Smoltz 2–2; R.Beck 0–0; B.Harvey 0–0; R.Johnson 0–0; J.McDowell 0–0; J.Key 0–0; J.Montgomery 0–0; R.Aguilera 0–0; D.Ward 0–0.

HBP: C.Fielder by J.Burkett.

WP: J.Smoltz 2

GAME DATA—T: 2:49; A: 48147; Temp: 95; Wind: To right, Speed: 8 mph

UMPIRES—HP: Jim McKean (AL), 1B: Bob Davidson (NL), 2B: Mike Reilly (AL), 3B: Gary Darling (NL), LF: Dale Scott (AL), RF: Mark Hirschbeck (NL)

STARTING LINEUPS

	National League	*American League*
1.	M.Grissom cf	R.Alomar 2b
2.	B.Bonds lf	P.Molitor dh
3.	G.Sheffield 3b	K.Griffey Jr. cf
4.	J.Kruk 1b	J.Carter rf
5.	B.Larkin ss	J.Olerud 1b
6.	M.Grace dh	K.Puckett lf
7.	D.Justice rf	C.Ripken ss
8.	D.Daulton c	W.Boggs 3b
9.	R.Sandberg 2b	I.Rodriguez c
	T.Mulholland p	M.Langston p

NL 1ST: M.Grissom popped to W.Boggs-3b in foul territory; B.Bonds doubled to right field; G.Sheffield homered to leftfield [B.Bonds scored]; J.Kruk flied to K.Puckett-lf; B.Larkin struck out; 2 R, 2 H, 0 E, 0 LOB. NL 2, AL 0.

AL 1ST: R.Alomar grounded out (G.Sheffield-3b to J.Kruk-1b); P.Molitor walked; K.Griffey Jr. grounded out (J.Kruk-1b unassisted) [P.Molitor to second]; J.Carter popped to B.Larkin-ss; 0 R, 0 H, 0 E, 1 LOB. NL 2, AL 0.

NL 2ND: M.Grace grounded out (R.Alomar-2b to J.Olerud-1b); D.Justice singled to center field; D.Daulton grounded out (M.Langston-p to J.Olerud-1b) [D.Justice to second]; R.Sandberg walked; M.Grissom struck out; 0 R, 1 H, 0 E, 2 LOB. NL 2, AL 0.

AL 2ND: J.Olerud grounded out (R.Sandberg-2b to J.Kruk-1b); K.Puckett homered to centerfield; C.Ripken grounded out (B.Larkin-ss to J.Kruk-1b); W.Boggs walked; I.Rodriguez flied to D.Justice-rf; 1 R, 1 H, 0 E, 1 LOB. NL 2, AL 1.

NL 3RD: R.Johnson replaced M.Langston (pitching); B.Bonds grounded out (C.Ripken-ss to J.Olerud-1b); G.Sheffield popped to C.Ripken-ss; Johnson's first pitch sailed far over Kruk's head; Kruk then bailed out on the next three pitches; J.Kruk struck out; 0 R, 0 H, 0 E, 0 LOB. NL 2, AL 1.

AL 3RD: A.Benes replaced T.Mulholland (pitching); R.Alomar homered to rightfield; P.Molitor flied to B.Bonds-lf; K.Griffey Jr. struck out; J.Carter singled to left field; J.Olerud forced J.Carter (B.Larkin-ss unassisted) [J.Olerud to first]; 1 R, 2 H, 0 E, 1 LOB. NL 2, AL 2.

NL 4TH: B.Larkin flied to J.Carter-rf; M.Grace grounded out (R.Johnson-p to J.Olerud-1b); D.Justice flied to K.Griffey Jr.-cf; 0 R, 0 H, 0 E, 0 LOB. NL 2, AL 2.

AL 4TH: K.Puckett grounded out (R.Sandberg-2b to J.Kruk-1b); C.Ripken struck out; W.Boggs lined to B.Bonds-lf; 0 R, 0 H, 0 E, 0 LOB. NL 2, AL 2.

NL 5TH: **J.McDowell replaced R.Johnson (pitching); C.Fielder replaced J.Olerud (playing 1b);** D.Daulton grounded out (C.Fielder-1b unassisted); R.Sandberg grounded out (C.Ripken-ss to C.Fielder-1b); M.Grissom flied to K.Griffey Jr.-cf; 0 R, 0 H, 0 E, 0 LOB. NL 2, AL 2.

AL 5TH: **J.Burkett replaced A.Benes (pitching); R.Kelly replaced M.Grissom (playing cf); J.Bell replaced R.Sandberg (playing 2b);** I.Rodriguez doubled to left field; R.Alomar grounded out (J.Bell-2b to J.Kruk-1b) [I.Rodriguez to third]; **A.Belle batted for P.Molitor;** A.Belle singled to right field [I.Rodriguez scored, A.Belle to second (error by D.Justice-rf)]; K.Griffey Jr. singled to right field [A.Belle scored, K.Griffey Jr. to second (on throw home)]; J.Carter struck out; C.Fielder was hit by a pitch; K.Puckett doubled to left field [K.Griffey Jr. scored, C.Fielder to third]; **S.Avery replaced J.Burkett (pitching);** C.Ripken grounded out (G.Sheffield-3b to J.Kruk-1b); 3 R, 4 H, 1 E, 2 LOB. NL 2, AL 5.

NL 6TH: **J.Key replaced J.McDowell (pitching); G.Vaughn replaced K.Puckett (playing lf); D.White replaced K.Griffey Jr. (playing cf); J.Gonzalez replaced J.Carter (playing rf); C.Baerga replaced R.Alomar (playing 2b); S.Cooper replaced W.Boggs (playing 3b); T.Steinbach replaced I.Rodriguez (playing c);** B.Bonds doubled to right field; G.Sheffield singled to left field [B.Bonds to third]; J.Kruk struck out; B.Larkin out on a sacrifice fly to D.White-cf [B.Bonds scored]; M.Grace grounded out (C.Fielder-1b unassisted); 1 R, 2 H, 0 E, 1 LOB. NL 3, AL 5.

AL 6TH: **B.Bonilla replaced B.Bonds (playing lf); A.Galarraga replaced J.Kruk (playing 1b); D.Hollins replaced G.Sheffield (playing 3b); J.Blauser replaced B.Larkin (playing ss);** S.Cooper flied to B.Bonilla-lf; T.Steinbach struck out; C.Baerga reached on an error by J.Blauser-ss [C.Baerga to first]; A.Belle walked [C.Baerga to second]; D.White doubled to right field [C.Baerga scored (unearned), A.Belle to third]; **J.Smoltz replaced S.Avery (pitching);** J.Smoltz threw a wild pitch [A.Belle scored (unearned), D.White to third]; J.Gonzalez walked; J.Smoltz threw a wild pitch [D.White scored (unearned), J.Gonzalez to second]; C.Fielder flied to B.Bonilla-lf; 3 R (0 ER), 1 H, 1 E, 1 LOB. NL 3, AL 8.

NL 7TH: **J.Montgomery replaced J.Key (pitching); T.Fryman replaced C.Ripken (playing ss);** D.Justice flied to J.Gonzalez-rf; D.Daulton struck out; J.Bell popped to S.Cooper-3b; 0 R, 0 H, 0 E, 0 LOB. NL 3, AL 8.

AL 7TH: **R.Beck changed positions (pitching); M.Piazza replaced D.Daulton (playing c); T.Gwynn replaced D.Justice (playing rf);**

G.Vaughn singled to left field; T.Fryman popped to J.Blauser-ss; S.Cooper struck out; T.Steinbach doubled to center field (R.Kelly-cf to J.Blauser-ss to D.Hollins-3b) [G.Vaughn scored, T.Steinbach out at third]; 1 R, 2 H, 0 E, 0 LOB. NL 3, AL 9.

NL 8TH: **R.Aguilera replaced J.Montgomery (pitching);** R.Kelly struck out; B.Bonilla singled to right field; D.Hollins doubled to right field [B.Bonilla to third]; A.Galarraga popped to T.Fryman-ss; J.Blauser struck out; 0 R, 2 H, 0 E, 2 LOB. NL 3, AL 9.

AL 8TH: **B.Harvey replaced R.Beck (pitching);** C.Baerga struck out; **F.Thomas batted for A.Belle;** F.Thomas singled to center field;

D.White forced F.Thomas (J.Blauser-ss to J.Bell-2b) [D.White to first]; D.White stole second; J.Gonzalez struck out; 0 R, 1 H, 0 E, 1 LOB. NL 3, AL 9.

NL 9TH: **D.Ward replaced R.Aguilera (pitching); G.Jefferies batted for M.Grace;** G.Jefferies struck out; T.Gwynn grounded out (T.Fryman-ss to C.Fielder-1b); M.Piazza struck out; 0 R, 0 H, 0 E, 0 LOB. NL 3, AL 9.

Final Totals	R	H	E	LOB
National League	3	7	2	5
American League	9	11	0	7

65

The "Crime Dog" Takes a Bite outta the AL

Talk around baseball in early July centered on the impending player strike, which started in mid-August and canceled the rest of the season, including the World Series for the first time since 1904. Fans needed a spectacular evening to remind them of the glories of the game on the field, and that's what they got. In a classic confrontation, the NL overcame a lead in the ninth inning and won in the tenth, 8–7.

The AL held a 7–5 lead as the bottom of the ninth started. Manager Cito Gaston of Toronto called on all-time save leader Lee Smith of the Orioles to close out what would have been the seventh straight AL win. The Expos' Marquis Grissom opened with a walk, and Astro Craig Biggio forced Grissom at second base. It looked like a double play, but third baseman Scott Cooper of Boston was slow getting the ball to the Twins' Chuck Knoblauch at second. NL Manager Jim Fregosi, who skippered the Phillies during the season, asked the Braves' Fred McGriff to pinch-hit for Cubs relief pitcher Randy Myers. Smith got ahead in the count and threw a fastball low and away that McGriff reached down and smacked over the left-center-field wall for a two-run, game-tying homer.

Smith remarked later, "I put that pitch where I wanted to put it, but he went down and got it. If I'd thrown that same pitch and Fred had hit into a double play, he'd have said, 'Smitty got me with a good pitch.' It wasn't in his wheelhouse. But I guess his wheelhouse is all over."

Indeed, McGriff, nicknamed "Crime Dog" by ESPN's Chris Berman, came into the game with more home runs (197) than any other player during the previous five years. It was a dream match-up, with the leading home run slugger facing the save leader. Smith came into the break with 430 career saves, including 29 in the first half of 1994 in thirty-three chances.

McGriff, who was named the game's MVP, said,

"He made a good pitch, but I got it. This is a nice little feeling. It's the stuff you dream about." Smith's teammate Cal Ripken Jr. commented on the match-up: "Lee is a low fastball pitcher, and McGriff is a low fastball hitter. It was like a collision out there." McGriff's homer was the fifteenth by a pinch hitter in the All-Star Game.

In the top of the tenth, the AL got two base runners when Oakland's Ruben Sierra and Ranger Ivan Rodriguez singled. However, the Phillies' Doug Jones induced Detroit's Travis Fryman to hit a fly ball and struck out Knoblauch to end the inning.

In the NL half of the tenth, Tony Gwynn of the Padres, in his tenth All-Star Game, greeted new pitcher Jason Bere of the White Sox with a single to center field. The Expos' Moises Alou, in the first at bat of his first All-Star Game, doubled to the wall in left-center. The thirty-four-year-old Gwynn raced around from first and slid under the tag, getting his foot between Ivan Rodriguez's legs for the winning tally.

Ironically, the last time the NL had won, in 1987, Smith had been the winning pitcher. The 1994 game was Smith's first AL All-Star performance, sixth overall, and he had yet to record a save in the midsummer classic. He was named to the AL squad in 1995 for the last time but did not pitch. Doug Jones was credited with the win and became the first Phillies pitcher to register a win in All-Star competition since Ken Raffensberger in 1944, despite the fact that the team had been represented by Robin Roberts, Curt Simmons, and Steve Carlton through the years.

Each team scored a run in the first inning. In the bottom of the third, the NL took the lead as Houston's Jeff Bagwell singled, the Cardinals' Gregg Jefferies was hit by a pitch, and Gwynn doubled to right, scoring Jefferies, who slid around Rodriguez's tag.

The Junior Circuit pulled even in the sixth as Blue Jay Roberto Alomar singled and stole second. Seattle's Ken Griffey Jr., the player with the most votes overall, singled to center field to score Alomar but was out trying to stretch the hit into a double. Pale Hose first baseman Frank Thomas singled, and Joe Carter of Toronto hit a grounder to Matt Williams. The Giants third sacker threw wildly past second into right field, allowing Thomas to score and Carter to reach third base. Minnesota's Kirby Puckett then plated Carter with a single to center.

The NL got one run back in the bottom half of the frame on a Grissom homer to right. However, the AL scored three more times in the seventh. Rodriguez singled, and Tiger Mickey Tettleton walked. Cardinals shortstop Ozzie Smith dove to his right to snare Knoblauch's grounder up the middle and threw to Biggio while still on his knees to force Tettleton at second, while Rodriguez moved to third. It was a classic stop by Smith, who had received the most votes of any NL player. Scott Cooper doubled Rodriguez home, and Indians center fielder Kenny Lofton singled to score Knoblauch, setting up the ninth-inning fireworks.

Matt Williams of the Giants and Griffey led their respective leagues in home runs at the break. Each had clouted thirty-three long balls and seemed to have a legitimate chance to reach Roger Maris's record total of sixty-one by season's end. Frank Thomas was only one behind Griffey in the AL. However, the player strike saved Maris's mark for another year.

The Pirates hosted the All-Star Game for the fourth time, and it was the second at Three Rivers Stadium (the first had been held in 1974). It was the ninth extra-inning contest, all of which have been won by the NL.

Moises Alou joined his dad, Felipe, as the eighth father-son combination to play in an All-Star Game. There were actually three sons of former All-Stars in this game, with Ken Griffey Jr. and Barry Bonds each representing a second-generation All-Star.

Only two rookies were named to the teams: Pirate Carlos Garcia and Astro John Hudek. Hudek had been released in July 1993 by the Tigers but had come into the 1994 break with fifteen saves for Houston. Paul Molitor played in his sixth and last game, having been named seven times.

Moises Alou, who had missed much of the 1993 season with a broken leg, started his career with the Pirates, which made his game-winning hit special for him and his former manager Jim Leyland.

This was the second straight year that the elected NL center fielder missed the game due to injury. In 1993, Andy Van Slyke had suffered a broken collarbone, and this year the Phillies' Lenny Dykstra had an appendectomy, which prevented him from playing.

Wade Boggs became the fifth American Leaguer to play in ten straight All-Star contests. Brooks Robinson appeared in fifteen, Yogi Berra in fourteen, this was Ripken's twelfth, and Mickey Mantle appeared in ten straight.

Although Tony Gwynn was the lone San Diego Padre to be named to the NL team, there were six ex-Padres on the two contingents: Roberto Alomar and Joe Carter (Blue Jays), McGriff (Braves), Ricky Bones (Brewers), Randy Myers (Cubs), and Ozzie Smith (Cardinals). AL manager Cito Gaston also played for the Padres. Ozzie Smith performed his fan-pleasing back flip as he took the field at the start of the game.

After the game, Gwynn summed up everyone's feelings: "This is what baseball is all about."

	AL		NL	
P	Jimmy Key	NYA	Greg Maddux	ATL
C	Ivan Rodriguez	TEX	Mike Piazza	LAN
1B	Frank Thomas	CHA	Gregg Jefferies	SLN
2B	Roberto Alomar	TOR	Mariano Duncan	PHI
3B	Wade Boggs	NYA	Matt Williams	SFN
SS	Cal Ripken	BAL	Ozzie Smith	SLN
OF	Joe Carter	TOR	Barry Bonds	SFN
OF	Ken Griffey	SEA	Lenny Dykstra +	PHI
OF	Kirby Puckett	MIN	Dave Justice	ATL
	Wilson Alvarez	CHA	Moises Alou	MON
	Albert Belle	CLE	Jeff Bagwell	HOU
	Jason Bere	CHA	Rod Beck	SFN
	Ricky Bones	MIL	Rich Becker	MIN
	Will Clark	TEX	Dante Bichette	COL
	David Cone	KCA	Craig Biggio	HOU
	Scott Cooper	BOS	Ken Caminiti	HOU
	Chili Davis	CAL	Jeff Conine	FLO
	Travis Fryman	DET	Wil Cordero	MON
	Pat Hentgen	TOR	Doug Drabek	HOU
	Randy Johnson	SEA	Darrin Fletcher	MON
	Chuck Knoblauch	MIN	Carlos Garcia	PIT
	Kenny Lofton	CLE	Marquis Grissom	MON
	Paul Molitor	TOR	Tony Gwynn	SDN
	Mike Mussina	BAL	Ken Hill	MON
	Paul O'Neill	NYA	John Hudek	HOU
	Ruben Sierra	OAK	Danny Jackson	PHI
	Lee Smith	BAL	Doug Jones	PHI
	Mickey Tettleton	DET	Barry Larkin +	CIN
			Fred McGriff	ATL
			Randy Myers	CHN
			Jose Rijo +	CIN
			Bret Saberhagen	NYN

+ player replaced on roster

```
American League    100  003  300  0-  7
National League    103  001  002  1-  8  (10)
     0 outs when winning run was scored.
```

AMERICAN LEAGUE

	ab	r	h	bi	bb	so	po	a
R.Alomar, 2b	3	1	1	0	0	0	0	0
C.Knoblauch, 2b	3	1	0	0	0	2	1	2
W.Boggs, 3b	3	1	1	0	0	2	0	2
S.Cooper, 3b	2	1	1	1	0	0	0	2
K.Griffey Jr., cf	3	0	2	1	0	0	2	0
K.Lofton, cf	2	0	1	2	0	1	1	0
F.Thomas, 1b	2	1	2	1	1	0	6	0
W.Clark, 1b	2	0	2	0	0	0	7	0
J.Carter, lf	3	1	0	0	0	0	1	0
A.Belle, lf	2	0	0	0	0	0	1	0
K.Puckett, rf	3	0	1	1	0	0	1	0
R.Sierra, rf	2	0	1	0	0	0	1	0
C.Ripken, ss	5	0	1	0	0	2	1	2
I.Rodriguez, c	5	1	2	0	0	1	5	0
J.Key, p	0	0	0	0	0	0	0	0
P.Molitor, ph	1	0	0	0	0	0	0	0
D.Cone, p	0	0	0	0	0	0	0	0
C.Davis, ph	1	0	0	0	0	0	0	0
M.Mussina, p	0	0	0	0	0	0	0	0
R.Johnson, p	0	0	0	0	0	0	0	1
M.Tettleton, ph	0	0	0	0	1	0	0	0
P.Hentgen, p	0	0	0	0	0	0	0	0
P.O'Neill, ph	1	0	0	0	0	0	0	0
W.Alvarez, p	0	0	0	0	0	0	0	0
L.Smith, p	0	0	0	0	0	0	0	0
T.Fryman, ph	1	0	0	0	0	0	0	0
J.Bere, p	0	0	0	0	0	0	0	0
Totals	44	7	15	6	2	8	27	9

BATTING

2B: K.Griffey Jr. (off G.Maddux); S.Cooper (off D.Jackson); C.Ripken (off R.Beck).

2-out RBI: K.Puckett.

RBI, scoring position, less than 2 outs: C.Knoblauch 0–1; S.Cooper 1–1; K.Griffey Jr. 1–1; K.Lofton 2–2; F.Thomas 1–1; J.Carter 0–1; A.Belle 0–2; I.Rodriguez 0–1; P.O'Neill 0–1; T.Fryman 0–1.

BASERUNNING

SB: R.Alomar (2nd base off D.Drabek/M.Piazza); K.Lofton (Double SB 3rd base off R.Beck/M.Piazza); W.Clark (Double SB 2nd base off R.Beck/M.Piazza).

Team LOB: 9

FIELDING

DP: (1). C.Ripken-W.Clark.

NATIONAL LEAGUE

	ab	r	h	bi	bb	so	po	a
G.Jefferies, 1b	1	2	1	0	0	0	6	0
K.Hill, p	0	0	0	0	0	0	1	0
D.Bichette, ph	1	0	1	0	0	0	0	0
D.Drabek, p	0	0	0	0	0	0	0	0
J.Hudek, p	0	0	0	0	0	0	0	0
D.Jackson, p	0	0	0	0	0	0	0	0
W.Cordero, ss	2	0	0	0	0	0	1	1
T.Gwynn, cf-rf	5	2	2	2	0	0	2	0
B.Bonds, lf	3	0	0	1	0	2	1	0
M.Alou, lf	1	0	1	1	0	0	0	0
M.Piazza, c	4	0	1	1	0	0	6	0
D.Fletcher, c	0	0	0	0	0	0	3	0
M.Williams, 3b	3	0	0	0	0	2	0	1
K.Caminiti, 3b	1	0	0	0	0	0	0	0
D.Justice, rf	2	0	0	0	0	0	1	0
M.Grissom, cf	1	1	1	1	1	0	2	1
M.Duncan, 2b	1	0	0	0	0	0	0	2
C.Garcia, 2b	2	0	1	0	0	0	0	1
C.Biggio, 2b	1	1	0	0	0	0	2	1
O.Smith, ss	3	0	1	0	0	0	1	2
R.Beck, p	0	0	0	0	0	0	0	0
R.Myers, p	0	0	0	0	0	0	0	0
F.McGriff, ph-1b	1	1	1	2	0	0	0	0
G.Maddux, p	0	0	0	0	0	0	1	1
J.Bagwell, ph-1b	4	1	2	0	0	1	3	2
D.Jones, p	0	0	0	0	0	0	0	0
Totals	36	8	12	8	1	5	30	12

BATTING

2B: G.Jefferies (off J.Key); T.Gwynn (off D.Cone); M.Alou (off J.Bere).

HR: M.Grissom (6th inning off R.Johnson, 0 on, 1 out); F.McGriff (9th inning off L.Smith, 1 on, 1 out).

2-out RBI: M.Piazza.

RBI, scoring position, less than 2 outs: T.Gwynn 2–2; B.Bonds 1–2.

SF: B.Bonds.

GDP: W.Cordero.

BASERUNNING

Team LOB: 4

FIELDING

E: M.Williams (throw).

Outfield assist: M.Grissom (K.Griffey Jr. at 2B).

DP: (1). G.Maddux-G.Jefferies.

PITCHING	ip	h	r	er	bb	so
American League						
J.Key	2.0	1	1	1	0	1
D.Cone	2.0	4	3	3	0	3
M.Mussina	1.0	1	0	0	0	1
R.Johnson	1.0	2	1	1	0	0
P.Hentgen	1.0	1	0	0	0	0
W.Alvarez	1.0	0	0	0	0	0
L.Smith (BS)	1.0	1	2	2	1	0
J.Bere (L)	0.0	2	1	1	0	0
National League						
G.Maddux	3.0	3	1	1	0	2
K.Hill	2.0	0	0	0	1	0
D.Drabek (BS)	0.2	4	3	1	0	1
J.Hudek	0.2	1	2	2	1	1
D.Jackson (BS) *	0.0	3	1	1	0	0
R.Beck	1.2	1	0	0	0	1
R.Myers	1.0	1	0	0	0	1
D.Jones (W)	1.0	2	0	0	0	2

* Pitched to 3 batters in 7th

Inherited Runners—Scored:
D.Cone 0–0; M.Mussina 0–0; R.Johnson 0–0; P.Hentgen 0–0; W.Alvarez 0–0; L.Smith 0–0; J.Bere 0–0; K.Hill 0–0; D.Drabek 0–0; J.Hudek 1–0; D.Jackson 2–2; R.Beck 2–0; R.Myers 0–0; D.Jones 0–0.
HBP: G.Jefferies by D.Cone.

GAME DATA—T: 3:14; A: 59568; Temp: 83; Wind: To left, Speed: 9 mph

UMPIRES—HP: Paul Runge (NL), 1B: John Shulock (AL), 2B: Jerry Layne (NL), 3B: Rocky Roe (AL), LF: Bill Hohn (NL), RF: Jim Joyce (AL)

STARTING LINEUPS

	American League	National League
1.	R.Alomar 2b	G.Jefferies 1b
2.	W.Boggs 3b	T.Gwynn cf
3.	K.Griffey Jr. cf	B.Bonds lf
4.	F.Thomas 1b	M.Piazza c
5.	J.Carter lf	M.Williams 3b
6.	K.Puckett rf	D.Justice rf
7.	C.Ripken ss	M.Duncan 2b
8.	I.Rodriguez c	O.Smith ss
9.	J.Key p	G.Maddux p

AL 1ST: R.Alomar grounded out (O.Smith-ss to G.Jefferies-1b); W.Boggs singled to center field; K.Griffey Jr. doubled to left-center [W.Boggs to third]; F.Thomas singled to center field [W.Boggs scored, K.Griffey Jr. to third]; J.Carter lined into a double play (G.Maddux-p to G.Jefferies-1b) [F.Thomas out at first]; 1 R, 3 H, 0 E, 1 LOB. AL 1, NL 0.

NL 1ST: G.Jefferies doubled to left field; T.Gwynn grounded out (F.Thomas-1b unassisted) [G.Jefferies to third]; B.Bonds out on a sacrifice fly to K.Puckett-rf [G.Jefferies scored]; M.Piazza lined to F.Thomas-1b; 1 R, 1 H, 0 E, 0 LOB. AL 1, NL 1.

AL 2ND: K.Puckett grounded out (M.Williams-3b to G.Jefferies-1b); C.Ripken grounded out (M.Duncan-2b to G.Jefferies-1b); I.Rodriguez struck out; 0 R, 0 H, 0 E, 0 LOB. AL 1, NL 1.

NL 2ND: M.Williams struck out; D.Justice flied to K.Griffey Jr.-cf; M.Duncan grounded out (W.Boggs-3b to F.Thomas-1b); 0 R, 0 H, 0 E, 0 LOB. AL 1, NL 1.

AL 3RD: **P.Molitor batted for J.Key;** P.Molitor grounded out (G.Jefferies-1b unassisted); R.Alomar grounded out (M.Duncan-2b to G.Jefferies-1b); W.Boggs struck out; 0 R, 0 H, 0 E, 0 LOB. AL 1, NL 1.

NL 3RD: **D.Cone replaced P.Molitor (pitching);** Cone threw 40 pitches in 2 innings; O.Smith flied to K.Griffey Jr.-cf; **J.Bagwell batted for G.Maddux;** J.Bagwell singled to left field; G.Jefferies was hit by a pitch [J.Bagwell to second]; T.Gwynn doubled to right field [J.Bagwell scored, G.Jefferies scored]; B.Bonds struck out; M.Piazza singled to left-center [T.Gwynn scored]; M.Williams struck out; 3 R, 3 H, 0 E, 1 LOB. AL 1, NL 4.

AL 4TH: **J.Bagwell stayed in game (playing 1b); K.Hill replaced G.Jefferies (pitching); C.Garcia replaced M.Duncan (playing 2b);** K.Griffey Jr. grounded out (J.Bagwell-1b to K.Hill-p); F.Thomas walked; J.Carter flied to D.Justice-rf; K.Puckett grounded out (J.Bagwell-1b unassisted); 0 R, 0 H, 0 E, 1 LOB. AL 1, NL 4.

NL 4TH: D.Justice grounded out (W.Boggs-3b to F.Thomas-1b); C.Garcia grounded out (C.Ripken-ss to F.Thomas-1b); O.Smith singled to right field; J.Bagwell struck out; 0 R, 1 H, 0 E, 1 LOB. AL 1, NL 4.

AL 5TH: **M.Grissom replaced D.Justice (playing cf); T.Gwynn changed positions (playing rf);** C.Ripken flied to B.Bonds-lf; I.Rodriguez flied to M.Grissom-cf; **C.Davis batted for D.Cone;** C.Davis grounded out (C.Garcia-2b to J.Bagwell-1b); 0 R, 0 H, 0 E, 0 LOB. AL 1, NL 4.

NL 5TH: **M.Mussina replaced C.Davis (pitching); D.Bichette batted for K.Hill;** D.Bichette singled to left field; T.Gwynn flied to J.Carter-lf; B.Bonds struck out; M.Piazza popped to F.Thomas-1b in foul territory; 0 R, 1 H, 0 E, 1 LOB. AL 1, NL 4.

AL 6TH: **D.Drabek replaced D.Bichette (pitching);** R.Alomar singled to center field; W.Boggs struck out; R.Alomar stole second; K.Griffey Jr. singled to center field (M.Grissom-cf to J.Bagwell-1b to O.Smith-ss) [R.Alomar scored, K.Griffey Jr. out at second]; F.Thomas singled to center field; J.Carter reached on an error by M.Williams-3b [F.Thomas scored (unearned) (no RBI), J.Carter to third]; K.Puckett singled to center field [J.Carter scored (unearned)]; **J.Hudek replaced D.Drabek (pitching);** C.Ripken struck out; 3 R (1 ER), 4 H, 1 E, 1 LOB. AL 4, NL 4.

NL 6TH: **R.Johnson replaced M.Mussina (pitching); W.Clark replaced F.Thomas (playing 1b); C.Knoblauch replaced R.Alomar (playing 2b); S.Cooper replaced W.Boggs (playing 3b); A.Belle replaced J.Carter (playing lf); K.Lofton replaced K.Griffey Jr. (playing cf); R.Sierra replaced K.Puckett (playing rf);** M.Williams flied to R.Sierra-rf; M.Grissom homered to rightfield; C.Garcia singled to center field; C.Garcia was picked off first (R.Johnson-p to W.Clark-1b); O.Smith hit a ball over the lf fence only to see it hook foul; O.Smith grounded out (W.Clark-1b unassisted); 1 R, 2 H, 0 E, 0 LOB. AL 4, NL 5.

AL 7TH: **C.Biggio replaced C.Garcia (playing 2b); K.Caminiti replaced M.Williams (playing 3b);** I.Rodriguez singled to center field; **M.Tettleton batted for R.Johnson;** M.Tettleton walked [I.Rodriguez to second]; C.Knoblauch forced M.Tettleton (O.Smith-ss to C.Biggio-2b) [I.Rodriguez to third, C.Knoblauch to first]; O.Smith dived to his right and threw from his knees; **D.Jackson replaced J.Hudek (pitching);** S.Cooper doubled to left field [I.Rodriguez scored, C.Knoblauch to third]; K.Lofton singled to left field [C.Knoblauch scored, S.Cooper scored]; W.Clark singled to center field [K.Lofton to second]; **W.Cordero replaced D.Jackson (playing ss); R.Beck replaced O.Smith (pitching);**

K.Lofton stole third and W.Clark stole second; A.Belle reached on a fielder's choice (W.Cordero-ss to M.Piazza-c) [K.Lofton out at home, W.Clark to third]; R.Sierra popped to C.Biggio-2b; 3 R, 4 H, 0 E, 2 LOB. AL 7, NL 5.

NL 7TH: **P.Hentgen replaced M.Tettleton (pitching);** J.Bagwell singled to right field; W.Cordero grounded into a double play (C.Ripken-ss to W.Clark-1b) [J.Bagwell out at second]; T.Gwynn grounded out (W.Clark-1b unassisted); 0 R, 1 H, 0 E, 0 LOB. AL 7, NL 5.

AL 8TH: C.Ripken doubled to right-center; I.Rodriguez flied to M.Grissom-cf; **P.O'Neill batted for P.Hentgen;** P.O'Neill popped to W.Cordero-ss; C.Knoblauch struck out; 0 R, 1 H, 0 E, 1 LOB. AL 7, NL 5.

NL 8TH: **W.Alvarez replaced P.O'Neill (pitching);** B.Bonds flied to K.Lofton-cf; M.Piazza grounded out (C.Knoblauch-2b to W.Clark-1b); K.Caminiti flied to A.Belle-lf; 0 R, 0 H, 0 E, 0 LOB. AL 7, NL 5.

AL 9TH: **R.Myers replaced R.Beck (pitching); D.Fletcher replaced M.Piazza (playing c); M.Alou replaced B.Bonds (playing lf);** S.Cooper grounded out (C.Biggio-2b to J.Bagwell-1b); K.Lofton struck out; W.Clark singled to second base; A.Belle flied to T.Gwynn-rf; 0 R, 1 H, 0 E, 1 LOB. AL 7, NL 5.

NL 9TH: **L.Smith replaced W.Alvarez (pitching);** L.Smith threw 28 pitches in 1 inning; M.Grissom walked; C.Biggio forced M.Grissom (S.Cooper-3b to C.Knoblauch-2b) [C.Biggio to first]; **F.McGriff batted for R.Myers;** F.McGriff homered to left-center [C.Biggio scored]; J.Bagwell grounded out (C.Knoblauch-2b to W.Clark-1b); W.Cordero grounded out (S.Cooper-3b to W.Clark-1b); 2 R, 1 H, 0 E, 0 LOB. AL 7, NL 7.

AL 10TH: **F.McGriff stayed in game (playing 1b); D.Jones replaced J.Bagwell (pitching);** R.Sierra singled to center field; C.Ripken struck out; I.Rodriguez singled to right field [R.Sierra to second]; **T.Fryman batted for L.Smith;** T.Fryman flied to T.Gwynn-rf [R.Sierra to third]; C.Knoblauch struck out; 0 R, 2 H, 0 E, 2 LOB. AL 7, NL 7.

NL 10TH: **J.Bere replaced T.Fryman (pitching);** T.Gwynn singled to center field; M.Alou doubled to left-center [T.Gwynn scored]; 1 R, 2 H, 0 E, 1 LOB. AL 7, NL 8.

Final Totals	R	H	E	LOB
American League	7	15	0	9
National League	8	12	1	4

66

Back to Business

When the All-Star Game came to Texas in 1995, baseball was still trying to right itself after the disastrous strike in 1994 canceled the last third of the season and all of the postseason. "Last year we were talking about the strike coming. This year we're talking baseball," said Frank Thomas.

George W. Bush, who left the position of managing general partner of the Rangers to become the Texas governor, said, "This is a great event to get the game of baseball back on track. This is a celebration of baseball."

The talk of the town this year was the NL's starting hurler, rookie Hideo Nomo, who came into the break leading the NL with 119 strikeouts. He also compiled a 6-1 record with a 1.99 ERA for the first half of the season. The Tornado, as he was called in his native Japan, was the first rookie pitcher to start an All-Star contest since Dodger Fernando Valenzuela in 1981.

Three-time defending NL Cy Young Award winner Greg Maddux, who would win the award again at the end of the 1995 season, was out with a groin injury, which left the starting spot to Nomo. "I think more people want to watch him pitch than me, to be honest. He's unique. There's a certain mystique which I don't have," said Maddux. NL starting shortstop Ozzie Smith remarked, "He is what is good about baseball right now. That's why people are looking to him."

Nomo's mound opponent was Randy Johnson, the first Mariner hurler to start an All-Star Game. Like Nomo, Johnson was leading his league in strikeouts, with 152. The two starters performed as expected: they each struck out three of the six batters they faced in two innings and allowed only one to reach base. Nomo allowed a single to Carlos Baerga, while Johnson walked Lenny Dykstra. Both runners were caught stealing; thus, both Nomo and Johnson faced the minimum six batters. Each would end the 1995 season with an award: Nomo would be named the NL Rookie of

the Year, while Johnson would win the AL Cy Young Award.

The scoring started in the bottom of the fourth when Frank Thomas, who had been the American League MVP each of the previous two seasons, hit a two-run homer into the second deck in left field. The blast scored Baerga, who went three for three in the contest. Thomas was the first White Sox player to homer in an All-Star Game. His homer landed in a luxury suite rented by the Players' Association, and Alex Fehr, nine-year-old nephew of union head Donald, ended up with the ball.

The NL got its first hit and first run in the sixth when Craig Biggio also homered to left. This was the first of three consecutive innings in which the NL had a solo four-bagger. In the seventh, it was Mike Piazza's turn as he hit one to right field. In the eighth, Florida Marlin Jeff Conine pinch-hit for designated hitter Ron Gant and smashed the ball into the left-field seats, putting the NL ahead for good, 3–2.

Conine became the tenth player to homer in his first All-Star at bat and the sixteenth pinch hitter to launch one. Only two other players had performed both feats in the same at bat: George Altman in 1961 and Lee Mazzilli in 1979. Since Conine had never seen pitcher Steve Ontiveros of Oakland, injured Giant Matt Williams gave Conine a scouting report, telling him to look for a breaking ball. After taking a ball, Conine at first thought about taking another pitch but decided he might get one he could hit. He was correct because Ontiveros threw the breaking ball of Williams's report (a slider), and Conine launched it into the seats. After the game, Conine remarked, "My friends back in Florida told me to swing for the fences. I wasn't thinking about it at the time, but it worked out that way."

For his effort, Conine was named the game's MVP. It was an especially sweet moment for the Marlin player because he was the only 1994 All-Star who did not get into that game. Conine had a sympathetic manager in Montreal's Felipe Alou because Alou had been on four All-Star rosters but had only played twice. "I promised I would use him," said Alou. "I knew sometime in May that he was going to play in the game. I wanted to make sure he got into the game, and it paid off."

The NL got only three hits all night off the superb AL pitching staff, but they were all home runs. This was the first time in All-Star history that all of a team's hits were round-trippers. NL second baseman Craig Biggio, who would never be mistaken for a slugger despite his homer in the sixth, said, "You see a lot of strange things happen in this game, and that was definitely one of them." Asked whether he could win a homer-hitting contest, Biggio said, "I don't think so. If there was a bunting contest, I might win that."

The pitching for both teams was exceptional, recording seventeen strikeouts with only three walks. While the AL staff gave up only the three hits, their colleagues in the NL surrendered eight: six singles, Thomas's home run, and a double by Baerga. For the second consecutive year, a Phillies pitcher won the game after the contingent from the City of Brotherly Love had never registered a win in sixty-one years of All-Star play. This time the winner was Heathcliff Slocumb, who pitched one inning of scoreless ball after coming out of the bullpen in the seventh inning.

The AL stranded seven runners from the fifth inning on, helping the NL hurlers. Rookie pitcher Tyler Green started the fifth inning for the NL and was greeted by singles from Cal Ripken Jr. and Wade Boggs. However, Kirby Puckett, playing in his tenth and last All-Star contest, struck out, Ivan Rodriguez forced Boggs, and Kenny Lofton grounded out.

In the sixth, with Denny Neagle of the Pirates on the mound for the NL, Carlos Baerga doubled to right, and pinch runner Roberto Alomar stole third. He was stranded there as Edgar Martinez flied out, Mo Vaughn struck out, and Albert Belle grounded out to end the inning. Again in the seventh, the AL had runners on first and second with one out, but Rodriguez and Jim Edmonds both struck out.

After the game, Ripken said, "When you lose, you say, 'It's just an exhibition.' When you win you say, 'We took it seriously.' " Ripken was at 2,077 consecutive games played at the break, just 54 games from Lou Gehrig's mark, which he broke on September 6.

There were twenty-three first-time All-Stars on the rosters, including two rookies (Green and Nomo). This game marked the twelfth and last time that Ozzie Smith was elected by the fans to start.

Earlier in the day, former All-Star and Hall of Famer Mickey Mantle had spoken at a press conference at Baylor University Medical Center, where he was recovering from liver transplant surgery. This was Mantle's first public appearance since his operation on June 8. Mantle admitted that he had partied too much during his career. He told of flying from Dallas to Anaheim for the 1967 All-Star Game. He arrived at the park in time to pinch-hit for Jim McGlothlin in the fifth inning (striking out), and then he flew back to Texas to rejoin his friends at a bar.

On the day before the game, undercover Arlington police officers mounted a sting operation to catch people scalping tickets to the game. There was a new city ordinance making it a misdemeanor to sell tickets for more than their face value, and one of the people caught in the trap was Rangers relief pitcher Ed Vosberg, who allegedly was trying to sell complimentary tickets he had been given to the game.

Baseball used this occasion to remind the American public of the many positive aspects of the game and to further recover some of its former status as the national pastime. Seeing the best practitioners of the sport at their craft was a good way to divert attention from the unpleasantness of the previous year.

	AL		NL	
P	Randy Johnson	SEA	Hideo Nomo	LAN
C	Ivan Rodriguez	TEX	Mike Piazza	LAN
1B	Frank Thomas	CHA	Fred McGriff	ATL
2B	Carlos Baerga	CLE	Craig Biggio	HOU
3B	Wade Boggs	NYA	Matt Williams +	SFN
SS	Cal Ripken	BAL	Ozzie Smith +	SLN
OF	Albert Belle	CLE	Barry Bonds	SFN
OF	Ken Griffey +	SEA	Lenny Dykstra	PHI
OF	Kirby Puckett	MIN	Tony Gwynn	SDN
DH	Edgar Martinez	SEA	Ron Gant	CIN
	Roberto Alomar	TOR	Dante Bichette	COL
	Kevin Appier	KCA	Bobby Bonilla	NYN
	Gary Disarcina	CAL	Vinny Castilla	COL
	Jim Edmonds	CAL	Jeff Conine	FLO
	Chuck Finley	CAL	Darren Daulton	PHI
	Erik Hanson	BOS	Mark Grace	CHN
	Kenny Lofton	CLE	Tyler Green	PHI
	Dennis Martinez	CLE	Tom Henke	SLN
	Tino Martinez	SEA	Barry Larkin	CIN
	Mark McGwire +	OAK	Greg Maddux +	ATL
	Jose Mesa	CLE	Raul Mondesi	LAN
	Paul O'Neill	NYA	Mickey Morandini	PHI
	Steve Ontiveros	OAK	Randy Myers	CHN
	Manny Ramirez	CLE	Denny Neagle	PIT
	Kenny Rogers	TEX	Jose Offerman	LAN
	Kevin Seitzer	MIL	Carlos Perez	MON
	Lee Smith	CAL	Reggie Sanders	CIN
	Mike Stanley	NYA	Heathcliff Slocumb	PHI
	Mo Vaughn	BOS	John Smiley	CIN
	David Wells	DET	Sammy Sosa	CHN
			Todd Worrell	LAN

+ player replaced on roster

National League	000 001 110-	3		
American League	000 200 000-	2		

NATIONAL LEAGUE

	ab	r	h	bi	bb	so	po	a
L.Dykstra, cf	2	0	0	0	1	0	1	0
S.Sosa, cf	1	0	0	0	0	0	2	0
T.Gwynn, rf	2	0	0	0	0	0	1	0
R.Sanders, rf	1	0	0	0	0	1	0	0
R.Mondesi, rf	1	0	0	0	0	0	2	0
B.Bonds, lf	3	0	0	0	0	1	0	0
D.Bichette, lf	1	0	0	0	0	1	2	0
M.Piazza, c	3	1	1	1	0	0	6	1
D.Daulton, c	0	0	0	0	0	0	3	0
F.McGriff, 1b	3	0	0	0	0	2	5	0
M.Grace, 1b	0	0	0	0	0	0	1	0
R.Gant, dh	2	0	0	0	0	1	0	0
J.Conine, ph	1	1	1	1	0	0	0	0
B.Larkin, ss	3	0	0	0	0	0	2	3
J.Offerman, ss	0	0	0	0	0	0	0	0
V.Castilla, 3b	2	0	0	0	0	1	0	0
B.Bonilla, 3b	1	0	0	0	0	1	0	0
C.Biggio, 2b	2	1	1	1	0	0	2	1
M.Morandini, 2b	1	0	0	0	0	1	0	1
Totals	29	3	3	3	1	9	27	6

BATTING

HR: M.Piazza (7th inning off K.Rogers, 0 on, 2 out); J.Conine (8th inning off S.Ontiveros, 0 on, 0 out); C.Biggio (6th inning off D.Martinez, 0 on, 2 out).
2-out RBI: M.Piazza; C.Biggio.

BASERUNNING

CS: L.Dykstra (2nd base by R.Johnson/I.Rodriguez).
Team LOB: 0

AMERICAN LEAGUE

	ab	r	h	bi	bb	so	po	a
K.Lofton, cf	3	0	0	0	0	1	0	0
J.Edmonds, ph-cf	1	0	0	0	0	1	0	0
C.Baerga, 2b	3	1	3	0	0	0	1	2
R.Alomar, pr-2b	1	0	0	0	0	0	0	0
E.Martinez, dh	3	0	0	0	0	1	0	0
T.Martinez, ph	1	0	1	0	0	0	0	0
F.Thomas, 1b	2	1	1	2	0	0	5	1
M.Vaughn, 1b	2	0	0	0	0	2	4	0
A.Belle, lf	3	0	0	0	0	1	1	0
P.O'Neill, lf	1	0	0	0	0	0	0	0
C.Ripken, ss	3	0	2	0	0	0	2	1
G.DiSarcina, pr-ss	1	0	0	0	0	0	0	0
W.Boggs, 3b	2	0	1	0	0	0	0	1
K.Seitzer, ph-3b	2	0	0	0	0	0	0	0
K.Puckett, rf	2	0	0	0	0	1	2	0
M.Ramirez, ph-rf	0	0	0	0	2	0	2	0
I.Rodriguez, c	3	0	0	0	0	1	6	1
M.Stanley, c	1	0	0	0	0	0	3	0
Totals	34	2	8	2	2	8	26	6

BATTING

2B: C.Baerga (off D.Neagle).
HR: F.Thomas (4th inning off J.Smiley, 1 on, 2 out).
2-out RBI: F.Thomas 2.
RBI, scoring position, less than 2 outs: E.Martinez 0-1; M.Vaughn 0-1; K.Puckett 0-1; I.Rodriguez 0-2.

BASERUNNING

SB: R.Alomar (3rd base off D.Neagle/M.Piazza).
CS: C.Baerga (2nd base by H.Nomo/M.Piazza).
Team LOB: 7

PITCHING	ip	h	r	er	bb	so
National League						
H.Nomo	2.0	1	0	0	0	3
J.Smiley	2.0	2	2	2	0	0
T.Green	1.0	2	0	0	0	1
D.Neagle	1.0	1	0	0	0	1
C.Perez	0.1	1	0	0	1	0
H.Slocumb (w)	1.0	1	0	0	0	2
T.Henke	0.2	0	0	0	0	1
R.Myers (s)	1.0	0	0	0	1	0

Inherited Runners—Scored:
J.Smiley 0-0; T.Green 0-0; D.Neagle 0-0; C.Perez 0-0; H.Slocumb 2-0; T.Henke 1-0; R.Myers 0-0; K.Appier 0-0; D.Martinez 0-0; K.Rogers 0-0; S.Ontiveros 0-0; D.Wells 0-0; J.Mesa 0-0.

GAME DATA—T: 2:40; A: 50920; Temp: 101; Wind: From center, Speed: 10 mph

PITCHING	ip	h	r	er	bb	so
American League						
R.Johnson	2.0	0	0	0	1	3
K.Appier	2.0	0	0	0	0	1
D.Martinez	2.0	1	1	1	0	0
K.Rogers (BS)	1.0	1	1	1	0	2
S.Ontiveros (L)	0.2	1	1	1	0	1
D.Wells	0.1	0	0	0	0	1
J.Mesa	1.0	0	0	0	0	1

UMPIRES—HP: Durwood Merrill (AL), 1B: Charlie Williams (NL), 2B: Al Clark (AL), 3B: Mike Winters (NL), LF: Ted Hendry (AL), RF: Ed Rapuano (NL)

STARTING LINEUPS

	National League	American League
1.	L.Dykstra cf	K.Lofton cf
2.	T.Gwynn rf	C.Baerga 2b
3.	B.Bonds lf	E.Martinez dh
4.	M.Piazza c	F.Thomas 1b
5.	F.McGriff 1b	A.Belle lf
6.	R.Gant dh	C.Ripken ss
7.	B.Larkin ss	W.Boggs 3b
8.	V.Castilla 3b	K.Puckett rf
9.	C.Biggio 2b	I.Rodriguez c
	H.Nomo p	R.Johnson p

NL 1ST: L.Dykstra walked; T.Gwynn flied to A.Belle-lf; L.Dykstra was caught stealing second (I.Rodriguez-c to C.Ripken-ss); B.Bonds struck out; 0 R, 0 H, 0 E, 0 LOB. NL 0, AL 0.

AL 1ST: K.Lofton struck out; C.Baerga singled to right field; C.Baerga was caught stealing second (M.Piazza-c to C.Biggio-2b); E.Martinez struck out; 0 R, 1 H, 0 E, 0 LOB. NL 0, AL 0.

NL 2ND: M.Piazza grounded out (F.Thomas-1b to R.Johnson-p); F.McGriff struck out; R.Gant struck out; 0 R, 0 H, 0 E, 0 LOB. NL 0, AL 0.

AL 2ND: F.Thomas popped to M.Piazza-c in foul territory; A.Belle struck out; C.Ripken lined to T.Gwynn-rf; 0 R, 0 H, 0 E, 0 LOB. NL 0, AL 0.

NL 3RD: **K.Appier changed positions (pitching)**; B.Larkin grounded out (C.Baerga-2b to F.Thomas-1b); V.Castilla struck out; C.Biggio grounded out (C.Ripken-ss to F.Thomas-1b); 0 R, 0 H, 0 E, 0 LOB. NL 0, AL 0.

AL 3RD: **J.Smiley replaced H.Nomo (pitching)**; W.Boggs flied to L.Dykstra-cf; K.Puckett grounded out (J.Smiley-p to F.McGriff-1b); I.Rodriguez grounded out (B.Larkin-ss to F.McGriff-1b); 0 R, 0 H, 0 E, 0 LOB. NL 0, AL 0.

NL 4TH: L.Dykstra grounded out (C.Baerga-2b to F.Thomas-1b); T.Gwynn grounded out (F.Thomas-1b unassisted); B.Bonds grounded out (K.Appier-p to F.Thomas-1b); 0 R, 0 H, 0 E, 0 LOB. NL 0, AL 0.

AL 4TH: K.Lofton grounded out (C.Biggio-2b to F.McGriff-1b); C.Baerga singled to left field; E.Martinez popped to B.Larkin-ss; F.Thomas homered to leftfield [C.Baerga scored]; A.Belle popped to B.Larkin-ss; 2 R, 2 H, 0 E, 0 LOB. NL 0, AL 2.

NL 5TH: **D.Martinez replaced K.Appier (pitching)**; **M.Vaughn replaced F.Thomas (playing 1b)**; M.Piazza lined to C.Ripken-ss; F.McGriff flied to K.Puckett-rf; R.Gant popped to M.Vaughn-1b in foul territory; 0 R, 0 H, 0 E, 0 LOB. NL 0, AL 2.

AL 5TH: **T.Green replaced J.Smiley (pitching)**; **R.Sanders replaced T.Gwynn (playing rf)**;

C.Ripken singled to center field; W.Boggs singled to right field [C.Ripken to second]; K.Puckett struck out; I.Rodriguez forced W.Boggs (B.Larkin-ss to C.Biggio-2b) [C.Ripken to third, I.Rodriguez to first]; K.Lofton grounded out (T.Green-p to F.McGriff-1b); 0 R, 2 H, 0 E, 2 LOB. NL 0, AL 2.

NL 6TH: B.Larkin lined to C.Baerga-2b; V.Castilla grounded out (W.Boggs-3b to M.Vaughn-1b); C.Biggio homered to leftfield; L.Dykstra grounded out (D.Martinez-p to M.Vaughn-1b); 1 R, 1 H, 0 E, 0 LOB. NL 1, AL 2.

AL 6TH: **D.Neagle replaced T.Green (pitching)**; **B.Bonilla replaced V.Castilla (playing 3b)**; **S.Sosa replaced L.Dykstra (playing cf)**; C.Baerga doubled to right field; **R.Alomar ran for C.Baerga**; R.Alomar stole third; E.Martinez flied to S.Sosa-cf; M.Vaughn struck out; A.Belle grounded out (B.Larkin-ss to F.McGriff-1b); 0 R, 1 H, 0 E, 1 LOB. NL 1, AL 2.

NL 7TH: **R.Alomar stayed in game (playing 2b)**; **K.Rogers replaced D.Martinez (pitching)**; **P.O'Neill replaced A.Belle (playing lf)**; R.Sanders struck out; B.Bonds flied to K.Puckett-rf; M.Piazza homered to rightfield; F.McGriff struck out; 1 R, 1 H, 0 E, 0 LOB. NL 2, AL 2.

AL 7TH: **C.Perez replaced D.Neagle (pitching)**; **D.Daulton replaced M.Piazza (playing c)**; **M.Grace replaced F.McGriff (playing 1b)**; **M.Morandini replaced C.Biggio (playing 2b)**; **D.Bichette replaced B.Bonds (playing lf)**; **R.Mondesi replaced R.Sanders (playing rf)**; C.Ripken singled to left field; **G.Disarcina ran for C.Ripken**; **K.Seitzer batted for W.Boggs**; K.Seitzer flied to R.Mondesi-rf; **M.Ramirez batted for K.Puckett**; M.Ramirez walked [G.DiSarcina to second]; **H.Slocumb replaced C.Perez (pitching)**; I.Rodriguez struck out; **J.Edmonds batted for K.Lofton**; J.Edmonds struck out; 0 R, 1 H, 0 E, 2 LOB. NL 2, AL 2.

NL 8TH: **S.Ontiveros replaced K.Rogers (pitching)**; **M.Stanley replaced I.Rodriguez (playing c)**; **G.Disarcina stayed in game (playing ss)**; **K.Seitzer stayed in game (playing 3b)**; **M.Ramirez stayed in game (playing rf)**; **J.Edmonds stayed in game (playing cf)**; **J.Conine batted for R.Gant**; J.Conine homered to leftfield; B.Larkin grounded out (S.Ontiveros-p to M.Vaughn-1b); B.Bonilla struck out; **D.Wells replaced S.Ontiveros (pitching)**; M.Morandini struck out; 1 R, 1 H, 0 E, 0 LOB. NL 3, AL 2.

AL 8TH: **J.Offerman replaced B.Larkin (playing ss)**; R.Alomar flied to D.Bichette-lf; **T.Martinez batted for E.Martinez**; T.Martinez singled to right field; **T.Henke replaced H.Slocumb (pitching)**;

M.Vaughn struck out; P.O'Neill flied to S.Sosa-cf; 0 R, 1 H, 0 E, 1 LOB. NL 3, AL 2.

NL 9TH: **J.Mesa replaced D.Wells (pitching);** S.Sosa flied to M.Ramirez-rf; R.Mondesi flied to M.Ramirez-rf; D.Bichette struck out; 0 R, 0 H, 0 E, 0 LOB. NL 3, AL 2.

AL 9TH: **R.Myers replaced T.Henke (pitching);** G.DiSarcina flied to D.Bichette-lf; K.Seitzer grounded out (M.Morandini-2b to M.Grace-1b); M.Ramirez walked; M.Stanley lined to R.Mondesi-rf; 0 R, 0 H, 0 E, 1 LOB. NL 3, AL 2.

Final Totals	R	H	E	LOB
National League	3	3	0	0
American League	2	8	0	7

67

Piazza to Go

The 1996 season featured an offensive explosion that included more home runs than had ever been hit in the Majors. However, the AL players left their bats at home over the All-Star break as the NL hurlers threw the first shutout in the big game since 1990. It was the seventh shutout in All-Star history and the fifth by the NL. And for the first time in All-Star history, none of the fourteen pitchers who worked walked a batter.

"That wasn't a typical night for those American League batters, believe me," said NL manager Bobby Cox. "They can bomb the ball out of any ballpark. We just made some exceptional pitches tonight."

The NL started the scoring in the first inning. Lance Johnson, who replaced the injured Tony Gwynn on the roster, led off with a double and scored on two infield outs. The Senior Circuit scored two more in the next inning on a Mike Piazza solo homer into the upper deck and two singles by Chipper Jones and Henry Rodriguez.

The Senior Circuit continued plating runners in the third inning. Singles by Barry Larkin and Barry Bonds were followed by a double play in which Fred McGriff struck out and Bonds was caught stealing second. Then, a double by Piazza scored Larkin. The NL wrapped up the scoring in the sixth as Ken Caminiti homered to start the frame. The home run by Caminiti marked the first time a San Diego Padre had homered in All-Star competition. Dante Bichette doubled and moved to third on a strike-three wild pitch, which also put Ellis Burks on first base. Bichette scored as Craig Biggio forced Burks at second.

The AL got only one runner to third base with less than two outs. In the sixth, Kenny Lofton singled and stole second after a fly out by Wade Boggs. Roberto Alomar singled to shortstop, and Lofton moved over to third. However, Pedro Martinez struck out Albert Belle and induced Mo Vaughn to ground out to stop the threat.

The AL squad came into the game with a combined .314 average with 348 home runs, far better than the corresponding NL numbers, .303 and 288. However, the best performance for the AL came from Lofton, who had two singles in three trips to the plate and stole two bases. Lance Johnson ended with three hits for the NL, including his double.

Born in nearby Norristown, Pennsylvania, Piazza had been drafted mostly as a family favor by the Dodgers in the sixty-second round of the 1988 free-agent draft. Piazza's performance in this game earned him MVP honors. He had two hits in three attempts, with a double in addition to his homer. "I just didn't want to embarrass myself tonight," Piazza said. "I didn't think of any heroics. Every time I play in this park, it's a thrill for me because of my past. And for something like this to happen in Philadelphia is just unbelievable."

None of the five Junior Circuit pitchers came away unscathed; they each surrendered at least one hit. Chuck Finley struck out four of the eight NL batters he faced. Kevin Brown, Tom Glavine, Steve Trachsel, and Ricky Bottalico each pitched a perfect inning for the NL. John Smoltz started for the NL and was credited with the win after pitching two-hit shutout ball for two innings. He was the first Atlanta Braves pitcher to win; the last hurler for the franchise to win was Gene Conley of the Milwaukee team in 1955. Braves pitchers had started six of the last eight All-Star contests.

This was the third consecutive victory by the NL and the second game played at the Vet. The first had been played twenty years earlier during the bicentennial celebration.

Four of the elected starters—Ken Griffey Jr., Frank Thomas, Gwynn, and Matt Williams—were unable to play due to injuries. Griffey had received the most votes of any player, with Piazza leading the NL. One rookie was named to the squad, catcher Jason Kendall of the Pirates. Todd Hundley made it a family affair by playing (his dad, Randy, had played in 1969). The Hundleys became the ninth father-son duo to be named All-Stars.

The night's sentimental moment came when Ozzie Smith stepped to the plate in the seventh inning. Smith had already announced that he would retire at the end of the season, and this game was his fourteenth appearance in the All-Star classic. He had entered the contest as a defensive replacement in the sixth, and as he stepped to the plate, he received a minute-long standing ovation from the 62,670 fans in the stands. Fans elected Smith twelve times as a starter, which, with Cal Ripken Jr., is more than any other shortstop in history. "I got chills when that happened," Cox said. "I know Ozzie got very emotional at the plate. I didn't think he was going to be able to take his at bat. I was pleased he just made contact."

The most bizarre feature of the night was something that the fans didn't even know about. During the pregame team photo session, Ripken had his nose broken by an accidental slash of Roberto Hernandez's forearm. Ripken said later, "We were taking the team picture. Roberto stepped on the platform, and it tilted. He threw his arm back to catch his balance and hit my nose. It was a pretty vicious backhand."

Hernandez, a relief pitcher for the White Sox, had buzzed fastballs by Ripken in the past but had finally hit him by accident. Said Hernandez, "It was bleeding pretty bad. I offered him my shirt to help stop the bleeding. I got more nervous and panicky. Robbie [Alomar] and Brady [Anderson] offered to get me a bodyguard when I go to Baltimore."

Ripken, who had played 2,239 consecutive regular season games and thirteen consecutive All-Star contests, did not let the first broken nose of his life keep him out of the game. He did most of the work toward resetting the nose himself before the Phillies team physician arrived to help. "By the time the doctor got there, he had already pushed it back into place," Baltimore teammate Brady Anderson said. "The doctor just said, 'I can push it in further.'" Ripken played six innings with gauze stuffed up his nose. His reaction? "I wouldn't give it a second thought."

In Miami that day, it was announced that pitcher Rolando Arrojo of the Cuban National Team had defected while the team was in the United States preparing for the Atlanta Olympics. Two years later, he played in the 1998 All-Star contest.

	AL			NL		
P	Charles Nagy		CLE	John Smoltz		ATL
C	Ivan Rodriguez		TEX	Mike Piazza		LAN
1B	Frank Thomas	+	CHA	Fred McGriff		ATL
2B	Roberto Alomar		BAL	Craig Biggio		HOU
3B	Wade Boggs		NYA	Matt Williams	+	SFN
SS	Cal Ripken		BAL	Barry Larkin		CIN
OF	Albert Belle		CLE	Dante Bichette		COL
OF	Ken Griffey	+	SEA	Barry Bonds		SFN
OF	Kenny Lofton		CLE	Tony Gwynn	+	SDN
	Sandy Alomar		CLE	Jeff Bagwell		HOU
	Brady Anderson		BAL	Ricky Bottalico		PHI
	Jay Buhner		SEA	Kevin Brown		FLO
	Joe Carter		TOR	Ellis Burks		COL
	Chuck Finley		CAL	Ken Caminiti		SDN
	Travis Fryman		DET	Tom Glavine		ATL
	Roberto Hernandez		CHA	Mark Grudzielanek		MON
	Chuck Knoblauch		MIN	Todd Hundley		NYN
	Edgar Martinez		SEA	Lance Johnson		NYN
	Mark McGwire		OAK	Chipper Jones		ATL
	Jose Mesa		CLE	Jason Kendall		PIT
	Jeff Montgomery		KCA	Al Leiter		FLO
	Roger Pavlik		TEX	Greg Maddux		ATL
	Troy Percival		CAL	Pedro Martinez		MON
	Andy Pettitte		NYA	Henry Rodriguez		MON
	Alex Rodriguez		SEA	Gary Sheffield		FLO
	Greg Vaughn		MIL	Ozzie Smith		SLN
	Mo Vaughn		BOS	Steve Trachsel		CHN
	John Wetteland		NYA	Mark Wohlers		ATL
	Dan Wilson		SEA	Todd Worrell		LAN
				Eric Young		COL

+ player replaced on roster

RETROSHEET EXPANDED BOX SCORE Tuesday, 7/9/1996 American League at National League (N)

American League	000	000	000-	0	
National League	121	002	00x-	6	

AMERICAN LEAGUE

	ab	r	h	bi	bb	so	po	a
K.Lofton, cf	3	0	2	0	0	0	0	0
J.Carter, cf	1	0	1	0	0	0	1	0
W.Boggs, 3b	3	0	0	0	0	0	1	2
T.Fryman, ph-3b	1	0	0	0	0	1	0	1
R.Alomar, 2b	3	0	1	0	0	0	0	3
C.Knoblauch, 2b	1	0	1	0	0	0	3	1
A.Belle, lf	4	0	0	0	0	3	1	0
M.Vaughn, 1b	3	0	1	0	0	0	5	1
M.McGwire, 1b	1	0	1	0	0	0	2	1
I.Rodriguez, c	2	0	0	0	0	1	6	2
S.Alomar Jr., ph-c	2	0	0	0	0	0	1	0
C.Ripken, ss	3	0	0	0	0	0	1	1
T.Percival, p	0	0	0	0	0	0	0	0
R.Hernandez, p	0	0	0	0	0	0	1	0
D.Wilson, ph	1	0	0	0	0	0	0	0
B.Anderson, rf	2	0	0	0	0	0	0	0
R.Pavlik, p	0	0	0	0	0	0	0	0
A.Rodriguez, ph-ss	1	0	0	0	0	0	0	0
C.Nagy, p	0	0	0	0	0	0	1	0
E.Martinez, ph	1	0	0	0	0	0	0	0
C.Finley, p	0	0	0	0	0	0	0	0
J.Buhner, ph-rf	2	0	0	0	0	0	1	0
Totals	34	0	7	0	0	5	24	12

BATTING
2B: M.Vaughn (off J.Smoltz).
RBI, scoring position, less than 2 outs: W.Boggs 0–1; R.Alomar 0–1; A.Belle 0–1; I.Rodriguez 0–1; C.Ripken 0–1.
GDP: S.Alomar Jr..

BASERUNNING
SB: K.Lofton 2 (2nd base off J.Smoltz/M.Piazza; 2nd base off P.Martinez/M.Piazza).
Team LOB: 7

FIELDING
DP: (1). I.Rodriguez-C.Ripken.

NATIONAL LEAGUE

	ab	r	h	bi	bb	so	po	a
L.Johnson, cf	4	1	3	0	0	0	5	0
B.Larkin, ss	3	1	1	0	0	0	0	2
O.Smith, ss	1	0	0	0	0	0	0	3
B.Bonds, lf	3	0	1	1	0	0	2	0
P.Martinez, p	0	0	0	0	0	0	0	0
G.Sheffield, rf	1	0	0	0	0	0	2	0
F.McGriff, 1b	2	0	0	0	0	2	2	1
T.Glavine, p	0	0	0	0	0	0	0	0
K.Caminiti, 3b	2	1	1	1	0	1	0	0
T.Worrell, p	0	0	0	0	0	0	0	0
M.Wohlers, p	0	0	0	0	0	0	0	0
A.Leiter, p	0	0	0	0	0	0	0	0
M.Piazza, c	3	1	2	2	0	1	4	0
T.Hundley, c	1	0	0	0	0	0	1	0
J.Kendall, c	0	0	0	0	0	0	0	0
D.Bichette, rf	3	1	1	0	0	1	0	0
S.Trachsel, p	0	0	0	0	0	0	0	0
M.Grudzielanek, 3b	1	0	0	0	0	0	0	0
C.Jones, 3b	2	1	1	0	0	0	1	1
R.Bottalico, p	0	0	0	0	0	0	0	0
E.Burks, lf	2	0	1	0	0	1	1	0
C.Biggio, 2b	3	0	0	1	0	1	1	1
E.Young, pr-2b	1	0	0	0	0	0	2	1
J.Smoltz, p	0	0	0	0	0	0	1	0
H.Rodriguez, ph	1	0	1	1	0	0	0	0
K.Brown, p	0	0	0	0	0	0	0	0
J.Bagwell, 1b	2	0	0	0	0	1	5	0
Totals	35	6	12	6	0	8	27	9

BATTING
2B: L.Johnson (off C.Nagy); M.Piazza (off C.Finley); D.Bichette (off R.Pavlik).
3B: E.Burks (off R.Hernandez).
HR: K.Caminiti (6th inning off R.Pavlik, 0 on, 0 out); M.Piazza (2nd inning off C.Nagy, 0 on, 0 out).
2-out RBI: M.Piazza; H.Rodriguez.
RBI, scoring position, less than 2 outs: B.Larkin 0–2; B.Bonds 1–1; G.Sheffield 0–1; F.McGriff 0–1; E.Burks 0–1; C.Biggio 1–1.

BASERUNNING
SB: L.Johnson (2nd base off R.Pavlik/I.Rodriguez).
CS: L.Johnson (3rd base by R.Pavlik/I.Rodriguez); B.Bonds (2nd base by C.Finley/I.Rodriguez).
Team LOB: 5

FIELDING
E: K.Caminiti (fumble).
DP: (1). O.Smith-E.Young-J.Bagwell.

PITCHING	ip	h	r	er	bb	so
American League						
C.Nagy (L)	2.0	4	3	3	0	1
C.Finley	2.0	3	1	1	0	4
R.Pavlik	2.0	3	2	2	0	2
T.Percival	1.0	1	0	0	0	1
R.Hernandez	1.0	1	0	0	0	0
National League						
J.Smoltz (W)	2.0	2	0	0	0	1
K.Brown	1.0	0	0	0	0	0
T.Glavine	1.0	0	0	0	0	1
R.Bottalico	1.0	0	0	0	0	1
P.Martinez	1.0	2	0	0	0	1
S.Trachsel	1.0	0	0	0	0	0
T.Worrell	1.0	2	0	0	0	1
M.Wohlers	0.2	1	0	0	0	0
A.Leiter	0.1	0	0	0	0	0

Inherited Runners—Scored:
C.Finley 0–0; R.Pavlik 0–0; T.Percival 0–0; R.Hernandez 0–0; K.Brown 0–0; T.Glavine 0–0; R.Bottalico 0–0; P.Martinez 0–0; S.Trachsel 0–0; T.Worrell 0–0; M.Wohlers 0–0; A.Leiter 0–0.
WP: R.Pavlik

GAME DATA—T: 2:35; A: 62670; Temp: 77; Wind: To right, Speed: 10 mph

UMPIRES—HP: Randy Marsh (NL), 1B: Larry McCoy (AL), 2B: Charlie Reliford (NL), 3B: Joe Brinkman (AL), LF: Larry Poncino (NL), RF: Chuck Meriwether (AL)

STARTING LINEUPS

	American League	National League
1.	K.Lofton cf	L.Johnson cf
2.	W.Boggs 3b	B.Larkin ss
3.	R.Alomar 2b	B.Bonds lf
4.	A.Belle lf	F.McGriff 1b
5.	M.Vaughn 1b	M.Piazza c
6.	I.Rodriguez c	D.Bichette rf
7.	C.Ripken ss	C.Jones 3b
8.	B.Anderson rf	C.Biggio 2b
9.	C.Nagy p	J.Smoltz p

AL 1ST: K.Lofton singled to center field (it was the 2–1 pitch); K.Lofton stole second (it was the 1–1 pitch); W.Boggs popped to C.Jones-3b; R.Alomar flied to L.Johnson-cf [K.Lofton to third]; A.Belle struck out; 0 R, 1 H, 0 E, 1 LOB. AL 0, NL 0.

NL 1ST: L.Johnson doubled to left field (it was the first pitch); B.Larkin grounded out (R.Alomar-2b to M.Vaughn-1b) [L.Johnson to third]; B.Bonds grounded out (M.Vaughn-1b to C.Nagy-p) [L.Johnson scored]; F.McGriff struck out; 1 R, 1 H, 0 E, 0 LOB. AL 0, NL 1.

AL 2ND: M.Vaughn doubled to right field (it was the first pitch); I.Rodriguez popped to C.Biggio-2b; C.Ripken lined to B.Bonds-lf; B.Anderson grounded out (F.McGriff-1b to J.Smoltz-p); 0 R, 1 H, 0 E, 1 LOB. AL 0, NL 1.

NL 2ND: M.Piazza homered to deep leftfield (it was the 2–1 pitch); D.Bichette grounded out (R.Alomar-2b to M.Vaughn-1b); C.Jones singled to center field (it was the 1–0 pitch); C.Biggio grounded out (W.Boggs-3b to M.Vaughn-1b) [C.Jones to second]; **H.Rodriguez batted for J.Smoltz**; H.Rodriguez singled to right field (it was the 1–0 pitch) [C.Jones scored]; L.Johnson grounded out (R.Alomar-2b to M.Vaughn-1b); 2 R, 3 H, 0 E, 1 LOB. AL 0, NL 3.

AL 3RD: **K.Brown replaced H.Rodriguez (pitching); E.Martinez batted for C.Nagy**; E.Martinez grounded out (B.Larkin-ss to F.McGriff-1b); K.Lofton flied to L.Johnson-cf; W.Boggs grounded out (B.Larkin-ss to F.McGriff-1b); 0 R, 0 H, 0 E, 0 LOB. AL 0, NL 3.

NL 3RD: **C.Finley replaced E.Martinez (pitching)**; B.Larkin singled to center field (it was the 0–2 pitch); B.Bonds singled to rightfield (it was the 2–0 pitch) [B.Larkin to third]; F.McGriff was called out on strikes while B.Bonds was caught stealing second (I.Rodriguez-c to C.Ripken-ss); M.Piazza doubled to right-center (it was the 1–0 pitch) [B.Larkin scored]; D.Bichette struck out; 1 R, 3 H, 0 E, 1 LOB. AL 0, NL 4.

AL 4TH: **J.Bagwell replaced K.Brown (playing 1b); T.Glavine replaced F.McGriff (pitching)**; R.Alo-mar grounded out (C.Jones-3b to J.Bagwell-1b); A.Belle struck out; M.Vaughn grounded out (C.Biggio-2b to J.Bagwell-1b); 0 R, 0 H, 0 E, 0 LOB. AL 0, NL 4.

NL 4TH: C.Jones lined to A.Belle-lf; C.Biggio struck out; J.Bagwell struck out; 0 R, 0 H, 0 E, 0 LOB. AL 0, NL 4.

AL 5TH: **R.Bottalico replaced C.Jones (pitching); K.Caminiti replaced T.Glavine (playing 3b)**; I.Rodriguez struck out; C.Ripken flied to B.Bonds-lf; B.Anderson reached on an error by K.Caminiti-3b (it was the first pitch) [B.Anderson to first]; **J.Buhner batted for C.Finley**; J.Buhner lined to L.Johnson-cf; 0 R, 0 H, 1 E, 1 LOB. AL 0, NL 4.

NL 5TH: **R.Pavlik replaced B.Anderson (pitching); J.Buhner stayed in game (playing rf)**; L.Johnson singled to right-center (it was the 1–2 pitch); L.Johnson stole second (it was the first pitch); B.Larkin flied to J.Buhner-rf; L.Johnson was caught stealing third (it was the first pitch) (I.Rodriguez-c to W.Boggs-3b); B.Bonds grounded out (M.Vaughn-1b unassisted); 0 R, 1 H, 0 E, 0 LOB. AL 0, NL 4.

AL 6TH: **O.Smith replaced B.Larkin (playing ss); P.Martinez replaced B.Bonds (pitching); E.Burks replaced R.Bottalico (playing lf)**; K.Lofton singled to right field (it was the 2–0 pitch); W.Boggs flied to E.Burks-lf; K.Lofton stole second (it was the 1–2 pitch); R.Alomar singled to shortstop (it was the 2–2 pitch) [K.Lofton to third]; A.Belle struck out; M.Vaughn grounded out (O.Smith-ss to J.Bagwell-1b); 0 R, 2 H, 0 E, 2 LOB. AL 0, NL 4.

NL 6TH: **C.Knoblauch replaced R.Alomar (playing 2b); M.McGwire replaced M.Vaughn (playing 1b)**; K.Caminiti homered to very deep right-center (it was the 0–2 pitch); M.Piazza struck out; D.Bichette doubled to right field (it was the 1–2 pitch); E.Burks struck out while D.Bichette advanced to third on a wild pitch [E.Burks to first]; C.Biggio forced E.Burks (C.Ripken-ss to C.Knoblauch-2b) [D.Bichette scored, C.Biggio to first]; **E.Young ran for C.Biggio**; J.Bagwell forced E.Young (W.Boggs-3b to C.Knoblauch-2b) [J.Bagwell to first]; 2 R, 2 H, 0 E, 1 LOB. AL 0, NL 6.

AL 7TH: **E.Young stayed in game (playing 2b); S.Trachsel replaced D.Bichette (pitching); G.Sheffield replaced P.Martinez (playing rf); S.Alomar Jr. batted for I.Rodriguez**; S.Alomar Jr. popped to L.Johnson-cf; C.Ripken grounded out (O.Smith-ss to J.Bagwell-1b); **A.Rodriguez batted for R.Pavlik**; A.Rodriguez flied to G.Sheffield-rf in foul territory; 0 R, 0 H, 0 E, 0 LOB. AL 0, NL 6.

NL 7TH: **S.Alomar Jr. stayed in game (playing c); A.Rodriguez stayed in game (playing ss); T.Per-**

cival replaced C.Ripken (pitching); **J.Carter re-placed K.Lofton (playing cf)**; L.Johnson singled to center field (it was the first pitch); O.Smith grounded out (C.Knoblauch-2b to M.McGwire-1b) [L.Johnson to second]; G.Sheffield popped to C.Knoblauch-2b; K.Caminiti struck out; 0 R, 1 H, 0 E, 1 LOB. AL 0, NL 6.

AL 8TH: **T.Worrell replaced K.Caminiti (pitching); M.Grudzielanek replaced S.Trachsel (playing 3b); T.Hundley replaced M.Piazza (playing c)**; J.Buhner popped to E.Young-2b; J.Carter singled to shortstop (it was the 1–1 pitch); **T.Fryman batted for W.Boggs**; T.Fryman struck out; C.Knoblauch singled to left field (it was the 1–1 pitch) [J.Carter to second]; A.Belle lined to L.Johnson-cf; 0 R, 2 H, 0 E, 2 LOB. AL 0, NL 6.

NL 8TH: **T.Fryman stayed in game (playing 3b); R.Hernandez replaced T.Percival (pitching)**; T.Hundley flied to J.Carter-cf; M.Grudzielanek grounded out (T.Fryman-3b to M.McGwire-1b); E.Burks tripled to center field (it was the first pitch); E.Young grounded out (M.McGwire-1b to R.Hernandez-p); 0 R, 1 H, 0 E, 1 LOB. AL 0, NL 6.

AL 9TH: **J.Kendall replaced T.Hundley (playing c); M.Wohlers replaced T.Worrell (pitching)**; M.McGwire singled to center field (it was the 1–2 pitch); S.Alomar Jr. grounded into a double play (O.Smith-ss to E.Young-2b to J.Bagwell-1b) [M.McGwire out at second]; **A.Leiter replaced M.Wohlers (pitching); D.Wilson batted for R.Hernandez**; D.Wilson flied to G.Sheffield-rf; 0 R, 1 H, 0 E, 0 LOB. AL 0, NL 6.

Final Totals	R	H	E	LOB
American League	0	7	0	7
National League	6	12	1	5

68

Hometown Hero

It was a special night for the Alomar family as Sandy Jr. crushed a two-run, tie-breaking home run to left field in the seventh inning to lead his American League teammates to their first win in four years. Alomar, the Indians catcher who came into the contest with a thirty-game hit streak, had dedicated the game to his grandmother, who had died three days before in Puerto Rico.

"You only get one chance to play in front of your home crowd in an All-Star Game, if that," Alomar said. "I was just flying around the bases. I don't think I have ever run so fast on a homer." Both Sandy Jr. and his brother Roberto wore black ribbons on their jerseys during the game.

Sandy Jr., the AL's leading hitter at the break with a .375 average, became the first All-Star to hit a four-bagger in his home ballpark since Henry Aaron in 1972. He also became the first player named the Most Valuable Player of the All-Star Game in his own park.

Joe Torre, in his first stint as a manager in the All-Star Game, said, "It's a storybook ending. I feel very good for Sandy and Robbie." Torre also played in eight All-Star Games in his career (his first was in Cleveland in 1963) and became the twenty-fourth man to play in and manage an All-Star contest.

Edgar Martinez, who homered in the second inning off Greg Maddux, became the first designated hitter elected by the fans because this was the first year that the position appeared on the fan ballot. Rounding out the scoring was Javier Lopez's home run in the seventh that struck the left-field pole. Lopez was the eleventh player to homer in his first All-Star at bat.

Eight AL pitchers held the Senior Circuit to three hits, with only Lopez hitting for extra bases. Four of the hurlers (Justin Thompson, Pat Hentgen, Randy Myers, and Mariano Rivera) did not allow a base runner in their stint. For the NL, only eventual Cy Young Award winner Pedro Martinez

pitched a perfect inning as he struck out two of the three batters he faced.

White Sox outfielder Albert Belle asked Torre for permission to sit out the game. Belle had left the Indians at the end of 1996 to sign a $55 million contract. In his first trip to Cleveland as a member of the Pale Hose, fans had thrown objects at Belle, and he had responded with an obscene gesture, for which he was fined. Before the All-Star Game, Belle said, "I've had death threats here."

"Albert and I talked and he was a little uncomfortable playing here," Torre said. "So I wasn't going to play him unless I had to. With Frank Thomas out, he felt obligated to be here to represent the White Sox." Belle skipped the home run contest, batting practice, and the team photo in addition to the game.

Leading up to the game, a lot of media attention focused on the match-up between AL starting pitcher Randy Johnson and the Rockies' Larry Walker. Walker came into the game leading the NL in hitting at .398 with twenty-five homers and had sat out an interleague game in which Colorado faced the Mariners' six-foot-ten lefty. Johnson had been particularly tough on left-handed batters, and Walker's decision to sit out that day caused a lot of second-guessing from the media.

Walker came to bat with two outs in the second inning. At that point, Johnson had not allowed a base runner. The Big Unit's first pitch sailed about four feet over Walker's head to the backstop. Walker turned his batting helmet around backward and moved to the right-handed batter's box, where he took a high fastball for ball two. Walker then returned to his usual side of the plate and took a walk from Johnson on a 3-1 pitch. Torre suggested that perhaps the two planned the event, but Johnson and Walker both denied it.

"When he throws a pitch like that, you just hope it's high," said Walker. "I'm glad I'm only six-three and a half." Johnson said, "It was kind of humid out there. The ball just slipped out of my hand. You saw it. I went right to the resin bag. I guess it was kind of apropos that it slipped while Larry Walker was up." Told that Walker claimed that he and Johnson were friends, Johnson replied, "I don't remember getting a Christmas card from him last year." The two players were teammates in the Montreal minor league organization. This comedy was a reminder of the John Kruk incident in the 1993 All-Star Game.

Tony Gwynn came into the break with a .394 average, and both he and Walker had a shot at hitting .400 for the season. "Tony has a much better chance," said Walker. "He doesn't strike out much and puts the ball in play. It is frustrating, though, when you're hitting .398 and only leading the league in hitting by four points." By the end of the year, both players had the usual drop-off, as Gwynn led the NL at .372 with Walker the runner-up at .366. However, Walker's season earned him the NL MVP Award, even if he did "duck" Randy Johnson.

Mark McGwire of the Athletics, with thirty-one, and Ken Griffey Jr. of the Mariners, with thirty, led the AL in homers at the All-Star break, which prompted more talk of a run at Roger Maris's home run record. McGwire would be traded to the Cardinals on July 31, so Griffey led the AL with fifty-six homers. McGwire hit thirty-four in the AL and twenty-four for St. Louis to lead the majors with fifty-eight dingers, even though he did not come close to leading either league. Larry Walker led the NL with forty-nine big flies.

Cal Ripken Jr. received plenty of teasing from his teammates during the pregame team photo session, and six-foot-five Mark McGwire offered him protection while they posed. These antics were a result of the broken nose Ripken suffered during the 1996 pregame photo shoot.

For the second straight year, Griffey garnered the most votes. Also for the second consecutive year, Mike Piazza led the NL squad in votes. There were three rookies named to the teams: Jason Dickson, Tony Womack, and AL Rookie of the Year Nomar Garciaparra.

This was the first game at The Jake but the fifth time the Indians had hosted the spectacular (the other four games were played at Municipal Stadium). Cleveland has hosted more All-Star contests than any other team.

	AL		NL	
P	Randy Johnson	SEA	Greg Maddux	ATL
C	Ivan Rodriguez	TEX	Mike Piazza	LAN
1B	Tino Martinez	NYA	Jeff Bagwell	HOU
2B	Roberto Alomar	BAL	Craig Biggio	HOU
3B	Cal Ripken	BAL	Ken Caminiti	SDN
SS	Alex Rodriguez	SEA	Barry Larkin +	CIN
OF	Brady Anderson	BAL	Barry Bonds	SFN
OF	Ken Griffey	SEA	Kenny Lofton +	ATL
OF	Dave Justice +	CLE	Larry Walker	COL
DH	Edgar Martinez	SEA	Tony Gwynn	SDN
	Sandy Alomar	CLE	Moises Alou	FLO
	Albert Belle	CHA	Rod Beck	SFN
	Jeff Cirillo	MIL	Jeff Blauser	ATL
	Roger Clemens	TOR	Kevin Brown	FLO
	David Cone	NYA	Royce Clayton	SLN
	Joey Cora	SEA	Shawn Estes	SFN
	Jason Dickson	ANA	Steve Finley	SDN
	Nomar Garciaparra	BOS	Andres Galarraga	COL
	Pat Hentgen	TOR	Tom Glavine	ATL
	Chuck Knoblauch	MIN	Mark Grace	CHN
	Mark McGwire	OAK	Todd Hundley +	NYN
	Mike Mussina	BAL	Charles Johnson	FLO
	Randy Myers	BAL	Bobby Jones	NYN
	Paul O'Neill	NYA	Chipper Jones	ATL
	Mariano Rivera	NYA	Darryl Kile	HOU
	Jose Rosado	KCA	Ray Lankford	SLN
	Frank Thomas +	CHA	Javier Lopez	ATL
	Jim Thome	CLE	Pedro Martinez	MON
	Justin Thompson	DET	Denny Neagle	ATL
	Bernie Williams	NYA	Curt Schilling	PHI
			Tony Womack	PIT

+ player replaced on roster

RETROSHEET EXPANDED BOX SCORE Tuesday, 7/8/1997 National League at American League (N)

```
National League    000 000 100-  1
American League    010 000 20X-  3
```

NATIONAL LEAGUE

	ab	r	h	bi	bb	so	po	a
C.Biggio, 2b	3	0	0	0	0	1	0	4
T.Womack, 2b	1	0	0	0	0	0	1	0
T.Gwynn, dh	3	0	0	0	0	0	0	0
A.Galarraga, ph	1	0	0	0	0	1	0	0
B.Bonds, lf	2	0	0	0	1	1	2	0
S.Finley, lf	1	0	0	0	0	1	1	0
M.Piazza, c	1	0	0	0	1	0	2	0
J.Lopez, c	1	1	1	1	0	0	4	1
C.Johnson, c	1	0	0	0	0	1	2	0
J.Bagwell, 1b	3	0	0	0	0	0	8	1
M.Grace, 1b	1	0	0	0	0	0	1	0
L.Walker, rf	1	0	0	0	1	0	0	0
M.Alou, rf	2	0	1	0	0	0	1	0
K.Caminiti, 3b	2	0	0	0	0	0	0	0
C.Jones, 3b	1	0	0	0	0	0	0	1
R.Lankford, cf	2	0	0	0	1	1	0	0
J.Blauser, ss	2	0	1	0	0	0	1	1
R.Clayton, ss	1	0	0	0	0	1	0	1
Totals	29	1	3	1	4	7	23	9

BATTING
HR: J.Lopez (7th inning off J.Rosado, 0 on, 0 out).
RBI, scoring position, less than 2 outs: J.Bagwell 0–1.

BASERUNNING
SB: B.Bonds (2nd base off D.Cone/I.Rodriguez).
Team LOB: 5

FIELDING
PB: J.Lopez.

AMERICAN LEAGUE

	ab	r	h	bi	bb	so	po	a
B.Anderson, lf-rf	4	0	2	0	0	0	1	0
A.Rodriguez, ss	3	0	1	0	0	2	0	2
N.Garciaparra, ss	1	0	0	0	0	0	1	0
K.Griffey Jr., cf	4	0	0	0	0	2	0	0
T.Martinez, 1b	2	0	0	0	0	0	10	0
M.McGwire, 1b	2	0	0	0	0	2	4	0
E.Martinez, dh	2	1	2	1	0	0	0	0
J.Thome, ph	1	0	0	0	0	0	0	0
P.O'Neill, rf	2	0	0	0	0	1	1	0
B.Williams, lf	0	1	0	0	1	0	1	0
C.Ripken, 3b	2	0	1	0	0	0	0	3
J.Cora, pr-2b	1	0	0	0	0	0	0	1
C.Knoblauch, 2b	0	0	0	0	0	0	1	1
I.Rodriguez, c	2	0	0	0	0	0	3	1
S.Alomar Jr., c	1	1	1	2	0	0	4	0
R.Alomar, 2b	2	0	0	0	0	0	1	5
J.Cirillo, 3b	1	0	0	0	0	1	0	0
Totals	30	3	7	3	1	8	27	13

BATTING
2B: B.Anderson (off C.Schilling).
HR: E.Martinez (2nd inning off G.Maddux, 0 on, 0 out);
   S.Alomar Jr. (7th inning off S.Estes, 1 on, 2 out).
2-out RBI: S.Alomar Jr. 2.
RBI, scoring position, less than 2 outs: A.Rodriguez
   0–1; R.Alomar 0–1.

BASERUNNING
CS: E.Martinez (2nd base by C.Schilling/J.Lopez).
Team LOB: 4

PITCHING	ip	h	r	er	bb	so
National League						
G.Maddux	2.0	2	1	1	0	0
C.Schilling	2.0	2	0	0	0	3
K.Brown	1.0	1	0	0	0	0
P.Martinez	1.0	0	0	0	0	2
S.Estes (L)	1.0	1	2	2	1	1
B.Jones	1.0	1	0	0	0	2
American League						
R.Johnson	2.0	0	0	0	1	2
R.Clemens	1.0	1	0	0	0	0
D.Cone	1.0	0	0	0	2	0
J.Thompson	1.0	0	0	0	0	1
P.Hentgen	1.0	0	0	0	0	0
J.Rosado (W, BS)	1.0	2	1	1	1	1
R.Myers	1.0	0	0	0	0	2
M.Rivera (S)	1.0	0	0	0	0	1

Inherited Runners—Scored:
   C.Schilling 0–0; K.Brown 0–0; P.Martinez 0–0;
   S.Estes 0–0; B.Jones 0–0; R.Clemens 0–0;
   D.Cone 0–0; J.Thompson 0–0; P.Hentgen 0–0;
   J.Rosado 0–0; R.Myers 0–0; M.Rivera 0–0.
WP: C.Schilling; S.Estes

GAME DATA—T: 2:36; A: 44916; Temp: 81; Wind: Left to
right, Speed: 12 mph

UMPIRES—HP: Larry Barnett (AL), 1B: Gerry Davis (NL),
2B: Drew Coble (AL), 3B: Jeff Kellogg (NL), LF: Terry Craft
(AL), RF: Wally Bell (NL)

STARTING LINEUPS

National League	American League
1. C.Biggio 2b	B.Anderson lf
2. T.Gwynn dh	A.Rodriguez ss
3. B.Bonds lf	K.Griffey Jr. cf
4. M.Piazza c	T.Martinez 1b
5. J.Bagwell 1b	E.Martinez dh
6. L.Walker rf	P.O'Neill rf
7. K.Caminiti 3b	C.Ripken 3b
8. R.Lankford cf	I.Rodriguez c
9. J.Blauser ss	R.Alomar 2b
G.Maddux p	R.Johnson p

NL 1ST: C.Biggio struck out; T.Gwynn grounded out (R.Johnson-p to T.Martinez-1b); B.Bonds struck out; 0 R, 0 H, 0 E, 0 LOB. NL 0, AL 0.

AL 1ST: B.Anderson grounded out (C.Biggio-2b to J.Bagwell-1b); A.Rodriguez singled to right field; K.Griffey Jr. flied to B.Bonds-lf; T.Martinez grounded out (C.Biggio-2b to J.Bagwell-1b); 0 R, 1 H, 0 E, 1 LOB. NL 0, AL 0.

NL 2ND: M.Piazza grounded out (R.Alomar-2b to T.Martinez-1b); J.Bagwell grounded out (R.Alomar-2b to T.Martinez-1b); Johnson's first pitch to Walker sailed over and behind his head; Walker reversed his helmet and moved to the other batter's box for the next pitch then he returned to his norm side; L.Walker walked; K.Caminiti forced L.Walker (A.Rodriguez-ss to R.Alomar-2b) [K.Caminiti to first]; 0 R, 0 H, 0 E, 1 LOB. NL 0, AL 0.

AL 2ND: E.Martinez homered to leftfield; P.O'Neill grounded out (G.Maddux-p to J.Bagwell-1b); C.Ripken grounded out (C.Biggio-2b to J.Bagwell-1b); I.Rodriguez grounded out (G.Maddux-p to J.Bagwell-1b); 1 R, 1 H, 0 E, 0 LOB. NL 0, AL 1.

NL 3RD: **R.Clemens replaced R.Johnson (pitching);** R.Lankford grounded out (R.Alomar-2b to T.Martinez-1b); J.Blauser singled to center field; C.Biggio grounded out (R.Alomar-2b to T.Martinez-1b) [J.Blauser to second]; T.Gwynn grounded out (C.Ripken-3b to T.Martinez-1b); 0 R, 1 H, 0 E, 1 LOB. NL 0, AL 1.

AL 3RD: **C.Schilling replaced G.Maddux (pitching);** R.Alomar grounded out (J.Blauser-ss to J.Bagwell-1b); B.Anderson doubled to left field; C.Schilling threw a wild pitch [B.Anderson to third]; A.Rodriguez struck out; K.Griffey Jr. struck out; 0 R, 1 H, 0 E, 1 LOB. NL 0, AL 1.

NL 4TH: **D.Cone replaced R.Clemens (pitching);** B.Bonds walked; B.Bonds stole second; M.Piazza walked; J.Bagwell lined to P.O'Neill-rf [B.Bonds to third]; B.Bonds advanced to and M.Piazza was out trying to advance to second (I.Rodriguez-c to A.Rodriguez-ss to T.Martinez-1b); L.Walker

grounded out (R.Alomar-2b to T.Martinez-1b); 0 R, 0 H, 0 E, 1 LOB. NL 0, AL 1.

AL 4TH: **J.Lopez replaced M.Piazza (playing c);** T.Martinez grounded out (J.Bagwell-1b to C.Schilling-p); E.Martinez singled to left field; E.Martinez was caught stealing second (J.Lopez-c to J.Blauser-ss); P.O'Neill struck out; 0 R, 1 H, 0 E, 0 LOB. NL 0, AL 1.

NL 5TH: **J.Thompson replaced D.Cone (pitching);** K.Caminiti grounded out (C.Ripken-3b to T.Martinez-1b); R.Lankford struck out; J.Blauser grounded out (C.Ripken-3b to T.Martinez-1b); 0 R, 0 H, 0 E, 0 LOB. NL 0, AL 1.

AL 5TH: **K.Brown replaced C.Schilling (pitching); C.Jones replaced K.Caminiti (playing 3b); R.Clayton replaced J.Blauser (playing ss); M.Alou replaced L.Walker (playing rf);** C.Ripken singled to center field; **J.Cora ran for C.Ripken;** I.Rodriguez grounded out (C.Biggio-2b to J.Bagwell-1b) [J.Cora to second]; J.Lopez allowed a passed ball [J.Cora to third]; R.Alomar grounded out (K.Brown-p to J.Bagwell-1b); B.Anderson flied to B.Bonds-lf; 0 R, 1 H, 0 E, 1 LOB. NL 0, AL 1.

NL 6TH: **P.Hentgen replaced J.Thompson (pitching); M.McGwire replaced T.Martinez (playing 1b); J.Cora stayed in game (playing 2b); J.Cirillo replaced R.Alomar (playing 3b); B.Williams replaced P.O'Neill (playing lf); B.Anderson changed positions (playing rf); S.Alomar Jr. replaced I.Rodriguez (playing c);** C.Biggio popped to M.McGwire-1b in foul territory; T.Gwynn grounded out (J.Cora-2b to M.McGwire-1b); B.Bonds flied to B.Williams-lf; 0 R, 0 H, 0 E, 0 LOB. NL 0, AL 1.

AL 6TH: **P.Martinez replaced K.Brown (pitching); T.Womack replaced C.Biggio (playing 2b); S.Finley replaced B.Bonds (playing lf);** A.Rodriguez struck out; K.Griffey Jr. lined to M.Alou-rf; M.McGwire struck out; 0 R, 0 H, 0 E, 0 LOB. NL 0, AL 1.

NL 7TH: **J.Rosado replaced P.Hentgen (pitching); N.Garciaparra replaced A.Rodriguez (playing ss);** J.Lopez homered to leftfield; Lopez' first All-Star at bat and Rosado's first All-Star batter faced; J.Bagwell lined to N.Garciaparra-ss; M.Alou singled to right field; C.Jones flied to B.Anderson-rf; R.Lankford walked [M.Alou to second]; R.Clayton struck out; 1 R, 2 H, 0 E, 2 LOB. NL 1, AL 1.

AL 7TH: **S.Estes replaced P.Martinez (pitching); M.Grace replaced J.Bagwell (playing 1b); J.Thome batted for E.Martinez;** J.Thome grounded out (R.Clayton-ss to M.Grace-1b); B.Williams walked; J.Cora flied to S.Finley-lf; S.Estes threw a wild pitch [B.Williams to second]; S.Alomar Jr. homered to leftfield [B.Williams scored]; J.Cirillo struck out; 2 R, 1 H, 0 E, 0 LOB. NL 1, AL 3.

NL 8TH: **R.Myers replaced J.Rosado (pitching); C.Knoblauch replaced J.Cora (playing 2b);** T.Womack grounded out (C.Knoblauch-2b to M.McGwire-1b); **A.GAlarraga batted for T.Gwynn;** A.Galarraga struck out; S.Finley struck out; 0 R, 0 H, 0 E, 0 LOB. NL 1, AL 3.

AL 8TH: **B.Jones replaced S.Estes (pitching); C.Johnson replaced J.Lopez (playing c);** B.Anderson singled to left field; N.Garciaparra forced B.Anderson (C.Jones-3b to T.Womack-2b)

[N.Garciaparra to first]; K.Griffey Jr. struck out; M.McGwire struck out; 0 R, 1 H, 0 E, 1 LOB. NL 1, AL 3.

NL 9TH: **M.Rivera replaced R.Myers (pitching);** C.Johnson struck out; M.Grace grounded out (M.McGwire-1b unassisted); M.Alou lined to C.Knoblauch-2b; 0 R, 0 H, 0 E, 0 LOB. NL 1, AL 3.

Final Totals	R	H	E	LOB
National League	1	3	0	5
American League	3	7	0	4

69

A Mile-High Offensive Barrage

The first All-Star game in the Mountain Time Zone occurred during the "year of the homer," in which four players reached the All-Star break with at least thirty homers. Many observers expected that trend to spill into this clash due to Denver's mile-high elevation. What spectators saw was the most offense ever in one All-Star Game but not the expected homer barrage. The teams combined for twenty-one runs on thirty-one hits, tying a record. The AL tied two records by scoring thirteen runs itself, marking the third time the Junior Circuit has scored that many runs in a game, and getting nineteen hits. The AL also set a new standard for thievery in one game by swiping five bases. All of the offense added up to the longest nine-inning game in All-Star history, at three hours and thirty-eight minutes, as the AL won its second straight game.

Seven players had multiple-hit games, including Roberto Alomar, Ivan Rodriguez, and Devon White with three each. There were few bright spots for the pitchers, however. AL starter David Wells, who had pitched a perfect game May 17, allowed only one walk in two innings. This game marked the first time that a pitcher threw a perfecto and started the midseason classic in the same year. John Wetteland pitched a perfect seventh inning, including a three-pitch strikeout of Javier Lopez.

"When you watch the scoring in Denver, you always see big numbers," Roberto Alomar said. "In this ballpark, that's what you expect." NL Manager Jim Leyland said, "It was a Coors Field–type game. You saw some balls bloop in and some freak hits. Guys had to play deep in the outfield. Then they hit some out of the park."

The game was scoreless until the bottom of the third. Larry Walker opened with a walk, and Walt Weiss moved him to second with an 0-2 single to left. After Tom Glavine sacrificed, Craig Biggio was struck by a pitch, loading the bases. Tony Gwynn then hit a two-run single up the middle.

The lead was short-lived because the AL scored four times in the top of the fourth. Alex Rodriguez and Ivan Rodriguez each singled to start the inning, and Cal Ripken Jr. doubled them home. Damion Easley's infield hit and Roberto Alomar's walk loaded the bases for Ken Griffey Jr., who walked to force in the third run. Juan Gonzalez, who came into the game with 101 RBI, scored Easley with a sacrifice fly. Gonzalez's RBI total was the second highest ever at the break, behind Hank Greenberg's 103 in 1935, and much attention was focused on the eventual American League MVP. Hack Wilson's RBI record from 1930 seemed to be in jeopardy. The official record was listed at 190, but research by the Society for American Baseball Research and Retrosheet has since shown that Wilson actually had one more run driven in that year. In any case, Gonzalez never got close, ending with 157.

The American Leaguers scored in each inning from the fourth to the end of the game. They regained the lead in the top of the sixth even though they hit only one ball out of the infield. New NL pitcher Ugueth Urbina and catcher Javier Lopez seemed to have trouble working together throughout the inning. Lopez visited the mound several times during the inning, and the battery mates still had trouble communicating. Roberto Alomar greeted Urbina by beating out a hit off Biggio's glove near second base. Griffey, who had entered the break with thirty-five homers to lead the AL, tapped one between the mound and first base, and both runners were safe. After a Gonzalez strikeout, the runners pulled a double steal, and Jim Thome coaxed a walk to load the bases.

Lopez allowed the 2-2 pitch to go by for a passed ball and the first run of the inning. Lopez was also charged with a passed ball in the 1997 game and became the first catcher with two career passed balls in All-Star history. After the game, Lopez said, "His fastball is tough to hit, and it's tough to catch too. It sinks or cuts. Whenever I'd call for a fastball away, I'd have to guess whether it was going to sink or cut. I guessed wrong on the passed ball."

Derek Jeter struck out on the next pitch. Griffey scored on a wild pitch to Ivan Rodriguez, who then singled to left, scoring Thome.

Roberto Alomar led his team to victory with three hits, including a homer in the seventh off Padres closer Trevor Hoffman, who had not surrendered a dinger in 37.2 innings coming in to the game. Alomar took home MVP honors one year after his brother Sandy captured the award. The Alomars were the first brothers to win the award. "I'm more excited for him than I was for myself," said Sandy.

AL Manager Mike Hargrove said, "I played with their father and I've been fortunate enough to watch both of these young men play. They are very talented, and I don't think anyone should be surprised by what they can do."

This was the sixth time that the Alomar brothers had been named to All-Star teams in the same year. The only other brothers to accomplish this, Joe and Dom DiMaggio, played in six games together between 1941 and 1951. In other family matters, the Boones became the first three-generation All-Stars. Ray was named twice, Bob four times, and now Bret for the first time.

NL vote leader Mark McGwire came into the game leading the majors with thirty-seven homers, tying Reggie Jackson's 1969 total for most at the break. Jackson had more chances to get there, though, since the game in 1969 was not played until July 23. Homers in this game came from Alex Rodriguez and Barry Bonds, in addition to Roberto Alomar. The Bonds became the second father-son pair to each homer in All-Star competition. Bobby Bonds hit his in 1973, while the Ken Griffeys went deep in 1980 (Sr.) and 1992 (Jr.)

Bartolo Colon got the win for the AL even though he surrendered the biggest blast of the night in Bonds's three-run homer in the fifth inning. The ball struck a Giants banner hung from the upper deck in right field and just missed another banner that, if struck, would have given a million dollars to a fan as part of a promotion.

Colon was the first Cleveland hurler to win since Bob Feller in 1946.

The roster size was increased to thirty this year to accommodate two new teams. This was an increase by two over the standard set in 1969, which was also an expansion year. Only five of the sixty players named to the squads were not used. There were twenty-three first-time players named, including two rookies: Rolando Arrojo, who had defected from Cuba two years previously on All-Star day, and Ben Grieve, 1998 AL Rookie of the Year. The overall vote leader was Griffey, marking his third consecutive year as leader.

Ripken started his fifteenth consecutive game to set the record in that department, topping Willie Mays's mark of starting fourteen consecutive games in ten seasons from 1957 to 1966. Ripken had thirteen consecutive starts at shortstop before moving to third base in 1997.

Mike Piazza appeared in the game as a member of the New York Mets, having already played for the Los Angeles Dodgers and Florida Marlins in 1998. Piazza was the first player to play for three different clubs in the same season before being named to an All-Star squad. Perhaps more unusual was the situation of pitcher Jeff Shaw, who was traded by the Reds to Los Angeles two days before the All-Star Game. His first appearance in a Dodger uniform was in this game, which had never happened before, and he became the first player to pitch in an All-Star classic on his birthday. Four non-pitchers had already played on their birthdays: Billy Herman, Ted Simmons, Andre Dawson, and Robin Ventura.

For the seventh-inning stretch, a tape of Harry Caray singing "Take Me Out to the Ballgame" was shown on the scoreboard. Caray, the longtime announcer for the Cardinals, Athletics, White Sox, and Cubs, had died the previous February. Caray broadcast Major League games from 1945 through 1997 and in 1989 received the Ford C. Frick Award for excellence in broadcasting.

	AL		NL	
P	David Wells	NYA	Greg Maddux	ATL
C	Ivan Rodriguez	TEX	Mike Piazza	NYN
1B	Jim Thome	CLE	Mark McGwire	SLN
2B	Roberto Alomar	BAL	Craig Biggio	HOU
3B	Cal Ripken	BAL	Chipper Jones	ATL
SS	Alex Rodriguez	SEA	Walt Weiss	ATL
OF	Juan Gonzalez	TEX	Barry Bonds	SFN
OF	Ken Griffey	SEA	Tony Gwynn	SDN
OF	Kenny Lofton	CLE	Larry Walker	COL
	Sandy Alomar	CLE	Moises Alou	HOU
	Rolando Arrojo	TBA	Andy Ashby	SDN
	Scott Brosius	NYA	Dante Bichette	COL
	Roger Clemens	TOR	Bret Boone	CIN
	Bartolo Colon	CLE	Kevin Brown	SDN
	Ray Durham	CHA	Vinny Castilla	COL
	Damion Easley	DET	Andres Galarraga	ATL
	Darin Erstad	ANA	Tom Glavine	ATL
	Tom Gordon	BOS	Trevor Hoffman	SDN
	Ben Grieve	OAK	Jason Kendall	PIT
	Derek Jeter	NYA	Javier Lopez	ATL
	Pedro Martinez	BOS	Robb Nen	SFN
	Paul O'Neill	NYA	Rick Reed	NYN
	Dean Palmer	KCA	Edgar Renteria	FLO
	Rafael Palmeiro	BAL	Curt Schilling	PHI
	Troy Percival	ANA	Jeff Shaw	LAN
	Brad Radke	MIN	Gary Sheffield	LAN
	Manny Ramirez	CLE	Sammy Sosa +	CHN
	Aaron Sele	TEX	Ugueth Urbina	MON
	Mo Vaughn +	BOS	Greg Vaughn	SDN
	Omar Vizquel	CLE	Fernando Vina	MIL
	John Wetteland	TEX	Devon White	ARI
	Bernie Williams +	NYA		

+ player replaced on roster

American League	000	413	113-13
National League	002	130	020-8

AMERICAN LEAGUE

	ab	r	h	bi	bb	so	po	a
K.Lofton, lf	3	0	1	0	1	0	2	0
D.Erstad, lf-cf	2	1	0	0	0	0	3	0
R.Alomar, 2b	4	2	3	1	1	0	3	2
R.Durham, ph-2b	1	1	1	1	0	0	0	0
K.Griffey Jr., cf	3	1	2	1	1	0	0	0
P.O'Neill, lf	2	0	0	0	0	0	0	1
J.Gonzalez, rf	3	0	0	1	0	1	0	0
M.Ramirez, rf	1	0	0	1	0	0	0	0
J.Thome, 1b	2	1	0	0	2	1	4	0
R.Palmeiro, 1b	2	1	2	1	0	0	2	0
A.Rodriguez, ss	3	2	2	1	0	1	1	2
D.Jeter, ss	1	0	0	0	0	1	0	2
O.Vizquel, ph-ss	2	0	1	0	0	0	1	1
I.Rodriguez, c	4	1	3	1	0	0	5	0
S.Alomar Jr., c	1	0	1	1	0	0	5	0
C.Ripken, 3b	4	1	1	2	0	0	1	1
R.Arrojo, p	0	0	0	0	0	0	0	0
J.Wetteland, p	0	0	0	0	0	0	0	0
D.Palmer, ph	1	0	0	0	0	0	0	0
T.Gordon, p	0	0	0	0	0	0	0	0
T.Percival, p	0	0	0	0	0	0	0	0
D.Wells, p	1	0	0	0	0	0	0	0
R.Clemens, p	0	0	0	0	0	0	0	0
D.Easley, ph	1	1	1	0	0	0	0	0
B.Radke, p	0	0	0	0	0	0	0	0
B.Grieve, ph	0	0	0	0	1	0	0	0
B.Colon, p	0	0	0	0	0	0	0	0
S.Brosius, 3b	2	1	1	0	0	1	0	0
Totals	43	13	19	11	6	5	27	9

BATTING

2B: C.Ripken (off T.Glavine).

HR: R.Alomar (7th inning off T.Hoffman, 0 on, 2 out); A.Rodriguez (5th inning off A.Ashby, 0 on, 0 out).

2-out RBI: R.Alomar; R.Palmeiro; I.Rodriguez.

RBI, scoring position, less than 2 outs: K.Lofton 0–1; R.Durham 1–1; K.Griffey Jr. 0–1; P.O'Neill 0–2; J.Gonzalez 1–5; M.Ramirez 1–2; D.Jeter 0–2; S.Alomar Jr. 1–1; C.Ripken 2–1; D.Palmer 0–1.

SF: J.Gonzalez; M.Ramirez.

GDP: C.Ripken; D.Palmer.

BASERUNNING

SB: K.Lofton (2nd base off G.Maddux/M.Piazza); R.Alomar (Double SB 3rd base off U.Urbina/J.Lopez); R.Durham (2nd base off R.Nen/J.Lopez); K.Griffey Jr. (Double SB 2nd base off U.Urbina/J.Lopez); I.Rodriguez (2nd base off U.Urbina/J.Lopez); S.Brosius (2nd base off R.Nen/J.Lopez).

Team LOB: 11

FIELDING

E: K.Griffey Jr.; S.Brosius (fumble).

Outfield assist: P.O'Neill (F.Vina at HP).

DP: (2). A.Rodriguez-R.Alomar-J.Thome; O.Vizquel-R.Palmeiro.

NATIONAL LEAGUE

	ab	r	h	bi	bb	so	po	a
C.Biggio, 2b	3	0	0	0	0	3	2	4
T.Hoffman, p	0	0	0	0	0	0	0	0
J.Shaw, p	0	0	0	0	0	0	0	0
G.Vaughn, ph-lf	1	0	1	2	0	0	0	0
T.Gwynn, rf	2	0	1	2	0	0	0	0
D.White, cf	3	1	3	0	0	0	0	0
R.Nen, p	0	0	0	0	0	0	0	0
M.McGwire, 1b	2	1	0	0	1	1	6	0
A.Galarraga, 1b	2	0	0	0	0	0	7	0
B.Bonds, lf	2	1	1	3	1	0	1	0
D.Bichette, lf-rf	2	0	0	0	0	1	1	0
C.Jones, 3b	2	1	0	0	1	0	0	0
V.Castilla, 3b	2	0	0	0	0	0	0	2
M.Piazza, c	3	0	1	0	0	0	2	0
J.Lopez, c	1	0	0	0	0	1	3	0
J.Kendall, ph	1	0	1	0	0	0	0	0
L.Walker, cf-rf	1	1	0	0	1	0	2	0
M.Alou, ph-rf-cf	3	1	1	0	0	2	0	0
W.Weiss, ss	3	1	2	1	0	0	2	2
E.Renteria, ss	1	1	0	0	0	0	0	3
G.Maddux, p	0	0	0	0	0	0	0	1
T.Glavine, p	0	0	0	0	0	0	0	1
K.Brown, p	0	0	0	0	0	0	0	0
G.Sheffield, ph	1	0	0	0	0	0	0	0
A.Ashby, p	0	0	0	0	0	0	0	0
U.Urbina, p	0	0	0	0	0	0	0	0
F.Vina, ph-2b	1	0	1	0	1	0	1	1
Totals	36	8	12	8	5	8	27	14

BATTING

HR: B.Bonds (5th inning off B.Colon, 2 on, 0 out).

RBI, scoring position, less than 2 outs: G.Vaughn 2–2; T.Gwynn 2–2; M.McGwire 0–1; A.Galarraga 0–1; B.Bonds 1–1; L.Walker 0–1; W.Weiss 1–1; G.Sheffield 0–1.

S: T.Glavine.

GDP: A.Galarraga; C.Jones.

BASERUNNING

Team LOB: 8

FIELDING

E: F.Vina (fumble).

PB: J.Lopez.

DP: (2). E.Renteria-F.Vina-A.Galarraga; C.Biggio-W.Weiss-M.McGwire.

PITCHING	ip	h	r	er	bb	so
American League						
D.Wells	2.0	0	0	0	1	1
R.Clemens	1.0	2	2	2	1	1
B.Radke	1.0	2	1	1	1	1
B.Colon (w)	1.0	2	3	3	1	1
R.Arrojo	1.0	2	0	0	0	1
J.Wetteland	1.0	0	0	0	0	1
T.Gordon	1.0	3	2	1	1	0
T.Percival	1.0	1	0	0	0	2
National League						
G.Maddux	2.0	3	0	0	1	1
T.Glavine	1.1	5	4	4	3	0
K.Brown	0.2	0	0	0	0	1
A.Ashby	1.0	1	1	1	1	0
U.Urbina (L, BS)	1.0	3	3	3	1	2
T.Hoffman	1.0	1	1	1	0	1
J.Shaw	1.0	3	1	1	0	0
R.Nen	1.0	3	3	1	0	0

Inherited Runners—Scored:
R.Clemens 0–0; B.Radke 0–0; B.Colon 0–0; R.Arrojo 0–0; J.Wetteland 0–0; T.Gordon 0–0; T.Percival 0–0; T.Glavine 0–0; K.Brown 3–1; A.Ashby 0–0; U.Urbina 0–0; T.Hoffman 0–0; J.Shaw 0–0; R.Nen 0–0.

HBP: C.Biggio by R.Clemens.
WP: U.Urbina

GAME DATA—T: 3:38; A: 51267; Temp: 84; Wind: Right to left, Speed: 16 mph

UMPIRES—HP: Ed Montague (NL), 1B: Derryl Cousins (AL), 2B: Brian Gorman (NL), 3B: Rick Reed (AL), LF: Rich Rieker (NL), RF: Tim McClelland (AL)

STARTING LINEUPS

	American League	National League
1.	K.Lofton lf	C.Biggio 2b
2.	R.Alomar 2b	T.Gwynn rf
3.	K.Griffey Jr. cf	M.McGwire 1b
4.	J.Gonzalez rf	B.Bonds lf
5.	J.Thome 1b	C.Jones 3b
6.	A.Rodriguez ss	M.Piazza c
7.	I.Rodriguez c	L.Walker cf
8.	C.Ripken 3b	W.Weiss ss
9.	D.Wells p	G.Maddux p

AL 1ST: K.Lofton singled to left field (it was the 2–1 pitch); K.Lofton stole second (it was the first pitch); On a bunt R.Alomar singled to first base (it was the 0–1 pitch) [K.Lofton to third]; K.Griffey Jr. popped to M.McGwire-1b in foul territory; J.Gonzalez grounded out (G.Maddux-p to M.McGwire-1b) [R.Alomar to second]; broken bat; J.Thome walked; A.Rodriguez was called out on strikes; 0 R, 2 H, 0 E, 3 LOB. AL 0, NL 0.

NL 1ST: 25 pitches for Maddux in first; C.Biggio struck out; T.Gwynn flied to K.Lofton-lf; M.McGwire grounded out (A.Rodriguez-ss to J.Thome-1b); 0 R, 0 H, 0 E, 0 LOB. AL 0, NL 0.

AL 2ND: I.Rodriguez singled to right field (it was the 2–0 pitch); C.Ripken grounded into a double play (C.Biggio-2b to W.Weiss-ss to M.McGwire-1b) [I.Rodriguez out at second]; D.Wells grounded out (C.Biggio-2b to M.McGwire-1b); 0 R, 1 H, 0 E, 0 LOB. AL 0, NL 0.

NL 2ND: B.Bonds walked; C.Jones grounded into a double play (A.Rodriguez-ss to R.Alomar-2b to J.Thome-1b) [B.Bonds out at second]; M.Piazza popped to R.Alomar-2b; 0 R, 0 H, 0 E, 0 LOB. AL 0, NL 0.

AL 3RD: **T.Glavine replaced G.Maddux (pitching)**; K.Lofton walked; R.Alomar popped to C.Biggio-2b; K.Griffey Jr. singled to center field (it was the 2–1 pitch) [K.Lofton to third]; J.Gonzalez popped to C.Biggio-2b; J.Thome flied to B.Bonds-lf in foul territory; 0 R, 1 H, 0 E, 2 LOB. AL 0, NL 0.

NL 3RD: 24 pitches for Glavine; **R.Clemens replaced D.Wells (pitching)**; L.Walker walked; W.Weiss singled to left field (it was the 0–2 pitch) [L.Walker to second]; T.Glavine out on a sacrifice bunt (C.Ripken-3b to R.Alomar-2b) [L.Walker to third, W.Weiss to second]; C.Biggio was hit by a pitch (it was the 0–2 pitch); T.Gwynn singled to center field (it was the 2–1 pitch) [L.Walker scored, W.Weiss scored, C.Biggio to third]; bounced past Alomar; M.McGwire struck out; B.Bonds flied to K.Lofton-lf; 2 R, 2 H, 0 E, 2 LOB. AL 0, NL 2.

AL 4TH: 26 pitches for Clemens; A.Rodriguez singled to right field (it was the 2–2 pitch); I.Rodriguez singled to center field (it was the 0–2 pitch) [A.Rodriguez to second]; C.Ripken doubled to right field (it was the 1–0 pitch) [A.Rodriguez scored, I.Rodriguez scored]; **D.Easley batted for R.Clemens**; D.Easley singled to second base (it was the 1–0 pitch) [C.Ripken to third]; K.Lofton grounded out (T.Glavine-p to M.McGwire-1b) [D.Easley to second]; R.Alomar walked; K.Griffey Jr. walked [C.Ripken scored, D.Easley to third, R.Alomar to second]; 57 total pitches for Glavine; **K.Brown replaced T.Glavine (pitching)**; J.Gonzalez out on a sacrifice fly to L.Walker-cf [D.Easley scored]; J.Thome was called out on strikes; 4 R, 4 H, 0 E, 2 LOB. AL 4, NL 2.

NL 4TH: **B.Radke replaced D.Easley (pitching)**; C.Jones walked; M.Piazza singled to center field (it was the 1–1 pitch) [C.Jones to third (error by K.Griffey Jr.-cf)]; L.Walker popped to C.Ripken-3b in foul territory; W.Weiss singled to right field (it was the first pitch) [C.Jones scored, M.Piazza to second]; **G.Sheffield batted for K.Brown**; G.Sheffield popped to A.Rodriguez-ss; C.Biggio was called out on strikes; 1 R, 2 H, 1 E, 2 LOB. AL 4, NL 3.

AL 5TH: **A.Ashby replaced G.Sheffield (pitching)**; **L.Walker changed positions (playing rf)**; **D.White replaced T.Gwynn (playing cf)**; A.Rodriguez homered to right-center (it was the 1–1 pitch); I.Rodriguez flied to L.Walker-rf; C.Ripken grounded out (W.Weiss-ss to M.McGwire-1b); **B.Grieve batted for B.Radke**; B.Grieve walked; K.Lofton forced B.Grieve (C.Biggio-2b to W.Weiss-ss) [K.Lofton to first]; 1 R, 1 H, 0 E, 1 LOB. AL 5, NL 3.

NL 5TH: **D.Erstad replaced K.Lofton (playing lf)**; **D.Jeter replaced A.Rodriguez (playing ss)**; **B.Colon replaced B.Grieve (pitching)**; D.White tripled to center field (it was the 3–1 pitch); M.McGwire walked; B.Bonds homered to right-field (it was the 2–2 pitch) [D.White scored, M.McGwire scored]; off the Giants banner hanging from the upper deck; C.Jones grounded out (R.Alomar-2b to J.Thome-1b); M.Piazza grounded out (D.Jeter-ss to J.Thome-1b); **M.Alou batted for L.Walker**; M.Alou struck out; 3 R, 2 H, 0 E, 0 LOB. AL 5, NL 6.

AL 6TH: **M.Alou stayed in game (playing rf)**; **A.Galarraga replaced M.McGwire (playing 1b)**; **V.Castilla replaced C.Jones (playing 3b)**; **U.Urbina replaced A.Ashby (pitching)**; **J.Lopez replaced M.Piazza (playing c)**; R.Alomar singled to second base (it was the 0–2 pitch); K.Griffey Jr. singled to first base (it was the 0–2 pitch) [R.Alomar to second]; J.Gonzalez struck out; R.Alomar stole third and K.Griffey Jr. stole second (it was the 0–2 pitch); J.Thome walked; J.Lopez allowed a passed ball (it was the 2–2 pitch) [R.Alomar scored, K.Griffey Jr. to third, J.Thome to second]; D.Jeter struck out; U.Urbina threw a wild pitch (it was the 0–1 pitch) [K.Griffey Jr. scored, J.Thome to third]; I.Rodriguez singled to left field (it was the 3–2 pitch) [J.Thome scored]; I.Rodriguez stole second (it was the first pitch); C.Ripken grounded out (C.Biggio-2b to A.Galarraga-1b); 3 R, 3 H, 0 E, 1 LOB. AL 8, NL 6.

NL 6TH: **D.Erstad changed positions (playing cf); R.Palmeiro replaced J.Thome (playing 1b); P.O'Neill replaced K.Griffey Jr. (playing lf); M.Ramirez replaced J.Gonzalez (playing rf); R.Arrojo replaced C.Ripken (pitching); S.Brosius replaced B.Colon (playing 3b);** W.Weiss flied to D.Erstad-cf; **F.Vina batted for U.Urbina;** F.Vina singled to left field (it was the 1–2 pitch); C.Biggio struck out; D.White singled to center field (it was the 1–0 pitch) [F.Vina to second]; A.Galarraga flied to D.Erstad-cf; 0 R, 2 H, 0 E, 2 LOB. AL 8, NL 6.

AL 7TH: **F.Vina stayed in game (playing 2b); T.Hoffman replaced C.Biggio (pitching); D.Bichette replaced B.Bonds (playing lf); E.Renteria replaced W.Weiss (playing ss);** S.Brosius was called out on strikes; D.Erstad grounded out (E.Renteria-ss to A.Galarraga-1b); R.Alomar homered to rightfield down the line (it was the 3–2 pitch); P.O'Neill grounded out (V.Castilla-3b to A.Galarraga-1b); 1 R, 1 H, 0 E, 0 LOB. AL 9, NL 6.

NL 7TH: Harry Carey 'sang' 'Take Me Out to the Ballgame' via video tape; he had died in February; **S.Alomar Jr. replaced I.Rodriguez (playing c); J.Wetteland replaced R.Arrojo (pitching);** D.Bichette grounded out (D.Jeter-ss to R.Palmeiro-1b); V.Castilla popped to S.Alomar Jr.-c in foul territory; J.Lopez struck out; 0 R, 0 H, 0 E, 0 LOB. AL 9, NL 6.

AL 8TH: **J.Shaw replaced T.Hoffman (pitching);** M.Ramirez grounded out (V.Castilla-3b to A.Galarraga-1b); R.Palmeiro singled to left field (it was the 2–2 pitch); **O.Vizquel batted for D.Jeter;** O.Vizquel singled to center field (it was the 0–1 pitch) [R.Palmeiro to third]; S.Alomar Jr. singled to right field (it was the 0–1 pitch) [R.Palmeiro scored, O.Vizquel to third]; **D.Palmer bat-**

ted for J.Wetteland; D.Palmer grounded into a double play (E.Renteria-ss to F.Vina-2b to A.Galarraga-1b) [S.Alomar Jr. out at second]; 1 R, 3 H, 0 E, 1 LOB. AL 10, NL 6.

NL 8TH: **T.Gordon replaced D.Palmer (pitching); O.Vizquel stayed in game (playing ss);** M.Alou singled to right field (it was the first pitch); E.Renteria reached on an error by S.Brosius-3b (it was the 1–2 pitch) [M.Alou to second, E.Renteria to first]; F.Vina walked [M.Alou to third, E.Renteria to second]; **G.Vaughn batted for J.Shaw;** G.Vaughn singled to left field (it was the 1–1 pitch) [M.Alou scored, E.Renteria scored (unearned), F.Vina to second]; D.White singled to left field (it was the 1–1 pitch) (P.O'Neill-lf to S.Alomar Jr.-c) [F.Vina out at home, G.Vaughn to second]; A.Galarraga grounded into a double play (O.Vizquel-ss to R.Palmeiro-1b) [D.White out at second]; 2 R (1 ER), 3 H, 1 E, 1 LOB. AL 10, NL 8.

AL 9TH: **M.Alou changed positions (playing cf); D.Bichette changed positions (playing rf); G.Vaughn stayed in game (playing lf); R.Nen replaced D.White (pitching);** S.Brosius singled to center field (it was the 2–1 pitch); S.Brosius stole second (it was the first pitch); D.Erstad reached on an error by F.Vina-2b (it was the 1–0 pitch) [S.Brosius to third, D.Erstad to first]; **R.Durham batted for R.Alomar;** R.Durham singled to right field (it was the 0–1 pitch) [S.Brosius scored, D.Erstad to third]; R.Durham stole second (it was the 1–0 pitch); P.O'Neill grounded out (A.Galarraga-1b unassisted); M.Ramirez out on a sacrifice fly to D.Bichette-rf [D.Erstad scored (unearned)]; R.Palmeiro singled to center field (it was the 3–1 pitch) [R.Durham scored (unearned)]; O.Vizquel grounded out (E.Renteria-ss to A.Galarraga-1b); 3 R (1 ER), 3 H, 1 E, 1 LOB. AL 13, NL 8.

NL 9TH: **T.Percival replaced T.Gordon (pitching); R.Durham stayed in game (playing 2b);** D.Bichette struck out; V.Castilla lined to D.Erstad-cf; **J.Kendall batted for J.Lopez;** J.Kendall singled to center field (it was the 0–2 pitch); M.Alou struck out; 0 R, 1 H, 0 E, 1 LOB. AL 13, NL 8.

Final Totals	R	H	E	LOB
American League	13	19	2	11
National League	8	12	1	8

70

Love Fest in Boston

The All-Star Game returned to historic Fenway Park for the first time since 1961, and the pregame festivities were historic as well. Before the game, thirty-two members of Major League Baseball's All-Century Team were introduced on the field, including many Hall of Famers. The last player introduced was former Red Sox All-Star Ted Williams, who received a loud, emotional welcome from the fans as he rode in from center field, tipping his cap along the way. The All-Century Team players and the current All-Stars gathered around Williams in the center of the infield and were slow to leave the field, finally leaving only after a public address announcement requested that they do so. The game started fourteen minutes late due to the ceremonies.

Perhaps Phillies catcher Mike Lieberthal put Williams's stature best: "To get here, we came through a tunnel named for him. Now that's cool." One of the tunnels connecting Boston to Logan Airport is the Ted Williams Tunnel.

Fenway Park has long been known as a hitters' haven, but this All-Star Game belonged to the pitchers. The teams collected thirteen total hits — six singles by the AL and five singles and two doubles by the NL — while twenty-two batters struck out in the contest. The twenty-two punch-outs set a new record for both teams in one All-Star Game, beating the former record of twenty-one set in 1984. The twelve strikeouts by NL batters tied the mark for one team (the last to do so was the 1986 AL squad).

The runs and hits totals for the game contrasted with the averages for the first half of the season. In the NL, teams were averaging 10.1 runs and 18.6 hits per game, while the Junior Circuit teams averaged 10.4 runs and 19 hits per game. This was the third time in five years that the All-Star teams' combined run total was five or less, all in odd years in the smaller AL parks.

After the power-hitting display the previous eve-

ning in the Home Run Derby, it was understandable that the All-Star pitchers were reluctant to take the mound. NL starter Curt Schilling, who had been drafted by the Red Sox, came into the break with a 13-4 record for the 46-40 Phillies. He talked about pitching in this situation: "I'm honored to be chosen to get the start but, seeing the lineup they're throwing out there, it might not have bothered me throwing second or third. I'm as nervous for this as I've been for any game I've ever pitched."

AL manager Joe Torre selected Red Sox ace Pedro Martinez to start for the hosts. Martinez became the seventh pitcher to start an All-Star Game in his home ballpark. The previous players to accomplish this feat were Carl Hubbell (1934), Johnny Vander Meer (1938), Red Ruffing (1939), Don Drysdale (1959), Whitey Ford (1960), and Steve Rogers (1982).

Martinez had a 15-3 record at the break with a 2.10 ERA and 184 strikeouts. He led the AL in all three categories and the Majors in wins and ERA. Martinez had held opposing batters to a .213 average, also the best mark in the AL.

In the first inning, Martinez struck out Barry Larkin of Cincinnati, Larry Walker of the Rockies, and Sammy Sosa of the Cubs. It was the first time in All-Star history that the first three batters of the game struck out. After Sosa missed the third strike, the fans erupted and chanted "Pedro, Pedro" as the team left the field.

Martinez continued his domination in the second as he struck out home run champ Mark McGwire of the Cardinals, thus striking out the first four batters of the game. Arizona's Matt Williams hit the first pitch to second baseman Roberto Alomar of the Indians, who booted the easy grounder. Houston's Jeff Bagwell then stepped in, but Martinez struck him out, and Williams was doubled at second base on a stolen base attempt. The five strikeouts by Martinez came up one short of the record of six in a game, held by four NL pitchers: Hubbell (1934), Vander Meer (1943), Larry Jansen (1950), and Ferguson Jenkins (1967). Martinez tied the record for AL pitchers in one game, set by Billy Pierce (1956) and Boston's Dick Radatz (1963 and 1964).

Martinez was the second Red Sox pitcher to win an All-Star contest, following Roger Clemens, who had won the 1986 game. Jimmy Key had been the last pitcher to win an All-Star Game in his home park when he won in relief in 1991. Martinez was named the game's MVP, the second time a hometown player had been voted the honor (Sandy Alomar Jr. won the award in Cleveland in 1997). Martinez was named the AL Cy Young Award winner at the end of the season and placed second in the balloting for the AL MVP Award.

Torre talked about Martinez after the game:. "It's like hitting in a dark room. When you're facing a guy like Pedro and he's so pumped up in front of a crowd like this. . . . I'm glad he was on my side, that's for sure."

The AL batters struck for two runs in the first inning. Cleveland's Kenny Lofton hit a grounder to first baseman McGwire, and Lofton beat Schilling to the bag for a single. After the next two batters made outs, Lofton stole second. This marked the third time in the past four All-Star Games that Lofton had singled and stolen second in the first inning (he did not play in the 1997 game). This was Lofton's fifth career steal in All-Star competition, tying him for second place with Roberto Alomar behind Willie Mays, who stole six bases.

Lofton's Cleveland teammate Manny Ramirez followed the stolen base with a walk, and another Indian, Jim Thome, singled to center to score Lofton. Baltimore's Cal Ripken Jr., playing in his seventeenth All-Star Game, singled to right field to plate Ramirez.

In the third inning, David Cone of the Yankees replaced Martinez on the mound. Cone struck out Mike Piazza of the crosstown Mets, but Brewer Jeromy Burnitz doubled to right, and one out later, Larkin singled to score Burnitz with the only NL run of the game.

Cone got into trouble again in the fourth inning. With one out, McGwire walked, drawing boos from the crowd because they wanted to see a "Big Mac" blast into the left-field net. One out later, Bagwell and Piazza each singled to load the bases, but Burnitz grounded out to end the threat.

The AL scored the last runs of the game in the bottom of the fourth. Thome walked, and Ripken was hit by a Kent Bottenfield pitch. Thome scored, and Ripken moved to third on Rafael Palmeiro's single to right. After a strikeout, Roberto Alomar reached when Matt Williams misplayed his grounder at third base, scoring Ripken.

In the fifth inning, Baltimore's Mike Mussina went to the mound for the AL. Jay Bell of Arizona walked, and Larkin forced Bell. Arizona's Luis Gonzalez doubled to left, advancing Larkin to third, but Mussina struck out Sosa and McGwire to end the inning.

In the seventh, the NL threatened again but were denied by a brilliant play by Indians shortstop Omar Vizquel. Atlanta outfielder Brian Jordan walked but was caught stealing. Jeff Kent of the Giants then walked, and with two out, Boston second baseman Jose Offerman threw the ball away on a grounder by Luis Gonzalez, allowing Kent to go to third. Vladimir Guerrero hit a grounder up the middle that Vizquel dove to catch. While still on the ground, Vizquel flipped the ball from his glove hand to Offerman at second to force Gonzalez.

This was the third consecutive victory for the AL and the eighth in twelve games. In the previous games at Fenway Park, the AL had won in 1946, and the teams had played to the only tie in All-Star history in the second game of 1961. The NL has never homered at Fenway in All-Star competition.

Torre became the sixth manager to win his first two All-Star Games, following Red Schoendienst (1968–69), Tommy Lasorda (1978–79), Tom Kelly (1988 and 1992), Tony La Russa (1989–90), and Cito Gaston (1993–94).

For the first time since 1988, no batter collected more than one hit in the contest. In contrast, six pitchers struck out multiple batters. In addition to Martinez, Schilling and Cone each whiffed three batters, and Bottenfield and Mussina each struck out two. NL Cy Young Award winner (and strikeout champ) Randy Johnson pitched one perfect inning, striking out one batter.

Andy Ashby and Trevor Hoffman of the Padres and Mike Hampton and Billy Wagner of the Astros combined to pitch two perfect innings for the NL in the seventh and eighth, while Tampa Bay's Roberto Hernandez pitched a perfect eighth for the AL.

There were twenty-four first-time All-Stars on the rosters, seventeen of them in the NL. Baltimore outfielder B. J. Surhoff played in his first game at the age of thirty-four, the oldest of the new All-Stars. Also among the first-time players were three rookies: Cincinnati pitcher Scott Williamson, who was named the NL Rookie of the Year; Texas pitcher Jeff Zimmerman; and Marlins shortstop Alex Gonzalez. Gonzalez became the first rookie shortstop to play for the NL in the All-Star Game.

Roberto Alomar became the fifth player to represent four different teams in the All-Star Game, joining Walker Cooper, George Kell, Rich Gossage, and Lee Smith. Ripken's sixteenth consecutive start extended his own record in that department. Ivan Rodriguez, the controversial choice for American League MVP, made his seventh consecutive start as catcher for the AL. Johnny Bench started nine straight games and Yogi Berra eight, while Bill Freehan also started seven consecutive games as catcher.

Dave Nilsson of the Brewers became the first Australian native to play in an All-Star Game and was the last, record-setting strikeout of the night in the ninth inning. Six of the starters were Latino, with a total of fourteen on the two teams. In addition, this game marked the first time two Canadians appeared in the same All-Star Game. Larry Walker and Jeff Zimmerman were both born in British Columbia.

It had been thirty-seven years since the last game at Fenway Park, the longest span between All-Star Games for a park and a city. Baltimore had waited thirty-four years between 1958 and 1993 (Memorial Stadium and Camden Yards), while Comiskey Park had a thirty-three-year wait between games (1950 to 1983). The paid attendance of 34,187 was the smallest All-Star crowd since the previous game at Fenway Park in 1961.

Ken Griffey Jr. led all players in fan ballots, while Sosa led the NL. It was Griffey's fourth consecutive year leading all players in the voting. Rangers outfielder Juan Gonzalez refused to come because he had not been elected to start, and Yankees pitcher Mariano Rivera cited personal business at home in Panama and was replaced.

One of the most exciting memories of the All-Star gala came the night before the game, during the Home Run Derby. The event, which started out as a small side event in 1985, has grown to be one of the most important parts of the All-Star celebration. In the first round, Mark McGwire hit thirteen homers to set a new record for a round, including many over the left-field wall and screen. One shot cleared the light tower over the screen and landed in the parking lot across Ted Williams Way (the street behind left field.)

Red Sox shortstop Nomar Garciaparra edged out Derek Jeter of the Yankees as the starter at the end of the voting period. Boston had played eighteen games at home in June, and fan balloting during that time helped Garciaparra win the election. In the top of the fourth inning, Garciaparra took the field, but just before the inning was about to start, Torre sent Jeter out to replace him. It was a classy move by the skipper because Garciaparra left to thunderous applause. In the bottom of the inning, when Jeter came to bat, he imitated Garciaparra's routine in the batter's box. Garciaparra taps his toes as he waits for the pitch, and Jeter mimicked this action as a tribute to the hometown hero.

There was a lot of attention paid to the history of the game and the ballpark during this All-Star extravaganza. Larry Walker attended the postgame press conference with a piece of turf. "I hope the grounds crew doesn't get too mad, but I tore this piece of grass up from right field. I'm taking this baby home with me so that I can say I played right field at Fenway Park. When I was up hitting in the first, I had no feeling. I was in awe, looking at the sign that said 'Fenway Park' and the big wall in left field. I struck out at Fenway Park, and I'm proud of it."

	AL		NL	
P	Pedro Martinez	BOS	Curt Schilling	PHI
C	Ivan Rodriguez	TEX	Mike Piazza	NYN
1B	Jim Thome	CLE	Mark McGwire	SLN
2B	Roberto Alomar	CLE	Jay Bell	ARI
3B	Cal Ripken	BAL	Matt Williams	ARI
SS	Nomar Garciaparra	BOS	Barry Larkin	CIN
OF	Ken Griffey	SEA	Tony Gwynn +	SDN
OF	Kenny Lofton	CLE	Sammy Sosa	CHN
	Manny Ramirez	CLE	Larry Walker	COL
DH	Rafael Palmeiro	TEX	Jeff Bagwell	HOU
	Brad Ausmus	DET	Andy Ashby	SDN
	Harold Baines	BAL	Kent Bottenfield	SLN
	Jose Canseco +	TBA	Jeromy Burnitz	MIL
	David Cone	NYA	Paul Byrd	PHI
	Ron Coomer	MIN	Sean Casey	CIN
	Tony Fernandez	TOR	Alex Gonzalez	FLO
	Shawn Green	TOR	Luis Gonzalez	ARI
	Roberto Hernandez	TBA	Vladimir Guerrero	MON
	John Jaha	OAK	Mike Hampton	HOU
	Derek Jeter	NYA	Trevor Hoffman	SDN
	Mike Mussina	BAL	Randy Johnson	ARI
	Charles Nagy	CLE	Brian Jordan	ATL
	Jose Offerman	BOS	Jeff Kent	SFN
	Magglio Ordonez	CHA	Mike Lieberthal	PHI
	Troy Percival	ANA	Jose Lima	HOU
	Mariano Rivera +	NYA	Kevin Millwood	ATL
	Jose Rosado	KCA	Robb Nen +	SFN
	B.J. Surhoff	BAL	Dave Nilsson	MIL
	Omar Vizquel	CLE	Gary Sheffield	LAN
	John Wetteland	TEX	Ed Sprague	PIT
	Bernie Williams	NYA	Billy Wagner	HOU
	Jeff Zimmerman	TEX	Scott Williamson	CIN

RETROSHEET EXPANDED BOX SCORE Tuesday, 7/13/1999 National League at American League (N)

```
National League      001 000 000- 1
American League      200 200 00x- 4
```

NATIONAL LEAGUE

	ab	r	h	bi	bb	so	po	a
B.Larkin, ss	3	0	1	1	0	1	1	1
A.Gonzalez, ph-ss	1	0	0	0	0	0	1	0
L.Walker, rf	2	0	0	0	0	1	1	0
L.Gonzalez, lf	2	0	1	0	0	0	0	0
S.Sosa, cf	3	0	0	0	0	2	1	0
V.Guerrero, rf	1	0	0	0	0	0	1	0
M.McGwire, 1b	2	0	0	0	1	2	3	0
S.Casey, 1b	1	0	0	0	0	0	4	0
M.Williams, 3b	3	0	1	0	0	1	1	0
E.Sprague, 3b	1	0	0	0	0	0	0	0
J.Bagwell, dh	3	0	1	0	0	2	0	0
G.Sheffield, ph	1	0	0	0	0	0	0	0
M.Piazza, c	2	0	1	0	0	1	6	0
M.Lieberthal, c	1	0	0	0	0	0	1	0
D.Nilsson, c	1	0	0	0	0	1	3	0
J.Burnitz, lf-rf	2	1	1	0	0	0	0	0
B.Jordan, cf	1	0	1	0	1	0	0	0
J.Bell, 2b	1	0	0	0	1	1	0	1
J.Kent, 2b	1	0	0	0	1	0	1	2
Totals	32	1	7	1	4	12	24	4

BATTING
2B: J.Burnitz (off D.Cone); L.Gonzalez (off M.Mussina).
2-out RBI: B.Larkin.
RBI, scoring position, less than 2 outs: S.Sosa 0–2; J.Bell 0–1.
GDP: M.Lieberthal; J.Kent.

BASERUNNING
CS: M.Williams (2nd base by P.Martinez/I.Rodriguez); B.Jordan (2nd base by J.Zimmerman/B.Ausmus).
Team LOB: 8

FIELDING
E: M.Williams (fumble).

AMERICAN LEAGUE

	ab	r	h	bi	bb	so	po	a
K.Lofton, lf-cf	3	1	1	0	0	1	0	0
B.Williams, cf	1	0	0	0	0	1	0	0
N.Garciaparra, ss	2	0	0	0	0	0	0	0
D.Jeter, ss	1	0	0	0	0	1	1	0
O.Vizquel, ss	1	0	0	0	0	0	1	4
K.Griffey Jr., cf	2	0	0	0	0	1	0	0
B.Surhoff, lf	2	0	0	0	0	0	0	0
M.Ramirez, rf	1	1	0	0	1	1	0	0
S.Green, rf	1	0	1	0	0	0	0	0
M.Ordonez, rf	1	0	0	0	0	0	0	0
J.Thome, 1b	2	1	1	1	1	0	4	0
R.Coomer, 1b	1	0	0	0	0	1	4	0
C.Ripken, 3b	1	1	1	1	0	0	0	0
T.Fernandez, 3b	2	0	0	0	0	1	0	2
R.Palmeiro, dh	2	0	1	1	0	0	0	0
H.Baines, ph	1	0	1	0	0	0	0	0
J.Jaha, ph	1	0	0	0	0	1	0	0
I.Rodriguez, c	2	0	0	0	0	1	10	1
B.Ausmus, c	1	0	0	0	0	0	2	1
R.Alomar, 2b	2	0	0	1	0	1	2	2
J.Offerman, ph-2b	1	0	0	0	0	0	3	0
Totals	31	4	6	4	2	10	27	10

BATTING
2-out RBI: J.Thome; C.Ripken.
RBI, scoring position, less than 2 outs: K.Lofton 0–1; R.Palmeiro 1–1; I.Rodriguez 0–1; R.Alomar 1–1.

BASERUNNING
SB: K.Lofton (2nd base off C.Schilling/M.Piazza).
Team LOB: 6

FIELDING
E: R.Alomar (fumble); J.Offerman (throw).
DP: (3). I.Rodriguez-R.Alomar; T.Fernandez-R.Alomar-J.Thome; J.Wetteland-O.Vizquel-R.Coomer.

PITCHING	ip	h	r	er	bb	so
National League						
C.Schilling (L)	2.0	3	2	2	1	3
R.Johnson	1.0	0	0	0	0	1
K.Bottenfield	1.0	1	2	2	1	2
J.Lima	1.0	1	0	0	0	0
K.Millwood	1.0	1	0	0	0	1
A.Ashby	0.1	0	0	0	0	0
M.Hampton	0.2	0	0	0	0	0

Inherited Runners—Scored:
R.Johnson 0-0; K.Bottenfield 0-0; J.Lima 0-0; K.Millwood 0-0; A.Ashby 0-0; M.Hampton 0-0; T.Hoffman 0-0; B.Wagner 0-0; D.Cone 0-0; M.Mussina 0-0; J.Rosado 0-0; J.Zimmerman 0-0; R.Hernandez 0-0; J.Wetteland 0-0.
HBP: C.Ripken by K.Bottenfield.

PITCHING	ip	h	r	er	bb	so
National League *(continued)*						
T.Hoffman	0.1	0	0	0	0	1
B.Wagner	0.2	0	0	0	0	2
American League						
P.Martinez (w)	2.0	0	0	0	0	5
D.Cone	2.0	4	1	1	1	3
M.Mussina	1.0	1	0	0	1	2
J.Rosado	1.0	1	0	0	0	1
J.Zimmerman	1.0	0	0	0	2	0
R.Hernandez	1.0	0	0	0	0	0
J.Wetteland (s)	1.0	1	0	0	0	1

GAME DATA—T: 2:53; A: 34187; Temp: 68; Wind: Right to left, Speed: 10 mph

UMPIRES—HP: Evans, Jim (AL), 1B: Tata, Terry (NL), 2B: Ford, Dale (AL), 3B: Hernandez, Angel (NL), LF: Johnson, Mark (AL), RF: Vanover, Larry (NL)

STARTING LINEUPS

	National League	American League
1.	B.Larkin ss	K.Lofton lf
2.	L.Walker rf	N.Garciaparra ss
3.	S.Sosa cf	K.Griffey Jr. cf
4.	M.McGwire 1b	M.Ramirez rf
5.	M.Williams 3b	J.Thome 1b
6.	J.Bagwell dh	C.Ripken 3b
7.	M.Piazza c	R.Palmeiro dh
8.	J.Burnitz lf	I.Rodriguez c
9.	J.Bell 2b	R.Alomar 2b
	C.Schilling p	P.Martinez p

NL 1ST: B.Larkin struck out; L.Walker was called out on strikes; S.Sosa struck out; 0 R, 0 H, 0 E, 0 LOB. NL 0, AL 0.

AL 1ST: K.Lofton singled to first base (it was the 1–2 pitch); N.Garciaparra lined to L.Walker-rf; K.Griffey Jr. was called out on strikes; K.Lofton stole second (it was the 2–1 pitch); M.Ramirez walked; J.Thome singled to center field (it was the 1–0 pitch) [K.Lofton scored, M.Ramirez to second]; C.Ripken singled to right field (it was the first pitch) [M.Ramirez scored, J.Thome to second]; R.Palmeiro grounded out (M.McGwire-1b unassisted); 2 R, 3 H, 0 E, 2 LOB. NL 0, AL 2.

NL 2ND: M.McGwire struck out; M.Williams reached on an error by R.Alomar-2b (it was the first pitch) [M.Williams to first]; J.Bagwell struck out while M.Williams was caught stealing second (I.Rodriguez-c to R.Alomar-2b); 0 R, 0 H, 1 E, 0 LOB. NL 0, AL 2.

AL 2ND: five strikeouts for P.Martinez ties AL record; I.Rodriguez grounded out (J.Bell-2b to M.McGwire-1b); R.Alomar struck out; K.Lofton struck out; 0 R, 0 H, 0 E, 0 LOB. NL 0, AL 2.

NL 3RD: **D.Cone replaced P.Martinez (pitching);** M.Piazza struck out; J.Burnitz doubled to right field (it was the 2–2 pitch); J.Bell was called out on strikes; B.Larkin singled to center field (it was the 1–1 pitch) [J.Burnitz scored]; L.Walker grounded out (D.Cone-p to J.Thome-1b); 1 R, 2 H, 0 E, 1 LOB. NL 1, AL 2.

AL 3RD: **R.Johnson replaced C.Schilling (pitching);** N.Garciaparra popped to S.Sosa-cf; K.Griffey Jr. grounded out (M.McGwire-1b unassisted); M.Ramirez struck out; 0 R, 0 H, 0 E, 0 LOB. NL 1, AL 2.

NL 4TH: **B.Surhoff replaced K.Griffey Jr. (playing lf); K.Lofton changed positions (playing cf); D.Jeter replaced N.Garciaparra (playing ss); S.Green replaced M.Ramirez (playing rf);** S.Sosa popped to J.Thome-1b; M.McGwire walked; M.Williams struck out; J.Bagwell singled to right field (it was the 2–2 pitch) [M.McGwire to second]; M.Piazza singled to right field (it was the first pitch)

[M.McGwire to third, J.Bagwell to second]; J.Burnitz grounded out (J.Thome-1b unassisted); 0 R, 2 H, 0 E, 3 LOB. NL 1, AL 2.

AL 4TH: **L.Gonzalez replaced L.Walker (playing lf); J.Burnitz changed positions (playing rf); K.Bottenfield replaced R.Johnson (pitching);** J.Thome walked; C.Ripken was hit by a pitch (it was the 1–2 pitch) [J.Thome to second]; R.Palmeiro singled to right field (it was the first pitch) [J.Thome scored, C.Ripken to third]; I.Rodriguez struck out; R.Alomar reached on an error by M.Williams-3b (it was the 0–1 pitch) [C.Ripken scored, R.Palmeiro to second, R.Alomar to first]; K.Lofton popped to M.Williams-3b in foul territory; Jeter does a Garciaparra imitation in the batter's box; D.Jeter struck out; 2 R, 1 H, 1 E, 2 LOB. NL 1, AL 4.

NL 5TH: **T.Fernandez replaced C.Ripken (playing 3b); M.Mussina replaced D.Cone (pitching);** J.Bell walked; B.Larkin forced J.Bell (R.Alomar-2b to D.Jeter-ss) [B.Larkin to first]; L.Gonzalez doubled to left field (it was the 2–0 pitch) [B.Larkin to third]; S.Sosa was called out on strikes; M.McGwire struck out; 0 R, 1 H, 0 E, 2 LOB. NL 1, AL 4.

AL 5TH: **B.Jordan replaced J.Burnitz (playing cf); V.Guerrero replaced S.Sosa (playing rf); J.Kent replaced J.Bell (playing 2b); S.Casey replaced M.McGwire (playing 1b); M.Lieberthal replaced M.Piazza (playing c); J.Lima replaced K.Bottenfield (pitching);** B.Surhoff grounded out (S.Casey-1b unassisted); S.Green singled to second base (it was the 1–2 pitch); J.Thome flied to V.Guerrero-rf; T.Fernandez forced S.Green (J.Kent-2b to B.Larkin-ss) [T.Fernandez to first]; 0 R, 1 H, 0 E, 1 LOB. NL 1, AL 4.

NL 6TH: **B.Williams replaced K.Lofton (playing cf); B.Ausmus replaced I.Rodriguez (playing c); J.Rosado replaced M.Mussina (pitching);** M.Williams singled to left field (it was the 1–2 pitch); J.Bagwell struck out; M.Lieberthal grounded into a double play (T.Fernandez-3b to R.Alomar-2b to J.Thome-1b) [M.Williams out at second]; 0 R, 1 H, 0 E, 0 LOB. NL 1, AL 4.

AL 6TH: **K.Millwood replaced J.Lima (pitching); E.Sprague replaced M.Williams (playing 3b); H.Baines batted for R.Palmeiro;** H.Baines singled to center field (it was the 2–1 pitch); B.Ausmus forced H.Baines (B.Larkin-ss to J.Kent-2b) [B.Ausmus to first]; **J.Offerman batted for R.Alomar;** J.Offerman grounded out (K.Millwood-p to S.Casey-1b) [B.Ausmus to second]; B.Williams struck out; 0 R, 1 H, 0 E, 1 LOB. NL 1, AL 4.

NL 7TH: **J.Offerman stayed in game (playing 2b);**

M.Ordonez replaced S.Green (playing rf); O.Vizquel replaced D.Jeter (playing ss); R.Coomer replaced J.Thome (playing 1b); J.Zimmerman replaced J.Rosado (pitching); B.Jordan walked; B.Jordan was caught stealing second (it was the 1–0 pitch) (B.Ausmus-c to J.Offerman-2b); J.Kent walked; A.Gonzalez batted for B.Larkin; A.Gonzalez popped to J.Offerman-2b; first NL rookie ss to play in All-Star game; L.Gonzalez reached on an error by J.Offerman-2b (it was the 1–1 pitch) [J.Kent to third, L.Gonzalez to first]; V.Guerrero forced L.Gonzalez (O.Vizquel-ss to J.Offerman-2b) [V.Guerrero to first]; 0 R, 0 H, 1 E, 2 LOB. NL 1, AL 4.

AL 7TH: A.Gonzalez stayed in game (playing ss); A.Ashby replaced K.Millwood (pitching); Vizquel flipped ball from glove hand; O.Vizquel grounded out (S.Casey-1b unassisted); M.Hampton replaced A.Ashby (pitching); Surhoff is oldest of first-time players in 1999; B.Surhoff grounded out (J.Kent-2b to S.Casey-1b); M.Ordonez popped to A.Gonzalez-ss; 0 R, 0 H, 0 E, 0 LOB. NL 1, AL 4.

NL 8TH: R.Hernandez replaced J.Zimmerman (pitching); S.Casey grounded out (O.Vizquel-ss to R.Coomer-1b); E.Sprague grounded out (T.Fernandez-3b to R.Coomer-1b); G.Sheffield batted for J.Bagwell; G.Sheffield grounded out (O.Vizquel-ss to R.Coomer-1b); 0 R, 0 H, 0 E, 0 LOB. NL 1, AL 4.

AL 8TH: broken bat grounder by Sheffield; D.Nilsson replaced M.Lieberthal (playing c); T.Hoffman replaced M.Hampton (pitching); R.Coomer was called out on strikes; B.Wagner replaced T.Hoffman (pitching); T.Fernandez struck out; J.Jaha batted for H.Baines; J.Jaha was called out on strikes; 0 R, 0 H, 0 E, 0 LOB. NL 1, AL 4.

NL 9TH: J.Wetteland replaced R.Hernandez (pitching); D.Nilsson struck out; B.Jordan singled to right field (it was the 2–2 pitch); J.Kent grounded into a double play (J.Wetteland-p to O.Vizquel-ss to R.Coomer-1b) [B.Jordan out at second]; 0 R, 1 H, 0 E, 0 LOB. NL 1, AL 4.

Final Totals	R	H	E	LOB
National League	1	7	1	8
American League	4	6	2	6

All-Sub Stars

The major story before the seventy-first All-Star Game at Turner Field in Atlanta was the long list of injured players who would not be playing. The American League had three starters who were unable to play (third baseman Cal Ripken Jr., shortstop Alex Rodriguez, and outfielder Manny Ramirez), while the host National League had four (catcher Mike Piazza, first baseman Mark McGwire, and outfielders Barry Bonds and Ken Griffey Jr.). The seven replaced starters surpassed the previous record of four set in 1980.

In addition, Atlanta's Greg Maddux was injured after being named to the NL pitching staff. Boston's Pedro Martinez was hurt and never officially named to the AL squad, but he was at the game and was introduced with the other players. The official announcement was that Martinez "would be treated as if he was an All-Star" since he had been a unanimous pick of the AL managers. He did not appear on the official roster but does appear on the roster below.

With Mariners shortstop Alex Rodriguez out with a concussion, AL Manager Joe Torre selected New York's Derek Jeter, who had the second highest vote total at shortstop, to start the game. Jeter came through with three hits in three at bats and knocked in the two runs that gave the AL the lead in the fourth inning, a lead that they never surrendered. He was the unanimous MVP of the game, the first Yankee and fourth shortstop to win the trophy since the award was created in 1962. Previous shortstops to win were the Dodgers' Maury Wills in 1962, Cincinnati's Dave Concepcion in 1982, and Baltimore's Cal Ripken Jr. in 1991.

The starting pitcher match-up of Toronto's David Wells and Arizona's Randy Johnson featured two of the most dominating southpaws of recent years. Johnson, the 1999 NL Cy Young Award winner, entered the All-Star break with a 14-2 record and a 1.80 ERA. In 144 2/3 innings, Johnson had struck out 198 batters. His wins and

ERA both led the NL while his strikeout total led the majors. Johnson became the second pitcher to start the All-Star Game for each league, having started for the AL in 1997 and 1999 as a Seattle Mariner. Vida Blue started for the AL in 1971 and 1975 as a member of the Athletics and for the NL in 1978 representing the Giants.

David Wells came into the game with a 15-2 record to lead the majors in wins and was 13-0 on the road since September 1999. He had walked only eighteen batters in 128 1/3 innings pitched during the first half of the season, and had nine walkless games out of the nineteen he pitched.

In the first inning, Johnson threw only eight pitches, allowing one baserunner on a double by Jeter. Wells matched Johnson by throwing eleven pitches and surrendering one hit, a single to Chipper Jones. Danny Graves of the Reds replaced Johnson in the second inning and surrendered one single. However, Graves received some help from center fielder Jim Edmonds of the Cardinals, who replaced Griffey in the starting line-up. Boston's Carl Everett, the first batter Graves faced, laced the ball to deep left-center, and Edmonds made a spectacular over-the-shoulder basket catch on the warning track to deny Everett an extra-base hit.

Wells continued his dominance of the NL batters in the second. Edmonds knocked out a single, but Wells retired the other three batters he faced. Wells's two scoreless innings meant that AL starters had pitched 8 consecutive scoreless innings in four games since Charles Nagy surrendered two runs in 1996. Wells had not surrendered a run in 4 1/3 innings pitched in three All-Star games. By not surrendering a run in this game, Johnson's career ERA in All-Star competition was lowered to 1.00 with one run in nine innings pitched over six games.

One of the NL batters who Wells faced in the second, Braves first baseman Andres Galarraga, received the loudest ovation of the night from his home town fans. Galarraga missed the entire 1999 season with lymphoma but had returned to his old form in the first half of 2000. He entered the break with twenty homers and a .547 slugging average, and he replaced McGwire in the starting lineup. Jeter said of Galarraga: "That's a great story for him to come back and have the kind of year he is having, then to get a chance to start in the All-Star Game at home. He's a great person as well as a great player."

Dodgers hurler Kevin Brown replaced Graves on the mound for the NL in the third inning. After Orioles pinch hitter Mike Bordick was robbed of an extra base hit by another sensational catch by Edmonds, Brown quickly got ahead of Indians' second baseman Roberto Alomar 0-2. Alomar fouled off the next pitch, however, and Brown seemed to lose the plate as he threw four of the next five pitches out of the strike zone. Jeter singled to center for his second hit, and Yankees center fielder Bernie Williams forced Alomar on a grounder to Chipper Jones at third base, but the relay to first was late. Oakland first baseman Jason Giambi walked to fill the bases, and then Carl Everett received the fifth bases loaded walk in All-Star history to drive home the first run of the game.

In the bottom of the inning, with two outs, Chipper Jones homered on a 2-0 pitch to left center to the delight of the 51,323 partisan fans. Jones became the thirteenth player to homer in his own park in All-Star competition. In 1972, Braves' Hall of Famer Hank Aaron homered in the only other game played in Atlanta, at Atlanta Stadium. Jones was excited after the game: "It's not often that a player gets to play on his home field in an All-Star Game, much less start. To go out there and hit a home run, it was just awesome." This was a sweet moment for Jones as he had not been selected for the 1999 game, even though he was the NL MVP.

Al Leiter of the Mets took the mound for the NL in the fourth inning. After the Royals' Jermaine Dye walked and the Indians' Travis Fryman singled to start the inning, pinch hitter Mike Sweeney of the Royals hit what looked like a double play ball. Shortstop Barry Larkin booted the ball, however, and the bases were loaded with no one out. After Roberto Alomar popped out, Jeter hit his two-run single to center, scoring Dye and Fryman.

In the fifth inning, the NL scored another run to cut the AL's lead to 3–2. The Dodgers' Gary Sheffield walked, went to third on Chipper Jones's single to right, and scored on Braves center fielder Andruw Jones's single to center. It remained a one-run game until the ninth inning.

With Padres closer Trevor Hoffman pitching the ninth for the NL, White Sox second baseman Ray Durham singled to right, and BoSox shortstop Nomar Garciaparra singled to left, advancing Dur-

ham to third. Twins outfielder Matt Lawton drove in Durham with the third consecutive single of the inning and then stole second base. Garciaparra scored on White Sox right fielder Magglio Ordonez's sacrifice fly, which also advanced Lawton to third. With the infield playing in, Darin Erstad hit a grounder that Montreal second baseman Jose Vidro bobbled on the grass, scoring Lawton.

Yankees closer Mariano Rivera came on in the ninth to attempt to nail down the AL victory. The first batter he faced, Mike Lieberthal of the Phillies, hit a grounder up the middle that Garciaparra fielded on the right side of second base. His throw to first went into the stands behind the NL dugout, placing Lieberthal on second base. It was Garciaparra's second error of the game, as he had kicked a grounder by Brian Giles in the sixth inning. Garciaparra, playing in his third All-Star Game, was the first shortstop to commit two errors in a single All-Star game, and he tied the career record for shortstops held by Joe Cronin and Ernie Banks. After the errant throw, Steve Finley singled to center field to score Lieberthal with an unearned run, but Rivera got Edgar Renteria to ground into a double play to end the game.

There were quite a few defensive gems in the game in addition to Edmonds's spectacular catch in the second inning. In the fifth, Edmonds himself was the victim of a great play when Troy Glaus snagged his pop-up by reaching over the railing into the AL dugout. An inning later, Gold Glove catcher Ivan Rodriguez of the Rangers caught a Barry Larkin pop by reaching into the stands over first baseman Carlos Delgado's glove. Four batters later, Delgado reached into the NL dugout to make his own great catch of a pop-up.

Each team used eight pitchers. In addition to Wells, only the Cardinals' Darryl Kile pitched two innings. This was his first All-Star appearance after having been picked and not used in 1993 and 1997. Derek Lowe, Todd Jones, and Tim Hudson each pitched a perfect inning for the AL, while Tom Glavine and Bob Wickman performed the same feat for the NL. Jones, from nearby Marietta, Georgia, purchased forty-five game tickets for family and friends.

Jeter and Chipper Jones, each with three hits, were the only players with multihit games. The Braves representatives all played well. Galarraga, Chipper Jones, and Andruw Jones were a combined five for seven at the plate, collecting more than half of the NL's nine total hits. The trio had two of the three RBI for the team. Tom Glavine, the Braves lone pitching representative, struck out one batter in his perfect inning.

This was the fourth consecutive win for the AL and their tenth in thirteen years. Joe Torre won his third All-Star Game in three tries. He became the third manager to win his first three midsummer classics; Tommy Lasorda won in 1978, 1979, and 1982, while Tony La Russa won from 1989 through 1991.

Bobby Cox lost for the fourth time to give him a 1-4 record as All-Star manager. Cox became the fifth skipper to manage the All-Star game in his own park, a feat previously accomplished by Bill Terry (Polo Grounds, 1934), Joe McCarthy (Yankee Stadium, 1939), Del Baker (Briggs Stadium, 1941) and Billy Martin (Yankee Stadium, 1977).

The AL used twenty-nine of thirty players on the roster, tying the record for most players used by one team set by the NL in 1981. Pitcher Chuck Finley of the Indians was the only AL player not to see action, which came as no surprise to Finley, who had been told by Torre before the game that he would be held back for use as the "emergency" pitcher. With the twenty-seven players used by the NL, the combined fifty-six players tied the record for most total players used in one game, set in 1981 (twenty-nine by the NL and twenty-seven by the AL) and equaled in 1999 (twenty-eight by the NL and twenty-eight by the AL).

There were twenty-six first-time All-Stars on the rosters for the game, including fifteen for the AL and eleven for the NL. This is the second highest total for first-timers with the record set in 1988 when there were thirty-two first time All-Stars on the two rosters.

The squads in this game included eight players who have represented both leagues in the All-Star game: Roberto Alomar, Kevin Brown, Jeff Cirillo, Jim Edmonds, Randy Johnson, Fred McGriff, Ken Griffey Jr., and Mark McGwire. Ivan Rodriguez started at catcher for the eighth consecutive time, tying Yogi Berra for second place behind Johnny Bench, who started nine consecutive games.

Jeff Kent became the first Giants second baseman to start an All-Star game. Jason Kendall, named as the starter replacing Mike Piazza, became the first Pirate catcher to start since Smokey Burgess in 1961. Piazza was out with a concussion that he suffered three days before, when he was struck on the head by a Roger Clemens pitch, which the Mets claimed was intentional.

Cal Ripken Jr. did not play in the game for the first time after seventeen consecutive years in the game, including the last sixteen as a starter. This includes the 1996 game when Ripken's nose was broken during the pregame team photo session.

This was the first year that fans could vote for the All-Stars via the Internet. Ivan Rodriguez led all players in the voting, while Piazza led the NL players. It was the first time that a catcher led each league in voting. In addition, this was the first year since 1995 that Griffey did not lead in the balloting.

This was the fourth time the Braves had hosted an All-Star Game. The game was played in Boston in 1936, in Milwaukee in 1955, and in Atlanta in 1972. The NL had won all three previous games.

Pos	AL		Team		NL		Team
P	David Wells		TOR		Randy Johnson		ARI
C	Ivan Rodriguez		TEX		Mike Piazza	+	NYN
1B	Jason Giambi		OAK		Mark McGwire	+	SLN
2B	Roberto Alomar		CLE		Jeff Kent		SFN
3B	Cal Ripken	+	BAL		Chipper Jones		ATL
SS	Alex Rodriguez	+	SEA		Barry Larkin		CIN
OF	Jermaine Dye		KCA		Barry Bonds	+	SFN
OF	Manny Ramirez	+	CLE		Ken Griffey	+	CIN
OF	Bernie Williams		NYA		Sammy Sosa		CHN
	James Baldwin		CHA		Edgardo Alfonzo		NYN
	Tony Batista		TOR		Kevin Brown		LAN
	Mike Bordick		BAL		Jeff Cirillo		COL
	Carlos Delgado		TOR		Ryan Dempster		FLO
	Ray Durham		CHA		Jim Edmonds		SLN
	Darin Erstad		ANA		Steve Finley		ARI
	Carl Everett		BOS		Andres Galarraga		ATL
	Chuck Finley		CLE		Brian Giles		PIT
	Travis Fryman		CLE		Joe Girardi		CHN
	Nomar Garciaparra		BOS		Tom Glavine		ATL
	Troy Glaus		ANA		Danny Graves		CIN
	Tim Hudson		OAK		Vladimir Guerrero		MON
	Jason Isringhausen		OAK		Jeffrey Hammonds		COL
	Derek Jeter		NYA		Todd Helton		COL
	Todd Jones		DET		Trevor Hoffman		SDN
	Matt Lawton		MIN		Andruw Jones		ATL
	Derek Lowe		BOS		Jason Kendall		PIT
	Edgar Martinez		SEA		Darryl Kile		SLN
	Pedro Martinez	+	BOS		Al Leiter		NYN
	Fred McGriff		TBA		Mike Lieberthal		PHI
	Magglio Ordonez		CHA		Greg Maddux	+	ATL
	Jorge Posada		NYA		Edgar Renteria		SLN
	Mariano Rivera		NYA		Shane Reynolds		HOU
	Aaron Sele		SEA		Gary Sheffield		LAN
	Mike Sweeney		KCA		Jose Vidro		MON
					Bob Wickman		MIL

\+ player replaced on roster

RETROSHEET EXPANDED BOX SCORE Tuesday, 7/11/2000 American League at National League (N)

American League   001 200 003- 6
National League   001 010 001- 3

AMERICAN LEAGUE

	ab	r	h	bi	bb	so	po	a
R.Alomar, 2b	2	0	0	0	1	0	3	1
R.Durham, 2b	2	1	1	0	0	0	1	3
D.Jeter, ss	3	1	3	2	0	0	0	1
N.Garciaparra, ss	2	1	1	0	0	0	2	2
B.Williams, cf	3	0	0	0	0	0	0	0
M.Lawton, cf	2	1	1	1	0	0	0	0
J.Giambi, 1b	2	0	0	0	1	2	2	0
A.Sele, p	0	0	0	0	0	0	0	0
M.Ordonez, rf	1	0	1	1	0	0	1	0
C.Everett, lf	2	0	0	1	1	0	1	0
D.Erstad, lf	2	0	0	1	0	0	0	0
I.Rodriguez, c	3	0	1	0	0	0	3	0
J.Posada, c	2	0	0	0	0	1	2	0
J.Dye, rf	2	1	0	0	1	1	1	0
J.Isringhausen, p	0	0	0	0	0	0	0	0
D.Lowe, p	0	0	0	0	0	0	0	0
F.McGriff, 1b	2	0	0	0	0	1	5	0
T.Fryman, 3b	2	1	1	0	0	1	0	0
T.Glaus, 3b	1	0	0	0	0	0	2	0
T.Batista, ph-3b	1	0	0	0	0	1	0	0
D.Wells, p	0	0	0	0	0	0	0	0
M.Bordick, ph	1	0	0	0	0	0	0	0
J.Baldwin, p	0	0	0	0	0	0	0	0
M.Sweeney, ph	1	0	0	0	0	0	0	0
C.Delgado, 1b	1	0	1	0	0	0	4	0
T.Jones, p	0	0	0	0	0	0	0	0
E.Martinez, ph	1	0	0	0	0	0	0	0
T.Hudson, p	0	0	0	0	0	0	0	0
M.Rivera, p	0	0	0	0	0	0	0	1
Totals	38	6	10	6	4	7	27	8

BATTING
2B: D.Jeter (off R.Johnson); C.Delgado (off D.Kile); M.Ordonez (off D.Kile).
2-out RBI: C.Everett.
RBI, scoring position, less than 2 outs: R.Alomar 0–2; R.Durham 0–1; D.Jeter 2–2; B.Williams 0–3; M.Lawton 1–1; M.Ordonez 1–2; D.Erstad 1–2.
SF: M.Ordonez.

BASERUNNING
SB: M.Lawton (2nd base off T.Hoffman / M.Lieberthal).
Team LOB: 10

FIELDING
E: N.Garciaparra (fumble); N.Garciaparra (throw).
DP: (1). N.Garciaparra-R.Durham-F.McGriff.

NATIONAL LEAGUE

	ab	r	h	bi	bb	so	po	a
B.Larkin, ss	3	0	0	0	0	0	0	2
E.Renteria, ss	2	0	0	0	0	0	0	2
C.Jones, 3b	3	1	3	1	0	0	1	0
J.Cirillo, 3b	1	0	0	0	0	0	2	1
V.Guerrero, lf	2	0	1	0	0	0	1	0
A.Leiter, p	0	0	0	0	0	0	0	0
A.Jones, cf	2	0	1	1	0	1	2	0
S.Sosa, rf	3	0	0	0	0	1	1	0
D.Kile, p	0	0	0	0	0	0	0	1
B.Wickman, p	0	0	0	0	0	0	0	0
J.Vidro, ph-2b	1	0	0	0	0	0	0	0
J.Kent, 2b	2	0	0	0	0	0	0	0
E.Alfonzo, 2b	2	0	0	0	0	1	0	1
T.Hoffman, p	0	0	0	0	0	0	0	0
A.Galarraga, 1b	2	0	1	0	0	0	4	0
T.Helton, pr-1b	2	0	0	0	0	0	5	0
J.Edmonds, cf	2	0	1	0	0	0	3	0
M.Lieberthal, c	2	1	1	0	0	0	4	0
J.Kendall, c	2	0	0	0	0	1	3	1
T.Glavine, p	0	0	0	0	0	0	0	0
B.Giles, rf	2	0	0	0	0	0	0	0
R.Johnson, p	0	0	0	0	0	0	0	0
D.Graves, p	0	0	0	0	0	0	0	0
K.Brown, p	0	0	0	0	0	0	0	0
J.Hammonds, ph	1	0	0	0	0	0	0	0
G.Sheffield, lf	1	1	0	0	1	0	1	0
S.Finley, lf	1	0	1	1	0	0	0	0
Totals	36	3	9	3	1	4	27	8

BATTING
HR: C.Jones (3rd inning off J.Baldwin, 0 on, 2 out).
2-out RBI: C.Jones.
RBI, scoring position, less than 2 outs: A.Jones 1–1; S.Sosa 0–1; B.Giles 0–1; S.Finley 1–1.
GDP: E.Renteria.

BASERUNNING
Team LOB: 7

FIELDING
E: B.Larkin (fumble); J.Vidro (fumble).

PITCHING	ip	h	r	er	bb	so
American League						
D.Wells	2.0	2	0	0	0	2
J.Baldwin (w)	1.0	2	1	1	0	0
A.Sele	1.0	1	0	0	0	0
J.Isringhausen	1.0	2	1	1	1	0
D.Lowe	1.0	0	0	0	0	0
T.Jones	1.0	0	0	0	0	1
T.Hudson	1.0	0	0	0	0	1
M.Rivera	1.0	2	1	0	0	0
National League						
R.Johnson	1.0	1	0	0	0	1
D.Graves	1.0	1	0	0	0	1
K.Brown	1.0	1	1	1	3	0
A.Leiter (L)	1.0	2	2	1	1	1
T.Glavine	1.0	0	0	0	0	1
D.Kile	2.0	2	0	0	0	0
B.Wickman	1.0	0	0	0	0	1
T.Hoffman	1.0	3	3	3	0	2

Inherited Runners—Scored:
J.Baldwin 0–0; A.Sele 0–0; J.Isringhausen 0–0; D.Lowe 0–0; T.Jones 0–0; T.Hudson 0–0; M.Rivera 0–0; D.Graves 0–0; K.Brown 0–0; A.Leiter 0–0; T.Glavine 0–0; D.Kile 0–0; B.Wickman 0–0; T.Hoffman 0–0.

GAME DATA—T: 2:56; A: 51323; Temp: 86; Wind: Left to right, Speed: 5 mph

UMPIRES—HP: Reilly, Mike, 1B: Hirschbeck, Mark, 2B: Bell, Wally, 3B: Schrieber, Paul, LF: O'Nora, Brian, RF: Diaz, Lazaro

STARTING LINEUPS

	American League	National League
1.	R.Alomar 2b	B.Larkin ss
2.	D.Jeter ss	C.Jones 3b
3.	B.Williams cf	V.Guerrero lf
4.	J.Giambi 1b	S.Sosa rf
5.	C.Everett lf	J.Kent 2b
6.	I.Rodriguez c	A.Galarraga 1b
7.	J.Dye rf	J.Edmonds cf
8.	T.Fryman 3b	J.Kendall c
9.	D.Wells p	R.Johnson p

AL 1ST: injured starters: AL-Ripken, Alex Rodriguez, Manny Ramirez; NL-Piazza, McGwire, Bonds, Griffey Maddux and Pedro Martinez replaced; R.Alomar grounded out (B.Larkin-ss to A.Galarraga-1b); D.Jeter doubled to left field (it was the 1–1 pitch); B.Williams grounded out (B.Larkin-ss to A.Galarraga-1b); J.Giambi struck out; 0 R, 1 H, 0 E, 1 LOB. AL 0, NL 0.

NL 1ST: B.Larkin popped to J.Giambi-1b; C.Jones singled to center field (it was the 0–1 pitch); V.Guerrero lined to R.Alomar-2b; S.Sosa was called out on strikes; 0 R, 1 H, 0 E, 1 LOB. AL 0, NL 0.

AL 2ND: **D.Graves replaced R.Johnson (pitching);** C.Everett flied to J.Edmonds-cf; great catch by Edmonds falling on the warning track; I.Rodriguez singled to right field (it was the 1–2 pitch); J.Dye flied to V.Guerrero-lf; T.Fryman struck out; 0 R, 1 H, 0 E, 1 LOB. AL 0, NL 0.

NL 2ND: J.Kent grounded out (J.Giambi-1b unassisted); standing ovation for Galarraga—a cancer survivor and home town player; A.Galarraga lined to C.Everett-lf; J.Edmonds singled to right field (it was the 1–2 pitch); J.Kendall was called out on strikes; 0 R, 1 H, 0 E, 1 LOB. AL 0, NL 0.

AL 3RD: **K.Brown replaced D.Graves (pitching); M.Bordick batted for D.Wells;** M.Bordick lined to J.Edmonds-cf; R.Alomar walked; D.Jeter singled to center field (it was the first pitch) [R.Alomar to second]; B.Williams forced R.Alomar (C.Jones-3b unassisted) [D.Jeter to second, B.Williams to first]; J.Giambi walked [D.Jeter to third, B.Williams to second]; C.Everett walked [D.Jeter scored, B.Williams to third, J.Giambi to second]; fifth bases loaded walk in All-Star history Cox visited mound; I.Rodriguez lined to J.Edmonds-cf; 1 R, 1 H, 0 E, 3 LOB. AL 1, NL 0.

NL 3RD: **J.Baldwin replaced M.Bordick (pitching);** light rain starts and lasts about one inning; **J.Hammonds batted for K.Brown;** J.Hammonds flied to J.Dye-rf; B.Larkin popped to R.Alomar-2b; C.Jones homered to very deep left-center (it was the 2–0 pitch); V.Guerrero singled to left field (it was the first pitch); S.Sosa popped to R.Alomar-2b; 1 R, 2 H, 0 E, 1 LOB. AL 1, NL 1.

AL 4TH: **G.Sheffield replaced J.Hammonds (playing lf); A.Leiter replaced V.Guerrero (pitching);** J.Dye walked; T.Fryman singled to center field (it was the first pitch) [J.Dye to second]; **M.Sweeney batted for J.Baldwin;** M.Sweeney reached on an error by B.Larkin-ss (it was the 1–2 pitch) [J.Dye to third, T.Fryman to second, M.Sweeney to first]; R.Alomar popped to A.Galarraga-1b; D.Jeter singled to center field (it was the first pitch) [J.Dye scored, T.Fryman scored (unearned), M.Sweeney to second]; B.Williams grounded out (J.Kendall-c to A.Galarraga-1b) [M.Sweeney to third, D.Jeter to second]; J.Giambi struck out; 2 R (1 ER), 2 H, 1 E, 2 LOB. AL 3, NL 1.

NL 4TH: **C.Delgado replaced M.Sweeney (playing 1b); T.Glaus replaced T.Fryman (playing 3b); A.Sele replaced J.Giambi (pitching);** J.Kent grounded out (R.Alomar-2b to C.Delgado-1b); A.Galarraga singled to center field (it was the first pitch); **T.Helton ran for A.Galarraga;** J.Edmonds popped to T.Glaus-3b in foul territory; Glaus reached into the AL dugout to catch the ball; J.Kendall grounded out (D.Jeter-ss to C.Delgado-1b); 0 R, 1 H, 0 E, 1 LOB. AL 3, NL 1.

AL 5TH: **T.Helton stayed in game (playing 1b); A.Jones replaced A.Leiter (playing cf); E.Alfonzo replaced J.Kent (playing 2b); M.Lieberthal replaced J.Edmonds (playing c); T.Glavine replaced J.Kendall (pitching);** C.Everett grounded out (E.Alfonzo-2b to T.Helton-1b); I.Rodriguez flied to S.Sosa-rf; J.Dye struck out; 0 R, 0 H, 0 E, 0 LOB. AL 3, NL 1.

NL 5TH: **R.Durham replaced R.Alomar (playing 2b); N.Garciaparra replaced D.Jeter (playing ss); M.Ordonez replaced A.Sele (playing rf); D.Erstad replaced C.Everett (playing lf); J.Isringhausen replaced J.Dye (pitching);** G.Sheffield walked; B.Larkin popped to I.Rodriguez-c in foul territory; I. Rodriguez reached into the stands to catch the ball; C.Jones singled to right field (it was the 0–2 pitch) [G.Sheffield to second]; A.Jones singled to center field (it was the 1–0 pitch) [G.Sheffield scored, C.Jones to second]; S.Sosa flied to M.Ordonez-rf [C.Jones to third]; E.Alfonzo popped to C.Delgado-1b in foul territory; 1 R, 2 H, 0 E, 2 LOB. AL 3, NL 2.

AL 6TH: **J.Cirillo replaced C.Jones (playing 3b); D.Kile replaced S.Sosa (pitching); E.Renteria replaced B.Larkin (playing ss); B.Giles replaced T.Glavine (playing rf);** T.Glaus grounded out (E.Renteria-ss to T.Helton-1b); C.Delgado doubled to right field (it was the 3–2 pitch); R.Durham popped to J.Cirillo-3b in foul territory;

N.Garciaparra lined to G.Sheffield-lf; 0 R, 1 H, 0 E, 1 LOB. AL 3, NL 2.

NL 6TH: **M.Lawton replaced B.Williams (playing cf);** **J.Posada replaced I.Rodriguez (playing c);** **D.Lowe replaced J.Isringhausen (pitching);** T.Helton lined to N.Garciaparra-ss; M.Lieberthal popped to T.Glaus-3b in foul territory; B.Giles reached on an error by N.Garciaparra-ss (it was the 1–0 pitch) [B.Giles to first]; G.Sheffield grounded out (N.Garciaparra-ss to C.Delgado-1b); 0 R, 0 H, 1 E, 1 LOB. AL 3, NL 2.

AL 7TH: **S.Finley replaced G.Sheffield (playing lf);** M.Lawton grounded out (D.Kile-p to T.Helton-1b); M.Ordonez doubled to right field (it was the 3–2 pitch); one-hopper off the wall; D.Erstad grounded out (E.Renteria-ss to T.Helton-1b) [M.Ordonez to third]; J.Posada grounded out (J.Cirillo-3b to T.Helton-1b); 0 R, 1 H, 0 E, 1 LOB. AL 3, NL 2.

NL 7TH: **F.McGriff replaced D.Lowe (playing 1b);** **T.Jones replaced C.Delgado (pitching);** E.Renteria grounded out (R.Durham-2b to F.McGriff-1b); J.Cirillo popped to F.McGriff-1b in foul territory; A.Jones struck out; 0 R, 0 H, 0 E, 0 LOB. AL 3, NL 2.

AL 8TH: **B.Wickman replaced D.Kile (pitching);** F.McGriff popped to J.Cirillo-3b in foul territory; **T.Batista batted for T.Glaus;** T.Batista struck out; **E.Martinez batted for T.Jones;** E.Martinez lined to A.Jones-cf; 0 R, 0 H, 0 E, 0 LOB. AL 3, NL 2.

NL 8TH: **T.Batista stayed in game (playing 3b);** **T.Hudson replaced E.Martinez (pitching);** **J.Vidro batted for B.Wickman;** J.Vidro popped to

N.Garciaparra-ss; E.Alfonzo struck out; T.Helton grounded out (R.Durham-2b to F.McGriff-1b); 0 R, 0 H, 0 E, 0 LOB. AL 3, NL 2.

AL 9TH: **J.Vidro stayed in game (playing 2b);** **T.Hoffman replaced E.Alfonzo (pitching);** R.Durham singled to right field (it was the 3–1 pitch); N.Garciaparra singled to left field (it was the first pitch) [R.Durham to third]; M.Lawton singled to right field (it was the 2–2 pitch) [R.Durham scored, N.Garciaparra to third]; M.Lawton stole second (it was the 1–0 pitch); M.Ordonez out on a sacrifice fly to A.Jones-cf [N.Garciaparra scored, M.Lawton to third]; D.Erstad reached on an error by J.Vidro-2b (it was the 0–1 pitch) [M.Lawton scored (RBI), D.Erstad to first]; J.Posada struck out; F.McGriff struck out; 3 R, 3 H, 1 E, 1 LOB. AL 6, NL 2.

NL 9TH: **M.Rivera replaced T.Hudson (pitching);** M.Lieberthal singled to shortstop (it was the 1–1 pitch) [M.Lieberthal to second (error by N.Garciaparra-ss)]; Garciaparra's throw went into the stands behind the dugout; B.Giles grounded out (M.Rivera-p to F.McGriff-1b); S.Finley singled to center field (it was the 2–2 pitch) [M.Lieberthal scored (unearned)]; E.Renteria grounded into a double play (N.Garciaparra-ss to R.Durham-2b to F.McGriff-1b) [S.Finley out at second]; 1 R (0 ER), 2 H, 1 E, 0 LOB. AL 6, NL 3.

Final Totals	R	H	E	LOB
American League	6	10	2	10
National League	3	9	2	7

ALL-TIME
ROSTERS

PLAYERS (1,307 total players)

This lists all players named to a team, including those replaced due to injury. The number in parentheses represents the number of times named to an All-Star roster. For total games played, please see the career statistics for players.

Aaron, Hank (25) MIL NL 1955–1965; ATL NL 1966–1974; MIL AL 1975

Aase, Don (1) BAL AL 1986

Adams, Ace (1) NY NL 1943

Adcock, Joe (2) MIL NL 1960

Agee, Tommie (2) CHA AL 1966–1967

Aguilera, Rick (3) MIN AL 1991–1993

Aguirre, Hank (2) DET AL 1962

Alexander, Doyle (1) DET AL 1988

Alfonzo, Edgardo (1) NYN NL 2000

Allen, Dick (7) PHI NL 1965–1967; SLN NL 1970; CHA AL 1972–1974

Allen, Johnny (1) CLE AL 1938

Alley, Gene (2) PIT NL 1967–1968

Allison, Bob (3) WAS AL 1959; MIN AL 1963–1964

Alomar, Roberto (11) SDN NL 1990; TOR AL 1991–1995; BAL AL 1996–1998; CLE AL 1999–2000

Alomar Sr., Sandy (1) CAL AL 1970

Alomar Jr., Sandy (6) CLE AL 1990–1992, 1996–1998

Alou, Felipe (3) SFN NL 1962; ATL NL 1966, 1968

Alou, Matty (2) PIT NL 1968–1969

Alou, Moises (3) MON NL 1994; FLO NL 1997; HOU NL 1998

Altman, George (3) CHN NL 1961–1962

Alvarez, Wilson (1) CHA AL 1994

Alvis, Max (2) CLE AL 1965, 1967

Anderson, Brady (3) BAL AL 1992, 1996–1997

Andrews, Mike (1) BOS AL 1969

Andrews, Nate (1) BSN NL 1944

Andujar, Joaquin (4) HOU NL 1977, 1979; SLN NL 1984–1985

Antonelli, Johnny (6) NY NL 1954, 1956–1957; SFN NL 1958–1959

Aparicio, Luis (13) CHA AL 1958–1962; BAL AL 1963–1964; CHA AL 1970; BOS AL 1971–1972

Appier, Kevin (1) KCA AL 1995

Appling, Luke (7) CHA AL 1936, 1939–1941, 1943, 1946–1947

Armas, Tony (2) OAK AL 1981; BOS AL 1984

Armstrong, Jack (1) CIN NL 1990

Arnovich, Morrie (1) PHI NL 1939

Arrojo, Rolando (1) TBA AL 1998

Arroyo, Luis (2) SLN NL 1955; NYA AL 1961

Ashburn, Richie (6) PHI NL 1948, 1951, 1953, 1958; NYN NL 1962

Ashby, Andy (2) SDN NL 1998–1999

Atwell, Toby (1) CHN NL 1952

Ausmus, Brad (1) DET AL 1999

Averill, Earl (6) CLE AL 1933–1938

Avery, Steve (1) ATL NL 1993

Avila, Bobby (3) CLE AL 1952, 1954–1955

Azcue, Joe (1) CLE AL 1968

Baerga, Carlos (3) CLE AL 1992–1993, 1995

Bagby, Jim (2) CLE AL 1942–1943

Bagwell, Jeff (4) HOU NL 1994, 1996–1997, 1999

Bailey, Ed (6) CIN NL 1956–1957, 1960–1961; SFN NL 1963

Baines, Harold (6) CHA AL 1985–1987, 1989; OAK AL 1991; BAL AL 1999

Baker, Dusty (2) LAN NL 1981–1982

Baker, Gene (1) CHN NL 1955

Baldwin, James (1) CHA AL 2000

Bando, Sal (4) OAK AL 1969, 1972–1974

Banks, Ernie (14) CHN NL 1955–1962, 1965, 1967, 1969

Bannister, Floyd (1) SEA AL 1982

Barber, Steve (2) BAL AL 1963, 1966

Barfield, Jesse (1) TOR AL 1986

Barker, Len (1) CLE AL 1981

Bartell, Dick (2) PHI NL 1933; NY NL 1937

Bass, Kevin (1) HOU NL 1986

Batista, Tony (1) TOR AL 2000

Battey, Earl (5) MIN AL 1962–1963, 1965–1966

Bauer, Hank (3) NYA AL 1952–1954

Baylor, Don (1) CAL AL 1979

Beck, Rod (3) SFN NL 1993–1994, 1997

Becker, Rich (1) NYN NL 1994

Beckert, Glenn (4) CHN NL 1969–1972

Bedrosian, Steve (1) PHI NL 1987

Belanger, Mark (1) BAL AL 1976

Bell, Beau (1) SLA AL 1937

Bell, Buddy (5) CLE AL 1973; TEX AL 1980–1982, 1984

Bell, Gary (4) CLE AL 1960, 1966; BOS AL 1968

Bell, George (3) TOR AL 1987, 1990; CHN NL 1991

Bell, Gus (4) CIN NL 1953–1954, 1956–1957

Bell, Jay (2) PIT NL 1993; ARI NL 1999

Belle, Albert (5) CLE AL 1993–1996; CHA AL 1997

Bench, Johnny (14) CIN NL 1968–1980, 1983

Benedict, Bruce (2) ATL NL 1981, 1983

Benes, Andy (1) SDN NL 1993

Benton, Al (2) DET AL 1941–1942

Bere, Jason (1) CHA AL 1994

Berger, Wally (4) BSN NL 1933–1936

Berra, Yogi (18) NYA AL 1948–1962

Berry, Ken (1) CHA AL 1967

Bibby, Jim (1) PIT NL 1980

Bichette, Dante (4) COL NL 1994–1996, 1998

Bickford, Vern (1) BSN NL 1949

Biggio, Craig (7) HOU NL 1991–1992, 1994–1998

Billingham, Jack (1) CIN NL 1973

Blackwell, Ewell (6) CIN NL 1946–1951

Blair, Paul (2) BAL AL 1969, 1973

Blanton, Cy (2) PIT NL 1937; PHI NL 1941

Blasingame, Don (1) SLN NL 1958

Blass, Steve (1) PIT NL 1972

Blauser, Jeff (2) ATL NL 1993, 1997

Blue, Vida (6) OAK AL 1971, 1975, 1977; SFN NL 1978, 1980–1981

Bluege, Ossie (1) WAS AL 1935

Blyleven, Bert (2) MIN AL 1973; CLE AL 1985

Bochte, Bruce (1) SEA AL 1979

Boddicker, Mike (1) BAL AL 1984

Boggs, Wade (12) BOS AL 1985–1992; NYA AL 1993–1996

Bolling, Frank (4) MIL NL 1961–1962

Bonds, Barry (9) PIT NL 1990, 1992; SFN NL 1993–1998, 2000

Bonds, Bobby (3) SFN NL 1971, 1973; NYA AL 1975

Bones, Ricky (1) MIL AL 1994

Bonham, Tiny (2) NYA AL 1942–1943

Bonilla, Bobby (6) PIT NL 1988–1991; NYN NL 1993, 1995

Boone, Bob (4) PHI NL 1976, 1978–1979; CAL AL 1983
Boone, Bret (1) CIN NL 1998
Boone, Ray (2) DET AL 1954, 1956
Bordick, Mike (1) BAL AL 2000
Borowy, Hank (1) NYA AL 1944
Bottalico, Ricky (1) PHI NL 1996
Bottenfield, Kent (1) SLN NL 1999
Boudreau, Lou (7) CLE AL 1940–1944, 1947–1948
Bouton, Jim (1) NYA AL 1963
Bowa, Larry (5) PHI NL 1974–1976, 1978–1979
Boyer, Ken (11) SLN NL 1956, 1959–1964
Bradley, Phil (1) SEA AL 1985
Branca, Ralph (3) BRO NL 1947–1949
Brandt, Jackie (2) BAL AL 1961
Brantley, Jeff (1) SFN NL 1990
Brecheen, Harry (2) SLN NL 1947–1948
Brenly, Bob (1) SFN NL 1984
Bressoud, Eddie (1) BOS AL 1964
Brett, George (13) KCA AL 1976–1988
Brett, Ken (1) PIT NL 1974
Brewer, Jim (1) LAN NL 1973
Brewer, Tom (1) BOS AL 1956
Bridges, Rocky (1) WAS AL 1958
Bridges, Tommy (6) DET AL 1934–1937, 1939–1940
Brinkman, Ed (1) DET AL 1973
Brissie, Lou (1) PHA AL 1949
Brock, Lou (6) SLN NL 1967, 1971–1972, 1974–1975, 1979
Brooks, Hubie (2) MON NL 1986–1987
Brosius, Scott (1) NYA AL 1998
Brown, Chris (1) SFN NL 1986
Brown, Jimmy (1) SLN NL 1942
Brown, Kevin (5) TEX AL 1992; FLO NL 1996–1997; SDN NL 1998; LAN NL 2000
Brown, Mace (1) PIT NL 1938
Browning, Tom (1) CIN NL 1991
Brunansky, Tom (1) MIN AL 1985
Buckner, Bill (1) CHN NL 1981
Buford, Don (1) BAL AL 1971
Buhl, Bob (2) MIL NL 1960
Buhner, Jay (1) SEA AL 1996
Bumbry, Al (1) BAL AL 1980
Bunning, Jim (9) DET AL 1957, 1959, 1961–1963; PHI NL 1964, 1966
Burdette, Lew (3) MIL NL 1957, 1959
Burgess, Smoky (9) PHI NL 1954–1955; PIT NL 1959–1961, 1964
Burgmeier, Tom (1) BOS AL 1980
Burke, Tim (1) MON NL 1989
Burkett, John (1) SFN NL 1993
Burks, Ellis (2) BOS AL 1990; COL NL 1996
Burleson, Rick (4) BOS AL 1977–1979; CAL AL 1981
Burnitz, Jeromy (1) CIN NL 1999
Burns, Britt (1) CHA AL 1981
Burroughs, Jeff (2) TEX AL 1974; ATL NL 1978
Busby, Jim (1) CHA AL 1951
Busby, Steve (2) KCA AL 1974–1975
Butler, Brett (1) LAN NL 1991
Byrd, Paul (1) PHI NL 1999
Byrne, Tommy (1) NYA AL 1950
Calderon, Ivan (1) MON NL 1991
Callison, Johnny (4) PHI NL 1962, 1964–1965
Camilli, Dolph (2) BRO NL 1939, 1941

Caminiti, Ken (3) HOU NL 1994; SDN NL 1996–1997
Campanella, Roy (8) BRO NL 1949–1956
Campaneris, Bert (6) OAK AL 1968, 1972–1975; TEX AL 1977
Campbell, Bill (1) BOS AL 1977
Candelaria, John (1) PIT NL 1977
Cannizzaro, Chris (1) SDN NL 1969
Canseco, Jose (6) OAK AL 1986, 1988–1990, 1992; TBA AL 1999
Capra, Buzz (1) ATL NL 1974
Cardenas, Leo (5) CIN NL 1964–1966, 1968; MIN AL 1971
Carew, Rod (18) MIN AL 1967–1978; CAL AL 1979–1984
Carlton, Steve (10) SLN NL 1968–1969, 1971; PHI NL 1972, 1974, 1977, 1979–1982
Carrasquel, Chico (4) CHA AL 1951, 1953–1955
Carroll, Clay (2) CIN NL 1971–1972
Carter, Gary (11) MON NL 1975, 1979–1984; NYN NL 1985–1988
Carter, Joe (5) TOR AL 1991–1994, 1996
Carty, Rico (1) ATL NL 1970
Casanova, Paul (1) WAS AL 1967
Case, George (3) WAS AL 1939, 1943–1944
Casey, Sean (1) CIN NL 1999
Cash, Dave (3) PHI NL 1974–1976
Cash, Norm (5) DET AL 1961, 1966, 1971–1972
Castilla, Vinny (2) COL NL 1995, 1998
Caudill, Bill (1) OAK AL 1984
Cavarretta, Phil (3) CHN NL 1944, 1946–1947
Cedeno, Cesar (4) HOU NL 1972–1974, 1976
Cepeda, Orlando (11) SFN NL 1959–1964; SLN NL 1967
Cerv, Bob (1) KC AL 1958
Cey, Ron (6) LAN NL 1974–1979
Chalk, Dave (2) CAL AL 1974–1975
Chambliss, Chris (1) NYA AL 1976
Chance, Dean (2) LAA AL 1964; MIN AL 1967
Chandler, Spud (4) NYA AL 1942–1943, 1946–1947
Chapman, Ben (4) NYA AL 1933–1936
Chapman, Sam (1) PHA AL 1946
Charlton, Norm (1) CIN NL 1992
Cimoli, Gino (1) BRO NL 1957
Cirillo, Jeff (2) MIL AL 1997; COL NL 2000
Clancy, Jim (1) TOR AL 1982
Clark, Jack (4) SFN NL 1978–1979; SLN NL 1985, 1987
Clark, Will (6) SFN NL 1988–1992; TEX AL 1994
Clayton, Royce (1) SLN NL 1997
Clear, Mark (2) CAL AL 1979; BOS AL 1982
Clemens, Roger (7) BOS AL 1986, 1988, 1990–1992; TOR AL 1997–1998
Clemente, Roberto (15) PIT NL 1960–1967, 1969–1972
Clift, Harlond (1) SLA AL 1937
Coates, Jim (2) NYA AL 1960
Cochrane, Mickey (2) DET AL 1934–1935
Colavito, Rocky (9) CLE AL 1959; DET AL 1961–1962; KC AL 1964; CLE AL 1965–1966
Colbert, Nate (3) SDN NL 1971–1973
Colborn, Jim (1) MIL AL 1973
Coleman, Jerry (1) NYA AL 1950
Coleman, Joe (1) PHA AL 1948
Coleman, Joe (1) DET AL 1972
Coleman, Vince (2) SLN NL 1988–1989
Collins, Ripper (3) SLN NL 1935–1936; CHN NL 1937
Colon, Bartolo (1) CLE AL 1998
Concepcion, Dave (9) CIN NL 1973, 1975–1982

Cone, David (5) NYN NL 1988, 1992; KCA AL 1994; NYA AL 1997, 1999

Conigliaro, Tony (1) BOS AL 1967

Conine, Jeff (2) FLO NL 1994–1995

Conley, Gene (4) MIL NL 1954–1955; PHI NL 1959

Consuegra, Sandy (1) CHA AL 1954

Coomer, Ron (1) MIN AL 1999

Cooper, Cecil (5) MIL AL 1979–1980, 1982–1983, 1985

Cooper, Mort (3) SLN NL 1942–1943; BSN NL 1946

Cooper, Scott (2) BOS AL 1993–1994

Cooper, Walker (8) SLN NL 1942–1944; NY NL 1946–1949; CIN NL 1950

Cora, Joey (1) SEA AL 1997

Corbett, Doug (1) MIN AL 1981

Cordero, Wil (1) MON NL 1994

Coscarart, Pete (1) BRO NL 1940

Cramer, Doc (5) PHA AL 1935; BOS AL 1937–1940

Crandall, Del (11) MIL NL 1953–1956, 1958–1960, 1962

Cronin, Joe (7) WAS AL 1933–1934; BOS AL 1935, 1937–1939, 1941

Crosetti, Frankie (2) NYA AL 1936, 1939

Crowder, Alvin (1) WAS AL 1933

Crowe, George (1) CIN NL 1958

Cruz, Jose (2) HOU NL 1980, 1985

Cuccinello, Tony (2) BRO NL 1933; BSN NL 1938

Cuellar, Mike (4) HOU NL 1967; BAL AL 1970–1971, 1974

Cullenbine, Roy (2) SLA AL 1941; CLE AL 1944

Culp, Ray (2) PHI NL 1963; BOS AL 1969

Cunningham, Joe (2) SLN NL 1959

Cuyler, Kiki (1) CHN NL 1934

Dahlgren, Babe (1) PHI NL 1943

Daley, Bud (4) KC AL 1959–1960

Danning, Harry (4) NY NL 1938–1941

Dark, Al (3) NY NL 1951–1952, 1954

Darling, Ron (1) NYN NL 1985

Daulton, Darren (3) PHI NL 1992–1993, 1995

Davalillo, Vic (1) CLE AL 1965

Davenport, Jim (2) SFN NL 1962

Davis, Alvin (1) SEA AL 1984

Davis, Chili (3) SFN NL 1984, 1986; CAL AL 1994

Davis, Curt (2) PHI NL 1936; SLN NL 1939

Davis, Eric (2) CIN NL 1987, 1989

Davis, Glenn (2) HOU NL 1986, 1989

Davis, Jody (2) CHN NL 1984, 1986

Davis, Mark (2) SDN NL 1988–1989

Davis, Ron (1) NYA AL 1981

Davis, Tommy (3) LAN NL 1962–1963

Davis, Willie (2) LAN NL 1971, 1973

Dawley, Bill (1) HOU NL 1983

Dawson, Andre (8) MON NL 1981–1983; CHN NL 1987–1991

Dean, Dizzy (4) SLN NL 1934–1937

DeCinces, Doug (1) CAL AL 1983

Delgado, Carlos (1) TOR AL 2000

DeMaestri, Joe (1) KC AL 1957

Demaree, Frank (2) CHN NL 1936–1937

Dempster, Ryan (1) FLO NL 2000

Dent, Bucky (3) CHA AL 1975; NYA AL 1980–1981

Derringer, Paul (6) CIN NL 1935, 1938–1942

Diaz, Bo (2) CLE AL 1981; CIN NL 1987

Dibble, Rob (2) CIN NL 1990–1991

Dickey, Bill (11) NYA AL 1933–1934, 1936–1943, 1946

Dickson, Jason (1) ANA AL 1997

Dickson, Murry (1) PIT NL 1953

Dierker, Larry (2) HOU NL 1969, 1971

Dietz, Dick (1) SFN NL 1970

Dillinger, Bob (1) SLA AL 1949

DiMaggio, Dom (8) BOS AL 1940–1942, 1946, 1949–1952

DiMaggio, Joe (13) NYA AL 1936–1942, 1946–1951

DiMaggio, Vince (2) PIT NL 1943–1944

DiSarcina, Gary (1) CAL AL 1995

Dobson, Joe (1) BOS AL 1948

Dobson, Pat (1) BAL AL 1972

Doby, Larry (7) CLE AL 1949–1955

Doerr, Bobby (9) BOS AL 1941–1944, 1946–1948, 1950–1951

Donovan, Dick (5) CHA AL 1955; WAS AL 1961; CLE AL 1962

Dotson, Richard (1) CHA AL 1984

Downing, Al (1) NYA AL 1967

Downing, Brian (1) CAL AL 1979

Drabek, Doug (1) HOU NL 1994

Dravecky, Dave (1) SDN NL 1983

Dropo, Walt (1) BOS AL 1950

Drysdale, Don (9) LAN NL 1959, 1961–1965, 1967–1968

Duncan, Dave (1) OAK AL 1971

Duncan, Mariano (1) PHI NL 1994

Dunston, Shawon (2) CHN NL 1988, 1990

Duren, Ryne (4) NYA AL 1958–1959, 1961

Durham, Leon (2) CHN NL 1982–1983

Durham, Ray (2) CHA AL 1998, 2000

Durocher, Leo (3) SLN NL 1936; BRO NL 1938, 1940

Dye, Jermaine (1) KCA AL 2000

Dykes, Jimmy (2) CHA AL 1933–1934

Dykstra, Lenny (3) PHI NL 1990, 1994–1995

Early, Jake (1) WAS AL 1943

Easler, Mike (1) PIT NL 1981

Easley, Damion (1) DET AL 1998

Eckersley, Dennis (6) CLE AL 1977; BOS AL 1982; OAK AL 1988, 1990–1992

Edmonds, Jim (2) CAL AL 1995; SLN NL 2000

Edwards, Bruce (2) BRO NL 1947, 1951

Edwards, Johnny (3) CIN NL 1963–1965

Elliott, Bob (6) PIT NL 1941–1942, 1944; BSN NL 1947–1948, 1951

Ellis, Dock (1) PIT NL 1971

Ellis, Sammy (1) CIN NL 1965

Ellsworth, Dick (1) CHN NL 1964

Elston, Don (2) CHN NL 1959

Engle, Dave (1) MIN AL 1984

English, Woody (1) CHN NL 1933

Ennis, Del (3) PHI NL 1946, 1951, 1955

Erskine, Carl (1) BRO NL 1954

Erstad, Darin (2) ANA AL 1998, 2000

Estes, Shawn (1) SFN NL 1997

Estrada, Chuck (2) BAL AL 1960

Etchebarren, Andy (2) BAL AL 1966–1967

Evans, Darrell (2) ATL NL 1973; SFN NL 1983

Evans, Dwight (3) BOS AL 1978, 1981, 1987

Everett, Carl (1) BOS AL 2000

Evers, Hoot (2) DET AL 1948, 1950

Face, Roy (6) PIT NL 1959–1961

Fain, Ferris (5) PHA AL 1950–1952; CHA AL 1953–1954

Fairly, Ron (2) MON NL 1973; TOR AL 1977

Farmer, Ed (1) CHA AL 1980

Farrell, Turk (5) PHI NL 1958; HOU NL 1962, 1964–1965

Feller, Bob (8) CLE AL 1938–1941, 1946–1948, 1950

Fernandez, Sid (2) NYN NL 1986–1987

Fernandez, Tony (5) TOR AL 1986–1987, 1989; SDN NL 1992; TOR AL 1999

Ferrell, Rick (7) SLA AL 1933; BOS AL 1934–1937; WAS AL 1938, 1944

Ferrell, Wes (2) CLE AL 1933; BOS AL 1937

Ferriss, Dave (1) BOS AL 1946

Fette, Lou (1) BSN NL 1939

Fidrych, Mark (2) DET AL 1976–1977

Fielder, Cecil (3) DET AL 1990–1991, 1993

Fingers, Rollie (7) OAK AL 1973–1976; SDN NL 1978; MIL AL 1981–1982

Finigan, Jim (2) PHA AL 1954; KC AL 1955

Finley, Chuck (5) CAL AL 1989–1990, 1995–1996; CLE AL 2000

Finley, Steve (2) SDN NL 1997; ARI NL 2000

Finney, Lou (1) BOS AL 1940

Fisher, Eddie (1) CHA AL 1965

Fisk, Carlton (11) BOS AL 1972–1974, 1976–1978, 1980; CHA AL 1981–1982, 1985, 1991

Flanagan, Mike (1) BAL AL 1978

Fletcher, Darrin (1) MON NL 1994

Fletcher, Elbie (1) PIT NL 1943

Flood, Curt (3) SLN NL 1964, 1966, 1968

Foiles, Hank (1) PIT NL 1957

Ford, Whitey (10) NYA AL 1954–1956, 1958–1961, 1964

Fornieles, Mike (1) BOS AL 1961

Forsch, Ken (2) HOU NL 1976; CAL AL 1981

Fosse, Ray (2) CLE AL 1970–1971

Foster, George (5) CIN NL 1976–1979, 1981

Fox, Nellie (15) CHA AL 1951–1961, 1963

Fox, Pete (1) BOS AL 1944

Foxx, Jimmie (9) PHA AL 1933–1935; BOS AL 1936–1941

Franco, John (4) CIN NL 1986–1987, 1989; NYN NL 1990

Franco, Julio (3) TEX AL 1989–1991

Francona, Tito (1) CLE AL 1961

Frankhouse, Fred (1) BSN NL 1934

Freehan, Bill (11) DET AL 1964–1973, 1975

Fregosi, Jim (6) LAA AL 1964; CAL AL 1966–1970

French, Larry (1) CHN NL 1940

Frey, Lonny (3) CIN NL 1939, 1941, 1943

Friend, Bob (4) PIT NL 1956, 1958, 1960

Frisch, Frankie (3) SLN NL 1933–1935

Fryman, Travis (5) DET AL 1992–1994, 1996; CLE AL 2000

Fryman, Woodie (2) PHI NL 1968; MON NL 1976

Furillo, Carl (2) BRO NL 1952–1953

Gaetti, Gary (2) MIN AL 1988–1989

Galan, Augie (3) CHN NL 1936; BRO NL 1943–1944

Galarraga, Andres (5) MON NL 1988; COL NL 1993, 1997; ATL NL 1998, 2000

Gant, Ron (2) ATL NL 1992; CIN NL 1995

Garcia, Carlos (1) PIT NL 1994

Garcia, Damaso (2) TOR AL 1984–1985

Garcia, Mike (3) CLE AL 1952–1954

Garciaparra, Nomar (3) BOS AL 1997, 1999–2000

Garner, Phil (3) OAK AL 1976; PIT NL 1980–1981

Garr, Ralph (1) ATL NL 1974

Garrelts, Scott (1) SFN NL 1985

Garver, Ned (1) SLA AL 1951

Garvey, Steve (10) LAN NL 1974–1981; SDN NL 1984–1985

Gaston, Cito (1) SDN NL 1970

Gedman, Rich (2) BOS AL 1985–1986

Gehrig, Lou (7) NYA AL 1933–1939

Gehringer, Charlie (6) DET AL 1933–1938

Gentile, Jim (6) BAL AL 1960–1962

Giambi, Jason (1) OAK AL 2000

Gibson, Bob (9) SLN NL 1962, 1965–1970, 1972

Giles, Brian (1) PIT NL 2000

Gilliam, Jim (2) BRO NL 1956; LAN NL 1959

Girardi, Joe (1) CHN NL 2000

Giusti, Dave (1) PIT NL 1973

Glaus, Troy (1) ANA AL 2000

Glavine, Tom (7) ATL NL 1991–1993, 1996–1998, 2000

Gomez, Lefty (7) NYA AL 1933–1939

Gonzalez, Alex (1) FLO NL 1999

Gonzalez, Juan (2) TEX AL 1993, 1998

Gonzalez, Luis (1) ARI NL 1999

Gooden, Dwight (4) NYN NL 1984–1986, 1988

Goodman, Billy (2) BOS AL 1949, 1953

Goodman, Ival (2) CIN NL 1938–1939

Gordon, Joe (9) NYA AL 1939–1943, 1946; CLE AL 1947–1949

Gordon, Sid (2) NY NL 1948–1949

Gordon, Tom (1) BOS AL 1998

Goslin, Goose (1) DET AL 1936

Gossage, Rich (9) CHA AL 1975–1976; PIT NL 1977; NYA AL 1978, 1980–1982; SDN NL 1984–1985

Grabarkewitz, Billy (1) LAN NL 1970

Grace, Mark (3) CHN NL 1993, 1995, 1997

Grant, Jim (2) CLE AL 1963; MIN AL 1965

Graves, Danny (1) CIN NL 2000

Gray, Ted (1) DET AL 1950

Green, Shawn (1) TOR AL 1999

Green, Tyler (1) PHI NL 1995

Greenberg, Hank (4) DET AL 1937–1940

Greenwell, Mike (2) BOS AL 1988–1989

Grich, Bobby (6) BAL AL 1972, 1974, 1976; CAL AL 1979–1980, 1982

Grieve, Ben (1) OAK AL 1998

Griffey, Ken (3) CIN NL 1976–1977, 1980

Griffey Jr., Ken (11) SEA AL 1990–1999; CIN NL 2000

Griffin, Alfredo (1) TOR AL 1984

Grim, Bob (1) NYA AL 1957

Grimsley, Ross (1) MON NL 1978

Grissom, Lee (1) CIN NL 1937

Grissom, Marquis (2) MON NL 1993–1994

Grissom, Marv (1) NY NL 1954

Groat, Dick (8) PIT NL 1959–1960, 1962; SLN NL 1963–1964

Gross, Kevin (1) PHI NL 1988

Gross, Wayne (1) OAK AL 1977

Grote, Jerry (2) NYN NL 1968, 1974

Grove, Lefty (6) PHA AL 1933; BOS AL 1935–1939

Grove, Orval (1) CHA AL 1944

Grubb, John (1) SDN NL 1974

Gruber, Kelly (2) TOR AL 1989–1990

Grudzielanek, Mark (1) MON NL 1996

Gubicza, Mark (2) KCA AL 1988–1989

Guerrero, Pedro (5) LAN NL 1981, 1983, 1985, 1987; SLN NL 1989

Guerrero, Vladimir (2) MON NL 1999–2000

Guidry, Ron (4) NYA AL 1978–1979, 1982–1983

Guillen, Ozzie (3) CHA AL 1988, 1990–1991

Gumpert, Randy (1) CHA AL 1951

Gura, Larry (1) KCA AL 1980

Gustine, Frankie (3) PIT NL 1946–1948

Guzman, Juan (1) TOR AL 1992

Gwynn, Tony (15) SDN NL 1984–1987, 1989–1999

Haas, Bert (1) CIN NL 1947

Hack, Stan (4) CHN NL 1938–1939, 1941, 1943

Haddix, Harvey (3) SLN NL 1953–1955

Hafey, Chick (1) CIN NL 1933

Hall, Jimmie (2) MIN AL 1964–1965

Hallahan, Bill (1) SLN NL 1933

Haller, Tom (3) SFN NL 1966–1967; LAN NL 1968

Hammaker, Atlee (1) SFN NL 1983

Hammonds, Jeffrey (1) COL NL 2000

Hamner, Granny (3) PHI NL 1952–1954

Hampton, Mike (1) HOU NL 1999

Hansen, Ron (2) BAL AL 1960

Hanson, Erik (1) BOS AL 1995

Harder, Mel (4) CLE AL 1934–1937

Hargan, Steve (1) CLE AL 1967

Hargrove, Mike (1) TEX AL 1975

Harnisch, Pete (1) HOU NL 1991

Harper, Tommy (1) MIL AL 1970

Harrah, Toby (4) TEX AL 1972, 1975–1976; CLE AL 1982

Harrelson, Bud (2) NYN NL 1970–1971

Harrelson, Ken (1) BOS AL 1968

Harris, Mickey (1) BOS AL 1946

Hart, James (1) SFN NL 1966

Hartnett, Gabby (6) CHN NL 1933–1938

Harvey, Bryan (2) CAL AL 1991; FLO NL 1993

Hatton, Grady (1) CIN NL 1952

Hayes, Frankie (5) PHA AL 1939–1941, 1944; CLE AL 1946

Hayes, Von (1) PHI NL 1989

Haynes, Joe (1) CHA AL 1948

Hearn, Jim (1) NY NL 1952

Heath, Jeff (2) CLE AL 1941, 1943

Heaton, Neal (1) PIT NL 1990

Hegan, Jim (5) CLE AL 1947, 1949–1952

Hegan, Mike (1) SEA AL 1969

Helms, Tommy (2) CIN NL 1967–1968

Helton, Todd (1) COL NL 2000

Hemsley, Rollie (5) SLA AL 1935–1936; CLE AL 1939–1940;
    NYA AL 1944

Henderson, Dave (1) OAK AL 1991

Henderson, Rickey (10) OAK AL 1980, 1982–1984; NYA AL
    1985–1988; OAK AL 1990–1991

Hendrick, George (4) CLE AL 1974–1975; SLN NL 1980, 1983

Henke, Tom (2) TOR AL 1987; SLN NL 1995

Henneman, Mike (1) DET AL 1989

Henrich, Tommy (5) NYA AL 1942, 1947–1950

Henry, Bill (2) CIN NL 1960

Hentgen, Pat (3) TOR AL 1993–1994, 1997

Herbert, Ray (1) CHA AL 1962

Herman, Billy (10) CHN NL 1934–1941; BRO NL 1942–1943

Hernandez, Willie (3) DET AL 1984–1986

Hernandez, Keith (5) SLN NL 1979–1980; NYN NL 1984, 1986–
    1987

Hernandez, Roberto (2) CHA AL 1996; TBA AL 1999

Herr, Tom (1) SLN NL 1985

Herrmann, Ed (1) CHA AL 1974

Hershiser, Orel (3) LAN NL 1987–1989

Hickman, Jim (1) CHN NL 1970

Higbe, Kirby (2) PHI NL 1940; BRO NL 1946

Higgins, Mike (3) PHA AL 1934, 1936; DET AL 1944

Higuera, Teddy (1) MIL AL 1986

Hildebrand, Oral (1) CLE AL 1933

Hill, Ken (1) MON NL 1994

Hiller, John (1) DET AL 1974

Hinton, Chuck (1) WAS AL 1964

Hisle, Larry (2) MIN AL 1977; MIL AL 1978

Hoag, Myril (1) SLA AL 1939

Hoak, Don (1) CIN NL 1957

Hockett, Oris (1) CLE AL 1944

Hodges, Gil (8) BRO NL 1949–1955, 1957

Hoeft, Billy (1) DET AL 1955

Hoerner, Joe (1) PHI NL 1970

Hoffman, Trevor (3) SDN NL 1998–2000

Holland, Al (1) PHI NL 1984

Hollins, Dave (1) PHI NL 1993

Holmes, Tommy (1) BSN NL 1948

Holtzman, Ken (2) OAK AL 1972–1973

Honeycutt, Rick (2) SEA AL 1980; TEX AL 1983

Hooton, Burt (1) LAN NL 1981

Hopp, Johnny (1) BSN NL 1946

Horlen, Joe (1) CHA AL 1967

Horner, Bob (1) ATL NL 1982

Horton, Willie (4) DET AL 1965, 1968, 1970, 1973

Hough, Charlie (1) TEX AL 1986

Houtteman, Art (1) DET AL 1950

Howard, Elston (11) NYA AL 1957–1965

Howard, Frank (5) WAS AL 1962, 1968–1971

Howe, Steve (1) LAN NL 1982

Howell, Jack (1) CAL AL 1985

Howell, Jay (2) OAK AL 1987; LAN NL 1989

Howell, Roy (1) TOR AL 1978

Howser, Dick (2) KC AL 1961

Hoyt, Lamarr (1) SDN NL 1985

Hrbek, Kent (1) MIN AL 1982

Hubbard, Glenn (1) ATL NL 1983

Hubbell, Carl (8) NY NL 1933–1938, 1940–1941

Hudek, John (1) HOU NL 1994

Hudson, Sid (2) WAS AL 1941–1942

Hudson, Tim (1) OAK AL 2000

Hughson, Tex (3) BOS AL 1942–1944

Hume, Tom (1) CIN NL 1982

Hundley, Randy (1) CHN NL 1969

Hundley, Todd (2) NYN NL 1996–1997

Hunt, Ron (2) NYN NL 1964, 1966

Hunter, Billy (1) SLA AL 1953

Hunter, Jim (8) KC AL 1966–1967; OAK AL 1970, 1972–1974;
    NYA AL 1975–1976

Hurst, Bruce (1) BOS AL 1987

Hutchinson, Fred (1) DET AL 1951

Irvin, Monte (1) NY NL 1952

Isringhausen, Jason (1) OAK AL 2000

Jablonski, Ray (1) SLN NL 1954

Jackson, Bo (1) KCA AL 1989

Jackson, Danny (2) CIN NL 1988; PHI NL 1994

Jackson, Grant (1) PHI NL 1969

Jackson, Larry (5) SLN NL 1957–1958, 1960; CHN NL 1963

Jackson, Randy (2) CHN NL 1954–1955

Jackson, Reggie (14) OAK AL 1969, 1971–1975; NYA AL 1977–
    1981; CAL AL 1982–1984

Jackson, Travis (1) NY NL 1934

Jacoby, Brook (2) CLE AL 1986, 1990

Jaha, John (1) OAK AL 1999

Jansen, Larry (2) NY NL 1950–1951

Javery, Al (2) BSN NL 1943–1944

Javier, Julian (2) SLN NL 1963, 1968

Jay, Joey (2) CIN NL 1961

Jefferies, Gregg (2) SLN NL 1993–1994

Jenkins, Ferguson (3) CHN NL 1967, 1971–1972

Jensen, Jackie (3) NYA AL 1952; BOS AL 1955, 1958

Jeter, Derek (3) NYA AL 1998–2000

John, Tommy (4) CHA AL 1968; LAN NL 1978; NYA AL 1979–1980

Johnson, Alex (1) CAL AL 1970

Johnson, Bill (1) NYA AL 1947

Johnson, Bob (7) PHA AL 1935, 1938–1940, 1942; WAS AL 1943; BOS AL 1944

Johnson, Charles (1) FLO NL 1997

Johnson, Dave (4) BAL AL 1968–1970; ATL NL 1973

Johnson, Don (1) CHN NL 1944

Johnson, Howard (2) NYN NL 1989, 1991

Johnson, Lance (1) NYN NL 1996

Johnson, Randy (7) SEA AL 1990, 1993–1995, 1997; ARI NL 1999–2000

Jones, Andruw (1) ATL NL 2000

Jones, Bobby (1) NYN NL 1997

Jones, Chipper (4) ATL NL 1996–1998, 2000

Jones, Cleon (1) NYN NL 1969

Jones, Doug (5) CLE AL 1988–1990; HOU NL 1992; PHI NL 1994

Jones, Randy (2) SDN NL 1975–1976

Jones, Ruppert (2) SEA AL 1977; SDN NL 1982

Jones, Sam (2) CHN NL 1955; SFN NL 1959

Jones, Todd (1) DET AL 2000

Jones, Willie (2) PHI NL 1950–1951

Joost, Eddie (2) PHA AL 1949, 1952

Jordan, Brian (1) ATL NL 1999

Jose, Felix (1) SLN NL 1991

Josephson, Duane (1) CHA AL 1968

Joyner, Wally (1) CAL AL 1986

Judd, Oscar (1) BOS AL 1943

Jurges, Billy (3) CHN NL 1937; NY NL 1939–1940

Justice, Dave (3) ATL NL 1993–1994; CLE AL 1997

Kaat, Jim (3) MIN AL 1962, 1966; CHA AL 1975

Kaline, Al (18) DET AL 1955–1967, 1971, 1974

Kasko, Eddie (2) CIN NL 1961

Kazak, Eddie (1) SLN NL 1949

Keegan, Bob (1) CHA AL 1954

Kell, George (10) DET AL 1947–1952; BOS AL 1953–1954; CHA AL 1956; BAL AL 1957

Keller, Charlie (5) NYA AL 1940–1941, 1943, 1946–1947

Kellner, Alex (1) PHA AL 1949

Kelly, Roberto (2) NYA AL 1992; CIN NL 1993

Kelly, Pat (1) CHA AL 1973

Keltner, Ken (7) CLE AL 1940–1944, 1946, 1948

Kemp, Steve (1) DET AL 1979

Kendall, Jason (3) PIT NL 1996, 1998, 2000

Kennedy, Terry (4) SDN NL 1981, 1983, 1985; BAL AL 1987

Kennedy, Vern (2) CHA AL 1936; DET AL 1938

Kent, Jeff (2) SFN NL 1999–2000

Keough, Matt (1) OAK AL 1978

Kern, Jim (3) CLE AL 1977–1978; TEX AL 1979

Kerr, Buddy (1) NY NL 1948

Kessinger, Don (6) CHN NL 1968–1972, 1974

Key, Jimmy (4) TOR AL 1985, 1991; NYA AL 1993–1994

Kile, Darryl (3) HOU NL 1993, 1997; SLN NL 2000

Killebrew, Harmon (13) WAS AL 1959; MIN AL 1961, 1963–1971

Kiner, Ralph (6) PIT NL 1948–1953

Kingman, Dave (3) NYN NL 1976; CHN NL 1979–1980

Kittle, Ron (1) CHA AL 1983

Klein, Chuck (2) PHI NL 1933; CHN NL 1934

Kluszewski, Ted (4) CIN NL 1953–1956

Knepper, Bob (2) HOU NL 1981, 1988

Knight, Ray (2) CIN NL 1980; HOU NL 1982

Knoblauch, Chuck (4) MIN AL 1992, 1994, 1996–1997

Knoop, Bobby (1) CAL AL 1966

Knowles, Darold (1) WAS AL 1969

Konstanty, Jim (1) PHI NL 1950

Koosman, Jerry (2) NYN NL 1968–1969

Koufax, Sandy (7) LAN NL 1961–1966

Kralick, Jack (1) CLE AL 1964

Kramer, Jack (2) SLA AL 1946–1947

Kranepool, Ed (1) NYN NL 1965

Kreevich, Mike (1) CHA AL 1938

Kruk, John (3) PHI NL 1991–1993

Krukow, Mike (1) SFN NL 1986

Kubek, Tony (4) NYA AL 1958–1959, 1961

Kucks, Johnny (1) NYA AL 1956

Kuenn, Harvey (10) DET AL 1953–1959; CLE AL 1960

Kurowski, Whitey (4) SLN NL 1943–1944, 1946–1947

Laabs, Chet (1) SLA AL 1943

Labine, Clem (2) BRO NL 1956–1957

LaCoss, Mike (1) CIN NL 1979

Lamanno, Ray (1) CIN NL 1946

Landis, Jim (2) CHA AL 1962

Landreaux, Ken (1) MIN AL 1980

Langston, Mark (4) SEA AL 1987; CAL AL 1991–1993

Lanier, Max (2) SLN NL 1943–1944

Lankford, Ray (1) SLN NL 1997

Lansford, Carney (1) OAK AL 1988

Larker, Norm (2) LAN NL 1960

Larkin, Barry (11) CIN NL 1988–1991, 1993–1997, 1999–2000

LaRoche, Dave (2) CLE AL 1976–1977

Lary, Frank (3) DET AL 1960–1961

Latman, Barry (1) CLE AL 1961

Laudner, Tim (1) MIN AL 1988

Lavagetto, Cookie (4) BRO NL 1938–1941

Lavelle, Gary (2) SFN NL 1977, 1983

Law, Vance (1) CHN NL 1988

Law, Vern (2) PIT NL 1960

Lawrence, Brooks (1) CIN NL 1956

Lawton, Matt (1) MIN AL 2000

Lazzeri, Tony (1) NYA AL 1933

Lea, Charlie (1) MON NL 1984

Lee, Bill (2) CHN NL 1938–1939

Lee, Bill (1) BOS AL 1973

Lee, Bob (1) CAL AL 1965

Lee, Thornton (1) CHA AL 1941

Lefebvre, Jim (1) LAN NL 1966

LeFlore, Ron (1) DET AL 1976

Leiber, Hank (3) NY NL 1938; CHN NL 1940–1941

Leiter, Al (2) FLO NL 1996; NYN NL 2000

Lemanczyk, Dave (1) TOR AL 1979

Lemaster, Denny (1) ATL NL 1967

Lemon, Bob (7) CLE AL 1948–1954

Lemon, Chet (3) CHA AL 1978–1979; DET AL 1984

Lemon, Jim (2) WAS AL 1960

Leonard, Dutch (4) WAS AL 1940, 1943–1944; CHN NL 1951

Leonard, Jeff (2) SFN NL 1987; SEA AL 1989

Leppert, Don (1) WAS AL 1963

Lewis, Buddy (2) WAS AL 1938, 1947

Lieberthal, Mike (2) PHI NL 1999–2000

Lima, Jose (1) HOU NL 1999

Lindell, Johnny (1) NYA AL 1943

Litwhiler, Danny (1) PHI NL 1942

Lockman, Whitey (1) NY NL 1952

Loes, Billy (1) BAL AL 1957

Lofton, Kenny (6) CLE AL 1994–1996; ATL NL 1997; CLE AL
    1998–1999

Logan, Johnny (4) MIL NL 1955, 1957–1959

Lolich, Mickey (3) DET AL 1969, 1971–1972

Lollar, Sherm (9) SLA AL 1950; CHA AL 1954–1956, 1958–1960

Lombardi, Ernie (7) CIN NL 1936–1940; BSN NL 1942; NY NL
    1943

Lonborg, Jim (1) BOS AL 1967

Long, Dale (1) PIT NL 1956

Lopat, Eddie (1) NYA AL 1951

Lopata, Stan (2) PHI NL 1955–1956

Lopes, Davey (4) LAN NL 1978–1981

Lopez, Al (2) BRO NL 1934; PIT NL 1941

Lopez, Aurelio (1) DET AL 1983

Lopez, Javier (2) ATL NL 1997–1998

Lowe, Derek (1) BOS AL 2000

Lowrey, Peanuts (1) CHN NL 1946

Lumpe, Jerry (1) DET AL 1964

Luzinski, Greg (4) PHI NL 1975–1978

Lyle, Sparky (3) NYA AL 1973, 1976–1977

Lynn, Fred (9) BOS AL 1975–1980; CAL AL 1981–1983

Lyons, Ted (1) CHA AL 1939

Mack, Ray (1) CLE AL 1940

Maddux, Greg (8) CHN NL 1988, 1992; ATL NL 1994–1998,
    2000

Madlock, Bill (3) CHN NL 1975; PIT NL 1981, 1983

Maglie, Sal (2) NY NL 1951–1952

Mahaffey, Art (3) PHI NL 1961–1962

Maloney, Jim (1) CIN NL 1965

Malzone, Frank (8) BOS AL 1957–1960, 1963–1964

Mancuso, Gus (2) NY NL 1935, 1937

Mantilla, Felix (1) BOS AL 1965

Mantle, Mickey (20) NYA AL 1952–1965, 1967–1968

Manush, Heinie (1) WAS AL 1934

Marichal, Juan (10) SFN NL 1962–1969, 1971

Marion, Marty (7) SLN NL 1943–1944, 1946–1950

Maris, Roger (7) KC AL 1959; NYA AL 1960–1962

Marrero, Connie (1) WAS AL 1951

Marshall, Mike (2) LAN NL 1974–1975

Marshall, Mike (1) LAN NL 1984

Marshall, Willard (3) NY NL 1942, 1947, 1949

Martin, Billy (1) NYA AL 1956

Martin, Hersh (1) PHI NL 1938

Martin, Pepper (4) SLN NL 1933–1935, 1937

Martin, Stu (1) SLN NL 1936

Martinez, Dennis (4) MON NL 1990–1992; CLE AL 1995

Martinez, Edgar (5) SEA AL 1992, 1995–1997, 2000

Martinez, Pedro J. (5) MON NL 1996–1997; BOS AL 1998–2000

Martinez, Ramon (2) LAN NL 1990–1991

Martinez, Tino (2) SEA AL 1995; NYA AL 1997

Martinez, Tippy (1) BAL AL 1983

Masi, Phil (3) BSN NL 1946–1948

Masterson, Walt (2) WAS AL 1947–1948

Mathews, Eddie (12) MIL NL 1953, 1955–1962

Matlack, Jon (3) NYN NL 1974–1976

Matthews, Gary (1) ATL NL 1979

Mattingly, Don (6) NYA AL 1984–1989

Maxwell, Charlie (2) DET AL 1956–1957

May, Carlos (2) CHA AL 1969, 1972

May, Dave (1) MIL AL 1973

May, Lee (3) CIN NL 1969, 1971; HOU NL 1972

May, Pinky (1) PHI NL 1940

Mayberry, John (2) KCA AL 1973–1974

Mays, Willie (24) NY NL 1954–1957; SFN NL 1958–1972;
    NYN NL 1973

Mazeroski, Bill (10) PIT NL 1958–1960, 1962–1964, 1967

Mazzilli, Lee (1) NYN NL 1979

McAuliffe, Dick (3) DET AL 1965–1967

McBride, Bake (1) SLN NL 1976

McBride, Ken (3) LAA AL 1961–1963

McCarver, Tim (2) SLN NL 1966–1967

McCool, Billy (1) CIN NL 1966

McCormick, Frank (8) CIN NL 1938–1944; PHI NL 1946

McCormick, Mike (4) SFN NL 1960–1961

McCovey, Willie (6) SFN NL 1963, 1966, 1968–1971

McCullough, Clyde (2) CHN NL 1948, 1953

McDaniel, Lindy (2) SLN NL 1960

McDougald, Gil (6) NYA AL 1952, 1956–1959

McDowell, Jack (3) CHA AL 1991–1993

McDowell, Sam (6) CLE AL 1965–1966, 1968–1971

McGee, Willie (4) SLN NL 1983, 1985, 1987–1988

McGlothen, Lynn (1) SLN NL 1974

McGlothlin, Jim (1) CAL AL 1967

McGraw, Tug (2) NYN NL 1972; PHI NL 1975

McGregor, Scott (1) BAL AL 1981

McGriff, Fred (5) SDN NL 1992; ATL NL 1994–1996; TBA AL 2000

McGwire, Mark (12) OAK AL 1987–1992, 1995–1997; SLN NL
    1998–2000

McLain, Denny (3) DET AL 1966, 1968–1969

McLish, Cal (1) CLE AL 1959

McMahon, Don (1) MIL NL 1958

McMillan, Roy (2) CIN NL 1956–1957

McNally, Dave (3) BAL AL 1969–1970, 1972

McQuinn, George (6) SLA AL 1939–1940, 1942, 1944; NYA AL
    1947–1948

McRae, Hal (3) KCA AL 1975–1976, 1982

Medwick, Joe (10) SLN NL 1934–1940; BRO NL 1941–1942;
    NY NL 1944

Melton, Bill (1) CHA AL 1971

Melton, Cliff (1) NY NL 1942

Menke, Denis (2) HOU NL 1969–1970

Merritt, Jim (1) CIN NL 1970

Mesa, Jose (2) CLE AL 1995–1996

Messersmith, Andy (4) CAL AL 1971; LAN NL 1974–1975;
    ATL NL 1976

Michaels, Cass (2) CHA AL 1949–1950

Millan, Felix (3) ATL NL 1969–1971

Miller, Eddie (8) BSN NL 1939–1942; CIN NL 1943–1944,
    1946–1947

Miller, Stu (2) SFN NL 1961

Millwood, Kevin (1) ATL NL 1999

Milnar, Al (1) CLE AL 1940

Mincher, Don (2) CAL AL 1967; SEA AL 1969

Minoso, Minnie (9) CLE AL 1951; CHA AL 1952–1954, 1957;
    CLE AL 1959; CHA AL 1960

Minton, Greg (1) SFN NL 1982

Mitchell, Dale (2) CLE AL 1949, 1952

Mitchell, Kevin (2) SFN NL 1989–1990

Mize, Johnny (10) SLN NL 1937, 1939–1941; NY NL 1942, 1946–1949; NYA AL 1953

Mizell, Wilmer (1) SLN NL 1959

Molitor, Paul (7) MIL AL 1980, 1985, 1988, 1991–1992; TOR AL 1993–1994

Monbouquette, Bill (4) BOS AL 1960, 1962–1963

Monday, Rick (2) OAK AL 1968; LAN NL 1978

Mondesi, Raul (1) LAN NL 1995

Money, Don (4) MIL AL 1974, 1976–1978

Monge, Sid (1) CLE AL 1979

Montanez, Willie (1) ATL NL 1977

Montefusco, John (1) SFN NL 1976

Montgomery, Jeff (3) KCA AL 1992–1993, 1996

Moon, Wally (3) SLN NL 1957; LAN NL 1959

Moore, Donnie (1) CAL AL 1985

Moore, Gene (1) BSN NL 1937

Moore, Jo-Jo (6) NY NL 1934–1938, 1940

Moore, Mike (1) OAK AL 1989

Moore, Terry (4) SLN NL 1939–1942

Morales, Jerry (1) CHN NL 1977

Moran, Billy (2) LAA AL 1962

Morandini, Mickey (1) PHI NL 1995

Morgan, Joe (10) HOU NL 1966, 1970; CIN NL 1972–1979

Morgan, Mike (1) LAN NL 1991

Morris, Jack (5) DET AL 1981, 1984–1985, 1987; MIN AL 1991

Moryn, Walt (1) CHN NL 1958

Moseby, Lloyd (1) TOR AL 1986

Moses, Jerry (1) BOS AL 1970

Moses, Wally (1) PHA AL 1937

Mossi, Don (1) CLE AL 1957

Mota, Manny (1) LAN NL 1973

Mueller, Don (2) NY NL 1954–1955

Mueller, Ray (1) CIN NL 1944

Mulcahy, Hugh (1) PHI NL 1940

Mulholland, Terry (1) PHI NL 1993

Mullin, Pat (2) DET AL 1947–1948

Mumphrey, Jerry (1) HOU NL 1984

Muncrief, Bob (1) SLA AL 1944

Munger, Red (3) SLN NL 1944, 1947, 1949

Mungo, Van (4) BRO NL 1934–1937

Munson, Thurman (7) NYA AL 1971, 1973–1978

Murcer, Bobby (5) NYA AL 1971–1974; SFN NL 1975

Murphy, Dale (7) ATL NL 1980, 1982–1987

Murphy, Johnny (3) NYA AL 1937–1939

Murray, Eddie (8) BAL AL 1978, 1981–1986; LAN NL 1991

Musial, Stan (24) SLN NL 1943–1944, 1946–1963

Mussina, Mike (5) BAL AL 1992–1994, 1997, 1999

Myer, Buddy (2) WAS AL 1935, 1937

Myers, Randy (4) CIN NL 1990; CHN NL 1994–1995; BAL AL 1997

Nagy, Charles (3) CLE AL 1992, 1996, 1999

Narleski, Ray (2) CLE AL 1956, 1958

Neagle, Denny (2) PIT NL 1995; ATL NL 1997

Neal, Charlie (3) LAN NL 1959–1960

Nelson, Dave (1) TEX AL 1973

Nen, Robb (2) SFN NL 1998–1999

Nettles, Graig (6) NYA AL 1975, 1977–1980; SDN NL 1985

Newcombe, Don (4) BRO NL 1949–1951, 1955

Newhouser, Hal (6) DET AL 1942–1944, 1946–1948

Newman, Jeff (1) OAK AL 1979

Newsom, Bobo (4) SLA AL 1938–1939; DET AL 1940; PHA AL 1944

Nicholson, Bill (4) CHN NL 1940–1941, 1943–1944

Niekro, Joe (1) HOU NL 1979

Niekro, Phil (5) ATL NL 1969, 1975, 1978, 1982; NYA AL 1984

Nilsson, Dave (1) SLN NL 1999

Nokes, Matt (1) DET AL 1987

Nolan, Gary (1) CIN NL 1972

Nomo, Hideo (1) LAN NL 1995

Noren, Irv (1) NYA AL 1954

Norris, Mike (1) OAK AL 1981

Nuxhall, Joe (2) CIN NL 1955–1956

O'Dell, Billy (2) BAL AL 1958–1959

O'Donoghue, John (1) KC AL 1965

O'Doul, Lefty (1) BRO NL 1933

O'Neill, Paul (5) CIN NL 1991; NYA AL 1994–1995, 1997–1998

O'Toole, Jim (1) CIN NL 1963

Odom, Johnny (2) OAK AL 1968–1969

Offerman, Jose (2) LAN NL 1995; BOS AL 1999

Oglivie, Ben (3) MIL AL 1980, 1982–1983

Olerud, John (1) TOR AL 1993

Oliva, Tony (8) MIN AL 1964–1971

Oliver, Al (7) PIT NL 1972, 1975–1976; TEX AL 1980–1981; MON NL 1982–1983

Olson, Greg (1) ATL NL 1990

Olson, Gregg (1) BAL AL 1990

Ontiveros, Steve (1) OAK AL 1995

Ordonez, Magglio (2) CHA AL 1999–2000

Orosco, Jesse (2) NYN NL 1983–1984

Orta, Jorge (2) CHA AL 1975; CLE AL 1980

Osteen, Claude (2) LAN NL 1970, 1973

Osteen, Darrell (1) CIN NL 1967

Otis, Amos (5) KCA AL 1970–1973, 1976

Ott, Mel (11) NY NL 1934–1944

Owen, Mickey (4) BRO NL 1941–1944

Paciorek, Tom (1) SEA AL 1981

Pafko, Andy (4) CHN NL 1947–1950

Page, Joe (3) NYA AL 1944, 1947–1948

Pagnozzi, Tom (1) SLN NL 1992

Paige, Satchel (2) SLA AL 1952–1953

Palmeiro, Rafael (4) CHN NL 1988; TEX AL 1991; BAL AL 1998; TEX AL 1999

Palmer, Dean (1) KCA AL 1998

Palmer, Jim (6) BAL AL 1970–1972, 1975, 1977–1978

Pappas, Milt (3) BAL AL 1962, 1965

Parker, Dave (7) PIT NL 1977, 1979–1981; CIN NL 1985–1986; MIL AL 1990

Parnell, Mel (2) BOS AL 1949, 1951

Parrish, Lance (8) DET AL 1980, 1982–1986; PHI NL 1988; CAL AL 1990

Parrish, Larry (2) MON NL 1979; TEX AL 1987

Pascual, Camilo (7) WAS AL 1959–1960; MIN AL 1961–1962, 1964

Passeau, Claude (4) CHN NL 1941–1943, 1946

Patek, Freddie (3) KCA AL 1972, 1976, 1978

Pattin, Marty (1) MIL AL 1971

Pavlik, Roger (1) TEX AL 1996

Pearson, Albie (1) LAA AL 1963

Pearson, Monte (2) NYA AL 1936, 1940

Pena, Tony (5) PIT NL 1982, 1984–1986; SLN NL 1989

Pendleton, Terry (1) ATL NL 1992

Pepitone, Joe (3) NYA AL 1963–1965
Percival, Troy (3) CAL AL 1996; ANA AL 1998–1999
Perez, Carlos (1) MON NL 1995
Perez, Pascual (1) ATL NL 1983
Perez, Tony (7) CIN NL 1967–1970, 1974–1976
Perry, Gaylord (5) SFN NL 1966, 1970; CLE AL 1972, 1974;
    SDN NL 1979
Perry, Gerald (1) ATL NL 1988
Perry, Jim (3) CLE AL 1961; MIN AL 1970–1971
Pesky, Johnny (1) BOS AL 1946
Peters, Gary (2) CHA AL 1964, 1967
Peterson, Fritz (1) NYA AL 1970
Petrocelli, Rico (2) BOS AL 1967, 1969
Petry, Dan (1) DET AL 1985
Pettitte, Andy (1) NYA AL 1996
Phelps, Babe (3) BRO NL 1938–1940
Piazza, Mike (8) LAN NL 1993–1998; NYN NL 1999–2000
Pierce, Billy (7) CHA AL 1953, 1955–1959, 1961
Piersall, Jim (2) BOS AL 1954, 1956
Piniella, Lou (1) KCA AL 1972
Pinson, Vada (4) CIN NL 1959–1960
Pizarro, Juan (2) CHA AL 1963–1964
Plesac, Dan (3) MIL AL 1987–1989
Pocoroba, Biff (1) ATL NL 1978
Podres, Johnny (4) LAN NL 1958, 1960, 1962
Pollet, Howie (3) SLN NL 1943, 1946, 1949
Porter, Darrell (4) MIL AL 1974; KCA AL 1978–1980
Porterfield, Bob (1) WAS AL 1954
Posada, Jorge (1) NYA AL 2000
Powell, Boog (4) BAL AL 1968–1971
Power, Vic (6) KC AL 1955–1956; CLE AL 1959–1960
Presley, Jim (1) SEA AL 1986
Puckett, Kirby (10) MIN AL 1986–1995
Puhl, Terry (1) HOU NL 1978
Purkey, Bob (5) CIN NL 1958, 1961–1962
Quisenberry, Dan (3) KCA AL 1982–1984
Radatz, Dick (2) BOS AL 1963–1964
Radcliff, Rip (1) CHA AL 1936
Radke, Brad (1) MIN AL 1998
Raffensberger, Ken (1) PHI NL 1944
Raines, Tim (7) MON NL 1981–1987
Ramirez, Manny (4) CLE AL 1995, 1998–2000
Ramirez, Rafael (1) ATL NL 1984
Ramos, Pedro (1) WAS AL 1959
Randolph, Willie (6) NYA AL 1976–1977, 1980–1981, 1987;
    LAN NL 1989
Raschi, Vic (4) NYA AL 1948–1950, 1952
Rawley, Shane (1) PHI NL 1986
Ray, Johnny (1) CAL AL 1988
Raymond, Claude (1) HOU NL 1966
Reardon, Jeff (4) MON NL 1985–1986; MIN AL 1988; BOS AL
    1991
Reed, Rick (1) NYN NL 1998
Reed, Ron (1) ATL NL 1968
Reese, Peewee (10) BRO NL 1942, 1946–1954
Regan, Phil (1) LAN NL 1966
Reiser, Pete (3) BRO NL 1941–1942, 1946
Reitz, Ken (1) SLN NL 1980
Remy, Jerry (1) BOS AL 1978
Renteria, Edgar (2) FLO NL 1998; SLN NL 2000
Repulski, Rip (1) SLN NL 1956

Reuschel, Rick (3) CHN NL 1977; PIT NL 1987; SFN NL
    1989
Reuss, Jerry (2) PIT NL 1975; LAN NL 1980
Reynolds, Allie (5) NYA AL 1949–1950, 1952–1954
Reynolds, Craig (2) SEA AL 1978; HOU NL 1979
Reynolds, Harold (2) SEA AL 1987–1988
Reynolds, Shane (1) HOU NL 2000
Rhoden, Rick (2) LAN NL 1976; PIT NL 1986
Rice, Del (1) SLN NL 1953
Rice, Jim (8) BOS AL 1977–1980, 1983–1986
Richard, J.R. (1) HOU NL 1980
Richardson, Bobby (8) NYA AL 1957, 1959, 1962–1966
Richert, Pete (2) WAS AL 1965–1966
Riddle, Elmer (1) PIT NL 1948
Riggs, Lew (1) CIN NL 1936
Righetti, Dave (2) NYA AL 1986–1987
Rigney, Bill (1) NY NL 1948
Rijo, Jose (1) CIN NL 1994
Ripken, Cal (18) BAL AL 1983–2000
Rivera, Mariano (3) NYA AL 1997, 1999–2000
Rivers, Mickey (1) NYA AL 1976
Rizzuto, Phil (5) NYA AL 1942, 1950–1953
Roberts, Bip (1) CIN NL 1992
Roberts, Robin (7) PHI NL 1950–1956
Robinson, Aaron (1) NYA AL 1947
Robinson, Brooks (18) BAL AL 1960–1974
Robinson, Eddie (4) WAS AL 1949; CHA AL 1951–1952; PHA AL
    1953
Robinson, Frank (14) CIN NL 1956–1957, 1959, 1961–1962,
    1965; BAL AL 1966–1967, 1969–1971; CAL AL 1974
Robinson, Jackie (6) BRO NL 1949–1954
Rodriguez, Alex (4) SEA AL 1996–1998, 2000
Rodriguez, Ellie (2) KCA AL 1969; MIL AL 1972
Rodriguez, Henry (1) MON NL 1996
Rodriguez, Ivan (9) TEX AL 1992–2000
Roe, Preacher (4) BRO NL 1949–1952
Rogers, Kenny (1) TEX AL 1995
Rogers, Steve (5) MON NL 1974, 1978–1979, 1982–1983
Rojas, Cookie (5) PHI NL 1965; KCA AL 1971–1974
Rolfe, Red (4) NYA AL 1937–1940
Rollins, Rich (2) MIN AL 1962
Romano, John (4) CLE AL 1961–1962
Rosado, Jose (2) KCA AL 1997, 1999
Rosar, Buddy (5) NYA AL 1942; CLE AL 1943; PHA AL 1946–
    1948
Rose, Pete (17) CIN NL 1965, 1967–1971, 1973–1978; PHI NL
    1979–1982; CIN NL 1985
Roseboro, John (6) LAN NL 1958, 1961–1962; MIN AL 1969
Rosen, Al (4) CLE AL 1952–1955
Rowe, Schoolboy (3) DET AL 1935–1936; PHI NL 1947
Rudi, Joe (3) OAK AL 1972, 1974–1975
Ruffing, Red (6) NYA AL 1934, 1938–1942
Runnels, Pete (5) BOS AL 1959–1960, 1962
Rush, Bob (2) CHN NL 1950, 1952
Russell, Bill (3) LAN NL 1973, 1976, 1980
Russell, Jack (1) WAS AL 1934
Russell, Jeff (2) TEX AL 1988–89
Russo, Marius (1) NYA AL 1941
Ruth, Babe (2) NYA AL 1933–1934
Ruthven, Dick (2) ATL NL 1976; PHI NL 1981
Ryan, Connie (1) BSN NL 1944

Wilson, Don (1) HOU NL 1971
Wilson, Glenn (1) PHI NL 1985
Wilson, Jim (3) MIL NL 1954; BAL AL 1955–1956
Wilson, Jimmy (2) SLN NL 1933; PHI NL 1935
Wilson, Willie (2) KCA AL 1982–1983
Winfield, Dave (12) SDN NL 1977–1980; NYA AL 1981–1988
Wise, Rick (2) PHI NL 1971; SLN NL 1973
Witt, Mike (2) CAL AL 1986–1987
Wohlers, Mark (1) ATL NL 1996
Womack, Tony (1) PIT NL 1997
Wood, Wilbur (3) CHA AL 1971–1972, 1974
Woodeshick, Hal (1) HOU NL 1963
Woodling, Gene (1) BAL AL 1959
Worrell, Todd (3) SLN NL 1988; LAN NL 1995–1996
Wright, Clyde (1) CAL AL 1970
Wyatt, John (1) KC AL 1964
Wyatt, Whit (4) BRO NL 1939–1942
Wynegar, Butch (2) MIN AL 1976–1977

Wynn, Early (9) WAS AL 1947; CLE AL 1955–1957; CHA AL
    1958–1960
Wynn, Jim (3) HOU NL 1967; LAN NL 1974–1975
Wyrostek, Johnny (2) CIN NL 1950–1951
Yastrzemski, Carl (18) BOS AL 1963, 1965–1979, 1982–1983
York, Rudy (7) DET AL 1938, 1941–1944; BOS AL 1946–1947
Yost, Eddie (1) WAS AL 1952
Young, Eric (1) COL NL 1996
Young, Matt (1) SEA AL 1983
Youngblood, Joel (1) NYN NL 1981
Yount, Robin (3) MIL AL 1980, 1982–1983
Zachry, Pat (1) NYN NL 1978
Zak, Frankie (1) PIT NL 1944
Zarilla, Al (1) SLA AL 1948
Zernial, Gus (1) PHA AL 1953
Zimmer, Don (2) CHN NL 1961
Zimmerman, Jeff (1) TEX AL 1999
Zisk, Richie (2) CHA AL 1977; TEX AL 1978

Alou, Felipe	1–0	Montreal	NL 1995 (W)
Alston, Walter	1–2	Brooklyn	NL 1954 (L), 1956 (W), 1957 (L)
	6–0	Los Angeles	NL 1960–1 (W), 1960–2 (W), 1964 (W), 1966 (W), 1967 (W), 1975 (W)
Altobelli, Joe	0–1	Baltimore	AL 1984 (L)
Anderson, Sparky	3–1	Cincinnati	NL 1971 (L), 1973 (W), 1976 (W), 1977 (W)
	0–1	Detroit	AL 1985 (L)
Baker, Del	1–0	Detroit	AL 1941 (W)
Bauer, Hank	0–1	Baltimore	AL 1967 (L)
Berra, Yogi	1–0	New York	NL 1974 (W)
Bochy, Bruce	0–1	San Diego	NL 1999 (L)
Boudreau, Lou	1–0	Cleveland	AL 1949 (W)
Cochrane, Mickey	1–0	Detroit	AL 1935 (W)
Cox, Bobby	1–4	Atlanta	NL 1992 (L), 1993 (L), 1996 (W), 1997 (L), 2000 (L)
Craig, Roger	0–1	San Francisco	NL 1990 (L)
Cronin, Joe	1–0	Washington	AL 1934 (W)
	1–1	Boston	AL 1940 (L), 1947 (W)
Dark, Al	1–0	San Francisco	NL 1963 (W)
	0–1	Oakland	AL 1975 (L)
Dressen, Chuck	1–0	Brooklyn	NL 1953 (W)
Durocher, Leo	0–2	Brooklyn	NL 1942 (L), 1948 (L)
	2–0	New York	NL 1952 (W), 1955 (W)
Dyer, Eddie	0–1	St. Louis	NL 1947 (L)
Fregosi, Jim	1–0	Philadelphia	NL 1994 (W)
Frey, Jim	0–1	Kansas City	AL 1981 (L)
Frisch, Frank	0–1	St. Louis	NL 1935 (L)
Gaston, Cito	1–1	Toronto	AL 1993 (W), 1994 (L)
Green, Dallas	1–0	Philadelphia	NL 1981 (W)
Grimm, Charlie	1–1	Chicago	NL 1936 (W), 1946 (L)
Haney, Fred	1–2	Milwaukee	NL 1958 (L), 1959–1 (W), 1959–2 (L)
Hargrove, Mike	1–1	Cleveland	AL 1996 (L), 1998 (W)
Harris, Bucky	1–0	New York	AL 1948 (W)
Hartnett, Gabby	0–1	Chicago	NL 1939 (L)
Herzog, Whitey	0–3	St. Louis	NL 1983 (L), 1986 (L), 1988 (L)
Hodges, Gil	1–0	New York	NL 1970 (W)
Houk, Ralph	1–2	New York	AL 1962–1 (L), 1962–2 (W), 1963 (L)
Howser, Dick	1–0	Kansas City	AL 1986 (W)
Hutchinson, Fred	1–1	Cincinnati	NL 1962–1 (W), 1962–2 (L)
Johnson, Darrell	0–1	Boston	AL 1976 (L)
Johnson, Dave	1–0	New York	NL 1987 (W)
Kelly, Tom	2–0	Minnesota	AL 1988 (W), 1992 (W)
Kuenn, Harvey	1–0	Milwaukee	AL 1983 (W)
La Russa, Tony	3–0	Oakland	AL 1989 (W), 1990 (W), 1991 (W)
Lasorda, Tom	3–1	Los Angeles	NL 1978 (W), 1979 (W), 1982 (W), 1989 (L)
Lemon, Bob	0–1	New York	AL 1979 (L)
Leyland, Jim	0–1	Florida	NL 1998 (L)
Lopez, Al	0–1	Cleveland	AL 1955 (L)
	0–4	Chicago	AL 1960–1 (L), 1960–2 (L), 1964 (L), 1965 (L)
Mack, Connie	1–0	Philadelphia	AL 1933 (W)
Martin, Billy	0–2	New York	AL 1977 (L), 1978 (L)
	0–1	Oakland	AL 1982 (L)
Mauch, Gene	1–0	Philadelphia	NL 1965 (W)
McCarthy, Joe	4–3	New York	AL 1936 (L), 1937 (W), 1938 (L), 1939 (W), 1942 (W), 1943 (W), 1944 (L)
McGraw, John	0–1	New York (ret.)	NL 1933 (L)
McKechnie, Bill	1–1	Cincinnati	NL 1940 (W), 1941 (L)
McNamara, John	0–1	Boston	AL 1987 (L)
Mele, Sam	0–1	Minnesota	AL 1966 (L)
Murtaugh, Danny	2–0–1	Pittsburgh	NL 1961–1 (W), 1961–2 (T), 1972 (W)

O'Neill, Steve	1–0	Detroit	AL 1946 (W)
Owens, Paul	1–0	Philadelphia	NL 1984 (W)
Piniella, Lou	0–1	Cincinnati	NL 1991 (L)
Richards, Paul	0–1–1	Baltimore	AL 1961–1 (L), 1961–2 (T)
Sawyer, Eddie	1–0	Philadelphia	NL 1951 (W)
Schoendienst, Red	2–0	St. Louis	NL 1968 (W), 1969 (W)
Shotton, Burt	1–0	Brooklyn	NL 1950 (W)
Showalter, Buck	0–1	New York	AL 1995 (L)
Smith, Mayo	0–1	Detroit	AL 1969 (L)
Southworth, Billy	1–1	St. Louis	NL 1943 (L), 1944 (W)
	0–1	Boston	NL 1949 (L)
Stengel, Casey	4–6	New York	AL 1950 (L), 1951 (L), 1952 (L), 1953 (L), 1954 (W), 1956 (L), 1957 (W), 1958 (W), 1959–1 (L), 1959–2 (W)
Tanner, Chuck	1–0	Pittsburgh	NL 1980 (W)
Terry, Bill	1–2	New York	NL 1934 (L), 1937 (L), 1938 (W)
Torre, Joe	3–0	New York	AL 1997 (W), 1999 (W), 2000 (W)
Weaver, Earl	1–3	Baltimore	AL 1970 (L), 1971 (W), 1972 (L), 1980 (L)
Williams, Dick	0–1	Boston	AL 1968 (L)
	0–2	Oakland	AL 1973 (L), 1974 (L)
	1–0	San Diego	NL 1985 (W)

MOST GAMES

Casey Stengel, 10
Walter Alston, 9
Joe McCarthy, 7
Sparky Anderson, 5
Al Lopez, 5
Bobby Cox, 5
Leo Durocher, 4
Tom Lasorda, 4
Earl Weaver, 4
Dick Williams, 4

MOST WINS

Walter Alston, 7
Joe McCarthy, 4
Casey Stengel, 4
Sparky Anderson, 3
Tony La Russa, 3
Tom Lasorda, 3
Joe Torre, 3

MOST LOSSES

Casey Stengel, 6
Al Lopez, 5
Bobby Cox, 4
Whitey Herzog, 3
Billy Martin, 3
Joe McCarthy, 3
Earl Weaver, 3
Dick Williams, 3

**MOST GAMES
WITHOUT A LOSS**

Tony LaRussa, 3
Danny Murtaugh, 3 (1 tie)
Joe Torre, 3
Tom Kelly, 2
Red Schoendienst, 2

**MOST GAMES
WITHOUT A WIN**

Al Lopez, 5
Whitey Herzog, 3
Billy Martin, 3
Paul Richards, 2 (1 tie)

MANAGED BOTH LEAGUES

Sparky Anderson
Al Dark
Dick Williams

MANAGED IN HOME BALLPARK

Bill Terry, Polo Grounds, 1934
Joe McCarthy, Yankee Stadium, 1939
Del Baker, Briggs Stadium, 1941
Billy Martin, Yankee Stadium, 1977
Bobby Cox, Turner Field, 2000

NOTES

1936: Joe McCarthy managed because Mickey Cochrane had suffered a nervous breakdown
1940: Joe Cronin managed because Joe McCarthy was ill
1948: Leo Durocher managed because Burt Shotton had retired
1954: Walter Alston managed because Charlie Dressen had been fired
1961: Paul Richards managed because Casey Stengel was no longer with the Yankees
1964: Al Lopez managed because Ralph Houk was Yankees' GM
1965: Al Lopez managed because Yogi Berra had been fired, and Gene Mauch managed because Johnny Keane left the Cardinals for the Yankees
1974: Dick Williams managed as an Angel not Athletic
1995: Felipe Alou and Buck Showalter had the best records when a strike ended the 1994 season

PEOPLE WHO HAVE PLAYED IN AND MANAGED THE ALL-STAR GAME

Felipe Alou	Alvin Dark	Gabby Hartnett	Al Lopez
Hank Bauer	Leo Durocher	Gil Hodges	Billy Martin
Yogi Berra	Jim Fregosi	Fred Hutchinson	Lou Piniella
Lou Boudreau	Frank Frisch	Dave Johnson	Red Schoendienst
Mickey Cochrane	Cito Gaston	Harvey Kuenn	Bill Terry
Joe Cronin	Mike Hargrove	Bob Lemon	Joe Torre

Name	League	Team	Years
Alston, Walter	NL	Los Angeles	1971
Altobelli, Joe	AL	Baltimore	1983
Anderson, Sparky	NL	Cincinnati	1974
	AL	Detroit	1982, 1984, 1993
Baker, Del	AL	Detroit	1935, 1937, 1938, 1940
	AL	Boston	1947
Baker, Dusty	NL	San Francisco	1994, 1997
Bauer, Hank	AL	Baltimore	1966
Baylor, Don	NL	Colorado	1994, 1998
Bengough, Benny	NL	Philadelphia	1951
Bevington, Terry	AL	Chicago	1996
Blackburne, Lena	AL	Philadelphia	1939, 1943
Bochy, Bruce	NL	San Diego	1997
Boone, Bob	AL	Kansas City	1996
Boudreau, Lou	AL	Boston	1953
Bragan, Bobby	NL	Pittsburgh	1957
	NL	Milwaukee	1965
Bristol, Dave	NL	Cincinnati	1968, 1969
Carey, Max	NL	Brooklyn	1933
Chapman, Ben	NL	Philadelphia	1947
Collins, Eddie	AL	Boston	1933
Collins, Terry	NL	Houston	1995
Cooke, Dusty	NL	Philadelphia	1951
Corrales, Pat	AL	Texas	1979
	NL	Philadelphia	1983
	AL	Cleveland	1986
Corriden, John	NL	Chicago	1939
	AL	New York	1948
Cox, Bobby	AL	Toronto	1985
Craft, Harry	AL	Kansas City	1959
Craig, Roger	NL	San Francisco	1987, 1988, 1992
Crandall, Del	AL	Milwaukee	1975
Cronin, Joe	AL	Boston	1936, 1944
Crosetti, Frank	AL	New York	1950, 1957, 1961
Cuccinello, Tony	AL	Cleveland	1952, 1955
	AL	Chicago	1959, 1960, 1964
Daly, Tom	AL	Boston	1940
Dark, Al	NL	San Francisco	1961
	AL	Cleveland	1969
Dierker, Larry	NL	Houston	2000
Dickey, Bill	AL	New York	1950, 1951
Dressen, Chuck	NL	Cincinnati	1935, 1937
	AL	New York	1948
	AL	Washington	1956
Durocher, Leo	NL	Brooklyn	1941
	NL	New York	1954
	NL	Chicago	1969, 1970
Dyer, Eddie	NL	St. Louis	1948
Ermer, Cal	AL	Minnesota	1968
Fanning, Jim	NL	Montreal	1982
Fitzsimmons, Fred	NL	Philadelphia	1944
Fletcher, Art	AL	New York	1933, 1936, 1937, 1938, 1939, 1941, 1942, 1943, 1944
Fox, Charlie	NL	San Francisco	1972
Franks, Herman	NL	San Francisco	1966, 1967, 1968
Fregosi, Jim	AL	Chicago	1987
	NL	Philadelphia	1993, 1996
Frey, Jim	AL	Kansas City	1980
	NL	Chicago	1985
Frisch, Frank	NL	St. Louis	1937, 1938
	NL	Pittsburgh	1942, 1943
Garcia, Dave	AL	Cleveland	1981
Gardner, Billy	AL	Minnesota	1983
Garner, Phil	AL	Milwaukee	1995
Gaston, Cito	AL	Toronto	1991
Gomez, Preston	NL	San Diego	1971
Gonzalez, Mike	NL	St. Louis	1943, 1944
Grammas, Alex	AL	Milwaukee	1977
Grimm, Charlie	NL	Chicago	1935
	NL	Milwaukee	1954
Gutteridge, Don	AL	Chicago	1955, 1960, 1965
Haines, Jesse	NL	St. Louis	1937
Haney, Fred	NL	Pittsburgh	1955
Hargrove, Mike	AL	Cleveland	1994, 1997
Harris, Bucky	AL	Washington	1942
Harris, Lum	AL	Baltimore	1958
	NL	Atlanta	1970
Hartsfield, Roy	AL	Toronto	1979
Hemus, Solly	NL	St. Louis	1960
Henrich, Tommy	AL	New York	1951
Herman, Billy	NL	Brooklyn	1953
Herzog, Whitey	AL	Texas	1973, 1974
	AL	Kansas City	1978
Hitchcock, Billy	AL	Baltimore	1962
Hodges, Gil	AL	Washington	1964
Hornsby, Rogers	AL	St. Louis	1935
Houk, Ralph	AL	New York	1970
Howe, Art	NL	Houston	1991
	AL	Oakland	1998
Howser, Dick	AL	Kansas City	1982, 1985
Hunter, Billy	AL	Baltimore	1971
Hutchinson, Fred	AL	Detroit	1954
	NL	St. Louis	1956
	NL	Cincinnati	1960, 1964
Johnson, Darrell	AL	Seattle	1979
Johnson, Dave	NL	New York	1986
Johnson, Walter	AL	Cleveland	1934
Keane, Johnny	NL	St. Louis	1962
Kelly, Tom	AL	Minnesota	1991
Kennedy, Bob	NL	Chicago	1963
Lamont, Gene	AL	Chicago	1994
	NL	Pittsburgh	1998

Name	League	Team	Year(s)
Lanier, Hal	NL	Houston	1987
La Russa, Tony	AL	Chicago	1984
	AL	Oakland	1987
Lasorda, Tom	NL	Los Angeles	1977, 1983, 1984, 1986, 1993, 1996
Lavagetto, Cookie	NL	Brooklyn	1953
Lefebvre, Jim	AL	Seattle	1990
Lemon, Bob	AL	Kansas City	1972
	AL	Chicago	1977
Leyland, Jim	NL	Pittsburgh	1990, 1991, 1994
Lillis, Bob	NL	Houston	1985
Lopez, Al	AL	Cleveland	1952
Manuel, Jerry	AL	Chicago	1999
Marion, Marty	AL	Chicago	1954
Martin, Billy	AL	Detroit	1971
	AL	Texas	1975
Mauch, Gene	NL	Philadelphia	1961, 1963
	NL	Montreal	1973
	AL	Minnesota	1976
McKechnie, Bill	NL	Boston	1933, 1934, 1936
	NL	Cincinnati	1938, 1942, 1946
	AL	Cleveland	1949
McKeon, Jack	AL	Kansas City	1974
	NL	San Diego	1989
	NL	Cincinnati	1999
McNamara, John	NL	San Diego	1976
	NL	Cincinnati	1980, 1982
	AL	Boston	1986
McRae, Hal	AL	Kansas City	1992
Mele, Sam	AL	Minnesota	1963, 1965
Mills, Art	AL	Detroit	1946
Morgan, Joe	AL	Boston	1989
Murtaugh, Danny	NL	Pittsburgh	1959, 1971, 1975
O'Neill, Steve	AL	Detroit	1947
Oates, Johnny	AL	Baltimore	1993
	AL	Texas	1995, 1997
Ott, Mel	NL	New York	1947, 1948
Ozark, Danny	NL	Philadelphia	1976, 1977, 1978, 1979
Perkins, Cy	NL	Philadelphia	1951
Pesky, Johnny	AL	Boston	1963
Phillips, Lefty	AL	California	1970
Piniella, Lou	AL	Seattle	2000
Pitler, Jake	NL	Brooklyn	1950, 1953
Prothro, Doc	NL	Philadelphia	1940
Rader, Doug	AL	California	1989
Riggleman, Jim	NL	Chicago	1995, 1999
Rigney, Bill	NL	New York	1958
	AL	California	1967
Robinson, Frank	AL	Cleveland	1976
	AL	Baltimore	1980, 1990
Rodgers, Buck	NL	Montreal	1988, 1989
Rothschild, Larry	AL	Tampa Bay	2000
Ruel, Muddy	AL	Cleveland	1949
Sawyer, Eddie	NL	Philadelphia	1959
Schacht, Al	AL	Washington	1934
Scheffing, Bob	NL	Chicago	1957
Schoendienst, Red	NL	St. Louis	1972, 1974, 1975
Sewell, Luke	AL	St. Louis	1946
Shea, Merv	AL	Detroit	1941
Shellenback, Frank	NL	New York	1952
Shotton, Burt	NL	Brooklyn	1949
Showalter, Buck	AL	New York	1992
	NL	Arizona	2000
Sisler, Dick	NL	Cincinnati	1965
Smith, Mayo	NL	Philadelphia	1955, 1958
	AL	Detroit	1968
Southworth, Billy	NL	Boston	1946
Stanky, Eddie	NL	St. Louis	1952
	AL	Chicago	1967
Stengel, Casey	NL	Brooklyn	1934
	NL	Boston	1940
	NL	New York	1962, 1964
Stock, Mike	NL	Brooklyn	1950
Tanner, Chuck	AL	Chicago	1973
	NL	Pittsburgh	1978, 1979, 1982, 1984
Tebbetts, Birdie	NL	Cincinnati	1956
	AL	Cleveland	1966
Terry, Bill	NL	New York	1939
Torre, Joe	NL	Atlanta	1983
	NL	St. Louis	1992
	AL	New York	1998
Traynor, Pie	NL	Pittsburgh	1936
Trebelhorn, Tom	AL	Milwaukee	1988
Turner, Jim	AL	New York	1953, 1956, 1957, 1958
Valentine, Bobby	AL	Texas	1988
Vernon, Mickey	AL	Washington	1961, 1962
Virdon, Bill	NL	Pittsburgh	1973
	NL	Houston	1980, 1981
Wagner, Honus	NL	Pittsburgh	1944
Walker, Harry	NL	Pittsburgh	1966, 1967
Walters, Bucky	NL	Cincinnati	1949
Weaver, Earl	AL	Baltimore	1969, 1974
Williams, Dick	AL	Oakland	1972
	NL	Montreal	1981
Williams, Jimy	AL	Boston	1999
Williams, Ted	AL	Washington	1969
Wilson, Jim	NL	Chicago	1941
Zimmer, Don	AL	Boston	1978
	AL	Texas	1981
	NL	Chicago	1990

Note: Bristol replaced Durocher in 1968 due to illness.

UMPIRES

*plate umpire

Name	Lg	Gm	Years
Anthony, Merlyn	AL	1	1974
Ashford, Emmett	AL	1	1967
Ballanfant, Lee	NL	4	1938, 1942*, 1949, 1954
Barlick, Al	NL	7	1942, 1949*, 1952*, 1955*, 1959-1*, 1966*, 1970*
Barnett, Larry	AL	4	1973, 1980, 1988, 1997*
Barr, George	NL	2	1937*, 1944*
Basil, Steve	AL	2	1938, 1940
Bell, Wally	NL	1	1997
	ML	1	2000
Berry, Charlie	AL	5	1944, 1948*, 1952, 1956*, 1959-2
Boggess, Dusty	NL	5	1946, 1952, 1955, 1960-1*, 1960-2
Bonin, Greg	NL	1	1991
Boyer, Jim	AL	1	1947
Bremigan, Nick	AL	2	1979, 1985
Brinkman, Joe	AL	3	1977, 1991*, 1996
Brocklander, Fred	NL	1	1984
Burkhart, Ken	NL	4	1959-2, 1962-2, 1967, 1973
Chylak, Nestor	AL	6	1957, 1960-1, 1960-2*, 1964, 1973*, 1978
Clark, Al	AL	2	1984, 1995
Coble, Drew	AL	2	1985, 1997
Colosi, Nick	NL	2	1971, 1980
Conlan, Jocko	NL	6	1943, 1947*, 1950, 1953*, 1958*, 1962-2*
Cooney, Terry	AL	2	1979, 1989
Cousins, Derryl	AL	2	1987, 1998
Craft, Terry	AL	1	1997
Crawford, Jerry	NL	1	1989
Crawford, Shag	NL	3	1959-1, 1961-1, 1968*
Dale, Jerry	NL	2	1972, 1980
Darling, Gary	NL	1	1993
Dascoli, Frank	NL	2	1951, 1957*
Davidson, Bob	NL	2	1987, 1993
Davidson, Satch	NL	1	1976
Davis, Gerry	NL	2	1989, 1997
Deegan, Bill	AL	1	1978
DeMuth, Dana	NL	1	1990
Denkinger, Don	AL	3	1971, 1976, 1987*
Dezelan, Frank	NL	1	1970
Diaz, Lazaro	ML	1	2000
DiMuro, Lou	AL	4	1965, 1967, 1972, 1981
Dinneen, Bill	AL	1	1933*
Dixon, Hal	NL	1	1957
Donatelli, Augie	NL	4	1953, 1959-1, 1962-1, 1969
Drummond, Cal	AL	1	1961-1
Dunn, Tom	NL	1	1943*
Engel, Bob	NL	4	1966, 1973, 1981, 1989
Engeln, Bill	NL	1	1953
Evans, Jim	AL	3	1976, 1989*, 1999*
Flaherty, Red	AL	3	1956, 1961-2, 1969*
Ford, Dale	AL	2	1988, 1999
Forman, Al	NL	1	1962-2
Frantz, Art	AL	1	1974
Froemming, Bruce	NL	2	1975, 1986*
Garcia, Rich	AL	2	1980, 1992
Geisel, Harry	AL	2	1935, 1938
Goetz, Larry	NL	2	1939, 1946
Goetz, Russ	AL	2	1970, 1975
Gore, Artie	NL	2	1949, 1956
Gorman, Tom	NL	5	1954, 1958, 1960-1, 1960-2*, 1969
Gorman, Brian	NL	1	1998
Gregg, Eric	NL	1	1986
Grieve, Bill	AL	2	1941, 1949
Haller, Bill	AL	4	1963, 1970, 1975*, 1981*
Hallion, Tom	NL	1	1992
Harvey, Doug	NL	6	1963, 1964, 1971, 1977, 1982*, 1992*
Hendry, Ted	AL	2	1983, 1995
Henline, Butch	NL	1	1947
Hernandez, Angel	NL	1	1999
Hirschbeck, John	AL	1	1989
Hirschbeck, Mark	NL	1	1993
	ML	1	2000
Hohn, Bill	NL	1	1994
Honochick, Jim	AL	5	1951, 1954, 1960-1*, 1960-2, 1966*
Hubbard, Cal	AL	3	1939*, 1944, 1949
Hurley, Eddie	AL	3	1951, 1956, 1962-1*
Jackowski, Bill	NL	3	1956, 1959-2*, 1963
Johnson, Mark	AL	2	1990, 1999
Jorda, Lou	NL	2	1941, 1951
Joyce, Jim	AL	1	1994
Kaiser, Ken	AL	1	1991
Kellogg, Jeff	NL	1	1997
Kibler, John	NL	4	1965, 1974, 1980*, 1985
Kinnamon, Bill	AL	2	1962-2, 1968
Klem, Bill	NL	2	1933*, 1938*
Kolls, Lou	AL	1	1936
Kosc, Greg	AL	2	1981, 1992
Kunkel, Bill	AL	2	1972, 1977*
Landes, Stan	NL	3	1957, 1961-1*, 1972*
Layne, Jerry	NL	1	1994
Luciano, Ron	AL	1	1973
Magerkurth, George	NL	2	1935*, 1939*
Maloney, George	AL	3	1974, 1979*, 1983*
Marsh, Randy	NL	3	1985, 1988, 1996*
McClelland, Tim	AL	2	1986, 1998
McCoy, Larry	AL	3	1978, 1985*, 1996
McGowan, Bill	AL	4	1933, 1937*, 1942*, 1950*
McKean, Jim	AL	3	1980, 1982, 1993*

Name	Lg	Gm	Years	Name	Lg	Gm	Years
McKinley, Bill	AL	3	1953*, 1958, 1962–2	Soar, Hank	AL	4	1952, 1955, 1959–2, 1963*
McSherry, John	NL	3	1975, 1982, 1991	Springstead, Marty	AL	3	1969, 1975, 1982
Meriwether, Chuck	AL	1	1996	Stark, Dolly	NL	1	1934
Merrill, Durwood	AL	2	1984, 1995*	Steiner, Mel	NL	2	1962–1, 1968
Montague, Ed	NL	3	1982, 1990*, 1998*	Stello, Dick	NL	2	1977, 1987
Moriarty, George	AL	1	1934	Stevens, Johnny	AL	6	1950, 1953, 1957*, 1960–1, 1960–2, 1965*
Morrison, Dan	AL	1	1988				
Napp, Larry	AL	4	1953, 1957, 1961–2*, 1968	Stewart, Bill	NL	4	1936, 1940, 1948, 1954*
Neudecker, Jerry	AL	3	1966, 1972, 1976	Stewart, Bob	AL	2	1962–1, 1969
Odom, Jim	AL	1	1968	Stewart, Ernest	AL	1	1942
O'Donnell, Jake	AL	1	1971	Sudol, Ed	NL	3	1961–2, 1964*, 1974*
Olsen, Andy	NL	1	1976	Summers, Bill	AL	7	1936*, 1941*, 1946*, 1949*, 1952*, 1955*, 1959–2*
O'Nora, Brian	ML	1	2000				
Ormsby, Red	AL	1	1935*				
Owens, Brick	AL	1	1934*	Tata, Terry	NL	3	1978, 1988, 1999
Palermo, Steve	AL	1	1986	Tschida, Tim	AL	1	1992
Pallone, Dave	NL	1	1983	Umont, Frank	AL	4	1958, 1961–1, 1966, 1971*
Paparella, Joe	AL	4	1948, 1954, 1959–1*, 1964				
Passarella, Art	AL	2	1947*, 1951*	Valentine, Bill	AL	1	1965
Pelekoudas, Chris	NL	3	1961–2, 1967, 1975	Vanover, Larry	NL	1	1999
Pfirman, Cy	NL	1	1934*	Vargo, Ed	NL	4	1961–1, 1966, 1974, 1981
Phillips, Dave	AL	2	1977, 1990	Venzon, Tony	NL	3	1959–2, 1962–1, 1969
Pinelli, Babe	NL	4	1937, 1941, 1950*, 1956*	Voltaggio, Vic	AL	1	1987
Pipgras, George	AL	1	1940	Warneke, Lon	NL	1	1952
Poncino, Larry	NL	1	1996	Welke, Tim	AL	1	1990
Pryor, Paul	NL	3	1963, 1971, 1978*	Wendelstedt, Harry	NL	4	1968, 1976*, 1983, 1992
Pulli, Frank	NL	2	1977, 1988*	West, Joe	NL	1	1987
Quick, Jim	NL	3	1981, 1983, 1991	Weyer, Lee	NL	4	1965, 1972, 1979, 1984*
Quinn, John	AL	1	1937	Williams, Bill	NL	3	1965, 1973, 1979
Rapuano, Ed	NL	1	1995	Williams, Charlie	NL	2	1985, 1995
Reardon, Beans	NL	3	1936*, 1940*, 1948*	Winters, Mike	NL	1	1995
Reed, Rick	AL	2	1986, 1998	Young, Larry	AL	1	1991
Reilly, Mike	AL	2	1982, 1993				
	ML	1	2000*				

MOST YEARS UMPIRING ALL-STAR GAME

Barlick, Al	7
Summers, Bill	7
Chylak, Nestor	6
Conlon, Jocko	6
Harvey, Doug	6
Rommel, Eddie	6
Secory, Frank	6
Stevens, Johnny	6

Name	Lg	Gm	Years
Reliford, Charlie	NL	1	1996
Rennert, Dutch	NL	2	1979, 1984
Rice, John	AL	3	1959–1, 1962–2, 1970
Rieker, Rich	NL	1	1998
Rigler, Cy	NL	1	1933
Rippley, Steve	NL	1	1990
Robb, Scotty	NL	2	1950, 1951*
Roe, Rocky	AL	2	1984, 1994
Rommel, Eddie	AL	6	1939, 1943*, 1946, 1950, 1954*, 1958*
Rue, Joe	AL	1	1943
Runge, Ed	AL	4	1955, 1959–1, 1961–1*, 1967*
Runge, Paul	NL	3	1978, 1986, 1994*
Salerno, Al	AL	1	1964
Schrieber, Paul	ML	1	2000
Schwarts, Harry	AL	1	1962–1
Scott, Dale	AL	1	1993
Sears, Ziggy	NL	2	1935, 1944
Secory, Frank	NL	6	1955, 1958, 1961–2, 1964, 1967, 1970
Shulock, John	AL	2	1983. 1994
Smith, Al	AL	2	1961–2, 1963
Smith, Vinnie	NL	2	1960–1, 1960–2

MOST YEARS, HOME PLATE UMPIRE

Summers, Bill	7
Barlick, Al	6
Conlon, Jocko	4
McGowan, Bill	3
Reardon, Beans	3
Rommel, Eddie	3

NOTES

Until 1948, each league had two umpires on the field and one alternate in the stands. In 1949 the alternates were positioned along the left and right field lines. For many early years, the umpires shifted positions in mid-game.

In 2000, the league umpire crews were combined into one major league crew. Those umpires are designated as ML rather than AL or NL umpires.

Shag and Gerry Crawford are father and son.
Tom and Brian Gorman are father and son.
Mark and John Hirschbeck are brothers.
Jake O'Donnell was also a referee in the National Basketball
Association.
Ed and Paul Runge are father and son.
Lon Warneke was selected to five All-Star games as a player.

CAREER STATISTICS FOR ALL PLAYERS

BATTERS
*indicates game started

Year	Team	AB	R	H	D	T	HR	TB	BI	W	K	SB	CS

Hank Aaron

Year	Team	AB	R	H	D	T	HR	TB	BI	W	K	SB	CS
1955	MIL NL	2	1	2	0	0	0	2	1	1	0	0	0
1956	MIL NL	1	0	0	0	0	0	0	0	0	0	0	0
1957*	MIL NL	4	0	1	0	0	0	1	0	0	1	0	0
1958*	MIL NL	2	0	0	0	0	0	0	1	1	0	0	0
1959-1*	MIL NL	4	1	2	0	0	0	2	1	0	1	0	0
1959-2*	MIL NL	3	0	0	0	0	0	0	1	0	0	0	0
1960-1*	MIL NL	4	0	0	0	0	0	0	0	0	0	0	0
1960-2*	MIL NL	3	0	0	0	0	0	0	0	0	0	0	0
1961-1	MIL NL	1	1	1	0	0	0	1	0	0	0	0	0
1961-2	MIL NL	2	0	0	0	0	0	0	0	0	0	0	0
1962-2	MIL NL	3	0	0	0	0	0	0	0	0	0	0	0
1963*	MIL NL	4	1	0	0	0	0	0	0	0	0	0	0
1964	MIL NL	1	0	0	0	0	0	0	0	0	1	0	0
1965*	MIL NL	5	0	1	0	0	0	1	0	0	0	0	0
1966*	ATL NL	4	0	0	0	0	0	0	0	0	1	0	0
1967*	ATL NL	6	0	1	0	0	0	1	0	0	0	1	0
1968*	ATL NL	3	0	1	0	0	0	1	0	1	2	1	0
1969*	ATL NL	4	1	1	0	0	0	1	0	0	1	0	0
1970*	ATL NL	2	0	0	0	0	0	0	0	0	0	0	0
1971*	ATL NL	2	1	1	0	0	1	4	1	0	0	0	0
1972*	ATL NL	3	1	1	0	0	1	4	2	0	1	0	0
1973*	ATL NL	2	0	1	0	0	0	1	1	0	0	0	0
1974*	ATL NL	2	0	0	0	0	0	0	0	0	0	0	0
1975	MIL AL	1	0	0	0	0	0	0	0	0	0	0	0
Totals	24 Yr	68	7	13	0	0	2	19	8	3	8	2	0

Don Aase

Year	Team	AB	R	H	D	T	HR	TB	BI	W	K	SB	CS
1986	BAL AL	0	0	0	0	0	0	0	0	0	0	0	0

Joe Adcock

Year	Team	AB	R	H	D	T	HR	TB	BI	W	K	SB	CS
1960-1*	MIL NL	3	0	2	1	0	0	3	0	0	0	0	0
1960-2*	MIL NL	2	1	1	0	0	0	1	0	0	1	0	0
Totals	2 Yr	5	1	3	1	0	0	4	0	0	1	0	0

Tommie Agee

Year	Team	AB	R	H	D	T	HR	TB	BI	W	K	SB	CS
1966	CHA AL	0	0	0	0	0	0	0	0	0	0	0	0
1967	CHA AL	0	0	0	0	0	0	0	0	0	0	0	0
Totals	2 Yr	0	0	0	0	0	0	0	0	0	0	0	0

Rick Aguilera

Year	Team	AB	R	H	D	T	HR	TB	BI	W	K	SB	CS
1992	MIN AL	1	0	0	0	0	0	0	0	0	1	0	0

Hank Aguirre

Year	Team	AB	R	H	D	T	HR	TB	BI	W	K	SB	CS
1962-2	DET AL	2	0	0	0	0	0	0	0	0	2	0	0

Edgardo Alfonzo

Year	Team	AB	R	H	D	T	HR	TB	BI	W	K	SB	CS
2000	NYN NL	2	0	0	0	0	0	0	0	0	1	0	0

Dick Allen

Year	Team	AB	R	H	D	T	HR	TB	BI	W	K	SB	CS
1965*	PHI NL	3	0	1	0	0	0	1	0	0	1	0	0
1966	PHI NL	1	0	0	0	0	0	0	0	0	1	0	0
1967*	PHI NL	4	1	1	0	0	1	4	1	0	3	0	0
1970*	SLN NL	3	0	0	0	0	0	0	0	1	1	0	0

Dick Allen *continued*

Year	Team	AB	R	H	D	T	HR	TB	BI	W	K	SB	CS
1972*	CHA AL	3	0	0	0	0	0	0	0	0	0	0	0
1974*	CHA AL	2	0	1	0	0	0	1	1	0	1	0	0
Totals	6 Yr	16	1	3	0	0	1	6	2	1	7	0	0

Johnny Allen

Year	Team	AB	R	H	D	T	HR	TB	BI	W	K	SB	CS
1938	CLE AL	1	0	0	0	0	0	0	0	0	0	0	0

Gene Alley

Year	Team	AB	R	H	D	T	HR	TB	BI	W	K	SB	CS
1967*	PIT NL	5	0	0	0	0	0	0	0	0	3	0	0

Bob Allison

Year	Team	AB	R	H	D	T	HR	TB	BI	W	K	SB	CS
1963	MIN AL	1	0	0	0	0	0	0	0	0	1	0	0
1964*	MIN AL	3	0	0	0	0	0	0	0	1	2	0	0
Totals	2 Yr	4	0	0	0	0	0	0	0	1	3	0	0

Roberto Alomar

Year	Team	AB	R	H	D	T	HR	TB	BI	W	K	SB	CS
1990	SDN NL	1	0	0	0	0	0	0	0	0	0	0	0
1991*	TOR AL	4	0	0	0	0	0	0	0	0	0	0	0
1992*	TOR AL	3	1	1	0	0	0	1	0	0	0	2	0
1993*	TOR AL	3	1	1	0	0	1	4	1	0	0	0	0
1994*	TOR AL	3	1	1	0	0	0	1	0	0	0	1	0
1995	TOR AL	1	0	0	0	0	0	0	0	0	0	1	0
1996*	BAL AL	3	0	1	0	0	0	1	0	0	0	0	0
1997*	BAL AL	2	0	0	0	0	0	0	0	0	0	0	0
1998*	BAL AL	4	2	3	0	0	1	6	1	1	0	1	0
1999*	CLE AL	2	0	0	0	0	0	0	1	0	1	0	0
2000*	CLE AL	2	0	0	0	0	0	0	1	0	0	0	0
Totals	11 Yr	28	5	7	0	0	2	13	3	2	1	5	0

Sandy Alomar

Year	Team	AB	R	H	D	T	HR	TB	BI	W	K	SB	CS
1970	CAL AL	1	0	0	0	0	0	0	0	0	0	0	0

Sandy Alomar

Year	Team	AB	R	H	D	T	HR	TB	BI	W	K	SB	CS
1990*	CLE AL	3	1	2	0	0	0	2	0	0	0	0	0
1991*	CLE AL	2	0	0	0	0	0	0	0	0	0	0	0
1992*	CLE AL	3	0	1	0	0	0	1	0	0	0	0	0
1996	CLE AL	2	0	0	0	0	0	0	0	0	0	0	0
1997	CLE AL	1	1	1	0	0	1	4	2	0	0	0	0
1998	CLE AL	1	0	1	0	0	0	1	1	0	0	0	0
Totals	6 Yr	12	2	5	0	0	1	8	3	0	0	0	0

Felipe Alou

Year	Team	AB	R	H	D	T	HR	TB	BI	W	K	SB	CS
1962-1	SFN NL	0	0	0	0	0	0	0	1	0	0	0	0
1968	ATL NL	0	0	0	0	0	0	0	0	0	0	0	0
Totals	2 Yr	0	0	0	0	0	0	0	1	0	0	0	0

Matty Alou

Year	Team	AB	R	H	D	T	HR	TB	BI	W	K	SB	CS
1968	PIT NL	1	0	1	0	0	0	1	0	0	0	0	0
1969*	PIT NL	4	1	2	0	0	0	2	0	1	1	0	0
Totals	2 Yr	5	1	3	0	0	0	3	0	1	1	0	0

Moises Alou

Year	Team	AB	R	H	D	T	HR	TB	BI	W	K	SB	CS
1994	MON NL	1	0	1	1	0	0	2	1	0	0	0	0

Year	Team	AB	R	H	D	T	HR	TB	BI	W	K	SB	CS

Moises Alou *continued*

Year	Team	AB	R	H	D	T	HR	TB	BI	W	K	SB	CS
1997	FLO NL	2	0	1	0	0	0	1	0	0	0	0	0
1998	HOU NL	3	1	1	0	0	0	1	0	0	2	0	0
Totals	3 Yr	6	1	3	1	0	0	4	1	0	2	0	0

George Altman

Year	Team	AB	R	H	D	T	HR	TB	BI	W	K	SB	CS
1961-1	CHN NL	1	1	1	0	0	1	4	1	0	0	0	0
1961-2	CHN NL	1	0	0	0	0	0	0	0	0	0	0	0
1962-2	CHN NL	1	0	0	0	0	0	0	0	0	0	0	0
Totals	3 Yr	3	1	1	0	0	1	4	1	0	0	0	0

Wilson Alvarez

Year	Team	AB	R	H	D	T	HR	TB	BI	W	K	SB	CS
1994	CHA AL	0	0	0	0	0	0	0	0	0	0	0	0

Max Alvis

Year	Team	AB	R	H	D	T	HR	TB	BI	W	K	SB	CS
1965	CLE AL	1	0	0	0	0	0	0	0	0	0	0	0
1967	CLE AL	1	0	0	0	0	0	0	0	0	0	0	0
Totals	2 Yr	2	0	0	0	0	0	0	0	0	0	0	0

Brady Anderson

Year	Team	AB	R	H	D	T	HR	TB	BI	W	K	SB	CS
1992	BAL AL	3	0	0	0	0	0	0	0	0	0	0	0
1996*	BAL AL	2	0	0	0	0	0	0	0	0	0	0	0
1997*	BAL AL	4	0	2	1	0	0	3	0	0	0	0	0
Totals	3 Yr	9	0	2	1	0	0	3	0	0	0	0	0

Mike Andrews

Year	Team	AB	R	H	D	T	HR	TB	BI	W	K	SB	CS
1969	BOS AL	1	0	0	0	0	0	0	0	0	0	0	0

Joaquin Andujar

Year	Team	AB	R	H	D	T	HR	TB	BI	W	K	SB	CS
1979	HOU NL	0	0	0	0	0	0	0	0	0	0	0	0

Johnny Antonelli

Year	Team	AB	R	H	D	T	HR	TB	BI	W	K	SB	CS
1954	NY NL	0	0	0	0	0	0	0	0	0	0	0	0
1956	NY NL	1	0	0	0	0	0	0	0	0	1	0	0
1959-1	SFN NL	0	0	0	0	0	0	0	0	0	0	0	0
Totals	3 Yr	1	0	0	0	0	0	0	0	0	1	0	0

Luis Aparicio

Year	Team	AB	R	H	D	T	HR	TB	BI	W	K	SB	CS
1958*	CHA AL	2	1	0	0	0	0	0	0	0	0	0	0
1959-1*	CHA AL	3	0	0	0	0	0	0	0	0	1	0	0
1959-2*	CHA AL	3	0	0	0	0	0	0	0	1	1	1	0
1960-1	CHA AL	2	0	0	0	0	0	0	0	0	0	0	0
1961-2*	CHA AL	2	0	0	0	0	0	0	0	1	1	0	0
1962-1*	CHA AL	4	0	1	0	1	0	3	0	0	0	0	0
1962-2*	CHA AL	2	0	0	0	0	0	0	0	0	1	0	0
1963	BAL AL	1	0	0	0	0	0	0	0	0	0	0	0
1970*	CHA AL	6	0	0	0	0	0	0	0	0	2	0	0
1971*	BOS AL	3	1	1	0	0	0	1	0	0	0	0	0
Totals	10 Yr	28	2	2	0	1	0	4	0	2	6	1	0

Luke Appling

Year	Team	AB	R	H	D	T	HR	TB	BI	W	K	SB	CS
1936*	CHA AL	4	0	1	0	0	0	1	2	1	0	0	0
1940*	CHA AL	3	0	2	1	0	0	3	0	0	0	0	0
1946	CHA AL	1	0	0	0	0	0	0	0	0	0	0	0
1947	CHA AL	1	1	1	0	0	0	1	0	0	0	0	0
Totals	4 Yr	9	1	4	1	0	0	5	2	1	0	0	0

Tony Armas

Year	Team	AB	R	H	D	T	HR	TB	BI	W	K	SB	CS
1981	OAK AL	1	0	0	0	0	0	0	0	0	1	0	0

Jack Armstrong

Year	Team	AB	R	H	D	T	HR	TB	BI	W	K	SB	CS
1990*	CIN NL	0	0	0	0	0	0	0	0	0	0	0	0

Rolando Arrojo

Year	Team	AB	R	H	D	T	HR	TB	BI	W	K	SB	CS
1998	TBA AL	0	0	0	0	0	0	0	0	0	0	0	0

Richie Ashburn

Year	Team	AB	R	H	D	T	HR	TB	BI	W	K	SB	CS
1948*	PHI NL	4	1	2	0	0	0	2	0	0	1	1	0
1951*	PHI NL	4	2	2	1	0	0	3	0	1	0	0	0
1953	PHI NL	1	0	1	0	0	0	1	1	0	0	0	0
1962-2	NYN NL	1	1	1	0	0	0	1	0	0	0	0	0
Totals	4 Yr	10	4	6	1	0	0	7	1	1	1	1	0

Andy Ashby

Year	Team	AB	R	H	D	T	HR	TB	BI	W	K	SB	CS
1998	SDN NL	0	0	0	0	0	0	0	0	0	0	0	0

Brad Ausmus

Year	Team	AB	R	H	D	T	HR	TB	BI	W	K	SB	CS
1999	DET AL	1	0	0	0	0	0	0	0	0	0	0	0

Earl Averill

Year	Team	AB	R	H	D	T	HR	TB	BI	W	K	SB	CS
1933	CLE AL	1	0	1	0	0	0	1	1	0	0	0	0
1934	CLE AL	4	1	2	1	1	0	5	3	0	1	0	0
1936*	CLE AL	3	0	0	0	0	0	0	0	0	0	0	0
1937*	CLE AL	3	0	1	0	0	0	1	0	1	1	0	0
1938*	CLE AL	4	0	0	0	0	0	0	0	0	1	0	0
Totals	5 Yr	15	1	4	1	1	0	7	4	1	3	0	0

Bobby Avila

Year	Team	AB	R	H	D	T	HR	TB	BI	W	K	SB	CS
1952*	CLE AL	2	0	1	0	0	0	1	1	0	0	0	0
1954*	CLE AL	3	1	3	0	0	0	3	2	0	0	0	0
1955	CLE AL	1	0	0	0	0	0	0	0	1	1	0	0
Totals	3 Yr	6	1	4	0	0	0	4	3	1	1	0	0

Joe Azcue

Year	Team	AB	R	H	D	T	HR	TB	BI	W	K	SB	CS
1968	CLE AL	1	0	0	0	0	0	0	0	0	1	0	0

Carlos Baerga

Year	Team	AB	R	H	D	T	HR	TB	BI	W	K	SB	CS
1992	CLE AL	1	1	1	1	0	0	2	1	0	0	0	0
1993	CLE AL	2	1	0	0	0	0	0	0	0	1	0	0
1995*	CLE AL	3	1	3	1	0	0	4	0	0	0	0	1
Totals	3 Yr	6	3	4	2	0	0	6	1	0	1	0	1

Jeff Bagwell

Year	Team	AB	R	H	D	T	HR	TB	BI	W	K	SB	CS
1994	HOU NL	4	1	2	0	0	0	2	0	0	1	0	0
1996	HOU NL	2	0	0	0	0	0	0	0	0	1	0	0
1997*	HOU NL	3	0	0	0	0	0	0	0	0	0	0	0
1999*	HOU NL	3	0	1	0	0	0	1	0	0	2	0	0
Totals	4 Yr	12	1	3	0	0	0	3	0	0	4	0	0

Ed Bailey

Year	Team	AB	R	H	D	T	HR	TB	BI	W	K	SB	CS
1956*	CIN NL	3	0	0	0	0	0	0	0	1	0	0	0
1957*	CIN NL	3	1	1	0	0	0	1	0	0	0	0	0
1960-2	CIN NL	1	0	0	0	0	0	0	0	0	0	0	0
1963*	SFN NL	1	0	1	0	0	0	1	1	1	0	0	0
Totals	4 Yr	8	1	2	0	0	0	2	1	2	0	0	0

Harold Baines

Year	Team	AB	R	H	D	T	HR	TB	BI	W	K	SB	CS
1985	CHA AL	1	0	1	0	0	0	1	0	0	0	0	0
1986	CHA AL	1	0	0	0	0	0	0	0	0	0	0	0

Year	Team	AB	R	H	D	T	HR	TB	BI	W	K	SB	CS

Harold Baines *continued*

Year	Team	AB	R	H	D	T	HR	TB	BI	W	K	SB	CS
1987	CHA AL	1	0	0	0	0	0	0	0	0	0	0	0
1989*	CHA AL	3	1	1	0	0	0	1	1	0	1	0	0
1991	OAK AL	1	0	0	0	0	0	0	1	0	0	0	0
1999	BAL AL	1	0	1	0	0	0	1	0	0	0	0	0
Totals	6 Yr	8	1	3	0	0	0	3	2	0	1	0	0

Dusty Baker

Year	Team	AB	R	H	D	T	HR	TB	BI	W	K	SB	CS
1981	LAN NL	2	0	1	0	0	0	1	0	0	0	0	0
1982	LAN NL	2	0	0	0	0	0	0	0	0	0	0	0
Totals	2 Yr	4	0	1	0	0	0	1	0	0	0	0	0

Gene Baker

Year	Team	AB	R	H	D	T	HR	TB	BI	W	K	SB	CS
1955	CHN NL	1	0	0	0	0	0	0	0	0	0	0	0

James Baldwin

Year	Team	AB	R	H	D	T	HR	TB	BI	W	K	SB	CS
2000	CHA AL	0	0	0	0	0	0	0	0	0	0	0	0

Sal Bando

Year	Team	AB	R	H	D	T	HR	TB	BI	W	K	SB	CS
1969*	OAK AL	3	0	1	0	0	0	1	0	0	0	0	0
1972	OAK AL	2	0	0	0	0	0	0	0	0	0	0	0
1973	OAK AL	1	0	0	0	0	0	0	0	0	0	0	0
Totals	3 Yr	6	0	1	0	0	0	1	0	0	0	0	0

Ernie Banks

Year	Team	AB	R	H	D	T	HR	TB	BI	W	K	SB	CS
1955*	CHN NL	2	0	0	0	0	0	0	0	0	1	0	0
1957	CHN NL	3	0	1	0	0	0	1	1	0	1	0	0
1958*	CHN NL	3	0	0	0	0	0	0	0	0	1	0	0
1959-1*	CHN NL	3	1	2	2	0	0	4	0	1	1	0	0
1959-2*	CHN NL	4	0	0	0	0	0	0	0	0	2	0	0
1960-1*	CHN NL	4	2	2	1	0	1	6	2	0	0	0	0
1960-2*	CHN NL	3	0	1	0	0	0	1	0	0	0	0	0
1961-2	CHN NL	1	0	0	0	0	0	0	0	0	1	0	0
1962-1	CHN NL	2	0	0	0	0	0	0	0	0	0	0	0
1962-2	CHN NL	2	1	1	0	1	0	3	0	0	0	0	0
1965*	CHN NL	4	0	2	0	0	0	2	0	0	1	0	0
1967	CHN NL	1	0	1	0	0	0	1	0	0	0	0	0
1969	CHN NL	1	0	0	0	0	0	0	0	0	0	0	0
Totals	13 Yr	33	4	10	3	1	1	18	3	1	8	0	0

Floyd Bannister

Year	Team	AB	R	H	D	T	HR	TB	BI	W	K	SB	CS
1982	SEA AL	0	0	0	0	0	0	0	0	0	0	0	0

Jesse Barfield

Year	Team	AB	R	H	D	T	HR	TB	BI	W	K	SB	CS
1986	TOR AL	3	0	0	0	0	0	0	0	0	2	0	0

Len Barker

Year	Team	AB	R	H	D	T	HR	TB	BI	W	K	SB	CS
1981	CLE AL	0	0	0	0	0	0	0	0	0	0	0	0

Dick Bartell

Year	Team	AB	R	H	D	T	HR	TB	BI	W	K	SB	CS
1933*	PHI NL	2	0	0	0	0	0	0	0	0	1	0	0
1937*	NY NL	4	0	1	0	0	0	1	0	0	0	0	0
Totals	2 Yr	6	0	1	0	0	0	1	0	0	1	0	0

Kevin Bass

Year	Team	AB	R	H	D	T	HR	TB	BI	W	K	SB	CS
1986	HOU NL	1	0	0	0	0	0	0	0	0	0	0	0

Tony Batista

Year	Team	AB	R	H	D	T	HR	TB	BI	W	K	SB	CS
2000	TOR AL	1	0	0	0	0	0	0	0	0	1	0	0

Earl Battey

Year	Team	AB	R	H	D	T	HR	TB	BI	W	K	SB	CS
1962-1*	MIN AL	2	0	0	0	0	0	0	0	0	0	0	0
1962-2*	MIN AL	2	1	0	0	0	0	0	0	1	0	0	0
1963*	MIN AL	2	0	1	0	0	0	1	1	0	0	0	0
1965*	MIN AL	2	0	0	0	0	0	0	0	0	0	0	0
1966	MIN AL	1	0	0	0	0	0	0	0	1	1	0	0
Totals	5 Yr	9	1	1	0	0	0	1	1	2	1	0	0

Hank Bauer

Year	Team	AB	R	H	D	T	HR	TB	BI	W	K	SB	CS
1952*	NYA AL	3	0	1	0	0	0	1	0	0	1	0	1
1953*	NYA AL	2	0	0	0	0	0	0	0	1	1	0	0
1954*	NYA AL	2	0	1	0	0	0	1	0	0	1	0	0
Totals	3 Yr	7	0	2	0	0	0	2	0	1	3	0	1

Don Baylor

Year	Team	AB	R	H	D	T	HR	TB	BI	W	K	SB	CS
1979*	CAL AL	4	2	2	1	0	0	3	1	0	0	0	0

Rod Beck

Year	Team	AB	R	H	D	T	HR	TB	BI	W	K	SB	CS
1994	SFN NL	0	0	0	0	0	0	0	0	0	0	0	0

Glenn Beckert

Year	Team	AB	R	H	D	T	HR	TB	BI	W	K	SB	CS
1969	CHN NL	1	0	0	0	0	0	0	0	0	0	0	0
1970*	CHN NL	2	0	0	0	0	0	0	0	0	0	0	0
1971*	CHN NL	3	0	0	0	0	0	0	0	0	0	0	0
1972	CHN NL	1	0	0	0	0	0	0	0	0	0	0	0
Totals	4 Yr	7	0	0	0	0	0	0	0	0	0	0	0

Steve Bedrosian

Year	Team	AB	R	H	D	T	HR	TB	BI	W	K	SB	CS
1987	PHI NL	0	0	0	0	0	0	0	0	0	0	0	0

Mark Belanger

Year	Team	AB	R	H	D	T	HR	TB	BI	W	K	SB	CS
1976	BAL AL	1	0	0	0	0	0	0	0	0	0	0	0

Buddy Bell

Year	Team	AB	R	H	D	T	HR	TB	BI	W	K	SB	CS
1973	CLE AL	1	0	1	0	1	0	3	0	0	0	0	0
1980	TEX AL	2	0	0	0	0	0	0	0	0	1	0	0
1981	TEX AL	1	0	0	0	0	0	0	1	0	0	0	0
1982	TEX AL	3	0	0	0	0	0	0	0	0	2	0	0
1984	TEX AL	1	0	0	0	0	0	0	0	0	0	0	0
Totals	5 Yr	8	0	1	0	1	0	3	1	0	3	0	0

Gary Bell

Year	Team	AB	R	H	D	T	HR	TB	BI	W	K	SB	CS
1960-1	CLE AL	0	0	0	0	0	0	0	0	0	0	0	0
1960-2	CLE AL	0	0	0	0	0	0	0	0	0	0	0	0
Totals	2 Yr	0	0	0	0	0	0	0	0	0	0	0	0

George Bell

Year	Team	AB	R	H	D	T	HR	TB	BI	W	K	SB	CS
1987*	TOR AL	3	0	0	0	0	0	0	0	0	0	0	0
1990	TOR AL	2	0	0	0	0	0	0	0	0	1	0	0
1991	CHN NL	1	0	0	0	0	0	0	0	0	1	0	0
Totals	3 Yr	6	0	0	0	0	0	0	0	0	2	0	0

Gus Bell

Year	Team	AB	R	H	D	T	HR	TB	BI	W	K	SB	CS
1953*	CIN NL	3	0	0	0	0	0	0	0	0	0	0	0
1954	CIN NL	1	1	1	0	0	1	4	2	0	0	0	0
1956*	CIN NL	1	0	0	0	0	0	0	0	0	1	0	0
1957	CIN NL	1	0	1	1	0	0	2	2	1	0	0	0
Totals	4 Yr	6	1	2	1	0	1	6	4	1	1	0	0

Year	Team	AB	R	H	D	T	HR	TB	BI	W	K	SB	CS

Jay Bell

Year	Team	AB	R	H	D	T	HR	TB	BI	W	K	SB	CS
1993	PIT NL	1	0	0	0	0	0	0	0	0	0	0	0
1999*	ARI NL	1	0	0	0	0	0	0	0	1	1	0	0
Totals	2 Yr	2	0	0	0	0	0	0	0	1	1	0	0

Albert Belle

Year	Team	AB	R	H	D	T	HR	TB	BI	W	K	SB	CS
1993	CLE AL	1	2	1	0	0	0	1	1	1	0	0	0
1994	CLE AL	2	0	0	0	0	0	0	0	0	0	0	0
1995*	CLE AL	3	0	0	0	0	0	0	0	0	1	0	0
1996*	CLE AL	4	0	0	0	0	0	0	0	0	3	0	0
Totals	4 Yr	10	2	1	0	0	0	1	1	1	4	0	0

Johnny Bench

Year	Team	AB	R	H	D	T	HR	TB	BI	W	K	SB	CS
1968	CIN NL	0	0	0	0	0	0	0	0	0	0	0	0
1969*	CIN NL	3	2	2	0	0	1	5	2	1	0	0	0
1970*	CIN NL	3	0	0	0	0	0	0	0	0	3	0	0
1971*	CIN NL	4	1	2	0	0	1	5	2	0	0	0	0
1972*	CIN NL	2	0	1	0	0	0	1	0	0	0	0	0
1973*	CIN NL	3	1	1	0	0	1	4	1	0	0	0	0
1974*	CIN NL	3	1	2	0	0	0	2	0	1	1	0	0
1975*	CIN NL	4	0	1	0	0	0	1	1	0	0	0	0
1976*	CIN NL	2	0	1	0	0	0	1	0	0	1	0	0
1977*	CIN NL	2	0	0	0	0	0	0	0	0	1	0	0
1980*	CIN NL	1	0	0	0	0	0	0	0	0	0	0	0
1983	CIN NL	1	0	0	0	0	0	0	0	0	0	0	0
Totals	12 Yr	28	5	10	0	0	3	19	6	2	6	0	0

Bruce Benedict

Year	Team	AB	R	H	D	T	HR	TB	BI	W	K	SB	CS
1981	ATL NL	1	0	0	0	0	0	0	0	0	1	0	0
1983	ATL NL	1	0	1	0	0	0	1	0	0	0	0	0
Totals	2 Yr	2	0	1	0	0	0	1	0	0	1	0	0

Al Benton

Year	Team	AB	R	H	D	T	HR	TB	BI	W	K	SB	CS
1942	DET AL	1	0	0	0	0	0	0	0	0	0	0	0

Jason Bere

Year	Team	AB	R	H	D	T	HR	TB	BI	W	K	SB	CS
1994	CHA AL	0	0	0	0	0	0	0	0	0	0	0	0

Wally Berger

Year	Team	AB	R	H	D	T	HR	TB	BI	W	K	SB	CS
1933*	BSN NL	4	0	0	0	0	0	0	0	0	0	0	0
1934*	BSN NL	2	0	0	0	0	0	0	0	0	1	0	0
1935*	BSN NL	2	0	0	0	0	0	0	0	0	1	0	0
Totals	3 Yr	8	0	0	0	0	0	0	0	0	2	0	0

Yogi Berra

Year	Team	AB	R	H	D	T	HR	TB	BI	W	K	SB	CS
1949	NYA AL	3	0	0	0	0	0	0	0	0	0	0	0
1950*	NYA AL	2	0	0	0	0	0	0	0	0	0	0	0
1951*	NYA AL	4	1	1	0	0	0	1	0	0	0	0	0
1952*	NYA AL	2	0	0	0	0	0	0	0	0	0	0	0
1953*	NYA AL	4	0	0	0	0	0	0	0	0	0	0	0
1954*	NYA AL	4	2	2	0	0	0	2	0	1	0	0	0
1955*	NYA AL	6	1	1	0	0	0	1	0	0	0	0	0
1956*	NYA AL	2	0	2	0	0	0	2	0	0	0	0	0
1957*	NYA AL	3	0	1	0	0	0	1	1	1	0	0	0
1958	NYA AL	2	0	0	0	0	0	0	0	0	0	0	0
1959-2*	NYA AL	3	1	1	0	0	1	4	2	0	2	0	0
1960-1*	NYA AL	2	0	0	0	0	0	0	0	0	0	0	0
1960-2*	NYA AL	2	0	0	0	0	0	0	0	0	1	0	0
1961-1	NYA AL	1	0	0	0	0	0	0	0	0	0	0	0

Yogi Berra *continued*

Year	Team	AB	R	H	D	T	HR	TB	BI	W	K	SB	CS
1962-2	NYA AL	1	0	0	0	0	0	0	0	0	0	0	0
Totals	15 Yr	41	5	8	0	0	1	11	3	2	3	0	0

Ken Berry

Year	Team	AB	R	H	D	T	HR	TB	BI	W	K	SB	CS
1967	CHA AL	1	0	0	0	0	0	0	0	0	1	0	0

Jim Bibby

Year	Team	AB	R	H	D	T	HR	TB	BI	W	K	SB	CS
1980	PIT NL	0	0	0	0	0	0	0	0	0	0	0	0

Dante Bichette

Year	Team	AB	R	H	D	T	HR	TB	BI	W	K	SB	CS
1994	COL NL	1	0	1	0	0	0	1	0	0	0	0	0
1995	COL NL	1	0	0	0	0	0	0	0	0	1	0	0
1996*	COL NL	3	1	1	1	0	0	2	0	0	1	0	0
1998	COL NL	2	0	0	0	0	0	0	0	0	1	0	0
Totals	4 Yr	7	1	2	1	0	0	3	0	0	3	0	0

Vern Bickford

Year	Team	AB	R	H	D	T	HR	TB	BI	W	K	SB	CS
1949	BSN NL	0	0	0	0	0	0	0	0	0	0	0	0

Craig Biggio

Year	Team	AB	R	H	D	T	HR	TB	BI	W	K	SB	CS
1991	HOU NL	1	0	0	0	0	0	0	0	0	0	0	0
1992	HOU NL	2	0	0	0	0	0	0	0	0	1	0	0
1994	HOU NL	1	1	0	0	0	0	0	0	0	0	0	0
1995*	HOU NL	2	1	1	0	0	1	4	1	0	0	0	0
1996*	HOU NL	3	0	0	0	0	0	0	1	0	1	0	0
1997*	HOU NL	3	0	0	0	0	0	0	0	0	1	0	0
1998*	HOU NL	3	0	0	0	0	0	0	0	0	3	0	0
Totals	7 Yr	15	2	1	0	0	1	4	2	0	6	0	0

Ewell Blackwell

Year	Team	AB	R	H	D	T	HR	TB	BI	W	K	SB	CS
1946	CIN NL	0	0	0	0	0	0	0	0	0	0	0	0
1947*	CIN NL	0	0	0	0	0	0	0	0	0	0	0	0
1948	CIN NL	0	0	0	0	0	0	0	0	0	0	0	0
1949	CIN NL	0	0	0	0	0	0	0	0	0	0	0	0
1950	CIN NL	1	0	0	0	0	0	0	0	0	1	0	0
1951	CIN NL	0	0	0	0	0	0	0	0	0	0	0	0
Totals	6 Yr	1	0	0	0	0	0	0	0	0	1	0	0

Paul Blair

Year	Team	AB	R	H	D	T	HR	TB	BI	W	K	SB	CS
1969	BAL AL	2	0	0	0	0	0	0	0	0	0	0	0
1973	BAL AL	0	0	0	0	0	0	0	0	0	3	0	0
Totals	2 Yr	2	0	0	0	0	0	0	0	0	0	0	0

Cy Blanton

Year	Team	AB	R	H	D	T	HR	TB	BI	W	K	SB	CS
1937	PIT NL	0	0	0	0	0	0	0	0	0	0	0	0

Don Blasingame

Year	Team	AB	R	H	D	T	HR	TB	BI	W	K	SB	CS
1958	SLN NL	1	0	0	0	0	0	0	0	0	0	0	0

Steve Blass

Year	Team	AB	R	H	D	T	HR	TB	BI	W	K	SB	CS
1972	PIT NL	0	0	0	0	0	0	0	0	0	0	0	0

Jeff Blauser

Year	Team	AB	R	H	D	T	HR	TB	BI	W	K	SB	CS
1993	ATL NL	1	0	0	0	0	0	0	0	0	1	0	0
1997*	ATL NL	2	0	1	0	0	0	1	0	0	0	0	0
Totals	2 Yr	3	0	1	0	0	0	1	0	0	1	0	0

Year	Team	AB	R	H	D	T	HR	TB	BI	W	K	SB	CS

Vida Blue

Year	Team	AB	R	H	D	T	HR	TB	BI	W	K	SB	CS
1971*	OAK AL	0	0	0	0	0	0	0	0	0	0	0	0
1975*	OAK AL	0	0	0	0	0	0	0	0	0	0	0	0
1978*	SFN NL	0	0	0	0	0	0	0	0	0	0	0	0
1981	SFN NL	0	0	0	0	0	0	0	0	0	0	0	0
Totals	4 Yr	0	0	0	0	0	0	0	0	0	0	0	0

Ossie Bluege

Year	Team	AB	R	H	D	T	HR	TB	BI	W	K	SB	CS
1935	WAS AL	0	0	0	0	0	0	0	0	0	0	0	0

Bert Blyleven

Year	Team	AB	R	H	D	T	HR	TB	BI	W	K	SB	CS
1973	MIN AL	0	0	0	0	0	0	0	0	0	0	0	0
1985	CLE AL	0	0	0	0	0	0	0	0	0	0	0	0
Totals	2 Yr	0	0	0	0	0	0	0	0	0	0	0	0

Bruce Bochte

Year	Team	AB	R	H	D	T	HR	TB	BI	W	K	SB	CS
1979	SEA AL	1	0	1	0	0	0	1	1	0	0	0	0

Wade Boggs

Year	Team	AB	R	H	D	T	HR	TB	BI	W	K	SB	CS
1985	BOS AL	0	0	0	0	0	0	0	0	1	0	0	0
1986*	BOS AL	3	0	1	0	0	0	1	0	0	0	0	0
1987*	BOS AL	3	0	0	0	0	0	0	0	0	0	0	0
1988*	BOS AL	3	0	1	0	0	0	1	0	0	0	0	0
1989*	BOS AL	3	1	1	0	0	1	4	1	0	0	0	0
1990*	BOS AL	2	0	2	0	0	0	2	0	1	0	0	0
1991*	BOS AL	2	1	1	0	0	0	1	0	1	0	0	0
1992*	BOS AL	3	1	1	0	0	0	1	0	0	1	0	0
1993*	NYA AL	1	0	0	0	0	0	0	0	1	0	0	0
1994*	NYA AL	3	1	1	0	0	0	1	0	0	2	0	0
1995*	NYA AL	2	0	1	0	0	0	1	0	0	0	0	0
1996*	NYA AL	3	0	0	0	0	0	0	0	0	0	0	0
Totals	12 Yr	28	4	9	0	0	1	12	1	4	3	0	0

Frank Bolling

Year	Team	AB	R	H	D	T	HR	TB	BI	W	K	SB	CS
1961–1*	MIL NL	3	0	0	0	0	0	0	0	0	1	0	0
1961–2*	MIL NL	4	0	0	0	0	0	0	0	0	0	0	0
1962–1	MIL NL	2	0	0	0	0	0	0	0	0	0	0	0
1962–2	MIL NL	3	0	1	1	0	0	2	0	0	0	0	0
Totals	4 Yr	12	0	1	1	0	0	2	0	0	1	0	0

Barry Bonds

Year	Team	AB	R	H	D	T	HR	TB	BI	W	K	SB	CS
1990	PIT NL	1	0	0	0	0	0	0	0	1	0	0	0
1992*	PIT NL	3	1	1	1	0	0	2	0	0	0	0	0
1993*	SFN NL	3	2	2	2	0	0	4	0	0	0	0	0
1994*	SFN NL	3	0	0	0	0	0	0	1	0	2	0	0
1995*	SFN NL	3	0	0	0	0	0	0	0	0	1	0	0
1996*	SFN NL	3	0	1	0	0	0	1	1	0	0	0	1
1997*	SFN NL	2	0	0	0	0	0	0	0	1	1	1	0
1998*	SFN NL	2	1	1	0	0	1	4	3	1	0	0	0
Totals	8 Yr	20	4	5	3	0	1	11	5	3	4	1	1

Bobby Bonds

Year	Team	AB	R	H	D	T	HR	TB	BI	W	K	SB	CS
1971	SFN NL	1	0	0	0	0	0	0	0	0	1	0	0
1973	SFN NL	2	1	2	1	0	1	6	2	0	0	0	0
1975*	NYA AL	3	0	0	0	0	0	0	0	0	1	0	0
Totals	3 Yr	6	1	2	1	0	1	6	2	0	2	0	0

Bobby Bonilla

Year	Team	AB	R	H	D	T	HR	TB	BI	W	K	SB	CS
1988*	PIT NL	4	0	0	0	0	0	0	0	0	0	0	0

Bobby Bonilla *continued*

Year	Team	AB	R	H	D	T	HR	TB	BI	W	K	SB	CS
1989	PIT NL	2	0	2	0	0	0	2	0	0	0	0	0
1990	PIT NL	1	0	0	0	0	0	0	0	0	0	0	0
1991*	PIT NL	4	0	2	0	0	0	2	1	0	1	0	0
1993	NYN NL	1	0	1	0	0	0	1	0	0	0	0	0
1995	NYN NL	1	0	0	0	0	0	0	0	0	1	0	0
Totals	6 Yr	13	0	5	0	0	0	5	1	0	2	0	0

Bob Boone

Year	Team	AB	R	H	D	T	HR	TB	BI	W	K	SB	CS
1976	PHI NL	2	0	0	0	0	0	0	0	0	0	0	0
1978	PHI NL	1	1	1	0	0	0	1	2	0	0	0	0
1979*	PHI NL	2	1	1	0	0	0	1	0	0	0	0	0
1983	CAL AL	0	0	0	0	0	0	0	0	0	0	0	0
Totals	4 Yr	5	2	2	0	0	0	2	2	0	0	0	0

Ray Boone

Year	Team	AB	R	H	D	T	HR	TB	BI	W	K	SB	CS
1954*	DET AL	4	1	1	0	0	1	4	1	0	0	0	0
1956	DET AL	1	0	0	0	0	0	0	0	0	0	0	0
Totals	2 Yr	5	1	1	0	0	1	4	1	0	0	0	0

Mike Bordick

Year	Team	AB	R	H	D	T	HR	TB	BI	W	K	SB	CS
2000	BAL AL	1	0	0	0	0	0	0	0	0	0	0	0

Hank Borowy

Year	Team	AB	R	H	D	T	HR	TB	BI	W	K	SB	CS
1944*	NYA AL	1	0	1	0	0	0	1	1	0	0	0	0

Ricky Bottalico

Year	Team	AB	R	H	D	T	HR	TB	BI	W	K	SB	CS
1996	PHI NL	0	0	0	0	0	0	0	0	0	0	0	0

Lou Boudreau

Year	Team	AB	R	H	D	T	HR	TB	BI	W	K	SB	CS
1940	CLE AL	0	0	0	0	0	0	0	0	0	0	0	0
1941	CLE AL	2	0	2	0	0	0	2	1	0	0	0	0
1942*	CLE AL	4	1	1	0	0	1	4	1	0	0	0	0
1947*	CLE AL	4	0	1	0	0	0	1	0	0	1	0	0
1948*	CLE AL	2	0	0	0	0	0	0	1	0	0	0	0
Totals	5 Yr	12	1	4	0	0	1	7	3	0	1	0	0

Jim Bouton

Year	Team	AB	R	H	D	T	HR	TB	BI	W	K	SB	CS
1963	NYA AL	0	0	0	0	0	0	0	0	0	0	0	0

Larry Bowa

Year	Team	AB	R	H	D	T	HR	TB	BI	W	K	SB	CS
1974*	PHI NL	2	0	0	0	0	0	0	0	0	0	0	0
1975	PHI NL	0	1	0	0	0	0	0	0	0	0	0	0
1976	PHI NL	1	0	0	0	0	0	0	0	0	0	0	0
1978*	PHI NL	3	1	2	0	0	0	2	0	0	0	1	0
1979*	PHI NL	2	0	0	0	0	0	0	0	1	0	0	0
Totals	5 Yr	8	2	2	0	0	0	2	0	1	0	1	0

Ken Boyer

Year	Team	AB	R	H	D	T	HR	TB	BI	W	K	SB	CS
1956*	SLN NL	5	1	3	0	0	0	3	1	0	0	0	1
1959–1	SLN NL	1	1	1	0	0	0	1	0	0	0	0	0
1959–2*	SLN NL	2	0	0	0	0	0	0	0	1	0	0	0
1960–1	SLN NL	0	0	0	0	0	0	0	0	1	0	0	0
1960–2	SLN NL	1	1	1	0	0	1	4	2	0	0	0	0
1961–1	SLN NL	2	0	0	0	0	0	0	0	1	2	0	0
1962–1*	SLN NL	2	0	0	0	0	0	0	0	0	1	0	0
1962–2*	SLN NL	3	0	1	0	0	0	1	0	0	0	0	0
1963*	SLN NL	3	0	0	0	0	0	0	0	0	0	0	0

Ken Boyer continued

Year	Team	AB	R	H	D	T	HR	TB	BI	W	K	SB	CS
1964*	SLN NL	4	1	2	0	0	1	5	1	0	1	0	0
Totals	10 Yr	23	4	8	0	0	2	14	4	3	4	0	1

Phil Bradley

Year	Team	AB	R	H	D	T	HR	TB	BI	W	K	SB	CS
1985	SEA AL	1	0	0	0	0	0	0	0	0	1	0	0

Ralph Branca

Year	Team	AB	R	H	D	T	HR	TB	BI	W	K	SB	CS
1948*	BRO NL	1	0	0	0	0	0	0	0	0	0	0	0

Jackie Brandt

Year	Team	AB	R	H	D	T	HR	TB	BI	W	K	SB	CS
1961–1	BAL AL	1	0	0	0	0	0	0	0	0	1	0	0

Jeff Brantley

Year	Team	AB	R	H	D	T	HR	TB	BI	W	K	SB	CS
1990	SFN NL	0	0	0	0	0	0	0	0	0	0	0	0

Harry Brecheen

Year	Team	AB	R	H	D	T	HR	TB	BI	W	K	SB	CS
1947	SLN NL	1	0	0	0	0	0	0	0	0	0	0	0

Bob Brenly

Year	Team	AB	R	H	D	T	HR	TB	BI	W	K	SB	CS
1984	SFN NL	1	0	0	0	0	0	0	0	0	1	0	0

George Brett

Year	Team	AB	R	H	D	T	HR	TB	BI	W	K	SB	CS
1976*	KCA AL	2	0	0	0	0	0	0	0	1	0	0	0
1977*	KCA AL	2	0	0	0	0	0	0	0	1	0	0	0
1978*	KCA AL	3	1	2	1	0	0	3	2	0	0	1	0
1979*	KCA AL	3	1	0	0	0	0	0	1	0	0	0	0
1981*	KCA AL	3	0	0	0	0	0	0	0	0	2	0	0
1982*	KCA AL	2	0	2	0	0	0	2	0	0	0	0	0
1983*	KCA AL	4	2	2	1	1	0	5	1	0	1	0	0
1984*	KCA AL	3	1	1	0	0	1	4	1	0	1	0	0
1985*	KCA AL	1	0	0	0	0	0	0	1	1	0	0	0
1988	KCA AL	1	0	0	0	0	0	0	0	0	0	0	0
Totals	10 Yr	24	5	7	2	1	1	14	5	4	4	1	0

Ken Brett

Year	Team	AB	R	H	D	T	HR	TB	BI	W	K	SB	CS
1974	PIT NL	0	0	0	0	0	0	0	0	0	0	0	0

Jim Brewer

Year	Team	AB	R	H	D	T	HR	TB	BI	W	K	SB	CS
1973	LAN NL	0	0	0	0	0	0	0	0	0	0	0	0

Tom Brewer

Year	Team	AB	R	H	D	T	HR	TB	BI	W	K	SB	CS
1956	BOS AL	0	0	0	0	0	0	0	0	0	0	0	0

Tommy Bridges

Year	Team	AB	R	H	D	T	HR	TB	BI	W	K	SB	CS
1937	DET AL	1	0	0	0	0	0	0	0	0	1	0	0
1939	DET AL	1	0	0	0	0	0	0	0	0	1	0	0
Totals	2 Yr	2	0	0	0	0	0	0	0	0	2	0	0

Ed Brinkman

Year	Team	AB	R	H	D	T	HR	TB	BI	W	K	SB	CS
1973	DET AL	1	0	0	0	0	0	0	0	0	0	0	0

Lou Brissie

Year	Team	AB	R	H	D	T	HR	TB	BI	W	K	SB	CS
1949	PHA AL	1	0	0	0	0	0	0	0	0	0	0	0

Lou Brock

Year	Team	AB	R	H	D	T	HR	TB	BI	W	K	SB	CS
1967*	SLN NL	2	0	0	0	0	0	0	0	0	0	0	0
1971	SLN NL	1	0	0	0	0	0	0	0	0	0	0	0
1974	SLN NL	1	1	1	0	0	0	1	0	0	0	1	0
1975*	SLN NL	3	1	1	0	0	0	1	0	0	0	1	0
1979	SLN NL	1	0	1	0	0	0	1	0	0	0	0	0
Totals	5 Yr	8	2	3	0	0	0	3	0	0	0	2	0

Hubie Brooks

Year	Team	AB	R	H	D	T	HR	TB	BI	W	K	SB	CS
1986	MON NL	2	1	0	0	0	0	0	0	0	1	0	0
1987	MON NL	3	1	1	0	0	0	1	0	0	1	0	0
Totals	2 Yr	5	2	1	0	0	0	1	0	0	2	0	0

Scott Brosius

Year	Team	AB	R	H	D	T	HR	TB	BI	W	K	SB	CS
1998	NYA AL	2	1	1	0	0	0	1	0	0	1	1	0

Chris Brown

Year	Team	AB	R	H	D	T	HR	TB	BI	W	K	SB	CS
1986	SFN NL	2	1	1	1	0	0	2	0	0	0	0	0

Jimmy Brown

Year	Team	AB	R	H	D	T	HR	TB	BI	W	K	SB	CS
1942*	SLN NL	2	0	0	0	0	0	0	0	0	0	0	0

Kevin Brown

Year	Team	AB	R	H	D	T	HR	TB	BI	W	K	SB	CS
1992*	TEX AL	1	0	0	0	0	0	0	0	0	1	0	0
1996	FLO NL	0	0	0	0	0	0	0	0	0	0	0	0
1998	SDN NL	0	0	0	0	0	0	0	0	0	0	0	0
2000	LAN NL	0	0	0	0	0	0	0	0	0	0	0	0
Totals	4 Yr	1	0	0	0	0	0	0	0	0	1	0	0

Mace Brown

Year	Team	AB	R	H	D	T	HR	TB	BI	W	K	SB	CS
1938	PIT NL	1	0	0	0	0	0	0	0	0	1	0	0

Tom Brunansky

Year	Team	AB	R	H	D	T	HR	TB	BI	W	K	SB	CS
1985	MIN AL	1	0	0	0	0	0	0	0	0	0	0	0

Bill Buckner

Year	Team	AB	R	H	D	T	HR	TB	BI	W	K	SB	CS
1981	CHN NL	1	0	0	0	0	0	0	0	0	0	0	0

Don Buford

Year	Team	AB	R	H	D	T	HR	TB	BI	W	K	SB	CS
1971	BAL AL	1	0	0	0	0	0	0	0	0	1	0	0

Bob Buhl

Year	Team	AB	R	H	D	T	HR	TB	BI	W	K	SB	CS
1960–1	MIL NL	0	0	0	0	0	0	0	0	0	0	0	0

Jay Buhner

Year	Team	AB	R	H	D	T	HR	TB	BI	W	K	SB	CS
1996	SEA AL	2	0	0	0	0	0	0	0	0	0	0	0

Al Bumbry

Year	Team	AB	R	H	D	T	HR	TB	BI	W	K	SB	CS
1980	BAL AL	1	0	0	0	0	0	0	0	0	0	0	0

Jim Bunning

Year	Team	AB	R	H	D	T	HR	TB	BI	W	K	SB	CS
1957*	DET AL	1	0	0	0	0	0	0	0	0	0	0	0
1959–1	DET AL	0	0	0	0	0	0	0	0	0	0	0	0
1961–1	DET AL	0	0	0	0	0	0	0	0	0	0	0	0
1961–2*	DET AL	1	0	0	0	0	0	0	0	0	0	0	0
1962–1*	DET AL	0	0	0	0	0	0	0	0	0	0	0	0
1963	DET AL	0	0	0	0	0	0	0	0	0	0	0	0
1964	PHI NL	0	0	0	0	0	0	0	0	0	0	0	0
1966	PHI NL	0	0	0	0	0	0	0	0	0	0	0	0
Totals	8 Yr	2	0	0	0	0	0	0	0	0	0	0	0

Lew Burdette

Year	Team	AB	R	H	D	T	HR	TB	BI	W	K	SB	CS
1957	MIL NL	1	0	0	0	0	0	0	0	0	0	0	0

Lew Burdette *continued*

Year	Team	AB	R	H	D	T	HR	TB	BI	W	K	SB	CS
1959–1	MIL NL	1	0	0	0	0	0	0	0	0	1	0	0
Totals	2 Yr	2	0	0	0	0	0	0	0	0	1	0	0

Smoky Burgess

Year	Team	AB	R	H	D	T	HR	TB	BI	W	K	SB	CS
1954	PHI NL	0	0	0	0	0	0	0	0	0	0	0	0
1955	CIN NL	1	0	0	0	0	0	0	0	0	0	0	0
1959–2	PIT NL	1	0	0	0	0	0	0	0	0	0	0	0
1960–1	PIT NL	1	0	0	0	0	0	0	0	0	0	0	0
1960–2	PIT NL	2	0	0	0	0	0	0	0	0	1	0	0
1961–1*	PIT NL	4	0	1	0	0	0	1	0	0	0	0	0
1961–2*	PIT NL	1	0	0	0	0	0	0	0	0	1	0	0
Totals	7 Yr	10	0	1	0	0	0	1	0	0	2	0	0

Ellis Burks

Year	Team	AB	R	H	D	T	HR	TB	BI	W	K	SB	CS
1996	COL NL	2	0	1	0	1	0	3	0	0	1	0	0

Rick Burleson

Year	Team	AB	R	H	D	T	HR	TB	BI	W	K	SB	CS
1977*	BOS AL	2	0	0	0	0	0	0	0	0	0	0	0
1979	BOS AL	2	1	0	0	0	0	0	0	0	1	0	0
1981	CAL AL	1	0	0	0	0	0	0	0	0	0	0	0
Totals	3 Yr	5	1	0	0	0	0	0	0	0	1	0	0

Jeromy Burnitz

Year	Team	AB	R	H	D	T	HR	TB	BI	W	K	SB	CS
1999*	MIL NL	2	1	1	1	0	0	2	0	0	0	0	0

Jeff Burroughs

Year	Team	AB	R	H	D	T	HR	TB	BI	W	K	SB	CS
1974*	TEX AL	0	0	0	0	0	0	0	0	2	0	0	0

Jim Busby

Year	Team	AB	R	H	D	T	HR	TB	BI	W	K	SB	CS
1951	CHA AL	0	0	0	0	0	0	0	0	0	0	0	0

Steve Busby

Year	Team	AB	R	H	D	T	HR	TB	BI	W	K	SB	CS
1975	KCA AL	0	0	0	0	0	0	0	0	0	0	0	0

Brett Butler

Year	Team	AB	R	H	D	T	HR	TB	BI	W	K	SB	CS
1991	LAN NL	1	0	0	0	0	0	0	0	0	0	0	0

Ivan Calderon

Year	Team	AB	R	H	D	T	HR	TB	BI	W	K	SB	CS
1991*	MON NL	2	0	1	0	0	0	1	0	0	0	1	0

Johnny Callison

Year	Team	AB	R	H	D	T	HR	TB	BI	W	K	SB	CS
1962–1	PHI NL	1	0	1	0	0	0	1	0	0	0	0	0
1962–2	PHI NL	0	0	0	0	0	0	0	0	1	0	0	0
1964	PHI NL	3	1	1	0	0	1	4	3	0	0	0	0
Totals	3 Yr	4	1	2	0	0	1	5	3	1	0	0	0

Dolph Camilli

Year	Team	AB	R	H	D	T	HR	TB	BI	W	K	SB	CS
1939	BRO NL	1	0	0	0	0	0	0	0	0	1	0	0

Ken Caminiti

Year	Team	AB	R	H	D	T	HR	TB	BI	W	K	SB	CS
1994	HOU NL	1	0	0	0	0	0	0	0	0	0	0	0
1996	SDN NL	2	1	1	0	0	1	4	1	0	1	0	0
1997*	SDN NL	2	0	0	0	0	0	0	0	0	0	0	0
Totals	3 Yr	5	1	1	0	0	1	4	1	0	1	0	0

Roy Campanella

Year	Team	AB	R	H	D	T	HR	TB	BI	W	K	SB	CS
1949	BRO NL	2	0	0	0	0	0	0	0	1	1	0	0
1950*	BRO NL	6	0	0	0	0	0	0	0	0	2	0	0
1951*	BRO NL	4	0	0	0	0	0	0	0	0	0	0	0

Roy Campanella *continued*

Year	Team	AB	R	H	D	T	HR	TB	BI	W	K	SB	CS
1952*	BRO NL	1	0	0	0	0	0	0	0	0	1	0	0
1953*	BRO NL	4	1	1	0	0	0	1	0	0	1	0	0
1954*	BRO NL	3	0	1	0	0	0	1	0	1	1	0	0
1956	BRO NL	0	0	0	0	0	0	0	0	0	0	0	0
Totals	7 Yr	20	1	2	0	0	0	2	0	3	5	0	0

Bert Campaneris

Year	Team	AB	R	H	D	T	HR	TB	BI	W	K	SB	CS
1968	OAK AL	1	0	0	0	0	0	0	0	0	0	0	0
1973*	OAK AL	3	0	0	0	0	0	0	0	0	2	0	0
1974*	OAK AL	4	0	0	0	0	0	0	0	0	2	0	0
1975*	OAK AL	2	0	2	0	0	0	2	0	0	0	0	0
1977	TEX AL	1	1	0	0	0	0	0	0	1	1	0	0
Totals	5 Yr	11	1	2	0	0	0	2	0	1	5	0	0

Bill Campbell

Year	Team	AB	R	H	D	T	HR	TB	BI	W	K	SB	CS
1977	BOS AL	0	0	0	0	0	0	0	0	0	0	0	0

Jose Canseco

Year	Team	AB	R	H	D	T	HR	TB	BI	W	K	SB	CS
1988*	OAK AL	4	0	0	0	0	0	0	0	0	1	0	0
1990*	OAK AL	4	0	0	0	0	0	0	0	1	1	1	0
Totals	2 Yr	8	0	0	0	0	0	0	0	1	2	1	0

Leo Cardenas

Year	Team	AB	R	H	D	T	HR	TB	BI	W	K	SB	CS
1964	CIN NL	1	0	0	0	0	0	0	0	0	1	0	0
1965	CIN NL	0	0	0	0	0	0	0	0	0	0	0	0
1966*	CIN NL	2	0	0	0	0	0	0	0	0	0	0	0
1968	CIN NL	0	0	0	0	0	0	0	0	0	0	0	0
Totals	4 Yr	3	0	0	0	0	0	0	0	0	1	0	0

Rod Carew

Year	Team	AB	R	H	D	T	HR	TB	BI	W	K	SB	CS
1967*	MIN AL	3	0	0	0	0	0	0	0	0	1	0	0
1968*	MIN AL	3	0	0	0	0	0	0	0	0	0	0	0
1969*	MIN AL	3	0	0	0	0	0	0	0	0	0	0	0
1971*	MIN AL	1	1	0	0	0	0	0	0	2	0	0	0
1972*	MIN AL	2	0	1	0	0	0	1	1	1	0	0	0
1973*	MIN AL	3	0	0	0	0	0	0	0	0	0	0	0
1974*	MIN AL	1	1	0	0	0	0	0	0	1	0	1	0
1975*	MIN AL	5	0	1	0	0	0	1	0	0	1	0	0
1976*	MIN AL	3	0	0	0	0	0	0	1	0	1	0	0
1977*	MIN AL	3	1	1	0	0	0	1	0	0	0	0	0
1978*	MIN AL	4	2	2	0	2	0	6	0	0	0	0	1
1980*	CAL AL	2	1	2	1	0	0	3	0	1	0	1	0
1981*	CAL AL	3	0	1	0	0	0	1	0	0	1	0	1
1983*	CAL AL	3	2	2	0	0	0	2	1	1	0	0	0
1984*	CAL AL	2	0	0	0	0	0	0	0	0	1	0	0
Totals	15 Yr	41	8	10	1	2	0	15	2	7	4	3	2

Steve Carlton

Year	Team	AB	R	H	D	T	HR	TB	BI	W	K	SB	CS
1968	SLN NL	0	0	0	0	0	0	0	0	0	0	0	0
1969*	SLN NL	2	0	1	1	0	0	2	1	0	1	0	0
1972	PHI NL	0	0	0	0	0	0	0	0	0	0	0	0
1979*	PHI NL	0	0	0	0	0	0	0	0	0	0	0	0
1982	PHI NL	0	0	0	0	0	0	0	0	0	0	0	0
Totals	5 Yr	2	0	1	1	0	0	2	1	0	1	0	0

Chico Carrasquel

Year	Team	AB	R	H	D	T	HR	TB	BI	W	K	SB	CS
1951*	CHA AL	2	0	1	0	0	0	1	0	0	0	0	0
1953*	CHA AL	2	0	0	0	0	0	0	0	0	0	0	0
1954*	CHA AL	5	1	1	0	0	0	1	0	0	2	0	0

Year	Team	AB	R	H	D	T	HR	TB	BI	W	K	SB	CS

Chico Carrasquel *continued*

Year	Team	AB	R	H	D	T	HR	TB	BI	W	K	SB	CS
1955	CHA AL	3	0	2	0	0	0	2	0	0	0	0	0
Totals	4 Yr	12	1	4	0	0	0	4	0	0	2	0	0

Gary Carter

Year	Team	AB	R	H	D	T	HR	TB	BI	W	K	SB	CS
1975	MON NL	0	0	0	0	0	0	0	0	0	0	0	0
1979	MON NL	2	0	1	0	0	0	1	1	0	0	0	0
1980	MON NL	1	0	0	0	0	0	0	0	0	0	0	0
1981*	MON NL	3	2	2	0	0	2	8	2	0	0	0	0
1982*	MON NL	3	0	1	0	0	0	1	1	0	0	0	0
1983*	MON NL	2	0	0	0	0	0	0	0	0	0	0	0
1984*	MON NL	2	1	1	0	0	1	4	1	1	0	0	0
1986*	NYN NL	3	0	0	0	0	0	0	0	0	0	0	0
1987*	NYN NL	1	0	0	0	0	0	0	0	0	1	0	0
1988*	NYN NL	3	0	1	0	0	0	1	0	0	1	0	0
Totals	10 Yr	20	3	6	0	0	3	15	5	2	1	0	0

Joe Carter

Year	Team	AB	R	H	D	T	HR	TB	BI	W	K	SB	CS
1991	TOR AL	1	1	1	0	0	0	1	0	1	0	0	0
1992*	TOR AL	3	1	2	0	0	0	2	1	0	0	0	0
1993*	TOR AL	3	0	1	0	0	0	1	0	0	1	0	0
1994*	TOR AL	3	1	0	0	0	0	0	0	0	0	0	0
1996	TOR AL	1	0	1	0	0	0	1	0	0	0	0	0
Totals	5 Yr	11	3	5	0	0	0	5	1	1	1	0	0

Rico Carty

Year	Team	AB	R	H	D	T	HR	TB	BI	W	K	SB	CS
1970*	ATL NL	1	0	0	0	0	0	0	0	0	1	0	0

George Case

Year	Team	AB	R	H	D	T	HR	TB	BI	W	K	SB	CS
1943*	WAS AL	2	1	0	0	0	0	0	0	0	1	1	0

Sean Casey

Year	Team	AB	R	H	D	T	HR	TB	BI	W	K	SB	CS
1999	CIN NL	1	0	0	0	0	0	0	0	0	0	0	0

Dave Cash

Year	Team	AB	R	H	D	T	HR	TB	BI	W	K	SB	CS
1974	PHI NL	1	0	0	0	0	0	0	0	0	0	0	0
1975	PHI NL	1	0	0	0	0	0	0	0	0	0	0	0
1976	PHI NL	1	1	1	0	0	0	1	0	0	0	0	0
Totals	3 Yr	3	1	1	0	0	0	1	0	0	0	0	0

Norm Cash

Year	Team	AB	R	H	D	T	HR	TB	BI	W	K	SB	CS
1961-1*	DET AL	4	0	1	1	0	0	2	0	0	2	0	0
1961-2*	DET AL	4	0	0	0	0	0	0	0	0	1	0	0
1966	DET AL	2	0	0	0	0	0	0	0	0	0	0	0
1971*	DET AL	2	0	0	0	0	0	0	0	0	2	0	0
1972	DET AL	1	0	0	0	0	0	0	0	0	1	0	0
Totals	5 Yr	13	0	1	1	0	0	2	0	0	6	0	0

Vinny Castilla

Year	Team	AB	R	H	D	T	HR	TB	BI	W	K	SB	CS
1995*	COL NL	2	0	0	0	0	0	0	0	0	1	0	0
1998	COL NL	2	0	0	0	0	0	0	0	0	0	0	0
Totals	2 Yr	4	0	0	0	0	0	0	0	0	1	0	0

Bill Caudill

Year	Team	AB	R	H	D	T	HR	TB	BI	W	K	SB	CS
1984	OAK AL	0	0	0	0	0	0	0	0	0	0	0	0

Phil Cavarretta

Year	Team	AB	R	H	D	T	HR	TB	BI	W	K	SB	CS
1944*	CHN NL	2	1	2	0	1	0	4	0	3	0	0	0
1946	CHN NL	1	0	0	0	0	0	0	0	0	1	0	0

Phil Cavarretta *continued*

Year	Team	AB	R	H	D	T	HR	TB	BI	W	K	SB	CS
1947	CHN NL	1	0	0	0	0	0	0	0	0	1	0	0
Totals	3 Yr	4	1	2	0	1	0	4	0	3	2	0	0

Cesar Cedeno

Year	Team	AB	R	H	D	T	HR	TB	BI	W	K	SB	CS
1972	HOU NL	2	1	1	0	0	0	1	0	0	1	0	0
1973*	HOU NL	3	0	1	0	0	0	1	1	0	2	0	0
1974	HOU NL	2	0	0	0	0	0	0	0	0	1	0	0
1976	HOU NL	2	1	1	0	0	1	4	2	0	1	0	0
Totals	4 Yr	9	2	3	0	0	1	6	3	0	5	0	0

Orlando Cepeda

Year	Team	AB	R	H	D	T	HR	TB	BI	W	K	SB	CS
1959-1*	SFN NL	4	0	0	0	0	0	0	0	0	0	0	0
1960-1	SFN NL	1	0	0	0	0	0	0	0	0	1	0	0
1960-2	SFN NL	2	0	0	0	0	0	0	0	0	0	0	0
1961-1*	SFN NL	3	0	0	0	0	0	0	0	0	0	0	0
1961-2*	SFN NL	3	0	0	0	0	0	0	0	0	0	0	0
1962-1*	SFN NL	3	0	0	0	0	0	1	0	1	0	0	0
1962-2*	SFN NL	1	0	0	0	0	0	0	1	0	0	0	0
1964*	SFN NL	4	0	1	0	0	0	1	0	0	0	0	0
1967*	SLN NL	6	0	0	0	0	0	0	0	0	1	0	0
Totals	9 Yr	27	0	1	0	0	0	1	1	1	3	0	0

Bob Cerv

Year	Team	AB	R	H	D	T	HR	TB	BI	W	K	SB	CS
1958*	KC AL	2	0	1	0	0	0	1	0	1	0	0	0

Ron Cey

Year	Team	AB	R	H	D	T	HR	TB	BI	W	K	SB	CS
1974*	LAN NL	2	0	1	1	0	0	2	2	0	0	0	0
1975*	LAN NL	3	0	1	0	0	0	1	0	0	0	0	0
1976	LAN NL	0	0	0	0	0	0	0	0	0	0	0	0
1977*	LAN NL	2	0	0	0	0	0	0	0	1	1	0	0
1978	LAN NL	1	0	0	0	0	0	0	0	0	0	0	0
1979	LAN NL	1	0	0	0	0	0	0	0	1	0	0	0
Totals	6 Yr	9	0	2	1	0	0	3	2	2	1	0	0

Dave Chalk

Year	Team	AB	R	H	D	T	HR	TB	BI	W	K	SB	CS
1974	CAL AL	1	0	0	0	0	0	0	0	0	1	0	0

Chris Chambliss

Year	Team	AB	R	H	D	T	HR	TB	BI	W	K	SB	CS
1976	NYA AL	1	0	0	0	0	0	0	0	0	0	0	0

Dean Chance

Year	Team	AB	R	H	D	T	HR	TB	BI	W	K	SB	CS
1964*	LAA AL	1	0	0	0	0	0	0	0	0	0	0	0
1967*	MIN AL	0	0	0	0	0	0	0	0	0	0	0	0
Totals	2 Yr	1	0	0	0	0	0	0	0	0	0	0	0

Spud Chandler

Year	Team	AB	R	H	D	T	HR	TB	BI	W	K	SB	CS
1942*	NYA AL	1	0	0	0	0	0	0	0	0	0	0	0

Ben Chapman

Year	Team	AB	R	H	D	T	HR	TB	BI	W	K	SB	CS
1933*	NYA AL	5	0	1	0	0	0	1	0	0	1	0	0
1934	NYA AL	2	0	1	0	1	0	3	0	0	0	0	0
1935	NYA AL	0	0	0	0	0	0	0	0	0	0	0	0
1936	WAS AL	1	0	0	0	0	0	0	0	0	0	0	0
Totals	4 Yr	8	0	2	0	1	0	4	0	0	1	0	0

Sam Chapman

Year	Team	AB	R	H	D	T	HR	TB	BI	W	K	SB	CS
1946	PHA AL	2	0	0	0	0	0	0	1	0	0	0	0

Year	Team	AB	R	H	D	T	HR	TB	BI	W	K	SB	CS

Norm Charlton

Year	Team	AB	R	H	D	T	HR	TB	BI	W	K	SB	CS
1992	CIN NL	1	0	0	0	0	0	0	0	0	1	0	0

Gino Cimoli

Year	Team	AB	R	H	D	T	HR	TB	BI	W	K	SB	CS
1957	BRO NL	1	0	0	0	0	0	0	0	0	1	0	0

Jeff Cirillo

Year	Team	AB	R	H	D	T	HR	TB	BI	W	K	SB	CS
1997	MIL AL	1	0	0	0	0	0	0	0	0	1	0	0
2000	COL NL	1	0	0	0	0	0	0	0	0	0	0	0
Totals	2 Yr	2	0	0	0	0	0	0	0	0	1	0	0

Jim Clancy

Year	Team	AB	R	H	D	T	HR	TB	BI	W	K	SB	CS
1982	TOR AL	0	0	0	0	0	0	0	0	0	0	0	0

Jack Clark

Year	Team	AB	R	H	D	T	HR	TB	BI	W	K	SB	CS
1978	SFN NL	1	0	0	0	0	0	0	0	0	1	0	0
1979	SFN NL	1	0	0	0	0	0	0	0	0	0	0	0
1985	SLN NL	1	0	0	0	0	0	0	0	1	0	0	0
1987*	SLN NL	3	0	0	0	0	0	0	0	0	2	0	0
Totals	4 Yr	6	0	0	0	0	0	0	0	1	3	0	0

Will Clark

Year	Team	AB	R	H	D	T	HR	TB	BI	W	K	SB	CS
1988*	SFN NL	2	0	0	0	0	0	0	0	0	0	0	0
1989*	SFN NL	2	0	0	0	0	0	0	0	0	1	0	0
1990*	SFN NL	3	0	1	0	0	0	1	0	0	0	0	0
1991*	SFN NL	2	0	1	0	0	0	1	0	1	0	0	0
1992	SFN NL	2	1	1	0	0	1	4	3	0	1	0	0
1994	TEX AL	2	0	2	0	0	0	2	0	0	0	1	0
Totals	6 Yr	13	1	5	0	0	1	8	3	1	2	1	0

Royce Clayton

Year	Team	AB	R	H	D	T	HR	TB	BI	W	K	SB	CS
1997	SLN NL	1	0	0	0	0	0	0	0	0	1	0	0

Mark Clear

Year	Team	AB	R	H	D	T	HR	TB	BI	W	K	SB	CS
1979	CAL AL	0	0	0	0	0	0	0	0	0	0	0	0

Roger Clemens

Year	Team	AB	R	H	D	T	HR	TB	BI	W	K	SB	CS
1986*	BOS AL	1	0	0	0	0	0	0	0	0	1	0	0
1988	BOS AL	0	0	0	0	0	0	0	0	0	0	0	0
1992	BOS AL	0	0	0	0	0	0	0	0	0	0	0	0
1998	TOR AL	0	0	0	0	0	0	0	0	0	0	0	0
Totals	4 Yr	1	0	0	0	0	0	0	0	0	1	0	0

Roberto Clemente

Year	Team	AB	R	H	D	T	HR	TB	BI	W	K	SB	CS
1960-1	PIT NL	1	0	0	0	0	0	0	0	0	0	0	0
1960-2	PIT NL	0	0	0	0	0	0	0	0	1	0	0	0
1961-1*	PIT NL	4	1	2	0	1	0	4	2	0	1	0	0
1961-2*	PIT NL	2	0	0	0	0	0	0	0	0	0	0	0
1962-1*	PIT NL	3	0	3	1	0	0	4	0	0	0	0	1
1962-2*	PIT NL	2	0	0	0	0	0	0	0	0	1	0	0
1963	PIT NL	0	0	0	0	0	0	0	0	0	0	0	0
1964*	PIT NL	3	1	1	0	0	0	1	0	0	1	0	0
1965	PIT NL	2	0	0	0	0	0	0	0	0	0	0	0
1966*	PIT NL	4	0	2	1	0	0	3	0	0	0	0	0
1967*	PIT NL	6	0	1	0	0	0	1	0	0	4	0	0
1969	PIT NL	1	0	0	0	0	0	0	0	0	1	0	0
1970	PIT NL	1	0	0	0	0	0	0	1	0	0	0	0
1971	PIT NL	2	1	1	0	0	1	4	1	0	1	0	0
Totals	14 Yr	31	3	10	2	1	1	17	4	1	9	0	1

Jim Coates

Year	Team	AB	R	H	D	T	HR	TB	BI	W	K	SB	CS
1960-1	NYA AL	0	0	0	0	0	0	0	0	0	0	0	0

Mickey Cochrane

Year	Team	AB	R	H	D	T	HR	TB	BI	W	K	SB	CS
1934	DET AL	1	0	0	0	0	0	0	0	0	0	0	0

Rocky Colavito

Year	Team	AB	R	H	D	T	HR	TB	BI	W	K	SB	CS
1959-1*	CLE AL	3	0	1	0	0	0	1	0	0	1	0	0
1959-2	CLE AL	2	1	1	0	0	1	4	1	0	1	0	0
1961-1*	DET AL	4	0	0	0	0	0	0	1	0	0	0	0
1961-2*	DET AL	4	1	1	0	0	1	4	1	0	0	0	0
1962-1	DET AL	1	0	0	0	0	0	0	0	1	0	0	0
1962-2*	DET AL	4	1	1	0	0	1	4	4	0	1	0	0
1964	KC AL	2	0	1	1	0	0	2	0	0	0	0	0
1965*	CLE AL	4	0	1	0	0	0	1	1	0	0	0	0
1966	CLE AL	1	0	0	0	0	0	0	0	0	0	0	0
Totals	9 Yr	25	3	6	1	0	3	16	8	1	3	0	0

Nate Colbert

Year	Team	AB	R	H	D	T	HR	TB	BI	W	K	SB	CS
1971	SDN NL	1	0	0	0	0	0	0	0	0	1	0	0
1972	SDN NL	0	1	0	0	0	0	0	0	1	0	0	0
1973	SDN NL	1	0	0	0	0	0	0	0	0	0	0	0
Totals	3 Yr	2	1	0	0	0	0	0	0	1	1	0	0

Jerry Coleman

Year	Team	AB	R	H	D	T	HR	TB	BI	W	K	SB	CS
1950	NYA AL	2	0	0	0	0	0	0	0	0	2	0	0

Joe Coleman

Year	Team	AB	R	H	D	T	HR	TB	BI	W	K	SB	CS
1948	PHA AL	0	0	0	0	0	0	0	0	0	0	0	0

Vince Coleman

Year	Team	AB	R	H	D	T	HR	TB	BI	W	K	SB	CS
1988*	SLN NL	2	1	1	0	0	0	1	0	0	0	1	0
1989	SLN NL	0	0	0	0	0	0	0	0	0	0	0	0
Totals	2 Yr	2	1	1	0	0	0	1	0	0	0	1	0

Ripper Collins

Year	Team	AB	R	H	D	T	HR	TB	BI	W	K	SB	CS
1935	SLN NL	1	0	0	0	0	0	0	0	0	0	0	0
1936*	SLN NL	2	0	0	0	0	0	0	0	2	0	0	0
1937	CHN NL	1	0	1	0	0	0	1	0	0	0	0	0
Totals	3 Yr	4	0	1	0	0	0	1	0	2	0	0	0

Bartolo Colon

Year	Team	AB	R	H	D	T	HR	TB	BI	W	K	SB	CS
1998	CLE AL	0	0	0	0	0	0	0	0	0	0	0	0

Dave Concepcion

Year	Team	AB	R	H	D	T	HR	TB	BI	W	K	SB	CS
1975*	CIN NL	2	0	1	0	0	0	1	0	0	1	0	1
1976*	CIN NL	2	0	1	0	0	0	1	0	0	0	0	0
1977*	CIN NL	1	0	0	0	0	0	0	0	1	0	0	1
1978	CIN NL	0	1	0	0	0	0	0	0	1	0	0	0
1980	CIN NL	1	1	0	0	0	0	0	0	0	0	0	0
1981*	CIN NL	3	0	0	0	0	0	0	0	0	1	0	0
1982*	CIN NL	3	1	1	0	0	1	4	2	0	0	0	0
Totals	7 Yr	12	3	3	0	0	1	6	2	2	2	0	2

David Cone

Year	Team	AB	R	H	D	T	HR	TB	BI	W	K	SB	CS
1988	NYN NL	0	0	0	0	0	0	0	0	0	0	0	0
1992	NYN NL	0	0	0	0	0	0	0	0	0	0	0	0
1994	KCA AL	0	0	0	0	0	0	0	0	0	0	0	0
Totals	3 Yr	0	0	0	0	0	0	0	0	0	0	0	0

Year	Team	AB	R	H	D	T	HR	TB	BI	W	K	SB	CS

Tony Conigliaro

Year	Team	AB	R	H	D	T	HR	TB	BI	W	K	SB	CS
1967*	BOS AL	6	0	0	0	0	0	0	0	0	2	0	0

Jeff Conine

Year	Team	AB	R	H	D	T	HR	TB	BI	W	K	SB	CS
1995	FLO NL	1	1	1	0	0	1	4	1	0	0	0	0

Gene Conley

Year	Team	AB	R	H	D	T	HR	TB	BI	W	K	SB	CS
1954	MIL NL	0	0	0	0	0	0	0	0	0	0	0	0
1955	MIL NL	0	0	0	0	0	0	0	0	0	0	0	0
1959-2	PHI NL	0	0	0	0	0	0	0	0	0	0	0	0
Totals	3 Yr	0	0	0	0	0	0	0	0	0	0	0	0

Sandy Consuegra

Year	Team	AB	R	H	D	T	HR	TB	BI	W	K	SB	CS
1954	CHA AL	0	0	0	0	0	0	0	0	0	0	0	0

Ron Coomer

Year	Team	AB	R	H	D	T	HR	TB	BI	W	K	SB	CS
1999	MIN AL	1	0	0	0	0	0	0	0	0	1	0	0

Cecil Cooper

Year	Team	AB	R	H	D	T	HR	TB	BI	W	K	SB	CS
1979	MIL AL	0	0	0	0	0	0	0	0	1	0	0	0
1980	MIL AL	1	0	0	0	0	0	0	0	0	0	0	0
1982*	MIL AL	2	0	1	0	0	0	1	0	0	1	0	0
1983	MIL AL	1	1	1	0	0	0	1	0	0	0	0	0
1985	MIL AL	0	0	0	0	0	0	0	0	1	0	0	0
Totals	5 Yr	4	1	2	0	0	0	2	0	2	1	0	0

Mort Cooper

Year	Team	AB	R	H	D	T	HR	TB	BI	W	K	SB	CS
1942*	SLN NL	0	0	0	0	0	0	0	0	0	0	0	0
1943*	SLN NL	1	0	0	0	0	0	0	0	0	0	0	0
Totals	2 Yr	1	0	0	0	0	0	0	0	0	0	0	0

Scott Cooper

Year	Team	AB	R	H	D	T	HR	TB	BI	W	K	SB	CS
1993	BOS AL	2	0	0	0	0	0	0	0	0	1	0	0
1994	BOS AL	2	1	1	1	0	0	2	1	0	0	0	0
Totals	2 Yr	4	1	1	1	0	0	2	1	0	1	0	0

Walker Cooper

Year	Team	AB	R	H	D	T	HR	TB	BI	W	K	SB	CS
1942*	SLN NL	2	0	1	0	0	0	1	0	0	0	0	0
1943*	SLN NL	2	0	1	0	0	0	1	0	0	0	0	0
1944*	SLN NL	5	1	2	0	0	0	2	1	0	1	0	0
1946*	NY NL	1	0	1	0	0	0	1	0	0	0	0	0
1947*	NY NL	3	0	0	0	0	0	0	0	0	1	0	0
1948*	NY NL	2	0	0	0	0	0	0	0	0	0	0	0
Totals	6 Yr	15	1	5	0	0	0	5	1	0	2	0	0

Joey Cora

Year	Team	AB	R	H	D	T	HR	TB	BI	W	K	SB	CS
1997	SEA AL	1	0	0	0	0	0	0	0	0	0	0	0

Wil Cordero

Year	Team	AB	R	H	D	T	HR	TB	BI	W	K	SB	CS
1994	MON NL	2	0	0	0	0	0	0	0	0	0	0	0

Pete Coscarart

Year	Team	AB	R	H	D	T	HR	TB	BI	W	K	SB	CS
1940	BRO NL	1	0	0	0	0	0	0	0	0	1	0	0

Doc Cramer

Year	Team	AB	R	H	D	T	HR	TB	BI	W	K	SB	CS
1935	PHA AL	0	0	0	0	0	0	0	0	0	0	0	0
1938	BOS AL	2	0	0	0	0	0	0	0	0	0	0	0
1939*	BOS AL	4	0	1	0	0	0	1	0	0	1	0	0
Totals	3 Yr	6	0	1	0	0	0	1	0	0	1	0	0

Del Crandall

Year	Team	AB	R	H	D	T	HR	TB	BI	W	K	SB	CS
1955*	MIL NL	1	0	0	0	0	0	0	0	0	0	0	0
1958*	MIL NL	4	0	0	0	0	0	0	0	0	0	0	0
1959-1*	MIL NL	3	1	1	0	0	0	1	1	0	1	0	0
1959-2*	MIL NL	2	0	1	0	0	0	1	0	0	0	0	0
1960-1*	MIL NL	3	1	2	0	0	1	5	1	0	0	0	0
1960-2*	MIL NL	2	0	0	0	0	0	0	0	0	0	0	0
1962-1*	MIL NL	4	0	0	0	0	0	0	0	0	0	0	0
1962-2*	MIL NL	1	0	0	0	0	0	0	0	0	0	0	0
Totals	8 Yr	20	2	4	0	0	1	7	2	0	1	0	0

Joe Cronin

Year	Team	AB	R	H	D	T	HR	TB	BI	W	K	SB	CS
1933*	WAS AL	3	1	1	0	0	0	1	0	1	0	0	0
1934*	WAS AL	5	1	2	1	0	0	3	2	0	1	0	1
1935*	BOS AL	4	0	0	0	0	0	0	1	0	1	0	0
1937*	BOS AL	4	1	1	0	0	0	2	0	0	0	0	0
1938*	BOS AL	3	0	2	1	0	0	3	1	1	0	0	0
1939*	BOS AL	4	0	1	0	0	0	1	0	0	1	0	0
1941*	BOS AL	2	0	0	0	0	0	0	0	0	1	0	0
Totals	7 Yr	25	3	7	3	0	0	10	4	2	4	0	1

Frankie Crosetti

Year	Team	AB	R	H	D	T	HR	TB	BI	W	K	SB	CS
1936	NYA AL	1	0	0	0	0	0	0	0	0	1	0	0

General Crowder

Year	Team	AB	R	H	D	T	HR	TB	BI	W	K	SB	CS
1933	WAS AL	1	0	0	0	0	0	0	0	0	0	0	0

Jose Cruz

Year	Team	AB	R	H	D	T	HR	TB	BI	W	K	SB	CS
1985	HOU NL	1	0	0	0	0	0	0	0	2	0	1	0

Tony Cuccinello

Year	Team	AB	R	H	D	T	HR	TB	BI	W	K	SB	CS
1933	BRO NL	1	0	0	0	0	0	0	0	0	1	0	0

Mike Cuellar

Year	Team	AB	R	H	D	T	HR	TB	BI	W	K	SB	CS
1967	HOU NL	0	0	0	0	0	0	0	0	0	0	0	0
1971	BAL AL	0	0	0	0	0	0	0	0	0	0	0	0
Totals	2 Yr	0	0	0	0	0	0	0	0	0	0	0	0

Roy Cullenbine

Year	Team	AB	R	H	D	T	HR	TB	BI	W	K	SB	CS
1941	SLA AL	1	0	0	0	0	0	0	0	0	0	0	0

Ray Culp

Year	Team	AB	R	H	D	T	HR	TB	BI	W	K	SB	CS
1963	PHI NL	0	0	0	0	0	0	0	0	0	0	0	0
1969	BOS AL	0	0	0	0	0	0	0	0	0	0	0	0
Totals	2 Yr	0	0	0	0	0	0	0	0	0	0	0	0

Joe Cunningham

Year	Team	AB	R	H	D	T	HR	TB	BI	W	K	SB	CS
1959-2	SLN NL	1	0	0	0	0	0	0	0	0	0	0	0

Kiki Cuyler

Year	Team	AB	R	H	D	T	HR	TB	BI	W	K	SB	CS
1934*	CHN NL	2	0	0	0	0	0	0	0	0	0	0	0

Babe Dahlgren

Year	Team	AB	R	H	D	T	HR	TB	BI	W	K	SB	CS
1943	PHI NL	2	0	0	0	0	0	0	0	0	0	0	0

Bud Daley

Year	Team	AB	R	H	D	T	HR	TB	BI	W	K	SB	CS
1959-1	KC AL	0	0	0	0	0	0	0	0	0	0	0	0
1960-1	KC AL	0	0	0	0	0	0	0	0	0	0	0	0
Totals	2 Yr	0	0	0	0	0	0	0	0	0	0	0	0

Year | Team | AB | R | H | D | T | HR | TB | BI | W | K | SB | CS

Harry Danning

Year	Team	AB	R	H	D	T	HR	TB	BI	W	K	SB	CS
1940	NY NL	1	0	1	0	0	0	1	1	0	0	0	0
1941	NY NL	1	0	0	0	0	0	0	0	0	0	0	0
Totals	2 Yr	2	0	1	0	0	0	1	1	0	0	0	0

Al Dark

Year	Team	AB	R	H	D	T	HR	TB	BI	W	K	SB	CS
1951*	NY NL	5	0	1	0	0	0	1	0	0	0	0	0
1954*	NY NL	5	0	1	0	0	0	1	0	0	0	0	0
Totals	2 Yr	10	0	2	0	0	0	2	0	0	0	0	0

Darren Daulton

Year	Team	AB	R	H	D	T	HR	TB	BI	W	K	SB	CS
1992	PHI NL	3	1	0	0	0	0	0	0	0	0	0	0
1993*	PHI NL	3	0	0	0	0	0	0	0	0	1	0	0
1995	PHI NL	0	0	0	0	0	0	0	0	0	0	0	0
Totals	3 Yr	6	1	0	0	0	0	0	0	0	1	0	0

Vic Davalillo

Year	Team	AB	R	H	D	T	HR	TB	BI	W	K	SB	CS
1965*	CLE AL	2	0	1	0	0	0	1	0	0	0	0	0

Jim Davenport

Year	Team	AB	R	H	D	T	HR	TB	BI	W	K	SB	CS
1962–1	SFN NL	1	0	1	0	0	0	1	0	0	0	0	0

Alvin Davis

Year	Team	AB	R	H	D	T	HR	TB	BI	W	K	SB	CS
1984	SEA AL	1	0	0	0	0	0	0	0	0	1	0	0

Chili Davis

Year	Team	AB	R	H	D	T	HR	TB	BI	W	K	SB	CS
1984	SFN NL	1	0	0	0	0	0	0	0	0	0	0	0
1986	SFN NL	1	0	0	0	0	0	0	0	0	1	0	0
1994	CAL AL	1	0	0	0	0	0	0	0	0	0	0	0
Totals	3 Yr	3	0	0	0	0	0	0	0	0	1	0	0

Curt Davis

Year	Team	AB	R	H	D	T	HR	TB	BI	W	K	SB	CS
1936	CHN NL	0	0	0	0	0	0	0	0	0	0	0	0

Eric Davis

Year	Team	AB	R	H	D	T	HR	TB	BI	W	K	SB	CS
1987*	CIN NL	3	0	0	0	0	0	0	0	0	1	0	0
1989*	CIN NL	2	0	0	0	0	0	0	0	1	0	1	0
Totals	2 Yr	5	0	0	0	0	0	0	0	1	1	1	0

Glenn Davis

Year	Team	AB	R	H	D	T	HR	TB	BI	W	K	SB	CS
1986	HOU NL	1	0	0	0	0	0	0	0	0	0	0	0
1989	HOU NL	1	1	1	0	0	0	1	0	1	0	0	0
Totals	2 Yr	2	1	1	0	0	0	1	0	1	0	0	0

Jody Davis

Year	Team	AB	R	H	D	T	HR	TB	BI	W	K	SB	CS
1984	CHN NL	1	0	0	0	0	0	0	0	0	0	0	0
1986	CHN NL	1	0	1	0	0	0	1	0	0	0	0	0
Totals	2 Yr	2	0	1	0	0	0	1	0	0	0	0	0

Mark Davis

Year	Team	AB	R	H	D	T	HR	TB	BI	W	K	SB	CS
1988	SDN NL	0	0	0	0	0	0	0	0	0	0	0	0

Ron Davis

Year	Team	AB	R	H	D	T	HR	TB	BI	W	K	SB	CS
1981	NYA AL	0	0	0	0	0	0	0	0	0	0	0	0

Tommy Davis

Year	Team	AB	R	H	D	T	HR	TB	BI	W	K	SB	CS
1962–1*	LAN NL	4	0	0	0	0	0	0	0	0	0	0	0
1962–2*	LAN NL	1	0	0	0	0	0	0	0	0	0	0	0
1963*	LAN NL	3	1	1	0	0	0	1	0	1	0	0	0
Totals	3 Yr	8	1	1	0	0	0	1	0	1	0	0	0

Willie Davis

Year	Team	AB	R	H	D	T	HR	TB	BI	W	K	SB	CS
1971	LAN NL	1	0	1	0	0	0	1	0	0	0	0	0
1973	LAN NL	2	1	2	0	0	1	5	2	0	0	0	0
Totals	2 Yr	3	1	3	0	0	1	6	2	0	0	0	0

Bill Dawley

Year	Team	AB	R	H	D	T	HR	TB	BI	W	K	SB	CS
1983	HOU NL	0	0	0	0	0	0	0	0	0	0	0	0

Andre Dawson

Year	Team	AB	R	H	D	T	HR	TB	BI	W	K	SB	CS
1981*	MON NL	4	0	1	0	0	0	1	0	0	1	1	0
1982*	MON NL	4	0	1	0	0	0	1	0	0	0	0	0
1983*	MON NL	3	0	0	0	0	0	0	0	0	1	0	0
1987*	CHN NL	3	0	1	1	0	0	2	0	0	1	0	0
1988*	CHN NL	2	0	1	0	0	0	1	0	0	0	0	0
1989	CHN NL	1	0	0	0	0	0	0	0	0	0	0	0
1990*	CHN NL	2	0	0	0	0	0	0	0	0	1	0	0
1991*	CHN NL	2	1	1	0	0	1	4	1	0	0	0	0
Totals	8 Yr	21	1	5	1	0	1	9	1	0	4	1	0

Dizzy Dean

Year	Team	AB	R	H	D	T	HR	TB	BI	W	K	SB	CS
1934	SLN NL	1	0	0	0	0	0	0	0	0	0	0	0
1935	SLN NL	0	0	0	0	0	0	0	0	0	0	0	0
1936*	SLN NL	1	0	0	0	0	0	0	0	0	1	0	0
1937*	SLN NL	1	0	0	0	0	0	0	0	0	0	0	0
Totals	4 Yr	3	0	0	0	0	0	0	0	0	1	0	0

Doug DeCinces

Year	Team	AB	R	H	D	T	HR	TB	BI	W	K	SB	CS
1983	CAL AL	1	0	0	0	0	0	0	0	0	0	0	0

Carlos Delgado

Year	Team	AB	R	H	D	T	HR	TB	BI	W	K	SB	CS
2000	TOR AL	1	0	1	1	0	0	2	0	0	0	0	0

Frank Demaree

Year	Team	AB	R	H	D	T	HR	TB	BI	W	K	SB	CS
1936*	CHN NL	3	1	1	0	0	0	1	0	0	0	0	0
1937*	CHN NL	5	0	1	0	0	0	1	0	0	0	0	0
Totals	2 Yr	8	1	2	0	0	0	2	0	0	0	0	0

Bucky Dent

Year	Team	AB	R	H	D	T	HR	TB	BI	W	K	SB	CS
1975	CHA AL	1	0	0	0	0	0	0	0	0	1	0	0
1980	NYA AL	2	0	1	0	0	0	1	0	0	1	0	0
1981*	NYA AL	2	0	2	1	0	0	3	0	0	0	0	0
Totals	3 Yr	5	0	3	1	0	0	4	0	0	2	0	0

Paul Derringer

Year	Team	AB	R	H	D	T	HR	TB	BI	W	K	SB	CS
1935	CIN NL	0	0	0	0	0	0	0	0	0	0	0	0
1939*	CIN NL	1	0	0	0	0	0	0	0	0	1	0	0
1940*	CIN NL	1	0	0	0	0	0	0	0	0	1	0	0
1941	CIN NL	0	0	0	0	0	0	0	0	0	0	0	0
Totals	4 Yr	2	0	0	0	0	0	0	0	0	2	0	0

Bo Diaz

Year	Team	AB	R	H	D	T	HR	TB	BI	W	K	SB	CS
1981	CLE AL	1	0	0	0	0	0	0	0	0	1	0	0
1987	CIN NL	1	0	0	0	0	0	0	0	0	0	0	0
Totals	2 Yr	2	0	0	0	0	0	0	0	0	1	0	0

Rob Dibble

Year	Team	AB	R	H	D	T	HR	TB	BI	W	K	SB	CS
1990	CIN NL	0	0	0	0	0	0	0	0	0	0	0	0

Bill Dickey

Year	Team	AB	R	H	D	T	HR	TB	BI	W	K	SB	CS
1934*	NYA AL	2	1	1	0	0	0	1	0	2	1	0	0

Year	Team	AB	R	H	D	T	HR	TB	BI	W	K	SB	CS

Bill Dickey continued

Year	Team	AB	R	H	D	T	HR	TB	BI	W	K	SB	CS
1936	NYA AL	2	0	0	0	0	0	0	0	0	0	0	0
1937*	NYA AL	3	1	2	1	0	0	3	1	1	0	0	0
1938*	NYA AL	4	0	1	1	0	0	2	0	0	0	0	0
1939*	NYA AL	3	1	0	0	0	0	0	0	1	0	0	0
1940*	NYA AL	1	0	0	0	0	0	0	0	0	0	0	0
1941*	NYA AL	3	0	1	0	0	0	1	0	0	0	0	0
1946	NYA AL	1	0	0	0	0	0	0	0	0	1	0	0
Totals	8 Yr	19	3	5	2	0	0	7	1	4	2	0	0

Murry Dickson

Year	Team	AB	R	H	D	T	HR	TB	BI	W	K	SB	CS
1953	PIT NL	1	0	1	0	0	0	0	1	1	0	0	0

Larry Dierker

Year	Team	AB	R	H	D	T	HR	TB	BI	W	K	SB	CS
1969	HOU NL	0	0	0	0	0	0	0	0	0	0	0	0

Dick Dietz

Year	Team	AB	R	H	D	T	HR	TB	BI	W	K	SB	CS
1970	SFN NL	2	1	1	0	0	1	4	1	0	0	0	0

Bob Dillinger

Year	Team	AB	R	H	D	T	HR	TB	BI	W	K	SB	CS
1949	SLA AL	1	2	1	0	0	0	1	1	0	0	0	0

Dom DiMaggio

Year	Team	AB	R	H	D	T	HR	TB	BI	W	K	SB	CS
1941	BOS AL	1	0	1	0	0	0	1	1	0	0	0	0
1946*	BOS AL	2	0	1	0	0	0	1	0	0	0	0	0
1949*	BOS AL	5	2	2	1	0	0	3	1	0	1	0	0
1950	BOS AL	2	0	0	0	0	0	0	0	0	0	0	0
1951*	BOS AL	5	0	1	0	0	0	1	0	0	2	0	0
1952*	BOS AL	2	0	1	1	0	0	2	0	1	1	0	0
Totals	6 Yr	17	2	6	2	0	0	8	2	1	4	0	0

Joe DiMaggio

Year	Team	AB	R	H	D	T	HR	TB	BI	W	K	SB	CS
1936*	NYA AL	5	0	0	0	0	0	0	0	0	0	0	0
1937*	NYA AL	4	1	1	0	0	0	1	0	1	2	0	0
1938*	NYA AL	4	1	1	0	0	0	1	0	0	1	1	0
1939*	NYA AL	4	1	1	0	0	1	4	1	0	0	0	0
1940*	NYA AL	4	0	0	0	0	0	0	0	0	0	0	0
1941*	NYA AL	4	3	1	1	0	0	2	1	1	0	0	0
1942*	NYA AL	4	0	2	0	0	0	2	0	0	0	0	0
1947*	NYA AL	3	0	1	0	0	0	1	0	1	0	0	0
1948	NYA AL	1	0	0	0	0	0	0	1	0	0	0	0
1949*	NYA AL	4	1	2	1	0	0	3	3	0	0	0	0
1950	NYA AL	3	0	0	0	0	0	0	0	0	0	0	0
Totals	11 Yr	40	7	9	2	0	1	14	6	3	3	1	0

Vince DiMaggio

Year	Team	AB	R	H	D	T	HR	TB	BI	W	K	SB	CS
1943	PIT NL	3	2	3	0	1	1	8	1	0	0	0	0
1944	PIT NL	0	0	0	0	0	0	0	0	0	0	0	0
Totals	2 Yr	3	2	3	0	1	1	8	1	0	0	0	0

Gary Disarcina

Year	Team	AB	R	H	D	T	HR	TB	BI	W	K	SB	CS
1995	CAL AL	1	0	0	0	0	0	0	0	0	0	0	0

Larry Doby

Year	Team	AB	R	H	D	T	HR	TB	BI	W	K	SB	CS
1949	CLE AL	1	0	0	0	0	0	0	0	0	0	0	0
1950*	CLE AL	6	1	2	1	0	0	3	0	0	2	0	0
1951	CLE AL	1	0	0	0	0	0	0	0	0	0	0	0
1952	CLE AL	0	0	0	0	0	0	0	0	0	0	0	0
1953	CLE AL	1	0	0	0	0	0	0	0	0	0	0	0

Larry Doby continued

Year	Team	AB	R	H	D	T	HR	TB	BI	W	K	SB	CS
1954	CLE AL	1	1	1	0	0	1	4	1	0	0	0	0
Totals	6 Yr	10	2	3	1	0	1	7	1	0	2	0	0

Bobby Doerr

Year	Team	AB	R	H	D	T	HR	TB	BI	W	K	SB	CS
1941*	BOS AL	3	0	0	0	0	0	0	0	0	1	0	0
1943*	BOS AL	4	1	2	0	0	1	5	3	0	0	0	0
1944*	BOS AL	3	0	0	0	0	0	0	0	0	1	0	0
1946*	BOS AL	2	0	0	0	0	0	0	0	0	0	0	0
1947	BOS AL	2	1	1	0	0	0	1	0	0	0	1	0
1948	BOS AL	2	0	0	0	0	0	0	0	0	1	0	0
1950*	BOS AL	3	0	0	0	0	0	0	0	0	0	0	0
1951	BOS AL	1	0	1	0	0	0	1	0	1	0	0	0
Totals	8 Yr	20	2	4	0	0	1	7	3	1	3	1	0

Dick Donovan

Year	Team	AB	R	H	D	T	HR	TB	BI	W	K	SB	CS
1961-1	WAS AL	0	0	0	0	0	0	0	0	0	0	0	0
1962-1	CLE AL	0	0	0	0	0	0	0	0	0	0	0	0
Totals	2 Yr	0	0	0	0	0	0	0	0	0	0	0	0

Richard Dotson

Year	Team	AB	R	H	D	T	HR	TB	BI	W	K	SB	CS
1984	CHA AL	0	0	0	0	0	0	0	0	0	0	0	0

Al Downing

Year	Team	AB	R	H	D	T	HR	TB	BI	W	K	SB	CS
1967	NYA AL	0	0	0	0	0	0	0	0	0	0	0	0

Brian Downing

Year	Team	AB	R	H	D	T	HR	TB	BI	W	K	SB	CS
1979	CAL AL	1	0	1	0	0	0	1	0	0	0	0	0

Doug Drabek

Year	Team	AB	R	H	D	T	HR	TB	BI	W	K	SB	CS
1994	HOU NL	0	0	0	0	0	0	0	0	0	0	0	0

Dave Dravecky

Year	Team	AB	R	H	D	T	HR	TB	BI	W	K	SB	CS
1983	SDN NL	0	0	0	0	0	0	0	0	0	0	0	0

Walt Dropo

Year	Team	AB	R	H	D	T	HR	TB	BI	W	K	SB	CS
1950*	BOS AL	3	0	1	0	1	0	3	0	0	0	0	0

Don Drysdale

Year	Team	AB	R	H	D	T	HR	TB	BI	W	K	SB	CS
1959-1*	LAN NL	1	0	0	0	0	0	0	0	0	1	0	0
1959-2*	LAN NL	0	0	0	0	0	0	0	0	0	0	0	0
1962-1*	LAN NL	1	0	0	0	0	0	0	0	0	1	0	0
1963	LAN NL	0	0	0	0	0	0	0	0	0	0	0	0
1964*	LAN NL	0	0	0	0	0	0	0	0	0	0	0	0
1965	LAN NL	0	0	0	0	0	0	0	0	0	0	0	0
1967	LAN NL	0	0	0	0	0	0	0	0	0	0	0	0
1968*	LAN NL	1	0	0	0	0	0	0	0	0	0	0	0
Totals	8 Yr	3	0	0	0	0	0	0	0	0	2	0	0

Mariano Duncan

Year	Team	AB	R	H	D	T	HR	TB	BI	W	K	SB	CS
1994*	PHI NL	1	0	0	0	0	0	0	0	0	0	0	0

Shawon Dunston

Year	Team	AB	R	H	D	T	HR	TB	BI	W	K	SB	CS
1990	CHN NL	2	0	0	0	0	0	0	0	0	0	0	0

Ryne Duren

Year	Team	AB	R	H	D	T	HR	TB	BI	W	K	SB	CS
1959-1	NYA AL	1	0	0	0	0	0	0	0	0	1	0	0

Leon Durham

Year	Team	AB	R	H	D	T	HR	TB	BI	W	K	SB	CS
1983	CHN NL	2	0	0	0	0	0	0	0	0	1	0	0

Year	Team	AB	R	H	D	T	HR	TB	BI	W	K	SB	CS

Ray Durham

Year	Team	AB	R	H	D	T	HR	TB	BI	W	K	SB	CS
1998	CHA AL	1	1	1	0	0	0	1	1	0	0	1	0
2000	CHA AL	2	1	1	0	0	0	1	0	0	0	0	0
Totals	2 Yr	3	2	2	0	0	0	2	1	0	0	1	0

Leo Durocher

Year	Team	AB	R	H	D	T	HR	TB	BI	W	K	SB	CS
1936*	SLN NL	3	0	1	0	0	0	1	0	0	1	0	0
1938*	BRO NL	2	1	0	0	0	0	0	0	0	1	0	0
Totals	2 Yr	5	1	1	0	0	0	1	0	0	2	0	0

Jermaine Dye

Year	Team	AB	R	H	D	T	HR	TB	BI	W	K	SB	CS
2000*	KCA AL	2	1	0	0	0	0	0	0	1	1	0	0

Jimmy Dykes

Year	Team	AB	R	H	D	T	HR	TB	BI	W	K	SB	CS
1933*	CHA AL	3	1	2	0	0	0	2	0	1	0	0	0

Lenny Dykstra

Year	Team	AB	R	H	D	T	HR	TB	BI	W	K	SB	CS
1990*	PHI NL	4	0	1	0	0	0	1	0	0	0	0	0
1995*	PHI NL	2	0	0	0	0	0	0	0	1	0	0	1
Totals	2 Yr	6	0	1	0	0	0	1	0	1	0	0	1

Jake Early

Year	Team	AB	R	H	D	T	HR	TB	BI	W	K	SB	CS
1943*	WAS AL	2	1	0	0	0	0	0	0	1	1	0	0

Mike Easler

Year	Team	AB	R	H	D	T	HR	TB	BI	W	K	SB	CS
1981	PIT NL	1	1	0	0	0	0	0	0	1	0	0	0

Damion Easley

Year	Team	AB	R	H	D	T	HR	TB	BI	W	K	SB	CS
1998	DET AL	1	1	1	0	0	0	1	0	0	0	0	0

Dennis Eckersley

Year	Team	AB	R	H	D	T	HR	TB	BI	W	K	SB	CS
1977	CLE AL	0	0	0	0	0	0	0	0	0	0	0	0
1982*	BOS AL	1	0	0	0	0	0	0	0	0	0	0	0
1988	OAK AL	0	0	0	0	0	0	0	0	0	0	0	0
1990	OAK AL	0	0	0	0	0	0	0	0	0	0	0	0
1992	OAK AL	0	0	0	0	0	0	0	0	0	0	0	0
Totals	5 Yr	1	0	0	0	0	0	0	0	0	0	0	0

Jim Edmonds

Year	Team	AB	R	H	D	T	HR	TB	BI	W	K	SB	CS
1995	CAL AL	1	0	0	0	0	0	0	0	0	1	0	0
2000*	SLN NL	2	0	1	0	0	0	1	0	0	0	0	0
Totals	2 Yr	3	0	1	0	0	0	1	0	0	1	0	0

Bruce Edwards

Year	Team	AB	R	H	D	T	HR	TB	BI	W	K	SB	CS
1947	BRO NL	0	0	0	0	0	0	0	0	0	0	0	0

Johnny Edwards

Year	Team	AB	R	H	D	T	HR	TB	BI	W	K	SB	CS
1963	CIN NL	2	0	0	0	0	0	0	0	0	0	0	0
1964	CIN NL	1	1	0	0	0	0	0	0	1	1	0	0
Totals	2 Yr	3	1	0	0	0	0	0	0	1	1	0	0

Bob Elliott

Year	Team	AB	R	H	D	T	HR	TB	BI	W	K	SB	CS
1941	PIT NL	1	0	0	0	0	0	0	0	0	0	0	0
1942	PIT NL	1	0	1	0	0	0	1	0	0	0	0	0
1944*	PIT NL	3	0	0	0	0	0	0	0	0	0	0	0
1948	BSN NL	2	0	1	0	0	0	1	0	0	0	0	0
1951*	BSN NL	2	1	1	0	0	1	4	2	0	0	0	0
Totals	5 Yr	9	1	3	0	0	1	6	2	0	0	0	0

Dock Ellis

Year	Team	AB	R	H	D	T	HR	TB	BI	W	K	SB	CS
1971*	PIT NL	1	0	0	0	0	0	0	0	0	1	0	0

Don Elston

Year	Team	AB	R	H	D	T	HR	TB	BI	W	K	SB	CS
1959-1	CHN NL	0	0	0	0	0	0	0	0	0	0	0	0

Woody English

Year	Team	AB	R	H	D	T	HR	TB	BI	W	K	SB	CS
1933	CHN NL	1	0	0	0	0	0	0	0	0	0	0	0

Del Ennis

Year	Team	AB	R	H	D	T	HR	TB	BI	W	K	SB	CS
1946	PHI NL	2	0	0	0	0	0	0	0	0	2	0	0
1951*	PHI NL	2	0	0	0	0	0	0	0	0	1	0	0
1955*	PHI NL	1	0	0	0	0	0	0	0	0	1	0	0
Totals	3 Yr	5	0	0	0	0	0	0	0	0	4	0	0

Carl Erskine

Year	Team	AB	R	H	D	T	HR	TB	BI	W	K	SB	CS
1954	BRO NL	0	0	0	0	0	0	0	0	0	0	0	0

Darin Erstad

Year	Team	AB	R	H	D	T	HR	TB	BI	W	K	SB	CS
1998	ANA AL	2	1	0	0	0	0	0	0	0	0	0	0
2000	ANA AL	2	0	0	0	0	0	0	1	0	0	0	0
Totals	2 Yr	4	1	0	0	0	0	0	1	0	0	0	0

Chuck Estrada

Year	Team	AB	R	H	D	T	HR	TB	BI	W	K	SB	CS
1960-1	BAL AL	0	0	0	0	0	0	0	0	0	0	0	0

Darrell Evans

Year	Team	AB	R	H	D	T	HR	TB	BI	W	K	SB	CS
1973	ATL NL	0	0	0	0	0	0	0	0	1	0	0	0
1983	SFN NL	1	0	0	0	0	0	0	0	0	0	0	0
Totals	2 Yr	1	0	0	0	0	0	0	0	1	0	0	0

Dwight Evans

Year	Team	AB	R	H	D	T	HR	TB	BI	W	K	SB	CS
1978	BOS AL	1	0	0	0	0	0	0	0	0	1	0	0
1981	BOS AL	2	1	1	0	0	0	1	0	1	0	0	0
1987	BOS AL	2	0	2	0	0	0	2	0	1	0	0	0
Totals	3 Yr	5	1	3	0	0	0	3	0	2	1	0	0

Carl Everett

Year	Team	AB	R	H	D	T	HR	TB	BI	W	K	SB	CS
2000*	BOS AL	2	0	0	0	0	0	0	1	1	0	0	0

Hoot Evers

Year	Team	AB	R	H	D	T	HR	TB	BI	W	K	SB	CS
1948*	DET AL	4	1	1	0	0	1	4	1	0	1	0	0
1950*	DET AL	2	0	0	0	0	0	0	0	1	1	0	0
Totals	2 Yr	6	1	1	0	0	1	4	1	1	2	0	0

Roy Face

Year	Team	AB	R	H	D	T	HR	TB	BI	W	K	SB	CS
1959-1	PIT NL	0	0	0	0	0	0	0	0	0	0	0	0
1959-2	PIT NL	0	0	0	0	0	0	0	0	0	0	0	0
1960-1	PIT NL	0	0	0	0	0	0	0	0	0	0	0	0
1961-1	PIT NL	0	0	0	0	0	0	0	0	0	0	0	0
Totals	4 Yr	0	0	0	0	0	0	0	0	0	0	0	0

Ferris Fain

Year	Team	AB	R	H	D	T	HR	TB	BI	W	K	SB	CS
1950	PHA AL	3	0	1	0	0	0	1	0	0	0	0	0
1951*	PHA AL	3	0	1	0	1	0	3	1	0	1	0	0
1953	CHA AL	1	1	1	0	0	0	1	0	0	0	0	0
Totals	3 Yr	7	1	3	0	1	0	5	1	0	1	0	0

Ron Fairly

Year	Team	AB	R	H	D	T	HR	TB	BI	W	K	SB	CS
1973	MON NL	0	0	0	0	0	0	0	0	0	0	0	0

Ron Fairly *continued*

Year	Team	AB	R	H	D	T	HR	TB	BI	W	K	SB	CS
1977	TOR AL	1	0	0	0	0	0	0	0	0	1	0	0
Totals	2 Yr	1	0	0	0	0	0	0	0	0	1	0	0

Ed Farmer

Year	Team	AB	R	H	D	T	HR	TB	BI	W	K	SB	CS
1980	CHA AL	0	0	0	0	0	0	0	0	0	0	0	0

Turk Farrell

Year	Team	AB	R	H	D	T	HR	TB	BI	W	K	SB	CS
1958	PHI NL	0	0	0	0	0	0	0	0	0	0	0	0
1962-2	HOU NL	0	0	0	0	0	0	0	0	0	0	0	0
1964	HOU NL	0	0	0	0	0	0	0	0	0	0	0	0
1965	HOU NL	0	0	0	0	0	0	0	0	0	0	0	0
Totals	4 Yr	0	0	0	0	0	0	0	0	0	0	0	0

Bob Feller

Year	Team	AB	R	H	D	T	HR	TB	BI	W	K	SB	CS
1939	CLE AL	1	0	0	0	0	0	0	0	0	1	0	0
1940	CLE AL	1	0	0	0	0	0	0	0	0	1	0	0
1941*	CLE AL	0	0	0	0	0	0	0	0	0	0	0	0
1946*	CLE AL	0	0	0	0	0	0	0	0	0	0	0	0
1950	CLE AL	0	0	0	0	0	0	0	0	0	0	0	0
Totals	5 Yr	2	0	0	0	0	0	0	0	0	2	0	0

Sid Fernandez

Year	Team	AB	R	H	D	T	HR	TB	BI	W	K	SB	CS
1986	NYN NL	0	0	0	0	0	0	0	0	0	0	0	0
1987	NYN NL	0	0	0	0	0	0	0	0	0	0	0	0
Totals	2 Yr	0	0	0	0	0	0	0	0	0	0	0	0

Tony Fernandez

Year	Team	AB	R	H	D	T	HR	TB	BI	W	K	SB	CS
1986	TOR AL	0	0	0	0	0	0	0	0	0	0	0	0
1987	TOR AL	2	0	0	0	0	0	0	0	0	1	0	0
1989	TOR AL	1	0	0	0	0	0	0	0	0	0	0	0
1992	SDN NL	2	1	1	0	0	0	1	0	0	0	0	0
1999	TOR AL	2	0	0	0	0	0	0	0	0	1	0	0
Totals	5 Yr	7	1	1	0	0	0	1	0	0	2	0	0

Rick Ferrell

Year	Team	AB	R	H	D	T	HR	TB	BI	W	K	SB	CS
1933*	BOS AL	3	0	0	0	0	0	0	0	0	0	0	0
1936*	BOS AL	2	0	0	0	0	0	0	0	0	2	0	0
Totals	2 Yr	5	0	0	0	0	0	0	0	0	2	0	0

Lou Fette

Year	Team	AB	R	H	D	T	HR	TB	BI	W	K	SB	CS
1939	BSN NL	0	0	0	0	0	0	0	0	0	0	0	0

Mark Fidrych

Year	Team	AB	R	H	D	T	HR	TB	BI	W	K	SB	CS
1976*	DET AL	0	0	0	0	0	0	0	0	0	0	0	0

Cecil Fielder

Year	Team	AB	R	H	D	T	HR	TB	BI	W	K	SB	CS
1990	DET AL	1	0	0	0	0	0	0	0	0	1	0	0
1991*	DET AL	3	0	0	0	0	0	0	0	1	0	0	0
1993	DET AL	1	0	0	0	0	0	0	0	0	0	0	0
Totals	3 Yr	5	0	0	0	0	0	0	0	1	1	0	0

Rollie Fingers

Year	Team	AB	R	H	D	T	HR	TB	BI	W	K	SB	CS
1973	OAK AL	0	0	0	0	0	0	0	0	0	0	0	0
1974	OAK AL	0	0	0	0	0	0	0	0	0	0	0	0
1978	SDN NL	0	0	0	0	0	0	0	0	0	0	0	0
1981	MIL AL	0	0	0	0	0	0	0	0	0	0	0	0
1982	MIL AL	0	0	0	0	0	0	0	0	0	0	0	0
Totals	5 Yr	0	0	0	0	0	0	0	0	0	0	0	0

Jim Finigan

Year	Team	AB	R	H	D	T	HR	TB	BI	W	K	SB	CS
1955*	KC AL	3	0	0	0	0	0	0	0	0	1	0	0

Chuck Finley

Year	Team	AB	R	H	D	T	HR	TB	BI	W	K	SB	CS
1990	CAL AL	0	0	0	0	0	0	0	0	0	0	0	0
1996	CAL AL	0	0	0	0	0	0	0	0	0	0	0	0
Totals	2 Yr	0	0	0	0	0	0	0	0	0	0	0	0

Steve Finley

Year	Team	AB	R	H	D	T	HR	TB	BI	W	K	SB	CS
1997	SDN NL	1	0	0	0	0	0	0	0	0	1	0	0
2000	ARI NL	1	0	1	0	0	0	1	1	0	0	0	0
Totals	2 Yr	2	0	1	0	0	0	1	1	0	1	0	0

Lou Finney

Year	Team	AB	R	H	D	T	HR	TB	BI	W	K	SB	CS
1940	BOS AL	0	0	0	0	0	0	0	0	1	0	0	0

Eddie Fisher

Year	Team	AB	R	H	D	T	HR	TB	BI	W	K	SB	CS
1965	CHA AL	0	0	0	0	0	0	0	0	0	0	0	0

Carlton Fisk

Year	Team	AB	R	H	D	T	HR	TB	BI	W	K	SB	CS
1972	BOS AL	2	1	1	0	0	0	1	0	0	1	0	0
1973*	BOS AL	2	0	0	0	0	0	0	0	0	0	0	0
1976	BOS AL	1	0	0	0	0	0	0	0	0	0	0	0
1977*	BOS AL	2	0	0	0	0	0	0	0	0	1	0	0
1978*	BOS AL	2	0	0	0	0	0	0	1	0	0	0	0
1980*	BOS AL	2	0	0	0	0	0	0	0	0	2	0	0
1981*	CHA AL	3	1	1	0	0	0	1	0	0	1	0	0
1982*	CHA AL	2	0	0	0	0	0	0	0	0	1	0	0
1985*	CHA AL	2	0	0	0	0	0	0	0	0	0	0	0
1991	CHA AL	2	0	1	0	0	0	1	0	0	1	0	0
Totals	10 Yr	20	2	3	0	0	0	3	1	0	7	0	0

Darrin Fletcher

Year	Team	AB	R	H	D	T	HR	TB	BI	W	K	SB	CS
1994	MON NL	0	0	0	0	0	0	0	0	0	0	0	0

Elbie Fletcher

Year	Team	AB	R	H	D	T	HR	TB	BI	W	K	SB	CS
1943*	PIT NL	2	0	0	0	0	0	0	0	0	0	0	0

Curt Flood

Year	Team	AB	R	H	D	T	HR	TB	BI	W	K	SB	CS
1964	SLN NL	0	1	0	0	0	0	0	0	0	0	0	0
1966	SLN NL	1	0	0	0	0	0	0	0	0	0	0	0
1968*	SLN NL	1	0	0	0	0	0	0	0	0	2	0	0
Totals	3 Yr	2	1	0	0	0	0	0	0	0	2	0	0

Hank Foiles

Year	Team	AB	R	H	D	T	HR	TB	BI	W	K	SB	CS
1957	PIT NL	1	1	1	0	0	0	1	0	0	0	0	0

Whitey Ford

Year	Team	AB	R	H	D	T	HR	TB	BI	W	K	SB	CS
1954*	NYA AL	1	0	0	0	0	0	0	0	0	1	0	0
1955	NYA AL	1	0	0	0	0	0	0	0	0	1	0	0
1956	NYA AL	0	0	0	0	0	0	0	0	0	0	0	0
1959-1	NYA AL	0	0	0	0	0	0	0	0	0	0	0	0
1960-2*	NYA AL	0	0	0	0	0	0	0	0	0	0	0	0
1961-1*	NYA AL	1	0	0	0	0	0	0	0	0	0	0	0
Totals	6 Yr	3	0	0	0	0	0	0	0	0	2	0	0

Mike Fornieles

Year	Team	AB	R	H	D	T	HR	TB	BI	W	K	SB	CS
1961-1	BOS AL	0	0	0	0	0	0	0	0	0	0	0	0

Year	Team	AB	R	H	D	T	HR	TB	BI	W	K	SB	CS

Ken Forsch

Year	Team	AB	R	H	D	T	HR	TB	BI	W	K	SB	CS
1976	HOU NL	0	0	0	0	0	0	0	0	0	0	0	0
1981	CAL AL	0	0	0	0	0	0	0	0	0	0	0	0
Totals	2 Yr	0	0	0	0	0	0	0	0	0	0	0	0

Ray Fosse

Year	Team	AB	R	H	D	T	HR	TB	BI	W	K	SB	CS
1970	CLE AL	2	1	1	0	0	0	1	1	1	0	0	0

George Foster

Year	Team	AB	R	H	D	T	HR	TB	BI	W	K	SB	CS
1976*	CIN NL	3	1	1	0	0	1	4	3	0	0	0	0
1977*	CIN NL	3	1	1	1	0	0	2	1	0	1	0	0
1978*	CIN NL	2	1	0	0	0	0	0	0	2	1	0	0
1979*	CIN NL	1	0	1	1	0	0	2	1	0	0	0	0
1981*	CIN NL	2	0	0	0	0	0	0	0	0	0	0	0
Totals	5 Yr	11	3	3	2	0	1	8	5	2	2	0	0

Nellie Fox

Year	Team	AB	R	H	D	T	HR	TB	BI	W	K	SB	CS
1951*	CHA AL	3	0	1	0	0	0	1	0	0	0	0	0
1953	CHA AL	1	0	0	0	0	0	0	0	0	0	0	0
1954	CHA AL	2	0	1	0	0	0	1	2	0	1	0	0
1955*	CHA AL	3	1	1	0	0	0	1	0	0	0	0	0
1956*	CHA AL	4	1	2	0	0	0	2	0	0	0	0	0
1957*	CHA AL	4	0	0	0	0	0	0	0	0	0	0	0
1958*	CHA AL	4	1	2	0	0	0	2	1	0	0	0	0
1959-1*	CHA AL	5	1	2	0	0	0	2	0	0	1	0	0
1959-2*	CHA AL	4	1	2	0	0	0	2	1	1	0	0	0
1960-1	CHA AL	2	0	1	0	0	0	1	1	0	0	0	0
1960-2	CHA AL	3	0	1	0	0	0	1	0	0	0	0	0
1961-1	CHA AL	0	2	0	0	0	0	0	0	1	0	0	0
1963*	CHA AL	3	0	1	0	0	0	1	0	0	1	0	0
Totals	13 Yr	38	7	14	0	0	0	14	5	2	3	0	0

Jimmie Foxx

Year	Team	AB	R	H	D	T	HR	TB	BI	W	K	SB	CS
1934*	PHA AL	5	1	2	1	0	0	3	1	0	2	0	0
1935*	PHA AL	3	1	2	0	0	1	5	3	1	1	0	0
1936	BOS AL	2	1	1	0	0	0	1	0	0	1	0	0
1937	BOS AL	1	0	0	0	0	0	0	0	0	0	0	0
1938*	BOS AL	4	0	1	0	0	0	1	0	0	1	0	0
1940*	BOS AL	3	0	0	0	0	0	0	0	0	1	0	0
1941	BOS AL	1	0	0	0	0	0	0	0	0	1	0	0
Totals	7 Yr	19	3	6	1	0	1	10	4	1	7	0	0

John Franco

Year	Team	AB	R	H	D	T	HR	TB	BI	W	K	SB	CS
1987	CIN NL	0	0	0	0	0	0	0	0	0	0	0	0
1990	NYN NL	0	0	0	0	0	0	0	0	0	0	0	0
Totals	2 Yr	0	0	0	0	0	0	0	0	0	0	0	0

Julio Franco

Year	Team	AB	R	H	D	T	HR	TB	BI	W	K	SB	CS
1989*	TEX AL	3	0	1	0	0	0	1	0	0	0	0	0
1990	TEX AL	3	0	1	1	0	0	2	2	0	0	0	0
Totals	2 Yr	6	0	2	1	0	0	3	2	0	0	0	0

Fred Frankhouse

Year	Team	AB	R	H	D	T	HR	TB	BI	W	K	SB	CS
1934	BSN NL	1	0	0	0	0	0	0	0	0	0	0	0

Bill Freehan

Year	Team	AB	R	H	D	T	HR	TB	BI	W	K	SB	CS
1965	DET AL	1	0	1	0	0	0	1	0	1	0	0	0
1966*	DET AL	2	0	1	0	0	0	1	0	0	0	0	0
1967*	DET AL	5	0	0	0	0	0	0	0	0	2	0	0
1968*	DET AL	2	0	0	0	0	0	0	0	0	1	0	0

Bill Freehan *continued*

Year	Team	AB	R	H	D	T	HR	TB	BI	W	K	SB	CS
1969*	DET AL	2	1	2	0	0	1	5	2	0	0	0	0
1970*	DET AL	1	0	0	0	0	0	0	0	0	0	0	0
1971*	DET AL	3	0	0	0	0	0	0	0	0	0	0	0
1972*	DET AL	1	1	0	0	0	0	0	0	0	1	0	0
Totals	8 Yr	17	2	4	0	0	1	7	2	2	3	0	0

Jim Fregosi

Year	Team	AB	R	H	D	T	HR	TB	BI	W	K	SB	CS
1964*	LAA AL	4	1	1	0	0	0	1	1	0	1	0	0
1966	CAL AL	2	0	0	0	0	0	0	0	0	1	0	0
1967	CAL AL	4	0	1	0	0	0	1	0	0	2	0	0
1968*	CAL AL	3	0	1	1	0	0	2	0	0	1	0	0
1969	CAL AL	1	0	0	0	0	0	0	0	0	0	0	0
1970	CAL AL	1	0	0	0	0	0	0	0	0	0	0	0
Totals	6 Yr	15	1	3	1	0	0	4	1	0	5	0	0

Larry French

Year	Team	AB	R	H	D	T	HR	TB	BI	W	K	SB	CS
1940	CHN NL	0	0	0	0	0	0	0	0	0	0	0	0

Lonny Frey

Year	Team	AB	R	H	D	T	HR	TB	BI	W	K	SB	CS
1939*	CIN NL	4	0	1	1	0	0	2	1	0	0	0	0
1941*	CIN NL	1	0	1	0	0	0	1	0	0	0	0	1
1943	CIN NL	1	0	0	0	0	0	0	0	0	0	0	0
Totals	3 Yr	6	0	2	1	0	0	3	1	0	0	0	1

Bob Friend

Year	Team	AB	R	H	D	T	HR	TB	BI	W	K	SB	CS
1956*	PIT NL	0	0	0	0	0	0	0	0	0	0	0	0
1958	PIT NL	0	0	0	0	0	0	0	0	0	0	0	0
1960-1*	PIT NL	2	0	0	0	0	0	0	0	0	2	0	0
Totals	3 Yr	2	0	0	0	0	0	0	0	0	2	0	0

Frankie Frisch

Year	Team	AB	R	H	D	T	HR	TB	BI	W	K	SB	CS
1933*	SLN NL	4	1	2	0	0	1	5	1	0	0	0	0
1934*	SLN NL	3	3	2	0	0	1	5	1	1	0	0	0
Totals	2 Yr	7	4	4	0	0	2	10	2	1	0	0	0

Travis Fryman

Year	Team	AB	R	H	D	T	HR	TB	BI	W	K	SB	CS
1992	DET AL	1	1	1	0	0	0	1	1	1	0	0	0
1993	DET AL	1	0	0	0	0	0	0	0	0	0	0	0
1994	DET AL	1	0	0	0	0	0	0	0	0	0	0	0
1996	DET AL	1	0	0	0	0	0	0	0	0	1	0	0
2000*	CLE AL	2	1	1	0	0	0	1	0	0	1	0	0
Totals	5 Yr	6	2	2	0	0	0	2	1	1	2	0	0

Gary Gaetti

Year	Team	AB	R	H	D	T	HR	TB	BI	W	K	SB	CS
1988	MIN AL	1	0	0	0	0	0	0	0	0	0	0	0
1989	MIN AL	1	0	0	0	0	0	0	0	0	1	0	0
Totals	2 Yr	2	0	0	0	0	0	0	0	0	1	0	0

Augie Galan

Year	Team	AB	R	H	D	T	HR	TB	BI	W	K	SB	CS
1936*	CHN NL	4	1	1	0	0	1	4	1	0	2	0	0
1943	BRO NL	1	0	0	0	0	0	0	0	1	0	0	0
1944*	BRO NL	4	1	1	0	0	0	1	1	1	0	0	0
Totals	3 Yr	9	2	2	0	0	1	5	2	2	2	0	0

Andres Galarraga

Year	Team	AB	R	H	D	T	HR	TB	BI	W	K	SB	CS
1988	MON NL	2	0	0	0	0	0	0	0	0	1	0	0
1993	COL NL	1	0	0	0	0	0	0	0	0	0	0	0
1997	COL NL	1	0	0	0	0	0	0	0	0	1	0	0
1998	ATL NL	2	0	0	0	0	0	0	0	0	0	0	0

Andres Galarraga continued

Year	Team	AB	R	H	D	T	HR	TB	BI	W	K	SB	CS
2000*	ATL NL	2	0	1	0	0	0	1	0	0	0	0	0
Totals	5 Yr	8	0	1	0	0	0	1	0	0	2	0	0

Ron Gant

Year	Team	AB	R	H	D	T	HR	TB	BI	W	K	SB	CS
1992	ATL NL	2	0	0	0	0	0	0	0	0	0	0	0
1995*	CIN NL	2	0	0	0	0	0	0	0	0	1	0	0
Totals	2 Yr	4	0	0	0	0	0	0	0	0	1	0	0

Carlos Garcia

Year	Team	AB	R	H	D	T	HR	TB	BI	W	K	SB	CS
1994	PIT NL	2	0	1	0	0	0	1	0	0	0	0	0

Damaso Garcia

Year	Team	AB	R	H	D	T	HR	TB	BI	W	K	SB	CS
1984	TOR AL	1	0	0	0	0	0	0	0	0	0	0	0
1985	TOR AL	2	0	1	0	0	0	1	0	0	0	1	0
Totals	2 Yr	3	0	1	0	0	0	1	0	0	0	1	0

Mike Garcia

Year	Team	AB	R	H	D	T	HR	TB	BI	W	K	SB	CS
1953	CLE AL	0	0	0	0	0	0	0	0	0	0	0	0

Nomar Garciaparra

Year	Team	AB	R	H	D	T	HR	TB	BI	W	K	SB	CS
1997	BOS AL	1	0	0	0	0	0	0	0	0	0	0	0
1999*	BOS AL	2	0	0	0	0	0	0	0	0	0	0	0
2000	BOS AL	2	1	1	0	0	0	1	0	0	0	0	0
Totals	3 Yr	5	1	1	0	0	0	1	0	0	0	0	0

Phil Garner

Year	Team	AB	R	H	D	T	HR	TB	BI	W	K	SB	CS
1976	OAK AL	1	0	0	0	0	0	0	0	0	1	0	0
1980	PIT NL	2	1	1	0	0	0	1	0	1	1	1	0
1981	PIT NL	0	0	0	0	0	0	0	0	0	0	0	0
Totals	3 Yr	3	1	1	0	0	0	1	0	1	2	1	0

Ralph Garr

Year	Team	AB	R	H	D	T	HR	TB	BI	W	K	SB	CS
1974	ATL NL	3	0	0	0	0	0	0	0	0	0	1	0

Ned Garver

Year	Team	AB	R	H	D	T	HR	TB	BI	W	K	SB	CS
1951*	SLA AL	1	0	0	0	0	0	0	0	0	1	0	0

Steve Garvey

Year	Team	AB	R	H	D	T	HR	TB	BI	W	K	SB	CS
1974*	LAN NL	4	1	2	1	0	0	3	1	0	1	0	0
1975*	LAN NL	3	1	2	0	0	1	5	1	0	0	0	0
1976*	LAN NL	3	1	1	0	1	0	3	1	0	0	0	0
1977*	LAN NL	3	1	1	0	0	1	4	1	0	2	0	0
1978*	LAN NL	3	1	2	0	1	0	4	2	1	0	0	0
1979*	LAN NL	2	1	0	0	0	0	0	0	1	0	0	0
1980*	LAN NL	2	0	0	0	0	0	0	0	0	0	0	0
1981	LAN NL	2	0	1	1	0	0	2	0	0	0	0	0
1984*	SDN NL	3	1	1	0	0	0	1	0	0	0	0	0
1985*	SDN NL	3	0	1	0	0	0	1	1	0	0	0	0
Totals	10 Yr	28	7	11	2	2	2	23	7	2	3	0	0

Cito Gaston

Year	Team	AB	R	H	D	T	HR	TB	BI	W	K	SB	CS
1970	SDN NL	2	0	0	0	0	0	0	0	1	0	0	0

Rich Gedman

Year	Team	AB	R	H	D	T	HR	TB	BI	W	K	SB	CS
1985	BOS AL	1	0	0	0	0	0	0	0	0	1	0	0
1986	BOS AL	0	0	0	0	0	0	0	0	0	0	0	0
Totals	2 Yr	1	0	0	0	0	0	0	0	0	1	0	0

Lou Gehrig

Year	Team	AB	R	H	D	T	HR	TB	BI	W	K	SB	CS
1933*	NYA AL	2	0	0	0	0	0	0	0	2	1	0	0
1934*	NYA AL	4	1	0	0	0	0	0	0	1	3	0	0
1935*	NYA AL	3	1	0	0	0	0	0	0	1	0	0	0
1936*	NYA AL	2	1	1	0	0	1	4	1	2	0	0	0
1937*	NYA AL	4	1	2	1	0	1	6	4	0	2	0	0
1938	NYA AL	3	0	1	0	0	0	1	0	0	0	0	0
Totals	6 Yr	18	4	4	1	0	2	11	5	6	6	0	0

Charlie Gehringer

Year	Team	AB	R	H	D	T	HR	TB	BI	W	K	SB	CS
1933*	DET AL	3	1	0	0	0	0	0	0	2	0	1	0
1934*	DET AL	3	0	2	0	0	0	2	0	3	0	1	0
1935*	DET AL	3	0	2	1	0	0	3	0	1	0	0	0
1936*	DET AL	3	0	2	1	0	0	3	0	2	0	0	0
1937*	DET AL	5	1	3	0	0	0	3	1	0	0	0	0
1938*	DET AL	3	0	1	0	0	0	1	0	1	0	0	0
Totals	6 Yr	20	2	10	2	0	0	12	1	9	0	2	0

Jim Gentile

Year	Team	AB	R	H	D	T	HR	TB	BI	W	K	SB	CS
1960-1	BAL AL	2	0	1	0	0	0	1	0	0	1	0	0
1961-1	BAL AL	2	0	0	0	0	0	0	0	0	2	0	0
1962-1*	BAL AL	3	0	0	0	0	0	0	0	1	1	0	0
1962-2*	BAL AL	4	0	1	0	0	0	1	0	1	1	0	0
Totals	4 Yr	11	0	2	0	0	0	2	0	2	5	0	0

Jason Giambi

Year	Team	AB	R	H	D	T	HR	TB	BI	W	K	SB	CS
2000*	OAK AL	2	0	0	0	0	0	0	0	1	2	0	0

Bob Gibson

Year	Team	AB	R	H	D	T	HR	TB	BI	W	K	SB	CS
1962-2	SLN NL	0	0	0	0	0	0	0	0	0	0	0	0
1965	SLN NL	0	0	0	0	0	0	0	0	0	0	0	0
1967	SLN NL	0	0	0	0	0	0	0	0	0	0	0	0
1969	SLN NL	0	0	0	0	0	0	0	0	0	0	0	0
1970	SLN NL	0	0	0	0	0	0	0	0	0	0	0	0
1972*	SLN NL	0	0	0	0	0	0	0	0	0	0	0	0
Totals	6 Yr	0	0	0	0	0	0	0	0	0	0	0	0

Brian Giles

Year	Team	AB	R	H	D	T	HR	TB	BI	W	K	SB	CS
2000	PIT NL	2	0	0	0	0	0	0	0	0	0	0	0

Jim Gilliam

Year	Team	AB	R	H	D	T	HR	TB	BI	W	K	SB	CS
1959-2	LAN NL	2	1	1	0	0	1	4	1	1	0	0	0

Dave Giusti

Year	Team	AB	R	H	D	T	HR	TB	BI	W	K	SB	CS
1973	PIT NL	0	0	0	0	0	0	0	0	0	0	0	0

Troy Glaus

Year	Team	AB	R	H	D	T	HR	TB	BI	W	K	SB	CS
2000	ANA AL	1	0	0	0	0	0	0	0	0	0	0	0

Tom Glavine

Year	Team	AB	R	H	D	T	HR	TB	BI	W	K	SB	CS
1992*	ATL NL	0	0	0	0	0	0	0	0	0	0	0	0
1996	ATL NL	0	0	0	0	0	0	0	0	0	0	0	0
1998	ATL NL	0	0	0	0	0	0	0	0	0	0	0	0
2000	ATL NL	0	0	0	0	0	0	0	0	0	0	0	0
Totals	4 Yr	0	0	0	0	0	0	0	0	0	0	0	0

Lefty Gomez

Year	Team	AB	R	H	D	T	HR	TB	BI	W	K	SB	CS
1933*	NYA AL	1	0	1	0	0	0	1	1	0	0	0	0
1934*	NYA AL	1	0	0	0	0	0	0	0	0	1	0	0
1935*	NYA AL	2	0	0	0	0	0	0	0	0	1	0	0

Year	Team	AB	R	H	D	T	HR	TB	BI	W	K	SB	CS
Lefty Gomez *continued*													
1937*	NYA AL	1	0	0	0	0	0	0	0	0	1	0	0
1938*	NYA AL	1	0	0	0	0	0	0	0	0	0	0	0
Totals	5 Yr	6	0	1	0	0	0	1	1	0	3	0	0
Alex Gonzalez													
1999	FLO NL	1	0	0	0	0	0	0	0	0	0	0	0
Juan Gonzalez													
1993	TEX AL	1	0	0	0	0	0	0	0	1	1	0	0
1998*	TEX AL	3	0	0	0	0	0	0	1	0	1	0	0
Totals	2 Yr	4	0	0	0	0	0	0	1	1	2	0	0
Luis Gonzalez													
1999	ARI NL	2	0	1	1	0	0	2	0	0	0	0	0
Dwight Gooden													
1984	NYN NL	0	0	0	0	0	0	0	0	0	0	0	0
1986*	NYN NL	0	0	0	0	0	0	0	0	0	0	0	0
1988*	NYN NL	0	0	0	0	0	0	0	0	0	0	0	0
Totals	3 Yr	0	0	0	0	0	0	0	0	0	0	0	0
Billy Goodman													
1949	BOS AL	0	0	0	0	0	0	0	0	0	0	0	0
1953*	BOS AL	2	0	0	0	0	0	0	0	1	0	0	1
Totals	2 Yr	2	0	0	0	0	0	0	0	1	0	0	1
Ival Goodman													
1938*	CIN NL	3	0	0	0	0	0	0	0	0	1	1	0
1939*	CIN NL	1	0	0	0	0	0	0	1	0	0	0	0
Totals	2 Yr	4	0	0	0	0	0	0	1	1	1	0	
Joe Gordon													
1939*	NYA AL	4	0	0	0	0	0	0	0	0	1	0	0
1940*	NYA AL	2	0	0	0	0	0	0	0	0	2	0	0
1941	NYA AL	2	1	1	0	0	0	1	0	0	0	0	0
1942*	NYA AL	4	0	0	0	0	0	0	0	0	3	0	0
1946	NYA AL	2	0	1	1	0	0	2	2	0	0	0	0
1947*	CLE AL	2	0	1	1	0	0	2	0	0	1	0	0
1948*	CLE AL	2	0	0	0	0	0	0	0	0	0	0	0
1949	CLE AL	2	1	1	1	0	0	2	0	0	1	0	0
Totals	8 Yr	20	2	4	3	0	0	7	2	0	8	0	0
Sid Gordon													
1949	NY NL	2	0	1	1	0	0	2	0	1	0	0	0
Tom Gordon													
1998	BOS AL	0	0	0	0	0	0	0	0	0	0	0	0
Goose Goslin													
1936	DET AL	1	1	1	0	0	0	1	0	1	0	0	0
Rich Gossage													
1975	CHA AL	0	0	0	0	0	0	0	0	0	0	0	0
1977	PIT NL	0	0	0	0	0	0	0	0	0	0	0	0
1978	NYA AL	0	0	0	0	0	0	0	0	0	0	0	0
1980	NYA AL	0	0	0	0	0	0	0	0	0	0	0	0
1984	SDN NL	0	0	0	0	0	0	0	0	0	0	0	0
1985	SDN NL	0	0	0	0	0	0	0	0	0	0	0	0
Totals	6 Yr	0	0	0	0	0	0	0	0	0	0	0	0
Billy Grabarkewitz													
1970	LAN NL	3	0	1	0	0	0	1	0	0	0	0	0
Mark Grace													
1993*	CHN NL	3	0	0	0	0	0	0	0	0	0	0	0
1995	CHN NL	0	0	0	0	0	0	0	0	0	0	0	0
1997	CHN NL	1	0	0	0	0	0	0	0	0	0	0	0
Totals	3 Yr	4	0	0	0	0	0	0	0	0	0	0	0
Jim Grant													
1965	MIN AL	0	0	0	0	0	0	0	0	0	0	0	0
Danny Graves													
2000	CIN NL	0	0	0	0	0	0	0	0	0	0	0	0
Ted Gray													
1950	DET AL	0	0	0	0	0	0	0	0	0	0	0	0
Shawn Green													
1999	TOR AL	1	0	1	0	0	0	1	0	0	0	0	0
Hank Greenberg													
1939*	DET AL	3	1	1	0	0	0	1	0	1	0	0	0
1940	DET AL	2	0	0	0	0	0	0	0	0	0	0	0
Totals	2 Yr	5	1	1	0	0	0	1	0	1	0	0	0
Mike Greenwell													
1988	BOS AL	1	0	0	0	0	0	0	0	0	0	0	0
1989	BOS AL	0	0	0	0	0	0	0	0	0	0	0	0
Totals	2 Yr	1	0	0	0	0	0	0	0	0	0	0	0
Bobby Grich													
1972*	BAL AL	4	0	0	0	0	0	0	0	0	2	0	0
1974	BAL AL	3	0	1	0	0	0	1	0	0	0	0	0
1976*	BAL AL	2	0	0	0	0	0	0	0	0	0	0	0
1979	CAL AL	1	0	0	0	0	0	0	0	0	1	0	0
1980	CAL AL	0	0	0	0	0	0	0	0	0	1	0	0
1982*	CAL AL	1	0	0	0	0	0	0	0	0	1	1	0
Totals	6 Yr	11	0	1	0	0	0	1	0	2	4	0	0
Ben Grieve													
1998	OAK AL	0	0	0	0	0	0	0	0	1	0	0	0
Ken Griffey													
1976	CIN NL	1	1	1	0	0	0	1	1	0	0	0	0
1980	CIN NL	3	1	2	0	0	1	5	1	0	0	0	0
Totals	2 Yr	4	2	3	0	0	1	6	2	0	0	0	0
Ken Griffey													
1990*	SEA AL	2	0	0	0	0	0	0	0	1	0	0	0
1991*	SEA AL	3	0	2	0	0	0	2	0	0	0	0	0
1992*	SEA AL	3	2	3	1	0	1	7	2	0	0	0	0
1993*	SEA AL	3	1	1	0	0	0	1	1	0	1	0	0
1994*	SEA AL	3	0	2	1	0	0	3	1	0	0	0	0
1997*	SEA AL	4	0	0	0	0	0	0	0	0	2	0	0
1998*	SEA AL	3	1	2	0	0	0	2	1	1	0	1	0
1999*	SEA AL	2	0	0	0	0	0	0	0	0	1	0	0
Totals	8 Yr	23	4	10	2	0	1	15	5	2	4	1	0

Year	Team	AB	R	H	D	T	HR	TB	BI	W	K	SB	CS

Alfredo Griffin

Year	Team	AB	R	H	D	T	HR	TB	BI	W	K	SB	CS
1984	TOR AL	0	0	0	0	0	0	0	0	0	0	0	0

Bob Grim

Year	Team	AB	R	H	D	T	HR	TB	BI	W	K	SB	CS
1957	NYA AL	0	0	0	0	0	0	0	0	0	0	0	0

Lee Grissom

Year	Team	AB	R	H	D	T	HR	TB	BI	W	K	SB	CS
1937	CIN NL	0	0	0	0	0	0	0	0	0	0	0	0

Marquis Grissom

Year	Team	AB	R	H	D	T	HR	TB	BI	W	K	SB	CS
1993*	MON NL	3	0	0	0	0	0	0	0	0	1	0	0
1994	MON NL	1	1	1	0	0	1	4	1	1	0	0	0
Totals	2 Yr	4	1	1	0	0	1	4	1	1	1	0	0

Marv Grissom

Year	Team	AB	R	H	D	T	HR	TB	BI	W	K	SB	CS
1954	NY NL	0	0	0	0	0	0	0	0	0	0	0	0

Dick Groat

Year	Team	AB	R	H	D	T	HR	TB	BI	W	K	SB	CS
1959-1	PIT NL	0	0	0	0	0	0	0	0	0	0	0	0
1959-2	PIT NL	1	0	0	0	0	0	0	0	0	0	0	0
1960-1	PIT NL	0	0	0	0	0	0	0	0	0	0	0	0
1960-2	PIT NL	1	0	0	0	0	0	0	0	0	0	0	0
1962-1*	PIT NL	3	1	1	0	0	0	1	1	0	0	0	0
1962-2*	PIT NL	3	0	2	0	0	0	2	2	0	0	0	0
1963*	SLN NL	4	0	1	0	0	0	1	1	0	1	0	0
1964*	SLN NL	3	0	1	1	0	0	2	1	0	1	0	0
Totals	8 Yr	15	1	5	1	0	0	6	5	0	2	0	0

Kevin Gross

Year	Team	AB	R	H	D	T	HR	TB	BI	W	K	SB	CS
1988	PHI NL	0	0	0	0	0	0	0	0	0	0	0	0

Jerry Grote

Year	Team	AB	R	H	D	T	HR	TB	BI	W	K	SB	CS
1968*	NYN NL	2	0	0	0	0	0	0	0	0	1	0	0
1974	NYN NL	0	0	0	0	0	0	0	0	0	0	0	0
Totals	2 Yr	2	0	0	0	0	0	0	0	0	1	0	0

Lefty Grove

Year	Team	AB	R	H	D	T	HR	TB	BI	W	K	SB	CS
1933	PHA AL	1	0	0	0	0	0	0	0	0	0	0	0
1936*	BOS AL	1	0	0	0	0	0	0	0	0	1	0	0
1938	BOS AL	0	0	0	0	0	0	0	0	0	0	0	0
Totals	3 Yr	2	0	0	0	0	0	0	0	0	1	0	0

John Grubb

Year	Team	AB	R	H	D	T	HR	TB	BI	W	K	SB	CS
1974	SDN NL	1	0	0	0	0	0	0	0	0	0	0	0

Kelly Gruber

Year	Team	AB	R	H	D	T	HR	TB	BI	W	K	SB	CS
1990	TOR AL	1	0	0	0	0	0	0	0	1	0	2	0

Mark Grudzielanek

Year	Team	AB	R	H	D	T	HR	TB	BI	W	K	SB	CS
1996	MON NL	1	0	0	0	0	0	0	0	0	0	0	0

Mark Gubicza

Year	Team	AB	R	H	D	T	HR	TB	BI	W	K	SB	CS
1988	KCA AL	0	0	0	0	0	0	0	0	0	0	0	0

Pedro Guerrero

Year	Team	AB	R	H	D	T	HR	TB	BI	W	K	SB	CS
1981	LAN NL	1	0	0	0	0	0	0	0	0	1	0	0
1983	LAN NL	1	0	0	0	0	0	0	0	0	1	0	0
1987	LAN NL	1	0	0	0	0	0	0	0	0	0	0	0
1989*	SLN NL	2	0	0	0	0	0	0	0	0	0	0	0
Totals	4 Yr	5	0	0	0	0	0	0	0	0	2	0	0

Vladimir Guerrero

Year	Team	AB	R	H	D	T	HR	TB	BI	W	K	SB	CS
1999	MON NL	1	0	0	0	0	0	0	0	0	0	0	0
2000*	MON NL	2	0	1	0	0	0	1	0	0	0	0	0
Totals	2 Yr	3	0	1	0	0	0	1	0	0	0	0	0

Ron Guidry

Year	Team	AB	R	H	D	T	HR	TB	BI	W	K	SB	CS
1978	NYA AL	0	0	0	0	0	0	0	0	0	0	0	0
1979	NYA AL	0	0	0	0	0	0	0	0	0	0	0	0
Totals	2 Yr	0	0	0	0	0	0	0	0	0	0	0	0

Ozzie Guillen

Year	Team	AB	R	H	D	T	HR	TB	BI	W	K	SB	CS
1990	CHA AL	2	0	0	0	0	0	0	0	0	0	0	0
1991	CHA AL	0	0	0	0	0	0	0	0	0	0	0	0
Totals	2 Yr	2	0	0	0	0	0	0	0	0	0	0	0

Frankie Gustine

Year	Team	AB	R	H	D	T	HR	TB	BI	W	K	SB	CS
1946	PIT NL	1	0	0	0	0	0	0	0	1	1	0	0
1947*	PIT NL	2	0	0	0	0	0	0	0	0	0	0	0
1948	PIT NL	1	0	0	0	0	0	0	0	0	1	0	0
Totals	3 Yr	4	0	0	0	0	0	0	0	1	2	0	0

Juan Guzman

Year	Team	AB	R	H	D	T	HR	TB	BI	W	K	SB	CS
1992	TOR AL	0	0	0	0	0	0	0	0	0	0	0	0

Tony Gwynn

Year	Team	AB	R	H	D	T	HR	TB	BI	W	K	SB	CS
1984*	SDN NL	3	0	1	0	0	0	1	0	0	1	1	0
1985*	SDN NL	1	0	0	0	0	0	0	0	0	0	0	0
1986*	SDN NL	3	0	0	0	0	0	0	0	0	1	0	0
1987	SDN NL	1	0	0	0	0	0	0	0	0	0	0	0
1989*	SDN NL	2	1	1	0	0	0	1	0	1	1	1	0
1990	SDN NL	0	0	0	0	0	0	0	0	1	0	0	0
1991*	SDN NL	4	1	2	0	0	0	2	0	0	0	0	0
1992*	SDN NL	2	0	0	0	0	0	0	0	1	0	0	0
1993	SDN NL	1	0	0	0	0	0	0	0	0	0	0	0
1994*	SDN NL	5	2	2	1	0	0	3	2	0	0	0	0
1995*	SDN NL	2	0	0	0	0	0	0	0	0	0	0	0
1997*	SDN NL	3	0	0	0	0	0	0	0	0	0	0	0
1998*	SDN NL	2	0	1	0	0	0	1	2	0	0	0	0
Totals	13 Yr	29	4	7	1	0	0	8	4	3	3	2	0

Bert Haas

Year	Team	AB	R	H	D	T	HR	TB	BI	W	K	SB	CS
1947	CIN NL	1	0	1	0	0	0	1	0	0	0	0	0

Stan Hack

Year	Team	AB	R	H	D	T	HR	TB	BI	W	K	SB	CS
1938*	CHN NL	4	1	1	0	0	0	1	0	0	1	0	0
1939*	CHN NL	4	0	1	0	0	0	1	0	1	3	0	0
1941*	CHN NL	2	0	1	0	0	0	1	0	1	1	0	0
1943*	CHN NL	5	1	3	0	0	0	3	0	0	0	0	0
Totals	4 Yr	15	2	6	0	0	0	6	0	2	5	0	0

Harvey Haddix

Year	Team	AB	R	H	D	T	HR	TB	BI	W	K	SB	CS
1955	SLN NL	0	0	0	0	0	0	0	0	0	0	0	0

Chick Hafey

Year	Team	AB	R	H	D	T	HR	TB	BI	W	K	SB	CS
1933*	CIN NL	4	0	1	0	0	0	1	0	0	0	0	0

Jimmie Hall

Year	Team	AB	R	H	D	T	HR	TB	BI	W	K	SB	CS
1964	MIN AL	0	0	0	0	0	0	0	0	0	0	0	0
1965	MIN AL	2	1	0	0	0	0	0	0	1	1	0	0
Totals	2 Yr	2	1	0	0	0	0	0	0	1	1	0	0

Bill Hallahan

Year	Team	AB	R	H	D	T	HR	TB	BI	W	K	SB	CS
1933*	SLN NL	1	0	0	0	0	0	0	0	0	0	0	0

Tom Haller

Year	Team	AB	R	H	D	T	HR	TB	BI	W	K	SB	CS
1967	SFN NL	1	0	0	0	0	0	0	0	0	0	0	0
1968	LAN NL	2	0	0	0	0	0	0	0	0	1	0	0
Totals	2 Yr	3	0	0	0	0	0	0	0	0	1	0	0

Atlee Hammaker

Year	Team	AB	R	H	D	T	HR	TB	BI	W	K	SB	CS
1983	SFN NL	0	0	0	0	0	0	0	0	0	0	0	0

Jeffrey Hammonds

Year	Team	AB	R	H	D	T	HR	TB	BI	W	K	SB	CS
2000	COL NL	1	0	0	0	0	0	0	0	0	0	0	0

Granny Hamner

Year	Team	AB	R	H	D	T	HR	TB	BI	W	K	SB	CS
1952*	PHI NL	1	0	0	0	0	0	0	0	1	0	0	0
1953	PHI NL	0	0	0	0	0	0	0	0	0	0	0	0
1954*	PHI NL	3	0	0	0	0	0	0	0	0	0	0	0
Totals	3 Yr	4	0	0	0	0	0	0	0	1	0	0	0

Ron Hansen

Year	Team	AB	R	H	D	T	HR	TB	BI	W	K	SB	CS
1960-1*	BAL AL	2	0	1	0	0	0	1	0	0	1	0	0
1960-2*	BAL AL	4	0	2	0	0	0	2	0	0	0	0	0
Totals	2 Yr	6	0	3	0	0	0	3	0	0	1	0	0

Mel Harder

Year	Team	AB	R	H	D	T	HR	TB	BI	W	K	SB	CS
1934	CLE AL	2	0	0	0	0	0	0	0	0	1	0	0
1935	CLE AL	1	0	0	0	0	0	0	0	0	1	0	0
1936	CLE AL	0	0	0	0	0	0	0	0	0	0	0	0
1937	CLE AL	1	0	0	0	0	0	0	0	0	0	0	0
Totals	4 Yr	4	0	0	0	0	0	0	0	0	2	0	0

Mike Hargrove

Year	Team	AB	R	H	D	T	HR	TB	BI	W	K	SB	CS
1975	TEX AL	1	0	0	0	0	0	0	0	0	0	0	0

Tommy Harper

Year	Team	AB	R	H	D	T	HR	TB	BI	W	K	SB	CS
1970	MIL AL	0	0	0	0	0	0	0	0	0	0	0	1

Toby Harrah

Year	Team	AB	R	H	D	T	HR	TB	BI	W	K	SB	CS
1976*	TEX AL	2	0	0	0	0	0	0	0	0	0	0	0

Bud Harrelson

Year	Team	AB	R	H	D	T	HR	TB	BI	W	K	SB	CS
1970	NYN NL	3	2	2	0	0	0	2	0	0	0	0	0
1971*	NYN NL	2	0	0	0	0	0	0	0	0	0	0	0
Totals	2 Yr	5	2	2	0	0	0	2	0	0	0	0	0

Ken Harrelson

Year	Team	AB	R	H	D	T	HR	TB	BI	W	K	SB	CS
1968	BOS AL	1	0	0	0	0	0	0	0	0	0	0	0

Jim Ray Hart

Year	Team	AB	R	H	D	T	HR	TB	BI	W	K	SB	CS
1966	SFN NL	1	0	0	0	0	0	0	0	0	1	0	0

Gabby Hartnett

Year	Team	AB	R	H	D	T	HR	TB	BI	W	K	SB	CS
1933	CHN NL	1	0	0	0	0	0	0	0	0	1	0	0
1934*	CHN NL	2	0	0	0	0	0	0	0	0	0	0	0
1935	CHN NL	0	0	0	0	0	0	0	0	0	0	0	0
1936*	CHN NL	4	1	1	0	1	0	3	1	0	0	0	0
1937*	CHN NL	3	1	1	0	0	0	1	0	0	0	0	0
Totals	5 Yr	10	2	2	0	1	0	4	1	0	1	0	0

Frankie Hayes

Year	Team	AB	R	H	D	T	HR	TB	BI	W	K	SB	CS
1940	PHA AL	1	0	0	0	0	0	0	0	0	0	0	0
1941	PHA AL	1	0	0	0	0	0	0	0	0	0	0	0
1944	PHA AL	1	0	0	0	0	0	0	0	0	1	0	0
1946*	CHA AL	1	0	0	0	0	0	0	0	0	0	0	0
Totals	4 Yr	4	0	0	0	0	0	0	0	0	1	0	0

Von Hayes

Year	Team	AB	R	H	D	T	HR	TB	BI	W	K	SB	CS
1989	PHI NL	1	0	1	0	0	0	1	1	0	0	0	0

Jeff Heath

Year	Team	AB	R	H	D	T	HR	TB	BI	W	K	SB	CS
1941*	CLE AL	2	0	0	0	0	0	0	0	1	1	0	0
1943	CLE AL	1	0	0	0	0	0	0	0	0	0	0	0
Totals	2 Yr	3	0	0	0	0	0	0	0	1	1	0	0

Jim Hegan

Year	Team	AB	R	H	D	T	HR	TB	BI	W	K	SB	CS
1950	CLE AL	3	0	0	0	0	0	0	0	0	3	0	0
1951	CLE AL	1	0	1	1	0	0	2	0	0	0	0	0
Totals	2 Yr	4	0	1	1	0	0	2	0	0	3	0	0

Tommy Helms

Year	Team	AB	R	H	D	T	HR	TB	BI	W	K	SB	CS
1967	CIN NL	1	0	0	0	0	0	0	0	0	0	0	0
1968*	CIN NL	3	0	1	1	0	0	2	0	1	0	0	0
Totals	2 Yr	4	0	1	1	0	0	2	0	1	0	0	0

Todd Helton

Year	Team	AB	R	H	D	T	HR	TB	BI	W	K	SB	CS
2000	COL NL	2	0	0	0	0	0	0	0	0	0	0	0

Rollie Hemsley

Year	Team	AB	R	H	D	T	HR	TB	BI	W	K	SB	CS
1935*	SLA AL	4	1	1	0	1	0	3	0	0	0	0	0
1940	CLE AL	1	0	0	0	0	0	0	0	0	0	0	0
1944*	NYA AL	2	0	0	0	0	0	0	0	0	0	0	0
Totals	3 Yr	7	1	1	0	1	0	3	0	0	0	0	0

Dave Henderson

Year	Team	AB	R	H	D	T	HR	TB	BI	W	K	SB	CS
1991*	OAK AL	2	0	0	0	0	0	0	0	0	1	0	0

Rickey Henderson

Year	Team	AB	R	H	D	T	HR	TB	BI	W	K	SB	CS
1980	OAK AL	1	0	0	0	0	0	0	0	0	0	0	0
1982*	OAK AL	4	1	3	0	0	0	3	0	1	0	1	0
1983	OAK AL	1	0	0	0	0	0	0	1	0	0	0	0
1984	OAK AL	2	0	0	0	0	0	0	0	0	1	0	0
1985*	NYA AL	3	1	1	0	0	0	1	0	0	1	1	0
1986*	NYA AL	3	0	0	0	0	0	0	0	0	1	0	0
1987*	NYA AL	3	0	1	0	0	0	1	0	0	0	0	0
1988*	NYA AL	2	0	1	0	0	0	1	0	1	0	0	0
1990*	OAK AL	3	0	0	0	0	0	0	0	0	1	0	0
1991*	OAK AL	2	1	1	0	0	0	1	0	0	0	0	0
Totals	10 Yr	24	3	7	0	0	0	7	1	2	4	2	0

George Hendrick

Year	Team	AB	R	H	D	T	HR	TB	BI	W	K	SB	CS
1974	CLE AL	2	0	1	0	0	0	1	0	0	0	0	0
1975	CLE AL	1	1	1	0	0	0	1	0	0	0	1	0
1980	SLN NL	2	0	1	0	0	0	1	1	0	0	0	0
Totals	3 Yr	5	1	3	0	0	0	3	1	0	0	1	0

Tom Henke

Year	Team	AB	R	H	D	T	HR	TB	BI	W	K	SB	CS
1987	TOR AL	0	0	0	0	0	0	0	0	0	0	0	0

Tommy Henrich

Year	Team	AB	R	H	D	T	HR	TB	BI	W	K	SB	CS
1942*	NYA AL	4	1	1	1	0	0	2	0	0	1	0	0
1947	NYA AL	1	0	0	0	0	0	0	0	0	1	0	0
1948*	NYA AL	3	0	0	0	0	0	0	0	1	2	0	0
1950	NYA AL	1	0	0	0	0	0	0	0	0	0	0	0
Totals	4 Yr	9	1	1	1	0	0	2	0	1	4	0	0

Bill Henry

Year	Team	AB	R	H	D	T	HR	TB	BI	W	K	SB	CS
1960-2	CIN NL	0	0	0	0	0	0	0	0	0	0	0	0

Pat Hentgen

Year	Team	AB	R	H	D	T	HR	TB	BI	W	K	SB	CS
1994	TOR AL	0	0	0	0	0	0	0	0	0	0	0	0

Ray Herbert

Year	Team	AB	R	H	D	T	HR	TB	BI	W	K	SB	CS
1962-2	CHA AL	1	0	0	0	0	0	0	0	0	1	0	0

Billy Herman

Year	Team	AB	R	H	D	T	HR	TB	BI	W	K	SB	CS
1934	CHN NL	2	0	1	1	0	0	2	0	0	0	0	0
1934	CHN NL	2	0	1	1	0	0	2	0	0	0	0	0
1935*	CHN NL	3	0	0	0	0	0	0	0	0	0	0	0
1936*	CHN NL	3	1	2	0	0	0	2	0	1	0	0	0
1937*	CHN NL	5	1	2	0	0	0	2	0	0	0	0	0
1938*	CHN NL	4	0	1	0	0	0	1	0	0	2	0	0
1939	CHN NL	1	0	0	0	0	0	0	0	0	1	0	0
1940*	CHN NL	3	1	3	0	0	0	3	0	0	0	0	0
1941	BRO NL	3	0	2	1	0	0	3	0	0	0	0	0
1942	BRO NL	1	0	0	0	0	0	0	0	0	0	0	0
1943*	BRO NL	5	0	2	0	0	0	2	0	0	0	0	0
Totals	11 Yr	32	3	14	3	0	0	17	0	1	3	0	0

Guillermo Hernandez

Year	Team	AB	R	H	D	T	HR	TB	BI	W	K	SB	CS
1984	DET AL	0	0	0	0	0	0	0	0	0	0	0	0
1985	DET AL	0	0	0	0	0	0	0	0	0	0	0	0
Totals	2 Yr	0	0	0	0	0	0	0	0	0	0	0	0

Keith Hernandez

Year	Team	AB	R	H	D	T	HR	TB	BI	W	K	SB	CS
1979	SLN NL	1	0	0	0	0	0	0	0	0	1	0	0
1980	SLN NL	2	0	2	0	0	0	2	0	0	0	0	0
1984	NYN NL	1	0	0	0	0	0	0	0	0	1	0	0
1986*	NYN NL	4	0	0	0	0	0	0	0	0	0	0	0
1987	NYN NL	2	0	1	0	0	0	1	0	0	1	0	0
Totals	5 Yr	10	0	3	0	0	0	3	0	0	3	0	0

Roberto Hernandez

Year	Team	AB	R	H	D	T	HR	TB	BI	W	K	SB	CS
1996	CHA AL	0	0	0	0	0	0	0	0	0	0	0	0

Tom Herr

Year	Team	AB	R	H	D	T	HR	TB	BI	W	K	SB	CS
1985*	SLN NL	3	1	1	1	0	0	2	0	0	0	0	0

Orel Hershiser

Year	Team	AB	R	H	D	T	HR	TB	BI	W	K	SB	CS
1987	LAN NL	0	0	0	0	0	0	0	0	0	0	0	0
1988	LAN NL	0	0	0	0	0	0	0	0	0	0	0	0
Totals	2 Yr	0	0	0	0	0	0	0	0	0	0	0	0

Jim Hickman

Year	Team	AB	R	H	D	T	HR	TB	BI	W	K	SB	CS
1970	CHN NL	4	0	1	0	0	0	1	1	0	2	0	0

Kirby Higbe

Year	Team	AB	R	H	D	T	HR	TB	BI	W	K	SB	CS
1946	BRO NL	1	0	0	0	0	0	0	0	0	1	0	0

Mike Higgins

Year	Team	AB	R	H	D	T	HR	TB	BI	W	K	SB	CS
1936*	PHA AL	2	0	0	0	0	0	0	0	0	2	0	0
1944	DET AL	1	0	0	0	0	0	0	0	0	0	0	0
Totals	2 Yr	3	0	0	0	0	0	0	0	0	2	0	0

Teddy Higuera

Year	Team	AB	R	H	D	T	HR	TB	BI	W	K	SB	CS
1986	MIL AL	1	0	0	0	0	0	0	0	0	1	0	0

Ken Hill

Year	Team	AB	R	H	D	T	HR	TB	BI	W	K	SB	CS
1994	MON NL	0	0	0	0	0	0	0	0	0	0	0	0

Chuck Hinton

Year	Team	AB	R	H	D	T	HR	TB	BI	W	K	SB	CS
1964	WAS AL	0	0	0	0	0	0	0	0	0	0	0	0

Larry Hisle

Year	Team	AB	R	H	D	T	HR	TB	BI	W	K	SB	CS
1977	MIN AL	1	0	0	0	0	0	0	0	0	0	0	0
1978	MIL AL	1	0	1	0	0	0	1	0	0	0	0	0
Totals	2 Yr	2	0	1	0	0	0	1	0	0	0	0	0

Myril Hoag

Year	Team	AB	R	H	D	T	HR	TB	BI	W	K	SB	CS
1939	SLA AL	1	0	0	0	0	0	0	0	0	1	0	0

Don Hoak

Year	Team	AB	R	H	D	T	HR	TB	BI	W	K	SB	CS
1957*	CIN NL	1	0	0	0	0	0	0	0	0	0	0	0

Gil Hodges

Year	Team	AB	R	H	D	T	HR	TB	BI	W	K	SB	CS
1949	BRO NL	3	1	1	0	0	0	1	0	0	0	0	0
1951*	BRO NL	5	2	2	0	0	1	5	2	0	1	0	0
1953	BRO NL	1	0	0	0	0	0	0	0	0	0	0	0
1954	BRO NL	1	0	0	0	0	0	0	0	0	0	0	0
1955	BRO NL	1	0	1	0	0	0	1	0	0	0	0	0
1957	BRO NL	1	0	0	0	0	0	0	0	0	0	0	0
Totals	6 Yr	12	3	4	0	0	1	7	2	0	1	0	0

Trevor Hoffman

Year	Team	AB	R	H	D	T	HR	TB	BI	W	K	SB	CS
1998	SDN NL	0	0	0	0	0	0	0	0	0	0	0	0
2000	SDN NL	0	0	0	0	0	0	0	0	0	0	0	0
Totals	2 Yr	0	0	0	0	0	0	0	0	0	0	0	0

Dave Hollins

Year	Team	AB	R	H	D	T	HR	TB	BI	W	K	SB	CS
1993	PHI NL	1	0	1	1	0	0	2	0	0	0	0	0

Tommy Holmes

Year	Team	AB	R	H	D	T	HR	TB	BI	W	K	SB	CS
1948	BSN NL	1	0	0	0	0	0	0	0	0	0	0	0

Ken Holtzman

Year	Team	AB	R	H	D	T	HR	TB	BI	W	K	SB	CS
1973	OAK AL	0	0	0	0	0	0	0	0	0	0	0	0

Rick Honeycutt

Year	Team	AB	R	H	D	T	HR	TB	BI	W	K	SB	CS
1983	TEX AL	0	0	0	0	0	0	0	0	0	0	0	0

Burt Hooton

Year	Team	AB	R	H	D	T	HR	TB	BI	W	K	SB	CS
1981	LAN NL	0	0	0	0	0	0	0	0	0	0	0	0

Johnny Hopp

Year	Team	AB	R	H	D	T	HR	TB	BI	W	K	SB	CS
1946*	BSN NL	2	0	1	0	0	0	1	0	0	0	0	0

Bob Horner

Year	Team	AB	R	H	D	T	HR	TB	BI	W	K	SB	CS
1982	ATL NL	1	0	0	0	0	0	0	0	0	0	0	0

Year	Team	AB	R	H	D	T	HR	TB	BI	W	K	SB	CS

Willie Horton

Year	Team	AB	R	H	D	T	HR	TB	BI	W	K	SB	CS
1965*	DET AL	3	0	0	0	0	0	0	0	1	1	0	0
1968*	DET AL	2	0	0	0	0	0	0	0	0	0	0	0
1970	DET AL	2	1	2	0	0	0	2	0	1	0	0	0
1973	DET AL	1	0	0	0	0	0	0	0	0	1	0	0
Totals	4 Yr	8	1	2	0	0	0	2	0	2	2	0	0

Charlie Hough

Year	Team	AB	R	H	D	T	HR	TB	BI	W	K	SB	CS
1986	TEX AL	0	0	0	0	0	0	0	0	0	0	0	0

Art Houtteman

Year	Team	AB	R	H	D	T	HR	TB	BI	W	K	SB	CS
1950	DET AL	1	0	0	0	0	0	0	0	0	1	0	0

Elston Howard

Year	Team	AB	R	H	D	T	HR	TB	BI	W	K	SB	CS
1960-1	NYA AL	1	0	0	0	0	0	0	0	1	1	0	0
1961-1	NYA AL	0	0	0	0	0	0	0	0	0	0	0	0
1961-2	NYA AL	2	0	0	0	0	0	0	0	0	1	0	0
1962-2	NYA AL	2	0	0	0	0	0	0	0	0	2	0	0
1963	NYA AL	1	0	0	0	0	0	0	0	0	1	0	0
1964*	NYA AL	3	1	0	0	0	0	0	0	0	2	0	0
Totals	6 Yr	9	1	0	0	0	0	0	0	1	7	0	0

Frank Howard

Year	Team	AB	R	H	D	T	HR	TB	BI	W	K	SB	CS
1968*	WAS AL	2	0	0	0	0	0	0	0	0	1	0	0
1969*	WAS AL	1	1	1	0	0	1	4	1	1	0	0	0
1970*	WAS AL	2	0	0	0	0	0	0	0	0	1	0	0
1971	WAS AL	1	0	0	0	0	0	0	0	0	0	0	0
Totals	4 Yr	6	1	1	0	0	1	4	1	1	2	0	0

Steve Howe

Year	Team	AB	R	H	D	T	HR	TB	BI	W	K	SB	CS
1982	LAN NL	0	0	0	0	0	0	0	0	0	0	0	0

Jay Howell

Year	Team	AB	R	H	D	T	HR	TB	BI	W	K	SB	CS
1987	OAK AL	0	0	0	0	0	0	0	0	0	0	0	0

Roy Howell

Year	Team	AB	R	H	D	T	HR	TB	BI	W	K	SB	CS
1978	TOR AL	1	0	0	0	0	0	0	0	0	0	0	0

Dick Howser

Year	Team	AB	R	H	D	T	HR	TB	BI	W	K	SB	CS
1961-1	KC AL	1	0	0	0	0	0	0	0	0	1	0	0

LaMarr Hoyt

Year	Team	AB	R	H	D	T	HR	TB	BI	W	K	SB	CS
1985*	SDN NL	1	0	0	0	0	0	0	0	0	1	0	0

Kent Hrbek

Year	Team	AB	R	H	D	T	HR	TB	BI	W	K	SB	CS
1982	MIN AL	1	0	0	0	0	0	0	0	0	0	0	0

Glenn Hubbard

Year	Team	AB	R	H	D	T	HR	TB	BI	W	K	SB	CS
1983	ATL NL	1	0	1	0	0	0	1	0	0	0	0	0

Carl Hubbell

Year	Team	AB	R	H	D	T	HR	TB	BI	W	K	SB	CS
1933	NY NL	0	0	0	0	0	0	0	0	0	0	0	0
1934*	NY NL	0	0	0	0	0	0	0	0	0	0	0	0
1936	NY NL	1	0	0	0	0	0	0	0	0	0	0	0
1937	NY NL	0	0	0	0	0	0	0	0	0	0	0	0
1940	NY NL	0	0	0	0	0	0	0	0	0	0	0	0
Totals	5 Yr	1	0	0	0	0	0	0	0	0	0	0	0

John Hudek

Year	Team	AB	R	H	D	T	HR	TB	BI	W	K	SB	CS
1994	HOU NL	0	0	0	0	0	0	0	0	0	0	0	0

Sid Hudson

Year	Team	AB	R	H	D	T	HR	TB	BI	W	K	SB	CS
1941	WAS AL	0	0	0	0	0	0	0	0	0	0	0	0

Tim Hudson

Year	Team	AB	R	H	D	T	HR	TB	BI	W	K	SB	CS
2000	OAK AL	0	0	0	0	0	0	0	0	0	0	0	0

Tex Hughson

Year	Team	AB	R	H	D	T	HR	TB	BI	W	K	SB	CS
1943	BOS AL	0	0	0	0	0	0	0	0	0	0	0	0
1944	BOS AL	1	0	0	0	0	0	0	0	0	0	0	0
Totals	2 Yr	1	0	0	0	0	0	0	0	0	0	0	0

Tom Hume

Year	Team	AB	R	H	D	T	HR	TB	BI	W	K	SB	CS
1982	CIN NL	0	0	0	0	0	0	0	0	0	0	0	0

Randy Hundley

Year	Team	AB	R	H	D	T	HR	TB	BI	W	K	SB	CS
1969	CHN NL	1	0	0	0	0	0	0	0	0	1	0	0

Todd Hundley

Year	Team	AB	R	H	D	T	HR	TB	BI	W	K	SB	CS
1996	NYN NL	1	0	0	0	0	0	0	0	0	0	0	0

Ron Hunt

Year	Team	AB	R	H	D	T	HR	TB	BI	W	K	SB	CS
1964*	NYN NL	3	0	1	0	0	0	1	0	0	1	0	0
1966	NYN NL	1	0	0	0	0	0	0	0	0	0	0	0
Totals	2 Yr	4	0	1	0	0	0	1	0	0	1	0	0

Billy Hunter

Year	Team	AB	R	H	D	T	HR	TB	BI	W	K	SB	CS
1953	SLA AL	0	0	0	0	0	0	0	0	0	0	0	0

Catfish Hunter

Year	Team	AB	R	H	D	T	HR	TB	BI	W	K	SB	CS
1967	KC AL	1	0	0	0	0	0	0	0	0	1	0	0
1970	OAK AL	0	0	0	0	0	0	0	0	0	0	0	0
1973*	OAK AL	0	0	0	0	0	0	0	0	0	0	0	0
1974	OAK AL	0	0	0	0	0	0	0	0	0	0	0	0
1975	NYA AL	0	0	0	0	0	0	0	0	0	0	0	0
1976	NYA AL	0	0	0	0	0	0	0	0	0	0	0	0
Totals	6 Yr	1	0	0	0	0	0	0	0	0	1	0	0

Fred Hutchinson

Year	Team	AB	R	H	D	T	HR	TB	BI	W	K	SB	CS
1951	DET AL	0	0	0	0	0	0	0	0	0	0	0	0

Jason Isringhausen

Year	Team	AB	R	H	D	T	HR	TB	BI	W	K	SB	CS
2000	OAK AL	0	0	0	0	0	0	0	0	0	0	0	0

Ray Jablonski

Year	Team	AB	R	H	D	T	HR	TB	BI	W	K	SB	CS
1954*	SLN NL	3	1	1	0	0	0	1	1	0	0	0	0

Bo Jackson

Year	Team	AB	R	H	D	T	HR	TB	BI	W	K	SB	CS
1989*	KCA AL	4	1	2	0	0	1	5	2	0	1	1	0

Danny Jackson

Year	Team	AB	R	H	D	T	HR	TB	BI	W	K	SB	CS
1994	PHI NL	0	0	0	0	0	0	0	0	0	0	0	0

Larry Jackson

Year	Team	AB	R	H	D	T	HR	TB	BI	W	K	SB	CS
1957	SLN NL	0	0	0	0	0	0	0	0	0	0	0	0
1958	SLN NL	0	0	0	0	0	0	0	0	0	0	0	0
1960-2	SLN NL	0	0	0	0	0	0	0	0	0	0	0	0
1963	CHN NL	1	0	0	0	0	0	0	0	0	0	0	0
Totals	4 Yr	1	0	0	0	0	0	0	0	0	0	0	0

Year	Team	AB	R	H	D	T	HR	TB	BI	W	K	SB	CS

Randy Jackson

Year	Team	AB	R	H	D	T	HR	TB	BI	W	K	SB	CS
1954	CHN NL	2	0	0	0	0	0	0	0	0	0	0	0
1955	CHN NL	3	1	1	0	0	0	1	1	0	1	0	0
Totals	2 Yr	5	1	1	0	0	0	1	1	0	1	0	0

Reggie Jackson

Year	Team	AB	R	H	D	T	HR	TB	BI	W	K	SB	CS
1969*	OAK AL	2	0	0	0	0	0	0	0	1	0	0	0
1971	OAK AL	1	1	1	0	0	1	4	2	0	0	0	0
1972*	OAK AL	4	0	2	1	0	0	3	0	0	1	0	0
1973*	OAK AL	4	1	1	1	0	0	2	0	0	1	0	0
1974*	OAK AL	3	0	0	0	0	0	0	0	1	2	0	0
1975*	OAK AL	3	0	1	0	0	0	1	0	0	2	0	0
1977*	NYA AL	2	0	1	0	0	0	1	0	0	1	0	0
1979	NYA AL	1	0	0	0	0	0	0	0	1	0	0	0
1980*	NYA AL	2	0	1	0	0	0	1	0	1	1	0	0
1981*	NYA AL	1	0	0	0	0	0	0	0	0	0	0	0
1982*	CAL AL	1	0	0	0	0	0	0	1	0	0	0	0
1984*	CAL AL	2	0	0	0	0	0	0	0	0	1	0	0
Totals	12 Yr	26	2	7	2	0	1	12	3	4	9	0	0

Travis Jackson

Year	Team	AB	R	H	D	T	HR	TB	BI	W	K	SB	CS
1934*	NY NL	2	0	0	0	0	0	0	0	0	1	0	0

Brook Jacoby

Year	Team	AB	R	H	D	T	HR	TB	BI	W	K	SB	CS
1986	CLE AL	1	0	0	0	0	0	0	0	0	1	0	0
1990	CLE AL	1	0	0	0	0	0	0	0	0	0	0	0
Totals	2 Yr	2	0	0	0	0	0	0	0	0	1	0	0

John Jaha

Year	Team	AB	R	H	D	T	HR	TB	BI	W	K	SB	CS
1999	OAK AL	1	0	0	0	0	0	0	0	0	1	0	0

Larry Jansen

Year	Team	AB	R	H	D	T	HR	TB	BI	W	K	SB	CS
1950	NY NL	2	0	0	0	0	0	0	0	0	1	0	0

Al Javery

Year	Team	AB	R	H	D	T	HR	TB	BI	W	K	SB	CS
1943	BSN NL	0	0	0	0	0	0	0	0	0	0	0	0

Julian Javier

Year	Team	AB	R	H	D	T	HR	TB	BI	W	K	SB	CS
1963*	SLN NL	4	0	0	0	0	0	0	0	0	2	0	0
1968	SLN NL	0	0	0	0	0	0	0	0	0	0	0	0
Totals	2 Yr	4	0	0	0	0	0	0	0	0	2	0	0

Gregg Jefferies

Year	Team	AB	R	H	D	T	HR	TB	BI	W	K	SB	CS
1993	SLN NL	1	0	0	0	0	0	0	0	0	1	0	0
1994*	SLN NL	1	2	1	1	0	0	2	0	0	0	0	0
Totals	2 Yr	2	2	1	1	0	0	2	0	0	1	0	0

Ferguson Jenkins

Year	Team	AB	R	H	D	T	HR	TB	BI	W	K	SB	CS
1967	CHN NL	1	0	0	0	0	0	0	0	0	0	0	0
1971	CHN NL	0	0	0	0	0	0	0	0	0	0	0	0
Totals	2 Yr	1	0	0	0	0	0	0	0	0	0	0	0

Jackie Jensen

Year	Team	AB	R	H	D	T	HR	TB	BI	W	K	SB	CS
1952	WAS AL	0	0	0	0	0	0	0	0	0	0	0	0
1955	BOS AL	1	0	0	0	0	0	0	0	0	0	0	0
1958*	BOS AL	4	0	0	0	0	0	0	1	0	1	0	0
Totals	3 Yr	5	0	0	0	0	0	0	1	0	1	0	0

Derek Jeter

Year	Team	AB	R	H	D	T	HR	TB	BI	W	K	SB	CS
1998	NYA AL	1	0	0	0	0	0	0	0	0	1	0	0

Derek Jeter *continued*

Year	Team	AB	R	H	D	T	HR	TB	BI	W	K	SB	CS
1999	NYA AL	1	0	0	0	0	0	0	0	0	1	0	0
2000*	NYA AL	3	1	3	1	0	0	4	2	0	0	0	0
Totals	3 Yr	5	1	3	1	0	0	4	2	0	2	0	0

Tommy John

Year	Team	AB	R	H	D	T	HR	TB	BI	W	K	SB	CS
1968	CHA AL	0	0	0	0	0	0	0	0	0	0	0	0
1980	NYA AL	1	0	0	0	0	0	0	0	0	1	0	0
Totals	2 Yr	1	0	0	0	0	0	0	0	0	1	0	0

Alex Johnson

Year	Team	AB	R	H	D	T	HR	TB	BI	W	K	SB	CS
1970	CAL AL	1	0	0	0	0	0	0	0	0	0	0	0

Billy Johnson

Year	Team	AB	R	H	D	T	HR	TB	BI	W	K	SB	CS
1947	NYA AL	0	0	0	0	0	0	0	0	0	0	0	0

Bob Johnson

Year	Team	AB	R	H	D	T	HR	TB	BI	W	K	SB	CS
1935*	PHA AL	4	0	0	0	0	0	0	0	0	3	0	0
1938	PHA AL	1	0	0	0	0	0	0	0	0	1	0	0
1942	PHA AL	1	0	1	0	0	0	1	0	0	0	0	0
1943	WAS AL	0	0	0	0	0	0	0	0	0	0	0	0
1944*	BOS AL	3	0	0	0	0	0	0	0	1	1	0	0
Totals	5 Yr	9	0	1	0	0	0	1	0	1	5	0	0

Charles Johnson

Year	Team	AB	R	H	D	T	HR	TB	BI	W	K	SB	CS
1997	FLO NL	1	0	0	0	0	0	0	0	0	1	0	0

Dave Johnson

Year	Team	AB	R	H	D	T	HR	TB	BI	W	K	SB	CS
1968	BAL AL	1	0	0	0	0	0	0	0	0	1	0	0
1970*	BAL AL	5	0	1	0	0	0	1	0	0	1	0	0
1973	ATL NL	1	0	0	0	0	0	0	0	0	0	0	0
Totals	3 Yr	7	0	1	0	0	0	1	0	0	2	0	0

Howard Johnson

Year	Team	AB	R	H	D	T	HR	TB	BI	W	K	SB	CS
1989*	NYN NL	3	0	1	0	0	0	1	1	0	1	1	0
1991	NYN NL	2	0	0	0	0	0	0	0	0	1	0	0
Totals	2 Yr	5	0	1	0	0	0	1	1	0	2	1	0

Lance Johnson

Year	Team	AB	R	H	D	T	HR	TB	BI	W	K	SB	CS
1996*	NYN NL	4	1	3	1	0	0	4	0	0	0	1	1

Randy Johnson

Year	Team	AB	R	H	D	T	HR	TB	BI	W	K	SB	CS
1994	SEA AL	0	0	0	0	0	0	0	0	0	0	0	0
2000*	ARI NL	0	0	0	0	0	0	0	0	0	0	0	0
Totals	2 Yr	0	0	0	0	0	0	0	0	0	0	0	0

Andruw Jones

Year	Team	AB	R	H	D	T	HR	TB	BI	W	K	SB	CS
2000	ATL NL	2	0	1	0	0	0	1	1	0	1	0	0

Chipper Jones

Year	Team	AB	R	H	D	T	HR	TB	BI	W	K	SB	CS
1996*	ATL NL	2	1	1	0	0	0	1	0	0	0	0	0
1997	ATL NL	1	0	0	0	0	0	0	0	0	0	0	0
1998*	ATL NL	2	1	0	0	0	0	0	0	1	0	0	0
2000*	ATL NL	3	1	3	0	0	1	6	1	0	0	0	0
Totals	4 Yr	8	3	4	0	0	1	7	1	1	0	0	0

Cleon Jones

Year	Team	AB	R	H	D	T	HR	TB	BI	W	K	SB	CS
1969*	NYN NL	4	2	2	0	0	0	2	0	0	0	0	0

Year	Team	AB	R	H	D	T	HR	TB	BI	W	K	SB	CS

Doug Jones

Year	Team	AB	R	H	D	T	HR	TB	BI	W	K	SB	CS
1988	CLE AL	0	0	0	0	0	0	0	0	0	0	0	0
1992	HOU NL	0	0	0	0	0	0	0	0	0	0	0	0
1994	PHI NL	0	0	0	0	0	0	0	0	0	0	0	0
Totals	3 Yr	0	0	0	0	0	0	0	0	0	0	0	0

Randy Jones

Year	Team	AB	R	H	D	T	HR	TB	BI	W	K	SB	CS
1975	SDN NL	0	0	0	0	0	0	0	0	0	0	0	0
1976*	SDN NL	1	0	0	0	0	0	0	0	0	1	0	0
Totals	2 Yr	1	0	0	0	0	0	0	0	0	1	0	0

Ruppert Jones

Year	Team	AB	R	H	D	T	HR	TB	BI	W	K	SB	CS
1977	SEA AL	1	0	0	0	0	0	0	0	0	0	0	0
1982	SDN NL	1	1	1	0	1	0	3	0	0	0	0	0
Totals	2 Yr	2	1	1	0	1	0	3	0	0	0	0	0

Sam Jones

Year	Team	AB	R	H	D	T	HR	TB	BI	W	K	SB	CS
1955	CHN NL	0	0	0	0	0	0	0	0	0	0	0	0
1959-2	SFN NL	0	0	0	0	0	0	0	0	0	0	0	0
Totals	2 Yr	0	0	0	0	0	0	0	0	0	0	0	0

Todd Jones

Year	Team	AB	R	H	D	T	HR	TB	BI	W	K	SB	CS
2000	DET AL	0	0	0	0	0	0	0	0	0	0	0	0

Willie Jones

Year	Team	AB	R	H	D	T	HR	TB	BI	W	K	SB	CS
1950*	PHI NL	7	0	1	0	0	0	1	0	0	0	0	0
1951	PHI NL	2	0	0	0	0	0	0	0	1	1	0	0
Totals	2 Yr	9	0	1	0	0	0	1	0	1	1	0	0

Eddie Joost

Year	Team	AB	R	H	D	T	HR	TB	BI	W	K	SB	CS
1949*	PHA AL	2	1	1	0	0	0	1	2	1	0	0	0

Brian Jordan

Year	Team	AB	R	H	D	T	HR	TB	BI	W	K	SB	CS
1999	ATL NL	1	0	1	0	0	0	1	0	1	0	0	1

Felix Jose

Year	Team	AB	R	H	D	T	HR	TB	BI	W	K	SB	CS
1991	SLN NL	2	0	1	0	0	0	1	0	0	0	0	0

Duane Josephson

Year	Team	AB	R	H	D	T	HR	TB	BI	W	K	SB	CS
1968	CHA AL	0	0	0	0	0	0	0	0	0	0	0	0

Wally Joyner

Year	Team	AB	R	H	D	T	HR	TB	BI	W	K	SB	CS
1986*	CAL AL	1	0	0	0	0	0	0	0	0	0	0	0

Dave Justice

Year	Team	AB	R	H	D	T	HR	TB	BI	W	K	SB	CS
1993*	ATL NL	3	0	1	0	0	0	1	0	0	0	0	0
1994*	ATL NL	2	0	0	0	0	0	0	0	0	0	0	0
Totals	2 Yr	5	0	1	0	0	0	1	0	0	0	0	0

Jim Kaat

Year	Team	AB	R	H	D	T	HR	TB	BI	W	K	SB	CS
1966	MIN AL	0	0	0	0	0	0	0	0	0	0	0	0
1975	CHA AL	0	0	0	0	0	0	0	0	0	0	0	0
Totals	2 Yr	0	0	0	0	0	0	0	0	0	0	0	0

Al Kaline

Year	Team	AB	R	H	D	T	HR	TB	BI	W	K	SB	CS
1955*	DET AL	4	0	1	1	0	0	2	0	1	2	0	0
1956*	DET AL	3	0	1	0	0	0	1	0	0	0	0	0
1957*	DET AL	5	1	2	0	0	0	2	2	0	0	0	0
1958	DET AL	0	0	0	0	0	0	0	0	0	0	0	0
1959-1*	DET AL	3	1	1	0	0	1	4	1	0	1	0	0

Al Kaline *continued*

Year	Team	AB	R	H	D	T	HR	TB	BI	W	K	SB	CS
1959-2	DET AL	2	0	0	0	0	0	0	0	0	1	0	0
1960-1	DET AL	2	2	1	0	0	1	4	2	0	0	0	0
1960-2	DET AL	1	0	1	0	0	0	1	0	1	0	0	0
1961-1	DET AL	2	1	1	0	0	0	1	1	0	0	0	0
1961-2*	DET AL	4	0	2	0	0	0	2	0	0	0	1	0
1962-2	DET AL	0	1	0	0	0	0	0	0	0	0	0	0
1963*	DET AL	3	0	0	0	0	0	0	0	0	1	0	0
1965	DET AL	1	0	0	0	0	0	0	0	0	0	0	0
1966*	DET AL	4	0	1	0	0	0	1	0	0	0	0	0
1971	DET AL	2	1	1	0	0	0	1	0	0	1	0	0
1974	DET AL	1	0	0	0	0	0	0	0	0	0	0	0
Totals	16 Yr	37	7	12	1	0	2	19	6	2	6	1	0

Eddie Kasko

Year	Team	AB	R	H	D	T	HR	TB	BI	W	K	SB	CS
1961-2	CIN NL	1	0	1	0	0	0	1	0	0	0	0	0

Eddie Kazak

Year	Team	AB	R	H	D	T	HR	TB	BI	W	K	SB	CS
1949*	SLN NL	2	0	2	0	0	0	2	1	0	0	0	0

Bob Keegan

Year	Team	AB	R	H	D	T	HR	TB	BI	W	K	SB	CS
1954	CHA AL	0	0	0	0	0	0	0	0	0	0	0	0

George Kell

Year	Team	AB	R	H	D	T	HR	TB	BI	W	K	SB	CS
1947*	DET AL	4	0	0	0	0	0	0	0	0	2	0	0
1949*	DET AL	3	2	2	0	0	0	2	0	1	0	1	0
1950*	DET AL	6	0	0	0	0	0	0	2	0	1	0	0
1951*	DET AL	4	1	1	0	0	1	4	1	0	1	0	0
1953	BOS AL	1	0	0	0	0	0	0	0	0	0	0	0
1956*	BAL AL	4	0	1	0	0	0	1	0	0	0	0	0
1957*	BAL AL	2	0	0	0	0	0	0	0	0	0	0	0
Totals	7 Yr	24	3	4	0	0	1	7	3	1	4	1	0

Charlie Keller

Year	Team	AB	R	H	D	T	HR	TB	BI	W	K	SB	CS
1940*	NYA AL	2	0	0	0	0	0	0	0	0	1	0	0
1941	NYA AL	1	0	0	0	0	0	0	0	0	1	0	0
1946*	NYA AL	4	2	1	0	0	1	4	2	1	1	0	0
Totals	3 Yr	7	2	1	0	0	1	4	2	1	3	0	0

Bobby Kelly

Year	Team	AB	R	H	D	T	HR	TB	BI	W	K	SB	CS
1992	NYA AL	2	0	1	1	0	0	2	2	0	1	0	0
1993	CIN NL	1	0	0	0	0	0	0	0	0	1	0	0
Totals	2 Yr	3	0	1	1	0	0	2	2	0	2	0	0

Pat Kelly

Year	Team	AB	R	H	D	T	HR	TB	BI	W	K	SB	CS
1973	CHA AL	1	0	0	0	0	0	0	0	0	0	0	0

Ken Keltner

Year	Team	AB	R	H	D	T	HR	TB	BI	W	K	SB	CS
1940	CLE AL	1	0	0	0	0	0	0	0	0	1	0	0
1941	CLE AL	1	1	1	0	0	0	1	0	0	0	0	0
1942*	CLE AL	4	0	0	0	0	0	0	0	0	1	0	0
1943*	CLE AL	4	1	1	1	0	0	2	0	0	3	0	0
1944*	CLE AL	4	1	1	0	0	0	1	0	0	0	0	0
1946*	CLE AL	0	0	0	0	0	0	0	0	1	0	0	0
1948*	CLE AL	3	1	1	0	0	0	1	0	1	0	0	0
Totals	7 Yr	17	4	4	1	0	0	5	0	2	5	0	0

Steve Kemp

Year	Team	AB	R	H	D	T	HR	TB	BI	W	K	SB	CS
1979	DET AL	1	0	0	0	0	0	0	0	0	0	0	0

Year	Team	AB	R	H	D	T	HR	TB	BI	W	K	SB	CS

Jason Kendall

Year	Team	AB	R	H	D	T	HR	TB	BI	W	K	SB	CS
1996	PIT NL	0	0	0	0	0	0	0	0	0	0	0	0
1998	PIT NL	1	0	1	0	0	0	1	0	0	0	0	0
2000*	PIT NL	2	0	0	0	0	0	0	0	0	1	0	0
Totals	3 Yr	3	0	1	0	0	0	1	0	0	1	0	0

Terry Kennedy

Year	Team	AB	R	H	D	T	HR	TB	BI	W	K	SB	CS
1981	SDN NL	1	0	0	0	0	0	0	0	0	0	0	0
1985*	SDN NL	2	0	1	0	0	0	1	1	0	0	0	0
1987*	BAL AL	2	0	0	0	0	0	0	0	0	1	0	0
Totals	3 Yr	5	0	1	0	0	0	1	1	0	1	0	0

Jeff Kent

Year	Team	AB	R	H	D	T	HR	TB	BI	W	K	SB	CS
1999	SFN NL	1	0	0	0	0	0	0	0	1	0	0	0
2000*	SFN NL	2	0	0	0	0	0	0	0	0	0	0	0
Totals	2 Yr	3	0	0	0	0	0	0	0	1	0	0	0

Matt Keough

Year	Team	AB	R	H	D	T	HR	TB	BI	W	K	SB	CS
1978	OAK AL	0	0	0	0	0	0	0	0	0	0	0	0

Jim Kern

Year	Team	AB	R	H	D	T	HR	TB	BI	W	K	SB	CS
1977	CLE AL	0	0	0	0	0	0	0	0	0	0	0	0
1978	CLE AL	0	0	0	0	0	0	0	0	0	0	0	0
1979	TEX AL	0	0	0	0	0	0	0	0	0	0	0	0
Totals	3 Yr	0	0	0	0	0	0	0	0	0	0	0	0

Buddy Kerr

Year	Team	AB	R	H	D	T	HR	TB	BI	W	K	SB	CS
1948	NY NL	2	0	0	0	0	0	0	0	0	1	0	0

Don Kessinger

Year	Team	AB	R	H	D	T	HR	TB	BI	W	K	SB	CS
1968*	CHN NL	2	0	0	0	0	0	0	0	0	1	0	0
1969*	CHN NL	3	0	0	0	0	0	0	0	0	0	0	0
1970*	CHN NL	2	0	2	0	0	0	2	0	0	0	0	0
1971	CHN NL	2	0	0	0	0	0	0	0	0	0	0	0
1972*	CHN NL	2	0	0	0	0	0	0	0	0	0	0	0
1974	CHN NL	1	1	1	0	1	0	3	1	0	0	0	0
Totals	6 Yr	12	1	3	0	1	0	5	1	0	1	0	0

Jimmy Key

Year	Team	AB	R	H	D	T	HR	TB	BI	W	K	SB	CS
1985	TOR AL	0	0	0	0	0	0	0	0	0	0	0	0
1994*	NYA AL	0	0	0	0	0	0	0	0	0	0	0	0
Totals	2 Yr	0	0	0	0	0	0	0	0	0	0	0	0

Darryl Kile

Year	Team	AB	R	H	D	T	HR	TB	BI	W	K	SB	CS
2000	SLN NL	0	0	0	0	0	0	0	0	0	0	0	0

Harmon Killebrew

Year	Team	AB	R	H	D	T	HR	TB	BI	W	K	SB	CS
1959–1*	WAS AL	3	0	0	0	0	0	0	0	0	1	0	0
1961–1	MIN AL	2	1	1	0	0	1	4	1	0	0	0	0
1963	MIN AL	1	0	0	0	0	0	0	0	0	1	0	0
1964*	MIN AL	4	1	3	0	0	0	3	1	0	0	0	0
1965*	MIN AL	3	1	1	0	0	1	4	2	2	1	0	0
1966	MIN AL	1	0	1	0	0	0	1	0	0	0	0	0
1967*	MIN AL	6	0	0	0	0	0	0	0	0	2	0	0
1968*	MIN AL	1	0	0	0	0	0	0	0	0	0	0	0
1969	MIN AL	1	0	0	0	0	0	0	0	0	0	0	0
1970*	MIN AL	2	0	1	0	0	0	1	0	0	1	0	0
1971	MIN AL	2	1	1	0	0	1	4	2	0	0	0	0
Totals	11 Yr	26	4	8	0	0	3	17	6	2	6	0	0

Ralph Kiner

Year	Team	AB	R	H	D	T	HR	TB	BI	W	K	SB	CS
1948	PIT NL	1	0	0	0	0	0	0	0	0	0	0	0
1949*	PIT NL	5	1	1	0	0	1	4	2	0	0	0	0
1950*	PIT NL	6	1	2	1	0	1	6	1	0	1	0	0
1951	PIT NL	2	1	1	0	0	1	4	1	0	0	0	0
1953	CHN NL	1	0	0	0	0	0	0	0	0	1	0	0
Totals	5 Yr	15	3	4	1	0	3	14	4	0	2	0	0

Dave Kingman

Year	Team	AB	R	H	D	T	HR	TB	BI	W	K	SB	CS
1976*	NYN NL	2	0	0	0	0	0	0	0	0	1	0	0
1980*	CHN NL	1	0	0	0	0	0	0	0	0	1	0	0
Totals	2 Yr	3	0	0	0	0	0	0	0	0	2	0	0

Ron Kittle

Year	Team	AB	R	H	D	T	HR	TB	BI	W	K	SB	CS
1983	CHA AL	2	1	1	0	0	0	1	0	0	1	0	0

Chuck Klein

Year	Team	AB	R	H	D	T	HR	TB	BI	W	K	SB	CS
1933*	PHI NL	4	0	1	0	0	0	1	0	0	0	0	0
1934	CHN NL	3	0	1	0	0	0	1	1	0	0	0	0
Totals	2 Yr	7	0	2	0	0	0	2	1	0	0	0	0

Ted Kluszewski

Year	Team	AB	R	H	D	T	HR	TB	BI	W	K	SB	CS
1953*	CIN NL	3	0	1	0	0	0	1	0	0	0	0	0
1954*	CIN NL	4	2	2	0	0	1	5	3	0	0	0	0
1955*	CIN NL	5	1	2	1	0	0	3	0	0	0	0	0
1956	CIN NL	2	1	2	2	0	0	4	1	0	0	0	0
Totals	4 Yr	14	4	7	3	0	1	13	4	0	0	0	0

Bob Knepper

Year	Team	AB	R	H	D	T	HR	TB	BI	W	K	SB	CS
1981	HOU NL	0	0	0	0	0	0	0	0	0	0	0	0
1988	HOU NL	0	0	0	0	0	0	0	0	0	0	0	0
Totals	2 Yr	0	0	0	0	0	0	0	0	0	0	0	0

Ray Knight

Year	Team	AB	R	H	D	T	HR	TB	BI	W	K	SB	CS
1980	CIN NL	1	1	1	0	0	0	1	0	1	0	1	0
1982	HOU NL	3	0	0	0	0	0	0	0	0	1	0	0
Totals	2 Yr	4	1	1	0	0	0	1	0	1	1	1	0

Chuck Knoblauch

Year	Team	AB	R	H	D	T	HR	TB	BI	W	K	SB	CS
1992	MIN AL	1	0	0	0	0	0	0	0	1	0	0	0
1994	MIN AL	3	1	0	0	0	0	0	0	0	2	0	0
1996	MIN AL	1	0	1	0	0	0	1	0	0	0	0	0
1997	MIN AL	0	0	0	0	0	0	0	0	0	0	0	0
Totals	4 Yr	5	1	1	0	0	0	1	0	1	2	0	0

Bobby Knoop

Year	Team	AB	R	H	D	T	HR	TB	BI	W	K	SB	CS
1966*	CAL AL	2	0	0	0	0	0	0	0	0	1	0	0

Darold Knowles

Year	Team	AB	R	H	D	T	HR	TB	BI	W	K	SB	CS
1969	WAS AL	0	0	0	0	0	0	0	0	0	0	0	0

Jim Konstanty

Year	Team	AB	R	H	D	T	HR	TB	BI	W	K	SB	CS
1950	PHI NL	0	0	0	0	0	0	0	0	0	0	0	0

Jerry Koosman

Year	Team	AB	R	H	D	T	HR	TB	BI	W	K	SB	CS
1968	NYN NL	0	0	0	0	0	0	0	0	0	0	0	0
1969	NYN NL	0	0	0	0	0	0	0	0	0	0	0	0
Totals	2 Yr	0	0	0	0	0	0	0	0	0	0	0	0

Year	Team	AB	R	H	D	T	HR	TB	BI	W	K	SB	CS

Sandy Koufax

Year	Team	AB	R	H	D	T	HR	TB	BI	W	K	SB	CS
1961–1	LAN NL	0	0	0	0	0	0	0	0	0	0	0	0
1961–2	LAN NL	0	0	0	0	0	0	0	0	0	0	0	0
1965	LAN NL	0	0	0	0	0	0	0	0	0	0	0	0
1966*	LAN NL	0	0	0	0	0	0	0	0	0	0	0	0
Totals	4 Yr	0	0	0	0	0	0	0	0	0	0	0	0

Jack Kramer

Year	Team	AB	R	H	D	T	HR	TB	BI	W	K	SB	CS
1946	SLA AL	1	1	1	0	0	0	1	0	0	0	0	0

Mike Kreevich

Year	Team	AB	R	H	D	T	HR	TB	BI	W	K	SB	CS
1938*	CHA AL	2	0	0	0	0	0	0	0	0	0	0	0

John Kruk

Year	Team	AB	R	H	D	T	HR	TB	BI	W	K	SB	CS
1992	PHI NL	2	1	2	0	0	0	2	0	0	0	0	0
1993*	PHI NL	3	0	0	0	0	0	0	0	0	2	0	0
Totals	2 Yr	5	1	2	0	0	0	2	0	0	2	0	0

Mike Krukow

Year	Team	AB	R	H	D	T	HR	TB	BI	W	K	SB	CS
1986	SFN NL	0	0	0	0	0	0	0	0	0	0	0	0

Tony Kubek

Year	Team	AB	R	H	D	T	HR	TB	BI	W	K	SB	CS
1959–2	NYA AL	1	1	0	0	0	0	0	0	1	1	0	0
1961–1*	NYA AL	4	0	0	0	0	0	0	0	0	1	0	0
Totals	2 Yr	5	1	0	0	0	0	0	0	1	2	0	0

Harvey Kuenn

Year	Team	AB	R	H	D	T	HR	TB	BI	W	K	SB	CS
1953	DET AL	1	0	0	0	0	0	0	0	0	0	0	0
1955*	DET AL	3	1	1	0	0	0	1	0	0	0	0	0
1956*	DET AL	5	0	1	0	0	0	1	0	0	0	0	0
1957*	DET AL	2	0	0	0	0	0	0	1	1	0	0	0
1959–1	DET AL	1	1	0	0	0	0	0	0	1	0	0	0
1960–1	CLE AL	3	1	1	0	0	0	1	0	0	0	0	0
1960–2	CLE AL	1	0	0	0	0	0	0	0	0	0	0	0
Totals	7 Yr	16	3	3	0	0	0	3	1	2	0	0	0

Whitey Kurowski

Year	Team	AB	R	H	D	T	HR	TB	BI	W	K	SB	CS
1944	SLN NL	1	0	1	1	0	0	2	2	0	0	0	0
1946*	SLN NL	3	0	0	0	0	0	0	0	0	2	0	0
1947	SLN NL	2	0	0	0	0	0	0	0	0	1	0	0
Totals	3 Yr	6	0	1	1	0	0	2	2	0	3	0	0

Chet Laabs

Year	Team	AB	R	H	D	T	HR	TB	BI	W	K	SB	CS
1943*	SLA AL	3	1	0	0	0	0	0	0	1	1	0	0

Clem Labine

Year	Team	AB	R	H	D	T	HR	TB	BI	W	K	SB	CS
1957	BRO NL	0	0	0	0	0	0	0	0	0	0	0	0

Mike LaCoss

Year	Team	AB	R	H	D	T	HR	TB	BI	W	K	SB	CS
1979	CIN NL	0	0	0	0	0	0	0	0	0	0	0	0

Ray Lamanno

Year	Team	AB	R	H	D	T	HR	TB	BI	W	K	SB	CS
1946	CIN NL	1	0	0	0	0	0	0	0	0	0	0	0

Jim Landis

Year	Team	AB	R	H	D	T	HR	TB	BI	W	K	SB	CS
1962–1	CHA AL	1	0	0	0	0	0	0	0	0	1	0	0

Ken Landreaux

Year	Team	AB	R	H	D	T	HR	TB	BI	W	K	SB	CS
1980	MIN AL	1	0	0	0	0	0	0	0	0	0	0	0

Mark Langston

Year	Team	AB	R	H	D	T	HR	TB	BI	W	K	SB	CS
1987	SEA AL	0	0	0	0	0	0	0	0	0	0	0	0
1992	CAL AL	0	0	0	0	0	0	0	0	0	0	0	0
Totals	2 Yr	0	0	0	0	0	0	0	0	0	0	0	0

Ray Lankford

Year	Team	AB	R	H	D	T	HR	TB	BI	W	K	SB	CS
1997*	SLN NL	2	0	0	0	0	0	0	0	1	1	0	0

Carney Lansford

Year	Team	AB	R	H	D	T	HR	TB	BI	W	K	SB	CS
1988	OAK AL	1	0	0	0	0	0	0	0	0	0	0	0

Norm Larker

Year	Team	AB	R	H	D	T	HR	TB	BI	W	K	SB	CS
1960–1	LAN NL	1	0	0	0	0	0	0	0	0	0	0	0
1960–2	LAN NL	0	1	0	0	0	0	0	0	1	0	0	0
Totals	2 Yr	1	1	0	0	0	0	0	0	1	0	0	0

Barry Larkin

Year	Team	AB	R	H	D	T	HR	TB	BI	W	K	SB	CS
1988	CIN NL	2	0	0	0	0	0	0	0	0	1	0	0
1990	CIN NL	0	0	0	0	0	0	0	0	0	0	1	0
1991	CIN NL	1	0	0	0	0	0	0	0	0	0	0	0
1993*	CIN NL	2	0	0	0	0	0	0	1	0	1	0	0
1995*	CIN NL	3	0	0	0	0	0	0	0	0	0	0	0
1996*	CIN NL	3	1	1	0	0	0	1	0	0	0	0	0
1999*	CIN NL	3	0	1	0	0	0	1	1	0	1	0	0
2000*	CIN NL	3	0	0	0	0	0	0	0	0	0	0	0
Totals	8 Yr	17	1	2	0	0	0	2	2	0	3	1	0

Dave LaRoche

Year	Team	AB	R	H	D	T	HR	TB	BI	W	K	SB	CS
1977	CAL AL	0	0	0	0	0	0	0	0	0	0	0	0

Frank Lary

Year	Team	AB	R	H	D	T	HR	TB	BI	W	K	SB	CS
1960–1	DET AL	0	0	0	0	0	0	0	0	0	0	0	0
1960–2	DET AL	0	0	0	0	0	0	0	0	0	0	0	0
1961–1	DET AL	0	0	0	0	0	0	0	0	0	0	0	0
Totals	3 Yr	0	0	0	0	0	0	0	0	0	0	0	0

Tim Laudner

Year	Team	AB	R	H	D	T	HR	TB	BI	W	K	SB	CS
1988	MIN AL	1	0	1	1	0	0	2	0	0	0	0	0

Cookie Lavagetto

Year	Team	AB	R	H	D	T	HR	TB	BI	W	K	SB	CS
1940*	BRO NL	2	0	0	0	0	0	0	0	0	0	0	0
1941	BRO NL	1	0	0	0	0	0	0	0	0	0	0	0
Totals	2 Yr	3	0	0	0	0	0	0	0	0	0	0	0

Gary Lavelle

Year	Team	AB	R	H	D	T	HR	TB	BI	W	K	SB	CS
1977	SFN NL	0	0	0	0	0	0	0	0	0	0	0	0

Vance Law

Year	Team	AB	R	H	D	T	HR	TB	BI	W	K	SB	CS
1988	CHN NL	0	0	0	0	0	0	0	0	0	0	0	0

Vern Law

Year	Team	AB	R	H	D	T	HR	TB	BI	W	K	SB	CS
1960–1	PIT NL	0	0	0	0	0	0	0	0	0	0	0	0
1960–2*	PIT NL	1	0	0	0	0	0	0	0	0	0	0	0
Totals	2 Yr	1	0	0	0	0	0	0	0	0	0	0	0

Matt Lawton

Year	Team	AB	R	H	D	T	HR	TB	BI	W	K	SB	CS
2000	MIN AL	2	1	1	0	0	0	1	1	0	0	1	0

Charlie Lea

Year	Team	AB	R	H	D	T	HR	TB	BI	W	K	SB	CS
1984*	MON NL	0	0	0	0	0	0	0	0	0	0	0	0

Year	Team	AB	R	H	D	T	HR	TB	BI	W	K	SB	CS

Bill Lee

Year	Team	AB	R	H	D	T	HR	TB	BI	W	K	SB	CS
1938	CHN NL	1	0	0	0	0	0	0	0	0	0	0	0
1939	CHN NL	0	0	0	0	0	0	0	0	0	0	0	0
Totals	2 Yr	1	0	0	0	0	0	0	0	0	0	0	0

Thornton Lee

1941	CHA AL	1	0	0	0	0	0	0	0	0	0	0	0

Jim Lefebvre

1966*	LAN NL	2	0	0	0	0	0	0	0	0	0	0	0

Ron LeFlore

1976*	DET AL	2	0	1	0	0	0	1	0	0	1	0	0

Hank Leiber

1938	NY NL	1	0	0	0	0	0	0	0	0	0	0	0

Al Leiter

Year	Team	AB	R	H	D	T	HR	TB	BI	W	K	SB	CS
1996	FLO NL	0	0	0	0	0	0	0	0	0	0	0	0
2000	NYN NL	0	0	0	0	0	0	0	0	0	0	0	0
Totals	2 Yr	0	0	0	0	0	0	0	0	0	0	0	0

Bob Lemon

Year	Team	AB	R	H	D	T	HR	TB	BI	W	K	SB	CS
1950	CLE AL	0	1	0	0	0	0	0	0	1	0	0	0
1951	CLE AL	0	0	0	0	0	0	0	0	0	0	0	0
1952	CLE AL	1	0	0	0	0	0	0	0	0	0	0	0
1954	CLE AL	0	0	0	0	0	0	0	0	0	0	0	0
Totals	4 Yr	1	1	0	0	0	0	0	0	1	0	0	0

Chet Lemon

Year	Team	AB	R	H	D	T	HR	TB	BI	W	K	SB	CS
1978	CHA AL	0	0	0	0	0	0	0	0	0	0	0	0
1979	CHA AL	2	1	0	0	0	0	0	0	1	1	0	0
1984*	DET AL	2	0	1	0	0	0	1	0	0	1	0	0
Totals	3 Yr	4	1	1	0	0	0	1	0	1	2	0	0

Jim Lemon

1960-1	WAS AL	1	0	0	0	0	0	0	0	1	1	0	0

Dutch Leonard

1943*	WAS AL	1	0	1	0	0	0	1	0	0	0	0	0

Jeffrey Leonard

Year	Team	AB	R	H	D	T	HR	TB	BI	W	K	SB	CS
1987	SFN NL	2	0	0	0	0	0	0	0	0	0	0	0
1989	SEA AL	1	0	0	0	0	0	0	0	0	1	0	0
Totals	2 Yr	3	0	0	0	0	0	0	0	0	1	0	0

Buddy Lewis

Year	Team	AB	R	H	D	T	HR	TB	BI	W	K	SB	CS
1938*	WAS AL	1	0	0	0	0	0	0	0	0	0	0	0
1947*	WAS AL	2	0	0	0	0	0	0	0	0	0	0	0
Totals	2 Yr	3	0	0	0	0	0	0	0	0	0	0	0

Mike Lieberthal

Year	Team	AB	R	H	D	T	HR	TB	BI	W	K	SB	CS
1999	PHI NL	1	0	0	0	0	0	0	0	0	0	0	0
2000	PHI NL	2	1	1	0	0	0	1	0	0	0	0	0
Totals	2 Yr	3	1	1	0	0	0	1	0	0	0	0	0

Danny Litwhiler

1942	PHI NL	1	0	1	0	0	0	1	0	0	0	0	0

Whitey Lockman

1952*	NY NL	3	0	0	0	0	0	0	0	0	1	0	0

Billy Loes

1957	BAL AL	1	0	0	0	0	0	0	0	0	0	0	0

Kenny Lofton

Year	Team	AB	R	H	D	T	HR	TB	BI	W	K	SB	CS
1994	CLE AL	2	0	1	0	0	0	1	2	0	1	1	0
1995*	CLE AL	3	0	0	0	0	0	0	0	0	1	0	0
1996*	CLE AL	3	0	2	0	0	0	2	0	0	0	2	0
1998*	CLE AL	3	0	1	0	0	0	1	0	1	0	1	0
1999*	CLE AL	3	1	1	0	0	0	1	0	0	1	1	0
Totals	5 Yr	14	1	5	0	0	0	5	2	1	3	5	0

Johnny Logan

Year	Team	AB	R	H	D	T	HR	TB	BI	W	K	SB	CS
1955	MIL NL	3	0	1	0	0	0	1	1	0	1	0	0
1958	MIL NL	1	0	0	0	0	0	0	0	0	0	0	0
Totals	2 Yr	4	0	1	0	0	0	1	1	0	1	0	0

Mickey Lolich

Year	Team	AB	R	H	D	T	HR	TB	BI	W	K	SB	CS
1971	DET AL	0	0	0	0	0	0	0	0	0	0	0	0
1972	DET AL	1	0	0	0	0	0	0	0	0	1	0	0
Totals	2 Yr	1	0	0	0	0	0	0	0	0	1	0	0

Sherm Lollar

Year	Team	AB	R	H	D	T	HR	TB	BI	W	K	SB	CS
1956	CHA AL	2	0	1	0	0	0	1	0	0	0	0	0
1959-1	CHA AL	1	0	0	0	0	0	0	0	0	0	0	0
1959-2	CHA AL	0	0	0	0	0	0	0	0	1	0	0	0
1960-1	CHA AL	1	0	0	0	0	0	0	0	0	0	0	0
1960-2	CHA AL	2	0	1	1	0	0	2	0	0	0	0	0
Totals	5 Yr	6	0	2	1	0	0	3	0	1	0	0	0

Ernie Lombardi

Year	Team	AB	R	H	D	T	HR	TB	BI	W	K	SB	CS
1938*	CIN NL	4	0	2	0	0	0	2	1	0	0	0	0
1939*	CIN NL	4	0	2	0	0	0	2	0	0	0	0	0
1940*	CIN NL	2	0	1	0	0	0	1	0	0	0	0	0
1942	BSN NL	1	0	0	0	0	0	0	0	1	0	0	0
1943	NY NL	2	0	0	0	0	0	0	0	0	0	0	0
Totals	5 Yr	13	0	5	0	0	0	5	1	1	0	0	0

Dale Long

1956*	PIT NL	2	0	0	0	0	0	0	0	0	2	0	0

Eddie Lopat

1951	NYA AL	0	0	0	0	0	0	0	0	0	0	0	0

Stan Lopata

1955	PHI NL	3	0	0	0	0	0	0	0	0	1	0	0

Davey Lopes

Year	Team	AB	R	H	D	T	HR	TB	BI	W	K	SB	CS
1978	LAN NL	1	0	1	0	0	0	1	1	0	0	0	1
1979*	LAN NL	3	0	1	0	0	0	1	0	0	1	0	0
1980*	LAN NL	1	0	0	0	0	0	0	0	0	0	0	0
1981*	LAN NL	0	0	0	0	0	0	0	0	0	1	1	0
Totals	4 Yr	5	0	2	0	0	0	2	1	1	1	0	1

Al Lopez

Year	Team	AB	R	H	D	T	HR	TB	BI	W	K	SB	CS
1934	BRO NL	2	0	0	0	0	0	0	0	0	1	0	0
1941	PIT NL	1	0	0	0	0	0	0	0	0	0	0	0
Totals	2 Yr	3	0	0	0	0	0	0	0	0	1	0	0

Year	Team	AB	R	H	D	T	HR	TB	BI	W	K	SB	CS

Javier Lopez

Year	Team	AB	R	H	D	T	HR	TB	BI	W	K	SB	CS
1997	ATL NL	1	1	1	0	0	1	4	1	0	0	0	0
1998	ATL NL	1	0	0	0	0	0	0	0	0	1	0	0
Totals	2 Yr	2	1	1	0	0	1	4	1	0	1	0	0

Derek Lowe

Year	Team	AB	R	H	D	T	HR	TB	BI	W	K	SB	CS
2000	BOS AL	0	0	0	0	0	0	0	0	0	0	0	0

Peanuts Lowrey

Year	Team	AB	R	H	D	T	HR	TB	BI	W	K	SB	CS
1946	CHN NL	2	0	1	0	0	0	1	0	0	0	0	0

Greg Luzinski

Year	Team	AB	R	H	D	T	HR	TB	BI	W	K	SB	CS
1975	PHI NL	1	0	0	0	0	0	0	0	0	1	0	0
1976*	PHI NL	3	0	0	0	0	0	0	0	0	0	0	0
1977*	PHI NL	2	1	1	0	0	1	4	2	0	0	0	0
1978*	PHI NL	2	0	1	0	0	0	1	1	1	0	0	0
Totals	4 Yr	8	1	2	0	0	1	5	3	1	1	0	0

Sparky Lyle

Year	Team	AB	R	H	D	T	HR	TB	BI	W	K	SB	CS
1973	NYA AL	0	0	0	0	0	0	0	0	0	0	0	0
1977	NYA AL	0	0	0	0	0	0	0	0	0	0	0	0
Totals	2 Yr	0	0	0	0	0	0	0	0	0	0	0	0

Fred Lynn

Year	Team	AB	R	H	D	T	HR	TB	BI	W	K	SB	CS
1975	BOS AL	2	0	0	0	0	0	0	0	0	1	0	0
1976*	BOS AL	3	1	1	0	0	1	4	1	0	1	0	0
1977	BOS AL	1	1	0	0	0	0	0	0	1	0	0	0
1978*	BOS AL	4	0	1	0	0	0	1	0	0	1	0	0
1979*	BOS AL	1	1	1	0	0	1	4	2	0	0	0	0
1980*	BOS AL	3	1	1	0	0	1	4	2	0	1	0	0
1981	CAL AL	1	0	1	0	0	0	1	1	0	0	0	0
1982*	CAL AL	2	0	0	0	0	0	0	0	0	0	0	0
1983*	CAL AL	3	1	1	0	0	1	4	4	1	2	0	0
Totals	9 Yr	20	5	6	0	0	4	18	10	2	6	0	0

Ray Mack

Year	Team	AB	R	H	D	T	HR	TB	BI	W	K	SB	CS
1940	CLE AL	1	0	0	0	0	0	0	0	0	1	0	0

Greg Maddux

Year	Team	AB	R	H	D	T	HR	TB	BI	W	K	SB	CS
1992	CHN NL	0	0	0	0	0	0	0	0	0	0	0	0
1994*	ATL NL	0	0	0	0	0	0	0	0	0	0	0	0
1998*	ATL NL	0	0	0	0	0	0	0	0	0	0	0	0
Totals	3 Yr	0	0	0	0	0	0	0	0	0	0	0	0

Bill Madlock

Year	Team	AB	R	H	D	T	HR	TB	BI	W	K	SB	CS
1975	CHN NL	2	0	1	0	0	0	1	2	0	0	0	0
1981	PIT NL	1	0	0	0	0	0	0	0	0	0	0	0
1983	PIT NL	1	0	0	0	0	0	0	0	0	0	0	0
Totals	3 Yr	4	0	1	0	0	0	1	2	0	0	0	0

Sal Maglie

Year	Team	AB	R	H	D	T	HR	TB	BI	W	K	SB	CS
1951	NY NL	1	0	0	0	0	0	0	0	0	0	0	0

Art Mahaffey

Year	Team	AB	R	H	D	T	HR	TB	BI	W	K	SB	CS
1961–2	PHI NL	0	0	0	0	0	0	0	0	0	0	0	0
1962–2	PHI NL	0	0	0	0	0	0	0	0	0	0	0	0
Totals	2 Yr	0	0	0	0	0	0	0	0	0	0	0	0

Jim Maloney

Year	Team	AB	R	H	D	T	HR	TB	BI	W	K	SB	CS
1965	CIN NL	0	0	0	0	0	0	0	0	0	0	0	0

Frank Malzone

Year	Team	AB	R	H	D	T	HR	TB	BI	W	K	SB	CS
1957	BOS AL	2	0	0	0	0	0	0	0	0	0	0	0
1958*	BOS AL	4	1	1	0	0	0	1	0	0	1	0	0
1959–1	BOS AL	2	0	0	0	0	0	0	0	0	0	0	0
1959–2*	BOS AL	4	1	1	0	0	1	4	1	0	0	0	0
1960–1*	BOS AL	3	0	0	0	0	0	0	0	0	0	0	0
1960–2*	BOS AL	2	0	0	0	0	0	0	0	1	0	0	0
1963*	BOS AL	3	1	1	0	0	0	1	1	0	0	0	0
Totals	7 Yr	20	3	3	0	0	1	6	2	1	1	0	0

Gus Mancuso

Year	Team	AB	R	H	D	T	HR	TB	BI	W	K	SB	CS
1935	NY NL	1	0	0	0	0	0	0	0	0	0	0	0
1937	NY NL	1	0	0	0	0	0	0	0	0	0	0	0
Totals	2 Yr	2	0	0	0	0	0	0	0	0	0	0	0

Felix Mantilla

Year	Team	AB	R	H	D	T	HR	TB	BI	W	K	SB	CS
1965*	BOS AL	2	0	0	0	0	0	0	0	0	0	0	0

Mickey Mantle

Year	Team	AB	R	H	D	T	HR	TB	BI	W	K	SB	CS
1953*	NYA AL	2	0	0	0	0	0	0	0	1	0	0	0
1954*	NYA AL	5	1	2	0	0	0	2	0	0	1	0	0
1955*	NYA AL	6	1	2	0	0	1	5	3	0	1	0	0
1956*	NYA AL	4	1	1	0	0	1	4	1	0	3	0	0
1957*	NYA AL	4	1	1	0	0	0	1	0	1	1	0	0
1958*	NYA AL	2	0	1	0	0	0	1	0	2	0	0	0
1959–1	NYA AL	0	0	0	0	0	0	0	0	0	0	0	0
1959–2*	NYA AL	3	0	1	0	0	0	1	0	1	1	0	1
1960–1*	NYA AL	0	0	0	0	0	0	0	0	2	0	0	0
1960–2*	NYA AL	4	0	1	0	0	0	1	0	0	1	0	0
1961–1*	NYA AL	3	0	0	0	0	0	0	0	2	0	0	0
1961–2*	NYA AL	3	0	0	0	0	0	0	1	2	0	0	0
1962–1*	NYA AL	1	0	0	0	0	0	0	0	1	1	0	0
1964*	NYA AL	4	1	1	0	0	0	1	0	0	2	0	0
1967	NYA AL	1	0	0	0	0	0	0	0	1	0	0	0
1968	NYA AL	1	0	0	0	0	0	0	0	1	0	0	0
Totals	16 Yr	43	5	10	0	0	2	16	4	9	17	0	1

Heinie Manush

Year	Team	AB	R	H	D	T	HR	TB	BI	W	K	SB	CS
1934*	WAS AL	2	0	0	0	0	0	0	0	1	0	1	0

Juan Marichal

Year	Team	AB	R	H	D	T	HR	TB	BI	W	K	SB	CS
1962–1	SFN NL	0	0	0	0	0	0	0	0	0	0	0	0
1962–2	SFN NL	0	0	0	0	0	0	0	0	0	0	0	0
1964	SFN NL	0	0	0	0	0	0	0	0	0	0	0	0
1965*	SFN NL	1	1	1	0	0	0	1	0	0	0	0	0
1966	SFN NL	0	0	0	0	0	0	0	0	0	0	0	0
1967*	SFN NL	1	0	0	0	0	0	0	0	0	0	0	0
1968	SFN NL	0	0	0	0	0	0	0	0	0	0	0	0
1971	SFN NL	0	0	0	0	0	0	0	0	0	0	0	0
Totals	8 Yr	2	1	1	0	0	0	1	0	0	0	0	0

Marty Marion

Year	Team	AB	R	H	D	T	HR	TB	BI	W	K	SB	CS
1943*	SLN NL	2	0	0	0	0	0	0	0	0	0	0	0
1944*	SLN NL	3	1	0	0	0	0	0	0	0	2	0	0
1946*	SLN NL	3	0	0	0	0	0	0	0	0	2	0	0
1947*	SLN NL	2	0	1	0	0	0	1	0	0	0	0	0
1950*	SLN NL	2	0	0	0	0	0	0	0	0	0	0	0
Totals	5 Yr	12	1	1	0	0	0	1	0	0	4	0	0

Year	Team	AB	R	H	D	T	HR	TB	BI	W	K	SB	CS

Roger Maris

Year	Team	AB	R	H	D	T	HR	TB	BI	W	K	SB	CS
1959–2*	KC AL	2	0	0	0	0	0	0	0	0	1	0	0
1960–1*	NYA AL	2	0	0	0	0	0	0	0	0	1	0	0
1960–2*	NYA AL	4	0	0	0	0	0	0	0	1	0	0	0
1961–1*	NYA AL	4	0	1	0	0	0	1	0	1	2	0	0
1961–2	NYA AL	1	0	0	0	0	0	0	0	0	0	0	0
1962–1*	NYA AL	2	0	0	0	0	0	0	1	0	1	0	0
1962–2*	NYA AL	4	2	1	1	0	0	2	1	1	0	0	0
Totals	7 Yr	19	2	2	1	0	0	3	2	3	5	0	0

Mike Marshall

Year	Team	AB	R	H	D	T	HR	TB	BI	W	K	SB	CS
1974	LAN NL	1	0	0	0	0	0	0	0	0	0	0	0

Willard Marshall

Year	Team	AB	R	H	D	T	HR	TB	BI	W	K	SB	CS
1942	NY NL	1	0	0	0	0	0	0	0	0	0	0	0
1947	NY NL	1	0	0	0	0	0	0	0	1	1	0	0
1949*	NY NL	1	1	0	0	0	0	0	0	2	0	0	0
Totals	3 Yr	3	1	0	0	0	0	0	0	3	1	0	0

Billy Martin

Year	Team	AB	R	H	D	T	HR	TB	BI	W	K	SB	CS
1956	NYA AL	1	0	0	0	0	0	0	0	0	0	0	0

Pepper Martin

Year	Team	AB	R	H	D	T	HR	TB	BI	W	K	SB	CS
1933*	SLN NL	4	0	0	0	0	0	0	1	0	1	0	0
1934	SLN NL	0	1	0	0	0	0	0	0	1	0	0	0
1935*	SLN NL	4	0	1	0	0	0	1	0	0	2	1	0
Totals	3 Yr	8	1	1	0	0	0	1	1	1	3	1	0

Dennis Martinez

Year	Team	AB	R	H	D	T	HR	TB	BI	W	K	SB	CS
1990	MON NL	0	0	0	0	0	0	0	0	0	0	0	0
1992	MON NL	0	0	0	0	0	0	0	0	0	0	0	0
Totals	2 Yr	0	0	0	0	0	0	0	0	0	0	0	0

Edgar Martinez

Year	Team	AB	R	H	D	T	HR	TB	BI	W	K	SB	CS
1992	SEA AL	1	0	0	0	0	0	0	0	0	0	0	0
1995*	SEA AL	3	0	0	0	0	0	0	0	1	0	0	0
1996	SEA AL	1	0	0	0	0	0	0	0	0	0	0	0
1997*	SEA AL	2	1	2	0	0	1	5	1	0	0	0	1
2000	SEA AL	1	0	0	0	0	0	0	0	0	0	0	0
Totals	5 Yr	8	1	2	0	0	1	5	1	0	1	0	1

Pedro Martinez

Year	Team	AB	R	H	D	T	HR	TB	BI	W	K	SB	CS
1996	MON NL	0	0	0	0	0	0	0	0	0	0	0	0

Ramon Martinez

Year	Team	AB	R	H	D	T	HR	TB	BI	W	K	SB	CS
1990	LAN NL	0	0	0	0	0	0	0	0	0	0	0	0

Tino Martinez

Year	Team	AB	R	H	D	T	HR	TB	BI	W	K	SB	CS
1995	SEA AL	1	0	1	0	0	0	1	0	0	0	0	0
1997*	NYA AL	2	0	0	0	0	0	0	0	0	0	0	0
Totals	2 Yr	3	0	1	0	0	0	1	0	0	0	0	0

Phil Masi

Year	Team	AB	R	H	D	T	HR	TB	BI	W	K	SB	CS
1946	BSN NL	2	0	0	0	0	0	0	0	0	0	0	0
1947	BSN NL	0	0	0	0	0	0	0	0	0	0	0	0
1948	BSN NL	2	0	1	0	0	0	1	0	0	0	0	0
Totals	3 Yr	4	0	1	0	0	0	1	0	0	0	0	0

Walt Masterson

Year	Team	AB	R	H	D	T	HR	TB	BI	W	K	SB	CS
1947	WAS AL	0	0	0	0	0	0	0	0	0	0	0	0

Walt Masterson *continued*

Year	Team	AB	R	H	D	T	HR	TB	BI	W	K	SB	CS
1948*	WAS AL	0	0	0	0	0	0	0	0	0	0	0	0
Totals	2 Yr	0	0	0	0	0	0	0	0	0	0	0	0

Eddie Mathews

Year	Team	AB	R	H	D	T	HR	TB	BI	W	K	SB	CS
1953*	MIL NL	3	1	0	0	0	0	0	0	0	0	0	0
1955*	MIL NL	2	0	0	0	0	0	0	0	0	0	0	0
1957	MIL NL	3	0	0	0	0	0	0	0	0	1	0	0
1959–1*	MIL NL	3	1	1	0	0	1	4	1	0	1	0	0
1959–2	MIL NL	1	0	0	0	0	0	0	0	0	1	0	0
1960–1*	MIL NL	4	0	0	0	0	0	0	0	0	0	0	0
1960–2*	MIL NL	3	1	1	0	0	1	4	2	0	0	0	0
1961–1*	MIL NL	2	0	0	0	0	0	0	0	0	0	0	0
1961–2*	MIL NL	3	1	0	0	0	0	0	0	1	1	0	0
1962–2	MIL NL	1	0	0	0	0	0	0	0	0	1	0	0
Totals	10 Yr	25	4	2	0	0	2	8	3	1	5	0	0

Jon Matlack

Year	Team	AB	R	H	D	T	HR	TB	BI	W	K	SB	CS
1974	NYN NL	0	0	0	0	0	0	0	0	0	0	0	0
1975	NYN NL	0	0	0	0	0	0	0	0	0	0	0	0
Totals	2 Yr	0	0	0	0	0	0	0	0	0	0	0	0

Gary Matthews

Year	Team	AB	R	H	D	T	HR	TB	BI	W	K	SB	CS
1979	ATL NL	2	0	0	0	0	0	0	0	0	0	0	0

Don Mattingly

Year	Team	AB	R	H	D	T	HR	TB	BI	W	K	SB	CS
1984	NYA AL	1	0	0	0	0	0	0	0	0	0	0	0
1985	NYA AL	1	0	0	0	0	0	0	0	0	0	0	0
1986	NYA AL	3	0	0	0	0	0	0	0	0	2	0	0
1987*	NYA AL	1	0	0	0	0	0	0	0	0	2	0	0
1988	NYA AL	2	0	0	0	0	0	0	0	0	0	0	0
1989	NYA AL	1	0	1	1	0	0	2	0	0	0	0	0
Totals	6 Yr	9	0	1	1	0	0	2	0	2	2	0	0

Charlie Maxwell

Year	Team	AB	R	H	D	T	HR	TB	BI	W	K	SB	CS
1957	DET AL	1	0	1	0	0	0	1	0	0	0	0	0

Carlos May

Year	Team	AB	R	H	D	T	HR	TB	BI	W	K	SB	CS
1969	CHA AL	1	0	0	0	0	0	0	0	0	1	0	0

Dave May

Year	Team	AB	R	H	D	T	HR	TB	BI	W	K	SB	CS
1973	MIL AL	2	0	0	0	0	0	0	0	0	0	0	0

Lee May

Year	Team	AB	R	H	D	T	HR	TB	BI	W	K	SB	CS
1969	CIN NL	1	0	0	0	0	0	0	0	0	1	0	0
1971	CIN NL	1	0	0	0	0	0	0	0	1	0	0	0
1972*	HOU NL	4	0	1	0	0	0	1	1	0	0	0	0
Totals	3 Yr	6	0	1	0	0	0	1	1	1	1	0	0

Pinky May

Year	Team	AB	R	H	D	T	HR	TB	BI	W	K	SB	CS
1940	PHI NL	1	0	0	0	0	0	0	0	0	0	0	0

John Mayberry

Year	Team	AB	R	H	D	T	HR	TB	BI	W	K	SB	CS
1973*	KCA AL	3	0	1	1	0	0	2	0	1	0	0	0
1974	KCA AL	1	0	0	0	0	0	0	0	0	0	0	0
Totals	2 Yr	4	0	1	1	0	0	2	0	1	0	0	0

Willie Mays

Year	Team	AB	R	H	D	T	HR	TB	BI	W	K	SB	CS
1954	NY NL	2	1	1	0	0	0	1	0	0	0	0	0
1955	NY NL	3	2	2	0	0	0	2	0	0	1	0	0

Year	Team	AB	R	H	D	T	HR	TB	BI	W	K	SB	CS

Willie Mays *continued*

Year	Team	AB	R	H	D	T	HR	TB	BI	W	K	SB	CS
1956	NY NL	3	2	1	0	0	1	4	2	1	2	0	0
1957*	NY NL	4	2	2	0	1	0	4	1	0	1	0	0
1958*	SFN NL	4	2	1	0	0	0	1	0	0	0	1	0
1959–1*	SFN NL	4	0	1	0	1	0	3	1	0	1	0	0
1959–2*	SFN NL	4	0	0	0	0	0	0	0	0	0	0	0
1960–1*	SFN NL	4	1	3	1	1	0	6	0	0	0	0	0
1960–2*	SFN NL	4	1	3	0	0	1	6	1	0	0	1	1
1961–1*	SFN NL	5	2	2	1	0	0	3	1	0	1	0	0
1961–2*	SFN NL	3	0	1	0	0	0	1	0	1	0	0	0
1962–1*	SFN NL	3	0	0	0	0	0	0	0	1	0	1	0
1962–2*	SFN NL	2	0	2	0	0	0	2	0	0	0	0	0
1963*	SFN NL	3	2	1	0	0	1	2	1	1	2	0	0
1964*	SFN NL	3	1	0	0	0	0	0	0	1	0	1	0
1965*	SFN NL	3	2	1	0	0	1	4	1	2	1	0	0
1966*	SFN NL	4	1	1	0	0	0	1	0	0	1	0	0
1967	SFN NL	4	0	0	0	0	0	0	0	0	1	0	0
1968*	SFN NL	4	1	1	0	0	0	1	0	0	1	0	0
1969	SFN NL	1	0	0	0	0	0	0	0	0	0	0	0
1970*	SFN NL	3	0	0	0	0	0	0	0	0	1	0	0
1971*	SFN NL	2	0	0	0	0	0	0	0	0	0	0	0
1972*	NYN NL	2	0	0	0	0	0	0	0	0	1	0	0
1973	NYN NL	1	0	0	0	0	0	0	0	0	1	0	0
Totals	24 Yr	75	20	23	2	3	3	40	9	7	14	6	1

Bill Mazeroski

Year	Team	AB	R	H	D	T	HR	TB	BI	W	K	SB	CS
1958*	PIT NL	4	0	0	0	0	0	0	0	0	1	0	0
1959–1	PIT NL	1	0	1	0	0	0	1	1	0	0	0	0
1960–1*	PIT NL	2	0	1	0	0	0	1	1	0	0	0	0
1960–2*	PIT NL	2	0	0	0	0	0	0	0	0	0	0	0
1962–1*	PIT NL	2	0	0	0	0	0	0	0	0	0	0	0
1962–2*	PIT NL	1	0	0	0	0	0	0	0	0	0	0	0
1967*	PIT NL	4	0	0	0	0	0	0	0	0	0	0	0
Totals	7 Yr	16	0	2	0	0	0	2	2	0	1	0	0

Lee Mazzilli

Year	Team	AB	R	H	D	T	HR	TB	BI	W	K	SB	CS
1979	NYN NL	1	1	1	0	0	1	4	2	1	0	0	0

Dick McAuliffe

Year	Team	AB	R	H	D	T	HR	TB	BI	W	K	SB	CS
1965*	DET AL	3	2	2	0	0	1	5	2	0	0	0	0
1966*	DET AL	3	0	0	0	0	0	0	0	0	1	0	0
1967	DET AL	3	0	0	0	0	0	0	0	0	0	0	0
Totals	3 Yr	9	2	2	0	0	1	5	2	0	1	0	0

Ken McBride

Year	Team	AB	R	H	D	T	HR	TB	BI	W	K	SB	CS
1963*	LAA AL	1	0	1	0	0	0	1	1	0	0	0	0

Tim McCarver

Year	Team	AB	R	H	D	T	HR	TB	BI	W	K	SB	CS
1966	SLN NL	1	1	1	0	0	0	1	0	0	0	0	0
1967	SLN NL	2	0	2	1	0	0	3	0	0	0	0	0
Totals	2 Yr	3	1	3	1	0	0	4	0	0	0	0	0

Frank McCormick

Year	Team	AB	R	H	D	T	HR	TB	BI	W	K	SB	CS
1938*	CIN NL	4	1	1	0	0	0	1	0	0	0	0	0
1939*	CIN NL	4	0	0	0	0	0	0	0	0	1	0	0
1940	CIN NL	1	0	0	0	0	0	0	0	0	0	0	0
1941	CIN NL	0	0	0	0	0	0	0	0	0	0	0	0
1942	CIN NL	2	0	0	0	0	0	0	0	0	0	0	0
1946	PHI NL	1	0	0	0	0	0	0	0	0	0	0	0
Totals	6 Yr	12	1	1	0	0	0	1	0	0	1	0	0

Mike McCormick

Year	Team	AB	R	H	D	T	HR	TB	BI	W	K	SB	CS
1960–1	SFN NL	1	0	0	0	0	0	0	0	0	0	0	0
1961–1	SFN NL	0	0	0	0	0	0	0	0	0	0	0	0
Totals	2 Yr	1	0	0	0	0	0	0	0	0	0	0	0

Willie McCovey

Year	Team	AB	R	H	D	T	HR	TB	BI	W	K	SB	CS
1963	SFN NL	1	0	0	0	0	0	0	0	0	1	0	0
1966*	SFN NL	3	0	0	0	0	0	0	0	1	0	0	0
1968*	SFN NL	4	0	0	0	0	0	0	0	0	3	0	0
1969*	SFN NL	4	2	2	0	0	2	8	3	0	1	0	0
1970	SFN NL	2	0	1	0	0	0	1	1	0	0	0	0
1971*	SFN NL	2	0	0	0	0	0	0	0	0	1	0	0
Totals	6 Yr	16	2	3	0	0	2	9	4	1	6	0	0

Lindy McDaniel

Year	Team	AB	R	H	D	T	HR	TB	BI	W	K	SB	CS
1960–2	SLN NL	0	0	0	0	0	0	0	0	0	0	0	0

Gil McDougald

Year	Team	AB	R	H	D	T	HR	TB	BI	W	K	SB	CS
1952	NYA AL	1	0	0	0	0	0	0	0	0	0	0	0
1957	NYA AL	2	1	0	0	0	0	0	0	0	0	0	0
1958	NYA AL	1	0	1	0	0	0	1	1	0	0	0	0
1959–1	NYA AL	0	0	0	0	0	0	0	0	0	0	0	0
Totals	4 Yr	4	1	1	0	0	0	1	1	0	0	0	0

Jack McDowell

Year	Team	AB	R	H	D	T	HR	TB	BI	W	K	SB	CS
1992	CHA AL	0	0	0	0	0	0	0	0	0	0	0	0

Sam McDowell

Year	Team	AB	R	H	D	T	HR	TB	BI	W	K	SB	CS
1965	CLE AL	0	0	0	0	0	0	0	0	0	0	0	0
1968	CLE AL	0	0	0	0	0	0	0	0	0	0	0	0
1969	CLE AL	0	0	0	0	0	0	0	0	0	0	0	0
1970	CLE AL	0	0	0	0	0	0	0	0	0	0	0	0
Totals	4 Yr	0	0	0	0	0	0	0	0	0	0	0	0

Willie McGee

Year	Team	AB	R	H	D	T	HR	TB	BI	W	K	SB	CS
1983	SLN NL	2	0	1	0	0	0	1	0	0	0	0	0
1985	SLN NL	2	0	1	1	0	0	2	2	0	0	0	0
1987	SLN NL	4	0	0	0	0	0	0	0	0	0	0	0
1988	SLN NL	2	0	0	0	0	0	0	0	0	0	0	0
Totals	4 Yr	10	0	2	1	0	0	3	2	0	0	0	0

Lynn McGlothen

Year	Team	AB	R	H	D	T	HR	TB	BI	W	K	SB	CS
1974	SLN NL	0	0	0	0	0	0	0	0	0	0	0	0

Jim McGlothlin

Year	Team	AB	R	H	D	T	HR	TB	BI	W	K	SB	CS
1967	CAL AL	0	0	0	0	0	0	0	0	0	0	0	0

Tug McGraw

Year	Team	AB	R	H	D	T	HR	TB	BI	W	K	SB	CS
1972	NYN NL	0	0	0	0	0	0	0	0	0	0	0	0

Fred McGriff

Year	Team	AB	R	H	D	T	HR	TB	BI	W	K	SB	CS
1992*	SDN NL	3	0	2	0	0	0	2	1	0	0	0	0
1994	ATL NL	1	1	1	0	0	1	4	2	0	0	0	0
1995*	ATL NL	3	0	0	0	0	0	0	0	2	0	0	0
1996*	ATL NL	2	0	0	0	0	0	0	0	2	0	0	0
2000	TBA AL	2	0	0	0	0	0	0	0	1	0	0	0
Totals	5 Yr	11	1	3	0	0	1	6	3	0	5	0	0

Mark McGwire

Year	Team	AB	R	H	D	T	HR	TB	BI	W	K	SB	CS
1987	OAK AL	3	0	0	0	0	0	0	0	0	1	0	0

Mark McGwire *continued*

Year	Team	AB	R	H	D	T	HR	TB	BI	W	K	SB	CS
1988*	OAK AL	2	0	1	0	0	0	1	0	0	1	0	0
1989*	OAK AL	3	0	1	0	0	0	1	0	0	0	0	0
1990*	OAK AL	2	0	0	0	0	0	0	0	0	2	0	0
1992*	OAK AL	3	1	1	0	0	0	1	2	0	0	0	0
1996	OAK AL	1	0	1	0	0	0	1	0	0	0	0	0
1997	OAK AL	2	0	0	0	0	0	0	0	0	2	0	0
1998*	SLN NL	2	1	0	0	0	0	0	0	1	1	0	0
1999*	SLN NL	2	0	0	0	0	0	0	0	1	2	0	0
Totals	9 Yr	20	2	4	0	0	0	4	2	2	9	0	0

Denny McLain

Year	Team	AB	R	H	D	T	HR	TB	BI	W	K	SB	CS
1966*	DET AL	1	0	0	0	0	0	0	0	0	1	0	0
1968	DET AL	0	0	0	0	0	0	0	0	0	0	0	0
1969	DET AL	0	0	0	0	0	0	0	0	0	0	0	0
Totals	3 Yr	1	0	0	0	0	0	0	0	0	1	0	0

Cal McLish

Year	Team	AB	R	H	D	T	HR	TB	BI	W	K	SB	CS
1959-2	CLE AL	0	0	0	0	0	0	0	0	0	0	0	0

Roy McMillan

Year	Team	AB	R	H	D	T	HR	TB	BI	W	K	SB	CS
1956*	CIN NL	3	1	2	0	0	0	2	0	1	0	0	0
1957*	CIN NL	1	0	0	0	0	0	0	0	0	0	0	0
Totals	2 Yr	4	1	2	0	0	0	2	0	1	0	0	0

Dave McNally

Year	Team	AB	R	H	D	T	HR	TB	BI	W	K	SB	CS
1969	BAL AL	0	0	0	0	0	0	0	0	0	0	0	0
1972	BAL AL	0	0	0	0	0	0	0	0	0	0	0	0
Totals	2 Yr	0	0	0	0	0	0	0	0	0	0	0	0

George McQuinn

Year	Team	AB	R	H	D	T	HR	TB	BI	W	K	SB	CS
1944*	SLA AL	4	0	1	0	0	0	1	0	0	1	0	0
1947*	NYA AL	4	0	0	0	0	0	0	0	0	1	0	0
1948*	NYA AL	4	1	2	0	0	0	2	0	0	0	1	0
Totals	3 Yr	12	1	3	0	0	0	3	0	0	2	1	0

Hal McRae

Year	Team	AB	R	H	D	T	HR	TB	BI	W	K	SB	CS
1975	KCA AL	1	0	0	0	0	0	0	0	0	0	0	0
1976	KCA AL	1	0	0	0	0	0	0	0	0	0	0	0
1982	KCA AL	0	0	0	0	0	0	0	0	1	0	0	0
Totals	3 Yr	2	0	0	0	0	0	0	0	1	0	0	0

Joe Medwick

Year	Team	AB	R	H	D	T	HR	TB	BI	W	K	SB	CS
1934*	SLN NL	2	1	1	0	0	1	4	3	0	1	0	0
1935*	SLN NL	3	0	0	0	0	0	0	0	1	1	0	0
1936*	SLN NL	4	0	1	0	0	0	1	1	0	0	0	0
1937*	SLN NL	5	1	4	2	0	0	6	1	0	0	0	0
1938*	SLN NL	4	0	1	0	0	0	1	1	0	0	0	0
1939*	SLN NL	4	0	0	0	0	0	0	0	0	1	0	0
1940*	BRO NL	2	0	0	0	0	0	0	0	0	0	0	0
1941	BRO NL	1	0	0	0	0	0	0	0	0	0	0	0
1942*	BRO NL	2	0	0	0	0	0	0	0	0	0	0	0
1944	NY NL	0	0	0	0	0	0	0	0	0	0	0	0
Totals	10 Yr	27	2	7	2	0	1	12	6	1	3	0	0

Denis Menke

Year	Team	AB	R	H	D	T	HR	TB	BI	W	K	SB	CS
1969	HOU NL	1	0	0	0	0	0	0	0	0	1	0	0
1970	HOU NL	0	0	0	0	0	0	0	0	1	0	0	0
Totals	2 Yr	1	0	0	0	0	0	0	0	1	1	0	0

Jim Merritt

Year	Team	AB	R	H	D	T	HR	TB	BI	W	K	SB	CS
1970	CIN NL	0	0	0	0	0	0	0	0	0	0	0	0

Andy Messersmith

Year	Team	AB	R	H	D	T	HR	TB	BI	W	K	SB	CS
1974*	LAN NL	0	0	0	0	0	0	0	0	0	0	0	0

Cass Michaels

Year	Team	AB	R	H	D	T	HR	TB	BI	W	K	SB	CS
1949*	CHA AL	2	0	0	0	0	0	0	0	1	0	0	0
1950	WAS AL	1	1	1	1	0	0	2	0	0	0	0	0
Totals	2 Yr	3	1	1	1	0	0	2	0	1	0	0	0

Felix Millan

Year	Team	AB	R	H	D	T	HR	TB	BI	W	K	SB	CS
1969*	ATL NL	4	1	1	1	0	0	2	2	0	1	0	0
1971	ATL NL	0	0	0	0	0	0	0	0	0	0	0	0
Totals	2 Yr	4	1	1	1	0	0	2	2	0	1	0	0

Eddie Miller

Year	Team	AB	R	H	D	T	HR	TB	BI	W	K	SB	CS
1940	BSN NL	1	0	0	0	0	0	0	0	0	1	0	0
1941	BSN NL	0	0	0	0	0	0	0	0	0	0	0	0
1942*	BSN NL	2	0	0	0	0	0	0	0	0	1	0	0
1943	CIN NL	1	0	0	0	0	0	0	0	0	1	0	0
Totals	4 Yr	4	0	0	0	0	0	0	0	0	3	0	0

Stu Miller

Year	Team	AB	R	H	D	T	HR	TB	BI	W	K	SB	CS
1961-1	SFN NL	0	0	0	0	0	0	0	0	0	0	0	0
1961-2	SFN NL	0	0	0	0	0	0	0	0	0	0	0	0
Totals	2 Yr	0	0	0	0	0	0	0	0	0	0	0	0

Don Mincher

Year	Team	AB	R	H	D	T	HR	TB	BI	W	K	SB	CS
1967	CAL AL	1	0	1	0	0	0	1	0	0	0	0	0
1969	SEA AL	1	0	0	0	0	0	0	0	0	1	0	0
Totals	2 Yr	2	0	1	0	0	0	1	0	0	1	0	0

Minnie Minoso

Year	Team	AB	R	H	D	T	HR	TB	BI	W	K	SB	CS
1951	CHA AL	2	0	0	0	0	0	0	0	0	0	0	0
1952	CHA AL	1	1	1	1	0	0	2	0	0	0	0	0
1953	CHA AL	2	0	2	0	0	0	2	1	0	0	0	0
1954*	CHA AL	4	1	2	0	0	0	2	0	1	0	0	0
1957	CHA AL	1	0	1	1	0	0	2	1	0	0	0	0
1959-1*	CLE AL	5	0	0	0	0	0	0	0	0	2	0	0
1960-1*	CHA AL	3	0	0	0	0	0	0	0	0	0	0	0
1960-2*	CHA AL	2	0	0	0	0	0	0	0	1	1	0	0
Totals	8 Yr	20	2	6	2	0	0	8	2	2	3	0	0

Greg Minton

Year	Team	AB	R	H	D	T	HR	TB	BI	W	K	SB	CS
1982	SFN NL	0	0	0	0	0	0	0	0	0	0	0	0

Dale Mitchell

Year	Team	AB	R	H	D	T	HR	TB	BI	W	K	SB	CS
1949	CLE AL	1	0	1	1	0	0	2	1	0	0	0	0
1952*	CLE AL	1	0	0	0	0	0	0	0	0	1	0	0
Totals	2 Yr	2	0	1	1	0	0	2	1	0	1	0	0

Kevin Mitchell

Year	Team	AB	R	H	D	T	HR	TB	BI	W	K	SB	CS
1989*	SFN NL	4	1	2	0	0	0	2	1	0	2	0	0
1990*	SFN NL	2	0	0	0	0	0	0	0	0	1	0	0
Totals	2 Yr	6	1	2	0	0	0	2	1	0	3	0	0

Johnny Mize

Year	Team	AB	R	H	D	T	HR	TB	BI	W	K	SB	CS
1937*	SLN NL	4	0	0	0	0	0	0	0	1	0	0	0
1939	SLN NL	1	0	0	0	0	0	0	0	0	1	0	0

Johnny Mize *continued*

Year	Team	AB	R	H	D	T	HR	TB	BI	W	K	SB	CS
1940*	SLN NL	2	0	0	0	0	0	0	0	0	0	0	0
1941*	SLN NL	4	1	1	1	0	0	2	0	0	0	0	0
1942*	NY NL	2	0	0	0	0	0	0	0	0	0	0	0
1946*	NY NL	1	0	0	0	0	0	0	0	0	0	0	0
1947*	NY NL	3	1	2	0	0	1	5	1	1	0	0	0
1948*	NY NL	4	0	1	0	0	0	1	0	0	1	0	0
1949*	NY NL	2	0	1	0	0	0	1	0	0	1	0	0
1953	NYA AL	1	0	1	0	0	0	1	0	0	0	0	0
Totals	10 Yr	24	2	6	1	0	1	10	2	1	3	0	0

Paul Molitor

Year	Team	AB	R	H	D	T	HR	TB	BI	W	K	SB	CS
1985	MIL AL	1	0	0	0	0	0	0	0	0	1	0	0
1988*	MIL AL	3	0	0	0	0	0	0	0	0	1	0	0
1991	MIL AL	0	0	0	0	0	0	0	0	0	0	0	0
1992	MIL AL	2	0	1	0	0	0	1	0	0	1	0	0
1993*	TOR AL	1	0	0	0	0	0	0	0	1	0	0	0
1994	TOR AL	1	0	0	0	0	0	0	0	0	0	0	0
Totals	6 Yr	8	0	1	0	0	0	1	0	1	3	0	0

Bill Monbouquette

Year	Team	AB	R	H	D	T	HR	TB	BI	W	K	SB	CS
1960-1*	BOS AL	0	0	0	0	0	0	0	0	0	0	0	0

Rick Monday

Year	Team	AB	R	H	D	T	HR	TB	BI	W	K	SB	CS
1968	OAK AL	2	0	0	0	0	0	0	0	0	1	0	0
1978*	LAN NL	2	0	0	0	0	0	0	0	0	0	0	0
Totals	2 Yr	4	0	0	0	0	0	0	0	0	1	0	0

Raul Mondesi

Year	Team	AB	R	H	D	T	HR	TB	BI	W	K	SB	CS
1995	LAN NL	1	0	0	0	0	0	0	0	0	0	0	0

Don Money

Year	Team	AB	R	H	D	T	HR	TB	BI	W	K	SB	CS
1976	MIL AL	1	0	0	0	0	0	0	0	0	0	0	0
1978*	MIL AL	2	0	0	0	0	0	0	0	0	1	0	0
Totals	2 Yr	3	0	0	0	0	0	0	0	0	1	0	0

Willie Montanez

Year	Team	AB	R	H	D	T	HR	TB	BI	W	K	SB	CS
1977	ATL NL	2	0	0	0	0	0	0	0	0	1	0	0

John Montefusco

Year	Team	AB	R	H	D	T	HR	TB	BI	W	K	SB	CS
1976	SFN NL	0	0	0	0	0	0	0	0	0	0	0	0

Jeff Montgomery

Year	Team	AB	R	H	D	T	HR	TB	BI	W	K	SB	CS
1992	KCA AL	0	0	0	0	0	0	0	0	0	0	0	0

Wally Moon

Year	Team	AB	R	H	D	T	HR	TB	BI	W	K	SB	CS
1957	SLN NL	1	0	0	0	0	0	0	0	0	0	0	0
1959-1*	LAN NL	2	0	0	0	0	0	0	0	1	2	0	0
1959-2*	LAN NL	2	0	0	0	0	0	0	0	2	0	0	0
Totals	3 Yr	5	0	0	0	0	0	0	0	3	2	0	0

Donnie Moore

Year	Team	AB	R	H	D	T	HR	TB	BI	W	K	SB	CS
1985	CAL AL	0	0	0	0	0	0	0	0	0	0	0	0

Jo-Jo Moore

Year	Team	AB	R	H	D	T	HR	TB	BI	W	K	SB	CS
1935	NY NL	2	0	0	0	0	0	0	0	0	0	0	0
1937	NY NL	1	0	0	0	0	0	0	0	0	0	0	0
1940	NY NL	2	0	0	0	0	0	0	0	0	0	0	0
Totals	3 Yr	5	0	0	0	0	0	0	0	0	0	0	0

Terry Moore

Year	Team	AB	R	H	D	T	HR	TB	BI	W	K	SB	CS
1939	SLN NL	1	0	0	0	0	0	0	0	0	0	0	0
1940*	SLN NL	3	0	0	0	0	0	0	0	1	1	0	0
1941*	SLN NL	5	0	0	0	0	0	0	1	0	1	0	0
1942	SLN NL	1	0	0	0	0	0	0	0	0	0	0	0
Totals	4 Yr	10	0	0	0	0	0	0	1	1	2	0	0

Jerry Morales

Year	Team	AB	R	H	D	T	HR	TB	BI	W	K	SB	CS
1977	CHN NL	0	1	0	0	0	0	0	0	0	0	0	0

Billy Moran

Year	Team	AB	R	H	D	T	HR	TB	BI	W	K	SB	CS
1962-1*	LAA AL	3	0	1	0	0	0	1	0	0	1	0	0
1962-2*	LAA AL	4	0	1	0	0	0	1	0	0	0	0	0
Totals	2 Yr	7	0	2	0	0	0	2	0	0	1	0	0

Mickey Morandini

Year	Team	AB	R	H	D	T	HR	TB	BI	W	K	SB	CS
1995	PHI NL	1	0	0	0	0	0	0	0	0	1	0	0

Joe Morgan

Year	Team	AB	R	H	D	T	HR	TB	BI	W	K	SB	CS
1970	HOU NL	2	1	1	0	0	0	1	0	0	0	0	0
1972*	CIN NL	4	0	1	0	0	0	1	1	1	0	1	0
1973*	CIN NL	3	2	1	1	0	0	2	0	1	0	0	0
1974*	CIN NL	2	0	1	1	0	0	2	1	0	1	0	0
1975*	CIN NL	4	0	1	0	0	0	1	0	0	0	0	0
1976*	CIN NL	3	1	1	0	0	0	1	0	0	0	0	0
1977*	CIN NL	4	1	1	0	0	1	4	1	0	1	0	0
1978*	CIN NL	3	1	0	0	0	0	0	0	1	1	0	0
1979	CIN NL	1	1	0	0	0	0	0	0	1	1	0	0
Totals	9 Yr	26	7	7	2	0	1	12	3	4	4	1	0

Jack Morris

Year	Team	AB	R	H	D	T	HR	TB	BI	W	K	SB	CS
1981*	DET AL	0	0	0	0	0	0	0	0	0	0	0	0
1984	DET AL	0	0	0	0	0	0	0	0	0	0	0	0
1985*	DET AL	0	0	0	0	0	0	0	0	0	0	0	0
1987	DET AL	0	0	0	0	0	0	0	0	0	0	0	0
Totals	4 Yr	0	0	0	0	0	0	0	0	0	0	0	0

Lloyd Moseby

Year	Team	AB	R	H	D	T	HR	TB	BI	W	K	SB	CS
1986	TOR AL	0	0	0	0	0	0	0	0	1	0	1	0

Don Mossi

Year	Team	AB	R	H	D	T	HR	TB	BI	W	K	SB	CS
1957	CLE AL	0	0	0	0	0	0	0	0	0	0	0	0

Manny Mota

Year	Team	AB	R	H	D	T	HR	TB	BI	W	K	SB	CS
1973	LAN NL	1	0	0	0	0	0	0	0	0	0	0	0

Don Mueller

Year	Team	AB	R	H	D	T	HR	TB	BI	W	K	SB	CS
1954	NY NL	1	0	1	1	0	0	2	1	0	0	0	0
1955*	NY NL	2	0	1	0	0	0	1	0	0	0	0	0
Totals	2 Yr	3	0	2	1	0	0	3	1	0	0	0	0

Ray Mueller

Year	Team	AB	R	H	D	T	HR	TB	BI	W	K	SB	CS
1944	CIN NL	0	0	0	0	0	0	0	0	0	0	0	0

Pat Mullin

Year	Team	AB	R	H	D	T	HR	TB	BI	W	K	SB	CS
1948*	DET AL	1	0	0	0	0	0	0	0	1	1	1	0

Jerry Mumphrey

Year	Team	AB	R	H	D	T	HR	TB	BI	W	K	SB	CS
1984	HOU NL	1	0	0	0	0	0	0	0	0	1	0	0

Year	Team	AB	R	H	D	T	HR	TB	BI	W	K	SB	CS

Bob Muncrief

Year	Team	AB	R	H	D	T	HR	TB	BI	W	K	SB	CS
1944	SLA AL	0	0	0	0	0	0	0	0	0	0	0	0

Red Munger

Year	Team	AB	R	H	D	T	HR	TB	BI	W	K	SB	CS
1949	SLN NL	0	0	0	0	0	0	0	0	0	0	0	0

Van Mungo

Year	Team	AB	R	H	D	T	HR	TB	BI	W	K	SB	CS
1934	BRO NL	0	0	0	0	0	0	0	0	0	0	0	0
1937	BRO NL	0	0	0	0	0	0	0	0	0	0	0	0
Totals	2 Yr	0	0	0	0	0	0	0	0	0	0	0	0

Thurman Munson

Year	Team	AB	R	H	D	T	HR	TB	BI	W	K	SB	CS
1971	NYA AL	0	0	0	0	0	0	0	0	0	0	0	0
1973	NYA AL	2	0	0	0	0	0	0	0	0	1	0	0
1974*	NYA AL	3	1	1	1	0	0	2	0	1	0	0	0
1975*	NYA AL	2	0	1	0	0	0	1	0	0	0	0	0
1976*	NYA AL	2	0	0	0	0	0	0	0	0	0	0	0
1977	NYA AL	1	0	0	0	0	0	0	0	0	1	0	0
Totals	6 Yr	10	1	2	1	0	0	3	0	1	2	0	0

Bobby Murcer

Year	Team	AB	R	H	D	T	HR	TB	BI	W	K	SB	CS
1971*	NYA AL	3	0	1	0	0	0	1	0	0	1	0	0
1972*	NYA AL	3	0	0	0	0	0	0	0	0	0	0	0
1973*	NYA AL	3	0	0	0	0	0	0	0	1	0	0	0
1974*	NYA AL	2	0	0	0	0	0	0	0	0	0	0	0
1975	SFN NL	2	0	0	0	0	0	0	0	0	0	0	0
Totals	5 Yr	13	0	1	0	0	0	1	0	1	1	0	0

Dale Murphy

Year	Team	AB	R	H	D	T	HR	TB	BI	W	K	SB	CS
1980	ATL NL	1	0	0	0	0	0	0	0	0	0	0	0
1982*	ATL NL	2	1	0	0	0	0	0	0	1	0	0	0
1983*	ATL NL	3	0	1	0	0	0	1	1	0	1	0	0
1984*	ATL NL	3	1	2	0	0	1	5	1	1	0	0	0
1985*	ATL NL	3	0	1	1	0	0	2	0	0	1	0	0
1986*	ATL NL	2	0	0	0	0	0	0	0	0	0	0	0
1987	ATL NL	1	0	0	0	0	0	0	0	0	0	0	0
Totals	7 Yr	15	2	4	1	0	1	8	2	2	2	0	0

Eddie Murray

Year	Team	AB	R	H	D	T	HR	TB	BI	W	K	SB	CS
1981	BAL AL	2	0	0	0	0	0	0	0	0	0	0	0
1982	BAL AL	1	0	0	0	0	0	0	0	1	0	0	0
1983	BAL AL	2	0	0	0	0	0	0	0	0	0	0	0
1984	BAL AL	2	0	1	1	0	0	2	0	0	1	0	0
1985*	BAL AL	3	0	0	0	0	0	0	0	0	0	0	0
1991	LAN NL	1	0	0	0	0	0	0	0	0	1	0	0
Totals	6 Yr	11	0	1	1	0	0	2	0	1	2	0	0

Stan Musial

Year	Team	AB	R	H	D	T	HR	TB	BI	W	K	SB	CS
1943*	SLN NL	4	0	1	1	0	0	2	1	0	0	0	0
1944*	SLN NL	4	1	1	0	0	0	1	1	0	0	0	0
1946*	SLN NL	2	0	0	0	0	0	0	0	0	0	0	0
1947	SLN NL	1	0	0	0	0	0	0	0	0	0	0	0
1948*	SLN NL	4	1	2	0	0	1	5	2	1	1	0	0
1949*	SLN NL	4	1	3	0	0	1	6	2	1	0	0	0
1950*	SLN NL	5	0	0	0	0	0	0	0	1	0	0	0
1951*	SLN NL	4	1	2	0	0	1	5	1	1	0	0	1
1952*	SLN NL	2	1	0	0	0	0	0	0	0	2	0	0
1953*	SLN NL	4	0	2	0	0	0	2	0	0	1	0	0
1954*	SLN NL	5	1	2	0	0	0	2	0	0	0	0	0
1955	SLN NL	4	1	1	0	0	1	4	1	1	1	0	0

Stan Musial *continued*

Year	Team	AB	R	H	D	T	HR	TB	BI	W	K	SB	CS
1956*	SLN NL	4	1	1	0	0	1	4	1	0	1	0	0
1957*	SLN NL	3	1	1	1	0	0	2	0	1	0	0	0
1958*	SLN NL	4	1	1	0	0	0	1	0	0	0	0	0
1959-1	SLN NL	1	0	0	0	0	0	0	0	0	0	0	0
1959-2*	SLN NL	0	0	0	0	0	0	0	0	1	0	0	0
1960-1	SLN NL	1	0	1	0	0	0	1	0	0	0	0	0
1960-2	SLN NL	1	1	1	0	0	1	4	1	0	0	0	0
1961-1	SLN NL	1	0	0	0	0	0	0	0	0	0	0	0
1961-2	SLN NL	1	0	0	0	0	0	0	0	0	1	0	0
1962-1	SLN NL	1	0	1	0	0	0	1	0	0	0	0	0
1962-2	SLN NL	2	0	0	0	0	0	0	0	0	0	0	0
1963	SLN NL	1	0	0	0	0	0	0	0	0	0	0	0
Totals	24 Yr	63	11	20	2	0	6	40	10	7	7	0	1

Mike Mussina

Year	Team	AB	R	H	D	T	HR	TB	BI	W	K	SB	CS
1992	BAL AL	0	0	0	0	0	0	0	0	0	0	0	0
1994	BAL AL	0	0	0	0	0	0	0	0	0	0	0	0
Totals	2 Yr	0	0	0	0	0	0	0	0	0	0	0	0

Randy Myers

Year	Team	AB	R	H	D	T	HR	TB	BI	W	K	SB	CS
1990	CIN NL	0	0	0	0	0	0	0	0	0	0	0	0
1994	CHN NL	0	0	0	0	0	0	0	0	0	0	0	0
Totals	2 Yr	0	0	0	0	0	0	0	0	0	0	0	0

Charles Nagy

Year	Team	AB	R	H	D	T	HR	TB	BI	W	K	SB	CS
1992	CLE AL	1	1	1	0	0	0	1	0	0	0	0	0
1996*	CLE AL	0	0	0	0	0	0	0	0	0	0	0	0
Totals	2 Yr	1	1	1	0	0	0	1	0	0	0	0	0

Ray Narleski

Year	Team	AB	R	H	D	T	HR	TB	BI	W	K	SB	CS
1958	CLE AL	1	0	1	0	0	0	1	0	0	0	0	0

Charlie Neal

Year	Team	AB	R	H	D	T	HR	TB	BI	W	K	SB	CS
1959-2	LAN NL	1	0	0	0	0	0	0	0	0	0	0	0
1960-1	LAN NL	0	0	0	0	0	0	0	0	0	0	0	0
1960-2	LAN NL	1	0	0	0	0	0	0	0	0	0	0	0
Totals	3 Yr	2	0	0	0	0	0	0	0	0	0	0	0

Dave Nelson

Year	Team	AB	R	H	D	T	HR	TB	BI	W	K	SB	CS
1973	TEX AL	0	0	0	0	0	0	0	0	0	0	0	0

Robb Nen

Year	Team	AB	R	H	D	T	HR	TB	BI	W	K	SB	CS
1998	SFN NL	0	0	0	0	0	0	0	0	0	0	0	0

Graig Nettles

Year	Team	AB	R	H	D	T	HR	TB	BI	W	K	SB	CS
1975*	NYA AL	4	0	1	0	0	0	1	0	0	1	1	0
1977	NYA AL	2	0	0	0	0	0	0	0	0	1	0	0
1978	NYA AL	0	0	0	0	0	0	0	0	0	0	0	0
1979	NYA AL	1	0	1	0	0	0	1	0	0	0	0	0
1980*	NYA AL	2	0	0	0	0	0	0	0	0	0	0	0
1985*	SDN NL	2	0	0	0	0	0	0	0	0	0	0	0
Totals	6 Yr	11	0	2	0	0	0	2	0	0	2	1	0

Don Newcombe

Year	Team	AB	R	H	D	T	HR	TB	BI	W	K	SB	CS
1949	BRO NL	1	0	0	0	0	0	0	1	0	0	0	0
1950	BRO NL	0	0	0	0	0	0	0	0	0	0	0	0
1951	BRO NL	2	0	1	0	0	0	1	0	0	0	0	0
1955	BRO NL	0	0	0	0	0	0	0	0	0	0	0	0
Totals	4 Yr	3	0	1	0	0	0	1	1	0	0	0	0

Year	Team	AB	R	H	D	T	HR	TB	BI	W	K	SB	CS

Hal Newhouser

Year	Team	AB	R	H	D	T	HR	TB	BI	W	K	SB	CS
1943	DET AL	1	0	0	0	0	0	0	0	0	0	0	0
1944	DET AL	0	0	0	0	0	0	0	0	0	0	0	0
1946	DET AL	1	1	1	0	0	0	1	0	0	0	0	0
1947*	DET AL	1	0	0	0	0	0	0	0	0	0	0	0
1948	DET AL	0	0	0	0	0	0	0	0	0	0	0	0
Totals	5 Yr	3	1	1	0	0	0	1	0	0	0	0	0

Bobo Newsom

Year	Team	AB	R	H	D	T	HR	TB	BI	W	K	SB	CS
1940	DET AL	1	0	1	0	0	0	1	0	0	0	0	0
1944	PHA AL	0	0	0	0	0	0	0	0	0	0	0	0
Totals	2 Yr	1	0	1	0	0	0	1	0	0	0	0	0

Bill Nicholson

Year	Team	AB	R	H	D	T	HR	TB	BI	W	K	SB	CS
1940	CHN NL	2	0	0	0	0	0	0	0	0	0	0	0
1941*	CHN NL	1	0	0	0	0	0	0	0	0	1	0	0
1943*	CHN NL	2	0	0	0	0	0	0	0	0	0	0	0
1944	CHN NL	1	1	1	1	0	0	2	1	0	0	0	0
Totals	4 Yr	6	1	1	1	0	0	2	1	0	1	0	0

Phil Niekro

Year	Team	AB	R	H	D	T	HR	TB	BI	W	K	SB	CS
1969	ATL NL	0	0	0	0	0	0	0	0	0	0	0	0
1978	ATL NL	0	0	0	0	0	0	0	0	0	0	0	0
Totals	2 Yr	0	0	0	0	0	0	0	0	0	0	0	0

Dave Nilsson

Year	Team	AB	R	H	D	T	HR	TB	BI	W	K	SB	CS
1999	MIL NL	1	0	0	0	0	0	0	0	0	1	0	0

Matt Nokes

Year	Team	AB	R	H	D	T	HR	TB	BI	W	K	SB	CS
1987	DET AL	2	0	0	0	0	0	0	0	0	0	0	0

Irv Noren

Year	Team	AB	R	H	D	T	HR	TB	BI	W	K	SB	CS
1954	NYA AL	0	0	0	0	0	0	0	0	0	0	0	0

Mike Norris

Year	Team	AB	R	H	D	T	HR	TB	BI	W	K	SB	CS
1981	OAK AL	0	0	0	0	0	0	0	0	0	0	0	0

Joe Nuxhall

Year	Team	AB	R	H	D	T	HR	TB	BI	W	K	SB	CS
1955	CIN NL	2	0	0	0	0	0	0	0	0	0	0	0

Billy O'Dell

Year	Team	AB	R	H	D	T	HR	TB	BI	W	K	SB	CS
1958	BAL AL	0	0	0	0	0	0	0	0	0	0	0	0
1959-2	BAL AL	0	0	0	0	0	0	0	0	0	0	0	0
Totals	2 Yr	0	0	0	0	0	0	0	0	0	0	0	0

Lefty O'Doul

Year	Team	AB	R	H	D	T	HR	TB	BI	W	K	SB	CS
1933	NY NL	1	0	0	0	0	0	0	0	0	0	0	0

Paul O'Neill

Year	Team	AB	R	H	D	T	HR	TB	BI	W	K	SB	CS
1991	CIN NL	2	0	0	0	0	0	0	0	1	0	0	0
1994	NYA AL	1	0	0	0	0	0	0	0	0	0	0	0
1995	NYA AL	1	0	0	0	0	0	0	0	0	0	0	0
1997*	NYA AL	2	0	0	0	0	0	0	0	1	0	0	0
1998	NYA AL	2	0	0	0	0	0	0	0	0	0	0	0
Totals	5 Yr	8	0	0	0	0	0	0	0	2	0	0	0

Jim O'Toole

Year	Team	AB	R	H	D	T	HR	TB	BI	W	K	SB	CS
1963*	CIN NL	1	0	0	0	0	0	0	0	0	0	0	0

Johnny Odom

Year	Team	AB	R	H	D	T	HR	TB	BI	W	K	SB	CS
1968	OAK AL	0	0	0	0	0	0	0	0	0	0	0	0
1969	OAK AL	0	0	0	0	0	0	0	0	0	0	0	0
Totals	2 Yr	0	0	0	0	0	0	0	0	0	0	0	0

Jose Offerman

Year	Team	AB	R	H	D	T	HR	TB	BI	W	K	SB	CS
1995	LAN NL	0	0	0	0	0	0	0	0	0	0	0	0
1999	BOS AL	1	0	0	0	0	0	0	0	0	0	0	0
Totals	2 Yr	1	0	0	0	0	0	0	0	0	0	0	0

Ben Oglivie

Year	Team	AB	R	H	D	T	HR	TB	BI	W	K	SB	CS
1980*	MIL AL	2	0	0	0	0	0	0	0	1	1	0	0
1982	MIL AL	1	0	0	0	0	0	0	0	0	0	0	0
1983	MIL AL	1	0	0	0	0	0	0	0	0	1	0	0
Totals	3 Yr	4	0	0	0	0	0	0	0	1	2	0	0

John Olerud

Year	Team	AB	R	H	D	T	HR	TB	BI	W	K	SB	CS
1993*	TOR AL	2	0	0	0	0	0	0	0	0	0	0	0

Tony Oliva

Year	Team	AB	R	H	D	T	HR	TB	BI	W	K	SB	CS
1964*	MIN AL	4	0	0	0	0	0	0	0	0	1	0	0
1965	MIN AL	2	0	1	1	0	0	2	0	0	0	0	0
1966*	MIN AL	4	0	0	0	0	0	0	0	0	0	0	0
1967*	MIN AL	6	0	2	0	0	0	2	0	0	3	0	2
1968	MIN AL	1	0	1	1	0	0	2	0	0	0	0	0
1970	MIN AL	2	0	1	1	0	0	2	0	1	0	0	0
Totals	6 Yr	19	0	5	3	0	0	8	0	1	4	0	2

Al Oliver

Year	Team	AB	R	H	D	T	HR	TB	BI	W	K	SB	CS
1972	PIT NL	1	0	0	0	0	0	0	0	0	0	0	0
1975	PIT NL	1	1	1	1	0	0	2	0	0	0	0	0
1976	PIT NL	1	0	0	0	0	0	0	0	0	0	0	0
1980	TEX AL	1	0	0	0	0	0	0	0	0	0	0	0
1981	TEX AL	1	0	0	0	0	0	0	0	0	0	0	0
1982	MON NL	2	1	2	1	0	0	3	0	0	0	0	1
1983*	MON NL	2	1	1	1	0	0	2	0	1	0	0	0
Totals	7 Yr	9	3	4	3	0	0	7	0	1	0	0	1

Greg Olson

Year	Team	AB	R	H	D	T	HR	TB	BI	W	K	SB	CS
1990	ATL NL	1	0	0	0	0	0	0	0	0	1	0	0

Magglio Ordonez

Year	Team	AB	R	H	D	T	HR	TB	BI	W	K	SB	CS
1999	CHA AL	1	0	0	0	0	0	0	0	0	0	0	0
2000	CHA AL	1	0	1	1	0	0	2	1	0	0	0	0
Totals	2 Yr	2	0	1	1	0	0	2	1	0	0	0	0

Jesse Orosco

Year	Team	AB	R	H	D	T	HR	TB	BI	W	K	SB	CS
1983	NYN NL	0	0	0	0	0	0	0	0	0	0	0	0

Claude Osteen

Year	Team	AB	R	H	D	T	HR	TB	BI	W	K	SB	CS
1970	LAN NL	0	0	0	0	0	0	0	0	0	0	0	0
1973	LAN NL	0	0	0	0	0	0	0	0	0	0	0	0
Totals	2 Yr	0	0	0	0	0	0	0	0	0	0	0	0

Amos Otis

Year	Team	AB	R	H	D	T	HR	TB	BI	W	K	SB	CS
1970	KCA AL	3	0	0	0	0	0	0	0	0	0	0	0
1971	KCA AL	1	0	0	0	0	0	0	0	0	0	0	0
1973*	KCA AL	2	0	2	0	0	0	2	1	0	0	1	0
1976	KCA AL	1	0	0	0	0	0	0	0	0	1	0	0
Totals	4 Yr	7	0	2	0	0	0	2	1	0	1	1	0

Year	Team	AB	R	H	D	T	HR	TB	BI	W	K	SB	CS

Mel Ott

Year	Team	AB	R	H	D	T	HR	TB	BI	W	K	SB	CS
1934	NY NL	2	0	0	0	0	0	0	0	0	0	1	0
1935*	NY NL	4	0	0	0	0	0	0	0	0	1	0	0
1936	NY NL	1	0	1	0	0	0	1	0	0	0	0	0
1937	NY NL	1	0	1	1	0	0	2	0	0	0	0	0
1938*	NY NL	4	1	1	0	1	0	3	0	0	1	0	0
1939*	NY NL	4	0	2	0	0	0	2	0	0	0	0	0
1940	NY NL	0	1	0	0	0	0	0	0	1	0	0	0
1941	NY NL	1	0	0	0	0	0	0	0	0	1	0	0
1942*	NY NL	4	0	0	0	0	0	0	0	0	2	0	0
1943	NY NL	1	0	0	0	0	0	0	0	0	1	0	0
1944	NY NL	1	0	0	0	0	0	0	0	0	0	0	0
Totals	11 Yr	23	2	5	1	1	0	8	0	1	6	1	0

Mickey Owen

Year	Team	AB	R	H	D	T	HR	TB	BI	W	K	SB	CS
1941*	BRO NL	1	0	0	0	0	0	0	0	0	0	0	0
1942	BRO NL	1	1	1	0	0	1	4	1	0	0	0	0
Totals	2 Yr	2	1	1	0	0	1	4	1	0	0	0	0

Tom Paciorek

Year	Team	AB	R	H	D	T	HR	TB	BI	W	K	SB	CS
1981	SEA AL	1	0	1	0	0	0	1	0	0	0	0	0

Andy Pafko

Year	Team	AB	R	H	D	T	HR	TB	BI	W	K	SB	CS
1947	CHN NL	2	0	1	0	0	0	1	0	0	0	0	0
1948*	CHN NL	2	0	0	0	0	0	0	0	0	0	0	0
1949	CHN NL	2	0	1	0	0	0	1	0	1	1	0	0
1950	CHN NL	4	0	2	0	0	0	2	0	0	0	0	0
Totals	4 Yr	10	0	4	0	0	0	4	0	1	1	0	0

Joe Page

Year	Team	AB	R	H	D	T	HR	TB	BI	W	K	SB	CS
1947	NYA AL	0	0	0	0	0	0	0	0	0	0	0	0

Tom Pagnozzi

Year	Team	AB	R	H	D	T	HR	TB	BI	W	K	SB	CS
1992	SLN NL	1	0	0	0	0	0	0	0	0	0	0	0

Satchel Paige

Year	Team	AB	R	H	D	T	HR	TB	BI	W	K	SB	CS
1953	SLA AL	0	0	0	0	0	0	0	0	0	0	0	0

Rafael Palmeiro

Year	Team	AB	R	H	D	T	HR	TB	BI	W	K	SB	CS
1988	CHN NL	0	0	0	0	0	0	0	0	1	0	0	0
1991	TEX AL	0	0	0	0	0	0	0	0	1	0	0	0
1998	BAL AL	2	1	2	0	0	0	2	1	0	0	0	0
1999*	TEX AL	2	0	1	0	0	0	1	1	0	0	0	0
Totals	4 Yr	4	1	3	0	0	0	3	2	2	0	0	0

Dean Palmer

Year	Team	AB	R	H	D	T	HR	TB	BI	W	K	SB	CS
1998	KCA AL	1	0	0	0	0	0	0	0	0	0	0	0

Jim Palmer

Year	Team	AB	R	H	D	T	HR	TB	BI	W	K	SB	CS
1970*	BAL AL	1	0	0	0	0	0	0	0	0	0	0	0
1971	BAL AL	0	0	0	0	0	0	0	0	0	0	0	0
1972*	BAL AL	0	0	0	0	0	0	0	0	0	0	0	0
1977*	BAL AL	0	0	0	0	0	0	0	0	0	0	0	0
1978*	BAL AL	1	0	0	0	0	0	0	0	0	0	0	0
Totals	5 Yr	2	0	0	0	0	0	0	0	0	0	0	0

Milt Pappas

Year	Team	AB	R	H	D	T	HR	TB	BI	W	K	SB	CS
1962-1	BAL AL	0	0	0	0	0	0	0	0	0	0	0	0
1962-2	BAL AL	0	0	0	0	0	0	0	0	0	0	0	0

Milt Pappas *continued*

Year	Team	AB	R	H	D	T	HR	TB	BI	W	K	SB	CS
1965*	BAL AL	0	0	0	0	0	0	0	0	0	0	0	0
Totals	3 Yr	0	0	0	0	0	0	0	0	0	0	0	0

Dave Parker

Year	Team	AB	R	H	D	T	HR	TB	BI	W	K	SB	CS
1977*	PIT NL	3	1	1	0	0	0	1	0	0	1	0	0
1979*	PIT NL	3	0	1	0	0	0	1	1	1	1	0	0
1980*	PIT NL	2	0	0	0	0	0	0	0	0	1	0	0
1981*	PIT NL	3	1	1	0	0	1	4	1	0	1	0	0
1985	CIN NL	2	0	0	0	0	0	0	0	0	1	0	0
1986	CIN NL	2	0	1	0	0	0	1	0	0	0	0	0
Totals	6 Yr	15	2	4	0	0	1	7	2	1	5	0	0

Mel Parnell

Year	Team	AB	R	H	D	T	HR	TB	BI	W	K	SB	CS
1949*	BOS AL	1	0	0	0	0	0	0	0	0	1	0	0
1951	BOS AL	0	0	0	0	0	0	0	0	0	0	0	0
Totals	2 Yr	1	0	0	0	0	0	0	0	0	1	0	0

Lance Parrish

Year	Team	AB	R	H	D	T	HR	TB	BI	W	K	SB	CS
1980	DET AL	1	0	0	0	0	0	0	0	0	1	0	0
1982	DET AL	2	0	1	1	0	0	2	0	0	0	0	0
1983	DET AL	2	0	0	0	0	0	0	0	0	1	0	0
1984*	DET AL	2	0	0	0	0	0	0	0	0	2	0	0
1986*	DET AL	3	0	0	0	0	0	0	0	0	0	0	0
1988	PHI NL	1	0	0	0	0	0	0	0	0	0	0	0
1990	CAL AL	1	1	1	0	0	0	1	0	1	0	0	0
Totals	7 Yr	12	1	2	1	0	0	3	0	1	4	0	0

Larry Parrish

Year	Team	AB	R	H	D	T	HR	TB	BI	W	K	SB	CS
1979	MON NL	0	0	0	0	0	0	0	0	0	0	0	0
1987	TEX AL	1	0	1	0	0	0	1	0	0	0	0	0
Totals	2 Yr	1	0	1	0	0	0	1	0	0	0	0	0

Camilo Pascual

Year	Team	AB	R	H	D	T	HR	TB	BI	W	K	SB	CS
1961-2	MIN AL	1	0	0	0	0	0	0	0	0	0	0	0
1962-1	MIN AL	1	0	0	0	0	0	0	0	0	0	0	0
1964	MIN AL	0	0	0	0	0	0	0	0	0	0	0	0
Totals	3 Yr	2	0	0	0	0	0	0	0	0	0	0	0

Claude Passeau

Year	Team	AB	R	H	D	T	HR	TB	BI	W	K	SB	CS
1941	CHN NL	1	0	0	0	0	0	0	0	0	0	0	0
1942	CHN NL	0	0	0	0	0	0	0	0	0	0	0	0
1946*	CHN NL	1	0	0	0	0	0	0	0	0	1	0	0
Totals	3 Yr	2	0	0	0	0	0	0	0	0	1	0	0

Freddie Patek

Year	Team	AB	R	H	D	T	HR	TB	BI	W	K	SB	CS
1976	KCA AL	0	0	0	0	0	0	0	0	0	0	0	0
1978*	KCA AL	3	0	1	0	0	0	1	0	0	1	0	0
Totals	2 Yr	3	0	1	0	0	0	1	0	0	1	0	0

Roger Pavlik

Year	Team	AB	R	H	D	T	HR	TB	BI	W	K	SB	CS
1996	TEX AL	0	0	0	0	0	0	0	0	0	0	0	0

Albie Pearson

Year	Team	AB	R	H	D	T	HR	TB	BI	W	K	SB	CS
1963*	LAA AL	4	1	2	1	0	0	3	0	0	1	0	0

Tony Pena

Year	Team	AB	R	H	D	T	HR	TB	BI	W	K	SB	CS
1982	PIT NL	1	0	0	0	0	0	0	0	0	0	1	0
1984	PIT NL	0	0	0	0	0	0	0	0	0	0	0	0
1985	PIT NL	1	0	0	0	0	0	0	0	0	1	0	0

Year	Team	AB	R	H	D	T	HR	TB	BI	W	K	SB	CS

Tony Pena *continued*

Year	Team	AB	R	H	D	T	HR	TB	BI	W	K	SB	CS
1986	PIT NL	0	0	0	0	0	0	0	0	0	0	0	0
1989	SLN NL	2	0	0	0	0	0	0	0	0	0	0	0
Totals	5 Yr	4	0	0	0	0	0	0	0	0	1	1	0

Terry Pendleton

| 1992* | ATL NL | 2 | 0 | 1 | 0 | 0 | 0 | 1 | 0 | 0 | 0 | 0 | 0 |

Joe Pepitone

1963*	NYA AL	4	0	0	0	0	0	0	0	0	2	0	0
1964	NYA AL	0	0	0	0	0	0	0	0	0	0	0	0
1965	NYA AL	1	0	0	0	0	0	0	0	0	1	0	0
Totals	3 Yr	5	0	0	0	0	0	0	0	0	3	0	0

Troy Percival

1996	CAL AL	0	0	0	0	0	0	0	0	0	0	0	0
1998	ANA AL	0	0	0	0	0	0	0	0	0	0	0	0
Totals	2 Yr	0	0	0	0	0	0	0	0	0	0	0	0

Pascual Perez

| 1983 | ATL NL | 0 | 0 | 0 | 0 | 0 | 0 | 0 | 0 | 0 | 0 | 0 | 0 |

Tony Perez

1967	CIN NL	2	1	1	0	0	1	4	1	0	1	0	0
1968	CIN NL	0	0	0	0	0	0	0	0	0	0	0	0
1969	CIN NL	1	0	0	0	0	0	0	0	0	1	0	0
1970*	CIN NL	3	0	0	0	0	0	0	0	0	2	0	0
1974	CIN NL	1	0	0	0	0	0	0	0	0	1	0	0
1975	CIN NL	1	0	0	0	0	0	0	0	0	1	0	0
1976	CIN NL	0	0	0	0	0	0	0	0	0	1	0	0
Totals	7 Yr	8	1	1	0	0	1	4	1	1	6	0	0

Gaylord Perry

1966	SFN NL	0	0	0	0	0	0	0	0	0	0	0	0
1970	SFN NL	0	0	0	0	0	0	0	0	0	0	0	0
1972	CLE AL	0	0	0	0	0	0	0	0	0	0	0	0
1974*	CLE AL	0	0	0	0	0	0	0	0	0	0	0	0
1979	SDN NL	0	0	0	0	0	0	0	0	0	0	0	0
Totals	5 Yr	0	0	0	0	0	0	0	0	0	0	0	0

Gerald Perry

| 1988 | ATL NL | 1 | 0 | 0 | 0 | 0 | 0 | 0 | 0 | 0 | 0 | 0 | 0 |

Jim Perry

| 1970 | MIN AL | 0 | 0 | 0 | 0 | 0 | 0 | 0 | 0 | 0 | 0 | 0 | 0 |

Johnny Pesky

| 1946* | BOS AL | 2 | 0 | 0 | 0 | 0 | 0 | 0 | 0 | 0 | 0 | 0 | 0 |

Gary Peters

| 1967 | CHA AL | 0 | 0 | 0 | 0 | 0 | 0 | 0 | 0 | 0 | 0 | 0 | 0 |

Fritz Peterson

| 1970 | NYA AL | 0 | 0 | 0 | 0 | 0 | 0 | 0 | 0 | 0 | 0 | 0 | 0 |

Rico Petrocelli

1967*	BOS AL	1	0	0	0	0	0	0	0	0	0	0	0
1969*	BOS AL	3	0	1	1	0	0	2	0	0	1	0	0
Totals	2 Yr	4	0	1	1	0	0	2	0	0	1	0	0

Dan Petry

| 1985 | DET AL | 0 | 0 | 0 | 0 | 0 | 0 | 0 | 0 | 0 | 0 | 0 | 0 |

Babe Phelps

1939	BRO NL	1	0	0	0	0	0	0	0	0	0	0	0
1940	BRO NL	0	0	0	0	0	0	0	0	1	0	0	0
Totals	2 Yr	1	0	0	0	0	0	0	0	1	0	0	0

Mike Piazza

1993	LAN NL	1	0	0	0	0	0	0	0	0	1	0	0
1994*	LAN NL	4	0	1	0	0	0	1	1	0	0	0	0
1995*	LAN NL	3	1	1	0	0	1	4	1	0	0	0	0
1996*	LAN NL	3	1	2	1	0	1	6	2	0	1	0	0
1997*	LAN NL	1	0	0	0	0	0	0	0	0	1	0	0
1998*	NYN NL	3	0	1	0	0	0	1	0	0	0	0	0
1999*	NYN NL	2	0	1	0	0	0	1	0	0	1	0	0
Totals	7 Yr	17	2	6	1	0	2	13	4	1	3	0	0

Billy Pierce

1953*	CHA AL	1	0	0	0	0	0	0	0	0	1	0	0
1955*	CHA AL	0	0	0	0	0	0	0	0	0	0	0	0
1956*	CHA AL	0	0	0	0	0	0	0	0	0	0	0	0
1957	CHA AL	1	1	1	0	0	0	1	0	0	0	0	0
Totals	4 Yr	2	1	1	0	0	0	1	0	0	1	0	0

Jim Piersall

1954	BOS AL	0	0	0	0	0	0	0	0	0	0	0	0
1956	BOS AL	1	0	0	0	0	0	0	0	0	0	0	0
Totals	2 Yr	1	0	0	0	0	0	0	0	0	0	0	0

Lou Piniella

| 1972 | KCA AL | 1 | 0 | 0 | 0 | 0 | 0 | 0 | 0 | 0 | 0 | 0 | 0 |

Vada Pinson

1959-2	CIN NL	0	0	0	0	0	0	0	0	0	0	0	0
1960-1	CIN NL	1	0	0	0	0	0	0	0	0	1	0	0
1960-2	CIN NL	0	0	0	0	0	0	0	0	1	0	0	0
Totals	3 Yr	1	0	0	0	0	0	0	0	1	1	0	0

Juan Pizarro

| 1963 | CHA AL | 0 | 0 | 0 | 0 | 0 | 0 | 0 | 0 | 0 | 0 | 0 | 0 |

Dan Plesac

1987	MIL AL	0	0	0	0	0	0	0	0	0	0	0	0
1988	MIL AL	0	0	0	0	0	0	0	0	0	0	0	0
Totals	2 Yr	0	0	0	0	0	0	0	0	0	0	0	0

Biff Pocoroba

| 1978 | ATL NL | 0 | 0 | 0 | 0 | 0 | 0 | 0 | 0 | 0 | 0 | 0 | 0 |

Johnny Podres

1960-2	LAN NL	0	0	0	0	0	0	0	0	0	0	0	0
1962-2*	LAN NL	1	1	1	1	0	0	2	0	0	0	0	0
Totals	2 Yr	1	1	1	1	0	0	2	0	0	0	0	0

Howie Polle

| 1949 | SLN NL | 0 | 0 | 0 | 0 | 0 | 0 | 0 | 0 | 0 | 0 | 0 | 0 |

Darrell Porter

| 1978 | KCA AL | 1 | 0 | 0 | 0 | 0 | 0 | 0 | 0 | 0 | 0 | 0 | 0 |

Year	Team	AB	R	H	D	T	HR	TB	BI	W	K	SB	CS

Darrell Porter *continued*

Year	Team	AB	R	H	D	T	HR	TB	BI	W	K	SB	CS
1979*	KCA AL	3	0	1	1	0	0	2	0	0	0	0	0
1980	KCA AL	1	0	0	0	0	0	0	0	0	1	0	0
Totals	3 Yr	5	0	1	1	0	0	2	0	0	1	0	0

Bob Porterfield

Year	Team	AB	R	H	D	T	HR	TB	BI	W	K	SB	CS
1954	WAS AL	1	0	0	0	0	0	0	0	0	0	0	0

Jorge Posada

Year	Team	AB	R	H	D	T	HR	TB	BI	W	K	SB	CS
2000	NYA AL	2	0	0	0	0	0	0	0	0	1	0	0

Boog Powell

Year	Team	AB	R	H	D	T	HR	TB	BI	W	K	SB	CS
1968	BAL AL	2	0	0	0	0	0	0	0	0	2	0	0
1969*	BAL AL	4	0	1	0	0	0	1	0	0	1	0	0
1970*	BAL AL	3	0	0	0	0	0	0	0	0	0	0	0
Totals	3 Yr	9	0	1	0	0	0	1	0	0	3	0	0

Vic Power

Year	Team	AB	R	H	D	T	HR	TB	BI	W	K	SB	CS
1955	KC AL	1	0	0	0	0	0	0	0	0	0	0	0
1956	KC AL	2	0	1	0	0	0	1	0	0	0	0	0
1959-1	CLE AL	1	1	1	0	0	0	1	1	0	0	0	0
1959-2	CLE AL	1	0	0	0	0	0	0	0	0	0	0	0
1960-2	CLE AL	2	0	0	0	0	0	0	0	0	0	0	0
Totals	5 Yr	7	1	2	0	0	0	2	1	0	0	0	0

Kirby Puckett

Year	Team	AB	R	H	D	T	HR	TB	BI	W	K	SB	CS
1986*	MIN AL	3	0	1	0	0	0	1	0	1	0	1	0
1987	MIN AL	4	0	0	0	0	0	0	0	0	3	0	0
1988	MIN AL	1	0	0	0	0	0	0	0	0	0	0	0
1989*	MIN AL	3	1	1	0	0	0	1	0	0	0	0	0
1990	MIN AL	1	0	1	0	0	0	1	0	0	0	0	0
1991	MIN AL	1	0	0	0	0	0	0	0	0	0	0	0
1992*	MIN AL	3	1	1	0	0	0	1	0	0	1	0	0
1993*	MIN AL	3	1	2	1	0	1	6	2	0	0	0	0
1994*	MIN AL	3	0	1	0	0	0	1	1	0	0	0	0
1995*	MIN AL	2	0	0	0	0	0	0	0	0	1	0	0
Totals	10 Yr	24	3	7	1	0	1	11	3	1	5	1	0

Bob Purkey

Year	Team	AB	R	H	D	T	HR	TB	BI	W	K	SB	CS
1961-1	CIN NL	0	0	0	0	0	0	0	0	0	0	0	0
1961-2*	CIN NL	0	0	0	0	0	0	0	0	0	0	0	0
1962-1	CIN NL	0	0	0	0	0	0	0	0	0	0	0	0
Totals	3 Yr	0	0	0	0	0	0	0	0	0	0	0	0

Dan Quisenberry

Year	Team	AB	R	H	D	T	HR	TB	BI	W	K	SB	CS
1982	KCA AL	0	0	0	0	0	0	0	0	0	0	0	0
1983	KCA AL	0	0	0	0	0	0	0	0	0	0	0	0
Totals	2 Yr	0	0	0	0	0	0	0	0	0	0	0	0

Dick Radatz

Year	Team	AB	R	H	D	T	HR	TB	BI	W	K	SB	CS
1963	BOS AL	0	0	0	0	0	0	0	0	0	0	0	0
1964	BOS AL	1	0	0	0	0	0	0	0	0	1	0	0
Totals	2 Yr	1	0	0	0	0	0	0	0	0	1	0	0

Rip Radcliff

Year	Team	AB	R	H	D	T	HR	TB	BI	W	K	SB	CS
1936*	CHA AL	2	0	1	0	0	0	1	0	0	0	0	0

Brad Radke

Year	Team	AB	R	H	D	T	HR	TB	BI	W	K	SB	CS
1998	MIN AL	0	0	0	0	0	0	0	0	0	0	0	0

Ken Raffensberger

Year	Team	AB	R	H	D	T	HR	TB	BI	W	K	SB	CS
1944	PHI NL	0	0	0	0	0	0	0	0	0	0	0	0

Tim Raines

Year	Team	AB	R	H	D	T	HR	TB	BI	W	K	SB	CS
1981	MON NL	0	0	0	0	0	0	0	0	0	0	0	0
1982*	MON NL	1	0	0	0	0	0	0	0	1	1	1	0
1983*	MON NL	3	0	0	0	0	0	0	0	0	1	0	0
1984	MON NL	1	0	0	0	0	0	0	0	0	1	0	0
1985	MON NL	0	1	0	0	0	0	0	0	1	0	0	0
1986	MON NL	2	0	0	0	0	0	0	0	0	1	0	0
1987	MON NL	3	0	3	0	1	0	5	2	0	0	1	0
Totals	7 Yr	10	1	3	0	1	0	5	2	2	4	2	0

Manny Ramirez

Year	Team	AB	R	H	D	T	HR	TB	BI	W	K	SB	CS
1995	CLE AL	0	0	0	0	0	0	0	0	0	2	0	0
1998	CLE AL	1	0	0	0	0	0	0	1	0	0	0	0
1999*	CLE AL	1	1	0	0	0	0	0	0	1	1	0	0
Totals	3 Yr	2	1	0	0	0	0	0	1	3	1	0	0

Willie Randolph

Year	Team	AB	R	H	D	T	HR	TB	BI	W	K	SB	CS
1977*	NYA AL	5	0	1	0	0	0	1	1	0	2	0	0
1980*	NYA AL	4	0	2	0	0	0	2	0	0	0	0	0
1981*	NYA AL	3	0	1	0	0	0	1	0	0	1	0	0
1987*	NYA AL	1	0	0	0	0	0	0	0	0	0	0	0
1989	LAN NL	1	0	0	0	0	0	0	0	0	0	0	0
Totals	5 Yr	14	0	4	0	0	0	4	1	0	3	0	0

Vic Raschi

Year	Team	AB	R	H	D	T	HR	TB	BI	W	K	SB	CS
1948	NYA AL	1	0	1	0	0	0	1	2	0	0	0	0
1949	NYA AL	1	0	0	0	0	0	0	0	0	0	0	0
1950*	NYA AL	0	0	0	0	0	0	0	0	0	0	0	0
1952*	NYA AL	0	0	0	0	0	0	0	0	0	0	0	0
Totals	4 Yr	2	0	1	0	0	0	1	2	0	0	0	0

Johnny Ray

Year	Team	AB	R	H	D	T	HR	TB	BI	W	K	SB	CS
1988	CAL AL	1	0	0	0	0	0	0	0	0	0	0	0

Jeff Reardon

Year	Team	AB	R	H	D	T	HR	TB	BI	W	K	SB	CS
1985	MON NL	0	0	0	0	0	0	0	0	0	0	0	0

Ron Reed

Year	Team	AB	R	H	D	T	HR	TB	BI	W	K	SB	CS
1968	ATL NL	0	0	0	0	0	0	0	0	0	0	0	0

Pee Wee Reese

Year	Team	AB	R	H	D	T	HR	TB	BI	W	K	SB	CS
1942	BRO NL	1	0	0	0	0	0	0	0	0	0	0	0
1947	BRO NL	1	0	0	0	0	0	0	0	1	1	0	0
1948*	BRO NL	2	0	0	0	0	0	0	0	0	1	0	0
1949*	BRO NL	5	0	0	0	0	0	0	1	0	0	0	0
1950	BRO NL	3	0	0	0	0	0	0	0	1	1	0	0
1951	BRO NL	0	0	0	0	0	0	0	0	0	0	0	0
1952	BRO NL	1	0	0	0	0	0	0	0	0	0	0	0
1953*	BRO NL	4	0	2	1	0	0	3	2	0	0	0	0
Totals	8 Yr	17	0	2	1	0	0	3	2	3	3	0	0

Pete Reiser

Year	Team	AB	R	H	D	T	HR	TB	BI	W	K	SB	CS
1941*	BRO NL	4	0	0	0	0	0	0	0	0	2	0	0
1942*	BRO NL	3	0	1	0	0	0	1	0	0	0	0	0
Totals	2 Yr	7	0	1	0	0	0	1	0	0	2	0	0

Year	Team	AB	R	H	D	T	HR	TB	BI	W	K	SB	CS

Ken Reitz

Year	Team	AB	R	H	D	T	HR	TB	BI	W	K	SB	CS
1980*	SLN NL	2	0	0	0	0	0	0	0	0	0	0	0

Edgar Renteria

Year	Team	AB	R	H	D	T	HR	TB	BI	W	K	SB	CS
1998	FLO NL	1	1	0	0	0	0	0	0	0	0	0	0
2000	SLN NL	2	0	0	0	0	0	0	0	0	0	0	0
Totals	2 Yr	3	1	0	0	0	0	0	0	0	0	0	0

Rip Repulski

Year	Team	AB	R	H	D	T	HR	TB	BI	W	K	SB	CS
1956	SLN NL	1	0	0	0	0	0	0	0	0	0	0	0

Rick Reuschel

Year	Team	AB	R	H	D	T	HR	TB	BI	W	K	SB	CS
1977	CHN NL	0	0	0	0	0	0	0	0	0	0	0	0
1987	PIT NL	0	0	0	0	0	0	0	0	0	0	0	0
Totals	2 Yr	0	0	0	0	0	0	0	0	0	0	0	0

Jerry Reuss

Year	Team	AB	R	H	D	T	HR	TB	BI	W	K	SB	CS
1975*	PIT NL	1	0	0	0	0	0	0	0	0	0	0	0
1980	LAN NL	0	0	0	0	0	0	0	0	0	0	0	0
Totals	2 Yr	1	0	0	0	0	0	0	0	0	0	0	0

Allie Reynolds

Year	Team	AB	R	H	D	T	HR	TB	BI	W	K	SB	CS
1950	NYA AL	1	0	0	0	0	0	0	0	0	0	0	0
1953	NYA AL	0	0	0	0	0	0	0	0	0	0	0	0
Totals	2 Yr	1	0	0	0	0	0	0	0	0	0	0	0

Craig Reynolds

Year	Team	AB	R	H	D	T	HR	TB	BI	W	K	SB	CS
1979	HOU NL	2	0	0	0	0	0	0	0	0	0	0	0

Harold Reynolds

Year	Team	AB	R	H	D	T	HR	TB	BI	W	K	SB	CS
1987	SEA AL	3	0	0	0	0	0	0	0	0	0	0	0
1988	SEA AL	1	0	0	0	0	0	0	0	0	0	0	0
Totals	2 Yr	4	0	0	0	0	0	0	0	0	0	0	0

Rick Rhoden

Year	Team	AB	R	H	D	T	HR	TB	BI	W	K	SB	CS
1976	LAN NL	0	0	0	0	0	0	0	0	0	0	0	0

Jim Rice

Year	Team	AB	R	H	D	T	HR	TB	BI	W	K	SB	CS
1977	BOS AL	2	0	1	0	0	0	1	0	0	0	0	0
1978*	BOS AL	4	0	0	0	0	0	0	0	2	0	0	0
1979*	BOS AL	5	0	1	1	0	0	2	0	0	2	0	0
1983*	BOS AL	4	1	2	0	0	1	5	1	0	0	0	0
1984	BOS AL	1	0	0	0	0	0	0	0	0	1	0	0
1985*	BOS AL	3	0	0	0	0	0	0	0	1	2	0	0
1986	BOS AL	1	0	0	0	0	0	0	0	0	1	0	0
Totals	7 Yr	20	1	4	1	0	1	8	1	1	8	0	0

J.R. Richard

Year	Team	AB	R	H	D	T	HR	TB	BI	W	K	SB	CS
1980*	HOU NL	0	0	0	0	0	0	0	0	0	0	0	0

Bobby Richardson

Year	Team	AB	R	H	D	T	HR	TB	BI	W	K	SB	CS
1962–1	NYA AL	1	0	0	0	0	0	0	0	0	0	0	0
1962–2	NYA AL	0	1	0	0	0	0	0	0	0	0	0	0
1963	NYA AL	2	0	0	0	0	0	0	0	0	0	0	0
1964*	NYA AL	4	0	1	0	0	0	1	0	0	1	0	0
1965	NYA AL	2	0	0	0	0	0	0	0	0	0	0	0
1966	NYA AL	2	0	0	0	0	0	0	0	0	0	0	0
Totals	6 Yr	11	1	1	0	0	0	1	0	0	1	0	0

Pete Richert

Year	Team	AB	R	H	D	T	HR	TB	BI	W	K	SB	CS
1965	WAS AL	0	0	0	0	0	0	0	0	0	0	0	0
1966	WAS AL	0	0	0	0	0	0	0	0	0	0	0	0
Totals	2 Yr	0	0	0	0	0	0	0	0	0	0	0	0

Lew Riggs

Year	Team	AB	R	H	D	T	HR	TB	BI	W	K	SB	CS
1936	CIN NL	1	0	0	0	0	0	0	0	0	1	0	0

Dave Righetti

Year	Team	AB	R	H	D	T	HR	TB	BI	W	K	SB	CS
1986	NYA AL	0	0	0	0	0	0	0	0	0	0	0	0
1987	NYA AL	0	0	0	0	0	0	0	0	0	0	0	0
Totals	2 Yr	0	0	0	0	0	0	0	0	0	0	0	0

Bill Rigney

Year	Team	AB	R	H	D	T	HR	TB	BI	W	K	SB	CS
1948	NY NL	0	0	0	0	0	0	0	0	1	0	0	0

Cal Ripken

Year	Team	AB	R	H	D	T	HR	TB	BI	W	K	SB	CS
1983	BAL AL	0	0	0	0	0	0	0	0	1	0	0	0
1984*	BAL AL	3	0	0	0	0	0	0	0	0	0	0	0
1985*	BAL AL	3	0	1	0	0	0	1	0	0	0	0	0
1986*	BAL AL	4	0	0	0	0	0	0	0	2	0	0	0
1987*	BAL AL	2	0	1	0	0	0	1	0	0	0	0	0
1988*	BAL AL	3	0	0	0	0	0	0	0	1	0	0	0
1989*	BAL AL	3	0	1	1	0	0	2	0	0	0	0	0
1990*	BAL AL	2	0	0	0	0	0	0	0	0	0	0	0
1991*	BAL AL	3	1	2	0	0	1	5	3	0	0	0	0
1992*	BAL AL	3	0	1	0	0	0	1	1	0	0	0	0
1993*	BAL AL	3	0	0	0	0	0	0	0	1	0	0	0
1994*	BAL AL	5	0	1	1	0	0	2	0	0	2	0	0
1995*	BAL AL	3	0	2	0	0	0	2	0	0	0	0	0
1996*	BAL AL	3	0	0	0	0	0	0	0	0	0	0	0
1997*	BAL AL	2	0	1	0	0	0	1	0	0	0	0	0
1998*	BAL AL	4	1	1	1	0	0	2	2	0	0	0	0
1999*	BAL AL	1	1	1	0	0	0	1	1	0	0	0	0
Totals	17 Yr	47	3	12	3	0	1	18	7	2	5	0	0

Mariano Rivera

Year	Team	AB	R	H	D	T	HR	TB	BI	W	K	SB	CS
2000	NYA AL	0	0	0	0	0	0	0	0	0	0	0	0

Mickey Rivers

Year	Team	AB	R	H	D	T	HR	TB	BI	W	K	SB	CS
1976	NYA AL	2	0	1	0	0	0	1	0	0	1	0	0

Phil Rizzuto

Year	Team	AB	R	H	D	T	HR	TB	BI	W	K	SB	CS
1950*	NYA AL	6	0	2	0	0	0	2	0	0	1	0	0
1951	NYA AL	1	0	0	0	0	0	0	0	0	0	0	0
1952*	NYA AL	2	0	0	0	0	0	0	0	0	0	0	0
1953	NYA AL	0	0	0	0	0	0	0	0	0	0	0	0
Totals	4 Yr	9	0	2	0	0	0	2	0	0	1	0	0

Bip Roberts

Year	Team	AB	R	H	D	T	HR	TB	BI	W	K	SB	CS
1992	CIN NL	2	1	2	0	0	0	2	2	0	0	0	0

Robin Roberts

Year	Team	AB	R	H	D	T	HR	TB	BI	W	K	SB	CS
1950*	PHI NL	1	0	0	0	0	0	0	0	0	1	0	0
1951*	PHI NL	0	0	0	0	0	0	0	0	0	0	0	0
1953*	PHI NL	0	0	0	0	0	0	0	0	0	0	0	0
1954*	PHI NL	1	0	0	0	0	0	0	0	0	0	0	0
1955*	PHI NL	0	0	0	0	0	0	0	0	0	0	0	0
Totals	5 Yr	2	0	0	0	0	0	0	0	0	1	0	0

Year	Team	AB	R	H	D	T	HR	TB	BI	W	K	SB	CS

Brooks Robinson

Year	Team	AB	R	H	D	T	HR	TB	BI	W	K	SB	CS
1960–1	BAL AL	2	0	0	0	0	0	0	0	0	0	0	0
1960–2	BAL AL	1	0	0	0	0	0	0	0	0	0	0	0
1961–1*	BAL AL	2	0	0	0	0	0	0	0	0	0	0	0
1961–2*	BAL AL	3	0	1	0	0	0	1	0	0	1	0	0
1962–1	BAL AL	0	0	0	0	0	0	0	0	0	0	0	0
1962–2	BAL AL	1	1	0	0	0	0	0	0	1	0	0	0
1963	BAL AL	2	0	2	0	0	0	2	0	0	0	0	0
1964*	BAL AL	4	0	2	0	1	0	4	2	0	0	0	0
1965*	BAL AL	4	1	1	0	0	0	1	0	0	1	0	0
1966*	BAL AL	4	1	3	0	1	0	5	0	0	0	0	0
1967*	BAL AL	6	1	1	0	0	1	4	1	0	1	0	0
1968*	BAL AL	2	0	0	0	0	0	0	0	0	0	0	0
1969	BAL AL	1	0	0	0	0	0	0	0	0	1	0	0
1970	BAL AL	3	1	2	0	1	0	4	2	0	0	0	0
1971*	BAL AL	3	0	1	0	0	0	1	0	0	0	0	0
1972*	BAL AL	2	0	0	0	0	0	0	0	0	0	0	0
1973*	BAL AL	2	0	0	0	0	0	0	0	0	0	0	0
1974*	BAL AL	3	0	0	0	0	0	0	0	0	0	0	0
Totals	18 Yr	45	5	13	0	3	1	22	5	1	4	0	0

Eddie Robinson

Year	Team	AB	R	H	D	T	HR	TB	BI	W	K	SB	CS
1949*	WAS AL	5	1	1	0	0	0	1	1	0	0	0	0
1951	CHA AL	1	0	0	0	0	0	0	0	0	0	0	0
1952*	CHA AL	2	0	1	0	0	0	1	1	0	1	0	0
1953	PHA AL	1	0	0	0	0	0	0	0	0	0	0	0
Totals	4 Yr	9	1	2	0	0	0	2	2	0	1	0	0

Frank Robinson

Year	Team	AB	R	H	D	T	HR	TB	BI	W	K	SB	CS
1956*	CIN NL	2	0	0	0	0	0	0	0	0	2	0	0
1957*	CIN NL	2	0	1	0	0	0	1	0	0	0	0	0
1959–2	CIN NL	3	1	3	0	0	1	6	1	0	0	0	0
1961–1	CIN NL	1	0	1	0	0	0	1	0	0	0	1	0
1962–2	CIN NL	2	0	0	0	0	0	0	0	0	0	0	0
1965	CIN NL	1	0	0	0	0	0	0	0	0	1	0	0
1966*	BAL AL	4	0	0	0	0	0	0	0	0	1	0	0
1969*	BAL AL	2	0	0	0	0	0	0	0	0	1	0	0
1970*	BAL AL	3	0	0	0	0	0	0	0	0	2	0	0
1971*	BAL AL	2	1	1	0	0	1	4	2	0	0	0	0
1974	CAL AL	1	0	0	0	0	0	0	0	0	0	0	0
Totals	11 Yr	23	2	6	0	0	2	12	3	0	7	1	0

Jackie Robinson

Year	Team	AB	R	H	D	T	HR	TB	BI	W	K	SB	CS
1949*	BRO NL	4	3	1	1	0	0	2	0	1	0	0	0
1950*	BRO NL	4	1	1	0	0	0	1	0	0	0	0	0
1951*	BRO NL	4	1	2	0	0	0	2	1	1	0	0	1
1952*	BRO NL	3	1	1	0	0	1	4	1	0	1	0	0
1953	BRO NL	1	0	0	0	0	0	0	0	0	0	0	0
1954*	BRO NL	2	1	1	1	0	0	2	2	0	0	0	0
Totals	6 Yr	18	7	6	2	0	1	11	4	2	1	0	1

Alex Rodriguez

Year	Team	AB	R	H	D	T	HR	TB	BI	W	K	SB	CS
1996	SEA AL	1	0	0	0	0	0	0	0	0	0	0	0
1997*	SEA AL	3	0	1	0	0	0	1	0	0	2	0	0
1998*	SEA AL	3	2	2	0	0	1	5	1	0	1	0	0
Totals	3 Yr	7	2	3	0	0	1	6	1	0	3	0	0

Henry Rodriguez

Year	Team	AB	R	H	D	T	HR	TB	BI	W	K	SB	CS
1996	MON NL	1	0	1	0	0	0	1	1	0	0	0	0

Ivan Rodriguez

Year	Team	AB	R	H	D	T	HR	TB	BI	W	K	SB	CS
1992	TEX AL	2	0	0	0	0	0	0	0	0	1	0	0
1993*	TEX AL	2	1	1	1	0	0	2	0	0	0	0	0
1994*	TEX AL	5	1	2	0	0	0	2	0	0	1	0	0
1995*	TEX AL	3	0	0	0	0	0	0	0	0	1	0	0
1996*	TEX AL	2	0	0	0	0	0	0	0	0	1	0	0
1997*	TEX AL	2	0	0	0	0	0	0	0	0	0	0	0
1998*	TEX AL	4	1	3	0	0	0	3	1	0	0	1	0
1999*	TEX AL	2	0	0	0	0	0	0	0	0	1	0	0
2000*	TEX AL	3	0	1	0	0	0	1	0	0	0	0	0
Totals	9 Yr	25	3	7	1	0	0	8	1	0	5	1	0

Preacher Roe

Year	Team	AB	R	H	D	T	HR	TB	BI	W	K	SB	CS
1949	BRO NL	0	0	0	0	0	0	0	0	0	0	0	0

Steve Rogers

Year	Team	AB	R	H	D	T	HR	TB	BI	W	K	SB	CS
1978	MON NL	0	0	0	0	0	0	0	0	0	0	0	0
1979	MON NL	0	0	0	0	0	0	0	0	0	0	0	0
1982*	MON NL	0	0	0	0	0	0	0	0	0	0	0	0
Totals	3 Yr	0	0	0	0	0	0	0	0	0	0	0	0

Cookie Rojas

Year	Team	AB	R	H	D	T	HR	TB	BI	W	K	SB	CS
1965	PHI NL	1	0	0	0	0	0	0	0	0	0	0	0
1971	KCA AL	1	0	0	0	0	0	0	0	0	0	0	0
1972	KCA AL	1	1	1	0	0	1	4	2	0	0	0	0
1973	KCA AL	0	0	0	0	0	0	0	0	1	0	0	0
Totals	4 Yr	3	1	1	0	0	1	4	2	1	0	0	0

Red Rolfe

Year	Team	AB	R	H	D	T	HR	TB	BI	W	K	SB	CS
1937*	NYA AL	4	2	2	0	1	0	4	2	1	0	0	0
1939*	NYA AL	4	0	1	0	0	0	1	0	0	0	0	0
Totals	2 Yr	8	2	3	0	1	0	5	2	1	0	0	0

Rich Rollins

Year	Team	AB	R	H	D	T	HR	TB	BI	W	K	SB	CS
1962–1*	MIN AL	2	1	1	0	0	0	1	0	0	0	0	0
1962–2*	MIN AL	3	0	1	0	0	0	1	0	0	0	0	0
Totals	2 Yr	5	1	2	0	0	0	2	0	0	0	0	0

John Romano

Year	Team	AB	R	H	D	T	HR	TB	BI	W	K	SB	CS
1961–1*	CLE AL	3	0	0	0	0	0	0	0	0	1	0	0
1961–2*	CLE AL	1	0	0	0	0	0	0	0	0	0	0	0
1962–1	CLE AL	2	0	1	0	0	0	1	0	0	0	0	0
Totals	3 Yr	6	0	1	0	0	0	1	0	0	1	0	0

Buddy Rosar

Year	Team	AB	R	H	D	T	HR	TB	BI	W	K	SB	CS
1946	PHA AL	2	1	1	0	0	0	1	0	0	0	0	0
1947*	PHA AL	4	0	0	0	0	0	0	0	0	1	0	0
1948*	PHA AL	1	0	0	0	0	0	0	0	0	0	0	0
Totals	3 Yr	7	1	1	0	0	0	1	0	0	1	0	0

Pete Rose

Year	Team	AB	R	H	D	T	HR	TB	BI	W	K	SB	CS
1965*	CIN NL	2	0	0	0	0	0	0	0	1	2	0	0
1967	CIN NL	1	0	0	0	0	0	0	0	0	0	0	0
1969	CIN NL	1	0	0	0	0	0	0	0	0	0	0	0
1970	CIN NL	3	1	1	0	0	0	1	0	1	2	0	0
1971	CIN NL	0	0	0	0	0	0	0	0	0	0	0	0
1973*	CIN NL	3	1	0	0	0	0	0	0	1	0	0	0
1974*	CIN NL	2	0	0	0	0	0	0	0	0	1	0	0
1975*	CIN NL	4	0	2	0	0	0	2	1	0	0	0	0
1976*	CIN NL	3	1	2	0	1	0	4	0	0	0	0	0

Pete Rose *continued*

Year	Team	AB	R	H	D	T	HR	TB	BI	W	K	SB	CS
1977	CIN NL	2	0	0	0	0	0	0	0	0	0	0	0
1978*	CIN NL	4	0	1	1	0	0	2	0	0	0	0	0
1979	PHI NL	2	0	0	0	0	0	0	0	0	0	0	0
1980	PHI NL	1	0	0	0	0	0	0	0	0	0	0	0
1981*	PHI NL	3	0	1	0	0	0	1	0	0	0	0	0
1982*	PHI NL	1	0	0	0	0	0	0	1	0	0	0	0
1985	CIN NL	1	0	0	0	0	0	0	0	0	0	0	0
Totals	16 Yr	33	3	7	1	1	0	10	2	3	5	0	0

John Roseboro

Year	Team	AB	R	H	D	T	HR	TB	BI	W	K	SB	CS
1961–2	LAN NL	3	0	0	0	0	0	0	0	0	3	0	0
1962–2	LAN NL	3	1	1	0	0	1	4	1	0	1	0	0
1969	MIN AL	1	0	0	0	0	0	0	0	0	0	0	0
Totals	3 Yr	7	1	1	0	0	1	4	1	0	4	0	0

Al Rosen

Year	Team	AB	R	H	D	T	HR	TB	BI	W	K	SB	CS
1952*	CLE AL	1	1	0	0	0	0	0	0	1	0	0	0
1953*	CLE AL	4	0	0	0	0	0	0	0	0	0	0	0
1954*	CLE AL	4	2	3	0	0	2	9	5	1	1	0	0
1955	CLE AL	2	0	0	0	0	0	0	0	1	2	0	0
Totals	4 Yr	11	3	3	0	0	2	9	5	3	3	0	0

Schoolboy Rowe

Year	Team	AB	R	H	D	T	HR	TB	BI	W	K	SB	CS
1936	DET AL	1	0	0	0	0	0	0	0	0	0	0	0
1947	PHI NL	1	0	0	0	0	0	0	0	0	0	0	0
Totals	2 Yr	2	0	0	0	0	0	0	0	0	0	0	0

Joe Rudi

Year	Team	AB	R	H	D	T	HR	TB	BI	W	K	SB	CS
1972	OAK AL	1	0	1	1	0	0	2	0	0	0	0	0
1974	OAK AL	2	0	0	0	0	0	0	0	0	1	0	0
1975*	OAK AL	3	0	1	0	0	0	1	0	0	0	0	0
Totals	3 Yr	6	0	2	1	0	0	3	0	0	1	0	0

Red Ruffing

Year	Team	AB	R	H	D	T	HR	TB	BI	W	K	SB	CS
1934	NYA AL	1	0	1	0	0	0	1	2	0	0	0	0
1939*	NYA AL	0	0	0	0	0	0	0	0	0	0	0	0
1940*	NYA AL	1	0	0	0	0	0	0	0	0	0	0	0
Totals	3 Yr	2	0	1	0	0	0	1	2	0	0	0	0

Pete Runnels

Year	Team	AB	R	H	D	T	HR	TB	BI	W	K	SB	CS
1959–1	BOS AL	0	0	0	0	0	0	0	0	0	0	0	0
1959–2*	BOS AL	3	0	0	0	0	0	0	0	1	2	0	0
1960–1*	BOS AL	1	0	0	0	0	0	0	0	1	0	0	0
1960–2*	BOS AL	2	0	0	0	0	0	0	0	1	1	0	0
1962–2	BOS AL	1	1	1	0	0	1	4	1	0	0	0	0
Totals	5 Yr	7	1	1	0	0	1	4	1	3	3	0	0

Bob Rush

Year	Team	AB	R	H	D	T	HR	TB	BI	W	K	SB	CS
1952	CHN NL	1	0	0	0	0	0	0	0	0	0	0	0

Bill Russell

Year	Team	AB	R	H	D	T	HR	TB	BI	W	K	SB	CS
1973	LAN NL	2	0	0	0	0	0	0	0	0	0	0	0
1976	LAN NL	1	0	0	0	0	0	0	0	0	0	0	0
1980*	LAN NL	2	0	0	0	0	0	0	0	0	0	0	0
Totals	3 Yr	5	0	0	0	0	0	0	0	0	0	0	0

John Russell

Year	Team	AB	R	H	D	T	HR	TB	BI	W	K	SB	CS
1988	PHI AL	0	0	0	0	0	0	0	0	0	0	0	0

Babe Ruth

Year	Team	AB	R	H	D	T	HR	TB	BI	W	K	SB	CS
1933*	NYA AL	4	1	2	0	0	1	5	2	0	2	0	0
1934*	NYA AL	2	1	0	0	0	0	0	0	2	1	0	0
Totals	2 Yr	6	2	2	0	0	1	5	2	2	3	0	0

Dick Ruthven

Year	Team	AB	R	H	D	T	HR	TB	BI	W	K	SB	CS
1981	PHI NL	0	0	0	0	0	0	0	0	0	0	0	0

Connie Ryan

Year	Team	AB	R	H	D	T	HR	TB	BI	W	K	SB	CS
1944*	BSN NL	4	1	2	0	0	0	2	0	0	0	1	0

Nolan Ryan

Year	Team	AB	R	H	D	T	HR	TB	BI	W	K	SB	CS
1973	CAL AL	0	0	0	0	0	0	0	0	0	0	0	0
1979*	CAL AL	0	0	0	0	0	0	0	0	0	0	0	0
1981	HOU NL	0	0	0	0	0	0	0	0	0	0	0	0
1985	HOU NL	1	0	0	0	0	0	0	0	0	1	0	0
Totals	4 Yr	1	0	0	0	0	0	0	0	0	1	0	0

Bret Saberhagen

Year	Team	AB	R	H	D	T	HR	TB	BI	W	K	SB	CS
1987*	KCA AL	0	0	0	0	0	0	0	0	0	0	0	0
1990	KCA AL	0	0	0	0	0	0	0	0	0	0	0	0
Totals	2 Yr	0	0	0	0	0	0	0	0	0	0	0	0

Chris Sabo

Year	Team	AB	R	H	D	T	HR	TB	BI	W	K	SB	CS
1988	CIN NL	0	0	0	0	0	0	0	0	0	0	1	0
1990*	CIN NL	2	0	0	0	0	0	0	0	0	0	0	0
1991*	CIN NL	2	0	0	0	0	0	0	0	0	0	0	0
Totals	3 Yr	4	0	0	0	0	0	0	0	0	0	1	0

Johnny Sain

Year	Team	AB	R	H	D	T	HR	TB	BI	W	K	SB	CS
1947	BSN NL	0	0	0	0	0	0	0	0	0	0	0	0
1948	BSN NL	0	0	0	0	0	0	0	0	0	0	0	0
Totals	2 Yr	0	0	0	0	0	0	0	0	0	0	0	0

Joe Sambito

Year	Team	AB	R	H	D	T	HR	TB	BI	W	K	SB	CS
1979	HOU NL	0	0	0	0	0	0	0	0	0	0	0	0

Juan Samuel

Year	Team	AB	R	H	D	T	HR	TB	BI	W	K	SB	CS
1987	PHI NL	4	0	0	0	0	0	0	0	0	1	0	0
1991	LAN NL	1	0	1	0	0	0	1	0	0	0	0	0
Totals	2 Yr	5	0	1	0	0	0	1	0	0	1	0	0

Ryne Sandberg

Year	Team	AB	R	H	D	T	HR	TB	BI	W	K	SB	CS
1984*	CHN NL	4	0	1	0	0	0	1	0	0	1	1	0
1985	CHN NL	1	1	0	0	0	0	0	0	1	1	0	0
1986*	CHN NL	3	0	0	0	0	0	0	0	0	2	0	0
1987*	CHN NL	2	0	0	0	0	0	0	0	0	0	0	0
1988*	CHN NL	4	0	1	0	0	0	1	0	0	2	0	0
1989*	CHN NL	3	0	0	0	0	0	0	0	0	2	0	0
1990*	CHN NL	3	0	0	0	0	0	0	0	0	0	0	0
1991*	CHN NL	3	0	1	1	0	0	2	0	0	0	0	0
1992*	CHN NL	2	0	0	0	0	0	0	0	0	1	0	0
1993*	CHN NL	1	0	0	0	0	0	0	0	0	1	0	0
Totals	10 Yr	26	1	3	1	0	0	4	0	2	9	1	0

Reggie Sanders

Year	Team	AB	R	H	D	T	HR	TB	BI	W	K	SB	CS
1995	CIN NL	1	0	0	0	0	0	0	0	0	1	0	0

Jack Sanford

Year	Team	AB	R	H	D	T	HR	TB	BI	W	K	SB	CS
1957	PHI NL	0	0	0	0	0	0	0	0	0	0	0	0

Year	Team	AB	R	H	D	T	HR	TB	BI	W	K	SB	CS
Manny Sanguillen													
1972	PIT NL	2	0	1	0	0	0	1	0	0	0	0	0
Benito Santiago													
1989*	SDN NL	1	0	0	0	0	0	0	0	0	0	1	0	0
1991*	SDN NL	3	0	0	0	0	0	0	0	0	0	1	0	0
1992*	SDN NL	1	0	0	0	0	0	0	0	0	0	1	0	0
Totals	3 Yr	5	0	0	0	0	0	0	0	0	0	3	0	0
Ron Santo													
1963	CHN NL	1	0	1	0	0	0	1	1	0	0	0	0
1965	CHN NL	2	0	1	0	0	0	1	1	0	0	0	0
1966*	CHN NL	4	0	1	0	0	0	1	1	0	0	0	0
1968*	CHN NL	2	0	1	0	0	0	1	0	2	0	0	0
1969*	CHN NL	3	0	0	0	0	0	0	0	1	0	0	0
1971	CHN NL	1	0	0	0	0	0	0	0	0	0	0	0
1972	CHN NL	1	0	0	0	0	0	0	0	0	0	0	0
1973*	CHN NL	1	1	1	0	0	0	1	0	2	0	0	0
Totals	8 Yr	15	1	5	0	0	0	5	3	5	0	0	0
Hank Sauer													
1950*	CHN NL	2	0	0	0	0	0	0	1	0	0	0	0
1952*	CHN NL	2	1	1	0	0	1	4	2	0	1	0	0
Totals	2 Yr	4	1	1	0	0	1	4	3	0	1	0	0
Steve Sax													
1982	LAN NL	1	0	1	0	0	0	1	0	0	0	0	1
1983*	LAN NL	3	1	1	0	0	0	1	1	0	0	0	0
1986	LAN NL	1	0	1	0	0	0	1	1	0	0	1	0
1989	NYA AL	1	0	0	0	0	0	0	0	0	0	0	0
1990*	NYA AL	1	0	0	0	0	0	0	0	1	0	1	0
Totals	5 Yr	7	1	3	0	0	0	3	2	1	0	2	1
Richie Scheinblum													
1972	KCA AL	1	0	0	0	0	0	0	0	0	0	0	0
Mike Schmidt													
1974	PHI NL	0	1	0	0	0	0	0	0	2	0	0	0
1976	PHI NL	1	0	0	0	0	0	0	0	0	0	0	0
1977	PHI NL	0	0	0	0	0	0	0	0	0	0	0	0
1979*	PHI NL	3	2	2	1	1	0	5	1	0	0	0	0
1981*	PHI NL	4	1	2	1	0	1	6	2	0	1	0	0
1982*	PHI NL	1	0	0	0	0	0	0	0	0	0	0	0
1983*	PHI NL	3	0	0	0	0	0	0	0	1	0	0	0
1984*	PHI NL	3	0	0	0	0	0	0	0	2	0	0	0
1986*	PHI NL	1	0	0	0	0	0	0	0	1	0	0	0
1987*	PHI NL	2	0	1	0	0	0	1	0	0	0	0	1
Totals	10 Yr	18	4	5	2	1	1	12	3	3	4	0	1
Johnny Schmitz													
1948	CHN NL	0	0	0	0	0	0	0	0	0	0	0	0
Red Schoendienst													
1946*	SLN NL	2	0	0	0	0	0	0	0	0	0	0	0
1948*	SLN NL	4	0	0	0	0	0	0	0	0	0	0	0
1949	SLN NL	1	0	1	0	0	0	1	0	0	0	0	0
1950	SLN NL	1	1	1	0	0	1	4	1	0	0	0	0
1951	SLN NL	0	0	0	0	0	0	0	0	0	0	0	0
1953*	SLN NL	3	0	0	0	0	0	0	0	0	0	0	0
1954	SLN NL	2	0	0	0	0	0	0	0	0	0	0	1
Red Schoendienst *continued*													
1955*	SLN NL	6	0	2	0	0	0	2	0	0	0	0	0
1957	MIL NL	2	0	0	0	0	0	0	0	0	0	0	0
Totals	9 Yr	21	1	4	0	0	1	7	1	0	0	0	1
Hal Schumacher													
1935	NY NL	1	0	0	0	0	0	0	0	0	0	0	0
Don Schwall													
1961–2	BOS AL	1	0	0	0	0	0	0	0	0	0	0	0
Mike Scioscia													
1989	LAN NL	1	0	0	0	0	0	0	0	0	0	0	0
1990*	LAN NL	2	0	0	0	0	0	0	0	0	1	0	0
Totals	2 Yr	3	0	0	0	0	0	0	0	0	1	0	0
Herb Score													
1956	CLE AL	0	0	0	0	0	0	0	0	0	0	0	0
George Scott													
1966*	BOS AL	2	0	0	0	0	0	0	0	0	0	0	0
1975	MIL AL	2	0	0	0	0	0	0	0	0	2	0	0
1977	BOS AL	2	1	1	0	0	1	4	2	0	0	0	0
Totals	3 Yr	6	1	1	0	0	1	4	2	0	2	0	0
Mike Scott													
1986	HOU NL	0	0	0	0	0	0	0	0	0	0	0	0
1987*	HOU NL	0	0	0	0	0	0	0	0	0	0	0	0
Totals	2 Yr	0	0	0	0	0	0	0	0	0	0	0	0
Tom Seaver													
1967	NYN NL	0	0	0	0	0	0	0	0	0	0	0	0
1968	NYN NL	0	0	0	0	0	0	0	0	0	0	0	0
1970*	NYN NL	0	0	0	0	0	0	0	0	0	0	0	0
1973	NYN NL	0	0	0	0	0	0	0	0	0	0	0	0
1975	NYN NL	0	0	0	0	0	0	0	0	0	0	0	0
1976	NYN NL	1	0	0	0	0	0	0	0	1	0	0	0
1977	CIN NL	0	0	0	0	0	0	0	0	0	0	0	0
1981	CIN NL	0	0	0	0	0	0	0	0	0	0	0	0
Totals	8 Yr	1	0	0	0	0	0	0	0	1	0	0	0
Kevin Seitzer													
1987	KCA AL	2	0	0	0	0	0	0	0	1	0	0	0
1995	MIL AL	2	0	0	0	0	0	0	0	0	0	0	0
Totals	2 Yr	4	0	0	0	0	0	0	0	1	0	0	0
Aaron Sele													
2000	SEA AL	0	0	0	0	0	0	0	0	0	0	0	0
George Selkirk													
1936	NYA AL	0	0	0	0	0	0	0	0	1	0	0	0
1939*	NYA AL	2	0	1	0	0	0	1	1	2	0	0	0
Totals	2 Yr	2	0	1	0	0	0	1	1	3	0	0	0
Andy Seminick													
1949*	PHI NL	1	0	0	0	0	0	0	0	0	0	0	0
Rip Sewell													
1943	PIT NL	0	0	0	0	0	0	0	0	0	0	0	0
1944	PIT NL	1	0	0	0	0	0	0	0	1	0	0	0

Rip Sewell *continued*

Year	Team	AB	R	H	D	T	HR	TB	BI	W	K	SB	CS
1946	PIT NL	0	0	0	0	0	0	0	0	0	0	0	0
Totals	3 Yr	1	0	0	0	0	0	0	0	0	1	0	0

Bobby Shantz

Year	Team	AB	R	H	D	T	HR	TB	BI	W	K	SB	CS
1952	PHA AL	0	0	0	0	0	0	0	0	0	0	0	0

Mike Sharperson

Year	Team	AB	R	H	D	T	HR	TB	BI	W	K	SB	CS
1992	LAN NL	1	0	0	0	0	0	0	0	0	0	1	0	0

Bob Shaw

Year	Team	AB	R	H	D	T	HR	TB	BI	W	K	SB	CS
1962-1	MIL NL	0	0	0	0	0	0	0	0	0	0	0	0

Jeff Shaw

Year	Team	AB	R	H	D	T	HR	TB	BI	W	K	SB	CS
1998	LAN NL	0	0	0	0	0	0	0	0	0	0	0	0

Spec Shea

Year	Team	AB	R	H	D	T	HR	TB	BI	W	K	SB	CS
1947	NYA AL	1	0	0	0	0	0	0	0	0	0	0	0

Gary Sheffield

Year	Team	AB	R	H	D	T	HR	TB	BI	W	K	SB	CS
1992	SDN NL	2	0	0	0	0	0	0	0	0	0	0	0
1993*	FLO NL	3	1	2	0	0	1	5	2	0	0	0	0
1996	FLO NL	1	0	0	0	0	0	0	0	0	0	0	0
1998	LAN NL	1	0	0	0	0	0	0	0	0	0	0	0
1999	LAN NL	1	0	0	0	0	0	0	0	0	0	0	0
2000	LAN NL	1	1	0	0	0	0	0	0	1	0	0	0
Totals	6 Yr	9	2	2	0	0	1	5	2	1	0	0	0

Chris Short

Year	Team	AB	R	H	D	T	HR	TB	BI	W	K	SB	CS
1964	PHI NL	0	0	0	0	0	0	0	0	0	0	0	0
1967	PHI NL	0	0	0	0	0	0	0	0	0	0	0	0
Totals	2 Yr	0	0	0	0	0	0	0	0	0	0	0	0

Norm Siebern

Year	Team	AB	R	H	D	T	HR	TB	BI	W	K	SB	CS
1962-1	KC AL	1	0	0	0	0	0	0	0	0	0	0	0
1964	BAL AL	1	0	0	0	0	0	0	0	0	0	0	0
Totals	2 Yr	2	0	0	0	0	0	0	0	0	0	0	0

Dick Siebert

Year	Team	AB	R	H	D	T	HR	TB	BI	W	K	SB	CS
1943*	PHA AL	1	0	0	0	0	0	0	0	0	0	0	0

Sonny Siebert

Year	Team	AB	R	H	D	T	HR	TB	BI	W	K	SB	CS
1966	CLE AL	0	0	0	0	0	0	0	0	0	0	0	0

Ruben Sierra

Year	Team	AB	R	H	D	T	HR	TB	BI	W	K	SB	CS
1989*	TEX AL	3	1	2	0	0	0	2	1	1	0	0	0
1991	TEX AL	2	0	0	0	0	0	0	0	0	2	0	0
1992	TEX AL	2	2	1	0	0	1	4	2	0	0	0	0
1994	OAK AL	2	0	1	0	0	0	1	0	0	0	0	0
Totals	4 Yr	9	3	4	0	0	1	7	3	1	2	0	0

Roy Sievers

Year	Team	AB	R	H	D	T	HR	TB	BI	W	K	SB	CS
1956	WAS AL	1	0	0	0	0	0	0	0	0	0	0	0
1959-1	WAS AL	0	0	0	0	0	0	0	0	1	0	0	0
1961-2	CHA AL	1	0	0	0	0	0	0	0	0	1	0	0
Totals	3 Yr	2	0	0	0	0	0	0	0	1	1	0	0

Al Simmons

Year	Team	AB	R	H	D	T	HR	TB	BI	W	K	SB	CS
1933*	CHA AL	4	0	1	0	0	0	1	0	0	0	0	0
1934*	CHA AL	5	3	3	2	0	0	5	1	0	1	0	0

Al Simmons *continued*

Year	Team	AB	R	H	D	T	HR	TB	BI	W	K	SB	CS
1935*	CHA AL	4	0	2	1	0	0	3	0	0	2	0	0
Totals	3 Yr	13	3	6	3	0	0	9	1	0	3	0	0

Curt Simmons

Year	Team	AB	R	H	D	T	HR	TB	BI	W	K	SB	CS
1952*	PHI NL	0	0	0	0	0	0	0	0	0	0	0	0
1953	PHI NL	0	0	0	0	0	0	0	0	0	0	0	0
1957*	PHI NL	0	0	0	0	0	0	0	0	0	0	0	0
Totals	3 Yr	0	0	0	0	0	0	0	0	0	0	0	0

Ted Simmons

Year	Team	AB	R	H	D	T	HR	TB	BI	W	K	SB	CS
1973	SLN NL	1	0	0	0	0	0	0	0	0	1	0	0
1977	SLN NL	3	0	0	0	0	0	0	0	0	0	0	0
1978*	SLN NL	3	0	1	0	0	0	1	0	0	1	0	0
1981	MIL AL	1	0	1	0	0	0	1	1	0	0	0	0
1983*	MIL AL	2	0	0	0	0	0	0	0	0	0	0	0
Totals	5 Yr	10	0	2	0	0	0	2	1	0	2	0	0

Harry Simpson

Year	Team	AB	R	H	D	T	HR	TB	BI	W	K	SB	CS
1956	KC AL	1	0	0	0	0	0	0	0	0	1	0	0

Bill Singer

Year	Team	AB	R	H	D	T	HR	TB	BI	W	K	SB	CS
1969	LAN NL	0	0	0	0	0	0	0	0	0	0	0	0
1973	CAL AL	0	0	0	0	0	0	0	0	0	0	0	0
Totals	2 Yr	0	0	0	0	0	0	0	0	0	0	0	0

Ken Singleton

Year	Team	AB	R	H	D	T	HR	TB	BI	W	K	SB	CS
1977	BAL AL	0	0	0	0	0	0	0	0	0	0	0	0
1979	BAL AL	1	0	0	0	0	0	0	0	0	0	0	0
1981*	BAL AL	3	2	2	0	0	1	5	1	0	0	0	0
Totals	3 Yr	4	2	2	0	0	1	5	1	0	0	0	0

Dick Sisler

Year	Team	AB	R	H	D	T	HR	TB	BI	W	K	SB	CS
1950	PHI NL	1	0	1	0	0	0	1	0	0	0	0	0

Bob Skinner

Year	Team	AB	R	H	D	T	HR	TB	BI	W	K	SB	CS
1958*	PIT NL	3	0	1	0	0	0	1	1	0	0	0	0
1960-1*	PIT NL	4	1	1	0	0	0	1	1	0	1	1	0
1960-2*	PIT NL	3	0	1	0	0	0	1	0	0	1	0	0
Totals	3 Yr	10	1	3	0	0	0	3	2	0	2	1	0

Bill Skowron

Year	Team	AB	R	H	D	T	HR	TB	BI	W	K	SB	CS
1957	NYA AL	3	1	2	1	0	0	3	0	0	1	0	0
1958*	NYA AL	4	0	0	0	0	0	0	0	0	1	0	0
1959-1*	NYA AL	3	0	2	0	0	0	2	0	0	0	0	0
1960-1*	NYA AL	3	0	1	0	0	0	1	0	0	2	0	0
1960-2*	NYA AL	1	0	1	0	0	0	1	0	1	0	0	0
Totals	5 Yr	14	1	6	1	0	0	7	0	1	4	0	0

Enos Slaughter

Year	Team	AB	R	H	D	T	HR	TB	BI	W	K	SB	CS
1941	SLN NL	2	1	1	0	0	0	1	0	0	1	0	0
1942	SLN NL	2	0	1	0	0	0	1	0	0	0	0	0
1946	SLN NL	1	0	0	0	0	0	0	0	0	0	0	0
1947*	SLN NL	3	0	0	0	0	0	0	0	0	1	0	0
1948*	SLN NL	2	0	1	0	0	0	1	0	0	1	0	0
1949	SLN NL	1	0	0	0	0	0	0	0	0	0	0	0
1950*	SLN NL	4	1	2	0	1	0	4	1	1	0	0	0
1951	SLN NL	1	0	0	0	0	0	0	0	0	0	0	0
1952*	SLN NL	2	0	1	1	0	0	2	0	0	1	0	0

Enos Slaughter *continued*

Year	Team	AB	R	H	D	T	HR	TB	BI	W	K	SB	CS
1953*	SLN NL	3	2	2	0	0	0	2	1	1	0	1	0
Totals	10 Yr	21	4	8	1	1	0	11	2	4	2	1	0

Roy Smalley

Year	Team	AB	R	H	D	T	HR	TB	BI	W	K	SB	CS
1979*	MIN AL	3	0	0	0	0	0	0	0	1	0	0	0

Al Smith

Year	Team	AB	R	H	D	T	HR	TB	BI	W	K	SB	CS
1955	CLE AL	1	0	0	0	0	0	0	0	1	1	0	0
1960–1	CHA AL	1	0	0	0	0	0	0	0	0	0	0	0
1960–2	CHA AL	1	0	0	0	0	0	0	0	0	0	0	0
Totals	3 Yr	3	0	0	0	0	0	0	0	1	1	0	0

Dave Smith

Year	Team	AB	R	H	D	T	HR	TB	BI	W	K	SB	CS
1990	HOU NL	0	0	0	0	0	0	0	0	0	0	0	0

Eddie Smith

Year	Team	AB	R	H	D	T	HR	TB	BI	W	K	SB	CS
1941	CHA AL	0	0	0	0	0	0	0	0	0	0	0	0

Hal Smith

Year	Team	AB	R	H	D	T	HR	TB	BI	W	K	SB	CS
1959–2	NL	2	0	0	0	0	0	0	0	0	1	0	0

Lee Smith

Year	Team	AB	R	H	D	T	HR	TB	BI	W	K	SB	CS
1983	CHN NL	0	0	0	0	0	0	0	0	0	0	0	0
1987	CHN NL	1	0	0	0	0	0	0	0	0	1	0	0
1994	BAL AL	0	0	0	0	0	0	0	0	0	0	0	0
Totals	3 Yr	1	0	0	0	0	0	0	0	0	1	0	0

Lonnie Smith

Year	Team	AB	R	H	D	T	HR	TB	BI	W	K	SB	CS
1982	SLN NL	0	0	0	0	0	0	0	0	0	0	0	0

Ozzie Smith

Year	Team	AB	R	H	D	T	HR	TB	BI	W	K	SB	CS
1981	SDN NL	0	0	0	0	0	0	0	0	2	0	1	0
1982	SLN NL	0	0	0	0	0	0	0	0	0	0	0	1
1983*	SLN NL	2	1	1	0	0	0	1	0	0	0	0	0
1984*	SLN NL	3	0	0	0	0	0	0	0	0	0	1	0
1985*	SLN NL	4	0	0	0	0	0	0	0	0	0	0	0
1986*	SLN NL	1	0	0	0	0	0	0	0	0	0	0	0
1987*	SLN NL	2	0	0	0	0	0	0	0	0	0	0	0
1988*	SLN NL	2	0	0	0	0	0	0	0	1	0	0	0
1989*	SLN NL	4	0	1	0	0	0	1	0	0	0	0	1
1990*	SLN NL	1	0	0	0	0	0	0	0	0	0	0	0
1991*	SLN NL	1	0	0	0	0	0	0	0	0	1	0	0
1992*	SLN NL	3	0	1	1	0	0	2	0	0	1	0	0
1994*	SLN NL	3	0	1	0	0	0	1	0	0	0	0	0
1996	SLN NL	1	0	0	0	0	0	0	0	0	0	0	0
Totals	14 Yr	27	1	4	1	0	0	5	0	3	2	2	2

Reggie Smith

Year	Team	AB	R	H	D	T	HR	TB	BI	W	K	SB	CS
1969	BOS AL	2	1	0	0	0	0	0	0	0	0	0	0
1972	BOS AL	1	0	0	0	0	0	0	0	0	1	0	0
1974	SLN NL	2	1	1	0	0	1	4	1	0	0	0	0
1975	SLN NL	2	1	1	0	0	0	1	0	0	0	0	0
1977	LAN NL	1	0	1	0	0	0	1	0	0	0	0	0
1978	LAN NL	3	0	0	0	0	0	0	0	0	2	0	0
1980*	LAN NL	2	0	0	0	0	0	0	0	0	0	0	0
Totals	7 Yr	13	3	3	0	0	1	6	1	0	3	0	0

John Smoltz

Year	Team	AB	R	H	D	T	HR	TB	BI	W	K	SB	CS
1992	ATL NL	0	0	0	0	0	0	0	0	0	0	0	0

John Smoltz *continued*

Year	Team	AB	R	H	D	T	HR	TB	BI	W	K	SB	CS
1996*	ATL NL	0	0	0	0	0	0	0	0	0	0	0	0
Totals	2 Yr	0	0	0	0	0	0	0	0	0	0	0	0

Duke Snider

Year	Team	AB	R	H	D	T	HR	TB	BI	W	K	SB	CS
1950	BRO NL	1	0	0	0	0	0	0	0	0	0	0	0
1951	BRO NL	0	0	0	0	0	0	0	0	0	0	0	0
1953	BRO NL	0	1	0	0	0	0	0	0	1	0	0	0
1954*	BRO NL	4	2	3	1	0	0	4	0	1	0	0	0
1955*	BRO NL	2	0	0	0	0	0	0	0	0	1	0	0
1956	BRO NL	3	0	0	0	0	0	0	0	0	1	0	0
1963	NYN NL	1	0	0	0	0	0	0	0	0	1	0	0
Totals	7 Yr	11	3	3	1	0	0	4	0	2	3	0	0

Lary Sorensen

Year	Team	AB	R	H	D	T	HR	TB	BI	W	K	SB	CS
1978	MIL AL	0	0	0	0	0	0	0	0	0	0	0	0

Sammy Sosa

Year	Team	AB	R	H	D	T	HR	TB	BI	W	K	SB	CS
1995	CHN NL	1	0	0	0	0	0	0	0	0	0	0	0
1999*	CHN NL	3	0	0	0	0	0	0	0	0	2	0	0
2000*	CHN NL	3	0	0	0	0	0	0	0	0	1	0	0
Totals	3 Yr	7	0	0	0	0	0	0	0	0	3	0	0

Mario Soto

Year	Team	AB	R	H	D	T	HR	TB	BI	W	K	SB	CS
1982	CIN NL	0	0	0	0	0	0	0	0	0	0	0	0
1983*	CIN NL	1	0	0	0	0	0	0	0	0	0	0	0
1984	CIN NL	0	0	0	0	0	0	0	0	0	0	0	0
Totals	3 Yr	1	0	0	0	0	0	0	0	0	0	0	0

Warren Spahn

Year	Team	AB	R	H	D	T	HR	TB	BI	W	K	SB	CS
1947	BSN NL	0	0	0	0	0	0	0	0	0	0	0	0
1949*	BSN NL	0	0	0	0	0	0	0	0	0	0	0	0
1953	MIL NL	0	0	0	0	0	0	0	0	0	0	0	0
1954	MIL NL	0	0	0	0	0	0	0	0	0	0	0	0
1956	MIL NL	1	0	0	0	0	0	0	0	0	0	0	0
1958*	MIL NL	0	0	0	0	0	0	0	0	1	0	0	0
1961–1*	MIL NL	0	0	0	0	0	0	0	0	0	0	0	0
Totals	7 Yr	1	0	0	0	0	0	0	0	1	0	0	0

Chris Speier

Year	Team	AB	R	H	D	T	HR	TB	BI	W	K	SB	CS
1972	SFN NL	2	0	0	0	0	0	0	0	0	0	0	0
1973*	SFN NL	2	0	0	0	0	0	0	0	0	1	0	0
Totals	2 Yr	4	0	0	0	0	0	0	0	0	1	0	0

Stan Spence

Year	Team	AB	R	H	D	T	HR	TB	BI	W	K	SB	CS
1944*	WAS AL	4	0	2	0	0	0	2	0	0	0	0	0
1946	WAS AL	0	1	0	0	0	0	0	0	1	0	0	0
1947	WAS AL	1	0	1	0	0	0	1	1	0	0	0	0
Totals	3 Yr	5	1	3	0	0	0	3	1	1	0	0	0

Jim Spencer

Year	Team	AB	R	H	D	T	HR	TB	BI	W	K	SB	CS
1973	TEX AL	1	0	0	0	0	0	0	0	0	0	0	0

Ed Sprague

Year	Team	AB	R	H	D	T	HR	TB	BI	W	K	SB	CS
1999	PIT NL	1	0	0	0	0	0	0	0	0	0	0	0

Gerry Staley

Year	Team	AB	R	H	D	T	HR	TB	BI	W	K	SB	CS
1960–2	CHA AL	0	0	0	0	0	0	0	0	0	0	0	0

Year	Team	AB	R	H	D	T	HR	TB	BI	W	K	SB	CS

Eddie Stanky

Year	Team	AB	R	H	D	T	HR	TB	BI	W	K	SB	CS
1947	BRO NL	2	0	0	0	0	0	0	0	0	0	0	0

Bob Stanley

Year	Team	AB	R	H	D	T	HR	TB	BI	W	K	SB	CS
1979	BOS AL	0	0	0	0	0	0	0	0	0	0	0	0
1983	BOS AL	0	0	0	0	0	0	0	0	0	0	0	0
Totals	2 Yr	0	0	0	0	0	0	0	0	0	0	0	0

Mike Stanley

Year	Team	AB	R	H	D	T	HR	TB	BI	W	K	SB	CS
1995	NYA AL	1	0	0	0	0	0	0	0	0	0	0	0

Willie Stargell

Year	Team	AB	R	H	D	T	HR	TB	BI	W	K	SB	CS
1964	PIT NL	1	0	0	0	0	0	0	0	0	0	0	0
1965*	PIT NL	3	2	2	0	0	1	5	2	0	1	0	0
1966	PIT NL	1	0	0	0	0	0	0	0	0	0	0	0
1971*	PIT NL	2	1	0	0	0	0	0	0	0	2	0	0
1972*	PIT NL	1	0	0	0	0	0	0	0	1	0	0	0
1973	PIT NL	1	0	0	0	0	0	0	0	0	1	0	0
1978	PIT NL	1	0	0	0	0	0	0	0	0	0	0	0
Totals	7 Yr	10	3	2	0	0	1	5	2	1	4	0	0

Rusty Staub

Year	Team	AB	R	H	D	T	HR	TB	BI	W	K	SB	CS
1967	HOU NL	1	0	1	0	0	0	1	0	0	0	0	0
1968	HOU NL	1	0	0	0	0	0	0	0	0	0	0	0
1970	MON NL	1	0	0	0	0	0	0	0	0	0	0	0
1976*	DET AL	2	0	2	0	0	0	2	0	0	0	0	0
Totals	4 Yr	5	0	3	0	0	0	3	0	0	0	0	0

John Stearns

Year	Team	AB	R	H	D	T	HR	TB	BI	W	K	SB	CS
1977	NYN NL	0	0	0	0	0	0	0	0	0	0	0	0
1980	NYN NL	1	0	0	0	0	0	0	0	0	0	0	0
1982	NYN NL	0	0	0	0	0	0	0	0	0	0	0	0
Totals	3 Yr	1	0	0	0	0	0	0	0	0	0	0	0

Terry Steinbach

Year	Team	AB	R	H	D	T	HR	TB	BI	W	K	SB	CS
1988*	OAK AL	1	1	1	0	0	1	4	2	0	0	0	0
1989*	OAK AL	3	0	1	0	0	0	1	0	0	0	0	0
1993	OAK AL	2	0	1	1	0	0	2	1	0	1	0	0
Totals	3 Yr	6	1	3	1	0	1	7	3	0	1	0	0

Dave Stenhouse

Year	Team	AB	R	H	D	T	HR	TB	BI	W	K	SB	CS
1962-2*	WAS AL	0	0	0	0	0	0	0	0	0	0	0	0

Vern Stephens

Year	Team	AB	R	H	D	T	HR	TB	BI	W	K	SB	CS
1943*	SLA AL	3	0	1	0	0	0	1	0	0	1	0	0
1944*	SLA AL	4	0	1	0	0	0	1	0	0	1	0	0
1946	SLA AL	3	1	2	1	0	0	3	2	0	0	0	0
1948	BOS AL	2	0	1	0	0	0	1	0	0	1	0	0
1949	BOS AL	2	0	0	0	0	0	0	0	0	1	0	0
1951	BOS AL	1	0	0	0	0	0	0	0	0	1	0	0
Totals	6 Yr	15	1	5	1	0	0	6	2	0	5	0	0

Dave Stieb

Year	Team	AB	R	H	D	T	HR	TB	BI	W	K	SB	CS
1980	TOR AL	0	0	0	0	0	0	0	0	0	0	0	0
1981	TOR AL	1	0	0	0	0	0	0	0	0	1	0	0
1983*	TOR AL	0	0	0	0	0	0	0	0	0	0	0	0
1984*	TOR AL	0	0	0	0	0	0	0	0	0	0	0	0
1985	TOR AL	0	0	0	0	0	0	0	0	0	0	0	0
1988	TOR AL	0	0	0	0	0	0	0	0	0	0	0	0

Dave Stieb *continued*

Year	Team	AB	R	H	D	T	HR	TB	BI	W	K	SB	CS
1990	TOR AL	0	0	0	0	0	0	0	0	0	0	0	0
Totals	7 Yr	1	0	0	0	0	0	0	0	0	1	0	0

Kurt Stillwell

Year	Team	AB	R	H	D	T	HR	TB	BI	W	K	SB	CS
1988	KCA AL	0	0	0	0	0	0	0	0	0	0	0	0

Snuffy Stirnweiss

Year	Team	AB	R	H	D	T	HR	TB	BI	W	K	SB	CS
1946	NYA AL	3	1	1	0	0	0	1	0	0	1	0	0

Dean Stone

Year	Team	AB	R	H	D	T	HR	TB	BI	W	K	SB	CS
1954	WAS AL	0	0	0	0	0	0	0	0	0	0	0	0

Steve Stone

Year	Team	AB	R	H	D	T	HR	TB	BI	W	K	SB	CS
1980*	BAL AL	1	0	0	0	0	0	0	0	0	1	0	0

Bill Stoneman

Year	Team	AB	R	H	D	T	HR	TB	BI	W	K	SB	CS
1972	MON NL	1	0	0	0	0	0	0	0	0	1	0	0

Mel Stottlemyre

Year	Team	AB	R	H	D	T	HR	TB	BI	W	K	SB	CS
1966	NYA AL	0	0	0	0	0	0	0	0	0	0	0	0
1968	NYA AL	0	0	0	0	0	0	0	0	0	0	0	0
1969*	NYA AL	0	0	0	0	0	0	0	0	0	0	0	0
1970	NYA AL	0	0	0	0	0	0	0	0	0	0	0	0
Totals	4 Yr	0	0	0	0	0	0	0	0	0	0	0	0

Darryl Strawberry

Year	Team	AB	R	H	D	T	HR	TB	BI	W	K	SB	CS
1984*	NYN NL	2	0	1	0	0	0	1	0	0	1	1	0
1985*	NYN NL	1	2	1	0	0	0	1	0	1	0	1	0
1986*	NYN NL	2	0	1	0	0	0	1	0	0	1	0	0
1987*	NYN NL	2	0	0	0	0	0	0	0	0	0	0	0
1988*	NYN NL	4	0	1	0	0	0	1	0	0	1	0	0
1990	NYN NL	1	0	0	0	0	0	0	0	0	1	0	0
Totals	6 Yr	12	2	4	0	0	0	4	0	1	4	2	0

Dick Stuart

Year	Team	AB	R	H	D	T	HR	TB	BI	W	K	SB	CS
1961-1	PIT NL	1	0	1	1	0	0	2	0	0	0	0	0
1961-2	PIT NL	1	0	0	0	0	0	0	0	0	0	0	0
Totals	2 Yr	2	0	1	1	0	0	2	0	0	0	0	0

Frank Sullivan

Year	Team	AB	R	H	D	T	HR	TB	BI	W	K	SB	CS
1955	BOS AL	1	0	0	0	0	0	0	0	0	1	0	0

Jim Sundberg

Year	Team	AB	R	H	D	T	HR	TB	BI	W	K	SB	CS
1978	TEX AL	0	0	0	0	0	0	0	0	0	0	0	0
1984	MIL AL	1	0	0	0	0	0	0	0	0	0	0	0
Totals	2 Yr	1	0	0	0	0	0	0	0	0	0	0	0

B.J. Surhoff

Year	Team	AB	R	H	D	T	HR	TB	BI	W	K	SB	CS
1999	BAL AL	2	0	0	0	0	0	0	0	0	0	0	0

Rick Sutcliffe

Year	Team	AB	R	H	D	T	HR	TB	BI	W	K	SB	CS
1987	CHN NL	0	0	0	0	0	0	0	0	0	0	0	0

Bruce Sutter

Year	Team	AB	R	H	D	T	HR	TB	BI	W	K	SB	CS
1978	CHN NL	0	0	0	0	0	0	0	0	0	0	0	0
1979	CHN NL	0	0	0	0	0	0	0	0	0	0	0	0
1980	CHN NL	0	0	0	0	0	0	0	0	0	0	0	0
1981	SLN NL	0	0	0	0	0	0	0	0	0	0	0	0
Totals	4 Yr	0	0	0	0	0	0	0	0	0	0	0	0

Year	Team	AB	R	H	D	T	HR	TB	BI	W	K	SB	CS

Don Sutton

Year	Team	AB	R	H	D	T	HR	TB	BI	W	K	SB	CS
1972	LAN NL	0	0	0	0	0	0	0	0	0	0	0	0
1973	LAN NL	0	0	0	0	0	0	0	0	0	0	0	0
1975	LAN NL	0	0	0	0	0	0	0	0	0	0	0	0
1977*	LAN NL	0	0	0	0	0	0	0	0	0	0	0	0
Totals	4 Yr	0	0	0	0	0	0	0	0	0	0	0	0

Mike Sweeney

Year	Team	AB	R	H	D	T	HR	TB	BI	W	K	SB	CS
2000	KCA AL	1	0	0	0	0	0	0	0	0	0	0	0

Pat Tabler

Year	Team	AB	R	H	D	T	HR	TB	BI	W	K	SB	CS
1987	CLE AL	1	0	0	0	0	0	0	0	0	1	0	0

Frank Tanana

Year	Team	AB	R	H	D	T	HR	TB	BI	W	K	SB	CS
1976	CAL AL	0	0	0	0	0	0	0	0	0	0	0	0

Danny Tartabull

Year	Team	AB	R	H	D	T	HR	TB	BI	W	K	SB	CS
1991*	KCA AL	2	0	0	0	0	0	0	0	0	1	0	0

Tony Taylor

Year	Team	AB	R	H	D	T	HR	TB	BI	W	K	SB	CS
1960-1	PHI NL	0	0	0	0	0	0	0	0	0	0	0	0
1960-2	PHI NL	1	0	1	0	0	0	1	0	0	0	0	0
Totals	2 Yr	1	0	1	0	0	0	1	0	0	0	0	0

Birdie Tebbetts

Year	Team	AB	R	H	D	T	HR	TB	BI	W	K	SB	CS
1942*	DET AL	4	0	0	0	0	0	0	0	0	2	0	0
1948	BOS AL	1	1	0	0	0	0	0	0	2	1	0	0
1949*	BOS AL	2	0	2	1	0	0	3	1	0	0	0	0
Totals	3 Yr	7	1	2	1	0	0	3	1	2	3	0	0

Johnny Temple

Year	Team	AB	R	H	D	T	HR	TB	BI	W	K	SB	CS
1956*	CIN NL	4	1	2	0	0	0	2	1	1	2	1	0
1957*	CIN NL	2	0	0	0	0	0	0	0	0	1	0	0
1959-1*	CIN NL	2	0	0	0	0	0	0	0	0	0	0	0
1959-2*	CIN NL	2	1	1	1	0	0	2	0	0	0	0	0
1961-1*	CLE AL	3	0	0	0	0	0	0	0	0	0	0	0
1961-2*	CLE AL	2	0	0	0	0	0	0	0	1	1	0	0
Totals	6 Yr	15	2	3	1	0	0	4	1	2	4	1	0

Garry Templeton

Year	Team	AB	R	H	D	T	HR	TB	BI	W	K	SB	CS
1977	SLN NL	1	1	1	1	0	0	2	0	0	0	0	0
1985	SDN NL	1	0	1	0	0	0	1	0	0	0	0	0
Totals	2 Yr	2	1	2	1	0	0	3	0	0	0	0	0

Gene Tenace

Year	Team	AB	R	H	D	T	HR	TB	BI	W	K	SB	CS
1975*	OAK AL	3	1	0	0	0	0	0	0	1	1	0	0

Bill Terry

Year	Team	AB	R	H	D	T	HR	TB	BI	W	K	SB	CS
1933*	NY NL	4	0	2	0	0	0	2	0	0	0	0	0
1934*	NY NL	3	0	1	0	0	0	1	0	1	0	0	0
1935*	NY NL	3	0	1	0	0	0	1	1	0	0	0	0
Totals	3 Yr	10	0	4	0	0	0	4	1	1	0	0	0

Mickey Tettleton

Year	Team	AB	R	H	D	T	HR	TB	BI	W	K	SB	CS
1989	BAL AL	1	0	0	0	0	0	0	0	0	1	0	0
1994	DET AL	0	0	0	0	0	0	0	0	1	0	0	0
Totals	2 Yr	1	0	0	0	0	0	0	0	1	1	0	0

Bob Tewksbury

Year	Team	AB	R	H	D	T	HR	TB	BI	W	K	SB	CS
1992	SLN NL	0	0	0	0	0	0	0	0	0	0	0	0

Bobby Thigpen

Year	Team	AB	R	H	D	T	HR	TB	BI	W	K	SB	CS
1990	CHA AL	0	0	0	0	0	0	0	0	0	0	0	0

Frank Thomas

Year	Team	AB	R	H	D	T	HR	TB	BI	W	K	SB	CS
1954	PIT NL	1	0	0	0	0	0	0	0	0	1	0	0
1955	PIT NL	1	0	0	0	0	0	0	0	0	1	0	0
1958*	PIT NL	3	0	1	0	0	0	1	0	1	0	0	0
Totals	3 Yr	5	0	1	0	0	0	1	0	1	1	0	0

Frank Thomas

Year	Team	AB	R	H	D	T	HR	TB	BI	W	K	SB	CS
1993	CHA AL	1	0	1	0	0	0	1	0	0	0	0	0
1994*	CHA AL	2	1	2	0	0	0	2	1	1	0	0	0
1995*	CHA AL	2	1	1	0	0	1	4	2	0	0	0	0
Totals	3 Yr	5	2	4	0	0	1	7	3	1	0	0	0

Gorman Thomas

Year	Team	AB	R	H	D	T	HR	TB	BI	W	K	SB	CS
1981	MIL AL	1	0	0	0	0	0	0	0	0	0	0	0

Lee Thomas

Year	Team	AB	R	H	D	T	HR	TB	BI	W	K	SB	CS
1962-1	LAA AL	1	0	0	0	0	0	0	0	0	0	0	0
1962-2	LAA AL	0	0	0	0	0	0	0	0	0	0	0	0
Totals	2 Yr	1	0	0	0	0	0	0	0	0	0	0	0

Jim Thome

Year	Team	AB	R	H	D	T	HR	TB	BI	W	K	SB	CS
1997	CLE AL	1	0	0	0	0	0	0	0	0	0	0	0
1998*	CLE AL	2	1	0	0	0	0	0	0	2	1	0	0
1999*	CLE AL	2	1	1	0	0	0	1	1	1	0	0	0
Totals	3 Yr	5	2	1	0	0	0	1	1	3	1	0	0

Jason Thompson

Year	Team	AB	R	H	D	T	HR	TB	BI	W	K	SB	CS
1978	DET AL	1	0	0	0	0	0	0	0	0	0	0	0
1982	PIT NL	1	0	0	0	0	0	0	0	0	0	0	0
Totals	2 Yr	2	0	0	0	0	0	0	0	0	0	0	0

Bobby Thomson

Year	Team	AB	R	H	D	T	HR	TB	BI	W	K	SB	CS
1948	NY NL	1	0	0	0	0	0	0	0	0	1	0	0
1949	NY NL	1	0	0	0	0	0	0	0	0	0	0	0
1952*	NY NL	2	0	0	0	0	0	0	0	0	0	0	0
Totals	3 Yr	4	0	0	0	0	0	0	0	0	1	0	0

Dickie Thon

Year	Team	AB	R	H	D	T	HR	TB	BI	W	K	SB	CS
1983	HOU NL	3	0	1	0	0	0	1	0	0	0	0	0

Andre Thornton

Year	Team	AB	R	H	D	T	HR	TB	BI	W	K	SB	CS
1982	CLE AL	1	0	0	0	0	0	0	0	0	1	0	0
1984	CLE AL	1	0	1	0	0	0	1	0	0	0	0	0
Totals	2 Yr	2	0	1	0	0	0	1	0	0	1	0	0

Luis Tiant

Year	Team	AB	R	H	D	T	HR	TB	BI	W	K	SB	CS
1968*	CLE AL	0	0	0	0	0	0	0	0	0	0	0	0
1974	BOS AL	0	0	0	0	0	0	0	0	0	0	0	0
1976	BOS AL	0	0	0	0	0	0	0	0	0	0	0	0
Totals	3 Yr	0	0	0	0	0	0	0	0	0	0	0	0

Jim Tobin

Year	Team	AB	R	H	D	T	HR	TB	BI	W	K	SB	CS
1944	BSN NL	0	0	0	0	0	0	0	0	0	0	0	0

Joe Torre

Year	Team	AB	R	H	D	T	HR	TB	BI	W	K	SB	CS
1964*	MIL NL	2	0	0	0	0	0	0	0	0	0	0	0
1965*	MIL NL	4	1	1	0	0	1	4	2	0	0	0	0

Year	Team	AB	R	H	D	T	HR	TB	BI	W	K	SB	CS

Joe Torre *continued*

Year	Team	AB	R	H	D	T	HR	TB	BI	W	K	SB	CS
1966*	ATL NL	3	0	0	0	0	0	0	0	0	1	0	0
1967*	ATL NL	2	0	0	0	0	0	0	0	0	0	0	0
1970	SLN NL	1	0	0	0	0	0	0	0	0	0	0	0
1971*	SLN NL	3	0	0	0	0	0	0	0	0	1	0	0
1972*	SLN NL	3	0	1	0	0	0	1	0	0	1	0	0
1973	SLN NL	3	0	0	0	0	0	0	0	0	0	0	0
Totals	8 Yr	21	1	2	0	0	1	5	2	0	3	0	0

Steve Trachsel

Year	Team	AB	R	H	D	T	HR	TB	BI	W	K	SB	CS
1996	CHN NL	0	0	0	0	0	0	0	0	0	0	0	0

Alan Trammell

Year	Team	AB	R	H	D	T	HR	TB	BI	W	K	SB	CS
1980	DET AL	0	0	0	0	0	0	0	0	0	0	0	0
1985	DET AL	1	0	0	0	0	0	0	0	0	0	0	0
1987	DET AL	1	0	0	0	0	0	0	0	0	0	0	0
1990	DET AL	1	0	0	0	0	0	0	0	0	0	0	0
Totals	4 Yr	3	0	0	0	0	0	0	0	0	0	0	0

Cecil Travis

Year	Team	AB	R	H	D	T	HR	TB	BI	W	K	SB	CS
1940*	WAS AL	3	0	0	0	0	0	0	0	0	0	0	0
1941*	WAS AL	4	1	1	1	0	0	2	0	1	0	0	0
Totals	2 Yr	7	1	1	1	0	0	2	0	1	0	0	0

Pie Traynor

Year	Team	AB	R	H	D	T	HR	TB	BI	W	K	SB	CS
1933	PIT NL	1	0	1	1	0	0	2	0	0	0	0	0
1934*	PIT NL	5	2	2	0	0	0	2	1	0	0	1	0
Totals	2 Yr	6	2	3	1	0	0	4	1	0	0	1	0

Tom Tresh

Year	Team	AB	R	H	D	T	HR	TB	BI	W	K	SB	CS
1962–2	NYA AL	2	0	1	1	0	0	2	1	0	0	0	0
1963	NYA AL	0	0	0	0	0	0	0	0	0	0	0	0
Totals	2 Yr	2	0	1	1	0	0	2	1	0	0	0	0

Gus Triandos

Year	Team	AB	R	H	D	T	HR	TB	BI	W	K	SB	CS
1958*	BAL AL	2	0	1	0	0	0	1	0	0	0	0	0
1959–1*	BAL AL	4	0	1	1	0	0	2	2	0	0	0	0
Totals	2 Yr	6	0	2	1	0	0	3	2	0	0	0	0

Manny Trillo

Year	Team	AB	R	H	D	T	HR	TB	BI	W	K	SB	CS
1977	CHN NL	1	0	0	0	0	0	0	0	0	1	0	0
1981	PHI NL	2	0	0	0	0	0	0	0	0	0	0	0
1982*	PHI NL	2	0	1	0	0	0	1	0	0	0	0	0
1983*	CLE AL	3	1	1	0	0	0	1	0	0	0	0	0
Totals	4 Yr	8	1	2	0	0	0	2	0	0	1	0	0

Virgil Trucks

Year	Team	AB	R	H	D	T	HR	TB	BI	W	K	SB	CS
1949	DET AL	1	0	0	0	0	0	0	0	0	0	0	0
1954	CHA AL	0	0	0	0	0	0	0	0	0	0	0	0
Totals	2 Yr	1	0	0	0	0	0	0	0	0	0	0	0

Thurman Tucker

Year	Team	AB	R	H	D	T	HR	TB	BI	W	K	SB	CS
1944*	CHA AL	4	0	0	0	0	0	0	0	0	0	0	0

Bob Turley

Year	Team	AB	R	H	D	T	HR	TB	BI	W	K	SB	CS
1958*	NYA AL	0	0	0	0	0	0	0	0	0	0	0	0

Wayne Twitchell

Year	Team	AB	R	H	D	T	HR	TB	BI	W	K	SB	CS
1973	PHI NL	0	0	0	0	0	0	0	0	0	0	0	0

Ugueth Urbina

Year	Team	AB	R	H	D	T	HR	TB	BI	W	K	SB	CS
1998	MON NL	0	0	0	0	0	0	0	0	0	0	0	0

Ellis Valentine

Year	Team	AB	R	H	D	T	HR	TB	BI	W	K	SB	CS
1977	MON NL	1	0	0	0	0	0	0	0	1	0	0	0

Fernando Valenzuela

Year	Team	AB	R	H	D	T	HR	TB	BI	W	K	SB	CS
1981*	LAN NL	0	0	0	0	0	0	0	0	0	0	0	0
1982	LAN NL	0	0	0	0	0	0	0	0	0	0	0	0
1984	LAN NL	0	0	0	0	0	0	0	0	0	0	0	0
1985	LAN NL	0	0	0	0	0	0	0	0	0	0	0	0
1986	LAN NL	0	0	0	0	0	0	0	0	0	0	0	0
Totals	5 Yr	0	0	0	0	0	0	0	0	0	0	0	0

Andy Van Slyke

Year	Team	AB	R	H	D	T	HR	TB	BI	W	K	SB	CS
1988	PIT NL	2	0	0	0	0	0	0	0	0	0	0	0
1992*	PIT NL	2	0	0	0	0	0	0	0	0	0	0	0
Totals	2 Yr	4	0	0	0	0	0	0	0	0	0	0	0

Johnny Vander Meer

Year	Team	AB	R	H	D	T	HR	TB	BI	W	K	SB	CS
1938*	CIN NL	0	0	0	0	0	0	0	0	0	0	0	0
1942	CIN NL	0	0	0	0	0	0	0	0	0	0	0	0
1943	CIN NL	1	0	0	0	0	0	0	0	0	1	0	0
Totals	3 Yr	1	0	0	0	0	0	0	0	0	1	0	0

Arky Vaughan

Year	Team	AB	R	H	D	T	HR	TB	BI	W	K	SB	CS
1934	PIT NL	2	0	0	0	0	0	0	0	0	0	0	0
1935*	PIT NL	3	1	1	1	0	0	2	0	1	0	0	0
1937*	PIT NL	5	0	2	0	0	0	2	0	0	0	0	0
1939*	PIT NL	3	1	1	0	0	0	1	0	1	0	0	0
1940*	PIT NL	3	1	1	0	0	0	1	0	0	1	0	0
1941*	PIT NL	4	2	3	0	0	2	9	4	0	0	0	0
1942*	BRO NL	2	0	0	0	0	0	0	0	1	0	0	0
Totals	7 Yr	22	5	8	1	0	2	15	4	3	1	0	0

Greg Vaughn

Year	Team	AB	R	H	D	T	HR	TB	BI	W	K	SB	CS
1993	MIL AL	1	1	1	0	0	0	1	0	0	0	0	0
1998	SDN NL	1	0	1	0	0	0	1	2	0	0	0	0
Totals	2 Yr	2	1	2	0	0	0	2	2	0	0	0	0

Mo Vaughn

Year	Team	AB	R	H	D	T	HR	TB	BI	W	K	SB	CS
1995	BOS AL	2	0	0	0	0	0	0	0	0	2	0	0
1996*	BOS AL	3	0	1	1	0	0	2	0	0	0	0	0
Totals	2 Yr	5	0	1	1	0	0	2	0	0	2	0	0

Robin Ventura

Year	Team	AB	R	H	D	T	HR	TB	BI	W	K	SB	CS
1992	CHA AL	2	1	2	1	0	0	3	1	0	0	0	0

Emil Verban

Year	Team	AB	R	H	D	T	HR	TB	BI	W	K	SB	CS
1946	PHI NL	1	0	0	0	0	0	0	0	0	0	0	0
1947*	PHI NL	2	0	0	0	0	0	0	0	0	0	0	0
Totals	2 Yr	3	0	0	0	0	0	0	0	0	0	0	0

Mickey Vernon

Year	Team	AB	R	H	D	T	HR	TB	BI	W	K	SB	CS
1946*	WAS AL	2	0	0	0	0	0	0	0	0	0	0	0
1948	WAS AL	0	1	0	0	0	0	0	0	1	0	1	0
1953*	WAS AL	3	0	0	0	0	0	0	0	2	0	0	0
1954	WAS AL	1	0	0	0	0	0	0	0	1	0	0	0
1955*	WAS AL	5	0	1	0	0	0	1	1	1	2	0	0
1956*	BOS AL	2	0	0	0	0	0	0	0	0	0	0	0

Year	Team	AB	R	H	D	T	HR	TB	BI	W	K	SB	CS

Mickey Vernon *continued*

Year	Team	AB	R	H	D	T	HR	TB	BI	W	K	SB	CS
1958	CLE AL	1	1	1	0	0	0	1	0	0	0	0	0
Totals	7 Yr	14	2	2	0	0	0	2	1	2	5	1	0

Zoilo Versalles

Year	Team	AB	R	H	D	T	HR	TB	BI	W	K	SB	CS
1963*	MIN AL	1	0	1	0	0	0	1	0	1	0	0	0
1965	MIN AL	1	0	0	0	0	0	0	0	1	0	0	0
Totals	2 Yr	2	0	1	0	0	0	1	0	2	0	0	0

Jose Vidro

Year	Team	AB	R	H	D	T	HR	TB	BI	W	K	SB	CS
2000	MON NL	1	0	0	0	0	0	0	0	0	0	0	0

Fernando Vina

Year	Team	AB	R	H	D	T	HR	TB	BI	W	K	SB	CS
1998	MIL NL	1	0	1	0	0	0	1	0	1	0	0	0

Frank Viola

Year	Team	AB	R	H	D	T	HR	TB	BI	W	K	SB	CS
1988*	MIN AL	0	0	0	0	0	0	0	0	0	0	0	0
1990	NYN NL	0	0	0	0	0	0	0	0	0	0	0	0
Totals	2 Yr	0	0	0	0	0	0	0	0	0	0	0	0

Ozzie Virgil

Year	Team	AB	R	H	D	T	HR	TB	BI	W	K	SB	CS
1985	PHI NL	1	0	1	0	0	0	1	2	0	0	0	0
1987	ATL NL	2	1	1	0	0	0	1	0	0	0	0	0
Totals	2 Yr	3	1	2	0	0	0	2	2	0	0	0	0

Omar Vizquel

Year	Team	AB	R	H	D	T	HR	TB	BI	W	K	SB	CS
1998	CLE AL	2	0	1	0	0	0	1	0	0	0	0	0
1999	CLE AL	1	0	0	0	0	0	0	0	0	0	0	0
Totals	2 Yr	3	0	1	0	0	0	1	0	0	0	0	0

Joe Vosmik

Year	Team	AB	R	H	D	T	HR	TB	BI	W	K	SB	CS
1935*	CLE AL	4	1	1	0	0	0	1	0	0	0	0	0

Hal Wagner

Year	Team	AB	R	H	D	T	HR	TB	BI	W	K	SB	CS
1946	BOS AL	1	0	0	0	0	0	0	0	0	0	0	0

Leon Wagner

Year	Team	AB	R	H	D	T	HR	TB	BI	W	K	SB	CS
1962–1*	LAA AL	4	0	0	0	0	0	0	0	0	0	0	0
1962–2*	LAA AL	4	1	3	0	0	1	6	2	0	0	0	0
1963*	LAA AL	3	1	2	0	0	0	2	0	0	0	0	0
Totals	3 Yr	11	2	5	0	0	1	8	2	0	0	0	0

Eddie Waitkus

Year	Team	AB	R	H	D	T	HR	TB	BI	W	K	SB	CS
1948	CHN NL	0	0	0	0	0	0	0	0	1	0	0	0

Dick Wakefield

Year	Team	AB	R	H	D	T	HR	TB	BI	W	K	SB	CS
1943*	DET AL	4	0	2	1	0	0	3	1	0	1	0	0

Bob Walk

Year	Team	AB	R	H	D	T	HR	TB	BI	W	K	SB	CS
1988	PIT NL	0	0	0	0	0	0	0	0	0	0	0	0

Bill Walker

Year	Team	AB	R	H	D	T	HR	TB	BI	W	K	SB	CS
1935*	SLN NL	0	0	0	0	0	0	0	0	0	0	0	0

Dixie Walker

Year	Team	AB	R	H	D	T	HR	TB	BI	W	K	SB	CS
1943	BRO NL	1	0	0	0	0	0	0	1	0	0	0	0
1944*	BRO NL	4	0	2	0	0	0	2	1	0	0	0	0
1946*	BRO NL	3	0	0	0	0	0	0	0	0	0	0	0
1947*	BRO NL	2	0	0	0	0	0	0	0	0	0	0	0
Totals	4 Yr	10	0	2	0	0	0	2	2	0	0	0	0

Harry Walker

Year	Team	AB	R	H	D	T	HR	TB	BI	W	K	SB	CS
1943*	SLN NL	1	0	0	0	0	0	0	0	0	0	0	0
1947*	PHI NL	2	0	0	0	0	0	0	0	0	1	0	0
Totals	2 Yr	3	0	0	0	0	0	0	0	0	1	0	0

Jerry Walker

Year	Team	AB	R	H	D	T	HR	TB	BI	W	K	SB	CS
1959–2*	BAL AL	1	0	0	0	0	0	0	0	0	1	0	0

Larry Walker

Year	Team	AB	R	H	D	T	HR	TB	BI	W	K	SB	CS
1992	MON NL	1	0	1	0	0	0	1	0	0	0	0	0
1997*	COL NL	1	0	0	0	0	0	0	0	1	0	0	0
1998*	COL NL	1	1	0	0	0	0	0	0	1	0	0	0
1999*	COL NL	2	0	0	0	0	0	0	0	1	0	0	0
Totals	4 Yr	5	1	1	0	0	0	1	0	2	1	0	0

Tim Wallach

Year	Team	AB	R	H	D	T	HR	TB	BI	W	K	SB	CS
1984	MON NL	1	0	0	0	0	0	0	0	0	0	0	0
1985	MON NL	2	1	1	1	0	0	2	0	1	1	0	0
1987	MON NL	3	0	0	0	0	0	0	0	0	2	0	0
1989	MON NL	1	0	0	0	0	0	0	0	0	0	0	0
1990	MON NL	2	0	0	0	0	0	0	0	0	0	0	0
Totals	5 Yr	9	1	1	1	0	0	2	0	1	3	0	0

Lee Walls

Year	Team	AB	R	H	D	T	HR	TB	BI	W	K	SB	CS
1958	CHN NL	1	0	0	0	0	0	0	0	0	0	0	0

Bucky Walters

Year	Team	AB	R	H	D	T	HR	TB	BI	W	K	SB	CS
1937	PHI NL	0	0	0	0	0	0	0	0	0	0	0	0
1940	CIN NL	0	0	0	0	0	0	0	0	0	0	0	0
1941	CIN NL	1	1	1	1	0	0	2	0	0	0	0	0
1942	CIN NL	0	0	0	0	0	0	0	0	0	0	0	0
1944*	CIN NL	0	0	0	0	0	0	0	0	0	0	0	0
Totals	5 Yr	1	1	1	1	0	0	2	0	0	0	0	0

Paul Waner

Year	Team	AB	R	H	D	T	HR	TB	BI	W	K	SB	CS
1933	PIT NL	0	0	0	0	0	0	0	0	0	0	0	0
1934	PIT NL	2	0	0	0	0	0	0	0	1	0	0	0
1935	PIT NL	1	0	0	0	0	0	0	0	0	0	0	0
1937*	PIT NL	5	0	0	0	0	0	0	1	0	0	0	0
Totals	4 Yr	8	0	0	0	0	0	0	1	0	1	0	0

Gary Ward

Year	Team	AB	R	H	D	T	HR	TB	BI	W	K	SB	CS
1983	MIN AL	1	0	0	0	0	0	0	0	0	0	0	0
1985	TEX AL	1	0	0	0	0	0	0	0	0	0	0	0
Totals	2 Yr	2	0	0	0	0	0	0	0	0	0	0	0

Lon Warneke

Year	Team	AB	R	H	D	T	HR	TB	BI	W	K	SB	CS
1933	CHN NL	1	1	1	0	1	0	3	0	0	0	0	0
1934	CHN NL	0	0	0	0	0	0	0	0	0	0	0	0
1936	CHN NL	1	0	0	0	0	0	0	0	0	0	0	0
Totals	3 Yr	2	1	1	0	1	0	3	0	0	0	0	0

Claudell Washington

Year	Team	AB	R	H	D	T	HR	TB	BI	W	K	SB	CS
1975	OAK AL	1	0	1	0	0	0	1	0	0	0	1	1
1984	ATL NL	2	0	1	1	0	0	2	0	0	1	0	0
Totals	2 Yr	3	0	2	1	0	0	3	0	0	1	1	1

Bob Watson

Year	Team	AB	R	H	D	T	HR	TB	BI	W	K	SB	CS
1973	HOU NL	0	0	0	0	0	0	0	0	0	0	0	0

Bob Watson continued

Year	Team	AB	R	H	D	T	HR	TB	BI	W	K	SB	CS
1975	HOU NL	1	0	0	0	0	0	0	0	0	0	0	0
Totals	2 Yr	1	0	0	0	0	0	0	0	0	0	0	0

Walt Weiss

Year	Team	AB	R	H	D	T	HR	TB	BI	W	K	SB	CS
1998*	ATL NL	3	1	2	0	0	0	2	1	0	0	0	0

Bob Welch

Year	Team	AB	R	H	D	T	HR	TB	BI	W	K	SB	CS
1980	LAN NL	1	0	0	0	0	0	0	0	0	1	0	0
1990*	OAK AL	0	0	0	0	0	0	0	0	0	0	0	0
Totals	2 Yr	1	0	0	0	0	0	0	0	0	1	0	0

David Wells

Year	Team	AB	R	H	D	T	HR	TB	BI	W	K	SB	CS
1998*	NYA AL	1	0	0	0	0	0	0	0	0	0	0	0
2000*	TOR AL	0	0	0	0	0	0	0	0	0	0	0	0
Totals	2 Yr	1	0	0	0	0	0	0	0	0	0	0	0

Don Wert

Year	Team	AB	R	H	D	T	HR	TB	BI	W	K	SB	CS
1968	DET AL	1	0	1	1	0	0	2	0	0	0	0	0

Vic Wertz

Year	Team	AB	R	H	D	T	HR	TB	BI	W	K	SB	CS
1949	DET AL	2	0	0	0	0	0	0	0	0	0	0	0
1951*	DET AL	3	1	1	0	0	1	4	1	0	0	0	0
1957*	CLE AL	2	0	1	0	0	0	1	1	0	0	0	0
Totals	3 Yr	7	1	2	0	0	1	5	2	0	0	0	0

Max West

Year	Team	AB	R	H	D	T	HR	TB	BI	W	K	SB	CS
1940*	BSN NL	1	1	1	0	0	1	4	3	0	0	0	0

Sam West

Year	Team	AB	R	H	D	T	HR	TB	BI	W	K	SB	CS
1933	SLA AL	0	0	0	0	0	0	0	0	0	0	0	0
1934	SLA AL	0	0	0	0	0	0	0	0	0	0	0	0
1937*	SLA AL	4	1	1	0	0	0	1	0	0	0	0	0
Totals	3 Yr	4	1	1	0	0	0	1	0	0	0	0	0

Wally Westlake

Year	Team	AB	R	H	D	T	HR	TB	BI	W	K	SB	CS
1951	SLN NL	0	0	0	0	0	0	0	0	0	0	0	0

John Wetteland

Year	Team	AB	R	H	D	T	HR	TB	BI	W	K	SB	CS
1998	TEX AL	0	0	0	0	0	0	0	0	0	0	0	0

Lou Whitaker

Year	Team	AB	R	H	D	T	HR	TB	BI	W	K	SB	CS
1983	DET AL	1	1	1	0	1	0	3	2	0	0	0	0
1984*	DET AL	3	0	2	1	0	0	3	0	0	0	0	0
1985*	DET AL	2	0	0	0	0	0	0	0	0	0	0	0
1986*	DET AL	2	1	1	0	0	1	4	2	0	1	0	0
Totals	4 Yr	8	2	4	1	1	1	10	4	0	1	0	0

Bill White

Year	Team	AB	R	H	D	T	HR	TB	BI	W	K	SB	CS
1960-1	SLN NL	1	0	0	0	0	0	0	0	0	1	0	0
1960-2	SLN NL	1	0	0	0	0	0	0	0	0	0	0	0
1961-1*	SLN NL	3	0	1	0	0	0	1	1	0	1	0	0
1961-2*	SLN NL	4	0	2	1	0	0	3	1	0	0	0	0
1963*	SLN NL	4	1	1	0	0	0	1	0	0	0	1	0
1964	SLN NL	1	0	0	0	0	0	0	0	0	1	0	0
Totals	6 Yr	14	1	4	1	0	0	5	2	0	3	1	0

Devon White

Year	Team	AB	R	H	D	T	HR	TB	BI	W	K	SB	CS
1989	CAL AL	1	0	0	0	0	0	0	0	0	0	0	0
1993	TOR AL	2	1	1	1	0	0	2	1	0	0	1	0

Devon White continued

Year	Team	AB	R	H	D	T	HR	TB	BI	W	K	SB	CS
1998	ARI NL	3	1	3	0	1	0	5	0	0	0	0	0
Totals	3 Yr	6	2	4	1	1	0	7	1	0	0	1	0

Frank White

Year	Team	AB	R	H	D	T	HR	TB	BI	W	K	SB	CS
1978	KCA AL	1	0	0	0	0	0	0	0	0	0	0	0
1979*	KCA AL	2	0	0	0	0	0	0	0	0	0	0	0
1981	KCA AL	1	0	0	0	0	0	0	0	0	0	0	0
1982	KCA AL	1	0	0	0	0	0	0	0	0	1	0	0
1986	KCA AL	2	1	1	0	0	1	4	1	0	0	0	0
Totals	5 Yr	7	1	1	0	0	1	4	1	0	1	0	0

Roy White

Year	Team	AB	R	H	D	T	HR	TB	BI	W	K	SB	CS
1969	NYA AL	1	0	0	0	0	0	0	0	0	1	0	0

Burgess Whitehead

Year	Team	AB	R	H	D	T	HR	TB	BI	W	K	SB	CS
1935	SLN NL	0	0	0	0	0	0	0	0	0	0	0	0
1937	NY NL	0	0	0	0	0	0	0	0	0	0	0	0
Totals	2 Yr	0	0	0	0	0	0	0	0	0	0	0	0

Pinky Whitney

Year	Team	AB	R	H	D	T	HR	TB	BI	W	K	SB	CS
1936*	PHI NL	3	0	1	0	0	0	1	1	0	1	0	0

Ernie Whitt

Year	Team	AB	R	H	D	T	HR	TB	BI	W	K	SB	CS
1985	TOR AL	0	0	0	0	0	0	0	0	0	0	0	0

Bob Wickman

Year	Team	AB	R	H	D	T	HR	TB	BI	W	K	SB	CS
2000	MIL NL	0	0	0	0	0	0	0	0	0	0	0	0

Hoyt Wilhelm

Year	Team	AB	R	H	D	T	HR	TB	BI	W	K	SB	CS
1959-2	BAL AL	0	0	0	0	0	0	0	0	0	0	0	0
1961-1	BAL AL	1	0	0	0	0	0	0	0	0	0	0	0
Totals	2 Yr	1	0	0	0	0	0	0	0	0	0	0	0

Bernie Williams

Year	Team	AB	R	H	D	T	HR	TB	BI	W	K	SB	CS
1997	NYA AL	0	1	0	0	0	0	0	0	1	0	0	0
1999	NYA AL	1	0	0	0	0	0	0	0	0	1	0	0
2000*	NYA AL	3	0	0	0	0	0	0	0	0	0	0	0
Totals	3 Yr	4	1	0	0	0	0	0	0	1	1	0	0

Billy Williams

Year	Team	AB	R	H	D	T	HR	TB	BI	W	K	SB	CS
1962-2	CHN NL	1	0	0	0	0	0	0	1	0	0	0	0
1964*	CHN NL	4	1	1	0	0	1	4	1	0	0	0	0
1965	CHN NL	1	0	0	0	0	0	0	0	0	0	0	0
1968	CHN NL	1	0	0	0	0	0	0	0	0	0	0	0
1972	CHN NL	2	1	1	0	0	0	1	0	0	0	0	0
1973*	CHN NL	2	0	1	0	0	0	1	0	0	0	0	0
Totals	6 Yr	11	2	3	0	0	1	6	2	0	0	0	0

Davey Williams

Year	Team	AB	R	H	D	T	HR	TB	BI	W	K	SB	CS
1953	NY NL	0	0	0	0	0	0	0	0	1	0	0	0

Matt Williams

Year	Team	AB	R	H	D	T	HR	TB	BI	W	K	SB	CS
1990	SFN NL	1	0	0	0	0	0	0	0	0	1	0	0
1994*	SFN NL	3	0	0	0	0	0	0	0	0	2	0	0
1999*	ARI NL	3	0	1	0	0	0	1	0	0	1	0	1
Totals	3 Yr	7	0	1	0	0	0	1	0	0	4	0	1

Stan Williams

Year	Team	AB	R	H	D	T	HR	TB	BI	W	K	SB	CS
1960-2	LAN NL	0	0	0	0	0	0	0	0	0	0	0	0

Ted Williams

Year	Team	AB	R	H	D	T	HR	TB	BI	W	K	SB	CS
1940*	BOS AL	2	0	0	0	0	0	0	0	1	0	0	0
1941*	BOS AL	4	1	2	1	0	1	6	4	1	1	0	0
1942*	BOS AL	4	0	1	0	0	0	1	0	0	0	0	0
1946*	BOS AL	4	4	4	0	0	2	10	5	1	0	0	0
1947*	BOS AL	4	0	2	1	0	0	3	0	0	1	0	0
1948	BOS AL	0	0	0	0	0	0	0	0	1	0	0	0
1949*	BOS AL	2	1	0	0	0	0	0	0	2	1	0	0
1950*	BOS AL	4	0	1	0	0	0	1	1	0	1	0	0
1951*	BOS AL	3	0	1	0	1	0	3	0	1	1	0	0
1954	BOS AL	2	1	0	0	0	0	0	0	1	2	0	0
1955*	BOS AL	3	1	1	0	0	0	1	0	1	0	0	0
1956*	BOS AL	4	1	1	0	0	1	4	2	0	1	0	0
1957*	BOS AL	3	1	0	0	0	0	0	0	1	0	0	0
1958	BOS AL	2	0	0	0	0	0	0	0	0	1	0	0
1959–1	BOS AL	0	0	0	0	0	0	0	0	1	0	0	0
1959–2*	BOS AL	3	0	0	0	0	0	0	0	0	1	0	0
1960–1	BOS AL	1	0	0	0	0	0	0	0	0	0	0	0
1960–2	BOS AL	1	0	1	0	0	0	1	0	0	0	0	0
Totals	18 Yr	46	10	14	2	1	4	30	12	11	10	0	0

Maury Wills

Year	Team	AB	R	H	D	T	HR	TB	BI	W	K	SB	CS
1961–1*	LAN NL	5	0	1	0	0	0	1	0	0	0	0	0
1961–2*	LAN NL	2	0	1	0	0	0	1	0	0	0	0	0
1962–1	LAN NL	1	2	1	0	0	0	1	0	0	0	1	0
1962–2	LAN NL	1	0	0	0	0	0	0	0	0	0	0	0
1965*	LAN NL	4	0	1	0	0	0	1	0	0	0	0	0
1966	LAN NL	1	0	1	0	0	0	1	1	0	0	0	0
Totals	6 Yr	14	2	5	0	0	0	5	1	0	0	1	0

Dan Wilson

Year	Team	AB	R	H	D	T	HR	TB	BI	W	K	SB	CS
1996	SEA AL	1	0	0	0	0	0	0	0	0	0	0	0

Don Wilson

Year	Team	AB	R	H	D	T	HR	TB	BI	W	K	SB	CS
1971	HOU NL	0	0	0	0	0	0	0	0	0	0	0	0

Glenn Wilson

Year	Team	AB	R	H	D	T	HR	TB	BI	W	K	SB	CS
1985	PHI NL	1	0	0	0	0	0	0	0	0	1	0	0

Jim Wilson

Year	Team	AB	R	H	D	T	HR	TB	BI	W	K	SB	CS
1956	CHA AL	0	0	0	0	0	0	0	0	0	0	0	0

Jimmy Wilson

Year	Team	AB	R	H	D	T	HR	TB	BI	W	K	SB	CS
1933*	SLN NL	1	0	0	0	0	0	0	0	0	0	0	0
1935*	PHI NL	3	0	1	1	0	0	2	0	0	0	0	0
Totals	2 Yr	4	0	1	1	0	0	2	0	0	0	0	0

Willie Wilson

Year	Team	AB	R	H	D	T	HR	TB	BI	W	K	SB	CS
1982	KCA AL	2	0	0	0	0	0	0	0	0	1	0	0
1983	KCA AL	1	0	1	1	0	0	2	1	0	0	0	0
Totals	2 Yr	3	0	1	1	0	0	2	1	0	1	0	0

Dave Winfield

Year	Team	AB	R	H	D	T	HR	TB	BI	W	K	SB	CS
1977	SDN NL	2	0	2	1	0	0	3	2	0	0	0	0
1978	SDN NL	2	1	1	0	0	0	1	0	0	0	0	0
1979*	SDN NL	5	1	1	1	0	0	2	1	0	1	0	0
1980	SDN NL	2	0	0	0	0	0	0	1	0	0	0	0
1981*	NYA AL	4	0	0	0	0	0	0	0	1	0	0	0
1982	NYA AL	2	0	1	0	0	0	1	0	0	0	0	0
1983*	NYA AL	3	2	3	1	0	0	4	1	0	0	0	0

Dave Winfield *continued*

Year	Team	AB	R	H	D	T	HR	TB	BI	W	K	SB	CS
1984*	NYA AL	4	0	1	1	0	0	2	0	0	1	0	0
1985*	NYA AL	3	0	1	0	0	0	1	0	0	0	1	0
1986*	NYA AL	1	1	1	1	0	0	2	0	0	0	0	0
1987*	NYA AL	5	0	1	1	0	0	2	1	0	0	0	0
1988*	NYA AL	3	1	1	1	0	0	2	0	0	0	0	0
Totals	12 Yr	36	6	13	7	0	0	20	5	2	2	1	0

Rick Wise

Year	Team	AB	R	H	D	T	HR	TB	BI	W	K	SB	CS
1973*	SLN NL	0	0	0	0	0	0	0	0	0	0	0	0

Mark Wohlers

Year	Team	AB	R	H	D	T	HR	TB	BI	W	K	SB	CS
1996	ATL NL	0	0	0	0	0	0	0	0	0	0	0	0

Tony Womack

Year	Team	AB	R	H	D	T	HR	TB	BI	W	K	SB	CS
1997	PIT NL	1	0	0	0	0	0	0	0	0	0	0	0

Wilbur Wood

Year	Team	AB	R	H	D	T	HR	TB	BI	W	K	SB	CS
1972	CHA AL	0	0	0	0	0	0	0	0	0	0	0	0

Hal Woodeshick

Year	Team	AB	R	H	D	T	HR	TB	BI	W	K	SB	CS
1963	HOU NL	0	0	0	0	0	0	0	0	0	0	0	0

Gene Woodling

Year	Team	AB	R	H	D	T	HR	TB	BI	W	K	SB	CS
1959–2	BAL AL	1	0	0	0	0	0	0	0	0	0	0	0

Todd Worrell

Year	Team	AB	R	H	D	T	HR	TB	BI	W	K	SB	CS
1988	SLN NL	0	0	0	0	0	0	0	0	0	0	0	0
1996	LAN NL	0	0	0	0	0	0	0	0	0	0	0	0
Totals	2 Yr	0	0	0	0	0	0	0	0	0	0	0	0

Clyde Wright

Year	Team	AB	R	H	D	T	HR	TB	BI	W	K	SB	CS
1970	CAL AL	0	0	0	0	0	0	0	0	0	0	0	0

John Wyatt

Year	Team	AB	R	H	D	T	HR	TB	BI	W	K	SB	CS
1964	KC AL	0	0	0	0	0	0	0	0	0	0	0	0

Whit Wyatt

Year	Team	AB	R	H	D	T	HR	TB	BI	W	K	SB	CS
1940	BRO NL	1	0	0	0	0	0	0	0	0	1	0	0
1941*	BRO NL	0	0	0	0	0	0	0	0	0	0	0	0
Totals	2 Yr	1	0	0	0	0	0	0	0	0	1	0	0

Butch Wynegar

Year	Team	AB	R	H	D	T	HR	TB	BI	W	K	SB	CS
1976	MIN AL	0	0	0	0	0	0	0	0	1	0	0	0
1977	MIN AL	2	1	1	0	0	0	1	0	0	0	0	0
Totals	2 Yr	2	1	1	0	0	0	1	0	1	0	0	0

Early Wynn

Year	Team	AB	R	H	D	T	HR	TB	BI	W	K	SB	CS
1955	CLE AL	0	0	0	0	0	0	0	0	0	0	0	0
1956	CLE AL	0	0	0	0	0	0	0	0	0	0	0	0
1957	CLE AL	0	0	0	0	0	0	0	0	0	0	0	0
1958	CHA AL	0	0	0	0	0	0	0	0	0	0	0	0
1959–1*	CHA AL	1	0	0	0	0	0	0	0	0	1	0	0
1959–2	CHA AL	0	0	0	0	0	0	0	0	0	0	0	0
1960–2	CHA AL	0	0	0	0	0	0	0	0	0	0	0	0
Totals	7 Yr	1	0	0	0	0	0	0	0	0	1	0	0

Jim Wynn

Year	Team	AB	R	H	D	T	HR	TB	BI	W	K	SB	CS
1967	HOU NL	1	0	1	0	0	0	1	0	0	0	0	0
1974*	LAN NL	3	1	1	0	0	0	1	0	0	0	0	0

Year	Team	AB	R	H	D	T	HR	TB	BI	W	K	SB	CS

Jim Wynn *continued*

Year	Team	AB	R	H	D	T	HR	TB	BI	W	K	SB	CS
1975*	LAN NL	2	1	1	0	0	1	4	1	0	0	0	0
Totals	3 Yr	6	2	3	0	0	1	6	1	0	0	0	0

Johnny Wyrostek

Year	Team	AB	R	H	D	T	HR	TB	BI	W	K	SB	CS
1950	CIN NL	2	0	0	0	0	0	0	0	0	0	0	0
1951	CIN NL	1	0	0	0	0	0	0	0	0	0	0	0
Totals	2 Yr	3	0	0	0	0	0	0	0	0	0	0	0

Carl Yastrzemski

Year	Team	AB	R	H	D	T	HR	TB	BI	W	K	SB	CS
1963	BOS AL	2	0	0	0	0	0	0	0	0	1	0	0
1967*	BOS AL	4	0	3	1	0	0	4	0	2	1	0	0
1968*	BOS AL	4	0	0	0	0	0	0	0	0	2	0	0
1969	BOS AL	1	0	0	0	0	0	0	0	0	0	0	0
1970*	BOS AL	6	1	4	1	0	0	5	1	0	0	0	0
1971*	BOS AL	3	0	0	0	0	0	0	0	0	1	0	0
1972*	BOS AL	3	0	0	0	0	0	0	0	0	1	0	0
1974	BOS AL	1	0	0	0	0	0	0	0	1	0	0	0
1975	BOS AL	1	1	1	0	0	1	4	3	0	0	0	0
1976	BOS AL	2	0	0	0	0	0	0	0	0	0	0	0
1977*	BOS AL	2	0	0	0	0	0	0	0	0	1	0	0
1979*	BOS AL	3	0	2	0	0	0	2	1	0	0	0	0
1982	BOS AL	1	0	0	0	0	0	0	0	0	1	0	0
1983	BOS AL	1	0	0	0	0	0	0	0	0	1	0	0
Totals	14 Yr	34	2	10	2	0	1	15	5	4	8	0	0

Rudy York

Year	Team	AB	R	H	D	T	HR	TB	BI	W	K	SB	CS
1938	DET AL	1	0	0	0	0	0	0	0	0	1	0	0
1941*	DET AL	3	0	1	0	0	0	1	0	0	0	0	0
1942*	DET AL	4	1	1	0	0	1	4	2	0	1	0	0
1943	DET AL	3	0	1	0	0	0	1	0	0	2	0	0
1946	BOS AL	2	0	1	0	0	0	1	0	0	0	0	0
Totals	5 Yr	13	1	4	0	0	1	7	2	0	4	0	0

Eric Young

Year	Team	AB	R	H	D	T	HR	TB	BI	W	K	SB	CS
1996	COL NL	1	0	0	0	0	0	0	0	0	0	0	0

Matt Young

Year	Team	AB	R	H	D	T	HR	TB	BI	W	K	SB	CS
1983	SEA AL	0	0	0	0	0	0	0	0	0	0	0	0

Joel Youngblood

Year	Team	AB	R	H	D	T	HR	TB	BI	W	K	SB	CS
1981	NYN NL	1	0	0	0	0	0	0	0	0	0	0	0

Robin Yount

Year	Team	AB	R	H	D	T	HR	TB	BI	W	K	SB	CS
1980	MIL AL	2	0	0	0	0	0	0	0	0	0	0	0
1982*	MIL AL	3	0	0	0	0	0	0	0	1	1	0	0
1983*	MIL AL	2	1	0	0	0	0	0	1	1	1	0	0
Totals	3 Yr	7	1	0	0	0	0	1	2	2	0	0	

Al Zarilla

Year	Team	AB	R	H	D	T	HR	TB	BI	W	K	SB	CS
1948	SLA AL	2	0	0	0	0	0	0	0	0	0	0	0

Gus Zernial

Year	Team	AB	R	H	D	T	HR	TB	BI	W	K	SB	CS
1953*	PHA AL	2	0	1	0	0	0	1	0	0	1	0	0

Don Zimmer

Year	Team	AB	R	H	D	T	HR	TB	BI	W	K	SB	CS
1961-1	CHN NL	1	0	0	0	0	0	0	0	0	0	0	0

Richie Zisk

Year	Team	AB	R	H	D	T	HR	TB	BI	W	K	SB	CS
1977*	CHA AL	3	0	2	1	0	0	3	2	0	1	0	0
1978*	TEX AL	2	0	1	0	0	0	1	0	1	1	0	1
Totals	2 Yr	5	0	3	1	0	0	4	2	1	2	0	1

PITCHERS
*indicates game started

Year		Team	IP	R	ER	H	HR	BB	SO
Don Aase									
1986	S	BAL AL	0.2	0	0	0	0	0	0
Rick Aguilera									
1991		MIN AL	1.1	0	0	2	0	0	3
1992		MIN AL	0.2	1	1	1	1	0	0
1993		MIN AL	1	0	0	2	0	0	2
Totals		3 Yr	3	1	1	5	1	0	5
Hank Aguirre									
1962–2		DET AL	3	2	2	3	0	0	2
Johnny Allen									
1938		CLE AL	3	1	1	2	0	0	3
Wilson Alvarez									
1994		CHA AL	1	0	0	0	0	0	0
Joaquin Andujar									
1979		HOU NL	2	2	1	2	0	1	0
Johnny Antonelli									
1954		NY NL	2	3	3	4	1	0	2
1956	S	NY NL	4	0	0	4	0	0	1
1959–1	W	SFN NL	0.1	0	0	0	0	1	0
Totals		3 Yr	6.1	3	3	8	1	1	3
Kevin Appier									
1995		KCA AL	2	0	0	0	0	0	1
Jack Armstrong									
1990*		CIN NL	2	0	0	1	0	0	2
Rolando Arrojo									
1998		TBA AL	1	0	0	2	0	0	1
Andy Ashby									
1998		SDN NL	1	1	1	1	1	1	0
1999		SDN NL	0.1	0	0	0	0	0	0
Totals		2 Yr	1.1	1	1	1	1	1	0
Steve Avery									
1993		ATL NL	1	3	0	1	0	1	1
James Baldwin									
2000	W	CHA AL	1	1	1	2	1	0	0
Floyd Bannister									
1982		SEA AL	1	0	0	1	0	0	0
Len Barker									
1981		CLE AL	2	0	0	0	0	0	1

Year		Team	IP	R	ER	H	HR	BB	SO
Rod Beck									
1993		SFN NL	1	1	1	2	0	0	1
1994		SFN NL	1.2	0	0	1	0	0	1
Totals		2 Yr	2.2	1	1	3	0	0	2
Steve Bedrosian									
1987		PHI NL	1	0	0	0	0	2	0
Gary Bell									
1960–1		CLE AL	2	0	0	0	0	0	0
1960–2		CLE AL	1	2	2	2	1	2	0
Totals		2 Yr	3	2	2	2	1	2	0
Andy Benes									
1993		SDN NL	2	1	1	2	1	0	2
Al Benton									
1942	S	DET AL	5	1	1	4	1	2	1
Jason Bere									
1994	L	CHA AL	0	1	1	2	0	0	0
Jim Bibby									
1980		PIT NL	1	0	0	1	0	0	0
Vern Bickford									
1949		BSN NL	1	2	2	2	0	1	0
Ewell Blackwell									
1946		CIN NL	2.2	2	2	3	0	1	1
1947*		CIN NL	3	0	0	1	0	0	4
1948		CIN NL	3	0	0	2	0	3	1
1949		CIN NL	1	0	0	0	0	0	2
1950	W	CIN NL	3	0	0	1	0	0	2
1951	S	CIN NL	1	0	0	1	0	1	2
Totals		6 Yr	13.2	2	2	8	0	5	12
Cy Blanton									
1937		PIT NL	0.1	0	0	0	0	0	1
Steve Blass									
1972		PIT NL	1	1	1	1	0	1	0
Vida Blue									
1971*	W	OAK AL	3	3	3	2	2	0	3
1975*		OAK AL	2	2	2	5	2	0	1
1978*		SFN NL	3	3	3	5	0	1	2
1981	W	SFN NL	1	0	0	0	0	0	1
Totals		4 Yr	9	8	8	12	4	1	7
Bert Blyleven									
1973	L	MIN AL	1	2	2	2	0	2	0
1985		CLE AL	2	2	2	3	0	1	1
Totals		2 Yr	3	4	4	5	0	3	1

Year	Team	IP	R	ER	H	HR	BB	SO
Hank Borowy								
1944*	NYA AL	3	0	0	3	0	1	0
Ricky Bottalico								
1996	PHI NL	1	0	0	0	0	0	1
Kent Bottenfield								
1999	SLN NL	1	2	2	1	0	1	2
Jim Bouton								
1963	NYA AL	1	0	0	0	0	0	0
Ralph Branca								
1948*	BRO NL	3	2	2	1	1	3	3
Jeff Brantley								
1990	L SFN NL	0.1	2	2	2	0	0	0
Harry Brecheen								
1947	SLN NL	3	1	1	5	0	0	2
Ken Brett								
1974	W PIT NL	2	0	0	1	0	1	0
Jim Brewer								
1973	S LAN NL	1	0	0	0	0	1	2
Tom Brewer								
1956	BOS AL	2	3	3	4	1	1	2
Tommy Bridges								
1937	DET AL	3	3	3	7	0	0	0
1939	W DET AL	2.1	0	0	2	0	1	3
Totals	2 Yr	5.1	3	3	9	0	1	3
Lou Brissie								
1949	PHA AL	3	2	2	5	1	2	1
Kevin Brown								
1992*	W TEX AL	1	0	0	0	0	0	1
1996	FLO NL	1	0	0	0	0	0	0
1997	FLO NL	1	0	0	1	0	0	0
1998	SDN NL	0.2	0	0	0	0	0	1
2000	LAN NL	1	1	1	1	0	3	0
Totals	5 Yr	4.2	1	1	2	0	3	2
Mace Brown								
1938	S PIT NL	3	1	1	5	0	1	2
Bob Buhl								
1960−1	MIL NL	1.1	2	1	2	1	1	1
Jim Bunning								
1957*	W DET AL	3	0	0	0	0	0	1
1959−1	DET AL	1	2	2	3	0	0	1
1961−1	DET AL	2	0	0	0	0	0	2
1961−2*	DET AL	3	0	0	0	0	0	1
1962−1*	DET AL	3	0	0	1	0	0	2
1963	L DET AL	2	1	0	0	0	1	0
1964	PHI NL	2	0	0	2	0	0	4

Year	Team	IP	R	ER	H	HR	BB	SO
Jim Bunning *continued*								
1966	PHI NL	2	0	0	1	0	0	2
Totals	8 Yr	18	3	2	7	0	1	13
Lew Burdette								
1957	MIL NL	4	0	0	2	0	1	0
1959−1	MIL NL	3	1	1	4	1	0	2
Totals	2 Yr	7	1	1	6	1	1	2
Tim Burke								
1989	MON NL	2	0	0	2	0	0	1
John Burkett								
1993	L SFN NL	0.2	3	3	4	0	0	1
Steve Busby								
1975	KCA AL	2	1	1	4	0	0	0
Bill Campbell								
1977	BOS AL	1	0	0	0	0	1	2
Steve Carlton								
1968	SLN NL	1	0	0	0	0	0	1
1969*	W SLN NL	3	2	2	2	2	1	2
1972	PHI NL	1	0	0	0	0	1	0
1979*	PHI NL	1	3	3	2	1	1	0
1982	PHI NL	2	0	0	1	0	2	4
Totals	5 Yr	8	5	5	5	3	5	7
Bill Caudill								
1984	OAK AL	1	0	0	0	0	0	3
Dean Chance								
1964*	LAA AL	3	0	0	2	0	0	2
1967*	MIN AL	3	1	1	2	1	0	1
Totals	2 Yr	6	1	1	4	1	0	3
Spud Chandler								
1942*	W NYA AL	4	0	0	2	0	0	2
Norm Charlton								
1992	CIN NL	1	0	0	0	0	0	1
Jim Clancy								
1982	TOR AL	1	0	0	0	0	0	0
Mark Clear								
1979	CAL AL	2	1	1	2	0	1	0
Roger Clemens								
1986*	W BOS AL	3	0	0	0	0	0	2
1988	BOS AL	1	0	0	0	0	0	1
1991	BOS AL	1	1	1	1	1	0	0
1992	BOS AL	1	0	0	2	0	0	0
1997	TOR AL	1	0	0	1	0	0	0
1998	TOR AL	1	2	2	2	0	1	1
Totals	6 Yr	8	3	3	6	1	1	4
Jim Coates								
1960−1	NYA AL	2	0	0	2	0	0	0

Joe Coleman

Year		Team	IP	R	ER	H	HR	BB	SO
1948	S	PHA AL	3	0	0	0	0	2	3

Bartolo Colon

Year		Team	IP	R	ER	H	HR	BB	SO
1998	W	CLE AL	1	3	3	2	1	1	1

David Cone

Year		Team	IP	R	ER	H	HR	BB	SO
1988		NYN NL	1	0	0	0	0	0	1
1992		NYN NL	1	0	0	0	0	0	1
1994		KCA AL	2	3	3	4	0	0	3
1997		NYA AL	1	0	0	0	0	2	0
1999		NYA AL	2	1	1	4	0	1	3
Totals		5 Yr	7	4	4	8	0	3	8

Gene Conley

Year		Team	IP	R	ER	H	HR	BB	SO
1954	L	MIL NL	0.1	3	3	3	1	1	0
1955	W	MIL NL	1	0	0	0	0	0	3
1959-2		PHI NL	2	0	0	0	0	1	2
Totals		3 Yr	3.1	3	3	3	1	2	5

Sandy Consuegra

Year		Team	IP	R	ER	H	HR	BB	SO
1954		CHA AL	0.1	5	5	5	0	0	0

Mort Cooper

Year		Team	IP	R	ER	H	HR	BB	SO
1942*	L	SLN NL	3	3	3	4	2	0	2
1943*	L	SLN NL	2.1	4	4	4	1	2	1
Totals		2 Yr	5.1	7	7	8	3	2	3

General Crowder

Year		Team	IP	R	ER	H	HR	BB	SO
1933		WAS AL	3	2	2	3	1	0	0

Mike Cuellar

Year		Team	IP	R	ER	H	HR	BB	SO
1967		HOU NL	2	0	0	1	0	0	2
1971		BAL AL	2	0	0	1	0	1	2
Totals		2 Yr	4	0	0	2	0	1	4

Ray Culp

Year		Team	IP	R	ER	H	HR	BB	SO
1963		PHI NL	1	0	0	1	0	0	0
1969		BOS AL	1	0	0	0	0	0	2
Totals		2 Yr	2	0	0	1	0	0	2

Bud Daley

Year		Team	IP	R	ER	H	HR	BB	SO
1959-1		KC AL	0.2	0	0	0	0	0	1
1960-1		KC AL	1	0	0	0	0	1	2
Totals		2 Yr	1.2	0	0	0	0	1	3

Curt Davis

Year		Team	IP	R	ER	H	HR	BB	SO
1936		CHN NL	0.2	3	3	4	1	1	0

Mark Davis

Year		Team	IP	R	ER	H	HR	BB	SO
1988		SDN NL	0.2	0	0	1	0	0	0
1989		SDN NL	1	0	0	0	0	0	2
Totals		2 Yr	1.2	0	0	1	0	0	2

Ron Davis

Year		Team	IP	R	ER	H	HR	BB	SO
1981		NYA AL	1	1	1	1	1	0	1

Bill Dawley

Year		Team	IP	R	ER	H	HR	BB	SO
1983		HOU NL	1.1	0	0	1	0	0	1

Dizzy Dean

Year		Team	IP	R	ER	H	HR	BB	SO
1934		SLN NL	3	1	1	5	0	1	4
1935		SLN NL	1	0	0	1	0	1	1
1936*	W	SLN NL	3	0	0	0	0	2	3
1937*	L	SLN NL	3	2	2	4	1	1	2
Totals		4 Yr	10	3	3	10	1	5	10

Paul Derringer

Year		Team	IP	R	ER	H	HR	BB	SO
1935		CIN NL	1	0	0	1	0	0	1
1939*		CIN NL	3	0	0	2	0	0	1
1940*	W	CIN NL	2	0	0	1	0	1	3
1941		CIN NL	2	1	1	2	0	0	1
Totals		4 Yr	8	1	1	6	0	1	6

Rob Dibble

Year		Team	IP	R	ER	H	HR	BB	SO
1990		CIN NL	1	0	0	1	0	1	0
1991		CIN NL	1	0	0	0	0	1	1
Totals		2 Yr	2	0	0	1	0	2	1

Murry Dickson

Year		Team	IP	R	ER	H	HR	BB	SO
1953	S	PIT NL	2	1	1	3	0	0	0

Larry Dierker

Year		Team	IP	R	ER	H	HR	BB	SO
1969		HOU NL	0.1	0	0	1	0	0	0

Dick Donovan

Year		Team	IP	R	ER	H	HR	BB	SO
1961-1		WAS AL	2	0	0	4	0	0	1
1962-1		CLE AL	2	1	1	3	0	0	0
Totals		2 Yr	4	1	1	7	0	0	1

Richard Dotson

Year		Team	IP	R	ER	H	HR	BB	SO
1984		CHA AL	2	0	0	2	0	1	2

Al Downing

Year		Team	IP	R	ER	H	HR	BB	SO
1967		NYA AL	2	0	0	2	0	0	2

Doug Drabek

Year		Team	IP	R	ER	H	HR	BB	SO
1994		HOU NL	0.2	3	1	4	0	0	1

Dave Dravecky

Year		Team	IP	R	ER	H	HR	BB	SO
1983		SDN NL	2	0	0	1	0	0	2

Don Drysdale

Year		Team	IP	R	ER	H	HR	BB	SO
1959-1*		LAN NL	3	0	0	0	0	0	4
1959-2*	L	LAN NL	3	3	3	4	2	3	5
1962-1*		LAN NL	3	0	0	1	0	1	3
1963	S	LAN NL	2	0	0	1	0	0	2
1964*		LAN NL	3	1	0	2	0	0	3
1965		LAN NL	0.1	0	0	0	0	0	0
1967	W	LAN NL	2	0	0	1	0	0	2
1968*	W	LAN NL	3	0	0	1	0	0	0
Totals		8 Yr	19.1	4	3	10	2	4	19

Ryne Duren

Year		Team	IP	R	ER	H	HR	BB	SO
1959-1		NYA AL	3	0	0	1	0	1	4

Dennis Eckersley

Year		Team	IP	R	ER	H	HR	BB	SO
1977		CLE AL	2	0	0	0	0	0	1
1982*	L	BOS AL	3	3	3	2	1	2	1
1988	S	OAK AL	1	0	0	0	0	0	1

Year	Team	IP	R	ER	H	HR	BB	SO
Dennis Eckersley *continued*								
1990	S OAK AL	1	0	0	1	0	0	1
1991	S OAK AL	1	0	0	0	0	0	1
1992	OAK AL	0.2	2	0	3	0	0	2
Totals	6 Yr	8.2	5	3	6	1	2	7
Dock Ellis								
1971*	L PIT NL	3	4	4	4	2	1	2
Don Elston								
1959−1	S CHN NL	1	0	0	1	0	0	1
Carl Erskine								
1954	BRO NL	0.2	0	0	1	0	0	1
Shawn Estes								
1997	L SFN NL	1	2	2	1	1	1	1
Chuck Estrada								
1960−1	BAL AL	1	1	1	4	0	0	1
Roy Face								
1959−1	PIT NL	1.2	3	3	3	0	2	2
1959−2	PIT NL	2	1	1	1	1	0	2
1960−1	PIT NL	1.2	0	0	0	0	0	2
1961−1	PIT NL	0.1	2	2	2	0	0	1
Totals	4 Yr	5.2	6	6	6	1	2	7
Ed Farmer								
1980	CHA AL	0.2	0	0	1	0	0	0
Turk Farrell								
1958	PHI NL	2	0	0	0	0	1	4
1962−2	HOU NL	1	3	3	3	1	1	2
1964	HOU NL	2	1	1	2	0	1	1
1965	HOU NL	1	0	0	0	0	1	0
Totals	4 Yr	6	4	4	5	1	4	7
Bob Feller								
1939	S CLE AL	3.2	0	0	1	0	1	2
1940	CLE AL	2	1	1	1	0	2	3
1941*	CLE AL	3	0	0	1	0	0	4
1946*	W CLE AL	3	0	0	2	0	0	3
1950	CLE AL	0.2	0	0	0	0	1	1
Totals	5 Yr	12.1	1	1	5	0	4	13
Sid Fernandez								
1986	NYN NL	1	0	0	0	0	2	3
1987	S NYN NL	1	0	0	0	0	1	1
Totals	2 Yr	2	0	0	0	0	3	4
Lou Fette								
1939	BSN NL	2	0	0	1	0	1	1
Mark Fidrych								
1976*	L DET AL	2	2	2	4	0	0	1
Rollie Fingers								
1973	OAK AL	1	0	0	0	0	0	0
1974	OAK AL	1	2	2	1	0	1	0

Year	Team	IP	R	ER	H	HR	BB	SO
Rollie Fingers *continued*								
1978	SDN NL	2	0	0	1	0	0	1
1981	L MIL AL	0.1	2	2	2	1	2	0
1982	MIL AL	1	0	0	2	0	0	0
Totals	5 Yr	5.1	4	4	6	1	3	1
Chuck Finley								
1990	CAL AL	1	0	0	0	0	1	1
1996	CAL AL	2	1	1	3	0	0	4
Totals	2 Yr	3	1	1	3	0	1	5
Eddie Fisher								
1965	CHA AL	2	0	0	1	0	0	0
Whitey Ford								
1954*	NYA AL	3	0	0	1	0	1	0
1955	NYA AL	1.2	5	4	5	0	1	0
1956	NYA AL	1	2	2	3	1	1	2
1959−1	L NYA AL	0.1	2	2	3	0	0	0
1960−2*	L NYA AL	3	3	3	5	2	0	1
1961−1*	NYA AL	3	1	1	2	0	0	2
Totals	6 Yr	12	13	12	19	3	3	5
Mike Fornieles								
1961−1	BOS AL	0.1	1	1	2	1	0	0
Ken Forsch								
1976	HOU NL	1	0	0	0	0	0	1
1981	CAL AL	1	1	1	1	1	0	0
Totals	2 Yr	2	1	1	1	1	0	1
John Franco								
1987	CIN NL	0.2	0	0	0	0	0	0
1990	NYN NL	1	0	0	0	0	0	0
Totals	2 Yr	1.2	0	0	0	0	0	0
Fred Frankhouse								
1934	BSN NL	1	0	0	0	0	1	0
Larry French								
1940	CHN NL	2	0	0	1	0	0	2
Bob Friend								
1956*	W PIT NL	3	0	0	3	0	0	3
1958	L PIT NL	2.1	2	1	4	0	2	0
1960−1*	W PIT NL	3	0	0	1	0	1	2
Totals	3 Yr	8.1	2	1	8	0	3	5
Mike Garcia								
1953	CLE AL	2	1	1	4	0	1	2
Ned Garver								
1951*	SLA AL	3	1	0	1	0	1	1
Bob Gibson								
1962−2	SLN NL	2	1	1	1	0	2	1
1965	S SLN NL	2	0	0	2	0	1	3
1967	SLN NL	2	0	0	2	0	0	2
1969	SLN NL	1	1	1	2	0	1	2
1970	SLN NL	2	2	2	3	0	1	2

Bob Gibson continued

Year		Team	IP	R	ER	H	HR	BB	SO
1972*		SLN NL	2	0	0	1	0	0	0
Totals		6 Yr	11	4	4	11	0	5	10

Dave Giusti

Year	Team	IP	R	ER	H	HR	BB	SO
1973	PIT NL	1	0	0	0	0	0	0

Tom Glavine

Year		Team	IP	R	ER	H	HR	BB	SO
1991*		ATL NL	2	0	0	1	0	1	3
1992*	L	ATL NL	1.2	5	5	9	0	0	2
1996		ATL NL	1	0	0	0	0	0	1
1998		ATL NL	1.1	4	4	5	0	3	0
2000		ATL NL	1	0	0	0	0	0	1
Totals		5 Yr	7	9	9	15	0	4	7

Lefty Gomez

Year		Team	IP	R	ER	H	HR	BB	SO
1933*	W	NYA AL	3	0	0	2	0	0	1
1934*		NYA AL	3	4	4	3	2	1	3
1935*	W	NYA AL	6	1	1	3	0	2	4
1937*	W	NYA AL	3	0	0	1	0	0	0
1938*	L	NYA AL	3	1	0	2	0	0	1
Totals		5 Yr	18	6	5	11	2	3	9

Dwight Gooden

Year		Team	IP	R	ER	H	HR	BB	SO
1984		NYN NL	2	0	0	1	0	0	3
1986*	L	NYN NL	3	2	2	3	1	0	2
1988*	L	NYN NL	3	1	1	3	1	1	1
Totals		3 Yr	8	3	3	7	2	1	6

Tom Gordon

Year	Team	IP	R	ER	H	HR	BB	SO
1998	BOS AL	1	2	1	3	0	1	0

Rich Gossage

Year		Team	IP	R	ER	H	HR	BB	SO
1975		CHA AL	1	1	1	1	0	0	0
1977		PIT NL	1	2	2	1	1	1	2
1978	L	NYA AL	1	4	4	4	0	1	1
1980		NYA AL	1	0	0	1	0	0	0
1984	S	SDN NL	1	0	0	1	0	0	2
1985		SDN NL	1	0	0	0	0	1	2
Totals		6 Yr	6	7	7	8	1	3	7

Jim Grant

Year	Team	IP	R	ER	H	HR	BB	SO
1965	MIN AL	2	2	2	2	1	1	3

Danny Graves

Year	Team	IP	R	ER	H	HR	BB	SO
2000	CIN NL	1	0	0	1	0	0	1

Ted Gray

Year		Team	IP	R	ER	H	HR	BB	SO
1950	L	DET AL	1.1	1	1	3	1	0	1

Tyler Green

Year	Team	IP	R	ER	H	HR	BB	SO
1995	PHI NL	1	0	0	2	0	0	1

Bob Grim

Year		Team	IP	R	ER	H	HR	BB	SO
1957	S	NYA AL	0.1	0	0	0	0	0	0

Lee Grissom

Year	Team	IP	R	ER	H	HR	BB	SO
1937	CIN NL	1	1	1	2	0	0	2

Marv Grissom

Year	Team	IP	R	ER	H	HR	BB	SO
1954	NY NL	1.1	0	0	0	0	0	2

Kevin Gross

Year	Team	IP	R	ER	H	HR	BB	SO
1988	PHI NL	1	0	0	0	0	0	1

Lefty Grove

Year		Team	IP	R	ER	H	HR	BB	SO
1933	S	PHA AL	3	0	0	3	0	0	3
1936*	L	BOS AL	3	2	2	3	0	2	2
1938		BOS AL	2	2	0	3	0	0	3
Totals		3 Yr	8	4	2	9	0	2	8

Mark Gubicza

Year	Team	IP	R	ER	H	HR	BB	SO
1988	KCA AL	2	1	1	3	0	0	2
1989	KCA AL	1	0	0	0	0	0	1
Totals	2 Yr	3	1	1	3	0	0	3

Ron Guidry

Year	Team	IP	R	ER	H	HR	BB	SO
1978	NYA AL	0.1	0	0	0	0	0	0
1979	NYA AL	0.1	0	0	0	0	1	0
Totals	2 Yr	0.2	0	0	0	0	1	0

Juan Guzman

Year	Team	IP	R	ER	H	HR	BB	SO
1992	TOR AL	1	0	0	2	0	1	2

Harvey Haddix

Year	Team	IP	R	ER	H	HR	BB	SO
1955	SLN NL	3	1	1	3	0	0	2

Bill Hallahan

Year		Team	IP	R	ER	H	HR	BB	SO
1933*	L	SLN NL	2	3	3	2	1	5	1

Atlee Hammaker

Year	Team	IP	R	ER	H	HR	BB	SO
1983	SFN NL	0.2	7	7	6	2	1	0

Mike Hampton

Year	Team	IP	R	ER	H	HR	BB	SO
1999	HOU NL	0.2	0	0	0	0	0	0

Mel Harder

Year		Team	IP	R	ER	H	HR	BB	SO
1934	W	CLE AL	5	0	0	1	0	1	2
1935	S	CLE AL	3	0	0	1	0	0	1
1936		CLE AL	2	0	0	2	0	0	2
1937	S	CLE AL	3	0	0	5	0	0	0
Totals		4 Yr	13	0	0	9	0	1	5

Pete Harnisch

Year	Team	IP	R	ER	H	HR	BB	SO
1991	HOU NL	1	0	0	2	0	0	1

Bryan Harvey

Year	Team	IP	R	ER	H	HR	BB	SO
1993	FLO NL	1	0	0	1	0	0	2

Tom Henke

Year	Team	IP	R	ER	H	HR	BB	SO
1987	TOR AL	2.2	0	0	2	0	0	1
1995	SLN NL	0.2	0	0	0	0	0	1
Totals	2 Yr	3.1	0	0	2	0	0	2

Bill Henry

Year	Team	IP	R	ER	H	HR	BB	SO
1960–2	CIN NL	1	0	0	2	0	0	0

Pat Hentgen

Year	Team	IP	R	ER	H	HR	BB	SO
1994	TOR AL	1	0	0	1	0	0	0

Year	Team	IP	R	ER	H	HR	BB	SO
Pat Hentgen *continued*								
1997	TOR AL	1	0	0	0	0	0	0
Totals	2 Yr	2	0	0	1	0	0	0
Ray Herbert								
1962–2	W CHA AL	3	0	0	3	0	0	0
Guillermo Hernandez								
1984	DET AL	1	1	1	1	1	0	1
1985	DET AL	0.2	0	0	1	0	1	2
Totals	2 Yr	1.2	1	1	2	1	1	3
Roberto Hernandez								
1996	CHA AL	1	0	0	1	0	0	0
1999	TBA AL	1	0	0	0	0	0	0
Totals	2 Yr	2	0	0	1	0	0	0
Orel Hershiser								
1987	LAN NL	2	0	0	1	0	1	0
1988	LAN NL	1	0	0	0	0	0	0
Totals	2 Yr	3	0	0	1	0	1	0
Kirby Higbe								
1946	BRO NL	1.1	4	4	5	1	1	2
Teddy Higuera								
1986	MIL AL	3	0	0	1	0	1	2
Ken Hill								
1994	MON NL	2	0	0	0	0	1	0
Trevor Hoffman								
1998	SDN NL	1	1	1	1	1	0	1
1999	SDN NL	0.1	0	0	0	0	0	1
2000	SDN NL	1	3	3	3	0	0	2
Totals	3 Yr	2.1	4	4	4	1	0	4
Ken Holtzman								
1973	OAK AL	0.2	0	0	1	0	0	0
Rick Honeycutt								
1983	TEX AL	2	2	2	5	0	0	0
Burt Hooton								
1981	LAN NL	1.2	3	3	5	0	0	1
Charlie Hough								
1986	TEX AL	1.2	2	1	2	0	0	3
Art Houtteman								
1950	DET AL	3	1	1	3	1	1	0
Steve Howe								
1982	LAN NL	0.1	0	0	0	0	0	0
Jay Howell								
1987	L OAK AL	2	2	2	3	0	0	3
1989	LAN NL	1	0	0	1	0	0	1
Totals	2 Yr	3	2	2	4	0	0	4

Year	Team	IP	R	ER	H	HR	BB	SO
LaMarr Hoyt								
1985*	W SDN NL	3	1	0	2	0	0	0
Carl Hubbell								
1933	NY NL	2	0	0	1	0	1	1
1934*	NY NL	3	0	0	2	0	2	6
1936	NY NL	3	0	0	2	0	1	2
1937	NY NL	0.2	3	3	3	0	1	1
1940	S NY NL	1	0	0	0	0	1	1
Totals	5 Yr	9.2	3	3	8	0	6	11
John Hudek								
1994	HOU NL	0.2	2	2	1	0	1	1
Sid Hudson								
1941	WAS AL	1	2	2	3	1	1	1
Tim Hudson								
2000	OAK AL	1	0	0	0	0	0	1
Tex Hughson								
1943	S BOS AL	3	2	2	5	1	0	2
1944	L BOS AL	1.2	4	3	5	0	1	2
Totals	2 Yr	4.2	6	5	10	1	1	4
Tom Hume								
1982	S CIN NL	0.1	0	0	0	0	0	0
Catfish Hunter								
1967	L KC AL	5	1	1	4	1	0	4
1970	OAK AL	0.1	3	3	3	1	0	0
1973*	OAK AL	1.1	0	0	1	0	0	1
1974	OAK AL	2	1	1	2	1	1	3
1975	L NYA AL	2	2	2	3	0	0	2
1976	NYA AL	2	2	2	2	1	0	3
Totals	6 Yr	12.2	9	9	15	4	1	13
Fred Hutchinson								
1951	DET AL	3	3	3	3	1	2	0
Jason Isringhausen								
2000	OAK AL	1	1	1	2	0	1	0
Danny Jackson								
1994	PHI NL	0	1	1	3	0	0	0
Larry Jackson								
1957	SLN NL	2	0	0	1	0	1	0
1958	SLN NL	0.2	0	0	0	0	0	0
1960–2	SLN NL	1	0	0	1	0	2	0
1963	W CHN NL	2	2	2	4	0	0	3
Totals	4 Yr	5.2	2	2	6	0	3	3
Larry Jansen								
1950	NY NL	5	0	0	1	0	0	6
Al Javery								
1943	BSN NL	2	0	0	2	0	0	3

Ferguson Jenkins

Year	Team	IP	R	ER	H	HR	BB	SO
1967	CHN NL	3	1	1	3	1	0	6
1971	CHN NL	1	2	2	3	1	0	0
Totals	2 Yr	4	3	3	6	2	0	6

Tommy John

Year	Team	IP	R	ER	H	HR	BB	SO
1968	CHA AL	0.2	0	0	1	0	0	0
1980 L	NYA AL	2.1	3	3	4	1	0	1
Totals	2 Yr	3	3	3	5	1	0	1

Randy Johnson

Year	Team	IP	R	ER	H	HR	BB	SO
1993	SEA AL	2	0	0	0	0	0	1
1994	SEA AL	1	1	1	2	1	0	0
1995*	SEA AL	2	0	0	0	0	1	3
1997*	SEA AL	2	0	0	0	0	1	2
1999	ARI NL	1	0	0	0	0	0	1
2000*	ARI NL	1	0	0	1	0	0	1
Totals	6 Yr	9	1	1	3	1	2	8

Bobby Jones

Year	Team	IP	R	ER	H	HR	BB	SO
1997	NYN NL	1	0	0	1	0	0	2

Doug Jones

Year	Team	IP	R	ER	H	HR	BB	SO
1988	CLE AL	0.2	0	0	0	0	0	1
1989 S	CLE AL	1.1	0	0	1	0	0	0
1992	HOU NL	1	3	3	4	0	0	2
1994 W	PHI NL	1	0	0	2	0	0	2
Totals	4 Yr	4	3	3	7	0	0	5

Randy Jones

Year	Team	IP	R	ER	H	HR	BB	SO
1975	SDN NL	1	0	0	0	0	0	1
1976* W	SDN NL	3	0	0	2	0	1	1
Totals	2 Yr	4	0	0	2	0	1	2

Sam Jones

Year	Team	IP	R	ER	H	HR	BB	SO
1955	CHN NL	0.2	0	0	0	0	2	1
1959-2	SFN NL	2	1	0	1	0	2	3
Totals	2 Yr	2.2	1	0	1	0	4	4

Todd Jones

Year	Team	IP	R	ER	H	HR	BB	SO
2000	DET AL	1	0	0	0	0	0	1

Jim Kaat

Year	Team	IP	R	ER	H	HR	BB	SO
1966	MIN AL	2	1	1	3	0	0	1
1975	CHA AL	2	0	0	0	0	0	0
Totals	2 Yr	4	1	1	3	0	0	1

Bob Keegan

Year	Team	IP	R	ER	H	HR	BB	SO
1954	CHA AL	0.2	2	2	3	1	0	1

Matt Keough

Year	Team	IP	R	ER	H	HR	BB	SO
1978	OAK AL	0.1	0	0	1	0	0	0

Jim Kern

Year	Team	IP	R	ER	H	HR	BB	SO
1977	CLE AL	1	0	0	0	0	0	2
1978	CLE AL	0.2	0	0	1	0	1	1
1979 L	TEX AL	2.2	2	2	2	1	3	3
Totals	3 Yr	4.1	2	2	3	1	4	6

Jimmy Key

Year	Team	IP	R	ER	H	HR	BB	SO
1985	TOR AL	0.1	0	0	0	0	0	0
1991 W	TOR AL	1	0	0	1	0	0	1
1993	NYA AL	1	1	1	2	0	0	1
1994*	NYA AL	2	1	1	1	0	0	1
Totals	4 Yr	4.1	2	2	4	0	0	3

Darryl Kile

Year	Team	IP	R	ER	H	HR	BB	SO
2000	SLN NL	2	0	0	2	0	0	0

Bob Knepper

Year	Team	IP	R	ER	H	HR	BB	SO
1981	HOU NL	2	0	0	1	0	2	3
1988	HOU NL	1	1	1	2	0	1	0
Totals	2 Yr	3	1	1	3	0	3	3

Darold Knowles

Year	Team	IP	R	ER	H	HR	BB	SO
1969	WAS AL	0.2	0	0	0	0	0	0

Jim Konstanty

Year	Team	IP	R	ER	H	HR	BB	SO
1950	PHI NL	1	0	0	0	0	0	2

Jerry Koosman

Year	Team	IP	R	ER	H	HR	BB	SO
1968 S	NYN NL	0.1	0	0	0	0	0	1
1969	NYN NL	1.2	0	0	1	0	0	1
Totals	2 Yr	2	0	0	1	0	0	2

Sandy Koufax

Year	Team	IP	R	ER	H	HR	BB	SO
1961-1	LAN NL	0	0	0	1	0	0	0
1961-2	LAN NL	2	0	0	2	0	0	1
1965 W	LAN NL	1	0	0	0	0	2	1
1966*	LAN NL	3	1	1	1	0	0	1
Totals	4 Yr	6	1	1	4	0	2	3

Jack Kramer

Year	Team	IP	R	ER	H	HR	BB	SO
1946 S	SLA AL	3	0	0	0	0	1	3

Mike Krukow

Year	Team	IP	R	ER	H	HR	BB	SO
1986	SFN NL	1	0	0	0	0	0	0

Clem Labine

Year	Team	IP	R	ER	H	HR	BB	SO
1957	BRO NL	1	3	1	3	0	0	2

Mike LaCoss

Year	Team	IP	R	ER	H	HR	BB	SO
1979	CIN NL	1.1	0	0	1	0	0	0

Mark Langston

Year	Team	IP	R	ER	H	HR	BB	SO
1987	SEA AL	2	0	0	0	0	0	3
1992	CAL AL	1	1	1	2	0	0	1
1993*	CAL AL	2	2	2	3	1	1	2
Totals	3 Yr	5	3	3	5	1	1	6

Dave LaRoche

Year	Team	IP	R	ER	H	HR	BB	SO
1977	CAL AL	1	0	0	1	0	1	0

Frank Lary

Year	Team	IP	R	ER	H	HR	BB	SO
1960-1	DET AL	1	0	0	1	0	0	1
1960-2	DET AL	1	0	0	1	0	1	0
1961-1	DET AL	0	1	0	0	0	0	0
Totals	3 Yr	2	1	0	2	0	1	1

Year	Team	IP	R	ER	H	HR	BB	SO

Gary Lavelle

Year	Team	IP	R	ER	H	HR	BB	SO
1977	SFN NL	2	0	0	1	0	0	2

Vern Law

Year	Team	IP	R	ER	H	HR	BB	SO
1960–1 S	PIT NL	0.2	0	0	0	0	0	0
1960–2* W	PIT NL	2	0	0	1	0	0	1
Totals	2 Yr	2.2	0	0	1	0	0	1

Charlie Lea

Year	Team	IP	R	ER	H	HR	BB	SO
1984* W	MON NL	2	1	1	3	1	0	2

Bill Lee

Year	Team	IP	R	ER	H	HR	BB	SO
1938	CHN NL	3	0	0	1	0	1	2
1939 L	CHN NL	3	3	2	3	1	3	4
Totals	2 Yr	6	3	2	4	1	4	6

Thornton Lee

Year	Team	IP	R	ER	H	HR	BB	SO
1941	CHA AL	3	1	1	4	0	0	0

Al Leiter

Year	Team	IP	R	ER	H	HR	BB	SO
1996	FLO NL	0.1	0	0	0	0	0	0
2000 L	NYN NL	1	2	1	2	0	1	1
Totals	2 Yr	1.1	2	1	2	0	1	1

Bob Lemon

Year	Team	IP	R	ER	H	HR	BB	SO
1950	CLE AL	3	0	0	1	0	0	2
1951	CLE AL	1	0	0	2	0	1	1
1952 L	CLE AL	2	2	2	2	1	2	0
1954	CLE AL	0.2	0	0	1	0	0	0
Totals	4 Yr	6.2	2	2	6	1	3	3

Dutch Leonard

Year	Team	IP	R	ER	H	HR	BB	SO
1943* W	WAS AL	3	1	1	2	0	0	0

Jose Lima

Year	Team	IP	R	ER	H	HR	BB	SO
1999	HOU NL	1	0	0	1	0	0	0

Billy Loes

Year	Team	IP	R	ER	H	HR	BB	SO
1957	BAL AL	3	0	0	3	0	0	1

Mickey Lolich

Year	Team	IP	R	ER	H	HR	BB	SO
1971 S	DET AL	2	1	1	1	1	0	1
1972	DET AL	2	0	0	1	0	0	1
Totals	2 Yr	4	1	1	2	1	0	2

Eddie Lopat

Year	Team	IP	R	ER	H	HR	BB	SO
1951 L	NYA AL	1	3	3	3	2	0	0

Derek Lowe

Year	Team	IP	R	ER	H	HR	BB	SO
2000	BOS AL	1	0	0	0	0	0	0

Sparky Lyle

Year	Team	IP	R	ER	H	HR	BB	SO
1973	NYA AL	1	0	0	1	0	0	1
1977	NYA AL	2	2	2	3	0	0	1
Totals	2 Yr	3	2	2	4	0	0	2

Greg Maddux

Year	Team	IP	R	ER	H	HR	BB	SO
1992	CHN NL	1.1	1	1	1	1	0	0
1994*	ATL NL	3	1	1	3	0	0	2
1997*	ATL NL	2	1	1	2	1	0	0

Greg Maddux *continued*

Year	Team	IP	R	ER	H	HR	BB	SO
1998*	ATL NL	2	0	0	3	0	1	1
Totals	4 Yr	8.1	3	3	9	2	1	3

Sal Maglie

Year	Team	IP	R	ER	H	HR	BB	SO
1951 W	NY NL	3	2	2	3	2	1	1

Art Mahaffey

Year	Team	IP	R	ER	H	HR	BB	SO
1961–2	PHI NL	2	0	0	0	0	1	0
1962–2 L	PHI NL	2	3	3	2	2	1	1
Totals	2 Yr	4	3	3	2	2	2	1

Jim Maloney

Year	Team	IP	R	ER	H	HR	BB	SO
1965	CIN NL	1.2	5	5	5	2	2	1

Juan Marichal

Year	Team	IP	R	ER	H	HR	BB	SO
1962–1 W	SFN NL	2	0	0	0	0	1	0
1962–2	SFN NL	2	2	1	2	0	0	2
1964 W	SFN NL	1	0	0	0	0	0	1
1965*	SFN NL	3	0	0	1	0	0	0
1966	SFN NL	3	0	0	3	0	0	2
1967*	SFN NL	3	0	0	1	0	0	3
1968	SFN NL	2	0	0	0	0	0	3
1971	SFN NL	2	0	0	0	0	1	1
Totals	8 Yr	18	2	1	7	0	2	12

Mike Marshall

Year	Team	IP	R	ER	H	HR	BB	SO
1974	LAN NL	2	0	0	0	0	1	2

Dennis Martinez

Year	Team	IP	R	ER	H	HR	BB	SO
1990	MON NL	1	0	0	0	0	0	1
1991 L	MON NL	2	3	3	4	1	0	0
1992	MON NL	1	0	0	0	0	1	1
1995	CLE AL	2	1	1	1	1	0	0
Totals	4 Yr	6	4	4	5	2	1	2

Pedro Martinez

Year	Team	IP	R	ER	H	HR	BB	SO
1996	MON NL	1	0	0	2	0	0	1
1997	MON NL	1	0	0	0	0	0	2
1999* W	BOS AL	2	0	0	0	0	0	5
Totals	3 Yr	4	0	0	2	0	0	8

Ramon Martinez

Year	Team	IP	R	ER	H	HR	BB	SO
1990	LAN NL	1	0	0	0	0	2	1

Walt Masterson

Year	Team	IP	R	ER	H	HR	BB	SO
1947	WAS AL	1.2	0	0	0	0	1	2
1948*	WAS AL	3	2	2	5	1	1	1
Totals	2 Yr	4.2	2	2	5	1	2	3

Jon Matlack

Year	Team	IP	R	ER	H	HR	BB	SO
1974	NYN NL	1	0	0	1	0	1	0
1975 W	NYN NL	2	0	0	2	0	0	4
Totals	2 Yr	3	0	0	3	0	1	4

Ken McBride

Year	Team	IP	R	ER	H	HR	BB	SO
1963*	LAA AL	3	3	3	4	0	2	1

Mike McCormick

Year	Team	IP	R	ER	H	HR	BB	SO
1960–1	SFN NL	2.1	1	1	3	0	3	2

Year		Team	IP	R	ER	H	HR	BB	SO
Mike McCormick *continued*									
1961–1		SFN NL	3	1	1	1	1	1	3
Totals		2 Yr	5.1	2	2	4	1	4	5
Lindy McDaniel									
1960–2	S	SLN NL	1	0	0	1	0	0	0
Jack McDowell									
1991		CHA AL	2	0	0	1	0	2	0
1992		CHA AL	1	0	0	0	0	0	0
1993	W	CHA AL	1	0	0	0	0	0	0
Totals		3 Yr	4	0	0	1	0	2	0
Sam McDowell									
1965	L	CLE AL	2	1	1	3	0	1	2
1968		CLE AL	1	0	0	1	0	0	3
1969		CLE AL	2	0	0	0	0	0	4
1970		CLE AL	3	0	0	1	0	3	3
Totals		4 Yr	8	1	1	5	0	4	12
Lynn McGlothen									
1974		SLN NL	1	0	0	0	0	0	1
Jim McGlothlin									
1967		CAL AL	2	0	0	1	0	0	2
Tug McGraw									
1972	W	NYN NL	2	0	0	1	0	0	4
Denny McLain									
1966*		DET AL	3	0	0	0	0	0	3
1968		DET AL	2	0	0	1	0	2	1
1969		DET AL	1	1	1	1	1	2	2
Totals		3 Yr	6	1	1	2	1	4	6
Cal McLish									
1959–2	S	CLE AL	2	0	0	1	0	1	2
Dave McNally									
1969		BAL AL	2	0	0	1	0	1	1
1972	L	BAL AL	0.1	1	1	1	0	1	0
Totals		2 Yr	2.1	1	1	2	0	2	1
Jim Merritt									
1970		CIN NL	2	0	0	1	0	0	1
Jose Mesa									
1995		CLE AL	1	0	0	0	0	0	1
Andy Messersmith									
1974*		LAN NL	3	2	2	2	0	3	4
Stu Miller									
1961–1	W	SFN NL	1.2	1	0	0	0	1	4
1961–2		SFN NL	3	0	0	1	0	0	5
Totals		2 Yr	4.2	1	0	1	0	1	9
Kevin Millwood									
1999		ATL NL	1	0	0	1	0	0	1
Greg Minton									
1982		SFN NL	0.2	0	0	0	0	1	0
Bill Monbouquette									
1960–1*	L	BOS AL	2	4	4	5	2	0	2
John Montefusco									
1976		SFN NL	2	0	0	0	0	2	2
Jeff Montgomery									
1992		KCA AL	0.2	2	2	2	0	0	0
1993		KCA AL	1	0	0	0	0	0	1
Totals		2 Yr	1.2	2	2	2	0	0	1
Donnie Moore									
1985		CAL AL	2	0	0	0	0	0	1
Mike Moore									
1989		OAK AL	1	0	0	0	0	0	1
Mike Morgan									
1991		LAN NL	1	0	0	0	0	0	1
Jack Morris									
1981*		DET AL	2	0	0	2	0	1	2
1984		DET AL	2	0	0	2	0	1	2
1985*	L	DET AL	2.2	2	2	5	0	1	1
1987		DET AL	2	0	0	1	0	1	2
1991*		MIN AL	2	1	1	4	0	0	1
Totals		5 Yr	10.2	3	3	14	0	4	8
Don Mossi									
1957		CLE AL	0.2	0	0	1	0	0	1
Terry Mulholland									
1993*		PHI NL	2	1	1	1	1	2	0
Bob Muncrief									
1944		SLA AL	1.1	0	0	1	0	0	1
Red Munger									
1949		SLN NL	1	0	0	0	0	1	0
Van Mungo									
1934	L	BRO NL	1	4	4	4	0	2	1
1937		BRO NL	2	2	2	2	0	2	1
Totals		2 Yr	3	6	6	6	0	4	2
Mike Mussina									
1992		BAL AL	1	0	0	0	0	0	0
1994		BAL AL	1	0	0	1	0	0	1
1999		BAL AL	1	0	0	1	0	1	2
Totals		3 Yr	3	0	0	2	0	1	3
Randy Myers									
1990		CIN NL	1	0	0	1	0	2	0
1994		CHN NL	1	0	0	1	0	0	1
1995	S	CHN NL	1	0	0	0	0	1	0
1997		BAL AL	1	0	0	0	0	0	2
Totals		4 Yr	4	0	0	2	0	3	3

Year	Team	IP	R	ER	H	HR	BB	SO

Charles Nagy

Year	Team	IP	R	ER	H	HR	BB	SO
1992	CLE AL	1	0	0	0	0	0	1
1996*	L CLE AL	2	3	3	4	1	0	1
Totals	2 Yr	3	3	3	4	1	0	2

Ray Narleski

1958	CLE AL	3.1	0	0	1	0	1	0

Denny Neagle

1995	PIT NL	1	0	0	1	0	0	1

Robb Nen

1998	SFN NL	1	3	1	3	0	0	0

Don Newcombe

1949	L BRO NL	2.2	2	2	3	0	1	0
1950	BRO NL	2	2	2	3	0	1	1
1951	BRO NL	3	0	0	2	0	0	3
1955	BRO NL	1	0	0	1	0	0	1
Totals	4 Yr	8.2	4	4	9	0	2	5

Hal Newhouser

1943	DET AL	3	0	0	3	0	1	1
1944	DET AL	1.2	3	3	3	0	2	1
1946	DET AL	3	0	0	1	0	0	4
1947*	DET AL	3	0	0	1	0	0	2
Totals	4 Yr	10.2	3	3	8	0	3	8

Bobo Newsom

1940	DET AL	3	0	0	1	0	1	1
1944	PHA AL	0.1	0	0	0	0	0	0
Totals	2 Yr	3.1	0	0	1	0	1	1

Phil Niekro

1969	S ATL NL	1	0	0	0	0	0	2
1978	ATL NL	0.1	0	0	0	0	0	0
Totals	2 Yr	1.1	0	0	0	0	0	2

Hideo Nomo

1995*	LAN NL	2	0	0	1	0	0	3

Mike Norris

1981	OAK AL	1	1	1	2	1	0	1

Joe Nuxhall

1955	CIN NL	3.1	0	0	2	0	3	5

Billy O'Dell

1958	S BAL AL	3	0	0	0	0	0	2
1959-2	BAL AL	1	1	1	1	1	0	0
Totals	2 Yr	4	1	1	1	1	0	2

Jim O'Toole

1963*	CIN NL	2	1	1	4	0	0	1

Johnny Odom

1968	OAK AL	2	0	0	0	0	2	2
1969	OAK AL	0.1	5	4	5	1	0	0
Totals	2 Yr	2.1	5	4	5	1	2	2

Steve Ontiveros

1995	L OAK AL	0.2	1	1	1	1	0	1

Jesse Orosco

1983	NYN NL	0.1	0	0	0	0	0	1

Claude Osteen

1970	W LAN NL	3	0	0	3	0	1	0
1973	LAN NL	2	0	0	2	0	1	1
Totals	2 Yr	5	0	0	5	0	2	1

Joe Page

1947	S NYA AL	1.1	0	0	1	0	1	0

Satchel Paige

1953	SLA AL	1	2	2	3	0	1	0

Jim Palmer

1970*	BAL AL	3	0	0	1	0	1	3
1971	BAL AL	2	0	0	1	0	0	2
1972*	BAL AL	3	0	0	1	0	1	2
1977*	L BAL AL	2	5	5	5	3	1	3
1978*	BAL AL	2.2	3	3	3	0	4	4
Totals	5 Yr	12.2	8	8	11	3	7	14

Milt Pappas

1962-1	BAL AL	1	0	0	0	0	0	0
1962-2	S BAL AL	1	1	1	1	1	1	0
1965*	BAL AL	1	3	3	4	2	1	0
Totals	3 Yr	3	4	4	5	3	2	0

Mel Parnell

1949*	BOS AL	1	3	3	3	1	1	1
1951	BOS AL	1	1	1	3	1	0	1
Totals	2 Yr	2	4	4	6	2	1	2

Camilo Pascual

1961-2	MIN AL	3	0	0	0	0	1	4
1962-1	L MIN AL	3	2	2	4	0	1	1
1964	MIN AL	2	1	1	2	0	0	1
Totals	3 Yr	8	3	3	6	0	2	6

Claude Passeau

1941	L CHN NL	2.2	5	5	6	1	1	3
1942	CHN NL	2	0	0	1	0	0	1
1946*	L CHN NL	3	2	2	2	1	2	0
Totals	3 Yr	7.2	7	7	9	2	3	4

Roger Pavlik

1996	TEX AL	2	2	2	3	1	0	2

Troy Percival

1996	CAL AL	1	0	0	1	0	0	1
1998	ANA AL	1	0	0	1	0	0	2
Totals	2 Yr	2	0	0	2	0	0	3

Carlos Perez

1995	MON NL	0.1	0	0	1	0	1	0

Year	Team	IP	R	ER	H	HR	BB	SO

Pascual Perez

Year	Team	IP	R	ER	H	HR	BB	SO
1983	ATL NL	0.2	2	2	3	0	1	1

Gaylord Perry

Year	Team	IP	R	ER	H	HR	BB	SO
1966 W	SFN NL	2	0	0	1	0	1	1
1970	SFN NL	2	2	2	4	0	1	0
1972	CLE AL	2	2	2	3	1	0	1
1974*	CLE AL	3	1	1	3	0	0	4
1979	SDN NL	0	1	1	3	0	0	0
Totals	5 Yr	9	6	6	14	1	2	6

Jim Perry

Year	Team	IP	R	ER	H	HR	BB	SO
1970	MIN AL	2	1	1	1	0	1	3

Gary Peters

Year	Team	IP	R	ER	H	HR	BB	SO
1967	CHA AL	3	0	0	0	0	0	4

Fritz Peterson

Year	Team	IP	R	ER	H	HR	BB	SO
1970	NYA AL	0	0	0	1	0	0	0

Dan Petry

Year	Team	IP	R	ER	H	HR	BB	SO
1985	DET AL	0.1	2	2	0	0	3	1

Billy Pierce

Year	Team	IP	R	ER	H	HR	BB	SO
1953*	CHA AL	3	0	0	1	0	0	1
1955*	CHA AL	3	0	0	1	0	0	3
1956* L	CHA AL	3	1	1	2	0	1	5
1957	CHA AL	1.2	3	3	2	0	2	3
Totals	4 Yr	10.2	4	4	6	0	3	12

Juan Pizarro

Year	Team	IP	R	ER	H	HR	BB	SO
1963	CHA AL	1	0	0	0	0	0	0

Dan Plesac

Year	Team	IP	R	ER	H	HR	BB	SO
1987	MIL AL	1	0	0	0	0	0	1
1988	MIL AL	0.1	0	0	0	0	0	1
1989	MIL AL	0	0	0	1	0	0	0
Totals	3 Yr	1.1	0	0	1	0	0	2

Johnny Podres

Year	Team	IP	R	ER	H	HR	BB	SO
1960–2	LAN NL	2	0	0	1	0	3	1
1962–2*	LAN NL	2	0	0	2	0	0	2
Totals	2 Yr	4	0	0	3	0	3	3

Howie Pollet

Year	Team	IP	R	ER	H	HR	BB	SO
1949	SLN NL	1	3	3	4	0	0	0

Bob Porterfield

Year	Team	IP	R	ER	H	HR	BB	SO
1954	WAS AL	3	2	2	4	1	0	1

Bob Purkey

Year	Team	IP	R	ER	H	HR	BB	SO
1961–1	CIN NL	2	0	0	0	0	0	1
1961–2*	CIN NL	2	1	1	1	1	2	2
1962–1	CIN NL	2	1	1	2	0	0	1
Totals	3 Yr	6	2	2	3	1	2	4

Dan Quisenberry

Year	Team	IP	R	ER	H	HR	BB	SO
1982	KCA AL	2	1	1	3	0	0	1
1983	KCA AL	1	0	0	1	0	0	1
Totals	2 Yr	3	1	1	4	0	0	2

Dick Radatz

Year	Team	IP	R	ER	H	HR	BB	SO
1963	BOS AL	2	1	1	2	0	0	5
1964 L	BOS AL	2.2	4	4	2	1	2	5
Totals	2 Yr	4.2	5	5	4	1	2	10

Brad Radke

Year	Team	IP	R	ER	H	HR	BB	SO
1998	MIN AL	1	1	1	2	0	1	1

Ken Raffensberger

Year	Team	IP	R	ER	H	HR	BB	SO
1944 W	PHI NL	2	0	0	1	0	0	2

Vic Raschi

Year	Team	IP	R	ER	H	HR	BB	SO
1948 W	NYA AL	3	0	0	3	0	1	3
1949 S	NYA AL	3	0	0	1	0	3	1
1950*	NYA AL	3	2	2	2	0	0	1
1952*	NYA AL	2	1	1	1	1	0	3
Totals	4 Yr	11	3	3	7	1	4	8

Jeff Reardon

Year	Team	IP	R	ER	H	HR	BB	SO
1985	MON NL	1	0	0	1	0	0	1
1991	BOS AL	0.2	0	0	1	0	0	0
Totals	2 Yr	1.2	0	0	2	0	0	1

Ron Reed

Year	Team	IP	R	ER	H	HR	BB	SO
1968	ATL NL	0.2	0	0	0	0	0	1

Rick Reuschel

Year	Team	IP	R	ER	H	HR	BB	SO
1977	CHN NL	1	0	0	1	0	0	0
1987	PIT NL	1.1	0	0	1	0	0	1
1989*	SFN NL	1	2	2	3	2	0	0
Totals	3 Yr	3.1	2	2	5	2	0	1

Jerry Reuss

Year	Team	IP	R	ER	H	HR	BB	SO
1975*	PIT NL	3	0	0	3	0	0	2
1980 W	LAN NL	1	0	0	0	0	0	3
Totals	2 Yr	4	0	0	3	0	0	5

Allie Reynolds

Year	Team	IP	R	ER	H	HR	BB	SO
1950	NYA AL	3	0	0	1	0	1	2
1953 L	NYA AL	2	2	2	2	0	1	0
Totals	2 Yr	5	2	2	3	0	2	2

Rick Rhoden

Year	Team	IP	R	ER	H	HR	BB	SO
1976	LAN NL	1	0	0	1	0	0	0

J.R. Richard

Year	Team	IP	R	ER	H	HR	BB	SO
1980*	HOU NL	2	0	0	1	0	2	3

Pete Richert

Year	Team	IP	R	ER	H	HR	BB	SO
1965	WAS AL	2	0	0	1	0	0	2
1966 L	WAS AL	0.1	1	1	2	0	0	0
Totals	2 Yr	2.1	1	1	3	0	0	2

Dave Righetti

Year	Team	IP	R	ER	H	HR	BB	SO
1986	NYA AL	0.2	0	0	2	0	0	0
1987	NYA AL	0.1	0	0	1	0	0	0
Totals	2 Yr	1	0	0	3	0	0	0

Mariano Rivera

Year	Team	IP	R	ER	H	HR	BB	SO
1997 S	NYA AL	1	0	0	0	0	0	1

Year	Team	IP	R	ER	H	HR	BB	SO
Mariano Rivera continued								
2000	NYA AL	1	1	0	2	0	0	0
Totals	2 Yr	2	1	0	2	0	0	1
Robin Roberts								
1950*	PHI NL	3	1	1	3	0	1	1
1951*	PHI NL	2	1	1	4	0	0	1
1953*	PHI NL	3	0	0	1	0	1	2
1954*	PHI NL	3	4	4	5	2	2	5
1955*	PHI NL	3	4	4	4	1	1	0
Totals	5 Yr	14	10	10	17	3	5	9
Preacher Roe								
1949	BRO NL	1	0	0	0	0	0	0
Kenny Rogers								
1995	TEX AL	1	1	1	1	1	0	2
Steve Rogers								
1978	MON NL	2	0	0	2	0	0	2
1979	MON NL	2	0	0	0	0	0	2
1982*	W MON NL	3	1	1	4	0	0	2
Totals	3 Yr	7	1	1	6	0	0	6
Jose Rosado								
1997	W KCA AL	1	1	1	2	1	1	1
1999	KCA AL	1	0	0	1	0	0	1
Totals	2 Yr	2	1	1	3	1	1	2
Schoolboy Rowe								
1936	DET AL	3	2	2	4	1	1	2
Red Ruffing								
1934	NYA AL	1	3	3	4	0	1	0
1939*	NYA AL	3	1	1	4	0	1	4
1940*	L NYA AL	3	3	3	5	1	0	2
Totals	3 Yr	7	7	7	13	1	2	6
Bob Rush								
1952	W CHN NL	2	2	2	4	0	1	1
Jeff Russell								
1988	TEX AL	1	0	0	1	0	1	0
1989	TEX AL	1	1	1	1	0	1	0
Dick Ruthven								
1981	PHI NL	0.1	0	0	0	0	0	0
Nolan Ryan								
1973	CAL AL	2	2	2	2	1	2	2
1979*	CAL AL	2	3	3	5	0	1	2
1981	HOU NL	1	0	0	0	0	0	1
1985	HOU NL	3	0	0	2	0	2	2
1989	W TEX AL	2	0	0	1	0	0	3
Totals	5 Yr	10	5	5	10	1	5	10
Bret Saberhagen								
1987*	KCA AL	3	0	0	1	0	0	0
1990	W KCA AL	2	0	0	0	0	0	1
Totals	2 Yr	5	0	0	1	0	0	1
Johnny Sain								
1947	L BSN NL	1	1	1	2	0	0	1
1948	BSN NL	1.2	0	0	0	0	0	3
Totals	2 Yr	2.2	1	1	2	0	0	4
Joe Sambito								
1979	HOU NL	0.2	0	0	0	0	1	0
Jack Sanford								
1957	PHI NL	1	1	1	2	0	0	0
Curt Schilling								
1997	PHI NL	2	0	0	2	0	0	3
1999*	L PHI NL	2	2	2	3	0	1	3
Totals	2 Yr	4	2	2	5	0	1	6
Johnny Schmitz								
1948	L CHN NL	0.1	3	3	3	0	1	0
Hal Schumacher								
1935	NY NL	4	1	1	4	0	1	5
Don Schwall								
1961–2	BOS AL	3	1	1	5	0	1	2
Herb Score								
1956	CLE AL	1	0	0	0	0	1	1
Mike Scott								
1986	HOU NL	1	1	1	1	1	0	2
1987*	HOU NL	2	0	0	1	0	0	1
Totals	2 Yr	3	1	1	2	1	0	3
Tom Seaver								
1967	S NYN NL	1	0	0	0	0	1	1
1968	NYN NL	2	0	0	2	0	0	5
1970*	NYN NL	3	0	0	1	0	0	4
1973	NYN NL	1	0	0	0	0	1	0
1975	NYN NL	1	3	3	2	1	1	2
1976	NYN NL	2	1	1	2	1	0	1
1977	CIN NL	2	3	2	4	0	1	2
1981	CIN NL	1	1	1	3	1	0	1
Totals	8 Yr	13	8	7	14	3	4	16
Aaron Sele								
2000	SEA AL	1	0	0	1	0	0	0
Rip Sewell								
1943	PIT NL	1	0	0	0	0	0	0
1944	PIT NL	3	0	0	0	0	1	2
1946	PIT NL	1	4	4	4	1	0	0
Totals	3 Yr	5	4	4	4	1	1	2
Bobby Shantz								
1952	PHA AL	1	0	0	0	0	0	3
Bob Shaw								
1962–1	S MIL NL	2	0	0	1	0	1	1

Year		Team	IP	R	ER	H	HR	BB	SO

Jeff Shaw

Year		Team	IP	R	ER	H	HR	BB	SO
1998		LAN NL	1	1	1	3	0	0	0

Spec Shea

| 1947 | W | NYA AL | 3 | 1 | 1 | 3 | 1 | 2 | 2 |

Chris Short

1964		PHI NL	1	2	2	3	0	0	1
1967		PHI NL	2	0	0	0	0	1	1
Totals		2 Yr	3	2	2	3	0	1	2

Sonny Siebert

| 1966 | | CLE AL | 2 | 0 | 0 | 0 | 0 | 0 | 1 |

Curt Simmons

1952*		PHI NL	3	0	0	1	0	1	3
1953		PHI NL	2	0	0	1	0	1	1
1957*	L	PHI NL	1	2	2	2	0	2	0
Totals		3 Yr	6	2	2	4	0	4	4

Bill Singer

1969		LAN NL	2	0	0	0	0	0	0
1973		CAL AL	2	3	3	3	2	1	2
Totals		2 Yr	4	3	3	3	2	1	2

Heathcliff Slocumb

| 1995 | W | PHI NL | 1 | 0 | 0 | 1 | 0 | 0 | 2 |

John Smiley

1991		PIT NL	0	1	1	1	0	0	0
1995		CIN NL	2	2	2	2	1	0	0
Totals		2 Yr	2	3	3	3	1	0	0

Dave Smith

| 1990 | | HOU NL | 0.2 | 0 | 0 | 1 | 0 | 2 | 1 |

Eddie Smith

| 1941 | W | CHA AL | 2 | 2 | 2 | 2 | 1 | 0 | 2 |

Lee Smith

1983		CHN NL	1	2	1	2	0	0	1
1987	W	CHN NL	3	0	0	2	0	0	4
1994		BAL AL	1	2	2	1	1	1	0
Totals		3 Yr	5	4	3	5	1	1	5

John Smoltz

1989	L	ATL NL	1	1	1	2	0	0	0
1992		ATL NL	0.1	0	0	1	0	0	0
1993		ATL NL	0.1	0	0	0	0	1	0
1996*	W	ATL NL	2	0	0	2	0	0	1
Totals		4 Yr	3.2	1	1	5	0	1	1

Lary Sorensen

| 1978 | | MIL AL | 3 | 0 | 0 | 1 | 0 | 0 | 0 |

Mario Soto

1982		CIN NL	2	0	0	3	0	0	4
1983*	L	CIN NL	2	2	0	2	0	2	2
1984		CIN NL	2	0	0	0	0	0	1
Totals		3 Yr	6	2	0	5	0	2	7

Warren Spahn

1947		BSN NL	2	0	0	0	0	1	1
1949*		BSN NL	1.1	4	0	4	0	2	3
1953	W	MIL NL	2	0	0	0	0	1	2
1954		MIL NL	0.2	1	1	4	0	1	0
1956		MIL NL	2	3	3	4	2	0	1
1958*		MIL NL	3	2	1	5	0	0	0
1961-1*		MIL NL	3	0	0	0	0	0	3
Totals		7 Yr	14	10	5	17	2	5	10

Gerry Staley

| 1960-2 | | CHA AL | 2 | 1 | 1 | 2 | 1 | 0 | 0 |

Bob Stanley

1979		BOS AL	2	1	1	1	0	0	0
1983		BOS AL	2	0	0	2	0	0	0
Totals		2 Yr	4	1	1	3	0	0	0

Dave Stenhouse

| 1962-2* | | WAS AL | 2 | 1 | 1 | 3 | 0 | 1 | 1 |

Dave Stewart

| 1989* | | OAK AL | 1 | 2 | 2 | 3 | 0 | 2 | 0 |

Dave Stieb

1980		TOR AL	1	1	0	1	0	2	0
1981		TOR AL	1.2	0	0	1	0	1	1
1983*	W	TOR AL	3	1	0	0	0	1	4
1984*	L	TOR AL	2	2	1	3	1	0	2
1985		TOR AL	1	0	0	0	0	1	2
1988		TOR AL	1	0	0	1	0	0	0
1990		TOR AL	2	0	0	0	0	1	1
Totals		7 Yr	11.2	4	1	6	1	6	10

Dean Stone

| 1954 | W | WAS AL | 0.1 | 0 | 0 | 0 | 0 | 0 | 0 |

Steve Stone

| 1980* | | BAL AL | 3 | 0 | 0 | 0 | 0 | 0 | 3 |

Bill Stoneman

| 1972 | | MON NL | 2 | 2 | 2 | 2 | 1 | 0 | 2 |

Mel Stottlemyre

1966		NYA AL	2	0	0	1	0	1	0
1968		NYA AL	0.1	0	0	0	0	0	1
1969*	L	NYA AL	2	3	2	4	1	0	1
1970		NYA AL	1.2	0	0	0	0	0	2
Totals		4 Yr	6	3	2	5	1	1	4

Frank Sullivan

| 1955 | L | BOS AL | 3.1 | 1 | 1 | 4 | 1 | 1 | 4 |

Rick Sutcliffe

1987		CHN NL	2	0	0	1	0	1	0
1989		CHN NL	1	2	2	4	0	0	0
Totals		2 Yr	3	2	2	5	0	1	0

Bruce Sutter

| 1978 | W | CHN NL | 1.2 | 0 | 0 | 0 | 0 | 0 | 2 |

Year	Team	IP	R	ER	H	HR	BB	SO
Bruce Sutter *continued*								
1979	W CHN NL	2	0	0	2	0	2	3
1980	S CHN NL	2	0	0	0	0	1	1
1981	S SLN NL	1	0	0	0	0	0	1
Totals	4 Yr	6.2	0	0	2	0	3	7
Don Sutton								
1972	LAN NL	2	0	0	1	0	0	2
1973	LAN NL	1	0	0	0	0	0	0
1975	LAN NL	2	0	0	3	0	0	1
1977*	W LAN NL	3	0	0	1	0	1	4
Totals	4 Yr	8	0	0	5	0	1	7
Greg Swindell								
1989	CLE AL	1.2	0	0	2	0	0	3
Frank Tanana								
1976	CAL AL	2	3	3	3	1	1	0
Bob Tewksbury								
1992	SLN NL	1.2	4	4	4	1	1	0
Bobby Thigpen								
1990	CHA AL	1	0	0	0	0	0	1
Justin Thompson								
1997	DET AL	1	0	0	0	0	0	1
Luis Tiant								
1968*	L CLE AL	2	1	0	2	0	2	2
1974	L BOS AL	2	3	2	4	0	1	0
1976	BOS AL	2	0	0	1	0	0	1
Totals	3 Yr	6	4	2	7	0	3	3
Jim Tobin								
1944	S BSN NL	1	0	0	0	0	0	0
Steve Trachsel								
1996	CHN NL	1	0	0	0	0	0	0
Virgil Trucks								
1949	W DET AL	2	2	2	3	0	2	0
1954	S CHA AL	1	0	0	0	0	1	0
Totals	2 Yr	3	2	2	3	0	3	0
Bob Turley								
1958*	NYA AL	1.2	3	3	3	0	2	0
Wayne Twitchell								
1973	PHI NL	1	0	0	1	0	0	1
Ugueth Urbina								
1998	L MON NL	1	3	3	3	0	1	2
Fernando Valenzuela								
1981*	LAN NL	1	0	0	2	0	0	0
1982	LAN NL	0.2	0	0	0	0	2	0
1984	LAN NL	2	0	0	2	0	0	3
1985	LAN NL	1	0	0	0	0	1	1

Year	Team	IP	R	ER	H	HR	BB	SO
Fernando Valenzuela *continued*								
1986	LAN NL	3	0	0	1	0	0	5
Totals	5 Yr	7.2	0	0	5	0	3	9
Johnny Vander Meer								
1938*	W CIN NL	3	0	0	1	0	0	1
1942	CIN NL	3	0	0	2	0	0	4
1943	CIN NL	2.2	1	0	2	0	1	6
Totals	3 Yr	8.2	1	0	5	0	1	11
Frank Viola								
1988*	W MIN AL	2	0	0	0	0	0	1
1990	NYN NL	1	0	0	1	0	0	0
1991	NYN NL	1	0	0	0	0	1	0
Totals	3 Yr	4	0	0	1	0	1	1
Billy Wagner								
1999	hou NL	0.2	0	0	0	0	0	2
Bob Walk								
1988	PIT NL	0.1	0	0	0	0	0	0
Bill Walker								
1935*	L SLN NL	2	3	3	2	1	1	2
Jerry Walker								
1959-2*	W BAL AL	3	1	1	2	0	1	1
Bucky Walters								
1937	PHI NL	1	0	0	2	0	0	0
1940	CIN NL	2	0	0	0	0	0	0
1941	CIN NL	2	1	1	3	0	2	2
1942	CIN NL	1	0	0	0	0	0	1
1944*	CIN NL	3	1	1	5	0	0	1
Totals	5 Yr	9	2	2	10	0	2	4
Duane Ward								
1993	TOR AL	1	0	0	0	0	0	2
Lon Warneke								
1933	CHN NL	4	1	1	6	0	0	2
1934	CHN NL	1	4	4	3	0	3	1
1936	S CHN NL	2.1	0	0	1	0	3	2
Totals	3 Yr	7.1	5	5	10	0	6	5
Bob Welch								
1980	LAN NL	3	2	2	5	1	1	4
1990*	OAK AL	2	0	0	1	0	0	1
Totals	2 Yr	5	2	2	6	1	1	5
David Wells								
1995	DET AL	0.1	0	0	0	0	0	1
1998*	NYA AL	2	0	0	0	0	1	1
2000*	TOR AL	2	0	0	2	0	0	2
Totals	3 Yr	4.1	0	0	2	0	1	4
John Wetteland								
1998	TEX AL	1	0	0	0	0	0	1
1999	S TEX AL	1	0	0	1	0	0	1
Totals	2 Yr	2	0	0	1	0	0	2

Year	Team	IP	R	ER	H	HR	BB	SO

Bob Wickman
Year	Team	IP	R	ER	H	HR	BB	SO
2000	MIL NL	1	0	0	0	0	0	1

Hoyt Wilhelm
Year	Team	IP	R	ER	H	HR	BB	SO
1959–2	BAL AL	1	0	0	1	0	0	0
1961–1 L	BAL AL	1.2	2	2	3	0	1	1
Totals	2 Yr	2.2	2	2	4	0	1	1

Mitch Williams
Year	Team	IP	R	ER	H	HR	BB	SO
1989	CHN NL	1	0	0	0	0	1	1

Stan Williams
Year	Team	IP	R	ER	H	HR	BB	SO
1960–2	LAN NL	2	0	0	2	0	1	2

Don Wilson
Year	Team	IP	R	ER	H	HR	BB	SO
1971	HOU NL	2	0	0	0	0	1	2

Jim Wilson
Year	Team	IP	R	ER	H	HR	BB	SO
1956	CHA AL	1	1	1	2	0	0	1

Rick Wise
Year	Team	IP	R	ER	H	HR	BB	SO
1973* W	SLN NL	2	1	1	2	0	0	1

Mark Wohlers
Year	Team	IP	R	ER	H	HR	BB	SO
1996	ATL NL	0.2	0	0	1	0	0	0

Wilbur Wood
Year	Team	IP	R	ER	H	HR	BB	SO
1972	CHA AL	2	1	1	2	0	1	1

Hal Woodeshick
Year	Team	IP	R	ER	H	HR	BB	SO
1963	HOU NL	2	0	0	1	0	1	3

Todd Worrell
Year	Team	IP	R	ER	H	HR	BB	SO
1988	SLN NL	1	0	0	0	0	0	0
1996	LAN NL	1	0	0	2	0	0	1
Totals	2 Yr	2	0	0	2	0	0	1

Clyde Wright
Year	Team	IP	R	ER	H	HR	BB	SO
1970 L	CAL AL	1.2	1	1	3	0	0	0

John Wyatt
Year	Team	IP	R	ER	H	HR	BB	SO
1964	KC AL	1	2	2	2	2	0	0

Whit Wyatt
Year	Team	IP	R	ER	H	HR	BB	SO
1940	BRO NL	2	0	0	1	0	0	1
1941*	BRO NL	2	0	0	0	0	1	0
Totals	2 Yr	4	0	0	1	0	1	1

Early Wynn
Year	Team	IP	R	ER	H	HR	BB	SO
1955	CLE AL	3	0	0	3	0	0	1
1956	CLE AL	1	0	0	0	0	0	1
1957	CLE AL	0.1	2	2	3	0	0	0
1958 W	CHA AL	1	0	0	0	0	0	0
1959–1*	CHA AL	3	1	1	2	1	1	3
1959–2	CHA AL	2	1	1	1	1	3	1
1960–2	CHA AL	2	0	0	0	0	0	2
Totals	7 Yr	12.1	4	4	9	2	4	8

Matt Young
Year	Team	IP	R	ER	H	HR	BB	SO
1983	SEA AL	1	0	0	0	0	0	1

Jeff Zimmerman
Year	Team	IP	R	ER	H	HR	BB	SO
1999	TEX AL	1	0	0	0	0	2	0

4

CAREER
AND GAME
STATISTICAL
LEADERS

CAREER BATTING LEADERS

GAMES

24	Stan Musial
	Willie Mays
	Hank Aaron
18	Ted Williams
	Brooks Robinson
17	Cal Ripken
16	Mickey Mantle
	Al Kaline
	Pete Rose
15	Yogi Berra
	Rod Carew
14	Roberto Clemente
	Carl Yastrzemski
	Ozzie Smith
13	Nellie Fox
	Ernie Banks
	Tony Gwynn
12	Johnny Bench
	Reggie Jackson
	Dave Winfield
	Wade Boggs
11	Billy Herman
	Mel Ott
	Joe DiMaggio
	Frank Robinson
	Harmon Killebrew
	Roberto Alomar
10	14 players tied

AT BATS

75	Willie Mays
67	Hank Aaron
63	Stan Musial
47	Cal Ripken
46	Ted Williams
45	Brooks Robinson
43	Mickey Mantle
41	Yogi Berra
	Rod Carew
40	Joe DiMaggio
38	Nellie Fox
37	Al Kaline
36	Dave Winfield
34	Carl Yastrzemski
33	Ernie Banks
	Pete Rose
32	Billy Herman
31	Roberto Clemente
29	Tony Gwynn
28	Luis Aparicio
	Johnny Bench
	Steve Garvey
	Wade Boggs
	Roberto Alomar

27	Joe Medwick
	Orlando Cepeda
	Ozzie Smith
26	4 players tied

RUNS

20	Willie Mays
11	Stan Musial
10	Ted Williams
8	Rod Carew
7	Joe DiMaggio
	Jackie Robinson
	Nellie Fox
	Al Kaline
	Hank Aaron
	Joe Morgan
	Steve Garvey
6	Dave Winfield
5	Arky Vaughan
	Yogi Berra
	Mickey Mantle
	Brooks Robinson
	Johnny Bench
	Fred Lynn
	George Brett
	Roberto Alomar
4	15 players tied

HITS

23	Willie Mays
20	Stan Musial
14	Billy Herman
	Ted Williams
	Nellie Fox
13	Hank Aaron
	Brooks Robinson
	Dave Winfield
12	Al Kaline
	Cal Ripken
11	Steve Garvey
10	Charlie Gehringer
	Mickey Mantle
	Ernie Banks
	Roberto Clemente
	Carl Yastrzemski
	Rod Carew
	Johnny Bench
	Ken Griffey
9	Joe DiMaggio
	Wade Boggs
8	Arky Vaughan
	Enos Slaughter
	Yogi Berra
	Ken Boyer
	Harmon Killebrew
7	12 players tied

DOUBLES

7	Dave Winfield
3	Al Simmons
	Joe Cronin
	Billy Herman
	Joe Gordon
	Ted Kluszewski
	Ernie Banks
	Tony Oliva
	Al Oliver
	Cal Ripken
	Barry Bonds
2	20 players tied

TRIPLES

3	Willie Mays
	Brooks Robinson
2	Rod Carew
	Steve Garvey
1	26 players tied

HOMERS

6	Stan Musial
4	Ted Williams
	Fred Lynn
3	Ralph Kiner
	Willie Mays
	Rocky Colavito
	Harmon Killebrew
	Johnny Bench
	Gary Carter
2	Frankie Frisch
	Lou Gehrig
	Arky Vaughan
	Al Rosen
	Mickey Mantle
	Eddie Mathews
	Al Kaline
	Hank Aaron
	Frank Robinson
	Ken Boyer
	Willie McCovey
	Steve Garvey
	Roberto Alomar
	Mike Piazza
1	91 players tied

GRAND SLAMS

Fred Lynn CAL AL 1983

PINCH-HIT HOMERS

Mickey Owen	BRO NL	1942	(Claude Passeau-P)
Larry Doby	CLE AL	1954	(Dean Stone-P)
Gus Bell	CIN NL	1954	(Marv Grissom-P)
Willie Mays	NY NL	1956	(Gus Bell-CF)
Stan Musial	SLN NL	1960–2	(Stan Williams-P)

PINCH-HIT HOMERS *CONTINUED*

Harmon Killebrew	MIN AL	1961–1	(Dick Donovan-P)
George Altman	CHN NL	1961–1	(Mike McCormick-P)
Pete Runnels	BOS AL	1962–2	(Dave Stenhouse-P)
Reggie Jackson	OAK AL	1971	(Vida Blue-P)
Cookie Rojas	KCA AL	1972	(Rod Carew-2B)
Willie Davis	LAN NL	1973	(Don Sutton-P)
Carl Yastrzemski	BOS AL	1975	(Jim Kaat-P)
Lee Mazzilli	NYN NL	1979	(Gary Matthews-LF)
Frank White	KCA AL	1986	(Lou Whitaker-2B)
Fred McGriff	ATL NL	1994	(Randy Myers-P)
Jeff Conine	FLO NL	1995	(Ron Gant-DH)

LEAD-OFF HOMERS

Frankie Frisch	SLN NL	1934
Lou Boudreau	CLE AL	1942
Willie Mays	SFN NL	1965
Joe Morgan	CIN NL	1977
Bo Jackson	KCA AL	1989

HOMERS IN EXTRA INNINGS

Red Schoendienst	SLN NL	1950	14
Stan Musial	SLN NL	1955	12
Tony Perez	CIN NL	1967	15

BACK-TO-BACK HOMERS

1954	AL	Al Rosen	Ray Boone
1956	AL	Ted Williams	Mickey Mantle
1975	NL	Steve Garvey	Jim Wynn
1989	AL	Bo Jackson	Wade Boggs

HOMERING IN FIRST ALL-STAR AT BAT

Max West	BSN NL	1940
Hoot Evers	DET AL	1948
Jim Gilliam	LAN NL	1959–2
George Altman	CHN NL	1961–1
Johnny Bench	CIN NL	1969
Dick Dietz	SFN NL	1970
Lee Mazzilli	NYN NL	1979
Terry Steinbach	OAK AL	1988
Bo Jackson	KCA AL	1989
Jeff Conine	FLO NL	1995
Javier Lopez	ATL NL	1997

HOMERING IN HOME BALLPARK

Joe DiMaggio	1939	Yankee Stadium
Ted Williams	1946	Fenway Park
Stan Musial	1948	Sportman's Park
Vic Wertz	1951	Briggs Stadium
George Kell	1951	Briggs Stadium
Al Rosen	1954	Municipal Stadium
Larry Doby	1954	Municipal Stadium
Jim Gilliam	1959	Memorial Coliseum
Harmon Killebrew	1965	Metropolitan Stadium
Frank Howard	1969	RFK Stadium
Hank Aaron	1972	Atlanta Stadium
Sandy Alomar	1997	Jacobs Field
Chipper Jones	2000	Turner Field

MOST HOME RUNS BEFORE THE ALL-STAR BREAK

Batter	Game Date	Before	Year
Reggie Jackson	07/23/1969	37	47
Mark McGwire	07/07/1998	37	70
Ken Griffey	07/07/1998	35	56
Frank Howard	07/23/1969	34	48
Roger Maris	07/11/1961	33	61
Mark McGwire	07/14/1987	33	49
Matt Williams	07/12/1994	33	43
Ken Griffey	07/12/1994	33	40
Sammy Sosa	07/07/1998	33	66
Frank Thomas	07/12/1994	32	38
Sammy Sosa	07/13/1999	32	63

MOST HOME RUNS AFTER THE ALL-STAR BREAK

Batter	Game Date	After	Year
Mark McGwire	07/13/1999	37	65
Hank Greenberg	07/06/1938	36	58
Albert Belle	07/11/1995	36	50
Mark McGwire	07/07/1998	33	70
Sammy Sosa	07/07/1998	33	66
Ralph Kiner	07/08/1947	31	51
Ralph Kiner	07/12/1949	31	54
Albert Belle	07/07/1998	31	49
Sammy Sosa	07/13/1999	31	63
Harmon Killebrew	07/10/1962	30	48

RUNS BATTED IN

12	Ted Williams
10	Stan Musial
	Fred Lynn
9	Willie Mays
8	Hank Aaron
	Rocky Colavito
7	Steve Garvey
	Cal Ripken
6	Joe Medwick
	Joe DiMaggio
	Al Kaline
	Harmon Killebrew
	Johnny Bench
5	Lou Gehrig
	Nellie Fox
	Al Rosen
	Dick Groat
	Brooks Robinson
	Carl Yastrzemski
	Gary Carter
	George Brett
	George Foster
	Dave Winfield
	Ken Griffey
	Barry Bonds
4	15 players tied

SACRIFICE BUNTS

1	39 players tied

SACRIFICE FLIES (SINCE 1954)

3	George Brett
2	Hank Aaron
	Roberto Clemente
	Pete Rose
1	21 players tied

HIT BY PITCHES

1 29 players tied

WALKS

11	Ted Williams
9	Charlie Gehringer
	Mickey Mantle
7	Stan Musial
	Willie Mays
	Rod Carew
6	Lou Gehrig
5	Ron Santo
4	Bill Dickey
	Enos Slaughter
	Carl Yastrzemski
	Reggie Jackson
	Joe Morgan
	George Brett
	Wade Boggs
3	20 players tied

INTENTIONAL WALKS
(SINCE 1954)

1 21 players tied

STRIKEOUTS

17	Mickey Mantle
14	Willie Mays
10	Ted Williams
9	Roberto Clemente
	Reggie Jackson
	Ryne Sandberg
	Mark McGwire
8	Joe Gordon
	Hank Aaron
	Ernie Banks
	Carl Yastrzemski
	Jim Rice
7	Jimmie Foxx
	Stan Musial
	Frank Robinson
	Elston Howard
	Dick Allen
	Carlton Fisk
6	Lou Gehrig
	Mel Ott
	Al Kaline
	Luis Aparicio
	Harmon Killebrew
	Norm Cash
	Willie McCovey
	Tony Perez
	Johnny Bench
	Fred Lynn
	Craig Biggio
5	18 players tied

STEALS

6	Willie Mays
5	Roberto Alomar
	Kenny Lofton
3	Rod Carew

2	Charlie Gehringer
	Hank Aaron
	Lou Brock
	Rickey Henderson
	Ozzie Smith
	Tim Raines
	Steve Sax
	Tony Gwynn
	Darryl Strawberry
	Kelly Gruber
1	55 players tied

CAUGHT STEALING

2	Tony Oliva
	Rod Carew
	Dave Concepcion
	Ozzie Smith
1	25 players tied

GROUND INTO DP

3	Joe DiMaggio
	Orlando Cepeda
	Pete Rose
2	Arky Vaughan
	Yogi Berra
	Luis Aparicio
	Bobby Richardson
	Earl Battey
	Willie McCovey
	Joe Torre
1	68 players tied

MOST AT BATS
WITHOUT A HIT

10	Terry Moore
9	Elston Howard
8	Wally Berger
	Jose Canseco
	Paul O'Neill
	Paul Waner
7	Glenn Beckert
	Robin Yount
	Sammy Sosa
6	George Bell
	Jack Clark
	Tony Conigliaro
	Darren Daulton
5	Gene Alley
	Rick Burleson
	Eric Davis
	Del Ennis
	Rick Ferrell
	Cecil Fielder
	Pedro Guerrero
	Jackie Jensen
	Tony Kubek
	Wally Moon
	Jo-Jo Moore
	Joe Pepitone
	Bill Russell
	Benito Santiago
4	24 players tied

ON BASE + SLUGGING (OPS)
(15 Plate Appearances minimum)

1.264	Fred Lynn
1.255	Charlie Gehringer
1.254	Steve Garvey
1.200	Ralph Kiner
1.154	Mike Piazza
1.132	Ken Griffey
1.122	Arky Vaughan
1.114	Gary Carter
1.091	Ted Williams
1.079	Johnny Bench
1.048	Mike Schmidt
1.032	Ken Boyer
1.029	Stan Musial
1.028	Lou Gehrig
1.011	Jackie Robinson
	Harmon Killebrew
1.004	Enos Slaughter
.986	Billy Herman
.967	Bill Skowron
.951	Dave Winfield
.938	George Brett
.899	Willie Mays
	Rocky Colavito
.889	Al Kaline
.888	Ernie Banks

ON BASE AVERAGE
(15 Plate Appearances minimum)

.655	Charlie Gehringer
.500	Ron Santo
.480	Enos Slaughter
	Ken Griffey
.471	Stan Hack
.467	Bill Skowron
.455	Billy Herman
.440	Arky Vaughan
.439	Ted Williams
.433	Steve Garvey
.423	Ken Boyer
.417	Lou Gehrig
.406	Wade Boggs
.400	Jackie Robinson
	Kenny Lofton
	Nellie Fox
	Johnny Bench
.395	Dave Winfield
.394	Stan Musial
.391	Bill Dickey
.389	Mike Piazza
	Dom DiMaggio
.381	Mike Schmidt
.375	Al Kaline
	Dick Groat

SLUGGING AVERAGE
(15 Plate Appearances minimum)

.933	Ralph Kiner
.900	Fred Lynn
.821	Steve Garvey
.765	Mike Piazza

.750 Gary Carter
.682 Arky Vaughan
.679 Johnny Bench
.667 Mike Schmidt
.654 Harmon Killebrew
.652 Ted Williams
     Ken Griffey
.640 Rocky Colavito
.635 Stan Musial
.611 Jackie Robinson
     Lou Gehrig
.609 Ken Boyer
.600 Charlie Gehringer
.583 George Brett
.563 Willie McCovey
.556 Dave Winfield
.550 Barry Bonds
.548 Roberto Clemente
.545 Ernie Banks
.533 Dale Murphy
     Willie Mays

MOST MULTIPLE HIT GAMES

6 Willie Mays
5 Billy Herman
  Stan Musial
4 Nellie Fox
  Charlie Gehringer
  Ken Griffey
  Brooks Robinson
3 Ernie Banks
  Johnny Bench
  George Brett
  Rod Carew
  Roberto Clemente
  Steve Garvey
  Ted Kluszewski
  Ted Williams
  Carl Yastrzemski
2 Hank Aaron
  Richie Ashburn
  Yogi Berra
  Bobby Bonilla
  Ken Boyer
  Joe Cronin
  Joe DiMaggio
  Jimmie Foxx
  Frankie Frisch
  Tony Gwynn
  Al Kaline
  Ernie Lombardi
  Mickey Mantle
  Minnie Minoso
  Cal Ripken
  Ivan Rodriguez
  Pete Rose
  Mike Schmidt
  Al Simmons
  Bill Skowron
  Enos Slaughter
  Arky Vaughan
  Leon Wagner
  Dave Winfield

MOST TIMES PLAYING ON WINNING TEAM

17 Hank Aaron
   Willie Mays
15 Pete Rose
13 Stan Musial
11 Roberto Clemente
   Cal Ripken
10 Johnny Bench
   Steve Garvey
   Ted Williams
9 Joe Morgan
8 Ernie Banks
  Ken Boyer
  Mike Schmidt
  Tom Seaver
7 Roberto Alomar
  Wade Boggs
  Gary Carter
  Orlando Cepeda
  Dave Concepcion
  Joe DiMaggio
  Don Drysdale
  Joe Gordon
  Ken Griffey
  Tony Perez
  Kirby Puckett
  Ron Santo
  Ozzie Smith
  Joe Torre
  Dave Winfield

MOST TIMES PLAYING ON LOSING TEAM

15 Brooks Robinson
13 Rod Carew
12 Carl Yastrzemski
11 Reggie Jackson
   Mickey Mantle
10 Al Kaline
   Harmon Killebrew
   Stan Musial
9 Yogi Berra
  Carlton Fisk
  Nellie Fox
  Johnny Mize
8 George Brett
  Tony Gwynn
  Billy Herman
  Fred Lynn
  Ted Williams
7 Bill Freehan
  Mel Ott
  Frank Robinson
  Ryne Sandberg
  Ozzie Smith
6 Hank Aaron

Will Clark
Rocky Colavito
Jim Fregosi
Bobby Grich
Catfish Hunter
Harvey Kuenn
Barry Larkin
Willie Mays
Joe Medwick
Minnie Minoso
Tony Oliva
Cal Ripken
Enos Slaughter
Arky Vaughan

CONSECUTIVE GAMES PLAYED

	Player	From		To
24	Willie Mays	1954	to	1973
	Stan Musial	1943	to	1963
18	Brooks Robinson	1960–1	to	1974
17	Cal Ripken	1983	to	1999
14	Hank Aaron	1962–2	to	1975
13	Mickey Mantle	1953	to	1962–1
12	Wade Boggs	1985	to	1996
	Ozzie Smith	1981	to	1992
	Dave Winfield	1977	to	1988
11	Roberto Alomar	1990	to	2000
	Roberto Clemente	1960–1	to	1967
	Nellie Fox	1953	to	1961–1
	Mel Ott	1934	to	1944
10	Hank Aaron	1955	to	1961–2
	Johnny Bench	1968	to	1977
	Yogi Berra	1949	to	1958
	Billy Herman	1934	to	1943
	Al Kaline	1955	to	1961–2
	Kirby Puckett	1986	to	1995
	Pete Rose	1973	to	1982
	Ryne Sandberg	1984	to	1993
9	Harmon Killebrew	1963	to	1971
	Fred Lynn	1975	to	1983
	Joe Medwick	1934	to	1942
	Ivan Rodriguez	1992	to	2000
	Ted Williams	1954	to	1960–2

CONSECUTIVE GAMES STARTED

	Player	From		To
16	Cal Ripken	1984	to	1999
14	Willie Mays	1957	to	1966
11	Wade Boggs	1986	to	1996
10	Hank Aaron	1965	to	1974
	Ozzie Smith	1983	to	1992
9	Johnny Bench	1969	to	1977
8	Yogi Berra	1950	to	1957
	Rod Carew	1971	to	1978
	Ivan Rodriguez	1993	to	2000
	Ryne Sandberg	1986	to	1993
7	Barry Bonds	1992	to	1998
	Joe DiMaggio	1936	to	1942
	Bill Freehan	1966	to	1972
	Steve Garvey	1974	to	1980
	Joe Medwick	1934	to	1940
	Joe Morgan	1972	to	1978
	Stan Musial	1948	to	1954
6	Hank Aaron	1957	to	1960–2

Walker Cooper	1942	to	1948
Nellie Fox	1955	to	1959–2
Charlie Gehringer	1933	to	1938
Mickey Mantle	1953	to	1958
Mickey Mantle	1959–2	to	1962–1
Mike Piazza	1994	to	1999
Dave Winfield	1983	to	1988

CONSECUTIVE GAMES WITH A HIT

7	Dave Winfield	1982	to	1988
6	Johnny Bench	1971	to	1976
	Willie Mays	1954	to	1959–1
	Joe Morgan	1972	to	1977
	Stan Musial	1953	to	1958
5	Wade Boggs	1988	to	1992
	Nellie Fox	1958	to	1960–2
	Steve Garvey	1974	to	1978
	Charlie Gehringer	1934	to	1938
	Mickey Mantle	1954	to	1958
	Brooks Robinson	1963	to	1967
4	Yogi Berra	1954	to	1957
	Walker Cooper	1942	to	1946
	Ken Griffey	1991	to	1994
	Dick Groat	1962–1	to	1964
	Al Kaline	1960–1	to	1961–2
	Ted Kluszewski	1953	to	1956
	Fred Lynn	1978	to	1981
	Willie Mays	1960–1	to	1961–2
	Mel Ott	1936	to	1939
	Jackie Robinson	1949	to	1952
3	Hank Aaron	1967	to	1969
	Hank Aaron	1971	to	1973
	Roberto Alomar	1992	to	1994
	George Brett	1982	to	1984
	Joe Carter	1991	to	1993
	Will Clark	1990	to	1992
	Del Crandall	1959–1	to	1960–1
	Joe Cronin	1937	to	1939
	Joe DiMaggio	1937	to	1939
	Nellie Fox	1954	to	1956
	Jimmie Foxx	1934	to	1936
	Lou Gehrig	1936	to	1938
	Billy Herman	1936	to	1938
	Reggie Jackson	1971	to	1973
	Al Kaline	1955	to	1957
	Harmon Killebrew	1964	to	1966
	Ralph Kiner	1949	to	1951
	Ernie Lombardi	1938	to	1940
	Joe Medwick	1936	to	1938
	Minnie Minoso	1952	to	1954
	Johnny Mize	1947	to	1949
	Dale Murphy	1983	to	1985
	Mike Piazza	1994	to	1996
	Kirby Puckett	1992	to	1994
	Cal Ripken	1997	to	1999
	Al Simmons	1933	to	1935
	Vern Stephens	1943	to	1946
	Darryl Strawberry	1984	to	1986
	Bill Terry	1933	to	1935
	Frank Thomas	1993	to	1995
	Arky Vaughan	1939	to	1941

Maury Wills	1961–1	to	1962–1
Dave Winfield	1977	to	1979
Rudy York	1941	to	1943

CONSECUTIVE GAMES WITH A HOMER

3	Ralph Kiner	1949	to	1951
2	Hank Aaron	1971	to	1972
	Frankie Frisch	1933	to	1934
	Lou Gehrig	1936	to	1937
	Fred Lynn	1979	to	1980
	Mickey Mantle	1955	to	1956
	Stan Musial	1948	to	1949
	Stan Musial	1955	to	1956
	Mike Piazza	1995	to	1996

CONSECUTIVE GAMES WITH AN EXTRA-BASE HIT

5	Steve Garvey	1974	to	1978
3	Reggie Jackson	1971	to	1973
	Ralph Kiner	1949	to	1951
	Ted Kluszewski	1954	to	1956
	Willie Mays	1960–1	to	1961–1
	Stan Musial	1955	to	1957
	Dave Winfield	1986	to	1988
2	Hank Aaron	1971	to	1972
	Barry Bonds	1992	to	1993
	George Brett	1983	to	1984
	Joe Cronin	1937	to	1938
	Bill Dickey	1937	to	1938
	George Foster	1976	to	1977
	Jimmie Foxx	1934	to	1935
	Frankie Frisch	1933	to	1934
	Charlie Gehringer	1935	to	1936
	Lou Gehrig	1936	to	1937
	Joe Gordon	1946	to	1947
	Fred Lynn	1979	to	1980
	Mickey Mantle	1955	to	1956
	Willie Mays	1956	to	1957
	Joe Morgan	1973	to	1974
	Dale Murphy	1984	to	1985
	Stan Musial	1948	to	1949
	Al Oliver	1982	to	1983
	Mel Ott	1937	to	1938
	Mike Piazza	1995	to	1996
	Brooks Robinson	1966	to	1967
	Al Simmons	1934	to	1935
	Lou Whitaker	1983	to	1984
	Ted Williams	1946	to	1947
	Dave Winfield	1983	to	1984

CONSECUTIVE GAMES WITH A RUN

6	Steve Garvey	1974	to	1979
5	Willie Mays	1954	to	1958
	Stan Musial	1954	to	1958
4	Lou Gehrig	1934	to	1937
	Mickey Mantle	1954	to	1957
	Willie Mays	1963	to	1966
	Joe Morgan	1976	to	1979
	Jackie Robinson	1949	to	1952
	Ted Williams	1954	to	1957
3	Roberto Alomar	1992	to	1994
	Joe DiMaggio	1937	to	1939
	George Foster	1976	to	1978

Nellie Fox	1958	to	1959–2
Jimmie Foxx	1934	to	1936
Ralph Kiner	1949	to	1951
Ted Kluszewski	1954	to	1956
Willie Mays	1960–1	to	1961–1
Brooks Robinson	1965	to	1967
Arky Vaughan	1939	to	1941
2 Hank Aaron	1971	to	1972
Carlos Baerga	1992	to	1993
Johnny Bench	1973	to	1974
Yogi Berra	1954	to	1955
Craig Biggio	1994	to	1995
Wade Boggs	1991	to	1992
Barry Bonds	1992	to	1993
Bob Boone	1978	to	1979
George Brett	1978	to	1979
George Brett	1983	to	1984
Lou Brock	1974	to	1975
Hubie Brooks	1986	to	1987
Rod Carew	1977	to	1978
Joe Carter	1991	to	1992
Joe Cronin	1933	to	1934
Nellie Fox	1955	to	1956
Frankie Frisch	1933	to	1934
Ken Griffey	1992	to	1993
Gabby Hartnett	1936	to	1937
Billy Herman	1936	to	1937
Ken Keltner	1943	to	1944
Harmon Killebrew	1964	to	1965
Fred Lynn	1976	to	1977
Fred Lynn	1979	to	1980
Stan Musial	1948	to	1949
Stan Musial	1951	to	1952
Al Oliver	1982	to	1983
Mike Piazza	1995	to	1996
Kirby Puckett	1992	to	1993
Cal Ripken	1998	to	1999
Ivan Rodriguez	1993	to	1994
Babe Ruth	1933	to	1934
Reggie Smith	1974	to	1975
Duke Snider	1953	to	1954
Frank Thomas	1994	to	1995
Jim Thome	1998	to	1999
Leon Wagner	1962–2	to	1963
Dave Winfield	1978	to	1979
Jim Wynn	1974	to	1975

CONSECUTIVE GAMES WITH RBI

5	Steve Garvey	1974	to	1978
4	Dick Groat	1962–1	to	1964
3	Hank Aaron	1958	to	1959–2
	Hank Aaron	1971	to	1973

George Brett	1983	to	1985
Ken Griffey	1992	to	1994
Ralph Kiner	1949	to	1951
Fred Lynn	1979	to	1981
Joe Medwick	1936	to	1938
Mike Piazza	1994	to	1996
2 Roberto Alomar	1998	to	1999
Sandy Alomar	1997	to	1998
Earl Averill	1933	to	1934
Craig Biggio	1995	to	1996
Lou Boudreau	1941	to	1942
Gary Carter	1981	to	1982
Roberto Clemente	1970	to	1971
Rocky Colavito	1961–1	to	1961–2
Joe Cronin	1934	to	1935
Joe DiMaggio	1948	to	1949
George Foster	1976	to	1977
Nellie Fox	1959–2	to	1960–1
Jimmie Foxx	1934	to	1935
Frankie Frisch	1933	to	1934
Lou Gehrig	1936	to	1937
George Kell	1950	to	1951
Harmon Killebrew	1964	to	1965
Greg Luzinski	1977	to	1978
Mickey Mantle	1955	to	1956
Roger Maris	1962–1	to	1962–2
Willie Mays	1956	to	1957
Willie Mays	1960–2	to	1961–1
Willie McCovey	1969	to	1970
Dale Murphy	1983	to	1984
Stan Musial	1943	to	1944
Stan Musial	1948	to	1949
Stan Musial	1955	to	1956
Rafael Palmeiro	1998	to	1999
Kirby Puckett	1993	to	1994
Cal Ripken	1991	to	1992
Cal Ripken	1998	to	1999
Jackie Robinson	1951	to	1952
Ron Santo	1965	to	1966
Frank Thomas	1994	to	1995
Dixie Walker	1943	to	1944
Bill White	1961–1	to	1961–2
Dave Winfield	1979	to	1980

CONSECUTIVE GAMES WITH A STEAL

2	Hank Aaron	1967	to	1968
	Roberto Alomar	1994	to	1995
	Lou Brock	1974	to	1975
	Charlie Gehringer	1933	to	1934
	Kenny Lofton	1998	to	1999
	Willie Mays	1963	to	1964
	Darryl Strawberry	1984	to	1985

CAREER PITCHING LEADERS

GAMES

8	Tom Seaver
	Juan Marichal
	Don Drysdale
	Jim Bunning
7	Dave Stieb
	Early Wynn
	Warren Spahn
6	Randy Johnson
	Roger Clemens
	Dennis Eckersley
	Rich Gossage
	Catfish Hunter
	Bob Gibson
	Whitey Ford
	Ewell Blackwell
5	Kevin Brown
	Tom Glavine
	David Cone
	Jack Morris
	Fernando Valenzuela
	Rollie Fingers
	Nolan Ryan
	Jim Palmer
	Steve Carlton
	Gaylord Perry
	Robin Roberts
	Bob Feller
	Bucky Walters
	Lefty Gomez
	Carl Hubbell
4	23 players tied

WINS

3	Lefty Gomez
2	Bruce Sutter
	Vida Blue
	Juan Marichal
	Don Drysdale
	Bob Friend
1	57 players tied

LOSSES

2	Dwight Gooden
	Luis Tiant
	Catfish Hunter
	Whitey Ford
	Mort Cooper
	Claude Passeau
1	58 players tied

SAVES

3	Dennis Eckersley
2	Bruce Sutter
	Mel Harder
1	39 players tied

INNINGS PITCHED

19.1	Don Drysdale
18	Juan Marichal
	Jim Bunning
	Lefty Gomez
14	Robin Roberts
	Warren Spahn
13.2	Ewell Blackwell
13	Tom Seaver
	Mel Harder
12.2	Jim Palmer
	Catfish Hunter
12.1	Early Wynn
	Bob Feller
12	Whitey Ford
11.2	Dave Stieb
11	Bob Gibson
	Vic Raschi
10.2	Jack Morris
	Billy Pierce
	Hal Newhouser
10	Nolan Ryan
	Dizzy Dean
9.2	Carl Hubbell
9	Randy Johnson
	Vida Blue
	Gaylord Perry
	Bucky Walters
8.2	3 players tied

HITS ALLOWED

19	Whitey Ford
17	Robin Roberts
	Warren Spahn
15	Tom Glavine
	Catfish Hunter
14	Jack Morris
	Tom Seaver
	Gaylord Perry
13	Red Ruffing
12	Vida Blue
11	Jim Palmer
	Bob Gibson
	Lefty Gomez
10	Nolan Ryan
	Don Drysdale
	Tex Hughson
	Bucky Walters
	Dizzy Dean
	Lon Warneke
9	Greg Maddux
	Early Wynn
	Don Newcombe
	Claude Passeau
	Tommy Bridges
	Mel Harder

	Lefty Grove
8	8 players tied

RUNS ALLOWED

13	Whitey Ford
10	Robin Roberts
	Warren Spahn
9	Tom Glavine
	Catfish Hunter
8	Vida Blue
	Jim Palmer
	Tom Seaver
7	Atlee Hammaker
	Rich Gossage
	Mort Cooper
	Claude Passeau
	Red Ruffing
6	Gaylord Perry
	Roy Face
	Tex Hughson
	Van Mungo
	Lefty Gomez
5	Dennis Eckersley
	Nolan Ryan
	Steve Carlton
	Johnny Odom
	Jim Maloney
	Dick Radatz
	Sandy Consuegra
	Lon Warneke
4	22 players tied

EARNED RUNS

12	Whitey Ford
10	Robin Roberts
9	Tom Glavine
	Catfish Hunter
8	Vida Blue
	Jim Palmer
7	Atlee Hammaker
	Rich Gossage
	Tom Seaver
	Mort Cooper
	Claude Passeau
	Red Ruffing
6	Gaylord Perry
	Roy Face
	Van Mungo
5	Nolan Ryan
	Steve Carlton
	Jim Maloney
	Dick Radatz
	Sandy Consuegra
	Warren Spahn
	Tex Hughson
	Lefty Gomez

	Lon Warneke
4	18 players tied

HOMERS

4	Vida Blue
	Catfish Hunter
3	Jim Palmer
	Steve Carlton
	Tom Seaver
	Milt Pappas
	Whitey Ford
	Robin Roberts
	Mort Cooper
2	20 players tied

HIT BATSMEN

1	29 players tied

WALKS

7	Jim Palmer
6	Dave Stieb
	Carl Hubbell
	Lon Warneke
5	Nolan Ryan
	Steve Carlton
	Bob Gibson
	Robin Roberts
	Warren Spahn
	Ewell Blackwell
	Dizzy Dean
	Bill Hallahan
4	Tom Glavine
	Jack Morris
	Jim Kern
	Tom Seaver
	Denny McLain
	Sam McDowell
	Mike McCormick
	Don Drysdale
	Turk Farrell
	Sam Jones
	Early Wynn
	Curt Simmons
	Vic Raschi
	Bob Feller
	Bill Lee
	Van Mungo
3	25 players tied

STRIKEOUTS

19	Don Drysdale
16	Tom Seaver
14	Jim Palmer
13	Catfish Hunter
	Jim Bunning
	Bob Feller

STRIKEOUTS *CONTINUED*

12 Sam McDowell
   Juan Marichal
   Billy Pierce
   Ewell Blackwell
11 Johnny Vander Meer
   Carl Hubbell
10 Dave Stieb
   Nolan Ryan
   Dick Radatz
   Bob Gibson
   Warren Spahn
   Dizzy Dean
 9 Fernando Valenzuela
   Stu Miller
   Robin Roberts
   Lefty Gomez
 8 Pedro Martinez
   Randy Johnson
   David Cone
   Jack Morris
   Early Wynn
   Vic Raschi
   Hal Newhouser
   Lefty Grove
 7 10 players tied

GAMES STARTED

 5 Don Drysdale
   Robin Roberts
   Lefty Gomez
 4 Jim Palmer
 3 Randy Johnson
   Greg Maddux
   Jack Morris
   Vida Blue
   Jim Bunning
   Whitey Ford
   Billy Pierce
   Warren Spahn
 2 David Wells
   Tom Glavine
   Dwight Gooden
   Dave Stieb
   Steve Carlton
   Dean Chance
   Juan Marichal
   Bob Friend
   Curt Simmons
   Vic Raschi
   Mort Cooper
   Bob Feller
   Paul Derringer
   Dizzy Dean
   Red Ruffing
 1 70 players tied

GAMES FINISHED

 6 Rich Gossage
 4 Dennis Eckersley
   Mel Harder
 3 Bruce Sutter

Rollie Fingers
Ewell Blackwell
Bob Feller
 2 Mariano Rivera
   Doug Jones
   Guillermo Hernandez
   Phil Niekro
   Dick Radatz
   Milt Pappas
   Juan Marichal
   Stu Miller
   Bud Daley
   Bucky Walters
   Lefty Grove
   Carl Hubbell
 1 93 players tied

HIGHEST ERA
(9 Innings pitched minimum)

9.00 Whitey Ford (12.0 IP)
8.00 Vida Blue (9.0 IP)
6.43 Robin Roberts (14.0 IP)
6.39 Catfish Hunter (12.2 IP)
6.00 Gaylord Perry (9.0 IP)
5.68 Jim Palmer (12.2 IP)
5.54 Tom Seaver (13.0 IP)
4.50 Nolan Ryan (10.0 IP)
3.38 Billy Pierce (10.2 IP)
3.27 Bob Gibson (11.0 IP)

LOWEST ERA
(9 Innings pitched minimum)

0.00 Mel Harder (13.0 IP)
0.50 Juan Marichal (18.0 IP)
0.73 Bob Feller (12.1 IP)
0.77 Dave Stieb (11.2 IP)
1.00 Jim Bunning (18.0 IP)
     Randy Johnson (9.0 IP)
1.32 Ewell Blackwell (13.2 IP)
1.40 Don Drysdale (19.1 IP)
2.00 Bucky Walters (9.0 IP)
2.45 Vic Raschi (11.0 IP)
2.50 Lefty Gomez (18.0 IP)

CONSECUTIVE GAMES PITCHED

6	Ewell Blackwell	1946	to	1951
	Early Wynn	1955	to	1959–2
5	Juan Marichal	1964	to	1968
4	Dizzy Dean	1934	to	1937
	Mel Harder	1934	to	1937
	Catfish Hunter	1973	to	1976
	Hal Newhouser	1943	to	1947
	Bruce Sutter	1978	to	1981
3	Rick Aguilera	1991	to	1993
	Kevin Brown	1996	to	1998
	Jim Bunning	1961–1	to	1962–1
	Paul Derringer	1939	to	1941
	Don Drysdale	1963	to	1965
	Dennis Eckersley	1990	to	1992
	Roy Face	1959–1	to	1960–1
	Bob Feller	1939	to	1941
	Whitey Ford	1954	to	1956

CONSECUTIVE GAMES PITCHED *CONTINUED*

Lefty Gomez	1933	to	1935
Trevor Hoffman	1998	to	2000
Randy Johnson	1993	to	1995
Jim Kern	1977	to	1979
Frank Lary	1960–1	to	1961–1
Bob Lemon	1950	to	1952
Dennis Martinez	1990	to	1992
Jack McDowell	1991	to	1993
Sam McDowell	1968	to	1970
Don Newcombe	1949	to	1951
Jim Palmer	1970	to	1972
Billy Pierce	1955	to	1957
Dan Plesac	1987	to	1989
Bob Purkey	1961–1	to	1962–1
Vic Raschi	1948	to	1950
Robin Roberts	1953	to	1955
Tom Seaver	1975	to	1977
Rip Sewell	1943	to	1946
Mario Soto	1982	to	1984
Dave Stieb	1983	to	1985
Mel Stottlemyre	1968	to	1970
Fernando Valenzuela	1984	to	1986
Bucky Walters	1940	to	1942

CONSECUTIVE GAMES STARTED (PITCHER)

3	Lefty Gomez	1933	to	1935
	Robin Roberts	1953	to	1955
2	Jim Bunning	1961–2	to	1962–1
	Mort Cooper	1942	to	1943
	Dizzy Dean	1936	to	1937
	Paul Derringer	1939	to	1940
	Don Drysdale	1959–1	to	1959–2
	Whitey Ford	1960–2	to	1961–1
	Tom Glavine	1991	to	1992
	Lefty Gomez	1937	to	1938
	Greg Maddux	1997	to	1998
	Jim Palmer	1977	to	1978
	Billy Pierce	1955	to	1956
	Robin Roberts	1950	to	1951
	Red Ruffing	1939	to	1940
	Dave Stieb	1983	to	1984

CONSECUTIVE GAMES FINISHED (PITCHER)

4	Mel Harder	1934	to	1937
3	Dennis Eckersley	1990	to	1992
	Bruce Sutter	1979	to	1981
2	Ewell Blackwell	1950	to	1951
	Bob Feller	1939	to	1940
	Rollie Fingers	1973	to	1974
	Rich Gossage	1977	to	1978
	Rich Gossage	1984	to	1985
	Guillermo Hernandez	1984	to	1985
	Stu Miller	1961–1	to	1961–2
	Milt Pappas	1962–1	to	1962–2
	Dick Radatz	1963	to	1964

Games Played

CATCHER
14 Yogi Berra
11 Johnny Bench
10 Carlton Fisk
9 Gary Carter
   Ivan Rodriguez
8 Del Crandall
   Bill Freehan
7 Bill Dickey
   Roy Campanella
   Lance Parrish
   Mike Piazza
6 Walker Cooper
   Smoky Burgess
   Elston Howard
   Sandy Alomar
5 Gabby Hartnett
   Ernie Lombardi
   Earl Battey
   Thurman Munson
4 Frankie Hayes
   Ed Bailey
   Sherm Lollar
   Joe Torre
   Ted Simmons
   Bob Boone
   Tony Pena
3 10 players tied

FIRST BASE
10 Steve Garvey
9 Mark McGwire
8 Johnny Mize
7 Rod Carew
6 Lou Gehrig
   Frank McCormick
   Eddie Murray
   Will Clark
5 Mickey Vernon
   Bill Skowron
   Orlando Cepeda
   Bill White
   Norm Cash
   Willie McCovey
   Don Mattingly
   Fred McGriff
4 Rudy York
   Gil Hodges
   Stan Musial
   Ted Kluszewski
   Vic Power
   Jim Gentile
   Harmon Killebrew
   Keith Hernandez

   Andres Galarraga
3 15 players tied

SECOND BASE
13 Nellie Fox
11 Roberto Alomar
10 Billy Herman
   Ryne Sandberg
9 Joe Morgan
8 Joe Gordon
   Bobby Doerr
   Red Schoendienst
   Rod Carew
7 Bill Mazeroski
6 Charlie Gehringer
   Johnny Temple
   Bobby Richardson
   Craig Biggio
5 Bobby Grich
   Willie Randolph
   Frank White
   Steve Sax
4 Jackie Robinson
   Frank Bolling
   Manny Trillo
   Davey Lopes
   Lou Whitaker
   Chuck Knoblauch
3 Bobby Avila
   Charlie Neal
   Dave Johnson
   Glenn Beckert
   Cookie Rojas
   Dave Cash
   Phil Garner
   Carlos Baerga
2 15 players tied

THIRD BASE
18 Brooks Robinson
12 Wade Boggs
10 Ken Boyer
9 Eddie Mathews
   Mike Schmidt
   George Brett
8 Ron Santo
7 Frank Malzone
6 Ken Keltner
   George Kell
   Ron Cey
   Graig Nettles
5 Tim Wallach
4 Jimmie Foxx
   Stan Hack
   Bob Elliott
   Al Rosen

   Tony Perez
   Buddy Bell
3 Chipper Jones
   Whitey Kurowski
   Harmon Killebrew
   Sal Bando
   Joe Torre
   Bill Madlock
   Pete Rose
   Ken Caminiti
   Cal Ripken
2 21 players tied

SHORTSTOP
14 Ozzie Smith
   Cal Ripken
10 Luis Aparicio
8 Ernie Banks
   Barry Larkin
7 Joe Cronin
   Pee Wee Reese
   Dave Concepcion
6 Dick Groat
   Maury Wills
   Don Kessinger
5 Arky Vaughan
   Lou Boudreau
   Marty Marion
   Vern Stephens
   Jim Fregosi
   Bert Campaneris
   Larry Bowa
4 Eddie Miller
   Phil Rizzuto
   Chico Carrasquel
   Leo Cardenas
   Tony Fernandez
3 Harvey Kuenn
   Gil McDougald
   Bill Russell
   Bucky Dent
   Rick Burleson
   Robin Yount
   Alex Rodriguez
   Nomar Garciaparra
   Derek Jeter
2 20 players tied

LEFT FIELD
14 Ted Williams
9 Stan Musial
8 Joe Medwick
   Barry Bonds
7 Minnie Minoso
   Carl Yastrzemski
   Rickey Henderson

   Tim Raines
6 Jim Rice
5 Frank Robinson
   Pete Rose
   Dave Winfield
4 Ralph Kiner
   Orlando Cepeda
   Willie Stargell
3 Bob Johnson
   Hank Aaron
   Bob Skinner
   Al Kaline
   Rocky Colavito
   Tommy Davis
   Leon Wagner
   Billy Williams
   Willie Horton
   Joe Rudi
   Greg Luzinski
   Tony Gwynn
   Paul O'Neill
   Albert Belle
2 24 players tied

CENTER FIELD
22 Willie Mays
12 Mickey Mantle
8 Fred Lynn
   Ken Griffey
6 Joe DiMaggio
   Kirby Puckett
5 Larry Doby
   Duke Snider
   Al Kaline
   Andre Dawson
4 Earl Averill
   Stan Musial
   Dom DiMaggio
   Cesar Cedeno
   Dale Murphy
   Willie McGee
   Kenny Lofton
   Rickey Henderson
3 Wally Berger
   Al Simmons
   Terry Moore
   Andy Pafko
   Carl Yastrzemski
   Amos Otis
   Bobby Murcer
   George Foster
   Devon White
2 28 players tied

RIGHT FIELD

- 16 Hank Aaron
- 12 Roberto Clemente
- 11 Reggie Jackson
- 8 Dave Winfield
- 6 Mel Ott
- Enos Slaughter
- Stan Musial
- Al Kaline
- Dave Parker
- Darryl Strawberry
- Tony Gwynn
- 5 Rocky Colavito
- Tony Oliva
- 4 Joe DiMaggio
- Roger Maris
- Frank Robinson
- Reggie Smith
- Andre Dawson
- Ruben Sierra
- 3 Paul Waner
- Bill Nicholson
- Dixie Walker
- Hank Bauer
- Pete Rose
- Dwight Evans
- Dale Murphy
- Manny Ramirez
- Larry Walker
- 2 24 players tied

OUTFIELD
(ALL POSITIONS)

- 22 Willie Mays
- 20 Hank Aaron
- 14 Ted Williams
- Mickey Mantle
- Roberto Clemente
- 13 Al Kaline
- 12 Stan Musial
- Dave Winfield
- 11 Reggie Jackson
- 10 Joe DiMaggio
- Rickey Henderson
- Tony Gwynn
- Kirby Puckett
- 9 Carl Yastrzemski
- 8 Joe Medwick
- Enos Slaughter
- Minnie Minoso
- Frank Robinson
- Rocky Colavito
- Fred Lynn
- Andre Dawson
- Ken Griffey
- Barry Bonds
- 7 Mel Ott
- Dale Murphy
- Tim Raines
- 6 8 players tied

Games Started

CATCHER

- 11 Yogi Berra
- 10 Johnny Bench
- 8 Del Crandall
- Ivan Rodriguez
- 7 Bill Freehan
- Carlton Fisk
- Gary Carter
- 6 Bill Dickey
- Walker Cooper
- Mike Piazza
- 5 Roy Campanella
- 4 Earl Battey
- Joe Torre
- 3 Gabby Hartnett
- Ernie Lombardi
- Ed Bailey
- Thurman Munson
- Benito Santiago
- Sandy Alomar
- 2 Jimmy Wilson
- Rick Ferrell
- Rollie Hemsley
- Birdie Tebbetts
- Buddy Rosar
- Smoky Burgess
- Gus Triandos
- John Romano
- Ted Simmons
- Lance Parrish
- Terry Kennedy
- Terry Steinbach
- 1 11 players tied

FIRST BASE

- 9 Steve Garvey
- 8 Johnny Mize
- 7 Rod Carew
- 6 Mark McGwire
- 5 Lou Gehrig
- Orlando Cepeda
- 4 Mickey Vernon
- Stan Musial
- Bill Skowron
- Willie McCovey
- Will Clark
- 3 Bill Terry
- George McQuinn
- Ted Kluszewski
- Bill White
- Norm Cash
- Harmon Killebrew
- Dick Allen
- Fred McGriff
- 2 Jimmie Foxx
- Frank McCormick
- Rudy York
- Eddie Robinson
- Joe Adcock
- Jim Gentile

- Boog Powell
- Pete Rose
- Frank Thomas
- Jim Thome
- 1 38 players tied

SECOND BASE

- 9 Ryne Sandberg
- Roberto Alomar
- 8 Nellie Fox
- Rod Carew
- 7 Joe Morgan
- 6 Charlie Gehringer
- Billy Herman
- Johnny Temple
- Bill Mazeroski
- 5 Joe Gordon
- Bobby Doerr
- 4 Red Schoendienst
- Jackie Robinson
- Willie Randolph
- Craig Biggio
- 3 Davey Lopes
- Lou Whitaker
- 2 Frankie Frisch
- Lonny Frey
- Bobby Avila
- Pete Runnels
- Frank Bolling
- Billy Moran
- Glenn Beckert
- Bobby Grich
- Manny Trillo
- Steve Sax
- 1 24 players tied

THIRD BASE

- 11 Brooks Robinson
- Wade Boggs
- 9 George Brett
- 7 Eddie Mathews
- Mike Schmidt
- 6 George Kell
- Ken Boyer
- 5 Ken Keltner
- Frank Malzone
- 4 Stan Hack
- Ron Santo
- 3 Ron Cey
- Graig Nettles
- Cal Ripken
- Chipper Jones
- 2 Pepper Martin
- Jimmie Foxx
- Arky Vaughan
- Red Rolfe
- Cecil Travis
- Bob Elliott
- Al Rosen
- Harmon Killebrew
- Rich Rollins
- Dick Allen

- Joe Torre
- Pete Rose
- Chris Sabo
- Matt Williams
- 1 28 players tied

SHORTSTOP

- 13 Cal Ripken
- 11 Ozzie Smith
- 8 Luis Aparicio
- 7 Joe Cronin
- 6 Ernie Banks
- 5 Marty Marion
- Dave Concepcion
- Barry Larkin
- 4 Arky Vaughan
- Dick Groat
- Don Kessinger
- 3 Lou Boudreau
- Pee Wee Reese
- Chico Carrasquel
- Harvey Kuenn
- Maury Wills
- Bert Campaneris
- Larry Bowa
- 2 Dick Bartell
- Luke Appling
- Leo Durocher
- Vern Stephens
- Phil Rizzuto
- Al Dark
- Roy McMillan
- Ron Hansen
- Jim Fregosi
- Dick McAuliffe
- Rico Petrocelli
- Bucky Dent
- Robin Yount
- Alex Rodriguez
- 1 21 players tied

LEFT FIELD

- 12 Ted Williams
- 8 Joe Medwick
- 7 Barry Bonds
- 5 Stan Musial
- 4 Minnie Minoso
- Rickey Henderson
- 3 Frank Robinson
- Bob Skinner
- Tommy Davis
- Leon Wagner
- Carl Yastrzemski
- Willie Stargell
- Greg Luzinski
- Jim Rice
- Tony Gwynn
- 2 Bob Johnson
- Ralph Kiner
- Wally Moon
- Orlando Cepeda
- Rocky Colavito

Willie Horton
Lou Brock
Pete Rose
Frank Howard
George Foster
Tim Raines
Kevin Mitchell
Kirby Puckett
Albert Belle
Kenny Lofton
1 45 players tied

CENTER FIELD

18 Willie Mays
12 Mickey Mantle
8 Ken Griffey
6 Joe DiMaggio
Fred Lynn
5 Andre Dawson
3 Wally Berger
Al Simmons
Earl Averill
Stan Musial
Dom DiMaggio
Carl Yastrzemski
Bobby Murcer
George Foster
Dale Murphy
Rickey Henderson
2 Mel Ott
Pete Reiser
Harry Walker
Richie Ashburn
Duke Snider
Gus Bell
Al Kaline
Roger Maris
Jim Wynn
Dave Winfield
Kirby Puckett
Lenny Dykstra
Tony Gwynn
Kenny Lofton
1 29 players tied

RIGHT FIELD

14 Hank Aaron
9 Reggie Jackson

7 Roberto Clemente
5 Al Kaline
Dave Winfield
Darryl Strawberry
4 Roger Maris
Dave Parker
Tony Gwynn
3 Joe DiMaggio
Enos Slaughter
Dixie Walker
Hank Bauer
Rocky Colavito
Frank Robinson
2 Babe Ruth
Mel Ott
Ival Goodman
Charlie Keller
Bill Nicholson
Stan Musial
Tony Oliva
Dale Murphy
Andre Dawson
Joe Carter
Dave Justice
Kirby Puckett
Larry Walker
1 41 players tied

OUTFIELD
(ALL POSITIONS)

18 Willie Mays
16 Hank Aaron
13 Mickey Mantle
12 Ted Williams
10 Stan Musial
Reggie Jackson
9 Joe DiMaggio
Tony Gwynn
8 Joe Medwick
Dave Winfield
Ken Griffey
7 Al Kaline
Roberto Clemente
Rickey Henderson
Andre Dawson
Barry Bonds
6 Frank Robinson
Roger Maris

Carl Yastrzemski
Fred Lynn
Kirby Puckett
5 Enos Slaughter
Rocky Colavito
George Foster
Dale Murphy
Darryl Strawberry
4 7 players tied

TOTAL GAMES
STARTED
(ANY POSITION)

18 Willie Mays
17 Hank Aaron
16 Cal Ripken
15 Rod Carew
14 Stan Musial
13 Mickey Mantle
12 Ted Williams
11 Yogi Berra
Brooks Robinson
Ozzie Smith
Wade Boggs
10 Johnny Bench
Reggie Jackson
Tony Gwynn
9 Joe DiMaggio
Steve Garvey
George Brett
Ryne Sandberg
8 Joe Medwick
Johnny Mize
Nellie Fox
Del Crandall
Luis Aparicio
Pete Rose
Dave Winfield
Ken Griffey
Roberto Alomar
7 15 players tied

GAME BATTING LEADERS

AT BATS

7	Willie Jones	PHI NL	1950	(14 inn)
6	Carl Yastrzemski	BOS AL	1970	(12 inn)
	Luis Aparicio	CHA AL	1970	(12 inn)
	Tony Conigliaro	BOS AL	1967	(15 inn)
	Harmon Killebrew	MIN AL	1967	(15 inn)
	Tony Oliva	MIN AL	1967	(15 inn)
	Brooks Robinson	BAL AL	1967	(15 inn)
	Orlando Cepeda	SLN NL	1967	(15 inn)
	Hank Aaron	ATL NL	1967	(15 inn)
	Roberto Clemente	PIT NL	1967	(15 inn)
	Red Schoendienst	SLN NL	1955	(12 inn)
	Yogi Berra	NYA AL	1955	(12 inn)
	Mickey Mantle	NYA AL	1955	(12 inn)
	George Kell	DET AL	1950	(14 inn)
	Larry Doby	CLE AL	1950	(14 inn)
	Phil Rizzuto	NYA AL	1950	(14 inn)
	Roy Campanella	BRO NL	1950	(14 inn)
	Ralph Kiner	PIT NL	1950	(14 inn)
5	49 players tied			

RUNS

4	Ted Williams	BOS AL	1946
3	Jackie Robinson	BRO NL	1949
	Joe DiMaggio	NYA AL	1941
	Frankie Frisch	SLN NL	1934
	Al Simmons	CHA AL	1934
2	51 players tied		

HITS

4	Carl Yastrzemski	BOS AL	1970	(12 inn)
	Ted Williams	BOS AL	1946	
	Joe Medwick	SLN NL	1937	
3	Chipper Jones	ATL NL	2000	
	Derek Jeter	NYA AL	2000	
	Devon White	ARI NL	1998	
	Ivan Rodriguez	TEX AL	1998	
	Roberto Alomar	BAL AL	1998	
	Lance Johnson	NYN NL	1996	
	Carlos Baerga	CLE AL	1995	
	Ken Griffey	SEA AL	1992	
	Tim Raines	MON NL	1987	(13 inn)
	Dave Winfield	NYA AL	1983	
	Rickey Henderson	OAK AL	1982	
	Carl Yastrzemski	BOS AL	1967	(15 inn)
	Brooks Robinson	BAL AL	1966	(10 inn)
	Harmon Killebrew	MIN AL	1964	
	Leon Wagner	LAA AL	1962–2	
	Roberto Clemente	PIT NL	1962–1	
	Willie Mays	SFN NL	1960–2	
	Willie Mays	SFN NL	1960–1	
	Frank Robinson	CIN NL	1959–2	
	Ken Boyer	SLN NL	1956	
	Al Rosen	CLE AL	1954	
	Bobby Avila	CLE AL	1954	
	Duke Snider	BRO NL	1954	
	Stan Musial	SLN NL	1949	

	Vince DiMaggio	PIT NL	1943
	Stan Hack	CHN NL	1943
	Arky Vaughan	PIT NL	1941
	Billy Herman	CHN NL	1940
	Charlie Gehringer	DET AL	1937
	Al Simmons	CHA AL	1934
2	186 players tied		

SINGLES

3	Ivan Rodriguez	TEX AL	1998	
	Rickey Henderson	OAK AL	1982	
	Carl Yastrzemski	BOS AL	1970	(12 inn)
	Harmon Killebrew	MIN AL	1964	
	Ken Boyer	SLN NL	1956	
	Bobby Avila	CLE AL	1954	
	Stan Hack	CHN NL	1943	
	Billy Herman	CHN NL	1940	
	Charlie Gehringer	DET AL	1937	
2	109 players tied			

DOUBLES

2	Barry Bonds	SFN NL	1993
	Ernie Banks	CHN NL	1959–1
	Ted Kluszewski	CIN NL	1956
	Joe Medwick	SLN NL	1937
	Al Simmons	CHA AL	1934
1	171 players tied		

TRIPLES

2	Rod Carew	MIN AL	1978
1	34 players tied		

HOMERS

2	Gary Carter	MON NL	1981
	Willie McCovey	SFN NL	1969
	Al Rosen	CLE AL	1954
	Ted Williams	BOS AL	1946
	Arky Vaughan	PIT NL	1941
1	141 players tied		

TOTAL BASES

10	Ted Williams	BOS AL	1946
9	Al Rosen	CLE AL	1954
	Arky Vaughan	PIT NL	1941
8	Gary Carter	MON NL	1981
	Willie McCovey	SFN NL	1969
	Vince DiMaggio	PIT NL	1943
7	Ken Griffey	SEA AL	1992
6	Chipper Jones	ATL NL	2000
	Roberto Alomar	BAL AL	1998
	Mike Piazza	LAN NL	1996
	Kirby Puckett	MIN AL	1993
	Mike Schmidt	PHI NL	1981
	Rod Carew	MIN AL	1978
	Bobby Bonds	SFN NL	1973
	Leon Wagner	LAA AL	1962–2
	Willie Mays	SFN NL	1960–2

TOTAL BASES *CONTINUED*

	Player	Team	Year	
	Ernie Banks	CHN NL	1960–1	
	Willie Mays	SFN NL	1960–1	
	Frank Robinson	CIN NL	1959–2	
	Ralph Kiner	PIT NL	1950	(14 inn)
	Stan Musial	SLN NL	1949	
	Ted Williams	BOS AL	1941	
	Lou Gehrig	NYA AL	1937	
	Joe Medwick	SLN NL	1937	
5	37 players tied			

RUNS BATTED IN

	Player	Team	Year	
5	Al Rosen	CLE AL	1954	
	Ted Williams	BOS AL	1946	
4	Fred Lynn	CAL AL	1983	
	Rocky Colavito	DET AL	1962–2	
	Ted Williams	BOS AL	1941	
	Arky Vaughan	PIT NL	1941	
	Lou Gehrig	NYA AL	1937	
3	Barry Bonds	SFN NL	1998	
	Will Clark	SFN NL	1992	
	Cal Ripken	BAL AL	1991	
	George Foster	CIN NL	1976	
	Carl Yastrzemski	BOS AL	1975	
	Willie McCovey	SFN NL	1969	
	Johnny Callison	PHI NL	1964	
	Mickey Mantle	NYA AL	1955	(12 inn)
	Ted Kluszewski	CIN NL	1954	
	Joe DiMaggio	NYA AL	1949	
	Bobby Doerr	BOS AL	1943	
	Max West	BSN NL	1940	
	Jimmie Foxx	PHA AL	1935	
	Joe Medwick	SLN NL	1934	
	Earl Averill	CLE AL	1934	
2	96 players tied			

SACRIFICE BUNTS

	Player	Team	Year	
1	Tom Glavine	ATL NL	1998	
	Ozzie Guillen	CHA AL	1991	
	Harold Reynolds	SEA AL	1987	(13 inn)
	Tony Fernandez	TOR AL	1987	(13 inn)
	Matt Nokes	DET AL	1987	(13 inn)
	Dave Stieb	TOR AL	1983	
	Bruce Bochte	SEA AL	1979	
	Don Sutton	LAN NL	1977	
	Gaylord Perry	CLE AL	1974	
	Claude Osteen	LAN NL	1973	
	Chris Speier	SFN NL	1972	(10 inn)
	Jim Palmer	BAL AL	1972	(10 inn)
	Sam McDowell	CLE AL	1970	(12 inn)
	Jim Fregosi	CAL AL	1967	(15 inn)
	Bill Freehan	DET AL	1967	(15 inn)
	Bill Mazeroski	PIT NL	1967	(15 inn)
	Ron Hunt	NYN NL	1966	(10 inn)
	Pete Rose	CIN NL	1965	
	Jim Bunning	DET AL	1963	
	Bill Henry	CIN NL	1960–2	
	Dick Groat	PIT NL	1959–1	
	Billy O'Dell	BAL AL	1958	
	Nellie Fox	CHA AL	1957	
	Bob Friend	PIT NL	1956	
	Billy Pierce	CHA AL	1955	(12 inn)

	Player	Team	Year	
	Bobby Avila	CLE AL	1955	(12 inn)
	George Kell	DET AL	1951	
	Joe Coleman	PHA AL	1948	
	Joe Medwick	NY NL	1944	
	Marty Marion	SLN NL	1944	
	Stan Musial	SLN NL	1944	
	Jake Early	WAS AL	1943	
	Vern Stephens	SLA AL	1943	
	Al Lopez	PIT NL	1941	
	Stan Hack	CHN NL	1941	
	Larry French	CHN NL	1940	
	Frank McCormick	CIN NL	1940	
	Leo Durocher	BRO NL	1938	
	Rick Ferrell	BOS AL	1933	

SACRIFICE FLIES

	Player	Team	Year	
1	Magglio Ordonez	CHA AL	2000	
	Manny Ramirez	CLE AL	1998	
	Juan Gonzalez	TEX AL	1998	
	Barry Bonds	SFN NL	1994	(10 inn)
	Barry Larkin	CIN NL	1993	
	Harold Baines	OAK AL	1991	
	Terry Steinbach	OAK AL	1988	
	George Brett	KCA AL	1985	
	Lou Whitaker	DET AL	1983	
	George Brett	KCA AL	1983	
	Robin Yount	MIL AL	1983	
	Pete Rose	PHI NL	1982	
	Reggie Jackson	CAL AL	1982	
	Buddy Bell	TEX AL	1981	
	Dave Parker	PIT NL	1979	
	Carlton Fisk	BOS AL	1978	
	George Brett	KCA AL	1978	
	Pete Rose	CIN NL	1975	
	Joe Morgan	CIN NL	1974	
	Roberto Clemente	PIT NL	1970	(12 inn)
	Ray Fosse	CLE AL	1970	(12 inn)
	Jim Fregosi	LAA AL	1964	
	Rocky Colavito	DET AL	1962–2	
	Roger Maris	NYA AL	1962–1	
	Felipe Alou	SFN NL	1962–1	
	Bill White	SLN NL	1961–1	(10 inn)
	Roberto Clemente	PIT NL	1961–1	(10 inn)
	Hank Aaron	MIL NL	1959–2	
	Hank Aaron	MIL NL	1958	
	Bobby Avila	CLE AL	1954	

HIT BY PITCHES

	Player	Team	Year	
1	Cal Ripken	BAL AL	1999	
	Craig Biggio	HOU NL	1998	
	Gregg Jefferies	SLN NL	1994	(10 inn)
	Cecil Fielder	DET AL	1993	
	Darryl Strawberry	NYN NL	1985	
	Chet Lemon	CHA AL	1979	
	Ken Singleton	BAL AL	1977	
	Jerry Morales	CHN NL	1977	
	Thurman Munson	NYA AL	1975	
	Larry Bowa	PHI NL	1975	
	Willie Stargell	PIT NL	1971	
	Denis Menke	HOU NL	1970	(12 inn)
	Elston Howard	NYA AL	1964	
	Zoilo Versalles	MIN AL	1963	

HIT BY PITCHES *CONTINUED*

	Player	Team	Year	Note
	Dick Groat	PIT NL	1962–2	
	Brooks Robinson	BAL AL	1962–1	
	Rich Rollins	MIN AL	1962–1	
	Orlando Cepeda	SFN NL	1961–2	(10 inn)
	Frank Robinson	CIN NL	1961–1	(10 inn)
	Bill Mazeroski	PIT NL	1960–1	
	Ernie Banks	CHN NL	1958	
	Al Kaline	DET AL	1955	(12 inn)
	Eddie Mathews	MIL NL	1953	
	Stan Musial	SLN NL	1952	(5 inn)
	Andy Seminick	PHI NL	1949	
	George Case	WAS AL	1943	
	Jimmy Brown	SLN NL	1942	
	Pinky May	PHI NL	1940	
	Ival Goodman	CIN NL	1938	

WALKS

	Player	Team	Year	Note
3	Phil Cavarretta	CHN NL	1944	
	Charlie Gehringer	DET AL	1934	
2	Jim Thome	CLE AL	1998	
	Manny Ramirez	CLE AL	1995	
	Don Mattingly	NYA AL	1987	(13 inn)
	Jose Cruz	HOU NL	1985	
	Ozzie Smith	SDN NL	1981	
	George Foster	CIN NL	1978	
	Mike Schmidt	PHI NL	1974	
	Jeff Burroughs	TEX AL	1974	
	Ron Santo	CHN NL	1973	
	Rod Carew	MIN AL	1971	
	Ron Santo	CHN NL	1968	
	Curt Flood	SLN NL	1968	
	Carl Yastrzemski	BOS AL	1967	(15 inn)
	Harmon Killebrew	MIN AL	1965	
	Willie Mays	SFN NL	1965	
	Mickey Mantle	NYA AL	1960–1	
	Wally Moon	LAN NL	1959–2	
	Mickey Mantle	NYA AL	1958	
	Willard Marshall	NY NL	1949	
	Ted Williams	BOS AL	1949	
	Birdie Tebbetts	BOS AL	1948	
	George Selkirk	NYA AL	1939	
	Ripper Collins	SLN NL	1936	
	Lou Gehrig	NYA AL	1936	
	Charlie Gehringer	DET AL	1936	
	Bill Dickey	NYA AL	1934	
	Babe Ruth	NYA AL	1934	
	Lou Gehrig	NYA AL	1933	
	Charlie Gehringer	DET AL	1933	
1	339 players tied			

INTENTIONAL WALKS

	Player	Team	Year
1	Rafael Palmeiro	TEX AL	1991
	Ken Griffey	SEA AL	1990

	Player	Team	Year	Note
	Wade Boggs	BOS AL	1990	
	Tim Wallach	MON NL	1985	
	Robin Yount	MIL AL	1983	
	Rod Carew	CAL AL	1983	
	Reggie Jackson	NYA AL	1979	
	Roy Smalley	MIN AL	1979	
	Dave Parker	PIT NL	1979	
	George Foster	CIN NL	1978	
	Willie Horton	DET AL	1970	(12 inn)
	Willie McCovey	SFN NL	1966	(10 inn)
	Johnny Edwards	CIN NL	1964	
	Bob Cerv	KC AL	1958	
	Granny Hamner	PHI NL	1952	(5 inn)
	Stan Musial	SLN NL	1950	(14 inn)
	Roy Campanella	BRO NL	1949	
	Stan Spence	WAS AL	1946	
	George Selkirk	NYA AL	1939	
	Ival Goodman	CIN NL	1939	
	Charlie Gehringer	DET AL	1934	

STRIKEOUTS

	Player	Team	Year	Note
4	Roberto Clemente	PIT NL	1967	(15 inn)
3	Craig Biggio	HOU NL	1998	
	Albert Belle	CLE AL	1996	
	Kirby Puckett	MIN AL	1987	(13 inn)
	Johnny Bench	CIN NL	1970	(12 inn)
	Willie McCovey	SFN NL	1968	
	Tony Oliva	MIN AL	1967	(15 inn)
	Gene Alley	PIT NL	1967	(15 inn)
	Dick Allen	PHI NL	1967	(15 inn)
	John Roseboro	LAN NL	1961–2	(10 inn)
	Mickey Mantle	NYA AL	1956	
	Jim Hegan	CLE AL	1950	(14 inn)
	Ken Keltner	CLE AL	1943	
	Joe Gordon	NYA AL	1942	
	Stan Hack	CHN NL	1939	
	Bob Johnson	PHA AL	1935	
	Lou Gehrig	NYA AL	1934	
2	118 players tied			

STEALS

	Player	Team	Year
2	Kenny Lofton	CLE AL	1996
	Roberto Alomar	TOR AL	1992
	Kelly Gruber	TOR AL	1990
	Willie Mays	SFN NL	1963
1	86 players tied		

CAUGHT STEALING

	Player	Team	Year	Note
2	Tony Oliva	MIN AL	1967	(15 inn)
1	31 players tied			

GROUND INTO DP

	Player	Team	Year
2	Bobby Richardson	NYA AL	1963
1	89 players tied		

HITS ALLOWED

	Player	Team	Year	
9	Tom Glavine	ATL NL	1992	(1.2 inn)
7	Tommy Bridges	DET AL	1937	(3 inn)
6	Atlee Hammaker	SFN NL	1983	(0.2 inn)
	Claude Passeau	CHN NL	1941	(2.2 inn)
	Lon Warneke	CHN NL	1933	(4 inn)
5	Tom Glavine	ATL NL	1998	(1.1 inn)
	Jack Morris	DET AL	1985	(2.2 inn)
	Rick Honeycutt	TEX AL	1983	(2 inn)
	Burt Hooton	LAN NL	1981	(1.2 inn)
	Bob Welch	LAN NL	1980	(3 inn)
	Nolan Ryan	CAL AL	1979	(2 inn)
	Vida Blue	SFN NL	1978	(3 inn)
	Jim Palmer	BAL AL	1977	(2 inn)
	Vida Blue	OAK AL	1975	(2 inn)
	Johnny Odom	OAK AL	1969	(0.1 inn)
	Jim Maloney	CIN NL	1965	(1.2 inn)
	Don Schwall	BOS AL	1961–2	(3 inn)
	Whitey Ford	NYA AL	1960–2	(3 inn)
	Bill Monbouquette	BOS AL	1960–1	(2 inn)
	Warren Spahn	MIL NL	1958	(3 inn)
	Whitey Ford	NYA AL	1955	(1.2 inn)
	Sandy Consuegra	CHA AL	1954	(0.1 inn)
	Robin Roberts	PHI NL	1954	(3 inn)
	Lou Brissie	PHA AL	1949	(3 inn)
	Walt Masterson	WAS AL	1948	(3 inn)
	Harry Brecheen	SLN NL	1947	(3 inn)
	Kirby Higbe	BRO NL	1946	(1.1 inn)
	Bucky Walters	CIN NL	1944	(3 inn)
	Tex Hughson	BOS AL	1944	(1.2 inn)
	Tex Hughson	BOS AL	1943	(3 inn)
	Red Ruffing	NYA AL	1940	(3 inn)
	Mace Brown	PIT NL	1938	(3 inn)
	Mel Harder	CLE AL	1937	(3 inn)
	Dizzy Dean	SLN NL	1934	(3 inn)
4	56 players tied			
	Tex Hughson	BOS AL	1944	(1.2 inn)
	Mort Cooper	SLN NL	1943	(2.1 inn)
	Van Mungo	BRO NL	1934	(1 inn)
	Lon Warneke	CHN NL	1934	(1 inn)
	Lefty Gomez	NYA AL	1934	(3 inn)
3	55 players tied			

RUNS ALLOWED

	Player	Team	Year	
7	Atlee Hammaker	SFN NL	1983	(0.2 inn)
5	Tom Glavine	ATL NL	1992	(1.2 inn)
	Jim Palmer	BAL AL	1977	(2 inn)
	Johnny Odom	OAK AL	1969	(0.1 inn)
	Jim Maloney	CIN NL	1965	(1.2 inn)
	Whitey Ford	NYA AL	1955	(1.2 inn)
	Sandy Consuegra	CHA AL	1954	(0.1 inn)
	Claude Passeau	CHN NL	1941	(2.2 inn)
4	Tom Glavine	ATL NL	1998	(1.1 inn)
	Bob Tewksbury	SLN NL	1992	(1.2 inn)
	Rich Gossage	NYA AL	1978	(1 inn)
	Dock Ellis	PIT NL	1971	(3 inn)
	Dick Radatz	BOS AL	1964	(2.2 inn)
	Bill Monbouquette	BOS AL	1960–1	(2 inn)
	Robin Roberts	PHI NL	1955	(3 inn)
	Robin Roberts	PHI NL	1954	(3 inn)
	Warren Spahn	BSN NL	1949	(1.1 inn)
	Rip Sewell	PIT NL	1946	(1 inn)
	Kirby Higbe	BRO NL	1946	(1.1 inn)

EARNED RUNS

	Player	Team	Year	
7	Atlee Hammaker	SFN NL	1983	(0.2 inn)
5	Tom Glavine	ATL NL	1992	(1.2 inn)
	Jim Palmer	BAL AL	1977	(2 inn)
	Jim Maloney	CIN NL	1965	(1.2 inn)
	Sandy Consuegra	CHA AL	1954	(0.1 inn)
	Claude Passeau	CHN NL	1941	(2.2 inn)
4	Tom Glavine	ATL NL	1998	(1.1 inn)
	Bob Tewksbury	SLN NL	1992	(1.2 inn)
	Rich Gossage	NYA AL	1978	(1 inn)
	Dock Ellis	PIT NL	1971	(3 inn)
	Johnny Odom	OAK AL	1969	(0.1 inn)
	Dick Radatz	BOS AL	1964	(2.2 inn)
	Bill Monbouquette	BOS AL	1960–1	(2 inn)
	Robin Roberts	PHI NL	1955	(3 inn)
	Whitey Ford	NYA AL	1955	(1.2 inn)
	Robin Roberts	PHI NL	1954	(3 inn)
	Rip Sewell	PIT NL	1946	(1 inn)
	Kirby Higbe	BRO NL	1946	(1.1 inn)
	Mort Cooper	SLN NL	1943	(2.1 inn)
	Van Mungo	BRO NL	1934	(1 inn)
	Lon Warneke	CHN NL	1934	(1 inn)
	Lefty Gomez	NYA AL	1934	(3 inn)
3	48 players tied			

WALKS

	Player	Team	Year	
5	Bill Hallahan	SLN NL	1933	(2 inn)
4	Jim Palmer	BAL AL	1978	(2.2 inn)
3	Kevin Brown	LAN NL	2000	(1 inn)
	Tom Glavine	ATL NL	1998	(1.1 inn)
	Dan Petry	DET AL	1985	(0.1 inn)
	Jim Kern	TEX AL	1979	(2.2 inn)
	Andy Messersmith	LAN NL	1974	(3 inn)
	Sam McDowell	CLE AL	1970	(3 inn)
	Johnny Podres	LAN NL	1960–2	(2 inn)
	Mike McCormick	SFN NL	1960–1	(2.1 inn)
	Don Drysdale	LAN NL	1959–2	(3 inn)
	Early Wynn	CHA AL	1959–2	(2 inn)
	Joe Nuxhall	CIN NL	1955	(3.1 inn)
	Vic Raschi	NYA AL	1949	(3 inn)
	Ewell Blackwell	CIN NL	1948	(3 inn)
	Ralph Branca	BRO NL	1948	(3 inn)
	Bill Lee	CHN NL	1939	(3 inn)
	Lon Warneke	CHN NL	1936	(2.1 inn)
	Lon Warneke	CHN NL	1934	(1 inn)
2	62 players tied			

STRIKEOUTS

	Player	Team	Year	
6	Ferguson Jenkins	CHN NL	1967	(3 inn)
	Larry Jansen	NY NL	1950	(5 inn)

STRIKEOUTS *CONTINUED*

	Player	Team	Year	
	Johnny Vander Meer	CIN NL	1943	(2.2 inn)
	Carl Hubbell	NY NL	1934	(3 inn)
5	Pedro Martinez	BOS AL	1999	(2 inn)
	Fernando Valenzuela	LAN NL	1986	(3 inn)
	Tom Seaver	NYN NL	1968	(2 inn)
	Dick Radatz	BOS AL	1964	(2.2 inn)
	Dick Radatz	BOS AL	1963	(2 inn)
	Stu Miller	SFN NL	1961–2	(3 inn)
	Don Drysdale	LAN NL	1959–2	(3 inn)
	Billy Pierce	CHA AL	1956	(3 inn)
	Joe Nuxhall	CIN NL	1955	(3.1 inn)
	Robin Roberts	PHI NL	1954	(3 inn)
	Hal Schumacher	NY NL	1935	(4 inn)
4	Chuck Finley	CAL AL	1996	(2 inn)
	Lee Smith	CHN NL	1987	(3 inn)
	Dave Stieb	TOR AL	1983	(3 inn)
	Mario Soto	CIN NL	1982	(2 inn)
	Steve Carlton	PHI NL	1982	(2 inn)
	Bob Welch	LAN NL	1980	(3 inn)
	Jim Palmer	BAL AL	1978	(2.2 inn)
	Don Sutton	LAN NL	1977	(3 inn)
	Jon Matlack	NYN NL	1975	(2 inn)
	Andy Messersmith	LAN NL	1974	(3 inn)
	Gaylord Perry	CLE AL	1974	(3 inn)
	Tug McGraw	NYN NL	1972	(2 inn)
	Tom Seaver	NYN NL	1970	(3 inn)
	Sam McDowell	CLE AL	1969	(2 inn)
	Catfish Hunter	KC AL	1967	(5 inn)
	Gary Peters	CHA AL	1967	(3 inn)
	Jim Bunning	PHI NL	1964	(2 inn)
	Camilo Pascual	MIN AL	1961–2	(3 inn)
	Stu Miller	SFN NL	1961–1	(1.2 inn)
	Don Drysdale	LAN NL	1959–1	(3 inn)
	Ryne Duren	NYA AL	1959–1	(3 inn)
	Turk Farrell	PHI NL	1958	(2 inn)
	Frank Sullivan	BOS AL	1955	(3.1 inn)
	Ewell Blackwell	CIN NL	1947	(3 inn)
	Hal Newhouser	DET AL	1946	(3 inn)
	Johnny Vander Meer	CIN NL	1942	(3 inn)
	Bob Feller	CLE AL	1941	(3 inn)
	Red Ruffing	NYA AL	1939	(3 inn)
	Bill Lee	CHN NL	1939	(3 inn)
	Lefty Gomez	NYA AL	1935	(6 inn)
	Dizzy Dean	SLN NL	1934	(3 inn)
3	69 players tied			

INNINGS PITCHED

	Player	Team	Year
6	Lefty Gomez	NYA AL	1935
5	Catfish Hunter	KC AL	1967
	Larry Jansen	NY NL	1950
	Al Benton	DET AL	1942
	Mel Harder	CLE AL	1934
4	Lew Burdette	MIL NL	1957
	Johnny Antonelli	NY NL	1956
	Spud Chandler	NYA AL	1942
	Hal Schumacher	NY NL	1935
	Lon Warneke	CHN NL	1933
3.2	Bob Feller	CLE AL	1939
3.1	Ray Narleski	CLE AL	1958
	Joe Nuxhall	CIN NL	1955
	Frank Sullivan	BOS AL	1955
3	138 players tied		

TEAM PITCHING TOTALS

American League Teams

STARTS

ANA (0) None
BAL (7) Jerry Walker (1959–2)
Milt Pappas (1965)
Jim Palmer (1970, 1972, 1977, 1978)
Steve Stone (1980)
BOS (6) Lefty Grove (1936)
Mel Parnell (1949)
Bill Monbouquette (1960–1)
Dennis Eckersley (1982)
Roger Clemens (1986)
Pedro Martinez (1999)
CAL (2) Nolan Ryan (1979)
Mark Langston (1993)
CHA (4) Billy Pierce (1953, 1955, 1956)
Early Wynn (1959–1)
CLE (5) Bob Feller (1941, 1946)
Luis Tiant (1968)
Gaylord Perry (1974)
Charles Nagy (1996)
DET (8) Hal Newhouser (1947)
Jim Bunning (1957, 1961–2, 1962–1)
Denny McLain (1966)
Mark Fidrych (1976)
Jack Morris (1981, 1985)
KC (0) None
KCA (1) Bret Saberhagen (1987)
LAA (2) Ken McBride (1963)
Dean Chance (1964)
MIL (0) None
MIN (3) Dean Chance (1967)
Frank Viola (1988)
Jack Morris (1991)
NYA (18) Lefty Gomez (1933, 1934, 1935, 1937, 1938)
Red Ruffing (1939, 1940)
Spud Chandler (1942)
Hank Borowy (1944)
Vic Raschi (1950, 1952)
Whitey Ford (1954, 1960–2, 1961–1)
Bob Turley (1958)
Mel Stottlemyre (1969)
Jimmy Key (1994)
David Wells (1998)
OAK (5) Vida Blue (1971, 1975)
Catfish Hunter (1973)
Dave Stewart (1989)
Bob Welch (1990)
PHA (0) None
SEA (0) None
SEA (2) Randy Johnson (1995, 1997)
SLA (1) Ned Garver (1951)
TBA (0) None
TEX (1) Kevin Brown (1992)
TOR (3) Dave Stieb (1983, 1984)
David Wells (2000)

WAS (2) Dutch Leonard (1943)
Walt Masterson (1948)
WAS (1) Dave Stenhouse (1962–2)

WINS

ANA (0) None
BAL (1) Jerry Walker (1959–2)
BOS (2) Roger Clemens (1986)
Pedro Martinez (1999)
CAL (0) None
CHA (5) Edgar Smith (1941)
Early Wynn (1958)
Ray Herbert (1962–2)
Jack McDowell (1993)
James Baldwin (2000)
CLE (3) Mel Harder (1934)
Bob Feller (1946)
Bartolo Colon (1988)
DET (3) Tommy Bridges (1939)
Virgil Trucks (1949)
Jim Bunning (1957)
KC (0) None
KCA (2) Bret Saberhagen (1990)
Jose Rosado (1997)
LAA (0) None
MIL (0) None
MIN (1) Frank Viola (1988)
NYA (6) Lefty Gomez (1933 1935 1937)
Spud Chandler (1942)
Frank Shea (1947)
Vic Raschi (1948)
OAK (1) Vida Blue (1971)
PHA (0) None
SEA (0) None
SEA (0) None
SLA (0) None
TBA (0) None
TEX (2) Nolan Ryan (1989)
Kevin Brown (1992)
TOR (2) Dave Stieb (1983)
Jimmy Key (1991)
WAS (2) Dutch Leonard (1943)
Dean Stone (1954)
WAS (0) None

LOSSES

ANA (0) None
BAL (3) Hoyt Wilhelm (1961–1)
Dave McNally (1972)
Jim Palmer (1977)
BOS (7) Lefty Grove (1936)
Tex Hughson (1944)
Frank Sullivan (1955)
Bill Monbouquette (1960–1)
Dick Radatz (1964)
Luis Tiant (1974)
Dennis Eckersley (1982)

LOSSES *CONTINUED*

CAL (1)	Clyde Wright (1970)
CHA (2)	Billy Pierce (1956)
	Jason Bere (1994)
CLE (4)	Bob Lemon (1952)
	Sam McDowell (1965)
	Luis Tiant (1968)
	Charles Nagy (1996)
DET (4)	Ted Gray (1950)
	Jim Bunning (1963)
	Mark Fidrych (1976)
	Jack Morris (1985)
KC (1)	Catfish Hunter (1967)
KCA (0)	None
LAA (0)	None
MIL (1)	Rollie Fingers (1981)
MIN (2)	Camilo Pascual (1962–1)
	Bert Blyleven (1973)
NYA (10)	Lefty Gomez (1938)
	Red Ruffing (1940)
	Ed Lopat (1951)
	Allie Reynolds (1953)
	Whitey Ford (1959–1, 1960–2)
	Mel Stottlemyre (1969)
	Catfish Hunter (1975)
	Goose Gossage (1978)
	Tommy John (1980)
OAK (2)	Jay Howell (1987)
	Steve Ontiveros (1995)
PHA (0)	None
SEA (0)	None
SEA (0)	None
SLA (0)	None
TBA (0)	None
TEX (1)	Jim Kern (1979)
TOR (1)	Dave Stieb (1984)
WAS (0)	None
WAS (1)	Pete Richert (1966)

TEAM RECORDS

ANA	0–0	NYA	6–10
BAL	1–3	OAK	1–2
BOS	2–7	PHA	0–0
CAL	0–1	SEA	0–0
CHA	5–2	SEA	0–0
CLE	3–4	SLA	0–0
DET	3–4	TBA	0–0
KC	0–1	TEX	2–1
KCA	2–0	TOR	2–1
LAA	0–0	WAS	2–0
MIL	0–1	WAS	0–1
MIN	1–2		

National League Teams

STARTS

ARI (1)	Randy Johnson (2000)
ATL (6)	Tom Glavine (1991, 1992)
	Greg Maddux (1994, 1997, 1998)
	John Smoltz (1996)
BRO (2)	Whit Wyatt (1941)
	Ralph Branca (1948)
BSN (1)	Warren Spahn (1949)
CHN (1)	Claude Passeau (1946),
CIN (9)	Johnny Vander Meer (1938)
	Paul Derringer (1939, 1940)
	Bucky Walters (1944)
	Ewell Blackwell (1947)
	Bob Purkey (1961–2)
	Jim O'Toole (1963)
	Mario Soto (1983)
	Jack Armstrong (1990)
COL (0)	None
FLO (0)	None
HOU (2)	J.R. Richard (1980)
	Mike Scott (1987)
LAN (11)	Don Drysdale (1959–1, 1959–2, 1962–1, 1964, 1968)
	Johnny Podres (1962–2)
	Sandy Koufax (1966)
	Andy Messersmith (1974)
	Don Sutton (1977)
	Fernando Valenzuela (1981)
	Hideo Nomo (1995)
MIL (0)	None
MLN (2)	Warren Spahn (1958, 1961–1)
MON (2)	Steve Rogers (1982)
	Charlie Lea (1984)
NY (1)	Carl Hubbell (1934)
NYN (3)	Tom Seaver (1970)
	Dwight Gooden (1986, 1988)
PHI (10)	Robin Roberts (1950, 1951, 1953, 1954, 1955)
	Curt Simmons (1952, 1957)
	Steve Carlton (1979)
	Terry Mulholland (1993)
	Curt Schilling (1999)
PIT (5)	Bob Friend (1956, 1960–1)
	Vern Law (1960–2)
	Dock Ellis (1971)
	Jerry Reuss (1975)
SDN (2)	Randy Jones (1976)
	LaMarr Hoyt (1985)
SFN (4)	Juan Marichal (1965, 1967)
	Vida Blue (1978)
	Rick Reuschel (1989)
SLN (9)	Bill Hallahan (1933)
	Bill Walker (1935)
	Dizzy Dean (1936, 1937)
	Mort Cooper (1942, 1943)
	Steve Carlton (1969)
	Bob Gibson (1972)
	Rick Wise (1973)

WINS

ARI (0)	None	
ATL (1)	John Smoltz (1996)	
BRO (0)	None	
BSN (0)	None	
CHN (5)	Bob Rush (1952)	
	Larry Jackson (1963)	
	Bruce Sutter (1978, 1979)	
	Lee Smith (1987)	
CIN (3)	Johnny Vander Meer (1938)	
	Paul Derringer (1940)	
	Ewell Blackwell (1950)	
COL (0)	None	
FLO (0)	None	
HOU (0)	None	
LAN (6)	Sandy Koufax (1965)	
	Don Drysdale (1967, 1968)	
	Claude Osteen (1970)	
	Don Sutton (1977)	
	Jerry Reuss (1980)	
MIL (0)	None	
MLN (2)	Warren Spahn (1953)	
	Gene Conley (1955)	
MON (2)	Steve Rogers (1982)	
	Charlie Lea (1984)	
NY (1)	Sal Maglie (1951)	
NYN (2)	Tug McGraw (1972)	
	Jon Matlack (1975)	
PHI (3)	Ken Raffensberger (1944)	
	Doug Jones (1994)	
	Heathcliff Slocumb (1995)	
PIT (4)	Bob Friend (1956, 1960–1)	
	Vern Law (1960–2)	
	Ken Brett (1974)	
SDN (2)	Randy Jones (1976)	
	LaMarr Hoyt (1985)	
SFN (6)	Johnny Antonelli (1959–1)	
	Stu Miller (1961–1)	
	Juan Marichal (1962–1, 1964)	
	Gaylord Perry (1966)	
	Vida Blue (1981)	
SLN (3)	Dizzy Dean (1936)	
	Steve Carlton (1969)	
	Rick Wise (1973)	

LOSSES

ARI (0)	None
ATL (2)	John Smoltz (1989)
	Tom Glavine (1992)

BRO (2)	Van Mungo (1934)	
	Don Newcombe (1949)	
BSN (1)	Johnny Sain (1947)	
CHN (4)	Bill Lee (1939)	
	Claude Passeau (1941,1946)	
	Johnny Schmitz (1948)	
CIN (1)	Mario Soto (1983)	
COL (0)	None	
FLO (0)	None	
HOU (0)	None	
LAN (1)	Don Drysdale (1959–2),	
MIL (0)	None	
MLN (1)	Gene Conley (1954)	
MON (2)	Dennis Martinez (1991)	
	Ugueth Urbina (1998)	
NY (0)	None	
NYN (3)	Dwight Gooden (1986, 1988)	
	Al Leiter (2000)	
PHI (3)	Curt Simmons (1957)	
	Art Mahaffey (1962–2)	
	Curt Schilling (1999)	
PIT (2)	Bob Friend (1958)	
	Dock Ellis (1971)	
SDN (0)	None	
SFN (3)	Jeff Brantley (1990)	
	John Burkett (1993)	
	Shawn Estes (1997)	
SLN (5)	Bill Hallahan (1933)	
	Bill Walker (1935)	
	Dizzy Dean (1937)	
	Mort Cooper (1942, 1943)	

TEAM RECORDS

ARI	0–0		MIL	0–0
ATL	1–2		MLN	2–1
BRO	0–2		MON	2–2
BSN	0–1		NY	1–0
CHN	5–4		NYN	2–3
CIN	3–1		PHI	3–3
COL	0–0		PIT	4–2
FLO	0–0		SDN	2–0
HOU	0–0		SFN	6–3
LAN	6–1		SLN	3–5

APPENDIX 1
HOME RUN DERBY

The Home Run Derby has grown from an accidental event to one of the highlights of the All-Star break. Thousands of fans pay to attend the player workout on the day preceding the game, primarily to watch the sluggers from each league try to hit the ball the farthest off a batting-practice pitcher.

In 1979 in Seattle, ten thousand fans were allowed into Kingdome at no charge for batting practice the day before the All-Star Game. They were treated to a great show as players hit one blast after another into the seats of the American League's most homer-friendly stadium that season.

By 1985, Major League Baseball had learned the lesson of that day in Seattle. For the first time, an official home run–hitting contest was held on the day before the All-Star Game, and more than forty-six thousand fans paid $2 each to watch batting practice at the Metrodome in Minneapolis. Five players were chosen from each circuit to compete in the interleague contest. The players had two "innings" of five swings each, and the American League won the contest 17–16. Dave Parker of the Reds hit the most home runs, crashing six big flies and setting the individual record, which would not be eclipsed until 1991.

In 1986 at Houston's Astrodome, a "skills competition" featuring a relay throw from outfielder to infielder to catcher was held in addition to the Home Run Derby. In the derby, the National Leaguers hit eight homers to beat their counterparts in the Junior Circuit by one dinger. Darryl Strawberry of the Mets paced the NL, and California's Wally Joyner led the AL, each hitting four homers.

The 1987 contest at Oakland Coliseum was the lowest-scoring derby to date, with the NL taking the honors, 6–2. Andre Dawson of the Cubs led the field with four homers. The match was part of the expanded skills competition, which also featured a catcher's accuracy throw, a relay throw, and hitting for accuracy.

Rain prevented the players from competing in 1988 at Riverfront Stadium in Cincinnati.

At Anaheim Stadium in 1989, the NL beat the AL for the third consecutive time, 9–5, in the Home Run Derby. The AL had not won since the first year. Eric Davis of Cincinnati and Ruben Sierra of Texas led their respective teams, each hitting three home runs.

The 1990 workout day featured only the Home Run Derby. Because the derby was held at Wrigley Field in Chicago, a high-scoring event was anticipated. However, weather conditions kept the players in the park for most of the competition. Hometown hero Ryne Sandberg of the Cubs set the pace with three shots out of the "friendly confines," but five of the eight participants hit no homers. The NL won for the fourth consecutive time, 4–1.

The American Leaguers won the Home Run Derby for only the second time in six tries at SkyDome in 1991, easily defeating their opponents, 20–7. The format of the event changed, with each contestant receiving ten outs instead of five to collect runs for his team. Baltimore's Cal Ripken Jr. hit twelve long balls in twenty-two swings, doubling Dave Parker's record of six, which was set in the first event in 1985. In fact, Ripken's total was more than any team had hit since that first year. Three of Ripken's blasts landed in the third deck or higher in left field.

The scene shifted to San Diego in 1992. Mark McGwire of Oakland hammered a total of twelve long balls to equal Ripken's derby record set the previous year. McGwire hit seven home runs on seven consecutive pitches during one stretch. The Mariners' Ken Griffey Jr. added seven of his own as the AL cruised to an easy victory, 27–13.

The AL won for the third consecutive year at Oriole Park at Camden Yards in 1993. Seattle's Griffey and the Rangers' Juan Gonzalez hit seven homers each during the competition and then faced each other in a playoff. They each hit four in the first playoff, thus forcing a second round, which Gonzalez finally won by hitting one home run to Griffey's none. However, the numbers do not tell the whole story of this exciting event. For the first time ever, a player hit the warehouse that contains the Orioles offices. Griffey blasted one pitch 445 feet over the right-field fence, the patio behind it, and Eutaw Street (a fan walkway) to strike the building on the fly. Gonzalez hit three of the longest blasts of the day, including one that landed in the upper deck in left field, an estimated distance of 473 feet.

In 1994 at Three Rivers Stadium in Pittsburgh, Griffey continued his torrid hitting in the Home Run Derby as he smashed seven big flies to lead the AL to victory, 17–11. It was the fourth consecutive win for the AL after losing four in a row. One dinger by Frank Thomas of the White Sox was estimated to have traveled 519 feet, the longest distance ever recorded in the short time that estimates have been made in the Home Run Derby.

The Home Run Derby format was changed in 1995 from a team competition to a three-round individual one. Eight participants hit in the first round, with the top four advancing to the second round (regardless of league affiliation), and the field was cut in half once more for the third round. Advancement (and winning the event) was based on homers hit in that round, not on a running total. The first round was a ten-out frame, with the players receiving five outs in the other two rounds. Thomas won the event by outhitting Cleveland's Albert Belle in the last round, 3–2, although Belle had a higher overall total, 16–15. Belle's total set a new one-year record, beating the twelve home runs by both Ripken in 1991 and McGwire in 1992.

In 1996 at Veterans Stadium in Philadelphia, the format changed slightly, with ten participants in the first round. The participants were the players with the top five home run totals at the break in each league. Barry Bonds of San Francisco emerged as the champion by hitting three line drive shots to right field in the last round to beat McGwire, who hit two high flies to left in the finals. Bonds also accumulated the top overall total, hitting seventeen home runs, with McGwire second (with fifteen) and Baltimore's Brady Anderson third (with eleven). Bonds set a new record high for one derby, beating Belle's total of sixteen from the previous year.

The competition in Cleveland's Jacobs Field in 1997 featured ten players, including a rookie for the first time. Before the main event, a Rookie Home Run Derby was held, in which Boston's Nomar Garciaparra hit three homers to beat Jose Guillen (Pittsburgh), Scott Rolen (Philadelphia), and Scott Spiezio (Oakland) and advance to the Home Run Derby. In the Derby, Colorado's Larry Walker hit the most homers (nineteen) but lost in the finals to Tino Martinez of the Yankees, whose total of sixteen included three in the last round to Walker's one. Martinez participated only because his manager, Joe Torre, talked him into it. Walker's nineteen homers topped the previous high for one year, seventeen by Bonds in 1996.

The mile-high atmosphere of Denver's Coors Field was the location of the 1998 event. Once again, the fans anticipated an awesome demonstration of power since the baseball world's attention had been focused on the long ball for a couple of years, and Coors Field had developed a reputation for high-octane offense. Added to this were the staggering regular season home run totals of the participants. Mark McGwire, now of the Cardinals, led a pack of four players who had at least thirty homers at the break with his own thirty-seven. The primary attention was on McGwire's chase of Roger Maris's single-season homer record, which McGwire would go on to break in September.

Seattle's Ken Griffey Jr. caused a furor by initially deciding not to participate in the 1998 derby. When he was presented with the trophy for the most fan votes for the All-Star Game, he was booed by the crowd. Hall of Famer Frank Robinson then spoke to Griffey about competing, as did some of his American League teammates. Griffey changed his mind and subsequently won the event with nineteen total homers, beating Jim Thome of the Indians in the finals, 3–2. Thome also hit nineteen total dingers in the Derby, seven into the upper deck in right field. The nineteen homers by the two sluggers tied Walker's record for one derby, set the previous year. McGwire did not make it out of the first round this time, but one of his shots traveled an estimated 510 feet to center field. That ball was only the second to be estimated at over 500 feet in the history of the Home Run Derby, 9 feet shorter than a Frank Thomas poke in 1994.

In 1999, the show moved to Fenway Park in Boston. The star of the night was McGwire in the first round, who hit thirteen blasts in twenty-three swings. Most of them cleared the wall *and* the screen in left field, with one shot traveling over the light tower and across the street into a parking lot, landing an estimated 488 feet away from home plate. Five of McGwire's shots flew more than 470 feet.

Griffey once again was doubtful for the contest until the day of the event. He barely made it into round two, having hit only one homer with one out to go in the first round. He took over after that, however, hitting ten in the second frame and beating Milwaukee's Jeromy Burnitz in the final round, 3–2. Griffey thus won for the second consecutive year and the third time overall. That odd final round featured two left-handed swingers in a park more suited to righties. Griffey and McGwire tied with the most overall at sixteen, and Burnitz ended with fourteen. Griffey passed McGwire for the top career total in the Home Run Derby, with fifty-nine to McGwire's fifty-six.

Turner Field proved to be anything but a "launching pad" (as the Braves former home was called) for the 2000 event. Two of the top home run hitters of the first half, Mark McGwire and Barry Bonds, missed the event due to injuries, and most of the players who participated did not fare well. Carl Everett and Vladimir Guerrero each hit one ball into the upper deck in left field, but the eventual winner, Sammy Sosa, hit eight balls off the face of or into the upper deck. Some of Sosa's shots were to left center field, but the blast that proved Sosa's superiority that night was a shot that carried over the camera area in center field and was estimated at 508 feet. The crowd cheered and chanted "Sammy! Sammy!" as Sosa pounded the ball time after time. The ten longest shots of the contest were all by Sosa, and his total of twenty-six set a new Derby record, easily topping the previous one-year record of nineteen held by multiple players.

Home Run Derby Results

Note – all distances are estimates.

1985—METRODOME, MINNEAPOLIS—AL 17, NL 16

Player	Team	Total HRs
AMERICAN LEAGUE		
Jim Rice	Boston	4
Eddie Murray	Baltimore	4
Carlton Fisk	Chicago	4
Tom Brunansky	Minnesota	4
Cal Ripken Jr.	Baltimore	1
NATIONAL LEAGUE		
Dave Parker	Cincinnati	6
Dale Murphy	Atlanta	4
Steve Garvey	Los Angeles	2
Ryne Sandberg	Chicago	2
Jack Clark	St. Louis	2

1986—ASTRODOME, HOUSTON—NL 8, AL 7

Player	Team	Total HRs
AMERICAN LEAGUE		
Wally Joyner	California	4
Jesse Barfield	Toronto	2
Jose Canseco	Oakland	1
NATIONAL LEAGUE		
Darryl Strawberry	New York	4
Dave Parker	Cincinnati	3
Hubie Brooks	Montreal	1

1987—OAKLAND COLISEUM, OAKLAND—NL 6, AL 2

Player	Team	Total HRs
AMERICAN LEAGUE		
George Bell	Toronto	1
Mark McGwire	Oakland	1
NATIONAL LEAGUE		
Andre Dawson	Chicago	4
Ozzie Virgil	Atlanta	2

1988—RIVERFRONT STADIUM, CINCINNATI—CANCELED DUE TO RAIN

1989—ANAHEIM STADIUM, ANAHEIM—NL 9, AL 5

Player	Team	Total HRs
AMERICAN LEAGUE		
Ruben Sierra	Texas	3
Mickey Tettleton	Detroit	1
Bo Jackson	Kansas City	1
Gary Gaetti	Minnesota	0
national league		
Eric Davis	Cincinnati	3
Glenn Davis	Houston	2
Howard Johnson	New York	2
Kevin Mitchell	San Francisco	2

1990—WRIGLEY FIELD, CHICAGO—NL 4, AL 1

Player	Team	Total HRs
AMERICAN LEAGUE		
Mark McGwire	Oakland	1
Ken Griffey Jr.	Seattle	0
Jose Canseco	Oakland	0
Cecil Fielder	Detroit	0
NATIONAL LEAGUE		
Ryne Sandberg	Chicago	3
Matt Williams	San Francisco	1
Bobby Bonilla	Pittsburgh	0
Darryl Strawberry	New York	0

1991—SKYDOME, TORONTO—AL 20, NL 7

Player	Team	Total HRs
AMERICAN LEAGUE		
Cal Ripken Jr.	Baltimore	12
Cecil Fielder	Detroit	4
Joe Carter	Toronto	2
Danny Tartabull	Kansas City	2
NATIONAL LEAGUE		
Paul O'Neill	Cincinnati	5
George Bell	Chicago	2
Chris Sabo	Cincinnati	0
Howard Johnson	New York	0

1992—JACK MURPHY STADIUM, SAN DIEGO—AL 27, NL 13

Player	Team	Total HRs
AMERICAN LEAGUE		
Mark McGwire	Oakland	12
Ken Griffey Jr.	Seattle	7
Joe Carter	Toronto	4
Cal Ripken Jr.	Baltimore	4
NATIONAL LEAGUE		
Larry Walker	Montreal	4
Gary Sheffield	San Diego	4
Fred McGriff	San Diego	3
Barry Bonds	Pittsburgh	2

1993—ORIOLE PARK AT CAMDEN YARDS, BALTIMORE—AL 21, NL 12

Player	Team	Total HRs
AMERICAN LEAGUE		
Juan Gonzalez	Texas	7
Ken Griffey Jr.	Seattle	7
Cecil Fielder	Detroit	4
Albert Belle	Cleveland	3

1993 CONTINUED

Player	Team	Total HRs
NATIONAL LEAGUE		
Barry Bonds	San Francisco	5
Bobby Bonilla	New York	5
David Justice	Atlanta	2
Mike Piazza	Los Angeles	0

PLAYOFF #1: Griffey Jr.—4, Gonzalez—4
PLAYOFF #2: Gonzalez—1, Griffey Jr.—0

1994—THREE RIVERS STADIUM, PITTSBURGH—
AL 17, NL 11

Player	Team	Total HRs
AMERICAN LEAGUE		
Ken Griffey Jr.	Seattle	7
Ruben Sierra	Oakland	4
Frank Thomas	Chicago	4
Albert Belle	Cleveland	2
NATIONAL LEAGUE		
Fred McGriff	Atlanta	5
Jeff Bagwell	Houston	3
Dante Bichette	Colorado	3
Mike Piazza	Los Angeles	0

1995—THE BALLPARK IN ARLINGTON, TEXAS

Player	Team	Round 1	Round 2	Round 3	Total
AMERICAN LEAGUE					
Frank Thomas	Chicago	8	4	3	15
Albert Belle	Cleveland	7	7	2	16
Mo Vaughn	Boston	3	3	—	6
Manny Ramirez	Cleveland	3	—	—	3
NATIONAL LEAGUE					
Ron Gant	Cincinnati	3	3	—	6
Raul Mondesi	Los Angeles	2	—	—	2
Reggie Sanders	Cincinnati	2	—	—	2
Sammy Sosa	Chicago	2	—	—	2

1996—VETERANS STADIUM, PHILADELPHIA

Player	Team	Round 1	Round 2	Round 3	Total	Longest
AMERICAN LEAGUE						
Mark McGwire	Oakland	4	9	2	15	460
Brady Anderson	Baltimore	5	6	—	11	433
Jay Buhner	Seattle	6	2	—	8	426
Joe Carter	Toronto	2	—	—	2	433
Greg Vaughn	Milwaukee	0	—	—	0	—
NATIONAL LEAGUE						
Barry Bonds	San Francisco	4	10	3	17	451
Henry Rodriguez	Montreal	3	—	—	3	437
Jeff Bagwell	Houston	2	—	—	2	460
Ellis Burks	Colorado	1	—	—	1	405
Gary Sheffield	Florida	0	—	—	0	—

1997—JACOBS FIELD, CLEVELAND

Player	Team	Round 1	Round 2	Round 3	Total	Longest
AMERICAN LEAGUE						
Tino Martinez	New York	5	8	3	16	436
Mark McGwire	Oakland	5	2	—	7	456
Brady Anderson	Baltimore	4	—	—	4	451
Ken Griffey Jr.	Seattle	3	—	—	3	451
Nomar Garciaparra	Boston	0	—	—	0	—
Jim Thome	Cleveland	0	—	—	0	—
NATIONAL LEAGUE						
Larry Walker	Colorado	9	9	1	19	479
Jeff Bagwell	Houston	4	1	—	5	413
Chipper Jones	Atlanta	3	—	—	3	429
Ray Lankford	St. Louis	2	—	—	2	424

1998—COORS FIELD, DENVER

Player	Team	Round 1	Round 2	Round 3	Total	Longest
AMERICAN LEAGUE						
Ken Griffey Jr.	Seattle	8	8	3	19	468
Jim Thome	Cleveland	7	10	2	19	477

Player	Team	Round 1	Round 2	Round 3	Total	Longest
Rafael Palmeiro	Baltimore	7	3	—	10	477
Alex Rodriguez	Seattle	5	—	—	5	452
Damion Easley	Detroit	2	—	—	2	443
NATIONAL LEAGUE						
Vinny Castilla	Colorado	7	5	—	12	475
Moises Alou	Houston	7	—	—	7	463
Javy Lopez	Atlanta	5	—	—	5	474
Mark McGwire	St. Louis	4	—	—	4	510
Chipper Jones	Atlanta	1	—	—	1	420

Alou was eliminated in the first round due to a tie breaker: fewer regular season homers.

1999 — FENWAY PARK, BOSTON

Player	Team	Round 1	Round 2	Round 3	Total	Longest
AMERICAN LEAGUE						
Ken Griffey Jr.	Seattle	3	10	3	16	460
Nomar Garciaparra	Boston	2	—	—	2	414
B.J. Surhoff	Baltimore	2	—	—	2	416
Shawn Green	Toronto	2	—	—	2	451
John Jaha	Oakland	1	—	—	1	418
NATIONAL LEAGUE						
Jeromy Burnitz	Milwaukee	6	6	2	14	436
Mark McGwire	St. Louis	13	3	—	16	488
Jeff Bagwell	Houston	5	1	—	6	398
Larry Walker	Colorado	2	—	—	2	405
Sammy Sosa	Chicago	1	—	—	1	371

2000 — TURNER FIELD, ATLANTA

Player	Team	Round 1	Round 2	Round 3	Total	Longest
AMERICAN LEAGUE						
Sammy Sosa	Chicago	6	11	9	26	508
Ken Griffey Jr.	Cincinnati	6	3	2	11	424
Carl Everett	Boston	6	6	—	12	447
Carlos Delgado	Toronto	5	1	—	6	443
Vladimir Guerrero	Montreal	2	—	—	2	454
Chipper Jones	Atlanta	2	—	—	2	412
Edgar Martinez	Seattle	2	—	—	2	432
Ivan Rodriguez	Texas	1	—	—	1	423

Second round pairings: Sosa vs. Everett; Griffey vs. Delgado.

Most Homers in One Derby

Player	Year	Total	Player	Year	Total
Sammy Sosa	2000	26	Rafael Palmeiro	1998	10
Larry Walker	1997	19	Jay Buhner	1996	8
Jim Thome	1998	19	Ken Griffey Jr.	1992	7
Ken Griffey Jr.	1998	19	Juan Gonzalez	1993	7
Barry Bonds	1996	17	Ken Griffey Jr.	1993	7
Albert Belle	1995	16	Ken Griffey Jr.	1994	7
Tino Martinez	1997	16	Mark McGwire	1997	7
Ken Griffey Jr.	1999	16	Moises Alou	1998	7
Mark McGwire	1999	16			
Frank Thomas	1995	15			
Mark McGwire	1996	15			
Jeromy Burnitz	1999	14			
Cal Ripken Jr.	1991	12			
Mark McGwire	1992	12			
Vinny Castilla	1998	12			
Carl Everett	2000	12			
Brady Anderson	1996	11			
Ken Griffey Jr.	2000	11			

Most Homers in Career

Player	Career Total	Years	Average
Ken Griffey Jr.	70	8	8.8
Mark McGwire	56	7	8.0
Sammy Sosa	29	3	9.7
Larry Walker	25	3	8.3
Barry Bonds	24	3	8.0
Albert Belle	21	3	7.0
Frank Thomas	19	2	9.5
Jim Thome	19	2	9.5
Cal Ripken Jr.	17	3	5.7
Tino Martinez	16	1	16.0
Jeff Bagwell	16	4	4.0
Brady Anderson	15	2	7.5
Jeromy Burnitz	14	1	14.0
Vinny Castilla	12	1	12.0
Carl Everett	12	1	12.0
Rafael Palmeiro	10	1	10.0
Dave Parker	9	2	4.5
Jay Buhner	8	1	8.0
Fred McGriff	8	2	4.0
Cecil Fielder	8	3	2.7
Joe Carter	8	3	2.7
Juan Gonzalez	7	1	7.0
Moises Alou	7	1	7.0
Ruben Sierra	7	2	3.5

APPENDIX 2
GENERAL REFERENCE

Day	Times	Years
July		
6	4	1933, 1938, 1942, 1983
7	5	1936, 1937, 1959–1, 1964, 1998
8	7	1935, 1941, 1947, 1952, 1958, 1980, 1997
9	7	1940, 1946, 1957, 1963, 1968, 1991, 1996
10	6	1934, 1951, 1956, 1962–1, 1984, 1990
11	10	1939, 1944, 1950, 1960–1, 1961–1, 1967, 1978, 1989, 1995, 2000
12	5	1949, 1955, 1966, 1988, 1994
13	10	1943, 1948, 1954, 1960–2, 1965, 1971, 1976, 1982, 1993, 1999
14	4	1953, 1970, 1987, 1992
15	2	1975, 1986
16	1	1985
17	1	1979
19	1	1977
23	2	1969, 1974
24	1	1973
25	1	1972
30	1	1962–2
31	1	1961–2
August		
3	1	1959–2
9	1	1981

ALL-STAR GAMES BY DAY OF THE WEEK

After World War II, the All-Star Game day settled on Tuesday. A few games have been played on other days of the week since then for various reasons.

The following are the 14 games of the 71 game series that were played on days other than Tuesday.

Sunday (1)	1981
Monday (6)	1935, 1942, 1959–2, 1960–1, 1961–2, 1962–2
Wednesday (6)	1937, 1938, 1940, 1960–2, 1969, 1983
Thursday (1)	1933

ALL-STAR GAME VENUES

Anaheim	Anaheim Stadium	1967, 1989
Atlanta	Atlanta Stadium	1972
	Turner Field	2000
Baltimore	Memorial Stadium	1958
	Oriole Park at Camden Yards	1993
Boston	National League Park	1936
	Fenway Park	1946, 1961–2, 1999
Brooklyn	Ebbets Field	1949
Chicago	Comiskey Park I	1933, 1950, 1983
	Wrigley Field	1947, 1962–2, 1990
Cincinnati	Crosley Field	1938, 1953
	Riverfront Stadium	1970, 1988
Colorado	Coors Field	1998
Cleveland	Municipal Stadium	1935, 1954, 1963, 1981
	Jacobs Field	1997

Detroit	Briggs Stadium (Tiger Stadium)	1941, 1951, 1971
Houston	Astrodome	1968, 1986
Kansas City	Municipal Stadium	1960–1
	Royals Stadium	1973
Los Angeles	Memorial Coliseum	1959–2
	Dodger Stadium	1980
Milwaukee	County Stadium	1955, 1975
Minnesota	Metropolitan Stadium	1965
	Metrodome	1985
Montreal	Olympic Stadium	1982
New York	Polo Grounds	1934, 1942
	Shea Stadium	1964
	Yankee Stadium	1939, 1960–2, 1977
Oakland	Oakland Coliseum	1987
Philadelphia	Shibe Park	1943, 1952
	Veterans' Stadium	1976, 1996
Pittsburgh	Forbes Field	1944, 1959–1
	Three Rivers Stadium	1974, 1994
St. Louis	Sportsman's Park (Busch Stadium I)	1940, 1948, 1957
	Busch Stadium II	1966
San Diego	San Diego Stadium (Jack Murphy Stadium)	1978, 1992
San Francisco	Candlestick Park	1961–1, 1984
Seattle	Kingdome	1979
Texas	The Ballpark in Arlington	1995
Toronto	SkyDome	1991
Washington	Griffith Stadium	1937, 1956
	DC Stadium (RFK Stadium)	1962–1, 1969

SELECTION PROCESS

1933–1934	Fans vote but managers not strictly bound by that vote
1935	Managers select entire team
1936	Fans select 16 players; managers select five
1937	Managers select team based on recommendations from other managers
1938–1946	Managers select entire team
1947–1957	Fans vote for eight starting positions; managers pick rest of the team
1958–1969	All players, managers and coaches vote for eight starters; managers pick the rest
1970-present	Fans select the eight starters; managers pick the rest of the team

ROSTER SIZE (PER TEAM)

1933	18
1934–1935	20
1936	21
1937–1938	23
1939–1968	25
1969–1997	28
1998-present	30

In 1959, 1961 and 1962, the rosters were expanded to 28 for the second game.
In 1960, when the games were played in a three-day span, the rosters were 30 for both games.

Year	Player	Team	Pos	Year	Player	Team	Pos
1962–1	Maury Wills	LAN NL	SS	1981	Gary Carter	MON NL	C
1962–2	Leon Wagner	LAN AL	LF	1982	Dave Concepcion	CIN NL	SS
1963	Willie Mays	SFN NL	CF	1983	Fred Lynn	CAL AL	CF
1964	Johnny Callison	PHI NL	RF	1984	Gary Carter	MON NL	C
1965	Juan Marichal	SFN NL	P	1985	LaMarr Hoyt	SDN NL	P
1966	Brooks Robinson	BAL AL	3B	1986	Roger Clemens	BOS AL	P
1967	Tony Perez	CIN NL	3B	1987	Tim Raines	MON NL	LF
1968	Willie Mays	SFN NL	CF	1988	Terry Steinbach	OAK AL	C
1969	Willie McCovey	SFN NL	1B	1989	Bo Jackson	KCA AL	LF
1970	Carl Yastrzemski	BOS AL	CF-1B	1990	Julio Franco	TEX AL	2B
1971	Frank Robinson	BAL AL	RF	1991	Cal Ripken, Jr.	BAL AL	SS
1972	Joe Morgan	CIN NL	2B	1992	Ken Griffey, Jr.	SEA AL	CF
1973	Bobby Bonds	SFN NL	RF	1993	Kirby Puckett	MIN AL	LF
1974	Steve Garvey	LAN NL	1B	1994	Fred McGriff	ATL NL	1B
1975	Bill Madlock	CHN NL	3B	1995	Jeff Conine	FLO NL	PH
	Jon Matlack	NYN NL	P	1996	Mike Piazza	LAN NL	C
1976	George Foster	CIN NL	CF-RF	1997	Sandy Alomar, Jr.	CLE AL	C
1977	Don Sutton	LAN NL	P	1998	Roberto Alomar	BAL AL	2B
1978	Steve Garvey	LAN NL	1B	1999	Pedro Martinez	BOS AL	P
1979	Dave Parker	PIT NL	RF	2000	Derek Jeter	NYA AL	SS
1980	Ken Griffey, Sr.	CIN NL	LF				

Notes:

The MVP trophy is named for Arch Ward, who conceived of the All-Star game concept. During the period 1970–1984 it was called the Commissioner's Trophy.

Two players have been selected MVP from the losing team, both from the American League: Brooks Robinson (1966) and Carl Yastrzemski (1970). Three National League players have won the award twice: Willie Mays (1963 and 1968), Steve Garvey (1974 and 1978) and Gary Carter (1981 and 1984). The 1974 award is particularly outstanding as Garvey was a write-in member of the team. Ken Griffey, Sr. (1980) and Ken Griffey, Jr. (1992) are the only father son pair to win the award. Brothers Sandy, Jr. and Roberto Alomar won the award in back-to-back years (1997–1998). Only two players have won the award in their home park: Sandy Alomar, Jr. in 1997 and Pedro Martinez in 1999.

REPLACEMENT PLAYERS

The 36 players chosen to participate in the first All-Star Game were at Comiskey Park, in uniform and ready to play that day in 1933. However, in most years since, one or more players was forced, or in some cases chose, to miss the game. Following is a complete list of those replacements. (**Bold print** indicates elected starter.)

Year	Team	Replacement	Replaced
1933	None		
1934	NL	OF Kiki Cuyler CHN	OF **Jo-Jo Moore** NY
1935	AL	OF Doc Cramer PHA	OF Earl Averill CLE
	NL	P Bill Walker SLN	P Van Mungo BRO
1936	AL	P Vern Kennedy CHA	P Tommy Bridges DET
1937	AL	P Johnny Murphy NYA	P Monty Stratton CHA
	AL	OF Sam West SLA	OF **Gee Walker** DET
1938	AL	P Johnny Murphy NYA	1B Hank Greenberg DET
	NL	C Harry Danning NY	C Babe Phelps BRO
1939	NL	SS Eddie Miller BSN	3B Cookie Lavagetto BRO
1940	AL	3B Cecil Travis WAS	3B **Red Rolfe** NYA
	NL	SS Eddie Miller BSN	SS Billy Jurges NY
	NL	OF Bill Nicholson CHN	OF Hank Leiber CHN
1941	NL	1B Frank McCormick CIN	1B Dolph Camilli BRO
	NL	OF Joe Medwick BRO	OF Hank Leiber CHN
1942	AL	C Hal Wagner BOS	C Bill Dickey NYA
	NL	P Ray Starr CIN	P Paul Derringer CIN
1943	AL	OF Dick Wakefield DET	OF Charlie Keller NYA
	NL	1B Elbie Fletcher PIT	1B Frank McCormick CIN
	NL	P Ace Adams NY	P Howie Pollett SLN

Year	Team	Replacement	Replaced
1944	AL	OF Pete Fox BOS	OF George Case WAS
	NL	SS Frankie Zak PIT	SS Eddie Miller CIN
	NL	P Jim Tobin BSN	P Red Munger SLN
	NL	P Bill Voiselle NY	P Max Lanier SLN
1946	NL	1B Frank McCormick PHI	SS Pee Wee Reese BRO
	NL	2B Emil Verban PHI	SS Eddie Miller CIN
1947	AL	P Early Wynn WAS	P Bob Feller CLE
	AL	OF Tommy Henrich NYA	OF Charlie Keller NYA
	NL	SS Pee Wee Reese BRO	SS **Eddie Miller** CIN
	NL	3B Whitey Kurowski SLN	3B **Bob Elliott** BOS
1948	AL	P Joe Dobson BOS	P Bob Feller CLE
	NL	2B Bill Rigney NY	2B **Eddie Stanky** BSN
	NL	SS Buddy Kerr NY	SS Marty Marion SLN
1949	None		
1950	None		
1951	None		
1952	AL	3B Gil McDougald NYA	3B George Kell BOS
	NL	P Jim Hearn NY	P Preacher Roe BRO
1953	NL	C Clyde McCullough CHN	C Del Crandall MLN
	NL	C Wes Westrum NY	C Del Rice SLN
1954	AL	P Dean Stone WAS	1B Ferris Fain CHA
	AL	1B Mickey Vernon WAS	3B George Kell CHA
	AL	P Sandy Consuegra CHA	P Mike Garcia CLE
	AL	OF Irv Noren NYA	P Allie Reynolds NYA
	NL	P Jim Wilson MLN	P Harvey Haddix SLN
1955	NL	C Stan Lopata PHI	C **Roy Campanella** BRO
1956	AL	P Herb Score CLE	P Ray Narleski CLE
	NL	C Stan Lopata PHI	C Del Crandall MLN
1957	None		
1958	None		
1959–1	NL	P Don Elston CHN	P Wilmer Mizell SLN
1959–2	AL	P Pedro Ramos WAS	P Camillo Pascual WAS
1960–1	AL	OF Jim Lemon WAS	P Camillo Pascual WAS
1960–2	None		
1961–1	None		
1961–2	None		
1962–1	AL	P Milt Pappas BAL	P Hoyt Wilhelm BAL
	NL	P Warren Spahn MLN	OF Hank Aaron MLN
1962–2	AL	P Ray Herbert CHA	P Ken McBride LAA
1963	AL	P Bill Monbouquette BOS	P Steve Barber BAL
	NL	2B Julian Javier SLN	2B **Bill Mazeroski** PIT
1964	AL	SS Eddie Bressoud BOS	SS Luis Aparicio BAL
	AL	OF Rocky Colavito KC	OF Al Kaline DET
1965	AL	C Bill Freehan DET	OF Carl Yastrzemski BOS
	AL	1B Joe Pepitone NYA	1B **Bill Skowron** CHA
	AL	OF Tony Oliva MIN	OF Mickey Mantle NYA
1966	AL	P Sonny Siebert CLE	P Sam McDowell CLE
	NL	P Phil Regan LAN	P Bob Gibson SLN
	NL	2B Jim Lefevbre LAN	2B **Joe Morgan** HOU
1967	AL	OF Ken Berry CHA	OF **Frank Robinson** BAL
	AL	OF Tony Oliva MIN	OF **Al Kaline** DET
	NL	P Chris Short PHI	P Denny Lemaster ATL
1968	AL	P Gary Bell BOS	P Jose Santiago BOS
	NL	OF Billy Williams CHN	OF **Pete Rose** CIN
	NL	SS Leo Cardenas CIN	SS Gene Alley PIT
1969	AL	2B Mike Andrews BOS	2B Dave Johnson BAL
	AL	OF Roy White NYA	OF Tony Oliva MIN
	AL	1B Don Mincher SEA	OF Mike Hegan SEA

Year	Team	Replacement	Replaced
1970	AL	2B Dave Johnson BAL	2B **Rod Carew** MIN
	NL	2B Joe Morgan HOU	2B Felix Millan ATL
1971	AL	C Dave Duncan OAK	C **Ray Fosse** CLE
	AL	1B Norm Cash DET	1B **Boog Powell** BAL
	AL	P Wilbur Wood CHA	P Sam McDowell CLE
	AL	OF Reggie Jackson OAK	OF **Tony Oliva** MIN
	NL	P Don Wilson CIN	P Larry Dierker HOU
1972	AL	SS Toby Harrah TEX	SS **Luis Aparicio** BOS
	AL	SS Bobby Grich BAL	SS Toby Harrah TEX
	AL	SS Bert Campaneris OAK	SS Freddie Patek KCA
	AL	P Ken Holtzman OAK	P Joe Coleman DET
	NL	P Ferguson Jenkins CHN	P Gary Nolan CIN
1973	AL	1B Jim Spencer TEX	1B Carl Yastrzemski BOS
	AL	OF Pat Kelly CHA	1B **Dick Allen** CHA
	NL	SS Bill Russell LAN	SS Dave Concepcion CIN
1974	AL	C Ed Hermann CHA	C **Carlton Fisk** BOS
	AL	C Jim Sundberg TEX	C Ed Hermann CHA
	AL	3B Don Money MIL	3B Sal Bando OAK
1975	AL	SS Toby Harrah TEX	2B Jorge Orta CHA
1976	AL	2B Phil Garner OAK	2B Willie Randolph NYA
1977	AL	P Nolan Ryan CAL	P Frank Tanana CAL
	AL	P Dennis Eckersley CLE	P Nolan Ryan CAL
	AL	P Jim Kern CLE	P Mark Fidrych DET
	AL	P Jim Slaton MIL	2B Don Money MIL
	AL	3B Wayne Gross OAK	P Vida Blue OAK
	NL	P Rich Gossage PIT	P Bruce Sutter CHN
1978	AL	2B Jerry Remy BOS	SS Rick Burleson BOS
	AL	OF Dwight Evans BOS	OF Carl Yastrzemski BOS
	AL	3B Graig Nettles NYA	OF **Reggie Jackson** NYA
	AL	OF Larry Hisle MIL	3B Graig Nettles NYA
	AL	C Darrell Porter KCA	C Thurman Munson NYA
	NL	C Biff Pocoroba Atl	C **Johnny Bench** CIN
1979	AL	1B Cecil Cooper MIL	1B **Rod Carew** CAL
	NL	1B Keith Hernandez SLN	OF Dave Kingman CHN
	NL	3B Larry Parrish MON	SS Dave Concepcion CIN
	NL	C Johnny Bench CIN	C **Ted Simmons** SLN
	NL	C John Stearns NYN	C Johnny Bench CIN
	NL	SS Craig Reynolds HOU	SS Gary Templeton SLN
1980	AL	OF Al Bumbry BAL	OF **Jim Rice** BOS
	AL	3B Graig Nettles NYA	3B **George Brett** KCA
	AL	2B Bobby Grich CAL	2B **Paul Molitor** MIL
	NL	3B Ray Knight CIN	3B **Mike Schmidt** PHI
	NL	P Ed Whitson SFN	P Vida Blue SFN
1981	AL	P Ron Davis NYA	P Rich Gossage NYA
1982	AL	1B Andre Thornton CLE	1B Rod Carew CAL
1983	AL	OF Ben Oglivie MIL	OF **Reggie Jackson** CAL
	AL	P Tippy Martinez BAL	P Ron Guidry NYA
1984	AL	SS Alfredo Griffin TOR	SS Alan Trammell DET
	NL	P Fernando Valenzuela LAN	P Joaquin Andujar SLN
1985	AL	C Rich Gedman BOS	C **Lance Parrish** DET
	NL	OF Glenn Wilson PHI	OF Pedro Guerrero LAN
	NL	C Terry Kennedy SDN	C **Gary Carter** NYN
	NL	P Ron Darling NYN	P Joaquin Andujar SLN
1986	AL	3B Brook Jacoby CLE	3B **George Brett** KCA
1987	AL	2B Harold Reynolds SEA	2B Lou Whitaker DET
	AL	3B Kevin Seitzer KCA	3B George Brett KCA
1988	AL	SS Kurt Stillwell KC	SS Ozzie Guillen CHA
	AL	SS Cal Ripken, Jr.	SS **Alan Trammell** DET
	NL	P Bob Walk PIT	2B Robby Thompson SFN

Year	Team	Replacement	Replaced
1989	AL	OF Ruben Sierra TEX	OF **Jose Canseco** OAK
	NL	P Rick Sutcliffe CHN	P Mike Scott HOU
	NL	OF Eric Davis CIN	OF **Darryl Strawberry** NYN
	NL	3B Howard Johnson NYN	3B **Mike Schmidt** PHI
1990	AL	IF Brook Jacoby CLE	OF Ellis Burks BOS
	NL	C Mike Scioscia LAN	C **Benito Santiago** SDN
1991	AL	1B Rafael Palmeiro TEX	1B Mark McGwire OAK
	NL	OF Ivan Calderon MON	OF **Darryl Strawberry** LAN
	NL	P Mike Morgan LAN	P Ramon Martinez LAN
1992	AL	OF Joe Carter TOR	OF **Jose Canseco** OAK
1993	NL	OF Marquis Grissom MON	OF **Andy Van Slyke** PIT
1994	NL	SS Wil Cordero MON	SS Barry Larkin CIN
	NL	P Rod Beck SFN	P Jose Rijo CIN
	NL	OF Marquis Grissom MON	OF **Lenny Dykstra** PHI
1995	AL	1B Tino Martinez SEA	1B Mark McGwire OAK
	AL	OF Kenny Lofton CLE	OF **Ken Griffey** SEA
	NL	P John Smiley CIN	P Greg Maddux ATL
	NL	SS Barry Larkin CIN	SS **Ozzie Smith** SLN
	NL	3B Vinny Castilla COL	3B **Matt Williams** SFN
1996	AL	OF Brady Anderson BAL	OF **Ken Griffey** SEA
	AL	None	1B **Frank Thomas** CHA
	NL	OF Henry Rodriguez MON	OF **Tony Gwynn** SDN
	NL	3B Ken Caminiti SDN	3B **Matt Williams** SFN
1997	AL	1B Jim Thome CLE	1B Frank Thomas CHA
	AL	Paul O'Neill NYA	OF **David Justice** CLE
	NL	OF Steve Finley SDN	OF **Kenny Lofton** ATL
	NL	SS Royce Clayton SLN	SS **Barry Larkin** CIN
	NL	C Charles Johnson FLO	C Todd Hundley NYN
1998	AL	1B Rafael Palmeiro BAL	1B Mo Vaughn BOS
	AL	OF Manny Ramirez CLE	OF Bernie Williams NYA
	NL	2B Bret Boone CIN	OF Sammy Sosa CHN
1999	AL	P Charles Nagy CLE	P Mariano Rivera NYA
	AL	DH Harold Baines BAL	DH **Jose Canseco** TBA
	NL	P Scott Williamson CIN	P Robb Nen SFN
	NL	OF Jeromy Burnitz MIL	OF **Tony Gwynn** SDN
2000	AL	SS Mike Bordick BAL	3B **Cal Ripken** BAL
	AL	3B Tony Batista TOR	SS **Alex Rodriguez** SEA
	AL	OF Carl Everett BOS	OF **Manny Ramirez** CLE
	NL	SS Edgar Renteria SLN	1B **Mark McGwire** SLN
	NL	C Joe Girardi CHN	C **Mike Piazza** NYN
	NL	OF Jeffrey Hammonds COL	OF **Barry Bonds** SFN
	NL	OF Steve Finley ARI	OF **Ken Griffey Jr.** CIN
	NL	P Danny Graves CIN	P Greg Maddux

ALL-STARS WHO PLAYED FOR MULTIPLE TEAMS DURING SEASON
*—team represented

Ed Bailey	1961	CIN SFN*		Walker Cooper	1949	NY CIN*
Harold Baines	1989	CHA* TEX		Walker Cooper	1950	CIN BSN*
Harold Baines	1999	BAL* CLE		Curt Davis	1936	PHI CHN*
Bert Blyleven	1985	CLE* MIN		Ryne Duren	1961	NYA LAA*
Bobby Bonilla	1995	NYN* BAL		Bruce Edwards	1951	BRO CHN*
Mike Bordick	2000	BAL* NYN		Rick Ferrell	1933	SLA BOS*
Smoky Burgess	1955	PHI CIN*		Rick Ferrell	1937	BOS WAS*
Smoky Burgess	1964	PIT* CHA		Wes Ferrell	1937	BOS WAS*
Jose Canseco	1992	OAK* TEX		Phil Garner	1981	PIT* HOU
Ben Chapman	1936	NYA WAS*		Frankie Hayes	1946	CLE CHA*
David Cone	1992	NYN* TOR		Billy Herman	1941	CHN BRO*

Player	Year	Teams
Rick Honeycutt	1983	TEX* LAN
Jackie Jensen	1952	NYA WAS*
George Kell	1952	DET BOS*
George Kell	1954	BOS CHA*
George Kell	1956	CHA BAL*
Ralph Kiner	1953	PIT CHN*
Dave LaRoche	1977	CLE CAL*
Willie Mays	1972	SFN NYN*
Mark McGwire	1997	OAK* SLN
Joe Medwick	1940	SLN BRO*
Cass Michaels	1950	CHA WAS*
Minnie Minoso	1951	CLE CHA*
Johnny Mize	1949	NY* NYA
Bobo Newsom	1939	SLA DET*
Lefty O'Doul	1933	BRO NY*
Mike Piazza	1998	LAN FLO NYN*
Rick Reuschel	1987	PIT* SFN
Frank Robinson	1974	CAL* CLE
Ray Scarborough	1950	WAS CHA*
Red Schoendienst	1957	NY MLN*
Tom Seaver	1977	NYN CIN*
Jeff Shaw	1998	CIN LAN*
Gary Sheffield	1993	SDN FLO*
Gary Sheffield	1998	FLO LAN*
Ruben Sierra	1992	TEX* OAK
Lee Smith	1993	SLN* NYA
Jim Spencer	1973	CAL TEX*
Tony Taylor	1960	CHN PHI*
Manny Trillo	1983	MON CLE*
Greg Vaughn	1996	MIL* SDN
Emil Verban	1946	SLN PHI*
Harry Walker	1947	SLN PHI*
David Wells	1995	DET* CIN
Vic Wertz	1952	DET* SLA
Wally Westlake	1951	PIT SLN*
Pinky Whitney	1936	BSN PHI*
Hoyt Wilhelm	1970	ATL* CHN
Jim Wilson	1956	BAL CHA*
Rudy York	1947	BOS CHA*

PLAYERS SELECTED IN BOTH LEAGUES

Aaron, Hank
Allen, Dick
Alomar, Roberto
Arroyo, Luis
Bell, George
Blue, Vida
Bonds, Bobby
Boone, Bob
Brown, Kevin
Bunning, Jim
Burks, Ellis
Burroughs, Jeff
Cardenas, Leo
Cirillo, Jeff
Clark, Will
Cone, David
Cuellar, Mike
Culp, Ray
Davis, Chili
Diaz, Bo
Edmonds, Jim
Fairly, Ron
Fernandez, Tony
Fingers, Rollie
Forsch, Ken
Garner, Phil
Gossage, Rich
Griffey Jr., Ken
Harvey, Bryan
Hendrick, George
Henke, Tom
Howell, Jay
John, Tommy
Johnson, Dave
Johnson, Randy
Jones, Doug
Jones, Ruppert
Justice, Dave
Kelly, Roberto
Kennedy, Terry
Leonard, Dutch
Leonard, Jeff
Lofton, Kenny
Martinez, Dennis
Martinez, Pedro J.
McGriff, Fred
McGwire, Mark
Messersmith, Andy
Mize, Johnny
Monday, Rick
Murcer, Bobby
Murray, Eddie
Myers, Randy
Nettles, Graig
Niekro, Phil
O'Neill, Paul
Offerman, Jose
Oliver, Al
Palmeiro, Rafael
Parker, Dave
Parrish, Lance
Parrish, Larry
Perry, Gaylord
Randolph, Willie
Reardon, Jeff
Reynolds, Craig
Robinson, Frank
Rojas, Cookie
Roseboro, John
Rowe, Schoolboy
Ryan, Nolan
Saberhagen, Bret
Sain, Johnny
Sax, Steve
Simmons, Ted
Singer, Bill
Smith, Lee
Smith, Reggie
Staley, Gerry
Staub, Rusty
Sutcliffe, Rick
Temple, Johnny
Thompson, Jason
Trillo, Manny
Vaughn, Greg
Viola, Frank
Washington, Claudell
Welch, Bob
White, Devon
Wilhelm, Hoyt
Wilson, Jim
Winfield, Dave

PLAYERS WHO REPRESENTED THREE OR MORE TEAMS

Allen, Dick	PHI, SLN, CHA
Alomar, Roberto	SDN, TOR, BAL, CLE
Alou, Moises	MON, FLO, HOU
Aparicio, Luis	CHA, BAL, BOS
Baines, Harold	CHA, OAK, BAL
Brown, Kevin	TEX, FLO, SDN, LAN
Burgess, Smoky	PHI, CIN, PIT
Colavito, Rocky	CLE, DET, KC
Cone, David	NYN, KCA, NYA
Cooper, Walker	SLN, NY, CIN, BSN
Donovan, Dick	CHA, WAS, CLE
Eckersley, Dennis	CLE, BOS, OAK
Fingers, Rollie	OAK, SDN, MIL
Galarraga, Andres	MON, COL, ATL
Gossage, Rich	CHA, PIT, NYA, SDN
Hemsley, Rollie	SLA, CLE, NYA
Jackson, Reggie	OAK, NYA, CAL
John, Tommy	CHA, LAN, NYA
Johnson, Bob	PHA, WAS, BOS
Jones, Doug	CLE, HOU, PHI
Kell, George	DET, BOS, CHA, BAL
Lombardi, Ernie	CIN, BSN, NY
McGriff, Fred	SDN, ATL, TBA
Medwick, Joe	SLN, BRO, NY
Messersmith, Andy	CAL, LAN, ATL
Mize, Johnny	SLN, NY, NYA
Myers, Randy	CIN, CHN, BAL

Newsom, Bobo	SLA, DET, PHA
Oliver, Al	PIT, TEX, MON
Palmeiro, Rafael	CHN, TEX, BAL
Parker, Dave	PIT, CIN, MIL
Parrish, Lance	DET, PHI, CAL
Perry, Gaylord	SFN, CLE, SDN
Reardon, Jeff	MON, MIN, BOS
Reuschel, Rick	CHN, PIT, SFN
Robinson, Eddie	WAS, CHA, PHA
Robinson, Frank	CIN, BAL, CAL
Rosar, Buddy	NYA, CLE, PHA
Ryan, Nolan	CAL, HOU, TEX
Sheffield, Gary	SDN, FLO, LAN
Smith, Lee	CHN, SLN, BAL, CAL
Smith, Reggie	BOS, SLN, LAN
Stanky, Eddie	BRO, BSN, NY
Staub, Rusty	HOU, MON, DET
Trillo, Manny	CHN, PHI, CLE
Vernon, Mickey	WAS, BOS, CLE
Wells, David	DET, NYA, TOR
White, Devon	CAL, TOR, ARI
Wilhelm, Hoyt	NY, BAL, ATL
Wilson, Jim	MIL, BAL, CHA
Wynn, Early	WAS, CLE, CHA
York, Rudy	DET, BOS, CHA

HALL OF FAME ALL-STARS

Aaron, Hank	Foxx, Jimmie
Aparicio, Luis	Frisch, Frankie
Appling, Luke	Gehrig, Lou
Averill, Earl	Gehringer, Charlie
Banks, Ernie	Gibson, Bob
Bench, Johnny	Gomez, Lefty
Berra, Yogi	Goslin, Goose
Boudreau, Lou	Greenberg, Hank
Brett, George	Grove, Lefty
Brock, Lou	Hafey, Chick
Campanella, Roy	Hartnett, Gabby
Carew, Rod	Herman, Billy
Carlton, Steve	Hubbell, Carl
Clemente, Roberto	Hunter, Catfish
Cochrane, Mickey	Irvin, Monte
Cronin, Joe	Jackson, Reggie
Cuyler, Kiki	Jackson, Travis
Dean, Dizzy	Jenkins, Ferguson
Dickey, Bill	Kaline, Al
DiMaggio, Joe	Kell, George
Doby, Larry	Killebrew, Harmon
Doerr, Bobby	Kiner, Ralph
Drysdale, Don	Klein, Chuck
Durocher, Leo	Koufax, Sandy
Feller, Bob	Lazzeri, Tony
Ferrell, Rick	Lemon, Bob
Fingers, Rollie	Lombardi, Ernie
Fisk, Carlton	Lopez, Al
Ford, Whitey	Lyons, Ted
Fox, Nellie	Mantle, Mickey

Manush, Heinie	Ryan, Nolan
Marichal, Juan	Schmidt, Mike
Mathews, Eddie	Schoendienst, Red
Mays, Willie	Seaver, Tom
McCovey, Willie	Simmons, Al
Medwick, Joe	Slaughter, Enos
Mize, Johnny	Snider, Duke
Morgan, Joe	Spahn, Warren
Musial, Stan	Stargell, Willie
Niekro, Phil	Sutton, Don
Ott, Mel	Terry, Bill
Paige, Satchel	Traynor, Pie
Palmer, Jim	Vaughan, Arky
Perry, Gaylord	Waner, Lloyd
Reese, Pee Wee	Waner, Paul
Rizzuto, Phil	Wilhelm, Hoyt
Roberts, Robin	Williams, Billy
Robinson, Brooks	Williams, Ted
Robinson, Frank	Wynn, Early
Robinson, Jackie	Yastrzemski, Carl
Ruffing, Red	Yount, Robin
Ruth, Babe	

BROTHERS SELECTED AS ALL-STARS

Alomar, Roberto & Sandy Jr.
Alou, Felipe & Matty
Brett, George & Ken
Cooper, Mort & Walker
DiMaggio, Joe, Dom & Vince
Ferrell, Rick & Wes
Grissom, Lee & Marv
May, Carlos & Lee
Niekro, Joe & Phil
Perry, Gaylord & Jim
Walker, Dixie & Harry
Waner, Lloyd & Paul
Martinez, Pedro & Ramon

FATHER/SON ALL-STARS

Alomar, Sandy Sr. & Roberto & Sandy Jr.
Alou, Felipe & Moises
Bell, Gus & Buddy
Bonds, Bobby & Barry
Boone, Ray & Bob
Boone, Bob & Bret
Coleman, Joe & Joe
Griffey, Ken & Ken Jr.
Hegan, Jim & Mike
Hundley, Randy & Todd
Law, Vern & Vance

GRANDFATHER/GRANDSON ALL-STARS

Boone, Ray & Bret

GAMES OF MORE OR LESS THAN NINE INNINGS

Game	Inn	Winner
1950	14	NL
1952	5	NL
1955	12	NL
1961–1	10	NL
1966	10	NL
1967	15	NL
1970	12	NL
1972	10	NL
1987	13	NL
1994	10	NL

DESIGNATED HITTERS IN THE ALL-STAR GAME

Jeff Bagwell	1999
Harold Baines	1989, 1991, 1999
Albert Belle	1993
Bobby Bonilla	1989, 1991
Jeff Conine	1995
Andres Galarraga	1997
Ron Gant	1995
Mark Grace	1993
Pedro Guerrero	1989
Tony Gwynn	1997
John Jaha	1999
Gregg Jefferies	1993
Jeff Leonard	1989
Edgar Martinez	1995, 1997
Tino Martinez	1995
Paul Molitor	1993
Rafael Palmeiro	1999
Gary Sheffield	1999
Danny Tartabull	1991
Frank Thomas	1993
Jim Thome	1997

FIRST ALL-STAR HOMERS BY EACH TEAM

NYA AL	Babe Ruth	1933
SLN NL	Frankie Frisch	1933
PHA AL	Jimmie Foxx	1935
CHN NL	Augie Galan	1936
BSN NL	Max West	1940
PIT NL	Arky Vaughan	1941
BOS AL	Ted Williams	1941
DET AL	Rudy York	1942
CLE AL	Lou Boudreau	1942
BRO NL	Mickey Owen	1942
NY NL	Johnny Mize	1947
CIN NL	Ted Kluszewski	1954
MLN NL	Eddie Mathews	1959–1
LAN NL	Jim Gilliam	1959–2
SFN NL	Willie Mays	1960–2
MIN AL	Harmon Killebrew	1961–1
LAA AL	Leon Wagner	1962–2
PHI NL	Johnny Callison	1964
BAL AL	Brooks Robinson	1967
WAS AL	Frank Howard	1969
OAK AL	Reggie Jackson	1971
ATL NL	Hank Aaron	1971
KCA AL	Cookie Rojas	1972
HOU NL	Cesar Cedeno	1976
NYN NL	Lee Mazzilli	1979
MON NL	Gary Carter	1981
CAL AL	Fred Lynn	1983
SEA AL	Ken Griffey	1992
TEX AL	Ruben Sierra	1992
FLO NL	Gary Sheffield	1993
TOR AL	Roberto Alomar	1993
CHA AL	Frank Thomas	1995
SDN NL	Ken Caminiti	1996

INJURIES

The worst thing that can happen in an All-Star game is for a player to be injured. The ceremony and excitement that surround the contests can make us forget that the possibility always exists for a player to be hurt. Serious injuries to Dizzy Dean in 1937 and Ted Williams in 1950 are part of the lore of the All-Star game, and the collision between Pete Rose and Ray Fosse in 1970 is famous, although little damage was done. Below is a brief summary of 17 instances in which players were injured either during or just before the game with the damage serious enough to keep them from playing. All of these are recounted in more detail in the essay for that game.

1933
    Bill Dickey of the Yankees hurt his thumb in pre-game batting practice.

1937
    Dizzy Dean of the Cardinals suffered a broken toe on a line drive by Cleveland's Earl Averill.

1939
    Ival Goodman of the Reds dived for a sinking line drive hit by George Selkirk of the Yankees and dislocated his shoulder.

1940
    In the top of the second, Max West of the Boston Bees bruised his hip running into right field wall trying to catch double hit by Luke Appling of the White Sox.

1947
    Emil Verban, Schoolboy Rowe, and coach Ben Chapman were hurt on the train coming to the game.

1950
    Ted Williams of the Red Sox broke his elbow making great catch against the scoreboard against Ralph Kiner of the Pirates.

1955
   Eddie Mathews of the Braves was hit on the wrist by a line drive from Al Kaline of the Tigers. There was no break.
1956
   Stan Musial of the Cardinals twisted his knee making a catch on Ted Williams of the Red Sox in the 8th.
   Yogi Berra of the Yankees was hurt on a foul tip by Ted Kluszewski of the Reds.
1958
   Bob Cerv of the Athletics reinjured a broken toe while crashing into the wall while making a catch on a ball hit by Milwaukee's Del Crandall in the 6th.
1963
   Willie Mays of the Giants hurt his leg on the center field fence making a catch to end 8th inning against Joe Pepitone of the Yankees.
1968
   Harmon Killebrew of the Twins ruptured his hamstring stretching for a throw.
1970
   Pete Rose of the Reds bowled over Ray Fosse of the Indians as he scored the winning run in the bottom of the 12th inning.
1973
   Catfish Hunter of the A's suffered a broken right thumb on a line drive by Billy Williams of the Cubs.
1981
   Fred Lynn of the Angels hurt his knee sliding into second base in the 6th inning as he was forced out following his pinch-hit single.
1991
   Jack Morris of the Tigers was hit by a line drive from Bobby Bonilla in the first inning.
1996
   Cal Ripken of the Orioles broke his nose in a freak accident during the pregame photo session but played anyway.

PRESIDENTIAL APPEARANCES

Franklin D. Roosevelt	1937
John Kennedy	1962–1
Lyndon Johnson	1962–1 (VP)
Richard Nixon	1959–1 (VP), 1960 (VP), 1970
Gerald Ford	1976, 1978 (former President)
Jimmy Carter	2000 (former President)
Ronald Reagan	1989 (former President)
George Bush	1981 (VP), 1988 (VP), 1991, 1992

In 1991, Canadian Prime Minister Brian Mulroney attended the game in Toronto with President Bush. In 1992, Mexican President Carlos Salinas de Gortari accompanied President Bush in San Diego. Also, Vice-President Spiro Agnew attended the 1969 game.

TEAM ABBREVIATIONS

ANA	AL	Anaheim Angels	1997-current
ARI	NL	Arizona Diamondbacks	1998-current
ATL	NL	Atlanta Braves	1966-current
BAL	AL	Baltimore Orioles	1954-current
BOS	AL	Boston Red Sox	1933-current
BRO	NL	Brooklyn Dodgers	1933–1934, 1936–1957
BSN	NL	Boston Braves	1933–1952
CAL	AL	California Angels	1965–1996
CHA	AL	Chicago White Sox	1933-current
CHN	NL	Chicago Cubs	1933-current
CIN	NL	Cincinnati Reds	1933, 1935-current
CLE	AL	Cleveland Indians	1933-current
COL	NL	Colorado Rockies	1993-current
DET	AL	Detroit Tigers	1933-current
FLO	NL	Florida Marlins	1993-current
HOU	NL	Houston Astros	1962-current

KC	AL	Kansas City A's	1955–1967
KCA	AL	Kansas City Royals	1969-current
LAA	AL	Los Angeles Angels	1961–1964
LAN	NL	Los Angeles Dodgers	1958-current
MIL	AL	Milwaukee Brewers	1970–1997
MLN	NL	Milwaukee Braves	1953–1965
MIL	NL	Milwaukee Brewers	1998-current
MIN	AL	Minnesota Twins	1961-current
MON	NL	Montreal Expos	1969-current
NY	NL	New York Giants	1933–1957
NYA	AL	New York Yankees	1933-current
NYN	NL	New York Mets	1962-current
OAK	AL	Oakland Athletics	1968-current
PHA	AL	Philadelphia Athletics	1933–1954
PHI	NL	Philadelphia Phillies	1933, 1935-current
PIT	NL	Pittsburgh Pirates	1933-current
SDN	NL	San Diego Padres	1969-current
SEA	AL	Seattle Pilots	1969
SEA	AL	Seattle Mariners	1977-current
SFN	NL	San Francisco Giants	1958-current
SLA	AL	St. Louis Browns	1933–1953
SLN	NL	St. Louis Cardinals	1933-current
TBA	AL	Tampa Bay Devil Rays	1998-current
TEX	AL	Texas Rangers	1972-current
TOR	AL	Toronto Blue Jays	1977-current
WAS	AL	Washington Senators	1933–1960
WAS	AL	Washington Senators	1961–1971

SOURCES

Atlanta Constitution
Baltimore Sun
Boston Globe
Chicago Daily News
Chicago Tribune
Cincinnati Enquirer
Cleveland Plain Dealer
Conine, Jeff (interview, 7–7-1999)
Detroit Free Press
Gerlach, Larry
Houston Post
Los Angeles Times
Major League Baseball
Milwaukee Journal
New York Times
New York World-Telegram
Palm Beach Post
Philadelphia Inquirer
Pittsburgh Post Gazette
Pittsburgh Press
St. Louis Globe Democrat
St. Louis Post-Dispatch
Spalding's Official Baseball Guide
The Sporting News
The Sporting News Baseball Guide
USA Today
USA Today Baseball Weekly
Washington Post

INDEX